CW00447850

THE GREENHILL
DICTIONARY
OF
GUNS AND GUNMAKERS

THE GREENHILL
DICTIONARY
OF
GUNS AND GUNMAKERS

From Colt's First Patent to the Present Day, 1836–2001
Military small-arms, sporting guns and rifles, air and gas guns, designers,
manufacturers, inventors, patentees, trademarks, brandnames and monograms

by John Walter

Greenhill Books, London
Stackpole Books, Pennsylvania

Greenhill Books

DEDICATION

To ARW and ADW;
to the memory of the pioneering work of
Colonel Robert E. Gardner (1893–1970);
and to Ian Hogg and the many thousands of enthusiasts
who have helped in the compilation of this work.

The Greenhill Dictionary of Guns and Gunmakers
first published by Greenhill Books, Lionel Leventhal Limited, Park House, 1 Russell Gardens, London NW11 9NN
and
Stackpole Books, 5067 Ritter Road, Mechanicsburg, PA 17055, USA

British Library Cataloguing in Publication Data
Walter, John, 1951–
The Greenhill Dictionary of Guns and Gunmakers : from Colt's first patent to the present day, 1836–2001
1. Firearms - Dictionaries 2. Firearms - History - Dictionaries 3. Gunsmiths - Dictionaries
4. Gunsmiths - History - Dictionaries
I. Title II. Dictionary of guns and gunmakers III. Guns and gunmakers
683.4'003

ISBN 1-85367-392-7

Library of Congress Cataloging-in-Publication Data available

Designed and edited by Ian Penberthy

Printed in Spain

CONTENTS

List of Illustrations

Introduction

THE GREENHILL DICTIONARY OF GUNS AND GUNMAKERS seeks to identify in a single volume as many brandnames, trademarks and gunmakers' monograms as possible; to date the activities of individual manufacturers from changes of corporate structure or address; to provide brief details of individual guns and, particularly, to direct the reader to sources of detailed information. The origins of the dictionary lie partly in habitual list-making begun during my childhood, partly on information accumulated over the past thirty years, and partly on links forged with collectors and enthusiasts around the world.

The book concentrates largely on the machine-made breech-loader at the expense of the single-shot cap-lock. However, if the beginning of the modern era is defined as the patenting of the first Colt revolver in the USA in 1836, cap-locks thereafter retained universal importance for several decades; indeed, in remote areas of Africa (and even the most distant backwaters of the USA) the scarcity of self-contained metallic-case ammunition ensured the survival of the cap-lock rifle into the twentieth century.

It is, of course, impossible to include every known brandname and trademark, or to attempt detailed summaries of the career of every known gunsmith and gun dealer. Writing in October 1970 in *Shooting Times & Country Magazine*, the late Gough Thomas claimed to have information about more than 4,000 British gunmakers; Gardner's *Small Arms Makers* itself contains nearly 400,000 words devoted to just one small part of the subject of guns and gunmaking; and there are several studies of individual gunmakers that each approach a half-million words.

Fortunately, several ready-made constraints exist. The days of American gunmakers steeped in the traditions of eighteenth-century Long Rifle smiths, who could make every gun component, were numbered by the machine-made sporting gun. Steadily improving distribution networks – the railways, in particular – were soon taking the products of Remington, Sharps, Winchester, Colt, Smith & Wesson, Iver Johnson, Lefever, the Crescent Arms Company and uncounted others to the farthest corners of the USA.

The output of the largest manufacturers, numbered in millions, finally undermined the need for individual craftsmanship. Consequently, gunmakers working in the USA prior to 1880 are rarely included unless they have a proven connection with multi-shot or breech-loading firearms.

The gunmaking fraternities in Europe, however, and especially in Britain, worked very differently from their North American counterparts prior to the First World War. Mass-production was confined largely to military establishments, and to aggressive government-supported private conglomerates, such as Waffenfabrik Mauser AG and Österreichische Waffenfabriks-Gesellschaft, whose output was more military than sporting.

The British had a particularly durable tradition of craftsmanship that had never been entirely subordinated to the machine. This could also be said of most other European gunmaking centres, until the unprecedented demands made by the First World War put a premium on quantity at the expense of quality.

The claims of individual nineteenth-century European gunmakers to inclusion in *The Greenhill Dictionary of Guns and Gunmakers* are often difficult to dismiss. Although many men bought components from specialist gun-lock makers, barrel riflers and stock makers, assembly and finishing were still undertaken personally. Thus many provincial British gunmakers have been included on the grounds that multi-shot handguns and breech-loading sporting guns have been (or may still be) found with appropriate marks.

Directory entries have been consciously biased toward Anglo-American affairs and, therefore, pay less detailed attention to the gunmakers operating in Brescia, Eibar, Ferlach, Liège, Saint-Étienne, Suhl and Weipert. However, an acknowledgment of the most important European makers will still be found, and a note on additional sources of information has been included in the introductory notes to the directory.

Inventors and patentees have been included where possible, although space limitations mean that priority has been given to designs that were exploited commercially at the expense of 'paper projects'. Some designers achieved stupendous totals of individual designs, particularly during the twentieth century, when the 'catch-all' patents of the 1860s had given way to the separate registry of each major component of a design.

Andrew Burgess, among the most versatile of gun designers, was granted no fewer than 836 firearms-related patents during his career; John Browning (perhaps the greatest of the great) is said to have received about 950, mostly for automatic weapons. Yet, in September 1957, *The Gun Report* related a claim made by the otherwise overlooked Crawford Loomis – who spent most of his working life with Remington – to have held 'more assignable patents than any other gun designer'.

I have tried to identify as many trademarks and brandnames as possible, although there some that still defy interpretation. A special effort has also been made to unravel monograms, which, at their most complex, can seem bafflingly obscure. The principles under which these have been analysed are described in greater detail in the directory entries entitled 'Monograms', 'National markings' and 'Trademarks and brandnames'.

When I began working on this book more than five years ago, I rashly sought an overall 'success rate' of fifty per cent: I felt that the reader should have one chance in two of finding what is sought. Once I began enlarging entries to include product details, even in shorthand form, content grew so rapidly that a book originally conceived as 80,000 words was approaching 500,000 when eventually 'time' was called.

To put this total in context, I estimate my published output to be a little over 3,000,000 words in a career spanning thirty years, and I'm sure that my good friend Ian Hogg has far exceeded even this. Consequently, although this book is genuinely ecletic, I realise that some topics are represented in far greater detail than others.

The owner of a brandname found on a Spanish 6.35mm Browning-type pocket pistol or an American Suicide Special revolver will find greater success than an enthusiast hunting a description of each of the hundreds of individual patents granted to Andrew Burgess or John Browning. Equally, it will be much easier to identify a shotgun-cartridge brandname than a military headstamp. However, where I am conscious of a shortfall in this, I have tried to provide alternative sources of information.

No one-volume guide to the worldwide gunmaking industry can hope to be comprehensive, of course, but all projects reach the point of 'publish and be damned' – where it may be better to offer the benefits of the best possible, but nonetheless incomplete, research than wait for decades until every last piece of information has been sifted.

If, indeed, this book is also what one of my friends classed as 'un-put-downable' – you look for a particular topic, but then spend time looking at unconnected things instead of focusing on the original entry – then it will have served an additional purpose very well.

Coverage will be expanded in due course, and readers wishing to help are encouraged to make contact through the Publishers or by e-mail (details of which can be found from the website http://www.gunsdictionary.fsnet.co.uk).

John Walter
Hove, England
2001

The Directory

THE DIRECTORY has been organised on as logical an alphabetical basis as can be compatible with its goals, although punctuation, ampersands and some word breaks have been ignored. In addition, some businesses and many brandnames (especially on shotgun ammunition) have always considered a prefatory 'The' as part of their title; these have been listed as 'Arms & Ammunition Company Ltd [The]' to minimise confusion.

Company names may cause problems if they are listed as 'Smith, James, & Sons Ltd', which could be a partnership of 'Smith' and 'James', or a business that had been started originally by a sole trader called 'James Smith' and subsequently expanded to include his sons. The style 'James Smith & Company' has been preferred throughout *The Greenhill Dictionary of Guns and Gunmakers*, even though it appears to disrupt alphabetical progression. The basis of classification, therefore, is effectively:

> Smith
> Smith [&] Company
> Smith [&] Son
> A.A. Smith
> A.A. Smith [&] Company
> A.A. Smith [&] Son
> A.B. Smith
> Smith [&] Brown
> Smith Carbine
> Smith Pistol
> Smith Rifle
> Smith, White [&] Company

Cross-references are indicated in several manners. Most simply say, 'Sharps (q.v.)' or '*see* Garand'. It is obvious in these cases that the keyword is 'Sharps' or 'Garand'. Where this is not so obvious, particularly as there is great scope for confusion in corporate names, an asterisk prefixes the keyword (e.g. 'James Paris ★Lee', 'Lee-★Enfield'). This is only used if the keyword is something other than the first one.

Particular care is necessary with monograms, which can be difficult to decipher, but the problems are summarised in the relevant directory entry, and the most confusing examples have been listed under every combination of their individual letters!

Brandnames and trademarks have been listed wherever possible, but numerical designations have been ignored anywhere other than in the section devoted to an individual manufacturer. Thus details of the Remington Model 700 bolt-action rifle will be found in 'Remington, rifles, bolt-action', but not under 'Model'. Numerical designations do not always appear on guns, and those that do are often easily identified by referring to sources of information listed in the individual directory entries.

Some of the best-known ammunition makers are also included, alongside many headstamp codes. However, only the surface of this complex subject has been scratched.

Proof marks may be identified from letters accompanying them, but no attempt has been made to explain the abbreviations used by military formations, except in an occasional general comment (e.g. 'German military unit marks'). There are many sources of additional information on these topics. Similarly, inspectors' marks have been ignored, with the exception of American examples. US government firearms inspectors customarily applied marks that are easily deciphered and can be used to date otherwise anonymous items.

Terminology and corporate structure

The introduction of limited liability, where the risks taken by promoters were restricted in law, brought a series of new abbreviations. Limited partnerships were formed by a general partner, who accepted complete liability, and a number of sleeping partners, whose risk was limited only to their capital investment – but only if they took no part in the running of the business. These were known as *Société en commandité* in France, frequently abbreviated to 'S.N.C.'; as *Società in accomandita* ('S.I.A.') In Italy; and as *Kommanditgesellschaft* ('KG') in Germany.

True limited-liability operations in Britain were distinguished by 'Ltd' or 'Company Ltd', although since 1977 public companies have been identified as 'plc' (public limited company). Similar businesses in the Netherlands are *naamloze vennootschap* ('NV'), and are *Aktiebolag* ('AB') in Sweden; Danish and Norwegian equivalents are usually identified as 'AS' or 'A/S'.

Public companies in France and Belgium are classed as *Société anonyme* ('SA'), the latter often gaining the additional qualification '*Belge*' ('SAB'); comparable terms include *Società per azioni* ('SPA', SpA) in Italy, and *Aktiengesellschaft* ('AG') in Germany.

Private companies, each formed in accordance with its own national rules, include *Société à responsabilité limitée* ('SARL', 's.a.r.l.') in France, *Gesellschaft mit beschränkter Haftung* ('GmbH') in Germany, and *Società a responsabilità limitata* ('SRL', 's.r.l.') in Italy. Any French company described as *Société Mixte* ('SM') is a partnership of private individuals and government agencies.

Additional information may appear in the form of 'Brothers' (often rendered simply as 'Bros.') and equivalents such as *Fratelli* ('F.lli', Italy), *Frères* (France and Belgium) and *Gebrüder* (Germany). Among the variants of 'Son' are *Sohn* (plural *Söhne*, German), *Zoon* (plural *Zonen*, Dutch), *fils* (French and Belgian), *Figlio* (plural *Figli*, Italian) and *Hijo* (plural *Hijos*, Spanish). Abbreviations for 'Propietor', often itself listed simply as 'Prop.', include *Inhaber* ('owner', German – *Inhaberin* if female). The terms *Witwe* ('German) and *Veuve* (French) both mean 'widow'.

The spelling of 'Liége' was altered officially to 'Liège' in 1946, reflecting changes in local pronunciation. The modern form is preferred throughout this book, although 'Liégeois' and 'Liégeoise' (both still in use) are unaffected.

CRITICAL BIBLIOGRAPHY AND NOTE ON SOURCES

References to sources of additional information have been provided in many entries. Further details will be found in the 'Bibliography' pages of the website: http://www.gunsdictionary.fsnet.co.uk/

General studies. *Firearms Past & Present* by Jaroslav Lugs, which has been published in Czech (1955), German (1962) and English (Grenville Publishing, London, 1973) is an underrated source of information, particularly as it takes a different perspective to the customary Anglo-American viewpoints. It has an excellent bibliography.

Gunmakers. Other studies of individual gunmakers include Johan Støckel's *Haandskydevaabens Bedømmelse* (second edition, Copenhagen, 1962), reprinted in 1992 by Journal-Verlag Schwend of Schwäbisch Hall (as *Der Neue Støckel*), with a third volume contributed by Eugen Heer. Although rarely intruding into the 'modern era', it is indispensable.

Colonel Robert E. Gardner's *Small Arms Makers* (Bonanza Books, New York, 1963), understandably biased toward US topics, was a pioneering and greatly underrated study that represents nearly 50 years of research. Its coverage may be inconsistent and occasionally frustrating, with comparatively little attention paid to individual products, but these are minor flaws.

Cataloguing British gunmaking has benefited greatly from the scholarly work of the late Howard Blackmore, whose *A Dictionary of London Gunmakers 1350–1850* (Phaidon-Christies, London, 1997) and 1999-vintage supplement are indispensable – particularly when supported by *English Gunmakers* ('The Birmingham and Provincial Gun Trade in the 18th and 19th century') by D.W. Bailey and D.A. Nie (Arms & Armour Press, London, 1978). The latter desperately needs reprinting in an enlarged and revised form. *Boothroyd's Revised Dictionary of British Gunmakers* (published privately, 1997), by Geoffrey Boothroyd and his daughter, Susan, is another invaluable source of information.

Yves Cadiou's *Grands Noms de l'Armurerie* (Crépin-Leblond, Paris, 1999), and John A. Belton's *Canadian Gunsmiths from 1608* (Museum Restoration Service, Bloomfield, 1992) are helpful, while Claude Gaier's *Five Centuries of Liège Gunmaking* (Éditions du Perron, 1996) is as attractive as its scholarship is excellent – even though it lacks an adequate directory of Liégeois gunsmiths!

Company histories. With the exception of an occasional sponsored, self-promotional or commemorative review (e.g., *F.N, 1889–1964* and the fiftieth-anniversary history of DWM) – and reprinted catalogues that give snapshots of individual activities – comparatively little information is available regarding any but the best-known makers. Colt and Winchester are served almost to saturation, whereas the activities of BSA and Savage (to name but two) hardly receive a mention.

Individually-sponsored studies of lesser manufacturers, which are often excellent in themselves, merely highlight the difficulty of balancing manufacturing history with the details sought by individual collectors.

Excellent examples of 'one-company' studies are Lieutenant-Colonel William S. Brophy's *Marlin Firearms* (Stackpole Books, Harrisburg, 1989), which delves into its subject in meticulous detail, and Harold F. Williamson's *Winchester. The Gun that Won the West* (A.S. Barnes, South Brunswick, 1962), which accepts that the history of a gunmaker is not simply that of the guns. Ellsworth S. Grant, in *The Colt Armory* (Mowbray Publishing, Lincoln, 1995), goes behind the scenes to show not only how the guns were made, but also how the manufactory operated.

The guns. So many books deal with individual topics that it is impossible to recommend more than a few. Particularly useful, however, are the all-enveloping *Small Arms of the World* (Stackpole Books, Harrisburg, eleventh edition, 1977), compiled by W.H.B. Smith, Joseph E. Smith and Edward C. Ezell; *The Greenhill Military Small Arms Data Book*, by Ian V. Hogg (1999); and

Military Small Arms of the World (Krause Publications, Iola, seventh edition, 2000) by Ian Hogg and Colonel John S.Weeks. *The Handgun*, by Geoffrey Boothroyd (Cassell, London, 1976), and *Handguns of the World*, by Edward C. Ezell (Stackpole Books, Harrisburg, 1981), present detailed overviews, whereas *Pistols of the World*, by Ian V. Hogg and John S.Weeks (DBI, Inc., Northfield, third edition, 1992), and *Rifles of the World*, by John Walter (Krause Publications, Iola, second edition, 1998), take a directory approach.

Detailed gun-by-gun listings, such as the *Gun Trader's Guide* (John E. Traister, ed., Stoeger Publishing Company, South Hackensack) and S.P. Fjestad's *The Blue Book of Used Gun Values* (Investment Rarities, Inc., Minneapolis), are published annually in the USA. Although these subordinate history to observational details, they represent invaluable sources of information.

Airguns. There is still no reliable directory of this particular subject, despite steadily growing interest. W.H.B. Smith's *Gas, Air and Spring Guns of the World* (1957) is out of date, and John Walter's *The Airgun Book* (the third edition of 1984 was the most historically orientated) has been out of print for many years. Only the recent editions of Dennis Hiller's *Air Rifles and Air Pistols* (published privately in Britain) have much to offer.

Cartridges and ammunition. There are several excellent sources of information concerning the history and identification of ammunition, not least being the work of Jakob H. Brandt and Horst H. Hamann in *Identifizierung von Handfeuer-Waffen-Munition* (Journal-Verlag Schwend, Schwäbisch Halle, 1971). I am concerned mainly with recording aids to identification; thus works such as *The Cartridge Guide*, by Ian Hogg (Arms & Armour Press, London, 1982), are invaluable. I would also like to single out *Collecting Shotgun Cartridges*, by Ken Rutterford (Stanley Paul, London, 1987), for particular praise; although this would benefit from critical review, the book offers so much information that it cries out for a

A

'a', 'A' – 1. 'A' in a seven-point star. A mark applied by an inspector working in the *Lithgow small-arms factory in New South Wales, Australia. Superseded by 'MA'; *see also* British military inspectors' marks. 2. 'A', often cursive, beneath a crown. Found on Belgian weapons: the mark of King Albert (1909–34). *See also* Cyphers, imperial and royal. 3. 'A' in a cross. A trademark found on *Gem-type airguns sold in Britain by Adolph *Arbenz of Birmingham. 4. Usually as 'a'. Found on parts for the Kar. 98k made during the Second World War by Nähmatag-Nähmaschinenteile AG of Dresden, Germany. 5. 'A', apparently above an inverted '2' forming the crossbar of the letter. An Arabic mark applied by the Iraqi Republican Guard. 6. As 'A', sometimes with an owl trademark. Found on small Browning-type autoloading pistols made by Gaspar *Arizaga of Eibar, Spain. 7. As 'A', often encircled. A *headstamp identifier associated with the *American Metallic Cartridge Company 8. A *headstamp found on rimfire and possibly other cartridges made by the *American Cartridge Company for sale in North America by *Gamble Stores. It may be accompanied by 'Airway'.

'AA' – 1. Beneath a crown. This mark will be found in the headstamps of Danish military ammunition made by the Ammunitionsarsenalet in Copenhagen during 1950–52. *See also* 'AMA'. 2. Monogram. A trademark found on automatic pistols made by *Azanza y Arrizabalaga of Eibar, Spain. 3. Monogram, 'S'-shape. Found on guns made by Fábrica de Armas SA *Alkartasuna of Guernica, Spain. 4. Applied to US military stores – including .30 Spnngfield rifles and .45 M1911A1 *Government Model pistols – refurbished by Augusta Arsenal, Georgia.

'AAA' – 1. Monogram. A trademark associated with handguns made by *Azanza y Arrizabalaga of Eibar, Spain. 2. Usually accompanied by a knight's helm. A trademark found on guns made by A. *Aldazabal of Eibar, Spain. 3. Found on a Spanish *Browning-type automatic pistol made by A. Aldazabal of Eibar, Guipúzcoa, in several patterns: (1) 6.35mm; six rounds, hammer fired; some guns may be marked 'Model 1919'. (2) 7.65mm; seven rounds, hammer fired; often marked 'Model 1916'.

'AA Auto Pistol'. Found on Browning-pattern 6.35mm and 7.65mm semi-automatic pistols made by *Azanza y Arrizabalaga of Eibar, Guipúzcoa, Spain.

'AAC' – 1. Monogram. A trademark associated with the products of the *American Arms Company of Boston, Massachusetts. 2. Found on guns made in Eibar, Spain, by *Azanza y Arrizabalaga.

AACO, 'A.A.Co.' – 1. Found in the headstamps of the products of the *American Ammunition Co. of Oak Park, Chicago and Muscatine, USA. 2. A *Suicide Special revolver made by the T.J. *Ryan Pistol Mfg. Co. of Springfield, Massachusetts, USA, in the late nineteenth century. 3. A superimposition-type monogram with 'A', 'A' and 'C' of near-equal dominance. A mark found on the grips of revolvers made by the *American Arms Company.

AAI Corporation. *See* ArmaLite.

'A-Airway'. *See* Airway.

'aak'. This mark will be found on pistols, rifles, machine-guns and components made during the German occupation of Czechoslovakia by Waffenwerke Brünn AG of Prague. They date from the Second World War.

'AAW'. *See* A.A. *White.

'AB' – 1. *See* A. *Buckminster. 2. Monogram. A trademark associated with the products of *Bersaluce Arieto-Aurtena y Cia of Eibar, Spain (actually 'BA').

'aba', 'ABA' – 1. As 'aba'; a trademark found on barrel-insert components made for *Erma by *Alig & Baumgärtel of Aschaffenburg, Germany. 2. As 'ABA', sometimes as a monogram with 'B' dominant. Used prior to c. 1920 by August Blatt of Albrechts bei Suhl in Thüringen, Germany.

Abadie was apparently a gunmaker, possibly an employee of the *Nagant brothers. His 1874-patent loading-gate is found on some Nagant revolvers made in the period 1878–90. Opening the gate allows the trigger to rotate the cylinder without needing to overcome the pressure of the mainspring, the hammer being disconnected. This facilitates ejecting spent cases or reloading the gun. (Note: Abadie is often mistakenly identified as a Portuguese army officer, as the 'Système à Abadie' is found on Portuguese guns in addition to Serbian issue.)

Abakan. A codename applied to a competition held in the USSR (subsequently in Russia) to find a replacement for the venerable *Kalashnikov assault rifle. The trials apparently began in the late 1980s and continued to 1995 or later. The name has often been (mistakenly) applied specifically to the 5.45mm *Nikonov or NSM rifle.

Abas, Abas Major. These names were applied to a .177-calibre spring-air pistol designed in 1944/45 by A.A., A.H. and S.C. Brown, protected by British Patent 604,411 and made in Birmingham by A.A. *Brown & Sons from 1947 until the early 1950s. The Abas Major was cocked by pulling down on the trigger guard, and loaded through a tap at the rear of the spring cylinder.

Abawerke. *See* Alig & Baumgärtel.

'ABB'. *See* A.B. *Blackington.

Abbey – 1. Usually found as 'The Abbey', on shotgun cartridges marketed by C.H. *Smith & Sons of Birmingham. They seem to have borne headstamps identifying *Nobel Industries or *Eley Kynoch. 2. Edmund Abbey, Newport Pagnell, Buckinghamshire. This English country gunmaker was listed in High Street in 1852, and in nearby John Street from 1862 until about 1870. His marks have been reported on self-cocking *pepperboxes and cap-lock revolvers. 3. F.J. Abbey & Company was a partnership of Frederick J. Abbey and Thomas H. Foster, who made cap-lock sporting guns – including rifles, shotguns and pistols – plus break-action cartridge shotguns from 43 South Clark Street, Chicago, Illinois, USA. The shotgun patented by Frederick J. Abbey seems to have been made until the late 1870s, when the company was sold to E. ★Thomas, Jr. **4.** Frederick J. Abbey, a gunmaker/inventor of 43 South Clark Street, Chicago, Illinois, was active from 1853 to 1879. He received US Patent 114,081 on 25 April 1871 to protect a shotgun-style breech locked by two lateral pins entering a recess in the barrel-block. Frederick Abbey made cap-lock target rifles before becoming a founding partner of F.J. Abbey & Company. **5.** George T. Abbey. Working from 1858 to 1874 in Chicago, Illinois, USA, George Abbey designed a breech-loading shotgun in the late 1860s, receiving US patent 87,814 on 16 March 1869. A vertical post-lock in the rear of the action was operated by either an under-lever or a catch ahead of the trigger guard. The under-lever lock comprised lugs on the bolt-head, while the catch relied on a pin pushed up into the barrel-block. There were also two lugs beneath the barrel. George Abbey is believed to have been the son of Frederick J. Abbey. **6.** Abbey Gun & Ammunition Company [The], Goring upon Thames and Wallingford, Oxfordshire; and Reading, Berkshire, England. This was a trading style of what later became the Abbey Supply Company, adopted in 1974. The company specialised in gun lubricants, but also imported Chinese-made airguns and Danish Pallet airgun ammunition into Britain. The move to Mill Lane, Wallingford took place in 1976, and to Great Knollys Street in Reading in 1981. Operations ceased in the early 1990s. **7.** Abbey Improved Chilled Shot Company Ltd; Newcastle upon Tyne, Northumberland, England. This metalworking business advertised itself as a manufacturer of 'Improved Chilled Shot…and…Hard and Patent Shot' as well as the loader of Abbeyrite shotgun cartridges. An advertisement in the 1910 edition of W.W. ★Greener's *The Gun and Its Development* noted that Abbey was then supplying more than twenty sizes of shot, ranging from 'LC' to 'D' – respectively six and 2,600 to the ounce. It is suspected that Greener had something to do with the Abbey company (the book notes that 'Exporters [should] apply to W.W. Greener…for prices'), but the operations were acquired by ★Eley Brothers shortly before the First World War.

Abbeyrite. A name associated with shotgun cartridges supplied to the gun trade prior to 1913/14 (wholesale only) by the ★Abbey Improved Shot Company Ltd.

'A.B.C.' Found in the headstamps of cartridges made in West Haven, Connecticut, USA, by the ★American Buckle & Cartridge Company.

Abercrombie & Fitch Company. Founded in 1892 by Ezra H. Fitch (1865–1930) and David T. Abercrombie (1867–1931), this purveyor of equipment for explorers, huntsmen, fishermen and sportsmen – including guns and ammunition – traded from 53–57 West 36th Street, New York, until the Abercrombie & Fitch Building was erected in 1916/17 on the corner of Madison Avenue and 45th Street. Prior to the emergence of ★Stoeger as the sole agency, Abercrombie & Fitch distributed refurbished 7.65mm Swiss-style Lugers; these were apparently assembled in Germany, but exported to the USA by ★Hämmerli. Most had Hämmerli-made barrels. The quantities involved remain in dispute, estimates ranging from an implausibly small forty-nine to an undoubtedly optimistic 1,500. Abercrombie & Fitch purchased ★Von Lengerke & Detmold of New York in 1928, and Von Lengerke & Antoine of Chicago a year later.

Subsequently, retail outlets were established throughout the USA: in Oakbrook, Illinois; Short Hills, New Jersey; Palm Beach and Bal Harbor, Florida; Troy, Michigan; Colorado Springs, Colorado; and San Francisco, California. The business traded profitably until the early 1970s, but filed a bankruptcy petition in August 1975 and effectively ceased to exist at the end of a close-down sale on 20 November 1977. Most of the guns and accessories sold by Abercrombie & Fitch can be identified by the distinctive cursive 'AFCo.' trademarks. *See also* Roger J. Bender, *Luger Holsters and Accessories of the 20th Century*.

Abergavenny Ace [The]. Found on shotgun cartridges sold in Wales by ★Bevan & Evans, then Bevan & Pritchard of Abergavenny.

Abesser – 1. Paul Abesser; Suhl in Thüringen, Germany. Listed in the directories as a sales agency, 1920. **2.** Abesser & Merkel; Suhl in Thüringen, Germany. Listed as a gunsmith during 1920–30, owned by Paul Abesser & Ernst Merkel.

Abingdon – 1. Abingdon Works Company [The]. This business was much less important than the Abingdon Works Company Ltd, the relationship being in name only. It was operated by members of the Cartland family from c. 1891 until the beginning of the twentieth century. **2.** Abingdon Works Company Ltd [The]. Trading from 94–97 Bath Street and Shadwell Street in Birmingham, Warwickshire, England, this business was incorporated in 1875. The principal shareholders were William M. ★Scott and Thomas Mabbutt, together with the partners of the earlier Abingdon Works trade association (founded 1872): Thomas Bentley, William Bourne, Charles Cooper, John Dent Goodman, Charles Playfair, Charles ★Pryse, Richard Redman, Joseph Smith, John Field ★Swinburn, Joseph ★Wilson and F. & H. Woodward. Many advertisements placed in the Birmingham directories in 1876 described the business as 'Manufacturers of Snider, Chassepot, Martini, and (Sole Manufacturers) of The "Swinburn" Breech Actions' – as well as military and sporting-gun nipples, roller skates, nipple wrenches, turn-screws, cleaning rods and lock vices. The Abingdon Works Company Ltd went into voluntary liquidation in 1889.

'ABL'. Often accompanied by a date (e.g. '1953'), this property mark was applied to Belgian service weapons – 'Armée Belge–Belge Leger' (i.e. 'Belgian Army' in French and Flemish). It has often been mistakenly listed as the designation of the ★SAFN rifle, but may be encountered on stores ranging from clothing to machine-guns.

'ac', 'A.C.' – 1. Usually as 'A.C.' or 'A C'. A designation mark found on British ★Snider and ★Martini-pattern artillery carbines. **2.** As 'ac'. Found on submachine-guns, pistols, rifles, signal pistols and parts made during the Second World War for the German Army by Carl ★Walther Waffenfabrik AG of Zella-Mehlis. **3.** As 'AC'. *See* Alexander ★Cameron.

ACAO. A superimposition-type monogram with 'A', 'C' and 'A' of near-equal dominance. Correctly 'AACO' (q.v.); used by the ★American Arms Company.

'A.C.C.' [The] – 1. Found on 12-bore shotgun cartridges retailed by ★Armstrong of Newcastle upon Tyne, England. The mark is believed to represent 'Armstrong & Co. Cartridge'. **2.** Also as 'A.C.Co.' Found in the headstamps of ammunition made by the ★Austin Cartridge Company of Cleveland, Ohio, USA.

Accelerating Firearms Company. This was an unsuccessful – and short-lived – promotional agency for a breech-loading gun designed by Azel Lyman. Its activities seem to have been confined to 1861–69.

Accelerator. A mechanism, usually consisting of a lever, that increases the rearward velocity of the recoiling bolt to separate it more effectively from a recoiling barrel. Accelerators are often found in machine-guns, where the purpose is to increase the rate of fire. They may also be encountered in auto-loading rifles, often simply to increase the power of the operating stroke and enhance reliability.

Accles – 1. James G. Accles was born of Irish stock in 1850 in Bendigo, then in the Australian state of Victoria (now in New South Wales). His parents moved to the USA in 1861, where he was educated. After an engineering apprenticeship with ★Colt's Patent Fire Arms Manufacturing Company, Accles moved to Britain in 1872. By 1874, he was employed as an engineer by Richard Jordan ★Gatling, helping to set up fifteen ammunition and machine-gun factories for the company prior to 1887. Accles left Gatling in 1888 to take part in an ill-fated venture, The ★Gatling Arms & Ammunition Company Ltd, which sought to develop markets for the distinctive machine-guns in Europe. When this project collapsed, Accles became a partner in ★Grenfell & Accles, to which much of the business and stock of The Gatling Arms & Ammunition Company had passed. Grenfell & Accles made machine-guns, revolvers and similar weapons. When the company also failed, about 1894, Accles formed the Accles Arms & Ammunition Manufacturing Company Ltd (sometimes known simply as Accles, Ltd) to make bicycles and ammunition. Accles' business failed again in 1899 and, after a brief association with Accles & Pollock Ltd (1901–03), he worked for the ★Birmingham Small Arms Company Ltd on a freelance basis, securing several patents in collusion with BSA and George ★Norman. Then he moved on to Accles & Shelvoke, described below. Accles is best known for his work with machine-guns. British Patent 5436/81 was granted in 1881 to protect a rotary magazine-feeder and a Gatling-type machine-gun. At the time, Accles was living at 41 Craven Street, Strand, London, and in Hartford, Connecticut, USA. A comparable US Patent, 290,622 of 18 December 1883, was sought from Hartford and assigned to the Gatling Gun Company. US Patent 348,180, protecting a machine-gun carriage, was sought from an address in Hartford and granted on 31 August 1886. Patents granted to protect the Accles Gun are listed in the following entry. British Patent 17,993/81 was granted jointly with H.H. Grenfell to protect a double-action simultaneous-extraction revolver, whereas 18,858/99 was granted on 3 September 1899 to protect a method of cooling machine-gun barrels. **2.** Accles Arms & Ammunition Manufacturing Company Ltd [The], Perry Barr, Birmingham, Warwickshire, England, c. 1894–99. Formed by the inventor James George Accles, this company succeeded to the firm of ★Grenfell & Accles, to which much of the business and stock of The Gatling Arms & Ammunition Company had passed. Grenfell & Accles had made machine-guns, revolvers, shotgun cartridges and similar items until it failed. About 1894, Accles formed a business of his own (sometimes known simply as Accles, Ltd) to make bicycles and ammunition in the Holford Works, which had been passed down through the various companies in the series. Trading ceased in 1899. **3.** Accles Gun, or Accles-Gatling Gun. British Patent 9455/88 was granted on 28 June 1888 to protect the Accles crank-operated rotating-barrel machine-gun (a modification of the Gatling). Its US equivalent, 426,356 of 22 April 1890, was sought from London. US Patent 487,238 of 6 December 1892 – a feed mechanism for machine-guns – was sought from Birmingham, England. The US Navy bought about 100 of these, adapted from the Gatling design by the latter's one-time employee James G. Accles. They were made in Britain by Grenfell & Accles, and purchased from the Driggs Ordnance Company of Washington, D.C. **4.** Accles & Pollock, Oldbury, England. This tube maker and general engineering company manufactured a vast number of parts for British small-arms, including ★Lee-Enfield rifles. For example, 100,000 'Barrels, .303 rifle, Mk 3' were supplied in 1944 to the Royal Ordnance Factory, ★Maltby, for assembly into Lee-Enfield No. 4 rifles. The rifling was formed by compressing the blanks on to a mandrel, the chamber being formed separately. Accles & Pollock often used the code 'M 1'. *See also* British military manufacturers' marks. **5.** Accles Positive Feed. Patented in 1882, this was fitted to some Gatling Guns. It held large quantities of ammunition (e.g., 104 .45-70 rounds) in a large vertical ring magazine. A propellor plate, connected to the gun-feed mechanism, drove the cartridges down through the body under the guidance of helical grooves in the end-plates. Unfortunately, this magazine was cumbersome, complex and easily damaged. Its problems were only partly solved by the advent of a quick-loader in 1886, and success was short-lived. Side-mounted Accles Positive Feeds were made for Danish fortress Gatlings, but as far as the US Army was concerned, the improved ★Bruce Feed was preferable. **6.** Accles & Shelvoke Ltd, Talford Street Engineering Works, Birmingham, Warwickshire. Founded in 1913 by James Accles and George Shelvoke, this business initially made humane cattle killers in accordance with the patents of Accles and Charles Cash. However, links were also forged with Frank ★Clarke, and it is suspected that Accles & Shelvoke made the prototypes of his ★Titan. The ★Warrior – patented by Clarke in association with Edwin ★Anson – was made in quantity in the early 1930s, and the ★Acvoke, designed by John ★Arrowsmith, followed post-war. As late as 1960, the business was still being listed as 'humane killer manufacturers'.

'A.C. County' [The]. A mark found on shotgun cartridges handled in southern England by A. ★Chamberlain of Salisbury.

Accuracy International Ltd. Based in Portsmouth, Hampshire, England, this company is best known as an importer of Walther firearms and airguns (succeeding ★Milbro). It was formed in the 1970s by Malcolm Cooper and his wife, Sarah. After making front-sight inserts and accessories under the 'AI' trademark, the company developed the purpose-built PM sniper rifle, adopted by the British Army – as the L96A1 – after trials lasting several years. The PM featured a bolt with a fully enclosed head and a sixty-degree throw. Two stock sides, moulded from olive-drab plastic, were bolted on to the aluminium chassis supporting the action to overcome warping in woodwork. The basic design has now become the AW (Arctic Warfare) after successful tests in Sweden.

'**Accuratus' [The].** A name associated with shotgun cartridges marketed by W.P. *Jones of Birmingham prior to the First World War.

Accu-Tek, Inc., Chino, California, USA. Maker of the AT-32 and AT-380 pocket pistols in 7.65mm Auto and 9mm Short respectively.

'**ACD'.** A monogram found on pistols made in Spain by Domingo *Acha y Compañía of Ermua. It should actually be read as 'DAC'.

ACDW. A concentric-type monogram with all four letters of equal significance. Correctly 'WDAC' (q.v.); used by the *Warner-Davis Arms Corporation.

Ace – **1.** Found on *Langenhan made Millita-type airguns imported into Britain. Possibly used by Frank *Dyke & Company Ltd of London, as it is usually accompanied by a shamrock. **2.** Often accompanied by 'The'. Found on shotgun ammunition made by the *Mullerite Cartridge Works of Birmingham as 'The Ace' or 'The Ace Long Range'. **3.** About 11,000 of these simplified *Government Model Colt semi-automatic pistols were made from 1931 to 1941 and during 1946/47. The use of .22 rimfire ammunition allowed recoil operation to be eschewed in favour of simple *blowback. Colt also offered a .45/.22 kit, which enabled a standard M1911A1 to be converted to fire rimfire ammunition. Made from 1938 to 1954, with a break during the Second World War, the kit had Stevens sights prior to 1947, and Colt Master patterns thereafter; it included a slide, a barrel and bushing, a return spring, a magazine, an ejector and a slide-stop. There were also a few .22/.45 kits, little more than 100 being made during 1938–42. *See also* Service Ace.

ACF. A shield-borne monogram consisting of 'A' and 'F' crossed diagonally, with 'C' (and sometimes a concentric 'o') superimposed. Correctly 'AFC' (q.v.); associated with Auguste Francotte et Cie.

ACG. A concentric-type monogram, with the 'G' and 'A' prominent. Correctly 'GAC' (q.v.); used by *Garate, Anitua y Cia.

Acha – **1.** Acha Hermanos y Compañía, Ermua, Guipúzcoa, Spain. Active from 1916 until 1927, this gun-making business was responsible for the *Atlas, *Ermua Model 1924 and *Looking Glass pistols. Some of the products may also bear the marks of Fabrique d'Armes de *Grande Précision. **2.** Domingo Acha y Compañía. Trading from the small Spanish town of Ermua, this company succeeded *Acha Hermanos c. 1927 and continued to market *Atlas and *Looking Glass pistols until the end of the Spanish Civil War in 1939. **3.** Domingo Acha y Compañía, Vizcaya, Spain. A maker of *Ruby-pattern semi-automatic pistols for the French Army during the First World War.

'**Achilles' [The].** A shotgun cartridge made in Britain by *Eley Bros. prior to the acquisition of the company by Explosives Trades Ltd in 1918.

Acier Comprimé. A French term ('compressed steel'), often found on revolvers made in France and Belgium during the last quarter of the nineteenth century. Also misleadingly used on revolvers made in Spain by *Apaolozo Hermanos of Zumorraga.

Ackermann. Jasper L. Ackermann, a gun designer resident in Monon, Indiana, USA, received US Patent 633,939 of 26 September 1899 (protecting a safety interlock for breech-loading guns) and US Patent 667,051 of 29 January 1901 for a break-action gun lock.

Acland. Francis E.D. Acland, an inventor resident in London, was the co-grantee of US Patent 472,244 of 5 April 1892 (sought jointly with Carl Holmstrom), protecting a gun lock, and US Patent 536,591 of 2 April 1895 (sought jointly with Louis Silverman and B. Orman) for a cartridge-belt loading machine. The latter was subsequently assigned to the *Maxim-Nordenfelt Guns & Ammunition Company Ltd.

'**ACM'.** *See* Alfred C. *Manning.

'**Acme' [The]** – **1.** A shotgun cartridge made in Britain by *Eley Bros. prior to the acquisition of the company by Explosives Trades Ltd in 1918, and thereafter by *Eley-Kynoch Ltd. **2.** A ribbed airgun slug made by *Cox & Sons of Aston juxta Birmingham, Warwickshire, England, from 1909 until the beginning of the First World War in 1914, although work may have been continued elsewhere as late as 1935. **3.** Found on a knife pistol. *See* Joseph *Rodgers. **4.** Associated with revolvers made in the 1890s by *Hopkins & Allen of Norwich, Connecticut, USA, for *Hulbert Bros. & Company. Essentially, they were similar to the enclosed-hammer *Forehand Model.

'**ACP', 'A.C.P.'** – **1.** An abbreviation of 'Automatic Colt Pistol', first applied in the early twentieth century, now customarily used to distinguish the proprietary Colt-Browning cartridges – .25 (6.35mm Auto), .32 (7.65mm Auto), .38 (9mm Short), .38 Super and .45. **2.** On US military firearms – *see* A.C. *Perrin. **3.** 'AC' above 'P', in a shield. Applied by inspectors working in the *Lithgow small-arms factory in New South Wales, Australia. *See also* British military inspectors' marks.

Acra. A brandname associated with *Mauser-pattern bolt-action rifles made in the USA by Reinhart *Fajen. 'Acraglas' was applied by Fajen and other gunsmiths to identify an early form of synthetic wood used in rifle stocks.

'**ACT'.** *See* A.C. *Treago.

Action – **1.** A general term for the portion of a gun (of practically any type) containing the principal operating parts, particularly the locking mechanism and the trigger unit. Popularly associated with rifles and shotguns, sometimes it is synonymous with 'frame'. **2.** A compact Spanish Browning-type pistol made in Eibar, Guipúzcoa, by Modesto *Santos; 6.35mm, six rounds, striker fired.

Acvoke. A spring-air pistol designed in Britain in the mid-1940s by John *Arrowsmith and made by *Accles & Shelvoke, 1948–54. An unwieldy gun with a concentric barrel and air cylinder, it was cocked by a butt-strap lever. As many as 20,000 may have been made, although the serial numbers seem to begin at something other than '1'.

ACW. A concentric-type monogram with all three letters equally dominant. Correctly 'WAC' (q.v.); used by the *Warner Arms Company.

ACWD. A concentric-type monogram with all four letters of equal significance. Correctly 'WDAC' (q.v.); used by the *Warner-Davis Arms Corporation.

'**A.C. Wiltshire' [The].** Encountered on shotgun cartridges handled by A. *Chamberlain of Salisbury, Wiltshire, England.

'**ad'.** A mark associated with German military small-arms and ammunition components made during the Second World War by Patronen-, Zündhütchen- und Metallwarenfabrik of Schönebeck an der Elbe.

Adams – **1.** Arthur Adams. A British gun-barrel maker. *See* Adams & Tait. **2.** F.W. Adams. An inspector of military rifles in 1904, using an 'FWA' mark. *See also* US arms inspectors' marks. **3.** Henry Adams. A London gunmaker occupying premises – successively – at 18, 51 and 54 Gray's Inn Lane (1858–78), Adams was granted British Patent 1827/73 of 1873 to protect an automatic hammer safety system that locked the mechanism unless the butt was gripped tightly. *See also* Adams & Company, perhaps his successor. **4.** Henry W. Adams was the designer of the breech-loading firearm protected by US Patent 11,685, granted on 19 September 1854 while he was domiciled in New York. When a crank handle was turned, the disc-breech rotated until a hole bored through it gave access to the chamber; when the handle was returned, the chamber was effectively sealed by the forward disc-wall. **5.** James S. Adams was an inspector of US military rifles and hand-guns from 1894 until 1904, using a 'JSA' mark. He held the position of Assistant Foreman of the Assembling Room in the *Springfield Armory for much of this peri-od. *See also* US arms inspectors' marks. **6.** John Adams was the younger brother of Robert Adams, with whom he appears to have been in partnership from c. 1845 until the formation of *Deane, Adams & Deane in 1851. His breech-loading cartridge revolver was subsequently adopted by the British government, whereupon Adams left the *London Armoury Company to form the Adams Patent Small Arms Company. Protection granted to John Adams for his revolvers included British Patent 2824/57 of 7 November 1857, for a rammer and lock details. The patent records his domicile as Queen's Road, Dalston, Middlesex. British Patent 1758/61, granted on 12 July 1861, protected a gun with a one-piece barrel/frame forging and an optional pinfire cylinder. At that time, Adams was living at 14 St Paul's Road, Camden Square, London. US Patent 30,602, similar to British Patent 1758/61, was granted on 6 November 1860 and assigned to Thomas *Poultney of Baltimore, Maryland. British Patent 1959/66 of 28 July 1866 protected an improve-ment of the 1861-type revolver frame and a method of loading metal-case centrefire cartridges from the front of the cylinder. British Patent 2961/67 was granted on 22 October 1867, for an improved loading-gate and rod ejector; and US Patent 85,350 followed on 28 December 1868 to protect many of the features originally included in British Patents 1959/66 and 2961/67. British Patent 2258/72 of 1872 was granted to protect an improved rod ejector with a swivel-mount attached to the revolver frame. **7.** John S. Adams, a gun designer in Taunton, Massachusetts, USA, was granted several US Patents in the 1860s. They included no. 39,455, granted on 11 August 1863, to protect a firearm in which the barrel piv-oted downward around 'false trunnions' (the major point of claim) and a 'packing piece' was added to combat wear. US Patent 44,377 of 27 September 1864 covered a gun with a tip-up chamber operated by the trigger guard 'tongued and grooved' to the breech block so that it could be slid backward to operate the extractor. US Patent 45,010 – granted on 30 May 1865 – protected a method of compressing a cartridge around a ball. **8.** P. Adams was the joint patentee, with S. Adams and John Simmons, of a magazine rifle: US Patent 275,085 of 3 April 1883, sought from Antioch, California. **9.** Robert Adams, born in 1809, traded in London from about 1830 until 1845, then became the manager of the business of George & John *Deane. Robert Adams participated in *Deane, Adams & Deane from 1851 until selling his gun-

making interests in 1856 to the *London Armoury Company (which subsequently he managed). However, he returned to independent trading in 1858 and occupied a warehouse in Henry Street, Bermondsey, from 1858; retail premises were maintained at 76 King William Street, London, during 1859–65. Then the business was bankrupted, but reappeared in a different form at 40 Pall Mall in 1866, and continued virtually until Adams died in 1870. Robert Adams, like many others of his family, was a prolific inventor, obtaining many patents and registered designs. He is known to have made airguns and air canes in addition to firearms, but is best known for his distinc-tive self-cocking cap-lock revolver (*see below*), patented in 1851. British Patents 1954/1854 and 285/60 protected breech-loading rifles, while British Patents 2725/1867 and 3216/1867 were granted for extractor designs. Among Adams' ammunition designs were British Registered Designs 3033/1851 and 3277/1852 for pro-jectiles, and British Patent 1/1852 for a cartridge. British Patent 2000/1854 was granted to protect barrel-boring and rifling machinery. **10.** S. Adams was the joint paten-tee, with his brother P. Adams and John Simmons, of a magazine gun protected by US Patent 275,085 of 3 April 1883. **11.** Samuel Adams. This US arms inspector, active immediately before the American Civil War, accepted rifle-muskets and cap-lock revolvers distinguished with his 'SA' mark. *See also* US arms inspectors' marks. **12.** Walter Adams the Younger. The son of Walter Adams the Elder, who had traded in Birmingham, England, from 1805, this gunsmith became an integral member of his father's company in 1865 – but, after trading under Adams & Son, reverted to his own name in 1869. Operations seem to have moved from Upper Priory, Birmingham, to 47 Whittall Street (1867–72) and latterly 281/2 Newton Street (1873–78). Sporting guns, includ-ing breech-loaders, have been found with his marks. **13.** Adams Bros. & Burnley Ltd, Harrow Street Metal Works, Harrow, Middlesex, England. A maker of British rifle-type 'Dischargers, Grenade, 21/2-inch, No. 2 Mk 1', 1943. Also supplied six experimental all-metal *Lee-Enfield No. 4 rifles, 1943. Adams Bros. & Burnley used the code 'S 3'. *See also* British military manufacturers' marks. **14.** Adams & Company, the well-known London gunmaking business, owned by Henry Adams, traded at 9 Finsbury Place South, EC, during 1870–80. A move to 32 Finsbury Pavement occurred in 1881, and thence to 22 Denmark Street, Soho, between 1894 and 1897. Trading ceased in 1899. Henry Adams patented an automatic hammer safety system in 1873, and his company is known to have made pin- and centrefire revolvers – probably including many of those that bore the name of John Adams. Shotgun cartridges were also among his products. **15.** Adams Patent Small Arms Company Ltd [The]. This gunmaking business was established at 391 Strand, London, England, on 15 August 1864, with John Adams as its managing director and (in addition to Adams) F. Mortimore, J.W. and J.S. Rooth, P. Browne, E.M. Ricketts and J.F. Shattock holding the shares. The origi-nal company was dissolved in July 1881, but immediately reconstituted under the aegis of William Watts Locke & Company and traded as 'Adams's Patent Small Arms Manufacturing Company', W. Watts Locke & Company, Proprietors until April 1894. Flare pistols were made in addition to revolvers. Toward the end of this period, a

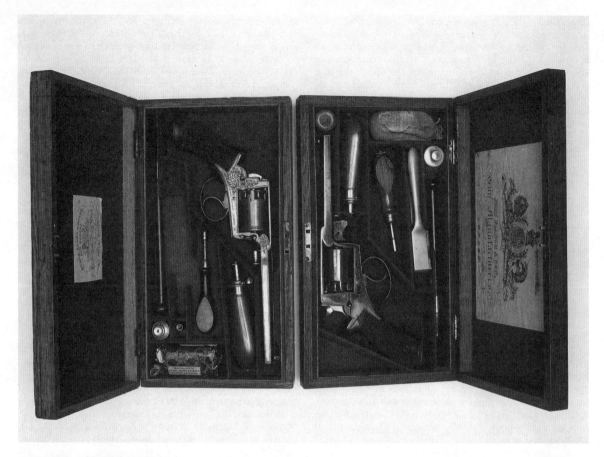

ADAMS REVOLVER

Adams (16)

This double-action design was successfully exhibited at the 1851 Great Exhibition, at the Crystal Palace in London, as a product of *Deane, Adams & Deane. The master protection was English Patent no. 13,527 (rifles, locks, breech-loaders and revolvers), granted on 24 February 1851, but comparable protection was sought elsewhere (e.g., US Patent 9694 of 3 May 1853, Belgian Patent 5061/794 and French Patent 12,247). British Patent 2712/53 was granted on 22 November 1853 to protect the Hesitating Revolver Lock; British Patent 2645/54 of 15 December 1854 protected a rammer system and additional lock details. These improvements were also embodied in US Patents of 3 June 1856 and 7 April 1857.

British Patent 50/64 of 8 January 1864 was intended to protect a cartridge revolver with an exchangeable cap-lock cylinder, but provisional protection was refused. The guns were manufactured by a variety of contractors: a licence was even granted in the United States to the *Massachusetts Arms Company. They were also produced in Belgium, and by a handful of British gunmakers.

The rammer was originally carried separately, but later was replaced by pivoting levers mounted on the gun; these were patented by (among others) John *Rigby, Robert Adams, John *Kerr and Joseph Brazier. The Kerr rammer, patented in July 1855, was commonly incorporated on military-issue guns; Brazier's rammer of April 1855 was probably the most efficient, but was confined only to the products of a few individual gunsmiths. Adams revolvers enjoyed popularity in British circles, but the absence of a single-action feature soon led to the introduction of the *Beaumont-Adams.

Cased Adams (left) *and Beaumont-Adams* (right) *revolvers, the latter being identifiable by the spurred hammer.*
Courtesy of Wallis & Wallis, Lewes.

move occurred to 40–42 Crampton Street, London. The suffix 'Ltd' was dropped in 1892. **16.** Adams revolver. *See* panel, facing page. **17.** Adams Revolving Arms Company. This agency was formed in New York City during the American Civil War, to promote the revolvers designed in Britain by Robert ★Adams, Frederick ★Beaumont and John ★Kerr. The .31 Pocket and .36-calibre Navy guns were made under licence by the ★Massachusetts Arms Company, but only the smaller pattern bears 'Adams' marks. **18.** Adams & Tait. A partnership between Arthur Adams and Joseph Henry Tait, this made barrels for, among other guns, Alexander ★Henry's rifles and the ★Hill & Williams airgun. The workshop was sited at 46 Price Street, Birmingham, England, from 1862 to 1864, after which it moved to 1 Price Street. City directories list it at 1 New Buildings, Price Street, between 1865 and 1899, where operations are believed to have continued until 1929. **19.** Adams & Westlake, founded in 1847 in Chicago, Illinois, USA, was best known for its 'Adlake'-brand oil lamps. The partnership has been linked with the production of simple .22 rimfire rifles and the ★Columbia push-in barrel BB Gun in the early 1900s, but it seems much more likely that these were given away to encourage young, enthusiastic and gullible sales agents.

Adamy. Gebrüder Adamy, Suhl in Thüringen, Windeweg 2 (1941). Listed as a maker of 'hunting weapons' (*Jagdwaffen*). Known to have included sporting rifles and – particularly – three-barrel guns (★*Drillinge*) among its products, this partnership of Franz and Albert Adamy ceased operations at the end of the Second World War.

Adasa. *See* Armamento de Aviación SA.

Adcock. G.T. Adcock. This English gunsmith maintained a sales office in London at 3 Gray's Inn Lane, W.C. (1861–63), and later at 22 Gray's Inn Road (1864–78).

ADCW. A concentric-type monogram with all four letters of equal significance. Correctly 'WDAC' (q.v.); used by the ★Warner-Davis Arms Corporation.

Adgey. Willam Adgey, an Irish gunmaker trading in Belfast prior to the First World War, marked sporting guns and ammunition. These included shotgun cartridges sold under the brandname Favourite.

Adirondack Fire Arms Company, Plattsburgh, New York State. Manufacturer of ★Robinson patent breech-loading magazine rifles, succeeding A.S. ★Babbitt. The business may have been purchased by the ★Winchester Repeating Fire Arms Company in 1874, or may simply have ceased trading when Winchester bought rights to the Robinson patents.

Adjustable Ranging Telescope ['ART']. One of the first military-issue sights with graduations allowing the firer to improve accuracy by using an internal man-height/distance correlation grid, this telescope pattern was the work of the Leatherwood Optical Company. *See* Sights, optical.

'ADK'. *See* A.D. ★King.

Adkin – 1. Henry Adkin established his gunmaking business in Offa Street, Bedford, in 1849, and traded there for at least twenty years. Marks applied by his successor – Henry Adkin & Sons – have been recorded on sporting guns, airgun ammunition, and a selection of shotgun cartridges sold under brandnames such as Ajax, Demon and Reliance. Usually confined to 12-bore, these normally prove to have been made by ★Eley or the Eley Division

of IMI. Trading is believed to have ceased in 1937. **2.** Henry Adkin was listed in London directories in 1850–59 and possibly later as a gunsmith and agent for John ★Smith & Son, at 4 Thavie's Inn, Holborn, W.C.

ADL. A designation applied to sporting rifles made by the ★Remington Arms Company (Model A̲, D̲e L̲uxe), distinguishing guns that had stocks with chequering and high combs. The 'ADL' stock subsequently became the standard pattern, although the term has never been dropped. *See also* BDL.

Adler – 1. A brandname found on shotgun ammunition made by W. ★Güttler of Reichenstein, Germany. **2.** Adler GmbH, Waffen- und Maschinenfabrik. Listed in Germany in the period between the wars, this gunsmithing business may have been a successor to Adlerwaffenwerke (q.v.). **3.** Adler pistol. A 7mm-calibre ★blowback semi-automatic patented in Germany on 22 August 1905 (no. 176,909) and in Britain on 25 October 1906 (no. 14,023/06) in the name of Max Hermsdorff. Markings on the guns suggest the involvement of Haeussler and Engelbrecht & Wolff, possibly Paul ★Häussler and the successors to Hermsdorff respectively. Only a few guns were made prior to about 1910. The receivers bear a distinctive trademark on the right side, consisting of a displayed eagle, clasping a riband in its talons, over an encircled 'MHZ'. *See* Karl Pawlas, 'Die "Adler-Pistole", eine interressante Konstruktion', in *Waffen-Revue* no. 9 (June 1973). **4.** Adlerwaffenwerk(e). This gunmaking establishment was formed in Zella St Blasii, Germany, about 1905–06 to exploit patents granted to Max Hermsdorff, making 7mm Adler pistols prior to 1910–11. The original company may have failed very quickly: surviving guns all bear Hermsdorff's trademark (an eagle and an encircled 'MHZ'), but invariably are marked as the products of Adlerwaffenwerke, Engelbrecht & Wolff.

'Admiral' [The]. Found on shotgun ammunition loaded by William ★Powell & Son of Birmingham, using ★Eley-Kynoch components. *See also* General.

Adolph. Fred Adolph, Genoa, New York State, and New York City. This US gunsmith-engineer, active from the early 1900s, was a champion of high-velocity rifle ammunition. Catalogues produced in the early 1920s showed cartridges ranging from '.22 Long Range Pistol' to '.40 Newton Express', but Adolph (who designed an automatic rifle in 1913/14) lost interest in guns and retired in 1924 to concentrate on music.

'A&D PATENT'. Found on shotguns, acknowledging use of the patents granted to ★Anson & Deeley.

Adrianson. John Adrianson, an inventor domiciled in Chicago, Illinois, USA, patented a 'revolver attachment for guns' on 1 January 1907 (US no. 839,978) and an 'extensible jacket for revolvers' on 4 June 1907 (no. 855,439).

Adsett. Thomas Adsett & Son operated a gunmaking business, trading from 101 High Street, Guildford, Surrey. Subsequently, the business was moved to 90 High Street, where work continued until the beginning of the Second World War.

ADWC. A concentric-type monogram with all four letters of equal significance. Correctly 'WDAC' (q.v.); used by the ★Warner-Davis Arms Corporation.

'AE' – 1. A trademark found on automatic pistols made by ★Echave y Arizmendi of Eibar, Spain, which should be read as 'EA'. **2.** A superimposition-type monogram, sometimes encircled, with neither letter prominent. Found on *Colt- and *Smith & Wesson-type swinging-cylinder revolvers made in Spain by Antonio *Errasti of Eibar.

Aegir. A brandname registered on 11 June 1927 (no. 370,176) by Louis *Bader, Valt. Sohn, of Zella-Mehlis, Germany, specifically for use on airguns.

'aek'. Found on pistols and small-arms components made by F. *Dušek of Opočno, working in German-occupied Czechoslovakia during the Second World War.

'AEP', 'A.E.P.' Often encircled, cursive, or in the form of a monogram. A trademark associated with the products of Anciens Établissements *Pieper of Herstal-lèz-Liège, Belgium. It will be encountered on a variety of military and sporting rifles, shotguns, pistols, revolvers and ammunition.

Aerosport. A brandname encountered on spring-airguns made by Maschinen- und Apparätebau *'Wagria' GmbH & Co., of Ascheberg/Holstein, Germany. The Aerosport 58 was a simple 4.5mm-calibre barrel-cocker, whereas the Aerosport 59 was a 5.5mm version intended for export. Production had ceased by 1960.

Aerostyle. The British military authorities acquired eighty .180 Air Gun Sets from Aerostyle Ltd in 1944. These are believed to have been used for gunnery training, but details are lacking.

Aeschbacher. Jacob G Aeschbacher, or 'Aeschbacker', an inventor living in Rosario, Santa Fé, Argentina, was granted US Patent 640,070 on 26 December 1899 to protect a firearm.

Aetna – **1.** A small *Suicide Special revolver manufactured by Harrington & Richardson of Worcester, Massachusetts, USA, in the 1880s. **2.** Aetna Arms Company. This spurious manufacturer's name was used by *Harrington & Richardson to disguise a selection of cheap pre-1917 revolvers.

'AF'. Often floriated, this monogram-trademark was used by August *Francotte & Companie of Liège, Belgium.

Afanasev. Nikolai Mikhailovich Afanasev, born in 1916 in Petrograd, Russia, is best known for a double-barrel aircraft machine-gun designed while he was serving with the Red Army during the Second World War. Afanasev subsequently became regarded as a leading expert in the design of aircraft weapons, particularly the gas-operated A-12.7 machine-gun.

AFAP. *See* Ateliers de Fabrication des Armes Portatives.

'AFC' – **1.** A shield-borne monogram consisting of 'A' and 'F' crossed diagonally, with 'C' (and sometimes a concentric 'o') superimposed. Used by Auguste Francotte & Co., notably on the grips of *vest-pocket pistols made c. 1912–14. **2.** A US inspector's mark. *See* A.F. *Cameron. **3.** Also found as 'AF&CO', a superimposition-type monogram with 'A' and 'F' of equal prominence. Found on the grips of double-action safety revolvers made by (or possibly for) Andrew *Fyrberg & Company of Hopkinton, Massachusetts, USA. **4.** Also encountered as 'AFCo' or 'A.F.Co.' A mark used by the *Abercrombie & Fitch Company of New York on a range of sporting goods, including holsters and accessories. It is rarely found on guns.

'AFM'. Associated with the *American Firearms Manufacturing Company of San Antonio, Texas, USA.

African – **1.** Or M81 African. This *Parker-Hale Mauser sporting rifle – in .300 H&H Magnum, .308 Normag,

.375 H&H Magnum or 9.3x62 – featured folding-leaf *Express back sights on a quarter rib, and an additional recoil lug. **2.** Found on guns made by Manufacture Française d'Armes et Cycles of Saint-Étienne, France. **3.** A Mauser-action sporting rifle made by Paul *Jaeger of the USA. Chambered for .375 H&H, .416 Taylor or .458 Winchester Magnum cartridges, it had a distinctive graphite-reinforced synthetic stock. **4.** African Magnum. Chambered only for .375 H&H Magnum, .404 Jeffrey or .458 Winchester Magnum ammunition, these *Parker-Hale Mausers (also known as the 1100M African Magnum) had a heavy barrel and a stock containing an additional recoil bolt. **5.** African Plains Rifle, or Model 700 APR. This bolt-action *Remington sporter was introduced in 1995 in chamberings ranging from 7mm Remington to .375 H&H Magnum. The stock is a wood-laminate pattern with a black rubber shoulder pad.

'AG' – **1.** A superimposition-type monogram. Used by Fabrique d'Armes de Guerre de Haute Précision Armand Gavage of Liège on semi-automatic pistols. **2.** Monogram. Associated with *Garate, Anitua y Compañía of Eibar, Spain. Correctly read as 'GA'. **3.** Accompanied by a crown and a crescent. A trademark used by *Arizmendi y Goenaga of Eibar, Spain. **4.** Usually accompanied by 'The'. On shotgun cartridges loaded by, or perhaps for E.J. *Churchill of London. The abbreviation is said to represent 'Accuracy Guaranteed'.

Aga, AGA. A mark applied to a sub-calibre training system marketed by the Swedish manufacturer, Autogen-Gas-Akumulatoren (*sic*). *See also* Stephens, Smith & Company.

'AGB'. *See* American Gun Barrel Company and A.G. *Bennett.

'AGC'. A concentric-type monogram, with the 'G' and 'A' prominent. It may be found on handguns, rifles, shotguns and accessories made by, or sometimes for, *Garate, Anitua y Compañía of Eibar, Spain, and is correctly read as 'GAC'.

'AGE' [The]. Found on shotgun cartridges made by *Eley-Kynoch and sold by Alex *Martin of Glasgow. Widely used as a trademark, it is said to represent 'Aberdeen-Glasgow-Edinburgh': Martin's three workshops in this particular period

Agency for Foreign Patent Solicitors ('AFPS'). *See* Theodor *Hornhauer.

Agent – **1.** Derived from the *Cobra, this .38 Special revolver was made by the Firearms Division of *Colt Industries in 1955–73. It had a 2in barrel and a short rounded butt; most guns were sold with hammer shrouds to prevent snagging clothing during a 'quick draw'. An alloy-frame version with a shrouded ejector rod, made in 1973–86, was often advertised as the Agent Lightweight. **2.** Correctly 'l'Agent'. A .25-calibre pistol made by *Manufacture Française d'Armes et Cycles of Saint-Étienne, France.

Ager. Wilson Ager & Company. A patentee of agricultural machinery and an agricultural implement supplier, Ager is remembered for his involvement with the *Billingshurst Requa Battery Gun of the American Civil War period. Representation was being maintained in London in 1868 at 4 Railway Place, E.C.

Agnew & Son. A gunsmithing and sporting goods business trading from 79 South Street, Exeter, Devon, England, in the twentieth century. Appropriate marks have been found on sporting guns and shotgun cartridges known as The Devonia.

Agniel et Cie, Place Chavanelle 16, Saint-Étienne, France. Listed in 1892 as a gunmaker.

'AGP'. *See* Anson G. ★Perkins.

Aguirre – 1. Aguirre y Aranzabal. Founded in Eibar in 1927 and now owned by the Aguirre brothers (Aguirre Hermanos y Cia), this company has become pre-eminent among Spanish shotgun makers. About 25,000 AYA guns have been made annually in recent years, ranging from plain box-lock patterns to the finest side-locks. **2.** Aguirre y Compañía. A gunmaker trading in Ermua from 1928 to 1937, specialising in Smith & Wesson-type revolvers. The company was a casualty of the Spanish Civil War. **3.** Aguirre, Zamacolas y Compañía; Eibar, Guipúzcoa, Spain. Makers of the ★Basculant and ★Le Dragon pistols.

Aguro. A brandname used on firearms made by ★Erquiaga, Muguruzu y Compañía of Eibar, Spain.

'AH' – 1. Monogram. Found on products of Hispano Argentino Fábrica de Automoviles SA of Buenos Aires, Argentina (actually 'HA'). **2.** Monogram. Found on pistols made by ★Apaolozo Hermanos of Zumorraga, Spain. **3.** Monogram. Associated with the products of ★Acha Hermanos of Ermua, Spain. **4.** On US military weapons; *see* Asabel ★Hubbard.

A & H. A superimposition-type monogram with 'A' and 'H' of equal dominance. Correctly 'H & A' (q.v.); used by ★Hopkins & Allen.

'AHC', 'AHF', 'AHGL', 'AHK', 'AHN', 'AHT'. Marks found on US military firearms and equipment. *See* Archibald H. ★Ceiley and Albert H. ★Clark; A.H. ★Forsythe; A.H.G. ★Lewis; Albert H. ★Kirkham; A.H. ★North; and Albert H. ★Thompson respectively.

'AI', 'A.I.' – 1. A mark associated with sight-inserts and other articles marketed in Britain by ★Accuracy International Ltd. **2.** A designation applied to the Romanian Cugir-made copy of the Soviet ★Kalashnikov assault rifle. **3.** A superimposition-type monogram, with neither letter dominant, customarily found on a shield. *See* 'IA'; found on Spanish break-open ★Smith & Wesson-style revolvers.

'A.I.D.', 'A I D'. Found on rifle and other small-arms components inspected by the Armaments Inspection Department, Enfield Lock.

Ailsa Craig. Found on airguns made by F. ★Langenhan or ★Mayer & Grammelspacher, and sold by ★Clyde's Game & Gun Mart of Glasgow.

AIM. Made by the Romanian arms factory in Cugir, this is a copy of the Soviet ★AKM, distinguished by an auxiliary pistol grip made integrally with the fore-end.

Aiming Tube. *See* sub-calibre adaptor.

Ainsworth. O.W. Ainsworth, often listed as 'Ainsworth', was the US government arms inspector who accepted weapons ranging from cap-lock and .44 Smith & Wesson revolvers to ★Gatling Guns. Active from 1831 into the 1870s, he used an 'OWA' mark. See also US arms inspectors' marks.

Air, Air... – 1. Air Arms Ltd. Trading from Hailsham in East Sussex, England, Air Arms has been responsible for perpetuating the ★Jackal series of airguns after the demise of ★Sussex Armoury. The company – part of the engineering group NSP – went on to make derivatives of the basic sidelever-cocking design (e.g. Combat, Rapide, Shamal and Supra) before introducing pre-

charged pneumatics. **2.** Air Ducts Ltd, Great West Road, Brentford, Middlesex, England. Makers of 3,750 'Mountings, Twin, Vickers .303 Machine-Gun, with Anti-Aircraft Sights' during the Second World War. The company may have used the code 'S 135' instead of its name. *See also* British military manufacturers' marks. **3.** Air Logic Ltd. This company was formed to promote the Whisperer silencer, designed by J.R. Spencer, and subsequently progressed to the Genesis pneumatic rifle before being absorbed into Scalemead. **4.** Air Match SrL. Founded by Giacomo ★Cagnoni in 1978, this airgun and pistol manufacturer is responsible for the Air Match CU400, CU600 and CU900 pneumatic pistols, in addition to cartridge-firing target pistols. Until the early 1980s, the guns were exported by the IGI marketing organisation and the manufacturer's name was all but unknown. *See also* Italguns.

Aircraft & General Engineering Co. Ltd, Albion Works, Park Way, Edgware, Middlesex, England. Makers of .303 ★Vickers machine-gun tripods during the Second World War, possibly marked with the code 'S 136' instead of the company name. *See also* British military manufacturers' marks.

Aircrewman – 1. A name applied to a version of the ★Smith & Wesson Model 12 ★Military & Police ★Airweight swing-cylinder revolver, acquired by the USAF in 1953/54. **2.** Aircrewman Special. Made by ★Colt's Patent Fire Arms Manufacturing Company for the USAF in 1951, in .38 Special only, this double-action revolver had a 2in barrel, fixed sights and chequered walnut grips.

Airgun. *See* panel, pp. 22/23.

Airgunaid. Founded by Eddie Barber in 1977, this small business traded from Springfield Road, Chelmsford, Essex, until the premises were burned down in 1981. The marks will be found on airguns based, for the most part, on ★Milbro Diana components.

Airlite. A mark associated with cartridge revolvers made by ★Gabilondo y Compañía of Eibar, Spain.

Airis. This brandname will be found on a small break-barrel 4.5mm air rifle made in the early 1960s by ★Valmet of Finland.

Airline. A tradename used on ammunition made by the ★Federal Cartridge Company of Minneapolis.

Airship or 'Airship Brand'. A mark found on packaging distinguished with an airship logo, usually containing airgun pellets made by W.H ★Darlow Ltd of Bradford, Yorkshire, England.

Airsporter. *See* panel, p. 24.

Air-Trol. A brandname associated with pneumatic guns made by the ★Crosman Arms Company, referring specifically to a patented air-valve.

Airway. Sometimes found as 'A-Airway', this ★headstamp was applied to ammunition sold throughout the USA by ★Gamble Stores. The source usually proves to have been the ★American Cartridge Company.

Airweight. A name applied by ★Smith & Wesson to a variety of swing-cylinder revolvers with aluminium-alloy frames, although the original alloy cylinders proved to be too weak and were replaced by steel items. The Model 12 ★Military & Police Airweight (1952–86) had a 2in barrel and a round-heel butt. A few were purchased by the USAF as the Model 13 Aircrewman, and a variant known as the Model 45 was developed for the US Postal

Service. The ★Chiefs' Special Airweight, or Model 37 from 1957, was introduced on the basis of an aluminium-alloy J-frame in 1952. A square-butt option was added a year later, and a steel cylinder replaced the alloy version from the beginning of 1954. The Model 637 Chiefs' Special Airweight – confined to 1990 – had a steel cylinder, a steel barrel and an alloy frame. The .38 ★Bodyguard Airweight, known as the Model 38 after 1957 and built on the J-frame, was essentially a ★Chiefs' Special with a shrouded hammer-enveloping frame designed to prevent the hammer spur from snagging clothing; the Model 638 Bodyguard Airweight, made in small numbers in 1990, combined a stainless-steel cylinder and barrel with an alloy frame The ★Centennial Airweight revolver of 1952–74, known as the Model 42 from 1957 onward, had an enclosed hammer and a safe-ty let into the backstrap. The earliest guns had alloy cylinders as well as alloy frames, but a steel cylinder was adopted in May 1954.

AIS – **1**. A variant of the Romanian AIM or ★Kalashnikov rifle with a folding butt. **2**. A superimposition-type mono-gram without dominant letters. Correctly 'SIA' (q.v.); found on revolvers distributed by ★Security Industries of America, Inc.

Aisthorpe. John Aisthorpe (active 1850–65) was born in 1827 and apprenticed to Henry Godsall before trading as a gun-barrel maker. He received British Patent 409/1864 for polygonal rifling while trading from 1 Grosvenor Mews, Marylebone, London, England.

'AJ'. Monogram. A trademark used by José ★Aldazabal of Eibar. The mark is correctly read as 'JA'.

'A.J. Aubrey'. A brandname used on guns and shooting

AIRGUN

By the 1850s, the traditional externally-charged designs – with their reservoirs filled by separate pumps – had lost favour for all applications except walking-stick and cane guns. Filling ball-, butt- or barrel reservoirs with air had proved to be protracted, arduous and often dangerous. Their replacements, in central Europe at least, took several forms.

Some of the earliest relied on a pair of spring-loaded bellows in the butt, betraying seventeenth-century origins, but the perfected guns contained a piston that was driven forward by a volute spring when released by the sear. Some guns were cocked by a combination of a crank handle and a toothed rack (★*Kurbelspanner*); others employed cocking levers combined with trigger guards (★*Bugelspanner*); attempts were even made to use rubber bands (*see* John ★Shaw, Lightning and Henry M. ★Quackenbush).

Although power was low, restricting them largely to shooting-gallery and indoor use, they were easy to operate and could be surprisingly accurate. Most examples fired darts from smooth-bored barrels, but a few were capable of firing larger-calibre lead balls. A growing use of double volute springs, customarily counter-wound and separated by a spacer, increased utility.

The traditional ★Gallery Gun, taken to North America by German and Bohemian gunmakers in the 1860s, laid the basis for designs pioneered in the USA in the 1870s by ★Havilland & Gunn and Quackenbush, the best of them offering not only good construction, but also appreciable power. Some of the largest, indeed, were 'convertibles' patented in the USA in 1872 by John Hannah, which could also fire .22 rimfire ammunition when required.

The unsuccessful prototype of what has now become known generically as a ★Gem, customarily credited to Asa ★Pettengill, was a classical receiver-cylinder design; the successful Haviland & Gunn pattern combined the air cylinder with the butt, reducing overall length while simultaneously providing greater air capacity. The Gallery Gun also inspired the ★BB Gun, an inexpensive ball-firer originating in the USA in the 1880s. However, it evolved into the perfected barrel-cocking spring-piston airgun, which, after briefly taking the form of the ★push lever design, reverted to the original Pettengill layout with the barrel formed as a lineal extension of the cylinder or piston chamber.

Guns of this type were made in great numbers from 1900 onward, particularly in Germany prior to 1914, and are still being offered in profusion. They were joined after 1907 by sturdier fixed-barrel guns, developed in Britain by Lincoln ★Jeffries, which relied on a separate under-type cocking lever and a rotary tap to receive a pellet or ball.

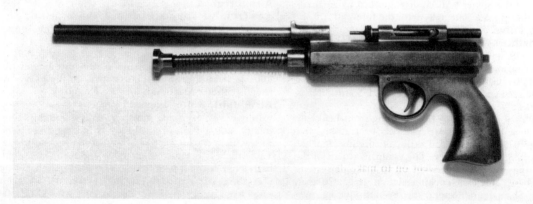

accessories sold during the early twentieth century by the US wholesaling business of *Sears, Roebuck & Company. Apparently, the name was that of the manager of Sears' manufacturing interests in Norwich, Connecticut. *See also* Albert J. *Aubrey and Ted *Williams.

Ajax [The]. A brandname associated with shotgun cartridges manufactured by *Nobel Explosives Ltd of Glasgow prior to 1918 and the purchase by Explosives Trades Ltd.

'AJB'. *See* Aldige J. *Bessette and A.J. *Bristol.

'ajf'. A mark found on submachine-guns and small-arms components made by Junker & Ruh AG of Karlsruhe in Baden, Germany, during the Second World War.

'AJG'. Monogram. A mark employed by J.G. Anschütz of Zella St Blasii and Zella-Mehlis, Germany, to be read as 'JGA'.

'AJH', 'AJM'. Applied to US military firearms and accessories by A.J. *Hall, Andrew J. *Harwood and Albert J. *Meyers.

'ak', AK – 1. As 'ak'. A mark found on some small-arms ammunition and components made in the German-occupied Vlasim (Czechoslovakia) factory of Munitions-fabriken vormals *Sellier & Bellot during the Second World War. **2.** As 'AK'. An abbreviated form of *Avtomat *Kalashnikova (Kalashnikov assault rifle), originating in the USSR and now specifically applied to the AK-47 (7.62mm) and AK-74 (5.45mm). *See also* AKM, AKMS, AKMSU and AKS.

Akah, AKAH. A brandname/trademark used by Albrecht *Kind of Berlin, Nürnberg and Hunstig bei Dieringshausen.

AKB. A modified version of the *Kalashnikov in bullpup

Jeffries-type rifles were popular in the period between the world wars, when most of the developmental strides concerned pistols such as the *Webley, designed by *Fearn & Johnstone, with its barrel (doubling as the cocking lever) along the top of the air cylinder. The *Parker pistol was cocked with a crank; the *Haenel was a barrel cocker; and the *Tell and the *Zenit relied on separate top-levers.

The earliest post-1945 developments centred on pre-war prototypes. However, the BSA *Airsporter was a notable attempt to improve balance and style; guns such as the *Weihrauch HW35 began a quest for the additional power that would allow the airgun to become a hunting weapon; and the introduction of truly recoilless spring-air designs – begun in the late 1950s by the *Giss-patent *Diana guns made by Mayer & Grammelspacher – has made airguns fit for competitive international shooting.

Underlever-cocking designs have gradually given way to side-lever patterns, much greater use has been made of synthetic components, and sights have been refined. The target-shooting market is currently dominated by the products of *Anschütz, *Feinwerkbau, *Hämmerli and others, although pre-charged pneumatics and *gas-guns have steadily gained favour. The advent of readily-available supplies of compressed air has enabled the reservoir airgun, out of favour since the nineteenth century, to return to popularity. Guns of this type, although lacking the self-contained advantages of spring-piston rivals, are entirely free from vibration and can be fired continuously until the pressure of air in the reservoir eventually declines far enough to affect power.

It is difficult to do justice to the history of the airgun in a few paragraphs. Unfortunately, although much detail has been published in magazines, few books provide other than a sketchy overview. W.H.B. Smith's *Gas, Air & Spring Guns of the World* (1958, reprinted many times) and the introduction to the third (1984) edition of *The Airgun Book* by John Walter give populist views; *Air Guns and other Pneumatic Arms* by Arne Hoff (1971) presents an academic approach. *See also* BB Gun, Gallery Gun and Gas gun.

This Polish-made Lucznik Predom 4.5mm Kl. 187 rifle is typical of the traditional spring-and-piston patterns. Note the trigger adjusting screw that runs through the front of the trigger-guard bow.

Facing page: *A typical Pope spring-and-piston air pistol, made under contract by Quackenbush during the 1880s.*

AIRSPORTER

This underlever-cocking spring-air rifle was the first post-war *BSA design to develop any real power. Its design is usually credited to Josef *Veselý, Claude Perry and Roger *Wackrow. The Airsporter was descended from the pre-war *Jeffries Pattern BSAs, but considerable thought had been given to the layout of the pivots, and the cocking mechanism was contained entirely in the half-length fore-end.

The system has sometimes erroneously been credited to *Föhrenbach, makers of the *Falke-brand guns, but the BSA was introduced some time before Föhrenbach had even begun trading. The unique conical piston-head of the Airsporter was patented by Claude Perry in 1946. The .22-calibre rifle reached the commercial market in 1948, accompanied by a short-action .177 derivative known as the *Club.

The Mk 1 rifle, with serial numbers prefixed 'G', 'GA', 'GB' or 'GC', was made from 1948 until 1958. It was followed by the Mk 2, made from 1959 until 1967 in .177 ('EE', 'EF', 'EG' numbers) and .22 ('GD', 'GE', 'GF', 'GG'); the Mk 4 of 1967–71 ('EK' and 'GI'); the Mk 5 of 1971–77 ('EL' and 'EN', 'GJ' and 'GL'); and the Mk 6 of 1977 onward ('EN' and 'GL'). The Airsporter S ('EP', 'GM') was introduced in 1981, followed by a Mk 2 in 1984. There has also been a carbine and a *Stutzen, made until the remnants of BSA were acquired by *El Gamo.

The rifle made to celebrate the centenary of the registry of the BSA Piled Arms trademark had a three-quarter-length stock and the lever contained entirely within the fore-end.

configuration, credited to Bulgarian engineer Georgiy Balakov. It was exhibited for the first time in 1997.

AKD. *See* Kalashnikov.

AKK, AKKS. The indigenous designations for the fixed- and folding-butt versions of the Modernised Kalashnikov or *AKM, produced by the Arsenal small-arms factory in Bulgaria.

AKM, AKMS, AKMSU. Applied to a modernised version of the 7.62mm Soviet *Kalashnikov assault rifle, or AK. The AKMS was a folding-butt version, whereas the AKMSU was the short-barrelled submachine-gun derivative.

AKR. Also known as the 'Krinkov', apparently after its designer, this is a short-barrelled derivative of the Soviet AKMSU-type *Kalashnikov.

Akrill – 1. Esau Akrill (active 1833–58 and later). A gunsmith with premises in Market Place, Beverley, Yorkshire, England, Akrill also apparently maintained a branch at 25 Blackfriar Gate, Hull, from 1847 to 1852. Among other guns, he made breech-loading self-priming rifles of the type patented by John *Gilby. Exhibited without conspicuous success in Paris in 1855, and London in 1862, the Gilby Self-Priming System could also be fitted to cannon. **2.** Henry Esau Akrill. The son of Esau Akrill, this gunsmith traded from 18 Market Place in the Yorkshire town of Beverley until 1914 or later. Akrill marked sporting guns and a wide variety of shotgun ammunition. Cartridges have been recorded bearing marks such as 'Collector', 'County' and 'Holderness'.

AKS. Applied to the folding-butt version of the original *Kalashnikov assault rifle.

'AL' – 1. *See* A. *Lavigne. **2.** A *headstamp associated with ammunition made by the *Federal Cartridge Company.

Alamo Ranger. An unidentified tradename found on a Spanish-made revolver.

Alard. H. Alard fils & Companie, a Belgian gunmaking

business based in Liège, had offices in Rotterdam and Maastricht, the Netherlands (1892–1937), and also, briefly, in London at 61 Great Tower Street, E.C., from 1896 to 1900.

Alaska. A sheath-trigger *Suicide Special revolver made in the USA by the *Hood Firearms Company of Norwich, Connecticut, in the late nineteenth century.

Alaskan – 1. See Mark X. **2.** A Mauser-action sporting rifle made by Paul *Jaeger of the USA. Chambered for 7mm Remington, .300 Winchester or .338 Winchester Magnum rounds, it had a walnut stock and a Douglas Premium barrel. **3.** Alaskan Model. A version of the *Colt *Double Action Army & Frontier revolver ordered by the US Army in 1902, with extended trigger guard to admit a thickly-gloved finger. **4.** Alaskan Wilderness Rifle, or Model 700 AWR. Made by *Remington, this bolt-action sporting rifle dates from 1994. Its matt-grey stock is made of fibreglass, graphite and Kevlar, the barrel is stainless steel and the action is satin-blue. Chamberings range from 7mm Remington to .375 H&H.

Albee. Inventor George E. Albee, from New Haven, Connecticut, USA, patented a magazine firearm on 14 December 1886 (US no. 354,371) and a firearm sight on 30 April 1907 (no. 852,152). Both patents were assigned to the *Winchester Repeating Arms Company.

'Albemarle' [The]. A brandname associated with shotgun cartridges sold by *Harrison & Hussey of London.

Alben. S. Alben's Sons (active in 1908) were listed in the *US Commercial Directory* as 'Arms makers' in Greenfield, Massachusetts.

Albini. An officer in the Italian Navy, eventually an admiral, Augusto Albini developed a lifting-block action that was perfected with the assistance of Francis *Braendlin – associated with Albini in British patents of 1866/67. The Albini-Braendlin rifle was tested throughout Europe, but was adopted only in Belgium. The breech embodied a locking bolt attached to the hammer-body. Rotating the hammer to half cock withdrew the bolt and allowed the breech-block handle to be lifted, extracting a spent case that was tipped from the feedway. Once the gun had been reloaded, the breech block was closed and the hammer thumbed back to full cock. Pressing the trigger allowed the hammer to fly forward, whereupon the locking bolt entered the back of the breech block and struck the firing pin. After testing different rifles, including the Remington, the Belgians selected the Albini-Braendlin breech because of the ease with which existing rifle-muskets could be converted. Apparently, the service weapons were made in Liège by *Fabrique d'Armes de l'État, and possibly also by Henri *Pieper & Company. The short rifles were the work of *Dresse-Laloux & Company, and perhaps also Pieper.

Albion – 1. Albion Motors Ltd, Glasgow, Scotland. Makers of about 42,500 British .38 *Enfield 'Pistols, Revolver, No. 2' during 1940–43. The company was allocated the code 'N 1' during the Second World War. See also British military manufacturers' marks. **2.** Usually found as 'The Albion' on shotgun cartridges loaded by the *Schultze Gunpowder Company. 'Albion' is an alternative name for England.

Albrecht – 1. Fritz Albrecht was a sporting gunmaker of Suhl, Thüringen, Germany, active prior to 1919. Succeeded by Rudolf Albrecht. **2.** Rudolf Albrecht. The son of Fritz Albrecht, above, this gunmaker traded until the end of the Second World War as 'Fritz Albrecht, Rud. Sohn'.

Albright. Louis Albright (active 1859–63), a gunmaker of Ottawa, Putnam County, Ohio, USA, received US Patent 38,366 on 5 May 1863 to protect a breech-loading firearm.

Aldasoro. Gunsmith Juan Aldasoro of Eibar, Spain, made firearms in the mid-nineteenth century. They included cap-lock rifle-muskets, short rifles and carbines for the Spanish Army. Revolvers were also made in the 1860s. See Berdan.

Alday y Gabilondo. This company made cheap, low-grade *Smith & Wesson-pattern revolvers in Placencia, Spain, from 1920 to 1932. The business may have been superseded by Alday y Compañía (c. 1932–37).

Aldazabal – 1. A. Aldazabal, Eibar, Guipúzcoa, Spain. Manufacturer of the 'AAA' automatic pistol (q.v.). **2.** Hijos de José Aldazabal, Eibar, Guipúzcoa, Spain. This gunmaking business was responsible for *Imperial pistols, often misleadingly marked as products of Fabrique d'Armes de Précision.

Alden. J.W. Alden, an inspector of US military firearms in 1905/06, used a 'JWA' mark. See also US arms inspectors' marks.

Alderman. Edward M. Alderman, an inventor of Sharon, Pennsylvania, USA, patented an electro-magnetic gun on 4 May 1908 (US Patent no. 920,709).

Aldis. Aldis Bros. Ltd of Birmingham, Warwickshire, England, manufactured optical equipment prior to 1918 – including signal lamps, and telescope sights used on Mk III *Lee-Enfield and P/14 sniper rifles. A typical 2.5x sight featured a range drum calibrated '1' to '6' (100–600yd).

Aldrich – 1. James T. Aldrich. Domiciled in Norwich, Connecticut, USA, this patentee of a revolving firearm – US no. 283,185 of 14 August 1883 – assigned rights to himself and W.H. Babcock. James Aldrich was also responsible for the revolving firearm protected by US Patent 308,231 of 18 November 1884. **2.** Waley Aldrich, or 'Wales Aldrich'. This inventor patented a breech-loading firearm on 12 May 1863 (US no. 38,455). The specification records his residence as Cleveland, Ohio, USA.

Aldridge. Edward Aldridge, a gunmaker trading from Hyde Park Corner, Ipswich, Suffolk, England, sold his own shotgun cartridges under brandnames such as Crown, Hyde Park and Anglian.

Alekhin, St Petersburg, Russia. A gun dealer operating prior to the 1917 Revolution.

Alert. A cheap *Suicide Special revolver made by the *Hood Firearms Company of Norwich, Connecticut, in the late nineteenth century.

Alessi. Federico Alessi of New York City invented the machine-gun protected by US Patents 672,690 of 23 April 1901 and 683,240 of 24 September 1901.

Alex. Another of the many sheath-trigger *Suicide Special revolvers made by the *Hopkins & Allen Arms Company of Norwich, Connecticut, in the late nineteenth century.

Alexander, Alexanders – 1. Charles W Alexander. Domiciled in Moorfield, Virginia, USA, Alexander patented a breech-loading rifle on 25 May 1858 (US no. 20,315). Subsequently, he sought Confederate Patent no. 163 on 18 April 1863. However, although a pattern gun was made at the Confederate States Armory (Richmond,

Virginia) in 1862, series production was never undertaken. **2.** Alexander & Duncan Leominster, Herefordshire. The name of this English provincial gunmaking business has been recorded on sporting guns and shotgun cartridges. **3.** Alexanders. The marks of this English gunmaking business, trading in Fordingbridge, Hampshire, have been reported on shotgun cartridges marketed under the brandname Fordingbridge.

Alexia. A typically inexpensive *Suicide Special revolver manufactured by the *Hood Firearms Company of Norwich, Connecticut, during the late nineteenth century.

Alexis. A *Suicide Special revolver made by the *Hood Firearms Company of Norwich, Connecticut, in the late nineteenth century.

Alfa, ALFA – 1. A brandname used on guns and accessories by A.L. *Frank of Hamburg. Sometimes encountered in the form of a monogram trademark, it was eclipsed in the 1920s by the 'WUM' of Georg *Frank. **2.** A break-open three-barrel 6.35mm repeating pistol, locked by a top lever and fired by a sequencing striker, marketed prior to 1914 by A.L. Frank of Hamburg **3.** A linear monogram, often encircled, with 'A' and 'F' dominant. Found on handguns, including Smith & Wesson-type break-open revolvers, made by Armero Especialistas Reunidas 'Alfa' of Eibar, Spain.

Alfson. Andrew Alfson of Chicago, Illinois, USA, was the designer of a magazine gun protected by US Patent no. 638,677 of 5 December 1899.

'A.L.H.' – 1. Found in the headstamps of cartridges made by A.L. *Howard & Company of New Haven. **2.** On US military weapons; see A.L. *Hallstrom.

Alig & Baumgärtel, Abawerke GmbH (Germany, 1933–84), was trading from Müllerstrasse 27/31 in Aschaffenburg when the code 'fqx' was allocated in June 1941. The business is believed to have made parts for the *Erma sub-calibre barrel inserts (*Einsteckläufe*) in c. 1938–41. Sometimes mistakenly claimed to have been a subsidiary of Simson & Company, Alig & Baumgärtel entered the local commercial register in June 1933 as a maker of 'precision machines and precision measuring equipment'. The business was succeeded by Schlief- und Maschinenfabrik 'aba' GmbH at the end of 1984.

Alkar – 1. Found on revolvers made by *Manufactura de Armas de Fuego and (or?) Sociedad *Alkartasuna Fábrica de Armas of Guernica. **2.** A small Browning-inspired automatic pistol made in Eibar by Fábrica de Armas *Alkartasuna SA: (a) 6.35mm, six or seven rounds, hammer fired; (b) 7.65mm, seven or nine rounds, hammer fired. Some guns may be marked 'Armas de Fuego'.

Alkartasuna. SA Alkartasuna, Fábrica de Armas, Eibar. This Spanish gunmaking business was formed in 1915 by ex-employees of *Esperanza y Unceta. In addition to guns of its own, the company supplied *Ruby pistol components during the First World War to *Gabilondo y Urresti. The proprietary *Alkar pistol may be encountered with 'Armas de Fuego' marks.

al-Khardj. The principal Saudi Arabian ordnance factory.

All, All... – 1. All-American or 'All-American Model 2000'. A double-action semi-automatic pistol with a roller-bearing trigger, designed by C. Reed Knight and introduced by *Colt's Manufacturing Company, Inc., in 1991, this features a recoil operated rotating-bolt lock and a fifteen-round magazine. The slide is made of steel, but the frame may be aluminium-alloy or polymer. **2.** All Round. Usually found as 'The All Round' on shotgun cartridges, which were sold in Bntain by J. *Collis. **3.** All British [The]. Found on 12-bore shotgun cartridges loaded by T. *Stensby & Company, Manchester, from components supplied by Eley-Kynoch. **4.** All-British Extra Special [The]. Associated with shotgun ammunition loaded by Charles *Smith & Sons of Newark. **5.** All Metal Products Company. Trading in Wyandotte, Michigan, USA, this metalworking business received the *Upton airgun-making machinery from Sears, Roebuck & Company in 1927, and continued to make the Upton M40 BB Gun – a simplified *Sterling – until 1929. Then the tools and fixtures were sold to the *King Rifle Company for $1, but were dumped in the Detroit River shortly after. *See also* Ranger and Wyandotte.

Allan Scottish gunmaker Arthur Allan, trading from 3 West Nile Street, Glasgow, is known to have rnarked shotgun cartridges with the 'Super A.A.' and 'Three Star' names.

Allen – 1. A *Suicide Special revolver made by the *Hopkins & Allen Arms Company of Norwich, Connecticut, in the late nineteenth century. **2.** Usually as 'Allen 22'. A small revolver made by *Forehand & Wadsworth of Worcester, Massachusetts. **3.** Cyrus B. Allen (active 1836–41). A gunmaker-metalsmith of Springfield, Massachusetts, maker of the Cutlass Pistols patented by George *Elgin, Allen also produced the Monitor revolvers patented by John W. *Cochran. The business was succeeded by Allen & Falls. **4.** E. Allen & Company; see Ethan Allen. **5.** Enos G. Allen. A native of Boston, Massachusetts, USA, at least according to patent applications – and also, presumably, a relation (a cousin perhaps?) of Ethan Allen. Enos Allen's US patents included no 39,024 of 30 June 1863, for progressive or gain-twist rifling. US Patent 41,590 of 16 February 1864 protected metal-case cartridges, and US Patent 45,306 of 6 December 1864 was for a 'Bullet for Small Arms'. **6.** Ethan Allen. Born in Bellington, Massachusetts, USA, on 2 September 1806, Allen had established his workshop in Grafton, Massachusetts, by 1835. There he patented his double-action pepperbox in 1837. Ethan Allen and his brother-in-law, Charles Thurber, initially made pepper-boxes in Grafton under the trading style Allen & Thurber. In 1842, however, the partnership left for Norwich, Connecticut, where it traded for five years before settling in the small Massachusetts town of Worcester as Allen, Thurber & Company. Charles Thurber resigned in 1855 in favour of another of Ethan Allen's brothers-in-law, Thomas P. *Wheelock. The company was renamed Allen & Wheelock, but the junior partner died in 1863. Allen's sons-in-law, Sullivan *Forehand and Henry C. *Wadsworth, became associated with the firm in 1865. During the American Civil War, in December 1861, the Federal government had purchased 198 Allen revolvers from a dealer – William *Read & Son of Boston – although no large-scale purchases were made directly from the maker. Ethan Allen died in 1871. Allen & Wheelock became *Forehand & Wadsworth in 1872, and operated, latterly as the Forehand Arms Company, until 1902. *See also* Edward A. *Prescott. Among Allen's US Patents for long-arms were 30,033 of 18 September 1860, granted for 'breech-loading firearms'. Double-barrelled hammer shotguns were made in accordance with US

ALLEN & WHEELOCK

Allen (17)

Worcester, Massachusetts, USA. The products of this partnership included solid-frame revolvers patented by Ethan ★Allen in 1857, ranging from .28, .31 and .34 five-shot double-action bar-hammer guns to a .44 six-shot Army pattern. They all featured cranked side hammers and a rammer that formed the major part of the trigger guard. Six-shot .36 Navy and .44 Army centre-hammer guns were manufactured in 1861, and a .36-calibre sheath-trigger single-action gun was also developed

during the early 1860s for the police department in Providence, Rhode Island.

A few centre-hammer revolvers were chambered for rimfire cartridges in the 1860s, but this infringed the Rollin ★White patent, and ★Smith & Wesson soon forced production to cease. Allen & Wheelock also made .32 and .44 ★lip-fire infringements of ★Smith & Wesson's rights – based on the company's cap-locks – with bored-through chambers, central hammers and a cylinder-axis pin entering from the front of the frame. Production continued until the business became Allen & Company in 1863.

A .36-calibre cap-lock Navy Model revolver made by Allen & Wheelock. Note the side-hammer and how the cylinder-axis pin runs through the back of the frame.

Patent 49,491 of 22 August 1865. The hinged breech block was locked by a pivoting latch set into the right side. The patent also showed a ratchet extractor operated by a finger-ring, but a sliding trigger guard was used on guns made from 1868 to 1871. US Patent 49,491 of 22 August 1865 and US Patent 84,929 of 15 December 1868 both protected breech-loading guns. One of the most important of all Ethan Allen's many designs was the double-action pepperbox protected by a US Patent granted on 11 August 1837. The patent was reissued in January 1840 (no. 60) and again in August 1844 (no. 64). US Patent 3998 was granted on 16 April 1845 for an improved pistol (pepperbox), and among the many patents granted to Ethan Allen for 'revolving firearms' were two protecting the revolver generally associated with Allen & Wheelock – 16,637 of 13 January 1857 and 18,836 of 15 December 1857. US Patent 21,400 added a method of reducing the effects of fouling by using a projection on the cylinder to deflect propellant cases away from the cylinder-axis pin. Other relevant patents were US 22,005 of 9 November 1858, 28,951 of 3 July 1860 and 33,328 of 24 September 1861. US Patent 33,509 of 22 October 1861 was granted to protect improvements in revolver design, embodied in the ★Bull Dog and other revolvers introduced in the late 1870s by ★Forehand &

Wadsworth. US Patent 35,067 of 29 April 1862 was another granted for improvements in revolver design. US Patent 15,454 of 29 July 1856 protected 'Moulds for hollow projectiles'; US Patent 30,109 of 25 September 1860 was granted for metallic-cartridge designs; and US Patent 47,688 of 16 May 1865 allowed claims to be made for improvements in metallic cartridges. Ethan Allen also made contributions to manufacturing techniques, as his US Patent 2919 of 1843 protected a 'Mode of engraving on flat, round, or cylindrical surfaces'. US Patent 27,415 of 13 March 1860 was granted for a method of constructing firearms. US Patent 36,760 of 28 October 1862 protected a back sight, while US Patent 46,617 of 7 March 1865 featured a 'cartridge retractor for breech-loading firearms'. US Patent 48,249 of 20 June 1865 was granted for 'construction of gun barrels', and US Patent 55,596 (19 June 1866) protected a method of heating and soldering gun barrels. **7.** Frank H. Allen of Norwich, Connecticut, USA, received US Patents 239,634 of 5 April 1881 and 273,335 of 6 March 1883 to protect 'Revolving Fire Arms'. The patents were exploited by the ★Minneapolis Fire Arms Company. **8.** Frederick Allen; *see* Allen, Brown & Luther. **9.** G.B. Allen. An inspector of US martial arms from 1894 to 1902, using a 'GBA' mark. *See also* US arms inspectors' marks. **10.** G.T. Allen. An inspector of military firearms in 1898, using a 'GTA' mark. Perhaps the same as preceding entry. **11.** Hiram J. Allen. An inventor domiciled in Arkadelphia, Arkansas, USA, grantee of US Patent 113,963 of 25 April 1871 to protect a breech-loading rifle. **12.** Lucius C. Allen. The cursive 'LCA' mark of this government arms inspector will be found on ★Beaumont-Adams revolvers purchased by the Federal government in 1861. **13.** Martin van Buren Allen, New York City. This US domiciled gunmaker-inventor received US Patent 741,754 of 20 October 1903 for a 'firearm safety-lock'; US Patent 793,382 of 13 June 1905 for a 'hammer-lock for firearm'; US Patent 793,381 of 13 June 1905 for a 'gunlocking device'; and US Patent 849,825 of 9 April 1907 for an improved hammer-lock firearm. **14.** Richard Allen, Birmingham, Warwickshire. An English gunsmith, specialising in 'revolving pistols', who occupied premises successively at 1 New Sumner Street (from 1853 to c. 1855) and 17 Steelhouse Lane (to 1866 or later). **15.** S. Allen's Sons. A gunsmithing business trading from Greenfield, Massachusetts, USA, from 1860 to 1868; possibly successors to S. Allen, active in the mid nineteenth century. **16.** Allen & Company, Worcester, Massachusetts. A successor to Allen & Wheelock, working from 1863 onward in a factory adjoining South Worcester railway station, Allen continued to market the .32 and .44 ★lip-fire revolvers until they could be replaced with .22 and .32 rimfire side-hammer patterns. The .22 rimfire single-shot Allen target pistols were also made in this period. **17.** Allen & Wheelock; *see* panel, p. 27. **18.** Allen Patent Fire-Arms Manufacturing Company. *See* Charles E. ★Bailey. **19.** Allen, Brown & Luther, Worcester, Massachusetts, USA. A partnership of Frederick Allen, Andrew J. Brown and John Luther, trading from 1848 to 1852. The business made musket and rifle barrels, employing, among others, Horace ★Smith and Daniel ★Wesson. **20.** Allen, Thurber & Company, Worcester, Massachusetts. Trading from 1847 until c. 1856, the principal stakeholder in this gunmaking business was Ethan Allen.

Allendorf. A.W. Allendorf of Schönebeck an der Elbe is said to have used 'AWA' ★headstamps on rimfire cartridges made prior to 1900. Confirmation is lacking.

Alleley. Richard Alleley, described in the local directories as a 'Maker of Air Guns and Air Canes', traded first from 86½ (1855–61) and later from 15 Weaman Street (1862–69), Birmingham, Warwickshire, England.

Allgemeine Elektrizitäts-Gesellschaft ('AEG') – now the world-renowned AEG-Telefunken engineering group – has become associated with small-arms largely through the manufacture, in 1917–18, of drum magazines for the ★Parabellum pistol (*Trommelmagazine 08*, 'TM. 08') and the ★Bergmann Maschinenpistole ('TM. 18'). Research in archives in Stuttgart has been used to support a claim that the drums were made in the Ackerstrasse factory in Berlin, but this was the company's head office and it seems more likely that the work was undertaken in Nürnberg. A trademark compnsing three hexagons within a fourth distinguished AEG-made magazines from those made by Gebr. ★Bing and ★Vereinigte-Automaten-Fabrik.

Allies – **1.** A Browning-type automatic pistol made by ★Bersaluce Arietio-Aurtena y Compañía of Eibar, Guipúzcoa, Spain, in at least two patterns: (a) 6.35mm, six rounds, hammer fired; (b) 7.65mm, six rounds, hammer

fired. The 7.65mm guns may also be marked 'Model 1924'. **2.** A small semi-automatic pistol made by Domingo ★Acha y Compañía of Ermua, Spain.

Allin – **1.** Erskine S. Allin. An inspector of US martial arms in c. 1850–65, using an 'ESA' mark (*see also* US arms inspectors' marks), Allin was approached in 1864 by the US Chief of Ordnance (General Alexander Dyer) in an attempt to find an efficient means of converting existing rifle-muskets. Allin, then a Master Armorer at the National Armory in ★Springfield, was asked to develop a gun on behalf of the Federal government. **2.** Lucius C. Allin. Possibly the brother of Erskine S. Allin, this government inspector accepted a variety of cap-lock revolvers from ★Colt, the ★Massachusetts Arms Company and the ★Starr Arms Company – made shortly before the American Civil War. His mark was 'LCA'. *See also* US arms inspectors' marks.

'Allington' [The]. A mark found on the cases of 12-bore shotgun ammunition sold by ★Sanders of Maidstone. It is believed that the cartridges, or at least their constituents, were supplied by ★Eley Bros. The name was apparently that of a local hunt.

Alloni, 12 boulevard Valbenoîte, Saint-Étienne. Listed in 1951 as a gunmaker.

Allport – **1.** Henry Allport, Cork, Ireland. The marks of this gunmaker have been reported on self-cocking ★pepperboxes dating from the middle of the nineteenth century. **2.** Herbert J. Allport. Active 1896–1914 and possibly later, this gunmaker is believed to have been the son of Thomas F. Allport (below) – succeeding to the Paddington premises in 1896. **3.** Samuel Blackmore Allport. A maker of guns, pistols, barrels, furniture and accessories, working in Birmingham, Warwickshire, England. Premises were occupied at 3 Weaman Row until c. 1838, when Allport moved to 50 Whittall Street. Master of the Birmingham Proof House from 1892 onward, he died on 23 October 1899. **4.** Thomas F. Allport. This English gunmaker traded from 3 Ashland Place, Paddington, London W., from 1889 to 1895. He was succeeded by his son (?) Herbert. Possibly the brother of Henry S. Allport.

Alltham & Son. English gunsmiths and ironmongers trading in the small Cumbrian town of Penrith early in the twentieth century, this business is known to have marked Eley Pegamoid shotgun ammunition.

'ALM', often in a triangle. This trademark is associated with L. ★Ancion-Marx of Liège, Belgium, but should be read as 'LAM'.

'Alma' [The]. Found on shotgun ammunition loaded for H. ★Clarke & Sons of Leicester.

'Almac' [The]. A shotgun cartridge manufactured by ★Eley-Kynoch.

Alpha... – **1.** Alpha Alaskan. Introduced in 1985, this bolt-action rifle by Alpha Arms of Dallas had a stainless-steel barrelled action, other metal parts being coated with a durable synthetic varnish called Nitex. The stock was usually a laminated pattern. **2.** Alpha Arms, Dallas, Texas, USA. This company made a limited range of sporting rifles designed by Homer ★Koon under the names Alpha Alaskan, Alpha Custom, Alpha Grand Slam and Alpha Model 1. All were based on a three-lug bolt mechanism with a sixty-degree throw, but production was confined to 1982–89. The Model 1 was offered during 1982–89 in .243 Winchester, 7mm-08 or .308 Winchester only. **3.**

Alpha Custom. A bolt-action rifle made by Alpha Arms of Dallas from 1985 to 1989, in chamberings ranging from .243 Winchester to .308 Winchester. **4. Alpha Grand Slam.** This rifle duplicated the Alpha Custom pattern, but had a stock of 'AlphaWood' – a composite of fibreglass and wood pulp.

'Alphamax' [The]. A mark found on cartridges made by *Eley-Kynoch Ltd and by *Irish Metal Industries Ltd.

Alpine – 1. A brandname associated with *Mauser-action sporting rifles made in Britain by *Firearms Company Ltd from the early 1960s until 1991 or later in Standard, Custom and Supreme grades. Chamberings have ranged from .22-250 to 8mm Remington Magnum. **2.** A bolt-action rifle made in the USA by *Dakota Arms.

Al Quds. A name associated with an Iraqi copy of the Yugoslavian M72B1 *Kalashnikov-type light machine-gun. *See also* Tabuk.

Alsop – 1. Charles Alsop, Middletown, Connecticut, USA. The designer of a shoulder-stock sometimes found with the *Savage cap-lock revolver, protected by US Patent 28,433 of May 1860. **2.** Charles H. Alsop, Middletown, Connecticut, USA. This gunsmith, apparently the son of Charles R. Alsop, sought protection for movable revolver-cylinder chambers to facilitate a gas-seal. This resulted in US Patent 33,770 of 26 November 1861. **3.** Charles R. Alsop, Middletown, Connecticut, USA. Alsop was granted protection for a cap-lock revolver, including US Patent 29,213 of 17 July 1860 and 34,226 of 21 January 1862. A rotary cam pressed the cylinder forward over the breech as the elongated hammer spur was thumbed back. **4. Alsop Repeating Firearms Company.** This gunmaking business, trading from Middletown, Connecticut, made a few .31- and .36-calibre revolvers to the designs of Charles H. and Charles R. Alsop in 1862/63 – even though members of the Alsop family held a stake in the *Savage Repeating Fire-Arms Company. They embodied the gas-seal features that had been patented in 1860/62.

Altenburger. Ernst Altenburger, Germany. *See* Mauser and Heckler & Koch.

Altendorf & Wright, trading from 20 & 24 Russell Street, Birmingham, acted as agent for revolvers incorporating a spring safety patented by A. *Fagnus et Cie of Liège in 1874 (British Patent 3,353/74). Their activities seem to have been confined to 1873–98.

'ALW'. *See* A.L. *Woodworth.

'am', 'AM' – 1. As 'AM'. A mark used by *Manufacture Française d'Armes et Cycles of Saint-Étienne, France, often in the form of a monogram (correctly 'MAF'). **2.** As 'am'. Found on small-arms ammunition and components made during 1940–45 by *Gustloff-Werke, in what had formerly been Otto Eberhardt Patronenfabrik at Hirtenberg in German-annexed Austria. **3.** An angular 'A' above an equally angular 'M', usually encircled. A mark associated with August *Menz of Suhl, found on the grips of *Liliput pistols. **4.** A superimposition-type monogram with both letters equally prominent. Found on the pistols made by August Menz of Suhl, Germany. **5.** A superimposition-type monogram, usually encircled, with 'M' splayed to accommodate 'A' and often with a small ring-target set between its feet. Used by August Menz of Suhl on sporting guns and accessories. **6.** A superimposition-type monogram, usually enwreathed, with neither letter

prominent. Used by August Menz of Suhl on sporting guns and accessories.

'AMA', beneath a crown. This mark will be found in the headstamps of Danish military ammunition made by the Ammunitionsarsenalet in Copenhagen during 1953–58. *See also* 'AA'.

'AMAC'. *See* American Military Arms Corporation.

'Amateurs' [The]. A mark found on shotgun cartridges loaded by the *Chamberlain Cartridge Company of Cleveland, Ohio, USA.

'AMB'. Monogram This mark will be found on pistols made in Spain by Martin A. *Bascaran of Eibar (*see* 'MAB').

Ambassadeur. Offered by Société Anonyme Continentale pour la Fabrication des Armes à Feu *Lebeau-Courally in 9.3x74R, with additional 20-bore shotgun barrels, this over/under Double Rifle has a distinctive three-piece fore-end with the fillets alongside the barrels. The side locks, breech, trigger guard and top lever are engraved with gold-inlaid oak leaves and high-relief game scenes on a blackened steel ground. Double triggers are standard fittings, and the butt generally has a straight wrist.

Ambassador Executive. A side-lock shotgun made by *Società Armi Bresciane to the designs of Renato *Gamba, with two 70cm 12-bore barrels, a *Purdey-style action and *Holland & Holland lockwork adapted by Gamba. Most of the guns have straight-wrist English butts, slender detachable fore-ends, and engraving that can range from 'Ambassador Black & Gold' to finest English-style bordered bouquet and floral scrollwork.

Amberg, or Königlich bayerische Gewehrfabrik (Royal Bavarian small-arms factory). This was founded in 1801 to make muskets and rifles for the state army. The 'crown over AMBERG' marks will be found on a variety of firearms dating prior to 1871, including the *Lindner breech-loading transformation of *Podewils-type rifle-muskets. *Werder rifles were also made in the Amberg factory in the 1870s, largely from subcontracted components; apart from a few experimental rifles and carbines, however, the later *Mauser rifles were made elsewhere. The Amberg factory has also been linked with the *Parabellum pistol, but undertook nothing other than repairs to Pistolen 1908. Operations ceased at the end of the First World War, when the factory was demilitarised. The Allied occupation authorities subsequently distributed much of the gunmaking machinery as war reparations, but sufficient remained of the facilities to allow the formation of 'Deprag'–Deutsche Präzisions-Werkzeuge AG.

Amberite. A smokeless propellant used by *Eley and others in shotgun ammunition prior to 1914.

'AMC'. *See* A.M. *Cooley.

'AMD'. A prefix applied to *Mauser bolt-action sporting rifles made by *Masquelier of Liège, Belgium.

America. A revolver made by the *Norwich Falls Pistol Company of Norwich, Connecticut, USA. Often found with the marks of *Merwin, Hulbert & Company.

American, American... – 1. Generally found as 'The American' on a selection of *Suicide Special revolvers. Apparently, some were made by *Ely & Wray of Springfield, Massachusetts; others were sheath-trigger guns made by Harrington & Richardson of Worcester, Massachusetts. They date from the 1880s. **2.** Generally as 'The American': a solid-framed double-action revolver, made by *Harrington & Richardson from the mid-1880s onward. It was offered as a six-shot .32, five-shot .38 or five-shot .44. **3.** Usually found as 'The American' on a revolver made in Springfield, Massachusetts, by *Smith & Wesson. **4.** A single-barrel box lock shotgun, with an exposed central hammer, made from 1876 until 1908 by *Hyde & Shatuck, then C.S. *Shatuck & Company. **5.** Usually found as 'American 38' on a revolver made by *Ely & Wray of Worcester, Massachusetts, USA, in the 1880s. Despite their marks, the guns may have been the work of *Harrington & Richardson. **6.** American Ace. A mark associated with ammunition made by the *American Cartridge Company of Kansas City. **7.** American Ammunition Company, Oak Park, Illinois, and Muscatine, Iowa, USA. Backed by Frederick Biffar & Company of Oak Park and Chicago, this business distributed shotgun cartridges under the headstamp 'A.A.Co.' and brandnames such as Jack Rabbit and Red Devil. **8.** American Arms Company [The]. Based in Chicopee Falls, Massachusetts, USA, this promotional business was formed by *Poultney & Trimble and the *American Machine Works. Work concentrated initially on the *Smith carbine after production had been withdrawn from the *Massachusetts Arms Company. Subsequently, the American Arms Company made the cartridge derringers patented by Henry F. *Wheeler, which had relied on a rotating two-barrel monoblock to give access to the breech. They were produced in a variety of chamberings from .22 to .45 during 1865–66. **9.** American Arms Company [The], Boston, Massachusetts (1872–93), and Milwaukee, Wisconsin (1893–1901). This gunmaking partnership of George *Fox and Henry *Wheeler is said to have been founded as early as 1872, exhibiting shotguns at the Centennial Exposition of 1876. Products included Wheeler derringers, Fox & Wheeler revolvers, and Fox semi-hammerless shotguns in 12-, 16- and 20-bore. The patented shotgun mechanism was cocked by a thumb lever on the right side of the breech; the revolvers, made in accordance with a patent granted in 1890 to George Fox and Henry Wheeler, had a hammer that could be rotated to full cock, then released by a second pull on the trigger – although a selector on the side of the frame enabled conventional double-action to be used at will. Trading was being undertaken from 103 Milk Street, Boston, in 1890, but a move to Milwaukee was made in 1893. George Fox died in 1900 and the assets of the business were purchased a year later by *Marlin Firearms Company. **10.** American Automatic Arms Company, Saco, Maine, USA. This short-lived business was formed to promote the guns designed by Franklin Young and J.E. Sheriff. **11.** American Automatic Pistol. Used misleadingly on a pistol made in Spain by Gregorio *Bolumburu of Eibar. **12.** American Ball Company. Trading in Providence, Rhode Island, USA, this business was granted British Patent 20,479/1905 for airgun slug and pellet-making machinery. A factory in Providence, on the corner of Eagle Street and Kinsley Avenue, was occupied until the assets of the company were acquired by *Daisy in 1939. **13.** American Boy. Used by Bliss & Goodyear of New Haven, Connecticut, USA, on revolvers made in the 1880s. **14.** American Buckle & Cartridge Company. West Haven, Connecticut, USA. A maker of ammunition, including shotgun cartridges. **15.** American Buldock [The]. Encountered on compact six-shot double-action .380 revolvers, derived

from the Webley *Bulldog. Made in Belgium prior to 1914, few are signed; they have short bird's-head butts. **16.** American Bull Dog. Found on an 1882-vintage five-shot double-action .32 or .38 revolver, made by *Johnson & Bye. The barrel was octagonal. **17.** American Cartridge & Ammunition Company, Hartford, Connecticut, USA. This ammunition-making business, which flourished briefly from 1901 to 1906, marked its products with 'A.M.C. & Co.' **18.** American Cartridge Company, Kansas City, Missouri. An ammunition-making business, said to have been founded c. 1924. Many of its products were marked simply 'A', although tradenames such as American Ace and Hiawatha Ace have been associated with it. **19.** American Classic. Introduced in 1975, this .177-calibre multi-stroke pneumatic rifle was made by the *Crosman Arms Company. Modelled on a *Remington auto-loading rifle of the 1960s, the Model 766 was charged by swinging the fore-end, and loaded either with pellets directly through the bolt channel or from a BB magazine in the butt. **20.** American Clay Bird [The]. A mark found on shotgun cartridges loaded by the *Chamberlain Cartridge Company of Cleveland, Ohio. **21.** American Dart Rifle. This was a version of the lever-action *Sterling BB Gun, with a cover beneath the barrel through which darts could be inserted in the breech. It was made by the *Upton Machine Company during 1912–15, although 'new' guns were apparently assembled from parts as late as the 1920s. **22.** American Derringer Corporation, Waco, Texas, USA. Makers of the .25-calibre Derringer Auto. **23.** American Eagle. A generic term applied to any *Luger pistol that displays the appropriate mark – the obverse (front) of the Great Seal of the Presidency – above its chamber. The mark usually signifies nothing other than commercial sale. Alternatively, associated with *Suicide Special revolvers made by the *Hopkins & Allen Arms Company of Norwich, Connecticut, in the late nineteenth century. **24.** American Electric Arms & Ammunition Company, New York City, USA. This was formed in the mid-1880s to exploit the electric-ignition patents granted to Samuel Russell. A relevant British Patent, 6305/86 of 1886, was even granted in the company name through the intermediacy of the London-based patent agent J.C. *Mewburn. However, although work continued for a decade (including the formation of the *Electric Arms & Ammunition Syndicate Ltd in London), nothing substantial ever came of the project. **25.** American Firearms Manufacturing Company, Inc., San Antonio, Texas, USA. Maker of the .25-calibre AFM Mark X automatic pistol. **26.** American Flask & Cap Company, Watertown, Connecticut. Founded in 1857 to make percussion caps, this business made self-contained cartridges from the 1870s onward. Business apparently ceased in or shortly after 1891. **27.** American Gun Company. This was a trading style used on firearms – notably shotguns, but possibly also on bought-in revolvers – handled by the H. & D. *Folsom Arms Company. **28.** American Gun Barrel Company. A specialist maker of shotgun barrels, working from 1914 until the early 1920s. The barrels may be marked 'AGB'. **29.** American Luger. Applied generically to any *Parabellum (Luger) pistol that displays the so-called *American Eagle mark above the chamber. Alternatively, applied specifically to the German-made Parabellum or Luger pistols distributed by *Stoeger between the two world wars. The term was also applied to the *Schimel pistol made in the 1950s by the *American Weapons Corporation. AWC was subsequently sued by Stoeger, proprietor of the *Luger tradename in North America since 1929, and the gas-operated Schimel became the Carbo-Jet. **30.** American Machine & Foundry Company [The], York, Pennsylvania, USA. This metalworking business converted Ml *Garand rifles to fire 7.62mm NATO cartridges, simply by firing two eight-round clips to expand a liner into the chamber wall. The first of these M1E14 rifles, later known by the US Navy as the Mk 2 Model 0, dated from 1964. **31.** American Machine Works, Springfield, Massachusetts, USA. Operated from 1843 until 1871 by Philos Tyler, this engineering business made *Smith carbines during 1863–65 – firstly for the *Massachusetts Arms Company, then under contract to *Poultney & Trimble. **32.** American Metallic Cartridge Company, South Coventry, Connecticut. The US ammunition-making business was founded c. 1865, but did not survive for long after the end of the American Civil War. It used a *headstamp consisting simply of 'A', often encircled, on rimfire cartridges ranging from .22 to .44. **33.** American Military Arms Corporation (AMAC), Jacksonville, Arkansas, USA. This succeeded to the business of Iver *Johnson in the early 1980s, but continued to use the earlier tradename. The company makes a copy of the .30 Ml Carbine as well as a series of long-range rifles (LRRS) in .338/416 Barrett or .50 Browning. These guns were introduced in 1987. Among other AMAC products are the .22 rimfire L'il Champ, a simple single-shot bolt-action rifle intended for juniors. German *Erma rimfire rifles have also been handled in the USA, under names such as US Carbine 22, Wagonmaster Lever Action and Targetmaster Pump Action. **34.** American Model. A term applied after the introduction of the *Russian Model to distinguish the original-pattern .44 No 3 *Smith & Wesson revolver. **35.** American Model Extra. A name found on a 7.65mm-calibre double-action revolver originating in Belgium prior to 1914. Manufacturer unknown. **36.** American Novelty Company. This metalworking business, trading in Chicago, Illinois, was responsible for the .22 Short *Defender and *Huntsman penknife-guns, 3in and 4in long respectively. Dating from c. 1921–28, they were similar to the *Rogers patterns, but relied on a radial firing lever set into the upper strap of the grip instead of a pivoting trigger latch. **37.** American Nut & Arms Company. Sometimes alternatively known as the American Nut & Tool Company, Boston, Massachusetts, USA. Established in 1867, with premises at 47 Kingston Street, this engineering business made breech-loading pistols in accordance with the patents granted to Henry F. *Wheeler. Business may have ceased in the early 1870s. **38.** American Pellet, 'Am-Pell'. Brandnames found on airguns and their ammunition, marketed by *Playtime Products, Inc., during the early 1970s. The guns were made in Canada and the USA, but most of the ammunition was imported from Europe. **39.** Amencan Repeating Rifle Company, Boston, Massachusetts, USA. This gunmaking business was formed in 1867 out of the *Fogerty Repeating Rifle Company, continuing to make the lever-action rifles designed by Valentine *Fogerty. Trading was brief; the assets and liabilities of the company were purchased by *Winchester in 1869, and operations ceased. **40.** American Settler. A name associated with a revolver sold in Belgium prior to c. 1910 by Charles *Clément. **41.**

American Standard Tool Company, Newark, New Jersey, USA. This metalworking business was responsible for the Hero pill-lock revolver, made from c. 1865 until 1872. **42.** American Tool Works, Chicago, Illinois, USA. Founded in the 1880s, this company made BB Guns from 1891 until declining sales led to near-insolvency in 1912. The business was sold to the *Upton Machine Works and production of the principal gun model, the *Sterling, continued for a few more years. **43.** American Trading Company, Springfield, Massachusetts. This business was the assignee of patents granted in 1868 to James Cranston, to protect improvements in cartridge design, but it is not known if ammunition of this type was ever made. **44.** American Weapons Corporation, Burbank, California, USA. Also known as *Hy Hunter, this business – which vanished in the 1970s – is best known for promoting the gas-operated *Schimel pistol (also known as the American Luger and Carbo-Jet). The guns were actually made by the A.C. *Swanson Company.

Americus. A *Suicide Special revolver made by the *Hopkins & Allen Arms Company of Norwich, Connecticut, in the late nineteenth century.

Ames – 1. Nathan Peabody Ames, born in September 1803 in Chelmsford, Massachusetts, succeeded to his father's gunmaking and metalsmithing business in 1829. Operations moved to Chicopee Falls in 1829, where the Ames Manufacturing Company was duly registered in 1834. Nathan died in 1847 without leaving an heir, his interests in the business passing to his brother, James Taylor Ames (1810–83). **2.** Ames Manufacturing Company or Ames Sword Company, Chicopee Falls, Massachusetts. Founded by Nathan P. and James T. Ames, this business prospered when orders for cannon and edged weapons were granted by the US Army from 1836 onward. Among the firearms made in the factory were a selection of 1842- and 1844-model *cap-lock pistols, 1,000 *Jenks rifles and 4,200 carbines during 1841–45, and *Lowell machine-guns in the 1870s. Ames also made *Protector turret pistols in c. 1889–95, and produced huge quantities of bayonets, swords and sabres; business continues today. The trading styles were interchangeable in the mid-nineteenth century, the marks being judged by the product, but the 'Sword Company' pattern has predominated since the 1880s.

'Amberite' [The]. This mark – the name of the propellant – will be found on shotgun cartridges loaded by or for *Curtiss & Harvey of London, prior to 1918.

'amf', 'Amf'. A mark found in the headstamps of Swedish military cartridges. It signifies *Arméförvaltningen* (army administration service).

Amiel. Tested in Spain in the 1860s, this was a 15mm-calibre *Snider-like conversion of a *Carabina de Cazadores Mo. 57/59* (a cap-lock short rifle), with the breech block axis pin on the left side of the breech block. A cranked lever pinned to the hammer body opened the breech and drew the extractor bar backward as the external hammer was retracted, and an L-shaped striking bar was let into the top of the breech block.

'amn'. Found on small-arms components made by the Neuwied factory of *Mauser-Werke KG during the Second World War.

'amo'. A mark found on small-arms components made in Germany during 1940–45 by the Waldeck Bezirk Kassel factory of *Mauser-Werke KG.

Amoskeag Manufacturing Company [The].
This gunmaking business, trading in Amoskeag and
Manchester, New Hampshire, USA, supplied the Federal
government with sizeable quantities of rifle-muskets during the American Civil War, but was also responsible for
some of the carbines and muskets produced in accordance
with the designs of Edward *Lindner.

AmPell, Am-Pell. See American Pellet.

Amthor – **1.** Arthur Amthor, Suhl in Thüringen,
Germany. Listed as a gunsmith, 1939. **2.** Franz Amthor,
Suhl in Thüringen, Germany. A barrel-blank maker list-
ed in 1939.

Amsler. Rudolf Amsler was a Swiss ballistician and gun
designer, associated during the twentieth century with
*Schweizerische Industrie-Gesellschaft of Neuhausen.

Anaconda. Introduced by *Colt's Manufacturing
Company, Inc., in 1990, this .44-calibre revolver is made
from satin-finish stainless steel. It is similar to the *King
Cobra, with a transfer-bar safety system, a ventilated-rib
barrel, a full-length ejector-rod shroud, and wrap-around
Neoprene grips. The Anaconda Hunter (1991) was essentially similar, but had an 8in barrel and a 2x Leupold telescope sight; it was sold in a fitted aluminium case.

Anciens Établissements. See Pieper.

Ancion – **1.** Jules Ancion & Cie, Liège. A Belgian gunmaker, a member of Le *Syndicat Anglais in the mid-
1850s. A member of the *Petit Syndicat, formed in
Herstal in 1870, then of the Grand Syndicat. A founder
member of les *Fabricants d'armes réunis, 1886, and a
founding shareholder in *Fabrique Nationale d'Armes de
Guerre in 1889, Ancion made *Comblain and other
rifles. **2.** L. Ancion-Marx, Liège, Belgium. A maker of
revolvers and sporting guns, particularly active prior to
the First World War. The guns included revolvers marked
'LAM' or 'L.A.M.'; some of these were chambered for
5.5mm *Velo-Dog cartridges, and others, following similar patterns (but advertised as Auto-Dog), for the
7.65mm Auto round.

'A. & N.C.S.L.' A mark found in the headstamps of cartridges made for the *Army & Navy Co-Operative Stores
Ltd prior to the First World War.

Anderson – **1.** John Anderson & Son. This gunsmithing
and sporting goods business with premises in the
Yorkshire town of Malton, possibly descended from
William Anderson (Market Place, Malton, 1840–67), is
known to have sold 12-bore shotgun cartridges under the
brandnames Derwent and Eclipse before the First World
War. At least some of these were imported by James R.
*Watson & Company of London, apparently from
Belgium. **2.** Anderson Brothers & Company, Plymouth,
Michigan, USA. This metalworking business was assigned
a half-share in a patent granted to Merritt *Stanley in
1891 and is believed to have made the prototype *Globe
BB Guns. See also Dubuar & Company, rnanufacturer of
the series-made Globe guns and a possible successor to
Anderson Bros.

André et Cie, 14 place Tardy, Saint-Étienne, France.
Listed in 1951 as a gunmaker.

Andreas. Hugo Andreas of Gotha was a retailer of
sporting guns and ammunition, active in Germany during 1941.

Andrews – **1.** Charles E. Andrews. Listed in directories
as a gunmaker, trading from 15 Swallow Street, Piccadilly,
London, England, in 1900. Possibly the son of the man

named in the next entry. **2.** C.W. Andrews. A London-
based gunmaker, listed at 6 Great Winchester Street,
E.C., from 1892 to 1900. Trading was undertaken as
C.W. Andrews Ltd from 1894 onward.

'Angler' [The]. This was the telegraphic codename of
John *MacPherson of Inverness, possibly used on shotgun
cartridges made by Kynoch prior to 1914.

Anglia. See H. & R. *Sneezum.

'Anglian' [The]. Found on 12-bore shotgun cartridges
sold in eastern England by Edward *Aldridge of Ipswich.
Apparently, they were made by *Rheinisch-Westfälische
Sprengstoff of Nürnberg, Germany.

Anglo Sure-Shot. 'Anglo Sure-Shot Mark 1' marks
may be encountered on *Britannia-pattern air rifles
retailed by *Ramsbottom & Company of Manchester in
the early 1900s. Similar marks will also be found on
*Millita-type Langenhans.

'ANGL. ZAKAZ'. A mark in Cyrillic (АНГЛ. ЗАКАЗ.)
distinguishing .455-calibre *Colt-Browning M1911 pistols delivered during the First World War for the Russian
government. Apparently, they were ordered through an
intemediary, perhaps taking over a contract originally
placed by Britain. It is an abbreviated form of *Angliskii
Zakaz* (English order).

Anitua. Gunmaker Gregorio Anitua of Eibar, Guipuzcoa, Spain, in partnership with Ignacio Charola, was
responsible for the *Charola y Anitua pistol of the 1890s.

Anschütz – **1.** A. Anschütz, Zella-Mehlis in Thüringen.
A master gunsmith listed in Germany in 1930. **2.** Bruno
Anschütz, Mehlis and Zella-Mehlis in Thüringen,
Germany. Listed during 1914–20 as a gunmaker, and in
1930 as a gun- and weapon maker. **3.** C.O. Anschütz,
Zella-Mehlis in Thüringen Germany. A weapon maker
listed in the *Deutsches Reichs-Adressbuch* for 1920. **4.** Curt
Anschütz, Zella-Mehlis in Thüringen, Germany. Listed
during 1930–45 as a gunmaker. **5.** Erdmann Anschütz,
Zella-Mehlis in Thüringen, Germany. A gunmaker listed
in 1920. **6.** Fridolin Anschütz, Mehlis in Thüringen,
Germany. Listed in 1900 as a gunmaker. **7.** H. Anschütz,
Zella St Blasii and Zella-Mehlis in Thüringen, Germany.
Listed in 1900–20 as a master gunsmith. **8.** J.G. Anschütz;
see panel, facing page. **9.** Otto Anschütz, Zella-Mehlis in
Thüringen, Germany. A specialist gun-stock maker listed
in directories in 1939–42. **10.** Reinhard Anschütz, Mehlis
in Thüringen, Germany. Listed in 1914 as a master gun-
smith. **11.** Richard Anschütz, Mehlis and Zella-Mehlis in
Thüringen, Germany. Listed in 1900–30 as a master gunsmith and gunmaker, specialising in 'target and hunting
rifles, and saloon rifles of all types'. The owner of the business in 1920–30 was Robert A. Anschütz. **12.** Udo
Anschütz, Zella St Blasii and Zella-Mehlis in Thüringen,
Germany. Listed in 1900–30 as a gun- and weapon maker.
Made target pistols and rifles under the brandname
*Rekord. Apparently, the business was acquired in the
1930s by Franz *Merkel, but traded under its own name
until the end of the Second World War. **13.** Anschütz &
Jehsert, Mehlis and Zella-Mehlis in Thüringen, Germany.
Listed in 1914 as weapons makers, and in 1920 as whole-
salers. Owned in 1920 by Hugo and Emil Anschütz.

Anson – **1.** E. Anson & Company, Birmingham,
Warwickshire, England. This gunsmithing business, run
by Edwin Anson (q.v.), was active from 1890 until the
end of the Second World War, when Anson's descendants
or executors allegedly sold it to *Curry & Keen. Premises

J.G. ANSCHÜTZ, GERMANIA-WAFFENWERK AG

Anschütz (8)

Mehlis and Zella-Mehlis in Thüringen, Germany. This gunsmithing business was founded by Johann Gottfried Anschütz in 1856. It soon attained a reputation for good-quality sporting guns, and by 1896 was employing a workforce of seventy-five. Anschütz was listed in the 1900 edition of the *Deutsches Reichs-Adressbuch* as a gunmaker, specialising in '[*]Flobert pistols, muzzle loaders, [*]Lefaucheux [pinfires], centre-fire guns, pocket pistols, revolvers. All sorts of small-calibre rifles, rifles and shotguns including first-class three-barrel rifles. Production in 1900: 75,000 items.'

More than 200 people were employed in 1914 and, in March 1915, a mark of a double-encircled 'JGA' was granted to 'J.G. Anschütz Germania-Waffenwerk' (no. 202,536) to supplement the head of *Germania, which had been used from the late 1890s. The owners in 1920 were noted as Fritz August and Otto Veit Anschütz; in 1930 they were Richard and Frau Alma Anschütz.

The 1925 edition of the *Deutsches Reichs-Adressbuch* lists the company's products as 'weapons of all types, including Flobert-, target and other pistols, revolvers of all types, air guns, all sorts of [*]Tesching, stalking and target rifles, double-barrel shotguns and [*]Drillinge.' Production of the *JGA air pistol began in this era, and perhaps also of the *Dolla; however, catalogues published in the early 1930s suggest that this was a period of distribution rather than manufacture. Trading ceased at the end of the Second World War.

In the 1950s, on the basis of a new bolt-action rimfire rifle (the Model 54), operations were rebuilt by Max and Rudolf Anschütz in Ulm am Donau. Shooting galleries were made for amusement-arcades in this period, and the first post-war airgun, the bolt-action LG275, was introduced in 1958. This was followed in 1959 by the first of the suppressed-recoil designs – the LG220 – and by several thousand training rifles modelled on the Egyptian Hakim auto-loader. Then the introduction of the improved Model 64 .22 rimfire bolt-action allowed the company to make the great success of its firearms-making business that Anschütz still enjoys.

Rifles have been made in huge numbers, most of them bearing numerical designations. A comprehensive list will be found in John Walter, *Rifles of the World* (second edition, Krause Publications, 1998), pp. 159–67. Patents granted to the company, particularly to protect its target guns (air and cartridge alike) are listed under their inventors' names. *See* Helmut *Liebmann, Arthur *Rauh, Dieter *Straube, August *Weisser, Hermann *Wild and Karl *Zimmermann.

The single-shot .22 Model 1807 bolt-action target rifle.
Courtesy of J.G. Anschütz GmbH, Ulm/Donau.

were occupied at 77 Slaney Street until 1895, but then a move to Steelhouse Lane took place. Birmingham city directories list the workshop successively at 14 (1913), 5 & 6 (1915) and 128 Steelhouse Lane (1921–28), perhaps indicating postal renumbering rather than constant moves. Anson is known to have distributed *Millita-type Langenhan rifles in the early 1900s. Prior to 1914, the company also marketed a distinctive air rifle of a design usually credited to Jacob *Mayer. This gun was known as the *Ansonia. Small numbers of *Firefly and underlever-cocking *Star pistols were made from 1922 to 1940, and a few were even assembled first by *Curry & Keen, and secondly by A. & A. *Brown & Sons immediately after the Second World War. **2.** Edwin Anson. Son of, and successor to, the renowned shotgun designer William Anson, Edwin Anson was the proprietor of E. Anson & Company. British Patent 24,837/1907 was granted to 'Edwin Anson, Gun & Rifle Manufacturer' to protect the *Highest Possible air pistol – manufacture of which, however, was entrusted to Westley *Richards. **3.** Edwin George Anson. Believed to have been the son of Edwin Anson (above), this gunsmith was granted British Patent 178,048 in 1921, protecting improvements to the Highest Possible air pistol with a concentric barrel/air cylinder system. The patent records Anson's home as '968 Warwick Road, Acocks Green, Birmingham, in the County of Warwickshire'. **4.** William Anson, Birmingham, Warwickshire, England. Anson was originally employed as foreman of Westley Richards' gun-action workshop, until starting out on his own account in 1877. Premises were occupied at 77 Slaney Street. The trading style became E. Anson & Company in 1891, and a move to Steelhouse Lane took place in 1896. Operations ceased in the 1940s. Among William Anson's British Patents were 3791/72 of 1872, protecting the fore-end catch that is still generally associated with his name. Patent 1756/75 of 1875 was obtained jointly with John *Deeley to protect the first commercially successful hammerless box-lock shotgun. This particular specification was filed while Anson was still employed as foreman of the Westley *Richards gun-action room. Shotguns and double rifles of this pattern are now known generically as Anson & Deeley. British Patents 4513/76 of 1876, 907/79 of 1879 and 4089/82 of 1882 were all granted for safety mechanisms; 1833/83 of 1883 (obtained jointly with John Deeley) protected modifications to the Anson & Deeley action; 15,299/84 of 1884 and 16,138/86 of 1886 were obtained for extractor or ejector designs; and 7274/88 of 1888 was granted for a 'drop-barrel gun'. **5.** Anson & Deeley; *see* panel, facing page.

'Ansonia' [The]. A brandname found on a barrel-cocking air rifle made in Birmingham by Edwin *Anson & Company, prior to 1914. As the gun seems to embody parts of Jacob *Mayer's British Patent 20,559 of 1901, the chronology of the Ansonia remains uncertain. Theories that it was imported from Germany, a pirated copy or made after the expiry of the Mayer patent all have their champions. There was also an Improved Ansonia with a Mayer & Grammelspacher-type barrel latch, which is usually marked as Anson's own product.

Ansorg – 1. A. Ansorg, Mehlis in Thüringen, Germany. Listed in 1914 as a gun-barrel maker. **2.** August H. Ansorg, Zella-Mehlis in Thüringen, Germany. Listed in the 1939 edition of the *Deutsches Reichs-Adressbuch* as a gun-barrel drawer. **3.** C.K. Ansorg, Zella-Mehlis in Thüringen, Germany. Listed in 1920 as a master gunsmith. **4.** Hermann Ansorg, Zella-Mehlis in Thüringen, Germany. Listed in 1920 as a weapon maker, in 1930 as a gunmaker, and in 1939 as a maker of guns and wholesaler of gun stocks. Trading ceased in 1945.

Anstey & Wilson, trading from Kenyon Street in Birmingham, Warwickshire, made 420,000 British No. 4 (*Lee-Enfield) rifle magazines during 1942/43. The code 'M 8' may have been used instead of the company name. *See* British military manufacturers' marks.

Antechaud-Bonnavion, rue Villeboeuf 6, Saint-Étienne, France. Listed in 1892 as a gunmaker.

'Anti-Recoil Cartridge' [The]. A mark applied to shotgun cartridges loaded by T. *Page-Wood of Bristol from components supplied by *Eley-Kynoch. There was also an Anti-Recoil Economic Cartridge, with a simpler crimp and possibly also a lighter load.

Antley. John Antley, an English gunmaker, was listed in directories at 37 Turner Street, Commercial Road, London E., 1864 and possibly later.

'Antrim' [The]. This was a shotgun cartridge sold in Ireland by *Cambridge & Company of Carrickfergus.

'AO', 'A-O'. Found on *M1 Carbine receivers made for International Business Machines by the *Auto-Ordnance Corporation.

'AP'. An abbreviation for *Armee-Pistole* (army pistol), found as 'Mod. AP' on the slides of the enclosed-hammer predecessor of the *Walther P. 38.

Apache – 1. This Belgian knuckleduster revolver was developed in the early 1870s by a gunmaker named Louis *Dolne. Named after the Parisian street gangs of the period, the barrelless pinfire revolver had a spurless hammer, a folding trigger, a swivelling knife blade on the lower edge of the frame, and a four-ring knuckleduster that doubled as a handgrip. The knuckle-bow folded upward beneath the frame to provide a compact weapon. Guns were made in Belgium or France, usually for 6mm pinfire cartridges,

although other chamberings are known. Genuine articles are marked 'L. DOLNE INVR.' on the frame, but others are marked with a crowned 'ML' of *Manufacture Liégeoise d'Armes à Feu **2.** A Browning-type automatic pistol made by *Ojanguren y Vidosa of Eibar, Guipúzcoa, Spain; 6.35mm, seven rounds, hammer fired. **3.** A dual-calibre BB/6.35mm pump-up pneumatic rifle made by the *National Cart Company of Pasadena, California, USA. Apparently, it dates from the late 1950s, but could not compete with *Crosman and *Sheridan designs, and rapidly disappeared. **4.** Or 'Nylon 77 Apache'. This was a version of the Nylon 66 rimfire auto-loading rifle, made in 1987 by the *Remington Arms Company specifically to rid the company of unwanted parts. They were sold exclusively by the K-Mart retail chain, distinguished by their bright green stocks and fore-ends. **5.** Apache Black. A name applied to a version of the *Remington *Nylon 66 auto-loading rifle with black synthetic butt and fore-end complemented by chrome-plated metalwork. *See also* Mohawk Brown and Seneca Green.

Apaolozo Hermanos were gunmakers trading in Eibar, and later Zumarraga, Guipúzcoa, Spain. They made the *Paramount and *Triomphe pistols.

APB. Applied to a silenced version of the Soviet 9mm *Stechkin pistol. *See also* APS.

'APC'. *See* A.P. *Casey and A.P. *Cobb.

Apex. A brandname associated with a proprietary .240 sporting-rifle cartridge introduced c. 1923 by *Holland & Holland of London, originally as the .240 Belted Rimless Nitro Express. It has also been associated with appropriately chambered *Mauser-action rifles.

'APP'. Found on a carbon-dioxide powered semi-automatic pistol made in Czechoslovakia in the 1960s by Zavodý Jan *Sverma. A modern-looking design with a seven-shot magazine and a gas cartridge in the butt, the APP achieved little success and rapidly disappeared.

Appleton. Gunmaker Henry M. Appleton traded from 51 London Wall, London E.C., England, 1869–72.

APR, or Model 700APR. *See* African Plains Rifle.

APS – 1. The abbreviated form of the designation of the Soviet 9mm *Stechkin pistol. *See also* APB. **2.** Sometimes mistakenly applied to the Soviet/Russian underwater submachine-gun designed by Vladimir *Simonov.

'APX'. An abbreviated form of Ateliers de *Puteaux. *See also* 'CTV'.

'Aquoid' [The]. A shotgun cartridge made by *Eley Bros. prior to the acquisition of the company by Explosives Trades Ltd in 1918.

'aqx'. Found on small-arms components made by the Berlin-Tegel (Germany) factory of *Rheinmetall-Borsig AG, 1940–45.

'ar', 'AR' – 1. As 'AR', cursive, beneath a crown. Found on the weapons of Saxony; the mark of King Albert (1873–1902). *See also* Cyphers, imperial and royal. **2.** As 'ar', associated with machine-guns, rifles and parts made in the Berlin-Borsigwalde factory of *Mauser-Werke KG during the Second World War. **3.** As 'AR'. A designation applied to the Israeli 5.56mm or 7.62mm *Galil Assault Rifle. **4.** As 'AR', beneath a crown. A mark associated with King Amadeo I of Spain, usually found above 'O' for Fábrica de Armas de *Oviedo. *See also* Royal cyphers and markings. **5.** As 'AR', on US military firearms. *See* Alexander *Reuben and Adam *Ruhlman.

Arbeitsgemeinschaft Haenel. *See* C.G. Haenel.

ANSON & DEELEY

Anson (5)

This name is given to a shotgun action patented in Britain in 1875 by William ★Anson and John ★Deeley. It was the first barrel-cocking hammerless design to enjoy commercial success, and had the lock mechanism mounted directly on the action instead of on separate side plates. Anson & Deeley's design was originally known as the Body Action, but subsequently it became much better known as a ★box-lock (cf. ★side-lock).

A safety lever mounted on the side of the action of the earliest guns was soon replaced by a sliding catch positioned on the tang behind the top lever.

The first guns were manufactured by Westley ★Richards of Birmingham, but subsequently the patent was licensed to several leading gunmakers and eventually – usually (but not always) after protection had lapsed – was simply copied far and wide.

Shotguns produced in accordance with the licensing agreements are normally marked 'A. & D. PATENT' somewhere on the action.

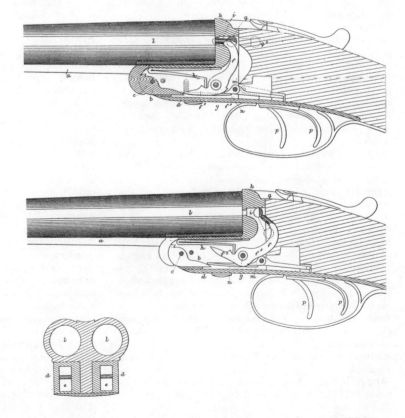

Virtually every modern box-lock shotgun, such as this Spanish-made Albrecht Kind 12-bore Model 20 (top), owes a great debt to Anson & Deeley. The drawings, from a British patent specification, show how compact the design had become.

Arbenz. Adolph(e) Arbenz and his successors, often listed as gunmakers, were merchants and wholesalers. However, as Arbenz was the communicant of British Patent 4413/86 of 1886, granted to Flurscheim & Bergmann (see Eisenwerke Gaggenau), it is clear that Arbenz's business had attained some importance. The patent notes the trading address in 1887 as 107 & 108 Great Charles Street, Birmingham, but a move had been made by 1914 to 33 Ludgate Hill, Birmingham. Arbenz survived into the post-1945 period, wholesaling ironmongery, but ceased trading c. 1959. The links with airguns had long since been severed.

Arbuthnot. Henry T. Arbuthnot of the Royal Artillery was the Assistant Superintendent of the *Royal Small Arms Factory, Enfield, from 1862 to 1866, and Superintendent – with the rank of colonel – from 1880 onward. He is best known for standing firm against the adoption of the Owen *Jones rifle, favouring the *Lee. This brought him into conflict with his superiors, and an allegation that he had accepted favours from the *Nordenfelt Arms & Ammunition Company (often in open competition with the Enfield factory) led to his resignation in October 1886. The Arbuthnot Stock, introduced to accompany the *Enfield-Martini rifle, was distinguished by a cutaway fore-end intended to prevent the underside of the barrel from rusting.

ARCO. A superimposition-type monogram with 'A' and 'R' equally dominant. Correctly 'RACO' (q.v.); used by the *Remington Arms Company.

Arcos. See José *Artes de Arcos SA.

Ardennes. Made by Société Anonyme Continentale pour la Fabrication des Armes à Feu *Lebeau-Courally, this *Anson & Deeley-type side-by-side box-lock (in 9.3x74R) has a distinctively scalloped rear edge to the frame. Fine English scroll engraving appears on the action and fences, while the action flats end in tear-drop finials. The gun has a double-trigger mechanism, a chequered pistol-grip butt and a folding back sight set into the tip of the double rib.

'Ardit' [The]. A corrupted form of 'Hard Hit', this mark will be found on shotgun cartridges handled by *Cogswell & Harrison.

Arendt. Henri Arendt of Liège manufactured pinfire revolvers, pistols and sporting guns during the 1870s and 1880s.

Argles. Alice Argles, the wife of a partner in the *Arms & Ammunition Manufacturing Company Ltd, was granted British Patent 4168/95 of 1895 to protect an airgun. The patent papers record her home address as 61 Alexander Road, Wimbledon, Surrey, and her profession as 'Gentlewoman'. Whether she was genuinely responsible for the patent (which would make her one of the few female inventors in this field) is not known; she may simply have been operating as a cover for her husband and his associates.

Argoud of Saint-Étienne, France, was listed in 1933 as a gunmaker.

'Argyll' [The]. A mark found on shotgun ammunition made by *Eley-Kynoch for Alex. *MacKay & Sons of Tarbert, Scotland.

Arisaka. See panel, facing page.

Aristocrat. A *Suicide Special revolver made by the *Hopkins & Allen Arms Company of Norwich, Connecticut, in the late nineteenth century.

Arizaga. Gunmaker Gaspar Arizaga of Eibar, Guipúzcoa, Spain, made the *Pinkerton pistols – which are sometimes marked simply 'Société d'Armes'. Arizaga also made the 6.35mm-calibre automatic pistols sold under the name *Mondial.

Arizmendi – 1. Francisco Arizmendi, Eibar. Manufacturer of the *Boltun, *Kaba Spezial, *Le Pistolet Automatique, *Roland, *Singer, *Victor and *Ydeal pistols. The Kaba Spezial was made specifically for Karl *Bauer of Berlin, and the Singer may have been supplied to *Arizmendi y Goenaga, although often marked as a product of Fabrique d'Armes de Précision. **2.** Norberto Arizmendi SA. Founded in Eibar in 1917 and owned in the 1980s by José Ignacio Arizmendi, grandson of the founder, this manufacturer of automotive components, metal goods and shotguns has also made air rifles and sporting guns. The workforce numbered 140 in 1980 and annual production capacity was some 60,000 guns. Arizmendi products are now sold under the brandname *Norica and trademark *NAC. **3.** F. Arizmendi y Goenaga, Eibar, Guipúzcoa, Spain. A maker of *Ruby-pattern semi-automatic pistols for the French Army during the First World War, and also of the *Teuf-Teuf, *Waldman and *Walman patterns.

ARM. A term distinguishing the Assault Rifle/Machine-gun variant of the *Galil, with a bipod and a folding carrying handle

Armada. A Spanish-language term signifying naval service – e.g. 'ARMADA ARGENTINA', found on *Colt revolvers acquired by the Argentinian Navy during the early twentieth century.

ArmaLite – 1. ArmaLite Corporation, Costa Mesa, California, USA. The manufacturer and distributor of the *ArmaLite AR-18 rifle, 1969–82. See also Chartered Industries of Singapore and Daewoo. **2.** ArmaLite Division of the Fairchild Engine & Airplane Corporation. This business was formed in 1954 to promote guns embodying aluminium-alloy parts and foam-filled synthetic furniture. The first gun, the .308 AR-3 designed by Eugene *Stoner, relied on a variation of the rotating-bolt locking system pioneered by Melvin *Johnson. Although the AR-3 was not particularly successful, it encouraged development of the AR-10. **3.** ArmaLite rifles. See panel, pp. 38/39. **4.** ArmaLite, Inc. See ArmaLite Division of Fairchild Engine & Airplane Corporation.

Armas... – 1. Armas El Corzo. See *El Corzo. **2.** Armas Juaristi. See Juaristi.

Armbruster Charles Armbruster. Listed in London directories of 1864/65 as a gunmaker, trading from 8 Vernon Place, Bloomsbury.

Armee... – 1. Armee-Pistole (AP, Army Pistol). An enlargement of the *Polizei-Pistole, made in the early 1930s by Carl *Walther Waffenfabrik of Zella-Mehlis, for German Army trials. The testers were sceptical of the value of blowback pistols chambered for the 9mm Parabellum cartridge, and the original AP was abandoned in favour of the locked-breech design described below. **2.** An enclosed-hammer forerunner of the Walther P. 38, made only in small numbers. See also Heeres Pistole. **3.** Armee- und Marinehaus, Inh. Deutscher-Offizier-Verein (DOV), Berlin-Charlottenburg, Hardenbergstrasse, Germany (1941). This business succeeded the *Warenhaus für Armee und Marine c. 1911, trading until the end of the Second World War. Rifles, shotguns, accessories and ammunition have been reported with

ARISAKA

This sturdy turning-bolt design was developed by a committee chaired by Colonel Nariake Arisaka to replace the *Murata. The perfected Meiji 38th Year Type rifle (adopted in 1906) was a modified version of the *Mauser, exceptionally strong and durable.

The earliest 6.5mm 'trials' or Meiji 29th Year Type rifle (1896) was followed by the refined Meiji 30th Year Type (M1897), which was actually adopted in February 1899, and then c. 1901 by a short-barrelled cavalry carbine. Next came the Meiji 35th Year Type rifle of 1902, an unsuccessful improvement on its predecessors; once the perfected 6.5mm-calibre Meiji 38th Year Type (M1905) rifles had been issued from 1907 onward, surviving 35th Year guns were reissued to the navy. The Meiji 44th Year Type cavalry carbine of 1911 was essentially similar to the 1905 pattern, but had a folding bayonet beneath the barrel.

Adopted in 1937, the Type 97 sniper rifle had a monopod beneath the fore-end, and the bolt handle bent downward. About 20,000 were made in the Kokura and Nagoya factories in 1938–41. When war with China began in 1937, the Japanese discovered that the 6.5mm cartridge was not powerful enough. The result was the 7.7mm semi-rimless Type 99 pattern, accompanied by a suitable Arisaka. Although a full-length rifle was made in small numbers, a shortened 'universal' pattern was preferred by 1940.

The Type 99 sniper rifle (1942) retained the basic features of the preceding Type 97, including the turned-down bolt and monopod. The earliest Kokura-assembled guns featured 2.5x sights, but the 10,000 or so Nagoya-made guns used the improved 4x Type 2. The Type 0 paratroop rifle was a standard Type 99 with the barrel and receiver joined by an interrupted thread, while the Type 1 (1941) was nothing more than a 38th Year Type carbine with a folding butt. The perfected Type 2, adopted in 1943, embodied a sliding wedge to lock the barrel and receiver together.

In 1943, attempts to conserve raw material led to the Substitute Type 99 rifle (also known as Type 99 Model 2 or Type 3), made of materials that steadily deteriorated as the war ran its course until the last guns made in 1945 were truly awful. Arisaka rifles were used in Britain, Burma, China, Indonesia, Korea, Russia and Siam. Finland employed some guns taken from the Russians, who had acquired many from Britain during the First World War. As the British guns had been purchased in Japan in 1914, it is possible to find a 38th Year Type rifle marked by four different countries.

Among the best sources of detailed information about the Japanese rifles is *Japanese Military Rifles* by Fred Honeycutt and J. Patt Anthony (Julin Books, 1983), although *Rifles of the World* by John Walter (second edition, Krause Publications, 1998) provides a useful summary. *See also* Heijo, Japanese small-arms designations, Koishikawa, Kokura, Mukden, Murata, Nagoya, Nanking, Simple Rifles, Special Navy Rifle, Tientsin, Tokyo Juki and Toyo Juki.

The 7.7mm Type 99 Arisaka sniper rifle, with its telescope sight, sight cover and monopod.

appropriate marks, which included the letter code 'jme' allocated in September 1941. **4.** Armee-Universal-Gewehr. A 5.56x45 auto-loading rifle made by *Steyr-Mannlicher GmbH. *See* AUG.

Armeria. *See* Fábrica de Armas de República Dominicana.

Armero Especialistas of Eibar, Guipúzcoa, Spain, made the *Omega pistol.

Armes... – 1. Armes Automatiques Lewis. *See* Lewis Gun. **2.** Armes et Materiales Militaires SA, also known as Armat. Manufacturers of machine-guns, hand-grenades, trench-mortars, ammunition and shells, Armat traded from Meir 24 in Antwerp, Belgium, between 1934 and 1939.

Armigas, or Armigas-Comega. A name associated with Atillio *Zanoletti, a maker of gas-powered guns in the 1960s.

Armi-Jager. *See* Jager-Armi di Armando Piscetta.

Armistead. American gunmaker Thomas E. Armistead, of Mazomanie, Wisconsin, patented a gun sight on 5 September 1893 (US no. 504,696).

Armit. Robert H. Armit, a patentee domiciled in London, England, was granted protection for a machine-gun on 17 February 1891 (US no. 446,807). A half-interest was assigned to T. McCulloch of London.

Armoury. A name found on *Mayer & Grammelspacher Diana airguns and airgun ammunition

ARMALITE RIFLES

ArmaLite (3)

Successfully tested in 1955, the AR-10K was followed in 1956 by fifty semi-production AR-10B rifles. Modified by James *Sullivan, they had a new gas tube above the barrel, an improved bolt carrier and a rifled steel liner inside an alloy barrel casing. ArmaLite had granted a licence to the Dutch state-owned *Artillerie-Inrichtingen, but retained the North American sales agency for itself; *Sidem International SA of Brussels was granted Europe and North Africa; *Cooper-Macdonald, Inc., of Baltimore, took charge of Australasia and the Far East; and *Interarms of Alexandria, Virginia, assumed responsibility for southern Africa and Central and South America.

AR-10 rifles were optimistically touted worldwide in 1959, but the best they could manage was to finish second to the FAL in South African trials of 1960. When the Dutch also rejected the ArmaLite in favour of the FAL, Artillerie-Inrichtingen lost interest, and all work in Zaandam stopped after only a few thousand had been made.

In 1957, to comply with a US Army specification for a lightweight small-calibre selective-fire rifle, ArmaLite engineers Robert *Fremont and James Sullivan altered the AR-10 to fire a modified .222 Remington round. About twenty of the first-pattern rifles were made, weighing just 6.12lb with a loaded 25-round magazine. Meanwhile, however, the US Army had increased the performance-at-range requirements, which ArmaLite answered simply by substituting the .222 Remington Special (known as .223 Remington from 1959) for the original .222 round.

Tests undertaken in 1958 showed that the small-calibre AR-15 and the rival *WLAR both performed better than the 7.62mm T44E4. Improvements were made to the AR-15, but the small-calibre high-velocity concept was encountering opposition from the Ordnance; although trials recommenced in December 1958, it had been decided that the T44 (later the M14) was the only rifle suitable for military use. Fairchild then lost interest in the ArmaLite and licensed it to *Colt.

The first Colt-made rifles (AR-15 Model 01, Colt Model 601) were completed in December 1959. ArmaLite, Inc., was formed in 1961 under the presidency of Charles Dorchester, but Fairchild had withdrawn, and Eugene *Stoner and his design team had joined the *Cadillac Gage Company. USAF trials of the AR-15 were encouraging, and, in January 1962, the 5.56mm Rifle AR-15 (later XM16, then M16) was classified as USAF standard.

In 1963, the Secretary of the Army recommended large-scale purchases of AR-15 rifles for army airborne units and special forces; on 4 November 1963, Colt received the first substantial government contract. Subsequently, a plunger designed by Foster *Sturtevant was added to the rear right side of the receiver, above the pistol grip, to allow the breech to be closed manually; and the improved XM16E1 became the M16A1 on 28 February 1967. On 30 June 1967, the US government bought manufacturing rights from Colt. In April 1968, therefore, contracts were agreed with the *Hydra-Matic Division of General Motors and *Harrington & Richardson.

In 1981, the US Marine Corps persuaded the managers of the Joint Services Small Arms Program to acquire fifty improved Colt-made rifles. Known as M16A1E1, these

---

(probably made by *Lanes Bros.) sold by Bertram *Webster & Company, The Southern Armoury, Newington Butts, London, in the 1920s.

Arms... – 1. Arms & Ammunition Manufacturing Company Ltd, London. Formed in 1891 and trading as a limited-liability company from 1895, initially this business was registered at 143 Queen Victoria Street, E.C. Apparently, representation was also maintained in Birmingham. It was sold to John R. *Watson in 1904, who may have been one of the original partners with William *Argles. The subsequent fate of the company is unknown, but it is presumed to have succumbed prior to 1914. Airguns and sporting rifles have been reported with its marks. **2.** Arms Corporation of South Africa Pty Ltd, or Armscor. The principal state-owned arms manufacturer in the Republic of South Africa, now known as Denel Pty, whose Vektor subsidiary now makes the small-arms. Armscor produced *Saive- and *Galil-type rifles, alongside *Browning machine-guns, artillery and armoured vehicles. **3.** Arms Corporation of the Philippines, Inc. A successor to *Squires, Bingham, retaining the Squibman brandname.

Armsby & Harrington, of Worcester, Massachusetts, USA, made rimfire cartridge rifles in accordance with Cyrus *Holden's patents of 1 April 1862 (no. 34,859) and 29 March 1864 (no. 42,139).

Armscor. *See* Arms Corporation of South Africa.

Armscorp. *See* Arms Corporation of the Philippines.

Armstrong – 1. Armstrong, Clonmel, Ireland. The marks of this gunmaker have been reported on self-cocking *pepperboxes dating from the middle of the nineteenth century. **2.** James W. Armstrong, Augusta, Kentucky, USA. The joint patentee, with John Taylor, of a breech-loading firearm on 25 November 1862 (no. 37,025). *See also* Armstrong & Taylor. **3.** John Armstrong, Terre Haute, Indiana, USA. Trading from 1882 to 1885, this gunmaker made single-shot sporting rifles. **4.** William Shaw Armstrong. An 'Agent for the sale of Wire Ropes, Boilers and Machinery', living at 75 Leopold Street in Leeds, Yorkshire, England, Armstrong patented an airgun in 1906 (British Patent 262/06). **5.** Armstrong & Company. Listed at 5 Newman Street, Oxford Street, London W., in 1897. **6.** Armstrong & Company. Trading in Newcastle upon Tyne, this English gunsmithing and sporting-goods business offered shotgun cartridges marked either 'Sporting Gun Depot' or *'A C C'. **7.** Armstrong & Taylor, Augusta, Kentucky. A partnership of James W. *Armstrong and John Taylor, who jointly patented a firearm in 1862. Apparently, the guns were made by the *Norwich Arms Company. **8.** Armstrongs (Gunmakers) Ltd. This business sold guns and sporting goods from premises on Carlton Hill, Nottingham, England. They included shotgun cartridges offered under a Sherwood brandname.

Army & Navy... – 1. Army & Navy Co-Operative Stores Ltd, London, England. Established in 1871, this

demonstrated such superiority that the M16A2 rifle was officially adopted in November 1983, with a new back sight, a heavy barrel and a three-shot burst mechanism.

Other ArmaLite rifles included the unsuccessful AR-16, designed by Eugene Stoner in 1961 specifically for tank and armoured-vehicle crewmen. In 1963, after Stoner had joined the Cadillac Gage Corporation, the AR-16 was scaled-down for the 5.56mm cartridge by Arthur *Miller to create the AR-18. Made largely of pressings, the gun was operated by a tappet-type piston

system in a tube above the barrel and had a seven-lug rotating bolt. Although tests undertaken in 1964–65 by the US Army were unsuccessful, a licence was granted to *Howa in Japan in 1969 and another to *Sterling Engineering in the mid-1970s.

The best source of information about ArmaLite rifles is unquestionably *The Black Rifle*, by the late Edward C. Ezell (Collector Grade Publications, 1987). *Rifles of the World* by John Walter (Krause Publications, second edition, 1998) provides a useful checklist.

The Colt-made 5.56mm M16A2 light machine-gun, derived from the standard AR-15 (M16) rifle, was an unsuccessful competitor in the US Army light squad automatic weapon trials won by the Belgian Minimi.

business retailed a vast range of military equipment, including uniforms, guns, edged weapons and ammunition. It was subsequently renamed Army & Navy Stores. Rifle and shotgun cartridges generally included 'A. & N.C.S.L.' in the headstamps and packaging, but were made elsewhere by companies such as *Eley Bros. and *Kynoch. **2.** Army & Navy Stores Ltd, London. A post-1913 (?) successor to the Army & Navy Co-Operative Stores Ltd, this business traded until recent times. Now it is part of the House of Fraser Group, but prior to 1945 specialised in uniforms, firearms, edged weapons, ammunition and ancillary goods required by military personnel. These included shotgun cartridges marked 'Coronation', 'Every Day', 'Eureka', 'Reliable' and 'Victoria'. The firearms and accessories were all made elsewhere.

Army Special Model. This gun replaced the Colt *New Model Army revolver in 1908. Renamed 'Official Police Model' in 1928, it was offered in several chamberings from .32-20 WCF to .41 Colt. The cylinder rotated clockwise and the *Positive Lock safety system was fitted.

Arnaiz. *See* Lopez de Arnaiz.

Arnaldi. Michele Arnaldi, then holding the rank of major in the Italian 31st infantry regiment, designed a breech-loading repeating action adaptable to the Swiss *Vetterli. About 300 M1870 Vetterli arms were converted in 1884, then issued for trials with the 7th Bersaglieri and 5th Alpini.

Arnold – 1. J. Arnold, Jr. An inspector of US martial arms c. 1868–71, using a 'JA' mark. *See also* US arms inspectors' marks. **2.** Remick K. Arnold. This arms inspector, active from 1862 to 1877 or later, used an 'RKA' mark. *See also* US arms inspectors' marks. **3.** William H. Arnold. Resident in Washington, D.C., USA, during 1857–60, Arnold received US Patent 23,538 on 12 April 1859 to protect 'projectiles for firearms'. He was also granted no. 26,076 on 15 November 1859 for a 'breech-loading firearm'.

'AR' above 'O'. Found, customarily beneath a crown, on Spanish military weapons. The mark combines the 'AR' of the king – Amadeo I Rex – with the 'O' of the Fábrica de Armas de *Oviedo.

Arostegui. *See* Arrostegui.

Aronson. Joseph N. Aronson, patentee of a breech-loading firearm on 13 November 1866 (no. 59,540), was domiciled in New York City.

Arquebusier. This name was given to a 6.35mm pocket pistol made by Ernest & François *Mayor. It was patented in 1919 by Ernst Rochat of Noyon.

Arrizabalaga – 1. Calixto Arrizabalaga, Eibar, Guipúzcoa, Spain. A gunmaker responsible for a range of sporting guns and semi-automatic pistols. **2.** Hijos de José Arrizabalaga, Eibar, Guipúzcoa, Spain. This gunmaking business traded in Eibar from 1915 until 1937, when it was a casualty of the Spanish Civil War. Maker of *Esmit revolvers and the *Terrible automatic pistol.

Arrostegui. The Spanish gun distributor Eulogio Arrostegui of Eibar, Guipúzcoa, marked a variety of firearms made elsewhere in Eibar, their origins often camouflaged with the names 'E.A.', 'Azul' and 'Super Azul' (the last being reserved for the Beistegui Hermanos *Royal MM31)

Arrow – 1. Impaled with an arrow. Found on a *Langenhan Millita-type gun; significance unknown, but believed to have been applied by a British distributor. 2. A 4.5mm break-barrel spring-air rifle made by the State Industry Factory in Shanghai, People's Republic of China, c. 1972–88, sold in Britain by the *Abbey Supply Company, David *Nickerson (Tathwell) Ltd and *Sussex Armoury. 3. A mark found on shotgun cartridges made in the Brimsdown (England) factory of the *Remington Arms–Union Metallic Cartridge Company. 4. Arrow Machinery Company, Philadelphia, Pennsylvania, USA. Trading from 234 North 3rd Street, this company was formed in 1922 by William *Heilprin and others to succeed *Heilprin's Manufacturing Company. It was liquidated in 1930.

Arrowsmith – 1. George A. Arrowsmith. Owner of a gunsmithing and metalworking business trading in Gold Street, New York City, Arrowsmith was the assignee of patents protecting a 'loaded ball' and a 'method of attaching a ball to a wooden cartridge'. These comprised the cartridge of the *Volition repeater, developed by Walter *Hunt, which was patented in England in December 1847, and subsequently in the USA in August 1849. Arrowsmith overreached himself financially, allowing the financier Courtlandt *Palmer to acquire rights to Hunt's patents for $100,000. See also Lewis *Jennings. 2. John Basil Arrowsmith. The co-patentee with *Accles & Shelvoke of the *Acvoke air pistol: British Patent 619,108, sought in November 1946. 3. Arrowsmith Manufacturing Company. A manufacturer of ammunition, trading in Niagara Falls in the early 1920s.

Arroyo y Echernagucia (sic). This Spanish gunsmithing and sporting-goods distribution business operated in Havana, Cuba, in the mid-1870s.

Artemis. This was a twenty-shot 8mm gas-powered rifle made by *Marocchi e Figli in the 1960s. The barrel was smooth-bored. The Artemis-S was a single-shot derivative in 4.5mm or 5.5mm, but was rarely seen outside Italy, and it is assumed that production was limited. All work seems to have ceased by 1970.

Artes. José Artes de Arcos SA of Madrid and Barcelona, Spain, made the *Setra AS2000 pneumatic rifles alongside sporting guns. Little else is known about its history.

Artex. This state-run Hungarian export agency, situated at Via Hadór 31, Budapest, in 1966, sold Hungarian-made sporting guns in the West. These included the Telly series of airguns, marketed in the UK by *Relum Ltd, and the FÉG pistols.

Artexim, Rambla Cataluña, Edificio Catalonia, Barcelona, Spain. An export agency for sporting and airguns – and also, perhaps, a small-scale gunmaker.

Artillerie-Inrichtingen. The principal state-owned Dutch ordnance factory in *Hembrug. See also ArmaLite.

Artillery Model – 1. A term applied in the modern era to the long-barrelled *Parabellum or Luger pistol, introduced in 1913 and correctly designated lang Pistole 1908. 2. Applied, without official status, to Colt-made M1873 *Single Action Army Revolvers converted by *Springfield Armory by shortening the barrel from 7.5in to 5.5in. The work was done in the 1890s, when the advent of the .38 M1892 allowed original full-length revolvers to be withdrawn from the US Cavalry for reissue to artillerymen; however, part numbers rarely match.

Artistic Arms Company. An engineering company that made a few *Sharps-Borchardt-type rifles in Hoagland, Indiana, USA, in the 1970s. The business failed to prosper, and Artistic Arms foundered after a mere handful of guns had been completed.

Art Metal Construction Company Ltd, Buckingham Palace Road, London SW1. A maker of magazines for the British 9mm *Sten Gun during the Second World War. The code 'S 311' may have been used instead of the company name. See also British military manufacturers' marks.

AS. A superimposition-type monogram, sometimes found encircled, with neither letter prominent. Correctly 'SA'; used by *Suinaga y Aramperri.

Asahi. An underlever-cocking spring-air rifle made in Japan by the *Kawaguchiya company c. 1948–55. Rarely seen outside the Far East, it was a copy of the pre-war *Jeffries Pattern BSA. The manufacturer produced a small number of modified guns with a modern-looking half stock, but had ceased work by the early 1960s.

'asb'. A mark found on cartridge clips, chargers, small-arms ammunition and components made in the Berlin-Borsigwalde factory of *Deutsche Waffen- und Munitionsfabriken AG.

'ASG'. See Albert S. *Granger.

Asgard Rifle. See Howth Rifle.

Ashcroft. E.H. Ashcroft of Boston, Massachusetts, USA, received a patent on a breech-loading firearm on 26 May 1863 (no. 38,645). He was also the assignee of a patent for an adjustable front sight granted on 29 March 1864 to John B. Learock (no. 42,091). See also Richard S. *Lawrence.

'Ashes [The]' or 'The Ashes Works'. Marks associated with gun-locks made in Wolverhampton, England, by Joseph *Brazier & Sons.

Ashley. George Ashley, Washingtonville, New York State, USA. A gunsmith trading in the early 1880s.

Ashton – 1. Dr Henry T. Ashton was the Superintendent of the *Royal Small Arms Factory, Enfield, from 1905 until 1909. He was also co-patentee with J.J. *Speed of the back sight used on the SMLE rifle, protected by British Patent 4776/06 of 27 February 1906. 2. T. Ashton. A gunsmith trading in London, England, in the middle of the nineteenth century. 3. Thomas R.R. Ashton, Deniliquin, New South Wales, 'in the Commonwealth of Australia'. Ashton received a selection of patents between 1895 and 1908. US Patent 537,858 of 23 April 1895, sought jointly with E.J. Kelly, protected a magazine firearm, while US no. 537,959 of 23 April 1895 (also with Kelly) protected a magazine. US Patent 589,684 of 7 September 1897 allowed claims for a 'magazine bolt gun', while US Patents 597,935 of 25 January 1898, 834,354 of 30 October 1906 and 931,983 of 24 August 1908 all protected 'magazine firearms'. The last two were sought from London, England. 4. J. Ashton & Company. This English gunmaker was listed at 1 Swallow's Gardens, Goodman's Fields, London E., in 1856/57. However, the directory entries for 1850–56 and 1858 all list the proprietor as Mrs Ashton. 5. William Ashton, Middletown, Connecticut, USA.

Patentee of a 'bullet mould with movable core, whereby hollow or Minie bullets are cast'. This was granted on 1 May 1855 (no. 12,774).

ASI – 1. A superimposition-type monogram without dominant letters, correctly 'SIA'; used by *Security Industries of America, Inc. **2.** ASI Ltd, Snape, Saxmundham, Suffolk, England. This company is best known as an importer of shotguns, sporting rifles, airguns and accessories, including the products of *AYA, *El Gamo and *Feinwerkbau. The El Gamo airguns have been marketed in Britain (from 1969 onward) under a range of distinctive names, including *Commando, *Paratrooper, *Rangemaster and *Sniper.

Asiatic – 1. A Browning-inspired pocket pistol, made by an unknown Spanish gunmaker, probably in the Eibar district; 6.35mm or 7.65mm Auto. **2.** 'Asiatic pistols'. This term was coined to categorise the all but unclassifiable selection of pistols made in China, Cambodia and other Far East states, c. 1910–50. It encompasses guns based, often loosely, on the Mauser C/96; others derived from the blowback *FN-Brownings; many that bear no relationship to any known design, with superfluous tangent-leaf sights or ventilated slides; and a few, customarily produced after the end of the Second World War, following the lines of the Browning GP-35 or *High Power. With the exception of pistols produced in Cambodia for the Cao-Dai rebels, which are surprisingly true to their .45 M1911A1 *Colt-Browning and GP-35 prototypes, quality is universally poor. Some guns bear spurious marks, particularly the well-known Mauser banner or FN monogram, although the engravers often made mistakes; working from right to left, for example, they regularly reversed letters (in particular, 'S') or misspelled words – e.g. 'PATDNT' instead of 'Patent' and 'EEU' for 'Feu'. Very few attempts have been made to catalogue these guns, but a good sequence of drawings appears in A.B. Zhuk's *The Illustrated Encyclopedia of Handguns* (Greenhill Books, London, 1995).

Askins. Charles Askins, USA. See Hoffman Arms Company.

Asociación Armera. An export agency with offices in Eibar, Guipúzcoa, Spain. Its marks may be encountered on the guns themselves.

A-Square Company, Inc., of Bedford, Kentucky, USA, has been making sporting rifles on the basis of a modified *Mauser bolt action from 1983 to date. They have been marketed under the names *Caesar and *Hannibal.

ASS – 1. A mark, perhaps still to be encountered as a monogram, used by August Schüler of Suhl, Germany. **2.** An abbreviated form of the designation of the Soviet/Russian silenced assault rifle or *Avtomat* designed by Serdyukov and Kraskov.

Assmuss. Inventor Albert Assmus of Chicago, Illinois, USA, was granted protection for a magazine firearm on 16 December 1873 (no. 145,748). A half-share was assigned to C. Assmus of Chicago.

Assonet Gun Factory, trading in Assonet, Massachusetts, USA, this was a short-lived gunmaking business that apparently made break-open single-barrel shotguns in 1893/94.

Aston – 1. This brandname is associated with a diabolo pellet with a distinctive low-set waist, introduced by *Cox & Son of Aston juxta Birmingham, England, some

time prior to 1909 and made until the beginning of the First World War. **2.** Henry Aston, Middletown, Connecticut, USA. A gunmaker trading in 1843–55. **3.** James Aston, Hythe, Kent. Aston was the Armourer to the British Army's School of Musketry from 1853 until 1870. He is regarded as having made important contributions to the design of the Pattern 1853 (Enfield) *cap-lock rifle-musket, and sold .45-calibre cap-lock target rifles on his own account. These were made by Hollis & Sheath or Isaac *Hollis & Sons of Birmingham. Aston also developed a falling-block breech-loading action, patented in the USA on 13 May 1873 (no. 138,837) and 12 March 1878 (201,216). **4.** R. & W. Aston [& Company]. This well-established English gunmaking business, based in Birmingham, was also listed at 38 Lime Street, London E.C., as 'Agents for G.S. Melland'. Subsequently, Richard & William Aston were listed at 26 Crosby Hill Chambers, London E.C., in 1869.

Astora. A brandname applied to shotguns, sporting guns and air rifles made by *Simson & Company of Suhl – subsequently part of *Berlin-Suhler Werke. The airguns included a military-style bolt-action repeating airgun with a cam-slot cocking stroke.

Astra – 1. A brandname found on the products of *Esperanza y Unceta of Guernica (*see below*). **2.** Astra Match. A six-shot .38-calibre target revolver made in Spain by Astra–Unceta y Cia SA, introduced in 1976. Derived from the *Cadix, it has a single-action trigger, adjustable sights and anatomical wooden hand-grips. The barrel is usually 15cm long. **3.** Astra pistols. See panel, p. 42. **4.** Astra revolvers. See panel, p. 43. **5.** Astra–Unceta [y Cia] SA, Guernica, Spain. Once the Second World War had ended, *Unceta y Cia abandoned the guns based on the Mauser C/96 and restricted work on those derived from the *Campo-Giro. Attempts to diversify led to the production of pneumatic drills and textile machinery, and the first shotguns were manufactured in 1954. The Astra name was officially incorporated in the company name in 1955, forming Astra–Unceta y Cia SA. The first new gun to be introduced was the *Cub pistol, followed by the *Camper and *Falcon pistols (1956), and the *Cadix revolver (1958). Work continued on a variety of improved designs, including the Walther-like *Constable, although most recent designations have tended to be numerical. *See also* Astra pistols (above).

AT, A.T. – 1. Found as 'A.T.' on British rifles, usually *Lee-Enfields, converted to chamber .23-centrefire *Aiming Tube ammunition. **2.** Usually as 'A&T'. See Adams & Tait. **3.** A superimposition-type monogram, with the letters equally dominant. It was used by Alois *Tomiška of Pilsen, Czechoslavakia, on 6.35mm and 7.65mm *Little Tom pistols.

Ateliers de Fabrication des Armes Portatives, 'A.F.A.P.', Calais, France. A name given to the small-arms repair workshops set up in 1914 by the Belgian Army fighting alongside British and French units·on the Western Front. The facilities were closed at the end of the First World War.

Atherton. Gunmaker William Atherton, of Northville in New York State, handled sporting guns and ammunition in the 1870s.

Atkin – 1. Henry Atkin. Among the best-known of the gunmakers working in London in the late nineteenth cen-

ASTRA PISTOLS

Astra (3)

Made by *Esperanza y Unceta, the first of these was simply a post-1914 *Victoria, offered in 6.35mm and 7.65mm. This 'Browning copy' acquired a grip safety in 1916, remained in production after the factory moved to Guernica in 1918, and was superseded in 1920 by the essentially similar Astra 200. When production ceased in 1967, nearly 160,000 of these 6.35mm-calibre blowbacks had been made.

Much better known is the 'tube-slide' 9mm Largo Astra 400 (or Modelo 1921), developed from the *Campo-Giro, which provided the basis for a range of handguns made until recent days. The Astra 300 was a small 400, chambered for the 7.65mm Auto or 9mm Short rounds; about 171,300 were made in 1923–47, including more than 85,000 delivered to Germany during the Second World War. Many of these were issued to Luftwaffe personnel and will bear appropriate inspectors' marks. The Astra 600 was a special short-barrelled Model 400 chambering the 9mm Parabellum cartridge; ordered by the Germans in 1943, only a quarter of an output of about 40,000 guns could be delivered before the liberation of France in 1944.

The Astra 900 and its derivatives were simplified adaptations of the Mauser C/96 (q.v.), with a detachable side-plate set into the frame. The Astra 901 was a selective-fire variant of the 900, retaining the ten-round integral magazine; the Astra 902 of 1928 was similar, but had a twenty-round magazine; the Astra 903 – introduced contemporaneously with the Mauser *Schnellfeuerpistole* – offered detachable magazines holding ten or twenty cartridges. The Modelo E was an Astra 903 improved in minor respects, and the Modelo F, known during development as the Astra 904, embodied a flywheel mechanism in the grip to reduce the cyclic rate from 950 rds/min to 350 rds/min.

Said to have been developed at the request of the Guardia Civil, the Modelo F was made only in small quantities. About 34,350 900-series guns were made before work ceased in 1937, during the Spanish Civil War; all but a few thousand had gone to China. Several thousand 900 and 903 examples were made for the Germans during the Second World War, and a last batch of Model 900 pistols was completed in 1955.

The .22LR or 6.35mm Auto Astra 7000, introduced in 1973, was an improved version of the *Cub, with neater external contours and a separate back sight dovetailed into the frame instead of a crude longitudinal groove. The 7.65mm or 9mm Short Astra 50 (A-50) was a simplified Constable, with the safety lever mounted on the frame instead of the slide, and the slide-release catch on the left side of the frame omitted; the .22 Astra TS-22 was similar, but had a long barrel within an extended slide, adjustable sights and an anatomical grip. The 9mm Short Astra 60 (A-60), introduced in 1987, is a derivative of the Constable with a thirteen-round staggered-column magazine and an ambidextrous safety catch on the slide.

The Astra 80 (A-80), the first of the modernised military-pattern semi-automatic pistols, incorporated a simplified *Colt-Browning barrel depressor, relying on a cam-finger instead of a pivoting link. The A-80 has a double-action trigger system embodying an external hammer and a de-cocking lever that can be mounted on the left or right side of the frame. Chambered for the 7.65mm Parabellum, 9mm Parabellum, .38 Super Auto or .45 ACP rounds, the A-80 has a staggered-column magazine with a capacity of fifteen (nine only in .45).

Introduced in 1985, the Astra 90 is a variant of the A-80 with a Walther-type rotary safety in the slide, and the magazine release catch moved from the butt-heel to a new position in the frame behind the trigger. *See also* Camper, Condor, Constable, Cub and Falcon.

The 7.65mm Astra Constable semi-automatic pistol was clearly inspired by the Walther Polizei-Pistole.

ASTRA REVOLVERS

Astra (4)

The earliest of these was the S&W-influenced ★Cadix, introduced in 1958. The first new revolver to be introduced after the introduction of the US Gun Control Act of 1968 was the Astra 357 (1972), with its frame strengthened to withstand the .357 Magnum cartridge, and barrel options ranging from 75mm to 215mm. The most important change, however, was the addition of a ★transfer-bar safety system. Contemporaneously, the basic Cadix was altered to become the ★New Cadix.

Other guns of this type include the Astra Z50 (1975–82), a snub-nose personal-defence revolver offered with a 50mm barrel in .22LR, .22 Magnum rimfire, .32 S&W Long and .38 Special; the Astra 357 Police, dating from 1980, a short-barrelled personal-defence gun with rudimentary sights; the Astra 680 of 1981, which was basically an improved 250; and the heavy-frame Astra 960 (introduced in 1973), a compact, double-action, six-shot .38 offered with barrels of 75mm, 100mm or 150mm.

Stainless-steel framed Inox variants of the models 250, 357 and 680 have also been manufactured in small numbers.

Three large-calibre revolvers – Astra 41, Astra 44 and Astra 45 – have been made on the same basic transfer-bar action, chambered for the .41 Magnum, .44 Magnum and .45 Long Colt cartridges respectively. Their barrels measure 150mm or 215mm.

This .357 Magnum Astra Police revolver can also fire 9mm Parabellum ammunition if a special cylinder is substituted and the rimless cartridges are held in a special spring clip.

---

tury, Atkin was listed at 43 Upper Manor Street, Chelsea, S.W., from 1862 to 1870; at 19 Oxenden Street, Haymarket, from 1877 to 1890 (Henry Atkin Ltd from 1877); and at 2 Jermyn Street for a few years from 1891. Based thereafter in 88 Jermyn Street, London SW1, the business moved in 1956 to 27 St James Street, and was amalgamated in the early 1960s to form Atkin, Grant & Lang. In addition to sporting guns and rifles, Henry Atkin handled shotgun ammunition marked with the brandnames Covert, Ever Ready, Gem and Raleigh (qq.v.). Most of these were made by ★Eley Bros. and ★Eley-Kynoch Ltd. An assortment of educational skeletonised actions were made for the British War Office during 1938–42, including long-arms and handguns that were often marked 'SKN'. Atkin – granted the code 'S 144' during the Second World War – also renovated more than 9,000 Mk IV and Mk V ★Lewis Guns in 1940/41. *See also* British military manufacturers' marks. **2.** Ralph Atkin, Painesville, Ohio, USA. The marks of this gunmaker have been reported on single-barrel shotguns dating from the 1880s, possibly made elsewhere. **3.** Atkin, Grant & Lang, St James's, London. This was a 1960s amalgamation of the businesses of Henry Atkin, Stephen ★Grant & Sons, and Joseph ★Lang & Son. Sporting guns of all types, including drop-barrel and bolt-action patterns have been made in quantity.

Atkins. Henry E. Atkins, a member of the English gun-making fraternity, is recorded as trading in 1874–87 from 877 Old Kent Road, London.

Atkinson – 1. James W. Atkinson, Milpitas, California, USA. Patentee of a spring gun on 28 June 1892 (no. 477,982) **2.** Joel Atkinson, Parkesburg, Kentucky, USA. Active in 1877–83, this gunmaker built double-barrel cap-lock sporting guns – with one rifled barrel and one smoothbore – and may also have made cartridge-firing derivatives. He was the father of Wyatt Atkinson **3.** T. Atkinson & Sons. The marks applied by this English gun-smithing business – trading from 19a Stricklandgate in the Cumbrian town of Kendal – have been reported on shot-gun cartridges with brandnames such as Kendal, Kendal Castle and Kent. These generally prove to have been made by ★Eley Bros. or ★Eley-Kynoch Ltd. **4.** William B. Atkinson, Bowling Green, Kentucky, USA. Atkinson received a patent protecting a magazine firearm on 11 April 1905 (US no. 787,257), a half-interest being assigned to E.R. Bagley. **5.** Wyatt Atkinson, Parkesburg, Kentucky, USA. Born in 1880, Wyatt Atkinson was the son of Joel (above). His marks have been reported on sporting guns. **6.** Atkinson & Company. These retailers of guns and sporting goods traded from 31 Oxford Street, Swansea, Glamorgan, Wales. Marks have been reported on sporting guns and shotgun cartridges with the brand-name ★Grand Finale.

Atlas – 1. A small 6.35mm Browning-type automatic pistol made by ★Acha Hermanos y Compañía of Ermua, Spain; six rounds, striker or hammer fired. **2.** A brand-name associated with a break-open repeating BB Gun designed by George P. ★Gunn and made by the Atlas Gun Company (below) in 1891–99. Three rods running parallel to the barrel provided a gravity-feed raceway for the ball ammunition. **3.** A lever-action repeating BB Gun designed by George W. ★Weaver in 1890 and made by the Atlas Gun Company, in two or more minor variants, from 1900 until all production ceased in 1906. **4.** Associated with a pump-up pneumatic rifle made by the Atlas Air Rifle Manufacturing Company in the 1950s. **5.** Atlas Air Rifle Manufacturing Company. Makers of the Atlas pneumatic rifle, this business operated in Ilion, New York State, USA. Production of the rifles seems to have begun in 1953, but ended in 1956; it was never large enough to assure the design a lasting place in airgun history, and the parent company had been liquidated by 1958. **6.** Atlas Gun Company. This US airgun manufacturer, like the later similar-sounding Atlas Air Gun Manufacturing Company, traded in the town of Ilion in New York State. It was founded in 1889 by Gilbert W. ★Warren and subsequently exploited some of the patents associated with George Gunn and George Weaver. The Atlas, ★Dandy and ★Victor BB Guns, together with a few unsophisticated cartridge rifles, were produced before Warren sold out to ★Daisy in 1906. **7.** Atlas Rifle Company, Ilion, New York State, USA. A maker of .22-calibre rifles in the 1890s. Possibly the same as the Atlas Gun Company.

'Atom' [The]. Found on shotgun cartridges sold prior to the First World War by ★Freeney's of Galway, Ireland.

A True Fit. A mark found on shotgun ammunition sold in Britain by ★Radcliffe of Colchester. Normally, it is accompanied by a drawing of a bowled-over rabbit.

Attila. A brandname associated with a small double-action semi-automatic pistol made in Hungary in the 1960s and 1970s by ★FÉG. Chambered for the 7.65mm Auto or 9mm Short cartridge, it was based on the Walther ★Polizei-Pistole, and essentially was a commercial variant of the Hungarian ★Walam or 48.M service pistol.

Atwater. John B. Atwater of Ripon, Wisconsin, USA, received US Patent 27,342 on 6 March 1860 to protect a rifled firearm. On 30 September 1862, he was granted another patent on a 'mode of rifling guns' (no. 36,592).

Atwood. Frederick J. Atwood, a lieutenant-colonel in the US Army, inspected .45 M1911A1 Colt pistols made in 1943–45 by the ★Ithaca Gun Company, ★Remington-Rand and ★Union Switch & Signal. They were marked 'FJA'. See also US arms inspectors' marks.

Aubrey – 1. A ★Suicide Special revolver made in the 1880s by the ★Meriden Arms Company of Meriden, Connecticut, USA. **2.** Albert J. Aubrey, Meriden, Connecticut, and Hopkinton, Massachusetts, USA. Among Aubrey's inventions was a gun sight protected by US Patent 835,091 of 6 November 1906, which was assigned to ★Sears, Roebuck & Company of Chicago. US Patent 839,535 (25 December 1906) also protected a gun sight, while 859,477 of 9 July 1907, 908,522 of 5 January 1908, 908,553 of 5 January 1908 and 911,362 of 2 February 1908 all allowed claims for 'firearms'. Aubrey was the manager of Sears' manufacturing facilities, and his name was used as a Sears brandname. See also Ted ★Williams.

'auc'. This mark was associated with components made in the Köln-Ehrenfeld (Germany) factory of ★Mauser-Werke KG in 1941–45.

Audax – 1. A 6.35mm six-shot ★Browning-type pocket pistol made in France prior to 1940 by ★Manufacture d'Armes des Pyrénées. Sometimes the guns are also marked 'UNIS', which thus far has defied interpretation. **2.** A 7.65mm French eight-shot personal-defence pistol, copied from the 1910-pattern ★FN-Browning by Manufacture d'Armes des Pyrénées.

Audley Safety Holster. This was patented in the USA by Francis H. Audley (1849–1916), a one-time NYC harness maker who, in 1905, had turned to police-supply from his shop at 8 Center Market Place. US Patent 1,113, 530 was granted on 13 October 1914, although an application had been made on 20 April 1912. The holster body contained an internal metal safety trigger-lock, which had to be released before the gun could be withdrawn. Made in small numbers in 1914–16, it was sold by ★Von Lengerke & Detmold, and ★Abercrombie, Fitch & Company in New York City; by E.K. ★Tryon in Philadelphia; and by ★Von Lengerke & Antoine in Chicago.

AUG. See panel, facing page.

Augezd. Adolf Freiherr von Odkolek von Augezd. See Adolf von ★Odkolek.

Aughenbaugh. Robert Martin Aughenbaugh, a gunsmith of Glenfield, Pennsylvania, USA, was the co-patentee with G.E. Ruffley of magazine firearms – US Patents no. 381,821 of 24 April 1888 and 399,464 of 12 March 1889.

Augusta Machine Works, based in Augusta, Georgia, Confederate States of America, during the American Civil War, made about 100 copies of the .36 six-shot ★Navy Model Colt with octagonal barrels and six (rare) or twelve cylinder-stop notches.

Aurora. A typical 6.35mm Browning-type pocket pistol, made by an unknown gunmaker, probably in the district centred on Eibar (Spain); six rounds, hammer fired.

Aury, rue du Chambon 9, Saint-Étienne, France. Listed in 1879 as a gunmaker.

Austin – 1. Edward B. Austin. An inspector of US .45 M1911 Colt automatic pistols accepted in 1917, using an 'EBA' mark. See also US arms inspectors' marks. **2.** Thomas K. Austin, New York City. Designer of an improvement in the cylinder-rotating mechanism of the ★Pettengill revolver made by ★Rogers & Spencer, protected by US Patent 21,730 in October 1858. See also E.A. ★Raymond and Charles ★Robitaille. **3.** Austin Cartridge Company, Cleveland, Ohio, USA. This was a subsidiary of the Austin Powder Company, formed in 1890 to make shotshells on machinery purchased from ★Chamberlain. Subsequently, the business was sold to the ★Western Cartridge Company in 1908. Generally, its products were distinguished by the headstamp 'A.C.C.' or 'A.C.Co.' **4.** Austin Motor Company Ltd, Longbridge Works, Birmingham, England. A maker of magazines for the British 9mm ★Sten Gun (box pattern) and the .303 ★Bren Gun (box and drum) during the Second World War. Some will be marked 'M 13'. See also British military manufacturers' marks.

Austro-Hungarian... – 1. Austro-Hungarian firearms. The principal manufacturing centre was once the small town of Ferlach, where 50,000 Lorenz rifle-muskets had been made for the Austrian Army prior to 1866. However, Ferlach had never recovered from economic depression at the end of the Napoleonic Wars and had survived only by making inexpensive Trade Guns for

AUG

Armee-Universal-Gewehr

Applied to a gas-operated bullpup 5.56mm assault rifle developed by ★Steyr-Mannlicher GmbH and adopted by the Austrian Army in 1977. The AUG is distinguished by its futuristic appearance, which envelops a 1.5x fixed-power optical sight in the carrying handle, while the butt and trigger unit are moulded in a single piece. Modular construction provides a choice of four different barrels, three trigger mechanisms and two receivers, allowing the creation of a selection of weapons, ranging from a short-barrel carbine to a light-support weapon with a bipod and an electro-optical sight; a conversion kit even permits a 5.56mm rifle to be transformed into a 9mm submachine-gun. Some guns are restricted to single-shots; others can fire multi-shot bursts in addition to conventional automatic fire.

The futuristic lines of this 5.56mm bullpup AUG assault rifle are evident in this view. Note the position of the magazine beneath the firer's chin, and the image-intensifying sight.

export to Africa and the Far East. Work thereafter was transferred to ★Steyr and Vienna, the imperial capital, where some of the best-known makers were to be found – understandably specialising in high-class sporting guns. Greater inventiveness was to be found in the northern province of Bohemia, where a group of gunsmiths worked in Prague and another in Weipert. The rise of mass production initially favoured Waffenfabrik Steyr, founded by Leopold ★Werndl, which rose to become first ★Osterreichische Waffenfabriks-Gesellschaft and then a major component of ★Steyr-Daimler-Puch. Other major gunmaking businesses included the ★Gasser establishment in Ottakring, and ★Wiener Waffenfabrik. Comparatively little information concerning Austro-Hungarian firearms is available in English, although Konrad Edeler von Kromar's *Repetier- und Handfeuerwaffen der systeme Ferdinand Ritter von Mannlicher* (1900) was reprinted in 1976. A summary may be found in John Walter, *Rifles of the World* (Krause Publications, second edition, 1998) and *Central Powers' Small Arms of World War One* (Crowood Press, 1999); Walter H.B. Smith's book *Mauser, Walther and Mannlicher Firearms* (combined edition, Stackpole Books, 1962) is also useful, although the Mannlicher section is basically a translation of Kromar's work. *See also* Fémaru Fegyver és Gépgyár, Ferlach, Fruwirth, Krnka, Kropatschek, Mannlicher, Škoda, Wanzl, Weipert and Werndl. **2.** Austro-Hungarian manufacturers' markings. Among the most distinctive identifiers on the Austro-Hungarian weapons were the marks applied by Fémaru Fegyver és Gépgyár of Budapest ('FGGY') and Österreichische Waffenfabriks-Gesellschaft of Steyr – often 'OEWG' or 'ŒWG', sometimes in one line, at other times in two. The guns generally lack the proliferation of inspectors' marks that characterise their German equivalents, although they do feature large displayed-eagle proof marks and acceptance marks such as 'W-n' and 'BP' accompanied by a two-digit date (e.g., 'W-n 18' showed that a gun had been accepted in Vienna in 1918). **3.** Austro-Hungarian military unit markings. The individual marks used by the k.u.k. Armée relied on identification letters, not unlike the German pattern (q.v.). However, they were far less complicated and are much easier to interpret. Line infantry regiments were distinguished by 'R.', with the so-called *Grenz-Regimenter* (Border regiments) using 'G.R.'; the *Kaiserjäger-Regiment* mark was 'J.R.' and the *Jäger-Bataillone* or riflemen used 'J.B.' Prefatory numbers distinguished the units from each other. The marks applied by the cavalry regiments were straightforward: 'D.R.' for the dragoons, 'H.R.' for the hussars, and 'U.R.' for the *Uhlanen* (lancers). Field-artillery regiments were distinguished by 'A.R.', and the garrison or fortress artillery battalions by 'F.B.'; the engineer units (*Genie Regimenter*) used 'Ge. R.', the pioneers had 'P.R.', and *Militär-Fuhrwesen-Korps* equipment sported 'F.K.' The marks were applied in a most distinctive fashion, with the major component above a short horizontal line and the lesser information, usually in the form of numbers, underneath. A typical example could read '27. R. 2. B.' above '6. 134.', separated by the line; this identified the 134th gun issued to *6. Kompagnie*, part of the second battalion of *27. Infanterie-Regiment*. A typical cavalry mark would be '4. U. R.' above 'R. 36.', applied by the *Reserve-Eskadron* of *4. Uhlanen-Regiment*; '36' was the individual gun number. Some marks will include additional letters, usually in the lower line. For example, '2. A. R.' stamped above '2. M. 34.' signified the 34th gun issued to the second munitions column (*Munitionskolonne*) of *2. Feld Artillerie-Regiment*. Landwehr marks will include 'L' in the top line, e.g. '3. L. U. R.' above '3. 9.' – the ninth gun issued to the third squadron of *3. Landwehr-Uhlanen-Regiment*. Landsturm markings almost always included 'LdSt.', 'Ld. St.' or 'LSt.'; 'I. LstB.' over '239' signified the 239th weapon issued to *I. Landsturm-Bataillon*. Austro-Hungarian marks of this type do not seem to be subject to the individual interpretations that characterise their German equivalents, particularly those of First World War vintage. The only exception seems to be the omission of 'R' for 'Regiment', which can mean that the stampings of hussar units, for example, can appear simply as 'H' instead of 'H.R.' Too little research has been undertaken in Austrian archives to discover whether this had any official significance.

Autechaud, Saint-Étienne, France. Listed in 1933 as a gunmaker.

Auto, Auto-, Auto... – 1. Auto-22, BAR-22 or Browning Auto-22. *See* Carabine Automatique Browning. **2.** Auto-Dog. A name that is associated with a ★Velo-Dog-style double-action revolver made in Belgium by ★Ancion-Marx of Liège prior to 1914. The guns had five-chamber cylinders and folding triggers. **3.** Auto Engineering (Croydon) Ltd, London Road, West Croydon, England. Fabricators of silencers for the Mk IIS ★Sten Gun, together with ★Braddick. The silencers may be marked 'S 7'. *See* British military manufacturers' rnarks. **4.** Auto-loading, also widely known as self-loading or semi-automatic. This is a mechanism which –

through force generated on firing – unlocks the breech (if appropriate), extracts and ejects the empty case, then recocks the firing mechanism and reloads so that the gun will fire when the trigger is pressed again. Strictly, all semi- and fully-automatic weapons are auto-loaders, although only guns in the latter group are auto-firing. **5.** Auto-Nine Corporation, Parma, Idaho, USA. Maker of the .22-calibre Auto Nine pistol in the 1980s. **6.** Auto-Ordnance Corporation of New York [The]. This entrepreneurial agency was formed in 1916 by John B. ★Blish, George Harvey, Thomas F. Ryan and John T. ★Thompson. Ryan was the financier, while Thompson had the political influence befitting a one-time Assistant Chief of Ordnance of the US Army. The administrative offices stood at 56 Pine Street in New York City, although most of the guns were made by ★Colt's Patent Fire Arms Manufacturing Company in Hartford, Connecticut. The object of attention was a series of weapons – in particular, a light automatic carbine or 'Sub-Machine Gun' – embodying a delayed-blowback system patented by Blish. Still a subject of great debate, this relied on the friction generated by differing metals sliding across each other under pressure. Submachine-guns and automatic rifles, often improved in accordance with patents granted to Theodore ★Eickhoff and Oscar ★Payne, were made for Auto Ordnance by ★Warner & Swasey (prototypes), Colt (series production), and are usually marked appropriately. Several different 'Tommy Guns' were made, culminating in a simplified blowback design that worked just as well as the complicated hesitation-lock pattern had done. Auto-Ordnance also promoted a gas-operated T10 machine-gun designed by William B. ★Ruger. The T10E2 would have been adopted by the US Army in 1942, but a decision was taken to standardise on only ★Browning-based guns. The army resurrected the T10E2 in 1944, as the T23, but although the perfected T23E2 showed merit once again, Browning production was accorded priority. The original business failed in the aftermath of the Second World War, but the name survives as a subsidiary of the Numrich Arms Corporation. It will be discovered on replica 'Tommy Guns' and M1911A1-pattern ★Colt-Browning pistols. *See also* John Taliaferro ★Thompson, Thompson submachine-gun.

Autocrat. A mark found on smokeless-propellant shotgun ammunition made by the ★Robin Hood Cartridge Company of Swanton, Vermont, prior to 1914.

'Autokill' [The]. Found on shotgun cartridges sold by ★Gray of Inverness, Scotland.

Auto-Mag. A large and powerful recoil-operated semi-automatic pistol, this was created in the 1960s by Max Gera of Sandford Arms, Pasadena, California, around the .44 Auto Magnum handgun cartridge. The gun was marketed from 1970 onward by the Auto-Mag Corporation of Pasadena, but this business was superseded within two years by the TDE Corporation, formed when the Thames Oil Company bought the patent rights. TDE also soon encountered problems, and control of the project passed to ★High Standard before reverting, in 1979, to Harry Sandford, one-time principal of the Sandford Arms Company! Before work stopped altogether, the AMT Corporation made a last batch with adjustable Behlert back sights. Owing to the custom-built qualities of the Auto-Mag, a variety of specially-marked models existed. These included the .41-calibre JMP, made for gunsmith

Lee Jurras, and names from Alaskan to Silhouette; details and chronology of these are not yet clear.

Automatic – 1. A generic term for any firearm capable of firing continuously (pistol, rifle or machine-gun), this is often mistakenly used interchangeably with ★semi-automatic, and may be confused with ★auto-loading. **2.** A name associated with a typical Spanish-made Browning-type pocket pistol, manufacturer unknown (but probably made in Eibar). Produced in at least two patterns: 6.35mm, generally six rounds, hammer fired. Some are marked 'Model 1911'; others display 'Model 1916'. **3.** A brandname found on an unidentifiable Spanish-made revolver, probably dating from the 1910–25 era. **4.** Automatic Arms Company, Buffalo, New York State. The assignees of automatic firearm patents granted to Samuel ★McLean, in succession to the ★McLean Arms & Ordnance Company of Cleveland, Ohio, which failed in 1909. Automatic Arms employed a retired US Army officer, Isaac N. ★Lewis, to adapt the ineffectual McLean designs into an efficient light machine-gun. **5.** Automatic Ejecting Model. Made in the USA by ★Harrington & Richardson, this .32 six-shot or .38 five-shot break-open revolver was introduced c. 1897. One version had a folding knife blade beneath the barrel. **6.** Automatic Ejector Model. A shotgun made by L.C ★Smith from about 1890 onward **7.** Automatic Hammerless. A brandname associated with a double-barrelled shotgun designed by Daniel ★Lefever. Identified by a thumb-catch on the tang, the double-trigger gun was made in seven grades ('F' to 'AA'), although an Optimus pattern appeared in c. 1892. **8.** Automatic Hammerless Model. This revolver was made in the 1890s by ★Harrington & Richardson, as a small-frame, five-shot .32; a large-frame, six-shot .32; or a five-shot .38. **9.** Automatic Model. This name was associated with an inexpensive US revolver made by ★Hopkins & Allen in 1885–98, and the Hopkins & Allen Arms Company in 1898–1907, with a simultaneous-ejection mechanism actuated when the barrel was tipped downward. **10.** Automatic Flareback Prevention Company. *See* W.D ★Smith. **11.** Automatic Guns, Inc., was formed in Washington, D.C., in 1939, possibly to assist the supply of weapons to Britain. The president was Major William R. Baldwin. However, no other details of its history are currently known. **12.** Automatic rifle. Applied to long-arms that will continue firing until either the trigger is released or the ammunition has been expended. **13.** Automatic Rifle Syndicate Ltd. This promotional agency had an office at 9 Queen Victoria Street, London S.W., England, from 1896 until 1900 or later. **14.** Automatic safety. *See* mechanical safety.

'auu'. Found on ammunition and components made in 1941–45 by Patronenhülsen- und Metallwarenfabrik AG in its Rokycany bei Pilsen factory in German-occupied Czechoslovakia.

'aux'. This code was used by the Magdeburg (Germany) factory of ★Polte-Werke, and will be found on cartridge clips and chargers, machine-gun belts and links, small-arms ammunition and associated components made during the Second World War.

'auy'. *See* 'aux'; this mark was used by Polte's Grüneberg (Nordbahn) factory in 1941–45.

'auz'. A mark used by the ★Polte-Werke factory in Arnstadt, Thüringen, on small-arms ammunition and components made during the Second World War.

'Avant-Tout' [The]. A brandname that will be found on shotgun ammunition handled by ★Cogswell & Harrison.

Avenger. A ★Suicide Special revolver made in the 1880s by the ★Hopkins & Allen Arms Company of Norwich, Connecticut.

Avengeur. *See* l'Avengeur.

Averill & Son, a gunsmithing business trading in Evesham, Worcestershire, England, marked shotgun cartridges as 'Averill's Express'.

Avery – 1. James L. Avery, Madison Court House, Florida, USA. Patentee of a method of mounting and setting guns, granted on 11 August 1874 (no. 153,924). The rights were assigned to Walter E. Avery. **2.** Stephen Avery. A gunmaker of North Anson, Maine, USA, active in the 1870s.

AVF. Applied to the Russian ★Fedorov automatic rifle, or *Avtomatischeskaia Vintovka Fedorova*, of 1916. *See* Avtomat.

Avion. A 6.35mm semi-automatic pistol, based on the ★FN-Browning, made by ★Azpiri y Compañia of Eibar, Guipúzcoa, Spain; six rounds, striker or hammer fired.

Avis Rifle Barrel Company, Springfield, Massachusetts, USA. A maker of barrels for the 1903-type US .30 service rifle during the Second World War

'avk'. Found on parts for the Kar. 98k made between 1941 and 1945 by Ruhrstahl AG, Presswerke Brackwede bei Bielefeld.

Avon [The]. A mark associated with shotgun cartridges assembled, or perhaps simply bought-in, by ★Nightingale & Son of Salisbury. The components seem to have originated outside Britain, but their origin is unclear.

Avramov. A Soviet/Russian weapons designer, now best-known as the co-developer of the ★RSA double-action revolver.

AVS, *Avtomaticheskaia Vintovka Simonova.* Associated with a rifle developed in the USSR in the 1930s by Sergei Simonov. Also known as AVS-36, after the year of adoption. *See* Simonov rifles.

'avt', AVT – 1. As 'avt'. Found on small-arms ammunition and parts made by Silva Metallwerke GmbH of Magdeburg, Germany, in 1941–45. **2.** As 'AVT'. An automatic rifle designed by F.V. ★Tokarev and introduced in 1940. *See also* 'SVT' and 'SNT'.

Avtomat. A Russian-language term ('Automat[ic]' in English), customarily applied to selective-fire assault rifles – particularly those designed by Vladimir ★Fedorov prior to 1916, and by Mikhail ★Kalashnikov after the end of the Second World War.

'avu'. Associated with the Genthin factory of Silva Metallwerke GmbH. Found on ammunition components made in Germany during the Second World War. *See also* 'avt'.

'AW', 'A.W.' – 1. Found on components for the No. 4 ★Lee-Enfield rifle made during the Second World War by Austey & Wilson. This company was also allocated the area-code 'M8', but often used its initials instead. **2.** An unidentified inspector's mark found on US Navy signal pistols dating from the early 1900s and on US military firearms. **3.** A monogram with an angular 'A' superimposed on 'W'. Correctly 'WA'; on revolvers made in the USA by Dan ★Wesson Arms.

'AWA'. Found in the ★headstamps of rimfire cartridges, said to have been made by A.W. Allendorff of Schönebeck an der Elbe.

'AWC', 'A.W.C.', 'A.W.Corp.' – 1. Trademarks and

brandnames associated with the *American Weapons Corporation. **2.** As 'AWC'. A concentric-type monogram with all three letters equally dominant. Correctly 'WAC' (q.v.); used by the *Warner Arms Company.

AWCD, AWDC. A concentric-type monogram with all four letters of equal significance. Correctly 'WDAC' (q.v.); used by the *Warner-Davis Arms Corporation.

'AWE'. *See* Arthur W. *Evans.

'AWG', 'A.W.G.' [The]. Found in the *headstamps and on the packaging of rim- and centrefire ammunition sold by A.W. *Gamage of London prior to 1914. The cartridges were made elsewhere.

'AWH'. *See* A.W. *Hatch.

'awj'. This codemark was allocated to the Yale & Towne Manufacturing & Company of Velbert, Rheinland (Germany), a maker of artillery components and small-arms magazines in 1941–44.

AWR, or Model 700AWR. *See* Alaskan Wilderness Rifle.

'awt'. Encountered on small-arms and associated components made during the Second World War by Württembergische Metallwarenfabrik AG in Geislingen-Steige, Germany. *See* Haenel.

'awz', 'AWZ', 'A.W.Z.' – 1. As 'AWZ' or 'A.W.Z.', sometimes accompanied by one or more six-point stars. Trademarks associated with Albin *Wahl of Zella-Mehlis, Thüringen, Germany, found on 6.35mm automatic pistols and dropping-block target rifles. *See also* Stern. **2.** As 'awz'. Found on parts made for the Kar. 98k during the Second World War by Dietrich Sasse's Söhne of Vienna.

'ax'. Used by Feinmechanische Werke GmbH of Erfurt, Germany, on rifles and small-arms components made during 1940–45.

Aydt. Carl Wilhelm Aydt, a German gunsmith, is associated with a distinctive dropping-block rifle usually (but not exclusively) made by *Haenel.

'aye'. A codemark found on German small-arms magazines made by Olympia Büromaschinenwerke AG of Erfurt during the Second World War.

'ayf' A mark found on submachine-guns, signal pistols and small-arms components made by *Erma-Werke, B. Geipel GmbH of Erfurt, Germany, in 1941–45.

'Ay-Jay-Effe' [The]. Found on shotgun cartridges sold in England by *Foster of Kidderminster.

Ayres – 1. John C. Ayres. An inspector of US martial arms – including Colt-made *Gatling Guns – in 1881–83, using a 'JCA' mark. *See also* US arms inspectors' marks. **2.** William G. Ayres, Brooklyn, New York, USA. Co-designer with G. Whittaker of a revolving firearm, the relevant patent being granted on 13 February 1877 (US no. 187,244).

Azanza y Arrizabalaga of Eibar, Guipúzcoa, Spain, made *Ruby-pattern semi-automatic pistols for the French Army during the First World War. Also commonly listed as the manufacturer of *Reims pistols.

Azimuth adjustment. This is found on a back sight to move the point of impact vertically. Sometimes mistakenly confused with windage.

Azpiri y Compañía of Eibar, Guipúzcoa, Spain, made the *Avion and *Colon semi-automatic pistols.

Azul. This tradename was found on handguns and possibly sporting rifles distributed in Spain by Eulogio *Arrostegui of Eibar before 1936. The basic Browning-type pistols were offered in two patterns: (a) 6.35mm, six rounds, hammer fired; and (b) 7.65mm, seven rounds, hammer fired.

B

'B' – 1. Encircled or within an encircled six-point star. A property mark found on Brazilian military weapons. 2. Beneath a crown. Found on Belgian weapons: the mark of King Baudoin (1950 to date). *See also* Cyphers, imperial and royal. 3. Stamped into the heel of British Bantam rifle butts, which were an inch (25mm) shorter than standard. 4. Beneath a crown, above a number. A mark applied by an inspector working in the British *Royal Small Arms Factory in Sparkbrook, Birmingham. Care should be taken to distinguish the upright or Roman letter 'B' of Sparkbrook from the cursive 'B' used by *BSA. *See also* 'SK' and British military inspectors' marks. 5. Beneath a crown, above a number. A mark applied by an inspector working in the *Birmingham Small Arms [& Metals] Company Ltd or *BSA Guns Ltd factories in Birmingham, Warwickshire, England. Care is necessary to distinguish the cursive 'B' used by *BSA from the upright or Roman letter 'B' of the Royal Small Arms Factory in Sparkbrook. *See also* British military inspectors' marks. 6. Beneath a crown. Found on Bulgarian weapons: Tsar Boris III (1918–43). *See also* Cyphers, imperial and royal. 7. An Art Nouveau or floriated letter found on the grips of pistols made for Theodor *Bergmann of Gaggenau prior to 1905, customarily by V.C. *Schilling & Company. 8. A cursive letter with the letter-tail curving back beneath the stem. Found on the grips of pistols made in the early 1920s by 'Theodor [*]Bergmann Gaggenau, Waffenfabrik Suhl'. Subsequently it was replaced by the company name. 9. Usually in an oval cartouche. Sometimes accompanied by a miner with a lamp, this is associated with the products of Theodor Bergmann. It will be found moulded into the grips of most Bergmann-Schmeisser pistols. 10. Beneath a crown. Found on Dutch weapons: the mark of Queen Beatrix (1980 to date). *See also* Cyphers, imperial and royal.

'ba', 'BA' – 1. Generally as 'BA'. A mark associated with *Lee-Enfield rifle and other small-arms components made by the Australian government factory in *Bathurst. 2. Generally as 'ba'. Used by Sundwiger Messingwerk vorm. Gebr. von der Becke KG of Sundwig Kreis Iserlohn, Germany, on small-arms ammunition made during the Second World War. 3. Generally as 'B.A.' Applied to US military stores – including .45 M1911A1 *Government Model pistols – refurbished by Benicia Arsenal.

'B & A'. This trademark was associated with the products of *Bolte & Anschütz of Zella-Mehlis, Germany. Found on sporting rifles and sub-calibre barrel inserts for the *Parabellum pistol, it often took the form of a cross containing 'B', 'B', 'A' and 'A' in the arms and the ampersand ('&') in the central void.

Babbitt – 1. A.S. Babbitt & Company; Plattsburgh, New York State. Manufacturer of *Robinson-patent breech-loading magazine rifles in 1870–72, until succeed-

ed by the *Adirondack Fire Arms Company. 2. Benjamin T. Babbitt. Giving his address as New York, Babbitt was granted several US Patents – including 34,472 of 25 February 1862 for 'the construction of ordnance', and 209,014 of 15 October 1878 to protect an airgun. He was undoubtedly associated with A.S. Babbitt & Company (above).

Babcock. N.L. Babcock of New Haven, Connecticut, USA, was granted US Patent 27,509 on 20 March 1860 to protect a breech-loading firearm.

Baby... – 1. 'Baby Browning' or 'FN-Baby'. A compact 6.35mm *blowback semi-automatic 'vest-pocket' pistol, perfected by the design department of Fabrique Nationale d'Armes de Guerre in 1932. 2. Baby Dragoon. This was the first of the .31 five-shot Colt pocket revolvers. Lacking rammers, they were reloaded by substituting cylinders. About 15,000 Baby Dragoons were made in 1848–50. 3. Baby Frommer. This was applied to a semi-automatic pistol made in Budapest (Hungary) by *Fegyvergyár Reszvenytársáság in 6.35mm, 7.65mm and 9mm Short. 4. Baby PA. This was a small .22-calibre automatic pistol made in Italy by Vincenzo *Bernardelli of Gardone Val Trompia. 5. Baby Russian. A term applied, apparently unofficially, to .38 break-open sheath-trigger single-action *Smith & Wesson revolvers of 1876–77, subsequently known as the .38 Single Action First Model. 6. Baby Sporting Carbine. *See* Remington rifles, rolling-block action.

Bachmann – 1. Adolf Bachmann, Gustav Sohn; Albrechts bei Suhl in Thüringen, Benshäusser Strasse 2 (1941). This business was listed in the *Deutsches Reichs-Adressbuch* (1939–41) as a maker of gun parts. 2. Friedrich H. Bachmann; Magdeburg, Germany. The joint grantee, with Richard Wagner of Suhl, of US Patent no. 568,289 of 22 September 1896. This protected a 'cocking mechanism for guns'. 3. Gustav Bachmann. A gunmaker listed in Suhl (Thüringen, Germany) directories for the period between the wars. He traded in Albrechts bei Suhl. 4. Bachmann & Goebel, also listed as Göbel, Albrechts bei Suhl in Thüringen. Owned by Wilhelm Bachmann and Wilhelm Goebel when the Second World War began, this gun-part manufacturing partnership specialised in airgun darts (*Luftgewehrbolzen*).

Back, Back... – 1. Back-action or Back-lock. An alternative method of construction to *side-lock, this originated in Europe in the nineteenth century and remained popular for the duration of the percussion-cap era. The principal distinguishing feature was the main spring, which lay behind the hammer. Even though it often weakened the wrist of the stock, the back-lock was particularly favoured on the earliest breech-loaders, as it freed the space ahead of the standing breech or action face for the barrel-locking mechanism. Eventually, locks of this type were superseded by the *box-lock. 2. Back Up. A small, but unusually powerful semi-automatic pocket pistol made in the USA by ★OMC. It chambered the .380 cartridge.

Bacon – **1.** A small ★Suicide Special revolver made by the Bacon Manufacturing Company of Norwich, Connecticut, in the late nineteenth century. **2.** A.N. Bacon; Washington, D.C., USA. Recipient of US Patent no. 56,846 of 31 July 1868, protecting a breech-loading firearm, Bacon part-assigned the protection to George E.H. Day. **3.** C.W. Bacon. A US government arms inspector active in the 1870s, using the initials 'CWB'. *See also* US arms inspectors' marks. **4.** George R. Bacon, Providence, Rhode Island, USA. On 21 July 1863, Bacon was granted US Patent 39,270 to protect a breech-loading firearm. Reissued on 15 March 1864, the patent was subsequently assigned to the ★Burnside Rifle Company. **5.** Thomas K. Bacon. *See* Bacon Arms Company. **6.** William S. Bacon. Assignee of patents granted to Frederick Smith (q.v.). **7.** Bacon Arms Company [The] or Bacon [Arms] Manufacturing Company, Norwich, Connecticut, USA. Established in 1858 by Thomas K. Bacon, this business made pepperboxes, single-shot pistols and a selection of revolvers, beginning with a modified .31-calibre open-frame ★Colt with detachable side-plates. Bacon had apparently undertaken sub-contract work for the ★Manhattan Fire Arms Company, although his own guns had a ball catch on the rammer-head instead of a Manhattan sliding wedge. Bacon revolvers will often be found with the marks of ★Fitch & Waldo; B.J. ★Hart & Brother; ★Tomes, Melvain & Company; the ★Union Arms Company; or the ★Western Arms Company. ★Hopkins & Allen purchased Bacon in 1867, continuing to make .31 side-plate revolvers and the .36-calibre ★Dictator. About 2,000 sheath-trigger solid-frame .31 five-chamber cap-lock revolvers were also made, occasionally under the Union Arms Company banner. Bacon produced a multi-barrel cartridge 'pepperbox derringer' in the 1860s, with a frame extending forward to the front of the elongated cylinder, as well as .22 and .32 rimfire infringements of the ★Smith & Wesson Model No. 1. Bacon's six-shot .32 and .38 rimfire Navy revolvers embodied a swinging cylinder patented on 27 May 1862 by Charles W. ★Hopkins (no. 35,419) and part-assigned to Henry ★Edgerton. The improved Briggs & Hopkins revolver was patented jointly by H.A. ★Briggs and Samuel S. Hopkins on 5 January 1864 (US no. 41,117), and assigned to themselves and Charles A. Converse. Alongside these revolvers, the Bacon Arms Company made single-shot .32 rimfire derringers loaded by swinging the barrel away from the breech. By 1888, a work force of twenty was making about 2,500 guns annually. Operations ceased shortly afterward, however, perhaps owing to the competition afforded by newer and more progressive manufacturers working in the New England states. *See also* Alonso ★Sweet and John H. ★Vickers. **8.** Bacon Manufacturing Company, Norwich, Connecticut, USA. Charles A. Converse and Samuel S. ★Hopkins assigned their breech-loading firearm patent (US no. 57,622 of 28 August 1866) to the 'Bacon Mfg. Co.' – assumed to have been a trading style of what was otherwise known as the Bacon Arms Company. **9.** Bacon & Curtis, or Curtiss. This partnership, trading from Poole, Dorset, England, marked sporting guns and ammunition. **Baden.** James T. Baden, a lieutenant in the Federal

Army, accepted small-arms marked 'JTB' during the American Civil War. *See also* US arms inspectors' marks.

'Badenoch' [The]. A brandname associated with shotgun ammunition sold by Robert ★MacPherson of Kingussie, Scotland. The cartridges were made by ★Eley-Kynoch.

Bader – **1.** Bernhard Bader, Mehlis in Thüringen, Germany. Listed in 1900–14 editions of the *Deutsches Reichs-Adressbuch* as a gun- and weapon-maker, specialising in 'officers', gendarmerie and police revolvers'. **2.** Emil Bader, Zella-Mehlis in Thüringen, Germany. Listed in 1939-vintage directories as a master gunsmith. **3.** Edmund Bader [& Söhne], Albrechts bei Suhl, Germany. Listed in the *Deutsches Reichs-Adressbuch* as a maker of sporting arms and gun parts (*Waffenteilefabrik*), 1927–39, and trading from Zellaer Strasse 49 in 1941. **4.** Hans Bader, Zella-Mehlis in Thüringen, Germany. Listed in 1930 as a maker of guns and weapons. **5.** Heinrich Bader, Mehlis and subsequently Zella-Mehlis in Thüringen, Germany. Listed in 1900 and again in 1920 as a gunmaker. **6.** Henry Bader, Saint Martinville, Louisiana. The patentee of a breech-loading firearm – US no. 216,012 of 3 June 1879. **7.** Louis Bader, Valt. Sohn; Mehlis and then Zella-Mehlis in Thüringen. Listed in Germany in 1919–20 as a gun- and weapon-maker, under the ownership of Franz Theodor, August and Kuno Bader. Listed in 1925 as a gunmaker, Bader was granted protection for trademark no. 370,476 – ★Aegir – in June 1927. Listed in 1930 as a gun- and weapon-maker, and in 1939 as a weapon maker (owner, Frau Ida Bader). *See also* ★Waffenwerk Mehlis. **8.** Louis August Bader, Zella-Mehlis in Thüringen, Germany. Listed in 1930–39 as a master gunsmith. Bader used an 'LB' mark, which sometimes took the form of a monogram. **9.** Robert Bader, Zella-Mehlis in Thüringen, Germany. Listed in 1920 as a gun-stock maker. **10.** W. Bader & Söhne, Mehlis and Zella-Mehlis in Thüringen, Germany. Listed in 1900–14 as a gunmaker, producing 'pocket pistols, pistols and revolvers for export, small-calibre rifles, etc.' Owned in 1919 by Robert Bader. The specialties of this long-established gunmaking business were listed in 1925 as '[★]Terzerole, pistols, revolvers for export, hunting carbines and ★Teschings, etc.' Listed in 1930 as a weapon-maker; in 1939 as a distributor of guns and ammunition; and in 1941 as a maker of sporting guns. **11.** Bader & Eck, vorm. Rob. Bader, Zella-Mehlis in Thüringen, Germany. A partnership of Richard Bader and Otto Eck, trading in 1930, specialising in the manufacture and wholesaling of gun-stocks.

Badger. American gunsmith George A. Badger of Quincy, Massachusetts, received US Patent 209,600 on 5 November 1878 to protect a 'registering attachment for firearms'.

Badinand – **1.** Badinand frères, place Chavanelle 6, Saint-Étienne, France. A gunmaker active in the late 1870s, but probably succeeded c. 1888 by Badinand fils, below. **2.** Badinand fils, rue Villeboeuf 22, Saint-Étienne, France. Listed in 1892 as a gunmaker, probably a successor to Badinand frères, above, c. 1888.

Badminton – **1.** Usually seen as 'The Badminton', a brandname found on shotgun cartridges loaded for ★Holland & Holland of London. **2.** Badminton School of Shooting [The]. This club, with its headquarters at 98 New Bond Street, London, England, in 1900, is believed to have maintained repair facilities of its own. Hence it qualifies for inclusion in H.J. Blanch's list 'The Gun Trade', published in *Arms & Explosives* in 1909.

Bad to Beat. Associated with a revolver sold in Belgium prior to c. 1910 by Charles *Clément, also known as the American Model 1887.

Baggett. William T. Baggett of San Francisco, California, USA, was granted US Patent 666,372 (22 January 1901) to protect a 'gun-alarm' of novel design.

Bagley. E.R. Bagley: *see* William B. *Atkinson.

Bagnall & Kirkwood, a distributor of guns, ammunition and sporting goods trading from 31 Westgate Road, Newcastle upon Tyne, England, handled ammunition with brandnames such as The Pointer and The Setter. The cartridges were bought from *Eley-Kynoch Ltd.

Bahco. Aktiebolaget Bahco ('AB Bahco'), Enköping and Stockholm, Sweden. This long-established metal-working business, specialising in bayonets and military equipment, made the gas-powered *Excellent rifles from 1906 to 1915 to the patents of Ewerlöf and *Blómen. The guns are clearly marked 'BAHCO', but the design of the 'H' has often been confused with 'M' and the company name, therefore, has often been mistakenly listed as Bamco.

Baikal. This trademark and brandname are associated with sporting rifles and airguns made by the *Izhevsk small-arms factory. The solitary break-barrel air rifle, known as the IZh-22, was sold in Britain as the *Milbro G530, in the USA as the *Hy-Score 870 Mark 3, and may also be encountered as the Vostok.

Baildham & Sons, a gunsmithing and ironmongery business trading in Stratford upon Avon, Warwickshire, England, handled shotgun ammunition marked 'The Duck Fowler'.

Bailey – 1. Charles E. Bailey, North Scituate, Massachusetts (1866–79), and Springfield, Massachusetts (1880–85). Charles Bailey was granted US Patent 72,777 of 31 December 1867 to protect a 'method of altering the caliber of muskets and other gun barrels'. The patent was assigned to the *Allen Patent Fire-Arms Manufacturing Company. Bailey subsequently developed a 'method of straightening and annealing gun barrels', the subject of US Patent no. 320,613 of 23 June 1885. **2.** Charles S. Bailey. The inventor of a 'gas check for central fire cartridges' with a thin metal disc over the primer, protected by a British Patent granted in 1882. Subsequently this was exploited by F. *Joyce & Company. **3.** Edmund C. Bailey. This government arms inspector, active during the American Civil War, was identified by the initials 'ECB'. *See also* US arms inspectors' marks. **4.** Elmer E. Bailey, Sinnamakoning, Pennsylvania, USA. Bailey is best remembered for his BB Guns, producing several designs in the late nineteenth century. Most of these were assigned to William *Heilprin. US Patent 487,169 of 29 November 1892 protected a lever-action design, heavy but mechanically very simple. US Patent 507,470 of 24 October 1893 was granted to protect an improvement of the earlier design. A half-share was granted to W.G. *Smith, who may have been either the manufacturer or a financier. US Patent no. 603,549 of 3 May 1899, sought in collaboration with Thomas A. *Monk, protected an improved lever-action BB Gun with a toggle link in the cocking mechanism and an unusual vertically-acting sear. **5.** Fortune L. Bailey, Indianapolis, Indiana, and possibly later Perham, Minnesota, USA. Bailey was granted two

US Patents protecting a manually operated machine-gun: 182,352 of 22 February 1876 and 206,852 of 13 August 1878. **6.** Lebbeus Bailey (also known as Lebbus, Lebbons or Libbons), Portland, Maine, USA. Joint patentee, with John B. Ripley and William B. Smith, of 'a percussion magazine rifle, waterproof'. The grant was made on 20 February 1839, but back-dated to 6 November 1838. **7.** Robert H. Bailey. The 'RHB' marks of this government arms inspector will be found on US-made rifle-muskets, *Remington rifles and *Sharps carbines accepted during 1870–77. *See also* US arms inspectors' marks. **8.** Thomas Bailey, 160½ Chartres Street, New Orleans, Louisiana, USA, in 1853. This maker of cap-lock rifles and revolvers received US Patent 24,274 on 7 June 1859 to protect a 'revolving firearm' and US Patent 24,437 on 14 June 1859 for a 'means for actuating moveable parts of firearms'. The Federal occupation of Louisiana during the American Civil War apparently put an end to Bailey's activities. **9.** Bailey's Gas Tight [The]. A brandname found on shotgun cartridges made by F. *Joyce & Company Ltd prior to 1907.

Baird – 1. John T. Baird, Olney, Illinois, USA. Recipient of US Patent 652,583 of 26 June 1900, to protect a folding gun. **2.** Samuel P. Baird. Working from c. 1860 until 1873, Baird, a lieutenant in the US Navy, accepted small-arms marked 'SPB'. They included *Starr and *Whitney revolvers and, apparently, some *Remington Rolling Block rifles. *See also* US arms inspectors' marks.

Baker – 1. Clyde Baker, later Baker & Main. Trading from 2100 East 59th Street, Kansas City, Missouri, USA, from 1921 to 1928, gunsmith Clyde Baker made sporting firearms and accessories. **2.** E. Baker & Son. This London-based gunmaker traded from Size Yard, Whitechapel Road, from 1850 to 1852; 49 Tenter Street in 1853–54; and 7 Union Street, Whitechapel, from 1854 until the early 1860s. Breech-loading guns have been reported with Baker's marks. **3.** Frank J. Baker, St Cloud, Minnesota, USA. Recipient of US Patents protecting magazine firearms: 783,851 of 28 February and 789,199 of 8 May 1905. **4.** Frank W. Baker. A government arms inspector active in 1909–17, this US Army major marked .45 Colt revolvers with 'FWB'. See also US arms inspectors' marks. **5.** Frederick Thomas Baker. The son of Thomas Kerslake Baker, this gunmaker continued to make sporting guns and rifles from premises at 88 Fleet Street, London, England, from 1858 until 1900 or later. London directories list additional premises at 21 Cockspur Street, S.W. (1882–98), and 29 Glasshouse Street (1899 and later). The name has also been reported on *Eley-made shotgun ammunition marked 'Baker's Best'. Trading may also have been undertaken in Birmingham. **6.** J.A. Baker, London, England. The marks of this gunmaker have been reported on self-cocking *pepperboxes dating from the middle of the nineteenth century. **7.** James Baker, Hereford. The marks of this English gunmaker – trading from Bye Street in 1841–61, and Elgin Street in 1862–68 – have been reported on sporting guns and self-cocking *pepperboxes dating from the mid-nineteenth century. **8.** James Thomas Baker. Trading from 103 Victoria Road, Darlington, County Durham, England, in the 1930s, Baker marked sporting guns and ammunition. **9.** John G. Baker, Philadelphia, Pennsylvania, USA. Patentee of a 'spring gun' on 15 June 1896 (US no. 343,560). **10.** Joseph Baker

& Son. An English gunmaking business with premises in the Norfolk town of Fakenham, Baker & Son marked shotgun cartridges (made by *Eley-Kynoch Ltd) with 'Baker's Special'. **11.** Thomas Baker. This gunmaker of Aston, Birmingham, was co-designer with William M. *Scott of a drop-barrel action and an improved vent – see British Patents 761/78 of 1878 and 617/82 of 1882, and a comparable US Patent (no. 264,773) of 19 September 1882. **12.** Thomas Kerslake Baker. This English gunmaker made a variety of firearms, including *pepperboxes and six-shot single-action cap-lock revolvers with a distinctive slotted hammer doubling as a back sight. These are usually marked 'Baker's Patent, Registered April 24, 1852'. Postal directories reveal Thomas Kerslake (or Kirslake) Baker successively at 34 St James's Street, London S.W., and 1 Stonecutter Street, E.C., in 1850; at 88 Fleet Street, E.C., in 1851–57; and at Blackhouse Court in 1853–56 only. Baker was succeeded in 1858 by his son, Frederick Thomas Baker. **13.** Walter Baker, Ilion, New York State, USA. Baker received US Patents protecting the manufacture of gun barrels (41,669 of 23 February 1864) and barrel-retaining bands (206,762 of 6 August 1878). **14.** W.H. Baker & Sons Company, Syracuse, New York, USA. This gunmaking business was founded in 1878 by William Baker to make Baker-patent side-lock shotguns, together with a few European-style combination guns with two smooth-bore barrels above a single rifled barrel. Work continued until 1880, when Lyman *Smith, one of its principals, bought the business. Subsequently this was operated as L.C. *Smith & Company, allowing Baker and Lyman Smith's brother, Leroy *Smith, to form the *Ithaca Gun Company. **15.** William Baker. Sometimes associated with Arthur Herbert *Marsh in the *Midland Gun Company, William 'Billy' Baker (1859–1934) was the patentee or co-patentee of several shotgun designs in the 1882–1909 era. He also obtained four patents protecting airguns, mostly refinements of the basic *Gem pattern. Baker is best known for a single-trigger system and the coil-spring Baker Ejector which, unlike the competing *Southgate type, would work when broken. He also designed a distinctive single-barrel semi-hammerless gun for *Vickers immediately after the end of the First World War, although ultimately the design was exploited by *Webley & Scott. His workshop originally stood in the Snow Hill area of Birmingham, but later Baker moved to Bath Street. Protection granted to William Baker included British Patent 5045/15 of 1915, accepted on 19 November 1915, to protect an airgun. British Patent 101,562, accepted on 5 October 1916, described another airgun. British Patent 160,057, sought with Arthur H. Marsh and accepted in 1920 to protect an improved airgun. British Patent 162,923 – also sought with Marsh – was granted on 12 May 1921 for yet another variation of the basic Gem-type airgun. **16.** William Baker was a commercial traveller living, so British Patent 13,203/06 of 1906 reveals, at Richmond House, Richmond Road, Caversham, Berkshire. He designed a padded catching box which – placed behind a target – was intended to catch airgun slugs so that they could be used over and over again. **17.** William Edward Baker. An English provincial gunmaker working from premises in Tavistock, Devon. **18.** William H. Baker, Lisle, New York State, USA. Born in 1835 and active in Lisle from shortly after the end of the American Civil War in 1865 to 1875, Baker is best known

as a shotgun designer, filing appropriate claims from the early 1860s onward. The earliest was granted on 8 December 1863 as US Patent 40,809, to protect a 'firearms lock'. This was followed on 31 August 1875 by US Patent 167,293, protecting a gun-lock opened by pressing the front trigger forward. Shotguns of this type were made by W.H. Baker & Sons Company of Syracuse. Baker then received protection for 'locks for firearms' – US Patents 199,773 of 29 January 1878 and 228,020 of 25 May 1880 – as well as the three 'breech-loading firearms' covered by 202,397 of 16 April 1878, 228,165 of 1 June 1880 and 248,249 of 11 November 1881. Guns embodying an improved box-lock action with a radial top lever were made in accordance with the 1880 patents. **19.** Baker Gun & Forging Company, Batavia, New York State, and 253 Church Street, New York City. Successors of the *Syracuse Forging Company in 1903, the year it was incorporated, this business continued to make single- and double-barrel exposed-hammer shotguns in accordance with the Baker patents. The first hammerless side-lock pattern had been introduced in 1899, followed by top lever box-lock Trap Guns in 1909 and an improved box lock in 1912. Many of the cheapest shotguns were sold under the *Batavia name, and a short-lived Batavia .22 auto-loading rifle appeared in 1911. However, the gunmaking division was sold in 1919 to H. & D. *Folsom Company of New York, and assembly of Baker-type guns did not cease until 1929; Folsom-assembled Bakers could be identified by their distinctive 'F' serial-number suffixes. The Baker Gun Company produced guns under a variety of brandnames, including Batavia, Batavia Leader, Black Diana and Paragon. *See also* Frank A. *Hollenbeck, George F. *Schafer and Edward *Watson. **20.** Baker & Marsh: *see* William Baker (above). **21.** Baker-Perkins, Birmingham, Warwickshire, England. A maker of British rifle-type 'Projectors, Grenade, No. 5 Mk 1/L', 1944. **22.** Baker's Best: *see* Frederick T. Baker. **23.** Baker's Special: *see* Joseph Baker & Son.

Balch. G.T. Balch, a US Army captain, accepted *Colt and *Savage revolvers during the American Civil War, marking them 'GTB'. *See also* US arms inspectors' marks.

Balcom. F. Balcom, Pittston, Pennsylvania, USA. Assignee of revolver patents granted to Thomas W. Bearcock (US 195,562), and to Bearcock and John Brooks (190,543). Both date from 1877.

Baldwin – **1.** Cyrus W. Baldwin, Boston, Massachusetts, USA. On 19 January 1869, Baldwin was granted US Patent 85,897 to protect the design of a breech-loading firearm. **2.** Eden A. Baldwin, Junior, Shelburne Falls, Massachusetts, USA. The executor of the estate of his father, Eden A. Baldwin, this 'mechanic' was granted US Patent 11,283 on 11 July 1854. Subsequently he established E.A. Baldwin & Company in Worcester, Massachusetts, to make firearms, but trading had ceased by the beginning of the American Civil War. **3.** William R. Baldwin (Major): *see* Automatic Guns, Inc.

Bales. George W. Bales of Ipswich, Suffolk, was an English gun- and bow-maker. He was listed in Tavern Street in 1838, and at 15 Cornhill in 1845–70, when his marks reportedly appeared on a few self-cocking *pepperboxes and cap-lock revolvers.

Ball – **1.** Albert Ball, one of the greatest of the mechanical geniuses to come out of the New England states. Ball's patents – more than a hundred of them – spanned a wide range of subjects. The first of the specifications relevant to firearms was US Patent 38,935 of 23 June 1863, granted to protect a 'self-loading fire-arm' made by the Windsor Manufacturing Company. A later US Patent, 43,827 of 16 August 1864, allowed claims for a 'breech-loading self-feeding firearm', also made by the Windsor Manufacturing Company. US Patent 45,307 (of 6 December 1864) protected a 'magazine fire-arm' with a tubular magazine that slid into the fore-end and was protected against accidental discharge caused by barrel-heat by insulation. US Patent 47,484 of 23 May 1865 covered a 'machine for lubricating bullets', and 60,664 of 1 January 1867 protected a 'cartridge retractor for breech-loading firearms'. A half-interest in 60,664 was assigned to the Windsor Manufacturing Company. *See also* Ball & Lamson and the E.G. ★Lamson Company. **2.** John Maxwell Ball. This 'engineer', living at 30 Coronation Street, Cheadle, Staffordshire, England, obtained two British Patents. However, as they were granted during the Second World War, there is no evidence that the guns were ever made. Patent 545,731 was accepted on 10 June 1942 for an auto-loading airgun design; Patent 563,757 followed on 29 August 1944 to protect an improvement of the earlier magazine. **3.** Ball & Lamson, Windsor, Vermont, USA. This partnership of

Albert Ball and Edward G. Lamson made Ball's 1863-patent magazine carbine, but failed shortly after the end of the American Civil War and was succeeded by the E.G. ★Lamson Company. **4.** Ball & Williams, Worcester, Massachusetts, USA. Active during the American Civil War, this partnership made sporting rifles, carbines and military long-arms in accordance with the 1861-vintage breech-mechanism patent granted to Charles H. ★Ballard. *See also* William A. ★Richardson.

Ballard – **1.** Alvin S. Ballard, Waterville, New York, USA. Recipient on 29 October 1878 of US Patent no. 209,444, protecting a firearm. **2.** Charles Ballard, Worcester, Massachusetts, USA. Ballard is best remembered for his distinctive breech-loading rifles and carbines, made in accordance with a patent granted in the USA on 5 November 1861 (no. 33,631). Ballard also patented a 'cartridge ejector for breech-loading firearms', the subject of US Patent 63,605 of 9 April 1867, and was responsible for the design of a single-barrel cartridge derringer patented on 22 June 1869. *See also* Ball & Williams, Ballard & Company, Ballard & Fairbanks, Merrimac Arms & Manufacturing Company, John M. ★Marlin, Joseph ★Merwin and Schoverling & Daly. **3.** John K. Ballard, Grayling, Michigan, USA. Recipient of US Patent 337,916, granted on 16 March 1886 to pro-

---

BALLARD RIFLE

Ballard (5)

Patented by Charles Ballard in November 1861, this distinctive US dropping-block design was very successful. The breech-block contained the hammer and the trigger mechanism, which automatically dropped the hammer to half-cock as the action opened. The first guns were made in 1862–63 by Dwight ★Chapin & Company of Bridgeport, Connecticut, under contract to Merwin & Bray.

Federal purchases in 1861–66 amounted to a mere thirty-five rifles and about 1,509 carbines, owing to the poor quality of Chapin's work. However, 600 rifles and 1,000 carbines were sold to Kentucky, where they were so well received that more orders followed; according to an inventory taken in

September 1864, the state cavalry and mounted infantry had 3,494 carbines, while the infantry had about 4,600 rifles.

Most of the Ballard rifles supplied to the Federal authorities incorporated an auxiliary cap-lock ignition system patented in January 1864 by Joseph ★Merwin & Edward Bray. Seemingly a backward step, this was useful in areas where ammunition was in short supply. Ballards were also made by ★Ball & Williams of Worcester, Massachusetts (1863–64, in .44, .46 and .56 rimfire); by R. ★Ball & Company of Worcester (1864–66); then by the ★Merrimack Arms & Manufacturing Company (1867–69) and the ★Brown Manufacturing Company (1869–73) of Newburyport, Massachusetts.

Rights were acquired by ★Schoverling & Daly of New York in 1873, and manufacture was licensed two years later to John

★Marlin of New Haven, Connecticut. Marlin-made rifles show many detail improvements on pre-1873 examples. Production eventually ceased at the beginning of the twentieth century. Model-names associated with the Ballards include Creedmoor, Hunter's, Long Range, Mid-Range, Montana, Off-Hand, Pacific, Perfection, Rigby, Schuetzen, Schuetzen Junior, Sporting and Union Hill, all of these being listed separately. Additional details will be found in *Rifles of the World* by John Walter (second edition, Krause Publications, 1998).

This example of the .44 rimfire Ballard single-shot dropping-block rifle dates from the American Civil War. The knob protruding beneath the fore-end activated the extractor once the breech had been opened.
Courtesy of Wallis & Wallis, Lewes.

tect a method of making gun barrels. **4.** Walter A. Ballard. This gunmaker was associated with the J. *Stevens Arms & Tool Company and the *Newton Arms Company. He designed the well-known Ballard loading tool, one of the earliest successful 'press' patterns, and died in Columbus, Ohio, in November 1941. **5.** Ballard rifle: *see* panel, p. 53. **6.** Ballard & Company (active c. 1860–72 and later), Jackson Street, Worcester, Massachusetts, USA. **7.** This small gunmaking business manufactured breech-loading firearms in accordance with a patent granted on 5 November 1861 to Charles H. Ballard. **8.** Ballard & Fairbanks, Worcester, Massachusetts, USA. This gunmaking partnership made Charles Ballard's 1869-patent .41 rimfire cartridge derringer, with a barrel that tipped down to expose the chamber after the catch on the barrel-block had been pressed forward. The ejector was operated by a toothed rack in the frame.

'Balliol' [The]. A mark associated with shotgun cartridges loaded by William *Richardson of Barnard Castle from *Eley-Kynoch components. The name associates with John de Balliol, a thirteenth-century king of Scotland.

Ballistic Bolt. This was an airgun projectile, developed by the *Sussex Armoury, which was introduced commercially in 1978 in .177 and .22. It consisted of a pointed metal nose set into a long, pliable synthetic four-fin shaft, intended to spin the dart in flight.

Ballou. This mark, perhaps a manufacturer's, was found on a *Gallery Gun of uncertain date. The gun was probably made in the southern states of the USA in the middle of the nineteenth century.

Balp, 3 cours Victor Hugo, Saint-Étienne, France (in 1951). Listed in 1933 and 1951 as a gunmaker.

Balsom. Frank Balsom of Omaha, Nebraska, USA, was granted protection for a gun-stock on 4 June 1907 (US Patent no. 856,016).

Baltimore Arms Company, Baltimore, Maryland, USA. This gunmaking business was responsible for shotguns, including hammerless doubles, made to the patents of Ansley *Fox. Operations were confined to 1896–1902, when rights to the patents were acquired by the *Philadelphia Arms Company.

Bamco. *See* Bahco.

Bandell & Neal. These men were employed by *Marlin, and were responsible for designing the Model 62 lever-action rifle.

Bandle. Jacob C. Bandle of Cincinnati, Ohio, USA, son of gunsmith P.C. Bandle, began operations at 260 Main Street in 1865. Work on guns and cutlery continued until 1891 or later, but had ceased by 1902. Bandle is chiefly remembered for light target rifles, but also made cap- or primer-propelled gallery guns to the designs of John H. *Krider. *See also* Christopher *Raquet.

Bandung. The principal Indonesian arms factory, on the island of Java, this was formerly the workshop of the Royal Netherlands Indies Army (*see* 'KNIL'). *Garand-type rifles, their *Beretta-type adaptations and FN-Browning GP-35 pistols have all been made there.

Banfield. J.C. Banfield & Sons, an English gunmaking and ironmongery business, operating from premises in Tenbury Wells, Worcestershire, is known to have marked shotgun ammunition made by *Eley-Kynoch Ltd.

Bang. Danish inventor-engineer Søren Hansen Bang, of Copenhagen, is best-known for semi-automatic rifle designs originating early in the twentieth century. These relied on propellant gas trapped by a muzzle cup to pull the operating rod forward. The goal was a softer action than the recoil-operated guns of the day, which often worked very harshly. However, although tested for many years, including during the Second World War on the German Gew. 41 (*Mauser and *Walther patterns), the muzzle-cup system ultimately proved unreliable and too susceptible to fouling.

Bango. This was an 'explosive' airgun pellet, properly known as Lane's Bango, made by *Lane Bros. from c. 1906 until the beginning of the First World War. A small charge of match compound was inserted in the slug-head, to be ignited through the combined effects of friction and force when the projectile struck a hard object. Although ineffective, owing to the minuscule explosive charge, Bango apparently succumbed to pressure brought by society. However, it is said to have had a surprisingly bright flash when fired at night.

Bang-Up. A cheap *Suicide Special revolver made in the USA by *Ely & Wray or *Harrington & Richardson.

Banker's Special or Banker's Special Model. Dating from 1926–40, this was a Colt *Police Positive with a full-size butt and a 2in barrel. Designed for ready concealment, it was advertised specifically for bank tellers and security officers; others were purchased to arm undercover policemen and railroad clerks. Total production of 35,000 included a few hundred guns with spurless hammers. The *Detective Special was similar.

Banks – 1. Benjamin Rodwell Banks designed distinctive airgun projectiles, a rotating or 'detachable' magazine, and a special cartridge inserter. Most of the patent specifications record his home address as 22 Elgin Road, East Croydon, Surrey, England. British Patent 12,742/92 of 1892 protects Banks' Patent Flanged Slug; British Patent 18,694/94 of 1894 protects Banks' Patent Shot Cartridge; and British Patent 22,930/94 protects the shotgun-cartridge inserting device. **2.** Banks & Company. This business was operated by the inventor Benjamin R. Banks (above) from Point Pleasant Works, Wandsworth, South London, England. Banks' patent airgun ammunition was made there from the early 1890s until 1911 or later, although trading seems to have ceased when the First World War began. **3.** Banks' Patent Flanged Slug. Patented in 1892 by Benjamin R. Banks, this airgun projectile had a rib or flange around its base to improve the air seal and enhance accuracy. It was somewhat similar to the modern *Sheridan slug, but had a markedly different nose. **4.** Banks' Patent Shot Cartridge. This consisted of a small reloadable open-ended, double-wadded tube of shot that could be inserted in the breech of an airgun. A few cartridges of this type have survived, but the effectiveness of the low-powered gun/shot combination was minimal.

Bannerman – 1. Francis Bannerman & Sons (subsequently Francis Bannerman Sons, Inc.), Brooklyn and New York City. Founded soon after the end of the American Civil War by Francis Bannerman (1851–1918), a Scottish emigré, this gun-dealing business grew rapidly. A move to Atlantic Avenue, Brooklyn, occurred in 1867, then to New York City and – successively – 118 Broad Street, 27 Front Street and 597 Broadway. Bannerman bought such huge quantities of military surplus that he was able to equip entire regiments during the

Spanish-American War of 1898, then bought so much more after hostilities had been concluded that an island in the Hudson river had to be purchased to store it! Frank Bannerman (1873–1945) and David Bannerman (1875–1957) had joined the business by the beginning of the twentieth century, forming Bannerman & Sons, and the purchase of 499 & 501 Broadway established the business as the doyen of military-surplus operations. Run in more recent times by Charles S. Bannerman, it moved to Blue Point, New York, in 1961. Although renowned largely as a dealer, Bannerman bought the assets of the *Spencer Rifle Company from *Pratt & Whitney and (despite a most acrimonious confrontation with Winchester) continued to make slide-action Spencer shotguns for some years. Production began in Brooklyn in 1893, the 1890-model Bannerman-Spencers being essentially similar to the original design. An improved pattern was introduced in 1900, but competition from better guns forced production to cease in 1901–02. **2.** Bannerman rifle. A thousand .303 rifles were made from a collection of Springfield, Krag and Mauser components, and sent to Britain in 1915 in acknowledgement of Bannerman's Scottish ancestry. Unfortunately, the guns failed inspection and were relegated to drill use.

'Banshee' [The]. Found on a shotgun cartridge sold by W.C. *Carswell of Liverpool, England.

Bantam – 1. A brandname applied to the 6.35mm M34 Bantam, a semi-automatic pocket pistol made by Pietro *Beretta of Gardone Val Trompia, Italy. **2.** A name given to the 5mm-calibre airgun slugs made by *Sheridan of Racine, Wisconsin, USA, for the pump-up pneumatic rifles introduced in 1949. The basic design had been anticipated more than fifty years previously by *Banks' Patent Flanged Slug. **3.** Applied to the shortest butt option fitted to British military rifles. It was 1in shorter than the standard pattern.

Bapty & Company is best known for providing a wide range of arms and equipment to film and television companies. Bapty originally sold sporting guns and accessories, including ammunition marked with the Bapty name, although apparently originating in Britain, Italy and the USA.

Bar, BAR – 1. See Browning Automatic Rifle. **2.** As Bär. A two-barrel four-shot repeating pistol designed by Burkard *Behr and made by J.P. *Sauer & Son of Suhl, Thüringen, Germany. **3.** As BAR-22. See Carabine Automatique Browning.

Barakuda – 1. Based on an old idea, this interesting booster was introduced in the early 1950s by Barakuda-Gesellschaft of Hamburg, Germany, in an attempt to boost the power of airguns. An auxiliary cylinder was used to inject a supposedly measured amount of ether into the air cylinder of a conventional rifle – the Weihrauch HW35 was preferred, owing to its strength. Additional power resulted when the heat generated by compression ignited the ether/air mixture in the air cylinder, but this 'controlled dieselling' proved to be very erratic and potentially dangerous. The fitting had been abandoned by 1958, but guns so fitted can be recognised by a slender auxiliary cylinder on the right side of the breech or by evidence that it was once fitted. **2.** Barakuda, Barracuda. A heavyweight *diabolo-type airgun pellet made by *Haendler & Natermann.

Barber – 1. Joseph Barber, Bridesburgh, Pennsylvania,

USA. Barber was granted US Patent 23,224 of 15 March 1859, jointly with P.C. Reinfried, to protect a breech-loading firearm. **2.** William H. Barber. This Federal government arms inspector, working in 1862, accepted cap-lock revolvers marked 'WHB'. See also US arms inspectors' marks.

Barberblade-Fabrik, Aalborg, Denmark. A razor-blade manufacturer also noted for a range of airgun pellets (the Abbey Diabolo, Black Box or *Pallet) developed in the late 1960s by Børge Naseby.

Barbier – 1. Pierre Barbier, place Polignais 10, Saint-Étienne, France. A gunmaker listed in 1879. **2.** Barbier-Gonon et Gaitte, rue Saint-Roch 7, Saint-Étienne, France. Listed in 1879 as a gunmaker.

Bardella. See Barella.

Barella – 1. H. Barella, Berlin. Founded in 1844, this 'Königl. Hof-Büchsenmacher' was trading in 1900 from Französischestrasse 25/26 in Berlin W8. Catalogues of the pre-1914 era proudly proclaimed the patronage of the Tsar of Russia, the kings of Italy and Romania, and an array of counts and grand dukes. They also claimed the grant of prize medals at exhibitions ranging from Stettin in 1863 to Königsberg in 1897. It is assumed that trading was restricted after 1920, but that work did not finally cease until the Russians took Berlin in 1945. **2.** R. Barella, Berlin and Suhl. Listed as a gunmaker in 1920 and as a distributor of weapons and ammunition in 1930. Sometimes wrongly listed as Bardella, and possibly also the same as the preceding entry (i.e. misreading 'H' as 'R').

Barford. Henry W. Barford & Company, trading from 14–16 Bishop Street, Coventry, Warwickshire, England, sold guns and sporting goods. Barford apparently commissioned *Eley-Kynoch shotgun cartridges marked 'Special Imperial'.

'Bargate' [The]. A mark found on shotgun ammunition made by *Kynoch prior to 1918 for John *MacPherson of Inverness, Scotland.

Barham. C.H. Barham, an English gunmaker trading from 95 Tilehouse Street, Hitchin, Hertfordshire, loaded shotgun ammunition marked 'The Challenge' and 'The Hert's Cartridge' (sic). Components were supplied after the First World War by *Eley-Kynoch Ltd.

Barkeep's Gun. A generic term for any short-barrel handgun, customarily a revolver, which could have been used behind a saloon bar – usually placed muzzle-down in a mug or glass.

Barker – 1. C.M. Barker, Albion, Michigan, USA. Joint recipient with William Dicer of US Patent 404,779, granted on 4 June 1889 to protect a breech-loading firearm. **2.** Milan S. Barker, Eugene, Oregon, USA. Designer of a distinctive *trap gun, patented on 28 November 1893 (US no. 509,716). **3.** T. Barker. A name found on shotguns handled by the H. & D. *Folsom Arms Company, possibly imported from Europe. **4.** Barker Gun Company. A brandname associated with shotguns made in the USA by the *Crescent Arms Company.

Barlow. John H. Barlow of New Haven, Connecticut, USA, was granted US Patent 659,953 of 16 October 1900 to protect a 'device for extracting shells from gun barrels'.

Barnekov. Kiel V. Barnekov (sometimes mistakenly listed as Barnskoy) of Cornwall, New York State, was granted US Patent 104,100 of 14 June 1870 to protect a breech-loading firearm. This was a very simple design, relying on a radial thumb-lever to retract the breech-block; an interlock between the block and the lever prevented the action flipping open as the gun fired.

Barnes – 1. A. Barnes. This provincial gunmaker, trading in Ulverston in Cumbria, north-west England, handled shotgun cartridges with the brandname Referendum. 2. Charles Barnes. An employee of the *Remington Arms Company, involved in the adaptation of the .30-calibre M1917 *Enfield rifle into a sporting rifle. 3. Frederick Barnes. A gunsmith established in premises at 3 Union Row, Tower Hill, London, England, as early as 1850, Barnes' marks have been reported on a wide variety of sporting guns, pepperboxes and revolvers. Directories published at the time of the Great Exhibition in 1851 list the business as Frederick Barnes & Son, with premises in London at 3 Union Row, 109 Fenchurch Street and 67 Minories (until 1856). By 1857, work was being concentrated at 109 Fenchurch Street, where it continued until 1914 or later. 4. John Barnes. This gunsmithing, ironmongery and sporting-goods business has been identified with Challenger-brand shotgun cartridges.

Barnett – 1. Barnett International. A well-established sporting-goods company, with branches in the USA and elsewhere, this is well-known for its crossbows. In 1981, however, Barnett's directors decided to diversify and began to distribute airguns such as the Barnett Spitfire – the Webley *Tracker under another name. 2. John Barnett, New Lexington, Ohio, USA. This inventor was granted US Patent 176,276 of 18 April 1876 to protect his breech-loading firearm. 3. John Barnett & Sons. Gunmaker John Edward Barnett first appears in the London, England, directories prior to 1850, trading in 1850–59 from 134 Minories in the heart of the city's gunmaking district. Additional premises were occupied in Brewhouse Lane, Wapping (1860–74) and Duncan Street, Leman Street, London E., from 1876 until c. 1912.

Barney. Everett H. Barney of Springfield, Massachusetts, designed a saluting gun patented in the USA on 15 October 1901 (no. 684,627).

Barning. Henry F. Barning of Jersey City, New Jersey, USA, was granted US Patent 794,770 (18 July 1905) to protect a 'breech-loading gun'.

'Barnite' [The]. A mark found on shotgun cartridges loaded by William *Richardson of Barnard Castle from *Eley-Kynoch components.

Barnitzke. Karl Barnitzke, Suhl in Thüringen, Wilhelm-Gustloff-Strasse 17 (1941). Listed in the Erfurt telephone directory as 'Ob.-Ing.' (*Oberingenieur*, senior engineer), Barnitzke has been linked not only with *Gustloff-Werke, but also with the design of the *Volksgewehr 1–5.

Barnum. Willis S. Barnum worked as a sporting-gun maker in Syracuse, New York State, trading first from 15 West Washington (1872–75), then 18 East Genesee (1875–82). Breech-loading shotguns have been reported with Barnum's marks, but these were simply bought in when required.

'Barnoid' [The]. This will be found on shotgun ammunition distributed in northern England by William *Richardson of Barnard Castle, loaded from *Eley-Kynoch components. It is assumed that the '-oid' suffix indicates a waterproof case.

Bar-O. A brandname associated with a patented adjustable rifle sight developed by the *Benjamin Rifle

Company. It was an aperture version of the open *Bar-V.

Baron – 1. J. Baron: see Randolph P *Cory. 2. Baron fils aîné, rue des Jardins 30, Saint-Étienne, France. Listed in 1879 as a distributor of and agent for arms and ammunition.

Barracuda. *See* Barakuda.

'Barrage' [The]. Associated with shotgun ammunition made by *Kynoch prior to 1918 for John *MacPherson of Inverness, Scotland.

Barrel – 1. The part of any gun containing the *bore, down which the bullet passes, and (usually) a *chamber in which the cartridge is inserted. 2. Barrel band, also known simply as band. This holds the barrel in the fore-end. It may be made in one piece or two, and retained by springs let into the fore-end (sprung band), or by screws or threaded bolts (screwed band). 3. Barrel extension. A frame attached to the barrel to carry the bolt or breech-block; alternatively, the part of the barrel behind the breech into which the bolt or breech-block may lock. 4. Barrel rib. A stiffener, forged or otherwise, attached to the upper surface of the barrel, into which the front sight blade is formed or fixed. This may be encountered on sporting rifles, although it is much more common on shotguns. The object is to give the barrel rigidity without adding as much weight as would be required if it had been forged with a greater diameter. Half- and quarter-ribs will be encountered on sporting guns, usually to carry the sights rather than stiffen the barrel.

Barrett – 1. Peter Barrett. A Gunner in the US Navy, Barrett accepted *Colt cap-lock revolvers in 1861–68, distinguished by 'PB' marks. *See also* US arms inspectors' marks. 2. Barrett Firearms Manufacturing, Inc., Murfreesboro, Tennessee. This gunmaking business has made a variety of sporting and military rifles, including the auto-loading .50-calibre *Light Fifty and Model 90 sniping rifles, introduced in 1983 and 1990 respectively.

Barry – 1. C.C.G. Barry. The designer of a safety catch for the Danish *Krag-Jørgensen service rifle. 2. R.P. Barry. This government arms inspector, a captain in the Federal Army working in 1861–64, accepted cap-lock revolvers marked 'RPB'. *Remington, *Rogers & Spencer, and *Starr patterns have been reported. *See also* US arms inspectors' marks.

Bartender's Model. *See* Sheriff's Model.

Barthelmes – 1. Alex. Barthelmes, Zella-Mehlis in Thüringen, Germany. Listed in the 1930 edition of the *Deutsches Reichs-Adressbuch* as a gunmaker. 2. Cuno Barthelmes, Zella-Mehlis in Thüringen, Germany. Listed in 1939 as a master gunsmith. 3. Engelhardt Barthelmes, Zella St Blasii and Zella-Mehlis in Thüringen, Germany. Listed in 1900–20 as a master gunsmith and gunmaker. Apparently owned in 1920 by Ernst & Fritz Barthelmes, this had changed by 1930 to Ernst Barthelmes alone. The business was listed as a weapon-maker in 1939. 4. Emil Barthelmes, Zella St Blasii and Zella-Mehlis in Thüringen, Germany. Founded in 1854, this business was described as a gunmaker in 1900–30. The directories list Barthelmes's specialties as 'hunting rifles, *Drillinge, stalking and hunting guns'. The *Deutsches Reichs-Adressbuch* for 1920–30 records the owner as M. Metzner. Use of the mark '[*]Diabolo' was granted in November 1927. The business was still trading in 1941, using a 'B' trademark. 5. Ernst Barthelmes, Zella St Blasii and Zella-Mehlis in Thüringen, Germany. Listed in 1914–20 as a gun- and weapon-maker. 6. Franz Barthelmes,

FRITZ BARTHELMES KG

Barthelmes (10)

Heidenheim Kreis Oggenhausen an der Brenz, Germany. Founded in 1948 by Fritz Barthelmes, but now operated by his son Martin, this metalworking business began making starting- and flare pistols in 1954. A patent for what became the first *FB Record air pistol (LP1) was sought unsuccessfully in 1967, but it is believed that objections made by *Mayer & Grammelspacher prevented acceptance. However, despite employing only twenty people, the Barthelmes company was making 40,000 guns annually by the mid-1980s.

The 4.5mm Barthelmes FB Record Jumbo is an air pistol; the rear of the barrel/receiver unit can be lifted once what appears to be the hammer (in reality a catch) has been released.

Zella-Mehlis in Thüringen, Germany. Listed in 1939 as a master gunsmith. **7.** Franz Barthelmes, Theod. Sohn, Zella-Mehlis in Thüringen, Germany. Listed as a gunmaker in 1930. **8.** Friedr. Theod. Barthelmes Sohn, Zella St Blasii in Thüringen, Germany. Listed in the 1900 edition of the *Deutsches Reichs-Adressbuch* as a gunmaker. **9.** Fritz Barthelmes. Born in Zella St Blasii in 1899, Barthelmes deserves to be remembered as the designer of the *Walther P.38, developed in the 1930s when he was chief engineer of Carl *Walther Waffenfabrik of Zella-Mehlis. The relevant British patent for the locking system is, after all, granted jointly to Barthelmes and Fritz Walther, and it is clear from the testimony of surviving employees that the concept was due more to Barthelmes than Walther. Fritz Barthelmes escaped from what was to be the Soviet Zone of a partitioned Germany in the summer of 1945, settling in the village of Heidenheim – where, ironically, Fritz Walther's fortunes also began a post-war recovery. There he formed Fritz Barthelmes KG (below) to make metal goods and, later, starting- and signal pistols. Barthelmes died in 1973. **10.** Fritz Barthelmes KG: *see panel, above.* **11.** Martin Barthelmes. Son of Fritz Barthelmes (above), and the owner since his father's death of Fritz Barthelmes KG. Martin Barthelmes designed the FB Record *Jumbo and magazine-feed Champion air pistols, in addition to improving the company's blank-firers.

Bartlett – 1. The A.F. Bartlett Company, Saginaw, Wisconsin, USA. Possibly the manufacturer of the *Crescent BB Gun, sharing the offices of the *Crescent Gun Company from 1904 until the latter disappeared in 1908 into its parent (the Crescent Salt Company). **2.** C.L. Bartlett. A government arms inspector active in 1904–10, using the initials 'CLB'. *See also* US arms inspectors' marks. **3.** W.W. Bartlett. This government arms inspector, working in 1899–1904, accepted small-arms marked 'WWB'. *See also* US arms inspectors' marks.

Barton. F. Barton & Company was a gunmaking business trading from 49 Lime Street, London E.C., England, from 1896 until the First World War.

Bartram. The marks of this retailer of sporting guns and ammunition have been reported on shotgun ammunition with the brandname Hard Hitters.

Bartsch. Emil Bartsch of Suhl in Thüringen, Germany. Listed as a gunmaker in 1930, and as a gunsmith in 1939.

Bar-V. A rarely seen, but interesting, rotary-bar elevating back sight offered by the *Benjamin Rifle Company of St Louis during the 1970s. It may be encountered on the Benjamin pneumatic rifles, being offered as an optional extra. The *Bar-O was a similar design with an aperture instead of an open V-notch.

Baryshev. Konstantin Aleksandrovich Baryshev was born in 1923 in Sosnovka, near Tambov, USSR. He graduated from the Dzherzhinsky Artillery Academy in 1946 and began working for the proving-ground authorities alongside many famous small-arms designers. During this period, Baryshev developed a 9mm pistol and a 7.62mm *Avtomat, and was also responsible for a mount for the *PKP machine-gun. Lieutenant-Colonel Baryshev retired from the army in 1974.

Bascaran – 1. C. y T. Bascaran SRC, Eibar, Guipúzcoa, Spain. Bascaran has made shotguns and airguns under the *Cometa brandname. The airguns included the Cometa V and VII, simple barrel-cockers briefly sold in Britain (in 1975–77) by *Parker-Hale Ltd. Subsequently, the guns reappeared under the *Lincoln brandname, owned by David *Nickerson (Tathwell) Ltd. **2.** Martin A. Bascaran of Eibar, Guipúzcoa, Spain, is recorded as the manufacturer of (among other firearms) the *Martian and *Thunder semi-automatic pistols.

Basculant – 1. A term associated with automatic pistols made by Nicholas *Pieper of Liège, Belgium, denoting tipping-barrel construction. *See also* Demontant. **2.** A small 6.35mm Browning-type automatic pistol made by

*Aguirre, Zamacolas y Compañía of Eibar, Spain; seven rounds, hammer fired.

Basque. A semi-automatic pistol manufactured by *Echave y Arizmendi of Eibar prior to the Spanish Civil War (1936–39).

Basson, 13 rue du Grand-Gonnet, Saint-Étienne, France. Described in directories dating from 1950–51 as a gunmaker.

Bästlein. Alfred Bästlein of Suhl in Thüringen, Germany, was listed in the *Deutsches Reichs-Adressbuch* (1939–42) as a gunsmith.

Basler – 1. John Basler, New York City. This gunmaker's name may simply disguise a sales office maintained by one of the partners in Basler & Denk or, more probably, indicate that the partnership had been split. St Louis-style *Gallery Guns are known with 'New York' markings. **2.** Basler & Denk. This maker of sporting guns and spring-air Gallery Guns traded in St Louis, Missouri, USA, in the 1860s. Many of the guns have been reported with the additional marks of Scharf & Son, but the relationship between the businesses is unclear.

Bassett. G.J. Bassett, a sporting-goods and ironmongery business trading from 4 Swan Street, Petersfield, Hampshire, England, sold shotgun cartridges branded 'Champion'.

Bastin. Henri Bastin of Liège, a maker of sporting guns and rifles, has been active in Belgium since the end of the Second World War.

Bâtard-Gevelot. *See* Gevelot.

Batavia. A brandname associated with the products of the *Baker Gun & Forging Co. of Batavia, New York. It was used on a range of inexpensive side-lock shotguns made from about 1905 onward, and on a .22 auto-loading rifle confined to 1911–14.

Bate. George Bate. Established in 1881 and still trading from 132 Steelhouse Lane, Birmingham, Warwickshire, England, in the 1930s, this gunmaker is recorded as having sold shotgun ammunition under the brandnames Game, Imperial and Leader. The cartridges (or perhaps simply components) were usually purchased from *Eley-Kynoch Ltd.

Bater. Inventor Charles Claude Bater, living in 1946 at 'Bungable', The Avenue, Finchley, London N3, was co-grantee with *Millard Brothers and George Arthur *Lee of British Patent 575,543 protecting a pump-up pneumatic airgun.

Bates – 1. Arthur Bates & Company. This gunmaking business had a shop at 22 Sun Street, Canterbury, Kent, England. Branches were also operated locally, in Sturry and Whitstable. **2.** Edward R. Bates. An English provincial gunmaker with premises in Canterbury, Kent, at 3 George Gate and 71 Burgate Street. **3.** George Bates. This gunsmithing business, trading prior to 1914 in Eastbourne, Sussex, England, handled shotgun cartridges marked 'The Eastbourne'. **4.** William L. Bates. This US government arms inspector, working in 1870–79, accepted Remington revolvers for the US Navy; the guns were marked 'WLB'. *See also* US arms inspectors' marks.

Batho. A name associated with round shot made by the Midland Gun Company in the 1930s.

Bath Street Gun Works; alternatively, Bath Gun Works: *see* *Midland Gun Company.

Bathurst, also known as Rifle Factory No. 2, Olympic Way and Stuart Street, Bathurst, New South Wales,

Australia. This was established in 1941 to supply SMLE components to the *Lithgow factory, but subsequently became a feeder for the *Orange establishment. Bathurst products were marked 'BA'.

Battue – 1. A form of snap-shooting at driven game. Usually undertaken with magazine rifles, or auto-loaders such as the *BAR; the requirements are usually a short barrel, a single direct-acting trigger and a fixed back sight at the front of a quarter-rib. **2.** Made in Liège by Société Anonyme Continentale pour la Fabrication des Armes à Feu *Lebeau-Courally, intended for use against driven game, in 9.3′74R only, this short-barrelled over/under rifle has double triggers, a pistol-grip butt, and a standing-block back sight let into the top of the quarter rib. Renaissance-style floral relief engraving, on the customary dark ground, is enhanced with gold inlaid vine-leaf and stem work. There are finely detailed hunting scenes on the side-plates and beneath the frame.

Bauer – 1. Bernh. Bauer, Mehlis and Zella-Mehlis in Thüingen, Germany. Listed in 1914–30 as a gun- and weapon-maker. **2.** Carl Bauer & Company: *see* Karl Bauer. **3.** Ernst Bauer, Suhl in Thüringen, Germany. Listed in 1914 directories as a gunmaker, Bauer specialised in repairs and re-stocking work. **4.** Fritz Bauer, Jena. A retailer of sporting guns, ammunition and accessories active in Germany in 1941. **5.** G. or Georg Bauer, Zella-Mehlis in Thüringen, Germany. Listed in 1930 as a master gunsmith. **6.** J. Bauer, Nachfolger, Zella-Mehlis in Thüringen, Germany. Listed in 1920–30 as a weapon-maker. **7.** Karl Bauer, Ka-Ba Waffenfabrik, Berlin, Breslau and Königsberg in Preussen, Germany, with factories in Suhl. Perhaps best known by the 'Ka-Ba' or 'Kaba' trademark, the guns distributed by this business included some Spanish-made 6.35mm automatic pistols. Bauer was established in Berlin in the early years of the twentieth century; directory entries customarily describe the operation as a *Waffengrosshandlung* (wholesaler) and it is not known whether manufacturing facilities were ever maintained. The Suhl branch was described in most 1920–30 editions of the *Deutsches Reichs-Adressbuch* as a 'weapon-maker' and in 1939 as 'master gunsmiths'. **8.** Bauer Firearms Corporation, Fraser, Michigan, USA. Maker of the Bauer 25 automatic pistol, based on the *Baby Browning.

Baumbach. Gunmaker Ferd. Baumbach the Younger (*der Jüngere*) traded in the period between the world wars in the village of Ebertshausen bei Suhl in the Thüringen district of Germany.

Bavaria – 1. A bolt-action hunting rifle, based on the 1898 Mauser, made in Belgium by Armes Ernest *Dumoulin SPRL. Offered in a variety of chamberings, the guns usually have double triggers and spatulate bolt handles. **2.** A brandname associated with airguns made in Erlangen – in Bavaria – by *Bayerische Sportwaffenfabrik. It was usually confined to English-speaking markets, 'Bayern' being substituted for European distribution. A similar mark will be found on paramilitary daggers made prior to 1945 by F. Barthelmes(s) of Muggendorf, but there is no connection between the two applications. **3.** A term applied by H. *Krieghoff GmbH to engraving patterns applied to the K-80 over/under shotgun. The designs show oval game-bird scenes and two small 'blind' oval panels within delicate floral scrolls. *See also* Bavaria-Suhl, Crown Grade, Danube, Gold Target and Parcours. Deluxe or custom versions may have gold inlays on blued grounds. **4.** Bavaria-Suhl. Another of the engraving patterns applied to K-80 and other guns made by H. ★Krieghoff GmbH. Similar to the standard Bavaria pattern (q.v.), it is much heavier; the blind panels are absent, and the panelling consists of acanthus leaves and tendrils. *See also* Crown Grade, Danube, Gold Target and Parcours.

Bayard, often accompanied by a mounted knight. A mark used by Anciens Établissements ★Pieper of Herstal-lèz-Liège, Belgium, on firearms ranging from ★Bergmann-Bayard pistols to a range of shotguns. *See also* Bergmann-★Mars.

Bayer. Gunsmith John Bayer made spring-air ★Gallery Guns in his workshop at 117 Prince Street, New York City, in 1869–73.

Bayerische Sportwaffenfabrik Hans Schütt oHG ('BSF') of Erlangen, Bavaria, Germany, was said to have been founded in 1935 to make airguns, although there is little evidence that anything other than prototypes were made prior to 1939. Series production did not commence until 1950, when the first of an extensive range of barrel- and underlever-cocking designs appeared. These included the Junior and Media barrel-cockers and the S54, which was little more than a variant of the ★Jeffries Pattern BSA with an elegant half-stock. Many will be found with the ★Wischo brandname of Wilsker & Co., the major export agency. BSF's products were soundly made, but lost ground to the more progressive approach of ★Feinwerkbau, ★Mayer & Grammelspacher and others in the 1970s. The company was hit particularly badly by the failure of its British agent in 1981, and the workforce of 130 in the Fuchsengarten factory in Erlangen was radically reduced. The company was sold in 1982 to Herbert Gayer, but the advent of improved products came too late to stave off the liquidation concluded in July 1985. Apparently, the stock of guns and components was purchased by ★Umarex and eventually marketed under a ★Mauser trademark.

Bayern. The German name for what is generally known in English as 'Bavaria', this has been specifically associated with airguns made by ★Bayerische Sportwaffenfabrik prior to 1989.

Bayet frères of Liège, inspired by the ★Dreyse, patented a bolt-action needle gun in Belgium in the 1850s, then offered it commercially for a few years. Unlike its Prussian prorotype, the Bayet gun was a self-cocker and generally had a straight slot for the bolt-handle base running the length of the receiver. Subsequently, revolvers were made from the 1870s until the First World War.

Baylis. Ebenezer Baylis & Son, sometimes listed as 'Bayliss', St Mary's Square, Birmingham, Warwickshire. Advertised in 1871 as 'Manufacturers of every description of Military and Sporting Implements for Breech & Muzzle-Loading Guns & Rifles. Contractors to the Honourable Board of Ordnance'. Baylis & Son also occupied premises at 42–44a Cannon Street, London, from 1874 to 1876.

Bayonet. This is a bladed weapon that can be attached to the muzzle of a rifle or musketoon, although not usually to a carbine. There are many different types. A socket bayonet is an all-metal pattern with a short cylindrical socket, which passes over the muzzle, and some method of locking the socket to the gun – a spring, a rotating collar or a sliding catch. A knife bayonet has a short straight blade, customarily defined as less than 250mm (11.8in)

long; a sword bayonet is essentially similar to a knife pattern, but has a blade exceeding 250mm. A sabre bayonet is usually a sword pattern with a curved or recurved (yataghan) blade. A rod bayonet normally slides in a channel beneath the muzzle, being carried on the gun at all times. Many books have been written about this particular subject. The best of them, commonly devoted to specific subjects (e.g., Japanese bayonets, British and Commonwealth bayonets), are excellent; perhaps the most useful of the general studies is Paul Kiesling's *World Bayonets* (Military Collectors Service, 1973–79), which has also been published in a much revised French edition.

Bazar. A tradename found on a knife-pistol made in Germany prior to the First World War, apparently on the basis of Springer-brand collar-lock knife parts purchased from Wilhelm ★Weltersbach of Solingen. The small pivoting barrel-block usually held a single .22 Short rimfire cartridge, and the spring-loaded striker was controlled by a small button trigger. The guns also often have auxiliary extractors for shotgun cartridges, marked 'C-12' or 'C-16' depending on gauge.

BB... – 1. BB Gun: *see* panel, p.60. **2.** BB Scout. A brandname associated with the Model 788 pneumatic BB Gun introduced by the ★Crosman Arms Company in 1977. The BB Scout has synthetic furniture, a 22-ball tube magazine and a swinging fore-end pump system.

BBF. See Bockbüchsflinte.

'BBL'. See B.B. ★Lombard.

'B.C.' A 6.35mm Browning-type pocket pistol made by Victor ★Bernedo y Compañía of Eibar, Spain. The magazine usually held six rounds.

'bcd'. A code allotted in 1941 to ★Gustloff-Werke, and used on rifles and small-arms components made in its Weimar (Germany) factory.

'BCP', with crossed sceptres and a crown. An abbreviated form of 'Birmingham Company Proof', applied by the Guardians of the Proof House in Birmingham, Warwickshire, England, from 1813 until replaced in 1904 by 'BP' (black powder) and 'NP' (nitro) proofs.

'bd'. Used in 1940–45 by F.A. Lange Metallwerke AG of Bodenbach an der Elbe, Germany, a maker of small-arms ammunition and components.

BDB. See Bockdoppelbüchse.

BDL. Associated with rifles made by the ★Remington Arms Company (Model B, De Luxe), distinguishing stocks with high-gloss finish, chequering of various types, and, usually, ★Monte Carlo-comb butts. *See also* ADL.

'be'. A mark used by Berndorfer Metallwarenfabrik Arthur Krupp AG on small-arms ammunition and components made during the Second World War.

'Beacon' [The]. Usually accompanied by a rabbit bounding over a foxglove, this mark was associated with shotgun cartridges made prior to the First World War by ★Kynoch for ★Shuffreys Lyd of Walsall.

Beals – 1. Fordyce Beals designed the ★Walking Beam revolver for ★Whitney, patented on 26 September 1856 ('revolving firearm', US no. 11,715), which relied on an oscillating bar to rotate the cylinder. A later design, patented on 24 June 1856 (US no. 15,167) and 26 May 1857 (17,359), was exploited by E. ★Remington & Son. Beals also patented a rammer, protected by 21,478 of 14 September 1858, which was used on the first .44 Remington Army-type revolvers. **2.** Robert P. Beals. Using the mark 'RB', this government arms inspector

BB GUN

BB… (1)

A term applied to a primitive form of *airgun, developed in the USA in the 1880s by companies such as *Markham and *Daisy. The primary goal was to provide a boy's gun inspired by the well-made (but expensive) *Gallery Guns and *Haviland & Gunn *Gems of the day, but firing .175in-diameter BB shot. Some of the earliest BB Guns consisted simply of a short smooth-bore liner in a crude wooden frame/stock unit, although even the first Daisy was made entirely of metal.

From these humble beginnings, the BB Gun has been made in huge quantities – production of the Daisy No. 25, designed by Charles *Lefever, alone exceeding 20,000,000 when work ceased in the 1970s. The market is currently dominated by the *Crosman Arms Company and the *Daisy Manufacturing Company, but the products have grown steadily in sophistication and now are often surprisingly good facsimiles of well-known firearms.

Owing to its hardness, BB shot is ideally suited to magazine feed; it has been used in a legion of spring-and-piston rifles cocked by rocking bolts, beginning with the *Haenel-made Sportmodell of 1933.

Typical of the legion of BB Guns is this Daisy Model 99 Champion, a simple spring-and-piston airgun cocked by pulling down on the trigger-guard lever.

Designed by Hugo *Schmeisser, subsequently this was copied in Germany, Czechoslovakia and Spain.

The best source of information about the US versions is *The American BB Gun* by Arni Dunathan (1976); W.H.B. Smith's *Gas, Air & Spring Guns of the World* (1958 and reprints) gives details of the bolt-cocking guns.

---

accepted *Colt revolvers during 1860–61. Then he changed to 'RPB' and continued to accept small-arms until 1880. *See also* US arms inspectors' marks.

Bear – 1. A brandname used by *Beeman's Precision Guns to identify .20-calibre flat-head diabolo airgun pellets made in Germany by *Haendler & Natermann. **2.** A Soviet/Russian brandname found on a semi-automatic sporting rifle. *See* Medved.

Bearcat. A .22 rimfire revolver introduced in 1966 by *Sturm, Ruger & Company, and made for about ten years. A simplified form of the *Single Six, it was made only in a single barrel length with fixed sights.

Bearcub. Another of the many brandnames used by *Beeman's Precision Guns, this was applied to round-nose 4.5mm and 5.5mm diabolo pellets made by *Haendler & Natermann.

Beardmore – 1. William Beardmore & Company Ltd, Parkhead Forge and Dalmuir Works, Glasgow, Lanarkshire, Scotland. Formed in 1886, superseding the partnership W. & I. Beardmore, this engineering business was best known prior to 1918 for warships, armour plate and heavy guns. After the First World War, however, seeking to diversify, Bearmore briefly promoted the Beardmore-Farquhar machine-gun (1919–27). **2.** Beardmore-Farquhar. Made by the Beardmore Engineering Company, in accordance with the patents of Moubray Gore *Farquhar and Arthur Henry *Hill, this light machine-gun was tested by the RAF in 1919, then by the British Army in the early 1920s. An unusual combination of gas and spring action allowed the weapon to be very lightly built by the standards of the day, weighing a mere $16\frac{1}{2}$lb with a 77-round pan magazine, but much of the operating mechanism was exposed to the elements. A handful of Improved Mark II Beardmore-Farquhar guns were offered from 1924 in .303, 7.65mm and 7x57, with pan or box magazines. A .5-calibre version weighing only 38lb was developed experimentally, but none of these innovative guns was successful.

Beardslee. Lester A. Beardslee, a lieutenant-commander in the Federal Navy, accepted *Starr cap-lock revolvers marked 'LAB' prior to 1861. *See also* US arms inspectors' marks.

Beasley. Benjamin Beasley was a gunmaker, registered at 4 St James's Street, London, England, in 1865.

Beatall. This name was given to conventional ribbed-skirt roundnose .177 and .22 diabolo airgun pellets made for many years by *Lanes Brothers (subsequently Lanes Ltd). They were exported to many countries worldwide and sold under a variety of other names, including *Precise Minuteman and National Pellets.

Beattie. The premises of London gunmaker James Beattie were listed at 205 Regent Street from at least 1850 to 1864, when the trading style changed to James Beattie & Son. Work continued from the same address until about 1880, when the formation of James Beattie & Company coincided with a move to 104 Queen Victoria Street, London E.C. Operations seem to have ceased in 1894.

'Beaufort' [The]. A brandname found on shotgun cartridges loaded for *Harrods of London, probably prior to 1939.

Beaumont – 1. Frans (de) Beaumont. A Dutch gunmaker, best known for the single-shot bolt-action rifle adopted by the Dutch Army in 1871. **2.** Frederick

Blackett Edward Beaumont, Upper Woodball, Barnsley, Yorkshire. This British Army officer (c. 1828–99), 'Late Royal Engineers', received British Patent no. 374/55 of 20 February 1855 to protect the trigger mechanism of a modified *Adams revolver, allowing it to be cocked manually. A comparable US Patent, no. 15,032, was granted on 3 June 1856.

Beaux. Leon Beaux (& Company) of Milan was one of Italy's leading ammunition makers prior to the emergence of *Fiocchi. Beaux made a variety of rifle, handgun and shotgun cartridges prior to c. 1920. They can be recognised by the inclusion in the headstamps of 'LB' or 'LBC'.

Beck. Johannes Beck designed the bolt-head of the perfected Dreyse *Zündnadelgewehr.

Becker & Hollander, established late in the nineteenth century in Suhl, in the Thüringen district of Germany, is best known for the *Beholla pistol. Rifles and shotguns were also made, but operations seem to have ceased at the end of the Second World War.

Beckwith – 1. Henry Beckwith. A gunsmith listed at 33 Fieldgate Street in 1858–65, and 58 Skinner Street, London E., from 1864 until 1868. **2.** William A. Beckwith. The name of this English gunsmith has been linked with firearms, apparently including an occasional self-cocking *pepperbox, made in the 1860s. Indeed, H.J. Blanch, writing in *Arms & Explosives* in 1909, lists Beckwith at a variety of London addresses in the mid-nineteenth century, culminating at 58 Skinner Street, London E., as late as 1868. However, William Beckwith had died in 1841; the business was continued in his name by widow Elizabeth and son Henry.

Bedford – 1. The American engineer Augustus Bedford, Boston, Massachusetts, USA. Bedford seems to have been the maker of the *Eureka, a .21-calibre spring-air pistol, which was basically a *Quackenbush design with an additional loading bolt patented by George A. *Walker in 1876. The gun had previously been made by *Pope, Brothers & Company. Production switched to the Quackenbush factory in Herkimer, New York State, in the 1880s and continued there until 1893. **2.** Bedford Brothers. This gunmaking partnership was listed at 11 Little Moorfields, London E.C., England, in 1867. **3.** Bedford & Walker. This gunmaking partnership apparently made air pistols in accordance with patents granted to George A. *Walker. *See* Augustus Bedford (above).

'Beecher's Bibles'. *See* John Brown Sharps.

Beeman Precision Guns, Inc., of San Anselmo and San Rafael, California, USA, was established on a commercial footing in 1972, having previously traded for some years as a hobby enterprise. It rose rapidly to become North America's largest distributor of European-style airguns, and has laid a justifiable claim to advances in the production of guns and ammunition, even though the former have often been based on Weihrauch components, and the latter on established *Haendler & Natermann designs. Beeman was responsible for the development of the R1 (made in Europe in a different form as the Weihrauch HW80), together with the Kodiak, Laser, Ram Jet and Silver Bear pellets. The great success provided by the airguns encouraged the company to expand into the firearms market in the 1980s, helped by the grant of exclusive agencies for the *Feinwerkbau and *Krico cartridge rifles.

Beesley. English gunmaker Frederick Beesley was first listed at 22 Queen Street, Edgware Road, London W., in 1879. He moved to 85 Edgware Road in 1892, then to 3 St James's Street in 1893. By 1900, Beesley occupied 2 St James's Street and 2 Pickering Place, London S.W.

Begueldre, Liège, Belgium. The marks of this gunmaker have been found on pistols and revolvers – *caplock and cartridge alike – dating from the second half of the nineteenth century.

Behelfspistole. A German term ('auxiliary pistol') used to denote the many non-regulation handguns that eventually found their way into official service during the First World War. Few of the *Behelfspistolen* were particularly powerful, but they did free Parabellums for frontline service. Material published later in the war indicates acquisition of a broad range of commercial designs, including tiny blowbacks seized after the invasion of Belgium.

Beholla. A small *blowback semi-automatic pistol made by *Becker & Hollander of Suhl, c. 1916–19. It seems to have had its origins, like the *FL-Selbstlader, in the 'Hindenburg Programm' of 1915. Designed specifically to meet German military requirements, the Beholla was chambered for the 7.65mm Auto cartridge and had a seven-round box magazine in the grip. Simple, reliable and easily made, guns of this type were also offered under the brandnames *Leonhardt, *Menta and *Stenda.

Behörden-Modell. A modernised version of the 7.65mm 1913- or Old Model pistol made by J.P. *Sauer & Sohn of Suhl, this was intended for police and paramilitary use (*Behörde*, authorities). The external changes were minimal, only a refinement in the shape of the handgrip distinguishing the 1930 from the 1913 pattern; however, the newer gun had a blade-like safety mechanism inserted into the trigger to ensure that the weapon would not fire accidentally. Too late to compete effectively with the Walther *Polizei-Pistole, the Behörden-Modell was replaced shortly before the Second World War began by the Sauer Modell 38.

Behr – 1. Burkhard Behr. The name of this Suhl-based gunsmith, whose operations lasted into the 1920s, is usually associated with the *Bär repeating pistol, made in small numbers by J.P. *Sauer & Sohn of Suhl, Thüringen, Germany, prior to 1914. His operations may have been succeeded eventually by Behrs Industrie-Gesellschaft. **2.** Behrs Industrie-Gesellschaft mbH. Formed in Suhl about 1930, this may have been a successor to the gunmaking business of Burkhard Behr (above). Apparently some of its wares were distinguished by the mark *Colonist.

Beistegui Hermanos of Eibar, Guipúzcoa, Spain, was a gunmaking business – formed in 1909 by Juan and Cosmé Beistegui – that achieved prominence during the First World War only as a sub-contractor for *Ruby-style pistols ordered from *Gabilondo y Urresti. These were marketed in the early 1920s under the name *Royal, alongside a variety of guns made for Fabrique d'Armes de *Grande Précision – including the *B.H., *Bulwark and *Libia. In 1926, however, the first of the Beistegui adaptations of the Mauser C/96 appeared, to be followed by an improved MM31. Production ceased in 1934; the factory was destroyed in 1937, during the Spanish Civil War; and the manufacture of bicycles and accessories began in Vittoria in 1939.

'bek'. A mark found on telescope sights and associated optical-instrument components made in Germany from 1940 to 1945 by Hensoldt-Werk Dr H. Hensoldt in Herborn/Dillkreis.

Bekeart Model. A distinctive *Smith & Wesson revolver originally made in 1912 to the order of gunsmith Philip Bekeart of San Francisco, California, USA. Essentially a .22 rimfire target revolver built on a .32 *Hand Ejector frame, it was made (with minor changes) until 1953.

Belgian... – **1.** Belgian Bull Dog, or Bulldog. A brand-name found on a selection of compact double-action .320 and .380 revolvers, based on the Webley *Bulldog, made in Belgium prior to 1914. Most have six-chamber cylinders and rounded or bird's-head butts; lanyard rings were optional. Not all give clues to their manufacturers, although some bear the 'A.F.' of *Francotte, and others have the crowned 'R' of *Rongé fils. **2.** Belgian Constable. Associated with double-action, six-shot .380 and .44 revolvers, similar to the Belgian Bulldogs (above), but larger. Originating in Belgium prior to 1914, they usually have squared butts and lanyard rings. Manufacturers' marks are often absent, although some guns display the 'A.F.' of *Francotte or the crowned 'R' of *Rongé fils.

Belknap. Theodore A. Belknap, a Federal arms inspector working during the American Civil War, marked cap-lock revolvers and possibly also breech-loading carbines with 'TAB'. *See also* US arms inspectors' marks.

Bell – **1.** George Bell: *see* Clyde's Game & Gun Mart. **2.** John A. Bell. A lieutenant in the US Navy, Bell accepted *Colt and *Smith & Wesson revolvers in 1902–03, marking them with the initials 'JAB'. *See also* US arms inspectors' marks. **3.** William L. Bell. This government arms inspector, a lieutenant in the US Army, accepted Colt pistols marked 'WLB' in 1937. *See also* US arms inspectors' marks. **4.** Bell-Craig. This was a break-barrel air rifle offered in the 1920s by *Clyde's Game & Gun Mart of Glasgow, but probably made in Germany by either Fr. *Langenhan or *Mayer & Grammelspacher. *See also* Ailsa-Craig.

Bellmore – **1.** Bellmore Gun Company. A brandname associated with shotguns made by the *Crescent Arms Company prior to 1917. **2.** Bellmore-Johnson Tool Company, Hamden, Connecticut. Maker of *Sharps-Borchardt actions for the *Sharps Arms Company.

Bellow & Son, an English gunsmithing and ironmongery business, had premises in Leominster, Hereford, Tenbury Wells and Bromyard prior to 1939.

Belmont – **1.** A name applied to a .250-calibre (No. 3 Bore) airgun introduced by C.G. Bonehill in 1908. Details of the design are not known, although it has been suggested as a prototype or variation of what subsequently became known as the *Improved Britannia. **2.** Belmont Gun Works, Belmont Gun & Gun Barrel Works; alternatively, Belmont Firearms Works: *see* C.G. *Bonehill.

Belt-buckle guns. A few nineteenth-century weapons of this type will be encountered, generally made with a short barrel pointing outward from an iron mounting plate on a stout leather belt. They are fired by a conventional hammer and nipple system, the direction of the strike being lateral. A lanyard attached to the arm or leg is normally used to release the cocked hammer. *See also* Disguised guns and Reuben *Goldberg.

Belted case. *See* cartridge case.

Bely et Durafour, rue de Chambin 17, Saint-Étienne, France. Listed in 1879 as a distributor of and agent for arms and ammunition.

Bendix. *See* George A. *Hyde.

Benemerita. Made by, or more probably for, D.F. *Ortega de Seija of Madrid, Spain, this 6.35mm Browning-type pocket pistol had a seven-round magazine and a hammer-pattern firing mechanism. The slide may be marked 'Model 1918'.

Benet, Benét – **1.** Laurence V. Benét. Son of Stephen Benét, one-time Chief of Ordnance of the US Army, this engineer settled in France to become a long-term employee of La Société Anonyme Établissements *Hotchkiss. Among his designs was the Hotchkiss light machine-gun, or Machine Rifle, developed in association with Henri Mercié. **2.** Benét-Mercié Machine Rifle (*Fusil Mitrailleur Mle. 1909*). Designed in 1907–09 by Laurence Benét and Henri Mercié, this was made in France by *Hotchkiss of Saint-Denis. The guns were issued in small numbers in Belgium and France, but were much more popular in the export markets. Purchasers included the US Army, in which the 'Benét-Mercié Machine Rifle, .30 Model 1909', after an allegedly poor showing in the border wars with Mexico, was unfairly castigated as the *'Daylight Gun' and rapidly withdrawn in favour of the *Lewis Gun.

Bengal. An inexpensive US-made *Suicide Special-type revolver; manufacturer unknown.

Benjamin – **1.** Henry Benjamin. A London-based successor to Benjamin & Burlez, trading initially from 20 St Mary Axe. By 1875, premises were being occupied at 36 St Mary Axe and 61½ Fore Street, E.C.; a move to 1 Moorfields took place in 1881, where Benjamin remained until at least 1900. **2.** M.P. Benjamin. This US government arms inspector, working in 1899–1909, accepted the small-arms marked 'MPB'. *See also* US arms inspectors' marks. **3.** W.A. Benjamin. This US government arms inspector, working in 1898, accepted small-arms marked 'WAB'. *See also* US arms inspectors' marks. **4.** W.E. Benjamin. Sometimes listed as working in the late 1890s, accepting small-arms marked 'WEB'; this may be a mistaken attribution of the mark of W.A. Benjamin (above). *See also* US arms inspectors' marks. **5.** Walter Rogers Benjamin, Jackson and Granite City, Illinois, then St Louis, Missouri, USA. This American airgun inventor began work in the 1890s, receiving his first patent in 1899. W.H.B. Smith, writing in 1958 in *Gas, Air & Spring Guns of the World*, dated Benjamin's earliest design to 1882. However, given the primitive nature of the 1899 patent, this seems much too optimistic. The earliest rifles were made by the *St Louis Rifle Company, which became the Benjamin Rifle Company in 1927. Among the protection granted to Benjamin was British Patent 12,824/99 of 1899, protecting a crude pneumatic rifle. The papers list Benjamin's address as Grand Tower Junction in Illinois. US Patent 693,823 of 25 February 1902 is essentially the British Patent of 1899; the US Patent Office customarily took several years to grant patents in this period. US Patent 695,025 of 11 March 1902 allowed claims for a pump-up gun with the barrel beneath the air chamber. Its British equivalent, 22,554/02 of 1902, lists the inventor's address as 212 Main Street, St Louis. US Patent 749,519 of 12 January 1904 protected

BENJAMIN RIFLE COMPANY

Benjamin (10)

St Louis, Missouri, and later Racine, Wisconsin, USA. Walter ★Benjamin, after trading briefly as the St Louis Rifle Company between 1899 and 1903, had licensed his patents to the Wissler Instrument Company of St Louis, which had been making his prototypes alongside theodolites and surveying equipment. Benjamin and Wissler formed a partnership, which soon prospered, and Aloys Spack

was employed as administrator from 1908 to 1916.

Wissler died in 1925 and, in 1927, Spack returned to gain control of what he re-registered as the Benjamin Air Rifle Company. Much pioneering work was done to cure persistent valve problems, and the first Benjamin pistol was announced in 1933. Vast numbers of pneumatic and gas-powered guns have since been made.

Although Benjamin gave the impression of a company struggling

to regain direction in the 1970s, it acquired ★Sheridan in 1982, and the fixtures and fittings necessary to make the British ★Sterling air rifle followed in 1983. Production has been concentrated since 1986 in the former Sheridan factory at Racine, Wisconsin.

Once made in St Louis, then in Racine by the combined Benjamin-Sheridan operations, the Model 342 (.22) and 347 (.177) pneumatic rifles are charged with air by swinging the pump-lever handle that doubles as a fore-end.

---

an improved pump-up airgun while 822,645 of 5 June 1906, sought from Granite City, protected an improved airgun and valve mechanism. **6.** Benjamin Brothers. A gunmaking partnership listed at 11 Little Moorfields, London E.C., England, in 1869–71. Possibly a short-lived predecessor of Henry Benjamin & Company. **7.** Benjamin & Burlez. This English gunmaking partnership was formed in 1861, trading from 20 St Mary Axe in London. Directory entries dating from 1867 onward list the business as Henry Benjamin or, more rarely, Henry Benjamin & Company. **8.** Benjamin Franklin. A brand-name associated with the products of the Benjamin Rifle Company. **9.** Benjamin Pistol Syndicate. Listed in 1898 at 24 Jewin Crescent, London E.C., England, the affairs of this agency remain mysterious. **10.** Benjamin Rifle Company: *see* panel, above.

Bennet, Bennett – **1.** W.A. Bennet or Bennett. This US government arms inspector, working in the 1890s, accepted small-arms marked 'WAB'. *See also* US arms inspectors' marks. **2** A.G. Bennett. The marks of this US government arms inspector – 'AGB' – will be found on ★Remington revolvers and ★Ward-Burton rifles accepted in 1868–79. *See also* US arms inspectors' marks. **3.** Charles H. Bennett was the first salesman to be employed by the Plymouth Iron Windmill Company of Plymouth, Michigan. This company subsequently became ★Daisy, and Bennett rose to the rank of general manager. Then he became president of Daisy, in 1920, and retained the honour until he died in 1956. **4.** Frederick F. Bennett. Son of Charles H. Bennett (above), Frederick Bennett invented a method of soldering the cast-iron frames of BB Guns to sheet-metal air cylinders – see US Patent 670,760 of 26 March 1901. **5.** Joseph Bennett, a gunmaker/engineer trading in Hartford, Connecticut, specialised in the manu-

facture of prototype weapons. Among them were guns made for Sir Charles ★Ross, to whom a US Patent granted to Bennett in February 1900 (no. 643,935) was ultimately assigned. **6.** Thomas Gray Bennett. Trained as a mechanic, Bennett (1845–1930) joined the ★Winchester Repeating Arms Company in 1870, becoming company secretary in 1871 and president in 1890. He was a prolific patentee, although it is possible that his name was often simply used by Winchester on designs emanating from the Model Room. US Patents granted for 'Breech-loading firearms' or simply 'Firearms' included 352,292 of 9 November 1906; 564,421 of 21 July 1896; 781,179 of 31 January 1905; and 836,554 of 20 November 1906. Three US Patents were granted to protect the design of 'bolt guns' – 632,090 of 29 August 1899; 782,716 of 14 February 1905; and 798,866 of 5 September 1905, with Frank F. Burton, to permit 'Krag or other rifles' to be converted to fire small-calibre ammunition. Among the many US patents granted to protect 'magazine firearms' were 188,844 of 27 March 1877; 190,264 of 1 May 1877, with William W. ★Wetmore; 209,748 of 12 November 1878; 224,366 of 10 February 1880 (also with Wetmore); 343,423 of 8 June 1886; 386,290 of 17 July 1888; 545,766 of 3 September 1895; 551,572 of 17 December 1895 (for a box-magazine gun); and 599,587 of 22 February 1898, with William Mason. US Patents 695,784 of 18 March 1902 and 710,660 of 7 October 1902, granted jointly with William ★Mason and Thomas C. ★Johnson respectively, protected designs for semi-automatic and automatic firearms. Among the lesser patents were three obtained in 1897 to protect locking catches for lever-action guns: 588,315 of 17 August, 598,201 of 31 August and 598,687 of 7 September. US Patents 487,465 and 487,466 of 6 December 1892 were 'take-down' systems; 537,598 of 26

April 1895 and 549,343 of 5 November 1895 protected 'recoil locking bars for bolt guns'. US Patent 223,797 was granted on 27 January 1880 for an improved 'Lock for Firearms'. US Patent 747,645 (22 December 1903) protected an extractor mechanism, whereas 564,420 of 21 July 1896 was obtained for a safety system. US Patent 557,947 of 7 April 1896 described a fore-end attachment system; 211,691 of 28 January 1879 was a magazine charger; 814,511 of 6 March 1906 protected a spreader for shot charges; and 355,121 of 28 December 1886 was granted for a proprietary sight design. **7.** V.L. Bennett. Active in the mid-1870s, this US arms inspector accepted small-arms marked 'VLB'. *See also* US arms inspectors' marks. **8.** William Bennett, New Haven, Connecticut, USA. The son of T.G. Bennett (above), this Winchester employee was granted US Patent 851,643 of 30 April 1907 to protect a cartridge deflector for top-ejecting guns. **9.** Bennett Model. A brandname applied to a thousand-shot BB Gun made by *Daisy in 1903–12. It was named after the company's general manager, Charles H. Bennett.

Benoit. Nathan L. Benoit, known to have been active in the early 1900s, accepted US military small-arms marked 'NLB'. *See also* US arms inspectors' marks.

Benson. Carl Benson, an engineer working for *Mossberg, was responsible, among other things, for the development of the company's centrefire bolt-action rifles.

Benthin, Liège, Belgium. This gunmaker was involved in the 1870s with le *Grand Syndicat.

Bentley – **1.** Joseph Bentley, Liversedge, Yorkshire, England. A gunsmith and ammunition maker trading from 309 Halifax Road, Bentley loaded shotgun cartridges from components supplied by *Greenwood & Batley. **2.** Joseph Bentley, Birmingham, Warwickshire, and Liverpool, Lancashire. This English gunmaker began trading from 11 Steelhouse Lane, Birmingham, in 1829. A move to 14 St Mary's Row took place about 1838, where operations continued until 1864. Premises were also maintained in Liverpool, at 143 Dale Street (1840); 12 South Castle Street (1842–51); 40 Lime Street and 6 South Castle Street (1852–57); and 6 South Castle Street and 37 Russell Street (1857–62). Bentley is best known for his 'Enclosed Central-fire Safety Gun, the Improved, Self Cocking, Revolving, Six-barrelled Pistol' (pepperbox), protected by English Patent 8024 granted jointly with George Stocker on 9 April 1839. Bentley's other patents included English 10,280 of 30 July 1844 for nipples placed parallel to the bore; English 960/52 of 4 December 1852 for a cap-lock revolver; British 768/54, granted on 4 April 1854 to protect improvements to revolvers; 780/56 of 1 April 1856 for a cap-lock breech-loader; and 2657/57 of 17 October 1857, for improvements in revolver and rammer design. **3.** Bentley & Playfair. This gunmaking business was based in Birmingham, Warwickshire, England, but maintained sales representation in London for many years. Postal directories list the premises at 20 High Holborn in 1885–89, 9 New Broad Street in 1891–92, and 60 Queen Victoria Street from 1893 until 1900 and later.

Benton. James G. Benton, an officer in the US Army, commanded the National Armory, *Springfield, from 1866 until relinquishing his post in 1881 with the rank of colonel. His personal marking is said to have been 'JGB'. *See also* John G. *Butler and US arms inspectors' marks.

Berdan – **1.** Hiram Berdan. A designer of a range of firearms, including bolt-action guns adopted in Russia and elsewhere. A prolific designer, he resigned his commission in the Federal Army in 1864, although the Civil War was still raging, and embarked on a new career. Among Berdan's US Patents were three granted on 10 January 1865: no. 45,898 protecting a method of rifling muzzle-loading smoothbores; 45,899 for a breech-loading firearm; and 45,901 for a bayonet-attachment system. Other 'breech-loading firearms' patents included 51,991 of 9 January 1866 and 52,925 of of 27 February 1866, both being assigned to the Berdan Fire-arms Manufacturing Company. The first protected extractors for a *rolling-block type breech, and the other was for a two-piece lifting-block design. Next came 85,162 of 22 December 1868, assigned to the company to protect a primitive form of bolt action. Additional patents included 88,486 of 30 March 1869, protecting the lifting-block Berdan I made in quantity by *Colt's Patent Fire Arms Manufacturing Company, under a sub-contract agreement, for the Russian government; 101,418 of 5 April 1870 for a modified two-part lifting block; 108,869 of 1 November 1870 for the bolt-action Berdan II; and 157,783 of 15 December 1874 for an improved form of bolt action. Berdan's last effort, 478,215 to protect a 'Method of operating submarine guns', was granted on 5 July 1892. US Patents 46,292 of 7 February 1865 and 52,818 of 27 February 1866 protected 'metallic cartridges for rifled breech-loading firearms', whereas 53,388 of 20 March 1866 was granted for a method of priming metallic cartridges. US Patent 82,587 of 29 September 1868, for a metallic cartridge, was also assigned to the Berdan Fire-arms Manufacturing Company. Hiram Berdan, successful and prosperous, died in March 1893. **2.** Berdan primer. Still used on many millions of the cartridges made each year, this, together with the essentially similar *Boxer pattern, was the earliest centrefire primer to be successful. A detachable cup, filled with priming compound, is inserted in a hole in the base of the *cartridge case. The impact of a firing pin or hammer-tip drives the thin cup material against an anvil placed in (or formed as part of) the case, compressing the priming compound until it ignites. The flash passes up through a central flash-hole to fire the main charge. The principal difference between the Berdan and the Boxer primers concerns the anvil, the former being made as part of the cartridge case and the latter supplied as part of the primer. Although Berdan is customarily given the credit for 'his' primer, there is some evidence that he exploited an idea he had seen in embryonic form on a visit to Frankford Arsenal. Certainly, there was a feeling in the US Army during the 1870s that the credit for the separately-primed cartridge case should really have been given to Stephen Benét. **3.** Berdan rifle, block-action. The block-action rifles were made in two basic patterns – conversions of rifle-muskets, distinguished by an external hammer, and a simplified newly-made version with a linear striker system. The conversions were most popular in Spain, where trials had been undertaken successfully in 1865. Spanish guns chambered 15mm-calibre rimmed cartridges, and had breech blocks that could be lifted up and forward by a small integral lever. Hammers remained external. The *Fusil para Infanteria Mo. 1867*, the standard infantry rifle, was converted from 1859-type rifle muskets by *Ybarzabal of Eibar, *Orbea Hermanos y Cia of Eibar, and *Euscalduna of Planencia. Marks on the lock plates included a crown over an 'AR' monogram, and 'O' for 'Oviedo'. The *Fusil para Cazadores Mo. 1867*, the short rifle, was similar to (but shorter than) the infantry pattern. Guns converted from Mo. 1857 short rifles had generous trigger-guard bows; Mo. 1857/59 examples had a notably cramped trigger guard. The artillery and engineer carbine, or *Carabina para Artilleria e Ingenieros Mo. 1867*, was a short-barrel weapon adapted from the rifled engineer carbine of 1858. Artillerymen carried a heavy-blade sword bayonet. A Mo. 1861 engineer carbine was also made in small numbers, and a few marine-infantry carbines (*Carabina para Infanteria de Marina, Mo. 1867*) were converted from Mo. 1858 cap-lock naval short rifles, made in 1860–61 by Juan ★Aldasoro of Eibar. The 1868-patent linear striker design was supplied in quantity only to Russia, where about 30,000 rifles and a few carbines made by ★Colt's Patent Fire Arms Manufacturing Company served for a few years. The breech-block could be lifted at the rear, exposing the chamber, once the striker had been withdrawn. A new cartridge was inserted, the block was closed, and the trigger was pressed to allow the striker to fly forward to lock the breech. **4.** Berdan rifle, bolt-action. Very successful in Russia, this was a conventional turning-bolt pattern relying on the sturdy bolt-handle rib to double as a locking lug. The earliest 'four-line' guns (the calibre was actually .42) were made by the ★Birmingham Small Arms Company, although work was soon started in Tula. Huge quantities of the M1870 infantry rifles had been made when production stopped in c. 1892; even in 1914, 362,000 10.6mm original and 7.62mm converted Berdans remained on the inventory. Carbines were made in small numbers, alongside a distinctive ball-trigger ★cossack rifle.

Beretta. *See* panel, p. 66.

Berezin – 1. Mikhail Evgenyevich Berezin was born in Goncharka, Russia, in 1905. He graduated from the Leningrad Military Mechanical Institute in 1934 and worked thereafter for the ★Tula ordnance factory. Transferred to the Tula design bureau in 1935, he developed the first of his machine-guns (q.v.). Twice honoured with the USSR State Prize, Berezin died in 1950. **2.** Berezin machine-gun. The first of these aircraft weapons was a 12.7mm prototype successfully test-fired in 1935. This provided the basis for the UB series – UBK, UBS and UBT.

Bergen. Alfred Bergen, USA: *see* National Carbine.

Berger – 1. 60 rue Mulatière, Saint-Étienne, France. Listed in 1951 as a gunmaker. **2.** François Berger, place Chavanelle 15, Saint-Étienne, France. Listed in 1879 as a gunmaker. **3.** M. Berger et Cie, Manufacture d'Armes, rue Villeboeuf 10, Saint-Étienne, France. Listed in 1892 as a maker of 'guns of all systems'. These included the hammerless shotguns branded ★'Phénix', auto-cocking guns offered as ★Nemrod, and 8mm Le Français revolvers. **4.** Pierre Berger, grande rue Saint-Roch 9, Saint-Étienne, France. Listed in 1879 as a gunmaker; possibly succeeded in the 1880s by M. Berger et Cie (above). **5.** Berger-Granger, rue Valbenoîte 13, Saint-Étienne, France. Listed in 1879 as a gunmaker.

Bergeron, trading from 5 rue Desflaches, Saint-Étienne, France, in 1951. Listed in 1933 and 1951 as a gunmaker.

Bergmann – 1. Theodor Bergmann is best known as an inventor of firearms, although apparently most of the cre-

ative work was undertaken by his long-time employee Louis ★Schmeisser. Together with a partner named Flürscheim, Bergmann founded ★Eisenwerke Gaggenau in 1877 to make metalware, railings, railway lines and lamp-posts. A series of patents was granted in the 1880s, usually to protect variations of the Haviland & Gunn ★Gem airgun. Individual specifications included German Patent 39,962 of 8 October 1886, its British equivalent 4413/86 of 1886, and German Patent 42,091 of 5 June 1887. Eisenwerke Gaggenau made substantial quantities of airguns, often distinguishable simply by the mark of 'E', 'G' and crossed pistols. Some were copies of the ★Quackenbush patterns, which had been licensed to Bergmann c. 1884. A few guns have been found with a mark of 'Th.B.' and crossed pistols. It is assumed that these were made after Bergmann left Eisenwerke Gaggenau in the early 1890s to exploit Schmeisser's automatic pistol patents. They may have been simply assembled from parts handed over to the new organisation, as there is no evidence that Bergmann was ever involved in large-scale airgun production after the split from Eisenwerk Gaggenau. *See also* Bergmanns Industriewerke (below). **2.** Theodor Bergmanns Erben GmbH, Berlin and Suhl in Thüringen, Germany. Bergmann was responsible for a selection of 6.35mm pocket automatics, including the Models 2 and 3, and their ★Einhand versions, the Models 2A and 3A. The business was still listed as a maker of weapons in 1939, and traded until the end of the Second World War. **3.** Bergmann-Bayard. Derived from the Bergmann-★Mars, chambered for the 9mm Bergmann-Bayard (9mm Bergmann No. 6) cartridge, this ★recoil-operated semi-automatic pistol – also known as the Mle 1908 – was supplied in quantity to Spain (as the Mo. 1903), Denmark (M/1910) and Greece prior to 1914. Although the Bayard pattern retained the exposed hammer of its Mars prototype and a detachable box magazine in the frame, its trigger aperture was approximately circular and the contours of the grip were refined. Production ceased in Belgium when the First World War began, although the Danes began work in the ★Hærens Tøjhus, Copenhagen, in the early 1920s. These guns, which served as M/1910/21, customarily had enlarged wooden grips and a circular knurled-head grip on the magazine base, which entered a semi-circular void in the frame. **4.** Bergmann machine-gun. This ★recoil-operated weapon was patented in the name of Theodor Bergmann in 1901, although the design was actually due to Louis ★Schmeisser. The Bergmann-MG. 02 was locked by a rising block, in the barrel extension, which engaged in the recess in the top surface of the bolt. The Bergmann deserved a better fate, but its failure was due entirely to a loss of production facilities (*see* ★Bergmanns Industriewerk). Work began again in 1908, probably under the supervision of Hugo ★Schmeisser – son of Louis – who had remained with Bergmann after his father's departure to work for ★Rheinische Metallwaaren-u. Maschinenfabrik. The Bergmann-MG. 10 was similar to its predecessors, firing from a closed bolt, but the feed mechanism was driven by the recoil of the barrel and barrel extension. Push-through belts were replaced by the standard withdrawal Maxim pattern, which allowed Austrian Keller-Ruszitska disintegrating-link metallic belts to be used when appropriate. The Bergmann had a fire-rate of 480–600 rds/min, owing to the short travel of the locking mechanism. A few guns were used in the First

PIETRO BERETTA SPA

Gardone Val Trompia, Brescia, and Rome. Claiming origins as early as the sixteenth century, Beretta made sporting guns prior to the confederation of Italy in 1860. By the 1870s, however, the business was powerful enough to tender successfully to make *Vetterli rifles, short rifles and carbines, many thousands being produced for the Italian Army prior to 1885.

During the 1930s, under the supervision of Tullio Marengoni, auto-loading rifles were made. By 1939, however, the Beretta had been rejected in favour of the *Revelli Armaguerra design. Production of automatic pistols began in earnest during the First World War, continuing most successfully through the 1930s until the present day; guns based on the M951 Brigadier and the many derivatives of the 92-series are now in service throughout the world – including the USA, where the 9mm Pistol M9 (Beretta 92F) is being made by Beretta USA in Accokeek, Maryland.

The small-calibre pistols have included the 6.35mm Model 1919 pocket pistol and, in later days, the M34 Bantam, M418 Panther, M951 Jetfire (all in 6.35mm) and Minx (.22). Automatic weapons of all types have been developed since the 1920s, including the pre-war Model 38 submachine-gun, and a selection of automatic rifles developed by Marengoni and others. Large numbers of *Garand and improved Garand-type (BM59) rifles were made from 1953 onward, and more recently work has concentrated on a 5.56mm 70/90-series of assault rifles, carbines and light machine-guns.

The history of Beretta is traced in greater detail in *Beretta, la dinastia industriale più antica del monde* by Held & Morin (Aquafresca Editrice, 1980), and in R.L. Wilson, *The World of Beretta. An International legend* (Greenhill Books, 2000).

Details of the handguns may be found in J.B. Wood's *Beretta Automatic Pistols* (Stackpole, 1985), and Michel Malherbe's *Les Pistolets Beretta* (Éditions Pardès, 1991).

In addition to assault rifles, handguns and bolt-action rifles, Beretta makes excellent shotguns – such as this ornate side-lock over-and-under example.

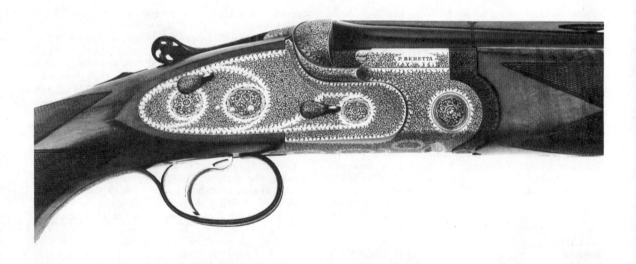

World War, adapted to standard mounts. The Bergmann-LMG. 15 was developed during the First World War, but was little more than a lightened air-cooled MG. 10. A pistol grip was added beneath the receiver, and a small shoulder plate was attached to the back of the receiver. The action was efficient enough in theory, but flaws in its design gave problems in aerial combat, and the Bergmann-LMG. 15 was relegated to ground roles. The original guns fired from an open bolt, but accuracy was poor and a much-modified pattern – the LMG. 15 neuer Art (LMG.15n.A.) – was substituted in 1916. **5. Bergmann-Mars.** Based on the breech-locking system patented in 1901 by Louis *Schmeisser, this semi-automatic pistol was customarily chambered for the 7.8mm No. 5 or 9mm Bergmann No. 6 cartridges. Distinguished by a detachable box magazine in the frame,

Schlitten 08 (Maxim) ahead of the trigger guard, it also had an exposed spur-hammer. The first guns were made for Theodor Bergmann by V.C. *Schilling u. Co., in Suhl, but the purchase of Schilling by *Krieghoff (1904) interrupted production just as the Spanish Army was showing interest. Work continued until the end of 1906, when a few 11.35mm guns were made for US Army trials, but the Mars was licensed to Anciens Établissements *Pieper in 1907 and re-emerged as the Bergmann-Bayard. **6. Bergmann pistols.** Details of the earliest Bergmann-Schmeisser pistols are given below. They were followed by the Bergmann No. 5, a fragile military-style semi-automatic, fed from a detachable box magazine ahead of the trigger guard and locked by displacing the tail of the breech-block laterally into the receiver wall. This method was patented in Germany in the Spring of 1898. Then

BERGMANN-SCHMEISSER PISTOLS

Bergmann (8)

The first pistol to be developed by Bergmann, based on a patent granted to a Hungarian watchmaker, Otto Brauswetter, was unsuccessful. It was followed by a series of pistols designed by Louis *Schmeisser, characterised by clip-loaded magazines, pivoting magazine cover plates and bolts reciprocating independently within an enveloping receiver.

The first few guns embodied a form of hesitation lock, but the perfected 1896 patterns were simple blowbacks lacking (at least initially) extractors; spent cases were expelled simply by residual gas pressure. The series included a tiny 5mm No. 1 with a folding trigger, a larger 5mm No. 2 with a small circular trigger guard, and a 6.5mm No. 3 holster pistol. They were successful enough to sell in the thousands, but were rapidly eclipsed by *Browning and other designs at the beginning of the twentieth century.

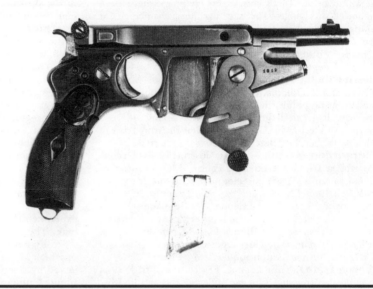

Among the earliest successful pocket pistols were the small Bergmann-Schmeisser designs. Dating from the late 1890s, this is a No. 2 New Model chambering a tiny 5mm cartridge. Courtesy of Masami Tokoi, Düsseldorf.

came the Bergmann-Mars (q.v.), but rights to the handguns were then sold to Anciens Établissements Pieper and it became the Bergmann-Bayard. Production of blowback semi-automatics resumed after the First World War, beginning in the early 1920s with the 6.35mm Models 2 and 3, with six- and nine-round magazines respectively, and the essentially similar Models 2A and 3A, which had one-hand (*Einhand*) cocking systems based on the *Chylewski patents. The earliest guns had wooden grips set with 'enricled B' medallions, but later guns had injection-moulded 'BERGMANN' plastic grips. Eventually, Bergmann's gunmaking business was acquired by AG *Lignose of Berlin, although the pistols retained their designations and were customarily marketed as Theodor Bergmann Erben (*Erben*, successors) to capitalise on the established Bergmann name. They included a version of the Menz *PB Special. **7.** Bergmann-Simplex. An 8mm-calibre semi-automatic pistol made for Theodor Bergmann in the early 1900s. The first guns may have been made in Germany by V.C. *Schilling & Co., but apparently later examples were made in Liège (or perhaps even in Saint-Étienne by *Manufacture Française d'Armes et Cycles) shortly before a liaison between Bergmann and Anciens Établissements Pieper was concluded c. 1907. The guns have exposed ring hammers and detachable box magazines ahead of the trigger; they are customarily marked only 'PAT.' over 'BREVETE' over 'D.R.G.M.' on the left side of the frame. **8.** Bergmann-Schmeisser pistols: *see* panel,

above. **9.** Bergmanns Industriewerke. Based in Gaggenau in Baden, Germany, the Bergmann operation is best known for the pistols produced to the designs of Louis *Schmeisser. The guns were sub-contracted to V.C. *Schilling of Suhl, but work in Germany ceased when the Schilling factory was purchased by *Sempert & Krieghoff in 1904. Later Bergmann-type pistols were made in Belgium by Anciens Établissements *Pieper. Machine-guns, rifles, airguns and possibly also shotguns will be found bearing the Bergmann name together with a miner-and-lamp trademark. The *Deutsches Reichs-Adressbuch* for 1914 and 1920 still listed 'Bergmanns Abteilung Suhl in Thüringen' as a gunmaker.

Bergstutzen. Applied in central Europe to guns with two rifled barrels of different chamberings, superposed. *See* Combination weapons.

Beriola. P. Beriola of 13 rue Louis-Blanc, Saint-Étienne, France, was listed in 1951 as a gunmaker.

Beristain. Armeria Beristain y Cia of Barcelona, Spain, distributed *Gabilondo-made Bufalo pistols in the 1920s, distinguished by their patented grip safety and loaded-chamber indicator. Operations seem to have ceased c. 1932, possibly owing to restrictions placed on the export of firearms by the Republican government.

Berjat. Paul Berjat of place Villeboeuf 1, Saint-Étienne, France, was listed as a gunmaker in 1879.

Berlin... – 1. Berlin-Lübecker Maschinenfabrik. A maker of components for the Gew. 41 and Gew. 43

*Walther rifles, usually identified by the code letters 'duv'. **2.** Berlin-Suhler Waffen- u. Fahrzeugwerke GmbH (BSW), Berlin, and Suhl in Thüringen, Germany. Listed as a maker of BSW-brand guns, weapons, sporting rifles, bicycles, motorcycles, Astora-brand freewheel hubs, prams and baby carriages, and fans (*Kuhlschranke*), 1939. W.H.B. Smith, writing in *Gas, Spring & Air Guns of the World*, links BSW with production of air-powered training rifles. However, the gun he pictures is actually a *Mars. BSW was renamed Gustloff-Werke in 1940, but ceased trading at the end of the Second World War.

Bernard – 1. L. Bernard, Liège. A gunmaker active in Belgium in the 1860s and 1870s. His marks have been reported on double-barrel sporting guns, chambered for pinfire or (later) centrefire cartridges. **2.** Walter Bernard, an 'electro-plate worker' was co-patentee, with John Fredrick *Bird, of an electrically-operated bell target. *See* British Patent 7340/08 of 1908.

Bernardelli. Vincenzo Bernardelli & Co. SNC of Gardone Val Trompia, Brescia, Italy, has made a variety of automatic pistols, including the .22 rimfire PA Baby. Bernardelli entered the SR or SR-556 assault rifle – a variant of the Israeli *Galil – in the Italian Army trials of the 1980s, but the *Beretta AR 70 was preferred.

Bernardon-Martin – 1. Établissements Bernardon-Martin et Cie, Saint-Étienne, France. Manufacturers of the 6.35mm and 7.65mm *Hermetic semi-automatic pistols, c. 1907–12. *See also* Société Française d'Armes Automatiques de Saint-Étienne. **2.** Bernardon-Martin pistols. These 6.35- and 7.65mm pocket/personal-defence guns were made by *Bernardon, Martin et Cie in 1906–12. Some slides are reportedly marked 'Société Française d'Armes Automatiques de St.-Étienne'.

Berne frères, Saint-Étienne, France. Listed in 1879 as a gunmaker, trading from rue Villeboeuf 4, and in 1892 at rue Villeboeuf 15.

Bernedo. Spanish gunmaker Vincenzo Bernedo (sometimes erroneously listed as Victor Bernedo), trading in Eibar, made *Ruby-pattern semi-automatic pistols for the French Army during the First World War. He has also been identified with the *B.C. and *Bernedo pistols, the latter being a 7.65mm Browning-type semi-automatic.

Bernerprobe. *See* BP monogram.

Berngard. F. Berngard & Co., formerly I. Shendrunev, was a Russian distributor with a specialist weapons department (*Oruzheinyi magazin*). Catalogues note his address as Moscow.

Berridge. I.L. Berridge & Company of Leicester, England, made 'Pistols, Signal, No. 1' (Mks III*, IV and V) from 1941 until the end of the Second World War. The code 'M 601' was often used instead of the company name. *See also* British military manufacturers' marks.

Berry – 1. Joseph Berry, 22 Bridge Street, Worksop, Nottinghamshire, England. The marks of this gunmaker (active in 1863–68) have been reported on sporting guns and cap-lock revolvers. **2.** Sharman West Berry, Market Place, Woodbridge, Suffolk, England. This gunmaker worked from 1845 until the early 1870s. His marks have been reported on sporting guns, self-cocking *pepperboxes, cap-lock revolvers, bows and airguns, and he entered a breech-loading 12-bore *Lefaucheux-type shotgun in the trials undertaken by *The Field* in 1866.

Bersa. Fabrica de Armas 'Bersa' SA, Ramos Meija,

Buenos Aires. One of the principal Argentinian manufacturers of semi-automatic pistols, Bersa has made a range of blowbacks customarily identified by numerical designations. The guns have included the single-action 7.65mm Model 85 and the 9mm Short Model 97, introduced in c. 1979–80, and a series of .22 rimfires including the Models 622, 644 and 844. A small pocket pistol called the Picolla was also once made. The mid-1980s brought the double-action Models 223, 224 and 226 (.22 rimfire), and 383 (9mm Short); the first two digits refer to calibre, and the last to barrel length in inches.

Bersaluce Arietio-Aurtena y Compañia of Eibar in the province of Guipúzcoa, Spain, made the *Allies semi-automatic pistol.

Berthier – 1. Adolphe V.P.M. Berthier, trained as a railway engineer and was working in Algeria when, in 1888, he submitted his first rifle to the French authorities. The guns proved to be very successful, although able only to loosen the hold of the inferior *Lebel on the French Army psyche. Berthier also experimented with automatic weapons, producing an effective light machine-gun prior to the First World War, but the failure of his efforts owed more to the antics of promoters than to inherent design flaws. The *Vickers-Berthier light machine-gun may have been adopted by the British Army had not the Czechoslovakian predecessor of the *Bren Gun intervened. **2.** Berthier rifles. The first ten experimental 8mm infantry rifles were made at the Ateliers de Puteaux in 1888. They were followed by an experimental artillery musketoon, then a cavalry carbine. The original infantry-pattern Berthier was superseded by ten Puteaux-made vertical-locking rifles, trials of which began in February 1890. These guns were followed by a series of rifles and short rifles (*Mousquetons*) adopted officially from 1890 to the end of the Firsr World War, largely owing to the inability of the French to provide an adaptation of the tube-magazine Lebel. Regulation patterns included cavalry, cuirassier and gendarmerie carbines (Mle 1890) and the artillery musketoon (Mle 92). The cavalry pattern lacked a bayonet, the cuirassier version had an extraordinary combless butt, the gendarmerie guns accepted a special épée bayonet with a groove in its white-metal hilt for the cleaning rod; the musketoon accepted a sword bayonet. The Berthier rifles of 1902 and 1907 were issued to French colonial troops as the *Fusil des Tirailleurs Indo-Chinois* and *Fusil des Tirailleurs Sénégalais* respectively, and the Modèle 1915 was adopted in desperation during the First World War. It was followed by the essentially similar Mle 1916, recognisable by a protruding magazine case for a five-round clip instead of the flush-fitting original three-round type. The Mle 92/16 musketoon also accepted the five-cartridge clips. Many surviving Berthier rifles were shortened in post-war days, and the musketoons were updated. However, experiments with new cartridges led to the standardisation of the *MAS 36 in the late 1930s. Additional details of the Berthier patterns will be found in John Walter, *Rifles of the World* (Krause Publications, second edition, 1998). **3.** Berthier Machine Rifle. Based on patents granted prior to 1914 and locked by a tilting bolt, this gas-operated weapon was offered as a light machine-gun or a heavy-barrelled automatic rifle. The Belgians took small numbers of 7.65x53 rifles prior to the First World War, the British rejected them in 1916, and the light machine-gun was adopted by the US Army as the .30 Model of 1917. However, the rickety structure of its promoter, the *United States Machine Gun Company, prevented delivery of any of the 7,000 guns ordered on behalf of the armed forces. The *Browning Automatic Rifle was preferred, and contracts for the Berthier were cancelled in 1918 after only prototypes had been made. Tests undertaken in 1919–20 with guns made by the US Machine Gun Company suggested that adoption had been too hasty, and the Berthier was abandoned. A modified form – the *Vickers-Berthier – subsequently enjoyed limited success in Britain and India, particularly as an aircraft gun.

Berthon, Saint-Étienne, France. Listed as a gunmaker in directories dating from 1933.

Bertois Frères, 40 rue des Armuriers, Saint-Étienne, France. Listed in 1951 as a gunmaker.

Bertoldo. *See* Vetterli-Bertoldo.

Bertrand – 1. A. Bertrand, Liège, Belgium. This gunmaker is known to have been responsible prior to 1914 for sporting guns and a range of inexpensive revolvers that included the Bushman, Companion, Courage, Destroyer, Graceful, Hunter, Murderer, Shatterer, Terrific and Western Boy. **2.** Jules Bertrand, Liège, Belgium. A maker of pistols and revolvers.

Bertschinger. Jacques Bertschinger was co-proprietor with Thommen and Wackernagel of *Hämmerli AG from 1946 until his death in 1979, and co-patentee of an airgun trainer. This well-known barrelled insert was made for guns such as the German Kar. 98k and the Swiss Schmidt-Rubin Kar 31.

Beryl – 1. Usually found as 'The Beryl' on shotgun ammunition distributed by W.R. *Pape of Newcastle

upon Tyne, being named after the gunsmith's wife. Apparently, the components were supplied by *Kynoch. **2.** An assault-rifle variant of the Radom-made Polish *Kalashnikov.

Besa – 1. A sustained-fire machine-gun made in Britain by *BSA Guns Ltd, in 7.92mm and 15mm. The small-calibre gun was based on the ZB53, developed by Československá Zbrojovka *Brno and known to the Czechoslovakian Army as the vz. 37. The Mark I, approved in June 1940, had a two-position selector lever on the receiver and a full-length barrel sleeve. The Mark II, approved on the same day, had a simplified receiver, a short barrel sleeve, changes in the action and a plain flash-hider. The Mark II★ was a simplified Mark II. The Marks III and III★ (August 1941) lacked the selector, fire-rates being set at 750 rds/min and 450 rds/min respectively. The Mark 3/2 (1952) and Mark 3/3 Besa (1954) were refurbished pre-1946 Mark III guns. The 3/2 version had a modified feed cover and a new mounting block, while the 3/3 had an improved barrel with a larger gas vent and a modified gas cylinder. **2.** Associated with .177 or .22 round-headed ribbed-body diabolo pellets made for BSA by *Lanes Ltd from the 1960s until the mid-1980s.

Besal. *See* panel, below.

Bessette. Aldige J. Bessette, a government arms inspector active in 1940, accepted .45 *Colt M1911A1 pistols marked 'AJB'. *See also* US arms inspectors' marks.

'Best of All' [The]. A brandname associated with shotgun ammunition made by the *Midland Gun Company of Birmingham.

Best Quality Magazine Rifle. This name was used by *Holland & Holland of London on sporting rifles made on the basis of *FN-Mauser actions in chamberings ranging from .240 Apex to .375 H&H Magnum. Straight

BESAL

This simplified .303 light machine-gun – somewhat *Bren-like externally – was developed by *BSA Guns Ltd, the work being credited to Harry Faulkner. The perfected design was cocked with the assistance of the sliding pistol-grip sub-assembly, inspired by the *Besa.

In the autumn of 1942, the Besal was adopted as the 'Gun, Light, Machine, Faulkner, .303-inch Mark I', but deliveries of Bren Guns from the Enfield *Royal Small Arms Factory, *Inglis and the *Monotype Scheme proved to be more than enough to meet demand. Approval of the Faulkner machine-gun was rescinded on 10 June 1943.

An example of the perfected .303 Besal light machine-gun, subsequently known as the Faulkner after its designer. This simplified substitute for the Bren Gun was approved for service, but never entered series production. Courtesy of Weller & Duffy, Birmingham.

combs were considered to be standard, with simple oval cheek pieces and round-tip fore-ends.

Betteridge. John Betteridge, a 'toolmaker', according to the papers of British Patent 15,769/06 of 1906, designed an adjustable front sight. Research in the Birmingham archives revealed that subsequently Betteridge followed a career in taxidermy – trading first from 140 Great Colmore Street and then (as John Betteridge & Son) from 55a Lee Crescent, Edgbaston.

Beuret, Liège, Belgium. A gunmaker involved in the 1870s with le *Grand Syndicat.

Beutegewehr (plural *Beutegewehre*). *See* panel, facing page.

Bevan & Evans traded in Abergavenny, Monmouthshire, Wales, until succeeded by Bevan & Pritchard (apparently in the 1930s). Shotgun cartridges have been seen with both of these trading styles and the brandname Abergavenny Ace.

Bevington. A. Bevington was listed as a member of the English gun trade at 298 Regent Street, London, in 1887; then at 12 Lime Street, London E.C., until 1900 or later.

'BFJ', 'BFL', 'BFQ'. Marks used on US military firearms and accessories by B.F. *James, Benjamin F. *Loughran and Benjamin F. *Quimby respectively.

BG. A superimposed-type monogram, with neither letter prominent. Correctly interpreted as 'GB' (q.v.), it was used by Gregorio *Bolumburu of Eibar.

'bh', 'B.H.' – 1. As 'bh'. Found on small-arms components made in 1940–45 by Brünner Waffenwerke AG of Brno, in German-occupied Czechoslovakia. 2. A superimposition-type 'BH' monogram, with neither letter prominent, found on the grips of *Beholla pistols made during the First World War by *Becker & Hollander of Suhl. 3. Usually as 'B.H.' A 6.35mm pistol, based on the tiny FN-Browning of 1905, made in Eibar, Spain, by *Beistegui Hermanos: six rounds, hammer fired. The guns were often marked by Fabrique d'Armes de *Grande Précision. 4. Found on US military weapons. *See* Benjamin *Hannis and Benjamin *Huger.

Bicentennial – 1. A brandname applied to the *Daisy M1776 lever-action BB Gun with a 500-shot gravity-feed magazine, introduced in 1966, but made in a special version in 1976–77 to celebrate the bicentennial of the Declaration of Independence. 2. Found on rifles made by *Remington to celebrate the 200th anniversary of the Declaration of Independence. The M760 Bicentennial was a variant of the Model 760 *Gamemaster slide-action rifle with an appropriately engraved receiver, whereas the Nylon 66 Bicentennial (a variant of the .22 rimfire Nylon 66 autoloader) had a logo etched into the left side of the receiver.

Bicycle... – 1. Bicycle-handlebar guns. Fears of danger posed to cyclists by wild dogs, wolves and petty criminals created a range of defensive weapons, ranging from the *Puppy and *Velo-Dog revolvers to the *Scheintod series. Among the most intriguing were the guns that were concealed within the bicycles themselves, almost always in the handlebars. Originating in France and Belgium, generally they were tiny pinfire pepperboxes with folding triggers and bar hammers. They were held in the end of the tubular handlebars by spring latches or a twist-lock. *See also* Disguised guns. 2. Bicycle Revolver or Bicycle Model. This was a double-action auto-ejecting revolver made in the USA by *Harrington & Richardson in the 1880s, as a seven-shot .22 or five-shot .32; it had a 2in barrel.

Big... – 1. Big Bag, usually encountered as 'The Big Bag'. This mark identified shotgun ammunition loaded by W. *Darlow from components supplied by *Kynoch or *Eley Kynoch. 2. Big Colt. A brandname applied unofficially in the early 1870s, by *Kittredge & Company of Cincinnati, to the .41 *New Line Colt revolver. 3. Big Five. Chambered for the .458 Winchester Magnum, this *Lebeau-Courally gun is a classic side-by-side side-lock with a straight-wrist butt, often accompanied by exchangeable .375 H&H Magnum barrels with telescope-sight mount blocks on the quarter rib. The decoration consists largely of acanthus leafwork and gold-line inlays, accompanying African game scenes. 4. Big Five, or Big 5. A brandname found on the firearms (including lever-action *Marlins) distributed by United Merchandising, Inc. 5. Big Game Rifle. *See* Bolt Action Big Game Rifle.

Bigelow – 1. Benjamin Bigelow, Rochester, New York State (to 1850), and Marysville, California (from 1850). This US gunmaker, one of many migrants enticed westward by the California Gold Rush, made sporting guns that included a few *Miller-type pinfire revolver rifles. 2. Bigelow & Haywood (or Hayward), Concord, Massachusetts, USA. These metalsmithing partners were listed in the late 1870s as 'gun, rifle and pistol manufacturers'.

Biggs. F.J. Biggs was listed by H.J. Blanch, writing in 1909, as a gunmaker trading from Ironmonger Lane, London E.C., in 1876. Subsequently he moved to 19 Gracechurch Street in 1877, then to Leadenhall Buildings in 1883; trading ceased in 1887.

Bighorn Rifle Company, Orem and American Fork, Utah, USA. This gunmaking business was responsible for sporting rifles made in 1983–87 on the basis of *FN Herstal or Spanish *Santa Barbara *Mauser actions, in chamberings ranging from .22–250 to medium-length Magnums.

Bijou – 1. A break-open BB Gun made by *Decker Manufacturing Company from 1893 until c. 1900. Guns made prior to 1895 had skeletal cast-iron stocks, but later examples were wood. 2. An American BB Gun, also known as the Bijou M1905 or simply 'B M1905', made by the *Hexagon Rifle Company (successors to Decker) in 1905–11. It differs from the Bijou (1) primarily in its markings.

Bildstein, Mommer & Co. KG, also known as Bimoco (q.v.), Gressenich über Stolberg, Rheinland, Germany. This lead and tin foundry was founded in 1924 by Kaspar Lück, Mathias Bildstein and Peter Mommer, entering the local commercial register in 1925. Production was interrupted in 1945 and recovered only slowly in the post-war era. The first airgun pellets were made in 1952, and this business proved such a great success that more than 200 people were being employed by 1974 – when Bimoco products were being exported to more than forty countries. However, competition from powerful manufacturers such as *Dynamit Nobel and *Haendler & Natermann proved too great; Bimoco was liquidated in the mid-1980s.

Billinghurst, often misleading listed as 'Billingshurst' – 1. William Billinghurst (1807–80), Rochester, New York State, USA. This gunsmith and agricultural implement maker was established in Stilson Street, Rochester, by 1843. US census returns indicate that he employed four

BEUTEGEWEHR

This term was used in Germany during the First World War to denote captured rifles that had been pressed into military service. *Kurze Beschreibung der an Ersatztruppen und Rekrutendepots verausgabten fremländischen Gewehre* ('A short description of the foreign rifles given to supplementary units and recruiting depots'), published in 1915, listed these rifles and carbines as the British Mks I and III SMLE (*Lee-Enfield); the Canadian *Ross M1910; the US single-shot *Remington and *Peabody; the Belgian *Albini-Braendlin, *Comblain and 1889-type *Mauser; the French Mle 66 *Chassepot, Mle 74 *Gras, Mle 78 Navy *Kropatschek, Mle 86/93 *Lebel, Mle 90 and Mle 92 *Berthier; the Italian *Vetterli-Vitali and *Mannlicher-Carcano; the Russian *Berdan and *Mosin-Nagant; the Austro-Hungarian M. 95 *Mannlicher rifle and Stutzen; and the Dutch *Beaumont, *Remington and 1895-type *Mannlicher.

German wholesalers had colossal stocks of military-surplus weaponry; in 1911, for example, A L *Frank alone had 250,000 Austro-Hungarian *Werndl rifles and 42,000 Italian *Vetterli rifles and musketoons. Shortages of Mauser rifles during the First World War forced an ever-increasing use of *Beutegewehre*. A 1915-vintage Baltic Naval Station (Kiel) inventory, for example, included 8,726 Mosin-Nagants.

Captured rifles were often altered for German service, many of the Russian examples having their magazines (but not their barrels) altered to accept the 7.9x57 service cartridge. Many Mosin-Nagants and a few ex-French Mle 86/93 Lebels had their fore-ends cut back to accept a sleeve-like bayonet adaptor designed in 1915 by Moritz *Magnus der Jüngere of Hamburg. *Beutegewehre* are usually easy to identify, as they will often bear German military proof or inspectors' marks, while an eagle within a 'DEUTSCHES REICH' cartouche may be struck into the butt.

The term 'Beutegewehre' was applied to foreign rifles impressed into German service during the First World War. This soldier, a driver attached to a field hospital of 5. Armee-Korps, holds an unaltered ex-Russian Mosin-Nagant.

men, working at 41 Main Street, Rochester, from the 1850s until work ceased about 1874. In addition to the battery gun described below, Billinghurst made target pistols, sporting guns, and a seven-shot pinfire revolver rifle with an additional shotgun barrel, two hammers and two triggers. **2.** Billinghurst & Requa Gun. Patented in the USA in September 1861 by William Billinghurst and Joseph Requa of Rochester, New York (no. 36,488), this Battery Gun was the first to use self-contained metallic cartridges, 25 being loaded into a flexible metal strip. A train of priming powder was laid in a trough behind the breech, flash from the *cap-lock firing mechanism reaching the propellant through holes in the cartridge-case heads. Unfortunately, Billinghurt-Requa guns were so susceptible to damp that they were customarily relegated to covered strongpoints and became known as Bridge Guns.

Billings & Spencer. *See* Ross.

Bimoco. This brandname, associated with the products of *Bildstein, Mommer & Co. KG, was applied in many forms. Bimoco Ball (or Präzisions-Rundkugel) identified standard lead shot, offered in many sizes and often copper- or nickel-coated. Bimoco Diabolo was a conventional airgun pellet, made with a round head and a ribbed body as the 4.5mm or 5.6mm *Engländer-Modell; as a 4.5mm or 5.5mm flathead with a ribbed skirt (*Gerrifelt*); and as a 4.5mm or 5.5mm flathead with a smooth body (*Glatt*). The 4.5mm Bimoco Elite was a flatheaded plain-body diabolo pellet made specifically for target shooting. Bimoco Meisterklasse pellets were specially selected versions of the Elite. Bimoco-Sheridan-Torpedo was a 5mm (.20) airgun slug with a sharply conical nose and a small flange around the base of the body. Bimoco Silver Streak was a 4.5mm diabolo pellet with a multi-flange head, produced to compete with the *Silver Jet. The distinctive Bimoco Spitz, or Bimoco Neue Spitz, was made in 4.5mm, 5.6mm and 6.35mm. A much-altered *diabolo, it had a plain skirt, a short parallel-side sub-calibre body and a semi-point head. It was developed specifically for short-barrelled guns.

Bing. Gebrüder Bing of Nürnberg, Germany, was one of the best known European toymakers. Founded by Ignaz and Adolph Bing in 1866, this metalsmithing business began to make tinplate toys in 1885 and embarked on a period of rapid expansion. The experience of sheet-metal work was used to good advantage in large numbers of drum magazines (TM. 08) made for the *Parabellum pistol during the First World War. These can be identified by the trademark of 'B' above 'N', separated by a short horizontal bar. The business became Bing-Werke in 1919, under the leadership of Stephan Bing, but encountered financial problems in the late 1920s and was purchased by a consortium of other toymakers in 1932. The manufacturing facilities may have continued to trade as Bing-Werke, making automotive components, but were incorporated in 'Nowag'–Noris-Werke AG in 1942 and became one of Germany's leading carburettor makers.

Bircham. Charles O. Bircham was an English gunsmith occupying premises in 124 Poplar High Street, London E.C., from 1867 until the turn of the century. The trading style became '& Son' from 1891 onward.

Bird – 1. John Frederick Bird. A machinist of 38 Lingard Street, Birmingham, Warwickshire, England, Bird was co-patentee with Walter Bernard of an electrically operated bell target. *See* British Patent 7340/08 of 1908. **2.** Bird Scaring Cartridge. A name given to a 4-bore 'shotgun' cartridge with a 10cm brass case, made by James *Pain & Sons of Salisbury. *See also* Brock's Explosives Ltd.

Birmingham – 1. *See* panel, below. **2.** Birmingham Gun Trade [The]. This association of Master Gunmakers and Master Gun Barrel Makers was formed in 1854 in an attempt to regulate what had become unruly trades, with tremendous variety in working practices, wages and selling

---

BIRMINGHAM

Birmingham (1)

The centre of the English provincial gunmaking industry, and of the first successful moves toward mechanisation. The environs of Birmingham, notably Coalbrookdale and the Ironbridge Gorge, were effectively the cradle of the Industrial Revolution; and it was natural that ironsmithing and associated trades should grow nearby.

Gunmaking had been organised as early as 1689, when the local member of Parliament petitioned King William III that his constituents be allowed to tender for Board of Ordnance contracts. A lengthy series of European and colonial wars ensured prosperity. Birmingham's affairs were refined by the establishment in Bagot Street in 1797 of a Proof and Viewing House for military arms. Then, owing to the provisions of the contemporaneous Gun Barrel Proof Act, an official Proof House was founded in 1813.

By the beginning of the nineteenth century, gunmakers, gun-stockers, gun-riflers and associated trades had come to dominate the area subsequently known as The Gun Quarter, bounded by Slaney Street, Shadwell Street, Loveday Street and Steelhouse Lane. Participating businesses rose from about fifty at the outbreak of the American War of Independence in 1776 to more than 500 in the 1850s. The census of 1851 recorded that 5,167 of the 7,731 gunsmiths and gun-workers recorded in England and Wales worked in Birmingham; in 1865, there were 174 gunmakers, 32 barrel-makers, 25 lock-makers, 61 implement-makers, and 600 retailers and distributors.

Production was stupendous. More than 7,000,000 guns, barrels and locks were made for the British government between 1804 and 1815, and the numbers of barrels successfully passing through the Proof House peaked at 961,459 in 1868. However, the loss of work to the *Royal Small Arms Factory, Enfield, and the advent of large-scale manufacturers such as *BSA, formed in 1861, threatened the livelihood of many independent smiths; by 1900, only 300 gunmakers were working in the Birmingham district.

Initially, the establishment of colonies of specialised trades in the environs of Birmingham was often due to, in the case of barrel-makers, reliance on sources of wind or water power. Consequently, lock-making centred on Darlaston, Wednesbury, Willenhall and Wolverhampton; and the barrel-makers congregated in Aston, Smethwick and West Bromwich.

One of the best sources of information about the Birmingham gunmaking industry is *English Gunmakers* (1978) by De Witt Bailey and Douglas A. Nie; also helpful is *The Gun Trade of Birmingham* by Keith Dunham (1955), produced by the City of Birmingham Museum and Art Gallery, and 'Birmingham's Gun Quarter and its Workshops' by D.M. Smith, published in the *Journal of Industrial Archaeology* (vol. 1, 1964/65).

Much of the Birmingham gunmaking industry remained comparatively primitive, except for companies such as BSA, Webley & Scott, and – latterly – Parker-Hale. However, the art of barrel-straightening remained the province of men; no machine has ever been developed to compete with them.

methods. The association was recognised by the Gun Barrel Proof Acts as that from which the fifteen Guardians of the Birmingham Proof House were elected. **3.** Birmingham Small Arms Company Ltd [The], also known simply as BSA, Steelhouse Lane and Armoury Road, Small Heath, Birmingham, Warwickshire, England. This gunmaking business was founded on 7 June 1861, when several leading Birmingham gunmakers purchased shares in a new company intended to be capitalised at £50,000. Principal shareholders included Isaac *Hollis, John F. *Swinburn, William *Tranter and Thomas *Turner. The goal of BSA was to mass-produce guns with fully interchangeable parts, in competition with the *London Armoury Company and the Royal Small Arms Factory at *Enfield Lock. After negotiating a terrible slump in the mid-1860s – when few armies were re-equipping – BSA obtained a lucrative British government contract to convert Enfield rifle-muskets to the *Snider system. About 156,000 guns were altered in 1867–68, and the first batches of 93,000 new guns were delivered in 1869. A lucrative contract for *Martini-Henry rifles was obtained in 1871, but the company was voluntarily liquidated in 1873 and re-emerged as the Birmingham Small Arms & Metal Company Ltd (below). The history of BSA in all its guises can be found in greater detail in John Walter, 'The Rise of the Piled Arms – A Short History of the Birmingham Small Arms Company' in *Guns Review*, 1983–84 and 1987. **4.** Birmingham Small Arms Company Ltd [The] (BSA), Armoury Road, Small Heath, Birmingham,

Warwickshire, England. The post-1901 reincarnation of BSA, having completed rifle contracts placed during the Boer War, also continued the bicycle-making operations begun by its immediate predecessor (BSA&MCo.). The first motorcycles were made in 1909, and, in 1910, BSA bought the British Daimler car manufacturer. However, increasing interest in airgun shooting in the early 1900s also prompted BSA to acquire production rights to an underlever-cocking rifle designed in 1904 by George Lincoln *Jeffries. Initially these guns were made under licence, alongside Lee-Enfields and a series of experimental auto-loading firearms. In 1907, however, BSA commenced production of airguns on its own acount and, helped by improvements due to Augustus Driver and George Norman, had made about 70,000 by 1914. A few training guns in *SMLE or Long Lee-Enfield guise had also been produced. By 1914, BSA was operating three factories in the Birmingham area – Small Heath, Sparkbrook and Coventry Road – and a fourth in nearby Redditch. Large numbers of weapons were produced during the First World War. In addition to the Lee-Enfields, BSA was also the British licensee of the light machine-gun credited to Isaac N. *Lewis. Many thousands of Lewis Guns had been delivered by 1918 to the British and Belgian Armies, for land and air service alike. In 1919, BSA, which had become too large to operate as a single unit, was split into three divisions: BSA Cycles Ltd, *BSA Guns Ltd and BSA Tools Ltd. The individual gun designs are considered separately under the names of their paten-

tees: John H. *Cox, Augustus H.M. *Driver, Lincoln *Jeffries and George *Norman. **5.** Birmingham Small Arms & Metals Company Ltd [The] (or BSA&MCo.), Armoury Road, Small Heath, Birmingham, Warwickshire, England. This 1873-vintage successor to the original Birmingham Small Arms Company Ltd (above) retained the Small Heath factory, but a sales office was also maintained in London at 6 Great Winchester Street from 1885 onward. Although BSA&MCo. enjoyed comparatively little success in the 1880s, its fortunes were partly restored by the adoption in British service of solid-drawn cartridge cases and the *Lee-Metford magazine rifle. However, in the middle of frantic War Office work, the company once again sought voluntary liquidation for the purposes of reconstruction (in 1897), emerging in 1901 to trade once again under its old name. In the intervening period, it had made substantial quantities of Lee-Metford Mk I, Mk I* and Mk II rifles, and Lee-Enfield Mks I and I* rifles. BSA&MCo. also offered .303 Lee-Metford and Lee-Enfield rifles commercially from 1892 onward, utilising actions taken from regular production runs. They had commercial proof marks and were marked 'LEE-SPEED PATENTS'. BSA&MCo. and its successor, the Birmingham Small Arms Company Ltd, also offered 'High-Velocity Sporting Patterns No. 1, No. 2 and No. 3' prior to 1914, chambered for cartridges ranging from 7x57 to .375 Flanged Nitro Express. There were also four different Magazine Sporting Pattern Carbines in 7x57, .303 and 8x51. Many other British gunmakers handled Lee-type sporters, usually bought wholesale from BSA. Normally these will bear a discreet *Piled Arms trademark on the action. **6.** Birmingham Small Arms Trade [The], Steelhouse Lane, Birmingham, Warwickshire. This British trading association was formed in 1854, during the Crimean War, by twenty of the area's leading gunmakers keen to share government contracts among themselves. Although discontent led to the formation of the Birmingham Small Arms Company by some of its participants, the Small Arms Trade association staggered on until 1878. Among the firearms made under its control were French Chassepot needle-guns and 1869-pattern Russian Krnka infantry rifles.

Birnie. Roger Birnie, Junior, ranked as a lieutenant in the US Army when he accepted small-arms marked 'RB' in 1879–80. *See also* US arms inspectors' marks.

Bishop – **1.** William Bishop, Billy Bishop or 'The Bishop of Bond Street'. Listed at 170 New Bond Street, London, from 1861 until 1870, this member of the English gun trade is best known as an agent for Westley *Richards of Birmingham. **2.** Usually found as 'The Bishop'. A name associated with shotgun ammunition made by *Eley Bros. prior to the First World War for the London gunmaker Charles *Riggs. It may be accompanied by a punning trademark in the form of a bishop's mitre atop a five-bar gate.

'Bishopsgate' [The]. A brandname associated with the shotgun ammunition sold by Alfred *Davis of London.

Bisley – **1.** Named after Britain's premier shooting range, this spring-air pistol was designed by Lincoln *Jeffries (Junior). The subject of British Patent 10,250/10 of 27 April 1910, it was cocked by a lever forming the back-strap of the air cylinder, which doubled as a butt. However, only a few hundred pistols of this pattern were made in 1912–13, before they were superseded by the

*Lincoln. **2.** A modified version of the *Single Six (rimfire) or *Blackhawk (centrefire) revolvers introduced by *Sturm, Ruger in 1986. Approximating with the original Colt patterns, the guns lie higher in the hand than the standard Rugers (owing to the repositioned grip) and the hammer spur is notably lower. Chamberings to date have included .22 LR rimfire, .32 H&R Magnum, .357 Magnum, .41 Magnum, .44 Magnum and .45 Long Colt. **3.** Bisley Model. This adaptation of the *Colt *Single Action Army revolver was made for target shooting from 1894 until 1915. It was easily recognised by the position of the grip, which had been moved upward in relation to the frame and barrel, and the low-spur hammer. The Bisley Flat-Top Target was similar, but had different sights. **4.** Bisley Model. Similar mechanically to the *Canberra, the *Parker-Hale M84 Mark II Bisley Model had plain right- or left-hand stocks. **5.** Bisley Works. The manufactory owned by A.G. *Parker & Company Ltd, then by *Parker-Hale Ltd, until the latter moved to Golden Hillock Road, Birmingham, in 1967.

Bissell. Thomas Bissell, an English gunsmith, was listed in London directories at various addresses in Tooley Street (1857–76) and at Star Corner (1876 only), London E.C., before a move to 75–77 Cranham Road, Rotherhithe New Road, London E.C., occurred in 1877. Business seems to have ceased temporarily in 1886, but reopened in new premises at 98 Hollydale Road, Peckham, in 1889. Work ceased in 1891, perhaps on Bissell's death or retirement.

Bitkov'. A.A. Bitkov' of Moscow was one of Russia's leading distributors of guns, ammunition, sporting goods, clothing and footware. Founded in 1889, the business traded until 1918 from an office located at 20 Bolsh. Lyubyanka Mosta, and warehouses situated in Bolsh. Lyubyanka and at Kyuzhnetskago Mosta 8.

Bittner. Gustav Bittner was one of the leading gunmakers operating in *Weipert, Bohemia. He was also one of the principal members of a co-operative formed in 1887 to produce components for the straight-pull *Mannlicher service rifle that had been adopted for the Austro-Hungarian Army. His workshop was particularly well equipped, with a range of machine tools driven by steam engines, but the scheme did not last. He is also renowned as the manufacturer of a mechanical repeating pistol developed by *Passler & Seidl. Operations seem to have ceased in the 1920s.

Bittorf. K. Bittorf of Suhl in Thüringen, Germany, made sporting guns in the 1930s, being listed in the *Deutsches Reichs-Adressbuch* for 1939.

Bizon. This is a 9mm Russian submachine-gun, based on some of the components of the *Kalashnikov assault rifle and made in *Izhevsk. A special helical-feed magazine protrudes beneath the barrel.

BJ. A superimposition-type monogram, 'J' within 'B', this is correctly interpreted as 'JB'. It was used by Manufacture Générale d'Armes et Munitions Jules *Bertrand.

'bk'. A mark associated with small-arms and ammunition components made by Metall-, Walz- und Plattierwerke Hindrichs Auffermann AG of Wuppertal-Barmen, Germany, during the Second World War.

BKIW. Berlin-Karlsruher Industrie-Werke: a trademark and trading style adopted in 1922 by *Deutsche Waffen- & Munitionsfabriken. It was used until 1936.

'bky'. Used on small-arms components made under

German supervision by the Ung. Brod factory of *Böhmische Waffenfabrik AG in 1941–45.

'BL'. *See* Benjamin *Lyon.

'bla'. A mark found on cartridge clips and chargers made by E.G. Leuner GmbH of Bautzen, Germany, during 1941–45.

Blachon. Pierre Blachon, a French gun designer, was the co-patentee of the *Le Français semi-automatic pistol. *See* Manufacture Française des Armes et Munitions.

Black, Black... – 1. John Black. A gunsmith trading in Bollington, Cheshire, England, Black loaded – or perhaps simply sold – shotgun cartridges under the brandname Bollin. **2.** Black Bird [The]. A brandname used by the *Chamberlain Cartridge Company of Cleveland, Ohio, USA, on shotgun ammunition. **3.** Black Box. A nickname, often claimed to be a brandname, associated with the Danish-made *Pallet airgun ammunition. **4.** Black Boy. An early diabolo-type airgun pellet, made by *Eley Bros. from 1910 until the beginning of the First World War. **5.** Black Forest Arms Factory, Germany. *See* Voetter & Co. **6.** Black Hills Rifle. Made by E. *Remington & Sons from 1875 until the early 1880s, this was a minor variant of the No. 1 Sporting Rifle. Usually it had a round barrel chambering the .45-70 Government cartridge. *See also* Remington rifles, rolling-block action. **7.** Black & Owen. A *Suicide Special revolver made by the *Hopkins & Allen Arms Company of Norwich, Connecticut, USA, in the late nineteenth century. **8.** Black Twenty, usually as 'The Black Twenty'. Found on shotgun cartridges made by *Eley Bros. prior to the acquisition of the company by Explosives Trades Ltd in 1918.

Blackadder. C.G. Blackadder. This gunsmith and ironmonger, trading in the small town of Castle Douglas in Kirkcudbrightshire, Scotland, offered shotgun ammunition under the brandname 'Castle Douglas'.

Blackhawk – 1. A modern single-action revolver, inspired by the Colt *Peacemaker, introduced by *Sturm, Ruger in 1955. The Blackhawk has a swinging loading gate and a reciprocating ejector rod in a case beneath the right side of the barrel, but relies exclusively on coil springs instead of the Colt-type leaves. Guns made after 1973, sometimes known as the New Model Blackhawk, incorporated a *transfer-bar safety system to comply with the Gun Control Act of 1968. They can be recognised by three axis-screw heads visible on the rght side of the frame instead of the original two. *See also* Super Blackhawk. **2.** Blackhawk Convertible. A variant of the standard revolver offered with an exchangeable cylinder. The standard pairings were 9mm/.357 Magnum and .45 Colt/.45 ACP. **3.** Blackhawk Flat-Top. A name given to a variant of the standard Ruger Blackhawk with a flat-top frame and an adjustable back sight. About 43,000 were made in 1955–63, exclusively in .357 Magnum, although barrel length varied from 4.625in to 10in. **4.** Blackhawk Flat-Top Magnum. This was an enlarged version of the .357 Blackhawk Flat-Top chambering .44 Magnum rounds. About 28,000 were made in 1956–63, with barrels ranging from 6.5in to 10in.

Blackington. A.B. Blackington. A US Federal government arms inspector active in the early 1860s, marking Starr and Colt revolvers with 'ABB'. *See also* US arms inspectors' marks.

Blackjack pistols. *See* truncheon guns.

'Blackmoor Vale' [The]. A brandname found on shotgun cartridges sold by H.C. *Little & Son of Yeovil, Somerset, England.

Blagdon – 1. Blagdon, Blagdonette [The]. Found on shotgun ammunition sold by *Cogswell & Harrison. **2.** Blagdon Schooting School [The]. A shooting club in Malden, Surrey, this had repair facilities of sufficient stature to be regarded by H.J. Blanch, writing in 1909, as a member of the English gun trade.

Blake – 1. James Blake. Trading from premises at 12 The Square, Kelso, Roxburghshire, Scotland, Blake handled shotgun ammunition under the Roxburgh brandname. **2.** John Blake of New York City designed a bolt-action rifle in the early 1890s, two .30 prototypes being tested by the US Army in 1891–93, although they were unable to challenge the Krag-Jørgensen. Both were stocked in military fashion and had spool magazines. Blake subsequently sought a patent, granted in July 1898, and rifles were advertised commercially in Grades 'A' (best) to 'D' (plain). The standard 'D'-grade rifle was offered in .236 (6mm Lee), 7x57, .30-40 Krag, .30-30 Winchester and proprietary .400 chamberings. **3.** John Alkin Blake, London. The marks of this gunmaker have been reported on self-cocking *pepperboxes dating from the middle of the nineteenth century. **4.** John A. Blake & Company. This gunmaking business, probably run by John Alkin Blake (above), began work prior to 1850, being listed in the 1851 census at 253 High Street, Wapping, London, England. Additional premises were opened at 35 Upper East Smithfield in 1853, the Wapping shop being closed shortly afterward. Trading continued until 1864. **5.** Blake Brothers & Company. This provincial ironmongery business, trading in the Herefordshire town of Ross-on-Wye, handled shotgun cartridges marked 'The Wye Valley'.

Blakemore. V. & R. Blakemore. This London-based company is perhaps best known for undertaking contracts to supply – among other items – *Swinburn-Henry rifles and carbines to the government of Natal. This suggests that Blakemore, trading from 46 Leadenhall Street in 1866–74, and 8 Lime Street in 1875–97, was more of a wholesaler and agent than a manufacturer. The marks have been mistakenly identified as N. & R. Blakemore.

Blanc – 1. Trading from rue Michelet 40, Saint-Étienne, France. Listed in 1892 as a gunmaker. **2.** Philippe Blanc, rue Traversière 9, Saint-Étienne. A gunmaker active in France in 1892.

Blanch – 1. John Blanch. This English gunmaker was active prior to 1812 – when he was trading in London from 39 Fish Street Hill – until at least 1848, when his son was taken into partnership. Pistols, muskets, pepperboxes and air canes were among Blanch's many products. **2.** John Blanch & Son. Formed in 1848 and trading from 29 Gracechurch Street, London E.C., until the First World War or later. Harold John (H.J.) Blanch is as well remembered for his assiduous collection of details concerning the English gun trade as for the excellent quality of his sporting guns, pepperboxes, revolvers, airguns and air canes. Eventually the company was taken over by Alfred Davis.

Blanchard-Grange, 67 rue Antoine-Durafour, Saint-Étienne, France (in 1951). Listed during 1933–55 as a gunmaker.

Blancheton, rue de la Comédie, Saint-Étienne, France. Listed in 1879 as a gunmaker.

Bland – 1. E.J. Bland. Listed at 17 Brook Street, London, in 1897–98, this English gunmaker may have been a member of Thomas Bland & Son (q.v.). **2.** Thomas Bland & Son. Bland's name was renowned among nineteenth-century London gunmakers, trading from the 1840s well into the present century. Operating in the 1860s from 4 & 5 King William Street, Bland traded thereafter from 106 Strand (1876–88), 430 Strand (1887–1900), and 2 King William Street from 1900 onward. Shotguns, sporting rifles, pistols, pump-up air canes and walking-stick guns were among the company's range of wares.

Blanks. William Blanks, Rochford, Essex. The marks of this English gunmaker, working from 1831 until 1869 or later, have been reported on sporting guns and self-cocking *pepperboxes from the middle of the nineteenth century.

Blanton. R. Blanton. A gunmaker trading in Market Place, Ringwood, Hampshire, England, Blanton is recorded as handling 'foreign-made' shotgun cartridges named Competitor and Imperial.

Blaser-Jagdwaffen GmbH, Isny/Allgau, Germany. A maker of a wide variety of break-open, dropping-block and bolt-action rifles, often embodying innovative design features. Additional details will be found in John Walter, *Rifles of the World* (Krause Publications, second edition, 1998).

Blatt. Aug. Blatt, Albrechts bei Suhl in Thüringen, Goldbach Strasse 37 (1941). Listed in the 1920s as a maker of gun and gun parts, when an 'ABA' mark was used. This metalworking business was specialising in gun-barrels when the Second World War began.

Blaze. John Blaze. Patentee, with Daniel *Wesson and John *Stokes, of the Wesson shotgun. *See* US Patents 72,434 of 17 December 1867 and 84,314 of 24 November 1868.

'Blazer' [The]. A name associated with shotgun ammunition sold by T. *Naughton of Galway; it was made by *Irish Metal Industries.

'blc'. Found on German military optical equipment made by Carl Zeiss of Jena in 1941–45.

Blickensdorfer – 1. John Blickensdorfer; St Louis, Missouri. Also listed as Johann Blickendoerfer, Blickendorffer and other variations, this German-born gunmaker, specialising in spring-air *Gallery Guns, is first recorded in the St Louis directories for 1864; by 1869, however, a partnership had been struck with Frederick Schilling. **2.** Blickensdorfer & Schilling. This partnership of John Blickensdorfer and Frederick Schilling traded from 12 South Third Street, St Louis, Missouri, from 1869 to c. 1875, having succeeded the earlier Blickensdorfer operations. A few breech-loading spring-air Gallery Guns may have been made in addition to sporting guns.

Blish. John Bell Blish (1860–1921) retired from the US Navy in 1905, ranking as commander, and applied his enthusiasm to the development of a breech-locking system that relied on the friction generated when two surfaces of different metal were made to slide across each other under pressure. Patented in the USA in 1913, subsequently the ideas were licensed to the *Auto-Ordnance Corporation and duly incorporated in the earliest *Thompson submachine-guns. However, the failure of the high-powered Thompson Automatic Rifles (which suffered from gas leaks and unacceptably harsh extraction)

and experience with the submachine-guns suggested that the complication was not justified by results. Guns made during the Second World War reverted to *blowback operation without performing notably badly.

Bliss. William Bliss, Norwich, Connecticut, USA. This gunsmith was granted US Patent 202,627 of 23 April 1878 to protect a 'firearm'; 283,854 of 28 August 1883 for a 'firearm safety lock'; and 313,048 of 3 March 1885 for a 'revolving firearm'. Sold by *Maltby, Curtis & Company and Maltby, Henley & Company of New York City, undoubtedly the guns were made elsewhere in New England.

Blissett – 1. John Blissett. A member of the English gun trade operating from 321–322 and then 322 High Holborn, London, in 1850–66. The trading style became John Blissett & Son in 1867, the business continuing from the same address until a move to 98 High Holborn occurred in 1876. The name changed again to John Blissett, Son & Tomes in 1878, but work continued only until 1883. Blissett is known to have made shotguns, sporting rifles, pepperboxes, pistols, airguns and air-canes. **2.** Thomas Blissett. A gunmaker listed in 1864 at 16 Water Lane, London E.C., England.

Blitz – 1. A brandname associated in the early 1950s with German bolt-action airgun trainers, which may prove simply to have been pre-war *Haenel Sportmodelle – or guns assembled from parts – being sold by wholesalers. **2.** A mark found on an Italian-made barrel-cocking spring-air pistol, otherwise known as the BBM or *BMB. **3.** Usually as Blitz-Gewehr (Lightning Rifle) – a nickname bestowed on the Bavarian *Werder rifle during the Franco-Prussian War.

Block... – 1. Block action: *see* panel, facing page. **2.** Block et Lévy, rue Tréfilerie 14, Saint-Étienne, France. Listed in 1892 as a gunmaker, by which time Veuve Block (widow Block) had succeeded her husband.

'Blocks the Sear'. A slogan associated with the *Infallible pistol, made in the USA by the *Warner Arms Company.

Blómen. Axel Linus Blómen, described in the earliest Swedish patent specifications as a 'clerk', was co-patentee with Per Samuel Ewerlöf of the *Excellent gas-powered rifle. The two men were the major shareholders in AB Våpenfabriken 'Excellent', formed about 1906. Blómen was the designer, while his partner, Ewerlöf, was the financier and administrator. The guns appear to have been made by AB *Bahco. The later patent specifications seem to suggest that Ewerlöf had lost interest in the project by 1910. Relevant protection included Swedish Patent 20,939 of 24 August 1904, granted to Ewerlöf and Blómen for the basic construction and valve mechanism of the 'Excellent' rifle. British Patent 25,579/05 of 1905 was comparable. Swedish Patent 20,423 of 31 December 1904 protected a variant of the valve and charging system, but was delayed in its progress through the Stockholm patent office and was not accepted until after 20,939. Swedish Patent 27,316 of 9 December 1907 was granted to Blómen and AB Excellent for a bolt-loading system, and 29,226 of 5 December 1908 (and British equivalent 28,192/09 of 1909) protected a gas-charging unit with an under-bench reservoir. Swedish Patent 33,298 of 23 January 1911 was granted to Blómen and AB Excellent to protect another modification to the valve and charging mechanism, whereas patent no. 51,181 of 17 November

BLOCK ACTION

Block (1)

A mechanism relying on a block placed behind the chamber to seal the breech, which may be encountered in many differing guises. Dropping or falling blocks slide vertically down through a mortise. The Farquharson, Sharps and Browning (Winchester) rifles are typical examples. Rising blocks – rarely encountered – should move vertically upward. Swinging blocks are common, although encountered in a variety of guises and difficult to categorise accurately. A few swing up and back. Some swing up and forward (e.g. Albini-Braendlin, Springfield-Allin). Some swing laterally backward (e.g. Restell) or forward (Milbank-Amsler). Many swing back and down (Remington Rolling Block, Spencer); others move down and back (Peabody, Martini). The Snider and similar breech-blocks swing laterally on a longitudinal pin.

Single-shot dropping-block rifles have regained importance in recent years, thanks to the reintroduction of guns such as the Sharps. This modern example of the genre, a Blaser BL820, shows its compact design.

1919 allowed a claim for a spring-air gun cocked by a top-lever along the butt wrist. Swedish Patent 60,763 of 1 July 1924, granted to Blómen alone, described a sliding-barrel system; 72,414 of 14 November 1929 (to Blómen and AB *Excellengeväret) depicted a spring-air pistol cocked – most unusually – by its sear bar.

Blondeau, Saint-Étienne, France. Listed in 1933 as a gunmaker, and at 7 place Villeboeuf in 1951.

Bloodhound. A cheap *Suicide Special revolver made in the late nineteenth century by *Ely & Wray of Springfield, Massachusetts, and the *Harrington & Richardson Arms Company of Worcester, Massachusetts.

Blow... – 1. Blowback. Also known as case projection, this relies on nothing but the inertia of a heavy breech-block, friction between sliding surfaces and the opposition of a powerful spring to delay the opening of the breech; delayed blowback adds elements such as swinging levers or multi-part breech-blocks to buy a little more time before the breech-block begins to move back. As the breech is not locked at the moment of discharge, operation of this type was initially confined to pistols and a few light automatic carbines chambering low-power cartridges. Few blowback auto-loading rifles, other than the *Winchesters designed by Thomas *Johnson, had been notably successful prior to 1914, as attempts to use military-pattern cartridges were generally doomed to failure. Extraction was customarily harsh unless the cartridges were lubricated – manufactured with a wax coating perhaps, or squirted with oil as they entered the chamber. Extractors were prone to tear through the case-rims or even rip the entire case head away, jamming the action. Although blowback operation was viewed with suspicion by most military ordnance authorities prior to 1945, views of this type have now been altered by the success of roller-locking systems. The first of these were used in a delayed blowback form by several experimental *Mausers tested in the closing stages of the Second World War, but have been featured more recently in many *CETME/*Heckler & Koch designs. The French AAT52 embodies a two-piece bolt and a lever-like 'retarder', and some of the SIG designs also rely on roller units. Most delayed-blowback guns still require fluted chambers, effectively floating cartridges on a cushion of gas in an attempt to improve extraction, but this complication (which prevents cartridges from being reloaded satisfactorily) is accepted in return for constructional simplicity. *See also* gas operation, delayed blowback, locked breech, operating systems and recoil operation. **2.** Blow-forward. The reverse of blowback operation (above), this relies on the barrel being projected forward by chamber pressure. The empty case is ejected before a spring returns the barrel to chamber a new cartridge. Although extraction and ejection are simplified, blow-forward has too many problems to attract rifle designers: the excessive weight of the moving parts disturbs aim too easily. The best known examples are the 1894-type Mannlicher pistol and the Schwarzlose pattern of 1908, which was made in surprisingly large numbers in Germany and the USA. SIG made a few AK-53 rifles in Switzerland in the early 1950s, but few other blow-forward rifles have ever encountered success.

'B.L.R.' Usually stencilled or painted on the butts of British military rifles: 'Beyond Local Repair' and thus destined to be returned to a major depot.

Blue... – 1. Blue Flash [The]. Found on shotgun cartridges loaded and sold by *Garrett of Evesham, Worcestershire, England. **2.** Blue Jacket. Three different *Suicide Special revolvers made in the USA in the late nineteenth century by the *Crescent Arms Company of Norwich, Connecticut; by the *Hopkins & Allen Arms Company of Norwich, Connecticut; and by *Johnson, Bye & Company and/or *Iver Johnson of Worcester and Fitchburg, Massachusetts. **3.** Blue Roc [The]. A brandname found on Kynoch-made shotgun cartridges sold by *Langley & Company (prior to 1914), *Langley & Lewis (in the 1920s and 1930s?) and Aubrey *Lewis (c. 1945–69). **4.** Blue Shell. This mark will be found on shotgun cartridges handled by John *Dickson of Edinburgh, Scotland. **5.** Blue Streak. A brandname used in recent times to distinguish the blued-finish .20-calibre pump-up pneumatic rifles made by *Sheridan of Racine, Wisconsin, USA, from its gaudier nickelled Silver Streak equivalents. **6.** Blue Whistler. A *Suicide Special revolver made by the *Hopkins & Allen Arms Company of Norwich, Connecticut, USA, in the late nineteenth century.

Blum. Budapest-based gunsmith Friedrich Blum is now generally credited with the design of the drum magazines (TM. 08 and TM für FSK) issued with the German *Parabellum pistols and *Mondragon rifles during the First World War. Blum was granted three relevant German patents in this period: 302,455, 305,074 and 305,564. *See also* Tatarek & von Benkö, and Trommelmagazin.

Blunt – 1. Stanhope English Blunt. Then a captain in the US Army, Blunt inspected the *Colt revolvers displaying an 'SEB' acceptance mark in 1889–90. *See also* US arms inspectors' marks. **2.** Blunt & Syms, New York City. This partnership between the inventor Orison *Blunt and the Syms brothers, William and Samuel, dated from 1848. Trading first from 44 Chatham Street, then 177 Broadway, the business made sporting guns, muskets and spring-air *Gallery Guns before the business passed to John G. *Syms.

BM. A floriated monogram, often superimposed on a sunburst motif. Found on the grips of *Hermetic semi-automatic pistols, made in France by Établissements *Bernardon-Martin et Cie of Saint-Étienne.

'BMB'. This trademark has been found on a barrel-cocking spring-air pistol, apparently Italian, which is also known as the BBM or Blitz. Any connection with *Breda Meccanica Bresciana is still open to debate.

'bmj'. Associated with optical equipment made during the Second World War by M. Hensoldt & Söhne of Wetzlar, Germany.

'bmz'. Marks of this type will be found on German small-arms and ammunition components made during the Second World War by Minerva Nähmaschinenfabrik AG of Boskowitz.

'B' above 'N', separated by a horizontal bar. A trademark used on *Parabellum drum magazines (TM. 08) made during the First World War by Gebr. *Bing of Nürnberg.

'bne'. Identifying small-arms ammunition and components made in the Second World War, this code was used by Metallwerke Odertal GmbH of Odertal Post Lautaberg/Harz, Germany.

'bnl'. Used during the Second World War by Ostmarkwerke GmbH of Gbell bei Prag on small-arms

components, made in German-occupied Czechoslovakia.

'BNP' and a crown. The definitive nitro-proof mark applied by the Guardians of the Proof House in Birmingham, Warwickshire, England, this replaced the 'BP' black powder and 'NP' nitro proofs in 1954.

'bnz'. Associated with the products of *Steyr-Daimler-Puch AG made in 1941–45, including machine-guns, pistols, rifles and relevant components.

Boa. Based on the proven Mark V action, these .357 Magnum revolvers were made in 1985 by the Firearms Division of *Colt Industries, for the Lew Horton Distribution Company of Southboro, Massachusetts. Only 1,200 guns were made, distinguished by 4 or 6in barrels with ejector-rod shrouds. There were also a hundred special cased two-barrel sets.

Boardman. Edward P. Boardman, Lawrence, Massachusetts, USA. Co-designer with Andrew Peavey of the *Little All Right revolver, protected by US Patent no. 172,243 of 18 January 1876.

Bobcat, Bob Cat – 1. Otherwise known as the G85/1, this was a .177-calibre barrel-cocking spring-air rifle made by *Milbro Ltd in 1979–82 for the juvenile market. **2.** A gas-powered rifle sold by *Precise Imports Corporation of Suffren, New Jersey, USA, but made in Japan by Taiyo Juki of Miroku.

Bobichon fils, rue Saint-Denis 1, Saint-Étienne, France. Listed in 1879 as a distributor of, and agent for, arms and ammunition.

Bock – 1. Oskar Bock, Dietzhausen in Thüringen, Hauptstrasse (1941). A maker of optical-sight mounts and associated components active in Germany early in the Second World War. **2.** Otto Bock, Berlin. This well-established German gunmaker, claiming to be one of the *Hoflieferanten* (purveyors to the Royal houshold) made sporting rifles embodying Oberndorf-made *Mauser actions. Many of these were chambered for the 9.3x62 cartridge developed by Bock in the early 1900s. **3.** Bockbüchsflinten. A term applied to guns with one rifled and one smoothbore barrel, superposed. *See* Combination weapons. **4.** Bockdoppelbüchse. A term applied to guns with two rifled barrels of the same chambering, superposed. *See* Combination weapons. **5.** Bockdrilling. A three-barrelled gun with a smoothbore above a large-calibre rifled barrel, with a small-calibre rifled barrel alongside the barrel block. *See* Combination weapons.

'Bodmin' [The]. A brandname found on shotgun cartridges sold prior to 1914 by *Jane of Bodmin, Corn-wall, England.

Bodson, Liège. A maker of sporting rifles in Belgium in the mid-nineteenth century.

Bodyguard or Model 49. A steel-frame version of the Bodyguard *Airweight, developed for the Massachusetts State Police, this .38-calibre swing-cylinder *Smith & Wesson revolver appeared in 1959. Most guns will be found with 2in barrels; a special variant with a stainless-steel cylinder was made for the Michigan State Police in the 1960s. An entirely stainless-steel version was introduced in 1986 as the Model 649.

Boecker. Ulrich Boecker, or Böcker. Residing at Wilhelmstrasse 15 in Hohenlimburg, Germany, this 'sporting goods maker' patented a double-spring airgun mechanism; *see* British Patent 380,036, accepted on 8 September 1932.

Bohemian design school, or simply Bohemian

School. A generic term coined to describe the repeaters made largely in the Weipert district by inventors such as *Bittner and *Passler & Seidl. *See also* Mechanical repeating pistol.

Bohlig & Eschrich. German gunmakers based in the Thüringian town of Zella St Blasii, and later in the Zella-Mehlis conurbation.

Böhme. Walter Böhme, Suhl in Thüringen, Germany. Listed in the 1930 edition of the *Deutsches Reichs-Adressbuch* as a sales agency.

Böhmer. Hermann Böhmer. A gunmaker trading in Zella St Blasii and Zella-Mehlis, Thüringen, Germany, early in the twentieth century.

Böhner. Hermann Böhner, Zella St Blasii in Thüringen. Listed in the 1900 edition of the *Deutsches Reichs-Adressbuch* as a gunmaker; this entry may have been a misprinted form of Hermann Böhmer (above).

Boissy. P. Boissy, rue de la Badouillère 34, Saint-Étienne, France. Listed in 1879-vintage directories as a gunmaker.

Boitard. Paul Boitard, grande rue Saint-Roch 4, Saint-Étienne, France. A gunmaker listed in 1879, still active in 1900.

Boker. Herman Boker, New York. A well-known distributor of firearms and edged weapons, Boker was sued in 1862 by *Smith & Wesson for selling revolvers made by the *Manhattan Fire Arms Company with bored-through chambers.

Bolen. John G. Bolen. Established at 104 Broadway, New York City, prior to 1837, Bolen sold a variety of guns and ammunition until the mid-1850s. He advertised himself – perhaps with licence! – as the manufacturer of a 'Patent Self-Cocking Pistol' and sold cased pairs of *pepperboxes as Bolen's Life Preservers; intriguingly, the pairs rarely matched, and could even be supplied by different manufacturers.

Bolles. Edward L. Bolles. A US government arms inspector active in 1902, identified by the initials 'ELB'. *See also* US arms inspectors' marks.

'Bollin' [The]. A mark found on shotgun cartridges sold by John *Black of Bollington.

Bolt – 1. This closes the breech of a gun. Used on practically all military rifles made from 1890 to 1940, it usually comprises a cylindrical body containing the firing pin and firing-pin spring. Several different types of bolt have been used, but most rely on lugs rotating into the receiver (or sometimes into the barrel extension) to lock the action securely. Some guns have the lugs on the bolt body; others have a detachable head. A few retract the lugs into the bolt during the opening stroke, and others may have a pivoting bar or locking strut. **2.** Bolt action: *see* panel, p. 80. **3.** Bolt Action Big Game Rifle. No purpose-built *Remington-Lee sporting rifles were offered in quantity until 1904, when a few of these were built on 1885-pattern Navy actions that had remained in store. They chambered the .43 Spanish, .44-77, .45-70 or .45-90 cartridges. **4.** Bolt carrier. A component or assembly that carries the bolt, commonly encountered in autoloaders. It may also control unlocking. **5.** Bolt plug, sleeve or shroud. This term is applied to a housing attached to the rear of the bolt, generally surrounding the cocking piece (q.v.). **6.** Bolt way. The portion of the receiver (q.v.) in which the bolt rides.

Bolte & Anschütz, Mehlis and Zella-Mehlis in Thüringen, Germany. Listed in 1900 as a weapon-maker and wholesaler, when owned by Fritz Reuss. Listed as a gun- and weapon-maker in 1914. The products included revolvers, pistols and small-calibre rifles among a wide range of other metal goods. Listed in 1920 as a wholesaler of guns and metalware, owned by F. Reuss and A. Spiess. By 1925, the products were being recorded as 'revolvers, *Flobert rifles and pistols, self-loading pistols'. The trademark of 'B & A' in a cross will be found on a variety of firearms and accessories, including sub-calibre barrel inserts for the Luger (protected by DRGM 1,364,272 of 1936) and the rimfire B.u.A.-Karabiner of the 1930s. Listed in 1930–39 as a gun- and weapon-maker; trading ceased in 1945.

Boltun. A small automatic pistol made by Francisco *Arizmendi of Eibar; 7.65mm, seven rounds, striker fired. It was based on the *FN-Browning of 1910, although a 6.35mm version based on the earlier Browning design of 1905 has also been reported.

Bolumburu. Gregorio Bolumburu, Eibar, Guipúzcoa, Spain. This gunmaking business is credited with making the *Bufalo, *Gloria, *Marina, *Regent, *Regina and *Rex automatic pistols. Regent guns may be marked by *Sociedad Española de Armas y Municiones (q.v.).

Bombrini, Parodi e Delfino, alternatively, Bombrini-Parodi-Delfino (BPD). This was one of Italy's leading ammunition manufacturers, identifying its products by the inclusion of 'B.P.D.' in headstamps – in a variety of forms. *See also* Mannlicher.

'Bomo' [The]. A shotgun cartridge loaded by the *Schultze Gunpowder Company Ltd prior to 1914.

Bonanza. A cheap *Suicide Special revolver made by the *Bacon Manufacturing Company of Norwich, Connecticut, USA, in the late nineteenth century.

'Bonax' [The]. Found on shotgun cartridges made by *Kynoch Ltd prior to the acquisition of the company by Explosives Trades Ltd in 1918, and in later years by *Eley-Kynoch Ltd.

Bond – 1. Edward & William Bond. This English gunmaking partnership was listed at 45 Cornhill and Hooper Square, Goodman's Fields, London E., in 1850–55. The Hooper Square address remained until 1861, although Cornhill gave way to 42 Leadenhall Street in 1856. The directory entries for 1862–70 are in the name of Edward P. Bond, but a reversion to Edward & William Bond – at 4 Northumberland Alley, Fenchurch Street, London E.C. – was made from 1871 until mention ceased in 1879. Edward Bond was the managing director of the *London Small Arms Company Ltd. for many years and is credited with the design of the Bolted Action for the Snider. **2.** George Edward Bond. This gunsmith continued to trade from Thetford, Norfolk, England, in succession to his father William Bond (1821–69). Trading continued until 1914 or later as G. Edward Bond & Sons; marks of this type have been found on shotgun cartridges sold under the brandname *Invincible. **3.** William Bond, Thetford, Norfolk. This gunmaker traded from the Old Market in 1821, the earliest recorded directory entry, and from St Magdalen Street in 1829–50. A move to Market Place occurred in 1851 or 1852, where work continued until the 1870s. Bond's marks have been seen on sporting rifles and self-cocking *pepperboxes dating from the middle of the nineteenth century, although the latter have sometimes been attributed to G.E. Bond of Thetford.

Bonehill – 1. Alfred M. Bonehill, Birmingham,

BOLT ACTION

Bolt (2)

A system of operation relying on a cylindrical bolt reciprocating to extract, eject, reload and cock the firing mechanism. Although the rudiments of the system may be seen in medieval cannon, the originator of the modern bolt-action rifle is generally agreed to have been the Prussian inventor Johann-Niklaus *Dreyse, a one-time apprentice of Samuel Pauly, whose *Zündnadelgewehr (needle rifle)

was adopted by the Prussian Army in 1840.

Straight-pull or rectilinear action simply requires a handle to be pulled backward, usually transmitting a rotary motion to the bolt head by way of lugs and helical cam-tracks. Associated with the later Austro-Hungarian Mannlicher service rifles and the Swiss Schmidt(-Rubin), this system may be operated quickly when clean and properly lubricated, but offers poor primary extraction.

Turning-bolt action requires a handle to be lifted or the bolt-body rotated to disengage locking lugs

before the backward movement can begin. Theoretically slower to operate than a straight-pull system, it offers more effective primary extraction and is less likely to be affected by variations in cartridge dimensions.

Many books and countless articles have been written on this particular topic. To date, there has been no good one-volume study, but Stuart Offeson's *The Bolt Action: A Design Analysis* (Winchester Press, 1976), and Frank de Haas's *Bolt-Action Rifles* (DBI Books, third edition, 1995) are helpful, as is D.B. Webster's *Military Bolt Action Rifles 1841–1918* (Museum Restoration Service, 1993).

See also Arisaka, Berthier, Lebel, Lee, Mannlicher, Mauser, Mosin-Nagant, Remington, Ross, Schmidt-Rubin, Springfield and Winchester.

Bolt-acton rifles come in many types. This is a German Blaser R-93, operated by pivoting the handle backward to retract the locking lugs that are just visible behind the bolt head. Designs of this type are sometimes classified as travelling blocks.

Warwickshire, England. In 1926, Bonehill succeeded his father Christopher to the ownership of Bonehill & Company, and continued to make sporting guns and rifles. The Birmingham directories list the business at 4 Prince Street from 1926 until 1961. **2.** Christopher George Bonehill, Birmingham. Bonehill was the owner of the Belmont Fire Arms Works in Birmingham from 1872 onward, apparently succeeding his father, and was himself succeeded by his son, Alfred, in 1926. Trading was originally centred on Charlotte and Morville Streets in Birmingham, but had moved to the Belmont Fire Arms Works, Belmont Row, by 1882. This may have coincided with the first order received by Bonehill for *Snider rifles. A move to 4 Price Street had been made by the end of the First World War. Bonehill was particularly interested in sporting guns, obtaining several relevant patents between 1877 and 1908. His shotguns were popular in the USA, where they were distributed by the H. & D. *Folsom Arms Company, among others. He is also remembered for the Bonehill *Britannia air rifle, designed by Frederick S. *Cox. Other relevant protection included British Patent 13,917/07 of 1907, sought with Henry *Homer to protect the *Improved Britannia air rifle, and 13,567/08 of 1908 (also with Homer) for a pellet-pusher.

3. Bonehill & Company. This gunsmithing business, best known as a 'merchant' or distributor began trading in Birmingham in 1851. The premises originally stood in Belmont Row, Birmingham, and consequently were known as Belmont Fire Arms Works or as the Britannia Gun Works. Christopher George Bonehill was listed as proprietor from 1872 onward, but was followed by his son, Alfred (q.v.).

Bonna. A brandname associated with a German 75-shot bolt-action repeating air rifle, first identified by W.H.B. Smith in *Gas, Air & Spring Guns of the World*. It has been suggested that these guns were pre-war Venuswaffenwerk *Mars examples (possibly assembled from surviving parts) being handled by a distributor active in the early 1950s – said to have been W. *Schlumper of Düsseldorf. Nothing further is known.

Bonnard, 34 rue du Musée, Saint-Étienne, France. Listed in 1951 as a gunmaker.

'Bonnaud' [The]. A name associated with shotgun cartridges made by F. *Joyce & Company Ltd of London prior to 1907.

Bonnavion frères, rue Villeboeuf 8, Saint-Étienne, France. Listed in 1879 as a gunmaking business.

Bonnet – 1. Trading in rue de Grand-Gonnet, Saint-

Étienne, France. Listed in 1892 as a gunmaker. **2.** A colonel in the French Army; *see* Lebel.

Bonnie & Clyde. A name given to a two-revolver set marketed in 1989–90 by the ★Charter Arms Corporation, commemorating the brief and bloody career of bank robbers Bonnie Parker and Clyde Barrow, which came to its end in Louisiana in 1934. The guns had six-round cylinders chambered for the .32 H&R Magnum (Bonnie) or .38 Special (Clyde) cartridges, the shrouded-ejector barrels measuring 2.5in. The grips were 'color co-ordinated wood laminate', and the set was accompanied by a gun-rug.

'Bono' [The]. A mark found on shotgun cartridges loaded by the ★Cogschultze Ammunition & Powder Company Ltd in 1911–14.

'Bon-Ton' [The]. Associated with shotgun ammunition sold by ★Graham of Inverness, Scotland.

Boom. A small ★Suicide Special revolver made in the USA by C.S. ★Shatuck of Hatfield, Massachusetts, in the late nineteenth century.

Boone Air Pistol. This was an interesting BB-calibre (.173) pistol made by the ★Target Products Corporation of Jackson, Michigan, shortly before the United States' entry into the Second World War in December 1941. It had a gravity feed, and a backward-moving piston cocked by pulling forward on a handle beneath the barrel.

Boot Gun. A generic term for a small pistol, usually a single-shot underhammer cap-lock, which could be carried tucked into the top of a riding boot.

Booth – 1. Howard R. Booth. A US government inspector of ★Colt revolvers in 1940, Booth used the marking 'HRB'. **2.** Pomeroy Booth. This US Federal government arms inspector, working in the early 1860s, accepted small-arms marked 'PB'. **3.** Thomas W. Booth. This government inspector, working for the Federal Army during the American Civil War, accepted ★Sharps and other carbines marked with 'TWB' in a cartouche. *See also* US arms inspectors' marks.

Boragine. Roberto Boragine, an Italian Army officer (then holding the rank of major), made improvements in the design of the ★Mannlicher-Carcano rifle in the 1940s.

Borchardt – 1. Hugo Borchardt was born in Magdeburg on 6 June 1844, but emigrated to the USA at the age of sixteen. He became superintendent of works for the short-lived Pioneer Breech-Loading Arms Company in c. 1871, moving to the Singer Sewing Machine Company, then briefly to ★Colt's Patent Fire Arms Manufacturing Company, before going on to ★Winchester. Borchardt was appointed factory superintendent of the ★Sharps factory on 1 June 1876, patenting the ★Sharps-Borchardt rifle and developing tooling for a prototype ★Lee-type bolt-action rifle. When the Sharps Rifle Company collapsed in the autumn of 1880, Hugo Borchardt returned to Europe in the autumn of 1882 to join ★Fegyver és Gépgyár Reszvenytársáság in Budapest. After returning briefly to the USA in 1891, Borchardt retraced his steps to Europe to perfect his pistol in association with first ★Ludwig Loewe & Company, then ★Deutsche Waffen- und Munitionsfabriken. Improved toggle-locked pistols and rifles were patented prior to 1914, but otherwise the life of this most versatile engineer passed without notice. All that is known with certainty is that Borchardt was living at Königgrätzer Strasse 66, in

Berlin, when his first patents were granted, and at Kantstrasse 31 in Berlin-Charlottenburg when he died on 8 May 1924. Protection granted to Borchardt included US Patent 153,310 of July 1874, for a method of machining lubricating grooves in hard lead bullets. US Patents 185,721 of 26 September 1876 and 206,217 of 23 July 1878, protecting elements of the Sharps-Borchardt rifle, were sought from Peekskill in New York State and assigned to the Sharps Rifle Company. Patent 197,319 of 20 November 1877 was granted for a gun sight; and 273,448 of 6 March 1883, for a 'detachable magazine for machine guns', was assigned to Joseph W. Frazier of New York City. Subsequently, Borchardt was granted nearly forty patents and sixty registered designs in Germany between 1893 and 1911. They included German Patent 75,837 of 9 September 1893, for the construction of the basic toggle-lock pistol; a patent of addition, 77,748 of 18 March 1894, made a specific claim for the roller used to break the toggle joint. British Patent 18,774/93 of 18 November 1893 and US Patent 561,260, granted on 10 November 1896, were broadly comparable with the two German specifications. German Patent 83,141 of 10 March 1895 protected a magazine with twin coil springs; and 91,998 of 10 October 1896 was granted for a modified magazine with a follower doubling as a hold-open. Later patents, such as British 17,678/07 of 2 August 1907, allowed claims for different methods of breaking a toggle-lock. German Patent 222,222 of 27 February 1909 protected an improved trigger mechanism for toggle-lock guns, similar specifications being accepted in Britain (29,622/09 of 17 December 1909) and the USA (987,543 of 21 March 1911). German Patent 227,078 of 27 February 1909 was granted for an improved ejector for toggle-lock pistols, and 215,811 of 30 April 1909 allowed the insertion of a short chain in the toggle assembly. Subsequently Borchardt patented an auto-loading rifle of this type in the USA – no. 1,160,832 of 1914 – but it was not successful. **2.** Borchardt-Luger: *see* panel, p. 82.

Borden. William A. Borden. This US government arms inspector, a lieutenant-colonel in the US Army, accepted Colt pistols marked 'WAB' in 1936–39. *See also* US arms inspectors' marks.

Border – 1. Generally found, as 'The Border', on shotgun cartridges sold by ★Forrest & Son of Kelso; by William ★McCall & Company of Dumfries; and by Robert ★Raine ('The Border Cartridge') of Carlisle prior to 1914. Their origins are not known, but are assumed to be ★Nobel. **2.** Border Patrol. Chambered for the .38 Special cartridge, 400 of these variant ★Police Positive Special revolvers were made in 1952 by ★Colt's Patent Fire Arms Manufacturing Company. They could be distinguished by a special heavyweight 4in barrel. About 6,500 additional guns were made in 1970–71 on the basis of Mark III ★Trooper frames.

Bore – 1. The axial hole through the barrel, usually rifled to spin the projectile. Bore diameter measurements usually exclude the depth of the rifling. *See also* Shot sizes. **2.** Bore sizes. The universal Anglo-American standard was laid down in the British Gun Barrel Proof Act of 1868, which regularised the sizes of shot from 'A' – with a diameter of 2in – to fifty-bore (a diameter of .453in), often listed as 50-gauge, or 50-gage in North America. The Imperial equivalents of the most popular bore sizes are ten-bore, .775; twelve-bore, .729; sixteen-bore, .662; twenty-bore, .615;

BORCHARDT-LUGER PISTOL

Borchardt (2)

The pistol popularly known as the Luger was developed from the *Borchardt pattern in the late 1890s. Although the Borchardt worked well enough when it was properly adjusted, the management of *Deutsche Waffen u. Munitionsfabriken realised that serious weaknesses in the design should be eliminated. The return spring was delicate, and the overhang of the spring housing behind the grip upset the balance when the gun was used in the hand.

Some time prior to trials held in Switzerland in the winter of 1898, Georg *Luger had developed a method of unlocking the toggle by using cam ramps on the frame instead of the Borchardt-type internal roller. The 7.65mm pistols that arrived in Switzerland in November 1898, therefore, were the first of the true Borchardt-Lugers. When the final eliminator began on

1 May 1899, DWM had submitted an improved Borchardt-Luger with a manually-operated safety lever set into the rear left side of the frame.

This easily won the trials, and, on 4 May 1900, the Borchardt-Luger was adopted by the Swiss Army. This encouraged DWM to offer the pistol commercially, and also to sell small quantities to countries such as Bulgaria, Portugal and the USA. The subsequent history of the gun is summarised under Parabellum (2).

The oldest known Borchardt-Luger is this experimental example supplied by Deutsche Waffen- & Munitionsfabriken to the Swiss Army trials of 1898.

and 28-bore, .550. The sizes below fifty-bore were regarded as 'small bore' in the 1868 Act, and customarily described in imperial measure. However, the cap-lock pistols and revolvers made in Britain prior to the 1860s were classified in smaller sizes – e.g. 84-bore or 120-bore. The bore-size equivalent can be calculated simply by cubing the dimension in inches, then dividing 4.6578 by the result. For a .410 shotgun, therefore, the answer proves to be 68-bore (0.410 x 0.410 x 0.410 = 0.06892; 4.6578 ÷ 0.06892 = 67.58). The method also works in reverse, as the equivalent of 84-bore is .381 (4.6578 ÷ 84 = 0.05545; $\sqrt[3]{0.05545}$ = 0.381). *See also* Teschner.

Boreham. J.S. Boreham, High Street, Colchester, Essex. This gunmaker traded from c. 1850 until he retired, selling the business to K.D. *Radcliffe in 1899.

Bormans. Alard Bormans, Belgium: *see* Fabrique Nationale d'Armes de Guerre.

Bornmann. Johann Bornmann. This gunsmith worked for the well-known *Teschner business in Frankfurt an der Oder before striking out on his own account in nearby Drossen. Among his patented innovations were an eccentric locking bolt for shotguns and double rifles, and an automatic pop-up back sight for the *Drilling or three-barrel gun. His operations were apparently confined to the 1860–1900 era.

Bornmüller. Richard Bornmüller, Suhl in Thüringen, Germany. Once a partner in Bornmüller, Simson & Luck, this gunmaker traded independently in Suhl in the twentieth century. Most of the directories list the business as a wholesaler of guns and ammunition. The entry in the

Deutsches Reichs-Adressbuch for 1900 lists the owners as 'Edm. R. & Ernst H. Bornmüller'; by 1914, however, it was being operated by Ernst Hilmar Bornmüller. The 1930 directory entry still lists 'Bornmüller & Co.', and the 1941 edition lists 'Richard Bornmüller u. Co.' as a gunmaker; operations ceased in 1945.

Boromet, Saint-Étienne, France. Listed in 1933 as a gunmaker.

Bortmess Gun Company, San Francisco, California. Founded by Dick Bortmess in the 1960s, this US gunmaking business has made the Ranger bolt-action rifle.

Boru, rue Neuve 32, Saint-Étienne, France. Listed in 1879 as a maker of gun parts and accessories.

Borzov. Boris Afanasevich Borzov was born in Tula, USSR, in 1944. He graduated as a mechanical engineer in 1967 and was appointed to the design bureau in the *Tula small-arms factory. He helped Petr Yakushev to create the *YakB multi-barrel machine-gun.

Boss – 1. J. Boss & Company. Trading successively in London in the twentieth century from 13 Dover Street, 41 Albemarle Street and, in more recent times, 13/14 Cork Street, Boss handled rifles, sporting guns and ammunition. About 3,900 *Lanchester submachine-guns were assembled during the Second World War, probably from parts made by the *Sterling Engineering Company. Boss also modified about 20,350 .303 No. 3 *Enfield rifles to Weedon Repair Standards (WRS) in the summer of 1939, and reconditioned about 1,100 .303 *Hotchkiss Mk I and Mk I* machine-guns in 1940. The code 'S 156' was allotted to J. Boss & Company in 1940, but does not seem to have been widely used. *See also* British military manufacturers' marks. **2.** Thomas Boss. One of the circle of 'Best' London gunmakers, Boss is known for high-quality sporting guns and rifles. Operations were listed at 73 St James's Street, London S.W., from prior to 1850 on into the twentieth century. The trading style changed to 'Thomas Boss & Son' in 1860. Boss claimed to have invented the single-trigger lock for shotguns, but the claim was contested by many other gunsmiths.

Bössel. Lorenz Bössel, Suhl in Thüringen, Germany. Listed in 1900 as a gunmaker, under the ownership of Carl Bössel.

Boston – 1. John Boston, Wood Street, Wakefield, Yorkshire, England. The marks of this gun- and fishing-tackle maker – trading from 1827 until about 1857 – have been reported on self-cocking *pepperboxes. Operations moved to nearby Branton in 1857 and continued there for at least eight years. **2.** Boston Bull Dog. A .22-, .32- or .38-calibre double-action Iver *Johnson revolver introduced in 1887. It was based on the earlier *American Bull Dog.

Boswell. Charles Boswell. Among the best known of the gunmakers operating in twentieth-century London, founded in 1884, Boswell traded from 126 Strand and – at a later date – from 15 Mill St, Hanover Square. Shotgun cartridges have been seen bearing the Strand address and the name Special Express.

Bosworth. John Bosworth. Listed at 47b Richard Street, London E., in 1864–65, this member of the English gun trade is believed to have made gun parts.

Bott. James Bott & Son. An English gunmaking business listed in London – at 38 Lime Street, E.C. – from 1890 until at least the time of the First World War.

Boucher, Saint-Étienne, France. Listed in 1933 as a gunmaker, and at 45 rue Mulatière in 1951.

Boudin et Gauthey, Saint-Étienne, France. Listed in 1933 as gunmakers.

Bougy fils, rue de la Loire 37, Saint-Étienne, France. Listed in 1879 as a distributor of, and agent for, arms and ammunition.

Boulet. Réné Boulet. Living at 11 Avenue Bugeaud, Paris, France, Boulet obtained British Patent 614,740 on 22 December 1948. Granted to protect 'Improvements in or relating to Pneumatic Devices for throwing small projectiles', this included the essence of the Milbro *Cub squeeze-bulb pistol. The British Patent contains the essence of two granted in France on 22 November 1945 and 23 May 1946, but the idea was by no means novel and had been preceded by a comparable US Patent in the 1860s.

Boult – 1. Alfred Julius Boult worked as a consulting engineer and patent agent from the 1880s, from chambers at 323 High Holborn, London, England. He entered a loose partnership with William P. *Thompson about 1890, but this had ended prior to the formation of Boult & Wade in 1896. **2.** Boult & Wade. This patent agency, a successor to Alfred Boult about 1896 (although Anthony Taylerson suggests 1902 in *The Revolver 1888–1914*), acted for Walter *Benjamin and David *Mefford. British Patents 830/96 of 1896 and 12,824/99 of 1899 are relevant. Boult & Wade was succeeded by Boult, Wade & Kilburn (1902–09), then, from 1910, by Boult, Wade & Tennant.

Bouniard et Barrière, 17 rue de l'Épreuve, Saint-Étienne, France. Listed in 1951 as gunmakers.

Bourbon. Philip Bourbon, US gunsmith: *see* Bouron.

Bourchez. A. Bourchez. Based in Liège, Belgium, this gunmaker employed Richard *Long of London as his British representative in 1867.

Bourderonnet, rue Villeboeuf 10, Saint-Étienne, France. Listed in 1879 as a gunmaker.

Bourdevaux. Peter Bourdeveaux. A member of the English gun trade listed at 34 Hart Street, Bloomsbury, London, in 1864–65.

Bourgaud et Cie, rue d'Annonay 9, Saint-Étienne, France. Working as early as 1838, making cap-lock pistols 'in Scottish style'. Listed in 1879 and again in 1892 as a gunmaker.

Bourne. Joseph Bourne, Birmingham, Warwickshire, England. Successor to Redfern & Bourne, this gunsmithing business – Joseph Bourne & Son from 1867 – traded from 5 Whittall Street in 1849–78 and 9 St Mary's Row from 1879 onward. Sporting guns, rifles, pistols and revolvers, often destined for the African trade, have been reported with its marks. Bourne also maintained offices in London, operating from 82 Mark Lane, London E.C., in 1877, and 4 Cullum Street in 1879–81.

Bouron. Philippe Bouron, New Orleans, Louisiana, USA. This maker of a breech-loading dart-gun with an under-barrel air reservoir is listed in Robert E. Gardner's *Small Arms Makers* at 257 Bayou Road, New Orleans, in 1853, and 534 Chartres Street in 1860. However, Gardner also lists 'Philip Bourbon' in New Orleans in 1870–75, and it is suspected that the two smiths are one and the same. Bouron's activities, therefore, spanned 1853–75 and possibly beyond.

Bourzat, petite rue Faure, Saint-Étienne, France. Listed in 1879 as a distributor of, and agent for, arms and ammunition.

Bowdler. William Bowdler, the inventor of a hand-held pellet magazine (British Patent 1114/07 of 1907), lived at Reeves Street Farm, Bloxwich, Staffordshire, England.

Bowe. George G. Bowe. This arms inspector, working during the American Civil War, accepted rifle and carbine stocks marked 'GGB'. *See also* US arms inspectors' marks.

Bowen – 1. George F. Bowen. Active in the late 1870s, this US arms inspector could be identified by the initials 'GFB'. *See also* US arms inspectors' marks. **2.** John Bowen. Trading in the Welsh town of Carmarthen, this gunsmith and ironmonger handled shotgun cartridges marked Myrddin.

Bowers. William J. Bowers. This US government arms inspector, working in 1938, accepted Colt pistols marked 'WJB'. *See also* US arms inspectors' marks.

Bown. James Bown & Son, Enterprise Gun Works, Wood Street, Pittsburgh, Pennsylvania, USA. The marks of this distributor, formed in 1871 by James and William H. Bown from the residue of Bown & Tetley (1842–70), will be found on a variety of firearms, including *Suicide Special revolvers and inexpensive shotguns. Trading ceased in 1884, when the assets were transferred to Bown & Hirth.

Boxer. Edward Mounier Boxer (1823–98), commissioned into the Royal Artillery in 1839, is best known as the developer of the primer that now bears his name (*see* cartridge). Boxer became superintendent of the Royal Laboratory, Woolwich, in the early 1860s and there developed a series of cartridges, fuzes and shells. The primer was distinguished by its own anvil, unlike the ★Berdan pattern, which had the anvil formed as part of the cartridge-case head. Ironically, Boxer primers have become more popular in North America than in Britain, where the Berdan version is preferred! Boxer was eventually forced out of the army, resigning his post in 1869 after a wrangle over the commercial exploitation of his patents.

Box lock. This term is given to a shotgun with the strikers, springs, tumblers and associated components fitted inside the action body instead of carried on detachable side-plates (cf. ★side lock). The earliest successful box-lock gun was patented in 1875 by William ★Anson and John ★Deeley, and made by Westley ★Richards of Birmingham. Box locks became universally popular when over-and-under shotguns grew in favour, but have never entirely displaced side locks on the best side-by-side doubles. Indeed, the construction of more than a few box locks has been disguised with false side-plates.

Boyd – 1. Edgar B. Boyd. A Federal government arms inspector identified by the initials 'EBB', active in 1862. *See also* US arms inspectors' marks. **2.** Francis E. Boyd, Hyde Park and Boston, Massachusetts, USA. This 'gun manufacturer', active 1866–73, was the co-designer with P.S. ★Tyler of the breech-loading shotguns protected by US Patents 73,494 and 88,540 of 21 January 1868 and 6 April 1869 respectively. The barrel-block pivoted on a longitudinal pin to expose the chambers. **3.** Boyd Breech-Loading Arms Company [The], Boston, Massachusetts, USA. This sales agency, operating from 81 Washington Street (1870) and 205 Broadway (1871–72), was formed to promote the shotgun patented in 1868–69 by Francis Boyd and P.S. Tyler. The 10- or 12-bore guns were made in Boyd's workshops in Hyde Park, Massachusetts, but had been overtaken by better designs when work ceased about 1873.

Boyer – 1. A. Boyer, Saint-Étienne, France. Listed in 1933 as a gunmaker, and in 1951 at rue du 11-Novembre. **2.** J.N. Boyer. This US arms inspector, working in 1905–06, accepted small-arms marked 'JNB'. *See also* US arms inspectors' marks.

Boyington. C.M. Boyington. An arms inspector identified by the initials 'CMB', active from 1901 until c. 1910. *See also* US arms inspectors' marks.

Boyle – 1. William Boyle. A gunmaker trading from 86 Leadenhall Street, London, England, in 1893–94. **2.** William Robert Boyle of 'The Chestnuts', Finham, Coventry, Warwickshire, England, was granted British Patent 711,542 (1954) to protect a lever-pumped airgun.

Boynton. William E. Boynton. This US government arms inspector, working in 1902–10, accepted small-arms marked 'WEB'. *See also* US arms inspectors' marks.

Boy's Choice. A ★Suicide Special revolver made in the USA by the ★Hood Firearms Company of Norwich, Connecticut, in the late nineteenth century.

Boy Scout's Rifle. An alternative designation for the Model 4S Military Model Remington rifle (rolling-block action) made by the ★Remington Arms Company from 1913 to 1933.

Bozard & Company. Listed as members of the English gun trade by H.J. Blanch, writing in *Arms & Explosives* in 1909, Bozard traded from 33 New Bond Street, London, in 1888–95, and 8 Bennett Street, London S.W., in 1896–97. Then the trading style changed briefly to Bozard, Bedingfield, Philip & Company of 4 Panton Street (1898), before reverting to Bozard & Company. Operations continued at the Panton Street workshop into the twentieth century.

'BP', 'B.P.' – 1. And a crown, encircled. This mark was applied by the Budapest proof house (Austria-Hungary, then Hungary) from 1891 until 1948, originally accompanied by an NPB nitro-proof mark, then simply appearing above 'FN'. *See also* 'F', encircled. **2.** And a crown, often encircled. The definitive black-powder proof mark applied by the Guardians of the Proof House in Birmingham, England, 1904–54. **3.** Often in the form of superimposed monograms. Marks associated with Bernhard ★Paatz of Mehlis and Zella-Mehlis, found on the grips of small open-frame revolvers, often with folding triggers, made prior to 1914. **4.** A monogram. This mark, with the letters back to back, was used by the ★Eidgenössische Waffenfabrik, Bern, Switzerland, as a proof mark. Known as the Bernerprobe, it had replaced a small Federal Cross in 1919.

'BPC' with crossed sceptres and a crown – *see* 'BCP'.

'bpd', 'BPD' – 1. Found as 'bpd' on optical equipment made in Vienna during the Second World War by C.P. Goerz GmbH. The equipment was used by the German armed forces. **2.** Found as 'BPD', 'B.P.D.' or 'B-P-D' in the headstamps of cartridges made by ★Bombrini, Parodi e Delfino.

'bpr'. This mark was used in 1941–45 by Johannes Grossfuss of Döbeln in Sachsen, on machine-guns and small-arms components made for the German armed forces.

'BR', beneath a crown, above a number. A mark applied by an inspector working in the ★Royal Small Arms Repair Factory in Birmingham. *See also* British military inspectors' marks.

Bradbury – 1. W.F. Bradbury. This government arms inspector, working in 1898–1902, accepted small-arms marked 'WFB'. **2.** William Bradbury. A US Federal government inspector working in the early 1860s, Bradbury accepted small-arms marked 'WB'. *See also* US arms inspectors' marks for both entries.

Braddell. James Braddell & Son. One of Ireland's best known gunmakers, trading from Arthur Street in Belfast, Braddell handled a wide range of guns and accessories. These included shotgun cartridges, which were sold under names such as Castle, J.B., Mors and Victory. The cartridge cases often display a trademark consisting of a 'JB' monogram on the Badge of the O'Neill family (the so-called 'Red Hand of Ulster'). Braddell also supplied substantial quantities of ★Winchester rifles to the British authorities in 1941.

Braddick Ltd. Fabricators of silencers for the British Mk IIS ★Sten Gun, together with ★Auto-Engineering. Location and manufacturer's code unknown.

Braeckers. Charles Braeckers & Cie, Liège, Belgium. A maker of gun parts, bayonets, sword-hilts and ironmongery, founded in the 1880s and trading until the First World War.

Braendlin – 1. Francis Augustus Braendlin, possibly of Belgian origin, worked for the Mont ★Storm Gun Works in 1863–65. Braendlin was the designer of a breech-loading rifle protected by British Patent 2147/63 of 31 August 1863, and co-patentee with William Mont ★Storm of a modification to the latter's breech-loading system protected by British Patent 708/65 of 14 March 1865. He was also the co-designer with Augusto ★Albini of the breech-loading system protected by British Patents 2243/66 of 30 August 1866, 2652/66 of 13 October 1866, and 460/67 of 20 February 1867. Braendlin was the senior partner in Braendlin & Sommerville, then associated with the Braendlin Armoury Company Ltd. **2.** Braendlin Armoury Company Ltd [The], 1–3 Lower Loveday Street, Birmingham, Warwickshire, England. This business was formed in 1871 to purchase the assets of Francis Augustus Braendlin, who had been trading as Braendlin & Sommerville. Among the major shareholders were several local gunmakers, including William ★Powell and his son. Initially managed by George Conrad Braendlin, son of Francis Augustus, the Armoury concentrated on the importation of Belgian-made rifles and shotguns. It was a licensee of patents granted to Friedrich von ★Martini – specifically British 2305/68 and 603/70 – and also of British Patent 1531/80, granted to A. ★Martini. This enabled the Martini-Marres-Braendlin ★Mitrailleuse pistol to be made in small quantities, but trading steadily declined and the Braendlin Armoury Company Ltd was liquidated voluntarily in 1888. **3.** Braendlin Armoury Company [The], Birmingham, England. This dealership in guns and ammunition, operated by Charles E. ★Greener, may have inherited either the Lower Loveday Street premises or the stock of the original Braendlin Armoury (above). Representation was maintained in London at 63 Cornhill (1886–95) and 13–14 Abchurch Lane (1896–98). It continued to trade on into the First World War, disappearing c. 1915. **4.** Braendlin & Sommerville, also known as Braendlin, Sommerville & Company. This partnership was formed in England in 1867, partly to promote rifle-muskets converted to the Albini-Braendlin breech-loading system, but also to make revolvers incorporating an extractor mechanism patented by ★Galand & Sommerville in 1868. Trading from 1–3 Lower Loveday Street, Birmingham, Braendlin & Sommerville were succeeded in 1871 by the Braendlin Armoury Company Ltd.

Braithwaite. John Braithwaite. Often recorded in Birmingham, apparently mistakenly, this English gunmaker was listed at 91 Briggate, Leeds, Yorkshire, in 1833–61.

Brand – **1.** C.A. Brand. This arms inspector, a US Navy lieutenant, accepted ★Smith & Wesson revolvers at the end of the nineteenth century. The guns were marked 'CAB'. *See also* US arms inspectors' marks. **2.** Richard Farmer Brand. Designer of the distinctive breech-loading carbine made in small numbers by ★Calisher & Terry. The gun was the subject of British Patent no. 1870 of 1853; made until c. 1860, it was distinguished by a large hinged ring on the rear of the breech behind the hammer.

Brandejs. Bedřich Brandejs. Born in 1851 in Prague, Bohemia, Brandejs was apprenticed to the gunmaker Lebeda, becoming manager of the gun-shop in 1871. He was granted patents in 1872 to protect improvements to shotguns and breech-loading rifles, but soon concentrated less on gunsmithing and more on journalism. His published works included *Die Moderne Gewehrfabrikation* (1886) and *Die Handhabung der Feuerwaffen* (1902); he was also responsible for the magazines *Český Střelec* (1884–86) and the much more influential *Der Waffenschmied* (Munich, 1881–90). Brandejs died in October 1918.

Brandname. *See* Trademarks and brandnames.

Brandon. Joel P. Brandon. Listed as a gunmaker, trading from 119a Oxford Street, London, England, in 1873–77.

'Brant' [The]. Found on shotgun cartridges loaded by the ★Chamberlain Cartridge Company of Cleveland, Ohio.

Bratt Colbran Ltd, Lancelot Road, Wembley, Middlesex, England. A maker of magazines for the British 9mm ★Sten Gun during the Second World War. The code 'S 159' may have been used instead of the company name. *See also* 'British military manufacturers' marks.

Braungardt – **1.** Leonhard Braungardt, Suhl in Thüringen, Germany. A gunsmith active in 1939. **2.** W. Braungardt, Suhl in Thüringen, Germany. A maker of sporting guns and accessories, founded in 1883. Listed in 1920 as a gunsmith, and in 1930–39 as 'Wilhelm Braungardt, gunsmith/gunmaker'. The owner was then Fr. Härting.

Bray – **1.** Alfred Bray & Son (also listed as A. Bray & Co.), Leicester, England. Makers of .303 ★Vickers machine-gun tripods during the Second World War. These may be marked simply 'M 602'. *See also* British military manufacturers' marks. **2.** Edward P. Bray, New York City. Co-designer with Joseph ★Merwin of an auxiliary cap-lock ignition system used on ★Ballard guns during the American Civil War. This was protected by US Patent no. 41,166, granted on 5 January 1864.

Brazier – **1.** Joseph Brazier [& Sons], Wolverhampton, Staffordshire, England. One of Britain's most prolific manufacturers of gun-locks, initially also listed as a gun and pistol maker, Joseph Brazier – perhaps the son of Benjamin Brazier (working c. 1815–30) – began his career in Great Brick-kiln Street in 1827, but claimed origins extending back to the middle of the eighteenth century, the factory being named 'The Ashes' in the early 1830s. A move to Lord Street occurred in the early 1880s, possibly after the Brazier family lost control, but the 'Ashes' name was retained. The trading style became '...& Son' in 1849, then '...& Sons' in 1874. J. & R. Brazier displayed gun-locks at the Great Exhibition held in London in 1851; Joseph was also the recipient of British Patent 760 of 1855, protecting a rammer for the ★Adams self-cocking revolver. British Registered Designs were granted for a spring clamp and a locking vice (1056 and 1068 of 1859 respectively). ★Anson & Deeley actions were made under licence from Westley ★Richards, from 1876 onward, and a patent granted in November 1896 (25,994/96) to G. Brazier and W. Cashmore, protecting a safety catch for hammerless sporting guns, was also used. The quality of the gun-locks could often be assessed from their markings – the cheapest may often have gone unmarked, or borne nothing but 'IS' or 'JS'; the next group bore Brazier's name; and the best included both the Brazier name and 'Ashes'. Work continued until the business was acquired by Edwin Chilton & Company in the 1920s. **2.** Thomas Brazier, Wolverhampton, Staffordshire. Listed in local directories as a gun-lock maker (1827–31), trading from Bloomsbury Street, then as a gun and pistol maker until 1872. He was probably a brother of Joseph, but confirmation is lacking. **3.** J. & R. Brazier, Wolverhampton. This is believed to have been an alternative trading style of what is better known as Joseph Brazier & Son.

BreakO, Break-O. A recoil-suppressing system fitted since the late 1980s to some of the rifles made by H. ★Krieghoff of Ulm/Donau.

Brecht. Gustavus V. Brecht or Breght, St Louis, Missouri, USA. A maker of butchers' knives and spring-air ★Gallery Guns active in 1864–75.

Breda. Ernesto Breda [Società Italiana Costruzione Meccaniche]. Based in Brescia, this sporting gunmaker was once renowned more for its heavy guns than small-arms. However, the Greek-type Mannlicher-Schönauer rifles used by the Austro-Hungarian Armies during the First World War were given to Italy in 1919, together with surviving spare parts. Subsequently they were refurbished and, ironically, shipped by Breda back to Greece. The name of Breda Meccanica Bresciana has been associated with crude BMB-brand spring-and-piston airguns, but it is not clear whether the two businesses are directly linked.

Breech, breech... – 1. The rear end of the action (q.v.), containing the breech-block and giving access to the chamber. *See also* receiver. **2.** Breech block, breech-block. Any non-cylindrical means of closing a breech. Breech-blocks may take a wide variety of forms – e.g. sliding vertically, pivoting laterally or tipping upward. **3.** Breech bolt. *See* bolt (above). **4.** Breech Loading Armoury Company Ltd. An English gunsmithing business registered at 4 Pall Mall, London, in 1861–64. Products unknown.

Breen. John J. Breen. A captain in the US Army, this arms inspector accepted *Colt revolvers marked 'JJB' in 1886. *See also* US arms inspectors' marks.

Breitenstein. J. Breitenstein, St Louis, Missouri, USA. A maker of sporting rifles and spring-air *Gallery Guns active in 1865–70.

Bren... – 1. Bren Gun: *see* panel, below. **2.** Bren Manufacturing Company, Gateshead, Northumberland, England. This gunmaking business, formed in 1942, made components for the Bren Gun. Coded 'N 10', they included piston parts and sears. Assembly of piston and breech-block units was also undertaken. **3.** Bren

Ten. This was a short-lived US adaptation of the *Česká Zbrojovka CZ 75, developed for the 10mm Norma cartridge by Jeff Cooper. The gun was introduced by Dornaus & Dixon in 1983, but, although offered in a range of options – Pocket Model, Military & Police Model, Dual-Master Presentation Model (10mm/.45 ACP) – had disappeared within a few years, owing to the failure of manufacturing facilities to match demand.

Brenier et Cie, 68 rue Antoine-Durafour, Saint-Étienne, France. Listed in 1951 as a gunmaker.

Brennan. Sydney J. Brennan. A gunmaker trading from 155 Upper Thames Street, London, England, from 1899 until the First World War.

Brenneke. Wilhelm Brenneke, Leipzig and Berlin. This German gunsmith was concerned more with development of ammunition than sporting guns, although rifles embodying Oberndorf *Mauser actions were made from 1912. They chambered the distinctive 7x64, 8x64 or 9.3x64 Brenneke cartridges introduced in 1912–24. The 8mm chambering reappeared in the late 1950s when W. Brenneke GmbH of Berlin-Schöneberg, a resurrection of the pre-1945 company, began to make sporting rifles on the basis of old war-surplus or new *FN Mauser actions.

Brescia arms factory. This government-owned arms factory made, among other equipment, 6.5mm *Mannlicher-Carcano service rifles marked 'FAB'.

Bretton, 6 cours Fauriel, Saint-Étienne, France. Listed in 1951 as a gunmaker, renowned for the Bretton and Baby Bretton shotguns made in small numbers by *Société Générale de Mechanique of Saint-Étienne. The lightweight Bretton had barrels that could slide forward on rails anchored in the frame. A radial locking lever lay on the right side of the breech. The barrels could be

BREN GUN

Bren (1)

The success of the *ZGB Improved Model 4 allowed the Bren light machine-gun (for Brno and Enfield) to be approved for issue in May 1935. A few guns were acquired from *Československá Zbrojovka of Brno, although the first of a 10,000-gun order placed with the *Royal Small Arms Factory, Enfield, was completed in September 1937. Enfield production was so slow that the last guns from the pre-war contracts were not delivered until 1942. Then a 5,000-gun order was given to the John *Inglis Company of Toronto in 1938, but the loss of vast quantities at Dunkirk soon reduced the inventory of Bren Guns to only 2,130.

Desperate steps were taken to simplify the basic design, which had a complicated drum-type back sight and a folding grip beneath the butt. The Mark I Modified (Mark I [M]),

accepted in the autumn of 1940, had a simpler receiver lacking the optical-sight bracket, and a new bipod. The Mark II (June 1941) had a leaf-pattern back sight, a simpler body, a fixed cocking handle and a stamped butt plate. The Mk III of May 1944 had a shortened barrel, a lighter receiver and a simplified butt; intended for paratroops, the contemporaneous Mk IV had even more metal removed from the receiver to save weight, and an ultra-short barrel.

Sometimes Bren Guns were issued with 100-round Mk I or II drum magazines instead of the customary thirty-round boxes. Nearly a million of these magazines were made, together with a few 200-round High Speed Drum units intended for anti-aircraft use. Many sub-contractors were recruited to accelerate production, the origin of their parts often being masked by letter-prefixed numerical codes (*see* British military manufacturers' codes).

Participants ranged from the

Austin Motor Company Ltd ('M 13') of Longbridge to Wilson & Mathieson Ltd of Leeds ('N 90'). Orders placed for Bren Guns between 3 September 1939 and 14 March 1944 amounted to 416,658, the principal manufacturers being the Royal Small Arms Factory, Enfield, John Inglis and the participants in the *Monotype Scheme.

Many surviving Bren Guns were converted for the 7.62x51mm NATO cartridge in the 1950s. These were known as the L4 series, beginning in 1957 with the 'Gun, Machine, Light, 7.62mm L4A1'. The perfected L4A4 was adopted in 1960.

The best source of information is Tom Dugelby's *The Bren Gun Saga* (Collector Grade Publications, 1986), although Miroslav Sada's *Československé ruční palné zbrane a kulomety* (Prague, 1971) is helpful if the language barrier can be overcome. A summary of helpful information can also be found in *Guns of the Empire* by George Markham (Arms & Armour Press, 1990).

removed from the mounting collar at will, allowing the firer to select different combinations.

Breuer. Eugène Breuer, Liège. A Belgian gunmaker, active in the 1850s and 1860s. The family gunmaking business also maintained an agency in Turin, managed by Alphonse Bormans, Breuer's brother-in-law.

Breuil – 1. Claude Breuil, 4 rue de Rozier, Saint-Étienne, France. Listed in 1951 as a gun-barrel maker. **2.** Jean Breuil, 13 rue Montesquieu, Saint-Étienne, France. Listed in 1951 as a gun-barrel maker.

Brewer – 1. Eugene Brewer. A member of the English gun trade, occupying premises at 37 Queen Street, London E.C. (1877–81), and 9 New Broad Street, London (1882–85). **2.** Nicholas Brewer. This gunmaker-inventor has been credited with the development of, among other things, the *Savage Model 110 bolt-action rifle. **3.** Roland L. Brewer. Recipient of US Patent no. 239,414 of 5 April 1881, protecting the construction of a 'base-pin catch for revolvers'. *Suicide Specials of this type were made before the grant of the patent by the *Pittson Arms Company, then by its successor, the Lee Arms Company of Wilkes-Barre, until 1889. **4.** Brewer & Son. An English patent agency with chambers at 33 Chancery Lane, London, and 7 East Parade, Leeds, Yorkshire, Brewer & Son advised William S. *Armstrong and Andrew *Forbes.

'brg'. Used in 1941–45 on Kar. 98k and other German small-arms components made by H.W. Schmidt of Döbeln in Sachsen.

Briden. George Briden. An English gunmaker listed by H.J. *Blanch among the many active in London in the fifty years from 1850 onward, Briden was trading from 30 Bow Street, London W.C., in 1856.

Bridesburg Machine Works. *See* Alfred *Jenks.

'Bridge Gun'. *See* Billinghurst & Requa Gun.

Briggs – 1. George W. Briggs, New Haven, Connecticut. Patentee on 16 October 1866 (US no. 58,937) of an improved magazine for the *Henry rifle, assigned to *Winchester. **2.** Henry A. Briggs, Norwich, Connecticut, USA. Co-patentee with Samuel *Hopkins of a 'revolving firearm', US Patent no. 41,117 of January 1864, assigned to themselves in association with Charles A. Converse. Briggs subsequently moved to Philadelphia, where he was granted US Patent 327,860 (October 1885) to protect a 'breech-loading firearm'. **3.** Horace A. Briggs, Norwich, Connecticut. Assumed to have been the son of Henry Briggs (above), this gunsmith was granted US Patent 429,110 of 3 June 1890 – jointly with William W. Armington – to protect a 'firearm'. He also received, jointly with Charles *W. Hopkins, son of Samuel Hopkins, US Patent 498,366 of January 1893. **4.** William Briggs, Main Street and later West Main Street, Norristown, Pennsylvania. Trading from the late 1840s until 1876, Briggs designed a 'Gun-Lock' and a lever-operated breech mechanism that slid the barrel forward to give access to the chamber: US Patents 25,244 of 30 August 1859 and 88,605 of 6 April 1869 respectively.

Bristol – 1. Found, often as 'The Bristol', on shotgun cartridges sold by George *Gibbs of Bristol, and on others loaded from *Eley-Kynoch components by T. *Page-Wood of Bristol. **2.** A.J. Bristol. This US government arms inspector accepted *Remington revolvers and *Sharps carbines in the 1870s, marking them 'AJB'. *See also* US arms inspectors' marks. **3.** Bristol Fire Arms Company, Bristol, Rhode Island, USA. In 1855, before the patent had been granted, Ambrose *Burnside had organised this gunmaking business in anticipation of success. Unfortunately, the army order of September 1858

This Czech-made .303 ZGB machine-gun was the prototype of the Bren. The sharp curve of the magazine, the absence of barrel fins and the position of the bipod all help to distinguish the Bren from the ZB vz.26/vz.30 series.

was small – 709 guns – and the absence of large-scale orders coincided with a severe economic depression that hit the New England firearms industry particularly badly in the autumn of 1857. In desperation, Burnside sold his patents to his creditors and the Bristol Fire Arms Company went into liquidation.

Britannia – 1. A spring-air rifle with the air cylinder in the butt, designed by Frederick S. *Cox in 1902–04. It was a greatly improved form of the *Gem. The barrel-cocking Britannia had the merits of compact design, particularly compared with its near-contemporary, the *Jeffries Pattern, but only about 4,000 were made in 1905–09 by C.G. *Bonehill. Although there was a weakness in the trigger mechanism, the Britannia probably failed because BSA marketed the Jeffries Pattern rifles with far greater resources than Bonehill could bring to Cox's design. The Cox-type Britannia was superseded by the *Improved Britannia of Bonehill & Homer, which was unarguably an inferior design. True Britannia rifles often bear retailer's brandnames, principally 'Anglo Sure-Shot Mark I' of *Ramsbottom of Manchester. **2.** Found on a telescoping-barrel pistol dating from the 1930s. Despite being marked 'Made in Britain', this may still prove to be a Mayer & Grammelspacher *Diana LP2. **3.** A brandname (often listed as The Britannia) associated with shotgun cartridges marketed by J. *Mather & Company of Newark and Southwell, but made by J.R. *Watson & Company of London.

British, British... – 1. 'British Bulldog', alternatively, 'British Bul-dog'. This mark will be encountered on compact six-shot double-action .320 and .380 revolvers, based on the Webley *Bulldog, but customarily made in Belgium prior to 1914. Most have rounded or bird's-head butts, lanyard rings being optional. Not all give clues to their manufacturers, although some bear either the crowned 'R' or the name of J.B. *Rongé fils. **2.** British Bull Dog. A brandname associated with a .38 single-action *Bull Dog-type revolver made in the USA by *Forehand & Wadsworth c. 1879–83. **3.** 'British Bull Dog'. Found on *Suicide Special revolvers made by the *Hopkins & Allen Arms Company of Norwich, Connecticut, USA, in the late nineteenth century. **4.** British Bull Dog. A double-action .38 and possibly also .41 revolver introduced in the USA by *Johnson & Bye in 1881. **5.** 'British Champion' [The]. Found on shotgun ammunition loaded by the *Mullerite Cartridge Works of Birmingham, England, c. 1925–35. **6.** 'British Constabulary', or 'British Constable'. This mark was associated with Belgian-made five- or six-shot .44 or .450 revolvers, similar to the British Bulldog, but larger. Dating prior to 1914, they have squared butts and lanyard rings. Few bear manufacturers' marks. **7.** British & Foreign Lee Arms Company Ltd. Registered at 23 Queen Victoria Street, London, from 1900 onward, this business was formed to look after the patent rights of the inventor James P. *Lee. **8.** British Lion. Airgun pellets apparently made by *Kynoch, possibly correctly known simply as 'Lion'. **9.** British Magazine Rifle Company Ltd. This business occupied premises at 13 Austin Friars, London, from 1896 until the early 1900s. **10.** British military inspectors' marks. Unlike their US counterparts, these cannot be linked with individuals merely by deciphering initials. The standard form was a crown above an identifier of the factory (e.g. 'E' for 'Enfield') above the number of the individual inspector. No list of numbers

and names has yet been published, but the agency codes were 'B' and 'SK' for the *Royal Small Arms Factory in Sparkbrook, Birmingham (Roman or upright); 'B' (cursive) for the *Birmingham Small Arms Company Ltd and *BSA Guns Ltd; 'BR' for the *Royal Small Arms Repair Factory in Bagot Street, Birmingham; 'E' for the *Royal Small Arms Factory, Enfield Lock; 'GRI' for the *Ishapore factory in India; 'S' for the Australian inspection facilities in Sydney; and 'X' for the *London Small Arms Company Ltd. Subsequently, the Ishapore mark was replaced by 'IS' after India gained independence, and the Sydney mark was superseded by those applied by the small-arms factories in *Lithgow ('ACP' on a shield, 'A' on a six-point star or 'L' above a broad arrow) and Orange ('O' above a broad arrow). The Canadian arms factory in Long Branch used 'IP' beneath crossed pennants under a crown. **11.** British military manufacturers' codes. The regional coding system was developed during the Second World War to disguise the identity of participants in the ordnance industries. The essence was a letter prefix – 'M', 'N' or 'S' – indicating whether the manufacturer concerned was in the Midlands, north or south of Britain; a number identified individual companies. More information will be found under 'M', 'N' and 'S'. **12.** British military proof marks. These normally consisted of crossed pennants, with 'P' in the lower quadrant and the monarch's initials beneath a crown in the upper quadrant (*see* Royal cyphers). The Royal Navy, however, used plain pennants above 'N' in the bottom quadrant; the Australian (Lithgow) mark had 'L' in the top quadrant and 'P' in the bottom; South Africa employed 'U' and 'P'; while India used a crowned 'GRI' in the top quadrant and 'P' in the bottom. The post-independence Indian mark substituted the four-tiger Asoka for the crowned 'GRI'. The Dominion of Canada also used crossed pennants, but the quadrant lettering was 'P' to the left, 'D' in the top and 'C' to the right; the fourth (bottom) quadrant was blank. **13.** British military unit markings. Only weapons issued for service from army stores were marked in accordance with *Regulations for Army Ordnance Services, Part One*. Magazine rifles and carbines bore the ordnance marks – number of the month and year of issue (e.g. 5/96) – together with the corps marks and consecutive numbers on the butt disc. On older guns with brass butt plates, only army ordnance marks were to be struck into the strap; corps marks did not appear. On guns with iron butt plates, the ordnance marks were to appear in the centre of the butt, 2in from the butt plate, with the corps marks between the two. Webley revolvers customarily bore the ordnance marks, corps marks and consecutive numbers on the 'upper part of the strap of stock'. The marks can identify some of the most famous regiments in the British Army – e.g. '8.03' over 'D.K.O.S.B.' over '128', on a butt disc would signify the 128th rifle retained by the reserve ('D') battalion of the King's Own Scottish Borderers after being issued in August 1903. Among the most desirable would be those marks applied by the premier line regiments of the British Army, including: 'A.& S.H.' for Princess Louise's Argyll & Sutherland Highlanders; 'C.G.' for the Coldstream Guards; 'G.G.' for the Grenadier Guards; 'GOR.' for the Gordon Highlanders; 'I.G.' for the Irish Guards; 'IN.F.' for the Royal Inniskilling Fusiliers; 'L.G.' for the Life Guards; 'R.B.' for The Rifle Brigade (The Prince Consort's Own); 'R.H.' for The Black Watch (Royal Highlanders); 'S.G.'

for the Scots Guards; and 'W.G.' for the Welsh Guards. Yeomanry regiments invariably display the identifier 'Y' above a line separating it from the county abbreviation, such as 'DVN.& CLL.' for Devon & Cornwall, 'LCK.' for Limerick, 'M.U.' for Mid-Ulster, 'STF.' for Staffordshire and 'Y.& D.' for Yorkshire & Durham. The senior (university) division of the Officers Training Corps applied marks, such as 'AYH.' for Aberystwyth and 'OXF.' for Oxford, below the 'O.T.C.' legend; the junior (schools) division displayed marks as diverse as 'HBY.' for Haileybury College and 'UPM.' for Uppingham. **14.** 'British Pioneer [The]'. Found on shotgun cartridges loaded for ★Harrods of London, probably prior to 1939. *See also* 'Pioneer'. **15.** British Smokeless. A shotgun cartridge made in Britain by ★Eley-Kynoch Ltd. **16.** British Tabulating Machine Company Ltd [The], Letchworth, Hertfordshire, England. This ★Monotype Scheme member made a variety of small parts for the ★Bren Gun in 1940–45. These sometimes bore the code 'S 162', although many of the pins were too small to be marked.

Briton – 1. Found, usually as 'The Briton', on shotgun cartridges sold by ★Grant & Lang of London. **2.** Apparently this telescoping-barrel .177-calibre spring-air pistol was British-made. Although the maker has yet to be properly identified, there has been speculation that T.J. ★Harrington & Company was involved. A bulldog trademark is also often present on the gun. *See also* Britannia.

Britte – 1. Théophile Britte (1874–1945), co-founder of Établissements Britte SA (below), patented the so-called ★Superbritte shotgun in 1931. **2.** Établissments Britte SA, Vivegnis-lèz-Liège, Belgium. Renowned for making the Superbritte shotgun, produced in small quantities in the early 1930s, this engineering business was established in 1897 by the brothers Théophile and Lambert Britte. Although small quantities of ★Holland & Holland-type double-barrelled shotguns had been made prior to 1914, the Superbritte (which appeared just as the Great Depression struck the Belgian gunmaking industry) represented the company's last foray into gunmaking. Éts. Britte instead concentrated on precision engineering.

Broadhurst. R. Broadhurst. An ironmongery business trading in Smithford Street, Coventry, Warwickshire, England, Broadhurst also handled sporting guns and ammunition. Shotgun cartridges made prior to 1914 by ★Eley Bros. Ltd have been seen with suitable markings.

Broadwell. Lewis Wells Broadwell, born in 1827 in New Orleans, Louisiana, is best known as a designer of guns and artillery, and for waging a long and unsuccessful campaign of words with Krupp. He was responsible for a 'breech-loading firearm' protected by US Patent 49,583 of 22 August 1865. Assigned to C.M. Clay, this protected a block that slid vertically through the frame as the trigger-guard was rotated laterally. Relying on two rapid-pitch threads, this was, in essence, little more than a two-part adaptation of ideas that had been tried since the early 1700s. Broadwell was also peripatetic, filing submissions from places as diverse as St Petersburg, Russia (1861), and Hietzing bei Wien (Austria, 1870s). Most of these protected improvements in breech-loading ordnance, but US Patent no. 110,338 of 20 December 1870 described a 'Feeder for Repeating Fire-arms' and 172,382 of 18 January 1876 protected a cartridge applicable to small-arms. Broadwell is also remembered for the Broadwell Drum, used with the ★Gatling Gun. He died in 1906.

Broberg. Waldemar Broberg. A US Army colonel, this arms inspector accepted ★Colt M1911A1 pistols during 1941. They were marked 'WB'. *See also* US arms inspectors' marks.

Brock's Explosives Ltd, Hemel Hempstead, Hertfordshire. This well-known English manufacturer of explosives and pyrotechnics has also marketed Bird Scaring Cartridges under its own name. The ammunition was made by ★Eley-Kynoch Ltd.

Broens. A. von Broens Witwe & Co., Zella St Blasii and Zella-Mehlis in Thüringen, Germany. Listed in 1900 as a gun- and weapon-maker. Still trading in 1920, but as a hardware distributor.

Brompetier. Applied to a small Spanish 6.35mm ★Browning-revolver made by ★Retolaza Hermanos of Eibar, probably prior to 1920.

Bronco. A compact pistol of Browning type, made by Echave y Arizmendi of Eibar: (a) 6.35mm, six rounds, hammer fired; (b) 7.65mm, six rounds, hammer fired. Both patterns may be marked 'Model 1918'.

Brong, also found as 'Le Brong'. This tradename was applied to Spanish ★Browning-revolvers made in Eibar by ★Crucelegui Hermanos, probably prior to 1920. Undoubtedly chosen for its similarity to 'Brng.' (a popular abbreviation of 'Browning'), Brong-Grand was a large pattern, chambered for 6mm ★Type Française rimfire, 6.35mm centrefire or 7.65mm centrefire cartridges; Brong-Petit was a small pattern restricted to 6.35mm.

Brooklyn Firearms Company, Brooklyn, New York City. Makers of the five-shot .32 rimfire revolver patented in 1863 by Frank ★Slocum. These had detachable sliding sleeves in each cylinder, which were pushed forward to allow rimfire cartridges to be inserted. Although a slot was cut through the chamber wall to accept the hammer nose, the cylinders were not bored-through and thus escaped the ire of ★Smith & Wesson.

Brooks – 1. Brooks & Son, 28 Russell Street, Birmingham, Warwickshire, England. This gunmaker exhibited 'Four-barrel Revolving Guns' and 'Six-barrel Revolving Pistols' at the Great Exhibition in London in 1851. **2.** Edward Brooks & Son. A gunsmithing business trading from 1 Fenchurch Street, London E.C., in 1853–54. Its marks have been reported on sporting guns, self-cocking ★pepperboxes and cap-lock revolvers. **3.** Henry M. Brooks. This US government inspector accepted ★Colt revolvers in 1902–06, marking them 'HMB'. **4.** John A. Brooks, Jr. A lieutenant-colonel in the US Army, Brooks accepted .45 ★Colt M1911A1 pistols in 1940, marking them with 'JAB'. **5.** P.H.M. Brooks. A US government arms inspector, working in 1909, Brooks accepted ★Colt revolvers marked 'PHMB'. *See also* US arms inspectors' marks for the last three entries. **6.** R. Brooks, Rockport, Massachusetts, USA. Designer of an air pistol protected by US Patent no. 99,754 of 1870. **7.** William F. Brooks, New York City. Promoter of the ★Gibbs breech-loading carbines during the American Civil War.

Broughton. S.H. Broughton. Working in 1899–1912, this arms inspector accepted small-arms marked 'SHB'. *See also* US arms inspectors' marks.

Brow. A tradename applied to Spanish ★Browning-revolvers made in Eibar by ★Ojanguren y Marcaido, probably prior to 1920. It was undoubtedly chosen for its similarity to a popular abbreviation of 'Browning'.

Brown – 1. Albert Arthur Brown. Senior partner in

A.A. *Brown & Sons, and co-patentee of the *Abas Major pistol with his sons Albert and Sidney. *See* British Patent 604,411, sought in January 1946 and accepted on 2 July 1948. **2.** Albert Henry Brown. Son of Albert Arthur Brown (above), and co-patentee with his father and younger brother Sidney of the Abas Major pistol. **3.** Alexander T. Brown, Syracuse, New York. Apparently L.C. *Smith's works superintendent, Brown was granted several US Patents for 'breech-loading firearms' – 261,663 of 25 July 1882 (half-assigned to H.H. Lincoln of Syracuse); 274,435 of 20 March 1883, for a rotary self-compensating locking bolt for shotguns; 291,288 of 1 January 1884 (half-assigned to L.C. Smith); and 367,089 of 26 July 1887. He was also granted three US patents for gun-locks: 234,749 of 23 November 1880; 289,062 of 27 November 1883 for an improved trigger mechanism; and 345,362 of 13 July 1886, for a 'concealed hammer' pattern. US Patent 350,109 of 5 October was obtained jointly with W.L. *Smith to protect a safety mechanism, and 381,109 of 17 April 1888 protected an airgun. Subsequently Brown became better known for the typewriter designs that formed the basis for L.C. Smith's later success. **4.** Charles L. Brown, New York City. The co-patentee with William H. Morris of a 'repeating firearm', protected by US Patent 26,919 of January 1860. The .41-calibre gun had a multi-chamber cylinder communicating with a series of separate throats radiating diagonally from the bore, but only a few examples were made shortly before the American Civil War by *Morris & Brown. **5.** Edward J. Brown & Company. Trading in Rotherham, Yorkshire, England, this gunsmithing and ironmongery business also sold sporting guns and ammunition. Pre-1914 *Kynoch-made shotgun cartridges have been reported with Brown's markings. **6.** John Brown [Sharps]: *see under* 'J'. **7.** Lucius C. Brown. This US government arms inspector marked small-arms accepted in the mid-1870s with 'LCB'. *See also* US arms inspectors' marks. **8.** O.H. Brown, Davenport, Iowa, USA. This inventor was responsible for a gas-powered pistol developed in the 1930s. Limited production of this gun, long and clumsy though it was, was undertaken in 1940–41 until stopped by the American entry into the Second World War. The gun received lavish praise in Leslie Wesley's *Air Rifles & Air Pistols* (1955), but the difficulties of providing solidified carbon-dioxide propellant charges could not be overcome. **9.** Sidney Charles Brown. Son of Albert Arthur Brown (above), and co-patentee with his father and elder brother Albert of the *Abas Major pistol. **10.** William Brown. This Federal government inspector accepted small-arms marked 'WB' in the early part of the American Civil War. *See also* US arms inspectors' marks. **11.** A.A. Brown & Sons Ltd, Abas Works, 4 Sand Street, Birmingham, Warwickshire, England. This metalworking company acquired small quantities of *Star air pistols from Curry & Keen, who had purchased the stock that had once belonged to Edwin *Anson. Ready sales encouraged Brown to produce the Abas Major, designed by A.A., A.H. and S.C. Brown in 1946. The Birmingham directories list Albert Arthur Brown as a gunsmith, trading from 27¹/₂ Whittall Street in 1930–35, and at 35¹/₂ Whittall Street in 1940. By 1945, however, the trading style A.A. Brown & Sons had been adopted (not A. & A. Brown & Sons, as sometimes is claimed), and lasted until the final directory entries were made in 1960. **12.** Brown & Brothers, 80 & 82 Chambers Street, New York City. Identified with the production of rimfire ammunition in the USA in the 1870s, although it seems that some of this may have been imported from Europe. An encircled 'G' *headstamp may betray the source as *Gevelot. Brown also marketed cartridges under the tradename Victor. One of the participants may have been the patentee Charles L. Brown. **13.** Brown Manufacturing Company [The], Newburyport, Massachusetts, USA. Makers of the *Southerner cartridge derringer in 1869–73, succeeding the *Merrimack Arms & Manufacturing Company. **14.** Brown Precision Company, Los Molinos, California, USA. This manufacturer was responsible for the High Country sporting rifle, c. 1975–83. Offered with a fibreglass stock, the rifle had a Model 700 Remington action and an internal magazine; chambering options included .243 Winchester, .25-06, .270 Winchester, 7mm Remington Magnum or .30-06. **15.** Brown Shoe Company, St Louis, Missouri, USA. This footwear manufacturer distributed *Warrior BB Guns as 'premiums' – incentives to encourage young and often gullible sales agents to reach their targets. When the goals were reached, the Buster Brown guns were simply handed over by the shoe company representatives. **16.** Brown Standard Fire Arms Company. This gunmaking business, based in New York, made self-cocking dropping-block rifles with a partially enclosed spurless hammer. Resembling the British enclosed-hammer Henry rifles of the early 1870s, the gun was patented in 1883 by John H. Brown. A few were sold commercially, but the venture seems to have failed by 1886. **17.** Brown & Mannett. A partnership with gunsmithing interests of some type, listed at 26 New City Chambers, London, England, from 1867 until 1874.

Browning – **1.** John M. Browning: *see* panel, pp. 92/93. **2.** Browning Arms Company, St Louis, Missouri, then Ogden, Utah, USA. Browning has offered or made a variety of pistols, sporting guns and rifles, including some built on FN-Mauser bolt actions from 1959 onward. These had a distinctive tang-mounted safety catch, and were offered in *Medallion Grade, *Olympian Grade and *Safari Grade, chambering cartridges ranging from .243 Winchester to .458 Winchester Magnum. Work stopped in 1974. **3.** Browning Automatic Carbine: *see* Carabine Automatique Browning. **4.** Browning Automatic Rifle [often known simply as BAR]: *see* panel, p. 94. **5.** Browning Automatic Sporting Rifle, or BAR. Made by FN Herstal SA from 1967 to date, this gas-operated rifle is locked by rotating seven lugs on the bolt head into the receiver. It is usually credited to Val Browning, son of John. Among its features are a patented hinged floor-plate/detachable box magazine unit. The standard rifle has an open back sight, and extensive chequering on the walnut pistol-grip butt and fore-end. The earliest deluxe examples had scroll engraving on the greyed receiver sides, gold-plated triggers and woodwork chosen for its figuring. Post-1985 guns were known as 'BAR Affût'. Chamberings have ranged from .243 Winchester to .30-06. The Battue (introduced in 1988) had a small folding-leaf back sight let into a quarter rib. Six hundred of the .30-06 Big Game Special Edition were made in 1987–88, with gold-plated triggers and engraved silver-grey receivers. The first BAR Magnums were introduced in 1969 in .300 Winchester Magnum chambering, a .338 Winchester option being added in 1988. **6.** Browning High-Power Semi-Automatic Rifle. This was made by Fabrique Nationale d'Armes de Guerre in accordance with a patent granted to John Browning in October 1900, which was also licensed to Remington. Consequently, the FN rifle was essentially similar to the Remington Model 8 (q.v.). The principal external differences lay in the solid matted rib above the barrel, and in the two-leaf back sight. Only about 4,910 guns were made in 1910–14 and 1921–31, all chambering the .35 Remington cartridge. **7.** Browning machine-gun: *see* panel, pp. 96/97. **8.** Browning pistols: *see* panel, p. 98. **9.** Browning repeating carbine: *see* Carabine à Répétition Browning. **10.** Browning-revolver. A term associated with a short-lived series of revolvers designed to capitalise on the success of the 1900-model Browning semi-automatic pistol introduced in Belgium by *Fabrique Nationale d'Armes de Guerre. The revolvers had their hammers enclosed in flat high-back frames, often overhanging a straight handgrip; many had folding triggers, and radial safety levers on the left side of the frame. The smallest versions often lacked rammers, enabling the frame-front to be shaped much more like a small pistol. The first guns were made in Belgium by Auguste *Francotte et Cie (mark: a crowned 'A.F.'), *Henrion Dassy et Heuschen ('HDH'), J.B. *Rongé fils, Établissements *Lebeaux, *Manufacture Liégeoise d'Armes à Feu (crowned 'ML'), and *Lepage et Cie; production ceased in 1914, although guns were available from wholesalers' stocks for many years. Others were made in Spain, where production started prior to the First World War and probably continued into the early 1920s; participants included the Eibar gunsmiths Francisco *Arizmendi, *Crucelegui Hermanos, *Ojanguren y Marcaido and *Retolaza Hermanos. A few guns were made in Germany by Friedrich *Pickert of Zella St Blasii, and the U.O.S. (q.v.) bears Italian markings. Many guns will be marked 'BROWNING', partly to indicate that they chamber the 6.35mm Browning pistol cartridge (or occasionally the 7.65mm version), but also, no doubt, to capitalise on the value of the designer's name. Spanish guns also often bear names such as *Brompetier, *Brong, *Brow and *Le Brong.

Bruce – 1. Edward W. Bruce. This US government inspector, working in 1875, accepted small-arms marked 'EWB'. *See also* US arms inspectors' marks. **2.** Lucien F. Bruce, Springfield, Massachusetts. Best known as the designer of the Bruce Feed, applied successfully to the *Gatling Gun, this engineer received several US patents for 'Cartridge Feeders for Machine Guns': 247,158 of 14 June 1881, 273,249 of 6 March 1883, 343,532 of 8 June 1886 and 351,960 of 2 November 1886, all assigned to *Colt's Patent Fire Arms Manufacturing Company. Bruce also developed a cartridge-charger for his feeders, US Patent 341,371 of 4 May 1886, and a series of magazines for breech-loading firearms (439,833, 462,298 and 708,311 of 4 November 1890, 3 November 1891 and 2 September 1902 respectively). A 'breech-loading magazine rifle', protected by US Patent 432,507 of 22 July 1890, was entered unsuccessfully in the trials that led to the adoption of the *Krag-Jørgensen in the USA.

Bruff, Brother & Seaver, New York City. These merchants sold 225 *Freeman-made *Joslyn revolvers to the Federal authorities in the winter of 1861.

Brühl. Wilhelm Brühl u. Co., Suhl in Thüringen. A small-scale gunmaking business (*Büchsenmacherei*), active in Germany prior to 1945.

Bruie. Henry Bruie. This English gunmaker, sometimes listed as either Bruce or Brucie, had a workshop at 13 Clayton Street, Caledonian Road, London, in 1855.

Brundett. W.H. Brundett. This US government inspector, working in 1898–1900, accepted Colt revolvers and other small-arms marked 'WHB'. *See also* US arms inspectors' marks.

Brun-Latrige, cours Fauriel 7, Saint-Étienne, France. Listed in 1892 as a gunmaker.

Brünn. Waffenwerk Brünn AG: *see* Československá Zbrojovka.

Bruno. A.E. Bruno. Co-designer with Walter *Scott of a rifle sight, protected by British Patent 3079/73 of 1873.

Brunon et Cie, place Mi-Carême 1, Saint-Étienne, France. Working as early as 1838 – as Brunon fils – making *Lefaucheux-style pinfire breech-loaders. Listed in 1879 as a distributor of, and agent for, arms and ammunition.

Brutus. A *Suicide Special revolver made in the USA by the *Hood Firearms Company of Norwich, Connecticut, in the late nineteenth century.

'BRW'. *See* B.R. *Whitcomb.

Bryce. James Bryce. A gunmaker working in Edinburgh, Scotland, from 1851 until 1874.

'BS' – 1. On German sporting guns: *see* Bergstutzen. **2.** On US military firearms: *see* Benjamin *Syrett.

BSA – 1. A trademark associated with the *Birmingham Small Arms Company Ltd and its successors. It was usually accompanied by a 'Piled Arms' mark of three stacked *Martini-Henry rifles, which was registered by the company in 1881. It will also be found in the headstamps of belted-case sporting rifle and handgun cartridges developed by BSA Guns Ltd in the 1920s, and also encountered on shotgun ammunition made for BSA by *Eley-Kynoch Ltd. **2.** BSA Break Action. This was associated with the company's first barrel-cocking air rifle, about 15,000 being made in 1932–39, in .177 and .22. **3.** B.S.A. Co., BSA Co. Used by the *Birmingham Small Arms Company Ltd – in various guises – in 1861–73 and 1897–1919. **4.** BSA Guns Ltd, Armoury Road, Small Heath, Birmingham, Warwickshire, England. The formation of this company from what had been Birmingham Small Arms Company Ltd coincided with a slump in the munitions business. Improved forms of the *Jeffries Pattern underlever-cocking airguns were made, production totalling about 109,000 in 1919–40 together with 15,000 simpler break-barrel guns (1932–39); experiments with *Thompson submachine-guns and automatic rifles proved to be fruitless. In the 1930s, however, BSA became a major participant in the production of the *Browning aircraft machine-gun while continuing to fulfil small orders for the .303 Rifle No. 1 (*Lee-Enfield). Production of airguns was suspended in 1940 to allow the factory facilities to concentrate on war work, which included reconditioning 1,580 .303 *Hotchkiss Mk I and Mk I* machine-guns pressed into emergency service as a result of the huge losses of arms and equipment at Dunkirk. No. 1 Mk III *Lee-Enfield rifles were made in Small Heath until 1943; about 1.5 million No. 4-type rifles were made between 1941 and 1945 in Small Heath and Studley Road, Redditch, as well as in a newly-built

JOHN M. BROWNING

Browning (1)

Son of the gunsmith Jonathan Browning (1805–79), John Moses Browning was born in Ogden, Utah, on 21 January 1855. He made his first gun in 1868, from parts discarded by his father, and (with his half-brother, Mathew S. Browning) succeeded to his father's business upon the latter's death. A Browning Brothers Hardware Company had been founded in 1875, the first of several retail outlets operating in Utah State.

John Browning was destined to become one of the greatest firearms inventors of all time, developing guns that ranged from single-shot rimfires to highly-efficient machine-guns.

Some of Browning's best-known designs (the BAR, his machine-guns and handguns) are listed separately, but he was an exceptionally prolific patentee in an era when patents tended to be all-embracing rather than split into separate applications. There are far too many patents to list individually (Robert E. Gardner's *Small Arms Makers* lists some), and attention is drawn here only to some of the best known. The total of US Patents alone has been said to have exceeded 950, although Ned

Schwing, in his magisterial *The Browning Superposed: John M. Browning's Last Legacy*, puts the total at a mere 128. However, it is not clear whether this includes the many patents that were granted outside the USA.

US Patent no. 220,271 was granted on 7 October 1879 to protect what became the single-shot *Winchester M1885 dropping-block rifle; 306,577 of 14 October 1884, assigned to the Winchester Repeating Arms Company, protected the 1884-pattern lever-action rifle. Patent 336,287 of 16 February 1886, another of the many assigned to Winchester, protected the M1887 lever-action shotgun; 441,390 (granted in the USA on 25 November 1890) depicted the M1893 Winchester pump-action shotgun, whereas no. 499,005 of 6 June 1893 and 524,702 of 21 August 1894 protected the Winchester M1892 and M1894 lever-action rifles respectively. Protection for a .22 rimfire single-shot bolt-action junior rifle (which became the Winchester M1900) was conferred by 632,094 of 29 August 1900.

Browning's sporting guns were exceptionally successful, but he is better known for his automatic weapons. The first relevant patent (US 471,782) dating from 29 March 1892 and protecting a gas-operated machine-gun, was the precursor of a

number that led ultimately to US Patents 544,657–544,659 of 20 August 1895: the M1895 or 'Potato Digger' (q.v.), made in quantity by *Colt's Patent Fire Arms Manufacturing Company and, ultimately, by *Marlin during the First World War.

Browning is also renowned for his semi-automatic pistols, the first patents (580,923–580,926) being granted in the USA on 20 April 1897. These protected a variety of designs, including a large-calibre military-type gun locked by tilting the barrel down at the breech (580,924) and a small-calibre *blowback (580,926). The former was soon exploited by *Colt's Patent Fire Arms Manufacturing Company, but the blowback was developed in Belgium by *Fabrique Nationale d'Armes de Guerre after Colt's management had failed to appreciate its commercial potential.

The semi-experimental 1899 pistol became the FN-Browning Mle 1900, the first of a series that incorporated the models of 1903 (9mm Browning), 1906 (6.35mm Auto, the first successful pocket semi-automatic) and 1910 (7.65mm Auto or 9mm Short) – not to mention a legion of Spanish-made 'Eibar' copies. Colt's locked-breech guns culminated in the US Army .45 M1911, or *Government Model, which embodied a perfected

---

factory in Shirley; and 81,330 No. 5 Mk 1 Jungle Carbines were made in Shirley in 1945–46. Output of automatic weapons included 468,100 .303 *Browning guns Mk I, Mk II and Mk II*, made in the Small Heath factory from 1937 until 1942, when air-raid damage caused much of the work to be dispersed to sub-contractors (including *Vickers-Armstrongs Ltd). More than 404,000 Mk II *Sten submachine-guns were made in the Tyseley factory from 1941 onward. The 7.92mm *Besa Guns Mk I, Mk II, Mk III and Mk III* were made in Redditch, and, after 1941, in supplementary factories in Leicester; production between 1939 and 1945, according to BSA figures, amounted to more than 59,300. There were also 3,200 15mm Besa Guns (1938–43). BSA Guns was also the sole manufacturer of the .55 Boys Mk I and Mk I* anti-tank rifles – 68,850 being made in 1936–43, initially at Small Heath, then dispersed to factories in Mansfield. Butts, bipods, cocking handles, magazines and other parts were made for the *Bren Gun during the Second World War, together with tripod mounts. BSA Guns made the ill-starred .303 *Besal machine-gun and the experimental 9mm *Veselý submachine-guns, eight of the latter being delivered in September 1944. BSA Guns Ltd was allotted a variety of manufacturing codes: Small

Heath used 'M 47A'; Redditch, 'M 47B'; Shirley, 'M 47C'; Leicester, 'M615'; and Mansfield, 'M 616'. By the end of the Second World War, more than sixty BSA-run factories were employing nearly 28,000 people. Commercial operations were rebuilt during the post-war period thanks to the introduction of airguns such as the Airsporter, Cadet, Cadet Major and Club (qq.v.), together with some efficient sporting guns built around a modified *Mauser bolt action and refinements of the pre-war Martini-action .22 target rifles. Although new designs continued to appear, including the *Meteor air rifle and some improved sporting firearms, the fortunes of BSA Guns Ltd declined until, in 1973, the remaining assets were acquired by Manganese Bronze Holdings. This enabled production to continue until, finally, in the 1980s, the original BSA Guns Ltd was liquidated. The assets were sold to BSA Guns (1984) Ltd, the sporting-rifle machinery was sold to Pakistan, and production of airguns continued in a new Armoury Road factory on a much smaller scale. In the early 1990s, what remained of BSA was acquired by the group controlling *El Gamo. Individual guns are considered separately, or under the names of their patentees: Robert P. *Cranston, Harold C. *Jones, Claude A. *Perry, Victor J. *Stohanzl, Josef

barrel lock protected by US Patent 984,519 of 14 February 1911.

Among the auto-loading sporting guns introduced prior to the First World War were a shotgun, protected by US Patent 659,507 of 9 October 1900, and a rifle (659,786 of 16 October 1900). The latter provided the basis for a *Carabine Automatique*, produced by Fabrique Nationale, and the Model 8, made by ★Remington Arms–UMC.

The First World War saw the introduction of both the M1917 Browning machine-gun and the Browning Automatic Rifle (BAR). The former was protected by a series of patents ranging from 768,934 of 23 June 1901 ('Recoil-operated Machine Gun') to 1,293,021 of 4 February 1919; the latter was protected by US 1,293,022. Another well-known product of this era was the Colt ★Woodsman .22 rimfire pistol, the subject of US Patent 1,276,716 of 27 August 1918.

Browning continued to refine his guns after the First World War, patenting a 37mm cannon in February 1925 (US Patents 1,525,065–1,525,067). The first protection for the efficient double-barrelled over/under, or Superposed, shotgun followed in March 1926 (1,578,638/9).

Unfortunately, the inventor suffered a heart attack on a visit to Fabrique Nationale and died in Herstal on 26 November 1926. Two of his best-known designs, the ★High Power pistol and the .50-calibre machine-gun, were patented posthumously on 22 February and 10 May 1927 respectively (US Patents 1,618,510 and 1,628,226).

There is no doubting John M. Browning's claims to fame. It may be argued that some of his ideas were perfected by others (e.g. Fabrique Nationale's Bureau d'Études, or Colt's technicians in Hartford), but no one has ever matched the diversity of Browning's designs.

It is strange that, with the exception of *John M. Browning,*

This prototype of the FN-Browning High Power pistol, John Browning's last handgun design, dated from late 1924. It has a unique permanently-attached folding butt.

American Gunmaker (1964), by John Browning and Curt Gentry, no comprehensive biography of Browning exists. Books, such as Ned Schwing's study of the Superposed shotgun, have been devoted to individual guns, but as yet there is no central source of information.

See also Colt and Fabrique Nationale d'Armes de Guerre.

★Veselý and Roger D. ★Wackrow. **5.** BSA Improved Model. Produced only in 1905–07, this was the first BSA made version of the underlever-cocking air rifle designed by Lincoln ★Jeffries. The Model B differs from its predecessor principally in the design of the loading tap and the tap-retainer plate. The Improved Model D of 1907 had the perfected loading tap, and generally bore the full patent number instead of just 'P.PAT.' Both the Improved Models were known by the generic term 'Standard Pattern'. **6.** BSA Juvenile Pattern or Junior Pattern. A diminutive version of the BSA Standard Pattern air rifle, introduced in 1909, but made only until the beginning of the First World War in .177. **7.** BSA Light Pattern. A short-barrel .177-calibre derivation of the BSA Standard Pattern air rifle, introduced in 1907 and made (as the No. 1 Light Model) until 1939. **8.** 'B.S.A. Ltd', 'BSA Ltd'. Marks used by BSA Guns Ltd from 1919 onward, usually accompanied by the ★Piled Arms trademark. **9.** BSA Military Model. Patented by Edwin ★Parsons and Leslie Bown ★Taylor of ★Westley Richards in 1906, this airgun duplicated the configuration of either the Territorial Long Lee-Enfield or the SMLE. It combined the action of the BSA Standard Pattern with a dummy bolt-handle, a military-style butt and a short wooden fore-end. The guns are rarely encountered in Britain, as most seem to have been sent to overseas colonies. **10.** B.S.A. & M. Co. Used by the ★Birmingham Small Arms & Munitions Company from 1873 until 1897, when the company reverted to its original name. **11.** BSA Standard Pattern. This generic term covers the original BSA derivatives of the Lincoln ★Jeffries air rifle, including the ★Improved Models B and D. The series contained guns in .177, .22 and .25 calibre (No. 1, No. 2 and No. 3 Bore respectively), and with a variety of detail differences explained in great detail in John Knibbs' book, *The Lincoln Jeffries Pattern BSAs.* The Standard Pattern was replaced after 1919 by the .177-calibre No. 1 or Club Model and the .22-calibre No. 2. **12.** BSA submachine-guns. These were tested in Britain in 1945–46, but were rejected as being needlessly complicated and expensive to make.

'BSF'. A mark associated with the products of ★Bayerische Sportwaffenfabrik of Erlangen. *See also* Bavaria and Wischo.

'BSW'. *See* Berlin-Suhler Werke.

Buccaneer. A barrel-cocking .177- or .22-calibre spring-air rifle, based on the ★Scorpion pistol, introduced by BSA Guns Ltd in 1979. It was easily distinguishable by its synthetic thumb-hole stock.

BROWNING AUTOMATIC RIFLE (BAR)

Browning (4)

Designed by John M. *Browning, a prototype of this squad automatic weapon was successfully demonstrated to the US Army Machine Gun Board in February 1917, and adopted as the 'Browning Machine Rifle, Caliber .30, Model of 1918'. Production was entrusted to *Colt's Patent Fire Arms Manufacturing Company, initially with technical assistance supplied by the *Winchester Repeating Arms Company; when work finished in 1919, more than 100,000 rifles had been made by Colt, Winchester, Marlin-Rockwell and their sub-contractors.

Developed by the Cavalry Board on the basis of combat experience gained in the First World War, the M1922 had a finned barrel and an optional tripod mount, allowing a greater volume fire of fire to be sustained before overheating. Only a few hundred guns were made before the M1918A1 was substituted. This was an adaptation of the M1918 with an improved gas system, a bipod and a shoulder-rest. Converted from A1 Brownings, the M1918A2 had a better bipod, a monopod beneath the butt and an adjustable buffer in the action to change the rate of fire. Colt also sold guns commercially as the Automatic Machine Rifle or Monitor.

In addition to the guns made by Colt, many others were made in Europe by *Fabrique Nationale d'Armes de Guerre. FN accepted a 10,000-gun contract placed by Poland in December 1927, then made alterations to the basic design by incorporating a rate-reducer (1930) and adding a readily-detachable barrel (1931). The work was undertaken by the company's Bureau d'Études, headed by Dieudonné *Saive.

US Army Lieutenant Val Browning, son of John M., demonstrates his father's automatic rifle, 1918. The apparent ease with which he has shouldered the gun disguises the fact that it weighs more than 16lb (7.25kg).

'Buccleuch' [The]. Named after a Selkirkshire (Scotland) place-name, and also possibly to honour the Duke of Buccleuch, this mark reportedly was found on a shotgun cartridge made by *Eley-Kynoch for George *Richardson of Dumfries.

Büchel – 1. Albin Büchel, Zella-Mehlis in Thüringen, Germany. Listed in 1939 as a master gunsmith. 2. Cuno Büchel: *see* Ernst Friedrich Büchel. 3. Ernst Friedrich Büchel, Mehlis and Zella-Mehlis in Thüringen, Germany. This gunmaking business was founded some time prior to 1887, and was still listed as a gunmaker in the *Deutsches Reichs-Adressbuch* for 1900–30 as a gunmaker, trading by 1930 as Ernst Friedr. Büchel GmbH. The business is best known for a series of target rifles and Free Pistols made under the *Luna brandname. 4. Ernst & Karl Büchel, Zella-Mehlis in Thüringen, Germany. Listed in 1930 as a master gunsmithy.

Büchner. O. & A. Büchner, Zella-Mehlis in Thüringen, Germany. Listed in 1920 as a weapon-maker.

Büchsflinten. A gun with one smooth and one rifled barrel, side by side. *See* Combination weapons.

Buckeye. A *Suicide Special revolver made in the USA by the *Hopkins & Allen Arms Company of Norwich, Connecticut, in the late nineteenth century.

Buckham. George T. Buckham. An employee of *Vickers, Sons & Maxim, and co-recipient – usually with A.T. *Dawson – of patent-protection for improvements in the *Maxim and Vickers-Maxim machine-guns.

Buckhorn. *See* Sights.

Buck Jones Special. This sixty-shot pump-action BB Gun was made by *Daisy between 1934 and 1941, complete with a compass and a sundial let into the left side of the butt. It was adapted from the No. 105 Daisy Junior Pump Gun and the Sears *Ranger, and was named after a popular film-star cowboy; also occasionally known as the No. 107.

Buckland. Cyrus E. Buckland, Springfield, Massachusetts. A gunmaker/engineer, factory superintendent of *Smith & Wesson, Buckland was involved in the formation of both *Smith, Hall & Buckland and the *Wesson Firearms Company.

Buckley-Hart Company. This short-lived successor to the *Hart Manufacturing Company and *Hart & Company may have continued to sell the *Matchless BB Guns. Trading seems to have been confined to 1903–04.

Buckmaster & Wood. Reportedly a gunsmithing and sporting-goods business trading in Wokingham, Berkshire, England.

Buckminster. A. Buckminster. This government inspector marked carbines with 'AB' in the years immediately prior to the American Civil War. *See also* US arms inspectors' marks.

Buco. This 'telescope' pistol consists of a short, large-diameter sheet-metal tube containing a coil spring, the firing mechanism and a small-diameter barrel. The knurled cap is rotated until two orange or red marks align, then removed to gain access to the breech. A special 10.6mm cartridge is inserted into the chamber, the barrel pulled forward until the sear engages, and the end-cap is replaced. The Buco can be fired merely by pressing the button protruding through the casing, which pivots the sear to release the barrel. The barrel flies backward under the influence of the spring, until the primer of the cartridge is slammed against a pin fixed on the inside of the end cap. The telescope guns, marked 'BUCO/D.R.G.M.', are thought to have been made by Richard Bornmüller & Co. of Suhl. The special ammunition has not yet been conclusively identified, but was probably loaded with a gas charge; lightweight construction suggests that the Buco could not have withstood the pressures developed by ball cartridges.

Budischowsky. Edgar Budischowsky. A German handgun designer. *See* Korriphila-Präzisionsmechanik GmbH.

Bufalo – **1.** A pocket pistol made by Gregorio *Bolumburu, Eibar: (a) 6.35mm, six rounds, hammer fired; (b) 7.65mm, seven rounds, striker fired. Based on the 1910-type *FN-Browning. **2.** A range of blowback semi-automatic pistols made by *Gabilondo y Cia of Elgoeibar for Armeria *Beristain y Cia of Barcelona prior to 1925. The smallest gun is a 6.35mm Auto variant of the FN-Browning of 1906, embodying a grip safety patented by Beristain c. 1919. The slides usually bear the patent numbers 62,004 and 67,577 – one referring to the safety mechanism and the other, apparently, to the registry of the tradename. The larger pistols, chambered for the 7.65mm Auto or 9mm Short cartridges, were based on the 1910-pattern FN-Browning and had the return spring concentric with the barrel. *See also* Danton.

Buffalo, Buffalo... – **1.** This bolt-action rifle, patented in France in 1897 by Pierre Blachon of *Manufacture Française d'Armes et Cycles, combined a bolt action with a travelling-block. A reciprocating breech-piece or *Culasse mobile* embodied a cylindrical collar containing the locking recesses; the locking lugs were formed in the periphery of the barrel. The mechanism proved to be simple, sturdy and durable, although the position of the extractor-operating extension prevented magazines from being used. Shotguns have been made in 12- and 14-bore, and rifles were still being made in the 1970s. Deluxe versions of all the sub-variants will be found with scalloped-edge woodwork and fluted or octagonal barrels. **2.** Buffalo Bill. A *Suicide Special revolver made in the USA by *Johnson, Bye & Company and/or *Iver Johnson of Worcester and Fitchburg, Massachusetts, in the late nineteenth century. **3.** Buffalo Bill or Buffalo Bill Model. A variant of the *Daisy M1894 Spittin' Image lever-action BB Gun, modelled on the *Winchester cartridge rifle of the same numerical designation. It displays a facsimile signature of William F. 'Buffalo Bill' *Cody on the receiver, a medallion let into the butt and a saddle ring on the barrel band. The first guns were made in 1969. **4.** Buffalo-Carabine. Made by *Manufacture Française d'Armes et Cycles and Manufrance SA, Saint-Étienne, c. 1900–77, this metre-long gun weighed a mere 2kg. Often fitted with a smooth-bore barrel, suited equally to ball or shot cartridges, it had a two-piece stock with a straight butt wrist. **5.** Buffalo-Champion. About 1.2m long and weighing 5.5kg, this gun had an adjustable trigger and micro-adjustable sights. The butt plate was customarily spurred, and a spherical palm-rest was fitted beneath the receiver ahead of the trigger. Champion rifles could be obtained in virtually any .22 chambering from Extra Short to Long Rifle. **6.** Buffalo-Concours. This target rifle had a heavy barrel, a pistol-grip butt with a cheek piece, a spurred butt plate and an adjustable tangent-leaf back sight. **7.** Buffalo-Eurêka. This usually combined a 9mm smooth-bore and a rifled 6mm rimfire pattern within a 'barrel' with a flattened oval cross-section. The guns measured about 1m long overall and weighed 2.4kg empty. Their sights were fixed. **8.** Buffalo-Mitraille, or Canadière Buffalo-Mitraille. This .22 (5.5mm) rimfire rifle, made by Manufacture Française d'Armes et Cycles, had three bores within a single large-diameter barrel. The cartridges were fired simultaneously to give a volley! The three-leaf back sight was used in conjunction with a bead on a band around the muzzle. **9.** Buffalo Newton Rifle Company, Buffalo, New York State, USA. *See* Newton. **10.** Buffalo-Pistolet, or Buffalo-Pistolet Stand. The handgun version of the basic action had a saw-handle grip, a spurred trigger guard and a tangent back sight. Offered only in .22 Long Rifle or 6mm *Type Française rimfire chamberings, the pistols weighed 1.3kg and were 42cm long. Engraving could be applied to order. **11.** Buffalo Rifle. Made by *Remington from 1874 until c. 1890, this was chambered for cartridges ranging from .40-50 Sharps to .50-70. Open Rocky Mountain sights were popular, but some guns had a sophisticated vernier sight mounted on the receiver tang behind the hammer. *See also* Remington rifles, rolling-block action. **12.** Buffalo-Scolaire (or Junior). A junior cadet rifle, offered by *Manufrance only in .22 Long Rifle and 6mm rimfire chamberings, this had a fore-end that extended almost to the muzzle. A nose-cap and an intermediate barrel band were fitted, and a grasping groove was cut in the fore-end beneath the adjustable back sight. **13.** Buffalo-Slave. Offered as the Modèle A (8mm rimmed French Mle 92 revolver cartridges) or Modèle B (.32-20 WCF). These

BROWNING MACHINE-GUN

Browning (7)

Adopted by the US Army after a sensational demonstration, the Model 1917 recoil-operated water-cooled gun was created by John M. *Browning on the basis of patents dating back to 1901. The Browning was much simpler than the *Vickers and *Hotchkiss equivalents, and a 15,000-gun contract was passed immediately to the *Remington Arms Company, while *Colt prepared the master drawings. By November 1918, more than 40,000 guns had been made by Colt, Remington and the *New England Westinghouse Company. When work ceased in 1919, production totalled 68,839. Combat experience had shown that there was a weakness in the bottom of the receiver, and a reinforcing plate was added in the 1920s.

The M1917A1 (1936) was an improved M1917, earlier guns being upgraded appropriately. The receiver was stronger, the feed mechanism was improved and the sights were changed. M1917A1 production continued throughout the Second World War, a steel water jacket replacing the original bronze version in 1942. The air-cooled M1918 Browning aircraft machine-gun, an unsuccessful transformation of the water-cooled M1917 ground gun, failed to reach service during the First World War.

Arriving too late to serve in the First World War, the M1918A1 aircraft gun had changes in the trigger and the mounting system compared with the M1917, but soon was replaced by the purpose-built M1919 aircraft gun. A variant developed for use in the Mark VIII battle-tank had a short barrel, a slotted barrel casing, an optical sight and a ball mount. Most M1919 tank guns were converted from water-cooled M1917 Brownings, but subsequently were altered to M1919A4 standards.

Limitations placed on funding persuaded the authorities to permit *Colt's Patent Fire Arms Manufacturing Company to continue development of the Browning on a commercial basis from 1922 onward. The first result was the adoption of the .30 Aircraft Machine Gun, M2 (1931), made in large numbers, but ultimately more popular in Britain than in US Army Air Corps service, where the .50-calibre version was preferred. The air-cooled M1919A1 (1931) was the first purpose-built ground gun since the M1917, with a front sight mounted on the trunnion block, a new tubular back sight and the removal of the ball mount. It was superseded by the M1919A2, an adaptation for vehicle or dismounted use with the front sight on the barrel casing, but virtually all M1919A2 guns had been altered to A4 standards by 1941. The M1919A3 (or E3) was a trial gun, similar to the M1919A2, but with the front sight on the trunnion block. The perfected M1919A4 had a short barrel, reducing the cyclic rate, but improving reliability.

The .50-calibre Browning owed its origins to the unexpected appearance of the 13mm German Mauser anti-tank rifle or *T-Gewehr. *Frankford Arsenal produced a cartridge simply by scaling-up the .30-06 pattern, but this was too powerful for an experimental enlargement of the M1917 to handle until a hydraulic buffer had been developed. Lack of funds prevented the perfected water-cooled .50 M1921 being acquired until 1925. The M1921A1 (1930) had a compound charging handle, which was eventually fitted to virtually all original 1921-type guns.

An M2 ground gun (1931) had a water jacket extending past the muzzle to cure the burn-out tendency of the M1921A1, but most were converted to air-cooled form during the Second World War. The .50 M1921 aircraft gun, which fed belts only from the left, was replaced by the convertible-feed M1923 and, in 1933, by the 'Caliber .50 Browning Machine Gun, Heavy Barrel, M2'. Barrel length was increased from 36in to 45in in 1938, slowing the cyclic rate and improving accuracy; older guns were modified when they were returned for repair. The .50 Browning was very successful, nearly 1.5 million .50 M2 aircraft guns being made by 1945. The original slotted barrel casings gave way during the Second World War to simple circular holes.

Mounts included the Tripods M1921 and M2; the Anti-aircraft Tripods M2, M3 and M43 (or navy Mk 21); the Elevator, Cradle M1; and the Anti-aircraft Mount M63 in addition to vehicle mounts. The M3 machine-gun (1944) was superficially similar to the M2, but changes made internally raised its cyclic rate from 800 to 1,200 rounds per minute. The newest guns of this type have Stellite barrel liners to increase bore life.

With the abandonment of the *Auto-Ordnance T10 machine-gun, efforts concentrated on lightened M1919A4 projects, but the decrease

---

guns had half-length fore-ends with grasping grooves and a three-leaf *Express-pattern back sight. They were 1.06m overall and weighed about 2.6kg. **14.** Buffalo-Sport. This half-stocked *Manufrance gun chambered .22 cartridges ranging from Extra Short to Long Rifle interchangeably. The back sight was usually a spring-leaf elevated by a slider. **15.** Buffalo-Stand. Distinguished by chequering on the woodwork, a crescent-shape butt plate, and an adjustable tangent-leaf back sight, this target rifle was offered by *Manufrance only in .22 rimfire chamberings ranging from Extra Short to Long Rifle. **16.** Buffalo-Super-Champion. The finest of the *Manufrance Buffalo range, this target rifle chambered .22 rimfire cartridges from .22 Short to the No. 7 or Extra Long pattern

favoured in Switzerland. Most examples have a double trigger mechanism with a setting lever, a separate palm-rest beneath the receiver, and an aperture sight attached to the left side of the receiver.

Bufferne. *See* Cannonier-Bufferne.

Buffington sight. Designed c. 1900 by Brigadier General A.R. Buffington (US Chief of Ordnance by 1910), this was fitted to some *Krag-Jørgensen rifles.

Bugbee – 1. Samuel F. Bugbee. A government inspector, working in 1900–10, Bugbee accepted small-arms marked 'SFB'. Probably the son of Samuel T. Bugbee (following). **2.** Samuel T. Bugbee. This inspector, working in 1861, accepted *Starr cap-lock revolvers for the Federal Army. They were marked 'STB'. He was proba-

in weight was matched by a reduction in strength. The .30 M1919A6 Browning – the M1919A5 was a tank gun derived from the M1919A4 – of 1943 had a shoulder stock and a bipod at the muzzle. Later examples had tripod adaptors, rotary carrying handles and synthetic furniture.

Many other countries used the Browning, particularly in its aircraft and vehicle applications. Indeed, guns of this general pattern were made in quantity in Belgium, Britain and Japan. The British Army was still

using .30 M1919A4 Brownings in the 1980s. The L3A3 variant was mounted in the Saladin and Saracen armoured cars, while the L3A4 was a tripod-mounted ground gun. The British also purchased small quantities of the .50 M2 HB Browning in the 1970s, as 'Guns, Machine, Browning, 12.7mm L1A1', placing them in store; 24 were sent to the Falklands in 1982 where, together with US M63 anti-aircraft mounts, they were used for local defence.

See also Colt machine-gun, 'Potato Digger'..

This .50-calibre Browning M2 HB, fitted with a Rank Pullin Controls SS86 crew-served weapon sight, shows the short open-sight radius, how the trigger pivots between the spade grips, and the buffer that protrudes from the back plate.

---

bly the father of Samuel F. Bugbee (above). *See also* US arms inspectors' marks.

Bügelspanner. A German-language term applied to airguns, generally taking *Gallery Gun form, which are cocked by pulling the trigger guard, combined with a lever, downward around a pivot in the butt-toe (cf.*Kurbelspanner). Popular in central Europe prior to 1914, they were still being made in small numbers in 1939, and one pattern was still available in the 1950s under the *Falke brandname.

Buglers, Ltd. The marks of this sporting-goods retailer trading in Ashford, Kent, have been reported on shotgun cartridges.

Bugnand, rue de Paris-Notre-Dame 10, Saint-

Étienne, France. Listed in 1892 as a distributor of, and agent for, arms and ammunition.

Bugnant fils, rue Villeboeuf 3, Saint-Étienne, France. Listed in 1879 as a maker of gun parts and accessories.

Buisson, rue Gambetta 21, Saint-Étienne, France. Listed in 1892 as a distributor of, and agent for, arms and ammunition.

Bul Dog. Encountered on compact six-shot double-action .320 and .380 revolvers, based on the Webley *Bulldog, but customarily made in Belgium prior to 1914. Most have rounded or bird's-head butts, lanyard rings being optional. Some bear either the crowned 'R' or the name of J.B. *Rongé fils.

Bulfighter. *See* Bull Fighter.

BROWNING PISTOLS

Browning (8)

The first handgun, with a top-mounted gas-operated flap-lock, was demonstrated to representatives of *Colt's Patent Fire Arms Manufacturing Company in the summer of 1895. The most important series of patents, however, was granted on 20 April 1897: US no. 580,923 protected the *gas-operated flap-lock gun; 580,924 protected a *recoil-operated gun with its barrel depressed by a double-link mechanism; 580,925 protected a recoil-operated gun with a rotating-barrel lock; and 580,926 protected the first *blowback design.

The locked-breech patents were licensed to Colt's Patent Fire Arms Manufacturing Company, although the first guns to be exploited in quantity were blowbacks protected by US Patent no. 621,747 of 21 March 1899, and made in Belgium by *Fabrique Nationale d'Armes de Guerre. Substantial quantities of a pre-production series of 7.65mm guns, now customarily known as the Mle 1899, were followed by the hugely successful Mle 1900. Production was rapid: the 100,000th gun was assembled on 4 August 1904.

Adopted by the Belgian Army and extremely popular commercially, the Mle 1900 gave way to the 9mm Mle 1903, with the barrel-return spring concentric with the barrel, then the 6.35mm M1906 pocket pistol that effectively laid the basis for the Spanish pistol-making industry in Eibar. Mle 1903 pistols

sold in quantity in Paraguay, Russia and Turkey, and were made in Sweden by *Husqvarna as the M/07. The introduction of the streamlined Mle 1910 pocket pistol, available in 7.65mm and 9mm Short, ensured that FN-Browning handgun sales reached a million on 31 January 1914.

Work began again in the early 1920s, with the advent of the Mle 10/22, developed for the army of the Kingdom of Croats, Serbs and Slovenes (Yugoslavia); popular also in the Netherlands, the Mle 10/22 was really little more than a long-barrelled Mle 1910. The standard slide was extended by means of a light sheet-steel shroud, and the grip was elongated to hold a large-capacity magazine.

The first of the recoil-operated Colt-Brownings appeared in 1900, being made in sporting and military guise. Although cumbersome, the .38 Model 1900 soon attracted the attention of the US Army and the US Navy alike, and small quantities were purchased for trials. Links at the muzzle and the breech pivoted the barrel downward as it recoiled, keeping its axis parallel to its locked position. Subject of additional patents granted on 9 September 1902 (708,794) and 19 December 1905 (808,003), protecting the slide hold-open stop and changes to the trigger system respectively, the .38 Model 1902 and .45 Model 1905 were essentially similar, but refined and more compact.

The Model 1909, developed to satisfy the US Army, had an improved single-link depressor system – John Browning's US Patent

984,519 of 14 February 1911 – that simply tipped the barrel downward at the breech to disengage circumferential locking lugs from the inside of the slide. Once a few alterations had been made to the M1909, it was adopted by the US Army as the 'Pistol, Semi-Automatic, Colt, Caliber .45, Model of 1911' – better known as the *Government Model. Markings on the slide acknowledged additional patents granted on 14 February 1911 and 19 August 1913. Most guns were made by Colt's Patent Fire Arms Manufacturing Company, but some were made in *Springfield Armory prior to the First World War. The principal contractors active in 1917–18 were Colt and the *Remington Arms–UMC Company; several other participants were recruited, but only the *North American Arms Company ever assembled pistols (and then only about a hundred in 1919).

An improved US service pistol, the M1911A1, followed in the early 1920s and laid the groundwork for innumerable variations on the same theme. Guns of this type were also made by a variety of contractors during the Second World War, including the *Ithaca Gun Company, *Remington-Rand, the *Singer Manufacturing Company and the *Union Switch & Signal Company.

The principle was copied by, among others, Fedor *Tokarev in the USSR; Charles Petter in Switzerland; and Wilniewczyc and Skryzpinski in Poland (see VIS). Others adapted US Patent 1,618,510, granted posthumously to John Browning in February 1927 – although sought in June 1923 – which became the Fabrique Nationale GP-35 or *High Power pistol. *See also* Glock, HAFDASA, Heckler & Koch, John *Inglis, Llama-Gabilondo, SACM, SIG, Star and Walther.

The perfected FN-Browning High Power pistol, also known as the GP-35, was simpler than the prototypes. This highly decorative Renaissance version has adjustable sports-type sights.

Bulkley. William H. Bulkley. This US Federal government inspector, working in 1862, accepted small-arms marked 'WHB'. *See also* US arms inspectors' marks.

Bull, *see also* John Bull – **1.** Freeman R. Bull. A civilian employee of the US National Armory, *Springfield, Bull was listed as a 'toolmaker' in 1863 and as an 'inspector for experimental arms' in 1865. His 'FRB' identifier will be found on *Laidley-Emery and other firearms, and he has also been credited with the adjustable sights fitted to the *Springfield-Allin Marksman's Rifle. Freeman Bull retired from service in 1899. *See also* US arms inspectors' marks. **2.** John Bull. A gunmaker trading in the High Street, Bedford, Bedfordshire, England, from 1846 until succeeded in 1868 by John Bull & Son. Bull was known as a maker of sporting guns and butt-reservoir airguns. **3.** William Bull: *see* Filser *Hopper.

Bullard – **1.** James H. Bullard, Springfield, Massachusetts. Co-designer with Daniel *Wesson of an improved retainer for revolver cylinders, protected by US Patent 187,269 of 20 February 1877. Bullard and Wesson also patented a rebounding hammer: 198,228 of 18 December 1877. An additional patent for a 'revolving firearm', protecting the Smith & Wesson *Double Action pattern, US no. 227,481, followed on 11 May 1880. After leaving Smith & Wesson, Bullard founded the Bullard Repeating Arms Company (below) to exploit protection accorded to a lever-action rifle by the US Patent Office on 16 August 1881 (no. 245,700). This design had been improved by 287,229 of 23 October 1883 before series production began. **2.** Bullard Repeating Arms Company [The], Springfield, Massachusetts, USA. Active 1885–89, this made the distinctive lever-action rifles in accordance with patents granted to James Bullard (above). However, despite excellent qualities, the Bullards were unable to withstand the challenge of Winchester, Marlin and others.

Bulldog, Bull Dog – **1.** A generic term for a small, large-calibre pocket revolver of a pattern originally introduced in the 1860s by Philip *Webley. **2.** A diabolo-type .177 or .22 airgun pellet made by *Lane Brothers from 1939 until the 1980s. **3.** A typically *Diana-type telescoping-barrel spring-air pistol of unknown provenance, probably dating from the 1920s. It is thought to have been distributed by Bertram *Webster & Company, trading as The Southern Armoury. **4.** Usually as two words: a .38-calibre five-shot single-action revolver, with a solid frame and a sheath trigger, made by *Forehand & Wadsworth in c. 1877–85 and also known as the *British Bull Dog, *Swamp Angel or *Terror. The design was based on patents granted to Ethan Allen in October 1861 and Forehand & Wadsworth in April 1875. **5.** Usually as two words: often marked by *Hopkins & Allen, this .44-calibre five-shot *Forehand & Wadsworth revolver had a double-action lock and a conventionally-guarded trigger. It superseded the earlier single-action .38 F&W *Bull Dog, apparently in the mid-1880s. **6.** Also known as Bulldozer. An angular cartridge derringer patented by Henry *Hammond in 1866 and made by the *Connecticut Arms Company until 1868 in chamberings ranging from .22 Short rimfire to .50. The barrel was released by a catch on the breech-top and pivoted to the left to expose the chamber. **7.** A five-shot double-action swing-cylinder revolver designed by Douglas McClenahan, and made in the USA by the *Charter Arms Corporation in .357 Magnum and .44 Special.

Barrels may be 2.5 or 3in, the latter being discontinued in 1988. Finish may be blue or stainless steel, and some guns (usually with 'P' suffix catalogue numbers) may be obtained with the snubbed Pocket Hammer. They also have wrap-around neoprene grips instead of wood. *See also* Police Bulldog and Target Bulldog. **8.** Bulldog Pug. Introduced by *Charter Arms in 1986, this is a variant of the Bulldog with a 2.5in barrel, fixed sights, a shrouded ejector and a broad hammer spur. **9.** Bulldog Tracker. Another variant of the *Charter Arms Bulldog, dating from c. 1982–86 and 1989 to date, this .357 Magnum revolver has adjustable sights, hand-filling wooden grips and barrels of 2.5–6in..

Bulldozer – **1.** A cartridge derringer patented in the USA by Henry *Hammond, better known as the Bulldog (q.v.). **2.** A selection of four different nineteenth-century *Suicide Special revolvers made in the USA by the *Crescent Arms Company of Norwich, Connecticut; the *Forehand & Wadsworth Arms Company of Worcester, Massachusetts; *Johnson, Bye & Company and/or *Iver Johnson of Worcester and Fitchburg, Massachusetts; and the *Norwich Arms Company and/or the *Norwich Falls Pistol Company of Norwich, Connecticut. Most of them have sheath triggers.

Bull Fighter, or Bulfighter. Associated with small .440 double-action five-shot revolvers made in Liège, c. 1890–1910; manufacturer unknown.

Bullock. Hanson B. Bullock. A Federal government inspector active in 1862, using the initials 'HBB'. *See also* US arms inspectors' marks.

Bullseye, Bull's Eye – **1.** A Langenhan-made *Millita rifle sold by the *Midland Gun Company, Birmingham, Warwickshire, England, prior to 1914. **2.** An English spring-air barrel cocking rifle made by, or for, the *Midland Gun Company of Birmingham; little more than a copy of the Langenhan-made Millita. **3.** Otherwise known as the *Gun Toys RO72, this Italian 4.5mm-calibre barrel-cocking spring-air pistol has been sold in Britain under brandnames such as *Panther. **4.** Usually as Bullseye. A *Suicide Special revolver made by Otis *Smith of Middlefield and Rock Fall, Connecticut, USA, in the late nineteenth century. **5.** A lever-action BB Gun, cocked by a rack-and-pinion system designed by Elbert *Searle, made by the Bull's Eye Rifle Company of Chicago, Illinois, USA, in 1907–17. **6.** A break-open BB Gun, using the butt as a cocking lever, made by the Bull's Eye Rifle Company of Chicago, USA, c. 1907–15. **7.** A double-barrel spring gun made by the Savage Arms Company in the 1930s, but really little more than a toy. **8.** Bullseye National Match. A variant of the *Gold Cup National Match Mark IV Series 80, introduced by *Colt's Manufacturing Company, Inc., in 1991. Specially hand-finished, it has Bomar sights. **9.** Bull's Eye Rifle Company, Chicago, Illinois, USA. This airgun manufacturer was founded c. 1906 to make a lever-action BB Gun designed by Elbert Searle, better known for the Savage automatic pistol. The airgun was the subject of US Patent 959,889 of 1910. A break-action version was also made, but trading had ceased by 1919.

Bully Bullets. *See* Lane Brothers.

Bulwark. A small *FN-Browning-type automatic pistol made by *Beistegui Hermanos in Eibar: 6.35mm, six rounds, striker fired. The guns were often marked by Fabrique d'Armes de *Grande Précision.

Bunge. Charles Bunge, Geneva, New York State, USA. The maker of repeating spring-air *Gallery Guns in the 1870s, Bunge obtained a US Patent in 1869 to protect a 'Revolving Spring Toy Gun'. He had been listed in the local directories since 1862/3 as a model builder, but from 1870 was described as a machinist or gunsmith. The last entries were made in 1894. Bunge also obtained US Patent 433,323 in 1890, for a gun sight, and made pill-lock revolver rifles before firearms chambering better cartridges overtook them.

Bunker. C.R. Bunker. This government inspector, working in 1875, accepted small-arms marked 'CRB'. *See also* US arms inspectors' marks.

Bunn. William Bunn. A gunsmith listed at 22 Chester Street, Kensington Cross, London, England, in 1857.

Buntline – 1. Buntline Scout. Made by *Colt's Patent Fire Arms Manufacturing Company (1959–64) and the Firearms Division of *Colt Industries (1964 onward), this was a variant of the *Frontier Scout with a 9.5in barrel instead of the standard 4.75in version. The original gun, factory model Q-2, chambered .22 Long Rifle rimfire ammunition; the F-2 pattern (introduced in 1960) was strengthened for .22 WRM; the K-2 pattern (1960) was a Q-2 with an alloy frame; and the P-2 was a blued K-2 with simulated staghorn grips. **2.** Buntline Special. Now associated with virtually any long-barrelled Colt *Single Action Army revolver, the term was coined by association with Edward Z.C. Judson, who wrote western fiction as 'Ned Buntline'. Judson claimed to have presented five such guns to leading lawmen, including Bat Masterson and Wyatt Earp. Although no trace of this order has ever been found, the myth is far too well established for the truth to have much effect. Colt's Patent Fire Arms Manufacturing Company made about 4,000 .45 Buntline Special Single Action Army revolvers between 1957 and 1975, distinguished by their 12in barrels.

Burbank. James K. Burbank. The marks of this government inspector, 'JKB', will be found on small-arms accepted in 1900–10. *See also* US arms inspectors' marks.

Burgess – 1. Andrew Burgess: *see* panel, facing page. **2.** Burgess Gun Company, Buffalo, New York State, USA. Incorporated in 1892, this manufacturer was responsible for 12-bore shotguns made in accordance with patents granted to Andrew Burgess in 1878–79. The guns were loaded by sliding the pistol grip down the underside of the butt, then returning it to chamber a fresh cartridge and close the bolt. The bolt opened automatically when the gun fired to eject the empty case. A few .30 and .44 slide-action rifles were made from 1896 onward, but production ceased when the business was sold to *Winchester in 1899.

Burgsmüller. H. Burgsmüller & Söhne. This German gunmaking business made two-barrel combination guns prior to 1914. These were based on Oberndorf *Mauser actions, but had a separate shotgun barrel beneath the rifled pattern. The breech of the shotgun, locked by a lever running forward beneath the fore-end, swung outward to the left for loading.

Burkardt. Franz Burkardt, Suhl in Thüringen, Germany. Listed in the district directories as a gunsmith, 1930.

'Burlington' [The]. Usually found as Burlington Cartridge or Burlington Express. A tradename associated with H. *Robinson of Bridlington, found on shotgun cartridges made by *Eley Kynoch.

Burns. John S. Burns. The 'JSB' mark of this government arms inspector will be found on small-arms accepted in 1898–1911. *See also* US arms inspectors' marks.

Burnside – 1. Ambrose Everett Burnside. Born in Liberty, Indiana, in 1824, Burnside rose to become an unexceptional general during the American Civil War, a state governor and the first president of the *National Rifle Association. He is also remembered as the designer of a breech-loading carbine, protected by US Patent 14,491 of 23 March 1856. The gun fired a unique conical cartridge inserted in the front of the breech-block before the action was closed. A small hole in the base of the cartridge case allowed a side-hammer cap-lock to be used. The inventor died in Bristol, Rhode Island, in 1881. **2.** Burnside Rifle Company, Providence, Rhode Island, USA. This business was formed in 1859 by a group, headed by Charles Jackson, to continue the work on the *'Burnside carbine. Tooling began in a new factory. Once again, the Civil War proved a boon: in July 1861, the Chief of Ordnance, Brigadier General James Ripley, passed Jackson a request for 800 Burnside carbines from Governor William Sprague of Rhode Island. These Second pattern carbines were finally delivered in March 1862. **3.** Burnside carbine: *see* panel, p. 102.

Burpee. Horace Burpee. Active during the American Civil War, this Federal government inspector accepted rifle-muskets marked 'HB'. *See also* US arms inspectors' marks.

Burroughs Adding Machine Company. Formed in 1905 in Detroit, Michigan, succeeding the Arithmometer Company. A contract for 250,000 .45 M1911 *Colt-Browning pistols was placed during the First World War, but no guns were ever made.

Burrow, Burrows, *see also* Burroughs – **1.** James Burrow or Burrows. A gunsmith and crossbow maker of this name traded from 26 Friargate, then 116 Fishergate, Preston, Lancashire, England, from 1817 until 1870/1. He is believed to have been succeeded by a similarly named son (trading from 46 Fishergate, Preston, and Lowther Street in Carlisle), who loaded – or perhaps simply sold – shotgun cartridges marked 'The Economic' prior to 1914. **2.** Edwin Burrows. A gunmaker listed by H.J. *Blanch at 110 Cannon Street, London, England, in 1878. **3.** William J. Burrows designed the first lever-action *Daisy BB Gun, protected by US Patent 765,270 of 19 July 1904. The specification records his residence in Plymouth, Michigan.

Burt. Addison M. Burt, New York City. A manufacturer of *Springfield rifle-muskets, delivering 11,495 against orders for 50,000 placed on 26 December 1861. Some surviving guns were converted to *Allin-system breech-loaders in the late 1860s.

Burton – 1. Usually as 'The Burton': associated with shotgun cartridges loaded by *Coltman of Burton upon Trent, Nottinghamshire, England. **2.** Bethel Burton, Brooklyn, New York. Active from the 1850s until his death in 1904, this firearms designer was granted a variety of US Patents. Beginning with no. 26,475 of 20 December 1859, granted to protect a 'breech-loading firearm' with an early form of segmental 'straight-pull' bolt, they included 81,059 of 11 August 1868 for a bolt-action 'breech-loading firearm' with interrupted-screw locking threads at the rear; 92,013 of 29 June 1869 for a similar bolt-action

ANDREW BURGESS

Burgess (1)

One of the least-known of leading firearms inventors, despite filing nearly 900 patents, Burgess was born on 16 January 1837 near Lake George (now Dresden) in New York State. He was apprenticed to the photographer Mathew Brady in 1855, became Brady's partner in 1863 and visited Europe on a photographic mission in 1870. There he became obsessed with firearms, receiving his first patents (US 119,115 and 119,218) in September 1871. These protected a variety of swinging-block rifles, and auxiliary magazines for the *Peabody and *Werndl rifles.

Andrew Burgess is best remembered for his lever-action rifles. The first was patented in the USA on 16 July 1872 (129,523), with a very simple one-piece actuating lever and breech-locking piece. An improved design followed in October 1875 (US no. 168,966), and guns were shown at the Centennial Exposition held in Philadelphia in 1876.

Rights to a stock-magazine were sold to Winchester, to avoid possible infringements in the *Hotchkiss rifle, but Burgess was also approached by Eli Whitney. The result was the .45-70 Whitney-Burgess rifle (1879–84), and a modified short-action derivative embodying a carrier patented by Samuel Kennedy (US no. 215,227). A series of bolt-action rifles followed, including magazine transformations of the German *Mauser and Russian *Berdan patterns. However, to claim that Burgess was the first inventor to succeed in combining the tube magazine and the bolt-action into a usable arm, as some enthusiasts have done, is misguided; *see* Vetterli.

An improved Whitney-Burgess rifle was introduced in 1886, chambered for the .32-40 (sporting) or .38-40 (military) cartridges, but Whitney was purchased by the *Winchester Repeating Arms Company in 1888 and work ceased.

This gun was the first to employ the radial 'drop lock' used in the Burgess shotgun, the Colt Lightning rifle and the Austrian M1886 *Mannlicher. The Austrians paid royalties on the Burgess patents – 235,204 (7 December 1880) and 209,393 (18 December 1883). In addition, Josef *Schulhof bought US Patent 210,182, which protected a mechanised butt magazine system.

Burgess's association with *Marlin began in 1880, when he was asked to design a new lever-action rifle. Burgess and Marlin jointly patented an improved carrier in 1881, and the basic action is still being used in lever-action Marlin rifles.

A liaison with *Colt's Patent Fire Arms Manufacturing Company led to the Colt-Burgess lever-action rifle, introduced in 1883, but abandoned two years later (under threat from Winchester) after only 6,403 had been made. The Colt featured a solid top link, instead of the split-link of earlier Burgess designs. Winchester had also purchased Patent 290,848 (25 December 1883), which protected an improvement to the weak Winchester M1873.

The most interesting of Andrew Burgess's firearms was the *Haveness, a slide-action half-automatic that brought patent-infringement conflicts with first Sylvester *Roper, then Christopher *Spencer. Made as shotguns (from 1893), rifles (1896) and take-down, or folding, rifles (1897), the action was cycled initially with a reciprocating pistol grip; after the first shot had been fired, however, the breech opened and ejected the spent cartridge automatically, leaving the firer with nothing to do but close the breech again.

Burgess and his partner, Charles Loomis, also built 12-bore side-by-side shotguns, fitted with damascus barrels imported from Liège, but the business was sold to Winchester in 1899. Burgess's last years were focussed on automatic weapons, but little had been achieved when he died in Florida on 19 December 1908. His last patent, US no. 822,851, had been granted on 5 June 1906 to protect a gas-operated pistol.

Taken from a patent granted in the USA in 1879 to Andrew Burgess, these drawings show a lever-operated action incorporated in the first successful Marlin rifle.

BURNSIDE CARBINE

Burnside (3)

The earliest or First Pattern guns, made by the *Bristol Firearms Company, lacked fore-ends and had a separate breech-lock lever curving beneath the hammer. The Second Pattern, usually credited to George Foster (foreman machinist in the Burnside Rifle Company factory in Providence), had an improved breech-block protected by US Patent 27,874 of 10 April 1860. The auxiliary locking lever and the *Maynard Tape Primer were discarded. Third Pattern guns were similar, but had short wooden fore-ends and stronger hammers. The Fourth Pattern Burnside was distinguished by an articulated breech-block patented in 1863 by Isaac *Hartshorn, Burnside's sales agent. The Fifth Pattern, based on the Hartshorn breech, had an additional pin-and-track system, designed by George *Bacon, to open the breech automatically; Hartshorn guns required two manual actions to be performed in the correct order, otherwise the breech-block would jam. Later guns also benefited from an improved bell-mouth cartridge that had been designed by Foster. These were made in a single piece, with a circumferential groove inside the case mouth containing lubricating wax. Largely because it relied on an external cap-lock, the Burnside system was popular with the military authorities. Total Federal purchases amounted to 55,567 between 1 January 1861 and 30 June 1866.

An example of the fifth, 1864 or last-pattern .54 Burnside carbine, incorporating the improvements made by Isaac Hartshorn and George Bacon.
Courtesy of Wallis & Wallis, Lewes.

gun with a tube magazine beneath the barrel; 143,614 of 14 October 1873, jointly with W.G. Burton, for an improved form of the 1869-patent magazine rifle; and 232,880 of 5 October 1880 for a 'magazine firearm'. US Patent 390,114 of 25 September 1888 was granted, while Burton was living in Britain, for an 'Automatic Machine Gun', whereas 622,443 of 4 April 1899, 640,627 of 2 January 1900 and 656,807 of 28 August 1900 were all granted to protect bolt-action magazine rifles. Burton's last effort, 785,085 of 21 March 1905, for an 'automatic firearm' was granted posthumously to the administrator of his estate, his son Henry C. Burton. Bethel Burton also designed waterproof percussion caps, self-contained cartridges, gun sights, and a combined bayonet and gun rest (613,241 of November 1898). *See* Lee-Burton and Ward-Burton. **3.** Burton's Patent Double Magazine Rifle. Developed by Bethel Burton in the mid 1880s, this attracted sufficient attention to be included in the British *Treatise on Military Small Arms and Ammunition* in 1888, but was too heavy and unnecessarily complicated.

'Burwood' [The]. A brandname found on shotgun cartridges handled by Charles *Hellis & Sons of London, England.

Bush & Field. *See* Sportsman Bush & Field.

Bushman. A brandname associated with a revolver made in Belgium prior to 1914 by A. *Bertrand.

Bushmaster – 1. A variant of the *Galway Fieldmaster pneumatic rifle, announced in 1984 and made in small numbers until 1988. **2.** This name was associated with a bolt-action rifle made by the *Winslow Arms Company, distinguished by the design of the stock. *See also* Plainsmaster.

Business Rifle, *see also* New Model Hammerless Business Rifle – **1.** Or Sharps' Business Rifle, 1874 pattern. This plain-looking gun appeared in the summer of 1876, with an octagonal barrel, a double set trigger, open sights and an oil-finished straight-wrist butt. Chamberings were restricted to .45-70 and .45-100. **2.** Made by E. *Remington & Sons in 1875–c. 1882, this was a minor variant of the No. 1 Sporting Rifle with a round barrel invariably chambering the .45-70 cartridge. *See also* Remington rifles, rolling-block action.

Bussey – 1. George Gibson Bussey. Designer of an air-gun protected by British Patent 526/76 of 1876, and proprietor of G.G. Bussey & Company (below). **2.** G.G. Bussey & Company, Museum Works, Rye Lane, Peckham, London SE. This sporting-goods manufacturing business was advertising Bussey's Patent Gyro Pigeon and Trap and Bussey's Improved Hawk Kites ('by the judicious use of which many a good Bag of Game may be secured') in 1871. Bussey also owned the Museum of Firearms, Peckham, where his wares were customarily exhibited. Remembered only as an airgun patentee, his factory in Peckham operated from 1870 until 1914, possibly later; the trading style changed from '...& Company' to '...& Company Ltd' in 1884. An advertisement in the 1910 edition of W.W. Greener's *The Gun and Its Development* indicates that at that time Bussey was making 'world famed cricket, golf, tennis, bowls, croquet [equipment]'. The trademark comprised 'GGB' pierced by a horizontal arrow.

Buster Brown Model. This was a minor variant of the *Warrior BB Gun, with a shot cup replacing the barrel-housing lug, made for the *Brown Shoe Company as a premium item between 1909 and c. 1912.

Butler – 1. Arthur Henry Butler. A 'clerk' of 51 Witton Road, Birmingham, Warwickshire, England, Butler was co-patentee with Frederick George *Clark of an airgun with a revolving cylindrical magazine: British Patent 4622/06 of 1906. **2.** John G. Butler. The 'JGB' marks of this arms inspector, a captain in the US Army, were applied to *Colt revolvers accepted in 1886. *See also* US arms inspectors' marks.

Butt – 1. The part of the stock extending backward against the firer's shoulder. It may be integral with the *fore-end, forming a one-piece stock, or a separate component. The upper edge of the butt is known as the *comb, which terminates at the shoulder in the heel. The toe is the lower tip of the butt, and the *grip – 'small' or 'wrist' – is the narrow portion immediately behind the action facilitating an effectual hand-grip. **2.** Zadock Butt. This government arms inspector, working in 1862, accepted small-arms marked 'ZB'. *See also* US arms inspectors' marks. **3.** Butt or shoulder plate. A fixture on the end of the butt, either to protect the wood or to ease the shock of firing on the firer's shoulder. The traditional metal pattern generally has a concave surface, known variously as rifle type or crescentic. Many sporting guns have been fitted with a straight or shotgun-type plate, while others, especially recent examples, have had plates of rubber or injection-moulded plastic. The most powerful sporting guns have compressible butt plates, often of ventilated pattern. Target rifles may have hooked or adjustable butt plates.

Butterfield – 1. Jesse Butterfield, Philadelphia, Pennsylvania, USA. Butterfield first achieved notoriety by copying the *Deringer, although his guns had a patented priming tube mounted vertically ahead of the hammer. Butterfield also developed a cap-lock revolver with a detachable tube of disc primers ahead of the trigger guard, protected by US Patent 12,124 of 1855, but only about 700 five-shot examples of these single-action Army patterns were completed by *Krider & Company in 1861–62. **2.** Butterfield & Marshall, Philadelphia, Pennsylvania. This gunmaking partnership of Jesse Butterfield and Simeon Marshall traded c. 1856–60. It was succeeded by Butterfield & Company.

Büttner – 1. A. Büttner, Zella St Blasii in Thüringen, Germany. Listed in 1900 as a gunmaker. **2.** Albert Büttner, Suhl in Thüringen, Germany. Listed as a gunmaker, 1930. **3.** Alf. Büttner, Suhl in Thüringen, Germany. Listed in the 1920 edition of the *Deutsches-Reichs Adressbuch* as a gunsmith, and in 1939 as '...& Söhne'. **4.** Gebr. Büttner. Owned in the 1920s by Ernst, Wilhelm and Max Büttner, this gunmaking business, in Suhl-Neundorf, may have succeeded to the operations of Ernst Büttner (above). **5.** Otto Büttner, Schmalkalden in Thüringen. A retailer of sporting guns and ammunition active in Germany in 1941.

Butts. William Mathews Butts was a wholesale merchant and partner with Austin *Wheeler in the *Grand Rapids Rifle Company. Wheeler and Butts were co-patentees with employees Caulkins and Lindberg of the first *Rapid BB Gun.

Buzz Barton Special. Otherwise known as the *Daisy No. 103, which had taken the *Markham/King No. 55 as its basis, production of this thousand-shot BB Gun was confined to 1934–36. The Buzz Barton Super Special Model, made by Daisy only in 1934, used the frame design of the obsolescent No. 3 Model B. It had a prominent sighting tube above the receiver.

'BV', and a crown, sometimes encircled. The view mark used by the Guardians of the Proof House in Birmingham, 1904–54.

'bye', Bye – 1. Found on small-arms ammunition components made in 1941–45 by 'Hanomag'–Hannover'sche Maschinenbau AG vorm. Georg Egestorff of Hannover-Linden, Germany. **2.** Martin Bye. This co-patentee of an air pistol protected by US Patents 176,003 and 176,004 of 1876 was also a partner of Iver *Johnson in *Johnson, Bye & Company of Worcester, Massachusetts. Both men were of Norwegian origin.

'byf'. Used by *Mauser-Werke KG of Oberndorf am Neckar, Württemberg, Germany, on machine-guns, pistols, rifles and components, this code was granted in February 1941 and used until the end of the Second World War.

Bylandt. Comte A. de Bylandt. Patentee of a repeating firearm with a cylindrical magazine containing 'false cartridges' (detachable chambers) loaded with powder and ball. The magazine was rotated by pulling upward on the top-lever, which pivoted around the rear of the action and cocked the hammer. Guns of this type were made in Liège in the late 1850s by the gunsmith *Decortis.

'bym'. Found on German small-arms components made during the Second World War by Genossenschafts Maschinenhaus der Büchsenmacher of Ferlach/Kärnten.

'bys'. Found on Kar. 98k barrels and other small-arms components made during the Second World War by Ruhrstal AG of Witten an der Ruhr, Germany.

'byw'. Associated with German small-arms components made between 1941 and 1945 by Stettiner Schraubenwerk Johannes Schäfer of Stettin.

'bzt'. Found on butts, pistol grips and other German small-arms components made in 1941–45 by Fritz Wolf, Rob. Sohn, of Zella-Mehlis.

'bzz'. Found on telescope sights and associated components made in 1941–45 by the camera and camera-lens factory of IG Farbenindustrie in Munich, Germany.

C

'C' – 1. Enclosing a Broad Arrow. A property mark, but also indicating small-arms and components made by *Canadian Arsenals Ltd in the Long Branch factory. The mark usually appears on guns made prior to 1945. 2. In an oval. Found on barrels of Canadian *Lee-Enfield rifles converted to 7.62mm for competition use. 3. Beneath a crown. A mark applied to Swedish military firearms made by *Carl Gustafs Stads Gevärsfactori of Eskilstuna.

'ca'. Associated with German military small-arms ammunition components made in 1940–45 by Vereinigte Deutsche Nickelwerke AG in Schwerte/Ruhr.

'CAAO'. A superimposition-type monogram with 'C', 'A' and 'A' of near-equal dominance. Correctly 'AACO' (q.v.); associated with the *American Arms Company.

'CAB'. See C.A. *Brand.

'C.A.C.' An abbreviated form of *Colonial Ammunition Company, found in the headstamps of cartridges made in New Zealand.

Caccia, *Concorde Caccia or *Daytona Caccia: see Hunting.

'C.A. Co.' A mark found on cartridges associated with the *Chicago Arms Company.

'cad'. Found on German military telescope sights and associated components made during 1940–45 by Karl Kahles of Vienna.

Cadet – 1. A barrel-cocking .177 spring-air gun made by *BSA Guns Ltd, the first being despatched from the Small Heath factory in Birmingham in December 1945. The Cadet was the first British airgun to have the breech-fork brazed to the air cylinder, a method of construction that has since become commonplace. A few minor changes were made to the Cadet, but otherwise the gun remained unchanged until the pattern was replaced by the *Meteor in 1959. About 150,000 Cadets had been made. 2. A *Suicide Special revolver made in the USA by Otis *Smith of Middlefield and Rock Fall, Connecticut, in the late nineteenth century. 3. Cadet Major. This .177-calibre barrel-cocking airgun, which appeared in 1947, was an enlargement of the Cadet with adjustable sights and an adjustable trigger. About 125,000 had been made when production ceased in 1957.

Cadillac Gage Company. See Stoner and ArmaLite.

Cadiot. Emmanuel H. Cadiot. This gunmaker, possibly a sales agency, briefly maintained an office at 72 Gracechurch Street, London E.C., in 1875. The name suggests French origin.

Cadix, or Astra Cadix. Introduced in 1958, this Spanish six-shot revolver, made by *Astra–Unceta y Cia, is based on Smith & Wesson swing-cylinder practice, but can easily be recognised by its streamlined appearance. The finish is customarily blue, although chrome, silver and gold plating will also be encountered. Some guns have also been engraved or damascened. Originally offered only in

.38 Special, with a five-chamber cylinder, subsequently the centrefire Cadix was chambered for the .32 S&W Long (six shots); a .22LR/.22 Magnum rimfire version, with a nine-chamber cylinder, appeared in 1969. Barrels measure 100mm or 150mm. The *New Cadix is an improved version. See also Astra Match.

'CADW'. A concentric-type monogram with all four letters of equal prominence. Correctly 'WDAC' (q.v.); used by the *Warner-Davis Arms Corporation.

Caesar – 1. A brandname used by *Excelsior Kinderschusswaffenfabrik GmbH of Schwabach bei Nürnberg, Germany. 2. A bolt-rifle made by *A-Square of Bedford, Kentucky, USA, from 1983 to date. Often made with synthetic stocks, the guns have been chambered for cartridges ranging from 7mm Remington Magnum to .500 A-Square Magnum.

'CAG', 'cag' – 1. Found as 'cag' on optical equipment made by D. *Swarovski in Wattens/Tirol during the Second World War. 2. A concentric-type monogram, with the 'G' and 'A' prominent. Correctly 'GAC' (q.v.); used by *Garate, Anitua y Cia.

Cagnoni. Giacomo Cagnoni. The designer of the *Air Match pneumatic pistol, and also the founder and managing director of Air Match SrL of Abbiategesso/Milano.

Cahen, Lyon & Cie. Although specialising in military weaponry, this French entrepreneurial business is best known for negotiating a licence for the needle-fire bolt system designed by Antoine *Chassepot. When the French government realised that the arsenals in Châtellerault, Saint-Étienne and Tulle could not cope with demand, Cahen, Lyon & Cie demanded the right to sub-contract work abroad. Consequently, Chassepot rifles will be found with British, Italian, Spanish and other marks. British representation was maintained through T. Christy & Company of 155 Fenchurch Street, London E.C., in 1868–73; most, if not all of the British-made Chassepots were ordered in Birmingham.

'CAL', 'C.A.L.' – 1. A mark associated with small-arms made in the Long Branch factory of *Canadian Arsenals Ltd. 2. See Carabine Automatique Leger.

Calderwood & Son, Dublin, Ireland (Eire). The marks of this gunmaker have been reported on self-cocking *pepperboxes dating from the middle of the nineteenth century.

Caldwell – 1. Homer Caldwell, Worcester, Massachusetts, USA. On 4 October 1887, this employee of *Harrington & Richardson received US Patent 370,926 to protect a revolver-cocking system. This could be actuated with the thumb, but only after the trigger had been pulled to raise the otherwise concealed hammer to half-cock. 2. William Caldwell. This government arms inspector, working immediately prior to the American Civil War, accepted .44 cap-lock Remington revolvers marked 'WC'. See also US arms inspectors' marks.

'Caledonia' [The]. Associated with shotgun ammunition sold in Britain by Alex. *Martin of Glasgow, but made by *Eley-Kynoch.

Caledonian – **1.** British .177 and .22-calibre diabolo airgun pellets made by *Milbro prior to 1982, and thereafter by *Milbro Caledonian Pellets Ltd. Ammunition of this type has also been made under the *Webley and *Kassnar brands. **2.** Caledonian Model. Applied to *Mauser-type sporting rifles made by John *Dickson & Sons in .243, .270 and .308 Winchester chamberings. Most examples have a typically British *Express back sight on a short rib.

Caliber, calibre. An expression of the internal diameter of a gun barrel, generally measured across the lands, but sometimes across the grooves or even – as a compromise – from the bottom of one groove to the land diametrically opposite. A calibre dimension is often an approximation and may depend on marketing strategy. The term is commonly used as a synonym for chambering (q.v.), but such misleading usage should be discouraged.

California Bull-Dog. A name associated with a revolver made in Belgium prior to 1914 by *Deprez.

Calisher – **1.** Henry Calisher. Partner of William *Terry in Calisher & Terry, and patentee of a bolt-action cap-lock breech-loader with an automatic cap-feed mechanism. *See* British Patent 1932/66 of 25 July 1866. **2.** Calisher & Terry. This gunmaking partnership entered the Birmingham, Warwickshire, directories in 1857, trading first from 116 Great Charles Street (1857–60), then 22–24 Whittall Street (1862–70). An 1862-vintage advertisement claims that Calisher & Terry were 'Manufacturers of Terry's Patent Breech Loading Rifles…Also of R. Adam's [sic] Patent Double Action Revolvers, Small Bore Breech Loading and Muzzle Loading Rifles of superior quality, and all other…Rifles, Guns and Pistols for Exportation'. The company also made a few breech-loading guns in accordance with a patent granted to Richard F. *Brand in 1853. Calisher & Terry maintained London offices at 28 Norfolk Street, Strand (1864–65) and 117–118 Leadenhall Street (1869–70), but then operations ceased.

Calkins. William Henry Calkins. A 'Salesman' and co-patentee of the spring-air BB Gun marketed by the *Rapid Rifle Company at the beginning of the twentieth century. US Patent 614,532 of 1898 and its British equivalent, 24,688/98 of 1898, attribute the design to Calkins, Charles A. Lindberg, William M. Butts and Austin K. Wheeler. *See also* Cycloid and Cyclone.

Callahan. John J. Callahan. This US government arms inspector, working in the early 1940s, accepted .45 M1911A1 Colt pistols marked 'JJC'. *See also* US arms inspectors' marks.

Calvert – **1.** John Calvert. An English gunmaker trading from the village of Walsden, near Todmorden in Yorkshire, Calvert is known to have handled sporting guns and ammunition (including *Eley-made shotgun cartridges dating prior to 1914). The family had previously been established in Leeds, where two generations of 'John Calverts' had worked in the nineteenth century. **2.** John W[illiam]. Calvert, Leeds, Yorkshire. The affairs of this gunmaker remain something of a mystery. John Calvert began trading in Kirkgate in 1797, moving to 34 Lowerhead Row by 1821, then to Commercial Street by 1827. Trading continued until the late 1860s. The problems lie in the listing of John & William Calvert in Briggate in 1804–22, then the appearance of William Calvert alone in 1827–30. It is suggested, therefore, that there were three generations of Calverts operating in this period: John, his son William and his grandson John William. Marks applied by J.W. Calvert (sic) have been found on self-cocking *pepperboxes dating from the middle of the nineteenth century.

Camargue. A derivative of the *Air Arms Supra sidelever-cocking spring-air rifle with the *Tyrolean-style stock.

Cambridge & Company. Based in Carrickfergus in Ireland, this gunsmithing business sold shotgun ammunition marked 'The Antrim', 'The County Down' and 'The Ulster'.

Cameron – **1.** A.F. Cameron. A US government arms inspector, working in 1875, who accepted small-arms marked 'AFC'. **2.** Alexander Cameron. This US government arms inspector, working in 1940, accepted Colt pistols marked 'AC'. *See also* US arms inspectors' marks for both previous entries. **3.** William Cameron & Company. This gun and ammunition distributor, trading in the Irish town of Ballymena, sold shotgun cartridges distinguished with the brandnames Cameronia and Cameron's Special.

'Cameronia' [The]. Found on shotgun cartridges sold by W. *Cameron & Company of Ballymena, Ireland.

Cammell. L.J. Cammell (Merseyside) Ltd, Moreton, Wirral, Cheshire. This British metalworking business is best known for its *Champion-brand airgun pellets. Founded by Louis Camilleri in the early 1960s, Cammell had concentrated largely on exports – in 1971, for example, its products were going to eighteen countries – and was particularly successful in the Middle East and South America. Champion pellets may also be encountered under the *Webley brandname.

Camo Synthetic. A version of the Remington M700 bolt-action rifle, also listed as M700 CS.

Camp – **1.** E.M. Camp. This Federal government arms inspector, working in the early 1860s, accepted Colt cap-lock revolvers marked 'EMC'. **2.** Francis Camp. A US government arms inspector, working in 1858–61, who accepted small-arms marked 'FC'. *See also* US arms inspectors' marks for both previous entries. **3.** Camp Perry. The Camp Perry Model was introduced in 1926 by *Colt's Patent Fire Arms Manufacturing Company. Named after the *National Rifle Association shooting range in Ohio, this was a single-shot .22 LR rimfire derivative of the *Officer's Model Target revolver with a pivoting chamber-block substituted for the cylinder and an 8 or 10in barrel. Sales were poor: only about 2,500 had been sold when work finished at the end of 1941.

Campbell. R. Campbell & Sons, sometimes listed as 'Cambell', Leyburn, Yorkshire, England. The name of this gunsmith has been found on shotgun cartridges, made by *Kynoch (or at least from Kynoch components) and sold under The Wensledale brand.

Campeon. A Spanish Browning-type automatic pistol made in Eibar by *Crucelegui Hermanos: (a) 6.35mm, six rounds; (b) 7.65mm, six rounds, hammer fired. Either gun may be marked 'Model 1919'.

Camper, or Astra Camper. This was a long-barrelled version of the *Cub pistol, made by Astra–Unceta y Cia SA in 1956–66. Production was comparatively meagre.

Campo-Giro – **1.** Don Venancio López de Ceballos y Aguirre, Condé del (Count of) Campo-Giro.

CAP-LOCK

A mechanism in which ignition was accomplished by striking a small portion of mercuric fulminate, developed by Scottish clergyman Alexander Forsyth (1768–1843) early in the nineteenth century, was the

first major advance from the flintlock. However, English Patent 3032/07 of 11 April 1807 had been drafted so skilfully that a stranglehold was applied to development of the percussion-ignition system for many years (cf. Colt's and then Rollin White's dominance of revolver

design in the middle of the nineteenth century).

Although the gunsmith Prélat claimed novelty in a copper cap patented in France in 1820, today credit for the discovery is customarily given to Joshua Shaw. The cap-lock had become sturdy and reliable once mass-manufacturing problems had been overcome and, although the message took some time to filter through to the military, experiments had begun in France by 1830. British trials began in 1831 with a tremendous variety of designs, but only Lovell's improved cap-lock, the 'common cap-lock', Manton's plug-lock and Eccles' cap-lock were selected for field trials in the Spring of 1836. The improved Lovell pattern was duly approved for service.

Cap-locks rapidly displaced flintlocks, largely as they were much less susceptible to damp, remaining in

This cased .36 Colt New Police revolver, dating from 1862, is typical of the guns that relied on percussion caps to ignite the charge. The caps were placed individually on nipples set into the rear of the cylinder.

Commissioned into the Spanish Artillery in the 1870s, the Count had been attached to the testing board that, in 1903, had accepted the *Bergmann-Mars pistol for service. However, he continued to work on pistols of his own, prototypes made in the *Oviedo small-arms factory in 1903–04 being followed by a small series of the so-called Modelo de 1904. Patents were granted in Spain on 7 October 1904 (no. 34,796) and in September 1910 (49,720), and development work continued until the Count was killed in a riding accident in 1919. An agreement with Juan *Esperanza, granting rights to Campo-Giro patents, was exploited posthumously to develop the 9mm *Astra. **2.** Campo-Giro pistol. The semi-experimental 1904-pattern guns were replaced by the Mo. 1910, twenty-five being made in Oviedo in 1910–11. Wood grips replaced the rubber, and the provision of a sliding wedge beneath the barrel delayed the opening of the breech. The Mo. 1910 Campo-Giro pistol was distinguished by its tubular slide, with retraction grooves above the trigger guard, and had an external hammer. A rod-type shoulder stock could be screwed into the heel of the butt when required. Tests suggested changes and, on 24 September 1912, the blowback 'Pistola automatica sistema Gampo-Giro Mo. 1913' was adopted. The locking wedge was abandoned in favour of a stronger barrel-return spring, and a production contract was given to *Esperanza y Unceta; about 1,000 pistols of this type were made, although only about 960 were accepted by the army. The Mo. 1913 had rubber grips, marked with a coronet above 'CAMPO-GIRO' and the manufacturer's 'EyU' monogram. It was superseded by the Mo. 1913–16,

with chequered wooden grips and a modified safety mechanism patented in Spain (no. 23,651 of 1913), Britain (no. 60,666/14) and the USA. The safety could be applied even if the gun had been cocked, and the magazine release, previously positioned immediately behind the trigger guard, was moved to the base of the butt. More than 13,000 guns had been made by 1919, but manufacturing problems (and the death of the inventor) led to the supersession of the Campo-Giro by the simplified Astra in 1921. With the exception of a few experimental prototypes, in 7.65mm Auto and .45 ACP, all guns of this type were chambered for the 9mm Largo (Bergmann-Bayard) cartridge.

'Camroid' [The]. Found on shotgun cartridges sold in Britain by *Gallyon & Sons.

Canada Tool & Specialty Company Ltd. See Ross.

Canadian... – **1.** Canadian Arsenals Ltd: see Long Branch. **2.** Canadian Industries Ltd, Brownsburg, Quebec. Founded in 1902 as the *Dominion Cartridge Company, this ammunition manufacturer has identified its products by the inclusion of 'C.I.L.' in the headstamps.

Canardier, Canardière. Terms associated with French-made duck (*canard*) guns. See Buffalo, Ideal, *Manufacture Française d'Armes et Cycles and Simplex.

Canberra. Derived from highly successful *Parker-Hale M82 and M83 military-pattern *Mauser-action sniping/target rifles, the M84 Mk II Canberra had aperture sights and an ambidextrous walnut stock.

Cane guns. Full, or rifle-length cane guns were made in surprisingly large numbers prior to 1914, including many pneumatic patterns. Handguns are rarely found in

107

front-line military service until c. 1870. By this time, inspired by lessons learned fom the American Civil War (1861–65), most armies were experimenting with self-contained metal case ammunition. However, the cap-lock retained popularity among sportsmen and target-shooters for some years, and cheap guns of this pattern were still being made in Birmingham and Liège for export to Africa, Asia and, indeed, parts of South America, when the Second World War began.

Most cap-locks were comparatively simple, consisting simply of a hammer, mounted externally on a lock plate, that was propelled by a leaf spring on the inside of the plate acting on the tumbler. The locks can be roughly categorised as back action or 'front action' (although the latter term is normally only implied by the absence

of a back-action qualification). The spring of a back-action lock lies behind the hammer, along with the majority of the lock plate. Locks of this type were greatly favoured in Europe, but were not so common in Britain, except on drop-barrel sporting guns.

Cap-locks are still being made in profusion, largely due to renewed interest in blackpowder shooting. Many are straightforward copies of the original nineteenth-century patterns, but some have been adapted to embody coil springs and roller bearings.

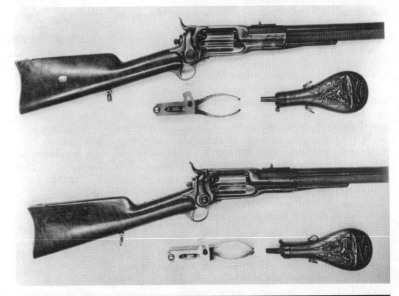

A matched pair of Colt Revolver Rifles, powder flasks and bullet moulds, presented by Samuel Colt to Russian Grand-Dukes Mikhail and Konstantin. Dating from 1857, the guns are in the Hermitage Museum in St Petersburg.

---

this form, however, with the exception of a small number of stick-handle pinfire pepperboxes of French or Belgian origin. These were often made with short fixed knife blades forged integrally with the cylinder-axis pin, and may be found in canes, umbrellas and walking sticks made throughout Europe prior to the First World War. The stick body had to be removed before the revolver could be fired. *See also* Disguised guns, Étoile and Heinrich ★Langenhan.

'Cannot be Beaten'. A mark found on shotgun cartridges made for Charles ★Naylor of Sheffield. The marks may read 'Naylor's Cannot be Beaten' and may be accompanied by a depiction of a cock pheasant.

Canonnier-Bufferne, grande rue Saint-Roch 5, Saint-Étienne, France. A specialist gun-barrel maker working in the late 1870s.

Canonnerie Stéphanoise, 13 rue de Vernay, Saint-Étienne, France. Listed in 1951 as a gun-barrel maker.

Cantabria – 1. A small Spanish Browning-type automatic pistol made by ★Garate Hermanos of Ermua: 6.35mm, seven rounds, hammer fired. May be marked 'Model 1918' or by Fabrique d'Armes de ★Grande Précision. **2.** A 6.35mm Spanish ★Browning-revolver, sharing the same general appearance as the 1900-pattern semi-automatic pistol made by ★Fabrique Nationale d'Armes de Guerre, but with a folding trigger and a five-chamber cylinder. Manufactured by Gregorio Bolumburu of Eibar, but often mistakenly credited to Garate Hermanos.

'Cantium', customarily cursive, above a riding crop. A mark found on cartridges distributed by the Kentish sporting-goods store ★Olby's.

Cantlow. William Cantlow, also listed as Cantalo or Cantelo. Arne Hoff listed a Girandoni-pattern airgun made by Cantalo, trading in Newport in the Isle of Wight in 1823–30. He was succeeded c. 1839 by his sons Charles, George and Edward, who were still trading at the same address in the 1840s. Pepperboxes, sporting rifles and airguns are said to exist with their marks.

'Canvas Back' [The]. Associated with shotgun ammunition loaded by the ★Chamberlain Cartridge Company of Cleveland, Ohio.

Cap-Chur. A brandname found on tranquilising equipment associated with the Palmer Chemical & Equipment Company of Douglasville, Georgia. The gas-powered dart guns – the subject of US Patent 2,854,925 – usually prove to have been made specially by the ★Crosman Arms Company, the original pistol being based on the Crosman Model 150, and the rifle on the Model 160. Both fired .45-calibre hypodermic darts and could be distinguished by their large-diameter bores.

'Capercaillie' [The]. A brandname said to have been found on shotgun cartridges sold in southern Scotland by ★Law of Castle Douglas. Its existence is unconfirmed.

Capital – 1. Found on shotgun ammunition marked in Scotland by John ★Dickson of Edinburgh. **2.** A name associated with smokeless-propellant shotgun ammunition made prior to the First World War by the ★Robin Hood Cartridge Company of Swanton, Vermont.

Cap-lock. *See* panel, above.

'Captain' [The]. Found on 12-bore shotgun cartridges loaded by the ★Schultze Gunpowder Company, apparently often on the basis of components supplied by ★Eley

Bros. The name honoured Hauptmann (Captain) Eduard Schultze, inventor of the propellant.

Captain Jack or 'Capt. Jack'. A *Suicide Special revolver produced by the *Hopkins & Allen Arms Company of Norwich, Connecticut, USA, in the late nineteenth century.

Carabina, carabine. A generic term for any short-barrelled firearm in Spanish and Italian (*carabina*) or French (*carabine*); cf. *mosqueton*. See also carbine.

Carabine... – 1. Carabine à Répétition Browning, Trombon. About 152,000 of these slide-action repeaters, derived from the Browning-designed external-hammer Winchester of 1890 (q.v.), were made by *Fabrique Nationale d'Armes de Guerre in 1921–74. It was externally similar to the .22 auto-loader, but had the magazine beneath the barrel instead of contained in the butt. The guns customarily had butts with shallow pistol grips, and circumferentially-ribbed slide handles enveloping the magazine tube. **2.** Carabine Automatique Browning, BAR-22 or Auto-22. This gun was made in accordance with patents obtained by John Browning in 1908, although production did not begin in Belgium until January 1913. The rifle had an enclosed hammer, a half-length fore-end, and a separate butt with a port cut in it to allow the magazine to be half-filled without opening the breech. The barrel and fore-end could be detached by releasing a catch and rotating the ribbed barrel collar through 90 degrees. The .22 LR rifle was more popular; the original .22 Short version was only made in small numbers. No sooner had production begun, than the Germans invaded Belgium and work ceased until 1920. Interrupted by the Second World War and its aftermath (1940–47), production ceased only when work passed to the *Miroku Firearms Company in Japan in the mid-1970s. Made until the mid-1960s, the basic .22LR or .22 Short Model A had a plain semi-pistol-grip butt and a slender fore-end. The Model B was an improved Model A with a chequered pistol-grip butt and a broad semi-beaver-tail fore-end. Deluxe examples (Grades III–V), introduced in 1971, have engraving on the receiver and woodwork specially selected for its attractive grain. Most were abandoned in 1974, although Grade VI did not appear until 1988. **3.** Carabine Automatique Légère, CAL or Light Automatic Carbine. About 30,000 of these were made by Fabrique Nationale d'Armes de Guerre, Herstal-lèz-Liège, in 1966–74. The first attempts to produce a satisfactory 5.56x45 rifle were made in 1963 by adapting the FAL, but the tilting-block locking system lacked the camming action to ease spent cases out of the chamber and extraction was unreliable. The prototypes of the CAL, demonstrated in 1967, retained the proven gas system and trigger of the FAL, but relied on a rotating bolt instead of a tilting block. Fixed- and folding-butt versions were produced, a fully-automatic capability usually being built into the trigger system. Series production began in 1969, but had ended by 1975 in favour of the FNC (q.v.). Gabon and Lebanon purchased a few in the early 1970s, but production was meagre compared with the FAL. **4.** Carabine La Reine. A French-made copy of the *King Model D BB Gun, although the name was also apparently found on some genuine US-made guns sold in France. The butts of the latter are often marked 'Card [sic] Armurier. Fab. Brevete. S.S.S. 15 Boulevard St. Denis. Paris', but nothing else is known. The name may prove to be 'Ricard'. **5.** Carabine Rover, Italy. See Rover.

Carbine – 1. A short firearm with a barrel measuring less than 20–22in, often lacking a bayonet (cf. musketoon). **2.** Carbine, .30 M1, USA. See M1 Carbine.

Carbo-Jet. This name was given to what had formerly been known as the *Schimel gas-powered pistol during the short period in which it was marketed by the *American Weapons Corporation.

Carbona. A term associated with the French *Giffard gas-powered guns, made in Saint-Étienne prior to 1914, first by *Escoffier, then by *Manufacture Française d'Armes et Cycles.

Carbon dioxide, carbonic anhydride. See Gas Gun.

Carcano. Salvatore Carcano. See Italian Mannlicher.

CARD, C.A.R.D. – 1. Acronyms associated with *Cardew Air Rifle Developments, found on ballistic pendulums, chronographs, targets and airgun accessories. **2.** Cardew Air Rifle Developments, Acocks Green, Birmingham, England. This business has been run since its inception by the experimenter Gerald Cardew – author of *The Airgun from Trigger to Muzzle* – making lubricants, measuring equipment, Chinaman targets, springs and accessories.

Caretta. Etore Caretta. Residing at Via Legnano 30, Torino, Caretta was granted British Patent 219,261 in 1924 to protect a gas-powered rifle similar to the Swedish *Excellent.

Carey. A.C. Carey, Malden, Massachusetts, USA. This man was the communicant on behalf of A.A. *Pope of British Patent 1381/76, protecting an airgun with a rotary magazine. Carey may have been the owner of the workshop where the prototype Pope pistols were made prior to the negotiation of licensing agreements with *Quackenbush.

Carl Gustaf, Carl Gustav. Carl Gustafs Stads Gevärsfactori, Eskilstuna. The Swedish government small-arms factory is best known for its *Mauser rifles, but has also made automatic rifles (see Ljungmann) and *Browning machine-guns. Target rifles (known as the Model 63) were made on the basis of the 1896-pattern Swedish *Mauser military action. The factory has also been linked with the *Excellent gas-powered training rifles, said to have been made in 1910–16 for the Swedish Navy, and with spring-air rifles. However, some of the latter are clearly being made in the People's Republic of China, and the Carl Gustav (sic) name seems to serve simply as a brandname. The Carl Gustaf factory was amalgamated with the *Husqvarna operation in 1970, forming *Forenade Fabriksverken.

'Caro' [The]. Associated with shotgun cartridges loaded with semi-smokeless propellant by the *Schultze Gunpowder Company of London prior to 1914. The derivation of the name (sometimes mistakenly listed as Cairo) is not known.

Carolina Arms Company or Carolina Gun Company. A brandname associated with shotguns made by the *Crescent Arms Company of Norwich, Connecticut, USA.

Caron Brothers Manufacturing Company, Montreal, Canada. Recipients of an order for 300,000 .45 M1911 Colt-*Browning pistols from the US government in 1917. However, no guns had been completed when the contract was cancelled immediately following the 1918 Armistice.

Carpenter. William Carpenter, USA. See Stevens.

Carr – 1. Carr Brothers. Gunsmiths and retailers of sporting goods trading in Huddersfield, Yorkshire, England. **2.** Edward P. Carr & Company. Trading prior to 1914 from Lower Parliament Street in Nottingham, England, Carr & Company handled sporting guns and ammunition. **3.** George Carr. A gunmaker, or perhaps wholesaler, with premises at 9 Chambers Street, Goodman's Fields, London E., in 1864–65. **4.** J.W. Carr. Supplier of 12-bore shotguns to the British military authorities, 1942. **5.** M.W. Carr. This US Federal government arms inspector, working during the American Civil War, accepted small-arms marked 'MWC'. **6.** Rinaldo A. Carr. The 'R.A.C.' marks of this inspector, a civilian employee of the US Ordnance Department, working from 1887 until 1910, will be found on Single Action Army Model *Colt revolvers, Colt-made *Gatling Guns and the .38-calibre Colt-*Browning pistols accepted for US Army trials in 1901. *See also* US arms inspectors' marks for the last two entries.

Carrington. *See* Hickman & Carrington.

Carswell. W.C. Carswell. This English gunmaker had premises at 4a Chapel Street in Liverpool, Lancashire; by the early 1900s, he had acquired the business of E. & G. *Higham and *Hooton & Jones, and was offering shotgun ammunition under the names *Banshee and Carswell's Special.

Carter – 1. Frederick W. Carter. Listed in 1898 as a gunmaker at 27a Ridinghouse Street, London W. **2.** Henry Carter was the co-patentee with George H. *Edwards of the Carter & Edwards bolt-action rifle, the subject of British Patents 2417/66, 2513/67, 2769/68 and 1767/69. **3.** John Carter, Britain. *See* Webley. **4.** Carter & Edwards Patent Breech-Loading Rifle Company. This business was formed to exploit patents granted to Henry Carter and George H. Edwards to protect a bolt-action rifle. An office was maintained at Gresham House, 209 Old Broad Street, London E.C., in 1869–70 only. Made in Birmingham, apparently by Walter W. *Scott, the gun was a surprisingly modern-looking design with an internal striker; it was entered in the British Army breech-loading rifle trials of 1868, but was disqualified when problems arose with other bolt-action guns. Small numbers of Carter & Edwards rifles and shotguns were made in the late 1860s, but without lasting success.

Cartridge... – 1. Cartridge case. This contains the propellant and a means of igniting it. There are two major categories – centrefire and rimfire, the former containing the primer centrally in the base of the case, and the latter around the inside of the case-rim. Some cases are straight, others may be necked (or 'bottle-necked') in an attempt to increase propellant capacity without affecting the case length. Belted cases have a raised rib or 'belt' around the body, ahead of the extraction groove, to position the cartridge accurately in the chamber. Belted cases are often very strong, and generally are confined to those rounds that develop high chamber pressures. Rimless cases have an extraction groove in the base, the rim being the same diameter as the case-head. They feed well from magazines, owing to the absence of projecting rims, but must be indexed on the case mouth and often suffer head-space problems. Rimmed cases have a protruding rim at the base of the case, which abuts the chamber face to position the cartridge. Consequently, they index very well, but are prone to rim-over-rim jams in the magazine. Semi-

rimmed cases have an extraction groove like a rimless (q.v.) pattern, in addition to a rim of slightly greater diameter than the case-head. Consequently, the rim can position the case correctly in the chamber, but is small enough to prevent interference in the magazine. **2.** Cartridge, shotgun: *see* panel, p. 110. **3.** Cartridge, small-arms: *see* panel, pp. 112/13. **4.** Cartridge Syndicate Ltd [The]. Registered at 20–23 Holborn, London E.C.1, this British distributor handled shotgun cartridges made by the *Trent Gun & Cartridge Works under the brandname Spartan.

Caruso, alternatively listed as Cruso. A brandname associated with shotguns made by the *Crescent Arms Company of Norwich, Connecticut.

Carver – 1. Alfred Carver. An English gunmaker with premises at 1 Graham Street, Pimlico, London, in 1889–93. **2.** Robert Carver. Listed by H.J. Blanch, writing in *Arms & Explosives* in 1909, as a member of the London gun trade working from 2 George Yard, Princes Street, Soho (1865–79). Possibly the father of Alfred Carver (above). **3.** William Henry Carver. This US Federal government arms inspector, working in 1861–62, during the American Civil War, accepted small-arms marked 'WHC'. *See also* US arms inspectors' marks.

Cary. G.R. Cary. A US airgun patentee, 1876. The piston moved backward.

Cascade Cartridge Company [The], 718 16th Street, Lewiston, Idaho, USA (in 1961). Owned by Elmer Imthurn and Kenneth *Wyatt, this ammunition-making business was the assignee of a patent granted to protect the Wyatt-Imthurn Target Luger.

Casey. A.P. Casey. Working immediately before the outbreak of the American Civil War, this US government arms inspector accepted Starr revolvers marked 'APC'. *See also* US arms inspectors' marks.

Cashmore – 1. Paul Cashmore, West Bromwich, Staffordshire. Listed in Church Field in 1849, trading as a gun- and pistol-maker, then at Newton Street Works until 1892. Cashmore was the co-patentee with Charles *Pryse of the so-called Pryse & Cashmore revolver, protected by British Patent 2018 of 1855, but now usually associated with George H. *Daw. Revolvers were supplied in the white to Pryse, who finished them in his Birmingham factory. Cashmore was advertising himself in 1872 as a 'maker of every description of Breech-Loading Revolver Actions, with Improved Self-Extractors'. He also claimed to have been 'the patentee of the Original Double Action' and to have designed the *Royal Irish Constabulary Pistol. **2.** William Cashmore, Birmingham, Warwickshire. Listed from 1847 as a gun- and pistol-maker, this metalsmith traded from Newton Street until 1857/8, then from Steelhouse Lane. He was granted British Patents 17,040 and 24,426 of 1895, protecting drop-barrel and single-trigger double sporting guns, and was co-patentee with George Brazier of a safety device for hammerless guns (British Patent 25,994 of 1895).

Ca-Si. A Spanish Browning-type pocket automatic made in Eibar, Guipúzcoa, by Fabrique d'Armes de *Grande Précision: 7.65mm, six rounds, hammer fired.

Cassady. *See* Thorsen & Cassady.

Castenholz. Wilhelm Castenholz, a retired German Army officer, was briefly a director of both *Deutsche Waffen- u. Munitionsfabriken and *Fabrique Nationale d'Armes de Guerre. Whether he then became the promoter of the short-lived *Rheinische Waffen- u.

SHOTGUN CARTRIDGE

Cartridge (2)

Most of the cartridges made prior to 1939 had cardboard bodies, often waterproofed with shellac or varnish, set into drawn-brass bases in the form of short, rimmed cylinders. The caps were almost always centrefire, although pin- and rimfire ammunition was made in small quantities in the earliest days of part-metallic ammunition. A few full-length metal cases were made, but never attained widespread distribution.

The case bodies were often printed with names, illustrations and decorations, whereas the base was usually *headstamped with the size designation (e.g. 'No. 12' for 12-bore) and the manufacturer's name or trademark. Shotgun ammunition made in Europe, as a general rule, had decoratively-printed bodies. However, British designs were very different; the ease with which the names of distributors could be added, even today, provides one of the most important sales tools a gunsmith or sporting-goods retailer can have. The ammunition manufacturers have always been quick to satisfy demand, so cartridges made by even small-scale commercial loaders have had the name of a gunsmith, an ironmonger or a sporting-goods dealer added at the printing stage.

*Eley, *Kynoch, *Eley-Kynoch and many other British-made cartridges, therefore, particularly cardboard-body/metal-head types, will be encountered with a bewildering profusion of markings; interestingly, however, illustrations – e.g. a running rabbit or a cock

These shotgun cartridges indicate the range of loads that can be expected, from small-diameter shot to buckshot, bullets, batons and CS gas.

pheasant – are often retained even though the cartridge name changes. This is simply because the etched or engraved illustration blocks could easily be retained in the printing press while the individual lead-block lettering was altered.

The increasingly widespread use of offset lithographic and comparable plastic printing techniques, characteristic of post-1960 ammunition, allowed illustrations to be changed with greater ease, and the stylistic content of the case body legends underwent a perceptible change; previously, only large-scale users paid the extra to have illustration blocks made.

Munitionsfabrik – associated with *Continental semi-automatic pistols – remains unknown.

Castle... – 1. Usually found as 'The Castle' on shotgun cartridges loaded by W. *Darlow from components supplied by *Kynoch or *Eley-Kynoch. A similar mark has also been found on ammunition handled by F.J. *Cole of Cirencester; James *Braddell & Son of Belfast; *Knight of Nottingham; William *Richards of Liverpool and Preston; H. *Robinson & Company of Bridgnorth; and Charles *Smith & Sons of Newark. Most of the components seem to have been supplied by *Eley-Kynoch, although at least some of the distributors loaded the cases on their own premises. **2.** 'Castle Douglas [The]'. This mark is associated with shotgun cartridges sold by C.G.

*Blackadder of Castle Douglas, Dumfriesshire, Scotland.

Cat. An airgun slug made by *Lane Bros. of Bermondsey, prior to 1914, although production continued on an intermittent basis into the 1960s.

Cataluña arms factory. *See* Tarrassa.

Cataract Tool & Optical Company. This US based manufacturing company supplied 8x telescope sights to the US Army early in 1901, for tests in conjunction with 1898-pattern Krag-Jørgensen infantry rifles. The trials were not successful enough to persuade the US Army to adopt Cataract sights, and the *Warner & Swasey pattern was eventually preferred.

Catterfeld – 1. Hugo Catterfeld, Mehlis and Zella-Mehlis in Thüringen, Germany. Listed in the *Deutsches-*

Reichs Adressbuch for 1900 as a gunmaker and in 1914–30 as a gun- and weapon maker. **2.** Ludwig Catterfeld, Zella St Blasii and Zella-Mehlis in Thüringen. Founded in 1865, this gunmaking business used the brandname Luca. It was listed in directories dating from 1900–30 as a gun- and weapon-maker.

Cavalier – 1. A name applied to the MAB Mle C pistol by its North American distributor. *See also* Manufacture d'Armes de Bayonne. **2.** Found on Yugoslavian/Serbian-made *Mauser-action rifles distributed in North America by *Interarms. *See* Mark X Cavalier.

Cave-Mérieux – 1. Cave-Mérieux fils, rue des Jardins 28, Saint-Étienne, France. Listed in 1879 as a distributor of, and agent for, arms and ammunition. **2.** Cave-Mérieux jeune [The Younger], rue Tarentaise 14, Saint-Étienne, France. Listed in 1879 as a distributor of, and agent for, arms and ammunition.

CAVIM. Compañía Anonima Venezolana de Industrias Militares. An outgrowth of the state-owned Venezuelan small-arms factory, this has marked about 10,000 Type 50-63 Para (FN *FAL) rifles supplied to the Guardia Nacional in 1974. The guns were assembled from Belgian-made parts.

'CAW' – 1. A concentric-type monogram with all three letters equally dominant. Correctly 'WAC' (q.v.); used by the *Warner Arms Company. **2.** Found on US military firearms. *See* C.A. *White.

'CAWD'. A concentric-type monogram with all four letters of equal prominence. Correctly 'WDAC' (q.v.); used by the *Warner-Davis Arms Corporation.

Cawdron. Herbert Cawdron. An English gunmaker trading from The Butlands, Wells-next-the-Sea, Norfolk, Cawdron sold shotgun ammunition marked 'The Holkham'.

'C.B.', 'CB' [The]. A shotgun cartridge made by *Kynoch Ltd prior to the acquisition of the company by Explosives Trades Ltd in 1918.

'C. & B.' Found in the headstamps of shotgun cartridges made in Germany by *Cramer & Buchholz prior to 1914.

'CBC', 'C.B.C.' – 1. An abbreviated form of *Companhia Brasiliero de Cartuchoes, a maker of small-arms ammunition and firearms. **2.** On US military firearms. *See* Calvin B. *Cross.

'CC', 'C.C.' – 1. As 'C.C.', a designation mark found on British-made *Martini-action cavalry carbines. **2.** A mark applied by the British ordnance authorities, denoting sale of surplus or obsolete weapons to county cadet corps. **3.** Found on the packaging of Standard British .303 ball ammunition packed in chargers. **4.** A superimposed-type monogram, with the letters back-to-back. Used by Charles Clément of Liège on pistols, revolvers and sporting guns. The lettering was often accompanied by two small diamonds. **5.** As 'CC', back-to-back, beneath a crown. Found on Romanian weapons: the mark of King Carol I (1881–1914) and also of Carol II (1930–40). *See also* Cyphers, imperial and royal.

'C.C.C.' – 1. This abbreviation of the name of the *Creedmore Cartridge Company of Barberton, USA, will be found in cartridge headstamps. **2.** Uncommonly found on the receivers of some of the first .30 *M1 Carbines made by Commercial Controls Corporation, one of the constituents of the *National Postal Meter group of sub-contractors.

'C.C.C.P.', usually accompanied either by a hammer-and-sickle or a five-point star. A mark applied to the weapons of the Soviet Army, ranging from the chamber-tops of *Mosin-Nagant rifles to the grips of *Tokarev pistols. The Cyrillic initials – 'SSSR' in Roman – represent Soyuz Sovetskikh Sotsialisticheskikh Respublik (Union of Soviet Socialist Republics).

'CCH'. *See* C.C. *Hubbard.

'CCM', 'C.C.M.' – 1. Found on components for the No. 4 *Lee-Enfield rifle made during the Second World War by the Canadian Cycle & Motor Company. **2.** Found on US military firearms. *See* Charles C. *Morrison.

CCMO. A superimposition-type monogram with 'C', 'C' and 'M' equally prominent. Correctly 'MCCO' (q.v.); used by *Maltby, Curtis & Company.

'C.C. & T. Co.' Found in the headstamps of ammunition made by the *Chamberlain Cartridge & Target Company of Cleveland, Ohio, USA.

'ccx'. On German military sights and optical equipment made by Optische und Feinmechanische Werke Hugo Meyer & Co. of Görlitz in 1941–45.

'CD'. *See* C. *Davis and C. *Drommer.

'CDAW'. A concentric-type monogram with all four letters of equal significance. Correctly 'WDAC' (q.v.); used by the *Warner-Davis Arms Corporation.

'CDL', 'C.D.L.', 'C...D...L'. *Headstamps associated with C.D. *Leet of Springfield, Massachusetts. Customarily found on rimfire ammunition.

'cdo', 'cdp'. Found on German military small-arms components made during the Second World War in the factories of Theodor *Bergmann & Co. KG in Velten ('cdo') and Bernau ('cdp').

CDWA. *See* 'CDAW'.

'ce'. On German pistols, rifles and small-arms components made during the Second World War by J.P. *Sauer & Sohn of Suhl in Thüringen.

'CEE'. *See* Charles E. *Evans.

Ceiley. Archibald H. Ceiley. This US Federal government arms inspector, working in 1862–63, accepted small-arms marked 'AHC'. *See also* US arms inspectors' marks.

Cei-Rigotti. Amerigo Cei-Rigotti. Italy. Designer of a gas-operated auto-loading rifle, first patented in 1895. A gun of this type was demonstrated at the British Royal Small Arms Factory, Enfield, in March 1901, without success; however, testing continued in Italy until at least 1905.

Celle, Saint-Étienne, France. Listed in directories from 1933 as a gunmaker.

Celta. A Spanish Browning-type pocket pistol made for a major distributor, Tómas de *Urizar of Barcelona: 6.35mm, six rounds. Probably made in Eibar.

Centaure. A brandname found on 6.35mm-calibre automatic pistols made by *Fabrique d'Armes Réunies of Liège. *See also* Dictator.

Centenary Rifle or Centenary Model. A thousand of these *Airsporter derivatives were made by *BSA Guns Ltd in 1982, celebrating the hundredth anniversary of the registration of the *Piled Arms trademark. They had three-quarter-length stocks with rosewood *schnabel fore-end tips, 'C'-prefix numbers and a special 'BSA Piled Arms Centenary – One of One Thousand' mark on top of the air cylinder.

Centennial – 1. A *Suicide Special revolver made by the *Hood Firearms Company of Norwich, Connecticut, USA, in the late nineteenth century. **2.** Or Centennial

SMALL-ARMS CARTRIDGE

Cartridge (3)

The word 'cartridge' derives from *charta*, a Latin word meaning 'paper', and originally acknowledged that a roll of stout paper (which often doubled as a wad) contained black powder and a lead ball. Many inventors tried to provide cartridges that were stronger or had better water-resistant qualities, but no real progress was made until the development of effective self-contained ammunition in the 1830s. Some of the earliest advances were made in France, where the *Robert cartridge – with a long priming tube protruding rearward – and the pinfire round were developed in the 1830s.

In its earliest form, the pinfire consisted of an annular metal base and a cardboard tube; the primer was ignited when a pin, protruding laterally, was driven downward by the gun-hammer. Cartridges of this type were made in Europe until the 1920s, in calibres ranging from 7mm to 20mm or more, but were too vulnerable to blows to gain widespread use.

The *Sharps and many others among the breech-loading guns made in the USA prior to the Civil War embodied self-contained cartridges, although most of these were made of skin, while others were of rubberised paper. The Prussian *Dreyse needle gun, adopted officially in 1840, and the French Chassepot (1867) fired combustible needle-fire cartridges with a pellet of fulminate held in either a papier-mâché sabot behind the bullet (Dreyse) or in the base of the elongated paper case (Chassepot). However, the *Burnside and *Maynard carbines used distinctive metal-case cartridges, even though ignition still relied on an external *cap-lock.

A major advance was made in the 1850s by *Smith & Wesson, whose perfection of a method of spinning priming compound into the internal periphery of case rims created the first .22 rimfire cartridge. The advent of patent-protected rimfire cartridges, even though the manufacturing processes were far from perfect, encouraged the development of a range of rival designs. However, as the majority of these were intended specifically to evade the protection granted to Smith & Wesson, most were cumbersome and often sources of great danger: teat-fire and lip-fire cartridges had vulnerable projections; some cartridges were manufactured with an annular belt of priming around the case body; and others had the priming in the form of a cup within the base of the cartridge case.

Rimfire ignition limited the size and power of cartridges, and progress was not made until the advent of the first centrefire priming systems. The first of these (e.g. Morse, Martin) were internal,

---

USA. A name associated with a revolver sold in Belgium prior to c. 1914 by A. *Rongé. **3.** Introduced in 1952 and known from 1957 as the Model 40, this swing-cylinder .38-calibre *Smith & Wesson revolver is easily recognisable by the enclosed hammer and a grip safety let into the backstrap of the butt. Guns made after 1968 have 'L'-prefix numbers, but interest in enclosed-hammer revolvers waned until the Model 40 (with its *Airweight equivalent) was abandoned in 1974. **4.** Centennial Model. This was a short-lived variant of the *Daisy M1894 lever-action BB Gun, 50,000 being ordered in 1970 by *Sears, Roebuck & Company to celebrate the centenary of the meeting of the transcontinental railroads. A replica of the Golden Spike rifle made for Sears by Winchester, the BB Guns had half-octagon barrels and a brass finish on the frame, fore-end cap and butt plate.

Center. An unusual 4.5mm underlever-cocking spring-air pistol made in Spain by *El Gamo. Its side-swinging breech-block was based on a Hungarian FÉG Telly prototype of the 1960s, but the articulated butt was unique. The *Falcón was a simplified Center.

Central Gun Company. A brandname associated with shotguns made by the *Crescent Arms Company.

Centrale... – **1.** Centrale Magazijn, Woerden. This Netherlands Indies Army (*KNIL) depot was known as the Centrale Werkplaatz until 1916. The facilities were subsequently used by the Indonesian Army after the Netherlands Indies gained independence in 1949. The mark 'C.M.' – usually accompanied by the date and inspector's initials – was applied to a variety of military stores, especially those made largely of wood or leather. **2.** Centrale Werkplaatz, Woerden. This was the main European depot and workshop of the Netherlands Indies Army (KNIL), renamed Centrale Magazijn in 1916. The mark 'C.W.' – usually accompanied by the date and inspector's initials – was applied to a variety of military stores, but particularly articles made largely of wood and leather. A typical example reads 'C.W.' over '10 12' (October 1912) and 'W.K.'

Centro de Estudios Técnicos de Materiales Especiales. *See* CETME.

Centurion. This name was used on Mauser-pattern sporting rifles made by the *Golden State Arms Corporation in the 1960s. The series included the standard Model 100 and deluxe Model 200, but a variety of styles was offered.

Century International Arms, Inc., St Albans, Vermont, USA. This distribution business has offered *Mauser-type sporting rifles built on Swedish Model 1896 or war-surplus Kar. 98k-type actions.

Čermak. Josef Čermak, Brno, Czechoslovakia. This engineer is credited with perfecting the vz. 58 assault rifle, an adaptation of the *Holek-designed ZB 530 chambering the Soviet 7.62x39 M43 cartridge intstead of the original long-case Czechoslovak version.

Certus. This tradename, also used as a telegraphic address, was linked with the products of *Cogswell & Harrison. It was associated specifically with a unique bolt-action system patented in 1900 by Edgar *Harrison and used for some years on rifles ranging from single-shot .22 rimfires up to magazine-fed .303 sporters. The action (which was also used on a few shotguns and apparently licensed to Westley *Richards) relied on a short stubby rotating bolt set into a block that could slide back on rails in the receiver. After the First World War, however, Certus sporting rifles were built on conventional *Mauser actions, either reconditioned from wartime manufacture or bought specially from Oberndorf. The

relying on the rim being folded over a suitable priming pocket, but the *Berdan and *Boxer replaceable-primer systems soon became universally popular. Boxer primers have separate anvils; Berdan primers rely on an integral anvil formed in the base of the case as part of the primer pocket.

These patterns are still used, although the British-designed Boxer system is more popular in North America than the American-designed Berdan…which is now commonplace in Europe. The old 'balloon-head' construction, with a primer pocket that protruded into the propellant space, has been superseded by the stronger 'solid-head' pattern with the floor of the propellant chamber flush with the top surface of the primer pocket.

With the exception of improvements in propellant and a constant search for an effective 'caseless' or consumable cartridge, the major twentieth-century advance has been the introduction of non-corrosive primers. It seems that most large-scale ammunition manufacturers were experimenting with primers of this type almost as soon as the First World War had ended, but the first to be perfected commercially was the Remington *Kleanbore system.

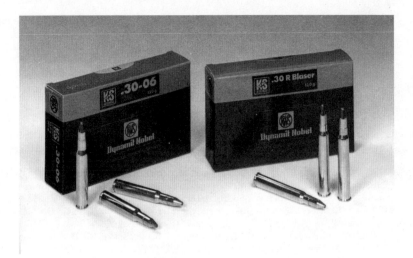

Made by Dynamit Nobel, these typical sporting-rifle cartridges – .30-06 (left) and .30R Blaser (right) – are usually marketed under the RWS brand.

name was also used on shotgun ammunition handled by Cogswell & Harrison, and the .177-calibre Certus spring-air pistol – another Harrison design, patented in Britain in 1929. Subsequently a few pistols were made in Cogswell & Harrison's Acton workshops, but the Certus was never able to challenge the Johnstone & Fearn-pattern *Webleys.

'CES'. *See* Charles E. *Sherman and Clarence E. *Simpson.

Česká Zbrojovka Akc. Spol., also known as ČZ or the Bohemian Arms Company Ltd, Prague. This Czechoslovakian gunmaking business was formed in 1922 by amalgamating *Hubertus and *Jinočeská Zbrojovka. The government transferred the manufacture of pistols from *Československá Zbrojovka of Brno to Prague in 1923, where subsequently vz. 24, vz. 27 and vz. 38 pistols were made in quantity, alongside vz. 28 and vz. 30 aircraft machine-guns and a bolt-action airgun known as the vz. 35. Patented in Britain in 1936 (no. 456,096), this served the Czechoslovak Army in a training role. After making MG. 34 components during the German occupation (1939–45), the Prague factory continued to make pistols – including the ČZ 50, ČZ 448 and vz. 52 – together with a variety of sporting guns and the ČZ 47 magazine-fed air rifle. A subsidiary factory in Uherský Brod (Závody Preshneho Strojirentsvi v Uherskem Brod) concentrated on .22 rimfire sporting guns and barrel-cocking airguns. Guns marked Narodny Podnik (State Enterprise) were made immediately after the seizure of the country by the Communists in 1948. In addition to firearms, the ČZ factories have also made machine tools (from 1928 onward), bicycles (from 1930) and motorcycles (from 1934). The company was renamed České Závody Motocyklové in 1955, in recognition of the growing importance of its automotive business. Československá Zbrojovka has also made handguns commercially, including the 6.35mm vz. 36 pocket pistol.

Československá Zbrojovka Akc. Spol., also known as ZB or the Czechoslovakian Arms Company Ltd, Brno, Czechoslovakia. This company was formed in 1923 to acquire the gunmaking business of ČSZ (below), although most of the shareholding remained in the hands of the Czechoslovakian government and large industrial giants such as Škoda. In addition to *Mauser-action military rifles, particularly the vz. 24 short pattern, sporting guns were also made in the early 1930s. The Model A was a half-stock rifle; Model B was a fully-stocked carbine. The later Model 21 (half-stock rifle) and Model 22 (fully-stocked carbine) had safety catches on the left side of the bolt shroud, and were offered in chamberings from 6.5x57 to 9x57. The Brno factory also inherited the *Praga M-24 light machine-gun. Once minor changes had been made, the M-24 became the ZB vz. 26 and series production began for the armed forces. The rifles and machine-guns were very successful, selling world-wide, and entire duplicate production lines were installed in Mosalsalasi (Persia), Cugir (Romania) and Kraguyevač (Yugoslavia) to make Mauser rifles – in the Persian factory only – and ZB 30 light machine-guns. Československá Zbrojovka survived the depression of the 1930s largely by perfecting the *Bren Gun in association with British technicians at the *Royal Small Arms Factory in Enfield, and by introducing the ZB 53 7.9mm and ZB 60 15mm belt-feed machine-guns. When the Germans occupied the factory, from 15 March 1939 onward, many technicians escaped to Britain to help produce the 7.9mm and 15mm *Besa guns during the Second World War. Operations began again after the Second World War, with guns such as the ZB vz. 52, vz. 52/57 and vz. 59 machine-guns. The

Brno company purchased several other businesses in the period between the world wars, including the long-established cartridge-making operations of Georg *Roth. This was managed as Československé Muniční a Korodělné Závody (Czechoslovakian Munitions and Metalworking Factory); stakes were also purchased in *Škoda and *Sellier & Bellot. Československá Zbrojovka N.P. is currently making sporting guns in Brno, production of military weapons being concentrated in Považske Strijírný and Dubniča nád Vahom.

Československé Závody na Výrobu Zbraní, also known as ČSZ or the Czechoslovakian Factory for Military Products, Brno. This state-owned small-arms factory was founded in March 1919 in what had been an Austro-Hungarian artillery depot. After refurbishing 100,000 Mauser and Mannlicher rifles for the Czechoslovakian Army, CSZ made a few 1895-pattern Mannlicher short rifles in 1921–22. However, a licensing agreement had been reached with Waffenfabrik *Mauser AG in 1921, and 42,000 sets of German-made rifle parts were assembled in Brno before production of 1898-type rifles began. These were superseded by the vz. 24 short rifle. However, constitutional difficulties were encountered in export markets, and the gunmaking operation of

ČSZ was sold in 1923 to *Československá Zbrojovka.

CETME. *See* panel, below.

'CEW', 'C.E.W.' – 1. Found on components for the British No. 4 *Lee-Enfield rifle made during the Second World War by C.E. Welstead. This company was also allocated the area code 'S127', but often used its initials instead. **2.** Found on US military firearms. *See* Charles E. *Wilson.

'CF', 'cf' – 1. Found as 'CF' on cartridges, usually in the form of a superimposed-letter monogram and often encircled. Associated with the products of Cartoucherie Française. **2.** Used as 'cf' by Westfälisch-Anhaltische Sprengstoff AG of Oranienburg on small-arms ammunition components made for the German forces during the Second World War.

'C.F.C. Co.' Associated with ammunition made by C.F. *Cook & Company.

'CFD'. *See* Charles F. *Dupee.

CFDO. 'FD' within 'C' with a small 'o' in its jaws. Correctly 'FD CO.' (q.v.); used by Fabrique d'Armes F. *Delu et Cie.

'CFL'. *See* C.F. *Lewis.

'C.F.M.'. Found on components for the British No. 4 *Lee-Enfield rifle made during the Second World War by

---

CETME

This Spanish agency is best known for the successful development of ideas originating in Germany during the Second World War. Inspired by the MG. 42, *Mauser-Werke engineer Wilhelm *Stähle began work in 1942 on weapons embodying a roller-locked breech operated by a conventional gas-piston unit. By 1943, however, experiments had shown that the mechanism worked satisfactorily without the piston assembly. Deep-seated official suspicion slowed progress with the delayed-blowback Gerät 06.H, and thirty locked-breech assault rifles (Gerät 06 or StG.45 [M]) had only just been commissioned when the war ended. Once the Mauser factory in Oberndorf had fallen into French hands, work was transferred to the Mulhouse factory of *SACM and continued for some time under the supervision of a Mauser engineer named Ludwig *Vorgrimmler. By 1951, however, attention had shifted to Spain. The Instituto Nacional de

Industrias had formed the Centro de Estudios Técnicos de Materiales Especiales (CETME) in Madrid, where, supervised by Vorgrimmler, the first assault-rifle prototypes were completed in 1952. Many changes were made to the guns and their ammunition until, in 1954, the Spanish government invited *Heckler & Koch to advise on series-production problems. Adopted in 1958, the 7.62mm Fusil de Asalto CETME and the 5.56mm 'L' variant (approved in 1984) have since been made in quantity in the factory of Empresa Nacional de Militares 'Santa Barbara' that had formerly been known as *Fábrica de Armas de Oviedo. The CETME rifle was licensed to *NWM in 1956, and, as the Germans had also become very interested, Heckler & Koch (q.v.) obtained production rights in the late 1950s.

An example of the 5.56mm Fusil de Asalto CETME Modelo LC on trial. Note how the bipod doubles as the fore-grip.

C.F. Moore & Son. This company was also allocated the area code 'S238', but often used its initials instead.

'CFR', 'CFU'. Found on US military firearms. *See* Charles F. *Rogers and Charles F. *Ulrich.

'cg'. Associated with German small-arms ammunition made by Finower Industrie GmbH of Finow/Mark in 1940–45.

'C.G.A.' – 1. Often within a buckler. A trademark associated with the British *Country Gentlemen's Association. **2.** 'CGA': a concentric-type monogram, with the letters 'G' and 'A' prominent. Correctly interpreted as 'GAC' (q.v.); used by *Garate, Anitua y Cia.

'CGC'. *See* Charles G. *Chandler and Charles G. *Curtis.

'CGH', 'C.G.H.' – 1. Often accompanied by crossed pistols. A mark associated with C.G. *Haenel of Suhl, found on rifles and bayonets made prior to the First World War. **2.** Found on US military firearms. *See* Charles G. *Howe.

'ch', 'CH', 'C.H.' – 1. Usually as 'ch'; associated with pistols, small-arms and components made by *Fabrique Nationale d'Armes de Guerre SA of Herstal-lèz-Liège during the German occupation of Belgium in 1940–44. **2.** An encircled superimposition-type monogram, with 'H' slightly dominant. Encountered on the frames of break-open *Smith & Wesson-style revolvers made in Spain prior to 1914 by *Crucelegui Hermanos of Eibar. **3.** As 'C.H.'; a Spanish 6.35mm Browning-type automatic pistol made by Crucelegui Hermanos in Eibar: eight rounds, hammer fired.

Chaffee – 1. Reuben S. Chaffee, Springfield, Massachusetts. An employee of the National Armory, Chaffee obtained several patents protecting 'magazine firearms' prior to 1900. They included US no. 161,480 of 30 March 1875, assigned in part to Bernard Stuve of Springfield; 211,887 of 4 February 1879 and 216,657 of 25 February 1879, the latter being assigned to J.N. Reece (q.v.) of Springfield; 314,363 of 24 March 1885, an improvement of 216,657 part-assigned to Reece; and 314,515 of 24 March 1885 for a 'Feeding Mechanism for Breech-Loading Fire Arms'. US Patent 342,328 ('Breech-Loading Firearm') was granted on 25 May 1886, one-tenth of the interest being assigned to the *Winchester Repeating Arms Company; 368,933 of 30 August 1887 (for a 'Magazine Firearm') was the last to be granted to Chaffee before he retired from the Armory. **2.** Chaffee-Reece rifle. This bolt-action design, the work of Reuben Chaffee and James *Reece, competed unsuccessfully against the Winchester-*Hotchkiss and the *Remington-Lee in the US Army trials of 1884. The butt contained an oscillating double-rack feed mechanism that proved to be unreliable and difficult to maintain, although it had the merit of separating the nose of one cartridge from the base of another. *Springfield Armory made 750 .45-70 Chaffee-Reece rifles in 1883–84 on machinery that had once been used to make the *Ward-Burtons. A solitary .30-calibre prototype – probably a conversion – was speedily eliminated from the trials of 1891, and the remaining .45 guns were sold to Francis *Bannerman & Sons shortly afterward.

Chaine. William Chaine. Usually listed as British, this inventor was granted British Patent 1905/95 of 26 January 1895 to protect a complicated revolver with a ring trigger and an auxiliary tubular magazine feeding cartridges into the cylinder.

Chaineux. A French gunmaker credited with perfecting the double-action lockwork encountered on *Lefaucheux pinfire revolvers of the 1850s.

Chalet, place Marengo 2, Saint-Étienne, France. Listed in 1879 as a gunmaker.

Challenge – 1. Usually as 'The Challenge'. Found on shotgun cartridges sold in Britain by C.H. *Barham of Hitchin; A. *Bates of Canterbury; E.R. *Bates of Canterbury; J. *Hobson of Leamington Spa; and *Marrow & Company of Halifax and Harrogate. Maker unknown. **2.** A break-action BB Gun made in the USA by *Thorsen & Cassady in the late 1890s.

Challenger – 1. Usually found as 'The Challenger', on shotgun cartridges sold in Scotland by John *Barnes of Ayr. **2.** *Suicide Special revolvers made in the USA by *Johnson, Bye & Company and/or *Iver Johnson of Worcester and Fitchburg, Massachusetts. They date from the late nineteenth century. **3.** A crude wood-body break-open BB Gun, with an inset brass barrel, made in the USA in 1886 by the *Markham Air Rifle Company. It was soon replaced by the *Improved Challenger. **4.** A name used by the Challenger Arms Corporation on a short-lived series of pneumatic pistols, rifles and shotguns. *See also* Plainsman; guns will also be encountered under the distributor's name, Goodenow. **5.** An alternative name for the *Challenge BB Gun. **6.** The most recent bearer of this particular name was a powerful .177-calibre spring-air rifle marketed in the USA by the *Crosman Arms Company from 1983 onward. Known in Europe as the *RWS 45, this gun was a *Mayer & Grammelspacher Diana LG 45 action fitted in a modified LG 35 stock. **7.** A simplified variant of the post-1948 *Woodsman Sport, 77,000 guns being made in 1950–55 by *Colt's Fire Arms Manufacturing Company. They had fixed sights, but lacked hold-opens and had the magazine release on the heel of the butt. The 4.5 and 6.5in barrels were tapered. The Challenger was replaced by the *Huntsman. **8.** Challenger Arms Corporation, Los Angeles, California, USA. This business made the Challenger and *Plainsman pneumatic pistols, rifles and shotguns in 1948–50, but was unable to compete satisfactorily with companies such as Benjamin and Crosman, and soon failed. Trading had certainly ceased by 1955.

Chambe, Saint-Étienne, France. Listed in 1933 as a gunmaker.

Chamber. The enlarged and shaped area of the interior of the gun barrel at the breech, into which the cartridge fits.

Chambering – 1. The act of cutting a chamber (q.v.) in the barrel. **2.** An indication of the cartridge a particular gun accepts: e.g. 'chambering .30-30 Winchester Central Fire', 'chambered for 7.62x51mm NATO cartridges'. It should not be confused with calibre (q.v.); the rifle chambering a .30-calibre cartridge may be any of several types. Thus the US Krag-Jørgensen M1892 (.30-40 Krag rimmed), Springfield M1903 (.30 M1903 or .30 M1906 rimless) and Winchester M1894 (.30-30 rimmed) may share the same calibre, but accept entirely different cartridges.

Chamberlain – 1. A. Chamberlain. An English gunmaker trading from 18 Queen Street, Salisbury, Wiltshire, Chamberlain offered shotgun ammunition marked 'A.C. County', 'A.C. Wiltshire', 'Command', 'Sarum', 'Stonehenge' and 'Wessex' prior to 1918. **2.** E.

Chamberlain. A gunmaker with shops in Andover and Basingstoke, Hampshire, England, Chamberlain handled guns and *Eley-made ammunition prior to 1914. **3.** George E. Chamberlain. This US government arms inspector, working in 1862–77, accepted small-arms marked 'GEC'. *See also* US arms inspectors' marks. **4.** John Chamberlain. A gunsmith trading from 23 Birchin Lane, London E.C., in 1869–76. He was succeeded by his son, Richard J. Chamberlain (below). **5.** Joseph F.E. Chamberlain. This US government arms inspector, working in 1875, accepted .45 S&W *Schofield revolvers marked 'JFEC'. *See also* US arms inspectors' marks. **6.** Martin J. Chamberlain, sometimes listed as Chamberlin, Springfield, Massachusetts, USA. This gunsmith received his first US Patent on 8 January 1867, when no. 60,998 was granted jointly with H.M. Chamberlain to protect a rifle with a radial breech-block swinging back and down. Subsequently, Martin Chamberlain developed breech-loading shotguns protected by US Patents 111,814 of 14 February 1871, 112,505 of 7 March 1871 (jointly with Dexter *Smith), 129,393 of 16 July 1872 and 135,405 of 4 February 1873. All of these protected radial breech-block systems, similar to the Remington Rolling Block, although the perfected version was locked by the tip of the sear. **7.** R.B. Chamberlain. This US government arms inspector, working in 1906, accepted small-arms marked 'RBC'. *See also* US arms inspectors' marks. **8.** Richard John Chamberlain, listed in 1875 at 9 Railway Approaches, London S.E. (probably his home), succeeded his father John Chamberlain in 1876/7. His gunsmith's shop was to be found in Birchin Lane until 1878, but it moved for two years to 81a Gracechurch Street, London E.C. No mention is made of Chamberlain in directories dated later than 1881. **9.** William G. Chamberlain. This US government arms inspector, working in 1858–73 and possibly later, accepted small-arms marked 'WGC'. *See also* US arms inspectors' marks. **10.** Chamberlain Cartridge Company, also recorded from 1894 as the Chamberlain Cartridge & Target Company or even – apparently mistakenly – as 'Chamberlin' (USA), 76 Superior Street, Cleveland, Ohio, USA. This business was formed in 1884 to exploit a patent granted to F.L. Chamberlain to protect a mechanically-driven 'Automatic Cartridge Loading Machine'. Operations continued until the Chamberlain Target & Trap Company was purchased by Remington–UMC in August 1933. Shotgun cartridges headstamped 'C.C. Co.' and later 'C.C. & T. Co.' were made under a variety of brandnames, including Amateurs, American Clay Bird, Black Bird, Brant, Canvas Back, Clay Pigeon, Mallard, Pintail, Point Shooting, Prairie Chicken, Quail, Red Head, Ruffed Grouse, Snipe, Sora, Squirrel, Taxidermist, Teal and Woodcock.

Chamberlin: a popular misrepresentation of *Chamberlain.

Chambers – 1. John Chambers. Listed as a gunmaker at 46 Lambeth Street, London E., from 1854 until about 1867. **2.** Septimus Chambers, a 'Gunmaker of Bristol, Cardiff & Shepton Mallet', designed an improved shotgun cartridge in the early years of the twentieth century. Based on pre-1914 Kynoch components, surviving examples are customarily marked 'Patent 15848' without identifying the year in question.

Chambert, rue Mulatière 27, Saint-Étienne, France. Listed in 1892 as a gunmaker.

Chambon – 1. Rue de Treuil 30, Saint-Étienne, France. Listed in 1879 as a distributor of, and agent for, arms and ammunition. **2.** Chambon Frères, 38 rue J.-B. David, Saint-Étienne, France. Listed in 1951 as a gunmaker.

Chamelot-Delvigne. Derived from the names of supposed inventors, this applied to a particular form of *double-action revolver lockwork. Guns of this type were popular in Belgium, the Netherlands, Italy and Switzerland (where improvements made by Rudolf *Schmidt created the so-called Chamelot-Delvigne & Schmidt sub-variant). At least one source credits the design of the Chamelot-Delvigne lock to the Frenchman Eugène *Lefaucheux, and the truth remains obscure. *See* A.W.F. Taylerson, *The Revolver, 1865–88* (Jenkins, London 1966).

Chamois. A *Mauser-pattern sporting rifle, made by Karl *Dschulnigg of Salzburg in the 1960s, this was similar to the *Ibex, but had a much more conventional stock.

Champion, Champion... – 1. Usually found as 'The Champion'. Brandnames Champion and Champion Long Range are associated with shotgun ammunition made by the *Mullerite Cartridge Works of Birmingham after 1922. The cartridges, which often bear a drawing of a cock pheasant, may also carry a variety of distributors' names – e.g. G.J. *Bassett of Petersfield, W.J. *Jeffrey of London, *Jewson of Halifax, *Palmer of Sittingbourne, and *Redmayne & Todd of Nottingham. **2.** A name applied generically to a range of airgun pellets made in Britain by L.J. *Cammell (Merseyside) Ltd in .177, .22 and .25. **3.** Champion: *see* Buffalo-Champion. **4.** A spring-air pistol patented by Iver *Johnson and Martin *Bye, but probably made in Herkimer, New York State, by, or for, the *Pope Manufacturing Company before a licence was agreed c. 1879 with *Quackenbush. Eldon Wolff records that boxes for Quackenbush felted darts and lead slugs were often labelled 'for...Excelsior and Hurricane Air Guns, Eureka, Champion's and Pope's Air Pistols'. The Quackenbush company made sixty-nine Champion pistols as late as 1884, but the contract arrangements (if any) are unclear. **5.** *Suicide Special revolvers made in the USA by *Johnson, Bye & Company and/or *Iver Johnson of Worcester and Fitchburg, Massachusetts. They date from the late nineteenth century. **6.** A sheath-trigger *Suicide Special revolver, made by the *Norwich Arms Company and/or the *Norwich Falls Pistol Company of Norwich, Connecticut, USA. **7.** Used on a single-barrel box-lock central-hammer shotgun made in 1885–90 by the John P. *Lovell Arms Company of Boston, Massachusetts, USA. Sometimes known as Lovell's Champion. **8.** A lever-action spring-air BB Gun made in the USA by *Daisy, otherwise known as the Model 99, Model 99 Target or Model 99 Target Special. **9.** Champion Hunter. A cone-point diabolo airgun pellet made in Britain by L.J. *Cammell (Merseyside) Ltd in .177 and .22. **10.** Champion of the World. A name associated with a revolver sold in Belgium prior to c. 1914 by A. *Rongé.

'Championship' [The]. Found on shotgun cartridges handled by Charles *Hellis & Sons of London.

Champlin. Champlin-Haskins Firearms, Inc., of Enid, Oklahoma, USA, made bolt-action rifles to the patents of Jerry Haskins in 1968–70. Distinguished by octagonal receivers and matching bolt shrouds, the rifles could be

CHARGER

A device for loading a magazine firearm, very common in military weapons, but much less popular on sporting guns. Cartridges are kept in a special holder, usually made of sheet metal and often containing a spring. The action is opened, the cartridge-holder positioned at the entrance to the magazine, and the cartridges are pressed downward by the thumb. This strips them from the charger and pushes them into the magazine box. Chargers are confusingly known as clips (q.v.) in North America, or sometimes as stripper clips to avoid problems of communication.

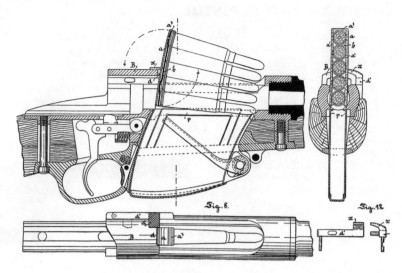

These drawings from Austro-Hungarian Privilegium (patent) 39/609 show how a charger works, and how it is customarily discarded automatically as the bolt closes.

chambered for practically any cartridge the purchaser specified. The manufacturer was reorganised to become Champlin Firearms, Inc., in 1971 and was still operating in the late 1990s.

Chandler – 1. Charles G. Chandler. This US Federal government arms inspector, working immediately prior to the American Civil War in 1861, accepted Colt and Remington cap-lock revolvers marked 'CGC'. **2.** Robert W. Chandler. This US government arms inspector, working during the First World War (1917–18), accepted .45 Colt and Smith & Wesson revolvers marked 'RWC'. **3.** William H. Chandler. A Federal government arms inspector, working during the American Civil War in 1862–64, this man accepted small-arms marked 'WHC'. *See also* US arms inspectors' marks for all three entries.

Chanson. Jean Chanson, 11 rue Basse-des-Rives, Saint-Étienne, France. Listed in 1951 as a gunmaker.

Chapeau-Delon, rue Violette 13, Saint-Étienne, France. Listed in 1879–92 as a gunmaker.

Chapel. A.E. Chapel, or A. & E. Chapel. A gunsmith reportedly working in Liverpool, Lancashire, England, in the nineteenth century, Chapel is said to have handled pepperboxes, cap-lock revolvers and air canes.

Chapin – 1. Dwight Chapin & Company, Bridgeport, Connecticut. A maker of *Ballard rifles. **2.** F.M. Chapin. This US government arms inspector, working in 1898, accepted small-arms marked 'FMC'. **3.** George W. Chapin. This Federal government arms inspector accepted .44 Starr cap-lock Army revolvers during the American Civil War. They were marked 'GWC'. *See also* US arms inspectors' marks for the last two entries.

Chaplin. B.E. Chaplin. The marks of this English gunmaker, trading from 6 Southgate Street, Winchester, Hampshire, have been found on shotgun ammunition marked 'Ideal' and 'Winton'. *See also* Howard A. *Davis.

Chapman – 1. E.E. Chapman. This US government arms inspector, a major in the US Army, accepted Remington-made M1911 (Colt) pistols in 1918–19. These were marked 'EEC'. **2.** William Chapman. This

US Federal government arms inspector, working in 1861–64, accepted small-arms marked 'WC'. *See also* US arms inspectors' marks.

Charco, Inc., Ansonia, Connecticut. A US-based gun-making business, 1992-vintage successors to the *Charter Arms Corporation.

Charger – 1. *See* panel, above. **2.** Charger guides. A method of positioning the charger to enable the firer to press cartridges into the magazine. Most charger-loading rifles have the guides on the front of the receiver bridge, although some early British Lee-Enfields had one guide on the bolt head, and some Mausers have the left guide formed by an upward extension of the bolt-stop. Mauser is usually credited with the introduction of the charger-loaded magazine, but elements of the system may be seen in some early quick-loading devices.

Charles Lancaster. A sporting rifle offered in the 1960s by *Atkin, Grant & Lang on a standard 1898-pattern Mauser action in .243 Winchester, .270 Winchester, .30-06 and .308 Winchester.

Charlier et Cie [Manufacture d'Armes], Liège. The Belgian-based maker of the *Wegria-Charlier or *WS pistols.

Charlin, 18 rue Béranger, Saint-Étienne, France. Listed in 1951 as a gunmaker.

Charola – 1. Ignacio Charola, Eibar. This Spanish gunmaker was the patentee and co-promoter with entrepreneur Gregorio Anitua of the Charola y Anitua automatic pistol. **2.** Charola y Anitua pistol: *see* panel, p. 118.

Charrin. This Liège based gunsmith patented a self-cocking dropping-block system in 1865. It was operated by lowering the combination operating lever/trigger guard (pivoted in a lug below the chamber) to push the striker back until it was held by the sear. Simultaneously, the breech-block, striker and trigger assembly dropped to expose the breech, and a pivoting extractor withdrew the spent case.

Chartron. J. Chartron; Saint-Étienne, France. Listed in 1933 as a gunmaker.

Charter – 1. George K. Charter or 'Carter'. This

CHAROLA Y ANITUA PISTOL

Charola (2)

One of the first successful semi-automatics, this pistol was patented in 1897 (although design work is said to have begun in 1895 or earlier). The action embodied a wedge-type breech-lock and, no doubt inspired by the *Mauser C/96, a box magazine lay ahead of the trigger. The earliest guns were remarkable for their tiny 5mm cartridge (now better known as 5mm Clément), but a more powerful 7mm version was introduced c. 1900. Production continued until about 1904, reaching perhaps 5,000. Charoly y Anitua pistols have a distinctive revolver-like butt and a safety lever extending back alongside the hammer. Many are found with Liège proof marks, and it is possible that they were actually made in Belgium for the promoters. Spanish markings and a winged-bullet trademark are customary, although short-safety pistols marked 'STANDART' on the left side of the frame are said to have been destined for Russia.

The recoil-operated Charola y Anitua, patented in Spain in 1897, was one of the earliest commercially successful semi-automatic pistols, even though originally it chambered a feeble 5mm cartridge. This example has Belgian proof marks.

Federal government arms inspector accepted Starr caplock Navy revolvers during the American Civil War. They were marked 'GKC'. *See also* US arms inspectors' marks. **2.** Charter Arms Corporation, Sniffens Lane, Stratford, Connecticut. Formed in the USA in 1964 to exploit a patent granted to Douglas McClenahan, this revolver-making business traded until succeeded in 1992 by *Charco, Inc. Success (measured by the production of a half-million guns by 1978) was built around a small five-shot double-action *Bulldog revolver with a yoke-mounted cylinder and an unbreakable copper/beryllium firing pin. Other claimed advantages included the small number of critical moving parts and a radial hammer-fall of a mere 55 degrees. Charter Arms also promoted a handgun version of the ArmaLite AR7 survival rifle, marketed as the Explorer (q.v.). *See also* Off-Duty, Pathfinder, Police Bulldog, Police Undercover, Target Bulldog, Undercover and Undercoverette.

Chartered Firearms Industries, Pty, and Chartered Industries of Singapore. Makers of automatic rifles. *See also* ArmaLite.

Chase. Luke B. Chase. This US government arms inspector, working shortly before the outbreak of the American Civil War, accepted small-arms marked 'LBC'. *See also* US arms inspectors' marks.

Chassepot – 1. Antoine Alphonse Chassepot (1833–1908), rising to *Contrôleur d'Armes* and a holder of the Cross of the Légion d'Honneur by the time he retired in 1886, was the son of an armourer. Chassepot began his career in the Mutzig factory in 1856, but was posted first to the central artillery depot, then to the Atelier de modèles de Saint-Thomas d'Aquin in Paris. He is best known as the inventor of the eponymous needle rifle used by the French Army during the war of 1870–71. This was the subject of several patents, including US no. 60,832 of 1 January 1867 and 91,167 of 23 November 1869 for a metallic-cartridge conversion. **2.** Chassepot needle rifle: *see* panel, facing page.

Châtellerault. Founded in 1819, the Manufacture d'Armes de Châtellerault made a wide range of French small-arms, including machine-guns, rifles and handguns, prior to closing in 1968. They included a few Mle 35S pistols, although apparently production was confined to 1946. The factory was also responsible for the MAC-50 service pistol, a 9mm Parabellum derivation of the Mle 35S M1 made from 1953 until 1963. *See also* Saint-Étienne and Tulle.

Chatham naval ordnance depot. Converter of some British *Lee-Enfield rifles to charger loading.

Chattaway. James Chattaway This Federal government arms inspector, working during the American Civil War, accepted small-arms marked 'JC'. *See also* US arms inspectors' marks.

Chauchat Machine Rifle. *See* CSRG.

Chaumont. M.J. Chaumont, Liège. A Belgian gunmaker, active during the mid-nineteenth century, Chaumont was known for his double-barrel sporting guns. Most were caplocks, but pinfire breech-loaders still survive.

Chausse – 1. Charles Chausse, Saint-Étienne, France. Listed in 1933 as a gunmaker, and in 1951 at 23 rue Charles-Rebour. **2.** Chausse jeune [the younger], Saint-Étienne, France. Listed in 1933 as a gunmaker, and in 1951 at 76 rue Antoine-Durafour.

Chavas (Veuve) et Sagnol, place Fourneyron, Saint-Étienne, France. Listed in 1892 as a distributor of, and agent for, arms and ammunition.

Chavot, 4 rue Clément-Forissière, Saint-Étienne, France. Listed in 1951 as a gunmaker.

Cheek piece. Found on the side of a gun butt to help the firer position his eye behind the sights. The Classic or Classical design was a plain oval, but many modern rifles have a Monte Carlo type with a high comb suited to optical sights. The Bavarian cheek piece has a squared lower edge, while the Tyrolean pattern (often wrongly called Swiss) has a distinctive concave surface with a curved comb.

Cheever & Burchard. A ★Suicide Special revolver made by the ★Ryan Pistol Company of Norwich, Connecticut, USA, in the late nineteenth century.

'Chelmsford' [The]. A name found on shotgun cartridges sold by ★Leech & Sons of Chelmsford.

'Chelt' [The]. A brandname found on shotgun ammunition sold by Aubrey ★Lewis of Luton.

Chenet-Royet, place Villeboeuf 10, Saint-Étienne, France. Listed in 1879 as a gunmaker.

Cherokee Gun Company. A brandname found on shotguns made by the ★Crescent Arms Company of Norwich, Connecticut, prior to 1920.

Chesapeake Gun Company. Another of the many brandnames associated with shotguns made in the twentieth century by the ★Crescent Arms Company.

Chevallier & Sanders. Designers of the auto-loading shotgun made by ★Sanders Small Arms Ltd, in accordance with British Patent 431,938 (*sic*) of 1935. Surviving guns also indicate that a patent of addition was sought in 1937 (application no. 4391/37).

Chevillard. Laurent Chevillard, rue d'Annonay 118, Saint-Étienne, France. Listed in 1892 as a gunmaker. Still trading in 1933.

CHASSEPOT NEEDLE RIFLE

Chassepot (2)

This was the first breech-loading rifle to be issued to the French Army, equipping many of the infantry regiments embroiled in the Franco-Prussian War of 1870–71. Derived from a patent granted in 1857, experimental bolt-action Chassepot rifles were being tested by the early 1860s. A few hundred experimental Camp de Chalôns rifles were made in 1865, perhaps in the government factory in Saint-Étienne, and the perfected *Fusil d'Infanterie Mle 1866* was adopted on 30 August 1866.

Guns were made initially in Saint-Étienne, but demands were so great that not only the other government factories in Châtellerault, Mutzig and Tulle, but also a private contractor – Cahen-Lyon & Cie – were added to the scheme. Cahen-Lyon purchased rifles in Belgium, Britain, Italy and Spain. When fighting began in the summer of 1870, more than a million Chassepot rifles had reached service. Work continued until 1875, when a halt was finally called in favour of the Gras pattern (q.v.).

Subsequently hundreds of thousands of needle rifles were

converted to fire metallic-case ammunition, as the Mle 1866/74, but unaltered examples served in the French colonies into the 1880s, and others were converted into sporting guns. The Prussian and Saxon Armies had each converted needle guns captured during the Franco-Prussian War of 1870–71 to replace obsolescent Dreyse carbines in the cavalry and Train.

The Chassepot had a higher muzzle velocity and a longer range than its rival, the Dreyse ★Zundnadelgewehr, but the heat of combustion rapidly destroyed the india-rubber sealing washer placed between the bolt head and the bolt body. A worn Dreyse would still fire effectively, even though the breech leaked propellant gas; the Chassepot, however, was virtually useless once the washer had distintegrated.

There were several Chassepot weapons: the standard infantry rifle had an 825mm barrel, a straight bolt handle, one iron barrel band and an iron nose-cap; the *Fusil pour la Cavallerie d'Afrique*, the colonial cavalry rifle, had an additional iron barrel band and the back swivel through the trigger-guard bow; and the *Carabine de Cavallerie* had a 700mm barrel, two brass bands, a

brass nose-cap, a swivel through the trigger guard and a spatulate bolt handle that turned down against the stock. The two *Carabines de Gendarmerie*, one for mounted (*à Cheval*) and one for dismounted (*à Pied*) units, were similar to the cavalry carbine; however, the former accepted a socket bayonet and the latter, with only a single barrel band and the back swivel beneath the butt instead of the trigger guard, accepted a sabre pattern. The *Mousqueton d'Artillerie*, or artillery musketoon (short rifle), had a 50cm barrel, a brass band, a brass nose-cap and a spatulate bolt handle turned downward. A large-calibre wall gun or *Fusil de Rempart* was also made in small numbers.

Additional details are best sought from sources such as Jean Martin, *Armes à Feu de l'Armée Française, 1860 à 1940* (Crépin-Leblond, 1974); John Walter, *The German Rifle* (Arms & Armour Press, 1979); and *Rifles of the World* (Krause Publications, second edition, 1998).

French Chassepot needle guns, captured in large numbers during the Franco-Prussian War, provided the basis for the Prussian metallic-cartridge conversion shown here. Note the additional eagle and cypher marks on the butt.

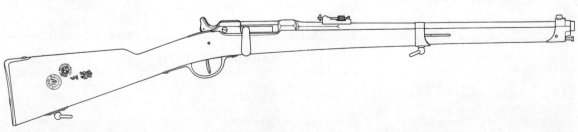

'CHH'. *See* C.H. *Hunt.

Chicago – 1. A wooden spring-air *BB Gun, also known as the Chicago Model, with double exposed cocking rods. Made in the USA by the *Markham Air Rifle Company in 1890–95, it was a break-open design with a brass or steel barrel liner. *See also* King New Chicago. **2.** Chicago Arms Company, Chicago, Illinois, USA. This distributor of guns and sporting goods sold cartridges with 'C.A. Co.' in their headstamps, but it is thought that actually they were made by one of the better known American manufacturers. The Chicago Fire Arms Company may have been a predecessor. **3.** Chicago Fire Arms Company, Chicago, Illinois, USA. This distributorship sold the *Protector turret pistol, patented by Jacques *Turbiaux. Made by the *Ames Sword Company, they usually have an automatic safety on the finger spur, which disengages when the trigger lever is squeezed. Apparently this was patented by Peter *Finnegan in 1893. A few guns may also be found with a double-ring finger guard patented by John *Norris about 1900. **4.** Chicago Protector, USA. *See* Protector. **5.** Chicago Rifle Manufacturing Company, Chicago, Illinois, active 1898–1900. Little is known about this short-lived manufacturer of the *Simplex BB Gun and a cap-firing derivative called the 'Defender'.

Chichester – 1. These were sheath-trigger *Suicide Special revolvers, made in the 1880s by the *Hood Firearms Company of Norwich, Connecticut, and the *Hopkins & Allen Arms Company of Norwich, Connecticut. **2.** 'Chichester Cross [The]'. Found on a shotgun cartridge sold in southern England by S. *Chitty of Chichester.

Chick. M.Y. Chick, New York City. Allegedly the submitter of the *Laidley-Emery breech-loading carbine to the US Army trials of 1865–66, but really no more than Theodore Laidley's pet name ('my chick') for his first carbine.

Chief's Special, Chiefs Special, Chiefs' Special. A small .38-calibre *Smith & Wesson swing-cylinder revolver, introduced in 1950 on the purpose-built J-frame and known since 1957 as the Model 36. The earliest guns had a rounded butt, but a square-heel version was substituted in 1952. A heavy-barrel variation, developed in 1967 for the New York Police Department, became standard in 1975. The Chiefs Special Target Model, with adjustable sights, was made in small quantities from 1955 until 1975; some guns were marked 'Model 36', but one batch made in the early 1970s was marked 'Model 50'. A Model 60 Stainless Steel Chiefs Special appeared in 1965, changing from bright- to satin-finish steel in 1966. *See also* Airweight.

Childs. Thomas L. Childs. The 'TLC' marks of this government arms inspector have been found on .45 M1911 (Colt) pistols dating from 1917. *See also* US arms inspectors' marks.

Chillingworth. Frederick Chillingworth. This US government arms inspector, working in the 1870s, accepted small-arms marked 'FC'. He was also responsible, in collaboration with Lieutenant E. *Rice, for the trowel bayonet developed for the .45-70 Springfield single-shot rifle. *See also* US arms inspectors' marks.

Chilton. Edwin Chilton, Wolverhampton, Staffordshire. Customarily listed as a gun-lock maker, Chilton was apprenticed to John *Stanton and began trading on his own account c. 1872. Business was undertaken from Low Street until, in the early 1880s, a move was made to Hampton House, 41 New Hampton Road West. Chilton made rebounding locks patented by Stanton, paying a royalty on each, in addition to locks for F. *Beesley and W.C. *Scott & Sons. The business, having enveloped Joseph Brazier & Sons after the First World War, finally closed in 1977.

China North Industries Corporation. *See* Norinco.

Chinese Lion. *See* Lion.

Chitty. Samuel Chitty. A gunmaker trading from 6 Lion Street, Chichester, Sussex, England, Chitty handled shotgun cartridges loaded by *Patstone's under the brand-names Chichester Cross and Wonder.

Chizhov. Ivan Ivanovich Chizhov, St Petersburg, Liteiniy Prospekt' 51. A distributor of guns and ammunition active in Russia prior to 1918.

Chobert. Louis Chobert et Cie. This Paris based gunsmithing business was responsible for transforming many thousands of obsolete *Lebel rifles into trench guns during the First World War.

Choke, or 'choke-bore'. *See* panel, facing page.

Chometon-Ponchon, grande rue Saint-Roch 15, Saint-Étienne, France. Listed in 1879 as a gunmaker; still listed in 1892 as Chometton at rue Saint-Roch 17.

'Chosen' [The]. Found on shotgun cartridges sold in Britain by *Fraser of Churchdown.

'CHP'. *See* C.H. *Parker.

Christmas. John K. Christmas. A lieutenant-colonel in the US Army, this government arms inspector accepted .45 M1911A1 (Colt) pistols made in 1942 by the Singer Manufacturing Company. They were marked 'JKC'. *See also* US arms inspectors' marks.

Christophe. Henri Christophe, Gallerie de la Reine, Brussels, and Fontaine l'Évêque, Liège. Heir to the gunmaking business founded by his father Louis l'Aîné in 1819, Christophe married the widow of Joseph *Montigny in the late 1860s and acquired the business of *Montigny & Mangeot. A variety of sporting guns and a few *Mitrailleuse volley-guns were made, and the business eventually passed to the younger Louis Christophe. It survived both world wars to make shotguns ranging from plain *Anson & Deeley box-locks to highly-decorative side-lock patterns, including a side-lock over/under design.

Christy. T. Christy & Company, Britain. *See* Cahen, Lyon & Cie.

Chuchu. Athanäse Chuchu, Bahia, Brazil. This gunmaker – active from 1875 until c. 1904 – is best known for an interesting block-action gendarmerie musketoon (*Mosquete do Policia*), unique to Brazil, which was made in Liège in the late 1870s for issue in Bahia. An operating lever on the right side of the breech was pulled back to cock the hammer, then outward to swing the entire breech-block laterally to the right. Chuchu received several US Patents, including 325,053 of 25 August 1885 for a 'repeating firearm'; 359,428 of 15 March 1887 for a 'firearm'; and 766,596 of 2 August 1904 for a 'breech-loading firearm'.

'Chulmleigh' [The]. Associated with shotgun cartridges distributed by A.J. *Stocker & Son and C. & E. *Stocker of Chulmleigh, Devon. They were made by *Eley-Kynoch, or, perhaps, loaded locally into *Eley-Kynoch cases and caps.

Churchill – 1. A brandname associated with *Mauser-

CHOKE

A term used to identify any firearm (most commonly a shotgun) with a constriction within the bore intended to concentrate the pattern of shot in an attempt to preserve performance at longer distances. Many systems of choking have been tried, including detachable muzzle extensions, but the most common is simply a short conical section of the bore just behind the muzzle.

Choke is usually defined by a name, hiding the extent of constriction. Guns without choke of any type are described as cylinder or cylinder bore. The most popular options are quarter choke (.010in smaller diameter than the bore measurement), half choke (.020in), three-quarter choke (.030in) and full choke (.040in). An assortment of intermediate stages has been offered, including improved-modified, improved cylinder and skeet bore. However, most of these vary according to the manufacturers' whims and are notoriously difficult to define.

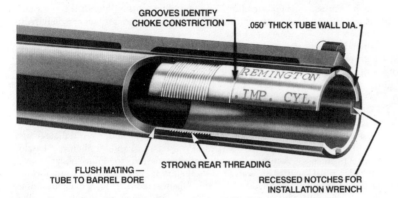

CUT-AWAY: "REM" CHOKE SEATING INSIDE BARREL

This cut-away drawing shows the construction of a Remington exchangeable choke. This particular example is 'improved-cylinder'.

pattern bolt-action rifles made in Italy by *FIAS, and sold in North America by *Kassnar. **2.** Charles Churchill. London directories list this member of the English gun trade at 16 Laurence Pountney Lane in 1869. He is believed to have been the father of E.J. Churchill (below). **3.** Churchill (Gunmakers) Ltd, London. A successor to Robert Churchill & Company, now owned by *Interarms, this gunmaking business has made rifles embodying *Mauser actions supplied by Zavodi *Crvena Zastava. These included the *One of One Thousand. **4.** E.J. Churchill. Renowned as one of London's leading gunmakers, Churchill traded from a shop in 8 Agar Street, Strand, from 1892 until 1900 or later. Then a move was made to Leicester Square, WC2, although a workshop was also occupied in nearby Orange Street. Among the brand-names applied to the shotgun cartridges handled by the business were 'A.G.', 'Express XXV', 'Field', 'Imperial', 'Pheasant', 'Premier', 'Prodigy' and 'Utility' (qq.v.). The components could be either British or European.
'CHW'. See C.H. *Wicker.
Chylewski. Witold Chylewski, then living in Austria-Hungary, was granted a patent in 1919 to protect a one-hand pistol cocking system. This relied on sliding the trigger guard backward – retracting the slide and cocking the hammer – then releasing the guard to run forward, allowing the slide to close and chamber a fresh cartridge. About 1,000 Chylewski pistols were made by *Schweizerische Industrie-Gesellschaft shortly after the First World War, but subsequently the design was exploited by *Bergmann and *Lignose under the brand-name *Einhand. A modern version is now being made in China.

'CI'. A superimposed monogram beneath a crown. Found on Portuguese weapons: the mark of Carlos I (1889–1908). See also Cyphers, imperial and royal.
Cigarette and cigar pistols. See Disguised guns.
CIJO. A monogram, partly concentric and partly superimposed, with 'I', 'J' and 'C' equally dominant. Correctly 'IJCO' (q.v.); found on revolvers made in the USA by Iver *Johnson.
'C.I.L.' Found in the headstamps of cartridges made by *Canadian Industries Ltd of Brownburg, Ontario, Canada.
Circular Hammer. A term that applies specifically to the New Model 1882 double-barrel hammer shotgun made by E. *Remington & Sons and the *Remington Arms Company.
Civil Guard Model. A name used in 1876 by E. *Remington & Sons and applied to a version of the standard military-style *rolling-block rifle chambering the 'Spanish or Russian Cartridge'; a sabre bayonet was a standard accessory. See also Egyptian Model, French Model and Spanish Model.
Cizeron. J.-M. Cizeron, rue Chapelon 12, Saint-Étienne, France. Listed in 1892 as a gunmaker.
'CJV'. See C.J. *Van Amburgh.
CJZ. A cursive superimposition-type monogram. Correctly read as 'JCZ' (q.v.); employed by *Jihočeská Zbrojovka of Prague.
'C.L.'. Found on sights of British Charger-Loading *Lee-Enfield rifles to show that they had been altered for .303 Mk VII ball ammunition.
Claborough – 1. Claborough Brothers, Birmingham, Warwickshire. This English gunmaking business, sometimes mistakenly listed as American (but see Claborough

& Golcher, below), was first listed in 1872 at 8 Whittall Street. It became J.P. Claborough & Brothers in 1882 – at 7¹/₂ St Mary's Row – then J.P. Claborough & Johnstone about 1893, when a London office was operated at 52 Leadenhall Street (1893–95 only). Trading continued until 1902 or later. **2.** Claborough & Golcher, 630 & 632 Montgomery Street, San Francisco, California, in the 1870s. This sales agency, formed during the great boom that followed the Californian Gold Rush of 1849, handled English-made Claborough Bros. shotguns among a range of firearms and sporting goods. Trading may have continued until 1890 or later.

'Clach' [The]. Often mistakenly recorded as 'Clack', this mark will be found on *Eley-Kynoch shotgun cartridges distributed by John *MacPherson of Inverness. The word means 'stone' in Gaelic (cf. Inverness placename Clachnacuddin, 'stone of the washer women').

Clair frères, rue de Lyon 118, Saint-Étienne, France. Listed in 1879 as a maker of gun-barrels, edged weapons and accessories, and also as a distributor of shooting accessories. Listed in 1892 as a maker of guns and edged weapons, with premises at rue de Lyon 126. The three Clair brothers – Benoît, Jean-Baptiste and Victor – made one of the first successful gas-operated shotguns, the subject of patents granted in several countries in 1889–90 (e.g. German no. 49,100). Benoît and Victor Clair were granted US Patent 483,539 of 4 October 1892 to protect a 'Firearm with Breech operated by the Gases of Explosion'. Gas was led back from a port in the bore to strike a piston, which in turn unlocked the breech. Much has been claimed for the Clairs, often without good foundation, but they deserve great credit for pioneering work in an era when the smokeless propellant on which their guns depended was still in its infancy.

Clancy. J. Clancy. This US government arms inspector, working in 1903–07, accepted small-arms marked 'JC'. *See also* US arms inspectors' marks.

Clark – **1.** Albert H. Clark. This US government arms inspector, working in 1860–79, accepted a range of small-arms including Springfield rifle-muskets. These were marked 'AHC'. **2.** C. Clark, London. The marks of this gunmaker have been reported on self-cocking *pepperboxes dating from the middle of the nineteenth century. **3.** David F. Clark. A US government arms inspector, working in 1861–85, Clark accepted small-arms marked 'DFC'. These included a range of cap-lock revolvers – Colt, Remington, Savage and Starr patterns – as well as Colt-made *Gatling Guns and Hotchkiss bolt-action rifles. **4.** Daniel F. Clark. The 'DFC' mark of this arms inspector is said to have been found on *Single Action Army Model Colts accepted for US Army service; *see also* David F. Clark (above). **5.** E.W. Clark. This US government arms inspector, working in 1873–80, accepted small-arms marked 'EWC'. **6.** Frederick George Clark. A 'Mechanic' of 64 Tennyson Road, Small Heath, Birmingham, Clark was the co-patentee with Arthur H. *Butler of a revolving cylindrical airgun magazine (British Patent no. 4622/06). Clark's address was sufficiently close geographically to the *Birmingham Small Arms Company factory in Small Heath to suggest that he was one of the company's employees, although no BSAs are known with this particular magazine. *See also* Joseph H. *Cox. **7.** George Clark & Company. Gunmakers, or perhaps merely distributors, working from 10 Craven

Buildings, Drury Lane, London, in 1870. **8.** William J. Clark. This government arms inspector, working in 1898, accepted US military small-arms marked 'WJC'. **9.** Clark, Sherrard & Company, Lancaster, Texas. This partnership made 500 copies of the *Navy Colt revolver, but completed them only after the American Civil War had ended. *See also* US arms inspectors' marks for most of the North American entries.

Clarke – **1.** Charles Clarke, Winchester Street, Salisbury, Wiltshire. This English gunmaker handled shotgun ammunition, loaded with amberite and marked 'The Original J.W.G.' – the significance of which remains unknown. The partnership of Clarke & Dyke is thought to have been a successor. **2.** Edward Clarke, Leicester, Leicestershire, England. The working life of this gunmaker lasted from 1834 until 1854 or later, successively from Market Place (1834–41), Gallowtree Gate (1846–49), then Hotel Street. Appropriate marks have been found on sporting guns and *pepperboxes. **3.** Frank Clarke, active from 1902 or earlier until 1955, was associated with Edwin *Anson and *Webley & Scott Ltd – although most of his airguns seem to have been made by *Accles & Shelvoke. Best known for the *Titan and *Warrior air pistols, Clarke has also been linked (less certainly) with smaller guns such as the *Firefly and *Whittall. *See also* Frank Clarke (Lead Products) Ltd and Stephen E. *Laszlo. Among the protection granted to Frank Clarke was British Patent 24,432/03 of 1903, sought from Gothic Arcade, Snow Hill, Birmingham, in which he describes his occupation as 'gunsmith'. This protected a spirally-fluted airgun slug. British Patent 110,999 was accepted in November 1917 for the prototype *Titan pistol, cocked by a push-in rod and subsequently made in small numbers by *Accles & Shelvoke. The patent gives Clarke's address as 6 Whittall Street, Birmingham. British Patent 208,341, accepted in December 1923, allowed improvements to be made in the Titan design. British Patent 231,557 of April 1925 was sought in collusion with John *Fearn and Douglas *Johnstone (co-patentees of the lifting-barrel cocking system embodied in the *Webley & Scott pistols) for a helical cocking system and a butt-mounted air cylinder. British Patent 351,268 of 1931 protected the sidelever-cocking Warrior pistol, designed jointly with Edwin Anson. Guns of this type were made in substantial quantities by Accles & Shelvoke. US Patent 538,057 was the equivalent of British 351,268. **4.** Frank Clarke. Trading from Thetford, Norfolk, England, Clarke was trading as an ironmonger prior to 1918. However, he also sold sporting guns, and shotgun cartridges identified by the brandnames Grafton and *Invincible. The ammunition was probably supplied by *Eley-Kynoch Ltd in a ready-loaded state. **5.** F. Clarke (Lead Products) Ltd. Founded by the airgun designer Frank Clarke (above), this business was co-patentee with its employee, William J. Walker, of two different air pistols. These were the subjects of British Patents 592,561 of 1947 and 623,860, although in each case applications had been made two years earlier. The Birmingham directories also record that F. Clarke (Lead Products) Ltd used the telegraphic address *Havoc. **6.** H. Clarke & Sons. British gunmakers trading in Leicester, Clarke & Sons offered shotgun cartridges under brandnames such as Alma and Midland. **7.** Clarke & Dyke, Salisbury, Wiltshire, and Southampton, Hampshire. This partnership, possibly a successor to

Charles Clarke, sold shotgun ammunition in southern England under the names J.W.G. and Salisbury. The cartridges were probably loaded by *Patstone's.

Clarkson. Ralph Clarkson. Employed by the *Winchester Repeating Arms Company, this designer/engineer is credited with creating the Winchester Light Automatic Rifle (*WLAR) to compete with the *ArmaLite AR-15 in the late 1950s.

Clarus. Bernard Clarus, Liège, Belgium. Designer of what became known as the *Clément pistol, patented in the USA on 27 July 1908 (no. 929,286).

Classic – 1. A brandname used for some years in the 1970s by *Classic Collections on Italian-made airguns. The basic Classic or Classic Standard Pistol was the 4.5mm-calibre *Gun Toys RO 71. The Classic Artillery Carbine was originally the *Gun Toys RO 72 pistol-carbine, with a wooden butt, but subsequently the designation was extended to include the standard long-barrelled RO 72 with a rod-type stock. The Classic Deluxe Model was the standard RO 72 (alias IGI 203), and the Classic Sniper's Carbine was an alternative name for the long-barrelled RO 72 with the rod-pattern stock. 2. Or M81 Classic. Introduced by *Parker-Hale Ltd in 1983, this Mauser-action sporting rifle had a straight-comb walnut stock. It has been chambered for a variety of cartridges, from .22-250 to .300 Winchester Magnum. 3. Or Classic Standard. A streamlined *box-lock *Double Rifle made by H. Krieghoff GmbH of Ulm/Donau, Germany, in chamberings ranging from 7x65R to 9.3x74R, this embodies a sliding self-adjusting locking wedge and an automatic hammer-release safety. The action is locked by a slide in the frame engaging two protrusions on the underside of the barrel-block and by an extension of the block entering the face of the standing breech. The side-by-side barrel units can be readily exchanged when required. 4. Classic Big Five. Intended to down the largest African game, this is simply a Krieghoff Classic (above) chambering high-power cartridges from .375 H&H to .500 Nitro Express 3in. The guns have 23.5in barrels, weigh about 9½lb, and usually have BreaKO recoil-reducers in the butt. The front trigger is hinged to protect a finger on the rear trigger from recoil. 5. Classic-S. This *Krieghoff Classic Standard variant, although built on the standard box-lock action, has side-plates to allow additional space for engraving. 6. A version of the Remington M700 bolt-action rifle, made from 1981 until 1998. It had a satin-finish walnut half-stock with a straight-comb butt. The fore-end was customarily round-tipped, although *schnabel-tip examples were made in small numbers. Post-1990 guns were offered on a very limited one-chambering-per-year basis – e.g. .220 Swift in 1992 and .375 H&H Magnum in 1996. 7. Or Magna Classic. Associated with *Magnum revolvers made by *Smith & Wesson. 8. Classic Collections, Fulham Palace Road, London NW6. Trading in the late 1970s, this short-lived operation sold Italian-made firearms and airguns under a number of Classic designations. Distribution seems to have ceased in 1981. 9. Classic Magnum. Dating from 1981–91, this was a variant of the Remington M700 Classic rifle chambered only for the 7mm Remington Magnum cartridge.

Claxton Rifle Battery. A multi-barrel volley or Battery gun, tested unsuccessfully in Britain in 1868.

Clay... – 1. E.E. Clay, Newton, Massachusetts.

Recipient, jointly with Alfred B. Ely, of US Patent no. 105,058 of 5 July 1870. This protected a breech-block that pivoted up and forward. *See also* Ely & Wray. 2. 'Clay Bird' [The]. Found on shotgun cartridges made by *Eley Bros. prior to the First World War for distributors such as Charles *Maleham of Sheffield, and William *Powell & Son of Birmingham. 3. 'Clay King', 'Clayking' [The]. This mark was associated with shotgun ammunition made by the *Mullerite Cartridge Works of Birmingham, Warwickshire, England. Sometimes they were marked 'Special Clay King'. 4. 'Clay Pigeon' [The]. Found on shotgun cartridges loaded in the USA by the *Chamberlain Cartridge Company of Cleveland, Ohio.

Clayton. W.H. Clayton. This government arms inspector, working in 1899–1901, accepted US military .38 Colt revolvers marked 'WHC'. *See also* US arms inspectors' marks.

'clb', 'CLB' – 1. Found as 'clb' on German military telescope sights and associated components made in 1940–45 by Optische Werke Dr F.A. Wöhler of Kassel. 2. Found on US military firearms as 'CLB'. *See* C.L. *Bartlett.

'Cleanfire'. On ammunition sold by Montgomery *Ward & Company, apparently distinguished by non-corrosive primers. Most of it was probably made by *Remington (cf. Kleanbore).

Clement, Clément – 1. Charles Clement. This gunmaker was listed in London directories for 1890–91 at 63 Queen Victoria Street. He is believed to have been the well-known Belgian Charles Ph. *Clément, although the entries do not make this particularly clear. 2. Charles Philibert Clément; Liège, Belgium. An exhibitor of military rifles and sporting guns at the World's Columbian Exhibition held in Chicago in 1893, Clément designed a concealed-hammer shotgun protected by US Patent 693,639, and sold a variety of revolvers prior to 1910 under brandnames such as American Settler, Bad to Beat (American Model of 1887), Washington and White House. He also promoted an eponymous 6.35mm pistol designed by Bernard *Clarus. The guns were made in Belgium in large numbers, were the subject of a patent of improvement granted in the USA to Clément on 13 September 1910, and were licensed to *Smith & Wesson in the USA. 3. William T. Clement, USA. *See* Samuel *Norris. 4. Clément pistol. These were made in a variety of chamberings, beginning in 1903 with 5mm Clément, which was little more than the cartridge chambered in the *Charola y Anitua; subsequently others were offered in 6.35mm and 7.65mm Auto versions. The guns had a fixed barrel, beneath a chamber containing the return spring, and a separate breech-block that slid backward until stopped by a vertical post in the breech. The original pattern had a barrel/receiver group that pivoted up and backward around a transverse pivot through the rear of the frame, but this feature was rapidly abandoned. Guns made in c. 1904–07 had small retraction grips at the front end of the breech-block and a frame that continued up at the back of the retraction-grip slot; those made in 1907–12 had breech-blocks, with retraction grooves along their length, that ran back in an open-back slot in the receiver. Although the 1912-pattern Clément pistol retained some of the distinctive internal features, it looked very much like an *FN-Browning externally. 5. Clément-Neumann rifle. Introduced prior to 1910, the Carabine Automatique Clément, chambering the .401 Winchester cartridge, was based on patents granted in 1903–08 to Charles Ph. Clément of Liège. It was based on the Clément pistols, although the breech-block reciprocated entirely within the receiver. The barrel was often octagonal, and the large slab-sided receiver had a five-round magazine in the trigger-guard housing. Clément's business was acquired in 1913 by *Neumann frères et Cie, and guns sold commercially after this date were marked 'Clément-Neumann'. Production ceased when the Germans invaded Belgium in 1914.

Clements & Son. A gunmaking business occupying 106a Fenchurch Street, London, in 1891–94.

Clerk. *See* Marks & Clerk.

Clerke Recreation Products. *See* Browning.

'Clermonite' [The]. A brandname associated with shotgun cartridges loaded by *Eley Bros., but referring specifically to their propellant loading, which was supplied by the *Clermont Explosives Company Ltd and *Muller & Company.

Clermont Explosives Company Ltd. A promotional agency formed in London by *Muller & Company, active from the early 1890s until c. 1905, this company supplied the semi-smokeless propellant known as Clermonite and Mullerite to shotgun-cartridge makers such as *Eley Bros. The mark 'M.C.' may be found on ammunition of this type.

Cleveland – 1. F.T. Cleveland. This government arms inspector, working in the mid-1870s, accepted US military Colt .45 Single Action Army revolvers marked 'FTC'. **2.** James T. Cleveland. This US government arms inspector, working from the mid-1850s until 1878 or later, accepted Colt, Savage and other cap-lock revolvers marked 'JTC'. *See also* US arms inspectors' marks.

Clifford. Russell Clifford; Miami, Florida. The inventor of the *LARC BB-firing submachine-gun, developed in the early 1970s. The gun was powered by pressurised freon, an inert gas.

Climax... – 1. Climax Cartridge [The]. An English 12-bore shotgun ammunition loaded from *Eley-Kynoch components by T. *Page-Wood of Bristol. **2.** Climax Rock Drill & Engineering Ltd, Carn Brea, Cornwall, England. This business, a member of the *Monotype Scheme, made barrels and other components for the *Bren Gun, often marking them with the code 'S 26'. Many of the guns assembled in the Monotype factory in Salfords were proved on the Carn Brea range.

Clinton – 1. Usually found as 'The Clinton' on shotgun ammunition loaded by Charles *Smith & Sons of Newark, possibly named after a local hunt. **2.** Clinton Cartridge Company, Chicago, Illinois. A manufacturer of ammunition, including rimfire patterns.

Clip – 1. A method of loading a magazine with several cartridges held in a special holder. The entire assembly is placed in the magazine, where a spring-loaded arm forces the cartridges upward so that a fresh cartridge is pushed into the chamber each time the bolt or breech-block reciprocates. As the last cartridge is loaded, the clip falls (or is ejected) from the weapon. Many early Mannlichers, the M1 Garand and other rifles have been clip-loaded. The system is much less flexible than a *charger, particularly in cases – such as the Garand – where the clip is essential to the action, yet cannot be

replenished with single rounds when in the magazine. **2.** Widely used in North America to describe a charger. It has also gained increasing (if exasperating) popularity among European sporting-rifle manufacturers to denote a detachable box magazine. **3.** Clip and Clip Magnum. These *Parker-Hale 1200-series rifles were identical with the *Super and Super Magnum patterns, but had detachable box magazines.

'Clipper'. Found on smokeless-propellant shotgun ammunition made prior to 1914 in Swanton, Vermont, by the *Robin Hood Cartridge Company.

Clitz. James M.B. Clitz. This government arms inspector, a captain in the US Navy, accepted Remington single-shot pistols dating from 1867. Their barrels were marked 'JMBC'. *See also* US arms inspectors' marks.

'C.L.L.E.' An abbreviated form of *Charger-Loading Lee-Enfield, encountered in designation marks found on pre-1918 British rifles.

Close. A French government arms inspector. *See* Kropatschek.

Clough – 1. George Clough & Sons, Bath, Somerset. The marks of these English gunmakers have been reported on self-cocking *pepperboxes, but the identification presents a problem. Clough traded from Old Bridge in 1815–22, adopting the style '...& Sons' by 1826. However, although premises had moved to 29 Southgate Street by 1832, work had ceased by 1837. It is much more likely, therefore, that the pepperboxes were sold by John Clough & Son (below). **2.** John Clough & Son, Bath, Somerset. Clough was listed in Claverton Place in 1825–27 and in Southgate Street – premises previously used by George Clough (above) – in 1841–44. Subsequent trading styles included John Clough & Son at 9 New Bond Street, in 1855–61; Thomas & John Clough in 1863; and Clough Bros. & Co. from 1865 until trading ceased in the 1870s. It seems most likely that the pepperboxes attributed to George Clough & Son were actually made by John Clough, although the possibility that the earlier trading name was perpetuated for some years should also be considered.

Cloverleaf – 1. A nickname applied to the *Colt *Patent House Pistol. **2.** Applied to sporting guns marked by the *Roper Repeating Rifle Company of Amherst, owing to the shape of their four-shot cylinders. The guns are more streamlined than their slam-fire predecessors (*see* Roper rifles) and are assumed to date from the mid-1870s. The front trigger withdraws the bolt and indexes the cylinder, allowing the case-mouth to move forward into the breech to make a seal when the rear trigger fires the gun. Series production was never undertaken, although elements of the two-trigger idea reappeared in the slide-action *Spencer-Roper guns (q.v.).

Clozet, rue Paul-Bert 31, Saint-Étienne, France. Listed in 1892 as a distributor of, and agent for, arms and ammunition.

Club – 1. A generic term applied in Britain prior to 1939 to almost any gun or airgun specifically intended for target shooting (i.e. Shooting Club). Lincoln *Jeffries, Langenhan *Millita, and Mayer & Grammelspacher *Diana airguns sold in Britain will all be found marked in this way. **2.** Only about 15,000 .177-calibre BSA Club air rifles were made from 1948 until 1958. Originally they were a special version of the .22 *Airsporter with a shorter piston stroke, but the distinction was soon blurred and all post-1959 guns of this general type were known as Airsporters regardless of calibre. **3.** 'Club Smokeless [The]'. This name was found on British shotgun ammunition, sold by *Jeffrey & Son of Guildford prior to 1914, and also by W.J. *Jeffrey of London.

Cloverine Salve Company. The name and location of this distributor of White Cloverine Brand Salve – and 'premium' rimfire rifles and BB Guns (the latter usually made by *Daisy) – have yet to be confirmed. Operations seem to have been confined to the period between the world wars.

Clyde – 1. Found on a variety of spring-air guns, including the pendant-lever Langenhan *Millita and barrel-cocking pistols, sold in Britain in the 1920s by Clyde's Game & Gun Mart of Glasgow. **2.** Clyde [The]. A brandname associated with shotgun cartridges made by *Nobel Explosives Ltd of Glasgow prior to 1918 and the purchase by Explosives Trades Ltd. **3.** Clyde Engineering Company, Scotland. *See* Clyde's Game & Gun Mart. **4.** Clyde's Game & Gun Mart. Trading from 46 Windsor Terrace, Glasgow, Scotland, this business was owned by George *Bell. Possibly a successor to the Clyde Engineering Company (but equally probably no more than a retailer), the Game & Gun Mart handled airguns, firearms, ammunition and accessories in addition to toys and sporting goods.

'CM', 'C.M.'. A mark applied by the central Netherlands Indies Army workshop, the *Centrale Magazijn, during 1916–49.

'CMAFO'. A superimposition-type monogram with 'M', 'F' and 'A' prominent. Correctly 'MFACO' (q.v.); found on revolvers made by the *Meriden Fire Arms Company.

'CMB'. *See* C.M. *Boyington.

'CMCO'. A superimposition-type monogram with 'C', 'M' and 'C' equally prominent. Correctly 'MCCO' (q.v.); used by *Maltby, Curtis & Company.

'CMFAO'. A superimposition-type monogram with 'M', 'F' and 'A' prominent. Correctly 'MFACO' (q.v.); found on revolvers made by the *Meriden Fire Arms Company.

'CMG'. *See* Costruzione Meccaniche *Zanoletti.

'cnd'. This mark will be found on German military magazines and small-arms components made by *National Krupp Registrier Kassen GmbH in its Berlin-Neukölln factory during the Second World War.

'CNG'. *See* Charles N. Goodrich.

'COA', sometimes in the form of a monogram. Found in the *headstamps of cartridges made by *Cartucheria Orbea, Argentina.

Coast to Coast Stores. *See* Marlin.

Cobb. A.P. Cobb. This government arms inspector, working in 1874, accepted small-arms marked 'APC'. *See also* US arms inspectors' marks.

Cobold. A term associated with a range of double-action revolvers, with round bird's-head butts, made in Liège prior to the First World War by *Henrion, Dassy et Heuschen (Fabrique d'Armes HDH). Fitted with five- or six-round cylinders, they may be chambered for 7.62mm Nagant, .320, .380, 9.4mm or .450 cartridges. *See also* Kobold.

Cobra. A lightweight version of the Detective Special, introduced in 1950 by *Colt's Patent Fire Arms Manufacturing Company, in .22LR rimfire, .32 New Police, .38 New Police and .38 Special chamberings, this double-action revolver originally offered a choice of 2 or

3in barrels and a round butt. Guns made in 1951–73, however, had 4in barrels and square-heel butts.

Cobray. *See* Ingram submachine-gun.

Cochran. Cochran's Breech-Loading Firearms Company. This business, registered at 43 Parliament Street, London S.W., in 1868, may have been formed to represent the American inventor John Webster Cochran in the British Army breech-loading rifle trials of the period. It encountered such limited success, however, that operations had ceased with a year.

Cocking piece. An attachment to the rear of the striker, carrying a knob or spur and the sear notches.

Cody Model. A brandname associated with the *Daisy Model 1894 *Spittin' Image BB Gun, distributed by the Cody Museum of Cody, Wyoming. The left side of the receiver displayed a picture of the Prince of Plainsmen, William F. 'Buffalo Bill' Cody (1846–1917), with a rope design and an appropriate 'Land of Buffalo Bill' slogan.

Coeur et Tyrode or Coeur-Tyrode, Saint-Étienne, France. Listed in 1933 as gunmakers.

'cof'. Associated with small-arms components made in Solingen in 1941–45 by Carl Eickhorn, better known for edged weapons.

Cofer. Thomas Cofer, Portsmouth and Norfolk, Virginia, Confederate States of America. This gunmaker was responsible for more than a hundred .36 Whitney Navy revolver copies – marked 'TWC' – with brass frames and spurred trigger guards. Originally these were designed to accept a special cartridge patented by Cofer on 12 August 1861. He remained active until 1877.

Coffee Mill – 1. Coffee Mill Gun. A nickname bestowed on the *Union Repeating Gun during the American Civil War (1861–65). **2.** Coffee Mill Sharps. Applied to the small quantity of *Sharps carbines made during the American Civil War with a small rotary mill let into the right side of the butt. This could be used to grind coffee beans and, if necessary, grain with the aid of a detachable handle.

Cogschultze Ammunition & Powder Company Ltd, London. A combination of the cartridge-making facilities of *Cogswell & Harrison and the propellant of the *Schultze Gunpowder Company, this business is said to have lasted only from 1909 until Schultze was purchased by Eley Bros. in 1911. A variety of brandnames was used on Cogschultze cartridges, including 'Bono', 'Farmo', 'Molto', 'Pluvoid', 'Ranger' and 'Westro'. Subsequently many of these were perpetuated by both *Eley and *Eley-Kynoch.

Cogswell – 1. Benjamin Cogswell. This English gunsmith/gun dealer operated at 224 Strand, London, from some time prior to 1845 until 1862, when he was succeeded by Cogswell & Harrison (below). Air canes, cased pistols, pepperboxes and *Tranter's Patent revolvers are known with Cogswell markings. His trade card claims origins as early as 1770, but this, it has been suggested, referred to the foundation of Cogswell's business by an antecedent named Essex. **2.** Cogswell & Harrison. This partnership succeeded to the business of Benjamin Cogswell (above) in 1862, trading in London from 224 Strand (sometimes listed as 223/4). Best known for sporting guns, C&H entered several 12-bore breech-loading shotguns in the trials sponsored in 1866 by *The Field*. At least one had a Dougall-patent *Lock Fast breech, and another was the Cogswell & Harrison's Patent Self-

Cocking Breech Loader. The directories record 224 Strand as the sole address until 1879/80, when an additional showroom, occupied only until 1894, was opened at 142 New Bond Street. By 1882, the Strand address had become no. 226, possibly simply a re-numbering expedient, and the Bond Street premises had been superseded by 1895 by a small workshop at 29a Gillingham Street. Eventually Cogswell & Harrison moved to 168 Piccadilly in 1917, with a factory at 21 Park Road, East Acton, London W3, and an office on the Avenue de l'Opéra in Paris, which lasted until 1956. The company modified about 14,300 British .303 No. 3 *Enfield rifles to Weedon Repair Standards (WRS) in the summer of 1939, and, in 1942, produced about 500 serviceable *Lee-Enfield No. 1 Mk III and No. 1 Mk III* rifles from a mixture of D.P. guns and spare parts. Some of these may have borne the code 'S 171'. *See also* British military manufacturer's marks. Cogswell & Harrsion has made *Mauser-pattern sporting rifles, originally on the basis of actions supplied from Oberndorf, but more recently on *FN patterns, after toying with the *Certus design prior to 1914. *See also* Longford and Special Model. Although best known for its patented sporting rifles and shotguns, Cogswell & Harrison also marked a range of shotgun cartridges. Some of these seem to have been made by the short-lived *Cogschulze company, but others came from *Eley, *Kynoch or the later *Eley-Kynoch business. Among the brandnames thus far identified are Ardit, Avant-Tout, Blagdon, Blagdonette, Certus, Huntic, Kelor, Konkor, Konor, Markor, Markoroid, Midget, Swiftsure and Victor. A few air canes were made in the nineteenth century. The Certus air pistol of the early 1930s is credited to Edgar *Harrison, who joined the company in 1874 and is credited with the establishment of the Gillingham Street factory. This raised the status of Cogswell & Harrison far above that of many rivals in the London Trade, but also led to accusations that the company had sold out its traditions 'to the machine'.

Coirer. B. Coirer. The name of this Paris based French gunsmith, or possibly retailer, has been reported on *Quackenbush-type airguns made in France or Belgium toward the end of the nineteenth century.

Cole – 1. Boston, Lincolnshire. The marks of a gunmaker of this name have been reported on self-cocking *pepperboxes dating from the middle of the nineteenth century. **2.** F.J. Cole, 171 Cricklade Street and 26 Castle Street, Cirencester, Gloucestershire. The marks of this English provincial gunsmithing business have been reported on shotgun ammunition marked 'Castle' and 'County Favourite'. **3.** John Cole's gunmaking business operated in West London from 1866–97, first from 29 Great Portland Street (1866–72), secondly from 13 Newman Street (1873–93), and lastly from 27a Ridinghouse Street. **4.** Cole & Son. This gunmaking business had branches in Devizes and Portsmouth prior to 1914, and possibly also in Chippenham and Windsor. Its marks have been reported on shotgun cartridges marked 'Crown', 'King Cole' and 'Signature'.

Colesby. Ephraim Colesby. A gunmaker listed in London at 1 Black Horse Alley, Fleet Street, E.C., in 1857–59.

Colgan, Limerick. The marks of this Irish gunmaker have been reported on self-cocking *pepperboxes dating from the middle of the nineteenth century.

Collath. Wilhelm Collath [Söhne], Frankfurt an der Oder. One of Germany's leading makers of rifles, sporting guns and proprietary cartridges, Collath succeeded Georg *Teschner in the 1890s. The company traded until the end of the Second World War.

'Collector' [The]. Found on 12-bore shotgun cartridges sold by Henry Esau *Akrill of Beverley, probably prior to 1914.

Colette. Henri Colette, Liège. This Belgian gunmaker is best known for a repeating saloon pistol, patented c. 1850, which had a magazine above the barrel that fed a 'charged ball' into the breech each time the hammer was retracted.

Henri Colleye, Liège, Belgium. A maker of pepperboxes, transitional revolvers, pin- and centrefire revolvers active c. 1835–80.

Collins – 1. Frederick Collins. A gunmakers' agent with premises at 7 Beaufort Buildings, Strand, London, in 1850–54. It is not known which companies Collins represented, nor whether any lineal connection with Collins Bros. can be made. **2.** James Collins. Listed as a gunmaker in 1850–54, trading from 115 Regent Street, London. Collins is recognised as a maker of pistols, including a few self-cocking *pepperboxes. **3.** Collins Bros. Successors to Bertram *Webster & Company, The Southern Armoury, this business traded from New Kent Road, London SE1, until the death of co-founder Tom Collins in the early 1990s. Many types of firearm and airgun have been sold over the years, as Collins Bros. were agents for many well-known manufacturers.

Collis. J. Collis. A gunmaker trading in Gravesend, Rochester and Strood, Kent, England, identified with shotgun cartridges marked 'All Round' and 'Famous Nulli Secundus'.

Colon. A Spanish pocket automatic pistol, based on the *FN-Browning, made in Eibar, Guipúzcoa, by *Azpiri y Compañía: 6.35mm, six rounds, hammer fired.

Coloney. Myron Coloney, US patentee: *see* J.H. *McLean.

Colonial – 1. A 6.35mm Browning-type automatic pistol made in Eibar, Guipúzcoa, Spain, by Fabrique d'Armes de *Grande Précision: six or seven rounds, hammer or striker fired. **2.** A cheap pressed-metal spring-airgun advertised in Britain by Martin *Pulvermann in the early years of the twentieth century. The guns were probably made by either F. *Langenhan or *Mayer & Grammelspacher, although surviving engravings suggest the latter source. **3.** Colonial Ammunition Company, Footscray, Melbourne, Victoria. This cartridge-making business, founded in 1888, was taken over by the Australian government in 1921 and renamed Ammunition Factory No. 1. *See also* Footscray. **4.** Colonial Ammunition Company, Auckland, New Zealand. Cartridges made by this company, including shotgun patterns, generally had headstamps marked 'C.A.C.' or 'N.Z.', the latter confined to 1938–45 only.

Colonist. A trademark associated with *Behr's Industrie-Gesellschaft of Suhl, Germany.

Colson. John Colson, Ipswich Street, Stowmarket, Suffolk. The marks of this English gunsmith, cutler and bow-maker, active 1843–70, have been reported on self-cocking *pepperboxes dating from the middle of the nineteenth century.

Colt – 1. Born in 1814, Samuel Colt is renowned as the

father of the revolver…even though preceded by Collier and others. His first guns were long-arms, made in Hartford and Baltimore in 1832–35. These worked well enough to encourage Colt to seek English Patent 6909, granted on 22 October 1835, and comparable US Patent 136 of 25 January 1836. Each claimed ease of loading, and rapidity of fire by connecting the hammer and cylinder-rotating pawl. A factory was founded in Paterson, New Jersey, but the venture failed in the early 1840s; not until the end of the decade, and an association with Captain Walker of the US Army, did Colt encounter success again. This was enabled first by an association with Eli *Whitney, then by the establishment of a factory in Hartford, Connecticut. Colt died in 1862, but not before some of the finest of all US-made *cap-lock revolvers had been developed. See also Colt revolvers (below). **2.** Colt-Burgess. A short-lived lever-action rifle made by *Colt's Patent Fire Arms Manufacturing Company in accordance with the patents of Andrew *Burgess. **3.** Colt-Browning pistol: see Browning pistols. **4.** Colt Gun & Carriage Company Ltd. Trading independently of *Colt's Patent Fire Arms Manufacturing Company, although with large-ly common ownership, this promotional agency for the *Browning-designed 'Potato Digger' machine-gun was listed at 34 Victoria Street, London S.W., for a few years after 1900. **5.** Colt Industries, Firearms Division, Hartford, Connecticut. See also ArmaLite, Mauser, Sako and Sauer. **6.** Colt Junior. A small exposed-hammer .22LR or .25 ACP pocket pistol sold in the USA prior to the implementation of the Gun Control Act of 1968; 73,075 guns were made in Spain by *Astra–Unceta y Cia SA. **7.** Colt machine-gun. The gas-operated 1895-pattern Colt Automatic Machine Gun was the work of John Browning. Protected by US Patents 471,783 and 544,661 (granted in March 1892 and August 1895 respectively), it relied on a radial operating lever pivoting downward to thrust the bolt back against its return spring. A clearance of 8in was required to ensure that the actuating lever did not bury itself in the ground on each stroke, a tendency that acquired the gun the nickname 'Potato Digger'. However, the Colt operated smoothly, and was simple and surprisingly reliable. The US Navy purchased guns in .236 and .30, the US Army and militia acquired .30-cali-bre examples, and others were sold to Russia. Subsequently many 1895-type guns were converted by *Marlin, forming the basis for several improved ground, armoured-vehicle and aircraft guns. **8.** Colt revolvers: see Colt's Patent Fire Arms Manufacturing Company; Colt Industries, Firearms Division; and Colt's Manufacturing Company, Inc. See also individual brandnames, such as Baby Dragoon, Dragoon Colt, Navy Colt, New Model Army, New Model Navy, New Model Pocket, New Model Police, Paterson Colt, Peacemaker, Pocket Colt, Root Colt, Walker Colt, Wells Fargo Colt, etc. **9.** Colt's Manufacturing Company, Inc., Hartford, Connecticut. Colt continues to make a variety of pistols, including the Junior (.25), Mustang 380 (9mm Short) and Mustang Plus Two (9mm Short). **10.** Colt's Patent Fire Arms Manufacturing Company: see panel, pp. 128/29.

Coltman & Company, Burton upon Trent. Trading from 49 Station Street, this English gunsmithing firm also specialised in loading shotgun cartridges. These were sold under a variety of brandnames, including Burton and K.C., although most of the marks prove to be generic (e.g.

Partridge, Pheasant, Rabbit). Coltman also loaded Governor cartridges for a retailer known only as 'J.S. & S.'

Colton. Edward K. Colton. This Federal arms inspector, working during the American Civil War (1861–65), accepted small-arms marked 'EKC'. See also US arms inspectors' marks.

Coltsman. This brandname was associated with the bolt-action sporting rifles sold by Colt in 1957-61, built on Mauser actions supplied by Fabrique Nationale. The rifles were offered in .300 H&H Magnum and .30-06 in Standard, Deluxe and Custom grades.

Columbia – 1. A brandname encountered on a barrel-cocking spring-air gun advertised by Casimir *Weber of Zürich, Switzerland, in 1908. It is assumed to have been a product of Fr. *Langenhan, *Mayer & Grammelspacher or Oskar *Will, and may also have been marketed under the name Colonial. **2.** A push-in barrel BB Gun sometimes attributed to *Adams & Westlake, but more probably made in the USA by W.G. *Smith & Company. See also Columbian. **3.** Columbia Armory, USA. See Otis *Smith.

Columbian – 1. A revolver made in the USA by the *Foehl & Weeks Manufacturing Company in the early 1890s. **2.** Or Columbian Air Gun. A spring-air BB Gun developed initially by Elmer E. *Bailey and thereafter in collaboration with Thomas E. *Monk. Made by the Columbian Air Gun Manufacturing Company, the origi-nal Model [18]99 was superseded by 1906 and 1908 pat-terns before operations ceased shortly before the First World War broke out in Europe in 1914. All three Columbians had 1,000-shot magazines, but they were not attractive enough to survive competition from more aggressive promoters such as *Daisy and *Markham. **3.** A lever-action BB Gun made to the patents of William *Heilprin, possibly after he had acquired the trading name previously associated with Bailey and Monk. The Columbian Model L was a single-shot lever-action gun designed by Heilprin and made in 1909–19; the Columbian Model M was a repeating version of the Model L, made in its original form in 1910–14, then in a simplified pattern until the end of production in 1919. **4.** Columbian Gun Company, New York. A brandname associated with shotguns made by the *Crescent Arms Company of Norwich, Connecticut.

Columbus – 1. A barrel-cocking spring-air gun adver-tised in the *ALFA catalogue of 1911. Apparently identi-cal with the US-made *Columbian, undoubtedly it orig-inated in Germany, even though its paternity is no longer clear. **2.** Columbus Fire Arms Company, Columbus, Georgia, Confederate States of America. Founded in 1862 by Louis & Elias Haiman, this gunmaking business pro-duced copies of the .36 *Navy Model Colt in 1863. Only about 100 guns had been made before the factory was sold to the government and moved to Macon, Georgia.

Colvin. Robert Colvin, Lancaster, Pennsylvania, USA. Colvin patented a revolver-sabre in March 1862. Originating during the Civil War, just one of many strange-looking weapons promoted enthusiastically across the USA, the Colvin sabre-revolver at least made the transition from patent-specification drawing to hardware. Unfortunately, its maker has never been identified conclusively, although there were many in the Lancaster area (the original home of the Pennsylvania Long Rifle) who could have been respon-sible. The gun part of the weapon was a five-shot cap-

COLT'S PATENT FIRE ARMS MANUFACTURING COMPANY

Colt (10)

Hartford, Connecticut. On the strength of the success of the *Whitney-made *Walker Colt revolver and the promise of a government contract for what became known as the *Dragoon, Samuel *Colt founded his own manufactory in 1848. Large numbers of cap-lock revolvers were made from the introduction of the Dragoon in 1848 to the last of the New Models of the early 1860s. These are listed separately (*see* Colt revolvers…). However, the company was so short of production capacity that a large contract for revolvers received from Russia in 1854 was passed on to gunsmiths in Liège.

The cap-lock Colt revolving shotgun was introduced about 1860, being little more than a smooth-bored revolver rifle in 10- or 20-bore. They had round barrels, *Root-patent creeping rammers, straight-wrist butts and short brass-tipped fore-ends. The guns were expensive, cumbersome and prone to chain-firing, and only about 1,000 were made.

The first cartridge pistols to be made were about 16,000 *Moore-designed National No. 1 and No. 2 knuckle-duster derringers produced in the Hartford factory after Colt had bought the *National Arms Company in 1870. These were followed by the .41 rimfire No. 3 derringer, designed by F. Alexander *Thuer, which lasted until 1912. After briefly considering acquiring a licence from *Smith & Wesson and

*Rollin White, Colt introduced the *Thuer conversion system, patented in 1868 and marketed in small numbers in 1869–70. This was unsuccessful, however, and soon was replaced by the *Richards and *Richards-Mason patterns of 1870–72. At least 30,000 Richards-Mason guns were made, the most numerous being .38 conversions of the .36 *New Police and *New Pocket Model cap-locks.

The .44-calibre *New Model Army revolver of 1872 was the first newly-made cartridge revolver to be offered, but production was comparatively meagre; within a year, it had been replaced by the *Peacemaker or *Single Action Army Model. The new gun was a huge success. Although the design was primitive compared with the double-action auto-ejecting revolvers introduced prior to 1900, the Peacemaker was sturdy, easy to use and simple to repair. By the time production had ceased for the first time in 1940 (it began again in the 1960s), nearly 380,000 guns had been made in a variety of chamberings and styles – e.g. *Bisley Model and *Flat Top Model.

Colt's first double-action revolvers, known colloquially as *Lightning or *Thunderer, were introduced in 1877. They embodied a trigger system designed largely by William *Mason, but while they were well liked by some of the gunfighters, they were notoriously weak and difficult to repair. Although 167,000 guns of this basic pattern were made, they were not regarded as particularly successful.

Based on patents granted to Andrew *Whitmore and William Mason, the 'Colt Breech-Loading Shotgun, Double barrel, Hammer Model 1878' – in 10- or 12-bore only – had side locks with rebounding hammers, Purdey-type under-lugs and a top lever. Work ceased in 1889, after about 22,700 shotguns had been made. There were also a few .45-calibre double rifles. The first hammerless shotgun was the 10- or 12-bore top-lever box-lock Model 1883, derived from patents issued in 1882 to Andrew Whitmore and William Mason. Production ceased in 1896, when only a little more than 7,000 had been made.

The cylinders of the first swinging-cylinder revolvers were carried on a yoke, unlocked by retracting the recoil shield on the left side of the frame. When the cylinder had been pulled out of the frame to the left, backward pressure on the cylinder-axis pin, to which the extractor plate was anchored, expelled the spent cases. However, the cylinder of the 1889-pattern Navy revolver rotated to the left, and, as the cylinder yoke also swung leftward, wear presented a serious problem in aligning the bore and chambers. Once this had been overcome and the perfected 1892-pattern Army revolver had appeared, the basic design remained unchanged for many years – apart from the addition of the *Positive Safety Lock in 1905.

Colt has also made a large number of automatic pistols, initially to the designs of John *Browning.

---

lock revolver rotated by a double-acting trigger within the crossguard of the sword.

Colvocressus. George M. Colvocressus or Colvocresses. A government arms inspector, holding the rank of commander in the Federal Navy, this man accepted *Whitney cap-lock revolvers during the American Civil War. These were marked 'GMC'. *See also* US arms inspectors' marks.

Comanche. A double-action *Smith & Wesson-type swinging-cylinder revolver made by *Llama–Gabilondo SA, 1977–82. It could be obtained with 100 or 150mm barrels, chambered for the .22 (Comanche I) or .38 Special (Commanche II). A few guns were made in 1986 in .22 Magnum. The Commanche III, introduced in 1975, is still being offered in .357 Magnum. Optional .22 rimfire chamberings and an 8.5in barrel were abandoned in 1986.

Comb. The upper edge of the *butt, extending backward from the grip (or wrist) to the heel. The classic comb is straight, but the popular Monte Carlo pattern curves upward at the heel – raising the line of sight – while the Bavarian (also known as Imperial or Hog's Back) comb has a noticeably convex curve from wrist to heel. A roll-over comb curves over the vertical toward the non-cheek side of the stock.

Combat – 1. Applied generically to a variety of automatic pistols, usually signifying plain military-style finish, sights or fittings. **2.** Usually encountered as 'The Combat'. A brandname found on British shotgun cartridges loaded by Russell *Hillsdon. **3.** Specifically associated with a short-barrel .22 air rifle (derived from the Sussex Armoury *Jackal) with a synthetic pseudo-military stock. It was made by *Air Arms of Hailsham in the early

See Hammerless Pocket Model. Rifles were marketed on FN-*Mauser Supreme actions in 1957–61 as the Coltsman series (q.v.). The company's only connection with powderless guns occurred in 1890 when, according to Walter Smith's *Gas, Air & Spring Guns of the World*, the unbelievable sum of a million dollars was paid for US rights to the *Giffard gas rifle. Much more successful militarily has been the Colt-*Browning machine-gun, and the *ArmaLite rifles and carbines made since an exclusive production licence was granted in 1959. Although the US government acquired rights in 1967 to produce ArmaLites for the US armed forces, Colt still controls commercial exploitation.

Representation was maintained in Britain for many years, beginning shortly after the successful showing of the revolvers at the Great Exhibition of 1851. In addition to the factory at Thames Bank, Pimlico, which operated in 1854–57 only, offices were maintained at 1 Spring Gardens in 1853, then at 14 Pall Mall (1857–91) and 37 Chandos Street (1858–60 only). Most directories list post-1863 entries for 'Colt's Patent Fire Arms Mfg Co., F. von Oppen…representative'). The agency moved to 26 Glasshouse Street, London S.W., in 1892 and stayed there for some years.

Millions of words have been written about Colt, some of the best known sources being listed in the Bibliography.

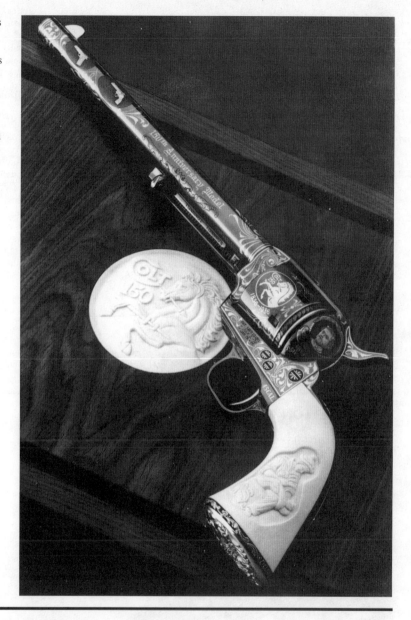

This exceptionally ornate .45-calibre Model P was made in 1986, celebrating the 150th anniversary of the grant of Samuel Colt's first patent.

1980s. **4.** Combat Commander. Service experience showed that the aluminium-alloy frame of the Colt *Commander pistol wore too quickly, forcing the Firearms Division of *Colt Industries to offer a steel alternative from 1971. Chambered for the 9mm Parabellum, .38 Super or .45 ACP cartridges, standard guns were finished in blue or satin nickel. A stainless steel version was introduced in 1991. **5.** Combat Elite. Destined for practical-pistol shooting, this variant of the .45 M1911A1 *Government Model Colt-*Browning offered an enlarged grip safety, a bevelled magazine aperture, and an enlarged ejection port. Three-dot sights, a stainless steel frame and wrap-around Neoprene grips were standard. The guns were made by the Firearms Division of *Colt Industries. **6.** Combat Magnum. The first revolver chambering .357 Magnum ammunition to be built on the medium or K-type frame, this *Smith & Wesson swing-cylinder pattern (also known as the Model 19 after 1957) was introduced commercially in 1955. It was the first of its type to feature a three-screw interlocking side-plate, and originally was made with large hand-filling wood grips (although the short-barrel option introduced in 1968 had a slender round-heel butt). A Stainless Steel Combat Magnum, or Model 66, was introduced in 1971. **7.** Combat Master. An improved form of the 1911A1-type Colt-Browning pistol in ultra-compact personal-defence guise, made in the USA by *Detonics. **8.** Combat Masterpiece. Derived from the *Masterpiece target revolvers, classic Smith & Wesson swing-cylinder patterns, these K-framed guns had 4in barrels and adjustable sights. Most were made in .22 and .38, from 1950 onward, although a few .32 examples were also made.

When numerical designations were introduced in 1957, the .22 Combat Masterpiece became the Model 18 (discontinued in 1985) and the .38 version became the Model 15. The Model 56, made specifically for the USAF in 1962, was a .38 Combat Masterpiece with a special 2in barrel. The Stainless Steel Combat Masterpiece, or Model 67, appeared in 1972; discontinued in 1988, it was reinstated in 1992.

Combi. *See* Kombi(-Handspanner).

Combination guns. *See* panel, below.

Comblain – 1. Hubert-Joseph Comblain (1813–93), a Liège *Armurier* (armourer), is best known for a single-shot dropping-block rifle patented in Belgium in 1870. Also made handguns and revolvers. **2.** Comblain rifle. The basic action comprised a sturdy receiver with a breech lever doubling as the trigger guard, which pivoted at the lower front edge. Pulling the lever lowered the breech-block – which contained the hammer, trigger and main spring – to disengage the locking shoulders. Adopted on 26 March 1870, the Carabine de la Garde Civique was made by the *Petit Syndicat in Liège. The Fusil d'Infanterie de la Garde Civique, adopted in 1882, was an improved form of the Mle 1870 with the hammer altered to allow the action to be uncocked at will. The Belgian Army used the Mousqueton Mle 1871, a short rifle adopted for regular cavalrymen on 15 July 1871. Subsequently many of these were modified for the pioneers and Train from 1883 (Mle 1871/83), gaining a new barrel band and a nose-cap. The standard Belgian-

pattern Comblain was exported to Greece in 1873 (8,000 rifles and 500 musketoons), then to Chile and Peru; a special pattern was made for Brazil. A few sporting guns were made in Liège in the 1870s, but were rapidly superseded by better designs. However, a limited number of guns were stocked and completed in Britain by E.M. *Reilly & Company of London. Edward Reilly had collaborated previously with the Belgian inventor in the Reilly-Comblain rifle of the mid-1860s.

Comega. *See* Armigas-Comega.

Comet – 1. Usually encountered as The Comet; a shotgun cartridge made by *Eley Bros. prior to the acquisition of the company by Explosives Trades Ltd in 1918. **2.** A brandname (originally Cometa) associated with spring-air guns made by C. y T. *Bascaran of Eibar. Only the Cometa V and Cometa VII have been exported in any numbers, but there is also a large Cometa pistol. The guns were sold in Britain in 1975–77 by *Parker-Hale Ltd, as Comets, and reappeared in the early 1980s under the 'Lincoln Comet' brandname of David Nickerson (Tathwell) Ltd. **3.** A *Suicide Special revolver made by the *Prescott Pistol Company of Hatfield, Connecticut, USA, in the late nineteenth century. **4.** A mark found on smokeless-propellant shotgun ammunition made by the *Robin Hood Cartridge Company of Swanton, Vermont, shortly before the First World War began.

Cometa. *See* Comet.

'Commanche'. Found on *Suicide Special revolvers

COMBINATION GUNS

Firearms history is littered with gun-maces, pistol-knives, knuckleduster-revolvers and comparable multiple-threat weapons. Few have been successful, apart, perhaps, from the pistols

fitted with auxiliary spring-bayonets. Patented by John Waters of Birmingham in 1781, these were made in substantial quantities until the end of the Napoleonic Wars.

As far as this book is concerned, the term 'combination firearm' has been reserved specifically for guns

that have, for example, one smoothbore barrel and one rifled barrel, and which are, therefore, effectively combinations of shotgun and rifle. Most of the guns of this type have been made in central Europe, specifically in Germany and Austria, by companies such as F.W. *Heym and *Krieghoff. However, a few have been made in Britain and the USA, most of the American examples being the work of Frank *Hollenbeck.

The majority of two-barrelled firearms are conventional shotguns or *Doppelflinten*, although the barrels may be side-by-side or one above the other (superposed). Guns with one smoothbore and one rifled barrel are known in German-speaking areas as *Büchsflinten* (side-by-side) or *Bockbüchsflinten* (superposed barrels); a *Doppelbüchse* or *Bockdoppelbüchse* has two rifled barrels, whereas a *Bergstutzen* has two superposed rifled barrels of

A typical German box-lock Sauer Model 3000 Drilling, with two shotgun barrels above a single central rifle. The selector lies on the left side of the butt.

made in the USA by the *Norwich Arms Company and/or the *Norwich Falls Pistol Company of Norwich, Connecticut. They date from the late nineteenth century.

'Command' [The]. Found on shotgun cartridges loaded by A. *Chamberlain of Salisbury.

Commander or Lightweight Commander. Introduced in 1949 by *Colt's Patent Fire Arms Manufacturing Company, this was a compact version of the M1911A1 *Government Model, with a 4.25in barrel, an aluminium-alloy frame and a steel slide. Post-1964 examples were the work of the Firearms Division of *Colt Industries. Most guns have been chambered for the .45 ACP cartridge, although .38 Special, 9mm Parabellum and 7.65mm Parabellum (.30 Luger) versions have also been offered. *See also* Combat Commander.

Commando – 1. A brandname applied by the British importers *ASI Ltd to the Spanish *Arizmendi Norica Mo. 73-T barrel-cocking spring-air rifle. Subsequently this was marketed by *Gunmark as the Phantom, a name that was once much better known. **2.** Or Colt Commando. About 50,000 of these revolvers were made during the Second World War by *Colt's Patent Fire Arms Manufacturing Company. They were little more than the Official Police Model, generally with 4in barrels and less care taken with finish. **3.** Applied to the Colt-made Model 609 CAR-15 purchased by the US Army in June 1966, but eventually reclassified – in improved form – as XM177 (Colt Model 649), or XM177E1 with the bolt-closing device in 1967. **4.** Commando Special. Made

in 1984–86 by the Firearms Division of *Colt Industries, this .38 Special revolver had a 2in barrel with a shrouded ejector rod, rubber grips and parkerised finish.

Commercial – 1. A *Suicide Special revolver made by C.S. *Shatuck of Hatfield, Massachusetts, USA, in the late nineteenth century. **2.** Commercial Controls Corporation, USA: *see* M1 Carbine and Winchester.

Commission Rifle. *See* Reichsgewehr.

Compagnie des Forges et Acieries de la Marine. *See* Saint Chamond.

Companhia Brasiliero de Cartuchoes, also known as CBC. A Brazilian maker of guns and ammunition. Products have ranged from airguns and revolvers to break-open shotguns and Double Rifles.

Compañía Anonima Venezolana de Industrias Militares, also known as CAVIM, Venezuela. *See* Saive.

Companion. A name associated with a revolver made in Belgium prior to 1914 by A. *Bertrand.

'Compeer'. A name found on shotguns made in the USA by the *Crescent Arms Company.

Competition. A generic term applied at some time to virtually every type of target gun, but specifically associated with the Competition SS (or Competitizione SS) gas-powered rifle made by *Marocchi e Figli.

'Competitor' [The]. Found on shotgun cartridges sold in southern England by *Blanton of Ringwood.

Compensator. A device on the muzzle of a firearm that diverts some of the emerging gas upward, so developing a downward thrust to counteract the rise of the

different calibres or chambering – usually a large centrefire and small rim- or centrefire pairing. A *Doppelbüchsbergstutzen* is similar, but has its barrels side-by-side.

Three-barrelled guns are usually known as *Drillinge*, the first hammerless pattern being patented by Friedrich Wilhelm Heym in 1891. The standard type has two shotgun barrels side-by-side above a rifled barrel; the *Flintendrilling* has three smoothbore barrels; the *Doppelbüchsdrilling* has two rifled barrels above a single smoothbore; and the *Kugeldrilling* has two barrels chambered for rifle ammunition above a rifled barrel chambering ball- or slug-type shotgun ammunition. A *Bockdrilling* has the smoothbore shotgun above the large-calibre rifled barrel, with a small-calibre rifled barrel set into the side of the barrel block (customarily to the right).

A few four-barrel guns – *Vierling*

– have also been made. Although most examples tend to be restricted to small-calibre rifle chamberings, 12-bore shotguns of this type have also been made in small numbers. Most of them have been too heavy and unwieldy to attract success.

The most common form of

combination firearm has a single rifled barrel and one smoothbore, actual combinations ranging from .22/.410 (popular in the USA) to much more powerful guns such as the *Tikka M07 .222 Remington/12-bore pattern. *See also* Disguised firearms.

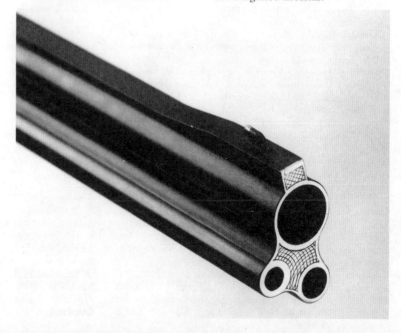

Typical of often bizarre barrel combinations is this Heym Bockdrilling. *This particular Model 35 has a 12-bore shotgun barrel above a .30-calibre rifle, with a .243 rifle to the right!*

muzzle during rapid firing. Originally the device was associated with the *Thompson submachine-gun, but had earlier origins. *See also* Cutts.

Compretta. Identified by W.H.B. Smith, writing in *Gas, Air & Spring Guns of the World* in 1958, with a series of Italian-made barrel-cocking airguns. The source of these remains unknown.

'con', 'CON' – 1. Used as 'con' by Franz Stock of Berlin-Neukölln on small-arms components made for the German armed forces during the Second World War. **2.** Found, as 'CON', on US Navy signal pistols dating from the mid-1890s: an unidentified inspector's mark.

Conant. Hezekiah Conant, Hartford, Connecticut. Granted a patent on 1 April 1856 (14,554) to protect an improved gas-seal for the *Sharps breech mechanism. The Sharps Rifle Company is said to have paid Conant $80,000 for rights to his invention, but it proved only partially effective. *See also* Richard *Lawrence.

Concorde – 1. A name given to a shotgun made in Italy by *Società Armi Bresciane SRL of Gardone. Essentially similar externally to the *Daytona, it has a *Boss-type box-lock action and a single-trigger mechanism patented by Renato *Gamba. Concorde guns are made in Double Trap, Hunting (Caccia), Skeet, Sporting Clays and Trap variants. All, except the 20-bore Trap, may be obtained in 12-bore, although the Hunting version has exchangeable barrels. **2.** Concorde Express. This is a double-rifle derivative of the Concorde shotgun described previously, with a prominent vertical rib between the 600mm barrels and a standing-block sight set into the front of the quarter rib. The pistol-grip butt usually has a cheek-piece and a low *Monte Carlo- or Bavarian-style comb. Chamberings are restricted to .30-06, 8x57 and 9.3x74R.

Concours. *See* Buffalo-Concours.

Condit. William Condit of Des Moines, Iowa, appears to have been a financier, receiving an interest in a variety of patents in return for investing in gun-related projects. The principal assignors were Elbert H. *Searle, inventor of the *Savage semi-automatic pistol, and Morris *Smith of the Standard Arms Company.

'COND.L.E.' An abbreviation of *Converted Lee-Enfield (not 'condemned'), encountered in British designation marks.

Condor – 1. A barrel-cocking spring-air rifle, based on the *Diana LG27, made by Mayer & Grammelspacher in the 1970s as the Model 226 and Model 228. **2.** A repeating BB Gun made by MMM–Mondial, Modesto *Molgora. The name was changed to Condo in the 1970s, presumably after complaints had been received from Mayer & Grammelspacher: *see* previous entry. **3.** Or Astra Condor, Model 8000. Derived from the tube-slide Astra 400, and ultimately from the *Campo-Giro, 11,432 examples this 9mm Short semi-automatic pistol were made in 1958–66. *See also* Falcon.

Cone. Samuel Cone, West Chesterfield, Massachusetts, USA. Cone made a six-shot solid-frame .32 rimfire revolver with a hinged loading gate behind the cylinder. Production ceased when this was classed as an infringement of the Rollin *White patent.

Conical Repeater. A name given to an unsuccessful repeating rifle patented in 1860 by Charles L. *Brown and William H. Morris, made in small numbers by *Morris & Brown of New York City. The gun had a

fixed cylinder, each chamber communicating with a separate throat leading to the bore.

Connacht. *See* Connaught [The].

'Connaught' [The]. A name associated with shotgun cartridges made by *Irish Metal Industries for sale by T. *Naughton of Galway. Possibly also found in its Erse spelling, Connacht.

Connecticut Arms & Manufacturing Company, Naubuc and later Glastonbury, Connecticut, USA. A maker of .28-calibre *cup-primer cartridge revolvers after the end of the American Civil War. The break-open sheath-trigger guns, distinguished by a spur-type extractor, were based on patents granted to Stephen *Wood in 1864–66. The company also made the *Bulldog or Bulldozer cartridge derringer patented by Henry *Hammond in 1866.

Connolly. J.E. Connolly, a government arms inspector, working in 1900–02, accepted US military small-arms marked 'JEC'. *See also* US arms inspectors' marks.

Conqueror – 1. Encountered on 12-bore shotgun ammunition loaded by the *Schultze Gunpowder Company, apparently using components supplied by *Eley Bros. The name is said to have been chosen as much for its association with William I of England (William the Conqueror) as its implications of success. **2.** A *Suicide Special revolver made in the USA by the *Bacon Manufacturing Company of Norwich, Connecticut, in the late nineteenth century.

Constable – 1. Popular as a name for small .320, .380 and .450 double-action revolvers of *Bulldog type, often used generically. However, most examples prove to have been made in Belgium prior to 1914 by Manufacture Liégeoise d'Armes à Feu, whose crowned 'ML' will usually be found on the frames. Many have a safety slider behind the hammer or on the left side of the frame; others rely on a *Reichsrevolver-type radial lever. **2.** Astra Constable or Astra 5000. Introduced in 1965, this double-action blowback semi-automatic pistol was *Astra–Unceta's equivalent of the *Walther PP. Chamberings were confined to .22LR, 7.65mm Auto and 9mm Short, the capacity of the detachable box magazines being ten, eight and seven rounds respectively. Chromed, damascened and engraved versions have all been made in small numbers, but most guns will be found with blued-steel frames. The .22LR Constable Sport (1968–80) was identical, but had a long barrel, adjustable sights and auxiliary weights. Comparatively unsatisfactory as a target pistol, it was superseded in 1979 by the TS-22 – which was effectively a modified Constable with an extended slide, better sights, and an anatomical wooden grip. *See also* Astra pistols.

Constablulary revolver, also known as Gendarmerie or Police. A generic term used to describe a particular class of revolver, derived from the original Webley Bulldog (q.v.). Constabulary revolvers customarily had longer barrels than true Bulldogs, but chambered similar large-calibre centrefire cartridges. The principal distinguishing feature was generally a metal butt cap and a ring for the lanyard that supposedly hung around a policeman's neck. Few of these revolvers, however, ever saw official use! A series of drawings illustrating these patterns may be found in A.B. Zhuk, *The Illustrated Encyclopedia of Handguns* (Greenhill Books, 1995).

Contest. A 4.5mm single-stroke pneumatic sporting gun,

a variant of the MC Super target rifle, made in Spain by ★El Gamo in the 1980s. Production was small, as the gun was too heavy for its purpose and offered too little power.

Continental – **1.** A name associated with two differing semi-automatic pistols, marketed in Germany prior to 1914 by ★Rheinische Waffen- u. Munitionsfabrik of Köln (marked in the pre-1920 form 'Cöln' on the slides). The simpler of the two is a 6.35mm ★Browning-type blowback, probably made in Spain in the early 1920s. The other, perhaps dating from c. 1912–13, resembles the British ★Webley & Scott Police Model of 1906; however, the contours of the frame differed, the safety catch was omitted, and changes were made in the dismantling system. The left side of the slide bore the brandname and a mysterious 'System ★Castenholz' allusion. **2.** A small Browning-type automatic pistol made in Eibar, Spain, for a major distributor/wholesaler, Tómas de ★Urizar of Barcelona: 6.35mm or 7.65mm, six or seven rounds, striker or hammer fired. Made elsewhere, the guns may bear the marks of Fabrique d'Armes de ★Grande Précision. Occasionally hammer-fired examples are marked 'Model 1920'. **3.** A name applied to 6.35mm pistols sold by Tómas de ★Urizar, but probably made by ★Garate, Anitua y Cia. **4.** A ★Suicide Special revolver made by the ★Hood Firearms Company of Norwich, Connecticut, USA, in the late nineteenth century. **5.** Continental Arms Company. Makers of a .22 rimfire five-shot sheath-trigger 'pepperbox derringer' in the 1860s. **6.** Continental Carbine, USA. See Mark X.

Contin-Souza [Établissements de], France. See Berthier.

'Contractile' [The]. Associated with shotgun cartridges handled prior to the First World War by ★Manton & Company, 'London and Calcutta'. Origins unknown.

Controlled Platform. A term applied to a pattern of rifle magazine where the follower can be depressed by the firer to allow cartridges to be dropped into the magazine body without the need to overcome the magazine spring as each cartridge is inserted. The best known patterns were developed by ★Edwards, ★Harris and ★Ross.

Converse. Lyman Converse, a Federal government arms inspector working in 1863, accepted Spencer repeating rifles marked 'LC'. See also US arms inspectors' marks.

Conway. Thomas Conway, Manchester, Lancashire, England. Conway began trading from 179 Chapel Street, Salford, about 1803. A move to 3 Market Street had occurred by 1815, and to 4 Black Friars by 1821. Conway died in 1853, but his executors worked on until 1869. Appropriate marks have been found on sporting guns (often imported from Liège), ★pepperboxes, cap-lock revolvers and crossbows dating from the middle of the nineteenth century.

Conyers. Arthur Conyers, a gunmaker trading in Blandford Forum, Dorset, England, loaded (or possibly simply handled) shotgun ammunition marked 'Dorset County'. Subsequently the business became Conyers & Sons, with additional branches in the Dorset villages of Driffield and Pocklington.

Cooden(s) A maker of magazines for the British 9mm ★Sten Gun during the Second World War, sometimes listed as Fricily Coodens (sic). A regional code may have been used instead of the company name, but even this is still subject to re-interpretation. May be the Cooden

Engineering Company of Cooden, Bexhill-on-Sea, Sussex (code, 'S 173').

Cook – **1.** C. Cook & Company. An English gunmaking business trading in Leighton Buzzard, Leicestershire, in the 1950s. **2.** C.F. Cook & Company. A US based manufacturer of ammunition headstamped 'C.F.C. Co.' Few other details are available. **3.** Edgar Parsons Cook. A native of Grantville, Ohio, USA, this 'Physician' was the patentee of the Cook Air Rifle (US Patent 1,116,675 of October 1913, and British Patent 26,329/12 of 1912) in addition to a long pellet with head flanges and a skirt at the base. **4.** John Cook, Bath, Somerset, England. A gunmaker of this name traded from Kingsmead Street in 1791–93 and Walcott Street in 1825–66, suggesting that a similarly-named son succeeded a father. Cook's marks have been found on sporting guns, including ★pepperboxes, dating from the mid-nineteenth century. **5.** J.T. Cook & Sons. Listed as gunmakers with premises at 6 Well Street, Wellclose Square, London, in the 1850s.

Cooley – **1.** A.M. Cooley, a US government employee, working in the first decade of the twentieth century, accepted small-arms marked 'AMC'. **2.** Henry B. Cooley. This Federal government arms inspector, working in the early 1860s, accepted cap-lock revolvers and other small-arms marked 'HBC'. **3.** J.B. Cooley. This government employee, working in 1898, accepted US military small-arms marked 'JBC'. Possibly the same as the next entry. **4.** J.S. Cooley. See previous entry; said to have accepted US military small-arms marked 'JSC' (1898). See also US arms inspectors' marks for all four entries.

Coombes – **1.** William Coombes. A gunsmith trading in Frome, Somerset, England, c. 1910–39. Shotgun cartridges – made by ★Kynoch or ★Eley-Kynoch – have been reported marked 'Coombes' Champion' and 'Eclipse'. **2.** Coombes' Champion. An ★Eley-Kynoch shotgun cartridge loaded, or perhaps simply sold, by William Coombes of Frome, Somerset, in the 1920s and 1930s.

Cooper – **1.** G.C. Cooper. A London gunmaker listed in 1890–93 at 131 High Holborn. **2.** James Cooper, Pittsburgh, Pennsylvania, USA. Designer of a double-action trigger mechanism of the Cooper Fire Arms Company revolver, protected by US Patents 29,684 of 4 September 1860 and 40,021 of 22 September 1863. **3.** Jeff Cooper: see Bren Ten. **4.** J.H. Cooper. This arms inspector, working in about 1870, accepted US military small-arms marked 'JHC'. They include single-shot Remington and .50-70 Springfield rifles, and .36 Remington cap-lock revolvers. **5.** J.R. Cooper & Company, 24 Legge Street, Birmingham, Warwickshire. Founded by Joseph Rock Cooper, this English gunmaking business maintained offices in London (at 52 Eastcheap, E.C.) in the early 1850s. 'Revolving Pistols' (pepperboxes) were exhibited at the Great Exhibition in London in 1851. **6.** Malcolm Cooper, Britain. See Accuracy International. **7.** Cooper Fire Arms Company, Philadelphia, Pennsylvania, USA. Despite external affinities with the open-frame Colts, the Cooper revolver had a double-action trigger system patented in 1860–63. After a few guns had been made in Pittsburgh, infringing ★Gruler & Reberty's patent, Cooper moved to Philadelphia. Five-shot .31 pocket and six-shot .36 Navy revolvers were made. The subsequent adoption of a double-diameter cylinder allowed the .31 pattern to include a sixth chamber. The marks on Cooper revolvers customarily acknowledged patents granted to

Stanhope *Marston in 1851, Josiah *Ells in 1854 and Charles *Harris in 1863, in addition to Cooper's own protection. **8.** Cooper & Goodman, one of the leading gunmakers in Birmingham, Warwickshire, traded in Woodcock, then Baggot Sheets from 1857 until succeeded in 1886 by C.H. Cooper trading alone. **9.** Cooper-Macdonald, Inc., Baltimore, Maryland, USA. Agents for the original ArmaLite AR-10 rifle in Australasia and the Far East, c. 1957–60.

Cop and Thug. *See* New Police Pistol.

Copenhagen arms factory. *See* Hærens Tøjhus.

Copperhead. A brandname used by the *Crosman Arms Company of Fairport, New York State, USA, on BBs, gas cartridges and accessories.

Coquet, sometimes listed, possibly erroneously, as 'Coquette', Liège, Belgium. A maker of revolvers active in the 1870s.

Corden. S.L. Corden. A gunsmith trading in Warminster, Wiltshire, England, Corden is known to have handled shotgun cartridges with the brandname Quickfire.

Cordier & Cie, Bellefontaine, Switzerland. This gunmaking business, better known for sporting guns, made a few thousand M1869 *Vetterli infantry rifles for the Swiss government in 1869–73.

A. Cordy & fils, Liège. A gunmaking business active in Belgium in the 1870s, renowned for double-barrelled rifles and shotguns.

Cornish. John Cornish & Company, Okehampton, Devon. The marks of this English gunsmithing business have been reported on shotgun cartridges sold under the Oakment brand.

'Cornubia' [The]. This mark will be found on shotgun cartridges loaded by the *Cornwall Cartridge Works of Liskeard.

Cornwall – 1. Cornwall Cartridge Works, Liskeard, Cornwall, England. This business loaded shotgun cartridges from components supplied by *Eley-Kynoch, using names such as Cornubia, Cornwall, Tamar and Trelawney. **2.** Usually encountered as 'The Cornwall': shotgun cartridges loaded by the Cornwall Cartridge Works of Liskeard.

Cornwell. John J. Cornwell This government arms inspector, a commander in the US Navy, accepted a range of small-arms marked 'JJC'. They date from 1848 to 1867. *See also* US arms inspectors' marks.

'Coronation' [The]. A shotgun cartridge made by *Eley-Kynoch Ltd. It has also been found with the marks of the *Army & Navy Stores Ltd of London.

Corto. Spanish for 'short', used to identify chamberings for the 9mm Corto (9mm Short, .380 ACP) pistol cartridge. *See also* Largo.

Cory. Randolph P. Cory, Union City, Indiana, and St Louis, Missouri, USA. Grantee of several patents protecting firearms (1881–1907), many assigned to J. *Baron.

Corzo. *See* Armas *El Corzo.

'cos'. Found on German small-arms components made in 1941–45 by *Merz-Werke Gebr. Merz of Frankfurt am Main.

Cosmopolitan – 1. Cosmopolitan Arms Company, Hamilton, Ohio. This US gunmaking business received a contract for about 1,140 *Gross-patent carbines to arm volunteers being mustered in neighbouring Illinois. Production began about 1862. **2.** Cosmopolitan carbine. The original .52-calibre Gross or Cosmopolitan guns had

a serpentine breech lever, doubling as a trigger guard, the tip of which recurved to lock into the back of the catch on the frame.

Cossack Rifle. A term applied to the long-arms carried by the Kazakh (Cossack) units of the Imperial Russian Army. The most distinctive features included a narrow-comb butt and a ball trigger; the latter was retained even by the *Berdan II breech-loaders of the 1870s. A cossack variant of the *Mosin-Nagant was also made, but this differed from the standard short-rifle or Dragoon pattern only in the design of the fore-end. However, it had a distinctive Cyrillic 'КАЗ' ('KAZ') serial-number prefix.

Coste-Blachon et Cie; rue Badouillère 21, Saint-Étienne, France. Listed in 1892 as a gunmaker.

Coster. G. Coster & Son, 145 West Nile Street, Glasgow. This Scottish gunsmithing business used the mark 'G.C. & S.' on guns and ammunition.

Costruzione Meccaniche Zanoletti. *See* Attilio *Zanoletti.

'Cotswold' [The]. Found on shotgun ammunition sold by Edwinson *Green of Gloucester. A similar mark has also been found on cartridges handled by *Evans of Burford, possibly supplied by Green.

Cotton – 1. Charles S. Cotton, a Federal government arms inspector holding the rank of lieutenant in the US Navy, accepted small-arms marked 'CSC' during the American Civil War. *See also* US arms inspectors' marks. **2.** Walter Cotton & Company. Trading in Coventry, Warwickshire, England, from the early 1900s until 1940. Shotgun ammunition has been reported with Cotton's marks.

Cottrell. S.P. Cottrell & Son, Buffalo, New York State, USA. This toolmaking business attempted to combine a firearm and flashlight in accordance with a US patent granted in 1923. A seven-shot .22LR double-action revolver, built into the top of the flashlight, could be fired with a folding trigger on the underside of the casing. The intention was to allow aim to be taken by light beam, as the bullet would go where the light pointed. However, the Cottrell two-cell flashlight-revolvers are now very rare.

Couch. John Couch, USA. *See* Game Shooter.

Cougar. This .177 or .22 barrel-cocking spring-air pistol, also known as the G5, was made by *Milbro Ltd from 1978 until 1982. It had distinctive ABS furniture and a rod-type sliding butt. A carbine variant was known as the Black Major.

Counet. Philippe Counet. This Liège based Belgian gunsmith was responsible for revolvers made in the 1870s, and also for a mechanically-repeating pistol.

Country, Country..., *see also* A.C. County and Town & Country **– 1.** Country Gentlemen's Association [The]. The marks of this group have been reported on shotgun ammunition made by *Kynoch Ltd prior to the First World War. Normally they took the form of 'C.G.A.' within a buckler. **2.** Usually encountered as 'The County': 12-bore shotgun cartridges sold by Henry Esau *Akrill of Beverley, probably prior to 1914. A similar brandname may be found on shotgun cartridges sold by *Johnson & Wright of Northampton, but usually this was accompanied by an illustration of the town's arms (two lions and a castle tower). **3.** 'County Cartridge' [The]. Found on shotgun cartridges sold in southern England by *Greenfield of Canterbury. **4.** 'County Down' [The]. Associated with shotgun cartridges handled by

*Cambridge & Company of Carrickfergus, Ireland. **5.** 'County Favourite' [The]. A mark associated with shotgun ammunition handled in Britain by F.J. *Cole of Cirencester, Gloucestershire.

Courage. A name associated with a revolver made in Belgium prior to 1914 by A. *Bertrand.

Courally, place de l'Hôtel-de-Ville 8, Saint-Étienne, France. Listed in 1892 as a gunmaker.

Courier. Confined to 1955–56, this was a variant of the *Cobra with a 3in barrel and a short rounded butt. Only a few thousand were made by *Colt's Patent Fire Arms Manufacturing Company, in .22 rimfire and .32 New Police centrefire.

Courtial – 1. Saint-Étienne, France. Listed in 1933 as a gunmaker, but succeeded c. 1946 by *Courtial et Debraye. **2.** Courtial et Debraye, 14 rue J.-B. David, Saint-Étienne. Listed in 1951 as a gunmaker, having succeeded to the business of Courtial (above) after the Second World War.

Coutts. William Coutts. According to London directories, this member of the English gun trade could be found in the Soho district at 58 King Street in 1871–75 and 11 Gerrard Street in 1876–84.

Coventry Ordnance Works [The]. Promoters of the *Laird-Mentayne light machine-gun in Britain prior to the First World War.

'Covert' [The]. A shotgun cartridge marked by Henry *Atkin of London.

Cow Boy. A Spanish Browning-type 6.35mm pocket pistol, made by an unknown gunmaker, probably in Eibar: six rounds, hammer fired. Some examples are misleadingly marked 'Fabrication Française'.

Cowe. *See* Snow & Cowe.

Cox – 1. Frederick Stanley Cox, a 'Gun Maker' of 6 Freer Road, Handsworth, Birmingham, designed the *Britannia air rifle – popularly, but mistakenly, ascribed to Christopher *Bonehill. The gun was the subject of British Patents 15,712/02 of 1902 and 9153/04 of 1904. It is possible that Cox was employed by Bonehill in the latter's Belmont Gun Works, but this is not known with certainty. **2.** John Cox, later Cox & Son. This English gunmaker began trading from 13 High Street, Southampton, Hampshire, in 1843. After a move to 7 Bernard Street in 1854, John Cox died in the early 1860s; business was carried on for a few years by his widow Mary-Ann, then by his son (also apparently named John). Cox & Son was still trading from 28 High Street at the turn of the century, when 'own-name' shotgun cartridges were being purchased from *Kynoch Ltd. Trading continued after the First World War as Cox & Clarke, then as Cox & MacPherson. Shotgun cartridges marked 'The Southampton' have been identified from this source. **3.** Joseph H. Cox. Proprietor of Cox & Son (below), J.H. Cox was granted British Patent 19,297/02 of 1902 to protect a variety of flanged and ribbed airgun slug subsequently sold under the name Acme. Cox was also responsible for a pan-type magazine protected by British Patent 4824/07 of 1907. Writing in *The Revolver 1888–1914*, Anthony Taylerson states that this design was 'assigned elsewhere' in 1912. Subsequently many enthusiasts have assumed that a licence was granted to *Haenel prior to the First World War, but Haenel did not enter the airgun business until 1925, and it seems more likely that Cox's pan magazine interested the *Birmingham Small Arms

Company Ltd. **4.** Cox & Clarke and Cox & MacPherson, Britain. *See* John Cox. **5.** Cox & Son. This foundry at 137a Guildford Street, Lozells, Aston juxta Birmingham, Warwickshire, was owned by Joseph H. *Cox. Trading from c. 1903 until the First World War, it made the *Acme, *Aston Villa and *Wonder airgun projectiles – all of which seem to have been introduced prior to 1907.

Coyle – 1. Joseph E. Coyle, a government arms inspector working in 1907, accepted US military small-arms marked 'JEC'. **2.** J.F. Coyle. An inspector of Krag-Jørgensen gallery-practice rifles in the late 1890s, using a 'JFC' mark. Perhaps the same as Joseph E. Coyle (above). *See* US arms inspectors' marks.

'CPH'. *See* Charles P. *Hill.

'cpj'. Allotted to Havelwerk GmbH of Brandenburg/Havel in 1941, this code was used on German artillery, machine-gun, rifle and ammunition components made during the Second World War.

'CPL'. *See* C.P. *Lynn.

'cpo'. Found on German military small-arms components made by *Rheinmetall-Borsig AG of Berlin-Marienfelde in 1941–45.

'cpq'. Used by the *Rheinmetall-Borsig AG factory, Guben, on machine-guns and small-arms components dating from the Second World War.

'CR'. *See* Cadwalader *Ringold.

'cra'. Granted in 1941 to Alkett-Altmärkische Kettenwerke GmbH of Berlin-Tegel, this codemark will be encountered on German machine-gun and small-arms components

Crabb. George Crabb. Recorded at 18 Brewer Street, Golden Square, London, in 1883, Crabb – a member of the English gun trade – may simply have been a merchant.

Craig, *see also* Ailsa Craig and Bell-Craig – **1.** J.B. Craig. This government arms inspector, working in 1897–1905, accepted military small-arms marked 'JBC'. Possibly the same as the succeeding entry. **2.** Joseph E. Craig. Said to have worked in 1898–1906, this inspector accepted small-arms marked 'JEC'. Possibly the same as the preceding entry. **3.** Joseph Edger Craig, a naval lieutenant, accepted small-arms for the Federal government during and immediately after the American Civil War. They were customarily marked 'JEC'. *See also* US arms inspectors' marks.

Cramer & Buchholz Pulverfabriken GmbH, Rönsahl and Hannover. This propellant- and ammunition-making business, founded in Germany in the 1870s, traded independently until the end of the First World War. Cartridges associated with its products include *Diana, Hussa and Krone brands (and probably also Silvanus), although most of the components were supplied by *Patronen-Hülsen-Fabriken Bitschweiler.

Cramer-Klett'schen Établissements, Nürnberg, Bavaria. Maker of *Werder rifles.

Crane – 1. J.H. Crane. A gunmaker trading successively from 2 Castle Court, Burchin Lane, London E.C. (1863); 3 Royal Exchange (1865–77); and 6 St Swithin's Lane (1878–79). He entered 12-bore *Lancaster-patent breech-loading shotguns in *The Field* trials in 1866. **2.** R.Z. Crane. This government arms inspector, working in 1935, accepted US military .45 M1911A1 (Colt) pistols marked 'RZC'. *See also* US arms inspectors' marks.

Cranston. Robert Peter Cranston. An employee of *BSA Guns Ltd and co-patentee with Harold *Jones and

Roger *Wackrow of the hammer and trigger mechanism of the *Scorpion air pistol.

'CRB'. *See* C.R. *Bunker.

Creamer. Robert Creamer, USA. *See* Winchester.

Creedmoor, *see also* Creedmore – **1.** Taken from a well-known rifle range at Creed's Farm on Long Island, this served as a brandname – particularly popular in the 1880s and 1890s – on Ballard, Hepburn, Peabody-Martini, Maynard, and Stevens rifles. *See also* Walnut Hill and What Cheer. **2.** Creedmoor Model, USA. *See* Long-Range Model. **3.** Creedmoor Target Rifle. Made by E. *Remington & Sons and the Remington Arms Company, in 1874–91, this embodied a specially finished No. 1 *rolling-block action and was among the finest rifles of its day. The 32in octagonal barrel could be chambered for .44-90, .44-100 or .44-105 Remington cartridges. Stocks were selected walnut, fore-ends terminated in pewter or German silver finials, and vernier peep-and-globe sights and spirit levels were customary. *See also* Improved Creedmoor Rifle, Long Range Military Creedmoor Rifle and Remington rifles, rolling-block action.

Creedmore, *see also* Creedmoor – **1.** A *Suicide Special revolver made by the *Hopkins & Allen Arms Company of Norwich, Connecticut, USA, in the late nineteenth century. **2.** Creedmore Cartridge Company, Barberton, Ohio, USA. Founded c. 1890, this short-lived business made rifle and shotgun ammunition with 'C.C.C.' in the headstamps.

Creighton. G. Creighton & Company. An English gunmaking business known to have been trading from 8 Warwick Road, Carlisle, Cumberland, prior to 1914.

Cremona arms factory. *See* Koucký and Mannlicher.

Crescent – **1.** A *Suicide Special revolver made by the Crescent Arms Company of Norwich, Connecticut, USA, in the late nineteenth century. **2.** Break-open BB Guns made by the Crescent Gun Company as a single-shot pattern (1904–08) or a repeater with a screw-head feed mechanism beneath the barrel (1905–08). **3.** Encountered on smokeless-propellant shotgun ammunition made c. 1910–15 by the *Robin Hood Cartridge Company of Swanton, Vermont. **4.** Crescent Arms Company, Norwich, Connecticut. Formed in 1892, this was one of the most prolific of all the North American makers of inexpensive shotguns – box-lock non-ejecting single- and double-barrel designs, hammer or hammerless, camouflaged by brandnames ranging from Faultless to Square Deal. The business was purchased in 1893 by H. & D. *Folsom Arms Company, but continued to trade under its own name until merged with the *Davis-Warner Corporation in 1930. Trading continued as the Crescent-Davis Corporation until the business was acquired by J. *Stevens Arms & Tool Company in 1932. **5.** Crescent-Davis Corporation, USA. *See* Crescent Arms Company. **6.** Crescent Gun Company, Saginaw, Michigan, USA. Owned by the Crescent Salt Company, this business made Crescent and *Dewey BB Guns from 1899 until c. 1908, although it is probable that production was undertaken by the A.F. *Bartlett Company (which shared the same officers and the same address from 1904). Production had ceased by 1909; it seems possible that the production machinery was sold subsequently to Japan, where the Crescent-like *Ozieh gun was introduced about 1912.

Cressall – **1.** Henry Cressall. Trading from 5 King Street, Holborn, London, in 1856–57, this English gunmaker was succeeded by his son William. **2.** William Cressall. Successor to his father Henry (above), trading from 45 Bedford Row, London, in 1858–73 or later.

Crieffel. A brandname associated with Richardson of Dunfermline, reportedly found on 12-bore shotgun cartridges of uncertain origin. Crieff is a town in Perthshire, Scotland.

Crighton. J.M. Crighton. This government arms inspector, working from 1895 until c. 1914, accepted US military small-arms marked 'JMC'. *See also* US arms inspectors' marks.

'Crimson Flash' [The]. A mark associated with shotgun cartridges loaded and sold by *Garrett of Evesham.

Crispin – **1.** Silas Crispin. A captain in the Federal Navy, this arms inspector accepted cap-lock Remington revolvers during the American Civil War. They were marked 'SC'. *See also* US arms inspectors' marks. **2.** Silas Crispin. This gunsmith – perhaps the same man as the previous entry – designed the hinged-frame revolver protected by US Patent 50,224 of 3 October 1865 and made by the *Smith Arms Company. The two-part cylinder accepted special cartridges with an annular priming band, loaded backward through the front section of the cylinder.

Crittenden & Tibbals Manufacturing Company, South Coventry, Connecticut. Ammunition manufacturers active during the American Civil War. The cartridges were often *headstamped 'CTM'.

'CRO'. A mark consisting of 'R' within a large 'C' containing a small 'o' in its jaws. Correctly read as 'RCO' (q.v.); used by *Robar & Co. of Liège.

Crockart – **1.** D. Crockart & Company, Stirling. A gunmaker trading in Scotland prior to the 1920s. Possibly succeeded by D.B. Crockart (below). **2.** D.B. Crockart & Company, Perth, Perthshire. This gunmaking business loaded, or perhaps simply handled, shotgun ammunition branded 'Perth' and 'Spotfinder'. The components were supplied by *Eley-Kynoch. **3.** J. Crockart & Son. This gunmaking business traded prior to 1939 in Blairgowrie, Perthshire. Some sporting guns and ammunition may be found with 'J.C. & S.' marks.

Crockett. Leroy Crockett, USA. *See* Winchester.

Crosby. Pierce Crosby, a commander in the US Navy, accepted single-shot Remington cartridge pistols and Whitney cap-lock revolvers in the 1860s. The guns will show 'PC' marks. *See also* US arms inspectors' marks.

Crosman Arms Company – **1.** Fairport, New York State. The origins of this maker of air- and gas guns lay in the grant of US Patent 1,512,993 (1924) to William A. McLean, chauffeur to the owner of the Crosman Seed Company. A gunmaking business was formed to exploit McLean's patent, but, after a promising start, its fortunes declined and it was sold in 1940 to Philp Y. Hahn. Fresh impetus after the Second World War enabled Crosman to market products ranging from the simplest of junior pneumatic and gas guns up to the Model 84 Olympic rifle and the Crosman-Skanaker competition pistol. Among the best known of Crosman's junior rifles have been the Model 766 American Classic, a Remington cartridge-rifle lookalike that could fire BB Shot and .177 diabolo pellets interchangeably; the lever-cocking Model 73 Saddle Pal; and a scaled-down slide-cocking version of the M1 Carbine. The Models 1322 Medalist and 1377 American

Classic pneumatic pistols have also been popular, although a gas-powered facsimile of the *Remington cap-lock revolver (the M1861 Shiloh) was less successful. Crosman sold substantial quantities of European-made spring-piston guns in North America in the 1980s and 1990s, often under the Challenger brandname. The guns were made by J.G. *Anschütz, *Bascaran and *Dianawerk Mayer & Grammelspacher. **2.** Crosman-Whaley, Britain. *See* Whaley's of North London Ltd.

Cross. Calvin Benjamin Cross, a Federal government arms inspector, working in 1862–63, accepted cap-lock revolvers and other small-arms marked 'CBC'. *See also* US arms inspectors' marks.

'Crow' [The]. A mark encountered on shotgun ammunition made in Britain for R. *Crowe Ltd of Great Baddow.

Crowe – 1. R. Crowe Ltd, 63 Maldon Road, Great Baddow, Essex. The marks of this British retailer of guns, ammunition and sporting goods will be encountered on shotgun ammunition (loaded by the *Hull Cartridge Company) sold under the name Crow in the 1970s. **2.** W.L. Crowe, listed alternatively as Crowl or Crowell. This government arms inspector, working in the early 1900s, accepted small-arms marked 'WLC'. *See also* US arms inspectors' marks.

Crown – 1. Usually encountered as 'The Crown'; on 12-bore shotgun cartridges distributed in Britain by gunsmiths and ironmongers such as Edward *Aldridge of Ipswich; *Cole & Son of Devizes and Portsmouth; *Jewson of Halifax; *Paragon Guns of Belfast; and Charles S. *Rosson of Norwich. **2.** An air rifle made by *Moritz & Gerstenberger; *see* Krone. **3.** A *Suicide Special revolver made by the *Harrington & Richardson Arms Company of Worcester, Massachusetts, USA, in the late nineteenth century. **4.** Crown Grade. A term applied by H. *Krieghoff GmbH to engraved patterns applied to the K-80 over/under shotgun. Game scenes of dogs and birds (often inlaid in gold) will be found on the receiver, edged with floral scrolls within a gold monoline border. *See also* Bavaria, Bavaria-Suhl, Danube, Gold Target and Parcours. **5.** Crown Grade. This name has been used by *Husqvarna on bolt-action sporting rifles made since the late 1950s in chamberings ranging from .243 Winchester to .308 Winchester. They have been offered in standard, deluxe and lightweight versions.

'crs', 'CRS' – 1. Used as 'crs' on small-arms components made during the Second World War by Paul Weyersberg & Co., Solingen, Germany. **2.** A superimposition-type monogram with 'R' dominant. Correctly 'SRC' (q.v.); associated with *Sears, Roebuck & Company. **3.** Found as 'CRS' on US military firearms; *see* Curtis R. *Sticknet.

Crucelegui – 1. A Spanish 6.35mm Browning-type pistol made in Eibar in the 1920s by *Crucelegui Hermanos: eight rounds, hammer fired. **2.** Crucelegui Hermanos, Eibar, Guipúzcoa, Spain. Makers of *Campeon, *C.H. and Crucelegui pistols.

Cruikshank & Fairweather. This patent agency had chambers at 65–66 Chancery Lane, London WC2, and 62 St Vincent Street, Glasgow, during the period it acted for Axel *Blómen & Per Ewerlöf and AB Våpenfabriken *Excellent. *See* British Patents 25,579/05 of 1905 and 28,192/09 of 1909.

Cruso. *See* Caruso.

Cruz. José Cruz, Spain; *see* Mugica.

Cruzen. George B. Cruzen, a Federal government arms inspector, working in the early 1860s, accepted Remington cap-lock revolvers marked 'GBC'. *See also* US arms inspectors' marks.

Crvena Zastava, Kragujevač. The Yugoslav (now Serbian) state firearms factory or Voini Tekhniki Zavod (VTZ) was formed from the former Serbian establishment in 1919, and equipped largely by *Fabrique Nationale d'Armes de Guerre in the early 1920s. In addition to Mauser rifles, the factory made *FN-Browning pistols and machine-guns. Nationalised in 1948 as Zavodi Crvena Zastava (Red Banner Works) or ZCZ, the facilities continued to make a range of weapons. These included a variety of *Simonov auto-loading carbines, *Kalashnikov-based assault rifles (*Automatská puška*) and light machine-guns (*Puškomitraljez*). Trading since 1990 has been undertaken as Zastava Arms, but the factory was seriously damaged by bombing in 1999, during the conflict between NATO and Serbia, and the current situation is unknown. Mausers, often simply in the form of barrelled actions, have been supplied to many gunmaking businesses. These included *Herter's of Waseca, Minnesota, prior to the involvement of *Interarms in the early 1970s. The ZCZ actions have many characteristics of the Belgian *FN Model 1924, as the original production machinery was installed by Fabrique Nationale as part of an agreement to supply technical assistance. However, the safety catch was moved to the right side of the receiver behind the bolt. These actions have been sold as the Herter J9 or Zastava 67, as well as the Interarms *Mark X brand. See also Whitworth Express Rifle.

'CS'. *See* Camo Synthetic and Clark *Swallow.

'CSC'. *See* Charles S. *Cotton.

'CSL'. *See* C.S. *Leonard and Charles S. *Lowell.

'csm'. This mark will be found on German machine-gun and small-arms components made by Knorr-Bremse AG of Berlin in 1941–45.

'CSR' – 1. A superimposition-type monogram with 'R' dominant. Correctly 'SRC' (q.v.); associated with *Sears, Roebuck & Company. **2.** A mark found on US military firearms and accessories. *See* Charles S. *Reed.

CSRG. *See* panel, pp. 138/39.

CSS. A superimposition-type monogram with 'S' dominant. Found on revolvers made by the C.S. *Shatuck Arms Company.

Cs.st.Z. An abbreviated form of *Československé statní Zbrojovka A.S., Brno.

'CSZ' – 1. Found on 6.35mm-calibre pocket pistols made c. 1920–21 by *Československé Závody na Vyrobu Zbraní. **2.** Found on the grips of Czechoslovakian 6.35mm Browning-type pistols made in the mid-1920s by *Československé statní Zbrojovka A.S. of Brno.

CTA. A superimposition-type monogram, sometimes encircled, with no letters prominent. Correctly 'TAC'; used by *Trocaola, Aranzabal y Cia.

'CTJ'. *See* C.T. *Judd.

'CTM'. A *headstamp found on rimfire cartridges made by the *Crittenden & Tibbals Manufacturing Company. Most of them date from 1864–68.

'cts'. Found on German small-arms ammunition components made during the Second World War by Märkisches Werk, H. Wilmsmann GmbH of Halver in Westfalen.

CTV. Prototype automatic rifles were developed by the French Commission Technique de Versailles (CTV) and

CSRG

Also known as the Chauchat, this rudimentary light machine-gun was adopted by the French Army during the First World War. Characterised by its semi-circular magazine, the 8mm

CSRG, or *Fusil Mitrailleur CSRG Mle 1915*, was simple and relatively easily made by poorly equipped factories. It is said to have been developed by three French government engineers (Chauchat, Sutter and Ribeyrolle) from a prototype submitted by the

*Gladiator manufactory. The US Army acquired nearly 13,000 8mm French-made rifles, then ordered 25,000 M1915 guns chambered for the .30 M1906 round. The American cartridge proved much too powerful, leading to jamming, case-head

the Établissment Technique de l'Artillerie de Puteaux (APX). They dated from 1903–10.

'cua'. On small-arms components made by *Röhm Gesellschaft of Zella-Mehlis, Thüringen, Germany, in 1941–45.

Cub – 1. A spring-air pistol sold in Britain, but made in Germany, probably by *Mayer & Grammelspacher. **2.** An air-bulb pistol, made by *Millard Bros. to the design of René Boulet in c. 1949–53; *see* British Patent 614,740 of 1948. **3.** Astra Cub, or Astra 2000. Chambered for the .22LR or 6.35 Auto rounds, this tiny blowback semi-automatic pistol derives from the *FN-Browning of 1906. It has an exposed hammer and rudimentary sights, but may be found with a variety of decorative finishes (*modelos de lujo*) and engraved or damascened. Grips may be plastic, wood, mother-of-pearl or ivory. The Cub was sold in the USA prior to 1968 as the *Colt Junior, but was superseded by the Astra 7000 in 1973. **4.** An alternative name for the Model 102 BB Gun made in the USA by *Daisy.

Cugir. The Romanian national small-arms factory, best known for the manufacture of machine-guns and *Kalashnikov assault rifles.

Cuinet. Alphonse Cuinet, rue de l'Industrie, Saint-Étienne, France. Listed in 1879 as a maker of gun parts and accessories.

Cuirasée. A tradename used by *Fabrique Nationale d'Armes de Guerre on shotgun ammunition loaded with large-diameter SG shot, c. 1932–40. It was customarily found with a metal cartridge case.

Cumberland – 1. Usually encountered as 'The Cumberland'; found on shotgun cartridges sold in Britain prior to 1914 by *Graham of Cockermouth. **2.** Cumberland Arms Company. A brandname associated with shotguns manufactured prior to the First World War

by the *Crescent Arms Company of Norwich, Connecticut, USA.

Cumming, Cummings – 1. William G. Cumming, sometimes listed as Cummings. A London based gunmaker and merchant trading at 135 Fenchurch Street in 1871 and 9 Railway Approach, London Bridge, in 1873–74. **2.** J.E. Cummings, a Federal government inspector working during the American Civil War (1861–65), accepted small-arms marked 'JEC'. *See also* US arms inspectors' marks.

Cunningham. Patrick Thomas Cunningham. This government arms inspector, a lieutenant in the Federal Navy, accepted military small-arms marked 'PTC' in 1864. *See also* US arms inspectors' marks.

Cuocq, rue Valbenoîte 16, Saint-Étienne, France. Listed in 1879 as a gunmaker; and in 1892, as Cuoq, at cours de l'Hôpital 14.

Cup-primer. Chambered in the *Plant revolvers, these *cartridges contained fulminate in a rearward extension of the cartridge case. A small hole bored in the rear of the cylinder-chamber allowed the hammer-nose to strike the priming pellet.

Curry – 1. James Curry. A 'Gun Implement Maker' of 13 Court, Price Street, Birmingham, Warwickshire, England, in the directories of 1913–20, James Curry is considered to have been either the father or brother of Joseph Curry (below). **2.** Joseph Curry. The relationship between Curry & Keen and this 'Gun Finisher', variously listed in Birmingham directories at 24, 27^1/2, 28 and 31^1/2 Whittall Street between 1915 and 1950 remains elusive. The trading style had become Joseph Curry Ltd by 1955, occupying premises at 6–18 Arthur Road, Birmingham 25, but operations had ceased by 1961. **3.** Curry & Keen are said to have purchased the business of Edwin *Anson in 1945. Small numbers of *Star pistols were assembled by A.A. *Brown & Sons,

separations and parts breakages. None of the .30 guns ever saw combat. The best source of information is undoubtedly *Honour Bound* by Gérard Demaison and Yves Buffetaut (Collector Grade Publications, 1995).

and allegedly sold by Curry & Keen into the early 1950s. However, a search of Birmingham directories failed to reveal Curry & Keen – leaving the possibility of a misrepresentation of Joseph Curry & Company (above) or a short-lived trader engaged in something other than the gun trade.

Curtis – 1. Charles G. Curtis, a Federal government arms inspector, accepted Henry repeating rifles in 1862–63. These were marked 'CGC'. **2.** George Curtis. This Federal government employee, working in 1860–62, accepted small-arms marked 'GC'. *See also* US arms inspectors' marks for each of the previous entries. **3.** Curtis's & Harvey Ltd, sometimes, especially in the early days, listed as Curtis & Hervey. One of the best known of all the British gunpowder and propellant makers, a successor to Curtis & André, this business was active in 1871, with manufacturing premises in Hounslow Mills and an office in Gracechurch Street, London E.C. Curtis's & Harvey amalgamated with John ★Hall & Company of Faversham, Kent, during the First World War, but became a constituent of ★Explosives Trades Ltd in November 1918. Among the products were shotgun cartridges sold under the brandnames Amberite, Diamond, Feather Weight, Marvel and Ruby. The major components were supplied by ★Eley Bros. Ltd.

'Curzon' [The]. A name associated with shotgun cartridges sold by ★Grant & Lang of London.

Cushing. Samuel Cushing. The 'SC' marks of this arms inspector, a lieutenant in the Federal Navy, have been found on flare pistols made in 1861–62. *See also* US arms inspectors' marks.

Custer – 1. Or Custer Commemorative; *see* General Custer. **2.** M.M. Custer. This US government arms inspector, working in 1905–12, accepted small-arms marked 'MMC'. *See also* US arms inspectors' marks.

Custom – 1. Usually found as 'Custom No. 1' and 'Custom No. 4'. Introduced by ★Parker-Hale Ltd of Birmingham in 1965, these conversions of .303 No. 1 and No. 4 Lee-Enfield rifles lacked charger guides and had the left wall of the receiver adapted to accept an optical-sight mount. The pistol-grip butts had ventilated recoil pads and the fore-end had an obliquely-cut tip. **2.** Custom Grade. A term applied to the ★Remington Model 700C bolt-action rifle, dating from 1965–89. The guns were made in four grades (I–IV), depending on the grain of the stock, the quality of the bluing and the amount of decoration. The term is currently reserved for the output of the Remington Gun Shop and is no longer restricted to variants of the Model 700.

Cut-off. Popular on early military repeating rifles, this restricts them to single-shot firing while holding the contents of the magazine in reserve. A typical lever-type example merely depresses the cartridges in the magazine so that the returning bolt can pass over them.

Cutter. C.N. Cutter, Worcester, Massachusetts. Joint applicant for protection for a 'breechloading firearm' with Franklin ★Wesson.

Cutts – 1. John H. Cutts. A gunmaker trading in Macclesfield, Cheshire, England, prior to 1918. **2.** Colonel Richard M. Cutts, USMC. Co-patentee, with his son Captain R.M. Cutts, Jr, of the 'Cutts Compensator' (q.v.). **3.** Cutts Compensator. Intended to stabilise lightweight weapons firing automatically, this consisted of a cylindrical extension to the muzzle with a series of slots or ports cut in its upper surface. These were intended to deflect part of the propellant gases that followed the bullet upward, creating an equal and opposite reaction that tended to push the muzzle down. In its original form, with ports on each side of the muzzle tube, the Cutts design had an unpleasant side blast that led to rejection by the US Army. However, once the ports had been moved to the top surface, the *compensator was adopted by *Auto-Ordnance in 1928 for use with the *Thompson submachine-gun. This was an expensive addition to what was already an expensive gun; few other gunmakers made use of Cutts' design, although many copied the general idea once the patent had lapsed.

'CV'. *See* Charles *Valentin'.

Cvackovec. Karl Cvackovec, Saalfeld in Thüringen. A retailer of sporting guns and ammunition active in Germany in 1941.

'cvl'. Used by WKC Waffenfabrik GmbH of Solingen-Wald on small-arms components made in 1941–45.

'CW', 'C.W.' – **1.** A superimposition-type monogram, with 'C' within 'W'. Associated with the pistols made in Germany prior to c. 1930 by Waffenfabrik Carl *Walther of Zella St Blasii and Zella-Mehlis. It is customarily found either moulded into the grips or on an inset cloisonné medallion. **2.** A mark applied prior to 1916 by the *Centrale Werkplaatz (the central storage depot of the Netherlands Indies Army). **3.** Found on US military stores; *see* Charles *Woodman.

'CWA'. A concentric-type monogram with all three letters equally dominant. Correctly 'WAC' (q.v.); used by the *Warner Arms Company.

'CWAD'. A concentric-type monogram with all four letters of equal significance. Correctly 'WDAC' (q.v.); used by the *Warner-Davis Arms Corporation.

'CWB'. *See* C.W. *Bacon.

'CWDA'. *See* 'CWAD'.

'CWH', 'CWK', 'CWS'. Used on US military firearms and accoutrements by C.W. *Hartwell, Christo W. *Kantany and C.W. *Snook.

'cxm'. Found on small-arms and ammunition components made in Germany during the Second World War by Gustav *Genschow & Co. AG in Berlin.

'cxn'. Associated with military gun sights and optical equipment made in Germany by Emil Busch AG of Rathenow, 1941–45.

Cycle – **1.** Or Cycle Model. Introduced in 1901, this was an Iver *Johnson *Hammer-the-Hammer gun. Made in exposed- or concealed-hammer forms, eventually it was chambered for .22, .32 and .38 ammunition. **2.** Cycle of operation: *see* operating cycle.

Cyclic rate. Also known as 'rate of fire', this is the theoretical continuous rate of fire of an automatic weapon, assuming an unlimited supply of ammunition – i.e. ignoring the need to reload, change magazines or replace the barrel. Theoretical cyclic rate can never be duplicated under service conditions, so the effective rate of fire is appreciably lower.

Cycloid. A spring-air BB Gun made to the patents of Calkins, Lindberg, *Wheeler & Butts by the *Rapid Rifle Company in c. 1898–1901. The name was also sometimes applied to a later gun, better known as the New Rapid, made to the patents of *Simonds, Fisher & Ross from 1902 until 1905.

Cyclone. An alternative name for *Cycloid.

Cylinder bore. *See* Choke.

Cyphers, imperial and royal. Although the small-arms of many armies bear distinctive *national markings, others are easier to identify by the markings applied by their kings, queens and emperors. Some cyphers were elaborate monograms; others were simply small crowned

Roman letters. They are listed here in alphabetical order, by country, then by mark. **1.** Bavaria. Kings Leopold II (1864–86), Otto (1886–1913) and Ludwig III (1913–18) used a crowned cursive 'L' or a crowned 'O'. **2.** Belgium. Kings Leopold II (1865–1909), Albert (1909–34), Leopold III (1934–50) and Baudoin (1950 to date) used the letters 'L', 'A', 'L' and 'B' respectively. The 'L' and 'A' marks are customarily cursive, whereas the 'B' is usually a Roman letter – often hatched horizontally in its largest sizes. **3.** Britain. Prior to the accession of Queen Elizabeth II ('E. II R.') in 1952, only three cyphers had been used since the 1830s: 'V.R.' (Victoria Regina) by Queen Victoria between 1837 and 1901; 'E.R.' (Edwardius Rex) by Edward VII, 1901–10, and Edward VIII (1936 only); and 'G.R.' by George V (1910–36) and George VI (1936–52). Date determines which is appropriate. The marks on small-arms consisted simply of crowns above Roman letters, although each monarch also had a cursive cypher that could take a very different form from the simple version. While cursive forms often graced the hilts of swords, uniforms and accoutrements, they have never been reported on firearms. **4.** Bulgaria. Prince Ferdinand I (Tsar from 1913) used a crowned 'F' from 1887 until superseded by Boris III (1918–43). Simeon II reigned from 1943 until 1946, but was deposed by pro-Communist forces before attaining his majority. **5.** Germany. The cyphers of Kaisers Wilhelm I (1871–88) and Wilhelm II (1888–1918) took the form of an imperial or squared-top crown above 'W'; it is thought that the 'F' of Kaiser Friedrich III, who reigned for a few months in 1888, may never have been applied to small-arms. Imperial cyphers were used only on the weapons of the navy and colonial-protection forces; the armies of Prussia, Bavaria, Saxony and Württemberg continued to apply their own royal cyphers. **6.** Netherlands. King Willem III (reigned 1849–1890) was succeeded by three queens – Wilhelmina (1890–1948), Juliana (1948–80) and Beatrix (1980 to date). Cyphers customarily take the form of a crowned 'W', 'J' or 'B'. In their larger applications, over the chambers of *Mannlicher rifles or on the slides of *FN-Browning pistols, for example, the letters were customarily outlined and hatched horizontally. Smaller versions, on the *Parabellum pistols or edged weapons, were often simply small cursive letters beneath crowns. **7.** Norway. The cyphers of King Haakon VII (1905–57) and King Olaf V (1957 to date) may be found on Krag-Jørgensen rifles and other military stores. They take the form of 'H' with '7' on the crossbar, or 'V' within 'O' respectively. **8.** Portugal. King Luis I (1861–89) used a crowned 'L Iº'; Carlos I (1889–1908) preferred an elaborate crowned 'CI' monogram, often found above the chambers of *Mauser-Vergueiro rifles; and Manuel II, deposed in the revolution of 1910, adopted a large crowned 'M' with a small '2' looped around the point. 'M2' marks will be found on 7.65mm army-type *Parabellum pistols. **9.** Prussia. King Friedrich Wilhelm IV used a crowned 'FW' mark. This was superseded by a simple 'W' when Wilhelm I gained the throne. The King of Prussia became Kaiser of Germany in 1871, reigning as Wilhelm I until 1888. He and his grandson, Wilhelm II (1888–1918) used crowned 'W' cyphers. There is no evidence that the mark of Friedrich III (1888) – presumably a crowned 'F' – was ever applied to small-arms. **10.**

Romania. Carol I (1881–1914) used an addorsed 'CC' monogram on behalf of himself and his consort, Charlotte of Luxembourg. Customarily encircled beneath a crown within a wreath of laurel, it will be found on machine-guns. Ferdinand (1914–27) is believed to have used a crowned 'F'; Míhaí I (1927–30 and 1940–47) adopted an elaborate monogram consisting of four crowned letters 'M', joining at their bases in the form of a cross. Carol II (1931–40) perpetuated the 'CC' monogram of his nineteenth-century predecessor. **11.** Saxony. The cyphers of Kings Albert (reigned 1873–1902), Georg (1902–04) and Friedrich August III (1904–18) took the form of cursive 'AR', 'GR' and 'FA' beneath crowns. **12.** Sweden. A black-letter 'C' beneath a crown appeared on many firearms made by the state ordnance factory is Eskilstuna, ★Carl Gustafs Stads Gevärsfaktori. This, however, should not be classed as a monogram; even though many Swedish kings have been named appropriately – e.g. Gustav V (1907–50), Carl XVI Gustaf (1950–73). Oskar II reigned from 1872–1907, during the period in which many ★Mauser rifles were made. **13.** Württemberg. Small-arms were marked simply with a crown over a Roman 'W', as King Wilhelm (1891–1918) shared his name with the Kaiser. However, a fraktur 'W' is commonly encountered on swords, uniforms and accoutrements, and may yet be reported on firearms.

'cyq'. Associated with the wartime products of Spreewerke GmbH of Berlin-Spandau, Germany, including P. 38 and small-arms components dating from 1941–45.

'cyw'. A mark found on components for the Kar. 98k and other small-arms made in Germany by Sächsische Guss-stahlwerke Döhlen AG in 1941–45.

'CZ', 'C.Z.' Often in the form of a concentric-type monogram, 'Z' within 'C'. Associated with the products of ★Česká Zbrojovka of Prague and Strakonice, commonly encountered on the slides and grips of semi-automatic pistols, above the chambers of rifles, or moulded into the butt plates of sporting guns.

Czar. Applied to two different types of sheath-trigger ★Suicide Special revolver, one made in the 1880s by the ★Hood Firearms Company of Norwich, Connecticut, and the other by the ★Hopkins & Allen Arms Company of Norwich, Connecticut.

D

'**D**' – 1. Associated with guns and components made in Britain by the *Royal Small Arms Factory, Enfield Lock, prior to 1988. **2.** A *headstamp associated with the *Dominion Cartridge Company of Montreal, Canada. **3.** Formed by the long tail of a stylised attenuated lion (or cat) stretching back over its upright head, customarily encircled. A trademark used by *Deutsche-Werke AG of Erfurt on *Ortgies pistols.

DA. Applied to the *Degtyarev light aircraft machine-gun, adopted by the Red Army in 1931. *See also* DP.

'**DACW**'. A concentric-type monogram with all four letters of equal significance. Correctly 'WDAC' (q.v.); used by the *Warner-Davis Arms Corporation.

Daewoo Precision Industries. Developer of firearms, including pistols and 5.56mm-calibre automatic weapons of the K-series intended to replace the M16A1 in Korean service. These are made in the former government-owned arms factory in Pusan, Republic of Korea, which was transferred to Daewoo in 1983.

Daffini. Libero Daffini. This Italian gunsmith began trading in August 1947, registering with the Brescia chamber of commerce in May 1949. Premises were maintained at Vicolo Tre Archi 9 in Brescia (1947–55), then in Frazione Mompiano, Villagio Montini, from 1955 until trading ceased in the early 1970s. Daffini built substantial quantities of sporting rifles on war-surplus *Mauser bolt actions in 1955–70. Made for the .30-06 or 8x57mm cartridges, they were sometimes identified by the mark *'Lida'. Shotguns, rifles and barrel-cocking airguns were also offered.

Dahlgren. John Adolphus Bernard Dahlgren (1809–70). Eventually retiring from the US Navy with Flag rank, Dahlgren is best known for his contributions to shipboard artillery. In 1861, however, his 'JAD' mark was applied to flare pistols. *See also* US arms inspectors' marks.

Daime. Jacques Louis Lemaire Daime. A 'Merchant', according to the British patent records, Daime sought protection for 'Improvements in Children's Air Guns and Pistols' in 1854–59. Applications for what would have been British Patents 2422/54 of 1854 and 157/59 of 1859 were filed, but the complete specifications were never presented and the substantive patents were never issued.

Daimler Motor Company Company Ltd [The], Coventry, Warwickshire, or possibly Burton-on-Trent, Nottinghamshire. This member of the *Monotype Scheme – using the code 'M 67' – made a few components, then assembled bodies for the *Bren Gun during the Second World War.

Dai-Nippon Heiki Kogyo, Notobe, Japan. A maker of 7.7mm Type 99 *Arisaka rifles, c. 1940–42.

Daisy – 1. A *Suicide Special revolver made in the USA by the *Bacon Manufacturing Company of Norwich, Connecticut, in the late nineteenth century. **2.** Daisy Manufacturing Company: *see* panel, facing page. **3.** Daisy Lever Action. A repeating BB Gun made in the USA by the *Daisy Manufacturing Company in 1912–13 to the

patents of William *Burrows. A 500-shot magazine tube was used. **4.** Daisy Repeater or Daisy Repeating Model. A term applied by *Daisy to a selection of BB Guns – Model A, a 350-shot lever-action design made in 1907–14; Model B, made as a 500-shot lever-action gun of 1904–12 and as a 1,000-shot version from 1905 until 1915; Model C, a 350-shot break-open pattern, made in 1912–14 only; No. 3 Model B, a 1,000-shot lever-action gun, modified from the Model B, made in 1915–34. **5.** Daisy Special. The 1,000-shot BB Gun, a blued deluxe version of the standard Model B or No. 3 Model B, made by Daisy in 1914–20. **6.** Daisy Standard. A name given to the Daisy No. 106, a 250-shot break-open BB Gun with a sliding breech cover. Production was undertaken in the USA in the Plymouth factory (1955–58) followed by limited assembly in Rogers (1959 only).

Dakota Arms, Inc., Sturgis, South Dakota. This US firearms-making business has made a variety of bolt-action rifles since 1988, usually chambered for cartridges ranging from .257 Roberts to .458 Winchester Magnum. The rifles are based on the Model 76 Classic action, essentially a modified Winchester Model 70 (Mauser) with a bolt-stop, gas shield and bolt guide patented in 1985 by Peter Grisel. The standard Classic Rifle has a straight-comb butt and a rounded fore-end, hand-cut chequering and a solid rubber shoulder pad. *See also* Alpine Rifle, Rigby Rifle, Safari Grade Rifle and Short Action Rifle.

'**DAL**'. *See* David A. *Lyle.

Daly. Charles Daly & Company, New York City. A distributor of guns, ammunition and sporting goods; *see also* Jäger.

Damon, Saint-Étienne, France. Listed in 1933 as a gunmaker. Still listed in 1951, trading from 7 rue des Francs-Maçons.

Dana. Henry Dana, a US Federal government arms inspector working in 1862–64, accepted small-arms marked 'HD'. *See also* US arms inspectors' marks.

'**Danatre**' [**The**]. Believed to be a version of the local elided pronunciation of the place-name ('Da'ntry'), this is associated with shotgun cartridges loaded by J.P. *Osborn of Daventry.

Dance Brothers, or Dance Bros. & Park, Columbia, Texas, Confederate States of America. Makers of a modified *Dragoon Colt in .36 and .44, lacking recoil shields behind the cylinder. Only about 500 guns were made.

Dandoy & Cie. Maillard Louis Dandoy was a French gunmaker, operating in the middle of the nineteenth century in Mauberge. His marks have been reported on breech-loading sporting guns and *pinfire revolvers.

Dandy. A break-open BB Gun made by the *Atlas Gun Company about 1897, for distribution by *Sears, Roebuck & Company. It may have been little more than the Atlas under another name, but unfortunately this theory is not proven.

Danks. Stephen Danks, a Federal arms inspector active

DAISY MANUFACTURING COMPANY

This well-known maker of BB Guns began life in 1882 as the *Plymouth Iron Windmill Company. Although the first two years were encouraging, profitability declined and the business only narrowly avoided being wound up at the 1888 general meeting. By that time, however, an all-metal BB Gun, designed by Clarence J. *Hamilton, had been shown to the company's president, Lewis C. Hough who, allegedly, exclaimed, 'Why Clarence, that's a daisy', and the name stuck. US Patent 320,297 was granted in 1888, and applications for two others had been made by the time small-scale production began.

The intention was to see whether the guns had potential as sales gimmicks, but demand was far greater than anyone had anticipated and the company was soon making much more money from guns than windmills. A proposal to make guns in quantity was presented to the board in January 1889 and finally, in 1895, the Daisy Manufacturing

Company was incorporated. Business grew under the direction of three generations of Houghs – Lewis, Edward and Cass – until Daisy was producing more guns than all of its rivals combined.

Among the greatest successes was the Daisy No. 25 Pump Gun, designed by Charles F. *Lefever in 1913–15: more than 20,000,000 had been made when production finally finished in 1975. The business was moved from Plymouth, Michigan, to Rogers in Arkansas in 1958, and control passed in 1960 from the Hough family to the Murchison brothers. The Murchisons, in turn, sold out to the Victor Comptometer Corporation (the name in which many post-1965 patents were granted), and Daisy was merged in 1974 with James Heddon's Sons Company. By 1978, Daisy and Victor Leisure had become part of the giant Kidde, Inc., empire.

In 1983, however, a consortium headed by Cass S. Hough regained control. Daisy has used countless

brandnames during its existence, earning a justified reputation for keeping up with the times: BB Guns have been named after cinema cowboys and cartoon-strip heroes, as well as real-life personalities such as Lewis Hough and *Buffalo Bill Cody.

Among the best sources of information are Cass Hough's *It's a Daisy!* (Daisy Division of Victor Comptometer Corp., 1976) and Arni Dunathan's *The American BB Gun* (Arco Publishing, 1971). The third edition of John Walter's *The Airgun Book* (Arms & Armour Press, London, 1984) contains a summary of individual models.

Although Daisy began life making some of the simplest BB Guns imaginable, attempts were made to modernise the product range from the late 1960s onward. This is a Model 881 multi-stroke pneumatic (introduced in 1974), charged by swinging the pump lever; the handle protrudes from the receiver ahead of the trigger guard.

during the American Civil War, accepted small-arms marked 'SD'. *See also* US arms inspectors' marks.

Dansk Rekylriffel Syndikat [DRS], Denmark. This gunmaking business was founded in 1896 to make an auto-loading rifle designed by Julius Rasmussen. Best known for the *Madsen light machine-gun, it became Dansk Industri Syndikat AS 'Madsen' (DISA) in 1936. Bolt-action rifles, an assault rifle (the LAR of 1962) and the Madsen-Saetter machine-gun were made after the Second World War, but work stopped in the early 1970s.

Danton. A name applied to a copy of the 1910-pattern *FN-Browning blowback semi-automatic pistol, made in Spain in the 1920s by *Gabilondo y Cia of Elgoeibar. It was little more than the Bufalo (q.v.) renamed after the agreement with Armeria *Beristain had lapsed. Originally all the guns relied only on a radial safety catch on the rear of the frame, but a grip safety was added in 1929. The 7.65mm and 9mm patterns were made in long-butt forms, with magazines holding as many as twelve rounds, but the range was abandoned in favour of the first *Llama pistols in the early 1930s. Some Danton

pistols are marked 'AUTOMATIC PISTOL WAR MODEL', together with the patent number 70,724 (which may have protected nothing but the registry of the tradename), yet there is no evidence that they were intended for military service.

Danube. A term applied by H. *Krieghoff GmbH to engraving patterns applied to the K-80 over/under shot-gun. The floral scroll and tendril design, almost English in its delicacy, has a central oval containing a matching design. *See also* Bavaria, Bavaria-Suhl, Crown Grade, Gold Target and Parcours.

Danuvia – 1. A term applied by the Germans to the Hungarian state firearms factory in Budapest. *See* FÉG. **2.** A small auto-loading pistol marketed in Hungary in the 1930s, possibly made in Spain.

Danzig arms factory. This Prussian establishment, which had been making guns since the eighteenth centu-ry, produced large quantities of *Mauser-action infantry rifles prior to 1918. These included the original 1871-pattern rifle, from 1873 onward; the M71/84 (the first examples being delivered in September 1885); and the

Gewhr 98, 140 being delivered daily by February 1901. In the period between the 1884- and 1898-pattern rifles, Danzig had made substantial quantities of the *Reichsgewehr (Gew. 88). The production machinery had been delivered in the autumn of 1888 from Ludwig *Loewe & Co., and the first deliveries followed in the summer of 1889. After the First World War, however, the Danzig manufactory was demilitarised. The rifle-making machinery was inherited by the Poles, who moved it to a new factory in *Radom.

'DAP'. See John Darby. A member of the English gun trade listed by H.J. Blanch in *Arms & Explosives* in 1909, with premises at 7 Ridinghouse Street, London (1866–70).

Dare Devil Dinkum. This cheap push-in barrel spring-air pistol was made from cheap castings, probably in Belgium, and sold by B. *Webster & Company, The Southern Armoury, and others prior to 1914. New guns continued to be sold from old stock well into the 1920s. Some are marked *'BREVETE' and *'S.G.D.G.', but the manufacturer has never been identified.

Darling. Benjamin & Barton Darling. These US based gunmakers have been credited with the first mechanically-operated revolver, possibly on flimsy grounds, although they certainly made pepperboxes.

Darlow. W. Darlow. This English gunmaking company began life in Bedford as 'W.W. Darlow' in the 1870s, but also maintained a branch at 8 Orford Hill, Norwich. It became W. Darlow Ltd in 1902 and was being managed by H.P. Darlow in 1930, when the business was described as an 'airgun ammunition manufacturer'. Darlow is best known for a variety of shotgun cartridges – including Big Bag, Castle and Orford – in addition to Airspeed and *Airship diabolo pellets, plus Bomber and Flight slugs. *Hubertus and Mayer & Grammelspacher *Diana air-guns, *EmGe blank firers, air canes, walking-stick guns and swordsticks were also available in the 1930s, and about 200 .22 No. 2 *Lee-Enfield trainers were made during the Second World War by re-tubing existing guns.

Darne – 1. R. Darne, rue du Désirée 14, Saint-Étienne, France (in the 1890s). Apparently founded in 1881 as F. Darne fils et Aîné; listed in 1892 as a gunmaker. This company, although it also made machine-guns, is best known for the distinctive Darne shotgun described below. By 1933, the business was trading as Manufacture d'Armes à Canons Fixés F. Darne fils aîné, E. Jallas et Cie, successeurs. Listed in 1951 at 71 cours Fauriel, and in 1970 at 65/79 Cours Fauriel as Établissements Darne SA; trading ceased in 1989. **2.** Darne machine-gun. The Darne company became involved in making the *Lewis Gun during the First World War. However, the Darne brothers realised that there was little point in producing complicated, well-finished weapons such as the Lewis if their service life was to be measured merely in weeks. The cheap, simple, robust and easily-made gas-operated 8mm Darne machine-gun was the result. However, although approved for service in 1918, none had reached service when the fighting ceased. While a few guns were issued to the French Army in the early 1920s, and others were tested on aircraft, the Darne was never able to establish itself in a way its good qualities deserved. **3.** Darne shotgun. Among the few fixed-barrel side-by-side designs ever to have found worldwide favour, more than 100,000 Darne shotguns had been made by 1928, and 300,000 by

1970. The essence of the action lies in a T-lever on top of the breech, which breaks the rigid lock as it rises, then retracts the sliding breech-block. As the action is closed, the lever forces the obturating discs hard against the base of the cartridges as the breech is closed, eliminating slack headspace and minimising recoil.

Dart Rifle. Often used as a generic term for any form of tranquiliser-dart gun (see Cap-Chur), but specifically for a BB Gun properly known as the *American Dart Rifle.

Dashwood Engineering Ltd, Empire Works, Croydon Road, Penge, London SE20. A maker of magazines for the British 9mm *Sten Gun during the Second World War. The regional code 'S 30' may have been used instead of the company name. See also British military manufacturers' marks.

'DAT' – 1. Found on US M1865 Spencer carbines: an unidentified inspector's mark. **2.** Found on other US military stores: see D.A. *Turner.

Daudetau – 1. Commandant Louis M.R. Daudetau, a French Army officer, was granted a selection of patents prior to the First World War. Among them were US no. 426,779 of 29 April 1890, granted jointly with M. Darmancier of Saint-Chamond to protect a 'breech-loading gun mechanism'. A series of US patents followed to protect magazine rifles and charger systems, including 458,824 (gun) and 458,825 (charger) of 1 September 1891; 473,827 of 26 April 1892; and 491,772 of 14 February 1893. These all list Daudetau's domicile as Vannes. **2.** Daudetau rifle. This bolt-action design was patented in Europe and the USA in the 1890s. Essentially similar to the *Lebel as far as its two-piece bolt was concerned, the Daudetau rifle had a magazine case formed integrally with the trigger guard and fed from a special (but hopelessly complicated) *charger. Presumably the first guns were chambered for the rimmed French 8x51 rifle cartridge, although those tested by the French services in the late 1890s accepted a 6.5x53.5 No. 12 semi-rimmed round. These guns are believed to have been assembled in Saint-Étienne from actions made by *Manufacture Française d'Armes et Cycles. However, although Uruguay selected the No. 12 cartridge for 1871-pattern 11mm Mauser rifles being converted in Saint-Denis c. 1900, the Daudetau rifle was not successful. A few sporting guns, sold under the name Rival (q.v.), were made from left-over actions in the 1920s.

Davenport – 1. William H. Davenport, Providence, Rhode Island, and Norwich, Connecticut. This gunmaker was best known for his shotguns. He was granted more than 25 US Patents for firearms (1881–1902). **2.** Davenport Arms Company, Norwich, Connecticut, USA. Makers of single-barrel shotguns with box-locks and central hammers, c. 1881–1900.

Davie. Francis Davie. A gunmaker trading in Elgin, Morayshire, Scotland, Davie was responsible for loading (or perhaps simply handling) shotgun cartridges marked *Moray. They probably date prior to 1914.

Davier, rue Villeboeuf, Saint-Étienne, France. Listed in 1892 as a gunmaker.

Davis – 1. Alfred Davis. Trading from 4 Bishopsgate Churchyard, Old Broad Street, London EC2, this gun-smithing agency handled shotgun cartridges – loaded by John *Blanch & Son – marked 'Bishopsgate'. They probably date prior to 1920. **2.** C. Davis. This government arms inspector, working in 1905, accepted US military small-arms marked 'CD'. *See also* US arms inspectors' marks. **3.** D.J. Davis. A US government arms inspector, working in 1905, responsible for accepting small-arms marked 'DJD'. *See also* US arms inspectors' marks. **4.** Howard A. Davis, 6 Southgate Street, Winchester, Hampshire. This English country gunmaker handled shotgun cartridges marked 'Flight' and 'Winton'. The business is said to have passed to B.E. Chaplin in the 1950s. **5.** N.R. Davis & Sons, Assonet, Massachusetts. Merged with *Warner Arms Company, 1917, to create Davis-Warner (below). **6.** Walter Davis. As late as December 1877, this Englishman, of 'Parkrange', Westbury Park, Durdham Down, Bristol, was granted protection for a combination weapon similar to the *Colvin revolver-sabre. Additional novelty lay in the sectional construction of the scabbard, which could be folded to act as a shoulder stock. **7.** Davis Industries, Mira Loma, California, USA. A maker of small automatic pistols in 7.65mm and 9mm Short in the 1980s. **8.** Davis-Warner Arms Corporation, Assonet, Massachusetts (to 1919), and Norwich, Connecticut, USA. Bought by H. & D. *Folsom and merged with Crescent Firearms Company, 1930, then sold in 1932 to the *Stevens Arms & Tool Company. *See* Warner Arms Company.

Daw – 1. George Henry Daw, one of the best known of the London gunmakers of the late nineteenth century, was first listed at 57 Threadneedle Street, E.C., in 1861. Trading continued from the Threadneedle Street premises until at least 1879, although the directories also list G.H. Daw & Company (below) at Sweeds Court, Great Trinity Lane, as early as 1870, and George H. Daw at an additional address – 2 New North Buildings, Chapel Street, E.C. – in 1876 and 1877. Daw became renowned for distributing double-action revolvers made in Birmingham by *Pryse & Redman (now better known as Daw Revolvers) and was among the first gunsmiths to offer centrefire shotgun cartridges, the earliest patent being granted in 1861. Subsequently he fought a celebrated court case against *Eley Bros. and Edward *Boxer, but lost. **2.** G.H. Daw & Company. A successor to the business of George H. Daw (above), first listed at 57 Threadneedle Street in 1880. The directories of 1888–89 list the business at 166 Fenchurch Street, London E.C., in 1888–89, then, as the Daw Gun Company, at 19 Great Winchester Street from 1890 until 1892.

'DAWC'. A concentric-type monogram with all four letters of equal prominence. Correctly 'WDAC' (q.v.); used by the *Warner-Davis Arms Corporation.

Dawson. Arthur Trevor Dawson. This engineer and one-time naval officer was associated with *Vickers, Sons & Maxim and *Vickers Ltd, rising to become managing director and, eventually, Chairman of the Board. Many of the patents protecting improvements to the Maxim, Vickers-Maxim and Vickers Guns (qq.v.) were granted in the name of Dawson and employees such as Louis Silverman and George Buckham. Among them were 19,714/98 of 1898, sought jointly with Silverman; 7161/06 of 1906, with Vickers, Sons & Maxim Ltd and Buckham; 3092/08 of 1908, with Vickers, Sons & Maxim Ltd and Buckham; 24,232/10, with Buckham; and 24,258/10 of 1910, also with Buckham. Virtually all were variations on the same theme: 'Improvements relating to Automatic Guns' or 'Improvements relating to Automatic and Similar Machine Guns'. Exceptions were provided by

14,966/08 of 1908, sought jointly with Carl A. Larsson to protect 'Improvements in Tripod and Similar Moutings for Automatic Guns', 11,233/11 of 1911, with Buckham, for 'Improvements in or relating to Gun Limbers'; 3559/13 of 1913 and 1688/14 of 1914, for mountings. In addition, Dawson's name could be found on 13,538/08 of 1908 and 16,370/08 of 1908, both of which were 'Communications from abroad by the Deutsche Waffen und Munitions Fabriken of Berlin'. Most of these patents were sought either from 32 Victoria Street, London, or Vickers House, Broadway, Westminster, London; those granted after 1910 usually describe Dawson as 'Sir A.T. Dawson, Knight, Lieutenant (Retired), RN' and as 'Superintendent of Ordnance Works'. He died in 1931.

Day. Frank Day. A gunmaker listed at 1 & 2 Fenchurch Street, London E.C., in 1878–80.

'Daylight Gun'. A nickname conferred on the US Army M1909 *Benét-Mercié Machine Rifles after a night raid by Pancho Villa on Columbus, New Mexico, in 1916. Civilian casualties were blamed on the machine-gunners, lapses in firing being mistaken for jams instead of lack of targets, and there being a belief that the feed-strips could not be loaded correctly in the dark. Official investigations revealed that the four guns had fired 20,000 rounds with very few jams, but the unfounded slander persisted for many years.

Daytona – 1. An over/under shotgun made in Italy by *Società Armi Bresciane to the designs of Renato *Gamba. The standard gun has a steel receiver, twin *Boss-type locking lugs, selective ejectors, internal hammers and a detachable trigger unit. Accessories include detachable chokes, interchangeable 12- and 20-bore barrel groups, and a butt with an adjustable comb. Double Trap, Hunting, Mono Trap, Skeet, Sporting Clays and Trap variants (qq.v) are available, the differences being in barrel length and butt profile. Engraving and associated decoration have been applied to order. **2.** Daytona SL. Similar to the standard Daytona (above), this has a sidelock instead of a box-lock action. It is made in Hunting, Skeet, Sporting Clays and Trap variants. **3.** Daytona SLHH. A variant of the Daytona SL, this is based on a Gamba-modified *Holland & Holland side lock, a straight-hand 'hog's belly' butt and a *schnabel-tip foreend. 12- and 20-bore chamberings can be supplied.

'D.B. Cartridge' [The], alternatively, 'Joyce's D.B. Cartridge'. Found on shotgun ammunition made by F. *Joyce & Company Ltd prior to 1907.

'dbg'. Used by *Dynamit AG of Düneberg on small-arms ammunition and components made for the German armed forces in 1941–45.

'D.B.H.' [The]. Found on British shotgun ammunition loaded by *Garrett of Evesham. The mark is said to represent 'Deadly-But-Humane'.

'DCAW'. A concentric-type monogram with all four letters of equal significance. Correctly 'WDAC' (q.v.); used by the *Warner-Davis Arms Corporation.

'DCC', 'D.C.C.', 'D.C.Co.' – 1. Found, in all three forms, in the headstamps of ammunition made in Ontario, Canada, by the *Dominion Cartridge Company. **2.** Found as 'D.C.Co.' in the headstamps of cartridges made late in the nineteenth century by the *Delaware Cartridge Company of Wilmington, Delaware, USA.

'DCG'. A monogram, the 'D' being dominant. A trademark associated with G.C. *Dornheim of Suhl.

'DCWA'. *See* 'DCAW'.

'DD'. *See* Daniel *Dunsmore.

'ddl'. Found on small-arms components made during the Second World War by Remscheider Hobelmesserfabrik Josua Corts Sohn of Remscheid.

'ddv'. Associated with German military optical sights and sight components manufactured in 1941–45 by Oculus of Berlin.

'ddx'. A mark associated with optical sights made in Germany by Voigtländer & Sohn AG of Braunschweig during the Second World War.

Dead Shot – 1. Encountered, as 'The Deadshot' or 'The Dead Shot', on shotgun cartridges sold in England by *Gill & Company of Oxford; by W.W. *Greener of Birmingham; by *Higgins of Tenbury Wells; by J. *Hobson of Leamington Spa; and by *Pinders of Salisbury. The ammunition may have been loaded by Frank *Dyke. 2. A *Suicide Special revolver made in the USA by the *Bacon Manufacturing Company of Norwich, Connecticut, in the late nineteenth century.

Deane – 1. George & John Deane. This gunmaking business was listed as trading from 30 King William Street, London, in the directories of 1850–51. Sporting guns, pepperboxes, revolvers and airguns are known from this source, which was superseded in 1852 by Deane, Adams & Deane. 2. John Deane & Son. Trading from 30 King William Street, London, from 1858 until 1872, this business succeeded Deane, Adams & Deane. 3. Deane, Adams & Deane. A partnership of George Deane, John Deane and Robert *Adams, this gunmaking business was formed specifically to promote the Adams self-cocking revolver. Trading was undertaken in London from 30 King William Street and 1 (later 2) New Weston Street, off Tooley Street, between 1854 and 1857. Then the company was split, allowing John Deane to go his own way.

Dearborn. J.R. Dearborn. This government arms inspector, working from 1894 until 1905 or later, accepted military small-arms marked 'JRD'. *See also* US arms inspectors' marks.

Debeaux frères, 'Hanoi, Mongtzé'. A retailer of guns and ammunition trading in French Indo-China prior to the First World War. Agents for, among others, Manufacture Française d'Armes et Cycles (Manufrance).

Debertshäuser. Oskar Debertshäuser, Suhl in Thüringen, Pfarrstrasse 26 (1940–41). Listed in 1939 as a gunsmith, and an ammunition and sales agency, but also regarded as a maker of *Kleinkalibergewehre* – rimfire sporting and target rifles.

Debrayle-Thevenon, Saint-Étienne, France. Listed in 1933 as gunmakers.

Dechambès. *See* Kropatschek.

Dechorin frères, rue des Jardins 29, Saint-Étienne, France. Listed in 1879 as a distributor of, and agent for, arms and ammunition.

Decker – 1. Frederick Decker. A partner in the *Hexagon Air Rifle Company, and possibly the son of George Decker (below). 2. Gebrüder Decker, Zella St Blasii and Zella-Mehlis in Thüringen, Germany. Listed in 1914–20 as a maker of gun parts. 3. George Decker, Detroit, Michigan, USA. Proprietor of the Decker Manufacturing Company, maker of the *Bijou BB Gun. 4. W. Decker, Zella St Blasii in Thüringen. Listed in 1914-vintage German trade directories as a gun- and weapon

maker. 5. Decker Electrical & Novelty Manufacturing Company, Detroit, Michigan. The proprietor of this business, George Decker, purchased rights to the *Magic BB Gun from the *Plymouth Air Rifle Manufacturing Company in 1893. Then trading continued as the Decker Manufacturing Company from 142 Brush Street, Detroit, until 1895/6, and 59–61 Woodbridge Street thereafter. Work ceased c. 1907, but not before two versions of the Bijou BB Gun had been made.

'DECO', 'DE Co.' Marks used by *Denecke u. Companie of Zella-Mehlis.

Decortis. G. Decortis or Decourts, Liège. A Belgian gunmaker renowned for making magazine guns in accordance with the patent of A. de *Bylandt. Although a few military-pattern rifles were made for trials in the 1850s, most survivors are stocked and decorated in sporting style. Made revolvers in the 1870s.

Deeley – 1. John Deeley, Birmingham, Warwickshire, England. Born in 1825, Deeley joined Westley *Richards of Birmingham in 1860 and, by 1871, had risen to the post of commercial manager. Beginning with 1422/73 of 1873, granted jointly with J.S. *Edge, Deeley obtained a variety of British Patents to safeguard the interests of Westley Richards. These included British Patent 1756/75 of 1875, with William *Anson, protecting a hammerless box-lock 'Anson & Deeley' shotgun; 1004/78 of 1878 (with Edge) for a dropping breech-block action; 907/79 of 1879 (with Anson), for a sliding breech-block action and safety mechanism; and 1241/81 and 3143/81 of 1881 (both with Edge) for sliding breech-block actions. Then came a series of patents protecting drop-barrel guns – 1833/83 of 1883 (with Anson), 14,526/84 of 1884, 5049/85 of 1885 (with F.J. Penn), 4289/86 of 1886, and 6913/88 of 1888 (with Penn). John Deeley was also co-designer with Penn of the improved bolt head adopted for the *Lee-Enfield rifle – British Patent 19,145/90 of 25 November 1890. Naturally this was assigned to Westley *Richards, and a royalty was paid on Lee-type guns made commercially by the *Birmingham Small Arms & Metals Company Ltd and the *London Small Arms Company Ltd. Deeley also had an interest in British Patent 12,324/92 for safety devices, obtained jointly with F.J. Penn; 21,346/95 of 1895 (also with Penn) for a single-trigger system for double-barrel guns; 17,731/97 of 1897 for a drop-barrel action (with Leslie B. *Taylor); and 3010/98 of 1898 for a safety mechanism, jointly with Penn. He retired in the early 1900s, being succeeded by Leslie Taylor, and died in 1913. 2. Deeley & Edge. Originally this single-shot falling-block rifle was an underlever pattern, introduced commercially in 1873 and improved several times in the late 1870s; most of the guns were made by Westley Richards & Company, John Deeley having become managing director of the business in 1872. Guns of this type were opened by pulling down on the spur of the trigger guard, which was offset to the right. In 1881, however, a modified or 'Improved' variant appeared; this was cocked by a radial thumb lever on the right side of the breech. 3. Deeley-Penn bolt head. *See* John Deeley and Lee-Enfield.

'**Deep Shell' [The].** A shotgun cartridge made by *Kynoch Ltd prior to the acquisition of the company by Explosives Trades Ltd in 1918, and thereafter by *Eley-Kynoch Ltd.

Deer – 1. A name associated with a simple barrel-cocking spring-air rifle emanating from the People's Republic of China, imported into Britain by the ★Abbey Supply Company. Made originally in the Tientsin Industry Factory, then in Peking, before being discontinued in the 1970s, the Model T-820 and Model 55 were the major 4.5mm- and 5.5mm-calibre versions of the basic design. Essentially similar guns were sold by ★Sussex Armoury (as the Hunter and Super Hunter) and by the Phoenix Arms Company as the Cougar. **2.** Deer Series. These ★Mauser-pattern sporting rifles were made in the USA by ★Rahn Gun Works, in .25-06, .270 Winchester and .308 Winchester. A deer's-head motif was engraved on the magazine floor plate.

Defender – 1. A name associated with a revolver sold in Belgium prior to 1914 by H. ★Ortmann, possibly with US origins (also advertised as the American Model of 1878). **2.** A compact 6.35mm automatic pistol made in France by ★Manufacture d'Armes de Bayonne in the 1960s. **3.** A US-made sheath-trigger .22, .32 or .38 ★Johnson & Bye revolver, with a 'Saw Handle' grip. It seems to have been introduced in 1875/76. **4.** A 1,000-shot lever-action BB Gun made in the USA by the ★Daisy Manufacturing Company in 1952–55, and also known as the No. 141. Originally introduced during the Korean War, explaining the name, the gun had a special shroud-

ed back sight and a wood (early) or synthetic (late) stock. **5.** A brandname applied to a .22-calibre pistol-knife made by the ★American Novelty Company in the 1920s. *See also* Huntsman. **6.** Defender Military Model. A 1,000-shot BB Gun made by ★Daisy in 1941, and also known as the No. 140. It had a two-piece hardwood stock, a dummy bolt, a screw-elevating back sight and even a rubber-tipped bayonet. The entry of the USA into the Second World War halted production after only small quantities had been made.

Defense. A compact 6.35mm-calibre Browning-pattern pistol, manufactured in Eibar, Guipúzcoa, Spain by an unidentified gunmaker. It probably dates from the early 1920s.

Defiance. A ★Suicide Special revolver made by the ★Norwich Arms Company and/or the ★Norwich Falls Pistol Company of Norwich, Connecticut, USA, in the late nineteenth century.

Dégat, rue de Lyon 47, Saint-Étienne, France. Listed in 1879 as a distributor of, and agent for, arms and ammunition.

Degrelle. *See* de ★Grelle.

Degtyarev – 1. Vasiliy Alekseyevich Degtyarev, born in Tula in 1880 into a family of gunsmiths, was among the most influential of all Soviet gun designers. Working in

DEGTYAREV MACHINE-GUN

Degtyarev (4)

The light 7.62x54R DP – *Degtyareva Pekhotniya obratsza* (Degtyarev, infantry pattern) – was adopted by the Red Army in 1927. It was distinguished by a pan magazine on top of the receiver, and by a gas-operated action locked by displacing the tail of the breech-block. Aircraft (DA) and armoured-vehicle (DT) versions were also made. The ★DPM and ★DTM were improved forms, developed during the Second World War.

The 7.62mm DS heavy machine-gun of 1939 was a failure, although eventually the 12.7mm DK, initially troublesome, was developed with the assistance of Georgiy ★Shpagin to become the reliable DShK. Degtyarev was responsible for the 7.62x39 M43 *Ruchnoi Pulemet Degtyareva* (RPD), developed in 1944–47, which served the Soviet Army for many years as a light squad automatic weapon – as well as being produced in China and some Soviet-bloc countries. The designer also made one of the first attempts to

provide a universal or general-purpose machine-gun for the Soviet Army. Submitted for trial in the late 1940s, this was derived from the 1944-type RPD. but was mounted on a light aluminium tripod.

The DP light machine-gun, introduced into Red Army service in 1928, was solid and dependable. The pan magazine ensured that the awkwardly-shaped Soviet 7.62x54R rifle cartridge fed efficiently, but was cumbersome and time-consuming to load.

the Tula factory from 1891 onward, eventually he was drafted into the Russian Army, being demobilised in 1906, after which he was transferred to the workshop attached to the Oranienbaum small-arms testing range – assisting Vladimir *Fedorov. Then he worked in the *Sestroretsk arms factory. Degtyarev is best known for the DP light machine-gun. However, after a run of great successes, a series of setbacks caused Degtyarev's star to wane. He died in 1949, highly decorated and with the rank of major-general. **2.** Degtyarev anti-tank rifle. Also known as the PTRD, this was developed in the USSR in 1941 to provide some defence against German armoured vehicles after the invasion of the Soviet Union. Chambered for a 14.5mm cartridge, it was a single-shot auto-ejecting bolt-action design. **3.** Degtyarev machine-gun: *see* panel, p. 147. **4.** Degtyarev rifle. The first of these gas-operated auto-loaders appeared in the late 1920s, and an obr. 1930g pattern was adopted officially in December 1931. However, the AVD was abandoned when the *Simonov proved to be a better design. **5.** Degtyarev submachine-guns. The original PPD, or *Pistolet-Pulemet Degtyareva*, was a blowback design developed in the 1930s. The first, or 1934, pattern fed from a detachable box magazine, but the perfected 1940 type could also accept a high-capacity drum inspired by the Finnish Suomi type.

De la Rue. Thomas De la Rue produced twenty sets of experimental Bakelite furniture for the No. 4 *Lee-Enfield rifle, 1937.

Delaunay-Belleville [Société Française]. *See* Daudetau.

Delaware Cartridge Company, Wilmington, Delaware, USA. Operating from 1876 until 1885, this ammunition-making business identified its products with a 'D.C. Co.' mark.

Delayed blowback. This is a blowback (q.v.) mechanism in which an additional restraint or brake is placed on the bolt or similar breech closure to delay or slow the opening movement. There is no positive breech lock. The system may also be described as hesitation or retarded blowback.

Delcour. Jean Delcour (1862–1931) was renowned as one of the greatest of the damascus barrelsmiths active in the Liège district prior to the First World War. After serving a lengthy apprenticeship, Delcour was given charge of the barrelmaking workshop operated in Nessonvaux by Henri *Pieper. When Pieper died in 1905, Delcour opened a small shop in Fraipont, in partnership with a colleague, but the invasion of Belgium by the Germans in 1914 brought the operations of Delcour-Dupont to a close.

Delfini. A popular misrepresentation of *Daffini.

Delhaxhe. Clearly influenced by the *Apache, this knuckleduster-revolver of the 1880s had an open-top frame and a fixed three-ring bow linking the trigger guard with the fixed bar-grip. Its knife blade swivelled laterally to project beneath the butt when required.

Delta – 1. Delta Elite. Chambered for the 10mm Auto Pistol cartridge, with an eight-round magazine, this was introduced by the Firearms Division of *Colt Industries in 1987. It was little more than a *Government Model in a different calibre, the principal external features being the slide marks and a triangular ('delta') logo set into the Neoprene grips. **2.** Delta Gold Cup. Offered by Colt from 1989 blued or in stainless steel, this had an Accro

back sight, a hand-honed trigger and a wrap-around Neoprene 'combat' grip.

De Luxe Model. *See* Special Model.

Delu. F. Delu et Cie, Fabrique d'Armes Delu, Liège, Belgium. Maker of a compact automatic 6.35mm pistol prior to the German invasion of Belgium in August 1914. The *Browning-type blowback was remarkable chiefly for its narrowness.

Delvigne – 1. Paris, France, and Liège, Belgium. A maker of revolvers active in the 1870s. **2.** Gustave Delvigne, Paris. A leading French ballistician of the nineteenth century, Delvigne served the French Army from 1820 onward. Beginning with the development of a rifled *cap-lock carbine (1827), when a lieutenant in the Royal Footguards, he progressed to a hollow-base cylindro-conoidal bullet (1841) and the *Carabine à Tige* (Pillar-breech, 1842) that paved the way for the work of Claude-Étienne *Minié. He appears to have resigned his commission in 1849 to pursue commercial gunmaking interests. *See also* Chamelot-Delvigne.

Demaret. Alexander Demaret. A member of the English gun trade listed in 1893 in London, at 4 St Mary Axe, E.C., but not apparently thereafter. Demaret may have been an agent, as the St Mary Axe address was shared by the Liège based gunmakers *Dresse, Laloux & Cie.

Demon – 1. A brandname used by the *Midland Gun Company, owner of the Demon Gun Works, on firearms and airguns, including a series of shotguns and spring-air guns of German origin, c. 1919–40. Some of the latter may prove to be Mayer & Grammelspacher *Dianas. **2.** Usually encountered as 'The Demon' on shotgun cartridges made prior to the Second World War by the Midland Gun Company in the Demon Gun Works, Birmingham. The mark may also be found on 12-bore shotgun cartridges generally attributed to H. *Adkin & Sons of Bedford, but probably also Midland Gun Company products. *See also* Double Demon. **3.** Usually found, as 'The Demon', on shotgun cartridges handled by *Helson of Exeter. They were made in France, rather than by the Midland Gun Company, and probably date from the 1950s. **4.** Or 'The Demon'. Airgun pellets made for the Midland Gun Company by *Lane Bros. and possibly others. The Improved Demon was Lane's Triumph under another name. **5.** A 6.35mm pocket pistol made in Spain by Manufactura de Armas 'Demon' (below) on the basis of the *FN-Browning pocket pistol of 1906: six rounds, hammer fired. **6.** Manufactura de Armas 'Demon', Eibar, Guipúzcoa. Maker of the *Demon pistol.

Demontant. A term associated with some of the semi-automatic pistols made in Liège, Belgium, by Nicholas *Pieper, with patented fixed-barrel 'dismantleable' construction. *See also* Basculant.

Demoulin Brothers & Company, also often listed as De Moulin or Dumoulin, Greenville, Illinois, USA. This business distributed the *Patent Masonic Institution Gun, a *Daisy Model B, No. 3 Model B or Model 30 modified to fire water. The guns were used in masonic initiation rites and customarily came in matched pairs, one of which was also capable of projecting water backward.

Deneke & Co., Mehlis and Zella-Mehlis in Thüringen, Germany. Listed in 1914 as a gun- and weapon maker, and in 1920 as a wholesaler when owned by Franz Denecke. Listed in directories published in 1930–39 as a gun- and weapon maker, and in 1941 as a gunmaker. This metalworking business often marked its products 'DECO' or 'DE Co.'

Dennis. Arthur Dennis, an English country gunmaker based in the village of Great Dunmow, Essex, handled guns, ammunition and accessories. Among his wares were shotgun cartridges marked 'Demon', acquired from the *Midland Gun Company.

Dennon – 1. K.M. Dennon. This government arms inspector, working in 1895–98, accepted US military small-arms marked 'KMD'. Possibly the same as R.M. Dennon (below). **2.** R.M. Dennon. A US government arms inspector, working in 1895–1902, who accepted small-arms marked 'RMD'. *See also* US arms inspectors' marks.

Denny. H.H. Denny. This government arms inspector, working in 1898, accepted military small-arms marked 'HHD'. *See also* US arms inspectors' marks.

Denver Air Rifle Company, Denver, Colorado, USA. This business made the Denver .22-calibre bolt-action air-gun patented by Richard Monner in the early 1940s. Series production during wartime was out of the question, and apparently the business was liquidated in 1946.

Denyer. Bernard Denyer. Trading as a gunmaker from 336 Oxford Street, London, in 1850, and thereafter from 131 Holborn Hill until c. 1875.

Deprez, Liège, Belgium. This gunsmith began making revolvers in the 1870s. Among the guns offered prior to 1914 were the Texas Bull-Dog, Western Boy and California Bull-Dog.

Deringer, derringer – 1. Henry Deringer, Philadelphia, Pennsylvania, USA. A gunmaker renowned for his single-shot cap-lock pocket pistol, although his output included holster pistols and sporting rifles. Henry Deringer died in 1867, leaving his executors to act against the many infringers of his name. **2.** Deringer or derringer pistol: *see* panel, below. **3.** Derringer Auto. A name associated with a .25-calibre pocket automatic pistol made in the USA in the 1980s by the *American Derringer Corporation.

Derington. *See* Derrington.

Derkenne. Établissements Derkenne, Mortier, Belgium. Makers of the *Le Novo pocket revolver, distributed in the late 1920s by *Dumoulin frères.

Derrington. Thomas Derrington & Son, Birmingham. This gun-rifling and pistol-making business succeeded Thomas Derington (*sic*), trading in Price Street, Birmingham, in 1834. It was listed in Reed's Buildings, Shadwell Street, in 1861. Ten years later, however, it had become a dealer in 'Gun and Pistol Stocks, Wholesale & Retail', with 'A large quantity of fine well-seasoned Gun Stocks always on hand'.

'Derwent' [The]. Found on 12-bore shotgun cartridges sold in Britain by John *Anderson & Son of Malton, possibly prior to the First World War.

Desborough & Son. This English gunsmith, based in Derby, sold shotgun cartridges marked 'Dovedale', apparently loaded using *Eley Bros. components.

Desert Eagle. Introduced in 1983, this bulky American-designed gas-operated pistol chambers .357 or .44 Magnum revolver ammunition. The bolt rotates to lock the breech. *See also* *Israeli Military Industries.

Desflaches. J. Desflaches, rue de la Charité 7, Saint-Étienne, France. Listed in 1879 as a gunmaker.

Despatch. A *Suicide Special revolver made by the *Hopkins & Allen Arms Company of Norwich, Connecticut, USA, in the late nineteenth century.

Dessart. Henri Dessart, Liège. The Belgian inventor and manufacturer of a shotgun with barrels that slid forward when the top-lever was opened, patented in 1907. One gun of this type was presented to Belgian King Albert in 1910, but production ceased in 1914 and surviving guns are rare.

Desservétaz, rue de la Loire 33, Saint-Étienne, France. Listed in 1892 as a distributor of, and agent for, arms and ammunition.

Destroyer – 1. Associated with a revolver made in Belgium prior to 1914 by A. *Bertrand. **2.** Spanish Browning-type pocket semi-automatics made by Isidro *Gaztañaga in Eibar: (a) 6.35mm, six rounds, with slides

---

DERINGER PISTOL

Deringer (2)

The classic Deringer was a tiny .41-calibre cap-lock, with 'DERINGER PHILADELᴬ' on the lock, pineapple-pattern escutcheons retaining the barrel key, and a false *damascus finish on the barrel. After the Californian Gold Rush of 1849, many other gunmakers copied the Deringer, including *Slotter & Company and A.J. *Plate of San Francisco, and even J. Deringer of Philadelphia – a tailor who allowed his name to be used by gunsmiths seeking spurious legitimacy. The term 'derringer', therefore, is applied generically to all compact single-shot pistols – cap-lock and cartridge alike – while 'Deringer' refers specifically to genuine Henry Deringer-made patterns.

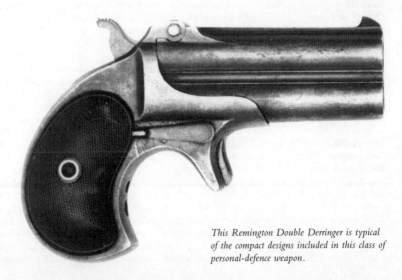

This Remington Double Derringer is typical of the compact designs included in this class of personal-defence weapon.

usually marked 'Model 1913' or 'Model 1918'; (b) 7.65mm, seven rounds, hammer fired, 'Model 1914', based on the 1905-type *FN-Browning; (c) 7.65mm, seven rounds, striker fired, based on the 1910-type *FN-Browning.

Destructor. A Spanish 7.65mm-calibre pocket pistol, based on the Browning design of 1906, made in Eibar by Iraola *Salaverria y Compañía: six rounds, hammer fired. Named after a British-made torpedo-gunboat launched on the Clyde in 1886.

Detective Special or Detective Special Model. This variant of the *Police Positive Special, with a 2in barrel, was introduced in 1926 in .32 New Police, .38 New Police and .38 Special chamberings. The original pattern lasted until 1972, when it was replaced by an improved version with a shrouded ejector rod and wrap-around wood grips; made only in .38 Special, the new version was produced until 1986. Pre-1964 guns were marked by Colt's Patent Fire Arms Manufacturing Company; post-1964 examples bear the marks of the Firearms Division of *Colt Industries. The cylinder length was reduced in 1966, and a few guns were made with hammer shrouds.

Detonics, Inc., Bellevue, Washington, USA. This gunmaking business owed its success to the sturdy M1911A1 Colt-*Browning pistol. The Service Master and Score Master were comparatively conventional full-length guns, but the ultra-compact Combat Master (1977) personal-defence weapon was shorter and lighter, incorporated a new muzzle seating system that discarded the old barrel-bush, and had a new spring assembly. The butt was shortened and the upper rear part of the slide was cut away so that the hammer spur could be recessed. A small double-action 9mm Parabellum (9x19) blowback known as the Pocket Nine appeared in 1984, but remained in production for only a very short time.

Deutsche... – 1. Deutsche Jagdpatronenfabrik, Rottweil am Neckar. A maker of ammunition, including shotgun cartridges, apparently founded in Germany in the 1870s and eventually purchased by *Dynamit Nobel in 1893. **2.** Deutsche Waffen- und Munitionsfabriken AG [DWM]: see panel, facing page. **3.** Deutsche-Werke AG, Erfurt, Thüringen. This engineering business, formed from the remnants of the Prussian government small-arms factory in Erfurt in 1919, made a range of military equipment prior to 1945. This included substantial quantities of *Ortgies pistols, dating from 1922–32, although pre-1922 examples, despite 'Ortgies & Co.' marks, may also have been made by Deutsche-Werke. A trademark 'D', taking the form of a highly stylised lion with its tail curled back over its head, will often be encountered on the slides and grips of the pistols.

Deville. A Belgian gunmaker, based in Liège, known for revolvers.

Devisme. Jean-Baptiste Devisme, 36 Boulevard des Italiens, Paris. A French gunmaker operating c. 1845–80, Devisme is known for a variety of sporting guns, pistols and *pinfire revolvers. Cartridge pepperboxes in the form of barrelless revolvers (*Pistolets de Poche* or *Coups de poing*) and a distinctive 12mm single-action revolver (*Pistolet d'Arçon*) were exhibited at the 1867 Paris Exposition, the latter being patented in France in 1869. Pressing a catch beneath the frame ahead of the cylinder pivots the barrel sideways to align the ejector rod with an individual chamber, while simultaneously allowing the frame to break downward around a transverse pivot immediately ahead of the trigger guard.

'Devonia' [The]. On 12-bore shotgun cartridges sold in south-west England by *Agnew & Son of Exeter and *Stanbury & Stevens of Exeter. Apparently they were made by *Eley-Kynoch and sometimes are listed, mistakenly, as The Devonian.

Dewaf. A typical Browning-inspired Spanish 6.35mm pocket pistol, manufacturer unknown, but probably emanating from Eibar. Some guns are also marked 'Model VI'.

Dewey. A single-shot break-open BB Gun made by the *Crescent Gun Company of Saginaw in the USA, from 1899 until c. 1904. It was named after Admiral Dewey, commander-in-chief of the US Naval forces and self-proclaimed hero of the Battle of Manila Bay during the Spanish-American War of 1898. **2.** Elbert H. Dewey. This government arms inspector, working in 1917, accepted .45 M1911 (Colt) pistols marked 'EHD'. See also US arms inspectors' marks.

'dfb'. Used by the Suhl factory of *Gustloff-Werke on German machine-guns and small-arms components dating from 1941–45.

'DFC'. See Daniel F. *Clark and David F. *Clark.

'DFM'. See Dexter F. *Mosman.

'DGC'. A monogram, the 'D' being dominant. A trademark associated with G.C. *Dornheim of Suhl.

'D.G.F.M.–(F.M.A.P.)'. Found on small-arms made in Argentina. See FMAP.

'DH'. A floriated superimposition-type cursive monogram. Correctly 'HD' (q.v.); associated with *Henrion & Dassy.

'dhp'. This code was granted in 1941 to H. *Burgsmüller & Söhne GmbH of Kreiensen/Harz, for use on small-arms components made for the German armed forces during the Second World War.

Diabolo. The popular name for a waisted airgun projectile derives from Spanish *diablo* (devil, fiend) by way of the popular child's game in which a wooden toy is whirled – 'like a devil' – on a guiding cord. The shape was mirrored in pellets designed to minimise the bore-contact area while allowing the base or skirt to expand into the bore to perfect an air seal. The origins of the diabolo pellet are still in doubt. References occur in manuals issued with Lincoln *Jeffries rifles in 1906, and it has been suggested that Jeffries himself should receive credit. Apparently, however, Jeffries' special pellet-making machinery was the work of an engineer named Boulton, who is also honoured sometimes. German claims can be discounted; diabolo pellets were not made there until 1914. The history of the diabolo since the First World War is tortuous, but there are recognisable landmarks, such as *Lane's Triumph. Modern designs have tended to conform to a standard skirt pattern, with the exception of the *Bimoco Spitz, and to confine novelty to the design of the head-bands or the shape of the head. **2.** A trademark registered prior to 1914 by Emil *Barthelmes of Zella-Mehlis in Thüringen, Germany.

Diamond – 1. Or 'Smokeless Diamond'. This mark will be found on shotgun cartridges loaded by, or for, *Curtis's & Harvey of London, prior to 1918. The name indicates the proprietary propellant loading. **2.** Diamond Arms. A *Suicide Special revolver made by the

DEUTSCHE WAFFEN- UND MUNITIONSFABRIKEN AG

Deutsche… (2)

Charlottenburg and Berlin-Borsigwalde. The history of this powerful gunmaking company began in 1872, when Henri Ehrmann & Companie was formed to make cartridge cases by the then-new extrusion process. Wilhelm Holtz & Companie succeeded to the Ehrmann operations in 1877, but sold the business within eighteen months to Wilhelm Lorenz. Lorenz re-registered his operations as Deutsche Metallpatronenfabrik Lorenz on 22 June 1878.

Trading continued profitably until, in February 1889, Lorenz sold his stake to Ludwig *Loewe & Co., for 5,000,000 marks. Then Loewe entered into an agreement with Pulverfabrik Rottweil-Hamburg and Vereinigte Rheinisch-Westfälische Pulverfabriken, and a succession of purchases and mergers ensued until – with effect from 4 November 1896 – the name Deutsche Waffen-und Munitionsfabriken (DWM) was adopted. This indicated that reliance on ammunition had been broadened to include firearms, the Martinikenfelde factory owned by Loewe in Charlottenburg being transferred to the new business and

bringing with it a licence to make the *Maxim machine-gun.

DWM was a beneficiary of a production agreement concluded with *Waffenfabrik Mauser AG, *Fabrique Nationale d'Armes de Guerre and *Österreichische Waffenfabriks-Gesellschaft (the Loewe family held stakes in all four businesses) to split contracts gained for Mauser rifles in the proportion 32.5:20:15:32.5. Consequently, many thousands of rifles were made prior to 1918 with DWM markings. By 1906, the monthly production capacity of the new DWM factory in the Wittenau district of Berlin was rated at 700 Mauser rifles and 120 Maxim machine-guns.

By early April 1915, the company was said to be making 1,400 Mauser rifles, 700 Parabellum pistols, ten machine-guns and 2,000,000 small-arms cartridges daily, together with 10,000 grenades, 5,000 fuzes and a large number of shell cases. Total

machine-gun production for DWM's 1915/16 financial year amounted to about 3,950. DWM purchased Waffenwerke Oberspree Kornbusch & Companie in 1916, continuing to make vast quantities of war material until the Armistice in November 1918.

The post-war slump hit hard, and the trading name changed on 30 May 1922 to *Berlin-Karlsruher Industrie Werke (BKIW) to hide the warlike origins of the business. A change to Berlin-Karlsruher Industrie Werke vormals DWM was made in June 1933, but the original name was readopted in 1936. Used until the end of the Second World War, it was finally replaced in 1949 by Industrie-Werke Karlsruhe (IWK).

DWM operated a variety of factories during the Second World War, their identities often hidden by codes. They included Berlin ('asb'), Karlsruhe ('faa'), Lübeck ('edq') and Posen ('eeo').

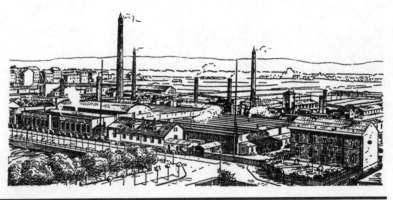

This drawing, taken from the company's fiftieth-anniversary history, shows the Karlsruhe factory as it would have been in the early 1890s.

---

*Hopkins & Allen Arms Company of Norwich, Connecticut, USA, in the late nineteenth century. **3.** Sometimes as a simple four-sided figure. A trademark and *headstamp associated with the *Western Cartridge Company of East Alton, Illinois.

Diamondback. Made by the Firearms Division of *Colt Industries in 1966–86, this .22 LR rimfire or .38 Special centrefire revolver has a short *Detective Special-style frame, a barrel with a *ventilated rib, a shrouded ejector rod and chequered walnut grips. Named after the venomous Western Diamondback Rattlesnake.

Diana – 1. A trademark used by Anciens Établissements *Pieper on shotguns marketed in Belgium prior to 1914. **2.** A brandname associated with airguns made in Britain by *Millard Brothers and *Milbro Ltd from 1949 until 1982, when the liquidation of Milbro allowed *Mayer & Grammelspacher (by then using *Original in Britain) to retrieve rights to a mark that had been 'confiscated' after

the Second World War. **3.** A trademark used on German spring-air guns made by Mayer & Grammelspacher of Rastatt/Baden, from c. 1905 to date. **4.** A brandname found on shotgun cartridges loaded in Germany by *Cramer & Buchholz, prior to 1914. **5.** A small 6.35mm automatic pistol of Browning type, made in Eibar, Spain, by, or perhaps for, Sociedad Española de Armas y Municiones (*SEAM). Possibly the product of *Erquiaga, Muguruzu y Compañía. **6.** Associated with a compact .25-calibre automatic pistol made in the USA by *Wilkinson Arms. **7.** Dianahaus, Suhl in Thüringen, Germany. A maker of hunting accessories (Inh. A. Emil Schlegelmilch), listed in the *Deutsches Reichs-Adressbuch* in 1914–20; a maker of hunting accessories (Inh. Hermann Ortloff), 1930. **8.** Dianawerk, Germany. *See* Mayer & Grammelspacher.

Diane – 1. Possibly French; a brandname found on a barrel-cocking spring-air gun, with a distinctive ring trigger, adapted from the ★Gem, but clearly made in France or possibly Belgium prior to 1914. Presumably the mark was chosen for its similarity to ★Diana. **2.** A 7.65mm-calibre Spanish semi-automatic pistol, with a seven-round box magazine, based on the Browning pattern of 1905, made in Eibar by ★Erquiaga, Muguruzu y Compañía.

Diard, Saint-Étienne, France. Listed in 1933 as a gunmaker. Trading in 1951 from 16 rue Clément-Forissier.

Dias. Luis C. Dias, Portugal. *See* Guedes.

Dick. Frederick R. Dick, Buffalo, New York State, USA. This gunsmith and maker of ★Gallery Guns was active successively from 181 Batavia Street (1857–60), 100 East Genesee Street (1863–67) and 945 Jefferson Street (1872–74).

Dickerman. Amos Dickerman, of New Haven, Connecticut, USA, was granted two US Patents to protect 'breech-loading firearms' – 323,501 of 4 August 1885 and 354,890 of 28 December 1886 – in addition to 369,437 of 6 September 1887 to protect a hammerless single-barrel shotgun. This was sold under the inventor's name, but undoubtedly manufacture was sub-contracted (perhaps to the ★Marlin Firearms Company).

Dickey. Arthur Vane Dickey. A 'Building Manager' of 301 Lowman Building, Seattle, Washington, USA, Dickey was granted British Patent 122,854 (1916) to protect the design of a reservoir airgun.

Dickinson – 1. E.L. Dickinson, Springfield, Massachusetts. This US gunmaker was responsible for a variety of ★Suicide Special revolvers, sold in the 1880s under names such as Earl Hood, Earthquake, Our Jake, Ranger, Sterling and Toledo Firearms Co. **2.** Henry Dickinson. Possibly the son of Herbert Dickinson (below), this gunsmith was granted British Patent 2724/14 of 1914 for practice bullets and pellets for airguns. **3.** Herbert Dickinson. This English gunmaker made his first appearance in the London directories in 1854, trading from 2 Little Prescot Street. Subsequently he was listed at 3 Little Prescot Street and 31 Frith Street, Soho, in 1858–61; at 2 Union Row, ★Minories, and 31 Frith Street, Soho, in 1862–71; and at 2 Union Row only from 1872 until 1907 or later (latterly under the charge of Henry Dickinson). Sporting guns, airguns and air canes are known from this source.

Dickson – 1. John Dickson & Son, Edinburgh, Midlothian, Scotland. John Dickson I was apprenticed to gunmaker James Wallace and began working on his own account c. 1831 from 63 Princes Street. Trading as John Dickson & Son from the early 1840s, subsequently the business was owned by John Dickson II, moving to 32 Hanover Street in 1928, then to Frederick Street in 1938. At this time, Dicksons acquired ★Mortimer & Son. Alex. ★Martin & Company followed in 1961. Dickson is best known for the ★Round Action shotguns and Double Rifles, but also offered bolt-action magazine guns and a range of ammunition. Among the many brandnames noted on shotgun cartridges are Blue Shell, Capital, Dickson's Favourite and Jubilee. Since the end of the Second World War, Dickson has made Mauser-type sporting rifles on the basis of old German or new FN actions. *See* Caledonian Model. **2.** Tracy C. Dickson, a US Army ordnance officer, designed a distinctive back sight used for a few years on the military Krag-Jørgensen rifle. **3.** Dickson's Favourite. Associated with shotgun cartridges handled by John Dickson of Edinburgh.

Dictator – 1. This name will be encountered on 6.35mm-calibre semi-automatic pistols made in Belgium by ★Fabrique d'Armes Réunies of Liège. *See also* Centaure. **2.** A .36-calibre open-frame cap-lock revolver, derived from the ★Colt, made c. 1867–72 by ★Hopkins & Allen in the former ★Bacon Manufacturing Company factory in Norwich, Connecticut, USA. Later examples were chambered for .38 rimfire ammunition.

Diemaco. *See* ArmaLite.

Diem, Diemb, *see also* Ziegenhahn & Diem – **1.** Franz Diem, Benshausen bei Suhl in Thüringen. This metal-smithing workshop made gun parts prior to 1945. **2.** Heinrich Diem, Benshausen bei Suhl in Thüringen. A maker of guns and gun parts listed in German trade directories in 1941. **3.** W. Diemb, Suhl in Thüringen, Germany. Trading in 1939 as a barrel-blank maker.

Diessner, Dießner. Erich Diessner & Co., Gera in Thüringen, Zeppelinstrasse 16. A retailer of guns and ammunition trading in Germany in 1941.

Diettrich. J.F. Diettrich & Company, St Louis, Missouri, USA. Gunmakers trading in 1840–56.

Diffley. Peter J. Diffley, a US Army lieutenant working in 1941, accepted .45 M1911A1 (Colt) pistols marked 'PJD'. *See also* US arms inspectors' marks.

Digonnet, rue Villeboeuf, Saint-Étienne, France. Listed in 1892 as a gunmaker.

'Diki-Diki'. A brandname found on blank-firing or ★Scheintod pistols made (probably prior to the First World War) by Adolf ★Niemeyer of Suhl.

Dill & Co. A maker of guns and gun parts trading in Zella-Mehlis in the 1920–30 period.

Dillingham. G. Dillingham, a government arms inspector working in 1875, accepted US military small-arms marked 'GD'. *See also* US arms inspectors' marks.

Dimick. H.E. Dimick & Company, St Louis, Missouri, USA. This gunsmith and distributor handled, among other things, .36-calibre open-top Colt-type revolvers made in 1864–65 by the ★Metropolitan Fire Arms Company.

Dinkum. *See* Dare Devil Dinkum.

Dinsmore. S.A. Dinsmore, a Federal government arms inspector, working during the American Civil War, accepted small-arms marked 'SAD'. *See also* US arms inspectors' marks.

Dippollito. M. Dippolito. This government arms inspector, working in 1939–40, accepted US martial .45 M1911 (Colt) pistols marked 'MD'. *See also* US arms inspectors' marks.

DISA-Madsen. *See* Dansk Industri Syndikat.

Disconnector. A component in the trigger mechanism that disconnects the trigger from the remainder of the firing train after each shot; the firer must release the trigger and take a fresh pressure to fire again. This prevents the gun from firing continuously after a single pressure on the trigger.

Disguised guns. Many different categories of these have been made: for example, ★bicycle-handlebar guns, ★cane guns, ★cigar and cigarette pistols, ★tool guns, and ★truncheon guns. The best sources of details are Lewis Winant's pioneering work *Firearms Curiosa* (1955), and *Secret Firearms* by John Walter (1997), which covers some of the same ground – specifically devoted to handguns – in less detail.

Dispersante. A tradename used by ★Fabrique Nationale d'Armes de Guerre on shotgun ammunition loaded with cube-shot, c. 1932–40.

Diss. Louis Diss of Ilion, New York State, spent much of his life working for E. *Remington & Sons. Many of his patents were granted to protect improvements to the *Remington-Lee bolt-action rifle, in particular to the design of the magazine. They included 295,563 of 25 March 1884 (obtained jointly with Lee), 304,712 of 26 August 1884 and 313,856 of 17 March 1885, all assigned to Remington; there were also 356,275 and 356,277 of 18 January 1887 and 367,199 of 26 July 1887, assigned to Brill & Russell (receivers of the liquidated Remington business). US Patent 383,108 of 22 May 1888 protected a 'Breech-loading Firearm' and was granted to Diss alone.

Distle. Maurice Distle, sometimes listed as Distel, a government arms inspector working in 1940, accepted .45 M1911A1 (Colt) pistols marked 'MD'. *See also* US arms inspectors' marks.

Distin. E. Distin & Company. An English country gunsmithing business working in Totnes, Devon, prior to the First World War. Distin's marks have been found on shotgun cartridges loaded with *Schultze propellant.

Ditzel. G. Hermann Ditzel, Zella-Mehlis in Thüringen, Germany. Listed in 1939–41 as a master gunsmith.

Divine. Associated with the .22-calibre *Crosman Model 2200 multi-stroke pneumatic rifle when it was being sold in Britain by the *Sussex Armoury. It has no official standing.

Dixon – 1. James Dixon & Sons, Cornish Place, Sheffield, Yorkshire, and 37 Ludgate Hill, London. Advertising in the 1870s as 'Manufacturers of the Best Sporting Apparatus for both Breech- and Muzzle-Loading Guns', Dixon is best known as a maker of powder flasks. However, the company also produced loading equipment, such as Horsley-patent cappers and turning, loading and closing machines for pin and centrefire ammunition. **2.** William Hall Manley Dixon, Britain. *See* Snider. **3.** Dixon & Company. This English gunsmithing business operated in Aston Common, Birmingham, Warwickshire, prior to 1914. Its marks have been found on shotgun cartridges loaded by *Kynoch.

'DJD'. *See* D.J. *Davis.

DK. *Degtyareva krupnokaliberniy* (Degtyarev large-calibre), applied to the earliest 12.7mm *Degtyarev heavy machine-gun; this was not successful in its original form, and was superseded by the *DShK pattern.

'dkl'. Found on military optical sights and associated components made in German in 1941–45 by Josef Schneider & Co. of Kreuznach.

'dlv'. Associated with German military small-arms components made prior to 1945 by the Remscheid factory of Deutsche Edelstahlwerke AG.

'D. & M.' Said to have been found on components for the British No. 4 *Lee-Enfield rifle made during the Second World War by Davis & Mawson Ltd.

'DMK'. *See* David M. *King.

'dmo'. A codemark used by Auto-Union AG of Chemnitz on German military small-arms components made in 1941–45.

'DMT'. *See* Daniel M. *Taylor.

'dnf'. This mark hides the identity of *Rheinisch-Westfälische Sprengstoff AG. It was used by the company's Stadeln bei Nürnberg factory on small-arms ammunition and components made for the German armed forces during the Second World War.

'dnh'. A mark used by the Durlach bei Karlsruhe factory of *Rheinisch-Westfälische Sprengstoff AG, on German military small-arms ammunition and components made during the Second World War.

Dobson & Rosson. An English gunsmithing partnership trading in Derby c. 1900, succeeded in due course by Charles *Rosson.

Dodge. William Dodge, Washington D.C., USA. The inventor of a simultaneous extraction system ('cartridge retractor for many-chambered firearm') protected by US Patent 45,912 of 17 January 1865, and a 'revolving firearm' protected by 45,983 of 24 January 1865. Subsequently both patents were assigned to *Smith & Wesson.

Dogg. Diabolo-type airgun pellets manufactured by *Stiga of Trånas.

Döll. Franz & Hugo Döll, Zella-Mehlis in Thüringen, Germany. Listed in 1939 as master gunsmiths.

Dolla. Found on German-made push-in barrel air pistols sold by – among others – *Darlow of Bedford and the *Midland Gun Company of Birmingham in the period between the world wars. The maker remains unidentified, although J.G. *Anschütz has been suggested.

Dolne. Louis Dolne. Trading in the 1870s from rue Janfosse in Liège, this Belgian gunmaker is best known for the *Apache knuckleduster-revolver of the 1870s.

Dolphin. A barrel-cocking spring-air rifle, practically identical with the *Ansonia, probably made c. 1901–10 by *Mayer & Grammelspacher and imported into Britain by the *Midland Gun Company. The barrel latch was an adaptation of Jacob *Mayer's British Patent 20,559/01 of 1901.

'dom'. Found on ammunition and small-arms components made in Germany in 1941–45 by Westfälische Metall-Industrie AG, Lippstadt.

Domingo Matheu. *See* FMAP.

Dominion – 1. Usually encountered as 'The Dominion'. Associated with shotgun cartridges loaded for *Holland & Holland of London prior to 1939. **2.** Dominion Cartridge Company. Founded in Canada in 1902, this made a variety of military and sporting ammunition until renamed *Canadian Industries Ltd in 1967. The products were often identified by 'DCC' or 'D.C.Co.' in the headstamps. **3.** Dominion Small Arms Factory Corporation, Canada. *See* *Long Branch.

'Don' [The]. Found on shotgun cartridges sold in England by *Gray of Doncaster and *Milburn & Son of Brampton. They were made by *Eley-Kynoch.

Donald, Atkey & Company. This English gunmaking business traded from 33 Cornhill, London E.C., in 1872–75.

Donaldson. William George Donaldson. A gunmaker trading in Grantown-on-Spey, Morayshire, probably prior to the First World War. Donaldson marked shotgun ammunition sold in Scotland under the brandname Triumph.

Donckier. Cl. Donckier, Liège. A maker of sporting rifles and shotguns active in Belgium prior to the First World War.

Donnet et Racodon, Saint-Étienne, France. Listed in 1933 as gunmakers; still trading as such in 1951, from 31 rue des Armuriers.

Dooley. William Dooley, Liverpool, Lancashire. The marks of this English gunmaker, trading in Line Street (1836–39) and Ranelagh Street (1846–64), have been reported on self-cocking *pepperboxes dating from the middle of the nineteenth century.

Doppman. J.L. Doppman, Jr. This government arms inspector, working in the mid-1930s, accepted .45 M1911A1 (Colt) pistols marked 'JLD'. *See also* US arms inspectors' marks.

Dorchester. Charles Dorchester, USA. *See* ArmaLite.

Dörmer. M. Willi Dörmer, Goldlauter bei Suhl, Germany. Listed in 1925 as a 'weapons maker', but not apparently mentioned in the Suhl directory for 1930.

Dormus. Georg [Ritter von] Dormus, Austria-Hungary. *See* Salvator-Dormus pistol, Škoda machine-gun.

Dornheim. G.C. Dornheim GmbH, Suhl in Thüringen (Zweig.). This wholesaler was founded in Suhl (then in Saxony) in 1863 and listed in the early years of the twentieth century as a sales agency and cartridge maker. The *Deutsches Reichs-Adressbuch* for 1925 credits Dornheim – brandname Gecado – with premises in Berlin, Hamburg, Köln, Lippstadt, Magdeburg, Nürnberg and Suhl, as well as a branch in Zwolle in the Netherlands. The products were listed as 'weapons, ammunition, propellant, hunting equipment and lead products. Manufacture, export and import'. The business was still being described as a 'weapons maker, sales agency' in 1930; as an ammunition and weapons maker in 1939; and as a supplier of 'weapons, ammunition, hunting and sporting equipment; manufacturing, wholesale, export...' in 1940–41. Dornheim may have been bought out by Gustav *Genschow in 1940, but continued trading under its own name until the end of the Second World War. *Mauser-pattern sporting guns were sold under the Gecado brand between the wars, but undoubtedly were made elsewhere. In addition to the gunmaking business in Suhl, Dornheim acquired the cartridge-loading facilities of Babette *Stahl in 1901, creating what became known as the Metall-Patronen-Hülsen-Fabrik Suhl, vorm. B. Stahl. The Dornheim name was revived in the 1950s by Albrecht *Kind (Akah), which now owns rights to the trademarks. Most of the Gecado airguns are made by *Mayer & Grammelspacher, but the origins of the modern *Mauser-action rifles are less clear.

'Dorset County' [The]. A brandname associated with shotgun cartridges handled in southern England by Arthur *Conyers of Blandford Forum.

'dot'. Used during the German occupation of Czechoslovakia by the Brno factory of Waffenwerke Brünn AG, this code (allocated in 1941) will be encountered on machine-guns, pistols, rifles, and small-arms components and ammunition

'dou'. A mark used in 1941–45 by Waffenwerke Brünn AG of Považská Bystrica on cartridge clips and chargers, small-arms and ammunition made under German supervision.

Double... – 1. Double Action. A mechanism in which the hammer or striker is cocked, then released by pulling through on the trigger (cf. Self-cocking). **2.** Double Action Army [Model]. Introduced in 1883 by *Merwin, Hulbert & Company, but made by *Hopkins & Allen, this .44-40 revolver had a double-action trigger system and a top strap above the cylinder. **3.** Double Action Army & Frontier Model. This was an improved 1878-vintage derivative of the *Lightning and *Thunderer, the first double-action revolvers to be made by *Colt's Patent Fire Arms Manufacturing Company. Chambering a range of cartridges from .32-20 WCF to .476 Eley, these large-frame guns had a trigger system made in accordance with

patents granted to William *Mason in 1881. A few of the short-barrel *Sheriff's or 'House' guns were made with spurless hammers. Production amounted to about 51,000 guns in 1878–1905. **4.** Double Action Frontier [Model]. This double-action *Smith & Wesson revolver was introduced in 1886 for the .44-40 WCF cartridge. Only a little over 15,000 had been made when work stopped in 1913. **5.** Double Action Model (or New Model Double Action): US-made revolvers. *See* Lightning and Thunderer. **6.** Double Action Pocket Army [Model]. A short-barrelled variant of the .44-40 *Double Action Army revolver made for *Merwin, Hulbert & Company by *Hopkins & Allen, introduced in 1884. **7.** Double-barrel, Double Barrel, or Double. Used as a generic term for any two-barrelled gun, usually, but not inevitably, shotguns (*see* Over and under, and Side by side). **8.** Double Barrel. A shotgun-type BB Gun made in the USA by the *Daisy Manufacturing Company in 1940–41, then as the Model 21 and Model 410 after the Second World War. The newest guns have synthetic butts and a painted finish. Each barrel was replenished simultaneously from two forty-eight-ball tube magazines. **9.** Double Crimp. Usually found as 'The Double Crimp' on shotgun cartridges loaded from *Eley-Kynoch components by T. *Page-Wood of Bristol. **10.** 'Double Demon [The]'. Found on shotgun ammunition made in Britain by the *Midland Gun Company of Birmingham. *See also* Demon. **11.** Double Deuce. Associated with a .22-calibre semi-automatic pistol made in the USA by *Steel City Arms. **12.** Double Eagle (also known as Series 90). A departure for Colt's Manufacturing Company, Inc., when it appeared in 1990, this was the first of the company's double-action adaptations of *Browning-type pistols. The 9mm Parabellum, .38 Special, 10mm Auto or .45 ACP Double Eagle was made largely of stainless steel. It had a de-cocking system and an internal firing-pin lock; the 'two-hand' trigger guard provided an external recognition feature. Variations have included the Double Eagle Combat Commander, introduced in 1991 with a 4.25in barrel chambering the .40 S&W or .45 ACP cartridges; the .45 ACP Double Eagle Officer's Model of 1991, with a 3.5in barrel; and the Double Eagle Officer's Lightweight Model, with an alloy frame. **13.** Double-Header. A *Suicide Special revolver made by the *Hopkins & Allen Arms Company of Norwich, Connecticut, USA, in the late nineteenth century. **14.** Double Repeating Deringer Pistol. *See* E. *Remington & Sons. **15.** Double rifle. Habitually applied to a shotgun-like weapon with two rifled barrels, popular in Britain prior to 1939 for big-game hunting, as it could chamber excessively lengthy cartridges with ease. **16.** Double Trap. *Concorde Double Trap or *Daytona Double Trap. 12-bore over/under shotguns made by *Società Armi Bresciane of Gardone Val Trompia, usually with anatomical pistol grips, beavertail fore-ends and single triggers. Barrels are normally 760mm long. **17.** Double Wing [The]. This brandname was associated with sporting guns and (particularly) shotgun ammunition sold in England by Charles *Maleham of Sheffield prior to 1914. The cartridges were made by *Eley Bros.

Doubling. The firing of one or more shots for a single pull of the trigger, usually as a result of the *disconnector failing.

Dougall. James Dalziel Dougall [& Sons]. This gunmaking business, based in Glasgow, claimed origins as early as the eighteenth century. James Dougall moved from Trongate to Gordon Street in 1850. He was granted British Patent 1128/60 of 1860 to protect the *Lock-Fast breech mechanism. Activating a side- or underlever allows a cam on the hinge pin to move the barrels forward off the breech discs before they can be dropped, in an attempt to overcome the major weakness of the *Lefaucheux-type 'single-bite' guns. Dougall enjoyed the patronage of the Prince of Wales and the Duke of Edinburgh. A London office was maintained for many years at 59 St James's Street (1864–82) and 8 Bennett Street, S.W., in 1883–93. The entries from 1888 onward generally record the trading style as James Dougall & Sons.

Douglas. Made in Spain by *Lasagabaster Hermanos of Eibar, this 6.35mm Browning-type pocket pistol had a hammer-type firing mechanism and a seven-round box magazine. It is sometimes marked 'Model 1914'.

Doumoulin & Fils, Milmort, near Liège. This Belgian gunmaking business built *Mauser-pattern sporting rifles on the basis of refurbished actions, the guns being sold as MR-2 (standard) and MR-5 (deluxe). Type A, in .375 H&H Magnum, and Type DM in chamberings from 7x57mm to 8x57mm were built on new FN actions.

Douplat frères, Saint-Étienne, France. Listed in 1933 as gunmakers; trading in 1951 from 38 rue Badouillère.

'dov'. This mark identifies machine-guns and small-arms components made under German supervision during the Second World War in the Wsetin factory of Waffenwerke Brünn AG.

'Dovedale' [The]. A brandname found on shotgun cartridges sold in England by *Desborough & Son of Derby.

'dow'. Reportedly found on optical equipment made under German supervision in 1941–45 by the Prerau factory of Waffenwerke Brünn AG, later known as Opticotechna GmbH.

Dowling – 1. Dublin. The marks of this Irish gunmaker have been reported on self-cocking *pepperboxes dating from the middle of the nineteenth century. **2.** Frederick Dowling. A gunmaker listed in 1865–69 at Castle Court, Castle Street East, London W. – probably his home – Dowling was co-patentee of the Grieve & Dowling rifle. The directories note him at 21 Eversholt Street, London N.W., in 1876–77.

Downie. R.C. Downie, a lieutenant-colonel in the US Army, accepted military .45 M1911A1 (Colt) pistols made by the *Union Switch & Signal Company in 1943. They were marked 'RCD'. *See also* US arms inspectors' marks.

'dox'. This mark identified the products of the Podbrezova factory of Waffenwerke Brünn AG, which made small-arms components under German supervision during the Second World War.

Doyle. J.H. Doyle, a government arms inspector working in 1894, accepted martial .38 Colt revolvers marked 'JHD'. *See also* US arms inspectors' marks.

DP, D.P. – 1. Applied to any British weapon that was reduced by damage or obsolescence to the status of 'Drill Purposes' only. Usually found on the *knoxform, receiver and woodwork of rifles. **2.** Degtyareva Pekhotniya (Degtyarev, infantry), applied to the *Degtyarev light machine-gun adopted by the Red Army in 1927. It was replaced by the DPM (q.v.). *See also* DA and DT.

'D', 'P' and 'C' with crossed pennants. A military proof mark – Dominion of Canada Proof. *See also* British military proof marks.

DPM. A designation applied to the modernised Soviet *Degtyarev light infantry machine-gun adopted in 1944. *See also* 'DA', 'DP' and 'DT'.

'DPS'. *See* Daniel P. *Strong.

'dpv'. Found on German military optical equipment made by Zeiss-Ikon AG of Dresden in 1941–45.

'dpw'. A codemark found on optical sights made in Germany by the Berlin-Zehlendorf or Goerzwerk factory of Zeiss-Ikon AG in 1941–45.

'dpx'. Associated with optical equipment made during the Second World War by the Contessawerk factory of Zeiss-Ikon AG in Stuttgart, Germany.

'dql'. Found on German military small-arms components made by Remo-Gewehr-Fabrik Gebrüder *Rempt of Suhl in 1941–45.

'DR'. *See* David *Rice.

Dragoon Colt. The first of these .44-calibre cap-lock revolvers, made in the USA in 1848–50, incorporated old Whitney parts. Improvements were soon made, resulting in a Second Model of 1850–51 (with squared cylinder-stop slots and pins between the nipples) and a Third Model of 1851–61 with a round-back trigger guard. About 20,000 were made between 1849 and 1855, virtually half of them being purchased by the US Army.

Dragunov – 1. Evgeniy Fedorovich Dragunov, born into a gunsmithing family in Izhevsk in 1920, worked in the local small-arms factory until 1945, when he was transferred to the design bureau staff. He is best known for the Dragunov sniper rifle (q.v.), but was also responsible for the development of sporting guns such as the auto-loading *Medved. Dragunov died in 1991. **2.** Dragunov rifle: *see* panel, p. 156.

Draper – 1. Lewis Draper, a government arms inspector working in 1875–78, accepted .45 Colt Single Action Army revolvers marked 'LD'. **2.** R.D. Draper. This government arms inspector, working in 1905, accepted small-arms marked 'RDD'. *See also* US arms inspectors' marks.

Drawn Steel Company, City Road, London. This promotional agency entered 12-bore *Lancaster-type breech-loading shotguns in the trials sponsored in Britain in 1866 by *The Field*.

Dreadnought – 1. Usually found as 'The Dreadnought' or 'The Dreadnought Cartridge'. A mark reported on shotgun cartridges made by *Eley-Kynoch for A.E. *Ringwood of Banbury. Normally it is accompanied by an illustration of a dreadnought-type battleship (but not the original *Dreadnought*) bow-on and making smoke. **2.** A *Suicide Special revolver made by the *Hopkins & Allen Arms Company of Norwich, Connecticut, USA, in the late nineteenth century.

Dresse-Laloux & Cie. Founded in 1862, this Liège based gunmaking business began transforming the rifle-muskets of the Belgian Army into *Albini-Braendlin breech-loaders in 1867. A member of the *Petit Syndicat, formed in Herstal in 1870, then of the Grand Syndicat. A founder member of les *Fabricants d'armes réunis, 1886, and a founding shareholder in *Fabrique Nationale d'Armes de Guerre in 1889. The agreement to form FN was signed by Alard Bormans on behalf of the company. Trading ceased shortly after the Germans invaded Belgium in 1914. Representation was maintained in London from 1881 until the First World War, from an

DRAGUNOV SNIPER RIFLE

Dragunov (2)

The 7.62x54R Soviet/Russian SVD, or *Snayperskaya Vintovka Dragunova*, has been made in Izhevsk since it was officially adopted in 1963. Credited to a design team led by Evgeniy Dragunov and Ivan Samoylov, the SVD is based on the turning-bolt *Kalashnikov action, with a short-stroke gas piston adapted from the *Tokarev automatic rifle. The cut-away butt/pistol-grip unit is most distinctive, and a PSO-1 optical sight clamps to a rail on the lower left side of the receiver. Ribs pressed into the sides of the box magazine improve the feed of the clumsy rimmed cartridges.

SVD rifles have been made in Bulgaria, the People's Republic of China, Egypt, Hungary and Poland; markings usually determine the country of origin. The current Russian guns, made by *Izhmash A/O, may be supplied with optical or electro-optical sights. For additional details, see *The AK-47* by Edward C. Ezell (Stackpole Books, 1976), and *Kalashnikov* by John Walter (Greenhill Military Manual series, 1999).

A typical Soviet 7.62x54R Dragunov sniper rifle, or SVD, showing the standard PSO-1 optical sight and the distinctive cut-away butt.

office at 47 Basinghall Street (1881–84) and 4 St Mary Axe (1897 onward). The latter was shared with Alexander *Demaret.

Drewry. Guy H. Drewry, active from 1930 until retiring in 1957 with the rank of brigadier-general in the US Army, inspected and accepted a variety of small-arms – M1 Garands, and Colt and Smith & Wesson revolvers – marked 'GHD'. *See also* US arms inspectors' marks.

Dreyfous. Samuel Dreyfous. This Paris based French inventor, wrongly placed by Eldon Wolff in London, designed an ambitious lung-powered airgun with a flexible tube connecting the user's mouth to the breech. It was the subject of British Patent 1182/64 of 1864, but no surviving examples have been identified.

Dreyse – 1. A brandname associated with firearms made by *Rheinische Metallwaaren- & Maschinenfabrik in accordance with patents granted to Louis *Schmeisser. They included 7.9mm-calibre machine-guns and a series of blowback pistols in 6.35mm, 7.65mm and 9mm. A 9mm light automatic carbine was made from c. 1907 until the beginning of the First World War, but with the exception of the 7.65mm pistol, none of the guns was successful. 2. Franz von Dreyse, son of the inventor of the Prussian needle gun, Johann-Niklaus von Dreyse (below), this gunsmith was born in Sömmerda in 1819. He is best remembered for designing a convertible needle-gun/centrefire bolt system, patented in Germany in 1874, and for attempting unsuccessfully to challenge the dominance of the *Mausers. Franz von Dreyse died in 1894. 3. Johann-Niklaus [von] Dreyse, renowned as the inventor of the Dreyse needle gun or *Zündnadelgewehr, was born in Sömmerda in 1787 and died there in 1867. The success of the experimental guns of the late 1830s was followed in 1840 by a Prussian government order for 60,000 infantry rifles, and the subsequent creation of Waffenfabrik von Dreyse (below). 4. Waffenfabrik von Dreyse. This gun-making business was set up in about 1842 by the inventor of the needle gun, Johann-Niklaus von Dreyse and super-

intended after about 1860 by his son, Franz. Although best known for the Dreyse-type needle guns, and for sporting guns and revolvers based on patents granted to Georg Kufahl, Waffenfabrik von Dreyse may also have made a few *Gallery Guns in the 1870s. Business declined steadily in the 1880s and, after the death of the younger Dreyse, it was clear that the once-famous company would not survive against more progressive rivals. While a few prototype *Mannlicher pistols were made in 1899–1900, the near-moribund Waffenfabrik von Dreyse was purchased by *Rheinische Metallwaaren- & Maschinenfabrik in 1901. Subsequently the *Dreyse brandname was retained for many small-arms. 5. Dreyse machine-gun. This had its origins in patents granted in 1909 to Louis *Schmeisser, designer of the *Bergmann machine-gun. The Dreyse was offered commercially from 1912 onward. The earliest water-cooled guns were mounted on light tube-leg tripods fitted with small pressed-steel wheels. Those that were being made at the outbreak of the First World War were seized by the German authorities, and, in 1915, RM&M is said to have been given a contract to supply modified guns with an additional bracket for the 08/15 bipod and provision for a shoulder stock. However, as RM&M soon switched to making MG. 08/15 *Maxims, it is thought that Dreyse guns did not work well enough under battle conditions. Eventually they were sent to Turkey for service in Mesopotamia. Tests showed that the mechanism had limited reserves of power, despite the inclusion of an *accelerator. A simple strut locked the bolt and barrel extension until disengaged during the recoil stroke, but proved to be too weak to compete with the Maxim and Bergmann machine-guns. 6. Dreyse needle gun: *see* Zündnadelgewehr. 7. Dreyse pistol: *see* panel, facing page.

'DRGM', 'D.R.G.M.' This German-language term, *Deutsches Reichs Gebrauchs Muster* (German Empire Utility Design), gave protection to designs in law – but rather less than 'D.R.P.' (q.v.), which signified a patent.

Driggs-Seabury Ordnance Company. *See* Savage.

Drilling. A generic term for a three-barrel *combination gun, first patented in Germany in 1891.

Drisket – 1. A. Drisket: *see* Drisket & Waroux. **2.** Drisket & Waroux. A Liège based Belgian gunmaking business with an agency in London, at 39 Monkwell Street, E.C., in 1870–72, and 1 Wood Street Square in 1873. Succeeded by A. Drisket & Company, at Wood Street Square until 1876.

Drissen – 1. Ferd. Drissen, Manufacture d'Armes de Chasse et de Tir, Liège, Belgium. Son of, and successor to, P. Drissen (below), this gunmaker traded until the Germans invaded Belgium in 1914. Representation was maintained in London in the nineteenth century, first at 19 Basinghall Street (in 1876), then successively at 115 Leadenhall Street (1877–78) and 21 Leadenhall Street in 1879. **2.** P. Drissen, Liège, Belgium. A gunmaker involved in the 1870s with le *Grand Syndicat.

Driver. Augustus Henry Murray Driver. A 'Consulting Engineer' and some-time works manager of the *Birmingham Small Arms Company Ltd, Driver was responsible for the design of several rifles and improvements in the BSA/Lincoln *Jeffries Pattern air rifles. Apart from patents in collusion with George *Norman, Driver was granted British Patent 11,817/05 of 1905 for a method of forging barrels and spring-chambers in a single piece, and British Patent 25,830/06 of 1906 for a spring-bolt to retain the cocking lever of an airgun until it was disengaged manually.

Drommer. C. Drommer. This government arms inspector, working between 1899 and c. 1912, accepted US martial small-arms marked 'CD'. *See also* US arms inspectors' marks.

Dror. This was a modified version of the 1944-pattern *Johnson-type light machine-gun made in 1949–52 for the Israeli Army. So many production problems arose in Israel, and so much trouble was encountered in sandy conditions, that the Dror was abandoned after a small quantity had been made. The most distinctive feature was the bottom-mounted magazine, which replaced the original lateral pattern.

'DRP', 'D.R.P.', 'D.R.Pa.' These marks signify protection by German *patents – *Deutsches Reichs-Patente* – representing the highest category of protection a design could be granted. Compare with 'D.R.G.M.' and 'D.R.W.Z.'

'D.R.P. Ang.', 'D.R.P. Angem.' These abbreviations, for *Deutsches Reichs-Patent Angemeldet*, indicate that a patent had been sought, but not yet granted. Normally they were used for a short time before being replaced with 'D.R.P.' (q.v.), and they can provide a dating aid.

'DRS'. A trademark, often in the form of a monogram, used on rifles and machine-guns made in Denmark by *Dansk Rekylriffel Syndikat AS 'Madsen' of Copenhagen.

'DRWZ', 'D.R.W.Z.', *Deutsches Reichs Waren-Zeichen* (Imperial German trademark). These should be compared with 'D.R.P.' and 'D.R.G.M.', which conferred patent and registered-design protection respectively.

DS. *Degtyareva stankoviya* (Degtyarev, heavy). This designation was applied to the belt-feed 7.62mm *Degtyarev

DREYSE PISTOL

Dreyse (7)

Patented in 1906–07 by Louis Schmeisser, the Dreyse pistol was made by *Rheinische Metallwaaren- & Maschinenfabrik of Sömmerda. It was introduced commercially c. 1908, chambering the 7.65mm Auto cartridge, and most (if not all) of the initial 1,000-gun production run went to the gendarmerie in Saxony, being marked 'K.S. Gend.' Dreyse pistols sold in substantial quantities prior to 1914 – the Berlin police used guns marked 'K.P.P.B.' – and remained in production throughout the First World War. The basic gun consisted of a fixed frame with a

separate slide/breech-block assembly, which recoiled backward on firing.

The design of the retraction grips at the front of the slide gives a clue to age: the original version had vertical grooves confined to the slide, but subsequently these were extended downward over the frame; then they became diagonal on the slide alone; and finally they took diagonal form on a squared backing.

Dreyse pistols were also made in small numbers in 6.35mm and 9mm, the former being a pocket model, whereas the latter represented an unsuccessful attempt, dating from 1912–13, to enlarge the basic design for the 1908-type service cartridge.

The unsuccessful 9mm Parabellum Dreyse pistol, introduced c. 1912, was a fiendish design; owing to the strength of the return spring, the entire top-plate had to be pivoted up and forward to cock the gun.

heavy machine-gun adopted by the Red Army in 1939, but soon abandoned when problems inherent in the design could not be overcome. It was replaced by the *Goryunov pattern.

Dschulnigg. Karl Dschulnigg, Salzburg, Austria. This custom gunsmith made sporting rifles on Mauser, Mannlicher and Sako actions, in virtually any chambering the customer requested. The Mausers have been sold under names such as *Chamois, *Ibex, *Ram, *Roebuck, *Tiger and *Top Hit.

'dsh'. Found on small-arms components made in the Teinitz foundry operated by Ing. F. *Janaček of Prag-Nusle during the German occupation of Czechoslovakia during the Second World War.

DShK, DshKM. Designations applied to a modification of the 12.7mm *Degtyarev heavy machine-gun, the DK, with a rotary feed-block mechanism designed by Georgiy *Shpagin. Eventually the original DShK was superseded by the modernised DShKM after the Second World War.

DT – 1. A designation applied to the Soviet 7.62mm *Degtyarev tank/vehicle machine-gun adopted in the early 1930s. The DTM of 1944 was an improved version. *See also* DA and DP. **2.** Found on US military firearms: *see* Daniel *Taylor.

DTM. Associated with Soviet machine-guns. *See* DT.

Duan. A Browning-type automatic pistol made by F. *Ormachea of Eibar, Spain: 6.35mm, six rounds, hammer fired.

DuBiel. Joseph DuBiel [DuBiel Arms Company], USA. Co-designer, with John Tyson, of a bolt-action rifle made in Sherman, Texas (1978–90).

Duboeuf père et fils, rue de la République 4, Saint-Étienne, France. Listed in 1879 as a gunmaker.

Dubuar – 1. James A. Dubuar or Du Buar. The proprietor of the Dubuar Manufacturing Company and the moving force behind production of the *Globe BB Guns. **2.** Dubuar Manufacturing Company, Northville, Michigan, USA. This woodworking and ships' tackle-making business made BB Guns designed by Merritt F. *Stanley after the inventor had moved to the Northville district from nearby Plymouth. Arni Dunathan, in *The American BB Gun,* dates this move to 1889 – although 1892 seems more plausible, as the earliest Globe guns bear the Plymouth address of *Anderson Bros. Production began in the East Main Street factory in 1892 and continued until Stanley's patents were sold to *Daisy in 1908. *See also* Globe Manufacturing Works.

Duchateau. Jean Duchateau, Liège. A Belgian gunmaker active in the period between the wars, known for good-quality sporting rifles and double-barrel shotguns.

Duchess. A *Suicide Special revolver made by the *Hopkins & Allen Arms Company of Norwich, Connecticut, USA, in the late nineteenth century.

'Duck Fowler' [The]. Found on shotgun ammunition sold in England by Baildham & Son of Stratford upon Avon, but probably made either by *Eley Bros. or by *Eley-Kynoch Ltd. The marks date from c. 1910–35.

Ductile Steel Company Ltd, Wednesbury, Staffordshire. This British engineering firm was the principal promoter of the unsuccessful *Hefah V light machine-gun of the early 1940s. Based on the *Lewis Gun, the Hefah was made only in small numbers.

Dudley. James S. Dudley, a lieutenant in the Federal Army, inspected and accepted Colt and Starr cap-lock revolvers during the American Civil War. These were marked 'JSD'. *See also* US arms inspectors' marks.

Duke – 1. A *Suicide Special revolver made by the *Hopkins & Allen Arms Company of Norwich, Connecticut, USA, in the late nineteenth century. **2.** R. & W. Duke. A gun- and airgun maker listed in Wilton Street, Aston, Birmingham, in 1854.

Dumoulin, *see also* DeMoulin – 1. Armes Ernest Dumoulin SPRL, Liège. Successors to Dumoulin & fils SA, apparently in the early 1970s. Makers of a range of high-quality sporting guns, including the bolt-action *Bavaria hunting rifle and the *Renaissance Drilling. **2.** F. Dumoulin & Companie. Based in Liège, this Belgian gunmaking business was represented in London in 1898–99. The office was at 9–11 Wilson Street. **3.** Dumoulin & Fils SA of Milmort, near Liège, made Mauser-type sporters in the early 1950s on refurbished war-surplus Kar. 98k-type actions. The MR-2 offered a straight-comb butt and a rounded fore-end tip of ebony, rosewood or horn; the MR-5 was an engraved deluxe version with a block-and-leaves back sight set into the front of a short rib stretching forward from the chamber. Later Type A rifles were built on new FN actions chambered for .375 H&H Magnum cartridges. They had Monte Carlo half-stocks, *Express sights let into quarter ribs and hinged magazine floor plates. Type DM rifles, for 7x57, 7.65x53 and 8x57 ammunition, usually exhibited an exaggerated pistol-grip cap, a notch-back Monte Carlo comb and basket-weave chequering. Dumoulin Fils have also made single-shot rimfire sporters since the end of the Second World War, including the single-shot Model 569 and the long-barrelled Model 570; TR models were similar, but had specially selected deluxe walnut woodwork. **4.** Dumoulin Frères & Cie, Liège. This Belgian gunsmithing business was founded in 1849 by André-Auguste Dumoulin, run by his widow after his early death and then by his sons. The Dumoulin brothers were founder members of les *Fabricants d'armes réunis, 1886, and founding shareholders in *Fabrique Nationale d'Armes de Guerre in 1889. The FN agreement was signed by Auguste Dumoulin on behalf of the company. Subsequently the firm participated in Le *Syndicat des Pièces interchangeables (1898), making large numbers of sporting guns on the basis of 'English Lever' or 'French Lever' actions. These relied on top levers behind the standing breech and radial levers beneath the fore-end respectively.

Dunbar. Edward F. Dunbar, a government arms inspector working in 1875, accepted small-arms marked 'EFD'. *See also* US arms inspectors' marks.

Duncan. S. Duncan & Sons. Operating from 62 Albany Road, Hull, Yorkshire, this English gunsmithing business marked shotgun cartridges with 'Duncan's Special Load' after the end of the Second World War. They were *Eley-Kynoch patterns.

'Dunmax' [The]. A mark found on shotgun ammunition made by *Eley and *Eley-Kynoch for *Mackenzie & Duncan of Brechin.

Dunsmore. Daniel Dunsmore. This government arms inspector, holding the rank of gunner in the US Navy, accepted single-shot Remington rifles during the late 1860s. They were marked 'DD'. *See also* US arms inspectors' marks.

Duo. A compact 6.35mm *Browning-type pocket pistols made in Czechoslovakia by František Dušek of Opočno, c. 1925–38. The Jaga and Perla were essentially similar.

Dupee – 1. Charles F. Dupee. This government arms inspector, working in the late 1930s, accepted .45 M1911A1 (Colt) pistols marked 'CFD'. **2.** George H. Dupee, a Federal government arms inspector working in 1862–63, during the American Civil War, accepted small-arms marked 'GHD'. *See also* US arms inspectors' marks for both entries.

Duplay, rue de la Loire 4, Saint-Étienne, France. Listed in 1892 as a gunmaker.

Dupont, 11 rue Cuvier, Saint-Étienne, France. Listed in 1951 as a gunmaker.

Dupuis & Warlow. A multi-barrel volley or Battery gun tested unsuccessfully in Britain in 1866.

Durafour – 1. Durafour et Crémérieux, rue du Chambon 17, Saint-Étienne, France. Listed in 1879 as a gunmaker. **2.** Durafour neveu et fils, cours Saint-Paul 4, Saint-Étienne, France. Listed in 1879–92 as a distributor of, and agent for, arms and ammunition.

Durham Ranger. A shotgun cartridge distributed by *Smythe of Darlington and Stockton-on-Tees, date and details unknown.

Durif et Descreux, rue de l'Herton, Saint-Étienne, France. Listed in 1892 as a gunmaker.

During. G. During. This government arms inspector, working from 1900 until 1911 or later, accepted US military small-arms marked 'GD'. *See also* US arms inspectors' marks.

Dušek. František Dušek, Opočno, Czechoslovakia. Maker of the 6.35mm *Duo, *Ideal, *Jaga and *Perla automatic pistols between the world wars.

Dussap jeune, rue Villeboeuf 20, Saint-Étienne, France. Listed in 1879 as a gunmaker.

Dustin. Edward N. Dustin, a Federal government arms inspector working during the American Civil War, accepted Burnside carbines marked 'END'. *See also* US arms inspectors' marks.

Durston. John S. Duston. This Federal government arms inspector working during the American Civil War of 1861–65, accepted small-arms marked 'JSD'. *See also* US arms inspectors' marks.

'DVB'. A monogram associated with guns handled by Verband deutscher Büchsenmacher, Waffen-, & Munitions-Handler e.V. of München, Germany, from 1912 until the end of the First World War.

'DW', usually cursive. A mark found on revolvers made in the USA by Dan *Wesson Arms. *See also* 'WA' monogram.

'DWA'. An acronym associated with *Deutsche-Werke AG of Erfurt.

'DWAC'. A concentric-type monogram with all four letters of equal significance. Correctly 'WDAC' (q.v.); used by the *Warner-Davis Arms Corporation.

'dwc'. Associated with German small-arms components made in 1941–45 by the Minden/Westfalen factory of Boehme & Co.

'DWCA'. *See* 'DWAC'.

'DWM'. *See* Deutsche Waffen- und Munitionsfabriken and D.W. *Massey.

'DWT'. *See* D. Waldo *Tyler.

Dyball. Edward Dyball. A member of the London gun trade listed at 24 Markham Street, Chelsea, from 1862 until 1867.

Dyke. Frank Dyke & Company Ltd. An important wholesaler of sporting guns and ammunition, and the principal distributor of *Mayer & Grammelspacher Diana guns since the 1920s, Frank Dyke began trading in 1883 from premises in Dowgate Hill, London E.C. Then the business moved successively to 21 Addle Street, Aldermanbury, E.C., in 1893–94; to 5, 6 & 7 St George's Avenue, Basinghall Street, E.C., in 1895; and to Union Street, London S.E., in 1908. Dyke had particularly unlucky experiences with ammunition, including a serious explosion in the Union Street premises in 1908. In addition to firearms and airguns, Dyke also handled shotgun cartridges marked 'Rabbit', 'Shamrock' and 'Yellow Wizard'. These were often loaded for small-scale clients and may not display identification. Some of the guns handled by Dyke prior to 1939 will be found with the brandname 'Shamrock' or simply a shamrock trademark. Despite the destruction of the warehouses during the Second World War, Dyke remained in London until 1966, when a move to Ernest Avenue, West Norwood, occurred.

Dykes. Arthur Henry Dykes. A gunsmith trading in Stowmarket, Suffolk, England, in the early part of the twentieth century. His marks have been reported on shotgun ammunition.

'dym'. Found on German optical sights and associated components made in 1941–45 by Runge & Kaulfuss of Rathenow.

Dynamite or 3B-Dynamite. The Triple-B pneumatic rifle/shotgun was made in small numbers by the *Ye-Wha company in the Republic of Korea.

Dynamit Nobel, vorm. Alfred Nobel & Co. This business was founded in 1877 by Alfred Nobel (1833–96), the Swedish-born inventor of dynamite, to succeed the 1865-vintage Alfred Nobel & Company. After an agreement had been concluded with IG-Farben in 1926, Dynamit AG's ammunition-making business grew so rapidly that it amalgamated with *Rheinisch-Westfälische Sprengstoff in 1931. Each part of the combine continued to trade independently until the end of the Second World War, when production ceased. Operations were rebuilt slowly after 1948, when the present trading style 'Dynamit Nobel AG Troisdorf' was adopted. A wide range of ammunition is currently being made under the RWS brand, including some of the world's best-known airgun pellets.

'dzl'. Associated with optical sights and similar equipment made by Optische Anstalt Oigee GmbH of Berlin-Schöneberg, Germany, from 1941 until the end of the Second World War.

E

'e', 'E' – 1. Found, as 'e', on German rifle and small-arms components made by Hermann Köhler AG of Altenburg in Thüringen in 1940–45. 2. Found as 'E' on the *knoxform of British rifle barrels with *Enfield-pattern rifling (Martini-Enfield and Lee-Enfield). 3. Beneath a crown, above a number. A mark applied by an inspector working in the *Royal Small Arms Factory in Enfield. See also British military inspectors' marks.

'E.A.', 'EA', 'E–A' – 1. Found on Argentine military weapons: Ejercito Argentino (Argentine Army). 2. A super-imposition-type monogram, sometimes encircled, with neither letter prominent. Correctly 'AE'; used by Antonio *Errasti. 3. A Spanish 6.35mm Browning-type automatic pistol made in Eibar by Eulogio *Arostegui: six rounds, hammer fired. Often marked 'Model 1916'. 4. Associated with *Echave y Arizmendi of Eibar. See 'EyA'.

'EAA', 'EAG'. Used on US military firearms by E.A. *Elliott, E.A. *Gowrie and E.A. *Graves.

Eagle – 1. The eagle has figured prominently in firearms advertising ever since the first trademarks were registered, and has also been featured in *proof marks applied in Germany since 1893. See also American Eagle and Desert Eagle. 2. On airgun ammunition made by *Slugs Ltd of Bromley from 1933 to the end of production c. 1954. 3. A pump-up pneumatic rifle made by the *Sharp Rifle Company of Tokyo, Japan. 4. A double-action six-shot solid-frame .38 revolver made in the USA by *Johnson & Bye from 1878 or 1879. 5. A *Suicide Special revolver made by the *Whitney Arms Company of Whitneyville, Connecticut, USA, in the 1880s. 6. A brandname associated with a BB Gun made in the USA by *Daisy, but better known as the *Golden Eagle. 7. Eagle Arms Co. A *Suicide Special revolver made by the *Harrington & Richardson Arms Company of Worcester, Massachusetts, USA, in the late nineteenth century. 8. Eagle Arms Company, New York, USA. Incorporated in November 1865, apparently this business was formed to sell *Plant revolvers. 9. Eagle Manufacturing Company, Norwich and Mansfield, Connecticut, USA. A gunmaking business active in 1861–65.

'EAH'. See Edward A. *Kingsbury.

Earl – 1. Hugh Earl, Britain. See Prometheus Pellets Ltd. 2. Earl Hood. A *Suicide Special revolver made by *E.L. Dickinson of Springfield, Massachusetts, USA, in the late nineteenth century.

Earthquake. *Suicide Special revolvers made in the USA by *E.L. Dickinson of Springfield, Massachusetts. They date from the late nineteenth century.

Easley. William Easley. This government arms inspector, working in 1902, accepted US military small-arms marked 'WE'. See also US arms inspectors' marks.

East. Edward East & Company (Britain). A gunmaker listed in London in 1874, trading at 1 & 2 Fenchurch Street.

'East Anglian' [The]. A brandname found on shot-gun cartridges sold in Suffolk and Norfolk – East Anglia, the eastern counties of England – by *Kerridge of Great Yarmouth.

'Eastbourne' [The]. Encountered on shotgun ammunition sold in south-eastern England by George *Bates of Eastbourne. Apparently the cartridges date from the 1920s.

Eaton – 1. William Eaton & Company. Listed as a member of the London gun trade in 1868, occupying premises at 35 Finsbury Circus and 98 London Wall, E.C. 2. Eaton & Kittredge, US gunmakers: see B. *Kittredge & Company.

'EAW'. See E.A. *Williams.

'EB', 'E.B.' – 1. Found on ammunition, including shot-gun cartridges, made in Britain by *Eley Bros. prior to the acquisition of the company by Explosives Trades Ltd in 1918. 2. A monogram found on spring-air guns made, or possibly only handled, by Emil *Barthelmes of Zella St Blasii and Zella-Mehlis, Thüringen, Germany, 1913–25.

'eba', EBA' – 1. As 'eba'. Associated with small-arms ammunition made in Germany by Metallwarenfabrik Scharfenberg & Teubert GmbH of Breitungen-Werra during the Second World War. 2. As 'EBA': see Edward B. *Austin.

'EBAC'. A 6.35mm six-shot *Browning-type pocket pistol made in France prior to 1940 by *Manufacture d'Armes des Pyrénées, apparently for the wholesaler Piot-Lepage of Paris.

'EBB'. See Edgar B. *Boyd.

Ebert. W. Ebert, Suhl in Thüringen. A weapons maker listed in the Deutsches Reichs-Adressbuch in 1930.

Eberwein. See Gerstenberger & Eberwein.

'E.B.L.' A shotgun cartridge made in Britain by *Eley Bros. prior to the acquisition of the company by Explosives Trades Ltd in 1918. Also used in cartridge headstamps, sometimes as 'E B' above 'L' within a shield.

'EBP'. See E.B. *Peck.

'EC', 'E.C.' Found on the back-sight leaves of British *Lee-Enfield carbines, showing that they had been regulated for Enfield-pattern rifling. A similar mark ('EC/88') was confined to Martini-Enfield carbines sent to New Zealand.

'Ecar' [The]. A shotgun cartridge made by *Eley Bros. prior to the acquisition of the company by Explosives Trades Ltd in 1918.

'ECB'. See Edmund C. *Bailey.

'Ecel' [The]. Found on shotgun cartridges sold in England by *Farmer of Leighton Buzzard, and Lightwood & Son of Birmingham (see Joseph Birks *Lightwood). Probably made by *Eley Bros. prior to the First World War, or by *Eley-Kynoch thereafter.

Echasa. A trademark associated with *Echave y Arizmendi of Eibar.

Echave y Arizmendi, later Echasa–Echave y Arizmendi y Cia SA'. Founded in Eibar in 1911, this Spanish gunmaking business is best known for a selection of simple Eibar-type semi-automatic pistols, offered prior to the Civil War (1936–39) under names such as Basque,

Bronco, Lightning, Pathfinder, Protecter (*sic*), Renard and Selecter (*sic*). The *Lur-Panzer and *Fast pistols date from the 1960s, although sporting rifles and shotguns may also have been made prior to the Spanish Civil War. Operations ended in liquidation in 1979. An 'EyA' trademark was used, often in the form of a monogram.

Echeverria – **1.** A. Echeverria [Hijos de], Eibar, Guipúzcoa, Spain. Maker of the *Vesta automatic pistol. *See also* Garate, Anitua y Cia. **2.** Bonifacio Echeverria y Compañia, Eibar, Guipúzcoa, Spain. This gunmaker succeeded his father, José-Cruz, and his brother, Julian, in 1910, at first making 6.35mm-calibre copies of the *Mannlicher pistol. Initially known by the model date, 1908, they had detachable magazines, while the trigger/trigger guard/front strap were formed as a single detachable unit. An improved 1914 pattern had projections on the slide to facilitate cocking. Guns of this general pattern, enlarged to handle the 7.65mm Auto cartridge, were made during the First World War alongside *Ruby (FN-Browning type) blowbacks for the French Army. The Echeverria pattern was known as the *Star, although the trademark was not registered formally until 1919, together with its Basque- and Spanish-language equivalents – Izarra and Estrella. *See also* Star–Bonifacio Echeverria. **3.** José-Cruz Echeverria, Eibar. A Spanish gunsmith, maker of sporting rifles and shotguns, who is best known for the exploits of his sons, Bonifacio and Julian Echeverria Orbea. With the departure of Julian in 1910, the family business underwent a transformation into Bonifacio Echeverria y Cia. **4.** Julio Echeverria, Eibar, Spain. A maker of sporting guns.

Eck. Richard & Otto Eck, Mehlis and Zella-Mehlis in Thüringen, Germany. Listed in directories dating from 1914 to 1920 as gun-stock makers.

'Ecko', 'ECKO'. Marks found on the products of Emil *Eckoldt of Suhl.

Eckoldt – **1.** Emil Eckoldt, Suhl in Thüringen, Schlageterstrasse 57. This German gunmaker began trading in 1876. In 1925, Eckoldt was still advertising himself as a maker of 'first-class hunting and target guns', which were often marked with 'EES' in a heart. By 1928, control had passed to Emil & Hugo Eckoldt and Rob. Schilling, and by 1939, according to the Suhl district directory, Hugo Eckoldt and Rob. Schilling alone were responsible for operations. Best known as a maker of signal pistols, Eckoldt also produced sporting guns. Trading finally ceased in 1945. **2.** F.W. Eckoldt, Suhl in Thüringen, Germany. A gunmaker trading in 1900.

Eckstein. August Eckstein, Suhl in Thüringen, Germany. Listed in the 1939 edition of the *Deutsches Reichs-Adressbuch* as a gunsmith.

Eclipse – **1.** Customarily found as 'The Eclipse' on shotgun cartridges sold in England by John *Anderson & Son of Malton, possibly prior to the First World War. The name will also be found on shotgun ammunition loaded, or perhaps simply sold, by William *Coombes of Frome; on shotgun cartridges loaded by William *Ford of Birmingham; and on ammunition sold by *Garden of Aberdeen, by T.J. *Hooke of York, by *Lane Bros. of Faringdon, and by Charles *Rosson of Derby. **2.** A *Suicide Special revolver made by *Johnson, Bye & Company and/or *Iver Johnson of Worcester and Fitchburg, Massachusetts, USA, in the late nineteenth century. **3.** A mark associated with smokeless-propellant shotgun ammunition made before the First World War by the *Robin Hood Cartridge Company of Swanton, Vermont.

École Normale de Tir, also known as ENT. The French Army marksmanship school was responsible for the development of a range of small-arms. These included a series of small-calibre bolt-action guns. Several different types of turning-bolt and straight-pull rifle were tested in 1896–1902. The École Normale also promoted a series of automatic rifles prior to the First World War. There were at least four gas-operated Rossignol designs with retractable locking lugs: two short-recoil Belgrand rifles; a Chezaud and a Vallarnaud, also operated by short recoil. None of these guns was particularly successful, as CTV and STA designs (q.v.) were preferred.

'Economax' [The]. A brandname found on shotgun cartridges loaded in northern Scotland by *Haygarth of Dunnet. Date unknown.

'Economic' [The]. This mark may be found on shotgun cartridges handled in northern England by J. *Burrow of Preston and Carlisle, apparently prior to 1939.

'Economist' [The]. A name encountered on shotgun ammunition handled by Charles *Hellis & Sons of London.

'Economy'. Found on shotgun ammunition made in the factory of the *Remington Arms–Union Metallic Cartridge Company in Brimsdown, Middlesex, England.

'ECP'. See Edward C. *Perry.

'E.C.' Powder Company, 40 Broad Street, London E.C. This propellant manufacturer began trading about 1905 and eventually was incorporated in *Explosives Trades Ltd in 1918. The business was registered as The Explosives Company, but the similarity of this to many rival operations caused the 'E.C.' trademark to be included in the trading style. Shotgun cartridges have been reported with suitable marks, which included 'E.C.' in a sunburst, or with claims such as 'Loaded with 'E.C.' Powder'.

'ECW'. See E.C. *Wheeler.

Eddystone – **1.** Usually as 'The Eddystone'. A brand of shotgun ammunition handled in south-west England by C.G. *Edwards & Son and *Jeffrey & Son of Plymouth. **2.** *See also* Remington Arms of Delaware.

'E. de M.' Encountered on military weapons. This mark represents *Ejercito de Mexico* (Mexican Army). *See also* 'E.M.'

Edenborough. Harold Edenborough, an 'Engineer' of 35 Oakley Crescent, Chelsea, London SW3, was granted British Patent 168,086 in 1920 to protect an air-gun magazine.

Eder. Josef Eder, 'vice-president, engineering' of *Erma-Werke, is credited with designing the Erma ELG 10 lever-action air rifle in the 1980s.

'edg'. A codemark found on German small-arms and small-arms ammunition components made in 1941–45 by J.A. Henckels Zwillingswerk of Solingen-Gräfrath.

Edgar Brothers Ltd, Catherine Street, Macclesfield, Cheshire. This British firearms distributor (still trading) is best known as an agency for Czechoslovakian products, including pistols, rifles made by *Československá Zbrojovka of Brno, and *Slavia-brand airguns. Weihrauch airguns have also been sold in considerable numbers.

Edge. John William Edge, Manchester, Lancashire. This name has been reported on British self-cocking *pepperboxes dating from the middle of the nineteenth century. There were two generations of 'John Edge', father and son, trading successively from 68 King Street (1827–34);

60 Bridge Street (1834–41); 6, then 15 Blackfriars (1844–50); 24 Ridgefield Street (1851); Russell Street (1854); and 43 Percy Street (1857–64). John Edge the Younger was granted British Patents 1688/60 of 13 July 1860, protecting a rifling system, and 821/62 of 25 March 1862 – jointly with W. Beaumont – to protect a mechanically adjustable back sight. He made rifles for Joseph *Whitworth in 1859–63, and was also associated with William *Deeley in the promotion of the *Deeley-Edge breech-loading rifle.

'Edgware' [The]. A brandname used by Charles *Hellis & Sons of London on shotgun ammunition.

Edie. John R. Edie, a captain in the US Army, inspected .45 Colt Single Action Army revolvers in 1874–75. Those accepted bore the mark 'JRE'. *See also* US arms inspectors' marks.

'Edmel' [The]. A brandname associated with shotgun ammunition sold in Britain by *Edwards & Melhiush, formed from the first syllable of the participants' names.

Edmonds. R.E. Edmonds. Based in Stalham, Norfolk, Edmonds was an ironmonger who doubled as a supplier of ammunition and shooting accessories. His marks have been found on Stalham and Stalham Superior shotgun cartridges.

'edq'. This code was alloted in 1941 to the Lübeck-Schlutup factory of *Deutsche Waffen- und Munitionsfabriken AG. It was used on small-arms ammunition and components made for the German armed forces prior to 1945.

'Edward' [The]. Associated with shotgun ammunition made by the *Midland Gun Company of Birmingham, Warwickshire, England, apparently only in 1937–39. It was introduced to mark the accession of Edward VIII.

Edwards – 1. The patentee of a series of magazines, including a variety of *controlled-platform types. *See* British Patents 4415/1901, 6062/1901, 9104/1901 and 13,124/1901. *See also* *Harris and Charles *Ross. **2.** Edwards & Company, Newport, Monmouthshire. The marks of this Welsh gunsmith have been found on shotgun cartridges bearing the brandname 'Newport'. They are believed to date from the period between the world wars. **3.** C.G. Edwards & Son. This English gunmaking business was trading in Plymouth, Devon, in 1907. It is known to have handled shotgun ammunition, probably made by *Eley Bros., identified by the brandnames Eddystone and Smeaton. **4.** George H. Edwards. Co-patentee with Henry *Carter of the *Carter & Edwards bolt-action rifle, the subject of British Patents 2417/66, 2513/67, 2769/68 and 1767/69 granted in 1866–69. **5.** William Edwards & Son, 63 St Aubyn Street, Devonport, Devon. The marks of this gunmaking business, active 1843–56, have been reported on sporting guns and self-cocking *pepperboxes. **6.** Edwards & Melhiush. Trading from Harborne, a village on the outskirts of Birmingham, this English gunmaking business handled shotgun cartridges marked 'Edmel'.

'eea'. A codemark allotted to the German gunmaker Hermann *Weihrauch of Zella-Mehlis in 1941, to be used on small-arms components made during the Second World War.

'EEC'. *See* E.E. *Chapman.

'eej'. Found on German small-arms and ammunition components made by Märkisches Walzwerk GmbH of Strausberg Bezirk Potsdam in 1941–45.

'eem'. Found on military small-arms and small-arms ammunition components made in Germany during the Second World War by Selve-Kronbiegel-Dornheim AG, Sömmerda.

'eeo'. Allotted to the Posen (Poznan) factory of *Deutsche Waffen- und Munitionsfabriken AG, for use on machine-guns and small-arms components made during the Second World War.

'eeu'. Associated with signal pistols made during the Second World War by Lieferungsgemeinschaft west-thüringische Werkzeug- und Metallwarenfabriken eGmbH, Schmalkalden in Thüringen.

'eev'. Found on German small-arms and small-arms ammunition components made in 1941–45 in the Tembach-Dietharz factory of Fr. Braun.

'eey'. Associated with the small-arms ammunition components made in Germany by Metallwarenfabrik Treuenbrietzen GmbH of Roederhof, 1941–45.

'EF'. *See* Edward *Ferrar and Edward *Flather.

'EFD' – 1. Used by the British *Royal Small Arms Factory at Enfield Lock, Middlesex. **2.** A US arms inspector's mark. *See* Edward F. *Dunbar.

'EFJ'. *See* E.F. Jarrard.

'EG', 'E.G.' Usually accompanied by two pistols in saltire. A mark associated with *Eisenwerke Gaggenau, Baden, used c. 1885–96.

'EGF'. *See* Edward G. *Fusger.

Egg – 1. Charles & Henry Egg. This partnership succeeded to the business of Joseph Manton & Son, trading from 6 Holles Street, Cavendish Square, in 1839–42 (initially as Joseph Egg & Company), and thereafter from 1 Piccadilly until 1850. Then Henry Egg continued operations alone, until he died in 1869 and was succeeded by his son, Henry William Egg. Trading finally ceased in 1880. **2.** Durs Egg. One of the best known of all the London gunmakers active in the first half of the nineteenth century – not least because of his liaison with Pauly and his ballooning exploits – Egg was born in Switzerland in 1748 and died in London in 1831. However, business was continued by his executors until 1837, and thereafter under the proprietorship of John Egg (c. 1797–1873). The directories still listed 'Durs Egg' at 4 The Colonnade, Pall Mall, as late as 1865, and sporting guns, pepperboxes and cap-lock revolvers have been seen with appropriate marks. **3.** Henry Egg, British gunsmith: *see* Charles & Henry Egg (above).

Eggars. Selmer Eggars, New Bedford, Massachusetts. A partner in Groudschos & Eggars in 1855–60, then trading alone until 1870 or later, Eggars specialised in whaling guns – altthough, paradoxically, he has also been identified with much more delicate spring-air *Gallery Guns.

Egan. Samuel George Egan, trading as a gunsmith, occupied premises at 157 Tachbrook Street, Pimlico, London, in 1887–93.

Egyptian Model. A name given in the 1870s by E. *Remington & Sons to a version of the standard military *rolling-block rifle chambering the 11mm 'Egyptian Cartridge'; a sabre bayonet was customary. *See also* Civil Guard Model, French Model and Spanish Model.

'EH'. *See* Ethan *Hancock and Edward *Hooker.

Ehbets. Carl J. Ehbets. An engineer employed by *Colt's Patent Fire Arms Manufacturing Company, eventually as the company's patent attorney. Ehbets was granted a US Patent on 5 August 1884 to protect a star-pattern ejector plate, and an improvement was allowed in

October 1884; both patents were assigned to Colt. He also received US no. 570,388 (27 October 1896) to protect a *gas-operated pistol with a *Bergmann-type clip-feed, and 580,935 (20 April 1896) for an aberrant *blow-forward design inspired by the *Mannlicher of 1894. Neither of these was successful. However, a grip-safety system, protected by US no. 917,723 of 6 April 1909, which withdrew the firing pin and blocked the sear, was combined with a similar system developed by George *Tansley and fitted to the .45 M1911 *Government Model pistol.

'EHD'. See Elbert H. *Dewey.

Ehmann. Ant. Ehmann, Suhl in Thüringen. Active in Germany as a gunsmith, according to the *Deutsches Reichs-Adressbuch*, in 1920.

'EHP'. See E.H. *Pearson and Edwin H. *Perry.

'Eichel', often accompanied by an acorn. This brand-name – 'acorn' in German – has been associated with sporting goods distributed by Albrecht *Kind.

Eickhoff. Theodore Eickhoff. Chief engineer of *Auto-

Ordnance, this man has been credited with developing the *Thompson submachine-gun to its perfected state. See also Oscar *Payne.

Eidgenössische... – 1. Eidgenössische Montier-Werkstätte, Bern. This Swiss state-owned ordnance factory made Federal-pattern M1869 (*Vetterli) rifles, M1871 short rifles and M1871 carbines from 1871 until 1875, when it was renamed Eidgenössische Waffenfabrik. **2.** Eidgenössische Waffenfabrik: see panel, below.

'EIG', 'E.I.G.' – 1. Crowned. Found on weapons owned by the British-controlled East India Government. They date from c. 1757–1857. Sometimes listed as 'E.I.C.' (East India Company). **2.** Encircled, superimposed on crosshairs. The mark of the EIG Corporation, a US importer of a variety of guns, including Japanese *Miroku revolvers.

'E. II R.', beneath a crown. Found on British weapons: the mark of Queen Elizabeth II (1952 to date). See also Cyphers, imperial and royal.

Einhand – 1. Or Einhandspanner, Einhandspannung.

EIDGENÖSSISCHE WAFFENFABRIK, BERN

Eidgenössische... (2)

Bern, Wylerstrasse and Stauffacherstrasse, Switzerland. The federal firearms factory was founded in 1871 as Eidg. Montierwerkstätte (q.v.), but was renamed four years later. The first large-scale work concerned the Swiss-pattern *Vetterli firearms, thousands of which were made between 1875 and 1887 – M1869 rifles, M1871 short rifles, M1878 rifles, M1878 short rifles, M1878 carbines and Border Guard carbines, and M1881 rifles and short rifles. A workforce numbering only forty-five had risen to nearly 1,000 by 1892.

The Vetterli rifles were followed

by the bolt-action *Schmidt-Rubins, the Parabellum (or *Luger) pistol, and a selection of *Maxim and other automatic weapons. A new factory was opened in Stauffacherstrasse in 1912, initially under the control of Louis von Stürler (director, 1894–1920), then of Adolf Fürrer (1921–40). Although the company employed nearly 1,350 men by 1942, operations were scaled down once production of the Schmidt-Rubin Kar. 31 had been slowed pending development of an automatic rifle and the SIG-Petter pistol had replaced the Luger. This allowed the old Wylerstrasse factory to be demolished in the late 1940s.

Products can often be identified

by a 'W+F' mark, which may take the form of a circular monogram, and also usually bear Swiss-style national or property marks. The Bern factory played an active role in the development of automatic weapons, making *Maxim and Fürrer machine-guns. The last guns to be made in quantity were the 7.5x55 MG. 51, derived from the wartime German MG. 42, which remained the standard Swiss general-purpose machine-gun until displaced in recent years by SIG roller-lock designs.

An aerial view of the Swiss state rifle factory, the Eidgenössische Waffenfabrik, Bern, taken in the early 1970s.

See one-hand cocking. **2.** A brandname associated with a range of small semi-automatic pistols offered between the world wars by Theodor *Bergmanns Erben and AG *Lignose, but now associated with virtually any design that could be cocked by sliding the trigger guard backward with one hand. The original gun of this type was patented by Witold *Chylewski and made in small numbers in the early 1920s by *Schweizerische Industrie-Gesellschaft, but the Bergmann/Lignose patterns were far more common. *See also* Jo-Lo-Ar and White-Merrill.

Einheitsmaschinengewehr. A German-language term ('all-purpose machine-gun') originating in the First World War with the Maxim-type MG. 16, but more commonly associated with the MG. 34 and MG. 42 of the Second World War. These could serve equally well as light support weapons, mounted on bipods, or to sustain fire from specially buffered tripods. Today the term is synonymous with *general-purpose machine-gun and *universal machine-gun.

Eisenwerke Gaggenau, Gaggenau in Baden. This general metalworking business was founded in 1879 to make household goods, metalware and railway lines. An assortment of sporting rifles, shotguns, pistols and airguns was developed by, or for, *Bergmann and Flürscheim, until operations were restructured in *Bergmanns Industriewerke in the late 1890s. The airgun patents are described more comprehensively in the Bergmann entry. Eisenwerke Gaggenau made large quantities of *Gem-type guns prior to 1914, together with small quantities of guns embodying the Hebelscheiber Verschluss – a push-lever lock dated by W.H.B. Smith in *Gas, Air & Spring Guns of the World* (1958) to c. 1905, but probably a decade or so older. Eisenwerke Gaggenau guns customarily bear an 'E.G.' trademark above crossed pistols.

Ejector – **1.** A device to throw empty cases out of a gun. It is usually a fixed bar or blade, which intercepts a spent case withdrawn from the breech by the *extractor. **2.** Associated with a wide variety of shotguns and, by extension, shotgun ammunition suited to them (the latter usually as 'The Ejector'). The name has been applied to cartridges made by practically every British source, including the *National Arms & Ammunition Company Ltd, the *Midland Gun Company, *Nobel Explosives Ltd of Glasgow and *Eley-Kynoch.

Ejercito. A Spanish-language term for 'army', customarily associated with firearms used in South America. *See also* Exercito and National markings.

'EJF', 'EJK', 'EJS'. *See* E.J. *Frost, E.J. *Kernan and Edward J. *Schoch.

'E K', 'E-K' – **1.** Found in the headstamps or on the bodies of cartridges made in Britain by *Eley-Kynoch Ltd. **2.** Cursive, in monogram form. Found on guns and accessories made – or possibly simply distributed – by Emil *Kerner of Suhl, Germany, 1903–14.

'EKC'. *See* Edward K. *Colton.

Eklund. Erik Eklund. A Swedish engineer: *see* Ljungmann.

'Ektor' [The], or 'Ektor Long'. Encountered on .410 shotgun cartridges sold by Charles S. *Rosson of Norwich; believed to be a corruption of 'Ejector'.

'ELB'. *See* Edward L. *Bolles.

El Cid. A Spanish 6.35mm Browning-type semi-automatic pistol made in Eibar by Casimir *Santos. Specimens may also be marked 'Model 1915'.

El Corzo. Armas El Corzo, Eibar, Guipúzcoa, Spain.

Allegedly a maker – or perhaps exporter – of sporting rifles, shotguns and spring-air guns active in the 1970s.

Elderkin & Son. Trading in Spalding, Lincolnshire, this English gunsmithing business marked sporting guns and shotgun cartridges.

Elector. A *Suicide Special revolver made by the *Hopkins & Allen Arms Company of Norwich, Connecticut, USA, in the late nineteenth century.

Electric, Electric... – **1.** A *Suicide Special revolver made by the *Forehand & Wadsworth Arms Company of Worcester, Massachusetts, USA, in the late nineteenth century. **2.** Electric Arms & Ammunition Syndicate Ltd [The]. This agency maintained an office at 35 Queen Victoria Street, London, in 1892–94. It is believed to have been formed to promote an electric-ignition sporting gun patented in the USA by Samuel Russell in 1884–86, and in Britain by the patent agent J.C. *Mewburn in 1886 on behalf of the *American Electric Arms & Ammunition Company of New York. This had been formed in the 1880s to promote the Russell gun, but nothing substantial was achieved.

Elevation adjustment. Found on sights, this makes alterations to vary the range – usually by raising or lowering the sight block. *See also* Azimuth adjustment and Sights.

Eley – **1.** Associated with centrefire rifle and shotgun cartridges made by *Eley Bros., generally prior to the acquisition of the company by Explosives Trades Ltd in 1918, although similar marks were used thereafter with the occasional addition of 'Kynoch', 'IMI' or the encircled *ICI trademark. **2.** Eley Brothers Ltd. Founded in London in 1828 as 'W. & C. Eley' by William Eley the Elder and Charles Eley, trading from 14 Charlotte Street, Fitzroy Square, subsequently this business passed to William's sons – William the Younger, Thomas, Charles and Henry. This occurred in 1841, when William Eley the Elder was killed in a fulminate explosion. Eley Brothers exhibited with distinction at the Great Exhibition of 1851, then issued £200,000 of public share capital in 1874 to form Eley Bros. Ltd. William Eley the Younger died in 1882, and Charles Eley in 1902, after which Henry Eley retired and the family ties were broken. A factory was erected in Angel Road, Edmonton, London, in 1905–07; by 1914, the company had purchased both the *Schultze Gunpowder Company and the *Abbey Improved Chilled Shot Company. Vast quantities of metal-case ammunition were made throughout Eley's existence in London and Edmonton, until the Explosive Trades take-over. This conglomerate, in turn, became Nobel Industries Ltd in 1920, then part of Imperial Chemical Industries in 1926. Thereafter, production of ammunition centred on the former *Kynoch Lion Works in the Witton district of Birmingham, and Eley Bros. Ltd was liquidated in 1928 – ironically, in its centenary year. In addition to metal-case cartridges, Eley has been in the forefront of shot and pellet making since the nineteenth century. Airgun slug-making machinery was installed as early as 1902, and by 1910 the *Black Boy and *Scout diabolo pellets were being offered. The Eley Division of IMI still makes pellets of this genre under its own brandname, *Wasp, although similar products have always been made under contract to others (e.g. the BSA *Pylarm). The brandnames used by Eley for shotgun cartridges were many and varied. They included Achilles, Acme, Aquoid, Black Twenty, Comet, E.B., E.B.L., Ecar, Eley, Ejector, Elite, Eloid, Erin-Go-Bragh,

Fourten, Grand Prix, Juno, Lancaster's Pygmies, Lightmode, Mars, Midget, Neptune, Parvo, Pegamoid, Pluto, Quail, Rocket, S.A., Thor, Titan, Tom Thumb, Universal, V.C., Vulcan and Zenith. In addition, many cartridges were loaded for individual gunmakers or by gunmakers using Eley components. Consequently, a variety of names will be found on otherwise standard Eley ammunition. The headstamps of these cartridges often give a clue to date. 'E.B.' or 'E.B.L' in the marks suggests an origin in the 1890s, whereas 'ELEY' was generally confined to 1900–19. **3.** Eley-Kynoch Ltd, ICI Metals Division. This business perpetuated many of the brand-names formerly associated with *Eley Brothers Ltd, *Kynoch Ltd and even *Nobel Explosives Ltd. They included 20th Century, Acme, Almac, Alphamax, Bonax, British Smokeless, Coronation, Deep Shell, Ejector, Empire, Extra Long, Fourlong, Fourten, G.P., Grand Prix, Hymax, Impax, Kyblack, Neoflak, Mettax, Nitrone, Noneka, Parvo, Primax, Rocket, Scarebird, Trapshooting, Universal, Velocity, Westminster, Wildfowling, Winchester Cannon, Yeoman and Zenith. Characteristic headstamps included the Eley name with 'N.I.' for 'Nobel Industries' (1920–25) and 'ELEY' and 'NOBEL', which were confined to the mid-1920s. After 1927, until the mid-1970s, most marks read 'ELEY-KYNOCH'; the encircled ICI trademark also appeared prior to c.1963.
'ELF'. See Elbert L. *Ford.
'ELG'. Usually crowned above a star within an oval border. The mark of the Belgian proof house in Liège – Épreuve Liégeois – used since 1813, but now regarded as the definitive proof applied under Proof Laws of 1888, 1923 and later. Normally it is accompanied by a 'PV' nitro-proof, a crowned 'R' rifled-barrel mark, the 'Perron' view-stamp and the mark of an inspector.
El Gamo. See panel, pp. 166/67.
Elgin – 1. George Elgin, USA. Patentee of the Elgin Cutlass Pistol (below). **2.** 'Elgin Arms'. Found on *Suicide Special revolvers made by the *Crescent Arms Company of Norwich, Connecticut, USA, in the late nineteenth century. **3.** Elgin Arms Company. A name associated with shotguns made in the USA prior to 1917 by the *Crescent Arms Company. **4.** Elgin Cutlass Pistol. Designed by George Elgin, this was originally conceived to accompany the South Seas Expedition of 1837, but was not successful – indeed, it is doubtful that any actually went with the US Navy explorers to the South Seas. Subsequently a few smaller examples were made for commercial sale, but failed to prosper and the principal promoters withdrew in disarray.
Elisco Tool Company. A maker of M16-type ArmaLite rifles in the Philippines, under licence from *Colt.
Elite – 1. Usually encountered as 'The Elite' on shotgun cartridges made in Britain by *Eley Bros., prior to the acquisition of the company by Explosives Trades Ltd in 1918. **2.** A match-grade 4.5mm diabolo airgun pellet made in Germany by *Bildstein, Mommer & Co. in 1970–82. **3.** The standard .22-calibre wood-stocked *Ensign bolt-action pneumatic cartridge air rifle, made in Britain by Saxby & Palmer and their successors. **4.** Micro-adjustable target sights made in Switzerland by *Grünig & Elmiger of Malters.
Elizarov. One of the designers – with Boris *Semin – of the Soviet 7.62mm short-case M43 cartridge, used in *Kalashnikov and other guns.

Elk Series. This comprised *Mauser-pattern sporting rifles made by *Rahn Gun Works in 6x57mm, 7mm Remington Magnum and .30-06. An elk's head appeared on the magazine floor plate.
Elkington & Company Ltd; Birmingham. A maker of magazines for the British 9mm *Sten Gun and .303 *Bren Gun (box pattern) during the Second World War. The regional code 'M 78' may have been used instead of the company name. See also British military manufacturers' marks.
Elleniki Biomekanika Oplon, also known as EBO, Greece. Makers of *Heckler & Koch rifles under licence for the Greek armed forces.
Ellicott. William Ellicott. An English country gunmaker based in Broad Street, Launceston, Cornwall, known to have handled sporting guns and ammunition between 1882 and 1914. He may have had a branch in South Wales, as shotgun cartridges are known with 'Ellicott-Cardiff' headstamps.
Elliot, Elliott – 1. E.A. Elliott, a government arms inspector working in 1895–1913, accepted small-arms marked 'EAA'. See also US arms inspectors' marks. **2.** Henry Elliott, Lowfield Street, Dartford, Kent. This gunsmith offered shotgun cartridges under the brandname Smasher. **3.** Henry Elliott, Birmingham, Warwickshire. This English gunsmith was granted British Patent 1782 of 1863, protecting a drop-barrel action for sporting guns 'on the windage system' made by Elliott & Sheldon (below). **4.** William H. Elliott, Plattsburg, New York State, and New York City. Occasionally listed as Eliot or Elliot, this man was a versatile designer, perhaps best remembered for his cartridge derringers. Among his US patents for 'revolving firearms' were 21,188 of 17 August 1858 and 28,460 of 29 May 1860, which protected the so-called *Zig-Zag derringer. US Patent 28,460 of 29 May 1860 protected the barrel cluster of the Remington-Elliott derringer, while 33,362 of 1 October 1861 allowed claims for its revolving striker mechanism. US Patent 68,292 of 27 August 1867 ('hammer for breech-loading firearms') was exploited in the single-barrel Remington Deringer. US Patent 51,440 was granted on 12 December 1865 to protect a 'many barrelled firearm', which became the Remington *Double Repeating Deringer Pistol. Elliott also designed the rammer fitted to Remington revolvers in 1861–63, the subject of US Patent 33,932 of December 1861. **5.** Elliott & Sheldon, 25 Whittall Street, Birmingham, Warwickshire, England. This gunmaking business entered 8-, 12- and 16-bore 'Patent Snap-Action Breech Loader' pinfire shotguns in the trials undertaken in 1866 by The Field. The guns were made in accordance with the patent granted to Henry Elliott (above).
Ellis – 1. Richard Ellis & Sons, a Birmingham gunmaking firm, traded from 13 St Mary's Row in 1897–98. Apparently representation was also maintained in London at that time. **2.** Willard Ellis. Co-designer with John *White of the *Plant revolver, protected by US Patents 24,726 of 12 July 1859 and 39,318 of 25 August 1863.
Ells. Josiah Ells. Grantee of US Patent 10,812 of 25 April 1854, protecting the extension around the cylinder-axis pin. See also Cooper Fire Arms Company.
Elmira Arms Company. A brandname associated with shotguns made by the *Crescent Arms Company of Norwich, Connecticut, prior to 1917.
'Eloid' [The]. A shotgun cartridge made in Britain by

INDUSTRIAS EL GAMO SL

San Baudilio de Llobregat, Barcelona, Spain. Founded by Don Antonio Casas the Elder in 1960 to make 'medium-high quality guns at medium-low prices', El Gamo has risen to become the major Spanish airgun manufacturer and has even acquired a controlling interest in *BSA Guns (UK) Ltd. A factory was also opened in Brazil in the early 1980s. A workforce numbering 250 in 1982 was making 1,000 guns and 4,000,000 diabolo pellets weekly in the Barcelona factory.

Products range from the simplest barrel-cocking rifle to the first single-stroke pneumatic target rifle (Sistema MC) to be manufactured in the Iberian Peninsula. El Gamo products, customarily identified by a stylised deer's-head trademark, have been distributed in Britain by *ASI. They have included the *Center and

*Eley Bros. prior to the company's acquisition by Explosives Trades Ltd in 1918.

'Elrco'. A mark found on *Mayer & Grammelspacher and other German-made spring-air guns sold in Britain by the East London Rubber Company in the 1920s.

Elvins. Amos Elvins. Listed as a member of the London gun trade by Harold J. Blanch, writing in 1909, Elvins was occupying part of 41 Queen's Road, Bayswater, in 1867.

'ELW'. See Edson L. *Wood and E.L. *Wunler.

Elwell. F.H. Elwell. Working in 1894–1909, this government arms inspector, accepted small-arms marked 'FHE'. See also US arms inspectors' marks.

Ely – 1. Alfred B. Ely operated in Newtown, Massachusetts, from shortly before the outbreak of the Civil War, in 1861, until c. 1875, when he may have become a partner in Ely & Wray (below). Ely was granted a patent in 1862, protecting chain-shot, and was co-grantee with E.C. Clay of protection for a lifting-block breech-loading rifle: US Patent 105,058 of 5 July 1870. More important, perhaps, was his role as assignee of Edgar M. *Stevens and Francis Vittum (1861), James W. Preston (1867) and A.L. *Varney (1869). 2. Franklin D. Ely, Plainfield, New Jersey. Possibly the son of A.B. Ely, this inventor of a 'firearm' was granted the protection of US Patent 908,892 on 5 January 1908. 3. Ely & Wray, Springfield, Massachusetts, USA. This gunmaking business has been linked with the production in the 1880s of *Suicide Specials named American, Bang-Up, Bloodhound, Panther and Tiger.

'EM', 'E.M.' – 1. On Mexican rifles and other small-arms: *Ejercito Mexicano* (Mexican Army). See also E. de M. 2. On US military small-arms and equipment: see Edwin *Martin and Edward *McCue.

'EMC'. See E.M. *Camp.

Emei, Em-Ei. This brandname was associated with the EM-45, a small sidelever-cocking 4.5mm-calibre spring-air rifle made in the People's Republic of China by the Jianshe Machine Tool Factory (part of *China North Industries Group). Distributed in Britain by the *Abbey Supply Company in the early 1980s, the Emei featured a near-foolproof pivoting-bar safety system. Its meagre dimensions and external resemblance to the *SKS carbine suggest that originally it was developed as a military trainer.

Emery. Charles A. Emery, Springfield, Massachusetts. An employee ('machinist') of the US government small-arms factory, *Springfield Armory, associated with Theodore Laidley (q.v.) in the development of the *Laidley-Emery rifle.

'Em-Ge', 'EMGE' – 1. Found on blank-firers, spring-air guns and the other products of *Moritz & Gerstenberger of Zella-Mehlis, Thüringen, Germany, c. 1922–45. The gas pistols included the 6mm Model 3A, which had a tipping two-barrel block, controlled by a slider on top of the frame, and a distinctive double-trigger system. The 6mm Model 2A took the form of a small automatic, although it had to be re-cocked manually after each of its six shots. The Model 5 was a sophisticated two-shot tipping-barrel design that could handle .320 blanks and tear-gas cartridges interchangeably. 2. Used on a variety of revolvers, blank-firers and spring-air pistols made in Germany since the late 1950s by *Gerstenberger & Eberwein, Em-Ge Sportgerate GmbH & Co. KG, of Gerstetten-Gussenstadt.

'EMK'. See E.M. *Kelsey.

'Emka', 'Em-Ka'. Names associated with the products of Max *Knoll of Suhl.

'EML'. See E.M. *Lovering.

Emme. John Emme. This English gunsmith was listed at 8 Carlisle Street, Soho, London, in 1860; at 25 Portland Street, Soho, and 6 Castle Court, Oxford Street, London W., in 1864–68; and at 29 Crown Street, Soho, in 1872–75.

Emonet, 12 rue Pierre-Termier, Saint-Étienne, France. Listed in 1951 as a gunmaker.

'emp'. Found on small-arms ammunition and associated components produced by *Dynamit AG of Empelde bei Hannover during the Second World War:

Empire – 1. A *Suicide Special revolver made by J. *Rupertus Patent Pistol Manufacturing Company of Philadelphia, Pennsylvania, USA, in the late nineteenth century. 2. Usually encountered as 'The Empire' on shotgun cartridges made in Scotland by *Nobel Explosives

*Falcón pistols, and the *Expo, *Expomatic, *Gamatic, *Gamo-68, Stamic and *Statical rifles – although some of these guns are better known by their British tradenames, such as Paratrooper (Gamo-68), Paratrooper Repeater (Gamatic), Rangemaster or Sniper (Expo), and Sniper Repeater (Expomatic).

The airguns made in Spain by El Gamo have included innovative designs such as the Gamatic (left), introduced in 1970. A tube magazine above the air cylinder feeds a pellet into the breech each time the action is cocked. In the UK, it was sold as the Paratrooper Repeater (right).

Ltd of Glasgow, prior to 1918, and later by *Eley-Kynoch Ltd. **3.** Empire Arms Company. A brandname associated with shotguns made by the *Crescent Arms Company of Norwich, Connecticut, prior to 1917.

Empresa Nacional de Militares, *See* Santa Barbara.

Emslie. David Emslie, trading in Elgin. Morayshire, Scotland, offered shotgun ammunition under the brandname Sniper.

'EMT'. *See* E.M. *Tinkham.

Encore. A version of the US-made *Johnson & Bye *Favorite revolver with a round barrel instead of an octagonal pattern.

'END'. *See* Edward N. *Dustin.

Enders' Oak Leaf. A brandname associated with shotguns made by the *Crescent Arms Company of Norwich, Connecticut, USA, prior to 1917.

Endter – 1. Aug. Endter & Söhne, Albrechts bei Suhl in Thüringen. A maker of gun and bicycle parts active c. 1922–45. **2.** Franz Endter, Albrechts bei Suhl, Thüringen, Germany. Listed in the 1925 edition of the *Deutsches Reichs-Adressbuch* as a maker of 'weapons and all kinds of gun parts'. **3.** Hermann Endter, Albrechts bei Suhl in Thüringen. A maker of components for sporting guns, active prior to 1945. Most post-1935 directories list him as Hermann Endter II, perhaps distinguishing a son from a similarly named father. **4.** Wilhelm Endter, a gunmaker or (more probably) a wholesaler has been described by W.H.B. Smith – in *Gas, Air & Spring Guns of the World* – as 'one of the most important manufacturers of airguns in pre-1918 Germany'. However, no Endter-marked gun has yet been authenticated, and no mention of a company of this name trading in the Thüringen district has been found in pre-1914 editions of the *Deutsches Reichs-Adressbuch*. There is, however, a possibility that 'Wilhelm Endter' is none other than Franz Endter (above).

Enfield – 1. Royal Small Arms Factory [often known simply as RSAF], Enfield Lock, Middlesex. Facilities on the River Lea, known as The Lock were leased by the British government to make gunpowder. A 'Small Arms Manufactory' was erected on the site during the Napoleonic Wars, in 1804, to assemble muskets. The site was purchased by the Crown in 1812, received the Lewisham gun-barrel-making machinery in 1816, saw the installation of barrel-rolling mills and waterwheels in 1852, and was entirely mechanised in the mid-1850s to make the P/1853 or Enfield rifle-musket. Much of the work was supervised by an American engineer, John H. Burton, and a substantial number of machine tools were supplied by *Robbins & Lawrence. The factory has made weapons ranging from swords and bayonets to 30mm cannon. Five hundred trials-pattern Lee-action rifles and carbines, made in 1888, were followed by .303 Lee-Metford Mk I, I*, II and II* rifles, and the .303 Mk I Carbine (totalling about 298,000 of all types), then by .303 long and short Lee-Enfield rifles, Mks I, I*, III, III*, V and VI, and Carbines Mks I and I* (3,080,000 of all types). By 1907, more than 2,000 men were being employed. Production of .303 No. 4 Lee-Enfields had amounted to 463,000 by 1945, but the factory also made .303 No 1 rifles by conversion from *Drill Purpose examples, and also returned 148,000 pre-1914 'Converted' guns to serviceable standards in May 1939. Four thousand .303 *Hotchkiss Mk I and Mk I* machine-guns were reconditioned in 1940. About 150,000 Pistols, Revolver, No. 2 were made in Enfield in 1936–45, the remainder being made by *Albion Motors, and substantial quantities of Pistols, Signal, No. 1 Mk III* were made in 1938–40. The *Sten Gun was also designed in the RSAF, most of the credit going to Reginald Shepherd and Harold Turpin. The name 'Sten' was derived from <u>S</u>hepherd, <u>T</u>urpin and <u>En</u>field. Many No. 4 *Lee-Enfields were converted in the 1960s to the 7.62mm L8 series (L8A1–L8A5, L39A1, L42A1). FN *Saive-type autoloading rifles (L1 series) and many other weapons have been made since the end of the Second World War, culminating in the 5.56mm L85A1 Individual Weapon and the L86 Light Support Weapon. Control of the factory passed to private hands in the 1970s, as *Royal Ordnance plc, and the facilities were moved to Nottingham in 1988. The Enfield site was sold for redevelopment. The prod-

This British .577 cap-lock (a P/1855 Royal Sappers & Miners Carbine) was made in the Royal Small Arms Factory, Enfield, in the late 1850s. Subsequently many of its type were converted to the Snider breech-loading

ucts of the Royal Small Arms Factory were customarily marked 'Enfield', 'Efd' or, in NATO days, 'UE'. **2.** Enfield Engager. A commercial name for the 5.56mm Light Support Weapon, issued in the British Army as the L86A1. The current version has its bipod on a long extension of the frame beneath the barrel, a cyclic rate averaging 775rds/min, and a 4x Sight, Unit, Small Arms, Trilux (★SUSAT) above the receiver. **3.** Enfield Envoy. Applied to commercial target-shooting/sniper derivatives of the British L42A1 Lee-Enfield sniper rifle, also known as the L39A1, offered by ★Royal Ordnance plc. **4.** Enfield-Lee. This name is normally applied to a prototype .402-calibre ★Lee-action rifle made in 1886 in the Royal Small Arms Factory, Enfield. It had a fixed box magazine loaded through the top of the action, but was replaced by the small-calibre prototypes of the ★Lee-Metford. **5.** Enfield-Martini. Applied to short-lived .402 ★Martini-type rifles tested in Britain in the mid-1880s prior to the adoption of the bolt-action Lee-Metford. **6.** Enfield Revolver. This name was applied to a quirky .476 double-action revolver designed by the Philadelphia-born mechanic Owen ★Jones, which, when the barrel was released to tip downward, pulled the cylinder forward along its axis pin to allow spent cases to fall clear of the breech. The Mark I was approved in August 1880, but problems with poor accuracy, misalignment between the rifled bore and the rifled chamber mouths, and constant flaking of the nickel-plated lockwork components soon became evident. A Mark II was approved in March 1882, followed in December 1888 by the Mark II 'with safety catch', but the Enfield was soon replaced with the much more efficient ★Webley pattern. **7.** Enfield Rifle: *see panel, pp. 170/71.*

Engelbrecht & Wolff. *See* Adlerwaffenfabrik.

Engh. Promoted by SA ★Manufacture Liégeoise d'Armes à Feu, guns of this pattern were entered in the Belgian Army trials of 1888–89. Production of military-test and sporting rifles is believed to have exceeded fifty, although survivors are rarely seen today. The straight-pull bolt action relied on a massive handle, protruding upward from the receiver, which could be pulled backward to rotate locking shoulders on the handle-base out of the receiver. Then the handle and the breech-block could be pulled straight back. The magazine spool of the earliest guns could be removed once its housing had been pivoted downward at the breech, and a cleaning rod was set into the left side of the fore-end of the two-piece stock. Later guns had a protruding single-column magazine case, a one-piece straight-wrist stock and a half-length hand guard running forward from the receiver ring to the barrel band.

Engländer-Modell. *See* English Model.

Engle – 1. Engle Spring Gun, USA. *See* Stephen D. Engle. **2.** Stephen D. Engle or Engel, Hazelton, Pennsylvania, USA. This inventor was granted US Patents 320,643 of 23 June 1885 and 334,575 of 19 January 1886 to protect 'Engle's Spring Gun'. This has been listed as a spring-air gun, but actually was a form of crossbow made in small numbers by the Engle Spring Gun Company. Engel received a later patent – 442,025 of 2 December 1890 – which was a true airgun, but it is not known whether this particular design was ever exploited.

English Markham Air Rifle Company. Trading in London in 1913–20, this is believed to have been a subsidiary of the parent American ★Markham airgun-making business.

English Model – 1. Employed as a generic term for anything specifically associated with the British gun trade, this has been applied to products as diverse as ribbed-skirt diabolo airgun pellets and – particularly prior to 1939 – the distinctive pistol-gripped Monk's Cowl or Monk's Hood butt introduced on ★Jeffries Pattern BSA air rifles. **2.** Used more recently (as 'English-model stock' or 'English stock') by Robert ★Beeman, among others, to distinguish otherwise conventional straight-wrist butts from the more popular ★Monte Carlo patterns. **3.** Applied to the 1875-pattern or English Model Sharps. Made by the Sharps Rifle Company, this mated a light-weight action with a slender butt and fore-end, and a particularly delicate hammer. The intention was to provide as heavy a barrel as possible within the limits imposed in off-hand shooting competitions, but the English Model, advertised from 1880 in three grades, was very unpopular. Eventually many unwanted actions were completed in John Lower's Sportsman's Depot in Denver, Colorado.

Enpen. Designed by the staff of the British ★Royal Small Arms Factory in Enfield, the 'Auxiliary Firing Device, Hand Held, Enpen Mark I' was made in quantity in 1944. It was little more than a short tube containing a bolt-like firing pin, locked in place by two small ball bearings until a pull on the pocket clip removed the locking rod and allowed the ball bearings to move inward to release the bolt. The Enpen was designed to be thrown away after use. However, a reloadable blank-firing version was made for training, and an improved Mark II could be replenished by unscrewing the barrel section. An essentially similar .38-calibre pen-pistol was chambered for tear-gas cartridges.

Ensign Arms Company. This short-lived business was founded to exploit bolt-action pneumatic cartridge air rifles associated with Saxby-Palmer. The Ensign Arms Company was a joint venture between Saxby & Palmer (Gunsmiths) Ltd and the optical-sight makers

Tasco, but traded only for three years before differences in marketing strategy caused an amicable split. *See also* Elite and Rapide.

'ENT'. *See* École Normale de Tir.

Entlarvt. *See* Scheintod.

Entwhistle. S. Entwhistle. A successor to Samuel *Troughton, perhaps about 1919, this gunsmith was trading in the 1930s from 151 Church Street, Blackpool, Lancashire. His marks have been reported on shotgun cartridges.

Envoy. *See* Enfield Envoy.

'eom'. Used in 1941–45 by H. Huck of Nürnberg on small-arms ammunition and components made for the German armed forces.

'EP'. Possibly an abbreviation of 'Extra Power'; a *headstamp found on ammunition sold by Montgomery *Ward & Company.

'E.R.', beneath a crown. Found on British weapons: the mark of King Edward VII (1901–10). *See also* Cyphers, imperial and royal.

Erben. Henry Erben. A commander in the US Navy, this arms inspector accepted single-shot Remington pistols in the late 1860s. They were marked 'HE'. *See also* US arms inspectors' marks.

Erfurt arms factory, Prussia/Germany. This gunmaking business was founded in 1815 in Saarn (near Düsseldorf), remaining in private hands until purchased by the Prussian government in 1851. The move to Erfurt occured in 1862. The factory made a variety of German small-arms, ranging from *Mauser rifles to *Parabellum (Luger) pistols. It was demilitarised after the First World War, under the terms of the Treaty of Versailles, and continued trading as *Deutsche-Werke AG.

Erfurter Maschinenfabrik B. Geipel GmbH. *See* Erma-Werke.

Erika – 1. An odd-looking 4.25mm semi-automatic pistol manufactured by *Pfannl of Krems an der Donau prior to the First World War. **2.** Found on children's guns made by *Mayer & Grammelspacher in 1904–14, and possibly later.

'Erin-Go-Bragh' [The]. A shotgun cartridge made by *Eley Bros. prior to 1914, specifically for sale in Ireland.

Erk. Walter Erk, Suhl in Thüringen, Germany. Listed as a gunsmith in 1939.

ERM, Poitiers, France. The French government marksmanship school, successor to the *École Normale de Tir: *see* MAS.

'ERMA', 'Er-Ma', 'Erma' – 1. Often encircled. Marks associated with the products of Erfurter Maschinenfabrik, B. Geipel GmbH of Erfurt. They will be found on subcalibre inserts (*Einsteckläufe*) made in the 1930s for the Kar. 98k and the *Parabellum pistol. The Parabellum unit was an auto-loader patented in 1927 by Richard Kulisch. Erma also made rimfire sporting and target rifles between the world wars. **2.** Often encircled. Used by Erma-Werke GmbH of München-Dachau (formerly Präzifix-Werke) on sub-calibre inserts made in the 1950s for *Interarms, and since the early 1950s on a series of handguns that includes revolvers, blank-firers and semi-automatic pistols based superficially on the *Parabellum, the *Colt-Browning, the *Walther PPK and even the little-known *Ortgies. **3.** Erma-Werke GmbH, München-Dachau, Johann Ziegler Strasse 13–15. Founded in southern Germany in 1948, as Präzifix-Werke, initially specialising

in refurbishing machine tools, then in the manufacture of slide- and roller-bearings, Erma is best known today for its firearms and blank-firers. These have included .22 blowback replicas of the M1 Carbine and the *Luger pistol, together with sturdily made S&W-type revolvers. A solitary airgun – the lever-action ELG 10 – was made as part of a programme encompassing .22 Winchester-lookalike lever-action rifles and an electronic training system. A recreation of the *Gallager carbine of American Civil War days has also been made in small numbers, and Erma has even offered an efficient centrefire target/sniping rifle.

Ermua – 1. A small 6.35mm-calibre Spanish Browning-type semi-automatic pistol, probably made by *Acha Hermanos y Compañía of Ermua, often marked 'Model 1924'. Attribution uncertain. **2.** A Browning-type pocket automatic pistol made for Tómas de *Urizar of Barcelona, Spain: 6.35mm, six rounds, hammer fired. This gun may be a version of the *Duan, made by F. *Ormachea of Eibar, and may also be marked 'Model 1925'.

'ern'. Found on small-arms components made by W.G. Dinkelmeyer of Kötzting, Germany, in 1941–45.

Ernst Thälmann Werke. *See* Haenel.

'ER' and 'P', with a crown and crossed pennants. A proof mark used in Britain during the reigns of Edward VII (1901–10) and Elizabeth II (1952 to date). *See also* British military proof marks.

Erquiaga – 1. Erquiaga y Cia, Eibar, Spain. A maker of *Ruby-pattern semi-automatic pistols for the French Army during the First World War. **2.** Erquiaga, Muguruzu y Compañía, Eibar, Guipúzcoa, Spain. Manufacturer of the Browning-type *Diane, *Fiel and *Marte blowback pocket/personal-defence pistols prior to the Spanish Civil War (1936–39). The company also made the 6.35mm Fiel No. 1, which was a proprietary design. **3.** Erquiaga Arms Company, Industry, California, USA. Active in 1964–65: *see* Ingram submachine-gun.

Errasti – 1. A small Browning-based pocket semi-automatic made in Eibar, Spain, by Antonio Errasti: (a) 6.35mm, six rounds, hammer fired; (b) 7.65mm, seven rounds, hammer fired. The guns date from the 1920s. **2.** Antonio Errasti, Eibar, Guipúzcoa, Spain. A maker of *Ruby-pattern semi-automatic pistols for the French Army during the First World War, and also of the eponymous semi-automatic pistol described previously.

Erskine – 1. James Erskine & Company. Listed in London in 1869, at 27 Finsbury Pavement, London E.C., Erskine presumably undertook the bulk of its trading elsewhere – perhaps even in Newton Stewart, Wigtownshire (below). **2.** James Erskine, Newton Stewart, Wigtownshire. A Scottish gunmaker active between 1866, when he entered an 'Improved *Lefaucheux' 12-bore breech-loading shotgun in the trials undertaken by *The Field*, and the First World War.

'ES'. A superimposition-type monogram, 'S' slightly dominant. Found on a *Smith & Wesson-type break-open revolver with Liège proof marks, made in Belgium or possibly Spain prior to 1914. Significance unknown.

E.S.A. – 1. Made in Eibar by Fábrica de Armas Automaticas 'E.S.A.', this was another of the many pocket semi-automatic pistols based on the *FN-Browning design of 1905: 6.35mm or 7.65mm, six rounds, usually hammer fired. **2.** A US inspector's mark: *see* Erskine S. *Allin. **3.** Fábrica de Armas Automaticas 'E.S.A.', Eibar, Guipúzcoa, Spain. Maker of the E.S.A. pistol (above).

ENFIELD RIFLE

Enfield (7)

A name given to a bolt-action design developed in Britain prior to the First World War, but made in quantity only in the USA. The genesis of the rifle lay in dissatisfaction with the *Lee-Enfield, which was felt by most ballisticians to be incapable of improvement. Most of the adverse opinions centred on the position of the locking lugs in the Lee system, which put most of the bolt body under stress at the instant of firing. As preference was clearly for a front-locking *Mauser-type action, the British developed the 'Rifle, Magazine, .276-inch Pattern 1913', and about 1,000 examples were made for trials.

These were still going on when the First World War broke out in the summer of 1914, but although most of the problems with the rifle had been overcome, the powerful cartridge was still giving some cause for concern.

A wholesale shortage of service rifles, temporarily alleviated by the acquisition of Japanese *Arisakas, was answered by ordering 'Rifles, Magazine, .303-inch, Pattern 1914' (essentially the experimental P/1913 adapted for the standard rimmed service round) from the *Remington Arms–Union Metallic Cartridge Company and the *Winchester Repeating Arms Company. The perfected Winchester-adapted rifle was accepted on 22 March 1915, and the first Ilion-made Remingtons were test-fired in October. Final assembly in the Winchester factory in New Haven began in January 1916, and three different non-interchangeable sub-variants were introduced into British service on 21 June.

Mark I (E) rifles were made in the Eddystone factory of the Remington Arms of Delaware Company, often with parts marked 'ERA'; Mark I (R) rifles were made by Remington–UMC in Ilion, with parts marked 'RA'; and Mark I (W) rifles were made by Winchester in New Haven, with many parts marked 'W'. An improved Mark I* rifle was approved in December 1916, with a longer left-side locking lug on the bolt and appropriate alterations to the seating in the receiver ring. Mk I* rifles with finely-adjustable back sights had a pattern mark with an additional 'F' suffix.

In the autumn of 1916, the British greatly reduced their orders. Winchester ceased work in December, although assembly in the Ilion (Remington) factory continued into 1917. Fortunately for the manufacturers, who had been put in a worrying position through the

---

Escoffier. Juste Escoffier [successors], rue Villeboeuf 7, Saint-Étienne, France. Listed in 1879 as a gunmaker. Owned by 1892 by J. *Rouchouse.

Escort. A compact semi-automatic pistol, also known as the M-61 Escort, made by *Smith & Wesson.

Escot et Allègre, 6 place Villeboeuf, Saint-Étienne, France. Listed in 1951 as gunmakers.

'Escuela'. A Spanish-language term meaning 'school', found on rifles and military stores used in Argentina: 'Escuela Militar' and 'Escuela Naval' were used by the military and naval academies, accompanied by a three-storey battlemented tower, and a crossed foul anchor and a breech-loading cannon respectively.

'ESF'. *See* Edward S. *Frost.

Esmit. A copy of the Colt *Police Positive made by *Arrizabalaga of Eibar.

'eso'. A mark found on German military optical sights made during the Second World War by Optische-Werke G. Rodenstock of München.

Esperanza y Unceta, Eibar and Guernica, Spain. Manufacturers of the *Campo-Giro and *Astra pistols. The business was founded in 1908 by gunmaker Juan Pedro de Unceta-Baerenechea and an engineer, Juan Esperanza, to make 'articles or manufactures of iron and steel' by 'mechanical fabrication'. Not satisfied merely with sub-contract work for other gunmaking businesses, Esperanza y Unceta began work on a gun of their own. Marketed first as the *Victoria, then as the Astra, this copy of contemporaneous FN-Brownings was followed by *Ruby-type guns made during the First World War for the French Army. The Astra trademark and name was adopted on 25 November 1914, and a move from Eibar to Guernica occurred in 1918, but Esperanza withdrew in 1926 and the business was renamed *Unceta y Cia. Production of Campo-Giro pistols began in 1914, leading to the 9mm Modelo 400 or M1921 and a range of deriv-atives described under 'Astra'. The business was also responsible for the *Fortuna, *Union, *Victoria and *Vite pistols, Union-brand guns being made exclusively for M. *Seytre of Saint-Étienne.

Essex – 1. A brandname associated with shotguns made in the USA by the *Crescent Arms Company of Norwich, Connecticut. The guns date prior to 1917. **2.** Usually encountered as 'The Essex County' on shotgun cartridges sold in south-eastern England by *Leech & Sons of Chelmsford, Essex.

Essiger. Ed. Essiger, Zella-Mehlis in Thüringen, Germany. Listed in 1939 as a gun-stock maker.

E.S.S. (Signs) Ltd, Feeder Road, Bristol. A maker of drum magazines for the British .303 *Bren Gun during the Second World War, often marking them with the code 'S 223' instead of the company name. *See also* British military manufacturers' marks.

'Estate' [The]. A mark associated with 12-bore and other shotgun cartridges distributed by *Oliver & Company of Hull. Their origins are not known.

Estrella. *See* Bonifacio *Echeverria.

Étoile. A name associated with a *cane gun (*canne-fusil*) made prior to the Second World War by *Manufacture Française d'Armes et Cycles. Offered in chamberings ranging from 6mm rimfire to 14mm centrefire, it had a screw-off horn handle containing a linear striker.

'E T L', 'E.T.L.' Found in the headstamps of ammunition made in the London (*Eley) and Birmingham (*Kynoch) factories of *Explosives Trades Ltd.

Etna. A Browning-type pocket pistol made in Spain by Santiago *Salaberrin of Eibar: 6.35mm, six rounds, hammer fired.

Eureka – 1. Usually encountered as 'The Eureka', on shotgun cartridges made in Scotland by *Nobel Explosives Ltd of Glasgow, prior to 1918 when the company was taken over by Explosives Trades Ltd. **2.** Eurêka:

drop in orders, the USA's entry into the First World War was accompanied by the realisation that only 740,000 Springfield and obsolete Krags were available. As a result, the Ordnance Department decided to re-chamber the P/1914 for the standard .30-06 rimless cartridge which, while longer than the .303 pattern, had a comparable body diameter.

The 'Rifle, Caliber .30, Model of 1917' (known in the USA as the Enfield to distinguish it from the Springfield) resembled its predecessor externally, but the rimless cartridge improved feed and the rifling unexpectedly resisted wear better than the Springfield type. By 11 November 1918, the Eddystone factory had made 1,181,910 rifles; Remington had supplied 545,540, and Winchester had contributed 465,980. Springfield Armory and Rock Island Arsenal had made only 313,000 M1903 rifles in the same period.

Almost a million refurbished .30-calibre rifles were placed in store in 1920, many survivors being sent to Britain in 1941 as part of the Lend-Lease program. Eventually a large number of these acquired red bands on the butts and red marks over the chambers to indicate that they chambered .30-06 ammunition instead of .303.

So many M1917 Enfield parts remained on hand at the end of the First World War that the Remington Arms Company was able to make a batch of 7x57 Model 40 rifles for Honduras. They were similar externally to the M1917, but lacked the eared back-sight protectors on the bridge of the receiver. What appears to be a Krag-type tangent-leaf sight can be seen on the top of the barrel.

---

see Buffalo-Eurêka. **3.** Found on children's guns made in 1905–45 by *Mayer & Grammelspacher, and possibly also in the early 1950s. **4.** A sheath-trigger *Suicide Special made in the USA in the 1880s by *Johnson, Bye & Company and/or *Iver Johnson of Worcester and Fitchburg, Massachusetts. **5.** A *Suicide Special revolver made by the *Harrington & Richardson Arms Company of Worcester, Massachusetts, USA, in the late nineteenth century. **6.** An air pistol made by *Bedford & Walker. **7.** Eureka Manufacturing Company (active 1867–80 and possibly later), Boston, Massachusetts, USA. Maker of a patented lathe and machine-tools. The company also produced Bedford's Eureka Air Pistol, designed by Bedford & Walker in the 1870s.

European... – **1.** A term applied to the *Remington Model 700BDL European bolt-action rifle, offered in 1993–95 with an oil-finish stock (instead of gloss varnish) in .243 Winchester, .270 Winchester, 7mm-08, 7mm Remington Magnum and .30-06. **2.** European Breech-Loading Firearms Company Ltd [The]. Listed in 1868 only, at 43 Parliament Street, London S.W., this agency was formed to promote some of the European rifles entered in trials that were being undertaken by the British Army at the time. The European Firearms Company Ltd (below) may have been a predecessor. **3.** European Firearms Company Ltd [The]. This promotional agency was listed at 3 Copthall Chambers, London, in 1865. It is thought that the European Breech-Loading Firearms Company Ltd (above) was a direct successor.

Euscalduna, Planencia, Spain. Maker of cap-lock rifles and short rifles in the middle of the nineteenth century. *See also* Remington.

Eusta. A brandname associated with air pistols distributed by Hans *Wrage & Company. The mark was registered in Germany on 13 October 1965, but the guns were short-lived and now are rarely seen.

Evans – **1.** Arthur W. Evans. This government arms inspector, a lieutenant in the US Army, accepted .45 M1911 (Colt) pistols made by Remington in 1917. They were marked 'AWE'. *See also* US arms inspectors' marks. **2.** Benjamin Evans & Company. Operating in Swansea, Glamorgan, this Welsh gunmaking business handled sporting guns and ammunition prior to 1939. **3.** C.A. Evans. An ironmonger and gunsmith trading in the Oxfordshire village of Burford, Evans sold shotgun cartridges marked 'Cotswold'. **4.** Charles E. Evans. This government inspector, working in 1905, accepted small-arms marked 'CEE'. *See also* US arms inspectors' marks. **5.** George F. Evans, Mechanic Falls, Maine. The son, or possibly younger brother, of Warren Evans, this engineer received four US Patents protecting improvements in gun locks and magazine firearms: 189,848 of 24 April 1877, 192,749 of 3 July 1877, 207,350 of 27 August 1878 and 213,455 of 25 March 1879. All are believed to have protected improvements to the Evans breech-loading rifle, distribution of which ceased in the early 1880s. **6.** Thomas John Evans. The marks of this gunmaker, working in Welshpool, have been found on guns and ammunition dating prior to 1914. **7.** Warren R. Evans, Thomaston and Mechanic Falls, Maine. Designer of the Evans repeating rifle, this engineer/gunsmith received several relevant US Patents, notably no. 84,685 of 8 December 1868. *See also* George F. Evans (above). **8.** William Evans. This London gunmaker was listed successively at 95a Buckingham Palace Road in 1883–84; at 4 Holden Terrace, Pimlico, in 1885–87; at 4 Pall Mall Place in 1888–95; and at 63 Pall Mall from 1896 until 1900 or later. The Pall Mall address has been reported on shotgun cartridges branded 'Mark Over', 'Marlboro', 'Pall Mall' and 'Sky High'. It is assumed that they were loaded by Evans with components supplied by *Eley Bros. **9.** Evans Repeating Rifle Company, Mechanic Falls, Maine, USA.

This was active in 1871–80, exploiting the magazine-rifle patents granted to Warren and (subsequently) George Evans. The rifle was a complicated mixture of the ★Spencer radial breech-block and a four-track Archimedean Screw tube magazine. Offered in military and sporting guise, and as a short-barrel carbine, with magazines holding as many as thirty-four .44 Evans Short cartridges, the original Patent Magazine Rifles were made until replaced in 1877 by an improved New Model. The latter had a semi-external hammer and a distinctive sliding ejection-port cover. About 1,000 New Model rifles are said to have been acquired by the Imperial Russian Navy in 1877, during the Russo-Turkish War, but the business was liquidated in 1880 after no more than 3,000 guns had been made. However, Evans had flourished sufficiently to maintain an office at 16 Worship Street, London E.C. (1878). **10.** J.E. Evans-Jackson, a British patent agent, acted for George ★Grant-Suttie and thus may have had chambers in Glasgow. *See* British Patents 154,662 and 156,423 of 1919–20. **11.** Evans, Gadd & Company. This distributor of guns, ammunition and accessories traded prior to the First World War in Exeter, Devon, England. Its marks have been reported on shotgun cartridges made by ★Eley Bros.

'Ever Ready' [The]. A shotgun cartridge marked by Henry ★Atkin of London.

'Every Day' [The]. Found on shotgun cartridges retailed in Britain by the ★Army & Navy Co-Operative Society Ltd and its successor, ★Army & Navy Stores Ltd of London, but made by ★Eley.

'EWC'. *See* E.W. ★Clark.

Ewen. J.W. Ewen. The marks of this Scottish gunmaker – of 45 The Green, Aberdeen – have been reported on sporting guns and shotgun cartridges marked 'The Ewen'. It is believed that these originated prior to 1914, but information is lacking.

Ewerlöf. Per Samuel Ewerlöf was the co-patentee with Axel ★Blómen of the ★Excellent gas-powered rifle. The British Patent papers describe Ewerlöf as a 'Merchant', living at Bergsgatan 23 in Stockholm, Sweden. Blómen is believed to have designed the rifle, while his partner financed the operations of AB Våpenfabriken 'Excellent' in the early 1900s.

Ewig – 1. J.H. Ewig. This government inspector, working in the late 1890s, accepted small-arms marked 'JHE'. **2.** J.W. Ewig. An arms inspector, working from 1898 until 1909 or later, this man is said to have accepted small-arms marked 'JWE'. This and the previous entry may refer to the same person, but with transcription errors. *See also* US arms inspectors' marks.

'E X D'. An abbreviated form of 'Examined', found on British small-arms ammunition reviewed at an annual inspection.

Executioner. A name associated with a revolver sold in Belgium prior to 1914 by A. ★Riga.

Excellent... – 1. *Excellentgevär* (Excellent rifle). This gas-powered rifle, patented in Sweden by ★Blómen & Ewerlöf from 1904 onward, was made for AB Våpenfabriken 'Excellent' by contractors in Germany and Sweden. Although the production history is difficult to determine, it seems most likely that the major components were made in Germany before being assembled at different times by AB ★Bahco, Carl Särenholm and even the Swedish government's firearms factory (★Carl Gustafs Stads

Gevärsfactori). The rifle is said to have been adopted by the Swedish Navy as a trainer in 1910, but no details are known. The original rifles had a distinctive half-stock, with the gas valve assembly projecting rearward above the trigger, and were charged from a separate reservoir. The tube connecting the gas tank and the gun breech often ran up through the pivot attaching the rifle to the shooting-booth bench. Subsequently some guns reverted to more conventional self-contained gas or air reservoirs mounted beneath the barrel. The calibre of most surviving guns seems to be 6mm. **2.** *Excellentpistoler* (Excellent pistols). These were made in Sweden, long after the demise of Aktiebolaget Våpenfabriken 'Excellent', for the similarly-named AB Excellentgeväret. The manufacturer is assumed to have been Carl Gustafs Stads Gevärsfactori, but confirmation is lacking. Products included a few top-lever-cocking 4.5mm pellet-firing pistols and 4.4mm-calibre trigger-guard-cocking ball firers known as the Excellent-Phantom-Repeterpistoler. About 5,000 of the latter, which were externally similar to the Walther ★Polizei-Pistole, were made between 1948 and 1953. **3.** AB Excellentgeväret was responsible for the Excellent pistols made in c. 1948–53 (above). Despite the similarities of name, apparently there were no links with the earlier Aktiebolaget Våpenfabriken 'Excellent'. **4.** AB Våpenfabriken 'Excellent' is believed to have been founded by Axel ★Blómen and Per Ewerlöf in 1906, to exploit patents granted to protect what became the Excellent gas-powered rifle. Trading from 5a Norra Blasiehommen, Stockholm, Sweden, in 1908–09, the company was liquidated in 1924.

Excelsior – 1. Associated with a light ★Gem-type spring-air gun, probably made by ★Mayer & Grammelspacher, sold in Britain by an unknown source prior to 1910. **2.** A ★Suicide Special revolver made by the ★Crescent Arms Company of Norwich, Connecticut, USA, in the late nineteenth century. **3.** 0 Grade Excelsior. A brandname associated with box-lock shotguns made in 1903–06 by D.M. ★Lefever, Sons & Company of Bowling Green, Ohio, USA. **4.** Excelsior Air Rifle. An unattributed ★Quackenbush-type airgun dating from, perhaps, 1870–85.

Exercito. A Portuguese-language term for 'army', customarily associated with firearms used in Angola, Brazil, Mozambique and Portugal. *See also* Ejercito and National markings.

'Exmoor' [The]. Found on shotgun cartridges said to have been sold in south-west England by ★Gliddon & Son of Williton.

Expanded Bullet, or Lane's Expanded No. 1 Gem Bullet: *see* Lane Brothers.

Expert – 1. A brandname associated with a pneumatic target rifle made by the ★Sharp Rifle Company of Tokyo, Japan, for three-positional shooting. Dating from 1962, it was replaced in the 1970s by the Model 700 Pan-Target 3P. **2.** A ★Suicide Special revolver made by the ★Hopkins & Allen Arms Company of Norwich, Connecticut, USA, in the late nineteenth century.

Explorateur-Mitraille. *See* 'L'Explorateur-Mitraille'.

Explosives Trades Ltd. *See* Eley Bros. Ltd, Eley-Kynoch and Kynoch Ltd.

Expo. Applied to a 4.5mm Spanish barrel-cocking spring-air rifle, also known as the Mo. 200, introduced by ★El Gamo in 1965 and known in Britain as the ★ASI ★Sniper. The Expomatic of 1970 offered an additional pellet tube above the air cylinder, a pellet being transferred mechanically into the breech each time the action was cocked.

Express – 1. Used to describe a wide variety of high-power rifles, shotguns and associated ammunition. The name has been applied to cartridges made by practically every British source, although only some of the shotgun cartridges made by the *National Arms & Ammunition Company Ltd seem to have displayed the mark. **2.** A massive Double Rifle made by *Manufacture Française d'Armes et Cycles de Saint-Étienne, usually with external-hammer back locks, although some guns dating from the 1930s had *Anson & Deeley box-locks. The standard action was locked by a sliding plate engaging two 'bites' (notches) in the under-lump, and by a top-lever engaging a doll's-head extension entering the standing breech (Triple Lock). Twin triggers, automatic ejectors and multi-leaf *Express sights were standard, while engraving could be added to order. Chamberings were restricted to 8x51R, .405 WCF and .450 No. 2 (.450 British); individual guns could weigh as much as 7kg. **3.** These Spanish Browning-type pistols were made – usually by *Garate, Anitua y Cia of Eibar – for the wholesaler Tómas de *Urizar of Barcelona. They came in at least two versions: (a) 6.35mm, six rounds, hammer fired, or five rounds, striker fired; (b) 7.65mm, six or seven rounds, striker or hammer fired. The 6.35mm guns may exhibit a grip safety mechanism, while the striker-fired 7.65mm examples are very rare. **4.** A *Suicide Special revolver made in the 1880s by the *Bacon Manufacturing Company of Norwich, Connecticut, USA. **5.** Usually found, as 'The Express XXV', on shotgun ammunition loaded by, or perhaps for, E.J. *Churchill of London. **6.** Express-Carabine. This name was applied to an over/under combination rifle-shotgun made by *Manufacture Française d'Armes et Cycles prior to c. 1930. The upper (smoothbore) barrel was usually 16-bore, whereas the lower (rifled) barrel chambered either 8mm Lebel or .32-40 Winchester cartridges. A pivoting back sight was let into the tang behind the action. **7.** Express Double Rifle. Made by Fabrique Nationale d'Armes de Guerre and FN Herstal SA, Herstal-lèz-Liège, generally chambering the 7x65R or 9.3x74R cartridges, this is a variant of the Browning-designed *Superposed shotgun with automatic compensation for wear in the breech and the top-lever system, and the frame strengthened to withstand the pressures generated by rifle ammunition. The standard gun has an engraved action, chequered woodwork, a single-trigger mechanism and a back sight set into a quarter-rib. The deluxe pattern is identical mechanically, but has a straight-wristed curved-belly butt and a three-piece fore-end. **8.** Express-Idéal. Based on the standard *Idéal side-by-side shotgun, this chambered cartridges ranging from 8mm Lebel to .450 British. An Express-type back sight was let into the top rib, and strengthening metallic fillets were bolted into the sides of the pistol grip. Guns of this pattern typically weighed about 4.5kg. **9.** Express-Mixte. This three-barrel combination gun, effectively a French-made *Drilling weighing 3.3–3.5kg, was the work of *Manufacture Française d'Armes et Cycles of Saint-Étienne. Two 12- or 16-bore smoothbore barrels were placed above a central rifled pattern chambered for .405 Winchester or similar cartridges. A safety catch was let into the upper tang, three triggers were fitted, and the action incorporated a *Greener cross-bolt. **10.** Express Rifle, Sharps-Borchardt. See New Model Hammerless Express Rifle.

Extezarraga y Abitua. See Fabrique d'Armes de Grande Précision.

Extra... – 1. Extra-Corps-Gewehr. Used in Austria-Hungary prior to 1918, this identified a short carbine-length firearm intended for pioneers, artillerymen and Train personnel. It could be distinguished from the essentially similar cavalry carbines by accepting the standard sword or knife bayonets. Guns of this type were made with *Mannlicher, *Wänzl and *Werndl-Holub breech mechanisms. **2.** Extra Long [The]. A shotgun cartridge made in Britain by *Eley-Kynoch Ltd. **3.** Extra Power. See 'EP'.

Extractor. This is customarily a claw, attached to the bolt or breech-block, which engages the rim or groove of a cartridge case to draw it from the chamber before presenting it to the ejector.

'exw'. Found on small-arms and small-arms ammunition components made in the Holleischen Kreis Mies factory of Metallwerke GmbH during the German occupation of Czechoslovakia in 1940–45.

'EWB' – 1. On Swiss military stores: Eidgenössische Waffenfabrik, Bern (q.v.). **2.** On US military firearms: see Edward W. *Bruce.

'EY.', 'E.Y.' Associated with British rifles, generally worn-out *Lee-Enfields or P/14 *Enfields, which were strengthened sufficiently (during and after the First World War) to fire grenades from cup-type dischargers. Their fore-ends were lashed with copper-wire reinforcement. A service rumour that the initials represented Edgar Youll (or Yule), allegedly the proposer of the alterations, lacks credence.

'EyA', 'EYA'. Marks found on guns made by *Echave y Arizmendi of Eibar, Spain. They may be encircled, and the 'Y' may be formed from three short radial lines.

'Eyeworth' [The]. Found on a 12-bore shotgun cartridge loaded by the *Schultze Gunpowder Company at a factory in Eyeworth Lodge in the New Forest, often with components supplied by *Eley Brothers.

Eyraud-Roussler, rue Saint-Louis 22, Saint-Étienne, France. Listed in 1879 as a gunmaker.

Eyring. Carl Eyring, Suhl in Thüringen. A German gunmaker, apparently active prior to 1914.

'E y U'. A superimposed-letter monogram. Found on some of the first handguns made in Spain by *Esperanza y Unceta of Guernica.

'EZ'. A part-superimposition monogram with slight prominence given to 'Z'. Used by Eduard *Zehner of Suhl, Germany, on the butt plates of sporting guns and the grips of 6.35mm Zehna pocket pistols.

F

'F' – **1.** Used during the Second World War by the British Royal Ordnance factory in Fazakerly. *See also* 'FY' and 'ROF[F]'. **2.** Beneath a crown. Found on Bulgarian weapons: the mark of Prince, later Tsar, Ferdinand I (1887–1918). *See also* Cyphers, imperial and royal. **3.** Encircled. Used in conjunction with the Hungarian *BP proof mark on foreign-made guns. **4.** Back-to-back, beneath a crown. Found on Romanian weapons: the mark of King Ferdinand I (1914–27). *See also* Cyphers, imperial and royal.

'fa', 'FA' – **1.** As 'FA'; a mark associated with *Lee-Enfield rifle parts and a few other small-arms components made by the Australian government 'feeder factory' in *Forbes. **2.** As 'fa'; found on German military ammunition and associated components made by Mansfeld AG in Hettstedt/Südharz during the Second World War. **3.** An abbreviated form of the Italian-language term *Fucile Automatico* (Automatic Rifle). *See also* 'FdA'. **4.** Cursive, beneath a crown. Found on the weapons of Saxony: the mark of King Friedrich August III (1904–18). *See also* Cyphers, imperial and royal. **5.** A mark identifying revolvers made in Spain by Francisco *Arizmendi of Eibar, including minuscule folding-trigger guns. A trademark of a five-pointed star above a horizontal crescent was also used. *See also* 'FAG'. **6.** As 'FA', 'F.A.' or 'F…A': *headstamps associated with the products of the US military ammunition factory in *Frankford Arsenal.

'faa'. This code, allotted in 1941 to the Karlsruhe factory of *Deutsche Waffen- und Munitionsfabriken AG, will be found on German small-arms ammunition.

'FAB'. Encircled, accompanied by a crown. Found on Italian military firearms, particularly Mo. 910 *Glisenti pistols, this signifies *Fabbrica d'Armi Brescia. A date of manufacture may also be included.

Fabbrica Armi Valle Susa. See Valle Susa di Guglielminotti.

Fabbrica d'Armi… A name given to the state-owned Italian small-arms factories in Brescia, Terni, Torino (Turin) and Torre Annunziata, active from the 1870s until the 1940s. They were known as 'Royal' (*Reale Fabbrica d'Armi*) until the declaration of a republic by Mussolini. Among the products were *Vetterli rifles, short rifles, carbines and the so-called 'Italian Mannlichers' (q.v.) credited to Salvatore Carcano. Markings included 'FA' ('FAB': Fabbrica d'Armi Brescia), but were often simply the initials of the factory within a crowned circular cartouche: 'TE' for Terni, 'TO' for Torino, and 'TA for Torre Annunziata.

Fabbrica Italiana Armi Sabatti [FIAS]. See Sabatti.

Fábrica… – **1.** Fábrica de Armas de Itajubá. This Brazilian arms factory is best known for the production of *Mauser-action magazine rifles. The Mo. 908/34 was a Brazilian-made version of the German 1908-pattern short rifle, chambering the US .30-06 cartridge; the similar Mo. 954 had a stamped-sheet 'boot' butt plate and a muzzle threaded to mount a grenade launcher. A licence was granted in the early 1960s by *Fabrique Nationale d'Armes de Guerre to allow work on the FAL to begin under the supervision of Industria de Material Belico de Brasil (Imbel). The receivers of the Mo. 964 (fixed butt) and Mo. 969A1 (folding butt) rifles usually display 'FABRICA DE ITAJUBA-BRASIL' and 'FZ. 7.62 M 964'. **2.** Fábrica de Armas de Republica Dominicana, San Cristobal. A maker of submachine-guns and automatic carbines in the Dominican Republic, c. 1949–75. Ex-Brazilian *Mauser rifles were refurbished in large number in the 1950s. **3.** Fábrica de Armas Neuhausen. A Spanish-language version of the company name found on *Mondragon auto-loading rifles. See SIG. **4.** Fábrica de Material de Guerra. See 'FAMAGUE'. **5.** Fábrica de Trubia, Spain: see La Rosa. **6.** Fábrica Militar de Armas Portatiles. See 'FMAP'. **7.** Fábrica Nacional de Armas [FNA]. See La Coruña and Oviedo.

Fabricants d'armes réunis [les], Herstal-lèz-Liège, Belgium. An association of gunmakers formed on 10 September 1886 to undertake the transformation of 30,000 rifle-muskets supplied by the Netherlands to the *Beaumont breech-loading system. The participants were *J. Ancion & Cie, *Dumoulin frères, *Dresse-Laloux & Cie, J. *Janssen, E. & L. *Nagant frères, *Pirlot-Frésart and A. *Simonis, joined in January 1887 by Henri *Pieper. After the initial contracts had been completed, however, the association was unable to compete with *Loewe, *Mauser and Österreichische Waffenfabriks-Gesellschaft and was disbanded. However, its existence led directly to the foundation of *Fabrique Nationale d'Armes de Guerre.

Fabrique… – **1.** Fabrique d'Armes de Grande Précision, Eibar, Spain: see Grande Précision. **2.** Fabrique d'Armes de l'État, Liège, Belgium: see Albini and Mauser. **3.** Fabrique d'Armes de Neuhausen, Neuhausen/Rheinfalls, Switzerland: see SIG. **4.** Fabrique d'Armes Réunies, Liège, Belgium. Maker of the 6.35mm-calibre *Centaure and *Dictator pocket pistols in the early twentieth century. **5.** Fabrique Nationale Carabine (FNC): see panel, facing page. **6.** Fabrique Nationale d'Armes de Guerre: see pp. 176/77. **7.** Fabrique Nationale rifles: see FN-Mauser, FN-Saive, FN-Sauer. **8.** Fabrique Nationale handguns: see FN-Browning pistols.

Fabryka… – **1.** Fabryka Bronie w Polska [FBP]: see Mauser. **2.** Fabryka Bronie w Radomu: see Radom.

'FA&CO'. A superimposition-type monogram with 'F' and 'A' of equal prominence. Correctly 'AF&CO' (q.v.); used by Andrew *Fyrberg & Co.

Fafschamps. See Mitrailleuse.

'FAG', 'F.A.G.', 'F.A. y G.' Marks identifying the handguns made by Francisco *Arizmendi y Goenaga of Eibar, Spain. A trademark of a five-pointed star above a horizontal crescent was also used.

Fagard, Liège, Belgium. A maker of revolvers active in the 1870s.

FNC SERIES

Fabrique... (5)

The successor to the ill-starred Carabine Automatique Leger (q.v.), the FNC was developed hurriedly in 1975–77 to participate in NATO standardisation trials. By 1980, most of the developmental problems had been overcome, and guns were entered in trials in Sweden in 1981–82. These performed well enough for the weapon to be adopted as the Automatkarabin 5 (Ak-5).

About 10,000 guns were sold to the Indonesian Air Force in 1982 and finally, in 1989, after issuing the FNC to airborne forces for some years, the Belgian government also accepted the 5.56mm gun. Several versions of the FNC have been made by FN Herstal SA. The original Model 90.00 had a folding tubular skeleton butt, although a fixed polyamide butt could be substituted. Barrels and chambers were chromed to minimise the effects of propellant fouling, and a three-round burst-fire mechanism was optional. The Model 92.00 was a short-barrelled carbine.

Then the designations were altered to distinguish between guns rifled for Belgian SS109 or US M193 ball ammunition. Consequently, the Model 90.00 became the Type 0000 if it was rifled for Belgian-type cartridges, and Type 2000 if adapted for US ammunition. The carbines were designated Type 6000 and Type 7000 respectively. The Type 6040 and Type 7030 were semi-automatic Law Enforcement carbines.

Currently guns are being made in Sweden, and production began in Indonesia in 1987. Indonesian rifles bear a Garuda mark on the receiver or magazine housing. Small batches may also have found their way into Africa, the Middle East, and South and Central America through dealers and intermediaries.

The 5.56x45 FN FNC, shown here on trial, is one of the leading general-purpose rifles available at the time of writing.

Fagnus. Albert Fagnus, Liège. A Belgian gunmaker active in the third quarter of the nineteenth century.

Fährmann. Georg Fährmann, Zella-Mehlis in Thüringen. A wholesaler of sporting guns, ammunition and accessories operating in Germany in 1939–41. Some of his goods were identified with 'G.F.Z.', sometimes in monogram form.

Fahner. Wilh. Fahner, Suhl in Thüringen. A gunmaker known to have been active in Germany in 1914–22.

Fairbrother. Henry Fairbrother & Company. This British patent agency – with chambers in London at 33 Cannon Street in 1909, and 30/32 Ludgate Hill by 1923 – acted for William *Heilprin and Fernand *Rocroy in obtaining British Patents 29,225/09 of 1909 and 254,976 of 1925.

Fairburn, Guisborough, Yorkshire. The name of this English gunmaker has been reported on shotgun cartridges made by *Eley Bros.

Fairchild Engine & Airplane Corporation. *See* ArmaLite.

Fairman. James Fairman. Originally an employee of William *Eley, Fairman worked as a 'Gunmaker & Manufacturer of Wire Cartridges' from 68 Jermyn Street, London, in 1843–52, and 23 Jermyn Street from 1853 until 1868.

Fajen. Reinhart Fajen Manufacturing Company, Inc., Warsaw, Missouri, USA. Fajen stocked and completed substantial quantities of *Acra S-24 rifles based on Spanish *Santa Barbara actions. They were bedded with synthetic Acraglass to enhance accuracy.

FAL. *See* Fusil Automatique Leger.

Falcon, *see also* Falke and Folgore – **1.** Usually found as 'The Falcon' on shotgun cartridges handled by Charles *Hellis & Sons of London. Date unknown. **2.** A .177 or .22-calibre barrel-cocking spring-air rifle made by *Webley & Scott Ltd from 1960 until replaced by the *Hawk in 1971. **3.** Astra Falcon, Astra 4000. Based on the *Astra 400 (Modelo 1921) and ultimately on the old tube-slide *Campo-Giro, this Spanish blowback pistol replaced the Astra 3000 in 1956. A detachable box magazine in the butt held eight 7.65mm Auto or seven 9mm Short cartridges, the barrel customarily measured 112mm long, and a special safety mechanism prevented the exposed ring-type hammer from slipping forward as it was cocked. *See also* Condor. **4.** As Falcón. This was a fixed-barrel underlever-cocking spring-air pistol made by *El

FABRIQUE NATIONALE D'ARMES DE GUERRE (FN)

Fabrique... (6)

This company owed its origins to a Belgian government decision, taken in 1888, to solicit tenders for 150,000 magazine rifles. Realising that this presented a huge threat to their individual livelihoods, some of the principal Liégeois gunmakers elected to band together.

Fabrique Nationale d'Armes de Guerre was founded on 3 July 1889. The principal subscribing gunmakers were Jules *Ancion & Cie, *Dresse-Laloux & Cie, *Dumoulin Frères & Cie, Auguste *Francotte, Joseph *Janssen, *Manufacture Liégeoise d'Armes à Feu, Émile & Léon *Nagant, Henri *Pieper, *Pirlot & Fresart and Albert *Simonis. The contract to make *Mauser rifles was signed in July 1889, a licence being negotiated with Waffenfabrik Mauser, and a factory was built at Herstal, on the edge of Liège. Tooling had begun by the end of January 1891 and, on 31 December, Fabrique Nationale delivered the first four Mausers to the Ministry of War.

The *Fusil à Répétition, système Mauser, Modèle de 1889* was formally adopted on 6 February 1892. By 30 June 1893, more than 40,000 Mle 89 rifles had been delivered to the army; daily production had stabilised at 250 rifles, 25,000 bullets and 25,000 cartridge cases. The last of the 150,000 rifles was delivered on 31 December 1894. Acquisition of export orders had persuaded Francotte and the Nagants, fearing the competition for their businesses, to sell their shares; a bigger problem was the threat posed by Mauser, which raised objections to a contract

placed with Fabrique Nationale by Chile. This involved the use of patents that had not been licensed in 1889. FN lost the court case, but Ludwig *Loewe bought out many of the original shareholders and, as Loewe also had a stake in Mauser, work continued.

A cartel formed in 1897 by Fabrique Nationale, Waffenfabrik Mauser, Deutsche Waffen- & Munitionsfabriken and Österreichische Waffenfabriks-Gesellschaft allowed substantial quantities of guns and ammunition to be made in Belgium prior to the First World War for export.

A decision to make .22 rimfire sporting rifles was taken in 1896 and, by the early 1900s, tens of thousands of parts-sets were being supplied annually to enable individual Liège gunmakers to assemble sporting guns of their own.

Fabrique Nationale also made substantial quantities of *Browning-designed pistols, resulting from an agreement signed in July 1897. These were exclusively blowbacks – the models 1899, 1900, 1903, 1906 and 1910 – but encouraging sales repaid any risks that had been taken in the 1890s many times over. The millionth handgun was assembled in July 1912. The liaison with John Browning was particularly fruitful; a licence to make 12-bore semi-automatic shotguns was signed in March 1903; the first .22 rimfire auto-loading rifle was completed in January 1913; and the first slide-action FN–Browning shotgun followed in December 1913.

In addition to ammunition, the company's cartridge-making facilities

also supplied millions of gas-bulbs (sold under the name 'Sparklet') to Aerators Company Ltd of London, a trade that, with breaks for two world wars, lasted from 1897 until 1954.

When the Germans invaded Belgium in August 1914, Fabrique Nationale d'Armes de Guerre was also making bicycles, vehicles and motorcycles alongside guns and ammunition. However, the company administration refused to comply with demands to make components for German service weapons and, after continual disputes, the Germans seized the Herstal factory in 1917. Two of the directors of Fabrique Nationale, Gustave Joassart and Alexander Galopin, escaped to France in 1915 to found *Manufacture d'Armes de Paris with the assistance of French industrialists.

When the First World War came to an end, however, the foundation of the Union Financière et Industrielle Liégeoise (UFIL) allowed the shares held in FN by German interests to be recovered, returning the company to Belgian ownership. Production of the 6.35mm 1906 and 7.65mm/9mm 1910-pattern pistols resumed alongside Mle 1922 Mauser rifles, but the operation was soon widened to encompass not only the Mle 10/22 pistol ordered by the Kingdom of Serbs, Croats and Slovenes (later Yugoslavia), but also the creation of a small-arms factory in Kraguyevač. Then an Mle 1924 Mauser-action short rifle proved to be a huge success, selling well throughout the world until 1940.

Production of a double-barrel *superposed shotgun designed by John Browning began in 1926, followed by work on a version of Browning Automatic Rifle ordered

Until disbanded in the 1980s, Fabrique Nationale had one of the finest engraving departments in the world (left). In addition, the company has made many guns under licence – including the 9mm Uzi submachine-gun (right) in the days before the Heckler & Koch MP5, which offered the accuracy of a rifle at short ranges, changed the focus of attention.

by Poland in 1927. A new cartridge-making factory was completed in Bruges in 1929, when the assets of Cartoucherie Belge SA were acquired. Design of the FN-Baby pistol was completed in 1932; series production of 7.65mm Browning machine-guns began in 1933; and the *Pistolet à Grande Puissance* – the legendary GP-35, or High Power – followed in 1935. The pistol had been created by John Browning soon after the end of the First World War, patented in the USA in 1923, and perfected in the FN Bureau d'Études after Browning's sudden death in Herstal in December 1926.

Business was rebuilt successfully after the Depression of the early 1930s and, by 1940, FN was once again supplying the needs of armies in Europe, the Americas and the Far East. The company history states that, in the period 1935–40 alone, 'an unknown quantity of equipment was made for China; FN had made 2062 [Browning] automatic rifles for Belgium; three thousand small-calibre machine-guns for Belgium, the Netherlands, Greece, Yugoslavia, Finland and Portugal; 4200 Browning aircraft machine-guns for France, Lithuania and Romania; 431 heavy machine-guns for Romania, Greece and the Netherlands; 56,500 "High Power" pistols, notably for Belgium, Lithuania, Estonia and Peru; 40,000 1922-pattern pistols for the Netherlands and Yugoslavia; 143,000 Mauser rifles for France, Greece, Lithuania, Venzeuela, Peru, Paraguay and the Yemen; 204 million "infantry cartridges"…in particular for Belgium, the Belgian Congo, France, Yugoslavia, Greece, Romania, Lithuania, Persia, the Yemen, Paraguay, Peru, Venezuela, Uruguay and Bolivia; eighteen million pistol cartridges for Lithuania, Peru and Bolivia; three million medium-calibre (12.7mm, 13.2mm) cartridges…and many millions of shells…'

A licence to make 40mm Bofors anti-aircraft guns had been purchased from Sweden in 1936, 150 units being supplied to the Belgian Army by 1939. The threat of war forced the evacuation of the Bruges and Zutendael factories to France, but the Herstal facilities were seized by the Germans when they invaded Belgium in May 1940. The factory was placed under the control of *Deutsche Waffen- & Munitionsfabriken (ironically, in view of pre-1914 history) and run as DWM Werk Lüttich until liberated in September 1944. During this period, Mle 10/22 and GP-35 pistols were made, alongside parts for the Kar. 98k, the P. 38 and the MK 108.

In 1941, Gustave Joassart and some of Fabrique Nationale's senior staff – René Laloux, Jean Vogels, Edouard Dufresne and Dieudonné Saive – had fled to Britain by way of Spain and Portugal, taking with them plans for an automatic rifle. Prototypes of this gun had been made in Herstal as early as 1937, and an improved version, known as the *SLEM, was made in small numbers at the British Royal Small Arms Factory in Enfield during the war. Eventually, the project became the *SAFN or Mle 1949 automatic rifle, then, after protracted development, the 7.62mm Fusil Automatique Leger, the *FAL or Light Automatic Rifle, which sold in huge numbers around the world for more than twenty years.

By 1964, guns of this type were serving the forces of 49 countries; 650,000 had been made in Belgium, together with more than 500,000 in Britain and by other licensees. The *MAG, designed by Ernest Vervier, appeared in 1957 and was adopted immediately in Belgium, Britain and Sweden. It has since become the preferred medium-support weapon of many armies. By 1964, production had amounted to 25,000 in Herstal, but others had been made in Britain and Sweden. By 1980, the armed forces of more than seventy countries had used the MAG.

Although the demand for Mauser-action military rifles receded greatly in the early 1950s, this was counterbalanced by an increase in interest in sporting derivatives. Browning-pattern pistols, rifles, shotguns and machine-guns have also been made in quantity, including a centrefire semi-automatic BAR sporting rifle designed by Val Allen Browning, and a .22 rimfire blowback pistol credited to Bruce Browning, introduced in 1950 and 1962 respectively. The two-millionth Browning-pattern auto-loading shotgun was completed in 1970.

FN took a large stake in Pietro *Beretta SpA in 1972 and acquired part of the stock of the *Browning Arms Company in 1977; Winchester followed in 1987. However, despite the successful introduction of the 5.56mm *FNC, the armament business lost impetus and, in October 1990, Société Générale Belgique (the principal shareholder) sold FN Herstal SA to *GIAT of France.

In 1997, the affairs of GIAT came under increasing pressure, and FN returned to Belgian hands once again. Work continues on a range of projects, including the new 5.7mm series of personal-defence weapons.

Gamo. Introduced in Britain in 1983, it is a simplified *Center with the same laterally-swinging loading port.

Falisse – 1. Louis Falisse, Liège, Belgium. A gunmaker involved in the 1870s with le *Grand Syndicat. **2.** Falisse & Trapmann, Liège, Belgium. This partnership, formed in 1832 and dissolved c. 1870, made gun nipples and percussion caps. Louis Falisse (q.v.) developed sophisticated gunmaking machinery in the early 1850s, much of it being installed in the *Manufacture d'Armes de l'État; a primer-making factory was built in Beufays; and a gunmaking factory, the Manufacturie Gravioule, was built in Liège in 1851–53 to pioneer the production in Europe of guns with interchangeable machine-made parts. Falisse also devised a bolt-action rifle c. 1862. In addition to providing a locking effect of its own against the split receiver bridge, the bolt handle engaged a locking lug in a slot in the receiver top and another in the bolt-way floor. A large knurled-edge disc screwed to the back of the bolt was most distinctive.

Falke. A brandname used on the spring-air guns made in Germany by Albert *Föhrenbach GmbH of Wennigsen bei Hannover c. 1950–59.

Falling Block Works, Troy, Michigan, USA. Makers of single-shot rifles based on a modernised form of the Winchester High Wall action. Production seems to have been confined to 1974–78, although, as the orders were processed individually, a tremendous variety of chamberings will be found.

FALO. *See* Fusil Automatique Lourd.

'FAMAE'. *See* FME.

'FAMAGUE'. The Colombian government small-arms factory in Bogota, F̲ábrica de M̲aterial de G̲uerra. Belgian-made *Mauser rifles were rebuilt there during 1960–75.

'FAMAP'. *See* FMAP.

'FAMAS'. *See* Manufacture d'Armes de *Saint-Étienne.

'FAMCO'. A superimposition-type monogram with 'M', 'F' and 'A' prominent. Correctly 'MFACO' (q.v.); found on revolvers made by the *Meriden Fire Arms Company.

Fanning. Leon B. Fanning, a government arms inspector working in the late 1930s, accepted .45 M1911A1 (Colt) pistols marked 'LBF'. *See also* US arms inspectors' marks.

'FAO'. The mark of Fábrica de Armas de *Oviedo.

'FAR'. Found on US military firearms and accessories. *See* Francis A. *Roe.

Fargo. *See* Wells, Fargo & Company.

Farley. J.P. Farley. A captain in the US Army, this arms inspector accepted small-arms marked 'JPF' in the mid-1870s. *See also* US arms inspectors' marks.

'Farm' [The]. This mark has been associated with shotgun cartridges sold in Britain by George *Gibbs of Bristol; and also handled by the *Hercules Arms Company of London.

Farmer, Leighton Buzzard, Bedfordshire. The name of this English gunmaker has been reported on shotgun cartridges made by *Kynoch and handled under the brandname Ecel.

'Farmo' [The]. Found on shotgun cartridges loaded by the *Cogschultze Ammunition & Powder Company Ltd of London in 1911–14.

'Farnford'. Derived from the location of the shops, Farnham and Guildford, this mark distinguishes *Remington-made shotgun cartridges distributed by *Tily & Brown.

Farquhar – 1. Moubray Gore Farquhar, a Scottish

'Gentleman', was the patentee (often in association with Arthur Henry *Hill) of the *Beardmore-Farquhar machine-gun and the Farquhar-Hill rifle. He received British Patents 28,587/1907, 17,211/1909 and 9118/1910 to protect the action of the gas-operated rifle (all with Hill), the oldest specification recording his residence as Aboyne, Aberdeenshire, and the last noting Monument Road, Edgbaston, Birmingham, 'in the County of Warwick'. US Patents 867,960 of 15 October 1906 and 920,301 of 4 May 1908 were also granted to protect the rifle. Later patents granted to Farquhar alone included British 127,957 and 183,225, both of which were incorporated in the Beardmore-Farquhar machine-gun. **2.** Farquhar-Hill rifle. This British auto-loader was patented jointly in 1907–10 by Moubray Gore Farquhar and the gunmaker Arthur Henry *Hill. It was exhibited in its original form at Bisley in 1909, and was tried in ever-improving forms into the 1920s without the British authorities ever being persuaded to adopt it. Apparently the later guns were made by *Webley & Scott, but the origins of the prototypes are less certain.

Farquharson. Gunmaker John Farquharson of Blairgowrie, Perthshire, Scotland, was renowned for the falling-block system patented in Britain in 1872. Strong and elegant, the action was operated by pulling down the combination cocking lever/trigger guard, simultaneously cocking the internal hammer and extracting a spent case. Most of the early Farquharson actions were made by George *Gibbs of Bristol, but other gunmakers (e.g. W.J. *Jeffrey) made them after the patents had expired. Interestingly, US Patent 193,759 of 31 July 1877 was assigned by the inventor to George Gibbs, Thomas Pitt and William Ellis *Metford. Cogswell & Harrison were still offering single-shot sporting rifles built on Farquharson actions in the mid-1920s, and a modern coil-spring revival is embodied in the *Ruger No. 1 and No. 3 rifles. Chambering can be practically any British sporting-rifle cartridge, ranging from small-calibre high-velocity rounds to the biggest game-stoppers; consequently, individual actions may differ greatly in size and weight.

Farrow. Milton Farrow. A gunmaker and marksman renowned in the USA for designing the butt plate fitted to *Ballard and other target rifles toward the end of the nineteenth century.

Fasan. A brandname ('pheasant' in German) associated with shotgun cartridges made prior to the First World War by *Pulverfabrik Hasloch.

Fasano, Saint-Étienne, France. Listed in 1933 as a gunmaker.

Fast – 1. A semi-automatic pistol made by *Echave y Arizmendi of Eibar prior to the Spanish Civil War (1936–39). **2.** Or Fast Model. Names applied to a series of blowback semi-automatic pistols made in Spain by *Echave y Arizmendi of Eibar on the basis of the Walther *PP. Chambered for .22LR rimfire, 6.35mm Auto, 7.65mm Auto and 9mm Short, the Fast Model 221 was sold in the USA as the Dickson Special Agent. It had a double-action trigger system, but was often very thinly blued and had plastic grips. The Fast Model 222 had walnut grips, and the chrome-plated deluxe Model 223 had pearlite grips. The last guns seem to have been made c. 1974.

'Faugh-a-Ballagh' [The]. A brandname found on shotgun ammunition sold in Ireland by *Keegan of Dublin.

Faulkner. Harry Faulkner, a designer employed by

*BSA Guns Ltd during the Second World War, is best known for the *Besal light machine-gun of 1942.

Faultless – **1.** Two different sheath-trigger *Suicide Special revolvers, one made in the 1880s by the *Crescent Arms Company of Norwich, Connecticut; the other by the *Hopkins & Allen Arms Company of Norwich, Connecticut, USA. **2.** A brandname associated with shotguns made prior to 1917 by the *Crescent Arms Company of Norwich, Connecticut, USA.

Faure – **1.** A. Faure, 17 rue Claude-Delaroa, Saint-Étienne, France. Listed in 1951 as a gunmaker. **2.** Henri Faure, 10 rue Clément-Forissier, Saint-Étienne, France. Listed in 1951 as a gunmaker.

Faurie, rue de la République 31, Saint-Étienne, France. Listed in 1892 as a gunmaker.

Favier, rue du Vernay 14, Saint-Étienne, France. Listed in 1879 as a distributor of, and agent for, arms and ammunition.

'Favorit' – **1.** A brandname found on airguns made in the period between the world wars; this has been the subject of considerable speculation and has been identified at different times with Oskar Will, Venuswaffenwerk and Langenhan. Now it is known that Favorit, German trademark no. 380,329, was granted to 'Firma Fr. Langenhan' of Zella-Mehlis on 20 January 1928 specifically for use on airguns. **2.** A *Mauser-pattern bolt-action rifle sold in Germany in the mid-1960s by Waffen-Frankonia, in chamberings ranging from .243 Winchester to 9.3x64. A distinctive double-trigger system was squeezed into the cramped military-style guard. A deluxe model was also offered, sometimes taking the form of a 2.8kg Leichtmodell instead of the 3.3kg Standardmodell. **3.** Favorit Safari. Similar to the standard Waffen-Frankonia Favorit listed previously, this had a single trigger, a ventilated rubber shoulder pad and an additional recoil bolt. It was chambered for high-power cartridges ranging from 8x68S to .458 Winchester. **4.** A typical Browning-inspired pocket pistol of unknown provenance, probably made in the Eibar district of Spain in the 1920s: 6.35mm, six rounds, hammer fired.

Favorite, Favourite – **1.** Favorite. A sheath-trigger revolver made by *Johnson & Bye of Worcester, Massachusetts, USA, in calibres ranging from .22 to .44. Similar to the *Tycoon, it was introduced c. 1873. **2.** Favorite. About 1,170 examples of this lightweight .44 *Smith & Wesson revolver, numbered in the same series as the standard double-action .44, were made in 1882–85. They can be recognised by the reduced diameter of the front section of the cylinder. **3.** Favorite Navy. A version of the *Johnson & Bye Favorite revolver with a round barrel instead of an octagonal pattern. **4.** 'The Favourite'. On 12-bore shotgun cartridges handled by William *Adgey of Belfast and *Hunter & Maddil of Belfast. The cases were made in England, but apparently loaded in Ireland.

'FAVS', 'F.A.V.S.' *See* Valle Susa di Guglielminotti.

Fawcett, Kirkby Lonsdale, Westmorland. The name of this English gunmaker has been reported on shotgun cartridges sold under the brandname Lunesdale.

Fay. Rimmon C. Fay, Ilion, New York State. This gunsmith was the patentee of a 'magazine firearm' and a 'cartridge lifter for firearms' (US 547,602 and 547,603 of 8 October 1895), as well as co-designer with George *Humphreys of the perfected hammerless shotguns made by the *Remington Arms Company. Fay is also said to have been responsible for the semi-hammerless single-

barrel Remingtons, relevant patents being granted on 30 October 1894, 16 June 1902 and 28 June 1904.

Fayard, Saint-Étienne, France. Listed in 1879 as a gun-maker, at rue de Foy 7, and again in 1892 at rue Mulatière 31. Listed in 1951 at 77 rue Antoine-Delafour, although possibly not in truly lineal succession.

Fayolle, rue du Vernay 37, Saint-Étienne, France. Listed in 1879–92 as a gunmaker.

Fazakerley. Royal Ordnance Factory [ROF], Fazakerley, Lancashire, England. A manufacturer of 619,900 No. 4 Mks 1, 1/2 and 1/3 British *Lee-Enfield rifles, about 2,250,000 Mks II, IIS and V *Sten submachine-guns, and 169,800 No. 5 Mk 1 Lee-Enfield Jungle Carbines during the Second World War. The guns were marked 'ROF[F]'. *See also* Lee-Enfield.

'FB', 'F.B.', 'fb' – **1.** Used as 'fb' by Mansfeld AG of Rothenburg/Saale on small-arms ammunition and components made for the German armed forces in 1940–45. **2.** Found as 'FB' or 'F.B.' on 'gas seal' revolvers, usually above 'RADOM': the mark of the Polish state firearms factory. Also the guns usually display stamps such as 'Ng. 27', indicating that they are *Nagants made in 1927.

'FB Record', 'FB Rekord', often in an irregular ten-pointed star. Associated with the products of Fritz *Barthelmes of Oggenhausen, Germany.

'FC' – **1.** A superimposed-letter monogram found in cartridge headstamps. Correctly 'CF': Cartoucherie Française. **2.** Found on US military firearms and accessories. *See* Francis *Camp and Frederick *Chillingworth.

'FCW'. Found on US military firearms and accessories. *See* Frank C. *Warner.

'fd'. Associated with German small-arms and small-arms ammunition components made by Stollberger Metallwerke KG von Asten, Lynen und Schleicher in 1940–45.

'FdA', 'F. d'A.'. Abbreviated forms of the Spanish- language term *Fusil de Asalto* and its Italian equivalent, *Fucile Asalto* (Assault Rifle).

'FDCO'. 'FD' within 'C' with a small 'o' in its jaws. A mark used on pistols made prior to the First World War by Fabrique d'Armes F. *Delu '& Co.', Liège.

'fde'. Found on small-arms ammunition components made in Germany in 1941–45 by the Förde factory of *Dynamit AG.

'FDH'. Found on US military firearms and accessories. *See* Filser D. *Horrert.

'FDL'. An unidentified inspector's mark found on *Joslyn carbines made for the Federal Army in 1862, during the American Civil War.

Fearn. John William Fearn, an employee of *Webley & Scott for many years, is best known as the co-patentee with Douglas *Johnstone of the distinctive and highly successful barrel-cocking Webley air pistols. His British patents included 219,872 of 1923 for the basic pistol action, 229,851 of 1924 for the original safety catch, and 231,270 of 1924 for a breech washer (all sought with Johnstone). British Patent 231,557 of 1924 was sought with Johnstone and Frank *Clarke to protect a butt-cylinder pistol with a helical cocking mechanism, and 251,651 of 1926, with Johnstone, protected metallic piston rings.

'Feather Weight' [The]. Associated with a brand of shotgun cartridges loaded by, or for, *Curtis's & Harvey of London, prior to 1918.

Federal... – **1.** Federal Cartridge Company, Minneapolis, Minnesota. Established in 1922 to make ammunition. *Headstamps have included 'AL', 'HP' and 'XL', with tradenames such as Airline and Monarch. **2.** Federal Stock Number (FSN). *See* Nato Stock Number.

Fedorov – 1. Vladimir Grigorevich Fedorov was born into the family of a school inspector in St Petersburg in 1874. Commissioned into the army in 1895, he graduated from the Mikhailovskoye artillery academy in 1900 with a burning desire to design firearms. This led to the work on a recoil-operated automatic rifle (1905–16) and, after the revolution, to a series of 'universal' machine-guns developed in collusion with his one-time assistant Vasily *Degtyarev. Electing to retire from weapons design in the early 1930s, Fedorov turned to education. He had already written *Osnovaniya chstroystva avtomaticheskogo oruzhiya* (*A history of automatic firearms*) in 1907, and his output in the 1930s did much to stimulate a new generation of small-arms designers. The best known of his books is undoubtedly *Evolutsiya Strelkovogo Oruzhiya* (*The evolution of small-arms*, Moscow, 1938), but Fedorov also published carefully researched monographs on early Russian military history and the development of artillery. Much decorated, Lieutenant-General Professor Vladimir Fedorov died in Moscow in 1966. **2.** Fedorov rifle. Development is said to have begun as early as 1905, but no working *recoil-operated prototypes seem to have been made in the *Sestroretsk small-arms factory until c. 1909. A series of pre-production 7.62x54R Fedorov rifles appeared in 1912–13, but the rimmed-case ammunition proved to be too powerful for the flap-lock mechanism and the Japanese 6.5x50 semi-rimmed round was substituted. Testing was still being undertaken when the First World War began. A lightened *Avtomat*, with an auxiliary grip ahead of the detachable 25-round box magazine, appeared in 1916; however, only a few hundred had been made when the October Revolution of 1917 brought work to an end. About 3,000 guns were made to a slightly modified design in the Kovrov machine-gun factory in the early 1920s, but the project was abandoned in favour of more promising designs on 1 October 1925. The rifles were recalled to store in 1928, although a few survivors were impressed into service during the 1939–40 Winter War with Finland. Modified *Avtomaty* appeared in the trials of 1926–27, without success, and Fedorov retired to teach. This left the field open for younger rivals, such as *Degtyarev, *Simonov and *Tokarev.

Feederle-Mauser. This designation may be applied to the Mauser C/96 pistol, acknowledging the part played in its creation by the Feederle brothers.

Feedway, feed-way. That part of a weapon where a cartridge, taken from the feed system, is positioned ready to be loaded into the chamber. Rarely seen in handguns, where the distance between the magazine and the chamber is generally very short, it is much more common in rifles and machine-guns.

FÉG, Fegyver... – 1. Fegyver é Gázkészülékgyár (FÉG), Budapest. The manufacturer of the Hungarian *Kalashnikov-type assault rifles and submachine-guns, AK-55, AKM-63, AKD-65 and NGM. **2.** Fegyvergyár Reszvenytársáság, Budapest. Maker of the Frommer *Baby pistol in 6.35mm Auto, 7.65mm Auto and 9mm Short, and of the 6.35mm Liliput.

Fehringer – 1. H. Fehringer. Zella-Mehlis in Thüringen, Germany. Listed in 1930 as a master gunsmith. **2.** Willi Fehringer, Zella-Mehlis in Thüringen.

Listed in the 1939 edition of the *Deutsches Reichs-Adressbuch* as a master gunsmith.

Feinmechanische Werke GmbH, Erfurt. A maker of German Kar. 98k (*Mauser) short rifles during the Third Reich, distinguished by 'S/27', '27' or 'ax' markings.

Feistel. Otto Feistel, jun., Gera in Thüringen, Werdauer Strasse 11. A retailer of sporting guns and ammunition active in Germany in 1941.

Feinwerkbau. *See* Westinger & Altenburger.

Feld. A multi-barrel volley or Battery Gun used during the Franco-Prussian War of 1870–71 (apparently unsuccessfully) by the Bavarian Army.

Feldmann. A brandname used on sporting guns distributed between the world wars by *Thieme & Schlegelmilch of Suhl. *See also* Parva.

Felstead. Thomas William Felstead, listed as a member of the London gun trade, occupied a workshop at 12 Haldon Street, Islington, in 1854–55. He was probably the son of Thomas Felstead, a gun-implement maker active in London in 1808–49.

Felton. Frederick Felton, an engineer employed by *Colt's Patent Fire Arms Manufacturing Company, developed the safety interlock of the M1894 .38 Army revolver. This prevented the trigger from releasing the hammer until the cylinder latch was properly seated.

Fémaru Fegyver és Gépgyár (FGGY). The Hungarian state firearms factory in Budapest.

'Fen' [The]. *See* Slingsby Guns.

Fennery. W.F. Fennery, often listed as Fennrery, was a government arms inspector, working in 1905, who accepted US military small-arms marked 'WFF'. *See also* US arms inspectors' marks.

'fer', 'FER' – 1. Found as 'fer' on German small-arms ammunition and components made by Metallwerke Wandhofen GmbH of Schwerte/Ruhr during the Second World War. **2.** Found as 'FER' on US military firearms. *See* F.E. *Randell.

Ferraciú. *See* Vetterli-Ferraciú.

Ferrar. Edward Ferrar, a government arms inspector working in 1861–68, accepted small-arms marked 'EF'. *See also* US arms inspectors' marks.

Ferrier. James Ferrier & Son, a gunsmithing business operating from 68 Mitchell Street, Glasgow, distributed sporting guns and ammunition. Its marks have been reported on shotgun cartridges made by *Eley Bros. prior to 1914.

Ferry. Lewis M. Ferry. This Federal inspector, working during the American Civil War, accepted small-arms marked 'LMF'. *See also* US arms inspectors' marks.

'FEW'. Found on US military firearms and accessories. *See* F.E. *Wilson and F.E. *Wyman.

Fez arms factory. The principal Moroccan small-arms factory, best known for *Beretta-type rifles.

'FFCO'. A floriated superimposition-type monogram: *see* JJCO.

'FFH'. Found on US military firearms and accessories. *See* F.F. *Hull.

FFV Ordnance, or Forsvarets Fabriksverken AS (Sweden); Husqvarna. This gunmaking conglomerate was created by an amalgamation of *Husqvarna and *Carl Gustavs Stads Gevärsfactori in the early 1970s. Also known as FFV–Viking Sport Arms, it has been part of the Bofors Ordnance group since 1993. Products have included the unsuccessful FFV-890C assault rifle, derived from the Israeli *Galil in the 1980s. This was entered in the Swedish Army rifle trials, but was beaten by the *FNC submitted by FN Herstal SA.

'FGGY', 'FG' above 'GY'. A mark associated with the products of *Fémaru Fegyver és Gépgyár.

'FH', 'FHE'. Found on US military firearms and accessories. *See* Frederick *Harvey, Frank *Heath, Frank *Hosmer and F.H. *Elwell.

'FHS' – 1. A mark found on guns made in Germany c. 1919–25 by Franz & Herbert *Schmidt of Zella-Mehlis. **2.** Found on US military firearms and accessories. *See* Frank H. *Schofield.

'FHT'. Found on US military firearms and accessories. *See* Feno H. *Traux.

'FIAS'. *See* Sabatti.

Fichtelmann. Friedr. Fichtelmann, Suhl in Thüringen, Germany. Listed as a gunsmith, 1920.

'FIE', 'F.I.E.'. A trademark associated with the *Firearms Import & Export Corporation, USA.

Fiel – 1. Fiel. A Spanish Browning-type semi-automatic pistol made by *Erquiaga, Muguruzu y Compañía of Eibar: 7.65mm, seven rounds, hammer fired. **2.** Fiel No. 1. This was a different proprietary 6.35mm design, with a six-round magazine and a hammer-type firing mechanism.

Field – 1. Usually encountered, as 'The Field', on shotgun cartridges handled by a variety of British gunsmiths and ironmongers, including E.J. *Churchill of London, and *Smythe of Darlington and Stockton-on-Tees. **2.** Alfred Field & Company. This gunsmithing business was listed at 77 Edmund Street, Birmingham, from 1891 until 1914 or later; a sales office was maintained in London in 1892–93, at '199a Bishopsgate Street, Without, E.C.' **3.** Frank Field, licensee of 'The Queen', 222 Sherlock Street, Birmingham, was granted British Patent 25,664/06 of 1906 to protect an improved Bell Target, which did not require a direct strike on the bell to operate. **4.** John P. Field & Company. A member of the English gun trade listed at 14 Upper Smithfield Street, London E., in 1862–66. **5.** William Field. This gunmaker, operating from 118 Unett Street, Birmingham, in 1881, was granted several British patents. These included no. 1927/77 for a single-shot breech-loading rifle, 2646/83 of 1883 for a drop-barrel action, and 7502/88 of 1888 (obtained jointly with C.H. Laubenburg). Three patents granted in 1898 – 4704/98 for a modification of the *Martini action incorporating a loading indicator; 11,468/98 protecting a magazine; and 23,477/98 for another Martini-type action – were granted to 'C.H. Engels, Trading as W. Field'. **6.** Field Rifle Company. Working in Birmingham from 2 King Alfred's Place (1885–96) and 2 Cambridge Street (1897–98), this gunmaking business was managed by William Field (q.v.). Products included the Field dropping-block rifle, cocked by a radial lever on the right side of the breech, and break-open shotguns. Trading seems to have ceased in 1898, when the assets of the company passed to C.B. Engels.

Fielding. W.C. Fielding, a government arms inspector working from 1897 until c. 1907, accepted small-arms marked 'WCF'. *See also* US arms inspectors' marks.

Fieldmaster – 1. A rifle with an under-barrel reservoir, operated by air or carbon dioxide, designed by Jack & John Fletcher and made in Britain by the *Galway Arms Company from 1983 until c. 1990. **2.** Also known as the Model 121A, this .22 rimfire slide-action rifle was made by the *Remington Arms Company between 1936 and 1954, with a protracted break during the Second World War. Based on *Pedersen, Garrison and Loomis patents, it had a plain pistol-grip butt, a finely-grooved slide handle and a three-quarter-length magazine. Abandoned in 1940, the Model 121S chambered the .22 Remington Special rimfire cartridge, whereas the smoothbore Model 121SB (1936–40) could fire ball and shot cartridges with equal facility. **3.** Also known as the Model 572. Introduced in 1959, this was a much-modernised form of the *Remington Arms Company's Model 121A (above) with a new slab-side receiver and a safety bolt running laterally through the rear web of the trigger guard. The butt was a plain straight-comb pattern, and the slide handle was grooved. Among the many variants were the 572BDL (1966–c. 1992), with chequered pistol grip and slide handle; the 572BT Lightweight (1958–62), with an anodised alloy frame and barrel sleeve coloured 'Buckskin Tan', and chrome-plating on the magazine tube, trigger lever and trigger guard; the 572CWB and 572TWB (1958–62) were similar to the 572BT, but in 'Crown Wing Black' and 'Teal Wing Blue' respectively; and the smoothbore 572SB, made only in small numbers in 1967–78. *See also* Sesquicentennial. **4.** A slide-action forty-five-shot BB Gun made in the USA by *Daisy from 1964 until c. 1973. Also known as the Model 26 and Model 572, it was based, with the manufacturer's permission, on the Remington Fieldmaster (above).

Field Model. This brandname was associated with *Mauser-pattern sporting rifles made in the USA in 1962–66 by the *High Standard Manufacturing Company, in .270 Winchester and .30-06. The basic rifle had a plain straight-comb hardwood stock, but a deluxe version was offered with a walnut *Monte Carlo stock.

Fifield & Richardson, Boston, Massachusetts, USA. An 1853-vintage catalogue of this distributor of firearms, accessories and sporting goods notes that the wares included 'air canes, saloon pistols…of English and French Manufacture'.

Finnegan. Peter H. Finnegan of Austin, Illinois, USA, was granted US Patent 504,154 in August 1893 for improvements in the design of the *Turbiaux Protector turret pistol.

Fiocchi. Guilio Fiocchi & C., Fiocchi Munizione SpA, Lecco. The best-known Italian ammunition-making business, Fiocchi has manufactured a range of military and sporting cartridges, identified by the presence of 'G.F.' in their headstamps. The company has also handled a range of blank-firers, and has promoted the Pardini-designed P10 pneumatic competition pistol. This was charged by an underlever and loaded through a Walther-type flip-up port. It was handled in Britain by the *Hull Cartridge Company.

Fiorini. Sestilio Fiorini, Italy. A designer of automatic rifles associated in the 1930s with *Breda.

Firearms… – 1. Firearms Company Ltd, Bridgwater, Somerset, England. This gunmaking business made *Alpine-brand *Mauser-action sporting rifles in 1960–75. Offered in a variety of stocks, with barrels of varying length, the original examples had actions retrieved from war-surplus guns; subsequently they were purchased from *Fabrique Nationale in Belgium and *Santa Barbara in Spain. **2.** Firearms Import & Export Corporation. Trading in 1977 from North West 21st Street in Miami,

Florida, FIE imported and distributed a wide range of European-made firearms and airguns. These included handguns made by *Tanfoglio and Forjas *Taurus, the Italian-made *Tiger air pistol, and a range of Czechoslovak and Hungarian products. The business moved to Hialeah Lakes, Florida, in 1982. Shotguns and black-powder guns were added to the range, but trading ceased in the early 1990s. **3.** Firearms International Corporation, Washington, D.C., USA. This business sold the *Musketeer rifle, built on an *FN-Mauser action.

Firebird. A name given to Hungarian-made pistols (*see* 'FÉG') sold in what was then West Germany by *Hege-Waffen of Schwäbisch Hall. Most prove to have been 9x19 Tokagypts (q.v.) with commercial-grade finish.

Firecat or Astra Firecat. A pocket pistol made in Spain by *Unceta y Compañía of Guernica, based on the *FN-Browning of 1905: 6.35mm, six rounds, hammer fired.

Firefly. This British pressed-metal push-in barrel .177 spring-air pistol is believed to have been made in Birmingham, either by Edwin *Anson or (more probably) by Frank *Clarke. Distributed by the *Midland Gun Company in 1925–33, the smoothbore Firefly is now quite rare.

Fire selector. *See* selective fire.

Firestar. A single-action semi-automatic pistol, derived from the *Colt-Browning, made by *Star–Bonifacio Echeverria SA. Introduced in 1990, the M40 Firestar chambers the .40 S&W cartridge; the M43 (1990) handles the 9mm Parabellum pattern; and the M45 (1992) uses the .45 ACP. All three versions have short barrels and single-column magazines. *See also* Megastar.

Firestone Tire & Rubber Company. *See* Marlin.

Firing mechanism. The trigger lever, sear(s), the hammer or striker, and all relevant pins, screws and springs.

Firing pin. *See* striker.

Firmin. H.G. Firmin. This government arms inspector, working from 1863 until 1881 or later, accepted a variety of small-arms marked 'HGF'. They included Enfield rifle-muskets, Remington cap-lock revolvers, Sharps and Spencer carbines and Remington rolling-block rifles. *See also* US arms inspectors' marks.

First Army Technical Research Institute, Tokyo. Developer of the Type 100 *Arisaka paratroop rifle.

Fischer – 1. Fritz Fischer, Suhl in Thüringen. Listed in the *Deutsches Reichs-Adressbuch* and similar pre-1945 directories as a maker of gun parts and gunsmiths' tools. **2.** Gustav Fischer, or Fisher, New York City. In his book *Small Arms Makers*, Robert E. Gardner describes this gunsmith as a maker of cap-lock rifles 'before and after 1860', but he survived long enough to make spring-air *Gallery Guns in the 1870s. **3.** Richard Fischer, junior, Gera in Thüringen. A retailer of sporting guns and ammunition trading in Germany in 1941. **4.** Willi Fischer, Zella-Mehlis in Thüringen, Germany. Listed in 1939 as a gun-stock maker.

Fisher – 1. Charles Fisher, a gunmaker and proprietor of an 'archery warehouse' was recorded at 8 Prince's Street, Soho, in 1826–78, and at 16 Wardour Street, London S.W., in 1879–81. **2.** Chauncey H. Fisher, Grand Rapids, Michigan, USA. Fisher was the co-patentee (with Frank Simonds and Hugh Ross) of the distinctive spring-air BB Gun made by the *Rapid Rifle Company in accordance with US Patent 614,532 of 13 December 1901. *See also* Calkins, Linderg, Butts & Wheeler. **3.** William Fisher.

This gunmaker, first recorded in Great Alie (*sic*) Street, London in 1816, operated from 1826 to 1833 in partnership with his father, Thomas, from 13 Mount Pleasant, Gray's Inn Lane. Subsequently he traded on his own account from 9 Belvedere Road, Lambeth (subsequently renamed Belvedere Crescent) until 1867.

Fisk. G.D. Fisk, a government arms inspector working in the mid-1870s, accepted small-arms marked 'GDF'. *See also* US arms inspectors' marks.

'Fist Revolver'. This term has been applied to a modification of the pepperbox (q.v.), consisting of an elongated cylinder mounted in an 'open-top' revolver-type frame. The idea was to produce a compact barrelless weapon that could be held in the palm to act either as a knuckleduster or simply to intensify a blow. It is said to have originated in Belgium, the invention of *Mariette. Some Liège-made open-frame revolvers could even be converted to fist patterns simply by detaching the barrel and rammer assembly.

Fitch… – 1. Fitch, Van Vechten & Company, New York City. Ammunition manufacturers active during the American Civil War, often marking their products 'FFV&Co.' **2.** Fitch & Waldo. A distributor of cap-lock revolvers made in the USA in the 1860s by the *Bacon Manufacturing Company of Norwich, Connecticut.

Fitzpatrick. T.J. Fitzpatrick. This government arms inspector, working in the late 1890s, accepted small-arms marked 'TJF'. *See also* US arms inspectors' marks.

'FJA'. Found on US military firearms and accessories. *See* F.J. *Atwood.

'FJ&CO'. An encircled monogram, with a dominant central 'J'. Correctly 'JF&CO.' (q.v.); used by *Janssen, fils & Co.

'FK'. Found on US military firearms and accessories. *See* Frank *Krack.

'FL', 'F.L.', 'F&L', 'F. & L.' – 1. As 'FL': a mark found on the grips of the F.L. Selbstlader or F.L. Armee-Modell, a 7.65mm semi-automatic pistol with the breech-block retained by a pivoting yoke locked by a thumb-screw. Designed in 1913, these weapons were made by Friedrich *Langenhan of Suhl during the First World War. A few short-barrelled/short-grip 7.65mm Modell I guns were also produced, apparently for commercial sale in 1919. The 6.35mm Modell II and the compact 6.35mm Modell III were similar to the Modell I, but the breech-block was locked by a lateral bolt. **2.** Generally found as 'F&L' or 'F.u.L.' Associated with the gunmaking business of *Franken & Lüneschloss, this mark is commonly encountered on single-shot dropping-block rifles made in Germany c. 1910–45. **3.** 'F' and 'L', often accompanied by two crossed airguns. A mark associated with Friedrich *Langenhan of Zella St Blasii and Zella-Mehlis, Thüringen, Germany, used from c. 1880 until 1914 or later.

Flachet. Jérôme Flachet, rue Saint-Louis 24, Saint-Étienne, France. Listed in 1879 as a gunmaker.

'Flag' [The]. A brandname associated with shotgun cartridges sold by *Gale of Barnstaple.

Flagg. J.G. Flagg, a government arms inspector working at the beginning of the twentieth century, accepted small-arms marked 'JGF'. *See also* US arms inspectors' marks.

Flanney Bolt Company. Manufacturer of barrels for the .45 M1911A1 *Government Model pistol during the Second World War.

Flare Projector, Caliber .45. *See* Liberator.

Flash-hider, flash suppressor. A muzzle attachment designed to minimise the effects of propellant flash, generally by using prongs or a pierced tube. It may be combined with a muzzle brake (q.v.), but is rarely particularly effective.

'Flash Junior' [The]. Found on shotgun cartridges loaded and sold in England by *Garrett of Evesham.

Flashlight pistol. *See* S.P. *Cottrell & Son and *Tool pistols.

Flather. Edward Flather, a Federal inspector working in 1862, accepted small-arms marked 'EF'. *See also* US arms inspectors' marks.

Flat-Top or Flat Top [Target] Model. This variant of the Colt *Single Action Army Revolver or Peacemaker was only made in small numbers; production amounted to less than 1,000 in 1888–96, in chamberings ranging from .22 Short rimfire to .476 Eley. A similar quantity of Flat Top Bisley guns was made in 1894–1913. *See also* Bisley Model.

'Fleet' [The]. Found on shotgun cartridges sold in Britain by William *Ford of Birmingham.

Fleetwood. Gustav Erik Fleetwood, one-time director of the government-owned *Husqvarna gun manufactory, 'improved' the Danish *Løbnitz air-powered machinegun. Unfortunately, the trials undertaken in 1846 were so disastrous that the device was speedily abandoned.

Fleischer – 1. Hugo Fleischer, Zella-Mehlis in Thüringen. Listed in the *Deutsches Reichs-Adressbuch* of 1939 as a gun-stock maker. **2.** K. Fleischer, Mehlis in Thüringen, Germany. Listed in 1900 as a gunmaker.

Fleischauer, Fleischhauer – 1. Ernst Fleischauer, Schleusingen in Thüringen. A gunsmith trading in Germany in 1941. **2.** E. Fleischhauer, Suhl in Thüringen, Germany. Listed in directories as a gunmaker, 1914–30.

Fleischmann. August Fleischmann, Suhl in Thüringen, Germany. A gunsmith trading in 1939.

Fletcher – 1. Edward Fletcher, Westgate Street, Gloucester, England. The name of this well-established gunmaking business, later renamed E. Fletcher & Son and Fletchers (Sports) Ltd, has been reported on shotgun cartridges made by *Eley-Kynoch. These also often bear the brandname Gloucester. **2.** J.H. Fletcher, a government inspector working in 1909, accepted US military small-arms marked 'JHF'. *See also* US arms inspectors' marks. **3.** Thomas Fletcher. Listed in 1866–72 as a gunsmith, trading from 42 Poultry, London E.C. Eldon Wolff, in *Air Guns* (1958), records Fletcher as a maker of air canes. **4.** Thomas Fletcher, 161 Westgate Street, Gloucester. This English gunmaker, known for sporting guns and selfcocking *pepperboxes, is listed in directories for 1841–59; then the entry changes to Mrs Elizabeth Fletcher until 1870. A 'Mr Fletcher of Gloucester' entered 12-bore patent snap-action breech-loading shotguns in the trials undertaken by *The Field* in 1866, so a son of Thomas may also have been involved. Details are lacking, however.

'FLH'. Found on US military firearms and accessories. *See* F.L. *Hosmer.

Fliegenschmidt. Max Fliegenschmidt. A gunsmith, or more probably gunmakers' agent, listed in London in 1887 at 44 Moorfields.

Flieger... – 1. Flieger-Gewehr [FG]. A designation applied to a half-stocked variant of the 1915-type *Mauser automatic rifle, tested by the Germans during the First World War. **2.** Flieger-Selbstlade-Karabiner [FSK]. A name applied to the Mexican-designed *Mondragon semi-automatic rifle, made in Switzerland by *SIG and used by the Germans during the First World War.

'Flight' [The]. A shotgun cartridge sold in southern England by Howard *Davis of Winchester.

Flobert. Nicholas Flobert, Paris. The name of this French gunsmith is customarily attached to the primer-propelled cartridge, patented in Europe in the 1840s,

---

FL-SELBSTLADER

This 7.65mm *blowback semi-automatic pistol was promoted by Friedrich *Langenhan of Suhl during the First World War. A separate breech-block was held in the slide by a pivoting yoke and a large knurled-head nut. A large ejection port weakened the slide, and as the lock-nut often worked loose after only a few rounds had been fired, the FL was never regarded as very efficient.

Many guns of this type display military inspectors' marks, and it is thought that most of the 85,000 made went to the army. Changes in the ejection port and trigger/disconnector mechanism were acknowledged in 1916 by the addition of a second *DRGM number to the slide mark.

The 7.65mm FL Selbstlader was made by Langenhan during the First World War. A major weakness was the screw that retained the breech-block which, if it became loose, could allow parts to be blown backward out of the gun.

and to a range of firearms chambering them. These included handguns and long-arms (almost always single-shot) locked by nothing other than the nose of the hammer entering a radially-pivoting breech-block. *See also* Saloon Gun.

FL-Selbstlader. *See* panel, p. 183.

Flürscheim. Michael Flürscheim, or Flürschein, Gaggenau in Baden, Germany. This man was the partner of Theodor *Bergmann in *Eisenwerke Gaggenau.

Fluted chamber. A chamber (q.v.) with longitudinal grooves extending into the bore, but not as far as the mouth. Propellant gas flows down these grooves to 'float' the case, counteracting pressure remaining inside the case. It is associated with actions in which the breech begins opening while the residual pressure is still high. If the chamber wall was plain, internal pressure would stick the body of the cartridge case firmly against the chamber; then any rearward movement of the bolt would tear the base off the cartridge. By floating the case, there is less resistance to movement and the bolt can begin opening without risk of premature damage. Fluted chambers are comparatively common in delayed-blowback military rifles (e.g. CETME, Heckler & Koch G3, Swiss Stgw.57).

'FLZ', 'F.L.Z', sometimes in a circle segmented by three radial lines. A mark associated with Friedrich *Langenhan

of Zella-Mehlis, Germany, used from c. 1922 until 1927 or later.

'FM'. Found on US military firearms and accessories. *See* F.A. *Massey.

'FMAP'. An abbreviated form of Fábrica Militar de Armas Portatiles 'Domingo Matheu' of Rosario, the principal Argentine small-arms factory.

'FMC'. Found on US military firearms and accessories. *See* F.M. *Chapin.

'FME'. A linear monogram with 'F' and 'E' sharing their top bars. Associated with the products of Fabrica de Material del Ejercito of Santiago, Chile. It will be found on the grips of 6.35mm FME or FAMAE Browning-type pistols, although the slides are often marked 'Fabrica de Material de Guerra'.

'FMR'. Found on US military firearms and accessories. *See* Francis M. Ramsey.

'FN', 'F N', 'F.N.', 'FN-...' – 1. Often in the form of a superimposition-type monogram, usually within an oval. Used by *Fabrique Nationale d'Armes de Guerre on firearms ranging from *Browning pistols to *Mauser rifles. Many pre-1905 examples were accompanied by an illustration of a 1900-pattern FN-Browning pistol. 2. Associated with the products of Fabrique Nationale Herstal SA. These have included machine-guns, rifles,

FN-MAUSER RIFLES

FN... (6)

By the middle of 1894, Fabrique Nationale had supplied Mauser rifles and cartridges to the Netherlands, Spain, Serbia, Brazil, Chile, Brazil, China, Norway and Costa Rica. In December, Chile approached the company to place an order for 60,000 *Mauser-system rifles, but Mauser objected to the fulfilment of non-Belgian orders, and the irritated Chileans placed the order with *Loewe. In December 1894, Mauser asked Fabrique Nationale to cease using the patents covering the 1893 or Spanish-pattern Mauser on the grounds that these were not part of the original 1891 agreement.

Fabrique Nationale tried to fight the injunction throughout 1895, but eventually it was decided at a high level in the government that there were no real grounds for objection. FN conceded the case. In February 1896, therefore, FN and Loewe negotiated a new contract with Mauser. Finally, in January 1897, a production agreement was signed by the principal manufacturers of Mauser rifles – FN, Mauser, DWM and OEWG – under which each was allocated a specific quota.

Contract work continued until August 1914, ceased for the duration

of the First World War, then resumed in 1919. Work continued between the wars; by 1940, FN-Mauser rifle production, excluding Belgian orders, had amounted to at least 517,000 since 1899. The Fusil d'Infanterie Modèle 1922 (1922–25), in 7x57, 7.65x53 and 7.9x57, was the first post-war Mauser to be made in the reconditioned and re-equipped Herstal factory. It was similar mechanically to the Gew. 98, but had a tangent-leaf back sight, a hand guard running forward from the receiver ring and a conventional bayonet attachment incorporating a muzzle ring. The barrel band was particularly narrow and the nose-cap was as simple as it could be.

Although guns of 1922 type were sold in quantity to Brazil, the Fusil Court Mle 1924 and Mle 1924/30 were much more successful. About 650,000 were made, customarily with a pistol-grip stock and a German H-pattern nose-cap. Production ceased when the Germans invaded Belgium in May 1940, although subsequently the Fabrique Nationale factory made parts for the Kar. 98k.

The Fusil Mle 1935 was also a standard 1898-pattern Mauser. The earliest examples were converted in the state arms factory – Manufacture d'Armes de l'État – from Gew. 98s received as reparations from Germany after First World War, but no sooner

had Fabrique Nationale begun to make new guns than the Germans invaded Belgium and work stopped. A few sniper rifles were distinguished by ring mounts above the chamber and on the receiver bridge, and by a special rubber cheek piece fitted in a metal cradle on the comb of the butt.

The Fusil Mle 35/46, made in small numbers once production had begun again after the Second World War, was a revision of existing Mle 35 service rifles for the US .30-06 cartridge. Alterations included a groove cut across the face of the chamber to accommodate the longer American cartridge, and the guides on the receiver recut to accept US chargers. Production of new .30-06 Mle 1950 rifles with an elongated magazine well eventually began in the Herstal factory.

A few sporters were made prior to the First World War, using actions that had been in stock since the 1890s. Chambered for 7x57 or 7.65x53 cartridges, they cocked on the closing stroke of the bolt and were stocked in minimal English fashion. Most of the guns made between the wars were based on the 1924-pattern military action, usually with a straight-comb half-stock.

Work began again in 1947, the earliest guns being assembled from a selection of pre-war and wartime parts. Bolt handles were swept

handguns and ammunition. **3.** FN-Baby. *See* Baby. **4.** FN-Browning. A trademark used by Fabrique Nationale d'Armes de Guerre and its successors, resulting from an agreement signed with John *Browning on 24 May 1907. **5.** FN-Carabine. The decision to make rimfire sporting guns was taken as early as November 1896, when the board of directors voted to make 50,000 simple .22 bolt-action sporting rifles. However, production did not begin until 1898. Available as a rifled .22 or smoothbore for .22 rimfire or 6mm Flobert cartridges, the most basic Fabrique Nationale sporting rifle was locked simply by turning the bolt handle down ahead of the receiver bridge. The plain half-stock had a short round-tipped fore-end, but lacked a butt plate. A deluxe version was also made, with a chequered walnut stock and improvements in the fittings. A .22-calibre military trainer had a full-length fore-end, a single barrel band, a simple nose-cap that could take a knife bayonet, and a leaf-and-slider back sight. The 9mm pattern was longer and heavier than the .22, and usually had a pivoting-lever extractor on the right side of the breech. **6.** FN-Mauser rifles: *see* panel, below. **7.** FN-Metallique, or Metallique-FN. A trade-name used by *Fabrique Nationale d'Armes de Guerre on shotgun ammunition, c. 1925–40. **8.** FN-Saive rifle (SAFN). This gas-operated auto-loader was originally developed in the late 1930s by Dieudonné *Saive, perhaps by adapting the *Tokarev, but the Germans invaded Belgium before preliminary work had been completed. Saive was one of several high-ranking FN technicians who escaped from Herstal in 1941 (taking blueprints with them) and eventually began working in Britain, where the first *SLEM rifles were made in *Enfield in 1943. These were refined in 1947–48, becoming Fusil Semi-automatique Mle 1949 (SAFN), often mistakenly listed as the *ABL. About 160,000 guns were made by Fabrique Nationale d'Armes de Guerre in Herstal-lèz-Liège, c. 1949–52, in 7x57, 7.65x53, 7.9x57 and .30-06. The Mle 49 had a tall squared receiver, carrying the back sight and its prominent guards, and the conventional pistol-grip stock held a single swivel-carrying band. Charger guides milled in the receiver top ahead of the back-sight base allowed the magazine to be reloaded through the open action. Muzzle brake/compensators were optional; semi-automatic and selective-fire versions could be made; and a sniper version with a telescope sight produced by Société Belge d'Optique et d'Instruments de Précision was issued in small numbers. Although guns had been exported in quantity to Colombia, Egypt, Indonesia and Luxembourg by 1952, the Mle 49 proved to be unsuitable for prolonged arduous use and was replaced by the FAL.

downward, although the first guns retained a simple military-style single-stage trigger. Chamberings were confined to 7x57, 8x57, .270 Winchester and .30-06. Changes were soon made: the trigger and magazine floor-plate release were improved, and the left wall of the receiver was raised. Chamberings ranging from .220 Swift to 10.75x68 were added. Guns intended for sale in North America had Monte Carlo-type stocks and Tri-Range back sights; most European examples had straight combs and folding two-leaf sights. Presentation-grade guns were introduced in the mid-1950s, with selected stocks and engraved metalwork, but they were discontinued in 1963.

Known as the Deluxe or Serie 200 after the introduction of the 300-pattern guns in 1957, the standard FN-Mauser action was discontinued in the early 1960s. A Magnum version appeared in 1953, with the magazine box and the bolt head altered to accommodate large-diameter cartridges. Chambered for a variety of *Holland & Holland and *Winchester cartridges, it was abandoned about 1963. A single-shot Bench Rest action was introduced in 1955, distinguished by a solid-base receiver and three different bolts to handle cartridges ranging from .222 Remington to belted magnums.

The Serie 300 action, introduced in Europe in 1956 and later known as the Supreme, had a radial safety behind the bolt handle, a smooth-topped receiver bridge, an improved trigger and a hinged magazine floor-plate. Actions of this type, used by *Colt, *Harrington & Richardson, *High Standard and *Marlin, were made in sizes ranging from No. 1 (for standard-length cartridges such as .270 Winchester and .30-06) to the No. 7 for magnums such as .264 and .338 Winchester. The Mle 30-11 sniper rifle was made c. 1975–87 in 7.62x51 and 7.9x57. It had a special heavy barrel and a butt with a rear

The FN-Mauser Model 30-11 sniper rifle, built on sporting-type bolt actions c. 1975–87, could be obtained in 7.62x51 and 7.9x57. This gun has a target-type aperture sight by Anschütz, but optical sights could be supplied to order. Note the unmistakable design of the adjustable butt.

section that could slide vertically. Most rifles were fitted with mounts for optical or electro-optical sights, and had a rail under the fore-end for a sling mount or a MAG-type bipod.

9. FN-Sauer rifle. FN Herstal SA made a small quantity of these in 1977–82 on the basis of the ★Sauer Model 80. They were distinguished by a massive forged-steel receiver separating the fore-end from the hog's-back butt. The woodwork was chequered, a ventilated rubber butt plate was standard, and chamberings ranged from .270 Winchester to 8x68S.

'FNA'. A linear monogram with 'F' and 'A' formed from the tails of 'N'. Associated with the products of Fabbrica Nazionale d'Armi of Brescia, makers of the Sosso pistols.

'FNAB'. *See* Fabbrica Nazionale d'Armi, Brescia.

FNC. An abbreviated form of Fabrique Nationale Carbine (or Carabine), a 5.56mm automatic rifle that replaced the unsuccessful ★CAL in the 1970s. It has been adopted by Sweden as the Ak-5, being made there by ★Forenade Fabriksverken AB.

'fnh'. This code, granted in 1941, will be found on pistols and small-arms components made by Böhmische Waffenfabrik AG in Prague during the German occupation of Czechoslovakia.

FN Herstal SA. Successor to Fabrique Nationale d'Armes de Guerre (q.v.).

Föckel. Hilmar Föckel, Pössneck in Thüringen. A retailer of sporting guns and ammunition trading in Germany in 1941.

Foehl – 1. Charles Foehl, a US gunmaker received US Patent 417,672 of 17 December 1889 to protect a readily detachable revolver cylinder. Foehl had been granted an earlier patent to protect the cylinder-rotating pawl incorporated in revolvers made briefly by Henry ★Deringer & Company of Philadelphia. **2.** Foehl & Weeks Manufacturing Company, Philadelphia, Pennsylvania, USA. This gunmaking business made solid-frame and break-open revolvers under names such as Columbian and Perfect in 1891–94. Some guns incorporated a removable cylinder system patented by Charles Foehl in December 1889.

Fogerty – 1. Valentine Fogerty of Boston, Massachusetts, was granted a series of US patents in the years immediately after the Civil War. They included no. 46,459 of 21 February 1865, 59,126 of 23 October 1866 (part-assigned to Paul Todd), and 82,819 of 6 October 1868, all protecting 'magazine rifles'. Two later patents – 86,520 and 117,398 of 2 February 1869 and 25 July 1871 respectively – protected a little-known single-shot bolt-action gun. **2.** Fogerty Arms Company, 'Corner of Harrison Avenue', Boston, Massachusetts, USA. Active in 1866–68, until succeeded by the ★American Repeating Rifle Company, this business made rifles in accordance with patents granted to Valentine Fogerty. The best-known version is the lever-action repeater protected by patents granted in 1865–68, with a tube magazine in the butt and a general overall resemblance to the ★Spencer. However, Fogerty also produced a small number of bolt-action rifles, patented in 1869–71. Production of the lever-action guns, chambered for .56-50 Spencer (military) or .40 rimfire (sporting) ammunition, ceased when the assets of the American Repeating Rifle Company were acquired by ★Winchester in 1869.

Föhrenbach. Albert Föhrenbach GmbH, Falke-Werke; Wennigsen bei Hannover, Germany. This metalworking company was founded in February 1949 to make and recondition conveyor-belt equipment, but began to make airguns and amusement-arcade shooting booths in 1950.

Spring-air rifles ranging from a junior barrel-cocker to a powerful underlever design were made until 1958, alongside a top-lever-cocking pistol and a single ★Bügelspanner Gallery Gun. Undoubtedly the Falke Model 80 and Model 90 were inspired by the BSA ★Airsporter, sharing a similar-looking underlever mechanism and a loading tap. It has often been claimed that BSA 'copied the Falke', but the Airsporter was in series production before Föhrenbach had even begun trading. Although the Falke guns offered good quality, they could not compete with the Mayer & Grammelspacher ★Dianas or the ★Weihrauch HW35; production ended in 1958 and, while guns continued to be sold for a short time, Föhrenbach was liquidated in 1961.

Follower. The mobile floor of the magazine that supports the cartridges.

Folger. William M. Folger. This government arms inspector, a lieutenant-commander in the US Navy, accepted Hotchkiss bolt-action rifles in 1879–80. They were marked 'WMF'. *See also* US arms inspectors' marks.

Folgore. This brandname, Italian for 'falcon', was used on a 4.5mm- or 5.5mm-calibre gas-powered rifle made in the 1960s by ★Armigas-Comega of Gardone Val Trompia.

Follett, Colyton and Seaton, Devon. The name of this English country gunmaker has been reported on sporting guns and ammunition dating from pre-1914 days.

Folsom. H. & D. Folsom Arms Company, New York City, USA. Founded 1860, this gunmaking business ultimately purchased such companies as the ★Crescent Arms Company. Trading from 314 Broadway, New York City, in 1916.

FOM. *See* Foreign Material Number.

Fontaney, rue Désirée 34, Saint-Étienne, France. Listed in 1879 as a maker of gun parts and accessories.

Fontvieille, rue d'Annonay 16, Saint-Étienne, France. Listed in 1892 as a gunmaker.

Foote. George B. Foote, a Federal government inspector working in 1862–63, accepted small-arms marked 'GBF'. *See also* US arms inspectors' marks.

Footscray. Ammunition Factory No. 1, Footscray, Melbourne, Victoria. Known prior to 1921 as the ★Colonial Ammunition Company, subsequently this cartridge-making factory was taken over by the Australian government. A variety of small-arms ammunition was made during the Second World War.

Forager. A 20-bore shotgun adaptation of the 1873-pattern Trapdoor ★Springfield rifle, 1,376 being made in Springfield Armory in 1881–85. They had distinctive short tapering fore-ends.

Forbes – 1. 'Feeder Factory', Lachlan Street, Forbes, New South Wales, Australia. This was established in 1942 to supply a few SMLE components to the ★Orange factory. Its products were marked 'FA'. **2.** Andrew Forbes, an 'Engineer' living at 136 Otley Road, Leeds, Yorkshire (according to British Patent 12,869/06 of 1906), designed an 'air-toy'. By stretching the imagination, this could be classed as an airgun. **3.** F.F. Forbes. A brandname associated with shotguns made in Norwich, Connecticut, by the ★Crescent Arms Company. Possibly a distributor.

Ford – 1. Elbert L. Ford, a lieutenant-colonel in the US Army, working in the late 1930s, inspected and accepted .45 M1911A1 (Colt) pistols marked 'ELF'. *See also* US arms inspectors' marks. **2.** Richard Ford. A gunsmith trading from 1, and later 2, Lambeth Street, Hooper

Square, London E., in 1860–68. **3.** William Ford, Eclipse Works, Birmingham, Warwickshire. Ford began trading at 23 Loveday Street in 1885 and had moved the Eclipse Works to 15 St Mary's Row by 1889. His marks have been reported on shotgun cartridges, loaded from *Kynoch or *Eley-Kynoch components. These were sold under a variety of brandnames, including Eclipse and Fleet. Ford is also known to have made, or marked, sporting guns and accessories.

'Fordingbridge' [The]. A mark found on 12-bore shotgun cartridges made by *Eley and sold in southern England by *Alexanders of Fordingbridge.

Fore-end. That part of the stock beneath the barrel. It may extend to the muzzle or, commonly in sporting patterns, only to half-length. A fore-end that flares outward to provide a better grip is known as a beaver-tail. The fore-end tip may be rounded; have a pronounced downward curl (schnabel tip); or display a curious parrot-beak derived from a pattern introduced by Alexander Henry in the 1870s.

Forehand – 1. Sullivan Forehand. This gunmaker was the co-designer with Henry C. *Wadsworth of a revolver protected by US Patent 162,162 of April 1875, and another gun – with a detachable side-plate – protected by US Patent 193,367 of 24 July 1877. These were made by Forehand & Wadsworth. **2.** Forehand Arms Company, Worcester, Massachusetts, USA. The trading style of Forehand & Wadsworth from c. 1894 to 1902. Simple single-barrel box-lock central-hammer and hammerless shotguns were made alongside inexpensive revolvers. **3.** Forehand Model or Forehand Model 1891. A brandname found on a solid-frame non-ejector five-shot revolver, similar to the *XL DA No. 6, made by *Hopkins & Allen for Forehand & Wadsworth. A safety catch was set into the back strap of the butt, and the hammer was often enclosed in the frame. **4.** Forehand & Wadsworth, Worcester, Massachusetts, USA. Sullivan Forehand and Henry Wadsworth joined Allen & Wheelock in the 1850s, but Wheelock died in 1863 and the business passed to Ethan *Allen. However, Allen died in 1871, and Forehand & Wadsworth was formed in 1872. The partnership began by making a .41 rimfire single-shot cartridge derringer, similar externally to the *Southerner, as well as solid-frame five-shot .32 and .38 pocket revolvers produced in accordance with a patent granted in 1877. The company also made simple single-barrel box-lock side-hammer, central-hammer and hammerless shotguns from 1887 onward. Work continued until the death of Forehand in 1898, Wadsworth having died six years earlier; as activity had been reduced to buying-in guns, the assets of what had become the Forehand Arms Company were acquired by Hopkins & Allen in 1902.

Foreign Material Number (FOM). A code used by US military and governmental agencies to identify arms and equipment originating outside the USA. They are comparable in some respects to the *Nato Standard Numbers, although the categorisation differs. The first component replicates that of the NSN (1005 for guns and small-arms with calibres of less than 30mm), but this is suffixed by a country designator, a matériel sub-category, the calibre and a specific-item identifier. Matériel sub-category numbers are: '1', handgun; '2', rifle; '3', submachine-gun; '4', machine-gun; '5', automatic cannon; and '6', grenade launcher. A typical FOM, for the original AK or *Kalashnikov assault rifle reads 1005-2-2-7.62-21; modifications are usually indicated by additional suffixes, the standard wood-butt AKM being 1005-2-2-7.62-21-2. A change in calibre customarily requires a new specific-item identifier, so the standard AK-74 became 1005-2-2-5.45-2. A more comprehensive list of FOM codes will be found in Edward C. Ezell, *Small Arms Today* (second edition), but it should be noted that the prefatory '0' in national identifiers is not always present.

Formost. A brandname used on firearms distributed in the USA by the J.C. *Penney Company.

Forrest & Sons, Kelso, Roxburghshire. The name of this Scottish gunmaking business has been reported on shotgun cartridges, loaded using *Eley-Kynoch components and sold under the brandnames Border and Tweed.

Forrester – 1. Harold J.C. Forrester, a British patent agent, had chambers at 75 New Street, Birmingham, and 88–90 Chancery Lane, London WC2. He acted for William *Baker & Arthur Marsh, and Alfred *Hale & Ernest Harris – see British Patents 160,057 and 166,759. The agency was renamed Forrester, Ketley & Company (following entry) in 1931. **2.** Forrester, Ketley & Company. Successor to Harold J.C. Forrester, this patent agency still retained the chambers in New Street and Chancery Lane (known as Central House and Jessel Chambers respectively) when it acted for *BSA and Claude *Perry. See British Patent 607,045.

Forsvarets Fabriksverken AB, Eskilstuna, Sweden. See FFV.

Forsyth. Alexander Forsyth & Company was formed in 1809 by the inventor of the percussion-ignition lock, Alexander Forsyth (1768–1843), and his partners James Brougham and C.B. Uther. It traded from 10 Piccadilly in succession to the Forsyth Patent Gun Company. Forsyth and Brougham withdrew in 1816, but Uther continued alone for some years from 8 Leicester Street, Leicester Square. However, although exhibiting guns at the Great Exhibition of 1851, trading had ceased within another year.

Forsythe. A.H. Forsythe. This government arms inspector, working during the First World War, accepted .45 M1911 (Colt) pistols marked 'AHF'. *See also* US arms inspectors' marks.

Fortuna – 1. Found in the headstamps of shotgun cartridges made in Germany prior to 1914, probably in the Karlsruhe factory of *Deutsche Waffen- und Munitionsfabriken. **2.** A small 6.35mm-calibre Spanish semi-automatic pistol, based on the *FN-Browning of 1905, made in Guernica by *Esperanza y Unceta: seven rounds, hammer fired.

Foss. Wilhelm Foss bought the *Venuswaffenwerk business of Oskar Will in 1921, continuing airgun production until the Second World War. He is best remembered as the designer of the *Tell III spring-air pistol, patented in Britain (no. 483,899) in 1938.

Foster – 1. Arthur James Foster, Sheffield House, The Bull Ring, Kidderminster, Worcestershire. This provincial gunmaking business – then being run by S. Foster – marked shotgun cartridges sold under the brandname Ay-Jay-Effe. **2.** Frank A. Foster, Norwich, Connecticut. Designer of a safety mechanism for break-open guns, protected by US Patent 545,355 of 27 August 1895, and an ejector for break-open guns protected by 645,705 of 20 March 1900. The latter was assigned to the *Crescent

Fire Arms Company. **3.** George F. Foster, Mohawk, New York State. This gunsmith was co-patentee with his father, George P. Foster (below), of a 'cartridge retractor for firearm' – US Patent 49,994 of 19 September 1865 – and a 'breechloading firearm', 56,399 of 17 July 1866. The patent drawings indicate that the latter was based on the *Burnside carbine. **4.** George P. Foster, Taunton, Massachusetts, and Bristol, Rhode Island. Trained as a gunsmith, active from about 1850 onward, Foster made *Klein-patent needle rifles and the *Howard breech-loading carbines. Subsequently he became works superintendent of the *Burnside Fire Arms Company in Rhode Island, where he was granted US Patent 27,791 of 10 April 1860 (protecting the perfected Burnside cartridge case) and 56,399 of 17 July 1866 for an improved Burnside-pattern breech-loading firearm. **5.** Richard Foster. An English gun, airgun and air-cane maker, active at 9 Loveday Street, Birmingham, in 1873–86, subsequently Foster moved to the 'Back of 132 Steelhouse Lane' and was still trading there when relevant directory entries ceased in 1892. **6.** Foster, Lott & Company, Dorchester, Dorset. The name of this English distributor of sporting guns, ammunition and accessories has been found on shotgun cartridges.

'Fourlong' [The]. Associated with a .410 shotgun cartridge made in Britain by *Eley-Kynoch Ltd.

Fournier – 1. Russel[l] J. Fournier. This government arms inspector, working in 1937–38, accepted military-issue .45 M1911A1 (Colt) pistols marked 'RJF'. *See also* US arms inspectors' marks. **2.** Fournier frères, aux Grandes Molières, Saint-Étienne. A specialist gun-barrel maker working in France in the late 1870s.

'Fourten' [The]. A mark associated with .410 shotgun ammunition loaded by the *New Explosives Company Ltd c. 1909–18, prior to the acquisition of the company by *Explosives Trades Ltd, and thereafter by *Eley-Kynoch Ltd.

'Fourtenner' [The]. Found on .410 shotgun ammunition manufactured by the *Mullerite Cartridge Works, Birmingham.

Foussard. Lucien Foussard, 7 place Villeboeuf, Saint-Étienne, France. Listed in 1951 as a gunmaker.

Fowler. T. Fowler, Dublin. The marks of this Irish gunmaker have been reported on self-cocking *pepperboxes dating from the middle of the nineteenth century.

Fox – 1. A compact Czechoslovakian 6.35mm semi-automatic pistol made first by Alois *Tomiška of Pilsen (folding-trigger pattern, 1919–21), then by *Jihočeská Zbrojovka of Prague (folding-trigger type, 1921–22) and finally, with a conventional trigger guard, by *Česká Zbrojovka AS of Prague (c. 1922–36). **2.** A.H. Fox Gun Company, Philadelphia, Pennsylvania, USA. This gunmaking business continued to make the hammerless top-lever box-lock shotguns that had been offered by the *Philadelphia Arms Company in 1902–05. Initially the Fox Gun Company traded from premises at the corner of Bristol and Wayne Streets, but Fox relinquished his interests in 1911. A move to 4600 North 18th Street followed. Some of the guns made after the First World War embodied a single trigger mechanism patented by Joseph Kautzky of Iowa. The assets and liabilities of the Fox Gun Company were acquired in 1930 by the *Savage Arms Company, which thereafter made Fox-type shotguns in its Utica factory until the beginning of the Second World War. **3.**

Ansley H. Fox. Born in Atlanta, Georgia, in 1875, Fox is best remembered as a shotgun designer. Relevant US Patents were 563,153 of 30 June 1896, sought from Baltimore; 714,688 of 2 December 1902 (assigned to the *Philadelphia Gun Company); 796,119 of 1 August 1905, for a barrel-locking device assigned to the A.H. Fox Gun Company; 801,862 of 17 October 1905; 810,046 of 16 January 1906 for a barrel-locking mechanism; and 921,220 of 11 May 1908, granted jointly with George A. *Horne. These top-lever box-lock guns were made by the *Baltimore Arms Company, the *Philadelphia Arms Company, the A.H. Fox Gun Company and the Savage Arms Company until 1941. Ansley Fox died in New York in 1948. **4.** Charles Fox, Canterbury, Kent. The name of this English country gunmaker has been reported on sporting guns and shotgun ammunition. **5.** George H. Fox. This gunmaker (c. 1831–1900) was granted US Patent 98,579 of 4 January 1870 to protect a shotgun with barrels that pivoted laterally to the right. Guns of this type were introduced in the mid-1870s by the *American Arms Company, but only a few had been made before an improved version was developed. Subsequent US Patents included 196,748 of 5 November 1877; 196,749 of 6 November 1877 (jointly with Henry F. *Wheeler); and 198,973 of 8 January 1878. Fox was also granted US Patents 255,274 of 21 March 1882 for a 'Firearm Lock'; 278,423 of 29 May 1883 for a fore-end attachment system; 278,424 of 29 May 1883 for an extractor mechanism; and 422,930 of 11 March 1890 (with Wheeler) for a revolver hammer that could be rotated to full-cock and released by a second pull on the trigger, or, selectively, by pulling through on the trigger. These guns were made by the American Arms Company.

'FP' – 1. A superimposition-type monogram, with both letters equally prominent and often placed diagonally. Associated with Franz *Pfannl of Krems an der Donau, maker of the *Erika pistol. **2.** A superimposed-type monogram, often encircled, with 'F' dominant and the tail of the 'P' projecting laterally. Used by Friedrich *Pickert of Zella St Blasii and Zella-Mehlis on a range of compact revolvers.

'F.P.D.F.' Found beneath a Brazilian enwreathed-star on small-arms used by the Força Policia Distrito Federal (federal district police force).

FPK. A sniper-rifle adaptation of the standard Romanian AIM or *Kalashnikov assault rifle, with a distinctive cutaway butt modelled on the *Dragunov or SVD design. Apparently it has been made only in small numbers.

'F.P.S.', 'FPS'. Marks used on sporting guns and shotgun ammunition distributed in the Isle of Wight by F.P. *Spencer of Newport.

'FR' – 1. A superimposed-type cursive monogram found on the grips of Belgian .44-calibre *Frontier revolvers, made by Felix *Raick of Liège prior to 1910. **2.** A superimposed-letter monogram. Found on French pistols: *see* 'RF' monogram. **3.** Found on US military firearms and accessories. *See* Frank *Richard, Frederick *Rogers and Franklin *Root.

Fraissenon, rue Badouillère, Saint-Étienne, France. Listed in 1879 as a gunmaker.

Franchi – 1. Luigi Franchi SpA, Fornaci, near Brescia, Italy. Better known for shotguns, Franchi made small numbers of the 7.62mm LF-59 in the early 1960s. The gas-operated rifle bore a superficial resemblance to the FN FAL, and was also locked by tilting the tail of the breech-block down against a transverse shoulder in the receiver. Fixed- and folding-butt versions were made, but the Italian Army preferred the *Beretta BM-59. **2.** Franchi-Llama SA, Portal de Gamarra, Vittoria, Spain. This export agency, specialising in sporting guns and handguns, is said to have handled airguns made by some of the smaller Spanish companies. None has yet been authenticated.

Francis – **1.** C. Francis & Son, Peterborough, Northamptonshire. The name of this gunmaker has been found on Demon-brand shotgun cartridges made by the *Midland Gun Company. **2.** Francis & Dean, St Mary's Hill, Stamford, Lincolnshire. The name of this gunmaking partnership has been recorded on Russian-made *Baikal shotgun cartridges dating from the 1960s. These bore the tradename 'Hy-Bird'.

Franck. Ern. Frederick Franck. Listed as a member of the London gun trade by H.J. Blanch, writing in *Arms & Explosives* in 1909, Franck is more likely to have been a representative for European (most probably German) interests. An office was maintained at 4 Cullum Street, London E.C., in 1879–80 only.

Francotte. Auguste *Francotte, Liège. A Belgian gunmaker, working in the 1830s and a member of the *Société des Anglais in the mid-1850s. A maker of *Adams-pattern double-action cap-lock revolvers prior to 1860; of pinfire cutlass revolvers in the early 1860s; and possibly also of the prototype &Le Mat revolvers popular in the Confederate States of America during the Civil War. Francotte also made about 4,000 M/69 *Werder carbines for the Bavarian Army in 1869–70, and others destined for gendarmerie use or commercial sale. Member of the *Petit Syndicat, formed in Herstal in 1870, then of the *Grand Syndicat. A founding shareholder in *Fabrique Nationale d'Armes de Guerre in 1889, when the signatory was Ernest Francotte. Offices were maintained in London in the late nineteenth century, initially at 110 Cannon Street, E.C., in 1877. The premises moved to 19 Basinghall Street in 1884, 130 London Wall in 1885, and lastly to 24 Great Winchester Street in 1889. No directory entries occur after 1893. Although never renowned as particularly innovative, Francotte made bolt-action and break-open sporting guns prior to 1939, often selling them in North America through agencies such as *Von Lengerke & Detmold and *Abercrombie & Fitch. Mauser-type rifles, often exquisitely decorated, were being offered in the 1990s – short, standard and magnum – for chamberings as diverse as .218 Bee and .505 Gibbs Magnum. Single- and double-barrelled box- and side-lock Double Rifles are also being promoted in chamberings including 6.5x50R and 7x65R. *See also* Marga and Martini-Francotte.

Frank. A.L. Frank Exportgesellschaft. Better known by the 'Alfa' acronym, thanks largely to a reprint of the impressive catalogue of 1911 in recent years, this Hamburg based trading company enjoyed great success prior to 1918. However, very little is known about its post-1918 history, except that Georg Frank seems to have been a successor. Trading probably ceased in the early 1930s.

Frankenau. Otto Frankenau. This German inventor, domiciled in Magdeburg, patented his 'Combination Pocket-Book & Revolver' (known in Britain as a Revolver Purse) in the autumn of 1877. Drawings accompanying British Patent 3375/1877 illustrate a pepperbox, but the finalised version incorporated a small

5mm six-shot double-action pinfire revolver. The gun was hidden inside a two-compartment sheet-metal case, one portion of which could be opened to contain coins. The trigger could be unfolded and pressed to fire the gun, automatically opening the muzzle flap before the shot was fired.

Franken & Lünenschloss, Suhl in Thüringen, Mühlplatz 4 am Wasser. Directories published in the 1920s list the principal wares of this partnership as 'hunting and best-quality guns of all types; ammunition'. Listed in 1930 as a weapons maker, when the business was owned by L. Mocker & H. Schaum; in 1939 as a weapons maker ('Inh. Hans Schaum'); and in 1940 as a *Waffenfabrik u. Grosshandlung* ('Weapons maker and Wholesaler'). Franken u. Lünenschloss made a range of small-calibre rifles marked 'F. & L.'; many of these incorporated the single-shot action now associated with Hermann *Weihrauch KG.

Frankford Arsenal, Frankford, Pennsylvania. The principal US Army small-arms ammunition factory, this was established in 1815. In addition to a wide range of cartridges – ranging from Civil War .56-50 *Spencer rimfires to .30-06 Springfields – Frankford has made small-arms and range-finders. The site was greatly enlarged shortly before the Second World War, increasing ammunition-making capacity greatly. Most cartridges can be identified by their 'FA' *headstamps.

Franklin. C.W. Franklin. A name found on shotguns handled in the USA by the H. & D. *Folsom Arms Company, prior to 1914, possibly imported from Europe. *See also* Benjamin Franklin.

Frankonia. *See* Waffen-Frankonia.

Fraser – **1.** Daniel Mackintosh Fraser began trading as a gunmaker in 1873, at 22 Greenside Place, Edinburgh, but had moved to 18 Leith Walk by 1874. He was granted a patent jointly with Alex. *Henry – to whom Fraser had been apprenticed – to protect an auxiliary fore-trigger for match rifles, but then entered into partnership with his younger brother to form D. & J. Fraser (below). Daniel Fraser was also granted British Patent 5111/79 of 13 December 1879 to protect a self-cocking drop-barrel action, and another to protect the Fraser dropping-block rifle. A patent was granted in 1885 for a telescope sight, in an offset mount on the left side of the breech, and another followed in 1895 for an improved short-pull trigger mechanism and an intercepting safety bar for bolt-action rifles. **2.** Daniel Fraser & Company. After the failure of D. & J. Fraser in 1889, Daniel Mackintosh Fraser continued trading under his own name with the assistance of his sons, Donald and James. The premises in Leith Street Terrace were supplemented by a workshop in Easter Road and a shooting ground near the village of Duddingston. Daniel Fraser died in 1901, leaving the business to be run by his sons. It became Daniel Fraser & Company Ltd in 1911, lasting until liquidated in the summer of 1917. The Frasers offered a range of sporting guns and rifles, the largest being marketed under the brand-name Velox, whereas the target rifles were usually marked 'Fraser's Special' or simply 'Special'. **3.** D. & J. Fraser, Edinburgh, Scotland. This partnership of Daniel Mackintosh and John Fraser was formed in 1878, trading from 4 Leith Street Terrace. It operated until 1889, when the brothers apparently went their own ways. **4.** Donald Fraser. Son of Daniel Fraser (above), this Scottish gunmaker was granted several British patents to protect an improved single-trigger mechanism (1903) and a telescope sight (1915). **5.** John Fraser. Listed at 1 Frederick Place, Edinburgh, this Scottish gun business operated briefly in 1890–98. It is believed to have been operated by the brother of Daniel Mackintosh Fraser, and to have been a distributor, simply marking the firearms that had been purchased elsewhere. Shotgun cartridges made by ★Eley Bros. have been found with appropriate marks. **6.** Norman Fraser. Trading from Station Road, Churchdown, Gloucestershire, this gunmaker offered shotgun cartridges made by ★Eley-Kynoch under the name 'Chosen'. **7.** Fraser Arms Company, Inc., Fraser, Michigan, USA. Maker of the Fraser 25 pocket pistol, a successor to the otherwise identical ★Bauer pattern.

'FRB'. Found on US military firearms and accessories. See Freeman R. ★Bull.

Freeman – 1. Austin T. Freeman, Binghampton, New York State, USA. Freeman was the grantee in December 1862 of US Patent 37,091, which protected a cylinder-axis pin/locking catch assembly that allowed the entire cylinder to be taken out of the left side of a revolver. **2.** William C. Freeman. Based first in New York City, then in Worcester, Massachusetts, this gunmaker was the agent for ★Joslyn rifles and carbines during the American Civil War. Production was sub-contracted to Asa ★Waters.

Freeney's, High Street, Galway, Ireland. The name of this gunmaker has been reported on shotgun cartridges sold under the brandname Atom. It is not known whether they pre-date the partition of Ireland in 1922.

Fremont. Robert Fremont, employed by the ★ArmaLite Division of the Fairchild Engine & Airplane Corporation, made improvements in the ArmaLite AR-10 and AR-15 rifles, 1956–58.

French... – 1. French Model. A name given in the 1870s by E. ★Remington & Sons to a version of the standard military ★rolling-block rifle chambering the French rimmed 11mm (Gras) cartridge; the French 1866-pattern sabre bayonet was customary. See also Civil Guard Model, Egyptian Model and Spanish Model. **2.** French & Son, Buckingham, Buckinghamshire. The name of this English country gunmaker has been reported on shotgun cartridges made by ★Nobel prior to 1914.

Freund – 1. A. & H. Freund, Suhl in Thüringen. A gunmaker active in Germany in 1914–20. **2.** Frank W. Freund, Cheyenne, Wyoming, and Denver Colorado. This gunsmith (active 1867–93) patented an improved Sharps-type action in August 1876. The round-topped breech-block was allowed to move backward as it dropped. When the breech lever was closed, the block moved up and forward to cam the cartridge-case forward into the breech. ★Wyoming Saddle Guns often had patented ★More Light sights.

Freyssinet, place Dorian 1, Saint-Étienne, France. Listed in 1892 as a gunmaker, formerly a partner in ★Schmitt et Freyssinet.

Friedrich – 1. A breech-loading rifle submitted to the Austro-Hungarian rifle trials of 1866. The ★Wänzl design was preferred. **2.** Carl Friedrich. A gunsmith active in Zella St Blasii in the 1860s, Friedrich is known to have made sporting firearms and spring-air ★Bügelspanner Gallery Guns.

Fritsch. O. Fritsch, Suhl in Thüringen. Listed as a gunmaker in Germany in 1900.

'FRM'. An unidentified US inspector's mark found on signal pistols made in 1861 for the Federal Army.

Froewis-Gragl. Josef Froewis-Gragl, Vorstadt in Feldkirch/Vorarlberg in 1979. This Austrian gunsmith has been listed as a maker of spring-air guns, perhaps in the 1950s, but nothing else is known.

Frohn. Adolf Frohn, Suhl in Thüringen. A German gunsmithing business claiming a foundation date of 1865. It was owned in 1914 and 1920 by Ad. Reinhäckel, and by Witwe H. Reinhäckel u. Kinder in 1930.

Frommer. Rudolf Frommer, born in Budapest on 4 August 1868, studied engineering before joining ★Fémaru Fegyver és Gépgyár in 1896. There he stayed until 1935, ultimately as managing director, but then was forced to retire by ill health, He died in Budapest on 1 September 1936. Frommer is best remembered for his ★recoil-operated semi-automatic pistols, the subject of a series of patents granted in 1902–13, but due at least partly to the work of Karel ★Krnka. The so-called 12.M pistol was adopted by the Honvéd, the Hungarian second-rank armed forces, and the ★Liliput version enjoyed a modest commercial success. Rudolf Frommer has also been credited with a series of recoil-operated rifles, but it is difficult to determine how much was due to his own skill as a designer and how much to his position as figurehead of FGGY. See also Georg ★Roth.

Frontier – 1. A mark found on a large .44-calibre Belgian-made revolver, probably dating prior to 1910. The guns also bear an 'FR' monogram on the grip, said to identify Felix ★Raick of Liège. **2.** A ★Suicide Special revolver made in the USA by the ★Norwich Arms Company and/or the ★Norwich Falls Pistol Company of Norwich, Connecticut, in the late nineteenth century. **3.** A brand-name associated with a gas-powered revolver made in the USA by the ★Crosman Arms Company, also known as the Frontier 36. **4.** Frontier Scout: see panel, facing page.

Frost – 1. Edward Frost, Bridlington, Yorkshire. The name of this English gunmaker has been reported on sporting guns and shotgun cartridges. **2.** Edward S. Frost, a Federal government inspector working during the American Civil War, accepted small-arms marked 'ESF'. **3.** E.J. Frost. This Federal government arms inspector, working in 1863–64, perhaps the same as the preceding entry, accepted gun barrels marked 'EJF'. See also US arms inspectors' marks.

'F.R.J.S.', usually accompanied by a five-pointed star: a misreading of 'S.F.R.J.' (q.v.); found on guns used in Yugoslavia.

Fruwirth – 1. Ferdinand Fruwirth. Shortly after the first ★Werndl rifles had been introduced, this Viennese gunsmith developed an 11mm bolt-action short rifle with a tube magazine beneath the barrel. Fruwirth began operations in the 1842, after serving an apprenticeship with ★Nowotny, but his business was purchased in 1870 by ★Österreichische Waffenfabriks-Gesellschaft. **2.** Fruwirth carbine. This small bolt-action firearm, the work of Ferdinand Fruwirth of Vienna (above), was issued for trials in 1869, being formally adopted for the Gendarmerie der Österreichischen Reichshälfle (Cisleithanischen Gendarmerie) and the Serecaner-Corps on 23 May 1872, then for the mounted gendarmerie in the Tirol and Dalmatia in 1874. The carbines were made by Österreichische Waffenfabriks-Gesellschaft of Steyr in 1872–75. The army tested the Fruwirth carbine in 1873 as a poten-

FRONTIER SCOUT

Frontier (4)

Introduced in 1957 in response to demands for a rimfire version of the *Single Action Army Revolver, this was made by *Colt's Patent Fire Arms Manufacturing Company (1958–64) and the Firearms Division of *Colt Industries (1964–70). The original gun, factory model Q, chambered .22 Long Rifle rimfire ammunition; an F-pattern, introduced in 1960, was suitably strengthened for .22

WRM. K-type guns (1960–70), confined to .22LR, had zamak-alloy frames; P-type guns, also known as Frontier Scout Model 62 (1962–70), had alloy frames, but their finish was blue and the grips were synthetic Staglite.

Production of Q and F Frontier Scouts had totalled about 246,000 when work stopped in favour of the rimfire *Peacemaker and *New Frontier; there were also about 44,000 K and 68,000 P guns. *See also* Buntline Scout.

A pair of .22-calibre rimfire New Frontier revolvers, dating from the 1970s. Essentially similar to the Frontier Scout, they were based on the Peacemaker, but offered adjustable target-type sights.

---

tial *Extra-Corps-Gewehr. The gun was popular in the gendarmerie, owing to its handiness and good rate of fire, but it was too fragile to withstand military service.

Fry, Marrian & Wells. Gunmakers' agents listed in 1900 at 3 Mincing Lane, London E.C.

'FS' – 1. In a broken oval cartouche. Found on the grips of Hungarian-made *Frommer Stop pistols. **2.** 'Fiberglass Stock'. A variant of the *Remington M700 bolt-action rifle.

'FSL', 'FSN'. Found on US military firearms and accessories. *See* Frederick S. *Leonard, F.S. *North and Nato Stock Number.

'F.S.R.J.', usually accompanied by a five-pointed star: a misreading of 'S.F.R.J.' (q.v.); found on guns used in Yugoslavia.

'FSS', 'FTC'. Found on US military firearms and accessories. *See* Frederick S. *Strong and F.T. *Cleveland.

'F.T.R.' Applied by the British armed forces to guns that have undergone a 'Factory Thorough Repair' (i.e. a complete rebuild).

FTL Marketing Corporation. A US maker of a compact semi-automatic pistol chambering the .25 ACP (6.35mm Auto) cartridge. The gun is believed to date from the 1980s.

Fuchs. Gebrüder Fuchs, Benshausen bei Suhl in Thüringen. A gunmaking business active in Germany prior to the First World War.

Fückert. Gustav Fückert, one of the leading gunmakers established in the Bohemian gunmaking centre of Weipert, was one of the principal members of a co-operative formed in 1887 to produce components for the straight-pull *Mannlicher service rifle that had been adopted for the Austro-Hungarian Army. Little else is known of his operations.

Fuery. George T. Fuery, sometimes listed as Fury, was a British patent agent who acted for Joseph *Cox, Ralph *Gilbert and George *Urry: *see* British Patents 4824/07 of 1907, 25,939/07 of 1907 and 19,417/07 of 1908. An office was maintained at 11 Burlington Chambers, New Street, Birmingham.

Fuller – 1. George Fuller began his gunmaking career at 2 Dean Street, Soho, in 1832. Recorded in the 1841 census in Caroline Street, St Pancras, he had moved to 104 Wardour Street by 1845; then 30 Southampton Street in 1846; 280 Strand in 1856 (where he claimed to be 'Gunmaker to H.R.H. The Prince Consort'); 15 Wynch Street in 1872; 6 Newcastle Street, Strand, in 1874; and 3 Waterloo Street in 1878. Trading finally ceased in 1880, when Fuller was approaching eighty. **2.** S.C. Fuller, South Street, Dorking, Surrey. The name of this English gunmaker, who began operations in 1897, has been reported on shotgun cartridges made by *Eley Bros. and sold under the brandname Long Shot.

'Füllhorn'. This brandname will be found on shotgun cartridges probably made in Germany prior to 1914 by *Munitionswerke Schönebeck.

Funk – 1. Carl Funk, Suhl in Thüringen, Germany. Listed in 1920 as a gunmaker. **2.** Christoph Funk, Suhl in Thüringen, Gothaer Strasse 18 (1940). A German gunmaking business operated in 1900 by Alb. & Osk. Funk, in 1914 by Ernst & Oskar Funk, and by Ernst Funk in 1920–39. Owned in 1940 by Emil Funk, the business specialised in 'hunting and sporting rifles' (*Jagd- u. Sportgewehre*). **3.** C.A. Funk & Co., Suhl in Thüringen, Rimbachstrasse 35 (1940). The affairs of this gunmaking business began in 1835. Although no specific mention was made in the 1920 edition of the *Deutsches Reichs-Adressbuch*, it is thought that the entry was actually that of

FUSIL AUTOMATIQUE LEGER (FAL)

Fusil... (2)

A prototype assault rifle made by *Fabrique Nationale d'Armes de Guerre, chambered for the German 7.9mm intermediate (Kurz) cartridge, was demonstrated in 1948 at the company's Zutendael proving range. Trials proved that *bullpup alternatives were unacceptable, so the standard or No. 1 rifle was enlarged in 1951 to chamber the semi-experimental British .280 (7x49) cartridge.

Rejection of the .280 round in 1952 persuaded FN to re-chamber the assault rifle for the .30 T65 pattern proffered by the Americans, the work being undertaken in Herstal under the supervision of Dieudonné *Saive and Ernest *Vervier. Small-scale series production began in 1953 to provide guns for field trials in the principal NATO armies, and the first of a great many export orders – for

Venezuela – was fulfilled with weapons chambered for the British .280 cartridge.

The perfected rifle was adopted by the Belgian Army in 1956. It had charger guides on the receiver; a smooth muzzle with neither grenade launcher nor flash suppressor; a nose-cap butt; and a plain butt plate without a trap. A tubular bayonet doubled as a flash suppressor/compensator if necessary, and the hand guard was usually injection-moulded plastic. Synthetic furniture replaced wood after 1963.

Among the variants have been the Type 50-00, a designation adopted in the 1970s to distinguish the standard or infantry-pattern selective-fire FAL. The Type 50-64 Para had a folding cocking handle and a repositioned breech-block return spring owing to the folding tubular-frame butt. The Type 50-63 Para was a short-barrelled version with a folding cocking handle and a

fixed battle sight. It lacked the hold-open and carrying handle of the 50-64.

Belgian-made FALs have been supplied to many military forces, ranging from Bahrain to Uganda, and have been made under licence in Austria, Argentina, Australia, Brazil, Britain, Canada and elsewhere. The FAL Compétition, or LAR Competition, intended for Military Match target-shooting, was a semi-automatic FAL made only in small batches from c. 1962 onward. Some have seen use as snipers' weapons, but this is not a role in which guns of this type customarily excel.

The Fusil Automatique Lourd, FALO or Heavy Barrel Light Automatic Rifle'(LAR HB) was introduced in 1958. The Type 50-41 was a special heavy-barrel FAL with a combination flash suppressor/muzzle brake and a folding bipod, but it was never particularly successful in heavy-support roles. Some champions of

---

Carl Funk (above). By the summer of 1925, however, C.A. Funk was advertising such specialties as 'sporting guns and pigeon guns'. Directories dated later than 1930 name the owners of the business as Karl & Lida Funk. Trading ceased at the end of the Second World War. **4.** Emil Funk, Suhl in Thüringen, Germany. A gunsmith operating in 1920. **5.** Franz Funk, Suhl in Thüringen. Listed in the 1930 *Deutsches Reichs-Adressbuch* as a gunsmith. **6.** Gottfried Funk & Söhne, Suhl in Thüringen. This German gunmaking business was owned in 1914 by G. Merkel. **7.** J. Aug. Funk, Nachfolger, Suhl in Thüringen, Germany. Listed as a gunmaker in 1900. **8.** Reinhard Funk, Suhl in Thüringen, Germany. Listed as a gunsmith, 1920. **9.** Richard Funk, Suhl in Thüringen. A gunsmith listed in the 1930 *Deutsches Reichs-Adressbuch*.

'Fur & Feather' [The]. A registered trademark found on shotgun cartridges sold by Edwinson *Green of Gloucester.

Furlong. Nicholas Furlong. First listed in London directories in 1836 at 124 Cock Hill, St Mary Ratcliff, Furlong makes his last appearance in the directories in 1857. By then he was trading from 26 Silver Street, Stepney.

Furor. A 7.65mm nine-shot *Browning-type personal-defence pistol made in France prior to 1940 by *Manufacture d'Armes des Pyrénées. Named after a British-built torpedo-boat sunk during the Battle of Manila Bay in the Spanish-American War. *See also* Destructor, Terror.

Fusger. Edwin G. Fusger, a government arms inspector working at the end of the nineteenth century, accepted military small-arms marked 'EGF'. *See also* US arms inspectors' marks.

Fusil – 1. A French- or Spanish-language term ('gun'), usually applied to a rifle or musket. **2.** Fusil Automatique

Leger, FAL, or Light Automatic Rifle: *see panel, above.* **3.** Fusil Automatique Lourd, FALO, or Heavy Barrel Light Automatic Rifle (LAR HB): *see* Fusil Automatique Leger. **4.** Fusil Saint-Nicolas. A name given to toy-like guns, usually capable of firing nothing other than caps, made by the Belgian firearms industry prior to the 1920s. Production usually peaked toward the end of the year – Saint Nicholas (Santa Claus) being synonymous in Europe with Father Christmas – and the guns made popular presents. They were modelled on virtually anything, ranging from revolvers to double-barrelled shotguns and Mauser bolt-action rifles.

Fussell's, Abergavenny, London, Newport and Port Talbot. The name of this Welsh gunmaker has been found on sporting guns and shotgun cartridges – normally loaded by Frank *Dyke in German cases. Typical examples give the premises as 55 Cross Street, Abergaveny; 118–119 Cheapside, London EC2; 2 Dock Street and 65 High Street, Newport (Monmouthshire); and 81 Station Road, Port Talbot. Trading is believed to have ceased in the 1950s.

'fva'. Found on small-arms ammunition components made in Germany in 1941–45 by Draht- und Metallwarenfabrik GmbH of Salzwedel.

'fvs'. Associated with military optical sights and associated components made in Germany in 1941–45 by Spindler & Hoyer, Göttingen.

'FW' Beneath a crown. Found on Prussian weapons: the mark of King Friedrich Wilhelm IV (1840–61). *See also* Cyphers, imperial and royal.

'F&W' – 1. A monogram with both letters of equal dominance, 'F' superimposed on 'W'. Moulded into the grips of revolvers made by *Forehand & Wadsworth. **2.** In a banner or cartouche, often with a 'stars and bars' shield. Another of the marks associated with Forehand & Wadsworth.

FAL-type rifles – Britain, for example – never used them; others soon withdrew them from front-line service.

The best source of information about the FAL and its derivatives is the three-volume set published in Canada by Collector Grade

Publications in 1995. This is essentially three books bound together – *North American FALs* by R. Blake Stevens (1979), *UK and Commonwealth FALs* by R. Blake Stevens (1987) and *The Metric FAL* by R. Blake Stevens and Jean E. van Rutten (1981).

This British L1A1 rifle, a modified FN FAL, made in the Enfield factory, shows the general lines of the many differing guns made to this general pattern. A Pilkington Snipe image-intensifying infantry-weapon sight is mounted above the receiver of this example.

'FWA'. Found on US military firearms and accessories. *See* F.W. ★Adams.

'FWB' – **1.** A mark used on cartridge, gas-powered, pneumatic and spring-air guns made by ★Feinwerkbau Westinger & Altenburger KG of Oberndorf am Neckar/Württemberg, c. 1963 to date. **2.** Found on US military firearms and accessories. *See* Frank W. ★Baker.

'FWM'. Found on US military firearms and accessories. *See* F.W. ★Macher.

'FWS'. Found on US military firearms and accessories. *See* F.W. ★Sanderson.

'fxo'. Allocated in 1941, this German military codemark was used on submachine-guns, machine pistols, magazines and small-arms components made by C.G. ★Haenel of Suhl.

'FY'. Used during the Second World War by the British Royal Ordnance factory in Fazakerly. *See also* 'F' and 'ROF[F]'.

Fyrberg. Andrew Fyrberg [& Company]. Trading in Worcester and Hopkinton, Massachusetts, USA, this gun-maker/inventor worked for several of the best-known New England gunsmithing businesses – including Iver ★Johnson – in a career spanning thirty years. Fyrberg received a selection of US Patents, beginning with 350,681 of 12 October 1886 (jointly with Iver Johnson) for a 'firearm'. Subsequent protection included 498,427 of 30 May 1893 and 574,409 of 5 January 1897 for 'break-down' guns, the former assigned to Charles S. ★Shatuck. Patents 624,321 and 624,322 of 2 May 1899 protected a 'firearm lock' and a 'shell ejector' respectively; 642,688 of 6 February 1900 was granted for a safety-

lock mechanism; and 669,520 of 12 March 1901 allowed claims for a breech-loading firearm. US Patent 735,490 of 4th August 1903 protected a 'top snap and cylinder catch for revolving firearms'. This was incorporated in the double-action break-open revolvers Fyrberg sold under his own name or 'A.F. Co.' marks in 1905–08, although they were probably made by Iver Johnson. He was also responsible for part of the ★Hammer-the-Hammer system. Later patents included 754,210 of 8 March 1904 for a 'firearm' and 841,240 of 15 January 1907 for an ejector mechanism; 869,967 of 5 November 1907 was granted for a 'breechloading gun', and 935,102 of 28 September 1908 for another 'firearm'.

'Fysche' [The]. A mark associated with shotgun cartridges made for Albert ★Pratt of Knaresborough; origins unknown.

'FZ'. This mark will be found on two-shot tipping-barrel ★Scheintod pistols styled after conventional pocket automatics. The barrels are locked with a sliding catch on the left side of the frame, and usually are marked 'D.R.G.M.' The manufacturer is believed to have been Fritz ★Zink of Suhl.

'fze'. Found on German small-arms components made during the Second World War by F.W. Höller of Solingen.

'fzg'. A mark found on optical sights and associated components made in Germany in 1941–45 by Feinmechanik eGmbH of Kassel.

'fzs'. A code allotted to Heinrich ★Krieghoff Waffenfabrik of Suhl, Germany, in June 1941. It will be found on machine-guns (MG. 81, MG. 131, MG. 151) and FG. 42 paratroop rifles made during the Second World War.

G

'G' – 1. And crossed pistols. A trademark associated with spring-air and other guns made by *Eisenwerke Gaggenau of Gaggenau in Baden. *See also* 'EG'. 2. A shield-shaped letter, often encircled. Used c. 1938–45 by *Gustloff-Werke of Suhl, on products that included small-calibre sporting rifles and semi-automatic pistols. 3. Often encircled; a *headstamp found on .22 rimfire cartridges associated with *Brown & Brothers of New York, but possibly made by *Gevelot. 4. A *headstamp associated with *Gamble Stores. The ammunition was made elsewhere in the USA.

'GA', 'ga' – 1. A superimposition-type monogram, correctly interpreted as 'AG' (q.v.). Used by Armand Gavage. 2. Used as 'ga' by Hirsch Kupfer- und Messingwerke AG of Finow/Mark on German military small-arms ammunition and components made in 1940–45.

Gabbett Fairfax. Hugh William Gabbett Fairfax, Leamington Spa, Warwickshire. Best known as the designer of the *Mars pistol, made in small numbers by *Webley & Scott early in the twentieth century, this English engineer was also associated with the development of semi-automatic rifles. Among his patents were two granted in the USA: 600,066 of 1 March 1898 and 684,055 of 8 October 1901, but none of the guns was successful, and it is thought that Gabbett Fairfax was bankrupted c. 1902. The *Mars Automatic Firearms Syndicate was formed in January 1904 to exploit Gabbett Fairfax's patents, but lasted just three years before itself entering liquidation. The inventor was active as late as 7 January 1919, when British Patent 141,128 was granted to protect an endless-chain magazine for auto-loading rifles.

Gabillot, rue Désirée 36, Saint-Étienne, France. Listed in 1892 as a gunmaker.

Gabilondo – 1. Gabilondo y Compañía, Elgoeibar, Spain. This gunmaking business was responsible for the *Danton and possibly also for the *Veritable Mosser Superior. More recently, it has been associated with the Llama series of automatic pistols, including the compact 6.35mm Model 17 and Model 18. 2. Gabilondo y Urresti, Spain. Founded in Guernica as 'Gabilondo cousins', this gunmaking business became Gabilondo y Urresti in 1909. Developers of the *Ruby-pattern pistols made in great numbers for the French (and subsequently also the Italian) Army during the First World War. The company was given an open-ended contract for 10,000 pistols monthly in the spring of 1915; subsequently this was trebled, forcing Gabilondo to recruit five additional contractors – SA Alkartasuna, Fábrica de Armas of Guernica; Beistegui Hermanos of Eibar; Eceolaza y Vicinai of Eibar; Hijos de Angel Echeverria of Eibar; and Bruno Salaverria y Cia of Eibar. Production is believed to have totalled 150,000–200,000 by November 1918. A move to Elgoeibar occurred in 1922; there, until the early 1930s, a series of 6.35mm, 7.65mm and 9mm Short blowback pistols, based on the FN-Brownings, were made under

names such as *Ruby, *Danton and *Bufalo. A variant of the Ruby with a large-capacity magazine (20–22 rounds), and often also a selective-fire capability, was made in small quantities in 1927–33 for export to China. At this time, however, a decision was taken to introduce copies of the locked-breech Colt-Browning. The first gun, the Llama Modelo IV, appeared commercially in 1931. Gabilondo also makes revolvers on the basis of the *Smith & Wesson swinging-cylinder system. Llama pistols will often be found with the names of distributors such as *Mugica and *Tauler, and have been sold in the USA in recent years by *Stoeger Industries of South Hackensack. *See also* Llama pistols and Llama revolvers.

Gabion – 1. Gabion aîné, rue Saint-Denis 5, Saint-Étienne, France. Listed in 1879 as a gunmaker. 2. Gabion jeune, rue Valbenoîte 17, Saint-Étienne, France. Listed in 1879 as a gunmaker. 3. Gabion-Fournel, rue Badouillère 22, Saint-Étienne, France. Listed in 1879 as a gunmaker.

'GAC'. A concentric-type monogram, with the 'G' and 'A' prominent. Found on Spanish break-open and swing-cylinder *Smith & Wesson-type revolvers, made in Eibar by *Garate, Anitua y Cia.

'G.A.G.' Found on the receivers of 11mm-calibre *Mauser-action carbines: Grenz-Aufseher-Gewehr, signifying guns made in the early 1880s specifically for the German border-guard and customs units by *Haenel and *Schilling of Suhl. Sometimes erroneously listed as Grenz-Aufsichts-Gewehr, they have bayonet lugs on the right side of the nose-cap.

'gal', 'GAL' – 1. Found, as 'gal' on German machine-gun, rifle and similar components made by Wagner & Co. GmbH of Mühlhausen in Thüringen during the Second World War. 2. Found as 'GAL' on US military firearms and accessories. *See* George A. *Lawrence. 3. Uziel Gal, an Israeli Army officer and engineer, was responsible for the *Uzi submachine-gun. Design work began in 1949 and was completed in 1951, when the perfected prototype was fired.

Galand. Charles François Galand, a Parisian gunsmith, was the co-designer with A. *Sommerville of a series of ejector levers for revolvers (British Patent 3039/68 of 5 October 1868) and a lock mechanism that could be dismantled without tools (British Patent 2308/72 of 1872). Galand received US Patent 140,028 of 17 June 1873, protecting the 'frame and stock for revolving firearms' and continued trading until 1889. An 1885-vintage catalogue records the Paris workshop address as 280 rue d'Hauteville – it had been at no. 13 in 1872 – and the existence of an office at 21 Whittall Street, Birmingham. At the time, Maison Galand was making muzzle-loading shotguns, single-barrelled break-open shotguns or *Fusils bascules*, double-barrelled shotguns, Express Rifles and a selection of revolvers.

Galaš. Otakar Galaš, born in Syrovice (Bohemia) in December 1904, joined *Československá Zbrojovka of

Brno after graduating in 1927 from the local state technical school. As an integral part of the small-arms research department, Galaš visited many countries where Czechoslovakian guns were being sold. After escaping to Britain in February 1940, during the Second World War, Galaš helped to organise production of ★Bren and ★Besa machine-guns and Oerlikon cannon in the ★BSA factories, on behalf of the Brno Arms Company Ltd of London. He returned to Czechoslovakia in 1945 to resume his pre-war career. Galaš has been credited with a series of sniper rifles, sporting guns and telescope-sight mounts, including the ★Mauser-type ZG 47 series and the vz. 54 military sniper rifle.

Gale. Edward Gale & Sons, Barnstaple and Bideford, Devon. The name of this English country gunmaking business has been found on a selection of shotgun cartridges with brandnames that include Flag and X.L. Trade directories list premises in Joy Street, Barnstaple, and at 2 & 3 Mill Street in Bideford.

Galef. J.L. Galef & Son, Inc., New York City. Distributors of guns and sporting goods, handling, among others, ★BSA rifles.

Galesi – 1. Rino Galesi, Rigarmi, Collobeato/Brescia, Italy. Maker of a range of compact blowback pistols in .22 rimfire and 6.35mm Auto. **2.** Industria Armi Galesi, Collobeato/Brescia. This Italian gunmaking business produced a series of 6.35mm-calibre semi-automatic pistols, known as the models of 1920, 1923 and 1930.

Galil rifle. An Israeli derivative of the ★Kalashnikov, developed in the late 1960s by way of the Finnish ★Valmet m/62 to replace the FAL. Named after the engineer responsible for the transformation, the Israeli rifle entered series production in 1971. However, the Galil has never entirely replaced US M16 series (★ArmaLite) rifles in military service. The basic patterns include the Assault Rifle, Machine-gun (ARM), with a bipod and a carrying handle; the Assault Rifle (AR); the Short Assault Rifle (SAR); and the Micro Assault Rifle (MAR). With the exception of the MAR, in 5.56mm only, the guns are all made by ★Israeli Military Industries of Ramat ha-Sharon in 5.56mm and 7.62x51. A Galil Sniper has also been offered, with a heavy barrel and a muzzle brake/compensator; and a semi-automatic police/sporting gun was introduced in 1987 in a one-piece hardwood stock as the Hadar II. Apart from the Hadar, virtually all Israeli Galils have been made with folding, but otherwise conventionally-shaped, wood butts. A copy of the Galil, differing largely in the elongation of the butt, was adopted by the South African forces in 1982 as the Rifle Type 4 (R 4). Made by ★Lyttleton Engineering Works of Pretoria, now known as Vektor, the R4 replaced the FN FAL in military service. The original full-length rifle has since been supplemented by the short R 5 and ultra-short R 6 derivatives. Galil-type rifles have also been made in Italy and Sweden, by Vincenzo ★Bernardelli (as the SR-556) and ★Forenade Fabriksverken (FFV-890C). Neither gun was successful in its trials, losing to the ★Beretta AR-70 and FN FNC respectively.

Galilean sight. This term was applied to a primitive form of optical sight, which was briefly popular during the First World War. The image and objective lenses were mounted separately, as far apart as possible, one at the muzzle and one on the receiver, but the delicacy of the unprotected components was such a great weakness that the stronger tube-type telescope sights were soon preferred. The principal British Galilean sights were the Gibbs, Lattey, Martin and Neill patterns. The Neill sight, the subject of British Patent 1850/15 of 1915 granted to Thomas Caldwell of Belfast, is also known as the Barnett or Ulster pattern.

Gallager – 1. Mahlon J. Gallager, Savannah, Georgia, USA. Patentee of a breech-loading carbine in July 1860. **2.** Gallager carbine. Made in Philadelphia by ★Richardson & Overman, this gun had a barrel that moved forward and tipped to give access to the chamber. The breech lever doubled as a trigger guard. The action would have presented fewer problems had not Gallager positioned half the chamber in the standing breech and the remainder in the barrel. Troops hated the Gallager, but the Federal government acquired nearly 23,000 of them. The .50-calibre side-hammer cap-lock pattern was supplemented by 5,000 'new pattern' guns chambering .56-50 Spencer cartridges, although these were delivered too late to see service.

Gallagher. William F. Gallagher, a captain in the US Army, accepted military small-arms marked 'WFG'. They date from 1940–41. *See also* US arms inspectors' marks.

Gallery Gun. Sometimes associated with any type of ★Saloon Gun, this term is often applied more strictly to classify spring-and-piston airguns originating in central Europe in the 1840s. They retained popularity until the First World War in Germany and Bohemia, and enjoyed a brief vogue in the USA in the decade that followed the Civil War of 1861–65. Scant attention has yet been paid to the cataloguing of European guns, although invariably they are either crank-wound (★Kurbelspanner) or cocked by a lever, pivoting in the butt-toe, which is customarily formed to double as the trigger guard (★Bügelspanner). The barrels tip downward – or, very rarely, turn laterally – to expose the breech. The guns made in the USA, conversely, have been subjected to detailed scrutiny. They were divided into five groups by Eldon Wolff, writing in *Air Guns* (1957), but his categorisation was based more on aesthetics and constructional details than cocking systems. Crank-wound New York City guns were made by David ★Lurch, August ★Mock and probably others, with essentially similar New England and Massachusetts types being made, as far as we know, only by Selmar ★Eggars of New Bedford and Joseph ★Tonks of Boston. Combinations of cocking lever and trigger guard were incorporated in St Louis guns, made in Missouri by John ★Blickensdoerfer, Gustavus Brecht and Edward Linzel; similar patterns were made in New York. A third, perhaps confined to Charles ★Bunge of Geneva, relied on a separate cocking lever that pivoted on the right side of the frame. Patented in 1869, the Bunge gun also embodied a revolving-cylinder magazine replenished (at least on the patent drawings) from a stationary hopper.

Gallia. A 6.35mm six-shot ★Browning-type pocket pistol made in France prior to 1940 by ★Manufacture d'Armes des Pyrénées. The slides usually display 'Fabrique à St. Étienne' in addition to the tradename.

Gallus. A compact Browning-type automatic pistol made by ★Retolaza Hermanos of Eibar: 6.35mm, six rounds, hammer fired. Apparently the guns date from the 1920s.

Gallyon & Sons, Cambridge, King's Lynn and Peterborough. Marks applied by this English country gunmaking business will be found on sporting guns, ammunition and accessories. These have included Eley- and Eley-Kynoch-made shotgun cartridges offered under brandnames such as Camroid, Granta, Granton, Kilham, Lynton and Sandringham.

Galopin. Alexander Galopin, Belgium. *See* Fabrique Nationale d'Armes de Guerre and Manufacture d'Armes de Paris.

Galway Arms Company [The], Medbourne, Leicestershire. Originally this British engineering business was renowned for its sound moderators, introduced in 1964, and for making the first silencers intended specifically for air rifles. Galway also made the *Fieldmaster pneumatic/gas-powered rifle, designed by Jack & John Fletcher and introduced commercially in 1983.

'GAM'. Found on US military firearms and accessories. *See* George A. *MacGruder.

Gamage. A.W. Gamage [Ltd], Holborn, London E.C. The name of Gamage is often associated with toys, but the company also sold large numbers of sporting guns, accessories and ammunition – particularly prior to the

1930s. These included shotgun cartridges marketed under the brandnames A.W.G., Holborn and Referee, as well as spring-air guns marked 'Holborn'.

Gamatic. A barrel-cocking repeating spring-air rifle, with a tube magazine above the air cylinder and a mechanical elevator system behind the breech, introduced by *El Gamo in 1970. Sold in Britain as the *ASI Paratrooper Repeater, it is basically a magazine-fed version of the Gamo-68 (below).

Gamba. Renato Gamba, Gardone Val Trompia. A designer of shotguns and accessories, best known for the range of guns made by *Società Armi Bresciane, but also for the Gamba Modell *Parabellums produced by Mauser Jagdwaffen GmbH in the late 1970s. Gamba still sells a version of the Mauser *HSc under his own name; the standard guns chamber the 7.65mm Auto Pistol cartridge, but the HSc Super is available only in 9mm Short. Most Gamba pistols will have either the distinctive eagle and 'RG' trademark, with the lettering in a decorative hand-drawn style, or the current eagle above 'Gr/rG' device.

Gamble Stores. A large retailing organisation estab-

GARAND RIFLE

Garand (2)

The original 1920-pattern primer-actuated rifle was replaced by the improved M1921 and M1922 rifles. Tests undertaken against the Thompson Auto Rifle PC in the summer of 1925 showed that the Garand had greater promise. The .30 M1924 rifle was tested at Fort Benning against ten Thompson Auto Rifles in 1926, but the report was inconclusive. Subsequently, however, the construction of the first gas-operated Garand was authorised.

Trials of these were undertaken throughout 1928 against .30 primer-actuation Garands, .30 Thompson Auto Rifles and .276 T1 Pedersen rifles, plus a .256 Bang, but the .30-calibre Garand was abandoned in February 1929 in

favour of the .276 T3 pattern. However, after testing throughout the summer of 1929, work on the .30 version began again. The first .30 T1E1 Garand appeared in the autumn of 1931, but broke its bolt on trial. It was retested successfully and followed by the .30 T1E2 in March 1932.

The 'Rifle, Semi-Automatic, Caliber .30, M1', was adopted on 9 January 1936, although delivery of the first series-made rifles was delayed until the late summer of 1937. Work was still under way to cure minor teething troubles when the Japanese attack on Pearl Harbor catapulted the US into the Second World War. Only Springfield Armory and Winchester were making rifles at this time.

Production ceased after the war, began again in 1951 during the conflict in Korea – when contracts were placed with

*Harrington & Richardson and the International Harvester Corporation – and finally ended in May 1957 after more than 6,000,000 guns had been made. Springfield Armory alone contributed more than 4,600,000 to the total. Production had been licensed to Pietro *Beretta in 1952, allowing a string of derivatives (especially the BM-59 series) to be manufactured into the 1970s. Italian-made Garands will be found with Indonesian, Nigerian and many other markings.

An automatic adaptation of the M1 Garand with a bipod and a detachable twenty-round box magazine, the T20, was tested in 1944. The perfected T20E2 was approved in 1945, and 100,000 were ordered for service in the Pacific, although hostilities ended before any could be made.

The M1 Garand was replaced

lished throughout the USA. Sporting guns and ammunition have been found with its marks, which included simple 'A' and 'G' *headstamps, and an 'Airway' (or 'A-Airway') brandname. Ammunition may be made by the *American Cartridge Company, the *Federal Cartridge Company or the *Winchester Repeating Arms Company.

Game, Game... – 1. Usually as 'The Game': a British shotgun cartridge, marked by, among others, George *Bate of Birmingham and *Stanbury & Stevens of Exeter. It seems to have been made by *Eley-Kynoch. **2.** Game & Gun Mart: see Clyde's Game & Gun Mart. **3.** Game Shooter. Patented in June 1859 by John *Couch and Henry *North, basically this was a six-barrel pepperbox with a single nipple. The barrel cluster could be slid forward against the pressure of a spring in the central axis-tube until it was held open by the sear. A volley of shots was fired by pulling on the muzzle rod or pressing the trigger, which enabled the trap gun to double as a personal-defence weapon if required. The Game-Shooter was hung from a branch, fence or similar anchor by a cord attached to the backstrap ring. Another cord was run from the muzzle rod to some

bait. When an animal tugged the bait strongly enough, the muzzle-rod released the sear, the barrel cluster sprang backward, and the gun fired. The earliest guns – with an unprotected trigger – were made by *North & Savage in Middletown, Connecticut, in 1859–60. Work seems to have been stopped by the Civil War, but began again about 1866. By then, North & Savage had become the *Savage Revolving Firearms Company. Post-war guns had flat-sided frames, sheathed triggers and a prominent top latch. A few chambered rimfire ammunition, but cap-locks seem to have predominated. Work seems to have ceased about 1870.

Gamemaster. Guns made by the *Remington Arms Company. – **1.** Also known as the Model 141A, this centrefire slide-action sporting rifle was made from 1936 until 1950. Replacing the Model 14A, made only for the rimless .30, .32 and .35 Remington cartridges, it had a five-round tube magazine beneath the barrel, a pistol-grip butt and a ribbed fore-end. **2.** Also known as the Model 760 (760A from 1953), this slide-action sporting rifle dates from 1952–82. A departure from the previous designs, it was locked by rotating lugs on the bolt into the

---

in US service by the M14, a 7.62x51 derivative known during development as the T44. After successful testing in competition with the Belgian FN *FAL (T48) and the British EM-2, the T44E4 was standardised as the M14 on 1 May 1957. Guns were made by Springfield Armory, Harrington & Richardson, the Winchester-Western Division of Olin Industries and Thompson-Ramo-Woolridge Inc., until work stopped in favour of the *ArmaLite M16 in 1964. Production in North America is estimated to have reached about 1,400,000, but the tooling was sold to Taiwan in 1968 and production continued in the Far East for many years. M14 and M21-type rifles can still be obtained from *Springfield Armory, Inc., of Geneseo.

The M15 heavy rifle was a variant of the standard M14, with a special heavy barrel, a bipod and a

shoulder-rest on top of the butt. It was not successful, and only a few hundred had been made when the project was abandoned in favour of the M14E2 (standardised as the M14A1 in 1960). The M14A1 was a selective-fire version of the standard M14, credited to Captain Durward Gosney of the US Army Infantry Board. It could be recognised by a folding forward handgrip, a vertical pistol grip behind the trigger, a stabiliser mounted over the compensator and a bipod with adjustable legs. The M14 NM of 1963 was a special National Match version, especially selected for accuracy, with fibreglass bedding and refined

sights. It was successful enough to encourage the introduction of the M21, adopted in 1975, which remained the standard sniper rifle of the US Army until superseded recently by the Remington Model 24 Sniper System.

Among the best sources of information are Julian S. Hatcher, *The Book of the Garand* (National Rifle Association of America, 1948); E.J. Hoffschmidt, *Know Your M1 Garand Rifles* (Blacksmith Corporation, 1975); Bruce N. Canfield, *A Collector's Guide to the M1 Garand and the M1 Carbine* (Andrew Mowbray, 1988); and R. Blake Stevens, *US Rifle M14* (Collector Grade Publications, 1991).

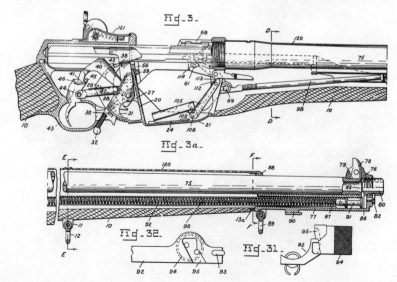

A modern Springfield Armory, Inc., version of the .30 Garand M1D sniper rifle (left) is contrasted with drawings from one of Garand's first patents protecting his perfected gas-operation system.

barrel extension and had a detachable box magazine. It could be distinguished from the Model 740 auto-loader by the fore-end, which exposed several inches of the barrel and operating rods. Chamberings ranged from .223 Remington to .35 Remington. Several variants have been made, including the 760ADL (1953–63), with better-quality woodwork; the 760BDL (1953–82) with high-gloss polyurethane finish on the woodwork and basketweave chequering; and the Model 760 Carbine (1962–80), made only in .270 Winchester, .280 Remington, .30-06 and .308 Winchester. *See also* Bicentennial, Peerless, Premier and Sesquicentennial.

Gamo. A brandname associated with the products of Industrias *El Gamo, the Spanish airgun-making business, but specifically applied to the Gamo-68 barrel-cocking spring-air rifle introduced in 1968 and known in Britain as the *ASI Paratrooper. Several versions of the basic design were made, including the Ranger with a folding stock, until the designation was advanced to Gamo-85 in the late 1980s.

Ganeard. W. Ganeard. This US government arms inspector, working at the beginning of the twentieth century, accepted Colt revolvers marked 'WG'. *See also* US arms inspectors' marks.

Gansevoort. Guert Gansevoort, a commander in the US Navy active from c. 1850 until the beginning of the American Civil War in 1861, accepted Colt, Remington and Whitney cap-lock revolvers marked 'GG'. *See also* US arms inspectors' marks.

Garage Gun. This was a simple emergency-pattern light machine-gun, said to have been made during the early stages of the Second World War in accordance with DD/E/2285 (Design Department, Enfield, drawing no. 2285). Details of its construction are unknown, although there is a theory that the Garage Gun and the *Besal were one and the same.

Garand – 1. John C. Garand. One of the best known of all firearms inventors (although by no means the most prolific), Jean Garand was a French-Canadian, born in 1887 in Saint-Rémi, Quebec. After completing an apprenticeship as a millwright, Garand moved to the USA in 1912 and founded a small engineering business. He

GARDNER GUN

Gardner (4)

Patented in 1874 by William Gardner, 'perfected' in 1876 and improved continually between 1882 and 1884, this mechanical machine-gun was made in the USA by *Pratt & Whitney of Hartford, Connecticut. It had five side-by-side barrels fired alternately by an oscillating feed. Each breech mechanism consisted of a crank and a reciprocating breech-block, and the gun was fired by a hammer. As the operating crank was rotated, the lock piece moved forward and rode over the ejector. When the breech was closed, the hammer was released automatically to hit the striker head and fire the chambered round.

Careful attention to development gradually increased the fire-rate of the basic Gardner mechanism until some of the barrels could be discarded. Eventually, single-barrel versions were made. A hundred guns were purchased by the US Navy following a successful test in Washington Navy Yard in 1879, but the Gardner did not offer sufficient improvement to displace the *Gatling.

In Britain, however, the Gardner was much more popular, and 350 were purchased in 1884 for the Royal Navy for experiments alongside the *Nordenfelt and the Gatling. In 1885, the Machine Gun Committee finally settled on a tripod-mounted single-barrel Gardner Gun for Land Service. The gun, mount and ammunition were to form a single mule-load weighing no more than 200lb. A two-barrel Gardner was recommended for special purposes.

Initially, guns were acquired from the Gardner Gun Company, although probably they were made in the USA; they were fitted on Enfield adaptations of two-wheeled Nordenfelt carriages supplied by *Temple & Company. Surviving examples of these 'Guns, Gardner, .4-inch, 2-barrel, Enfield Martini Chamber' were converted for the .45 solid-drawn Martini-Henry cartridge in the 1890s. They were still being used for instructional purposes as late as 1912, although they had been superseded long since in active use by the *Maxim and *Vickers Guns.

A British five-barrel .45 Gardner Gun, in this case dating from 1882, typified the manually-operated machine-guns that were popular before the Maxim Gun swept them all away.

anglicised his name on accepting US citizenship in 1914 and, when the First World War began, turned his attention to firearms. A design for a machine-gun brought him to the attention of the US military authorities in 1916, and eventually he was offered employment in the *Springfield Armory design office in 1919. Garand quickly rose to become a principal ordnance designer, remaining at Springfield until he retired in 1953. He died in 1974. The eponymous semi-automatic rifle remains his greatest work. **2.** Garand rifle: see panel, pp. 196/97.

Garanta. *See* Britannia.

Garate – 1. Garate Hermanos, Ermua, Spain. The *Cantabria pistol, made by this gunmaking partnership, was often marked as a product of Fabrique d'Armes de *Grande Précision. **2.** Garate, Anitua y Compañía, Eibar, Guipúzcoa, Spain. Makers of the *Sprinter and *Vesta automatic pistols, although it has been suggested that the earliest examples of the latter were made by Hijos de A. *Echeverria. **3.** Garate y Mendibe SA. Associated with sporting firearms and airguns, trading in Trespuentes (Alva), this Spanish business may have been little more than a distributor. No guns have yet been identified from this source.

Garcia – 1. García Saez, Spanish gunmaker and patentee. *See* Saez. **2.** Garcia Sporting Arms Corporation, a US gun distributing business: *see* Remington and Sako.

Garden – 1. Robert S. Garden. A London gunmaker listed at 200 Piccadilly in 1861–63, and 29 Piccadilly from 1864 to 1877. Robert Garden & Son was listed at 200 Piccadilly until 1886, then R.S. Garden – the son trading alone perhaps – from 1887 until the last entry in 1891. **2.** Walter Garden, Aberdeen. This Scottish gunmaker handled sporting guns and shotgun ammunition sold under the brandnames Eclipse, Granite City and Special Brown.

Gardener & Company, Chippenham, Wiltshire. This English gunmaking business is known to have handled sporting guns and shotgun ammunition.

Gardner – 1. Charles Gardner, a 'gunmaker's manager' living at 226 St Saviour's Road, Saltley, Birmingham, was co-patentee with Leslie *Taylor of an automatic loading tap for airguns – British Patent 2863/06 of 1906. He is believed, therefore, to have been employed by Westley *Richards. **2.** Henry Gardner & Company. A patent agency with chambers at 166 Fleet Street, London, acting for Alice *Argles in connection with British Patent 4168/95 of 1895. **3.** William Gardner, Toledo, Ohio. Born in 1844, Gardner arrived in Britain after serving in the US Army during the American Civil War, and he remained in England for much of his remaining life. His interest in firearms was evident in submissions of a magazine pistol to the British authorities in the early 1870s, in the development of the manually-operated machine-gun patented in 1874 (below), and in a quick-firing cannon that was still unfinished at the time of his sudden death in Henley Lodge, St Leonards on Sea, Sussex, on 20 January 1887. **4.** Gardner Gun: see panel, facing page. **5.** Gardner Gun Company (Ltd), London. Agents for the Gardner machine-gun, c. 1882–90.

Gardone – 1. One of the leading Italian gunmaking centres, the town of Gardone Val Trompia (near Brescia) has been the centre of activities for manufacturers such as *Beretta, *Bernardelli and others. **2.** Gardone Mechanical Works, Gardone Val Trompia, Italy. *See* Attilio *Zanoletti.

Garnet, Garnett. M. Garnett, Dublin. The name of

this Irish gunmaker (of Crampton Court and later 31 Parliament Street, Dublin) has been reported on shotgun cartridges sold under brandnames such as Kilquick and Suredeath. Some of these prove to have been loaded by *Irish Metal Industries.

Garnier, rue du Chambon 5, Saint-Étienne, France. Listed in 1879 and again in 1892 as a gunmaker. A Garnier was also listed in 1951 at 55 rue Claude-Delaroa.

Garrett. Frank Garrett, Evesham, Worcestershire. The name of this gunmaker, patentee of the Corona Wad, has been found on shotgun cartridges loaded and sold under brandnames such as Blue Flash, Crimson Flash, D.B.H., Flash Junior, Golden Flash and Tempest. Premises were also occupied in the Warwickshire town of Stratford-upon-Avon.

Garrick. Arthur Garrick, Sunderland, County Durham. The name of this retailer of sporting guns and ammunition has been reported on shotgun cartridges handled under the brandname *Sportsman.

Garrison. A *Suicide Special revolver made by the *Hopkins & Allen Arms Company of Norwich, Connecticut, USA, in the late nineteenth century.

Gartner. J. Gartner, also listed as 'Garner', Columbus, Ohio, USA. This man was recorded by Eldon Wolff in his book *Air Guns* (1958) as a maker of St Louis-pattern *Gallery Guns, but may have been no more than a retailer of guns made elsewhere.

Garvin. John Garvin, a lieutenant in the US Navy, was responsible for the acceptance of Colt Single Action Army revolvers in the mid-1870s. They were marked 'JG'. *See also* US arms inspectors' marks.

'GAS'. Found on US military firearms and accessories. *See* G.A. *Spooner.

Gas... – 1. Gas Gun: see panel, p. 200. **2.** Gas operation. This employs a tiny part of the gas generated by the propellant in the cartridge to operate the breech mechanism. Among the early attempts were the *Browning-designed Potato Digger (q.v.), made by *Colt's Patent Fire Arms Manufacturing Company, which relied on a radial lever; however, the most successful designs have embodied a piston. The piston usually lies beneath the barrel, connected with the bore by a small port through which gas can bleed. Gas-operated guns are customarily simpler and easier to make than recoil-operated equivalents, as they do not need carefully machined surfaces to ensure that parts slide smoothly. Gas operation was impossible if ammunition was loaded with black powder, as the fouling soon clogged the bore, the gas port and the piston chamber. However, the advent of smokeless propellant late in the nineteenth century gave an impetus to the development of gas-operated automatic weapons. The *Hotchkiss was among the most successful machine-guns made prior to 1914, but virtually all modern designs are gas-operated – with the exception of the recoil-operated *Brownings and delayed blowbacks derived from the German MG. 42. Early gas-operated firearms relied on intermediate rods or levers to operate the breech (indirect gas operation), but, inspired by the ArmaLite series, many modern designs lead gas straight back to strike the bolt or bolt carrier (direct gas operation). The direct method is simpler, but more prone to fouling. *See* panel, p. 201, *also* blowback, delayed blowback, locked breech, operating systems and recoil operation. **3.** Gas Ram, or gas-spring. A term coined to describe the action of the *Theoben

GAS GUN

Gas (1)

A term applied to rifles and pistols that rely on something other than air to propel a projectile. The first to make a contribution was Paul *Giffard, who attempted to promote gas guns as military weapons. While his designs were effective enough, and although *Colt was persuaded to invest heavily in the project, most surviving examples are Saloon Pistols, Saloon Guns and low-power hunting rifles made by *Rivolier et fils of Saint-Étienne.

Modern types normally resemble reservoir-type airguns or are replicas of well-known firearms (e.g. Colt Peacemaker and Beretta M92 pistol), but the power to propel the projectile is provided by a gas other than air. Carbon dioxide (originally known as carbonic anhydride) is preferred, although freon and others have been tried. The container may be an integral reservoir filled from a pressurised bottle, a replaceable cylinder or a small Sparklet bulb.

The rise of competitive airgun shooting in recent years has revived interest in gaseous propellant by failing to provide a strict definition of an airgun. Consequently, such manufacturers as *Feinwerkbau, *Hämmerli, *Steyr-Mannlicher and *Walther have offered high-quality competition guns alongside the more mundane 'recreational' pellet and BB firers made in huge numbers in the USA by *Crosman and *Daisy. See also 'Airgun'.

This .177 Hämmerli 480K target pistol, introduced in 1997, is typical of modern designs relying on carbon dioxide propellant.

airgun, a patented piston-operated design in which a charge of a suitable gas (originally sodium hexafluoride, but now nitrogen) replaces the customary coil spring. Originally the charge was sealed to prevent unauthorised tampering, but from 1987 onward, a Schräder valve was added to allow power to be adjusted. In addition to guns made in Britain by *Theoben Engineering, gas-ram patterns have been made under licence by *Weihrauch. **4. Gas-seal revolver.** This term is applied to designs in which the breech is sealed at the moment of discharge to prevent propellant gas from leaking past the cylinder/barrel joint. Among the first was an 8mm *Pieper design, produced in Belgium in small numbers from 1890 onward and possibly also licensed to Österreichische Waffenfabriks-Gesellschaft of Steyr. Some guns pushed the cartridge forward into the barrel at the moment of firing, and others, perhaps experimental, are believed to have slid the barrel backward to effect a seal. The most famous gas-seal design is undoubtedly the Belgian *Nagant, patented in Britain on 20 July 1894 (no. 14,010/94), which was adopted by Russia in 1895 and was still being made in Tula during the Second World War. This 7.62mm seven-shot solid-frame gun relied on a cam lever to press the cylinder forward over a rearward projection of the barrel; momentary expansion of the mouth of a special long-case brass cartridge-case was enough to seal the breech. The gains were not particularly great, but there is no doubt that the

mechanism worked. **5.** Gas-spring system. *See* Gas Ram. **6.** 'Gas-Tight' [The]. A mark associated with 12-, 16- and 20-bore shotgun ammunition assembled by the *New Normal Ammunition Company Ltd of Hendon, London, from components purchased in Europe. The propellant appears to have been German *Walsrode Jagdpulver. A similar mark was used by *Nobel's Explosives Company.

Gascoine. William Gascoine, also listed as Gas-coigne, Gascoyne or Gasquoine. This gunmaker, known to have manufactured sporting firearms and pumps for air canes, traded from Albert Street, Manchester, in 1857–69. The 1868 directory lists an additional address at 10 Market Place, which suggests that Gascoine succeeded Gascoine & Dyson (Blue Boar Court, 1846–62; Market Place, 1854–64).

Gaspard et Cie, 4 cours Fauriel, Saint-Étienne, France. Listed in 1951 as a gunmaker.

Gasser – 1. Johann Gasser. Best known for the large revolvers associated with the Gasser name, this gunsmith was born in Vienna on 6 June 1847 and succeeded his brother, Leopold (q.v.), on the latter's death. **2.** Leopold Gasser. Born in Spittal am Drau (Austria) on 31 March 1836, Gasser was apprenticed to a gunsmith. Striking out on his own, he moved to Vienna in 1858 and was admitted as a master of the gunsmiths' guild in 1862. The successful submission to the Austro-Hungarian military authorities of an open-frame revolver chambered for self-contained ammunition, in 1869, transformed Gasser's operations from an insignificant workshop to a major small-arms manufactory. However, Leopold Gasser died in Ottakring on 9 January 1871 without ever seeing the results of his labours. He was succeeded by his younger brother, Johann (q.v.). **3.** L. Gasser k.u.k. Hof- und Armee-Waffenfabrik, Ottakring. Initially this gunmaking business, founded by Leopold Gasser in 1862, made copies of the British *Adams cap-lock revolvers, but then concentrated on revolvers of its own – which, though generally believed to have been large and heavy, were actually made in far greater variety. Revolvers of this type were adopted by the Austro-Hungarian Army in 1870, and more than 100,000 had been made by 1884. By 1885, nearly 500 men were being employed in Ottakring and a newly-opened foundry in Sankt Polden. Operations continued until the partnership of *Rast & Gasser commenced formally in 1903, handguns being made alongside sewing machines and associated equipment. Many Gasser-made revolvers were distinguished by nothing other than a trademark of an apple impaled with an arrow. **4.** Gasser-Kropatschek rifle. This was a variant of the *Kropatschek bolt-action rifle with a loading gate on the right side of the receiver, which could be pressed inward (in similar fashion to the King-type gate associated with 1866-type *Winchesters) to allow cartridges to enter the tube magazine. This system was patented by the Viennese gunsmith Johann *Gasser in the late 1870s.

Gat. A small push-in barrel-cocking .177 spring-air pistol made by T.J. *Harrington & Company of Walton, Surrey, England, from c. 1948 until the company ceased trading on the death of its founder in 1996. The original version of the Gat lacked the safety catch found on guns made since in the 1980s, while the finishes have included baked enamel and nickel plating.

Gates. George Gates, Chicago, Illinois, USA. A printer and distributor of religious pictures, postcards, statuary and relics, Gates also distributed premium BB Guns. The *Sterling was the favoured item.

Gatling – 1. Richard Jordan Gatling was born in North Carolina and was widely, if unjustifiably, regarded as a Confederate sympathiser on the unlikely grounds that his Cincinnati factory was near enough to the demarcation line to supply either side if required! He was granted a selection of US patents, beginning with no. 36,836 of November 1862. **2.** Gatling Gun: *see* panel, pp. 202/03.

Gaucher – 1. Saint-Étienne, France. Listed in 1933 as a gunmaker, and in 1951 at rue du Docteur-Cordier. **2.** Gaucher-Bergeron frères, Saint-Étienne, France. Listed in 1879 as a gunmaker, with premises at rue des Creuses 12, rue Saint-Denis 41, and rue de la Badouillère 9. Still listed in 1892 at rue des Creuses 12 and rue Michelet 41.

Gaulois. A brandname associated with a repeating pistol made by *Manufacture Française d'Armes et Cycles of Saint-Étienne.

Gauthey, 20 rue Ferdinand, Saint-Étienne, France. Listed in 1951 as a gunmaker.

'GAW'. Found on US military firearms and accessories. *See* George A. *White and George A. *Woody.

Gaztañaga. Isidro Gaztañaga, Eibar, Guipúzcoa, Spain. A maker of *Ruby-pattern semi-automatic pistols for the French Army during the First World War, and also of the post-war *Destroyer series.

'GB' – 1. Usually accompanied by inspectors' marks in the form of capital letters surmounted by crowns or stars: a Belgian government property mark, *Gouvernement Belge*. **2.** A superimposed-type monogram, with neither letter prominent. Found on pistols, revolvers and sporting guns made in Spain by Gregorio *Bolumburu of Eibar.

'GBA', 'gba' – 1. Found as 'GBA' on US military firearms and accessories. *See* G.B. *Allen. **2.** Found as 'gba' on German rifle and other small-arms components made in 1941–45 by Adolf von Braucke of Ihmerterbach bei Westig in Westfalen.

'GBC', 'GBF', 'GC'. Found on US military firearms and accessories. *See* George B. *Cruzen, George B. *Foote and George *Curtis.

'GCA'. A concentric-type monogram, with the 'G' and 'A' prominent. Correctly 'GAC' (q.v.); used by *Garate, Anitua y Cia.

'GCD', 'G.C.D.', often in the form of a monogram with 'D' dominant. A trademark associated with the German gunsmithing business of G.C. *Dornheim of Suhl.

'GCS'. Found on US military firearms and accessories. *See* G.C. *Snell.

GAS OPERATION

Gas (2)

The basic principle is comparatively simple. Propellant gas is tapped from the bore by way of a small-diameter port, striking the head of piston 'a' before being vented to the atmosphere. Piston 'b', attached to a rod connected with the bolt carrier, pushes backward. This movement has the effect of pulling the locking shoulder on the top surface of the bolt 'd' from engagement with the top of the receiver 'e', thanks to the link between the bolt and bolt carrier.

The unlocked bolt continues backward to the limit of its

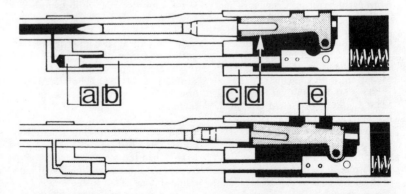

rearward travel, extracting the spent case, until the return spring reasserts itself. Then the bolt is propelled back into battery, stripping a new round into the chamber, and the link between the bolt carrier and bolt lifts the bolt back into engagement with the receiver.

GATLING GUN

Gatling (2)

Patented in the USA in November 1862, the original Gatling fired .58-calibre combustible cartridges inserted in integrally-capped carriers. The multi-barrel cluster had been introduced with the DeBrame Revolver Cannon (patented in December 1861), but Gatling's was the earliest gun of its type to be made in quantity. It achieved an impressive fire-rate by firing six times for each turn of the barrel cluster, although only one barrel (the uppermost) fired at a time.

The first Gatlings leaked gas badly and proved difficult to crank. By 1863, however, .58-calibre copper-case cartridges were being used in the separate cylindrical inserts. The first six Gatlings were made by Miles H. Greenwood & Company in the Eagle Iron Works, Cincinnati, Ohio, but were destroyed by fire before they could be completed – allegedly due to Confederate sabotage. Subsequently, backed by McWhinney & Rindge, thirteen more Gatlings were made by the Cincinnati Type Foundry Company; one was sold to the US Navy, and the remaining twelve were purchased for the Massachusetts Volunteers.

The American Civil War ended before much more could be done, although encouraging trials allowed development of a 1in-calibre Gatling to begin. The last .58 and the earliest 1in Gatlings were made in Philadelphia by the *Cooper Fire Arms Manufacturing Company, but, in August 1866, the US Army placed a 100-gun contract with the Gatling Gun Company. The order was sub-contracted immediately to *Colt's Patent Fire Arms Manufacturing Company.

The .50-70-405 Colt-made M1865 guns incorporated US Patent 47,631 of May 1865, protecting a camming sleeve inside the breech casing to retract the breech bolts as they revolved with the barrels. Subsequently all but five of them were converted to .45-70. The improved M1871 Gatling embodied an automatic oscillator and new breech bolts, patented in March 1871, which could be removed through the cascabel plate

for inspection or repair. The hopper would accept a curved box magazine or the Broadwell Drum (patented by L.M. *Broadwell in April 1872), which consisted of a cluster of twenty vertical twenty-round magazines in a single unit.

Only ten of these guns were acquired by the US Army. Others were made for export, including .42-calibre examples despatched to Russia (where they were known as the Gorlov). A production licence was granted as early as 1869 to Sir W.G. Armstrong & Company Ltd, and encouraging trials had been undertaken in Britain against field guns and the Montigny *Mitrailleuse. In October 1870, the British approved the Gatling for field and shipboard use, although the first order for .45- and .65-calibre Armstrong-made guns was not fulfilled until the beginning of 1874. All but twelve of them were given to the Royal Navy. The 'Gun, Gatling, .45 (Mark I)' was the first successful weapon of its type in British service. It was issued with the Trail Mk I and the Limber Mk I, together weighing about 1,450lb.

The .50-70 M1873 and .45-70 M1874 Gatling Guns were similar to their predecessors, but embodied bronze components; had breech bolts protected by US Patent 125,563 of 9 April 1872; and featured an improved oscillator (Patent no. 145,563). An improved feed hopper lay to the left of the gun's centre-line. The 'Musket length' gun generally had ten 32in barrels, mounted on a wheeled carriage; the so-called 'Camel Gun', mounted on a 40lb tripod, had 18in barrels.

The M1875 had a fixed front sight, an improved hopper feed with raised sidewalls and bevels on the leading edges of the bolt faces to improve the feed. The US Army bought an assortment of these guns, including four 'Camel' examples, and the US Navy purchased a variant with medium-length barrels encased in a bronze jacket. The M1876 had the magazine feed hopper on the centre-line, cartridge guides being added to the ends of the feed throat to facilitate the entry of cartridges. A new head-space adjusting lock was fitted, together with several internal improvements.

The 1877-pattern US Army guns, the last to incorporate an automatic oscillator, had feed hoppers with a small fluted drum at the base, improving feed to match the increased rate of fire. There was also a Bulldog Gatling, introduced in 1877, with short bronze-encased barrels and a crank-handle attached directly to the rear of the central axis rod protruding through the cascabel plate to increase the fire rate to 1,000rds/min. The M1879 had a special quickly-adjustable yoke elevator locked by a friction brake and ten 32in barrels. The US Army bought more than thirty, while the Navy took about twenty with bronze barrel casings.

The M1881 was equipped with the Bruce Feed, patented by Gatling Company employee Lucien F. *Bruce in September 1881 (US no. 247,158). This relied on a bronze frame with two T-slotted tracks accepting the cartridge rims. The feed system was also fitted to a few Gardner and Lowell guns. The US Army purchased twenty-seven ten-barrel M1881 guns, the first twelve accepting the Broadwell Drum or the original box magazines, whereas later deliveries were restricted to the Bruce Feed. Standard ten-barrel US Army guns weighed 260lb, plus 594lb for the wheeled carriage; US Navy guns usually had conical pedestal mounts.

Even the Bruce Feed failed to allow the Gatling Gun to work effectively if the angle of depression or elevation was excessive, so the *Accles Positive Feed, patented in 1882, was substituted. The M1883 Bulldog offered two crank positions, giving fire rates of 800 or 1,500rds/min. The bolts were altered and the extractors were strengthened, but the mechanism had an enduring reputation for case-head separations.

The Model 1885, Model 1886 and Model 1887 were difficult to distinguish externally, the US armed forces acquiring more than a hundred of them in 1883–87. The .45-70 ten-barrel M1889 reverted to exposed barrels, which the US Army preferred, and the Murphy Stop – a cocking switch – was added on the breech casing. Dual-feed adaptors accepted either the Bruce Feed or the old tin box magazines, and a yoke-and-socket mount replaced the previous turntable.

An electrically-powered Gatling Gun was tested by the US Navy in 1890, driven by an external Crocker-Wheeler motor. Even though the mechanism incorporated reduction gearing, a fire-rate of 1,500rds/min was easily attained. Then Gatling patented a gun with an integral motor in the receiver behind the breech-blocks (US no. 502,185 of 25 July 1893), achieving 3,000rds/min.

The M1891 and M1892 Gatlings resembled the 1889 pattern externally; more than fifty were purchased by the US Army. The M1893 was also similar, but chambered the .30 government (Krag-Jørgensen) cartridge and incorporated the Gatling Positive Feed system patented by Clement Broderick and John Vankeirsbilck in September 1893 (US no. 504,516). The US Army ordered eighteen guns, but the thin metal cartridge-strips of the Broderick-Vankeirsbilck feed were too fragile and the guns were converted to Bruce Feed in 1897–98 at the Gatling Company's expense.

Later US Army Gatlings included the M1895, with revised breech bolts, rebounding hammers, Bruce Feed, bronze parts painted olive drab and the remaining metalwork blackened: more than ninety guns were acquired between May and November 1898. The M1900 was little more than an M1895 with its hopper machined from solid bronze stock instead of being fabricated, although, for the first time, the bolts were interchangeable. Only about twenty were made for the army, plus a similar number of naval M1900 Mk 2 guns with bronze-encased barrel clusters. An improved Bruce Feed was standard.

Many of the US Gatlings were still in service in 1917, although most of them had been relegated to static use or to the militia. The advent of the *Maxim Gun and its competitiors had brought the era of the mechanically-operated machine-gun to an end. Yet the Gatling had sold well abroad – notably in France, Prussia and Japan – and had been particularly well received in Britain.

The best source of information is *The Gatling Gun*, by Paul Wahl and Donald Toppel (Arco Publishing, New York, 1976). *See also* James G. *Accles, Lucien F. *Bruce and Lewis W. *Broadwell.

Drawings of the 1875-pattern naval landing carriage for the US .45-70 Gatling Gun.

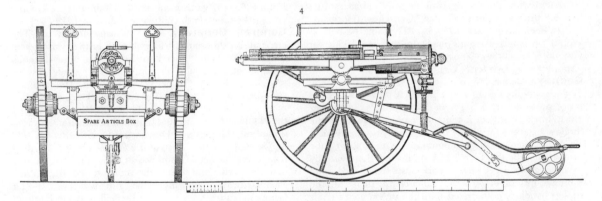

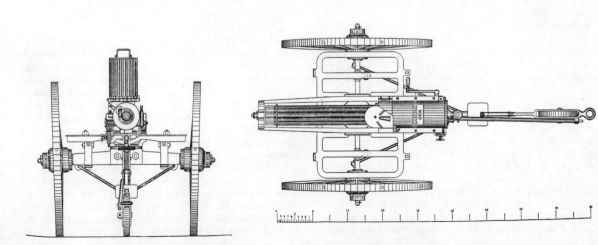

'G.C. & S.' *See* G. *Coster & Son.

'gcy'. Associated with German machine-guns and small-arms components made from July 1941 onward by L.O. Dietrich Vesta- Nähmaschinenwerke of Altenburg in Thüringen. Production lasted until the end of the Second World War.

'GD', 'GDF', 'GDG', 'GDL', 'GDR', 'GDS'. All found on US military firearms and accessories. *See* G. Dillingham and G. *During, G.D. *Fisk, Gilbert D. *Greason, George D. *Little, G.D. Ramsey, Jr, and George D. *Shattuck respectively.

'GEC'. Found on US military firearms and accessories. *See* George E. *Chamberlain.

'GECADO', 'Gecado' – 1. On a lozenge, customarily with 'C' enveloping 'A'. A trademark (Georg Carl Dornheim) used in the late 1930s by G.C. *Dornheim AG of Suhl. It will be found on a variety of guns, ammunition and accessories, including 6.35mm *Browning-type pocket pistols made in Spain. **2.** On a lozenge, customarily with 'C' enveloping 'A'. A trademark used since 1959 by *Dynamit Nobel on guns, ammunition and accessories, including airguns made by *Dianawerk, pistols made by *Reck, and *Mauser-action rifles supplied by a variety of contractors. **3.** Used in Germany since 1960 to distinguish *Mayer & Grammelspacher Diana airguns made for Albrecht *Kind.

Geco, GECO – 1. Sometimes in the form of a monogram 'G'+'eco'. An acronym, brandname and trademark associated with sporting firearms, airguns and accessories handled prior to 1959 by Gustav *Genschow, Germany. It has been used since 1959 by *Dynamit Nobel. **2.** Found on spring-air guns made in the late 1950s for Gustav *Genschow – now part of *Dynamit Nobel Troisdorf – by *Mayer & Grammelspacher.

Gedney. George W.B. Gedney, New York City. Gedney was the designer of a primitive low-powered air pistol protected by US Patent 33,344 of 24 September 1861. In the words of a contemporary encyclopedia, the 'hollow handle is formed of india-rubber or other flexible air-tight material, and communicates with a short tube placed beneath the barrel and connected therewith by means of a passage. A valve of cork closes the passage…and is pressed into its seat by a rod. To discharge the pistol, the rubber handle is compressed until the pressure of the air overcomes the adhesion of the valve to its seat, when it is driven back; the air then escapes into the tube and thence into the barrel, driving out the projectile.'

Gehmann. Walter Gehmann, Karlsruhe. This German gunsmith has made Mauser-type Original *Vom Hofe rifles on the basis of *Husqvarna actions. The guns usually had double triggers, twin recoil bolts and sharply curved pistols grips; chamberings were restricted in 1965 to the 5.6x61 Vom Hofe, 7x66 Vom Hofe and 6.5x68 RWS cartridges.

Geiger. Leonard Geiger, Hudson, New York State. Best known for the *Split-breech Remington carbine of the US Civil War era, Geiger submitted three different rifles to the US Army trials of 1865–66. Protected by US Patent 37,501 of 27 January 1863 (reissued as no. 2231 on 17 April 1866) and tested as Guns No. 8–10, they all relied on variations of the 'Split Breech' system. They had rounded receivers and separate fore-ends held by three sprung bands. In addition, E. *Remington & Sons submitted three similar carbines – Guns No. 46–8 – even

though experience had already shown the Geiger action to be weak. The Rider-patent Remington Carbine No. 57 was clearly preferable.

Geipel. Berthold Geipel, Germany. *See* Erma-Werke.

Gelly, rue Villeboeuf, Saint-Étienne, France. Listed in 1892 as a gunmaker.

Gem, 'GEM' – 1. Although often synonymous with an entire class of butt-cylinder airguns, this mark has also been found accompanying the 'E.G.' and crossed pistols of *Eisenwerke Gaggenau or the 'L.' and rifles of *Langenhan. It is believed to have been introduced prior to 1914 by a British importer, possibly *Lane Bros. **2.** An airgun slug made by Lane Bros. as Lanes' Perfect No. 1 Gem. **3.** Gem airguns: *see* panel, facing page. **4.** Usually encountered as 'The Gem' on 12-bore and other shotgun cartridges marked by Henry *Atkin of London. **5.** A *Suicide Special revolver made in the late nineteenth century by the *Bacon Manufacturing Company of Norwich, Connecticut, USA. **6.** Found on US military firearms and accessories. *See* George A. *Miller. **7.** Gem Rifle. An alternative name for the No. 2 Sporting Rifle made by E. *Remington & Sons and the *Remington Arms Company prior to 1910.

Gemmer. John P. Gemmer, St Louis, Missouri. Born in Germany in 1838, Gemmer emigrated to the USA in 1855. There he joined the gunsmithing business of Samuel *Hawken, whom Gemmer succeeded in 1861. Sporting guns, including spring-air *Gallery Guns dating from 1865–75, were made until Gemmer retired at the end of the nineteenth century. He died in 1919.

General, General… – 1. Usually found as 'The General' on shotgun cartridges loaded in the Birmingham shops of William *Powell & Son from *Eley-Kynoch components. *See also* Admiral. **2.** A Suicide Special revolver made by J. *Rupertus Patent Pistol Manufacturing Company of Philadelphia, Pennsylvania, USA, in the late nineteenth century. **3.** General Custer. A BB Gun made by the *Dubuar Company and presumably, therefore, a variation of the *Globe. Arni Dunathan dates it to 1898 or 1902 in *The American BB Gun*, but the former seems more likely unless the General Custer was a means of ridding Dubuar of unwanted guns after the collapse of the Globe Manufacturing Company. The gun was named after General George Armstrong Custer, killed at the Battle of the Little Big Horn in 1876. It may be no coinicidence that the 25th anniversary of his death occurred in 1901. **4.** General Motors was concerned with one of the silliest ordnance episodes of the Second World War, which centred on the T24 project, an adaptation of the German MG.42 captured in North Africa for the .30 M1906 cartridge, incorporating a rate-reducer to restrict the excessive cyclic rate of the German prototype. The ordnance authorities gave the project to the Saginaw Steering Gear Division of General Motors, which produced two T24 machine-guns for trial in October 1943. Initial tests were unsatisfactory, with a high proportion of jams that had not characterised the MG.42, but the guns duly arrived for a 10,000-round endurance trial at Springfield Armory in February 1944. After fifty jams in 1,483 rounds, the test was suspended and an investigation begun to discover the cause. This proved to be simply that the T24 designers had failed to allow for the additional length of the .30 M1906 cartridge compared with the German 7.9mm pattern, with the result that the bolt failed to recoil far enough to clear the ejection open-

GEM AIRGUNS

Gem (3)

Customarily used for any representative of the butt-cylinder pattern protected by US Patent 204,167 granted to Asa *Pettengill in 1878. This gun was licensed to Henry *Quackenbush c. 1884 and improved by George *Gunn, whose US Patent 337,395 (1886) allowed a claim for a gravity-feed ball magazine. Production began in Europe in the late 1880s, when it is assumed that Quackenbush licensed production to *Eisenwerke Gaggenau.

The first Quackenbush guns were known as No. 5 Combination, relying on two additional patents granted in 1887 – including Quackenbush's own 370,817 of 4 November 1887. However, the patent applications had been made some time earlier; production of the No. 5 was certainly under way by 1884, as thirty-eight of them had been made by the end of the year.

Production, never large, ceased on 3 May 1911, although new guns were still being despatched from the Herkimer warehouse in 1913.

The Quackenbush No. 5 had a replaceable striker unit, carried in a patch box in the butt, so that it could be used as an airgun or firearm. The piston-head struck the striker which, in turn, ignited the cartridge primer. Modified combination guns were made in Germany, Belgium and Britain prior to 1914, and usually can be identified by the presence of appropriate *proof marks.

Gem-type airguns were made by many manufacturers from 1885 until 1925, but are notoriously difficult to classify. Calibre may be .177, .21, .22 or .25. Among the known participants were *Eisenwerke Gaggenau, Fr. *Langenhan and *Mayer & Grammelspacher in Germany; an unidentified Belgian gunmaker using an encircled 'M' mark (which could be read as an 'OM' or 'MO' monogram); and a variety of British

retailers, among them *Arbenz of Birmingham and Sugg of Sheffield, their identities sometimes camouflaged by brandnames, one of which is *Laballe. Combination guns have also been seen with the marks of *Coirier of Paris and *Ancion-Marx of Liège, but are much scarcer than airguns.

Many relevant patents were granted to improve the Gem, most notably to Theodor *Bergmann, Fr. Langenhan, *Lane Bros., and William *Baker & Arthur Marsh. Some of these were dated as late as the 1920s, when the design was obsolete. The *Britannia – patented by Frederick *Cox in 1902–04 – remained the high point of Gem-type design.

A typical nickel-plated No. 1 Bore (.177) Gem butt-cylinder airgun, dating from the years immediately before the First World War.

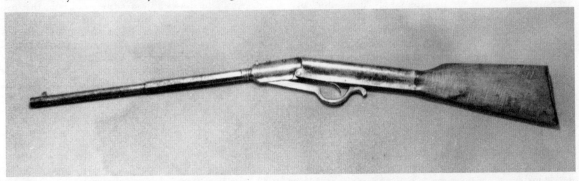

ing. The project was abandoned to avoid the expense of correcting the flaws. Springfield Armory reported that the T24 had some excellent features – particularly the barrel-change and the trigger mechanism – and that the rate reducer seemed efficient; on the debit side, the gun proved susceptible to clogging, had inadequate reserves of power in adverse conditions and was uncomfortable to fire. *See also* Hydra-Matic. **5. General Officer's Model.** Introduced in the 1970s, this was a shortened version of the .45 M1911A1 *Government Model Colt-*Browning semi-automatic pistol developed by Rock Island Arsenal. The magazine held six rounds instead of the customary seven. *See also* Officer's ACP Model. **6. General-purpose machine-gun**, or GPMG. Another name for a *universal machine-gun, adaptable to different roles simply by changing the mount, without altering the fabric of the gun. **7. General Service.** Associated with shotgun ammunition made by the *Mullerite Cartridge Works, Birmingham.
'Generally Useful' [The]. A brandname found on

shotgun cartridges sold in Britain by Charles *Lancaster & Company Ltd of London.
Genhardt. The gunmaker Heinrich Genhardt, operating in Liège, was granted a Belgian patent for his turret pistol on 31 August 1853; US Patent no. 16,477 of 27 January 1857 is comparable, and similar protection was sought in Britain and France. The guns relied on a sliding 'gas-seal' barrel and a magazine disc mounted horizontally. They were made in small numbers in Liège and elsewhere in 1855–60, but the advent of the revolver swept them away. Some guns were chambered for tube-primer cartridges; others handled conventional pinfire ammunition.
Genschow. Gustav Genschow & Co. AG (often known simply as Geco), Berlin SW68, Charlottenstrasse 6 in 1925. One of Germany's best-known manufacturers and distributors of 'weapons, ammunition and guns for sport, target shooting and practice', Genschow owned factories in Durlach, Wolfartsweier in Baden and Hachenburg in

Westerwald in 1925. Branches were maintained at this time in Hamburg, Hamm, Köln, Königsberg in Preussen, Suhl and Wien. Many of the goods were marked with the trademark 'Geco'. Genschow sold many Mauser-type sporters between 1920 and 1939, most of them being made elsewhere, even though substantial gunsmithing facilities were maintained in many of the Genschow branch offices. Mausers of this type often bore nothing but the well-known ★Geco trademark.

George – **1.** The marks of this London gunmaker have been reported on self-cocking ★pepperboxes dating from the middle of the nineteenth century. **2.** W.J. George, Dover, Kent. The name of this long-established gunmaker – known to have been trading as early as 1890 – has been reported on shotgun cartridges made by ★Kynoch. Sporting guns and airguns have also been found with George's marks.

Gerät. A German-language term: 'equipment'. Sometimes it was used prior to 1945 as a distinguishing prefix for small-arms, but generally was indicative of a design that had not reached service – e.g. Gerät 06 (H) and Gerät 040 were a Mauser-developed assault rifle and simplified pistol (★Volkspistole) respectively.

Gerest, place Villeboeuf 8, Saint-Étienne, France. Listed in 1879 and 1892 as a gunmaker.

Geriffelt. A German-language term applied generically either to rifled barrels or to indicate airgun pellets with ribbed bodies.

Gering. Hans Gering, Arnstadt in Thüringen (sic), Germany. A maker, or perhaps simply distributor, of 7.65mm ★Beholla-type pistols under the tradename Leonhardt. Operations seem to have failed by 1929, but nothing else is known. A link may exist with H.M. Gering & Co., a manufacturer of tongs and tools (Zangen- u. Werkzeugfabrik) trading in Heidersbach bei Suhl in 1940.

German... – **1.** German Army marks, pre-1918: see panel below. **2.** German Army marks, post-1920. Individual unit markings of this type used after 1923 were typically '2./J.R.15.5.', which would have indicated the fifth weapon issued to the second company of the fifteenth infantry regiment. The letter combinations 'A.R.', 'N.A.', 'Pi.' and 'R.R.' respectively signified artillery regiments, communications units, pioneer battalions and cavalry (Reiter) regiments; 'Kdtr.' was Kommandantur, a district command, and 'Ü.Pl.' signified the administrative staff of a training ground or Truppen-Übungsplatz. **3.** German colonial-service markings. Pre-1918 guns of this type were usually marked 'K.S.' (Kaiserliche Schutztruppe) until about 1911–12, after which each individual force applied its own marks – e.g. 'Sch.D.O.A.' applied by the Schutztruppe Deutsch-Ostafrika, the protective forces in German East Africa; or 'Sch.Tr.D.S.W.A.' for the smaller Schuztrupp Deutsch-Südwestafrika. **4.** German miscellaneous firearms markings. Documents such as the Vorschrift für die Stempelung der Pistole 08 nebst einer Zeichnung ('Regulation [telling] how to mark the Pistol 08, accompanied by a drawing') not only tell us how proof procedures were undertaken in respect of the Parabellum, or Luger, pistol, but also identify the purpose of individual inspectors' marks. This dispels many common myths, and can be used to date guns that lack their principal markings. The date stamp, or Jahreszahl, usually appeared above the chamber of Mauser rifles and Parabellum pistols alike. The Vorschriften also shows how to distinguish guns that had been refurbished or assembled from old parts. Refurbished guns had additional two-digit dates, such as '1909/13', over the chamber, showing the year of reconstruction; those assembled from parts had reversed dates in the form '1913/09' to signify a gun that had been

GERMAN ARMY UNIT MARKS, PRE-1918

German... (1)

These, when present, provide a very good means of linking guns with individual units, although the practice was suspended in 1916. They will be found in a variety of places, and the issue and re-issue of guns sometimes meant that the butt plate (for example) bore marks impressed by several different units. The markings were stamped on the butt marking disc of the Gew. 98 prior to November 1915, and thereafter on the top surface of the butt plate. ★Parabellum, or Luger, pistols usually have the marks on the front grip strap.

The marks can be difficult to decipher, particularly as the regimental armourers often failed to follow the regulations correctly. This became most obvious during the early stages of the First World War, when training fell below

normal peacetime standards. Infantry-regiment marks struck in this era by inexperienced or semi-literate personnel, for example, could read 'I.R.', 'J.R.' or 'Inf.R.' instead of the simple regulation 'R'.

The principal document governing the pre-1918 marks was *Vorschrift über das Stempeln der Handwaffen* (D.V.E. 185 in Prussia, D.V. 448 in Bavaria) of 1909, although many amendments (*Deckblätter*) were issued prior to the suspension of the scheme in 1916. Most common are the marks of the line infantry regiments ('R'). Next come the Bavarian line infantry regiments ('B...R.'), twenty-three of which existed in 1908 when the Prussians and their allies had 182. The many reserve infantry regiments used a cursive 'R', while the stampings applied by the regimental machine-gun companies ('...R.M.G...') are also commonplace.

There were fourteen Prussian rifle battalions, or *Jäger* ('J'), plus two Bavarian equivalents ('B...J.'). Appreciably less common are marks of the five regiments of foot guards ('G.R.') and five guard-grenadier units ('G.G.R.'), while stampings applied by the solitary Garde-Füsilier-Regiment ('G.F.R.'), Lehr-Infanterie-Bataillon ('L.I.B.'), Bavarian Leib-Regiment ('B.L.R.'), Garde-Jäger-Bataillon ('G.J.') or Garde-Schützen-Bataillon ('G.S.') are all very scarce.

Marks applied by cavalrymen will also be encountered, although they are scarcer – and thus more desirable – than line infantry equivalents. The establishment in 1908 included twenty-four line dragoon ('D.') regiments, seventeen line hussar ('H.') units, eight regiments of heavy cavalry (*Kürassiere*, 'K') and sixteen regiments of lancers (*Uhlanen*, 'U'). Even less common are the marks of two guard-dragoon regiments

assembled in 1913 from unmarked parts that were four years old. Letters identifying the state monarch or the emperor (*see* Cyphers, imperial and royal) may also lie on the left side of the barrel at the breech. Crowned military inspectors' stamps – the *Abnahmestempeln mit Krone* – were tiny fraktur letter punches, made in four sizes: 7mm, 4.2mm, 3.2mm and 2mm, measured from the base of the letter to the apex of the crown, being designated '*grosser*', '*mittlerer*', '*kleiner*' and '*kleinster*' *Abnahmestempel* respectively. Whole strings of these may be encountered on rifle parts, particularly alongside the breech. Some marks will be found in fraktur (gothic script), but others were cursive. All the letters of the alphabet were used, apparently excluding 'J', but the unusually high incidence of 'X' suggests that it may have been used as a substitute letter, perhaps identifying the junior of two or more inspectors whose surnames shared the same initial. A few marks have been encountered with a bar beneath the letter, which may indicate the junior of two inspectors with identical surnames. Although few individual inspectors have yet been identified, details of postings to the rifle factories can be gleaned from the *Militär-Wochenblatt* or the painstaking research undertaken by Horst Laumann and published over the last few years in the *Deutsches Waffen-Journal*. Manufacturers' and general markings (*Fabrik- und allgemeine Stempel*), including the DWM monogram trademark and the marks of the principal government factories – 'AMBERG' (Bavaria), 'DANZIG', 'ERFURT' or 'SPANDAU' beneath a crown – were not precisely defined in the regulations and can take a variety of forms depending on their size and the position on the gun. The DWM monogram found on Maxim machine-guns, for example, differs greatly from the designs associated with Mauser rifles and Parabellum pistols. The proof eagle (*Beschussadler*, or *Heraldischer Adler*) was customarily 3.2mm high and 2.9mm wide. Cartridges used for proof-firing – known as *Beschuss-Patrone* or *B-Patr.* – usually developed 75 per cent more pressure than normal. A calibre mark is usually to be found somewhere on the barrel near its joint with the receiver. The appearance of the 4.2mm and 2mm crown/'RC' marks of the Revisions-Commission in the pre-1914 regulations provide that these originated long before the Allied control commissions appeared in Germany after the Armistice. They will be found on otherwise serviceable pre-1918 guns that had failed inspection solely because of poor tolerances or external flaws. Rejected by the inspectors, these weapons were submitted to the Revisions-Commission for reappraisal. Those that were accepted for service were given marks to absolve individual inspectors of blame for subsequent service failures. Sequential serial numbers, *Gewehr- oder Pistolennummerstempel*, could be either 1.5mm or 2.1mm high. They usually appear in full on the left side of the barrel and receiver, and on the base of the bolt handle of the rifles, but the positions vary according to the type of gun. The guns seem to have been numbered on the basis of calendar years, although the governmental fiscal year ran from 1 April to 31 March. Letter suffixes were used after the introduction of the Gew. 88 to distinguish blocks of 10,000 guns. When the first block had been completed, numbers began again at 1a; when this was full, work recommenced at 1b. In the case of the Gew. 98 made during the First World War, the system reached 10000z (excluding the 'j'-block) and began again at 1aa. Parts of the serial number may be repeated on most of the components, including the bolt guide rib, the bolt head, the striker, the safety wing, the cocking piece, the striker head and the extractor. This is particularly true of pre-1888 rifles. **5.** German Navy unit marks. The most

('G.D.'), the guard hussars ('G.H.'), and three guard lancer regiments ('G.U.'). Marks indicating service in the Prussian royal bodyguard (Regiment der Gardes du Corps, 'G.d.C.') are particularly scarce. Other rarely-encountered marks indicate mounted riflemen (*Jäger zu Pferde*, 'J.P.'), Bavarian light horse (*Cheveaulegers*, 'B...Ch...'), Bavarian heavy cavalry regiments ('B...s.R...') and airmen ('F.A...' and 'F.E.A...').

The unreliability of many modern books has often done more harm than good to the transcription of German marks, although an honourable exception is provided by the painstakingly compiled *German Small-arms Markings from Official Documents* (1997) by Joachim Görtz and Don Bryans; another may be found in the bayonet books written and published in Britain by Anthony Carter, which deal with markings individually and give an exceptionally useful background history of pre-1918 German Army structure.

A typical German Army unit marking, on the butt strap of a Pistole 08 (Parabellum). This was applied by the machine-gun company of the second Bavarian reserve infantry regiment

common Marine identifier is a distinctive squared imperial crown above 'M' – the mark of the principal navy inspector responsible for the particular weapons. The most common unit markings (usually on the butt plates of rifles and the backstraps of pistol grips) include 'M.A.A.' for *Matrosen-Artillerie-Abteilung*, often prefixed by a roman numeral, 'M.D.' for *Matrosen-Division* (sailors division); 'S.B.' for *Seebataillon* (marines); 'St.S.B.' for the *Stamm-Seebataillon*; and 'T.D.' for the post-1908 *Torpedo-Division*. The 'U.A.' marks of the *Unterseeboot-Abteilung* are very rare, whereas the 'W.D.' of *Werft-Division* (comprising artificers, stokers, engine-room staff, etc), customarily prefixed by a roman numeral, is much more common. 'W.K.' indicates guns on the inventory of *Werft Kiel* (Kiel dockyard inventory) and 'W.W.' signifies *Werft Wilhelmshaven*. The most common of the post-1923 marks were property numbers incorporating the prefixes 'N.' or 'O.', for the *Nordsee* (North Sea) and *Ostsee* (Baltic) districts. **6.** German police marks, pre-1918. These identifiers included 'R.G.' applied by the *Reichsgendarmerie* operating in the province of Alsace-Lorraine, and 'K.Sächs.Gend.' or 'K.S.Gend.' for the Royal Saxon police. After the end of the First World War, however, important changes were made. **7.** German police marks, post-1920. The Prussian regulations of 1922 introduced the prefixes 'S', 'P' and 'L' for *Schutzpolizei*, police schools, and air-surveillance detachments respectively; 'S.Ar.II 2.15.', therefore, was the fifteenth weapon issued to second precinct of the second sub-district of the Arnsberg area command. 'S.D.' and 'S.S.' were the marks of the *Schutzpolizei* in Düsseldorf and Schneidemühl. The Bavarian Landespolizei applied marks such as 'M.5.15.' (the fifteenth gun issued to the fifth precinct of the München district). By 1932, however, the Prussian system had become 'K' for *Kriminalpolizei*, 'S' for *Schutzpolizei* and 'L' for *Landjägerei*: 'S.Br.II.15.' was the fifteenth gun issued to the second ('II') district of the *Schutzpolizei* of Breslau. Other marks included 'HP.' for the *Höhere Polizeischule* (central police school) in Berlin; 'PTV' for the *Polizeischule für Technik und Verkehr* (police institute for technology and transport) in Berlin; and 'RhP.' for the Rhine river police, or *Rheinpolizei*.

Germania – **1.** Protection for this brandname, accompanied by a suitable trademark, was granted to J.G. ★Anschütz in September 1907 (no. 50,666) and used into the 1930s, even though largely superseded by ★JGA. **2.** Germania-Waffenfabrik, Germany. *See* J.G. Anschütz.

Gerner. Charles Gerner was the co-designer, with Eli ★Whitney the Younger and Frank ★Tiesing, of the breech-loading shotgun protected by US Patent 93,149 of 27 July 1869.

Gerngross. Paul Gerngross, Suhl in Thüringen. A German gun-stocker, active in 1939.

Gerstenberger & Eberwein, Em-Ge Sport-gerätewerk, Gussenstadt. This metalworking business was a successor to ★Moritz & Gerstenberger, trading having ceased in Germany at the end of the Second World War. One of the original partners re-established operations in the early 1950s in West Germany, allowing the first of a range of airguns and blank-firers to be made. Products have since included cartridge revolvers, flare pistols, starting pistols, and a range of barrel-cocking spring-air pistols.

Gerster, rue Michelet 61, Saint-Étienne, France. Listed in 1892 as a gunmaker. Still trading in 1933 and also in 1951.

'GES'. Found on US military firearms and accessories. *See* 'George E. ★Saunders'.

'Ges. Gesch.', 'Ges. Geschützt'. These German-language abbreviations – 'Protected design' – will be found on a variety of equipment, signifying a level of protection below a patent or utility design (★DRP, ★DRGM), but better than simply a registered trademark (★DRWZ).

Geværfabrik Kjobenhavn. *See* Copenhagen.

Gevelot – **1.** Gevelot SA, France. *See* Société Française des Munitions. **2.** Gevelot & Cie, or Maisons Gevelot, later Gevelot & Gaupillat. This cartridge-making company – initially a maker of percussion caps – was formed in Paris in 1820, by Marin Bâtard-Gevelot. A factory was established in Issy-les-Moulineaux in 1826, but Gevelot died in 1846 and his successors formed an alliance in 1858 with Gaupillat, Illig, Gundorff & Masse. This arrangement led to the foundation in 1883 of Gevelot & Gaupillat, but the name was changed almost immediately to ★Société Française des Munitions. Cartridges made prior to 1883 can often be identified by a monogram consisting of two letters 'G' back to back, although this was perpetuated by SFM and care must be taken with dating.

'Gew', 'GEW' – **1.** As 'Gew.', often in fraktur (gothic script). Found on the receivers of German military firearms, this simply signifies *Gewehr* (rifle). **2.** Found as 'GEW' on US military firearms and accessories. *See* G.E. ★Worden.

'G.F.', 'G F', 'G-F'. These marks will be found in the headstamps of cartridges made in Italy by Guilio ★Fiocchi & C. (now Fiocchi Munizione SpA).

'GFB', 'GFG', 'GFM', 'GFT'. All found on US military firearms and accessories. *See* George F. ★Bowen, George F. ★Gray, George F. ★Morrison, and George F. ★Tucker respectively.

'GFZ', sometimes in the form of a monogram. A mark associated with Georg ★Fahrmann of Zella-Mehlis.

'GG' – **1.** Usually in the form of a monogram. This mark was used on ammunition made in France by ★Gevelot & Gaupillat and their successors, ★Société Française des Munitions. **2.** 'GG' beneath an eagle: *see* 'Gr rG'. **3.** Found on US military firearms and accessories. *See* Guert ★Gansevoort.

'GGB' – **1.** Pierced by a horizontal arrow. A trademark associated with George Gibson ★Bussey of Peckham, London. **2.** Found on US military firearms and accessories. *See* George G. ★Bowe.

'GGS'. Found on US military firearms and accessories. *See* G.G. ★Saunders.

'GH'. Found on US military firearms and accessories. *See* George ★Haines and George ★Hosmer.

Ghaye. A Liège gunsmith who, in the 1850s, developed a sliding-barrel system operated by an underlever ahead of the trigger. The original pattern was hinged at the tip of the fore-end, pulling the barrel forward by means of an intermediate link when the lever-grip was pulled down. Guns were made in many styles, although back-action locks were customary. Military prototypes usually have a barrel band and a nose-cap, whereas sporters and shotguns will have half-stocks or no fore-ends at all. Despite inherent weaknesses, the simple Ghaye system was popular in Belgium and France for many years, but the layout was often reversed so that the operating-lever pivot lay immediately ahead of the trigger. This allowed the breech-link to push the barrels away from the standing breech instead of pulling them; most of the rifles made in the 1860s by Jamar-Smits of Liège followed this pattern. Ghaye also manufactured revolvers in the 1870s.

'GHD'. Found on US military firearms and accessories. *See* Guy H. *Drewry and George H. *Dupee.

'ghf'. Allocated in 1941 to Fritz *Kiess & Co. GmbH of Suhl, for use on small-arms components made for the German armed forces.

'GHG', 'GHH', 'GHM'. Found on US military firearms and accessories. *See* George H. *Graham, George *Hubbard and G.H. *Munroe respectively.

'ghn'. Found on German rifle and other small-arms components made in 1941–45 by Carl Ullrich & Co. of Oberschönau in Thüringen.

'GHS'. Found on US military firearms and accessories. *See* Gustavus H. *Scott and Gilbert H. *Steward.

GIAT, Saint Cloud, France. Groupement Industriel des Armaments Terrestres, formed in 1950 and better known by its acronym, is responsible for the operations of the state-run ordnance factories (e.g. *MAS). The name was changed to GIAT Industries in 1990.

Gibbs – 1. George Gibbs [Ltd], Bristol, Gloucestershire. This English gunmaking business began trading in 1841 from 141 Thomas Street, succeeding the short-lived J. & G. Gibbs of Redcliffe Street. A move to 20 Clare Street took place in 1850, then to 29 Corn Street in c. 1860. By 1914, premises were being used in 37 Baldwin Street, Bristol, and 85 Savile Row, London. Gibbs was renowned for his single-shot match rifles, initially cap-locks, but then built on the *Farquharson action; however, the name will also be found on self-cocking *pepperboxes dating from the middle of the nineteenth century, *Lee-Metford and *Lee-Enfield rifles, and on a variety of shotguns. Shotgun cartridges were sold under such brandnames as Bristol and Farm. Mauser-type rifles were chambered for a selection of proprietary cartridges, including the .256 Gibbs Magnum (introduced c. 1913) and the .505 Rimless Magnum of 1910–11. Actions were bought from the Mauser factory in Oberndorf prior to 1914, although post-1920 guns showed greater variety. **2.** Lucius H. Gibbs, Oberlin, Ohio, and New York City. Grantee of US Patent 5316 of 2 October 1847, protecting a revolver; 14,057 of 8 January 1856 for a breech-loading carbine (q.v.); and 21,294 of 26 October 1858 for a method of patching ball ammunition. **3.** Gibbs Arms Company, New York City. Assignee of patents granted to Lucius H. Gibbs, responsible for the licensing of the Gibbs breech-loading carbine. Possibly a partnership of Lucius Gibbs and William Brooks, it had been dissolved by the time the Civil War ended in 1865. **4.** Gibbs carbine. Patented in January 1856, this was one of the lesser-known Civil War weapons. On 18 December 1861, the Ordnance Department contracted with William *Brooks of New York City for 10,000 Gibbs carbines at $28 apiece. Brooks sub-contracted most of the work to William *Marston's Phoenix Armory, but the factory was destroyed on 13 June 1863 during the New York Draft Riots, and the contract was terminated after only 1,052 guns had been accepted by the army. The .52-calibre Gibbs operated similarly to the Gallager (q.v.), as a lever, formed as the trigger guard, tipped the barrel forward and upward at the

breech to receive a new cartridge. Unlike the Gallager carbine, however, Gibbs' pattern fired a combustible paper cartridge. It had a distinctive underlever with a ring tip. **5.** Gibbs-Farquharson-Metford, Britain. *See* George *Gibbs and John *Farquharson. **6.** Gibbs Rifle Company, Martinsburg, West Virginia, USA. Owned by the *Navy Arms Company, this business succeeded to the rifle-making operations of *Parker-Hale in 1990, perpetuating many Parker-Hale Mauser rifles, but also introducing new patterns. *See also* Midland and Scout.

Gibson – 1. Abram Gibson, Worcester, Massachusetts, USA. Designer of a revolver with cylinder and barrel 'swinging away from the recoil shield', protected by US Patent 29,126 of 10 July 1860. Originally assigned in part to Joseph Hale, subsequently rights to the patent were acquired by *Smith & Wesson. **2.** Sidney L. Gibson, a lieutenant in the US Army, accepted US military High-Standard pistols in 1941. The guns were marked 'SLG'. *See also* US arms inspectors' marks.

Gidrol, rue Désirée 15, Saint-Étienne, France. Listed in 1892 as a gunmaker.

Gielgud. Henry Gielgud, often mistakenly listed as Grelgud: *see* Providence Tool Company.

Giffard – 1. Paul Giffard, born in Paris in 1837, died in 1897 after he had spent half his life perfecting pump-up pneumatic and gas-powered guns. Had the inventor not been determined to promote his designs as military weapons – clearly they had minimal offensive potential – and turned his attention to replacing the saloon rifles that were popular in his day, Giffard may have enjoyed great success. The gas guns (often advertised under the brand-name *Carbona) were made in Europe successively by *Rivolier fils of Liège, Sociéte *Stephanoise d'Armes of Saint-Étienne, and *Manufacture Française d'Armes et Cycles. Small numbers were made in Britain by the *International Giffard Gun & Ordnance Company Ltd, and *Colt's Patent Fire Arms Manufacturing Company is said to have acquired rights to the Giffard Gun for the staggering sum of 1,000,000 dollars. Protection obtained by Giffard included British Patent 2931/62, sought from 66 Boulevard des Batignolles, Paris, which was granted on 30 October 1862 to protect a pneumatic rifle charged by a longitudinally sliding pump under the barrel – precursor of the 1899-type *Benjamin. US Patent 41,500 of February 1864 was comparable. British Patent 21/72 of 3 January 1872 protected a gun accepting a separately-charged cartridge (the *Saxby-Palmer system in embryo), specifications being filed from 12 rue de la Pépinière, Paris. US Patent 136,315 of 25 February 1873 protected a gun with a detachable gas cylinder beneath the barrel, and 136,316 allowed claims for a gas-powered cane gun. British Patent 2077/86 of 7 January 1887 featured an improved self-contained gas cartridge and a single-shot rifle to chamber it. Giffard's address was listed then as Boulevard St Denis in Paris. British Patent 11,050/89 was granted on 21 September 1889 for an improved version of the single-shot gas gun patented in the USA in February 1873 (no. 136,315); US Patent 452,882 of May 1891 was essentially the same. British Patent 10,308/90 of 15 November 1891, the last relevant design to be protected by Giffard before he died, relates to another modified gas cylinder. Among the inventors who tried to make additional improvements to the basic Giffard concept were John *Wallace and Benjamin Thomson, patentees of the improved hammerless Giffard rifle made in Britain. **2.** Giffard Gun & Ordnance Company Ltd. Trading from Copthall House, Copthall Avenue, London E.C., this promotional agency was formed about 1894 to succeed the short-lived ★International (Giffard Gun) Company and continue the exploitation of patents granted to Paul Giffard and, eventually, for modifications made to Giffard's designs by John ★Wallace and Benjamin ★Thomson. The Giffard Gun & Ordnance Company Ltd was still trading in 1909 from Copthall Avenue, but the factory in North Finchley, London, was closed in 1913 after only a small number of hammerless gas-powered guns had been made.

Gifford. A.W. Gifford, Boston, Massachusetts, USA. Patentee of a method of securing the flights of airgun darts: see US Patent 177,932 of 1876, which Gifford assigned to A.A. ★Pope.

Gilbert – **1.** J.M. Gilbert. A lieutenant-colonel in the US Army, this arms inspector accepted .45 M1911 (Colt) pistols during the First World War. They were marked 'JMG'. See also US arms inspectors' marks. **2.** Ralph Benjamin Gilbert, a 'Gentleman' of 174 Victoria Road, Aston Manor, Birmingham, was the designer – British Patent no. 19,417/08 of 1908 – of an improved loading tap for the ★Jeffries Pattern BSA air rifles. Possibly only a prototype was ever made, although the advent of the First World War may have hindered exploitation.

Gilks. Charles H. Gilks. First mention of this English gunmaker occurred in 1857, when his addresses were listed as 3 Union Row, Tower Hill, London E., and 37 ★Minories. Trading was still being undertaken from the Union Row premises, together with 67 Minories and 327 Wapping High Street, when Gilks, Wilson & Company was formed in 1864. Thereafter the Union Road shop was the sole location. Gilks, Wilson & Company was succeeded by C.H. Gilks & Company, which traded until 1880.

Gill – **1.** Gill & Company, 5 High Street, Oxford. The marks of this English gunmaking business have been reported on shotgun cartridges made by ★Nobel and sold under the brandname Dead Shot. **2.** John Henry Gill, later John H. Gill & Sons and John H. Gill & Sons (Leeming Bar) Ltd, London. The name of this gunmaker has been reported on ★Greenwood & Batley shotgun cartridges sold under the brandname Sproxton.

'Gillingham' [The]. Found on 12-bore shotgun cartridges made by ★Kynoch Ltd for ★Strickland of Gillingham prior to the First World War.

Gillman. J. Gillman & Son, Birmingham, Warwickshire. This English gunmaking business, trading in the 1930s from the corner of Stafford Street and Corporation Street, is known to have handled sporting guns and ammunition.

Gillon. See A. ★Gilon.

Gilmore. L.G. Gilmore. This government arms inspector, working in 1895–1905, accepted small-arms marked 'LGG'. See also US arms inspectors' marks.

A. Gilon, Liège. A maker of ★Colt-copy cap-lock revolvers in the mid-nineteenth century, and (perhaps a son of the same name) ★Velo-Dog patterns at a later date. Trading is believed to have ceased shortly after the German army invaded Belgium in August 1914.

'Ginklu Fondas', and a stylised crown. A mark encountered on the chambers of ★Mauser-type rifles used by the Latvian Army prior to 1939. Apparently it means 'arms fund'.

Girard – **1.** C. Girard & Cie, Paris. Gunsmiths and gun dealers, renowned for supplying sporting guns and for their entrepreneurial role in the American Civil War, when countless thousands of inferior guns, purchased in Liège, were sent to the Federal Army. **2.** François Girard, Saint-Étienne, France. Listed in 1933 as a gunmaker. **3.** P. Girard, Saint-Étienne, France. Listed in 1933 directories as a gunmaker.

Giraudet, 23 rue de Terrenoire, Saint-Étienne, France. Listed in 1951 as a gunmaker.

Giraudon, boulevard Poincaré, Saint-Étienne, France. Listed in 1951 as a gunmaker.

Girodet. François Girodet, rue de la Paix 18, Saint-Étienne, France. Listed in 1879 as a distributor of, and agent for, arms and ammunition.

Giss. Kurt Giss. The designer and co-patentee with ★Mayer & Grammelspacher of the contra-piston recoil suppressing system embodied in a range of modern Diana airguns: the LP6 and LP10 pistols; the LG60, LG65, LG66, LG70 and LG72 barrel-cocking rifles; and the LG75 series of fixed-barrel sidelever cockers. Relevant protection included British Patent 803,028, sought in March 1956 and granted on 15 October 1958.

'GJM', 'GKC', 'GKJ'. All found on US military firearms and accessories. See G.J. ★McCallin, George K. ★Charter and G.K. ★Jacobs.

'gkp'. Associated with German optical sights and associated components made by the former Carl Schütz factory of Ruf & Co, Kassel, during the Second World War.

'GL' – **1.** A floriated monogram used to identify guns (usually ★Parabellum pistols) that had been produced under the personal supervision of Georg ★Luger. **2.** A trademark, often in the form of a monogram, associated with the products of Gebr. ★Luck of Suhl.

Gladiator. This name, applied to the French Chauchat or ★CSRG light machine-gun, is generally ascribed to one of its designers. However, it applies to the manufacturer – Fabrique des Cycles et Automobiles 'Gladiator', a producer of bicycles and motor vehicles in peacetime.

Glaser. W. Glaser, Zürich. The leading Swiss gun-distributing business of recent times, this was officially registered by Wilhelm Friedrich Glaser of Binningen in December 1908. Glaser sold target and sporting rifles, shotguns, pistols, sub-calibre barrel inserts and a wide variety of accessories. He even commissioned a small quantity of training pistols from ★Francotte prior to 1914; these had the general outline of a ★Parabellum, then the Swiss service pistol, but were blowbacks. Friedrich Aeschlimann and Heinrich Landis acquired the operation in 1934, but continued to trade as W. Glaser until stock was issued in 1957 and W. Glaser Waffen AG was formed. Premises were being occupied at Loewenstrasse 42 in the 1980s.

Glatt. A German-language term applied to a smooth-bore barrel or a smooth-skirted airgun pellet (cf. Gerrifelt, 'rifled').

Glaysher. John Glaysher or Glasier. A gunsmith trading in London from 2 George Yard, Prince's Street, Soho (1865–69), then 12 Denmark Street (1869–70).

Glenfield. A brandname associated with rifles produced by ★Marlin.

Gliddon & Son, Williton, Somerset. This distributor of agricultural equipment is said to have handled sporting guns and ammunition in south-west England under the brandname Exmoor.

Glisenti. A semi-automatic pistol used by the Italian Army prior to 1914. Said to have been designed largely by Abel ★Revelli, it was patented in 1906/07, promoted by Societá Siderugica Glisenti, and made in quantity by the Italian government factory in Brescia (FAB) as the 9mm M1910. Although a commercial variant was promoted by Metallurgica Bresciana Tempini SA (MBT) as the Brixia, the swinging-wedge breech-lock was found to be weak, and eventually the simple blowback ★Beretta was substituted.

Globe – 1. These spring-air BB Guns were initially made by ★Anderson Brothers Company of Plymouth, Michigan, USA, in accordance with a patent granted to Merritt F. ★Stanley on 28 January 1890. Later examples, however, were the work of the ★Dubuar Company of Northville, Michigan. Globe guns came in three versions. Made by Anderson in 1890–92, the oldest was a single-shot break-open pattern with a cast-iron frame and butt. Next came a similar gun made by Dubuar (usually dated to 1892–94, but possibly later) with a smaller frame and a hardwood butt. The third gun was a more ornate version of the second pattern, with a large 'G' cast integrally in the frame above the trigger guard. **2.** Globe Manufacturing Works, Northville, Michigan. Arni Dunathan, writing in *The American BB Gun*, states that this business had no connection with Dubuar, maker of the Globe-pattern BB Guns. However, it is difficult to conclude that no links existed with Merritt Stanley. The Globe Works burned down in 1899, and most of its workforce was transferred to Dubuar! It seems possible, therefore, that the Globe Works made the Globe guns after the split with Anderson Brothers, and that Dubuar was the third contractor instead of the second. This would mean that the Anderson-made Globe dates from 1890–92, the Globe version from 1892–99, and the Dubuar pattern from 1899 until c. 1902.

Glock GmbH, Deutsch-Wagram, Austria. Manufacturer of the Glock automatic pistols (q.v.). **2.** Glock pistol: *see panel, below.*

Gloria. A Spanish Browning-type pocket automatic made by Gregorio ★Bolumburu of Eibar in at least two patterns: (a) 6.35mm, six rounds, striker fired, sometimes marked 'Model 1913'; (b) 7.65mm, seven rounds, hammer fired, often marked 'Model 1915'.

GLOCK PISTOL

Glock (2)

The Model 17 semi-automatic pistol, designed by the Austrian engineer Gaston Glock, was introduced in 1983. Owing to the incorporation of many synthetic parts, the Glock became renowned – without reason – as the ★undetectable terrorist's gun, which could be taken through the X-ray surveillance equipment commonly encountered at airports and border crossings.

The most interesting feature of the pistol, which employs a variation of the ★Browning tipping-barrel lock, is the small auxiliary 'safety trigger' set into the trigger blade to ensure that the gun cannot be fired unless the firer deliberately pulls through on the trigger. Glocks have squared contours and are fired with the assistance of a striker inside the breech-block.

Among the many variants are the long-barrelled Model 17L, chambered for the 9mm Parabellum (9x19) cartridge; the Model 18C, a special 9x19 variant capable of fully automatic fire; the compact Model 19, with a short barrel and slide; the 10mm Auto Model 20; the .45 ACP Model 21; the .40 S&W Models 22 and 23, differing in size; and the 9mm Short/.380 Auto Model 25. The Model 24 is essentially a Model 17L chambering .40 S&W ammunition, and the otherwise identical Model 24C has a compensator fitted to the muzzle.

The Model 26 (9x19) and 27 (.40 S&W) Sub-Compact versions have short butts, restricted-capacity magazines and barrels that measure a mere 88mm long. In general, magazine capacities range from thirteen to seventeen rounds, depending on calibre; however, a thirty-three-round box can be obtained with the Model 18C.

This pistol has been one of the runaway successes of the modern gunmaking industry, rising from obscurity to notoriety in scarely more than a decade. The gun pictured is a 9mm Glock 19, with a fifteen-round magazine.

'Gloucester' [The]. A mark found on shotgun cartridges sold in England by Edward *Fletcher of Gloucester.

Glove pistols. *See* S.M. *Haight.

'GLP', 'GLW'. Found on US military firearms and accessories. *See* G.L. *Prentice and Grover L. *Wotkyns.

'GM'. A mark, often in monogram form, associated with the sporting guns made in Suhl by Gebr. *Merkel.

'GMC' – 1. In a diamond. A mark found on a .22-calibre semi-automatic pistol made in Argentina in the 1940s by Garbi, Moretti y Cia of Mar del Plata. **2.** Found on US military firearms and accessories. *See* George M. *Colvocressus.

'GMR'. Found on US military firearms and accessories. *See* George M. *Ransom.

Göcking. H. Göcking, Zella-Mehlis in Thüringen, Germany. Listed in 1939 as a master gunsmith.

Godins Ltd, Newport, Monmouthshire. Made box magazines for the British .303 *Bren Gun during the Second World War, often marking them with the code 'M 91' instead of the company name. *See also* British military manufacturers' marks.

Goedecke. C. Goedecke & Company. A gunmakers' representative, possibly German, listed in London directories for 1876/7 at 5 Grocer's Hall Court, E.C.

Goessl. Josef Goessl, Suhl in Thüringen, Gothaer Strasse 28. Listed in the *Deutsches Reichs-Adressbuch* for 1930–39 as a '*Gewehr- und Waffenfabrik*' ('gun and weapon maker'). The entry in the 1940 edition notes that Goessl made sporting guns and accessories, in addition to acting as 'weapons depot' (*Waffenlager*) for Stahlwerke Harkort-Eicken. Goessl used a 'J.G.S.' mark, some examples taking the form of a monogram.

Goff. Samuel F. Goff. This gunmaker was listed by H.J. Blanch, writing in *Arms & Explosives* in 1909, at 15 New Street, Covent Garden, London (1879). Goff traded from 17, 18 and 22 King Street, Covent Garden, in 1884–89 (latterly as Samuel F. Goff & Company), and from 32 Brompton Road (1889 only). Operations seem to have ceased in 1890. *See also* Gough.

Gold... – 1. George E. Gold, Castle Mill Street, Bristol, Gloucestershire. The name of this English country gunmaker has been reported on shotgun cartridges marked 'The Popular'. **2.** Gold Cup Commander. Introduced in 1991 by *Colt's Manufacturing Company, Inc., this had target sights, a bevelled magazine well, chequering and serrations on the grip straps, and an extra-wide grip safety. **3.** Gold Cup National Match. Dating from 1957–70, made by *Colt's Patent Fire Arms Manufacturing Company – prior to 1964 – and the Firearms Division of *Colt Industries, these .38 Super and .45 ACP target-shooting versions of *Government Model semi-automatic pistols had hand-fitted barrels and barrel bushings, honed components in the lockwork, relieved sears and lightened trigger blades in a quest for perfection. Most guns had 'NM'-suffix serial numbers and medallions set into their grips. The Mark III version (1961–74) was chambered specifically for .38 Special Mid-Range Wadcutter ammunition, whereas the Mark IV of 1970–83 – subsequently known as the Mark IV Series 70 – had a flat mainspring housing, a target hammer, an improved barrel bushing and a Colt-Elliason back sight. Two hundred 75th Anniversary National Match commemorative pistols were made in 1978, celebrating the first competition held at Camp Perry. The Gold Cup National Match

Mark IV Series 80 (1983 to date) had improvements in the trigger and sights, had hand-honed parts and could accept an eight-round magazine; a Stainless Gold Cup National Match followed in 1986. The advent of Colt's Manufacturing Company, Inc., brought two new guns in 1991: the *Bullseye National Match and the cased Presentation Gold Cup National Match, with a mirror-blued finish and jewelled parts. **4.** Gold Target. Applied by H. *Krieghoff GmbH to engraving patterns applied to the K-80 over/under shotgun. The design consists largely of boldly-cut acanthus leaves and tendrils, radiating from a central point on the receiver-side, within a gold monoline. *See also* Bavaria, Bavaria-Suhl, Crown Grade, Danube and Parcours Special.

Golden... – 1. Charles Golden, Bradford, Yorkshire. This gunmaker began trading on his own account in 1864, from 18 Cheapside, and worked until 1900 or later. His marks have been found on British shotgun cartridges loaded with *Schultze powder, and thus pre-dating 1914. **2.** William Golden, Huddersfield, Yorkshire. The name of this gunmaker has been reported on shotgun cartridges made by *Kynoch. Although Bailey & Nie, in *English Gunmakers*, record Golden only at 2 & 3 Cross Church Street in 1833–65, trading must have continued – possibly under the proprietorship of a similarly-named son – until 1900 or later. **3.** Golden Eagle. A 1,000-shot lever-action Model 50 made in the USA by *Daisy to commemorate fifty years of BB Gun production. Introduced in 1936 with a coppered finish and a tricolour eagle motif on the blacked wood butt, it was discontinued in 1949 (although little or no manufacturing had been done since 1941). **4.** Golden Eagle. Another 1,000-shot lever-action BB Gun, the No. 98 or Daisy Eagle, was made by Daisy from 1955 until 1961, with a paint finish, a fixed 2x telescope sight, gold frame decoration and an eagle impressed into the wood butt. It reappeared in 1975 with an embossed eagle medallion set in the synthetic butt, but lasted only until 1978. **5.** Golden Eagle. The 500-shot No. 104 lever-action BB Gun was made by *Daisy in the USA in 1966–67 with a plastic 'peep' telescope sight, but then became the Model 1776 (1968–73) before reverting in 1973–77 to Model 104 once a crossbolt safety catch had been added. **6.** Golden Eagle Rifles, Inc., of Houston, Texas, offered the Golden Eagle Model 7000 bolt-action rifle (c. 1976–82) in chamberings ranging from .22-250 to .458 Winchester Magnum. Locked by a distinctive five-lug mechanism, the guns were made in Japan by the *Nikko Firearms Manufacturing Company of Tochigi. **7.** 'Golden Flash' [The]. A brandname used by *Garrett of Evesham on shotgun cartridges sold in England. **8.** 'Golden Pheasant' [The]. A brandname found on British shotgun cartridges handled by *Hopkins of Leighton Buzzard. **9.** Golden State Arms Corporation, Pasadena, California, USA. This firearms manufacturer was responsible for a series of *Mauser-pattern sporting rifles made on *Santa Barbara actions in the 1960s. They were marketed as the *Centurion series.

Goldberg. 'Reuben Goldberg'. A patent granted in Britain in April 1934 to this inventor illustrated an 'improved belt-buckle gun' based on a twelve-shot pepperbox or barrelless revolver. This would have chambered weak short-case ammunition, such as 4mm Übungsmunition or .22 Short rimfire, but at least one 7.65mm-calibre belt buckle of a differing design was taken back to the

USA in 1945 as a war trophy. Its buckle-like case contains a hinged block of four barrels, which springs outward when the twin release catches are pressed. Each barrel has an independent hammer-and-trigger mechanism, although they can be fired as a volley if required. The name of the supposed inventor has been questioned, as 'Rube Goldberg' has been used in the USA for the promoters of gimcrack or unnecessarily complicated machinery (cf. 'Heath Robinson' in Britain), and it has been speculated that, in the case of the belt-buckle gun, it is little more than a pesudonym.

Golding – 1. G.E. Golding, Watton, Thetford, Norfolk. The name of this English country gunmaker has been reported on shotgun cartridges sold under the brandname Wayland. **2.** William Golding. This gunsmith began his career in London at 3 Marylebone Street, Piccadilly, in 1827. Subsequently he traded from 199 Oxford Street in 1829–31; 1 Duke Street, Grosvenor Square, in 1831–42; 27a Davies Street, Berkeley Square, in 1843–53; and lastly from 3 Mount Row, Berkeley Square from 1855 until his death in 1859.

Goldmark. Joseph Goldmark, New York City. Established in 1852, as a maker of caps, primers and cartridges, Goldmark produced rimfire ammunition during the American Civil War. These cartridges were usually *headstamped 'J.G.', often with a short underscore. However, soon after exhibiting at the Centennial Exposition held in Philadelphia in 1876, Goldmark ceased trading; the 1877 New York directory is the last in which an entry appears. He was granted US Patent 10,262 in November 1853 to protect a method of manufacturing percussion caps.

Goldsborough. John R. Goldsborough, also listed as Goldsboro. This Federal government arms inspector – holding captain's rank in the navy – accepted *Colt, *Savage and *Whitney cap-lock revolvers during the American Civil War. The guns were marked 'JRG'. *See also* US arms inspectors' marks.

Gonon – 1. Rue Mulatière 83, Saint-Étienne, France. Listed in 1892 as a gunmaker. **2.** G. Gonon, rue Badouillère 18, Saint-Étienne, France. Listed in 1892 as a gunmaker. **3.** Jean Gonon, grande rue Saint-Roch 1, Saint-Étienne, France. Listed in 1879 as a gunmaker. **4.** Régis Gonon, cours Jovin-Bouchard, Saint-Étienne, France. Listed in 1892 as a gunmaker. **5.** Gonon et Portafaix, Saint-Étienne, France. Listed in 1933 as gunmakers, and in 1951 at 8 rue Henri-Barbusse. **6.** Gonon Veuve et fils, rue Villeboeuf 15, Saint-Étienne, France. Listed in 1892 as a gunmaker.

Goodenow Manufacturing Company, Erie, Pennsylvania, USA. This was the original distributor and probable manufacturer of the gas-powered guns associated with the *Challenger Manufacturing Company and, later, of a similar range of guns offered under the *Plainsman name. Production seems to have been confined to 1953–58.

Goodrich. Charles N. Goodrich, a Federal government arms inspector working in 1863, accepted small-arms marked 'CNG'. *See also* US arms inspectors' marks.

'Goodwood' [The]. This name will be found on shotgun cartridges loaded by Russell *Hillsdon.

Goold. Lewis William Goold. A patent agent of 5 Corporation Chambers, Birmingham, who acted for Edwin *Anson and Lincoln *Jeffries & George Urry in 1906–21. *See* British Patents 20,744/06 and 21,324/06 of

1906, 24,837/07 of 1907, and 178,048 of about 1921. *See also* Sadler & Goold.

Goring. G.R. Goring. This government arms inspector, working in 1909–10, accepted US military small-arms marked 'GRG'. *See also* US arms inspectors' marks.

Görting. August Görting & Co., Mengersreuth-Hämmern bezirks Sonneberg. Listed in German trade directories in 1941 as a maker of weapons and assumed to have been a gunsmith.

Gorton. Walter T. Gorton. This government arms inspector, a major in the US Army, accepted .45 M1911 and M1911A1 (Colt) pistols marked 'WTG'. He was active from c. 1925 until the late 1930s. *See also* US arms inspectors' marks.

Goryunov – 1. Mikhail Mikhailovich Goryunov. The younger brother of Petr Goryunov, born in 1912, this gun designer worked on the land until joining the Kolomna engineering factory in 1930. Mikhail Goryunov moved to the Kovrov machine-gun factory in 1934, retiring in 1972 as deputy-director of production. With the assistance of Vasily *Voronkov, he was responsible for perfecting the SG machine-gun after the death of his brother Petr, and he received a USSR State Prize after the Second World War. **2.** Petr Maximovich Goryunov. Born in the village of Kamenka in 1902, the son of a peasant, Goryunov began work as a fitter in the Kolomna engineering factory at the age of ten. After serving in the Red Army during the Civil War, he returned to work in Kolomna until a move to the Kovrov machine-gun factory in 1930 brought him experience of small-arms design. He is best known as the designer of the Soviet SG or Goryunov machine-gun, finished by others after P.M. Goryunov's early death in 1943. A USSR State Prize was awarded posthumously in 1946. **3.** Goryunov machine-gun. Also known as the SG or SG-43, this gun was basically the work of Petr *Goryunov, although it was finished after his untimely death by Mikhail Goryunov and Vasiliy Voronkov. The 7.62mm gas-operated gun was locked by displacing the breech-block laterally; it was sturdy and, once teething troubles had been overcome, proved to be efficient. Large quantities of the basic SG, the improved SGM, and vehicle (SGMB) and tank (SGMT) versions were made, but eventually they were replaced by the *Kalashnikov-designed PK series.

Gosney. Durward Gosney, USA. *See* Garand.

Goth. Frederick Goth, USA. *See* Henry *McKenney.

Gould. H.G. Gould, a government arms inspector working in 1898, accepted US martial small-arms marked 'HGG'. *See also* US arms inspectors' marks.

Goutelle – 1. Goutelle-Berne, rue Saint-Roch 11, Saint-Étienne, France. Listed in 1879 as a gunmaker. **2.** Goutelle fils, rue Saint-Roch 3, Saint-Étienne, France. Listed in 1892 as a gunmaker. **3.** Goutelle-Thiver, rue Neuve 21, Saint-Étienne, France. Listed in 1879 as a gunmaker.

Government Model – 1. *See* panel, p. 214. **2.** Government Model 380. Introduced in 1984, chambering the ineffectual .380 ACP (9mm Short) cartridge, this was a reduced-scale version of the full-size .45 ACP pattern – retaining the tipping-barrel breech lock, but with a short-butt frame, a seven-round magazine and a barrel measuring only 3.5in long. The grip safety was omitted, although post-1988 examples had a firing-pin lock. The customary finish was blueing or nickel plate, but some

M1911 AND M1911A1 GOVERNMENT MODEL PISTOLS

Government...(1)

Derived from the experimental 1909-pattern *Browning pistol, the 'Pistol, Semi-Automatic, Colt, Caliber .45, Model of 1911' was adopted by the US Army on 29 March 1911. About 650,000 military-issue and 138,500 commercial guns, customarily distinguished by C-suffix numbers, were made in 1911–25. US military Colt-Browning pistols were made by a variety of contractors other than *Colt's Patent Fire Arms Manufacturing Company.

*Springfield Armory produced about 30,000 in 1914–15, before priorities were allocated elsewhere. When the First World War began, orders totalling 2,550,000 guns were placed as part of an attempt to accelerate production of all military stores. Licensees included the *Remington–UMC Company of Bridgeport, Connecticut; the *National Cash Register Company of Dayton, Ohio; the *North American Arms Company of Quebec, Canada; Caron Brothers of Montreal, Canada; the *Savage Arms Company of Utica, New York State; the Burroughs Adding Machine Company of Detroit, Michigan; the *Winchester Repeating Arms Company of New Haven, Connecticut; the *Lanston Monotype Company of Philadelphia, Pennsylvania; and the A.J. *Savage Munitions Company of San Diego, California.

However, when fighting ceased in November 1918, only Colt and Remington had completed any guns. Outstanding contracts were cancelled immediately, although the North American Arms Company assembled about 100 M1911 pistols in 1918–19, and the Savage Munitions Company delivered some slides.

About 20,000 of a .455 version with W-prefix numbers were supplied to Britain during the First World War, mostly for service with the Royal Flying Corps and, ultimately, the Royal Air Force. Guns were made under licence by *Kongsberg Våpenfabrikk in Norway, as the 11.25mm m/1912 and m/1914 (the latter with an extended slide-release catch); others were supplied to Argentina in 1917–25, as Mo. 1916; and a large contract, possibly 50,000, was placed by the Russians prior to the Revolution. These were supplied through intermediaries in Britain and have frames marked 'АНГЛ. ЗАКАЗ.' in Cyrillic (*Angliskii Zakazivat*, 'English Order').

The improved M1911A1, adopted in 1926, laid the groundwork for innumerable variations on the same theme. According to US Ordnance Board figures, 1,878,742 M1911A1 pistols were procured during the Second World War, although this figure is believed to have included refurbished pre-war guns and possibly unfulfilled orders. Other claims suggest that military production amounted only to about 1,643,000 guns (1925–70), plus those made for commercial sale: 76,500 prior to 1942, with C-suffix numbers, and 196,000 mostly C-prefix examples dating from 1947 to 1970.

Guns of this type were also supplied to Argentina, Brazil and Mexico, usually from commercial stores. Subsequently, however, the Argentine authorities made pistols of their own, as the '11.25mm Pistola Automatica Sistema Colt Mo. 1927', before proceeding to the Ballester Molina.

M1911A1 pistols were made during the Second World War by the *Ithaca Gun Company of Ithaca, New York; by *Remington-Rand, Inc., of Syracuse, New York State; by the *Union Switch & Signal Company of Swissvale, Pennsylvania; and by the *Singer Manufacturing Company, of Elizabethville, New Jersey. Use of subcontractors was also encouraged during this period when, for example, barrels were made by the *High Standard Manufacturing Company and the *Flanney Bolt Company.

Markings are usually self-explanatory. They include acknowledgements of patents granted to John *Browning and the manufacturer's name (with the exception of the Savage slides). Additional marks may have been applied to guns refurbished or reworked by military facilities such as Augusta Arsenal ('AA'), Benicia Arsenal ('BA'), *Rock Island Armory ('RIA') and *Springfield Armory ('SA').

This variant of the .45 Government Model, customised by Peter West of the British based Gunner One & Company in the 1990s, shows the interest that is still being taken in a design that is nearing its centenary. Extended muzzles with compensators, specially honed triggers, frame spurs and ambidextrous controls are just some of the many features found on guns adapted for Practical Pistol Shooting.

guns made in 1986–89 exhibited Coltguard electroless nickelling. A stainless-steel version dates from 1989, and a Government Model Pocketlite appeared in 1991 with an alloy frame.

Governor – **1.** Usually encountered as 'The Governor', accompanied by an illustration of a Watt flyball-type engine governor, this was to be found on English shotgun cartridges loaded by *Coltman of Burton upon Trent for an unidentified retailer with the initials J.S. & S. **2.** Two different sheath-trigger *Suicide Special revolvers made in the 1880s by the *Bacon Manufacturing Company and the *Hopkins & Allen Arms Company of Norwich, Connecticut, USA.

Gow. John R. Gow & Sons, Dundee, Angus. This Scottish gunmaking business sold sporting guns, accessories and ammunition – including shotgun cartridges marked 'Tayside'.

Gowling. Frederick Gowling. A gunsmith with premises at 21 Eversholt Street, Oakley Square, London N.W., in 1873–75.

Gowrie. E.A. Gowrie, a US government arms inspector working from 1903 to 1910 or later, accepted military small-arms marked 'EAG'. *See also* US arms inspectors' marks.

'GP', 'G.P.' – **1.** Found as 'The G.P.' ('The Grand Prix') on shotgun cartridges made in England by *Eley-Kynoch Ltd. **2.** Found as 'GP' on US military firearms and accessories. *See* George *Palmer and Giles *Porter.

'GPH'. Found on US military firearms and accessories. *See* George P. *Howland.

GPMG. *See* General-purpose machine-gun.

'gpt'. Used by Gustav *Bittner of Weipert, Bohemia, on signal pistols and small-arms components made during the German occupation of Czechoslovakia in 1940–45.

'gqm'. Found on German rifle and other small-arms components made in 1941–45 by Loch & Hartenberger of Idar/Oberstein.

'GR', 'G.R.' – **1.** As 'G. R.', beneath a crown. Found on British weapons: the mark of Kings George V (1910–36) and George VI (1936–52). *See also* Cyphers, imperial and royal. **2.** 'GR', cursive, beneath a crown. Found on the weapons of Saxony: the mark of King Georg (1902–04). *See also* Cyphers, imperial and royal.

Gräbner. Georg Gräbner, Rehberg bei Krems an der Donau, Austria. Distributor of the *Erika and *Kolibri pistols made by Franz *Pfannl in the 1920s.

Graceful. A brandname associated with a revolver made in Belgium prior to 1914 by A. *Bertrand.

'Grafton' [The]. Found on shotgun ammunition loaded in Britain for Frank *Clarke of Thetford and *Harrison & Hussey of London.

Grägl. *See* Froewis-Grägl.

Graham – **1.** George H. Graham. This Federal arms inspector, working during the American Civil War, accepted cap-lock revolvers and other small-arms marked 'GHG'. *See also* US arms inspectors' marks. **2.** G.P. Graham, Cockermouth, Cumberland. The name of this northern English gunmaker has been reported on shotgun ammunition sold under the brandname Cumberland. **3.** J. Graham & Company, Union Street, Inverness. The name of this Scottish gunmaking business will be found on sporting guns and ammunition, including shotgun cartridges sold under the brandnames Bon-Ton, Highland and Primo. The names are also often accompanied by the Inverness coat of arms, which are (most unusually) supported by a camel and an elephant. **4.** J.R. Graham. This government arms inspector, working in 1875, accepted US military small-arms marked 'JRG'. Possibly confused with O.R. Graham (below), but it is not known which version is correct. **5.** O.R. Graham, a government arms inspector working in 1875, accepted rifles and other small-arms marked 'ORG'. Possibly confused with J.R. Graham (above). *See also* US arms inspectors' marks.

Gramm. Otto Gramm, Zella-Mehlis in Thüringen, Germany. Listed in 1939 as a master gunsmith.

Grammelspacher. *See* Mayer & Grammelspacher.

Grand, Grand... – **1.** 'Grand Finale' [The]. Found on shotgun cartridges sold in Wales and south-west England by *Atkinson & Company of Swansea. **2.** Grand Prix, or The Grand Prix. Associated with 12-, 16- and 20-bore shotgun cartridges loaded by the *Schultze Gunpowder Company into cases supplied by *Eley Bros., Grand Prix ammunition is usually classed as an Eley product; additional confusion arises from the perpetuation of the name by Eley Bros., prior to the acquisition of the company by Explosives Trades Ltd in 1918, then by *Eley-Kynoch Ltd. **3.** Grand Syndicat [le], Herstal-lèz-Liège. This superseded the *Petit Syndicat in April 1870, inspired by the outbreak of the Franco-Prussian War and the scrabbling by the French for serviceable arms of almost any type. The participants were the members of the Petit Syndicat – *Ancion & Cie, *Dresse-Laloux & Cie, Auguste *Francotte and *Pirlot-Frésart – together with *Benthin, *Beuret, P. *Drissen, *Falisse, *Gulikers, E. *Malherbe, *Mordant, *Renkin frères and la *Société Liégeoise. The intention was to acquire orders that would be too large to be filled by any individual company, but which could be split between the participants. Operations ceased in 1876, but not before many thousands of *Chassepot rifles had been made for France, 100,000 Snider actions had been supplied to the government of the Ottoman Empire, 8,000 Comblain and 500 Comblain musketoons had been sent to Greece, 50,000 Buescu-system rifles and 10,000 musketoons had been delivered to Romania, and 4,000 revolvers had been produced for an unidentified power.

Grande, Grande... – **1.** Grande Précision. A Browning-pattern pocket automatic made by, or perhaps for, Fabrique d'Armes de *Grande Précision in Eibar, Guipúzcoa, Spain: 6.35mm, six rounds, hammer fired. Probably made by *Beistegui Hermanos. **2.** Fabrique d'Armes de Grande Précision, Extezarraga y Abitua, Eibar, Guipúzcoa. This business marked a wide range of guns, including automatic pistols bought in from smaller manufacturers in the district. They included *Ca-Si, *Colonial, *Grande Précision (probably made by Beistegui Hermanos), *Helvece, *Jubala (said to have been made by Larranaga y Elartza), *Jupiter, *Minerva, *Precision, *Princeps (some made made for Thieme y Edeler) and *Trust. **3.** Grande Puissance (*Pistolet à Grande Puissance*, GP): *see* High Power.

Graner. Louis Graner, Zella-Mehlis in Thüringen, Germany. Listed in the 1939 edition of the *Deutsches Reichs-Adressbuch* as a master gunsmith.

Grange, 13 rue des Armuriers, Saint-Étienne, France. Listed in 1951 as a gunmaker.

Granger – **1.** Rue Saint-Roch 21, Saint-Étienne, France. Listed in 1892 as a gunmaker. **2.** Albert S.

Granger. This Federal government arms inspector, work-ing during the American Civil War, accepted revolvers and other military small-arms marked 'ASG'. *See also* US arms inspectors' marks.

'Granite City' [The]. A name found on shotgun ammunition sold in northern Scotland by *Garden of Aberdeen.

Granjon. Jean-Michel Granjon, rue de Roanne 9, Saint-Étienne, France. Listed in 1879 as a distributor of, and agent for, arms and ammunition.

Granotier, Saint-Étienne, France. Listed in 1933 as a gunmaker.

Grant – 1. A *Suicide Special revolver made in the USA by William *Uhlinger of Philadelphia, Pennsylvania, in the late nineteenth century. **2.** Stephen Grant. This London gunmaker traded from 67a St James's Street from 1867 onward. The business became Stephen Grant & Sons in 1889, but amalgamated with Joseph *Lang & Sons in 1900. Grant's name has been reported on shotgun cartridges marked 'R.P.' **3.** Stephen Grant & Lang, 7 Bury Street, St James's, London SW1. The name of this gunmaking business has been reported on shotgun cartridges sold under the names Briton, Curzon, Grantbury, Instanter, Rocketer and Velogrant. After the amalgamation of Stephen Grant and Atkin & Son, the partnership of Grant & Lang acquired *Watson Bros. and Charles *Lancaster & Company. It also sup-plied about 2,500 *Winchester rifles to the British authorities in 1941. The code 'S 202' was allocated to Grant & Lang during the Second World War, but is

rarely (if ever) encountered. *See also* British military manufacturers' marks.

'Granta' [The]. A brandname associated with shotgun ammunition sold in England by *Gallyon & Sons.

'Grantbury' [The]. Used by *Grant & Lang of London on shotgun ammunition sold in Britain.

'Granton' [The]. Found on shotgun cartridges sold by *Gallyon & Sons, apparently in southern England even though the name could be regarded as having Scottish place-name connections.

Grant-Suttie. George Donald Grant-Suttie, a major in the Black Watch, listed his address as 'care of the Caledonian Club, St James's Square, London, S.W.1' when he sought what were to become British Patents 154,662 and 156,423 (1920) to protect reservoir-type air- and gas guns.

Granville. William Granville. A gunsmith trading in London in 1857, at 44 Holborn Hill.

'Grapevine'. A nickname applied to the *Gross-patent carbine made by the *Cosmopolitan Arms Company, owing to its serpentine operating lever.

Gras – 1. Basile Gras. Inventor of the metallic-cartridge Chassepot conversion adopted by the French government in 1874. **2.** Gras rifle: *see* panel, below.

Graves. E.A. Graves, a government arms inspector working in 1894–1902, accepted US martial small-arms marked 'EAG'. *See also* US arms inspectors' marks.

Gray – 1. D. Gray & Company, 30 Union Street, Inverness. The name of this Scottish gunmaking business has been reported on shotgun cartridges made by *Eley-

---

GRAS RIFLE

Gras (2)

This was the outcome of a series of trials held in France with the Dutch *Beaumont rifle and a conversion of the *Chassepot needle rifle submitted on 8 May 1873 by Basile Gras, who was then a captain serving in the French Army. The Gras was a simple bolt-action rifle, with a separate bolt head and a lock provided by the abutment of the bolt-handle base on the receiver bridge. No ejector was fitted, spent cases being removed from the feedway manually (or simply by inverting the rifle so that they fell clear). The *Fusil d'Infanterie Mle 1874* was adopted on 7 July 1874. Like its Chassepot predecessor, it had a slender one-piece stock with iron mounts, which included a

barrel band and a nose-cap. Many needle rifles were converted to Gras standards by boring out the breech to receive a liner chambered for the new metallic-case cartridges: these were known as Mle 1866/74; Mle 74/80 guns were improved by the addition of an annular gas-escape port in the bolt head and a relieving groove cut into the left side of the bolt-way.

The converted Mle 1866/74 and newly-made Mle 1874 *Carabines de Cavallerie* were similar to the infantry rifle, but had an additional barrel band and the bolt handle turned down against the stock. There were two patterns of Gendarmerie carbine and an artillery musketoon which, apart from chambering, duplicated the design of the earlier Chassepot variants. Subsequently the basic Gras action provided the basis for the

*Kropatschek and *Lebel designs, as well as the host for a number of magazine conversions attempted during the 1880s. Many of the guns that survived in 1914 were converted in the early months of the First World War to chamber the standard 8x51R Lebel rifle cartridge; others were adapted to fire grenades. The 8mm cartridge strained the Mle 74/80/14 actions to their limits. However, most of them were sent to the colonies where their weaknesses were unlikely to become liabilities.

The 11mm-calibre French Mle 1874 Gras infantry rifle was essentially a Chassepot needle rifle adapted to fire metal-case ammunition.

Kynoch and handled under names such as Autokill. **2.** George F. Gray. This US government arms inspector, working in 1905, accepted military small-arms marked 'GFG'. *See also* US arms inspectors' marks. **3.** Reginald Gray, Doncaster, Yorkshire. The name of this English provincial gunmaker has been reported on shotgun cartridges made by Frank *Dyke and sold under the brandname 'Don'. **4.** Samuel Gray. An English gunsmith and sword-cutler trading from 10 Marshall Street, Golden Square, London, in 1850–51.

Greason. Gilbert D. Greason, a Federal government arms inspector working in 1861–62, accepted small-arms marked 'GDG'. *See also* US arms inspectors' marks.

Great Western – 1. A *Suicide Special revolver made by the *Harrington & Richardson Arms Company of Worcester, Massachusetts, USA, in the late nineteenth century. **2.** Great Western Gun Works, Pittsburgh, Pennsylvania. Established by John H. Johnston in 1866, trading from 621 Smithfield Street in Pittsburgh, this gun-chandlery moved to 179 Smithfield Street when the original premises burned down in 1868. A further move to 285 Liberty Street took place in 1874. The Great Western Gun Works has been credited with the manufacture of shotguns, sporting rifles, revolvers and even St Louis-style *Gallery Guns, but virtually all of these were war-surplus, bought in from gunmaking businesses in North America or originating in Europe. Trading ceased in 1916.

Grebler. A. Grebler, or 'Grebles', Chicago, Illinois. This US gunsmith, sales agency or shooting-gallery owner has been linked with the manufacture of St Louis-style *Gallery Guns in the 1870s. Authentication is lacking.

Green, Green… – 1. Abram Green. This gunsmith was listed in Chamber Street, London, in 1847, and at 198 Whitechapel Road, London E., in 1859–60. **2.** Edwinson Charles Green, Gloucester and Cheltenham Spa, Gloucestershire. Green is perhaps best known for litigation with Webley over the origins of the stirrup-type locking system used on Webley revolvers. However, he also made sporting guns, and sold shotgun cartridges marked 'Cotswold', 'Fur & Feather' and 'Velox'. His name is associated with the *Webley-Green revolver, and also with a contentious claim to have invented the over/under shotgun. **3.** Geo. Green. This gunmaker, or possibly wholesaler, supplied *Winchester rifles to the British authorities in 1941. **4.** Samuel G. Green. A lieutenant-colonel in the US Army, Green accepted .45 M1911A1 (Colt) pistols marked 'SGG' in 1939–40. *See also* US arms inspectors' marks. **5.** William Green. A London gunmaker, originally of 22 Little Newport Street, Soho (1832–37), Green operated from 4 & 6 Leicester Square in 1838–55, then 138 New Bond Street in 1861–64. He was granted British Patent 2714/60 of 1860 to protect a breech-loading rifle with a tip-up block, and also advertised himself as 'Successor to Frederick *Prince and Sole Manufacturer of Prince's Breech-Loading Rifle'. **6.** William Charles Green. Listed in 1870 as a gunmaker, at 91 Wardour Street, London, and possibly also at 14 Coburn Road, London E., from 1883 to 1885. He may have been the son of William Green (above). **7.** 'Green Rival' [The]. This mark was associated with shotgun cartridges loaded in Britain by the *New Explosives Company Ltd during the period 1907–19. **8.** Green Seal. A shotgun cartridge made in Birmingham in the *Mullerite Cartridge Works. The name refers to the

colour of the case-crimp disc. *See also* 'Grey Seal', 'Red Seal' and 'Yellow Seal'.

Greenbat. A brandname associated with the products of *Greenwood & Batley of Leeds, including smokeless propellant.

Greene – 1. James Durrell Greene, Cambridge, Massachusetts, and Ann Arbor, Michigan, USA. This inventor was granted US Patent 11,157 of 27 June 1854 and 11,917 of 7 November 1854 to protect unsuccessful pivoting-barrel carbines. He soon progressed to a proprietary cartridge (US Patent 18,143 of September 1857) and an under-hammer bolt-action rifle – US Patent 18,634 of November 1857. Purchase of 100 guns was authorised on 5 August 1857, but the costs of tooling could not be recovered from so small an order and Greene preferred to travel to Europe, where a 3,000-gun order was obtained from Russia. Subsequently Greene patented an improvement to his bolt-action system (US Patent 34,422 of 18 February 1862), which was similar to the conversions supplied to Russia. He was also granted two patents after the American Civil War: 88,161 of 23 March 1869, for a 'breechloading firearm'; and 312,201 of 10 February 1885 for a magazine gun. **2.** W.H. Greene. This government arms inspector, working in 1902, accepted military small-arms marked 'WHG'. *See also* US arms inspectors' marks. **3.** Greene carbine. Protected by US Patent 11,157, granted to James Durrell Greene on 27 June 1854, this was made in small quantities between 1855 and 1857 by the *Massachusetts Arms Company. The breech was opened by pressing the front trigger, twisting the barrel to the right to disengage the locking lugs, sliding the barrel group forward and then finally to the right to expose the chamber. A hollow spike in the standing breech pierced the base of the combustible cartridge as the action was closed, allowing the flash from a percussion cap to reach the powder charge. **4.** Greene rifle. Nine hundred 1862-pattern under-hammer guns were ordered by the Federal authorities in January 1863. Made by *Milbury of Watertown, Massachusetts, they were still in store in March 1864. Rotating the bolt downward revolved two lugs into seats behind the chamber, rifling was *Lancaster oval-bore pattern, and the self-contained combustible cartridge carried a projectile in the base. The loaded Greene rifle, therefore, had one projectile ahead of the charge and a second bullet acting as a gas-seal. **5.** Greene Rifle Works, Worcester, Massachusetts. Active in 1864–67, this factory made the breech-loading rifles patented by James Durell Greene as well as the second or new-pattern *Warner carbines during the American Civil War.

Greener – 1. Charles Edward Greener. Son of William W. Greener (below), Charles Edward received British Patent 411,520 on 8 June 1934 to protect a lever-operated camming system intended to improve the seal between the breech face and barrel of airguns. It was used on the Greener Air Rifle of the 1930s, and a similar system has since been adopted by *Mayer & Grammelspacher and *Weihrauch. **2.** Harry Greener, St Mary's Square, Birmingham. This 'Gunmaker' and member of the powerful Greener dynasty received British Patent 9,644/03 of 1903 to protect the trigger mechanism of Lanes' *Musketeer spring-air rifle. **3.** William Greener, Birmingham. Born in Newcastle upon Tyne in 1806, where he set up his gunmaking business in 1829, Greener

moved to Birmingham in 1843 and traded there until his death in 1869. Representation was maintained in London by a succession of agents, beginning at 25 Gerrard Street, Soho, in 1846 and ending at 42 Eley Place, Holborn, in 1858. The last known agent was Daniel B. Harvey. Greener was a prolific inventor in several fields, among relevant protection being British Patent 2693/54 of 1854, for revolvers, breech-loaders and metallic-case cartridges; and 2349/64 of 1864 for a particular method of chambering barrels. He is also known as the author of such books as *The Gun* (1835) and *Gunnery* (1858). **4.** W.W. Greener & Company: *see* panel below. **5.** William W. Greener. 'Old William' retired in 1864, to be succeeded by his son, William Wellington Greener (1834–1921), best remembered for such books as *Modern Breech Loaders* (1871) and *The Gun and Its Development* (nine editions published prior to 1910). The younger Greener – never noted for his reticence! – claimed to have invented the air cane, which was patently untrue, although there is no doubt that he made invaluable contributions to the refinement and manufacture of the double-barrel sporting gun. **6.** Greener Cross-bolt. This was a method of locking the breech of a shotgun or double rifle, relying on a bar that, as the mechanism closed, was moved laterally by the top lever through a hole in the barrel-lump extension or Doll's head. **7.** 'Greener's Dwarf' [The]. Found on shotgun ammunition sold by W.W. ★Greener of Birmingham.
Greenfield. H.S. Greenfield [& Son], Canterbury, Kent. The marks of this English country gunmaking business, trading from 4 Upper Bridge Street, then 5 Dover Street in Canterbury, have been reported on sporting guns and ammunition. Shotgun cartridges marked 'The County Cartridge' have been seen with Greenfield's marks.
Greenleaf. William B. Greenleaf, Chicago, Illinois, USA. An employee of the ★Markham Air Rifle Company, Greenleaf was also co-patentee with Ernest S. ★Roe of BB Guns.
Greenwood – 1. Usually found as 'The Greenwood' on shotgun cartridges made by Greenwood & Batley. **2.** Greenwood & Batley, Leeds, Yorkshire, and Farnham, Surrey. Originally this engineering business, founded in 1856 by Thomas Greenwood and John Batley, was renowned for its machine tools, including gun- and ammunition-making equipment. Products of the Albion Foundry in Leeds equipped the ★Royal Small Arms Factory, Enfield, and the ★Birmingham Small Arms Company premises in Small Heath. Machine tools were supplied to, among others, the ★London Small Arms Company; the planned Macon Armory, which was never completed by the government of the Confederate States of America; ★Österreichische Waffenfabriks-Gesellschaft, Steyr; ★Manufacture de l'Armes de l'État, Liège, Belgium; and Waffenfabrik Neuhausen (subsequently ★SIG) in Switzerland. However, perhaps envious of the success of the Birmingham Small Arms Company, Greenwood & Batley diversified into the manufacture of guns and ammunition. Service-rifle and shotgun cartridges are known to have been made under a 'G B' headstamp together with brandnames such as Greenbat and Skyrack. Cartridges have also been reported with 'A.E.C. Grey Squirrel' and 'A.E.C. Pest Control' marks, but the significance of the 'A.E.C.' abbreviation is not yet known. *See also* Ludwig Loewe & Co. and Pratt & Whitney.

W.W. GREENER & COMPANY

Greener (4)

This was formed on the death of the elder Greener in 1869, becoming W.W. Greener Ltd in 1920, trading independently until acquired in 1965 by ★Webley & Scott Ltd. Premises were listed at 61 & 62 Loveday Street, Birmingham, in 1864–69, but then moved to St Mary's Square and stayed there for nearly 100 years. A London office was also maintained at 68 Haymarket.

An advertisement in the ninth edition of *The Gun and Its Development* (1910) lists branches at 19 Paragon Street, Hull; 63 & 65 Beaver Hall Hill, Montreal, Canada; and 44 Cortlandt Street, New York City. Later literature added 8 Avenue de l'Opéra in Paris; 176 Broadway in New York; and 38 Bolshaya Morskaya in St Petersburg. Trademarks included W.W.G. in many forms, and an elephant motif.

W.W. Greener entered a 12-bore Patent Wedge-Fast breech-loading shotgun in *The Field* trials of 1866.

The company also offered ★Lee-Enfield sporting and military rifles prior to 1914, but they were usually standard BSA-made guns with Greener marks. The No. 1 Sporting Rifle in .303 or .375 was the most popular pattern, being offered with 'sporting' or plain finish. Long Lee-Enfield rifles, 'specially sighted and tested for Match shooting', were also available. Martini-action sporting, miniature and target rifles were made in large numbers, and a Martini-action shotgun remained available into the 1970s.

Greener also handled shotgun cartridges displaying names such as 'Dead Shot', 'E-K', 'Greener's Dwarf', 'Paragon', 'Police Gun' and 'Sporting Life'. A few barrel-cocking air rifles were made in the 1930s, with the patented cam-lever breech seal, but sales were so slow that new guns were still being sold from stock in 1960.

About 39,400 British .303 No. 3 ★Enfield rifles were modified by Greener to Weedon Repair Standards (WRS) in the summer of 1939. A thousand .22 No. 2 ★Lee-Enfield training rifles and about 17,000 ★Lanchester submachine-guns were made in the early stages of the Second World War, the Lanchesters being assembled from parts made elsewhere (probably by the ★Sterling Engineering Company). Greener also supplied the British authorities with about 1,000 Martini-type rifles in 1940; 6,750 12-Bore Police Guns in 1942; about 2,300 Pistols, Signal, No. 1 Mk III★ in 1940; and a few hundred Horse Killers, .310, Mk 1. It is assumed that many bore the code 'M 94'. *See also* British military manufacturers' marks.

W.W. Greener was known for, among many other things, the variety of firearms he made on the basis of the Martini breech mechanism. They ranged from .230/.297 and .320 cadet rifles made prior to 1914 to single-barrel shotguns and the 12-bore (blank) line-throwing gun shown here.

Greer. John E. Greer. A US Army captain, this arms inspector accepted ★Colt and other revolvers in 1876–83, marking them 'JEG'. *See also* US arms inspectors' marks.

Greifelt – **1.** G.H. Greifelt, Suhl in Thüringen, Germany. Listed in the 1900 edition of the *Deutsches Reichs-Adressbuch* as a gunmaker. **2.** Greifelt & Co., Suhl in Thüringen. Founded in 1885 by Friedrich Greifelt and Emil Schlegelmilch, this gunmaking business was being run by Alfred Greifelt and Oskar Jung when the First World War broke out. An advertisement dating from 1925 extols the virtues of the company's 'hunting guns of various types'. The ownership remained unchanged in 1940, when premises were being occupied in Suhl at Lauwetter 25. At that time, products included sporting rifles, shotguns, gun-parts and accessories, being made under the superintendence of Richard Jung. Trading ceased at the end of the Second World War.

Grelgud. Henry Grelgud, Britain. *See* Gielgud.

Grelle. Charles de Grelle & Company, also listed as Degrelle and DeGrelle. Revealed in London directories in 1884–88, first at 19 Basinghall Street, and later at 130 London Wall, de Grelle is believed to have been a representative for the Belgian, or possibly French, gun trade and was clearly working earlier than the dates given in Blanch's *Arms & Explosives* article; de Grelle had entered the otherwise obscure single-shot Loron rifle in the British Army rifle trials of 1867–68.

Grendel, Inc., Rockledge, Florida. Maker of the innovative P-10 automatic in 9mm Short.

Grenfell. Grenfell & Accles, Ltd . An office was maintained briefly in London in 1892, at 7 Great St Helen's, E.C. *See* James G. ★Accles.

Greville. Harston C. Greville & Company. *See* Harston.

Grey, Grey… – **1.** William Grey. This gunmaker, trading from 41 (later 43) Old Bond Street, from 1858 until 1872, had previously been a partner in ★Moore & Grey. **2.** 'Grey Seal'. Found on shotgun cartridges made by the ★Mullerite Cartridge Works of Birmingham. The name refers to the colour of the case-crimp disc. *See also* 'Green Seal', 'Red Seal' and 'Yellow Seal'.

Greyer. W. Greyer, New York City. Active in 1865–72, Greyer is known to have made, or possibly sold, spring-air ★Gallery Guns.

'GRG', 'GRH'. Found on US military firearms and accessories. *See* G.R. ★Goring and George R. ★Harrington.

'GRI', beneath a crown, above a number. A mark applied by an inspector working in the Indian small-arms factory in ★Ishapore prior to the grant of independence in 1947. *See also* 'IS' and British military inspectors' marks.

Griessellich, Nebel & Company. This business is believed to have been a merchant and distributor, although sometimes listed as a member of the London gun trade. Operations were undertaken from 59 Basinghall Street in 1859–76, latterly as Henry Griessellich & Company.

Griffin & Howe, Inc., New York City. One of the best known of the custom gunmakers operating in the USA prior to the Second World War, this business was responsible for – among many others – ★Mauser sporting rifles built on Oberndorf actions.

Griffith, Griffiths – **1.** J.H. Griffith, a civilian arms inspector working for the Federal Navy, accepted small-arms marked 'JHG' during the American Civil War. *See also* US arms inspectors' marks. **2.** John A. Griffiths,

Cincinnati, Ohio, USA. An English-born gunmaker trading in the USA from 1834 until the end of the American Civil War in 1865, in partnership in the mid-1850s with Henry L. Siebert. Griffiths is best known for sporting guns, allegedly including a few breech-loaders, and his marks have also been found on *cap-lock revolvers made elsewhere. **3.** William Griffiths. A maker of 'Implements and Air Guns', according to his trade cards, Griffiths occupied premises at 61 Weaman Street, Birmingham, Warwickshire, in 1846–64. **4.** William Griffiths, Manchester, Lancashire. The name of this English provincial gunmaker has been reported on sporting guns and *Eley Bros. shotgun cartridges. A business of the name began trading in 1854 at 17 Erskine Street, Stretford New Road, and had moved to 42 Hyde Street by 1857. It is assumed that there were two similarly-named proprietors – father and son – and that trading continued at least until the outbreak of the First World War. **5.** William Griffiths, an 'Engineer' of Mossley House, Main Road, Bexley Heath, Kent, was the co-designer with Herbert *Woodgate of the Griffiths & Woodgate auto-loading rifle. This was protected by British Patents 21,282/91 of 5 December 1891 and 16,730/92 of 16 September 1892, granted for the basic action, and improvements in the safety and trigger arrangements respectively. **6.** Griffiths & Woodgate rifle. This auto-loader was patented by William Griffiths and Herbert *Woodgate in 1891–92. Offered to the British Army in 1893, it was rejected untried. Operated by recoil and locked by a turning bolt, the rifle was of sufficient interest to be included in Greener's *The Gun and Its Development* as late as 1910.

Grimard. Edgar Grimard, Liège. A Belgian agent, responsible for the supply of an assortment of guns from Belgium to the British War Office immediately prior to the German invasion in 1940. Apparently these included a batch of 7.92x57 *Vickers Guns on its way to Turkey.

Grimes. S.J. Grimes, Stamford, Lincolnshire. The name of this English gunmaker has been reported on shotgun cartridges made by Frank *Dyke in the 1920s, or more probably assembled from German-made components. These were sold under the brandname Stamford Champion.

Grimshaw. Thomas Grimshaw. A gunmaker listed in London at 48 Whiskin Street (1844–47); 6 Dorrington Street, Clerkenwell (1848–57); and 16 Penton Place, Pentonville Road (1858–59).

Grimwade & Company. Listed as a member of the London gun trade in 1880 only, trading from 54 Queen Victoria Street.

Grip – 1. A part of the butt (q.v.) between the action and the comb, also known as the wrist. **2.** A separate hand grip, either behind the trigger or beneath the fore-end, commonly fitted to compensate for the use of a straight-line stock, or to improve control in automatic fire.

'GRI' and 'P', with a crown and crossed pennants. A military proof mark used in India during the reigns as Emperor of George V (1910–36) and George VI (1936–47). *See also* British military proof marks.

Grisel. Peter Grisel, USA. *See* Dakota Arms.

Griswold & Gunnison, Griswoldville, Georgia, Confederate States of America. Makers in 1862–64 of about 3,500 .36 six-shot *Navy Colt-type revolvers with brass frames and round Dragoon-style barrels.

Grivolat père et fils, rue Villeboeuf 23, Saint-Étienne, France. Listed in 1892 as a gunmaker.

Groh. František Groh, born in the small Bohemian town of Kourim in January 1825, studied medicine in Prague and Vienna, graduating in 1846. Although best known as a leading and much decorated Austrian physician, Groh was also renowned as a writer on military matters and an inventor of breech-loading rifles. The best-known of the guns was a hinged side-locking action with an external hammer, patented in Germany in October 1871 (no. 17323).

Groom. Richard Groom. This gunmaker was first listed at 10 King Street, Commercial Road, London, in 1839. Subsequently he moved to Cock Hill, Stepney (c. 1840–46), then to 10 Wellington Passage, Stepney, by the time the last directory entry appeared in 1859.

Grosfils. Marcel Grosfils, Brussels, Belgium. Styled as *Arquebusier du Roi* ('Gunmaker to the King') and trading during the 1930s, this man seems to have bought many of the firearms in Liège, including shotguns made by Jean *Duchateau.

Gross, Groß – 1. Bruno Gross u. Co., Suhl-Neuendorf. A maker of parts for sporting guns and rifles, active in Germany during the 1930s. **2.** Henry Gross, Tiffin, Ohio, USA. Patentee of the Gross, or Cosmopolitan, carbine in August 1859 (no. 25,259). **3.** Gross carbine. This quirky firearm has acquired several different names: Gross, *Cosmopolitan and *Union. The carbine lacked a fore-end and was operated by pulling the breech lever down, pivoting the breech-block face upward as the rear of the breech swung down. A separate breech cover, with an integral loading groove, dropped to allow a combustible cartridge to be pushed into the chamber. The gun was fired by a conventional cap-lock. *See also* Gwyn & Campbell.

Groupement Industriel des Armements Terrestres. *See* GIAT.

'GR' and 'P', with a crown and crossed pennants. A British military proof mark used during the reigns of George V (1910–36) and George VI (1936–52). *See also* British military proof marks.

'Gr rG', beneath an eagle. This essentially circular mark, consisting of two jaw-to-jaw monograms beneath a displayed eagle, has been used by Renato *Gamba since the early 1990s on sporting guns made by *Società Armi Bresciane. *See also* 'RG'.

Gruber, Grüber – 1. A. Grüber, Suhl in Thüringen. Listed as a gunmaker in 1900. **2.** Chr. Grüber & Sohn, Suhl in Thüringen, Germany. A gunmaking business operated in 1900 by Ad. Frohn. **3.** Rob. Grüber, Suhl in Thüringen. A specialist gun-stocker trading in Germany in 1939.

Gruler. Joseph Gruler, Norwich, Connecticut. Co-grantee with August *Rebety of US Patent 25,259 of 27 December 1859, protecting the inclusion of safety notches on a revolver cylinder. This was exploited by the *Manhattan Fire Arms Company.

Grünel. A brandname used by Grünig & Elmiger.

Grünig & Elmiger, Jagd- & Sportwaffenfabrik & Mechanische Werkstätten, Malters, Switzerland. This long-established precision engineering business, which became Grunig & Elmiger AG in 1976, has made Grünel-brand sporting rifles and high-quality competition sights for many years. Grünig & Elmiger began to make the barrel inserts or Einsteckläufe designed by Walter Lienhard in 1962. Products are often marked with a concentric 'E' within 'G' monogram, although some older examples appear to have borne 'MA' within 'G'.

'GS', 'G.S.' A mark associated with the Geweermakers School in Bandung, Java. It will be found on replacement parts – including barrels, stocks and grips – fitted to weapons issued to the Netherlands Indies Army (*KNIL).

'GT', 'G.T.' – 1. Often in the form of a monogram. A trademark associated with *Gun Toys of Gardone Val Trompia, Italy. **2.** Found on US military firearms and accessories. *See* George *Talcott.

'GTA', 'GTB', 'GTR', 'GTW'. Found on US military firearms and accessories. *See* G.T. *Allen, G.T. *Balch, Garland T. *Rowland and George T. *Weaver respectively.

Guardian – 1. A name found on open-frame revolvers made in Belgium c. 1875–85 (some marked 'American Model 1878'). Perhaps the work of *Arendt of Liège, the larger guns chambered .380 cartridges; smaller ones generally accepted the .320 version, lacked the lanyard ring and had folding triggers. **2.** A *Suicide Special revolver made in the USA by the *Bacon Manufacturing Company of Norwich, Connecticut; late nineteenth century. **3.** Guardian 27C. A compact 6.35mm-calibre automatic pistol made in the USA by *Michigan Armament.

Guardia Rural. A generic term for virtually any rural gendarmerie raised in Spanish-speaking countries, this has been associated specifically with *Colt revolvers acquired by the Cuban gendarmerie at the end of the nineteenth century.

Guedes. A single-shot dropping-block rifle designed by Luis Guedes Dias in 1882–84 and adopted in 1885 by the Portuguese Army. Although made in large numbers by *Österreichische Waffenfabriks-Gesellschaft, the Guedes was soon replaced by the bolt-action *Kropatschek. It has been claimed that its breech-block (containing the trigger and hammer mechanism) was too weak for the 8x60R cartridge, and many unwanted guns were sold in the 1890s to Transvaal and the Orange Free State.

Guerreiro. Alessandro, or Alexander, Guerreiro of Genoa was granted British Patent 628/63 of 5 March 1863 – by way of agent William Clark – and US Patent 47,252 of 11 April 1865, each protecting a revolver with a cylinder that could be swung out to the right on a pivoting yoke. However, access to the chambers was possible only when a disc-like backplate had also been opened. Guerreiro revolvers were made in small numbers in Liège in the 1860s and 1870s, customarily chambering pinfire ammunition. Guns of this type may be marked 'SYSTÈME ITALIEN' on the frame. The British patent records note that an interest in the patent was granted in 1864 to Cauvin, Pavese, Williamson & Weiland.

'gug'. A codemark found on telescope sights and similar optical equipment made in 1941–44 by Ungarische Optische Werke AG of Budapest under contract to the German government.

Guglielminotti. *See* Valle Susa di Guglielminotti.

Guichard – 1. 66 cours Fauriel, Saint-Étienne, France. Listed in 1951 as a gunmaker. **2.** J. Guichard, rue de Lyon 46, Saint-Étienne, France. Listed in 1879 as a gunmaker. **3.** M. Guichard et Cie, 20 rue Montferré, Saint-Étienne, France. Listed in 1951 as a gunmaker.

Guide Lamp Division of General Motors, USA. Makers of the *Liberator pistol.

Guignand et Pailleux, 76 rue Antoine-Durafour, Saint-Étienne, France. Listed in 1951 as a gunmaker.

Guillot, Saint-Étienne, France. Listed in 1933 as a gunmaker. Still trading in 1951 from 11 place Villeboeuf.

Guinard. Albert Guinard, Paris. This entrepreneur, active prior to 1914, was the French agent for the British Gabbett Fairfax *Mars pistol in 1900–05. Some guns will be found with his name and address ('8 Avenue de l'Opera, Paris'), and French-language patent markings ('*Brevete *S.G.D.G.') .

Guiosson – 1. Guiosson aîné, rue de la Charité 9, Saint-Étienne, France. Listed in 1879–92 as a gunmaker. **2.** Rue Villeboeuf 22, Saint-Étienne, France. Listed in 1892 as a gunmaker.

Guisasola – 1. A Spanish 6.35mm-calibre Browning-type pocket pistol made by Guisasola Hermanos: six rounds, striker fired. **2.** Guisasola Hermanos, Eibar, Guipúzcoa. This Spanish gunmaking business was responsible for the Guisasola 6.35mm pistol, with a six-round box magazine.

'guj'. Associated with German military optical equipment made by Werner D. Kuehn of Berlin-Steglitz during the Second World War.

Gulikers, Liège, Belgium. A gunmaker involved in the 1870s with le *Grand Syndicat.

Gunn. George Peck Gunn, Herkimer, New York State. Gunn was the co-designer with Benjamin *Haviland of a spring-air pistol with the air cylinder in the butt (US Patent 126,954 of 1872). In addition, he and Haviland developed the *Pettengill system into what is now known as the *Gem. George Gunn also received protection for a magazine-fed derivative of the butt-cylinder airgun – US Patent 337,395 of 12 August 1885 and British Patent 3299/98 of 1886 – and for a felt-base airgun slug: US Patent 290,230 of 1883. The inventor reputedly joined the *Quackenbush organisation c. 1885, receiving US Patent 370,817 on 4 October 1887 and apparently assigning it to his master.

Günther – 1. Franz Günther, Suhl in Thüringen, Germany. A gunsmith/gun-stocker active in Suhl in 1939. **2.** Siegfried Günther, Suhl in Thüringen, Germany. A sales agency listed in the 1939 *Deutsches Reichs-Adressbuch*.

Gun Toys SpA, Gardone Val Trompia, Brescia, Italy. Best known as a maker of barrel-cocking spring-air pistols and pistol-carbines, Gun Toys has also made an extensive range of blank-firers. The products were distributed in Britain prior to 1982 by the *Sussex Armoury; thereafter by the *Phoenix Arms Company and Scalemead. The pistols have been sold in Britain as Hotshot and Panther, and also under the *IGI banner.

Günzel. A. Günzel, Suhl in Thüringen. A sales and promotional agency active in Germany in 1920–30.

Günzler. Otto Günzler, Suhl in Thüringen. A gunmaking business active in Germany, apparently between the world wars.

'guo'. Found on German small-arms components manufactured in the Hembrug/Zaandam factory of *Artillerie-Inrichtingen (NV Nederlandsche Maschinenfabrik) during the German occupation of the Netherlands in 1940–44.

Gurney. Henry Gurney. Listed as a gunmaker at 12a Gloucester Street, Commercial Road, East London, in 1854–55; and, as a partner in John & Henry Gurney, trading from 1 Red Lion Street, Holborn, London, in 1864–65.

Gurtys. Stanislaw Gurtys, Poznan. This engineer was granted German Patent 492,136 of 1926 to protect a selective-fire modification of the *Parabellum; at the time, Poznan (Posen) was then still in German territory. The modifications consisted of a new sear bar and an additional selector lever set in the trigger plate.

Gustloff-Werke, Berlin, Weimar and a regional office (*Zweigniederlassung*) in Suhl in Thüringen. Directories dating from 1940 listed two depots in Suhl – in Fritz-Sauckel-Strasse and Hohefeld Strasse – and a third in nearby Dietzhausen. There was a factory in Weimar, and another, the Rennsteigwerk, in Schmiedefeld am Rennstieg. Formerly trading as *Berlin-Suhler Werke (BSW), this German gunmaking business made automatic pistols and *Barnitzke-type automatic rifles during the Second World War.

Güttler. W. Güttler Pulverfabriken, Reichenstein, Germany. Maker of shotgun cartridges sold under the Adler brandname.

Guy. Charles Guy, Bell Street, Shaftesbury, Dorset. The marks of this English gunmaker (active 1841–59) have been reported on self-cocking *pepperboxes.

'GW'. Found on US military firearms and accessories. *See* George *Well and George *Wright.

'Gwalia' [The]. A brandname found on shotgun ammunition handled in Britain by *James of Newcastle Emlyn prior to 1939.

'GWC', 'GWH', 'GWM', 'GWP', 'GWR', 'GWS', 'GWW'. Found on US military firearms and accessories. *See* George W. *Chapin; George W. *Hagner and George W. *Hamlin; George W. *Morse and George W.

McKee; George W. *Patch; George W. *Rodgers; George W. *Schuman and G.W. *Smith; and George W. *Wassner respectively.

Gwyn & Campbell. These entrepreneurs simplified the action of the *Gross carbine (US Patent 36,709 of 21 October 1862) so that a grooved breech-block simply dropped at the front to expose the chamber. The gun resembled its predecessor, but the breech lever locked into the front of the catch on the underside of the butt, and the back sight was simplified. The Federal government purchased 9,342 Gross and Gwyn & Campbell carbines prior to 30 June 1866, but undoubtedly others were sold privately during the war.

Gye & Moncrieff. Best known for a patented sporting gun with the bar for the locking bolt running forward from the standing breech – instead of being part of the barrel-lump – this gunmaking partnership traded from 60 St James's Street, London, in 1876–85, then from 44 Dover Street until 1887.

Gypsy. A *Suicide Special revolver made by the *Crescent Arms Company of Norwich, Connecticut, USA, in the late nineteenth century.

'gyu'. Found on small-arms components made in 1941–45 by Gebr. Michera of Prague and Stara-Tura/Slowakei, working under German supervision during the occupation of Czechoslovakia.

'GZ'. Found on US military firearms and accessories. *See* George *Zauche.

H

'H', 'h' – 1. Found as 'H' on *knoxform and butts of .303 No. 1 *Lee-Enfield rifles fitted with Australian-pattern heavy barrels. 2. As 'H7', with '7' on the 'H' crossbar, beneath a crown. Found on Norwegian weapons: the mark of King Haakon VII (1905–57). *See also* Cyphers, imperial and royal. 3. In the form of a black-letter 'h', encircled and surmounted by a crown. A trademark associated with *Husqvarna Våpenfabrik, found on the grips of Swedish-made *FN-Browning and *Lahti pistols, as well as the chambers of many sporting rifles. 4. A *headstamp applied to rimfire ammunition made (originally for *Henry rifles) by the *New Haven Arms Company and its successor, the *Winchester Repeating Arms Company.

'HA', 'ha', 'H&A' – 1. A superimposition-type 'HA' monogram within a rhomboidal lozenge, with squared italic letters of equal prominence. Found on semi-automatic pistols (especially the .22 rimfire Hafdasa) made in Argentina by Hispano-Argentina Fábrica de Automviles SA. 2. Found as 'ha' on German small-arms ammunition components made by Wielandwerke AG of Ulm am Donau in 1940–45. 3. A superimposition-type monogram with 'H' and 'A' of equal dominance. A mark used by *Hopkins & Allen, customarily found on revolvers. 4. Usually as 'H&A', often encircled. Associated with the products of Hopkins & Allen.

Haaken-Plomdeur & Cie, Liège. Gunsmiths working in Belgium during the 1850s and 1880s, renowned for sporting rifles and shotguns.

Hackett. Edwin & George Hackett. This gunsmithing business was listed between 1876 and 1878 at 37 Gracechurch Street, London.

Hadar II. A derivative of the Israeli *Galil assault rifle, intended for police and sporting use. It can be distinguished by a one-piece wooden 'thumbhole' half-stock.

Haddan. Patent agents Herbert Haddan & Company, of 18 Buckingham Street, Strand, London, acted for a variety of inventors – including the Americans *Calkins, Lindberg, Wheeler and Butts (1898–1905).

Haemmerli. *See* Hämmerli.

Haendler & Natermann GmbH. August-Natermann-Platz, Hannover-Munden, Germany. Zacharias Haendler began trading in 1788, Haendler & Co. being formed when his daughter married Friedrich Natermann in 1817. Haendler & Natermann was founded on 1 January 1825, but was wholly owned by the Natermann family by 1835. Lead packaging material was made from 1840, lead shot from 1848, and production of lead balls, piping and zinc sheeting began in 1850. A fire destroyed much of the factory in 1888, but the business was speedily rebuilt by Kommerzienrat Johan August Natermann (1850–1922); 500 people were employed by 1898. Manufacture of bottle stoppers and wine-bottle seals was then in full swing. Haendler & Natermann AG was formed in 1923, registering with the chamber of commerce on 5 September, although ownership remained with the family. However, the principal male members died during or immediately after the Second World War, and directors were sought outside the family for the first time. Initially, post-war business was hindered by the dismantling of part of the factory, although operations improved quickly; very successful aluminium foil making, printing and packaging, for instance, began in 1954–56. H&N was sold to Metallgesellschaft AG and Vereinigte Deutsche Metallwerke AG in 1970. Metallgesellschaft sold its holding to Aluminium Walzwerk Singen GmbH three years later, and the company became Haendler & Natermann GmbH in 1977. By the mid-1980s, it was employing 750 people and making an incredible profusion of metal-foil packaging, containers, wine-bottle seals, shot, airgun pellets and muzzle-loading bullets. Haendler & Natermann also makes Z&S pellets, commemorating Zieh- und Stanzwerke Schedetal – bought by H&N in 1927. Trademarks have included a castle, 'HN', 'H-N' and 'H&N'.

'Haenel' – 1. Sometimes cursive. A mark often used by C.G. Haenel of Suhl between 1928 and 1933. It was superseded by 'Haenel' in an arrow, which was used until 1945. 2. C.G. Haenel, Waffen- & Fahrradfabrik, Suhl in Thüringen, Germany. *See* panel, pp. 224/25. 3. Haenel-Schmeisser. A brandname associated with automatic pistols made by C.G. Haenel.

'Hær', 'HÆR'. Found on Norwegian military stores; it simply means 'army' (cf. 'Heer').

Hærens... – 1. Hærens Krudtværk. The Danish state-owned ammunition factory apparently made sporting-rifle and shotgun cartridges distinguished by 'HK' in the headstamps. 2. Hærens Rustkammer, Hærens Tøjhus and Hærens Vaabenarsenal, Denmark. *See* Copenhagen.

Haeussler. Paul Haeussler: *see* Häussler.

Hafer. Thomas W. Hafer, a government employee, accepted firearms and accessories made for the US Army in 1941 by *Colt's Patent Fire Arms Manufacturing Company. Invariably they were identified by 'TWH', although this can be difficult to distinguish from an identical mark applied some years previously by T.W. *Holmes. *See also* US arms inspectors' marks.

Hagner. George W. Hagner, using a 'GWH' mark, accepted US military long-arms and accessories in 1845–46. However, these are difficult to distinguish from guns identified with George W. *Hamlin. *See also* US arms inspectors' marks.

Hahn – 1. Otto Hahn, Suhl in Thüringen, Germany. Another of the many sales agencies operating in the Suhl district in 1930–39. 2. Philip Y. Hahn Company, Fairport, New York State, USA. Maker of the gas-powered Hahn Super Repeater lever-action BB rifle, which would date from the period between 1930 – when Hahn left Crosman – and 1940, when he returned to buy out Crosman. The Hahn 45 gas-powered BB revolver was also made.

C.G. HAENEL, WAFFEN- & FAHRRADFABRIK

Based in Suhl in Thüringen, Germany, this gunmaking business was founded on 20 December 1840 by Carl Gottlieb Haenel (1804–57). After his death, the factory was run by his widow, Pauline-Henriette (1821–90), until their son, Carl (1855–1917), attained his majority. On the death of the younger Carl, control passed to his four children: Johanna, Charlotte, Gertrud and Herbert. Herbert Haenel (1891–1983) managed the operations from 1923 until the end of the Second World War.

A 1925 advertisement in the *Deutsches Reichs-Adressbuch* notes the principal products as 'Schmeisser pistols, 6.35mm-calibre, Haenel double-barrelled shotguns, Haenel hunting and sporting guns. Export agencies sought'. Most pre-1914 Haenel sporting rifles prove to be based on the Gew. 88 (*Reichsgewehr); huge quantities of carbines and short rifles, Kar. 88 and Gew. 91, had been made for the

German Army in the 1890s, and many thousands of actions would have been left over.

The 1907-pattern Haenel military rifle – originally offered to China in 6.8x57mm – was also based on the *Reichsgewehr, but had a pistol-grip stock and a patented quick-release magazine floor plate. A boss on the nose-cap accepted the bayonet, a suitable attachment lug lying on a plate extending back under the fore-end of the stock. Guns of this general pattern, but lacking the magazine system, were supplied to Paraguay in 1909; the few that remained in store in Germany were rebored for 7.9x57 S-Munition during the First World War. Actions of this type were also stocked in sporting guise, being advertised as the Model 1909.

The Suhl factory was instructed to begin making Gew. 98 (*Mauser rifles) for the German Army in 1915, but work stopped at the end of the war and fortunes declined.

That Haenel rose once again to a position of prominence within the German gunmaking industry was largely due to Hugo *Schmeisser, chief designer and technical director from 1928; his brother Hans served as sales director. Post-1918 products included the 6.35mm Models 1 and 2 Haenel-Schmeisser (HS) semi-automatic pistols, but Haenel turned to airguns in the late 1920s. These became a major contributor to the company's fortunes in the 1930s.

The airguns included a range of junior guns (X to XXXX) and models I–VIII prior to 1939; all were underlever-cocking fixed-barrel or simpler break-barrel guns, although some of the latter had a positive barrel lock. The Models 26, 27 and 28 pistols were designed by Hugo Schmeisser – who also developed the bolt-action Wehrsport Luftgewehr, later known as the *Sportmodell 33. There were also some cheap push-in barrel pistols. Most of the guns bore the trademark of the Haenel name within an arrow, which had been

---

Haight. S.M. Haight. The US naval intelligence service procured a glove pistol of this type, patented in 1938, although there was a link with the earlier *Juhasz sleeve pistol (q.v.). A single-barrel pistol attached to the back of a sturdy glove was fired simply by punching the target. This action depressed a cocking plunger, projecting above the barrel, then fired the gun in a single sweeping movement. The Mark 1 accepted .410 shotgun cartridges, but these were too bulky in relation to power, and the Mark 2 was redesigned to use a single .38 revolver cartridge.

'Hailsham Special' [The]. Associated with shotgun ammunition sold by A.F. *Smith of Hailsham, but apparently imported from Europe.

Haiman. Louis & Elias Haiman, USA. *See* Columbus Fire Arms Company.

Halang & Bachner, Suhl in Thüringen, Germany. This gunmaking partnership was being operated in 1900 by Benjamin Wilhelm Bachner.

Halali. Associated with shotgun cartridges made in Germany prior to 1914 by *Munitionswerke Schönebeck.

Halbe & Gerlich, Halger-Waffenfabrik, Kiel, later Hamburg. This German gunmaking partnership produced its first Mauser-type rifles c. 1923, chambered for the .244 Halger Magnum round. The range was later enlarged to encompass cartridges as large as the .404 Rimless Nitro Express. The guns often had half-octagonal barrels and a mount for an optical sight set forward on the barrel, ahead of the receiver ring. But their most distinctive feature – although not obvious externally – was a tapering bore.

Halbautomatische. *See* Half-automatic.

Hale – 1. Alfred Thomas Corbyn Hale, Britain. Co-patentee with Ernest Edwin *Harris of the Patent

Precision air pistol made in Britain by A.G. *Parker & Company Ltd of Birmingham. **2.** Joseph Hale, USA. *See* Abram *Gibson. **3.** Linus O. Hale accepted military firearms and accessories marked 'LOH' on behalf of the US Army; they date from 1902 to 1908. *See also* US arms inspectors' marks.

Haley. Richard Haley. A commander in the US Navy, this engineer is credited with a 7.62mm-calibre chamber adaptation for the *Garand.

Half... – 1. Half-automatic, in German, *Halbautomatische*: a term applied to single-shot guns that ejected spent cartridge cases automatically, usually by *blowback. Popular in Europe, although much less common in Britain and the USA, most guns of this type prove to have pre-1914 origins. **2.** Half-Breed. A *Suicide Special revolver made by the *Hopkins & Allen Arms Company of Norwich, Connecticut, USA, in the late nineteenth century. **3.** Half-Moon Clip. A name given to a small crescent-shaped spring-steel stamping, designed by Joseph H. *Wesson in 1917, which allowed the standard swing-cylinder *Colt *New Service and *Smith & Wesson *Hand Ejector revolvers acquired by the US government in 1917–18 to fire the rimless .45 ACP cartridge. Each clip held three rounds.

Halger. A brandname and trademark associated with *Halbe & Gerlich.

Hall – 1. A.J. Hall. The 'AJH' marks of this government inspector may be found on US Army firearms and accessories dating from 1904. *See also* US military inspectors' marks. **2.** Alexander Hall, New York City. This gunmaker, active 1854–73, made revolving-cylinder rifles. **3.** Frank Hall, Chesterfield, Derbyshire. The name of this English gunmaker has been found on shotgun cartridges

registered in Germany in June 1930.

By 1940, C.G. Haenel was making guns and bicycles in a factory at Strasse der Sturmabteilung 16 in Suhl, under the control of 'Herbert Haenel, Fabrikant'. A shooting range (Schießstand) was also maintained in the Suhl district. The production of airguns was suspended c. 1942, when Haenel, which received the code 'fxo' in 1941, was mobilised to make rifles, submachine-guns and similar items for the Wehrmacht. These included large quantities of P.08 magazines, although many were actually sub-contracted to August ★Menz and Reinhold ★Manteuffel.

The Suhl factory was seized by the Russians in 1945, after it had been transferred to the Russian Zone. The business was confiscated in June 1948 from the Haenel family by the DDR authorities, being integrated into the state-owned firearms industry of the German Democratic Republic. Vereinigte Metallwerke Ernst Thälmann, vorm. C.G. Haenel, Landes-Eigener Betrieb made ★Sportmodelle and other airguns, which may be found bearing a fir tree above 'L E B' over 'THÜRINGEN'. An encircled 'TW' monogram mark, with the 'T' formed by extending the centre of the 'W' upward, was also used. Eventually the former Sauer factory (then VEB-Fortunawerk) was

This Haenel Model 310 bolt-action airgun, derived from the Schmeisser-designed Sportmodell of the 1930s, has a tiny detachable box magazine for 4.4mm ball ammunition.

merged with Haenel to form VEB-Ernst Thälmann-Werk. Then it became Suhler Jagd- & Sportwaffenfabrik, continuing to make sporting guns and airguns until, unable to compete, it was finally liquidated (in controversial circumstances) in 1993.

sold under the brandname Hall-Right. **4.** John Hall & Son, 79 Cannon Street, London EC4, and Faversham Powder Mills, Faversham, Kent. A maker of black powder and, apparently, semi-smokeless propellant. Hall may also have loaded shotgun cartridges, although this has never been confirmed, and eventually amalgamated with ★Curtis's & Harvey. **5.** John Hancock Hall, Portland, Maine, USA. On 21 May 1811, Hall patented a distinctive breech-loading flintlock rifle, which soon attracted the attention of the US Army. The original 1819-pattern Hall was made for some years in Harper's Ferry Armory. The first Hall Carbine appeared in 1833; the first cap-lock introduced to the US Army, it had a distinctive sliding-rod bayonet beneath the barrel. Among the individual Hall models were .69 and .52 smoothbore carbines made for the Regiment of Dragoons in 1834; an 1836-model .69 smoothbore carbine for the Second Dragoons; and a .52-calibre rifled carbine believed to have been supplied to the Alabama State Militia. The 1840-model Hall Carbine had a folding elbow- (or L-shaped) breech lever, or a fishtail pattern – designed by Nahum ★Patch and James ★Huger respectively. Five hundred were delivered, but the elbow lever was disliked, and 6,000 were made with the Huger lever mechanism in 1840–43. About 2,500 improved Model 1841 cap-lock rifles were made at Harper's Ferry after Hall's death in 1840, with Huger-type breech levers. The last of the regulation-pattern Halls was the .52-calibre Model 1842 Carbine, with a Huger-pattern breech lever and brass furniture. Several thousand Hall rifles and carbines were returned to Federal store from state reserves during the Civil War, and a few even saw service with the Confederacy. **6.** Joseph Hall. A Federal government inspector, responsible for accepting

★Amoskeag rifle-muskets in 1864, during the American Civil War, marking them 'JH'. *See also* US arms inspectors' marks and John ★Hannis. **7.** Joseph Hall, Springfield, Massachusetts. One-time bookkeeper for ★Smith & Wesson, Hall was involved in the transformation of the gunmakers' ammunition-making business into ★Smith, Hall & Farmer and its successors, remaining with what had become Hall & Hubbard until operations ceased in the 1870s. **8.** Hall & Hubbard, Mill Street, Springfield, Massachusetts. This was the final development of what had once been ★Smith &Wesson's cartridge-making business, formed in 1869 when the facilities were sold to Joseph Hall, formerly the Smith & Wesson bookkeeper, and a partner named Hubbard. The operation was sold to C.D. ★Leet of Springfield, Massachusetts, in 1873. **9.** Hall-North. This name was associated with the Improved Model Carbine of 1840 (or M1843), with a side-mounted breech lever eventually patented in 1844 by ★North & Savage. About 11,000 were made by Simeon ★North between 1842 and 1850. **10.** 'Hall-Right', or 'Hall-Right Special' [The]. A brandname found on shotgun cartridges handled by Frank ★Hall of Chesterfield.

'Hallamshire' [The]. Associated with shotgun cartridges distributed by ★Roper, Son & Company of Sheffield. The name was provided by the local administrative district.

Halliday. B. Halliday & Company, 63 Cannon Street, London EC4. The name of this English gunmaking business has been found on shotgun cartridges made in the 1930s by ★Eley-Kynoch.

'ham'. Used by ★Dynamit AG of Hamm on small-arms ammunition and components made in Germany during the Second World War.

Hallstrom. A.L. Hallstrom is known to have accepted the US Army .45 Colt *M1911 pistols and *Smith & Wesson revolvers encountered with 'ALH' markings; they date from the period 1916–17. *See also* US arms inspectors' marks.

Hamburg-Amerikanischen Uhrenfabrik, Schramberg, Germany. Maker of drum magazines for the *Mondragon rifle (FSK. 15).

Hamilton – 1. C.J. Hamilton & Son. A partnership of Clarence and Coello Hamilton, trading as the Hamilton Manufacturing Company (below) in Plymouth, Michigan, USA. The company was the assignee of US Patents 696,962 ('Firearm Sight', 8 April 1902) and 704,962 ('Gun Barrel', 15 July 1902). **2.** Clarence J. Hamilton, Plymouth, Michigan, USA. This engineer designed the first of the *Daisy BB Guns in the late 1880s, but left the company in 1899 to manufacture rimfire cartridge rifles, largely from sheet-metal fabrications. These were comparatively unsuccessful, and work had ceased by 1910. Among Hamilton's US patents were 390,297 of 2 October 1888, for a shot seal and a loading port for BB Guns; 390,311 (jointly with Cyrus *Pinckney) for a gun cocked by a butt-mounted lever swinging down and forward; 408,971 of 13 August 1888 for a top-mounted cocking lever; 427,313 of 6 May 1890 for a 'Spring Air Gun barrel'; 455,942 of 14 July 1891 for a hinged-butt cocking system; 631,010 of 15 August 1899 for an airgun (assigned to the Daisy Manufacturing Company); and a selection of others, either granted in association with Coello Hamilton, or assigned to C.J. Hamilton & Son (above). Clarence Hamilton is said to have died in Plymouth in 1933. **3.** Coello Hamilton, Plymouth, Michigan. Son of Clarence Hamilton, this man was the co-patentee (with his father) of a method of rifling gun barrels and a simplified pressed-metal rifle: US Patents 660,725 of 30 October 1900, and 662,068 of 20 November 1900 respectively. **4.** Gustav Hugo Röhss Hamilton, or Count Hamilton. This Swedish nobleman, born in July 1874, was living at 28 Victoriagatan, Göteborg, when he designed the *Hamiltonpistol*. It was patented in Sweden on 11 December 1900 (no. 13,825), and in Britain on 11 May 1901 (no. 286/01), a few examples being made in the early 1900s by J. *Thorssin & Son for trials with the Swedish Army. The pistol chambered a variant of the 6.5mm Bergmann cartridge and had a unique curved breech-block, which ran back into the grip on recoil. Hamilton died in 1947. **5.** H.H. Hamilton, active during the American Civil War (1861–65), accepted cap-lock Sharps rifles marked 'HHH' on behalf of the Federal Army. *See also* Henry H. *Hartzell and US arms inspectors' marks. **6.** Hamilton Manufacturing Company [The], Plymouth, Michigan. Formed by Clarence Hamilton in 1899, after he had left *Daisy. Hamilton patented a sidelever-operated BB Gun c. 1900, but it is not known whether his company made any. It did, however, produce a few .22 rimfire rifles made largely of sheet-metal. Operations had failed by 1910. **7.** Hamilton Model. A spring-and-piston *BB Gun, cocked by a lever on top of the air cylinder, made in 1888–89 by the *Plymouth Iron Windmill Company of Plymouth, Michigan, to the designs of Clarence Hamilton.

Hamlin. George W. Hamlin accepted martial 1851-pattern *Colt revolvers in the mid-1850s, apparently on behalf of the US Army; they are said to have borne 'GMH' marks. *See also* US arms inspectors' marks and George W. *Hagner.

Hammer – 1. That part of a firing mechanism, usually working radially, that fires a chambered cartridge. **2.** 'Hammer the Hammer'. An advertising slogan used by Iver *Johnson from 1904 onward to promote a safety system used in some of the company's revolvers. A spacer was placed between the hammer and the firing pin to transmit a blow only when the trigger was deliberately pulled. An improved adjustable coil-spring version was introduced in 1908.

Hammerless, Hammerless... – 1. Truly hammerless guns rely on nothing but a striker to fire the primer cap; externally similar pseudo-hammerless designs may have a hammer inside the frame. **2.** Applied to *Sharps-Borchardt rifles dating from the period 1878–81. *See* New Model Hammerless. **3.** Hammerless Model. A name associated with a .25 automatic pistol made in the USA by *Harrington & Richardson. **4.** Hammerless Pocket Model. A 6.35mm automatic pistol made by *Webley & Scott Ltd of Birmingham, England. Also made in *Pocket Model form. **5.** Hammerless Pocket Model. Also listed as M1908 and Model M, this designation has been applied to three blowback semi-automatic pistols made by *Colt's Patent Fire Arms Manufacturing Company, beginning in 1903 with what was effectively a US-made FN-Browning chambered for the 7.65mm Auto (.32 ACP) cartridge. Work continued until the end of the Second World War, ceasing after more than 772,000 had been made. Production of the larger .380 version (1908–45) was less impressive, totalling a mere 128,000; about 410,000 of the .25 ACP version or Vest Pocket Hammerless Model, derived from the FN-Browning of 1906, were manufactured in 1908–41.

Hämmerli. *See* panel, facing page.

Hammerschmidt. C. Hammerschmidt, Weida. Listed as a retailer of sporting guns and ammunition in Germany in 1941.

Hammerstrom's Small Arms Company Ltd, Regina, Saskatchewan, Canada. An ammunition maker, or perhaps distributor, marking cartridges with the headstamp 'H.S.A.' Status uncertain.

Hammond – 1. Henry Hammond, Connecticut and Rhode Island, USA. This gunmaker was granted protection for a breech-loading carbine with a barrel that turned laterally, US Patent 44,798 of 25 October 1864 being sought from Providence, Rhode Island. However, Hammond is better known as the designer of the *Bulldog, or Bulldozer, derringer made by the *Connecticut Arms Company in accordance with US Patent 52,165 ('Cartridge Retractor for Fire Arms') of 23 January 1866. This particular specification records Hammond's domicile as Naubuc, Connecticut. He was also responsible for the design of shot and cartridge pouches (US Patents 54,147 of 24 April 1866, and 62,415 of 26 February 1867); gun sights (61,007 of 8 January 1867, and 175,702 of 4 April 1876); and a cartridge ejector mechanism (72,849 of 31 December 1867). US Patent 112,589, protecting a breech-loading firearm, was granted on 14 March 1871 and assigned to Lewis Hammond of Hartford. Like the original 1864 patent, this was sought from Providence, Rhode Island. **2.** Hammond Brothers, Winchester, Hampshire. The marks of this English gunmaking business, probably descendants of Isaac Hammond (active 1829–67 and possibly later), have been found on shotgun cartridges sold under the brandnames Reliance and Trusty Servant.

HÄMMERLI JAGD- & SPORTWAFFENFABRIK AG

Based in Lenzburg, Switzerland, this firearms manufacturer, best known for its high-grade target guns, was founded as a gun-barrel maker by Johann Ulrich Hämmerli (1824–91) in 1863. It became Hämmerli & Hausch in 1876, the Hausch family's interest coming to an end upon the foundation of Rudolf Hämmerli & Co. on 28 December 1921.

Rudolf Hämmerli – the grandson of the founder – continued alone after the death of his father, Johann 'Jeanot' Hämmerli, in 1934. His own death occurred in 1946, allowing control to pass to the triumvirate of Thommen, Wackernagel and Bertschinger, and the name changed first to Hämmerli & Co. AG, then to its present style. The shareholding was purchased by SIG in 1971, and now the business is often referred to as SIG-Hämmerli.

Hämmerli has always been renowned for the quality of its *Martini-action target rifles, for guns built on refurbished *Schmidt-Rubin actions, and for the Hammerli-*Walther and Hämmerli-International target pistols. The company also stocked military-surplus *Mauser actions until the late 1960s. Known as the 700.serie, they were chambered for a wide range of cartridges, from 6.5x55 to 10.3x60, and could be acquired in a variety of standard, deluxe and highly decorated forms. A gas-powered Hämmerli-Trainer was developed in 1955–58 and could be fitted to guns such as the Karabiner 98k and the Walther P38.

The Single and Rapid gas-powered BB pistols appeared in the same era. In the early 1960s, however, the Single was revised to fire diabolo pellets, and a superior match version, the 454 Master, was introduced. A series of gas-powered rifles also appeared during the 1960s, and sidelever-cocking spring-air rifles (1972–77) have also been marketed; these, like most of the Hämmerli air- and gas guns, were made by a subsidary in Tiengen/Oberrhein, Germany.

This single-shot .22 rimfire Model 106 Free Pistol is based on a much-modified Martini tilting-block action. The operating lever protrudes from the left grip above the trigger.

Hance. Sydney Hance, Britain: *see* Enfield.

Hancock – 1. Ethan Hancock accepted US Army firearms and accessories in 1918, during the First World War. They were marked simply 'EH', the period distinguishing them from the guns marked fifty years previously by Edward *Hooker. *See also* US arms inspectors' marks. **2.** W.J. Hancock & Company, a gunsmithing business working in London, was listed at 308 High Holborn in 1891–99, with an additional shop at 5 Pall Mall Place (1896–99 only). Appropriate marks have been found on sporting guns and shotgun ammunition.

Hand Ejector. *See* panel, pp. 228/29.

Hand Firing Device, Britain: *see* Welrod.

Handfeuerwaffen – 1. A German-language term: 'Small-arms'. **2.** Handfeuerwaffen-Productionsgenossenschaft, Suhl, Thüringen. A maker of 20,000 M/69 *Werder rifles for the Bavarian government, 1868–9.

Handmitrailleuse. *See* Mannlicher rifles, automatic and semi-automatic.

Handscombe. F.G. Handscombe, Bishop's Stortford, Hertfordshire, and Stansted, Essex. This English provincial gunmaker is known to have marked sporting guns and shotgun cartridges.

Handspanner. A German-language name given to any firearm that can be cocked manually, although now the term is normally restricted to those with hammers or strikers that are hidden internally. *See also* Kickspanner.

Handy. Probably made in Eibar, this is another of the many unattributable pocket pistols of Spanish origin: 9mm Short, seven rounds, striker fired. Based on the 1910-type FN-Browning, it is often marked 'Model 1917'.

Hannah. William W. Hannah, Hudson, New York State, USA. The patentee of a *Gallery Gun cocked by a combination of a swinging trigger guard and a rack-and-pinion mechanism. This was protected by US Patent 127,863 of 11 June 1872.

Hannibal. A bolt-rifle made by *A-Square of Bedford, Kentucky, from 1984 to date. A lighter version of the

HAND EJECTOR MODEL

Originally, this name graced a .32 *Smith & Wesson revolver, introduced in 1896 with a split-spring lock in the top strap above the six-chamber cylinder. Only about 20,000 guns had been made by 1903, when the basic pattern was improved by the addition of a thumb latch on the left side of the frame, behind the recoil shield. Production ceased in 1917, after about 263,000 Model 1903 guns had been had been made. They were superseded by the Third Model Hand Ejector, similar externally to the fifth-change M1903, with an additional hammer-block safety in the lock. About 26,000 .22 Hand Ejector revolvers were made in 1902–19, and 66,000 .32-20 Hand Ejectors were built on the medium frame shared with the .38 Hand Ejector *Military & Police pattern.

In addition to the .22, .32 and .38 patterns, Smith & Wesson built large .44-calibre swing-cylinder revolvers on the N-pattern frame. The earliest example, the Military Model of 1908, had an additional locking point between the cylinder-yoke and the extractor shroud, and, as a result, was known as the Triple Lock. Customarily offered only in .44 S&W Special and .44 S&W Russian chamberings, guns of this type were also made in .38-40 and .44-40 Winchester and .45 Colt. However, the additional complexity was not justified by sales, and the third locking point was abandoned after fewer than 16,000 .44 and 5,691 .455 revolvers (5,000 destined for British service) had been made.

The second model had a simpler ejector-rod shroud than its predecessor. Prior to September 1916, about 69,000 .455 guns were made for the British and 700 .45

Colt guns were supplied to Canada, apparently for the Royal Canadian Mounted Police. Production of second-model guns continued until 1940, with a break in 1917–20; however, when work stopped, only about 17,500 commercial examples had been sold.

A few thousand third-model .44 guns, which reverted to the heavy ejector-rod shroud of the earliest pattern (although lacking the third locking point), were made in 1926–40 and 1946–49. Five thousand of an adjustable-sight variant, known after 1957 as the Model 24, with a barrel rib and large grips, were made between 1950 and 1966.

The .45 Hand Ejector Model 1917, used by the US Army during the First World War alongside an essentially similar swing-cylinder Colt, was a .44 Hand Ejector with a 5.5in barrel and a lanyard ring at the

---

*Caesar pattern, normally the Hannibal is offered only with a wood stock.

Hannis – 1. Benjamin Hannis, a government inspector working during the American Civil War, accepted a variety of cap-lock revolvers on behalf of the Federal Army. They included the *Allen & Wheelock, *Colt, *Remington, *Savage and *Starr patterns, identified by 'BH' in a cartouche. Hannis's marks post-date those applied by Benjamin *Huger by several years. *See also* US arms inspectors' marks. **2.** John Hannis is said to have accepted firearms on behalf of the Federal Army, marking them 'JH'. Apparently they were confined to 1862; but *see also* 'James *Harris'.

Hanquet – 1. Jean-Baptiste Hanquet, Liège, Belgium. Father of Nicholas Hanquet (below), active as a gunmaker in 1849. Representation was maintained in London in 1870–71, at 6 Love Lane, E.C. Another son, Ferdinand, continued thereafter until 1878. **2.** Nicholas Hanquet, Liège. A Belgian gunmaker (1797–1858), son of Martin Hanquet, active in the mid-nineteenth century. Lived in Brazil for fifteen years; best known as the most important manufacturer of edged weapons to trade in Belgium in the mid-nineteenth century, Hanquet also made firearms, cutlery, harness and tableware. The business was still trading in 1925, making cap-lock Lazarinos for export, and *Types Brésilien* for Casa *Laport and other dealers in South America.

Hans. A.P. Hans, or A.P. Hans & Co. A gunmaker of Liège, Belgium, listed in London in 1886–89.

Hanson – 1. Charles Hanson, listed in 1829 in King Street, Huddersfield, Yorkshire, made *cap-lock sporting guns alongside butt- and pendant-ball reservoir airguns. He had moved to 160 High Holborn, London, by 1839, and was trading in 1857 from 1 Eaton Lane South. His 'London' marks have been reported on sporting guns, pistols, and self-cocking *pepperboxes. **2.** George Hanson, Baxter Gate, Doncaster, Yorkshire. The marks of this

English gunmaker, active from 1857 to 1868, have been reported on self-cocking *pepperboxes and cap-lock revolvers. Sometimes they have been recorded as 'S. Hanson', but the working career of Septimus Hanson of French Gate, perhaps the father of George, seems to have been confined to the pre-1830 era.

Hanyang. This Chinese arms factory made a substantial quantity of Mannlicher-type rifles, based on the German *Reichsgewehr. Normally these are known by the factory name.

Harding – 1. William Harding, London. This man seems to have been a clerk in the employment of the *London Armoury Company, at least in 1856–60. He was the patentee of the Deane-Harding *cap-lock revolver introduced (apparently accompanied by a long-barrelled revolver-carbine) by Deane & Son, King William Street, London Bridge, in the spring of 1859. Guns of this pattern, with a two-part frame/barrel unit and a simplified double-action lock, although often marked by Deane & Son, were made in Birmingham by *Tipping & Lawden, then by *Pryse & Redman. Harding received several British patents, including 1574/57 of 4 June 1857 for an 'Improvement in Pistol Holsters'; 669/58 of 29 March 1858, for 'Improvements in Revolver Firearms and in Apparatus for Manufacturing Projectiles'; and 1159/58 of 24 May 1858, for 'Improvements in Revolver Firearms'. Made in Army and Pocket versions, 54-bore and 120-bore respectively, Deane-Harding revolvers had five-chamber cylinders. **2.** Harding Brothers, Hereford, Herefordshire. Marks applied by this English gunmaking business have been found on shotgun cartridges sold under the name 'Rabbit Brand'.

Hard... – 1. Hard Pan. This name applies to two types of sheath-trigger *Suicide Special revolver of the 1880s: one made by the *Hood Firearms Company of Norwich, Connecticut, and the other by *Johnson, Bye & Company and/or *Iver Johnson of Worcester and Fitchburg, Massachusetts. **2.** 'Hard Hitters' [The]. Found on shotgun

base of the plain wooden grips; about 163,500 had been made prior to 11 November 1918, although not all had been issued. The most important feature was the use of ★Half-Moon Clips, invented by Joseph H. ★Wesson, to hold rimless .45 pistol cartridges in the cylinders. Each clip held three rounds. A few guns of this type were sold commercially, and 25,000 were supplied to Brazil in 1937; they bore ★national marks on the left side of the frame. Work finally ceased in 1949, but a few thousand .45 ACP and rarer .45 Colt Hand Ejector M1950 Target patterns (Model 26 after 1957) were offered until 1961.

A military-pattern gun (1951–66), known from 1957 as the Model 22, had a rebound-slide hammer block and chequered wooden grips, and lacked the lanyard ring of its predecessors; most guns chambered the .45 pistol

round, although a few hundred were made for the .45 rimmed Colt revolver cartridge. The perfected .45 Hand Ejector M1955, known since 1957 as the Model 25, had a heavy barrel, target grips and refinements in the lockwork. It was abandoned in 1991. *See also* Heavy Duty.

Features of the original Smith & Wesson Hand Ejector revolver are perpetuated in many of today's designs. This is a heavy-barrel version of the .38 Special Model 10 Military & Police revolver.

---

cartridges sold by Bartram of Hitchin, Hertfordshire, England, sometimes as 'Bartram's Hard Hitters'.

Hardy. Hardy Brothers, Alnwick, Northumberland. The name of this gunmaker has been found on shotgun cartridges sold under the brandname Hardy's Northern and Hardy's Reliance.

'Harewood' [The]. A mark found on shotgun ammunition made for E.M. ★Reilly of London by ★Eley Bros., apparently prior to 1900. It is assumed that the name refers to a hunt.

Harkom. Joseph Harkom. This Scottish gunmaker founded his business in 1840, at 21 West Register Street, Edinburgh, and moved to 32 Princes Street in 1855. The trading style became J. Harkom & Son in 1869, and the concern moved to 30 George Street in 1890, becoming part of ★Mortimer & Son in 1922.

Harlow Brothers, Birmingham, Warwickshire. Trading from 132 Bradford Street in 1864–67, this partnership of James T. and Edward Harlow made Wedge Bolt 12-bore pinfire breech-loading shotguns, which were entered in the trials sponsored by *The Field* in 1866. These were made in accordance with British Patent 2380 of 1863, granted to the brothers to protect two drop-barrel sporting-gun actions. A later patent granted to Edward Harlow alone, 2326 of 1860, illustrated six additional breech-loading systems.

Harnisch. Rudolf Harnisch, one of the best-known gunmakers established in the small Bohemian town of Weipert, was the proposer and a principal member of a co-operative formed in 1887 to produce components for the straight-pull ★Mannlicher service rifle that had been adopted for the Austro-Hungarian Army. Little else is known of his operations.

Harniss. Joseph Harniss. This name has been attributed to a US arms inspector, but is thought to have been confused with that of James Harris (q.v.).

Harold. Victor Harold & Company. A firm of mer-

chants and gunmakers' agents, listed at 9 Queen Street, Leicester Square, London, in 1857–58.

Harper's Ferry Armory, Virginia, USA. This government-owned gunmaking factory was authorised by an Act of Congress, on 2 April 1794, to be built on the site of a mill erected in the 1750s by Robert Harper. The facilities were completed in 1796. Output included ★Hall breech-loading rifles and carbines; in the financial year extending from 1 October 1841 to 30 September 1842, the factory made 3,105 muskets, 300 Hall rifles, 1,001 Hall carbines and an assortment of accessories, which included 501 'spring vices' and 1,999 wipers (ramrods). Work continued until the evening of 18 April 1861, at the beginning of the American Civil War, when men under the command of Lieutenant Roger Jones set fire to the Armory and retreated back across the Potomac river to prevent the production facilities from being captured by the Virginia Militia and exploited by the Confederacy.

Harrington – 1. George R. Harrington was a US government inspector, active in 1901. His 'GRH' marks have been reported on ★Colt revolvers and accessories. *See also* US arms inspectors' marks. **2.** T.J. Harrington & Sons Ltd, Walton, Surrey. The maker, in 1939–40 and again from 1947, of the ★Gat spring-air push-in barrel pistol and (from the mid-1980s) a similar rifle. **3.** Harrington & Richardson Arms Company, Worcester, Massachusetts. This business was formed to make the auto-ejecting pocket revolvers initially associated with ★Wesson & Harrington. A new revolver with a removable cylinder-axis pin was introduced in 1876, and the first double-action pattern appeared in 1878. By 1908, 3,000,000 guns had been made. After 1904, however, most of the guns were distinguished by model dates and pattern numbers instead of names. For example, three similar-looking models, introduced in 1904–06, were known as M1904 (.32 and .38), M1905 (.32) and M1906 (.22). *See also* [The] ★American, Automatic Ejecting Model, Automatic

Hammerless Model, Bicycle Revolver, H&R Bulldog, Premier, Police Automatic Model, Police Bicycle Model, Police Premier, Safety Hammer, Vest Pocket, Young America and Young America Bulldog. In addition to revolvers, Harrington & Richardson began to make hammerless *Anson & Deeley guns in 1881. The company also produced single-barrel hammer shotguns, including the Model 1900 in 12-, 16- and 20-bore, with a patented hinge pin, and the smaller, but otherwise similar, Model 1905 in an assortment of metric and imperial chamberings, ranging from .410 Eley to 24-bore. The Model 1908 was an improved 1900 pattern with a snap fore-end and a hook-type barrel retainer. In the first decade of the twentieth century, Harrington & Richardson turned to a *Webley & Scott-type automatic pistol. This was sold in .25 (as the .25 Hammerless Model) and in .32, but production was relatively meagre. Output between the world wars (and, indeed, from the resumption of production in 1946 until the end of trading) concentrated once again on inexpensive revolvers, although 5.56mm M16A1 rifles were made for the US armed forces after 1969. These ArmaLites clearly display the manufacturer's name and lion trademark on the receiver. Mauser-pattern rifles built on *FN actions were marketed from 1967 until 1982 in the *Ultra series, to be followed in 1982–84 by the 340 series (*Husqvarna Mauser actions), but the collapse of Harrington & Richardson brought work to an end.

Harris – 1. Charles Harris. Grantee of US Patent 39,771 of 1 September 1863 to protect a modified cylinder-locking bolt. See also Cooper Fire Arms Company. **2.** Ernest Edwin Harris, living in Duchess Road, Edgbaston, Birmingham, Warwickshire, was the co-patentee with Alfred T.C. *Hale of the Patent Precision air pistol made by A.G. *Parker & Company. See British Patent 162,923 of 1920, which notes that Harris was the works manager of the manufacturing company. **3.** Henry Harris, Congleton, Cheshire. Designer of a series of rifle magazines, including *controlled-platform patterns. See British Patents 10,239/1900, 16,284/1900, 14,640/1901 and 17,870/1901. Harris was also granted US Patents 675,004 of 28 May 1901 ('magazine firearm'), and 723,864 of 31 March 1903 ('firearm magazine'). Most of the patents were assigned to the Harris Rifle Magazine Ltd. See also Edwards and Charles *Ross. **4.** James Harris allegedly accepted Johnson and Waters single-shot cap-lock pistols and 1817-type Starr rifles for the US Army in 1838–45, marking them 'JH'. However, confusion reigns over the identification of a number of inspectors with similar names – e.g. John *Hannis, Joseph Hannis, James Harris and Joseph Harniss – operating in the same period, and also with James *Hawkins, who may have succeeded to the 'JH' mark. See also US arms inspectors' marks. **5.** Harris Gun Works: see McMillan Guns Works. **6.** Harris Products Company, Torrance, California, USA. See Marksman Products; Harris was the developer and initial marketer of the Marksman Repeater Pistol in 1955–57. **7.** Harris Rifle Magazine Ltd. Active in London from 1899 until 1905 or later, this company was the assignee of the rifle-magazine patents held by Henry Harris. None of these was particularly successful, except, in modified form, on some of the *Ross rifles.

Harrison – 1. Edgar Harrison, The Small Arms Factory, Feltham, Middlesex. This prolific patentee joined the family firm of *Cogswell & Harrison in 1874 and rose to become a director of the business. Edgar Harrison has been credited with the erection of a factory in Gillingham Street to 'make guns by machine', a move that brought sharp criticism from other London gunmakers. In addition to cocking mechanisms, back sights, safety systems and ejectors, often developed in collusion with others (e.g. Beesley, Jeffrey and Southgate), Harrison designed the *Certus air pistol in the late 1920s. **2.** George Harrison, London. An employee of the patent agents D. *Young & Company, named in specifications filed on behalf of John *Epensheid. **3.** Thomas & William Harrison, Carlisle, Cumberland. The name of this English provincial gunmaking business has been reported on sporting guns and shotgun ammunition. T. & W. Harrison succeeded Lancelot Harrison (active 1810–37), being listed at the same address – 10 Scotch Street – from 1847 until 1858. Trading continued at least until 1914. **4.** Harrison Arms Company. A name found on shotguns handled in the USA by the H. & D. *Folsom Arms Company, possibly imported from Europe. **5.** Harrison Brothers Ltd, Northfield. A maker of magazines for the British 9mm *Sten Gun during the Second World War. The code 'M 109' may have been used instead of the company name. See also British military manufacturers' marks. **6.** Harrison & Hussey, 41 Albemarle Street, London W. The name of this English gunmaking partnership has been reported on shotgun cartridges offered under such brandnames as Albemarle, Grafton and Stafford.

Harriss. Henry J. Harriss. A gunsmith trading from 9 Carlton Street, London S.W., in 1899.

Harrod's Stores Ltd. Trading from 1898 onward at 87–105 Brompton Road, Knightsbridge, London SW1, Harrod's was listed by H.J. Blanch, writing in Arms & Explosives in 1909, as a member of the gun trade. Presumably Harrod's, which undoubtedly sold guns and accessories, also maintained repair facilities. The name has been found on sporting guns and shotgun ammunition offered under brands such as Beaufort, British Pioneer, Kill-Sure and Pioneer.

'Harrogate' [The]. A brandname found on shotgun cartridges handled by R.T. *Hodgson of Harrogate.

Harston. Greville Harston & Company Ltd. This business, regarded by H.J. Blanch in his 1909 Arms & Explosives article as a member of the London gun trade, was listed in 1875 at 12 Queen Victoria Street, and 117 & 118 Bishopsgate Street Without in 1876. Subsequently Harston emigrated to Canada. It should be noted that, owing to the convoluted form of some indexes and directory entries, the business has often been listed mistakenly as Harston, Greville & Company Ltd.

Hart – 1. B.J. Hart & Brother. A distributor of cap-lock revolvers made in the USA in the 1860s by the *Bacon Manufacturing Company of Norwich, Connecticut. **2.** E.F. Hart, Clare, Suffolk. The name of this English gunmaker has been found on shotgun cartridges made by *Eley-Kynoch in the 1950s. **3.** Henry Hart. This gunsmith was listed at many addresses in Birmingham, Warwickshire, England – including 11 Fisher Street (1827–29), 3 Fisher Street (1830–33), 78 Lichfield Street (1834–37), then New Canal Street (1838–50). The trading style became Henry Hart & Company, at 54 New Canal Street in the early 1850s, but subsequently business may have continued at 21 Lower Priory (listed for 1853 only) and finally at 41 Pershore Road until 1873; Henry Hart & Sons & Company continued working until c 1885. **4.** Henry B. Hart, a government employee, accepted US Army firearms and accessories marked 'HBH'. They date from the mid-1870s. *See also* US Arms inspectors' marks. **5.** Henry C. Hart, Detroit, Michigan. Proprietor of the Hart Manufacturing Company, and the inventor of the *Matchless BB Gun protected by US Patent 437,491 of 30 September 1890. **6.** Henry P. Hart, Detroit. Younger son of the BB Gun inventor, Henry C. Hart. *See* Hart Manufacturing Company. **7.** Henry Hart Manufacturing Company, Detroit, Michigan, USA. This business began life in the 1880s, making railway, builders' and cabinet fittings, together with the Matchless BB Gun to the patent of Henry C. Hart. The Hart Manufacturing Company traded from 492–512 Franklin Street (renumbered 570–590 Franklin Street in 1894) until it moved to 74–78 Fort East Street in 1898. The trading style had become Hart & Company by 1896 (a partnership between Henry C. Hart, Robert W. Hart, Henry P. Hart and Michael W. Murray), but finally changed to Buckley-Hart Company in 1903. This disappeared in 1904–05. **8.** Robert W. Hart, Detroit. The elder son of the BB Gun inventor, Henry C. Hart. *See* Hart Manufacturing Company. **9.** Hart's Repeating Air Gun: the original name of the Matchless BB Gun, acknowledging the name of its manufacturer.

Hartford – **1.** Hartford Arms. A *Suicide Special revolver made by the *Crescent Arms Company of Norwich, Connecticut, USA, in the late nineteenth century. **2.** Hartford Arms Company. A brandname associated with shotguns made in the USA by the Crescent Arms Company of Norwich, Connecticut. **3.** Hartford Arms & Equipment Company, 618 Capitol Avenue, Hartford, Connecticut. This business was formed in 1929 to make .22 rimfire rifles and a selection of pistols, including a single-shot pattern and an elegant .22 blowback. Work ceased in 1932; the company was liquidated and the production machinery passed to *High Standard.

Hartley – **1.** Marcellus Hartley & Company, USA. *See* Lee. **2.** V. & H. Hartley, Oldham, Lancashire, made box and drum magazines for the British .303 *Bren Gun during the Second World War, often marking them with the code 'N 29' instead of the company name. *See also* British military manufacturers' marks. **3.** Hartley & Graham. A reorganisation of *Schuyler, Hartley & Graham, possibly in the 1880s.

Hartshorn. Isaac Hartshorn, Providence, Rhode Island. Recipient of US Patent 38,042 of 31 March 1863, protecting the improved breech-block used on the fourth-pattern *Burnside carbine.

Hartwell. C.W. Hartwell, a government arms inspector, accepted US Army firearms and accessories marked 'CWH' in 1831–50. *See also* US arms inspectors' marks.

Hartzell. Henry H. Hartzell is said to have accepted US Army firearms marked 'HHH', perhaps in the 1870s, but confirmation is lacking. *See also* H.H. *Hamilton and US arms inspectors' marks.

Harvard. A brandname associated with shotguns made in the USA – apparently prior to 1917 – by the *Crescent Arms Company of Norwich, Connecticut.

Harvey – **1.** Daniel B. Harvey, Britain. *See* William *Greener. **2.** Earle M. Harvey. Designer of the .30 T25

lightweight automatic rifle, in response to a specification issued by the US Office of the Chief of Ordnance in September 1945. Developed at *Springfield Armory, the T25 had a strut in the breech-block that pivoted down against a shoulder in the receiver. The rifle was characterised by a straight-line layout, a separate pistol grip and folding sights. It was not successful and was abandoned in 1951, although a modified version (the T47) lasted until 1953. **3.** Frederick Harvey, a Federal government inspector, accepted firearms and accessories during the American Civil War. Apparently they included the revolvers and cap-lock carbines, dating from c. 1862, that display 'FH' marks. The date distinguishes Harvey's guns from those accepted twenty years later by Captain Frank *Heath. *See also* US arms inspectors' marks. **4.** Harvey Guns, Great Yarmouth, Norfolk. The name of this English gunmaker has been found on shotgun cartridges sold in the 1970s.

Harys [von]. Karl von Harys, Suhl in Thüringen. A maker of sporting rifles and shotguns active in Germany prior to 1945. Some of the products will bear the brandname 'Inferno'.

'has'. Associated with the products of Pulverfabrik *Hasloch of Hasloch am Main in 1941–45. They included German military small-arms ammunition components.

Haschke. Henry Haschke, Britain: *see* L. *Lamblin & Company.

Hasdell. Thomas R. Hasdell. A gunsmith listed in 1862–66 at 150 St John Street Road, Clerkenwell, London. He entered 12-bore shotguns in the trials undertaken in 1866 by *The Field*: *Lefaucheux types chambering pin- or centrefire ammunition interchangeably, and a *Lancaster-patent gun restricted to centrefire.

Haseltine, Lake & Company, London W.C. Founded in 1869 by William Lake and Henry Haseltine, this patent agency was retained by many gunmakers. These included the *Daisy Manufacturing Company, William *Markham, Elbert *Searle, John S. *Wallace and Benjamin *Thompson. Normally the address is listed as 45 Southampton Buildings, but premises at 7 & 8 Southampton Buildings, chambers formerly occupied by Lake, may have been used for a few years in the 1870s.

Haskell. Philip Haskell, USA: *see* Remington.

Haskins. Jerry Haskins, USA: *see* Champlin.

Hasloch. A brandname associated with shotgun cartridges manufactured in Germany prior to 1914 by *Pulverfabrik Hasloch.

Hast – **1.** Frederick E.D. Hast. A gunmakers' agent trading in 1856–59 from 18 Aldermanbury, London. **2.** Philip Hast, Colchester, Essex. Listed in the High Street from 1805 until 1841, then under the name of Mrs Catherine Hast (widow) until 1849, this gunsmithing business passed into the hands of Philip Cockerell Hast (son) in 1850. Sporting guns and self-cocking *pepperboxes have been reported with Hast's markings, and Philip Hast the Younger entered a *Lancaster-patent 12-bore breech-loading shotgun in the trials undertaken in 1866 by *The Field*. Trading seems to have ceased in the 1870s.

Hastings. Henry D. Hastings, active c. 1862–63, during the American Civil War, accepted firearms and accessories on behalf of the Federal Army. They were marked 'HDH'. *See also* US arms inspectors' marks.

Hasuike Seisakusho KK, Higashinari-Ku, Osaka,

Japan. Since the 1970s, this company has made airgun pellets under the brandnames Jet, Lion, *Silver Jet and Zet.

Haswell. R. Haswell, London. Mentioned by H.J. Blanch in 1909 as a producer of the spring-air pistol 'on a new principle' – but as yet unidentified.

Hatch. A.W. Hatch accepted US Army firearms and accessories marked 'AWH', dating from c. 1903. *See also* US arms inspectors' marks.

Hatcher – 1. James L. Hatcher, brother of Julian S. Hatcher (author of *Hatcher's Notebook*), was responsible for accepting *Colt-made small-arms and machine-guns marked 'JAH' (readily distinguishable from firearms accepted for the US Navy many years earlier by James L. *Henderson). The Hatcher guns all date from 1938. At the time, he held the rank of major, but when he retired from military service it was with the rank of colonel. In addition to inspecting arms, James Hatcher designed the Hatcher-Bang rifle, based on the Danish *Bang. *See also* US arms inspectors' marks.

Hat guns. *See* Albert *Pratt.

Haub. Wilhelm Haub, Suhl in Thüringen, Germany. Listed in the *Deutsches Reichs-Adressbuch* as a gunsmith, 1939.

Häusser. Franz Häusser, Suhl in Thüringen, Germany. A gunmaker trading in 1930.

Häussler. Paul Häussler. The name of this Swiss gunsmith has been associated not only with the *Adler pistol, made in Germany prior to the First World War, but also with the *Glisenti. He was granted a patent in Switzerland in 1903 to protect a toggle-lock pistol.

Haveness. A term used by the inventor Andrew *Burgess to describe his distinctive sliding-pistol-grip shotguns.

Havens. P.B.B. Havens, working as a government inspector, accepted 1873-type Springfield rifles made in the mid-1870s, marking them 'PBBH'. *See also* US arms inspectors' marks.

Haviland. Benjamin Haviland, Herkimer and Ilion, New York State. Best known for his work with airguns, Haviland received a selection of US Patents, including 113,766 of 18 April 1871, for a drop-barrel pistol; 126,954 of 1872 (jointly with George P. *Gunn); and 290,230 of 1883 (also jointly with Gunn) for a felt-base airgun slug.

Haviland & Gunn. This partnership of Benjamin Haviland and George P. Gunn was responsible for the development of the *Pettengill spring-air gun. Rights to this were acquired by *Quackenbush in 1885 (although some sources date the assignment as early 1876), and subsequently it was made in the latter's factory.

Hawes Firearms Company, Los Angeles, California. Importer of a variety of guns and accessories from Europe, including 6.35mm *Reck P-8 and SM-11 pistols, marketed as La Fury 8 and La Fury 11 respectively.

Hawk – 1. Usually found as 'The Hawk'. Associated with shotgun ammunition made in Europe for James *Matthews of Ballymena. *See also* Kingfisher, Swift, and Wizard. **2.** 'Hawk Brand' [The]. A brandname found on shotgun cartridges handled by *Hawkes of Taunton. **3.** A .177/.22 barrel-cocking spring-and-piston air rifle made by *Webley & Scott in three different versions. The Mark I appeared in 1971, but was replaced in 1974 by the Mark 2. Each of these was characterised by an exchangeable barrel. The Mark 3, made from April 1977 to 1979 in both calibres, was a fixed-barrel derivative with the safe-

ty catch on the left side of the receiver cap instead of immediately behind it.

Hawker. Frank Hawker Ltd, Birmingham and Ironbridge. A maker of magazines for the British 9mm *Sten Gun during the Second World War. The code 'M 111' may have been used instead of the company name. *See also* British military manufacturers' marks.

Hawkes & Sons, Taunton, Somerset. This English country ironmonger sold sporting guns and ammunition, including shotgun cartridges marked 'Hawk Brand'. Apparently, these date from before the First World War.

Hawkesley. G. & J.W. Hawkesley, Carver Street, Sheffield, Yorkshire. Advertising in 1870 as 'Patentees & Manufacturers of Turnovers, Re-Cappers, Extractors, Cleaners and all kinds of Cartridge Implements, for both Pin and Central-fire Breech-loading Guns', this business also made powder flasks, shot punches and dram-bottles.

Hawkins – 1. James Hawkins accepted a few *Dragoon and *Navy-type Colt revolvers in 1849–55, identifying them with 'JH' in a cartouche. His use of this mark seems to have run on from James *Harris, but confusion still reigns. **2.** Samuel Hawkins. An inspector active on behalf of the Federal Army during the American Civil War, identifying firearms and accessories with 'SH'. Hawkins' work seems to have been confined to 1862. *See also* US arms inspectors' marks.

Hawks. Thomas B. Hawks, a government inspector active in 1862, accepted firearms and accessories for the Federal Army. They were marked 'TBH'. *See also* US arms inspectors' marks.

Hawley. Edmund H. Hawley, Kalamazoo, Michigan, USA. This inventor was granted US Patents 90,249 of 1 June 1869 for an 'Air Pistol Shooting Darts', and 118,886 of September 1871 (jointly with Charles H. *Snow) for an improved version of the 1869 design. Apparently guns of this type were made in small numbers by Snow & Cowe.

Hawthorne. A brandname associated with shotguns, *Crosman gas-powered guns and a variety of sporting goods sold in the USA by Montgomery *Ward & Company.

Hayden – 1. Orvin R. Hayden accepted firearms made by *Colt's Patent Fire Arms Manufacturing Company on behalf of the US Army, identifying them with 'ORH'. All seem to date from 1938. **2.** W.H. Hayden, a government inspector, accepted US Army firearms and accessories in 1901–05, marking them 'WHH'. *See also* US arms inspectors' marks.

Hayes. Joseph B. Hayes accepted .45 M1911A1 *Colt pistols on behalf of the US Army, work being confined to 1940. The guns bore 'JBH'. *See also* US arms inspectors' marks.

Haygarth. Colin Haygarth, trading from The Cottage Gunshop, Dunnet, Caithness, Scotland, has marked shotgun cartridges sold under the brandname Economax.

Hayward. S.E. Hayward [& Company], Tunbridge Wells, Kent, and Crowborough, Sussex. The name of this English gunmaker has been found on sporting guns and shotgun ammunition.

'HB' – 1. A superimposition-type monogram. Correctly read as 'BH' (q.v.); used by *Becker & Hollander of Suhl. **2.** Found on US military firearms and accessories. *See* Horace *Burpee.

'HBB', 'HBH', 'HBJ'. Found on US military firearms

and accessories. *See* Hanson B. ★Bullock, Henry B. ★Hart and H.B. ★Johnson.

'HBT'. An unidentified US inspector's mark found on 1860-type .44 Colt Army revolvers made for the Federal Army during the American Civil War.

'HC'. An encircled superimposition-type monogram, with the letter 'H' slightly dominant. Correctly 'CH' (q.v.); found on revolvers made by ★Crucelegui Hermanos.

'HCW'. Found on US military firearms and accessories. *See* H.C. ★Washburn.

'HD', 'H. & D.' – 1. A floriated superimposition-type cursive monogram. Found on semi-automatic pistols made by ★Henrion & Dassy of Liège, c. 1910–14. **2.** A brandname applied to revolvers made by Henrion & Dassy of Liège, Belgium; and also to 6.35mm-calibre pocket pistols made by ★Société d'Armes 'HDH'.

'HDH', 'H.D.H.' – 1. Found on Belgian-made firearms. *See* Henrion, Dassy et Heuschen and Société d'Armes 'HDH'. **2.** Found on US military firearms and accessories. *See* Henry D. ★Hastings.

HEADSTAMP

A term used to describe markings applied to the base, or 'head', of a ★cartridge case, usually identifying the manufacturer and date, and also often providing a description of the loading. The illustrations show typical marks, but the subject is very complicated, and detailed information should be sought from books on the subject, such as *The Cartridge Guide* by Ian Hogg (Arms & Armour Press, 1982), which includes more than 2,300 examples. However, although a few of the best-known marks are listed in the directory, I have concentrated more on shotgun ammunition. Unlike most rifle and handgun patterns, these include brandnames that may also be found on packaging and ephemera.

Military headstamps are often coded. In 1939, for example, British small-arms cartridges had purple primer annuli for ball and practice ammunition (no identification letter), green for armour-piercing ('W'), red for tracer ('G'), blue for incendiary ('B'), yellow for high-pressure proof rounds ('Q'), and black for observing and explosive ('O'). Blank ('L'), grenade-discharging ('H') and smoke-discharging ('E') rounds customarily had colourless annuli. Bullet tips were coloured only if the rounds were incendiary (blue), observing (black), armour-piercing (green) or tracer (red, white or grey).

Cartridges also bore the initials or recognised trade mark of the manufacturer of the case, the date of manufacture in full – or simply the last two digits – and a mark distinguishing the complete round (e.g. 'VII' identified Mk VII ball ammunition, and 'W Mk Iz' was a Mark I armour-piercing round loaded with nitrocellulose propellant.) However, these codes referred only to ammunition made and used in Britain, the British Empire and the British Commonwealth prior to the 1950s. Identical 7.7x56 (.303) ammunition was also used in Japan in the Second World War, where the primer-annuli codes were: black for ball ammunition; white for armour-piercing; green for incendiary; pink for tracer; and purple for high-explosive. The headstamps usually included at least one ideograph that indicated their Japanese origins.

Commercial headstamps usually identify little other than a manufacturer and the calibre or chambering. However, as some of the illustrations show, the maker's mark may be a monogram, a pictorial representation or an abstract symbol.

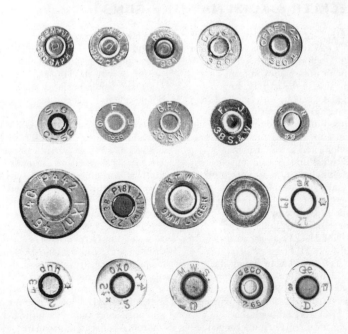

A typical selection of cartridge headstamps, showing the diversity that can be encountered.
Top row: 1. & 2. *Remington-UMC, USA*; 3. *Rheinisch-Westfalische Sprengstoff AG, German*; 4. *Defence Industries, Canada*; 5. *Cartucheria Orbea, Argentina.*
Second row: 1. *Pirotecnica di Capua, Italy*; 2. & 3. *Guilio Fiocchi, Italy*; 4. *Frank Joyce, Britain*; 5. *Fabrique Nationale d'Armes de Guerre, Belgium.*
Third row: 1. *Zieh- u. Stanzwerk GmbH, Germany*; 2. *Hugo Schneider AG (Hasag), Germany*; 3. *Kopsch-Turkus-Ward, USA*; 4. & 5. *Sellier & Bellot (Munitionsfabrik Vlasim), Czechoslovakia, under German suspervision.*
Bottom row: 1. *Rheinisch-Westfalische Sprengstoff, Germany*; 2. *Teuto-Metallwerke, Germany*; 3. *Metallwerke Schönebeck, Germany*; 4. & 5. *Gustav Genschow, Germany.*

'HDJ', 'HDW'. Found on US military firearms and accessories. See Henry D. *Jennings and H.D. *White.

Headstamp. See panel, p. 233.

Heal. W.E. Heal, Bampton Street, Tiverton, Devon. The name of this English ironmonger/gun dealer has been found on shotgun cartridges sold under the brand-name Tivvy.

Healthways, Inc., Los Angeles and Compton, California, USA. This company distributed a range of gas-powered BB pistols and rifles, the guns being made by specialist (and anonymous) sub-contractors. The *Plainsman pistol, designed by Kenneth R. *Pitcher and Richard M. *Kline, dated from 1955/56; see also Plainmaster and Top Score. Healthways traded from East Manville Street, Compton, in 1978–88, and has also promoted spring-powered revolvers and revolver-type pistols.

Heath. Frank Heath, a captain in the US Army, accepted military firearms and accessories in 1883–84, marking them 'FH'. The date distinguishes them from guns accepted twenty years earlier by Frederick *Harvey. See also US arms inspectors' marks.

'Heather' [The]. Found on shotgun cartridges sold by W.R. *Pape of Newcastle upon Tyne, the components being supplied by *Kynoch or *Eley.

Heathman. Thomas Heathman, Crediton, Devon. The name of this English country gunmaker has been found on shotgun cartridges made by *Kynoch prior to the First World War.

Heavy Duty, or Model 38/44 Heavy Duty. A name given to a .38-calibre variant of the N or large-frame swing-cylinder *Smith & Wesson revolvers, introduced in 1930. Temporarily discontinued in 1941, the guns were made again after 1946 with a new rebound-slide hammer block and S-prefix serial numbers. Renamed Model 20 in 1957, the Heavy Duty revolver lost ground so rapidly to .357 versions that it was abandoned in 1966. See also Outdoorsman.

Hebelscheiber Verschluss. See Push-lever lock.

Heberlein. Jorg, or George, Heberlein, St Louis, Missouri. Listed as a maker of St Louis-style spring-air *Gallery Guns in the early 1870s.

Hebler. Friedrich Wilhelm Hebler, often erroneously identified as an Austrian, was born in the small Swiss town of Rüschegg bei Bern on 6 March 1844, graduating as a mechanical engineer from the Swiss university system in 1866. Fascinated by ballistics, he began experimenting with small-calibre projectiles in 1874 and embarked on what became his life's work. Hebler has been credited with the use of a copper bullet jacket; he also developed a unique bullet with a central passage – intended to reduce wind resistance while simultaneously increasing range. Much of his work was undertaken in collaboration with Karel *Krnka. It included the introduction in 1892 of what may have been the first purpose-designed intermediate cartridge, approximately a third smaller than then-current rifle ammunition; this was developed for a Krnka carbine, which was also significantly smaller than rival designs. Best known for Das kleinste Kaliber oder das zukünftige Infanteriegewehr ('The smallest calibre or the Infantry Rifle of the Future'), published in several editions in the period 1886–91, Hebler died in Burgdorf on 30 January 1932.

Hebsacker. Wilhelm Hebsacker, Schwäbisch Hall, Germany: see Hege-Waffen.

Hecht & Company. This British merchanting business, known to have represented European firearms and edged-weapons makers, was listed at 58 Finsbury Pavement, London, in 1897–8.

Heckler & Koch – 1. Heckler & Koch GmbH, or H&K, was founded in Oberndorf in 1949 by Edmund Heckler and Theodor Koch, formerly employees of *Mauser-Werke. Initially, Heckler & Koch concentrated on specialised machine tools, but, after advising the

HECKLER & KOCH MACHINE-GUNS

The HK-Maschinengewehr Modell 11 (7.62x51) is essentially a G3 rifle with a bipod and a heavy barrel, which can be removed from the right side of the barrel casing. The HK11A1 may be distinguished by the design of the butt, which has a stepped under-edge to allow a left-hand grip, whereas the HK11E has an elongated barrel casing, an additional three-round burst-firing capability and a silent bolt-closure system. Guns of this pattern, designated EHK11A1, have been made in Greece by *Elleniki Biomekanika Oplon.

The HK12 was essentially similar to the HK11, but chambered the Soviet 7.62x39 M43 round; the HK13 and its derivatives accepted the 5.56x45 pattern. Alterations were made to the HK13 to approximate to the HK11A1, although the designation remained unchanged.

The HK13E, however, shared the extended barrel casing, optional fore-grip and three-round burst-firing capability with the HK11E. The HK13E is suited to the Belgian SS109 5.56mm bullet, but the outwardly identical HK13E1 is intended specifically to fire US M193 ball ammunition. The HK13C and HK13S of 1987 are variants of the HK13E with baked-on camouflage finish of 'forest green' (beige, brown, green, dark grey/black) or 'desert sand' – a sandy background with olive-drab patching.

The HK21 was an HK11 that accepted the German DM1 disintegrating-link or US M13 non-disintegrating belts instead of a box magazine. Mounts have included tripod, pillar and anti-aircraft/ground patterns. HK21A1 machine-guns had a stepped-edge butt and, ultimately, 'multiple-bullet' selector marks

instead of lettering. They could be altered to chamber 5.56x45 cartridges simply by changing the barrel, magazine and bolt, and a special 7.62x39 variant was made in small numbers. The HK21E offered an additional burst-firing capability and the extended barrel casing. H&K machine-guns have been made under licence in Greece by Elleniki Biomekanika Oplon (as EHK21A1), and in Portugal by Fábrica Militar de Braca de Prata.

The HK23A1 was the 5.56mm version of the HK21A1; and the HK23E, rifled for the SS109 bullet, offered an extended barrel casing and burst-firing capability. The HK23E1 was simply an HK23 adapted for the US M193 bullet. Introduced in 1987, the HK23C and HK23S had baked-on 'forest green' (C) or 'desert sand' (S) camouflage. Adapted from the HK23E, the short-lived HK73 embodied a patented linkless feed. It was

Spanish Army on mass-production techniques, became interested in weaponry. The licence for the *CETME rifle, which had been granted to *NWM, passed to Heckler & Koch, beginning a fruitful association with the roller-lock breech that continues to this day. Unfortunately for H&K, development of the caseless cartridge rifle, or G11, and its ultimate rejection by the Federal German government, put an enormous strain on finances; vulnerable to predators, Heckler & Koch was purchased in January 1991 by the British *Royal Ordnance plc, after the failure of a bid by *GIAT. Currently the business is owned by British Aerospace. Production of 5.56mm HK rifles has been moved to the Royal Ordnance factory in Nottingham, but the future remains far from clear. **2.** Heckler & Koch machine-guns: *see* panel, below. **3.** Heckler & Koch pistols: *see* panel, p. 236. **4.** Heckler & Koch rifles: *see* panel, pp. 236/37. **5.** Heckler & Koch submachine-guns: *see* panel, p. 238.

Hecla. This name graces two types of inexpensive sheath-trigger *Suicide Special revolver made in the USA in the 1880s: one by *Johnson, Bye & Company and/or *Iver Johnson of Worcester and Fitchburg, Massachusetts; the other by the T.J. *Ryan Pistol Company of Norwich, Connecticut.

'Hector'. This mark has been found on *Mayer & Grammelspacher Diana spring-air guns sold in Britain during the 1930s, but its significance remains uncertain.

'hee'. Associated with German machine-gun and small-arms components made during the Second World War by Ikaria-Werke GmbH of Velten/Mark.

Heer. A German-language term, meaning simply 'army' (cf. *Heereswaffen*, 'army weapons'; *Heereswaffenamt*, 'army weapons office').

Heeren. Christian A.F. Heeren, or Christian A.J.A. Heeren. This inventor was responsible for a compact dropping-block rifle, opened by pulling down on the trigger guard, which was pivoted – unusually – at the rear. Heeren is said to have been an officer in the state army of Baden, although a Paris address is customarily given in patent specifications (apparently the first was filed in Austria-Hungary); the breech mechanism proved particularly popular in Switzerland. The modern *Würthrich rifles incorporate a modernised Heeren-type block system. *See also* US Patent no. 239,496 of 29 March 1881.

Heeres-Pistole. German: 'Army Pistol' – a variant of the P. 38, made by Carl *Walther Waffenfabrik of Zella-Mehlis for commercial sale. However, some of the last guns to be marked 'Mod. HP' were impressed into military service at the beginning of the Second World War.

Hefah. The 'Gun, .303-inch, Machine, Hefah V' was a simplified .303 pan-feed *Lewis Gun, touted by the *Ductile Steel Company. However, it was never made in quantity and ultimately, even though provisionally adopted by the Royal Navy early in 1942, production amounted to little more than a handful of prototypes. *See also* Garage Gun.

Hege-Waffen GmbH, Schwäbisch Hall, Germany. Formerly trading as Wilhelm Hebsacker, this wholesaling and distribution business has handled a variety of firearms and sporting goods, including Hungarian-made FÉG pistols. Among these have been *Tokagypt examples sold as AP66 Firebird (c. 1967–75), and *Attila guns sold as the AP63. The company's marks will also be found on black-powder guns such as the Hege-Siber, a single-shot *caplock based on a target pistol made by a nineteenth-century Swiss gunsmith; a Hege-Manton coach pistol; and a re-creation of the Remington *New Army revolver.

'HEH'. Found on US military firearms and accessories. *See* H.E. *Hollister.

Heijo ordnance factory. Possibly functioning as a sub-plant or 'feeder' for *Jinsen arsenal, this Korean fac-

replaced in 1983 by the 5.56mm GR6, which was basically an HK21E with an integral 1.5x optical sight and an optional laser designator in the fore-end; guns of this type could accept box magazines, but were introduced with the linkless feed. The GR6C and GR6S variants were camouflaged. The 5.56mm GR9 and its camouflaged variants (GR9C and GR9S) were conventional belt-feed versions of the GR6, retaining the optical sight. The current G36 LSW is simply a heavy-barrelled version of the comparable rifle, fitted with a bipod.

The G3 assault rifle has provided the basis for a series of surprisingly effective support weapons, including this 7.62mm HK21A1. The belt-feed unit can be replaced with a box-magazine housing when required.

HECKLER & KOCH PISTOLS

The first of these was the HK4, a
*blowback semi-automatic offered
with four replaceable barrels (.22LR,
6.35mm, 7.65mm, 9mm Short).
Guns of this type were sold in the
USA by *Harrington & Richardson
of Worcester, Massachusetts, c.
1968–73, and may be marked
appropriately.

Next came the 9x19 P9,
credited to Herbert *Meidel, but
embodying a variation of the G3
roller-locking system. The single-
action P9 was soon joined by the
double-action P9S, in 9x19 and
.45, then by a P9 Sport. The large
blowback VP70 – later known as
the VP70M (for *Militärausführung*,
military pattern) – could fire fully

automatically only when its
holster-stock was attached; the
VP70Z (*Zivilausführung*, civilian
pattern) was a semi-automatic
commercial version.

The 9x19 *Polizei-Selbstlade-
Pistole*, or PSP, adopted in 1975 by
the German authorities as the *Pistole
7*, is a double-action delayed-
blowback design embodying a grip-
safety system. The P7M8 and
P7M13 differ in magazine capacity
(holding eight and thirteen rounds
respectively); the P7M45 was a .45
ACP version made in small numbers
in 1987–88; the P7M10 of 1988
chambered the .40 Smith & Wesson

cartridge; and a blowback P7K3 has
been offered in .22LR, 7.65mm
Auto and 9x17.

The P7 series was supplemented
in 1993 by the USP (*Universal-
Selbstlade-Pistole*), locked by a variant
of the *Browning cam-lock system
embodied in the FN *High Power
pistol. Originally conceived for the
.40S&W round, the USP is now
being offered in .40, .45 ACP and
9x19; the US Navy Mark 23 Model
0 is little more than a USP adapted
to accept a silencer.

H&K has also made the 26.7mm
P2A1 signal pistol and an electrically
ignited 7.62x36 P11-ZUB
*underwater pistol for Special
Forces use.

*The Heckler & Koch HK-4 pistol, inspired
by the pre-war Mauser HSc, could be
obtained with four interchangeable barrels:
.22, 6.35mm Auto, 7.65mm Auto and
9mm Short.*

HECKLER & KOCH RIFLES

Promising trials of the Spanish
*CETME rifle were undertaken in
Germany in 1955–56 and, in 1958,
the licence granted by CETME to
*NWM was transferred to Heckler
& Koch. Sufficient rifles were
purchased in Spain to permit field
trials to begin in 1959 and, in 1960,
the Gewehr 3 was adopted by the
Bundeswehr to replace the Gewehr
1 (*FAL).

The G3A1 (introduced in 1963)
had a retractable butt, sliding in
grooves pressed into the sides of the
receiver. The G3A2 (1962) had a
free-floating barrel, improving
accuracy; older guns rebuilt to the

same standards acquired an
additional 'FS' mark on the left side
of the magazine housing. The G3A3
(1964) had a solid synthetic butt
and, among other changes, a
modified NATO-standard flash
suppressor/muzzle brake. The G3A4
was a G3A3 with a retractable butt.
The G3A5 was a special semi-
automatic version made in
Oberndorf for Denmark; the G3A6
was exported to Iran, where
subsequently guns were made by the
*Mosalsalasi ordnance factory; and
the G3A7 – produced by *Makína
ve Kímya Endüstrísí Kurumu – was
developed for Turkey.

G3 Zf models, selected for
accuracy, have served as snipers'
weapons (Zf: *Zielfernrohr*, telescope
sight), but the G3 SG/1 of 1973,
with an optical sight and a special
set-trigger, is the preferred sniper
rifle, or *Scharfschützengewehr*. The G3
TGS (Tactical Group System, 1985)
has a single-shot HK79 grenade
launcher instead of the fore-
end/hand guard assembly and
supplementary sights; the G3
INKAS (1977) had an integral infra-
red laser-sighting projector built into
the cocking-handle tube.

Among other H&K rifles are the
HK32A2 (1965), chambered for the
7.62x39 Russian M43 round; the
HK32A3, with a retractable butt;

and the short-barrelled HK32KA1 of 1967. The HK33A2 (1965) was chambered for the 5.56x45 cartridge, the HK33A3 being a retractable-butt version, whereas the HK33 Zf was fitted with optical sights. The short-barrelled HK33KA1 was introduced in 1967. The HK33E (1983), a refined HK33A2, developed into guns with 'forest green' (HK33EC) or two-tone 'desert sand' camouflage (HK33ES). These C- and S-patterns may also be obtained in fixed-butt (A2) and retractable-stock (A3) guise. The HK33KC and HK33S are short-barrelled derivatives with retractable stocks.

The original HK36 was a 4.5x36 variant of the roller-lock design, made only in small numbers in the early 1970s before being abandoned to concentrate on the caseless-cartridge G11. The 5.56x45 G41, introduced in 1983 to replace the HK33 series, has an additional mechanical hold-open and a bolt-closing device. The G41A2 has a retractable butt, and the G41K is short-barrelled. TGS and INKAS variants of the G41 and G41K have also been made in small numbers. The design of the GR3, an adaptation of the G41, was finalised in 1988. The rifle has a small 1.5x optical sight on a permanent receiver-top mount, and can be obtained in 'forest green' (GR3C) or 'desert sand' (GR3S) camouflage finish; A2 guns have fixed butts, A3 versions have retractable butts, and K-types offer short barrels.

The *Präzisions-Scharfschützengewehr 1*, or PSG-1 (1985), is a 7.62mm G3 derivative

intended for ultra-accurate shooting. Its features include a detachable cheek piece, an anatomical pistol grip and a special heavy barrel. Developed specifically for the Bundeswehr and German police, the *Militär-Scharfschützengewehr 3*, or MSG-3 (1988), is a selected, but otherwise standard, G3 action with a specially honed trigger, a bolt-closing device, an adjustable butt and a fixed-leg bipod. The MSG-90 is simply an MSG-3 with a heavy barrel and a bipod with adjustable legs. The Bundeswehr — and some German police units — has also used modified 7.62mm HK11 and HK11E light machine-guns for sniping, designating them as rifles: G8 and G8A1 respectively.

Heckler & Koch rifles usually display their designation and maker's mark on the left side of the magazine housing, ahead of the serial number (e.g. 'G3 HK 12345') above the date of acceptance ('8/62' for August 1962). Guns made for the West Berlin police prior to the reunification of Germany were marked 'MAS' to avoid infringing treaty restrictions. Prior to c.1980, selectors were marked 'S' (*Sicher*, safe), 'E' (*Einzelfeuer*, single shots) and 'F' (*Feuer*, automatic fire); newer versions, however, are marked with multiple-bullet symbols, and greater use has been made of synthetic components.

One disadvantage of the roller lock is that the breech begins to open before the residual pressure inside the spent case has dropped sufficiently, leading, in extreme cases, to casehead separations. Common to almost all ★delayed

This short-barrelled 5.56mm Heckler & Koch G41K shows how the use of synthetic components has increased over the years in which rifles of this type have been made. Note the multi-bullet symbols on the ambidextrous selector.

blowbacks, this tendency is minimised in the H&K designs by fluting the chamber to 'float' the cartridge case on a cushion of gas. Although Heckler & Koch finally perfected the 4.73x33 caseless-cartridge rifle, issued in small quantities to German Special Forces in 1990 as the G11K3, the Federal government preferred the 5.56mm *Gewehr 36* (G36). Adopted in 1995, and outwardly similar to the G41, this gas-operated Heckler & Koch rifle is locked by a conventional rotating bolt and has an integral optical sight. Skeletal butts fold laterally. The G36K has a short barrel; the G36E and G36KE are export versions, with 1.5x sights instead of the 3x type.

Heckler & Koch has also made sporting rifles incorporating the roller-lock mechanism. These include the 5.56x45 SL-6 and 7.62x51 SL-7, introduced c. 1976, and a group of guns introduced in 1978: the HK-630 (.223 Remington), the HK-770 (.270 Winchester or .308 Winchester) and the HK-940 in .30-06 only. The .223 HK-91, once popular in North America, was little more than a 'sporting' version of the 5.56x45 HK33 limited to semi-automatic fire.

HECKLER & KOCH SUBMACHINE-GUNS

These have been made since 1964, chambering the 9x19 (9mm Parabellum) cartridge. The guns are customarily known as *Maschinenpistolen 5* (MP5), the original Bundeswehr designation. The MP5A2 has a fixed butt, whereas the MP5A3 has a retractable sliding pattern. All the guns can fire semi-automatically, but some made after c. 1983 had three-round burst capabilities, while others dating later than c. 1991 can fire two rounds for a single pull on the trigger.

The MP5SD series are silenced variants, with large-diameter barrel jackets. The 9x19 MP5SD1 lacks a butt, the MP5SD2 has a fixed butt and the MP5SD3 has a retractable sliding butt; burst-firing versions are designated MP5SD4, MP5SD5 and MP5SD6. The MP5K is an ultra-compact (*Kurz*) version, with a short barrel and a special fore-grip; the MP5KA1 is similar, but has a special smooth 'no-snag' receiver. The MP5KA4 and MP5KA5 are simply variants of the MP5K and MP5KA1 fitted with burst-firing units.

The MP5K PDW is a US-made Special Forces gun, with a butt that folds laterally and lugs on the muzzle to accept a silencer or grenade launcher. The MP5/10 and MP5/40 chamber the 10mm Auto and .40 S&W pistol cartridges respectively, whereas the HK53, although virtually the same size as the MP5, handles 5.56x45 rifle ammunition.

The 9mm MP5 submachine-gun has been outstandingly successful, offering a combination of short-range firepower and excellent accuracy that has proved irresistible to law-enforcement agencies worldwide. Clad in gas mask and body armour, this soldier is using image-intensifying goggles in conjunction with a laser designator attached to an MP5A3.

tory made ★Arisaka rifles under Japanese control during 1938–39.

Heilprin – 1. William Albert Heilprin, Philadelphia, Pennsylvania, USA. Patentee of a variety of ★BB Guns. Relevant US Patent specifications included 944,188 of 21 December 1909, for a gun fitted with a safety catch; 1,098,151 of 26 May 1914, for an improved BB Gun with a toggle-link in the cocking system; and 1,098,321 of 26 May 1914, for a break-butt cocking system. British Patent 29,225/09 of 1909 was comparable with US 944,188. **2.** Heilprin & Levy, USA. See Heilprin's Manufacturing Company. **3.** Heilprin's Manufacturing Company, Philadelphia, Pennsylvania. This business succeeded Heilprin & Levy in 1909 and made the ★Columbian BB Guns prior to c. 1919, when it returned to metal stamping until succeeded by the ★Arrow Manufacturing Company in 1928. Guns made under the Heilprin & Levy and Columbian banners may have been sub-contracted to the W.G. ★Smith Company.

Heim, *see also* Heym **– 1.** A trademark used by C.E. ★Heinzelmann of Plochingen am Neckar on sporting guns and ammunition. A few 6.35mm Heim pistols were made about 1930, combining features of the 1906-pattern FN-Browning and the vest-pocket (*Westentaschen*) pistols being made contemporaneously in nearby Oberndorf by ★Mauser-Werke AG. **2.** C. Heim, Suhl in Thüringen, Germany. This gunmaker is known to have been trading in Suhl between 1914 and 1920.

'Hei-Mo'. A trademark found on pistols and spring-air guns made, or more probably sold, by Heinrich ★Moritz of Zella St Blasii prior to 1919. *See also* 'He-Mo'.

Heimrich. E. Heimrich, Zella-Mehlis in Thüringen, Germany. Listed in the 1930 edition of the *Deutsches Reichs-Adressbuch* as a master gunsmith.

Hein. Arth. Otto Hein, Zella-Mehlis in Thüringen, Germany. Listed in 1939 as a master gunsmith.

Heinemann. Karl Heinemann. Designer of the ★Parabellum machine-gun and the ★Rheinmetall Rh. 28

and Rh. 29 auto-loading rifles. The rifles had distinctive lateral toggle-locks on the right rear of the receiver, box magazines protruding from the left side of the receiver, and *Bang-type muzzle cups to trap and divert propelling gases on to the actuating rod.

Heintz. Frederick W. Heintz. Listed as a gunmakers' agent in Britain in 1872–73, with shop premises at 102 London Wall.

Heintzmann & Rochussen. Gunmakers' agents and merchants, these partners operated in London from 9 Friday Street in 1865–66, and 23 Abchurch Lane in 1867–80. They represented, among others, Hermann *Lang of Solingen and *Manufacture Liégeoise d'Armes à Feu.

Heinzelmann. C.E. Heinzelmann, Plochingen am Neckar, Württemberg. This German gunmaking business made a few Heim-brand pistols in the 1930s, in addition to sporting rifles and shotguns. Trading had ceased by 1945, but details are lacking.

'Helepco'. This brandname will be found on 6.35mm-calibre automatic pistols made by *Manufacture d'Armes des Pyrénées Françaises for H. le *Personne & Company of London. See also Lepco.

Helfricht – 1. Gebrüder Helfricht, Zella St Blasii and Zella-Mehlis in Thüringen, Germany. Listed in 1914–20 as a gunmaker; owned in 1920 by Bruno Helfricht. **2.** Herm. Otto Helfricht, Mäbendorf. Listed in 1941 as a specialist supplier of gun-stock blanks. **3.** Hugo Helfricht, Zella-Mehlis in Thüringen, Germany. Listed in 1930 as a maker of guns and weapons. **4.** Karl Helfricht, Zella-Mehlis in Thüringen, Germany. Listed in 1930–39 as a gun-stock maker. **5.** Kuno Helfricht, Zella-Mehlis in Thüringen. Patentee of the Helfricht automatic pistols (below), although these may have been made by A *Krauser; see also Helkra. **6.** L. Helfricht, Zella-Mehlis in Thüringen, Germany. Listed in the 1939 *Deutsches Reichs-Adressbuch* as a master gunsmith. **7.** Otto Helfricht, Heinrich-Ehrhardt-Strasse, Zella-Mehlis in Thüringen, Germany. Listed in many 1939 trade directories as a specialist gun-stock maker. **8.** Otto Helfricht, Zella-Mehlis in Thüringen, Vorderhügel. Listed in 1939 as a gun-stock maker. Possibly the same as the preceding entry; the address may be his residence instead of a workshop. **9.** Traugott Helfricht, Zella-Mehlis in Thüringen. A maker of sporting rifles and shotguns active in Germany in the early twentieth century. **10.** Helfricht & Fischer, Zella St Blasii and Zella-Mehlis in Thüringen, Germany. Founded in 1859, listed in 1900–14 as gunmakers, and in 1919–20 as weapon makers. Owned in 1920–39 by Bruno Helfricht (gunmaker). **11.** Helfricht pistols. These 6.35mm pocket semi-automatics were based on patents granted in Germany in 1920 to Kuno Helfricht, whose 'KH' mark usually appears on the grips. The original guns (Models 1–3) had an abbreviated slide and a split ejection port; later Model 4 examples were more conventional. See also A. *Krauser.

Helkra. A version of the 6.35mm *Helfricht pocket pistol made by, or perhaps for, Alfred *Krauser of Zella-Mehlis, c. 1921–25.

Hellis. Charles Hellis [& Sons]. This gunmaking business was listed at 21 Shrewsbury Road, London N., in 1894–96, and thereafter at 119 Edgware Road, London W., from 1897 onward. It was supervised after 1902 by Charles and Clifford Hellis, sons of the founder, and even-

tually moved to larger premises at 121–3 Edgware Road. The company name will be found on a variety of sporting guns and shotgun cartridges sold under the tradenames Burwood, Championship, Economist, Edgware, Falcon, Highclere, Merlin, Service and Standard. Some of the pre-1914 cartridges were loaded in Belgium (or at least from Belgian-made parts), but generally post-1919 examples were the work of *Eley-Kynoch. Trading ceased in 1956, when *Hellis & Rosson was formed in Norwich.

Helmers. Franz Helmers, Suhl in Thüringen. A maker of hunting rifles and shotguns (*Jagdgewehr-Fabrikation*), active in Germany c. 1925–39.

Helmqvist. Stig Helmqvist, Sweden: see Stiga AB.

Helson. J. Helson, 84 Fore Street, Exeter, Devon. The name of this English country gunmaker has been found on shotgun cartridges sold under the brandnames *Demon and *Invincible.

Helvece. A compact Browning-type pocket pistol made by, or for, Fabrique d'Armes de *Grande Précision of Eibar, Guipuzcoa, Spain: 6.35mm, six rounds, hammer fired.

'HEM'. Found on US military firearms and accessories. See H.E. *Madden.

Hembrug. The Dutch state-owned arms factory, founded in the 1890s, was renowned for 6.5mm *Mannlicher rifles and *Schwarzlose machine-guns. Eventually it became part of Nederlandsch Wapen- en Munitiefabriek.

Hemenway. J.N. Hemenway, often listed as Hemingway and Henneway, accepted US military firearms and accessories marked 'JNH' in 1907. See also US arms inspectors' marks.

'He-Mo'. A trademark associated with Heinrich *Moritz of Zella-Mehlis, found on sporting guns, airguns and a few distinctive 7.65mm-calibre semi-automatic pistols made in the early 1920s. See also 'Hei-Mo'.

Henderson – 1. James L. Henderson, acting on behalf of the US Navy, accepted .36-calibre *Colt Navy revolvers, c. 1858–65. They bore a 'JLH' identifier, but are easily distinguished from guns accepted in the 1930s by James L *Hatcher. See also US arms inspectors' marks. **2.** Henderson & Company. The name of this Scottish ironmonger/gun dealer, based in Dundee, Angus, has been reported on *Eley shotgun cartridges. Apparently they date prior to the First World War.

'Hendon' [The]. Found on the bodies of 12-bore shotgun cartridges assembled in Hendon, London, by the *New Normal Ammunition Company Ltd, and the *Normal Improved Ammunition Company. The components were purchased in Europe and the USA.

Hendrick. E.A. Hendrick, active in 1904, accepted US military firearms and accessories marked 'EAH'. See also US arms inspectors' marks.

Hengelhaupt – 1. A. Hengelhaupt, Zella-Mehlis in Thüringen, Germany. Listed in 1930 as a master gunsmith and gunmaker. **2.** August Louis Hengelhaupt, Zella-Mehlis in Thüringen, Germany. Listed in the *Deutsches Reichs-Adressbuch* for 1939 as a master gunsmith. **3.** Hermann Hengelhaupt, Zella-Mehlis in Thüringen. Listed in German trade directories as a gun-stock maker, 1939. **4.** Richard Hengelhaupt, Zella-Mehlis in Thüringen. Listed in German directories as a gun-barrel drawer (1938–39)

Henkel. Adolf Henkel, Herges-Hallenberg. A maker of 'weapons', listed in the early 1940s in the gunmaking sections of German trade directories.

Henrion – 1. Henrion & Dassy [Fabrique d'Armes], Liège, Belgium. Makers of a wide variety of revolvers prior to c. 1895, when the trading style became Henrion, Dassy & Heuschen. 2. Henrion, Dassy et Heuschen, Liège, Belgium. This well-known gunmaking partnership made many sporting guns and different revolvers in the last few years of the ninetenth century. Then it was renamed *Société d'Armes 'HDH'.

Henrite Explosives Company Ltd, 97 Wilton Road, London S.W. The name of this propellant and explosives manufacturer – or, more probably importer – has been found on shotgun cartridges sold under the brandname Henrite prior to 1914. Some cases are also marked 'Made in Bavaria', possibly by *Utendörffer of Nürnberg.

Henry – 1. Alexander Henry, the well-known Scottish gunmaker, maintained premises in Glasgow, Edinburgh and London. The London office occupied 118 Pall Mall in 1877–86; 31 Cockspur Street, London S.W., in 1887–93; 23 Pall Mall in 1897–98; and 13a Charles Street, Haymarket, in 1899. The business was listed as Alex. Henry Ltd in 1897, and Alex Henry & Company [Ltd?] from 1898. Alexander Henry entered 12-bore pin- and centrefire breech-loading shotguns in *The Field* trials of 1866, and continued to make high-quality sporting, target and hunting rifles for many years. He is best known for the rifling of the *Martini–Henry rifle, protected by British Patent 2802/60. *See also* Henry Rifled Barrel Company (below). 2. Benjamin Tyler Henry: *see* panel, facing page. 3. Henry Repeating Rifle Company, New Haven, Connecticut. This seems to have been incorporated in 1865, after the collapse of the *New Haven Arms Company, but had itself been superseded within a year by the *Winchester Repeating Arms Company. It is assumed that Henry and Winchester had quarrelled. Even though Henry's 1860 patent was reissued in December 1868, the original had been assigned to Winchester. 4. Henry Arms Company. A name found on shotguns handled in the USA by the H. & D. *Folsom Arms Company, possibly imported from Europe prior to the First World War. 5. Henry Military Rifle Company [The]. This short-lived promotional agency for the Henry single-shot rifle operated in London in 1875–77, first from 39a King William Street, then from Chatham Buildings, New Bridge Street, E.C. 6. Henry Rifled Barrel Company Ltd [The], Blenheim Works, Eagle Wharf Road, Hoxton, London N. This gunmaking business was formed in 1875 to exploit the patents granted to the Scottish gunmaker Alex. Henry, whose single-shot rifle had performed so well in the British Army breech-loading rifle trials that its rifling design had been adopted for the *Martini–Henry rifle. The company was renamed Henry Rifled Barrel, Engineering & Small Arms Company Ltd in 1876, with additional premises at 2 Chatham Buildings, New Bridge Street, London E.C., and continued to trade until the early twentieth century. The principal product in the early days was gun barrels, but rifles and other small-arms were made from the 1880s. These were often identified solely by 'H.R.B.' ('Henry Rifled Barrel') marks.

Henser. Daniel Henser. A gunsmith listed at 1 Fowkes Buildings, London E.C., in 1880–89.

Henton. W.G. Henton & Sons, Lincoln. The name of this English country gunmaking business has been reported on sporting guns and shotgun ammunition.

Hepburn – 1. Lewis Lobdell Hepburn: *see* panel, p. 242.

2. Melvin Hepburn, New Haven, Connecticut. Son of Lewis Hepburn (above), recipient of US Patents 755,660 and 888,329, granted on 29 March 1904, and 888,329 of 19 May 1908 to protect 'take down' systems for shotguns. Both were assigned to the *Marlin Fire Arms Company. 3. Hepburn–Walker. A modification of the *Remington-Hepburn action, substituting an operating lever combined with the trigger guard for the sidelever. It was generally associated with the Remington No. 3 Match and No. 3 Schuetzen rifles (q.v.).

Heppleston. Thomas Heppleston, sometimes listed as Hepplestone, Manchester, Lancashire. This English gunmaker began trading in 1859 from 14 Thomas Street, Shude Hill, receiving British Patent 1278/60 of 23 May 1860 to protect cap-lock breech-loading systems. His name has also been found on British-made shotgun cartridges dating prior to 1914.

Heptinstall. William Heptinstall. This London gunsmith began trading from 6 Swan Street, *Minories, in 1830. Twice Master of the Gunmakers Company and a contractor to the East India Company, Heptinstall continued business alone from 18 Swan Street until William Heptinstall & Son was formed in 1856. Heptinstall senior died in 1866, but trading may have continued until 1868 or later.

Herbert & Company, 67 Strand, London. A patent agency retained by Henry Quackenbush, named as the grantees of British Patent 10,499/84.

Herbrüggen-Gewehrfabrik. *See* Al. *Schulte.

Hercules – 1. Generally found as 'The Hercules' on the products of the Hercules Arms Company of London, including sporting guns and ammunition. 2. Hercules Arms Company [The], 8 St Martin's, London WC2. This gunmaking business imported goods from Europe. Its marks have been reported on a variety of guns and accessories, including shotgun cartridges sold under the brandnames Farm and Hercules. These were probably loaded in London from German or Belgian components. 3. Hercules Cycle & Motor Company Ltd [The], Birmingham, Warwickshire. A member of the *Monotype Scheme, this bicycle-making business produced box magazines for the British .303 *Bren Gun during the Second World War, often marking them with the code 'M 117' instead of the company name. *See also* British military manufacturers' marks. 4. *See also* Herkules.

'Hereford' [The]. Found on shotgun cartridges distributed by P. *Morris & Son of Hereford, possibly the work of more than one manufacturer.

Herkules. A barrel-cocking 4.5mm-calibre air pistol made in Germany by *Moritz & Gerstenberger, c. 1937–39.

Hermann – 1. Of Liège. A Belgian gunsmith, designer of a 'revolver', 1839. This was a ring-trigger pepperbox, essentially identical to the better-known *Mariette. Still active in the 1870s, making revolvers. 2. Edwin Hermann. Listed in 1890 as a member of the London gun trade, with premises at 48 Marylebone Lane.

Hermetic. A group of French 6.35mm- and 7.65mm-calibre blowback semi-automatic pistols made c. 1907–12 by Établissements Bernardon-Martin et Cie. Some examples will be marked *'Société Française d'Armes Automatiques de Saint-Étienne', perhaps a successor to Bernardon-Martin.

Hermitage Arms Company, or Hermitage Gun Company. A brandname associated with shotguns made

BENJAMIN TYLER HENRY

Henry was born in Claremont, New Hampshire, on 22 March 1821. After serving an apprenticeship with J.B. Ripley & Company, patentees of a Waterproof Rifle, he was employed by Springfield Armory and Nicanor Kendall, then ★Robbins, Kendall & Lawrence. After working with several gunmaking companies in and around Connecticut, Henry became factory superintendent of the ★New Haven Arms Company.

Henry is renowned for designing the breech-loading magazine rifle protected by US Patent 30,446 of 16 October 1860, assigned to Oliver F. ★Winchester, which was not only exploited during the American Civil War as the Henry Repeating Rifle, but also provided the basis for the 1866-pattern Winchester. However, the inventor seems to have quarrelled with Winchester shortly after the demise of the New Haven Arms Company and became involved in different forms of engineering; he died in New Haven on 8 June 1898.

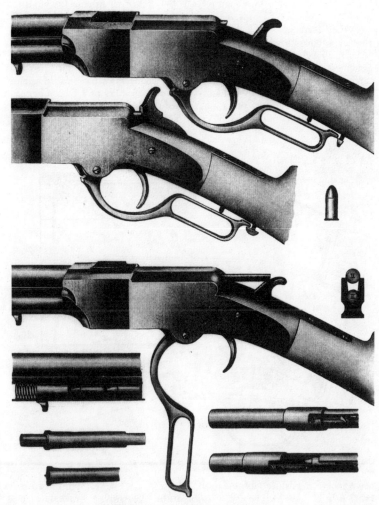

The 1860-pattern .44 rimfire Henry rifle (modern replica shown, above) provided the basis for the very successful lever-action Winchesters. It could be recognised by the absence of a fore-end. The drawings show how the trigger-guard lever actuates the sliding bolt which, in turn, pushes back the hammer until it can be retained on the sear.

---

in the USA prior to 1917 by the ★Crescent Arms Company of Norwich, Connecticut.

Hermsdorff. Max Hermsdorff, Germany. *See* Adlerwaffenfabrik.

Hero. – 1. A copy of a ★Daisy BB Gun, made in Japan in the early twentieth century. Manufacturer unknown. **2.** A ★Suicide Special revolver made in the 1880s by J. ★Rupertus Patent Pistol Manufacturing Company of Philadelphia, Pennsylvania, USA.

Herold. A brandname associated with rifles made in Germany by Franz ★Jäger of Suhl prior to 1939.

Heron Rogers & Company, London. A patent agency: *see* Francis Heron ★Rogers.

Herter's, Inc., Waseca, Minnesota, USA. A distributor of guns and sporting goods, including Mauser-action rifles made by Zavodi Crvena ★Zastava prior to c. 1974. They were marketed as Herters' J9 and Zastava 67. BSA-made guns, basically barrelled Monarch actions, were also sold in large numbers as Herters' U9.

Hertlein – 1. Alfred Hertlein & Co., Suhl in Thüringen, Germany. Listed in the *Deutsches Reichs-Adressbuch*, 1930–39 as a gunmaking business, owned by Alf. Hertlein, M. Zeth and J. Lümme. **2.** Franz Hertlein, Suhl in Thüringen, Germany. Listed as a gunsmith, 1939.

'Herts Cartridge' [The]. Found on shotgun cartridges sold in England by C.H. ★Barham of Hitchin, a

LEWIS LOBDELL HEPBURN

Born in Colton on 2 March 1832 and trained as a gunsmith, Hepburn made single-shot *cap-lock target rifles in the 1860s. However, his talents soon came to the attention of E. *Remington & Sons, where he became superintendent of sporting-gun production in the Ilion factory in 1871.

When Remington collapsed in 1886, Hepburn moved to the *Marlin Fire Arms Company and remained there for the rest of his career. Hepburn was an excellent shot, representing the USA in Elcho Shield challenge matches, and a prolific patentee. Among his US

Patents were a group protecting 'Breech-Loading Firearms': 220,285 of 7 October 1879 (for the *Remington-Hepburn target rifle) and 298,377 of 13 May 1884 for a lever-action magazine rifle, both assigned to Remington. Patents 434,062 of 12 August 1890 and 502,489 of 1 August 1893, assigned to Marlin, protected features of the Marlin M1891 and M1893 lever-action rifles respectively.

Others protected 'Firearms', 'Magazine Firearms' and 'Magazine Guns': 354,059 of 7 December 1886 for the Marlin M1888 rimfire lever-action rifle; 371,455 of 11 October

1887 and 400,679 of 2 April 1889 for the Marlin M1889 rimfire lever-action rifle; 463,832 of 24 November 1891 for an experimental lever-action rifle; 549,722 of 12 November 1895 for a lever-action shotgun; 560,032 of 12 May 1896 for a pump-action shotgun; 561,226 of 2 June 1886 for a shotgun take-down system; 584,177 of 8 June 1897 for the Marlin M1897 rifle; 776,243 of 29 November 1904, 882,563 of 24 March 1908 and 883,020 of 24 March 1908 for the Marlin Model 20 rifle; 918,447 of 13 April 1908 and 927,464 of 6 July 1908 for experimental semi-automatic rimfire rifles; and 943,828 of 21 December 1908 for a shotgun.

Virtually all of these had been assigned to Marlin. In addition, Hepburn received protection for 'Detachably Uniting Gun Barrels to Stocks' (534,691 of 26 February 1895) and a selection of safety systems. He died on 31 August 1914, having been bedridden since breaking his thigh in a fall on the way to the Marlin factory four years previously.

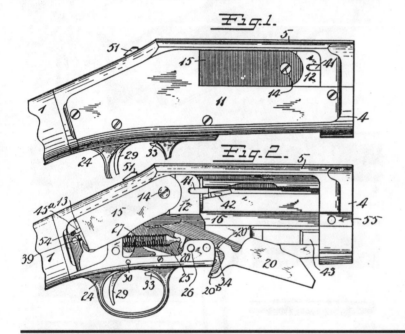

Lewis Hepburn's design for a hammerless slide-action shotgun, subsequently made by Marlin, from a US Patent granted in 1909.

---

town in Hertfordshire (abbreviation, 'Herts.').

Hervey. Thomas M. Hervey, a major in the US Army, was responsible for accepting guns made by *Colt's Patent Fire Arms Manufacturing Company; apparently confined to 1938, these bore the identifier 'TMH'. *See also* US arms inspectors' marks.

Hetherington. John Hetherington, Bridlesmith Gate, Nottingham. This English provincial gunmaker succeeded his father, also named John, in 1844 and traded for at least twenty years. Breech-loading sporting guns have been reported with his marks.

Heurtier, 26 rue Clément-Forissier, Saint-Étienne, France. Listed in 1951 as a gun-barrel maker.

Heuse. Ernest Heuse[-Lemoine] (1834–1926), a Belgian metalsmith, is renowned for the creation of damascus-twist gun barrels in his Nessonvaux workshop. Many of these were intended for the North

American market, where they were employed by gun-makers such as *Parker Brothers. Heuse has been credited by Claude Gaier with the creation of Boston and Washington twist-patterns.

'HEV', 'HEW'. Found on US military firearms and accessories. *See* Henry E. *Valentine and H.E. *Wallenberg respectively.

Hewett. Leslie Hewett Ltd, Upton Cross, Liskeard, Cornwall, England. This distribution company was founded in 1970 by M.J. Raymont, A.D. Rowe, L. Wakeham and T. Adams – three of whom were established international shots – to handle a variety of top-line shooting goods. Hewett distributed *RWS pellets and *RWS-Diana airguns among its impressive range of goods. The company was acquired by *Dynamit Nobel during the late 1980s, but continued to trade independently.

Hewitt. John Charles Edward Hewitt. A gunsmith listed at 84 Blackman Street, London E.C. (1862–90), and 24 Borough High Street, London S.E., from 1891 until trading ceased two years later.

Hewson. Thomas Hewson, London. The marks of this gunmaker have been reported on self-cocking *pepper-boxes dating from the middle of the nineteenth century.

Hexagon Air Rifle Company, Detroit, Michigan, USA. This partnership between George and Frederick Decker and Frank Trowbridge succeeded to production of the *Bijou BB Gun. The 1901-vintage *Hexagon – with a magazine under the butt and a hexagonal butt casing – was also made, but Trowbridge returned to forestry work in 1902, and George Decker died at much the same time. Frederick Decker moved to New York in 1903, where business may have been continued until c. 1910.

Heydt. Johs. Heydt, Albrechts bei Suhl in Thüringen, Zellaer Strasse 8 (1940). Listed in German trade directories as a maker of gun parts and accessories, owned in 1940–41 by Aug. Heym.

Heym – **1.** Conrad Heym, Suhl in Thüringen, Hohe Roder 7. Founded in 1876 and still listed in Germany in 1930–45 as a gunmaking business, then owned by Albert Heym and Otto Schröpfer the Younger. **2.** Franz Heym, Suhl in Thüringen, Germany. Registered as a gunsmith prior to 1920. **3.** Friedrich Wilhelm Heym, Suhl in Thüringen. This German gunmaking business, with origins stretching back to 1790, was founded in Suhl in 1865. It was listed prior to the First World War as specialising in shotguns and sporting rifles – owned in 1914–20 by Karl Adolf Heym; in 1930 by Karl Adolf and August Wilhelm Heym; and in 1939–45 by August Wilh. Heym. A workshop was occupied in Suhl at Schillingstrasse 7 (1939–45). Trading began again in Bavaria after the Second World War (below). Hunting and sporting guns have always been made, including the famous *Drilling, patented in Germany in 1891. **4.** Friedr. Wilh. Heym GmbH & Co., Münnerstadt, Bavaria, and Gleichamberg (Thüringen) from 1996. Heym made sporting guns and classic Mauser-type sporters for many years, the oldest being based on refurbished military-surplus actions, and later examples on FN-Mauser components. Heym progressed to the refined proprietary SR-20 action, but reverted in the 1990s to traditional Mauser actions for the largest chamberings. A few airguns were made in 1949–52, including about 3,000 LG 100 rifles; the LG 101 had a magazine, and the LG 102 was a junior rifle. The LP 103 was a push-in-barrel pistol. **5.** H. Heym. This gunmaking business, probably based in Suhl, was represented at 42 Poland Street, London W., in 1890–93. **6.** Karl Heym, Suhl in Thüringen, Germany. Operating as a gunsmith, 1930 and 1939. **7.** Max Heym, Suhl in Thüringen, Drusselstrasse 31 (1940). This gunmaking business began trading in 1865 and was still being listed in the *Deutsches Reichs-Adressbuch* in the period 1930–45. **8.** Rudolf Heym, Suhl in Thüringen, Germany. Trading in 1920–25 as a gunsmith. **9.** Stephan Heym, Suhl in Thüringen. Claiming origins in 1850, this gunmaking business was run by father and son (Stephan Heym d.J.) until the First World War. Trading is believed to have ceased in 1919. **10.** Gebrüder Heym, Suhl in Thüringen. Listed as a gunmaker in 1914; in 1920, owned by Richard and Emil Heym, and in 1930–39 by Richard and Bruno Heym. Makers of two-shot 12-, 16- and 20-bore Geha shotguns

from war-surplus Gew. 98, c. 1925–33. The business was listed in directories dating from the early years of the Second World War as a gunmaking business, trading in 1941 from Schlageterstrasse 43.

'Heyman Smokeless' [The]. Shotgun ammunition made in Birmingham by the *Mullerite Cartridge Company. Normally the name was accompanied by a trademark in the form of a male peacock in display.

'HFL'. Found on US military firearms and accessories. *See* Harry F. *Lynch.

'hgs'. A codemark found on German small-arms ammunition components made in 1941–45 by Gustav W.C. Burmester of Trittau Bezirk Hamburg.

'H. & H.', 'H&H'. Marks associated with the products of *Holland & Holland of London, England.

'HHH'. Found on US military firearms and accessories. *See* H.H. *Hamilton and Henry H. *Hartzell.

'hhv'. Allocated in 1941 to the Nibelungen/St Valentine factory of *Steyr-Daimler-Puch AG and subsequently used on German small-arms components made during the Second World War.

'hhw'. Used during the Second World War by Metallwerke Silberhütte GmbH of St. Andreasberg in Harz on small-arms ammunition components made for the German armed forces.

'Hiawatha Ace'. A mark associated with ammunition produced by the *American Cartridge Company of Kansas City.

Hibbard – **1.** A *Suicide Special revolver made by the *Crescent Arms Company of Norwich, Connecticut, USA, in the late nineteenth century. Undoubtedly it was intended to be sold by Hibbard, Spencer, Bartlett & Company (*see* following entry). **2.** Hibbard, Spencer, Bartlett & Company, Chicago, Illinois, USA. The largest and best-known of the pre-1914 hardware distributors, this business also sold guns and ammunition ranging from *Daisy BB Guns to shotguns. Sometimes the cartridges bore the company's initials – 'H.S.B. & Co.' – in their headstamps.

Hicks – **1.** Frederick Hicks, 67 High Street, Haverhill, Suffolk. The name of this English country gunmaker has been found on sporting guns and shotgun ammunition. **2.** William Cleveland Hicks, New Haven, Connecicut, and New York City. Recipient of US Patent 16,797 of 19 March 1857, to protect a 'nipple for…withdrawing cartridges from breech-loading firearms'; and 41,814 of 1 March 1864, protecting a breech-loading firearm assigned to Edward *Robinson and E. Chamberlain.

Hi-Compression. A name associated with .177 and .22 airgun pellets made in the USA by the *Benjamin Rifle Company.

Higgins – **1.** Harry Higgins, 46 & 48 Teme Street, Tenbury Wells, Worcestershire. The name of this gunmaker has been found on shotgun cartridges sold in south-west England under the brandnames Dead Shot and Harry Higgins Special. **2.** J.C. Higgins. A brandname associated with guns made in the USA (and elsewhere) for *Sears, Roebuck & Company.

High... – **1.** High-Power, or Hi-Power. A nickname applied to the Belgian FN-Browning 9mm Pistolet à Grande Puissance, Mle 35 (GP-35). Developed by John *Browning immediately after the First World War, it was perfected after his death in 1926 by Dieudonné *Saive and the staff of Fabrique Nationale d'Armes de Guerre. **2.** High Standard Manufacturing Company, New Haven and Hamden, Connecticut, USA. Formed in New Haven in 1926 by Gustave Beck and Carl ★Swebilius, trading from 131 East Street, this partnership intended to make gun-barrel drills. However, the chance purchase of machinery owned by the moribund ★Hartford Arms & Equipment Company allowed High Standard to enter the gunmaking business. The Hartford blowback semi-automatic pistol was put back into production as the Models A–E, differing largely in chamberings (the C-pattern was .22 Short) and barrel design. Exposed-hammer versions (HA–HE, although there was no HC) appeared in 1940, substantial quantities of Model-B US and Model USA-HD being made as trainers during the Second World War, while others went to the SOE and the OSS. Improvements made when work resumed in 1946 led to the G-series, introduced from 1947 onward, then to the Olympic (1950) and Supermatic (1951). A series of sporting designs followed: the Sport King and Field King in 1953, and the Flite King in 1954. Then came improved versions of the Supermatic series (Citation, Olympic, Tournament and Trophy), all dating from 1959. These were followed by the Olympic ISU (1964), Olympic ISU Military (1965), Supermatic Citation Military (1965), Supermatic Trophy Military (1965), Sharpshooter, Custom Target 10-X (1981), and Victor (1970). Nine-shot rimfire revolvers were made under names such as Camp Gun, Double Nine, Durango, High Sierra, Longhorn and Posse; the Crusader and Sentinel revolvers were principally centrefire, although rimfire versions of the latter could be obtained. The .22 Duramatic (1955–63 and 1972–74, also known as Plinker) was a blowback semi-automatic with a plastic butt unit, and the Derringer Model was a modernised form of the ★Remington Double Derringer Repeating Pistol. High Standard made barrels for the .45 M1911A1 ★Government Model pistol during the Second World War, and a few thousand High-Power rifles were made in 1962–66, based on ★Mauser actions purchased from ★Fabrique Nationale. They were known as the ★Field Model. Work ceased in the 1980s, but subsequently some of the pistols were resurrected by ★Mitchell Arms. **3.** 'High Velocity' [The]. A name encountered on shotgun cartridges sold in Britain by W.J. ★Jeffrey of London.

Higham – 1. Edward & George Higham, Liverpool, Lancashire. This English business claimed origins as early as 1795, when George Higham the Elder began trading in Warrington. Premises were still being occupied in Horsemarket Street, Warrington, as late as 1869. Edward and George Higham, presumably the sons of George the Elder, formed their partnership in Liverpool in c. 1857. Premises were occupied at 9 Ranelagh Street and 32 Berry Street (at least until 1870), but operations had moved to 4 Chapel Street by the end of the ninteenth century. Sporting guns and shotgun cartridges have been reported with appropriate marks. **2.** G.G. Higham, Oswestry, Shropshire. This English country gunmaker is believed to have been the grandson of George Higham, trading in Cross Street, Oswestry, in 1834–50. His marks have been found on shotgun cartridges under the brand-name Hi-Os.

'Highclere' [The]. This name is said to have been used on shotgun ammunition sold by Charles ★Hellis & Sons of London, for use on the Highclere estate of the Earl of Carnarvon. However, there is no evidence that anything other than the Earl's crest (on the wads) distinguished cartridges of this type.

'Highdown' [The]. A mark found on shotgun ammunition sold by ★Tilbury & Jeffries of Worthing. The name was provided by a nearby private estate and botanical garden owned by Sir Frederick Sterne.

Highest Possible. Associated with a curious spring-and-piston air pistol, with a break-grip cocking mechanism, made by Edwin ★Anson & Company under contract to Westley ★Richards of Birmingham. It was designed by Edwin Anson and patented in 1907, but only about 1,000 guns were made; the last had been sold by 1915. The name referred to the Highest Possible score in target shooting competitions.

'Highland' [The]. Associated with shotgun ammunition sold in northern Scotland by ★Graham of Inverness.

Highlander, or Churchill Highlander. A brandname associated with the Italian ★Sabatti Mauser-pattern sporting rifles sold in the USA by ★Kassnar Imports.

Highway Patrolman. Also known as the Model 28, this swing-cylinder ★Smith & Wesson revolver dates from the period 1954–86. Basically it is a .357 ★Magnum with a short barrel and a matt-top slide.

Hijo Militar. An Italian semi-automatic pistol made by Industrias Armi ★Galesi.

Hill – 1. A. Hill & Son, 9 Market Place, Horncastle, Lincolnshire. The name of this English country gunmaking business, formed in 1902 to acquire the assets of G.H. ★Wilson, has been found on a variety of shotgun cartridges. **2.** Arthur Henry Hill, Handsworth, Staffordshire. This 'Gunmaker', living in a suburb of Birmingham, was the co-recipient with Moubray ★Farquhar of British Patents 28,587/1907, 17,211/1909 and 9118/1910. These protected the action of the gas-operated ★Farquhar-Hill rifle, and list Hill's address as 28 Leyton Road, Handsworth. Hill was also involved in the development of airguns, receiving (jointly with Walter F. Williams) British Patent 25,222/05 of 16 July 1908, for the Hill & Williams air rifle (below). This particular specification lists Hill's address as 6 Cornwall Road, Hadsworth. British Patent 19,519/07, also with Williams and also accepted on 16 July 1908, protected a gun sight; two much later attempts – 425,555 and 425,755 of 18 and 20 March 1935 for 'improved air rifles' – record Hill's domicile as 68 Holliday Road, Handsworth. **3.** H.S. Hill accepted 1873-pattern ★Springfield-Allin rifles on behalf of the US Army. Confined to the mid-1870s, these are customarily marked 'HSH'. *See also* US arms inspectors' marks. **4.** John Hill. A London-based gunmaker, Hill began his career in 1808 at the ★Royal Small Arms Factory, Enfield. He began trading on his own account in Tower Hill in 1817, and was operating from 76 Tooley Street, Borough, by 1832. The directories listed additional premises at Essex Street and New Road, Whitechapel, from 1836 onward. Trading ceased in 1856. **5.** R.M. Hill, a major in the US Army, was responsible for accepting military firearms and accessories in the mid-1870s. Normally they display 'RMH' in a cartouche. *See also* US military inspectors' marks. **6.** William James Hill. Possibly the father of Arthur Hill, this airgun maker – in addition to being Vice-Consul for the Republic of Uruguay (1877–84) – occupied premises in Birmingham in St Mary's Row (1861–84) and Whittall Street (1885–90). According to advertisements, Hill made '…Needle Rifles,

Air Guns & Canes, and Powder Walking Stick Guns…' **7. William John Hill.** A member of the London gun trade operating in 1872 from 5 Bond Court, Walbrook, London E.C. (as W.J. Hill), and 1 & 2 Fenchurch Street in 1878–79 (as William J. Hill), this gunmaker may have been the son of John Hill. **8. Hill & Williams.** A partnership of Arthur Henry Hill (above) and Walter F. Williams, usually listed as the manufacturers of the 1905-patent Hill & Williams air rifle. **9. Hill & Williams air rifle.** Patented in 1905, but not made in quantity until 1908 or later, this .22-calibre gun was cocked by pulling upward on the barrel. It was probably too complicated and possibly also too expensive to compete with the ★Jeffries-pattern fixed-barrel underlever cocking rifles being made by the Birmingham Small Arms Company Ltd. Production had ended by 1911, having amounted to only a few hundred.

Hiller – 1. A. Hiller, Zella-Mehlis in Thüringen, Germany. Listed in 1930 as a master gunsmith. Perhaps the same as (or son of) the next entry. **2.** Albert Hiller, Mehlis in Thüringen, Germany. Listed in the 1914 edition of the *Deutsches Reichs-Adressbuch* as a gunmaker. **3.** Albert & Emil Hiller, Zella-Mehlis in Thüringen. Listed in 1939 German trade directories as master gunsmiths.

Hillig. Herman Hillig, Suhl in Thüringen, Germany. Operated as a gun-stocker in 1939.

Hillsdon – 1. Russell Hillsdon, Barnham, Chichester, Horsham and Worthing, Sussex. The name of this English gunmaker has been found on shotgun cartridges loaded under the brandnames Combat, Goodwood, Revenge, Sussex Champion and Sussex Express. **2.** Hillsdon & Stones. Gunmakers, or possibly merchants, listed at 149 Oxford Street, London, in 1897.

Himalayan Series. Mauser-action sporting rifles made by the ★Rahn Gun Works, chambered for 5.6x57 or 6.5x68S ammunition. Stocks were wood or fibreglass, and the magazine floor plate bore a yak's-head motif.

Hinde. W.R. Hinde, Whitehaven, Cumberland. The name of this English gunmaker has been found on shotgun ammunition.

Hines. W.J. Hines. This government employee, acting on behalf of the US Army, accepted firearms and accessories in 1904–11, marking them 'WJH'. *See also* US arms inspectors' marks.

Hinged frame. A gun in which the barrel forms a separate unit attached to the frame by a hinge bolt, so that by releasing a catch, the barrel can be tipped to expose the chambers. The barrel usually tips downward. The system is widely associated with shotguns and shotgun-type double rifles.

Hinsdale. A ★Suicide Special revolver made by the ★Hopkins & Allen Arms Company of Norwich, Connecticut, USA, in the late nineteenth century.

Hinton. George Hinton [& Sons], 5 Fore Street, Taunton, Somerset. The name of this English country gunmaker, active from 1900 (or earlier) until 1947, will be found on shotgun cartridges sold under the brandnames Special I.X.L., Standard and Taunton.

'Hi-Os', or 'HIOS' [The]. A brandname found on British shotgun cartridges made by ★Eley Bros. for Higham of Oswestry prior to 1914.

Hirtenberger Patronenfabrik. One of the leading Austro-Hungarian/Austrian ammunition manufacturers, this concern came into being when Ludwig & Siegfried Mandl founded a munitions-making business in 1860. Shares were issued for the first time in 1895, forming

Hirtenberger Patronen-, Zündhütchen- & Metallwaren-fabrik AG, and trading continued for forty years. After the German annexation of Austria in 1938 (the Anschluss), the Jewish-owned business was nationalised by the NSDAP and renamed Gustloff-Were AG, Otto Eberhardt, Patronenfabrik Hirtenberg; it supported the German war effort until the end of the Second World War. Operations began again under new management in 1955. Hirtenberg ammunition is customarily distinguished by 'H' or 'HP' monogram headstamps.

Hitchcock. J.E. Hitchcock, a Federal Army inspector, accepted military firearms and accessories in 1862–63, during the early stages of the American Civil War. Marked 'JEH', they can easily be distinguished by date from guns accepted by Jay E. ★Hoffer. *See also* US arms inspectors' marks.

'HJL', 'HJM'. Found on US military firearms and accessories. *See* H.J. ★Labonte and H.J. ★Meldrum respectively.

'HK', 'H.K.' – 1. Often accompanied by a crown. Found on Danish small-arms ammunition, apparently including sporting-rifle and shotgun cartridges, loaded by Hærens Krudtværk. **2.** Flanking a central sword-and-anchor device. A *Schwertanker* trademark registered in Germany by Henrich ★Krieghoff on 24 December 1928. Granted as no. 401,488, it will be found on sporting guns, rifles and ★Parabellum pistols made for the Luftwaffe in the late 1930s. **3.** Found on US military firearms and accessories. *See* Henry ★Kane and Henry ★Kirk. **4.** A mark, often encircled and found almost in monogram form, associated with ★Heckler & Koch of Oberndorf, Germany.

H&K. *See* Heckler & Koch.

'HKH'. Found on US military firearms and accessories. *See* Henry K. ★Hoff.

'hla'. Allotted in 1941 to the Sebaldushof factory of Metallwarenfabrik Treuenbrietzen GmbH, for use on components for German military small-arms ammunition.

'hlb'. Used from 1941 by the Selterhof factory of Metallwarenfabrik Treuenbrietzen GmbH on small-arms ammunition made for the German armed forces during the Second World War.

'hlc'. Associated with the products of Zieh- und Stanzwerk GmbH of Schleusingen/Thüringen, which included German military small-arms ammunition components made in 1941–45.

'HLL', 'HM. Found on US military firearms and accessories. *See* H.L. ★Lathorpe, and Henry ★Metcalfe and H. ★Murdock respectively.

'HM&CO'. A superimposition-type monogram with 'H' and 'M' equally prominent. Correctly 'MH&CO' (q.v.); used by ★Maltby, Curtis & Company.

'HMB'. *See* Henry M. ★Brooks.

'H.M. Co.' Found on components for the British No. 4 ★Lee-Enfield rifle made during the Second World War by H. Morris & Company. This company was also allocated the area code 'N49', but often used its initials instead.

'HMW'. A monogram correctly read as 'WHM', found on sporting guns and shotgun ammunition. *See* William H. ★Mark.

'HN'. Found on US military firearms and accessories. *See* Henry ★Nettleton.

'HN', 'H-N', H&N. Marks associated with ★Haendler & Natermann, commonly found on airgun ammunition.

'HO' – 1. A superimposition-type monogram with the axis of the letters set diagonally, usually encircled. Found on the grips of semi-automatic pistols patented in Germany in 1916–18 by Heinrich *Ortgies of Erfurt. **2.** A superimposition-type monogram, sometimes encircled, with neither letter prominent. Correctly 'OH'; used in Spain by *Orbea Hermanos. **3.** Found on US military firearms and accessories. *See* Herbert *O'Leary.

Hoard. C.B. Hoard's Armoury, Watertown, New York, USA. Maker of .44-calibre six-shot cap-lock Army revolvers in accordance with a patent granted to Austin *Freeman. Hoard was given a Federal government contract for 5,000 revolvers in 1864, but defaulted; subsequently the contract passed to *Rogers & Spencer.

Hobby. A name associated with lightweight 4.5mm and 5.5mm diabolo-type airgun pellets made in Germany by *Dynamit Nobel. Also known as RWS Hobby.

Hobe. Adolf Hobe, Langensalza. Listed as a retailer of sporting guns and ammunition in Germany during the early 1940s.

Hobson – 1. Frederick Hobson & Company. This English gunmaking business was listed in the London directories for 1896, trading from 34 Basinghall Street. **2.** J. Hobson, Leamington Spa, Warwickshire. The name of this English country gunmaker has been found on shotgun cartridges sold under the brandnames Challenge, Dead Shot and those listed in the next entry. **3.** 'Hobson's Choice', 'Hobson's Full Stop' [The]. Names used by J. *Hobson of Leamington Spa on shotgun cartridges sold in south-west England.

Hocke. Alfred Hocke, Zella-Mehlis in Thüringen, Germany. Listed in 1939 as a master gunsmith.

Hodge. J.T. Hodge, New York City. This gunmaker contracted to make 50,000 *Springfield rifle-muskets on 26 December 1861, but succeeded in delivering just 10,500 before the contract was rescinded. The factory is believed to have been destroyed in the New York Draft Riots, and rumours that breech-loading sporting guns were made after the American Civil War have never been authenticated satisfactorily.

Hodges – 1. Edwin Charles Hodges. Listed in the London directories as a gun-action maker, Hodges began working from 8 Florence Street, Islington, in 1860 and was still working there in 1900. In the intervening period, however, additional premises had been listed at 95 Mount Street, London W. (1879–81); 69 Ebury Street, London S.W. (1882–84); and 34 South Audley Street in 1885 only. **2.** Lionel Hodges. A member of the London gun trade listed at 249 Upper Street in 1899, and 18 Charterhouse Buildings, E.C., from 1900 onward. **3.** Richard Edward Hodges. Grantee of English Patent no. 12,623 of 1849 to protect the application of indiarubber to projectiles, Hodges made a variety of guns and bows with rubber strings. He traded from 44 Southampton Row, London, from 1852 until 1871. **4.** Hodges, Perrin & Company. A gunmaker, or possibly simply a distributor, listed in 1861 in Belvedere Road, South London.

Hodgson – 1. A.A. Hodgson, Louth, Lincolnshire. The name of this English country gunmaker – possibly the son of Jesse Hodgson (below) – has been found on shotgun cartridges sold under the brandname Luda. **2.** Henry Hodgson, Ipswich and Bury St Edmunds, Suffolk, England. This gunsmith and ironmonger acquired *Scotcher & Son in 1913, and traded until the beginning of the Second World War. **3.** Jesse Hodgson, Louth, Lincolnshire, and Bridlington, Yorkshire. The name of this

gunmaker, possibly the father of A.A. Hodgson (above), has been found on shotgun cartridges made prior to 1914 by *Kynoch Ltd. **4.** J. Hodgson, Lancaster, Lancashire. This English gunmaker is known to have marked shotgun cartridges sold under the brandname Lancaster. **5.** R.T. Hodgson, Station Bridge, Harrogate, Yorkshire. This gunmaker handled shotgun cartridges made in Britain prior to 1914 by *Kynoch and marked with the brandname 'Harrogate'. **6.** W. Hodgson, later W. Hodgson & Son, then R.C. Hodgson, Ripon, Yorkshire. The name of this gunmaking business has been found on shotgun cartridges sold under the brandname Rapido.

Hoff. Henry K. Hoff, using an 'HKH' mark on behalf of the Federal Navy, accepted a variety of firearms in the closing stages of the American Civil War. They included *Sharps & Hankins carbines and *Whitney revolvers. *See also* US arms inspectors' marks.

Hoffer. Major Jay E. Hoffer of the US Army accepted a variety of .38 *Colt revolvers and .30-calibre *Gatling Guns in the early 1900s, marking them 'JEH'; date and pattern distinguish these from guns accepted during the American Civil War by J.E. *Hitchcock. *See also* US arms inspectors' marks.

Hoffmann Arms Company, Cleveland, Ohio, and Ardmore, Oklahoma, USA. Hoffmann made sporting rifles on the basis of *Mauser actions, often chambering proprietary .276 or .300 cartridges. A few were fitted with the Howe-Whelen aperture back sight, which replaced the bolt shroud.

Hog's-back stock or comb. *See* stock.

Holborn. A brandname found on a selection of sporting guns, spring-air guns and shotgun cartridges sold by A.W. *Gamage Ltd of London prior to 1914. Most of the airguns were made in Germany.

Holden. Cyrus B. Holden, Worcester, Massachusetts, USA. This gunmaker was granted two US Patents to protect breech-loading firearms: 34,859 of 1 April 1862 and 42,139 of 29 March 1864, both being assigned jointly to the inventor and S.H. Bowker. Guns made by *Armsby & Harrington to the 1862 patent had an open-sided frame containing a block and a cocking slide (with suitable finger-holes), which were retracted manually after the trigger guard had been depressed. The 1864-patent gun had a sliding block pulled down with a finger-ring. Cyrus Holden continued to make drop-barrel and falling-block rifles on his own account from c. 1873 until shortly before his death in December 1906.

'Holderness' [The]. A 12-bore shotgun cartridge sold in northern England prior to 1914 by Henry Esau *Akrill of Beverley.

Holek – 1. Emanuel Holek, born in 1899, was apprenticed to the Prague gunmaker J. *Novotný before joining *Zbrojovka Praga in 1920. Thereafter concentrating on sporting guns, he collaborated with his brother, Václav (below) on the design of the *Praga machine-gun. After the collapse of the Praga business, Emanuel Holek worked for *Česká Zbrojovka of Strakonice – where he developed the ČZ auto-loading rifle – before joining Zbrojovka Brno in 1927. Subsequently he developed the ZH 29 and ZH 39 auto-loading rifles, but left Brno during the German occupation of Czechoslovakia to make Original Holek Automat sporting guns on his own account. He returned to Brno in 1955, to work for the Zavodý 'Jan Šverma', and has been credited with development of the ZH 101 over/under combination gun and a .22 rimfire sports pistol. **2.** František Holek, the younger brother of Václav, was born in 1894 and graduated from an engineering college before working in Moscow immediately after the Russian Revolution. He joined ★Zbrojovka Praga in 1919, rising to become chief designer in the production department, then worked briefly for ★Janeček before becoming manager of the ★Českolovenská Zbrojovka research department. František Holek has been credited with the conversion of the ★Schwarzlose machine-gun to 7.9mm; with development of a flash-suppressor for machine-guns (Czechoslovakian Patent 2774-29); and the design of a locked-breech machine-gun with an auxiliary lubricating pump (3764-28). He was also responsible for three automatic pistols, an assortment of sporting guns, the ZB 51 machine-gun and a 20mm cannon before his death in 1951. **3.** Václav Holek: *see panel, below.*

'Holkham' [The]. Encountered on shotgun cartridges sold by Herbert ★Cawdron of Wells-next-the-Sea, Norfolk, England.

Holland – 1. Albert Holland, Albrechts bei Suhl in Thüringen. A maker of gun parts, active in Germany in 1941. **2.** Harris John Holland, born in 1804, traded first as a tobacconist, then – from 1848 – as a gunmaker.

Business was initially undertaken from 9 King Street, London, but a move to 98 New Bond Street occurred in 1858. Holland was the co-patentee with Walter Payton of a pinfire breech-loader (1861), and from 1876 was the senior partner in Holland & Holland. Harris Holland has been suggested as the maker of ★Shaw's Patent India Rubber Gun; *see also* Henry Holland (below). He died in 1894, when approaching ninety. **3.** Henry Holland & Company, Birmingham, Warwickshire. This English gunsmith traded from 3 Princip Street (1833–46), 21 Steelhouse Lane (1847–59), 43½ Woodstock Street (1860) and, finally, 25 Steelhouse Lane (1863). Holland made 'Air & Percussion Cane & Stick' guns, in addition to Shaw's Patent India Rubber Gun (c. 1852) and revolving pistols, before being succeeded by Henry & Thomas Holland (8 Weaman Street North, 1853). This may suggest the existence of two generations of Henry Holland. **4.** James Holland [& Sons]. James Holland started trading from Gowers Walk, London in 1825. A move to 44 Great Prescott Street occurred in 1829, and the business became James Holland & Sons in 1850. Operations continued from Great Prescott Street until 1855 or 1856, when a new shop opened in 44 Tenter Street South. Trading ceased in 1868. **5.** Holland & Holland. Still one of London's leading sporting gunmak-

VÁCLAV HOLEK

Born in 1886, the eldest of the Holek brothers, Václav was apprenticed to a gunsmith in the town of Písek before joining Mulacz of Vienna in 1905. There he helped to develop the Holek-Schwarzenhuber rifle, a lever-action adaptation of the 1895-type straight-pull ★Mannlicher, which was rejected by the Austro-Hungarian Army because it could be fired too quickly. Holek returned to work for Novotný of Prague in 1910, concentrating on production of ★Holland & Holland-type shotguns. Joining ★Zbrojovka Praga in 1919, where he developed the 6.35mm and 7.65mm ★Praga pistols, he was responsible with his brother Emanuel for the Praga M-24 light machine-gun. Then Václav Holek moved to ★Československá Zbrojovka of Brno, where he played an important role in developing the experimental ★ZGB into the ★Bren Gun. He was also largely responsible for the belt-feed ZB 53 (or vz. 37) machine-gun, which was adopted subsequently in Britain as the ★Besa. Holek remained active after the Second World War, continuing to work on anti-tank rifles and submachine-guns until his death in 1954.

The Czechoslovakian 7.9x57 ZB 26 light machine-gun, designed by Václav Holek, not only was very successful, but it also provided the basis for the British Bren Gun.

ers, this partnership was formed in 1876 by Harris John Holland and his nephew, Henry William Holland. The premises at 98 New Bond Street, London W1, were retained; however, the trading style changed to Holland & Holland Ltd in 1899, and a move to 13 Bruton Street took place in 1960. The Holland & Holland name has been found on shotgun cartridges sold as Badminton, Dominion, Nitro Paradox, Recoilite, Royal and Twelve-Two. It will also be found on *Mauser rifles chambering proprietary cartridges ranging from .240 Belted Rimless Nitro Express (introduced c. 1923) to the .400/375 Belted Nitro Express (1905). Holland & Holland Ltd modified 179,200 British .303 No. 3 *Enfield rifles to Weedon Repair Standards (WRS) in the summer of 1939, then, during the early stages of the Second World War, converted 4,500 *Lee-Enfield No. 1 Mk III and No. 1 Mk III* rifles from D.P. guns and spare parts. Two thousand *Ross rifles were refurbished in September 1942, and 26,450 Lee-Enfield No. 4 Mk 1 (T) sniper rifles were assembled in 1943–45. On occasion, Holland & Holland used the wartime code 'S 51'. *See also* Apex, British military manufacturers' marks and Super Thirty.

Hollands. Edward Hollands. A gunsmith trading in London from 180 High Holborn (1864) and 55 Rupert Street, Haymarket, S.W., in 1870–75.

Hollenbeck – 1. Frank A. Hollenbeck, Syracuse and Batavia, New York State, USA. A one-time employee of the *Syracuse Gun Company and the *Baker Gun & Forging Company, Hollenbeck was granted several US patents for breech-loading firearms. These included 258,923 of 6 June 1882, 481,327 of 23 August 1892, and 505,794 of 26 September 1893, the last two apparently being assigned to the Syracuse Arms Company (although Gardner links the earlier with the Baker Gun & Forging Company). US Patent 446,166 of 10 February 1891 was granted for a safety mechanism; 461,182 of 13 October 1891 for a 'Firearm lock'; and 537,203 of 9 April 1894, assigned to the 'Syracuse Arms Co.', protected a cocking and ejecting mechanism. Hollenbeck remains best known for a three-barrel gun or *Drilling protected by US Patent 752,492 ('break-down firearm') of 1 March 1904 and originally made by the *Three Barrel Gun Company. **2.** Hollenbeck Gun Company, 131 West Water Street, Syracuse, New York. This was formed about 1910 to succeed the *Royal Gun Company, and made the distinctive Three Barrel Guns patented by Frank *Hollenbeck until 1913.

Höller. A. & E. Höller [& Co.]. Best known as a Solingen based maker of edged weapons, Höller also made guns and maintained agents in London in the nineteenth century. The directories list offices at 16 Gresham Street (1858) and 39 Monkwell Street, E.C., in 1868–70.

Hollis – 1. Isaac Hollis & Sons, Birmingham, Warwickshire. The name of this English gunmaking business has been reported on shotgun cartridges made by *Eley Bros. prior to 1914. Premises were also maintained in London, initially at 44a Cannon Street in 1870, then at 83 Cheapside (1872–78), latterly as Isaac Hollis & Son Ltd. Subsequently moves were made to 6 Great Winchester Street, E.C., in 1879; to 26 Billiter Buildings, E.C., in 1892; and to 101 Leadenhall Street in 1900. **2.** William Hollis, High Street, Cheltenham, Gloucestershire. The marks of this English country gunmaker, active between

1829 and 1856, have been found on sporting guns and *pepperboxes dating from the mid-nineteenth century.

Hollister. H.E. Hollister, active during the American Civil War (1861–5), accepted firearms and equipment on behalf of the Federal Army, marking them 'HEH'. *See also* US arms inspectors' marks.

Holme, Holmes – 1. Thomas T. Holme, Jr, ranking as a lieutenant in the US Army, was responsible for accepting *Colt-made firearms marked 'TTH'. They date from the period 1941–22. **2.** T.W. Holmes, a captain in the US Army, accepted .45 M1911A1 Colt pistols in the late 1920s, marking them 'TWH'. These are often difficult to distinguish from similar guns accepted in 1941 by Thomas W. *Hafer. *See also* US arms inspectors' marks.

Holt. G.F. Holt, USA: *see* Joseph C. *Marshall.

Holub. Carl [Karel] Holub. Born in Strakonice and trained as a locksmith, Holub saw out his military service in the Austrian state firearms factory in Vienna. There he met Josef *Werndl. Employed by the Werndl factory in Steyr after release from his military duties, Holub spent some time in the USA during the Civil War before returning to Steyr to perfect the drum-breech rifle that now customarily bears the Werndl name. This gun was adopted by the Austro-Hungarian Army in 1867 as the *Werndl-Holubsches Hinterladungs-Gewehr* (Werndl-Holub breech-loading rifle) and subsequently was made in huge quantities in the Steyr factory.

Homer. – 1. Frederick L. Homer. A merchant and gunmakers' agent, retained by P.J. *Malherbe of Liège in the 1850s. At the time, Homer's office was at 23 Crutched Friars in the City of London. **2.** Henry Homer of 6 Benett's Road, Washwood Heath, Birmingham, was the co-designer with Christopher *Bonehill of the *Improved Britannia air rifle, protected by British Patents 15917/07 of 1907 and 13,567/08 of 1908. It has often been suggested that the name was 'Horner' instead of Homer, but Bailey & Nie, in *English Gunmakers*, list no fewer than six Homers operating in the Birmingham area prior to 1900. It is assumed that he was employed by Bonehill in the Belmont Firearms Works (q.v.).

Hood – 1. Freeman W. Hood, Worcester and Boston, Massachusetts, and Norwich, Connecticut. Designer of a variety of firearms and related components, including a pivoting ejector, or discharger, protected by US Patent 44,953 of 8 November 1864. This was incorporated in some *Pond revolvers. Hood also received US Patent 116,593 of 4 July 1871 for an 'Improved Revolving Firearm', and 160,192 of 23 February 1875 for the five-shot revolver made by the Hood Arms Company. Additional 'revolving firearms' patents granted in the USA on 6 April 1875 (161,615) and 14 March 1876 (174,731) were each assigned to the Hood Firearms Company. However, neither of two later revolver patents (US 235,240 of 1880 and 268,489 of 1882), nor two related 'Firearm Lock' patents (241,804 of 1881 and 316,622 of 1885) were assigned in this way. Hood was also the co-assignee of a patent granted in 1881 to Henry *McGee. **2.** Hood Firearms Company, Norwich, Connecticut, USA. This short-lived manufacturing business, active c. 1875–79, made revolvers in accordance with the patent granted in 1875 to Freeman Hood (*see* previous entry).

Hooke. Thomas J. Hooke [& Sons], 38 & 39 The Pavement, Coppergate, York. The name of this English gunmaking business has been reported on shotgun cartridges sold under the brandname Eclipse.

Hooker. Edward Hooker, then a lieutenant-commander in the US Navy, accepted components for single-shot *Remington rolling-block pistols in 1867–68. They bore 'EH' marks, which can be distinguished by age from those applied during the First World War by Ethan *Hancock. *See also* US arms inspectors' marks.

Hookham. George Hookham, Birmingham, Warwickshire. Listed at 8 & 9 New Bartholomew Street, apparently this engineer was employed by *Kynoch. He developed an unsuccessful automatic rifle in 1899, but is better known for the *Swift air rifle, protected by British Patent 11,577/06 of 1906.

Hooton & Jones, 60 Dale Street, Liverpool, Lancashire. The name of this English gunmaking partnership has been found on a variety of goods, including sporting rifles, Smith & Wesson revolvers and a selection of shotgun cartridges. Trading continued until 1914 or later.

Hopkins – 1. Charles Hopkins. Grantee of US Patent no. 35,419 of 27 May 1862, protecting a 'revolving firearm', part-assigned to Henry *Edgerton. **2.** J.J. Hopkins. Trading from 2–4 Lake Street, Leighton Buzzard, Bedfordshire, this British ironmonger/gun dealer marked shotgun cartridges sold under the brandname Golden Pheasant. **3.** Hopkins & Allen. Founded by S.S. Hopkins, C.W. Hopkins and C.H. Allen in 1868, this US gunmaking business made a tremendous range of cheap sheath-trigger guns from *Acme to *Universal. H&A also offered a dropping-block shotgun in 12- and 16-bore into the 1880s. **4.** Hopkins & Allen Arms Company [The]. This was an 1898-vintage reorganisation of Hopkins & Allen. The assets of *Forehand & Wadsworth were acquired in 1902. In 1916, however, Hopkins & Allen was itself purchased by the *Marlin-Rockwell Corporation. Maker of about 8,000 Mle 1889 *Mauser rifles for the Belgian government during the First World War. **5.** Hopkins & Allen Noiseless. A brandname associated with a silencer or 'sound moderator' produced in the USA in the early twentieth century.

Hoppe – 1. Hermann Hoppe, Suhl in Thüringen, Germany. Listed as a gunsmith in the *Deutsches Reichs-Adressbuch* for 1939. **2.** Hermann Hoppe & Co. GmbH, Suhl in Thüringen. Listed in the 1920 edition of the *Deutsches Reichs-Adressbuch* as a gunmaker. Possibly the same as the previous entry.

Hopper. Filser Hopper (sometimes listed as *Horrert) was the co-grantee with Clarence Simpson and William Bull – employees of *Springfield Armory – of US Patent no. 2,108,817 of 1938, protecting the auxiliary carrier for rimfire cartridges that subsequently permitted the development of an effective machine-gun trainer for the US Army. Three patterns were used in quantity: the Trainer, Machine-gun, M3 for the .30 M1917 and M1917A1 water-cooled Brownings; the M4 for the air-cooled .30 M1919 series; and the M5 for the .30 M2 ground gun. The M2 aircraft-gun trainer, the T9, fired special sintered-iron disintegrating bullets. Prospective .50 Browning gunners had to be satisfied with the M9 trainer, which fired plastic pellets pneumatically at an aircraft model towed on a wire. *See also* MacGlashan Machine Gun Company.

Horne – 1. George A. Horne, Syracuse, New York State, USA. This shotgun designer received several US Patents for ejector systems, including 568,760 of 6 October 1896, 572,755 of 8 December 1896, and 731,904 of 23 June 1903. The last two of these, at least according to Robert E. Gardner, were assigned to the *Syracuse Gun Company. US Patent 690,955 of 14 January 1902 protected a 'recoil-operated firearm'; 754,564 of 15 March 1904 was granted for an improved safety mechanism; and 782,248 of 14 February 1905 was obtained for a 'breech-loading firearm'. US Patent 921,220 of May 1908 was obtained jointly with Ansley *Fox. **2.** William L. Horne, Meriden, Connecticut, USA. Possibly the brother of George A. Horne (above), this gunsmith was granted US Patents 357,960 of 15 February 1887 to protect an 'Electric Firearm', and 406,667 of 9 July 1889 for a 'Magazine Firearm'. The 1889 patent was obtained jointly with Joseph M. Reams of Meriden.

Hornet. – 1. A 5.5mm diabolo airgun pellet, also known as the MAG Hornet, made in the 1980s in Britain by L.J. Cammell & Company Ltd. It was sold exclusively by Manchester Air Guns (MAG). **2.** Associated with diabolo-type airgun pellets sold in the USA by *Stoeger or possibly *Hy-Score. Apparently they were made in Germany by *Rheinisch-Westfälische Sprengstoff prior to 1939, then by *Dynamit Nobel from the 1950s onward. **3.** A *Suicide Special revolver made by the *Prescott Pistol Company of Hatfield, Connecticut, in the late nineteenth century.

Hornhauer. Theodor Hornhauer, Schmiedegasse, Dresden, Saxony. This inventor of a spring-and-piston air pistol was granted British Patent 7932/95 of 1895.

Horrert. Filser D. Horrert was responsible for accepting .45 *Colt M1911A1 pistols for the US Army. Apparently confined to 1940, they bore 'FDH' marks. *See also* US arms inspectors' marks and Filser *Hopper.

'Horrido'. Found in the headstamps of shotgun cartridges advertised in 1911 by A.L. *Frank; maker unknown.

'Horsham Special' [The]. On shotgun ammunition sold in southern England by *Scott & Sargeant of Horsham. Origin unknown, although the cases and caps are believed to be European.

Horsley. Thomas Horsley [& Son], York. This English provincial gunmaker began trading at 48 Coney Street in 1833, where he was granted British Patents 374/62 of 12 February 1862, and 2410/63 of 1 October 1863 to protect breech-loading guns with drop-down barrels. He was still active in 1878, when a registered design was successfully sought for an alarm gun, but was succeeded shortly afterward by a son of the same name. Trading continued into the twentieth century from Micklegate, York, where Belgian-made shotgun ammunition was sold under the name Horsley's Smokeless Rabbit Cartridge.

Horton – 1. W. Horton, 199 Buchanan Street, Glasgow, Lanarkshire. The name of this Scottish gunmaker has been found on shotgun ammunition sold under such names as The Horton Cartridge and Horton Weatherproof. **2.** William Horton, Wyle Cop, Shrewsbury, Shropshire. The marks of this English country gunmaker have been reported on self-cocking *pepperboxes dating from the middle of the nineteenth century. Horton is known to have been active from 1827 until at least 1842, but the existence of the multi-barrel pistols must extend this range by at least ten years.

Hoskins. John Hoskins. A member of the London gun

trade listed in 1850–52 at 31 Frith Street, Soho, and in 1853 at 10 Grange Road, Bermondsey.

Hosmer – 1. Frank L. Hosmer. The 'FLH' mark of this government inspector – originally simply 'FH' – will be found on a variety of *Colt handguns accepted for service with the US Army, 1898–1923. They included a few .45 Single Action Army Model and .38 M1892 revolvers, in addition to .45 M1911 semi-automatic pistols. Frank Hosmer is believed to have been the son of George Hosmer (*see* following entry). **2.** George Hosmer accepted a variety of military firearms, including *Spencer carbines, *Remington rolling-blocks and *Ward-Burton rifles dating from c. 1862–72. Hosmer's marks can be confused with the similar 'GH' of George *Haines, although Haines was only active in 1861, prior to the American Civil War. **3.** W.E. Hosmer, a government employee working on behalf of the US Army, accepted a variety of .30-calibre *Springfield rifles and .45 M1911 *Colt pistols in 1905–17. The guns all have 'WEH' identifiers, although care must be taken to distinguish the Colts from M1911A1 guns subsequently accepted by William E. *House. *See also* US arms inspectors' marks.

Hotchkiss – 1. Benjamin Berkely Hotchkiss. Born on 1 October 1826 in Watertown, Connecticut, home of a US government arsenal, Hotchkiss was involved with guns and ammunition at an early age. In 1855, in collusion with his brother, Andrew, he demonstrated a cannon projectile to the US Navy without success. However, interest from Japan and Mexico supported the project until the Civil War began, whereupon an ordnance factory was established in New York and vast quantities of war *matériel* were supplied to the Federal government prior to 1865. Hotchkiss was a prolific inventor. Although most of his US patents were concerned with large-calibre ammunition – e.g. 'Canister Shot' (34,058 of 1862) and 'Time Fuze for Shells' (42,660 of 1864) – he was also granted US Patents 93,822 of 17 August 1869 and 99,898 of 15 February 1870 to protect single-shot bolt-action rifles derived from the French *Chassepot. Hotchkiss always maintained close links with France, and it is suspected that his family, like Maxim's, may have descended from Huguenot stock. Next came US Patent 122,465 of 2 January 1872, for a variation on the *Remington-style Rolling Block with a spring-assisted opening motion, then 169,641 of 9 November 1875 and 184,825 of 14 November 1876 for improved bolt-action rifles with a tube magazine in the butt. Substantial quantities of these weapons were made for the US Army and US Navy in 1878–85 by the *Winchester Repeating Arms Company; many others were sold commercially. However, although the Winchester-made rifles encountered limited success in North America, Hotchkiss became far better known for his mechanically-operated machine-guns. A few were made for rifle-calibre ammunition, but most guns were chambered either for 1in or 37mm ammunition. The revolver cannon remained popular into the twentieth century, particularly to give warships an effective means of close-range defence, but eventually they were replaced by large-calibre Maxims and similar automatic weapons. In 1882, Hotchkiss established a manufacturing business – Hotchkiss & Company – with its headquarters at 113 Chambers Street, New York City, and branches in Austria-Hungary, Britain, France, Germany, Russia and Italy. However, the inventor died suddenly in Paris on 14

February 1885 and the work he had begun was left for others to complete. **2.** Hotchkiss bolt-action rifle: *see* panel, facing page. **3.** Hotchkiss machine-guns: *see* panel, pp. 252/53. **4.** Hotchkiss Ordnance Company, New York and Washington D.C. *See* Benjamin Berkely Hotchkiss.

Hough – 1. Edward Cass Hough (1872–1959), the son of Lewis C. Hough, was a director of the *Daisy Manufacturing Company. He also designed a method of locking the barrel of a *BB Gun in its housing, using the front sight as a latch. *See* US Patent 903,092 of 3 November 1908. **2.** Lewis Cass Hough, Plymouth, Michigan, USA. One of the founders of the *Plymouth Iron Windmill Company and president of that company immediately prior to 1888, Lewis Hough (c. 1847–1902) subsequently became the first president of the Daisy Manufacturing Company. **3.** Hough Model. A name given to a lever-action single-shot BB Gun made by Daisy to the design of Edward Hough, produced from 1913 until c, 1920. A similar gun, known as the No. 11, lasted until 1937. **4.** Hough Model Repeater. Also known as the Model H, this lever-action 500-shot BB Gun was introduced in 1916 by the Daisy Manufacturing Company; comparatively unsuccessful, it lasted for little more than a year. Production was meagre.

Houllier. This Parisian gunmaker is credited with perfecting the *pinfire cartridge in 1846–47.

Hourat et Vie, Pau, France. The manufacturers of the 6.35mm *H-V pocket automatic pistol.

House – 1. William E. House, a captain in the US Army, accepted firearms (including M1911A1 pistols) purchased from *Colt's Patent Fire Arms Manufacturing Company in 1938. Marked 'WEH', the handguns should not be confused with M1911 examples accepted prior to the First World War by W.E. *Hosmer. *See also* US arms inspectors' marks. **2.** House of Imports. A trading style used by *Hy-Score of Brooklyn.

Howa Machinery Company, or Howa Machinery Limited, Nagoya. Best known as a contractor to the Japanese defence forces – making the 7.62mm Type 64 and 5.56mm Type 89 assault rifles – Howa produced the *Weatherby Vanguard actions from the early 1970s as well as the *ArmaLite AR-18 rifle in 1972–73.

Howard – 1. A.L. Howard & Company, New Haven, Connecticut, USA. An ammunition maker operating in the 1880s, Howard made rifle and shotgun cartridges identified by headstamps reading 'A.L.H.' **2.** Charles Howard of New York was granted US Patents 50,125 and 50.358 of 26 September and 10 October 1865 respectively to protect breech-loading firearms that essentially are improvements on Sebre Howard's design. He also received US Patent no. 54,728 of 15 May 1866 to protect a bayonet attachment for firearms. **3.** C.W. Howard, Hammonton, New Jersey. Patentee of a breech-loading rifle, US no. 39,232 of 14 July 1863. Probably Charles Howard (*see* previous entry). **4.** R. Howard. A patent for a revolver-sword was granted in 1882 to this Southampton based British designer. **5.** Sebre Howard, Elyria, Ohio. Patentee of a breech-loading firearm protected by US Patent 36,779 of 28 October 1862. Essentially the gun was the prototype of the *Thunderbolt, with a breech-block that slid backward in a tubular receiver as the trigger guard/underlever moved downward. **6.** Howard Arms. A *Suicide Special revolver made by the *Crescent Arms Company of Norwich,

HOTCHKISS RIFLES

Several patterns of this early butt-magazine design were made by the *Winchester Repeating Arms Company as a result of the exhibition of prototypes at the Centennial Exposition in 1876. The .45-70 Gun No. 19 was victorious in the US Army magazine rifle trials of 1878, and subsequently several hundred essentially similar M1878 Winchester-made actions stocked by Springfield Armory were acquired for trials. The US Navy purchased about 2,500 1879-pattern guns from Winchester, with repositioned safety catches and cut-off levers.

The US Army trials resulted in the *Remington-Lee beating the Winchester-Hotchkiss, with the *Chaffee-Reece in third place. However, as the margins of superiority were small, it was decided to acquire sufficient of each design for field trials. Late delivery of rifles delayed the trials until 1885, when the Lee still beat the improved 1883-pattern .45-70-405 Winchester-Hotchkiss (recognisable by a two-piece stock).

However, most respondents preferred the single-shot *Springfield-Allin rifle to any of the magazine patterns, and nothing more was done. Winchester attempted to cut its losses by advertising the Hotchkiss as a sporting rifle in .40-65 or .45-70, with options such as octagonal barrels, chequered pistol-grip butts, *schnabel-tip fore-ends, set triggers and engraved decoration, but the bolt-action rifles were unpopular on the Frontier. When production came to an end in 1899, little more than 60,000 third-pattern guns had been made.

The perfected Hotchkiss rifle, with a two-piece stock, was made in surprisingly large numbers by the Winchester Repeating Arms Company. This is an 1883-type .45-70 US Army trials gun.

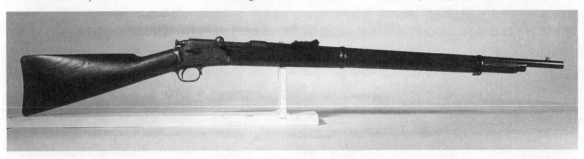

Connecticut, USA, in the late nineteenth century. **7.** Howard Arms Company. A brandname associated with shotguns made by the *Crescent Arms Company of Norwich, Connecticut, USA. **8.** Howard Brothers [Ltd], 240 St Ann's Road, Tottenham, London. The name of this gunmaking partnership has been found on shotgun cartridges. **9.** Howard Brothers & Company, Whitneyville and New Haven, Connecticut, USA. Distributors of hammerless *Thunderbolt rifles and shotguns designed by Sebre and Charles Howard. The guns were made by the *Whitney Arms Company.

Howarth – 1. F. Wise Howarth was a British patent agent, occupying chambers in 46 Lincoln's Inn Fields, London, when he acted for Oscar *Will in 1896. **2.** J.H. Howarth accepted firearms and accessories on behalf of the US Army in the period 1899–1910, using a 'JHH' identifier. The guns can be distinguished by date and pattern from those marked by Joseph H. *Hubbard more than thirty years previously. *See also* US arms inspectors' marks.

Howe. Charles G. Howe, a US Army lieutenant, was responsible for accepting the .45 *Colt revolvers and semi-automatic pistols marked 'CGH'. They all seem to date from 1917. *See also* US arms inspectors' marks.

Howell – 1. A. Howell & Son. A supplier of 12-bore shotguns to the British military authorities, 1942. **2.** John A. Howell, a commander in the US Navy, active in the late 1880s, accepted the 1882-pattern signal pistols marked 'JAH'. *See also* US arms inspectors' marks.

Howland. George P. Howland, a government inspector, accepted US Army *Colt .45 M1911A1 pistols in 1939.

They bore 'GPH' in a cartouche. *See also* US arms inspectors' marks.

Howth Rifle. A nickname applied to 1,500 11mm 1871-pattern *Mauser rifles, purchased shortly before the First World War to arm the Irish Citizen Army. Acquired in Hamburg with nearly 50,000 cartridges, probably from A.L. *Frank, they were transported in the yacht *Asgard* (owned by the novelist Erskine Childers) and landed in the harbour of Howth on 26 July 1914. They were conveyed the few miles to Dublin, quite openly, and later were used against the British in the Easter Rising of 1916. The guns are occasionally, but misleadingly, listed as Asgard Rifles.

'HP' – 1. An abbreviation for High-Power or Hi-Power, associated with the *Browning-designed Pistolet à Grande Puissance (GP), made by Fabrique Nationale d'Armes de Guerre and successors from the 1930s to date. **2.** An abbreviation for *Heeres-Pistole* (Army Pistol), found as 'Mod. HP' on the slides of the commercial variants of the *Walther P. 38. **3.** As 'HP' or 'H-P': *headstamps – 'Hi-Power' – associated with the *Federal Cartridge Company of Cincinnati.

'HR'. Found on US military firearms and accessories. See Harold *Richards.

'H&R', 'H. & R.' – 1. A *Suicide Special revolver made by the *Harrington & Richardson Arms Company of Worcester, Massachusetts, USA, in the late nineteenth century. **2.** A superimposition-type monogram with both letters equally dominant. Used by Harrington & Richardson on a variety of handguns, and also on the butt plates of shotguns. **3.** Accompanied by a pierced target. A

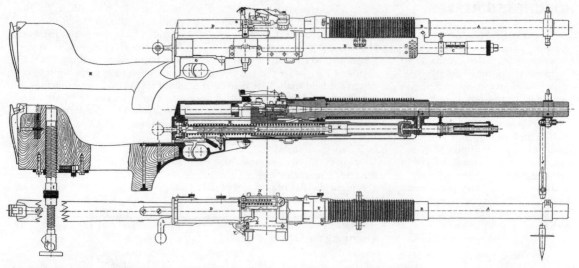

HOTCHKISS AND HOTCHKISS-ODKOLEK MACHINE-GUNS

The first Hotchkiss machine-gun – a five-barrel manually-operated gun similar externally to the Gatling – was invented by Benjamin B. Hotchkiss in the 1870s and was adopted immediately in France to replace the *Mitrailleuse. Made in the USA by *Pratt & Whitney, the subject of a reissue on 11 September 1877 of US Patent no. 7881 and improved by patents ranging from 211,737 of 28 January 1879 to 253,924 of 21 February 1882, the Hotchkiss Battery Gun was produced for many years in a variety of calibres.

No sooner had the rifle-calibre mechanical Hotchkiss been eclipsed by the *Maxim than the Paris office of Hotchkiss & Company was approached by an Austrian inventor, Adolf von *Odkolek. Hotchkiss' management immediately saw the potential of the Odkolek gun, and acquired rights. By the mid-1890s, the Odkolek had become the

Hotchkiss, and its inventor's name was soon forgotten.

Hotchkiss machine-guns of this period fed from distinctive metal strips. They had been tested by the French Army in 1897, upgraded to become the Mle. 00, but then 'improved' by government technicians to become the Mle. 05 (*Puteaux) and Mle. 07 (*Saint-Étienne). These were made in the French government arsenals, whereupon purchase from Hotchkiss virtually ceased.

The Hotchkiss company had also made small quantities of the Fusil Mitrailleur Mle. 09. Designed by Laurence Benét (son of General Stephen Benét, a former US Army Chief of Ordnance) and Henri Mercié, this light machine-gun featured an interrupted-screw locking collar. The feed-strips were inverted in an attempt to keep rainwater from the ammunition, but were more

difficult to load than the standard Hotchkiss 'cartridges-upward' type. The Benét-Mercié had been the best of the guns submitted to trials in the USA in 1908, and, being preferred to the *Madsen, was adopted as the 'Machine Gun Rifle, Caliber .30, Model of 1909', although eventually it became better known as the *Daylight Gun. Subsequently about 1,070 guns were made in *Springfield Armory and by *Colt's Patent Fire Arms Manufacturing Company for the US Army (670) and US Navy (400). The M1909 had a combined shoulder-stock/pistol grip, an ineffective butt monopod and a bipod. A spindly tripod mount was also available.

Hotchkiss guns were purchased by the British from 1914 onward, and a production line was installed in the *Royal Small Arms Factory at Enfield, beginning production in 1916. The 'Gun, Machine,

---

trademark registered by Harrington & Richardson of Worcester, Massachusetts, in May 1889.

'H.R.B.', 'HRB' – 1. A trademark associated with the *Henry Rifled Barrel, Engineering & Small Arms Company Ltd of London. **2.** Found on US military firearms and accessories. *See* Howard R. *Booth.

H&R Bulldog. Made by *Harrington & Richardson of Worcester, Massachusetts, USA, this was a double-action .32 (six-shot) or .38 (five-shot) revolver with a 2½-inch barrel. It dates from c. 1892–1910.

'hre'. Found on German military cartridge clips and chargers made during the Second World War by C.W. Motz & Co. of Brandenburg an der Havel.

'hrn'. This code was allocated in 1941 to Presswerk

GmbH of Metgethen in Ostpreussen, and used on small-arms ammunition components made for the German armed forces during the Second World War.

'HS', 'H.S.' – 1. A superimposition-type monogram with neither letter dominant, often encircled. Used by C.G. *Haenel of Suhl, Germany, notably on the grips of 6.35mm pocket pistols made in accordance with patents granted to Hugo *Schmeisser. It has been interpreted as 'Hugo Schmeisser', but is more likely to have been 'Haenel-Schmeisser'. The slides of later guns were marked 'Schmeisser's Patent', with 'SCHMEISSER' moulded into the grips. This mark was used from 1925 until c. 1928, when it was largely superseded, first by 'Haenel', then by 'Haenel' within an arrow. **2.** Sometimes

Hotchkiss, .303-inch, Mark I', officially adopted in June 1916, was supplemented after June 1917 by the Mark I★, made for infantry (Mk I★ No. 1) or tank use (Mk I★ No. 2). Renamed 'Gun, Machine, Hotchkiss, No. 2 Mk I★' in 1926, the weapon was eventually declared obsolete in June 1946. Hotchkiss Guns were exported in surprisingly large quantities prior to the First World War, most notably to Japan during the Russo-Japanese War of 1904–05. There their legacy remained, with the advent of the 6.5mm Taisho 3rd Year Type and 7.7mm Type 92 heavy machine-guns, until the end of the Second World War.

In the early 1920s, Hotchkiss promoted a series of light machine-guns with strip- or box-magazine feed. Customarily known as Mle. 22, these were tested in many countries without ever encountering real success, except in Greece, where small quantities of 6.5mm guns were acquired in 1926.

The drawings (above left) show the 1909-type Hotchkiss light machine-gun, or Fusil Mitrailleur. This was adopted by the British during the First World War, although the bipod was replaced by a ridiculously small-looking tripod (above). The strip-feed

Hotchkiss machine-gun remained surprisingly popular, particularly in the Far East. The 7.7mm Japanese Type 92 (1932) is the ultimate expression of the genre (below). The sockets on the tripod legs accept the poles that allow the gun to be manhandled into position.

as a superimposition-type monogram. Associated with the handguns – cartridge and blank-firing alike – made by Herbert ★Schmidt of Ostheim an der Rhön, Germany. **3.** Found on US military firearms and accessories. *See* Henry ★Saunders, Horace ★Scott, Harrison ★Shaler, Harris ★Smith, Howard ★Stockton and H. ★Syrett. **4.** Italic or slanted lettering, often in a circle. A trademark found on pistols made in the USA by the ★High Standard Manufacturing Company.

'HSa', HSA', 'H.S.A.' – **1.** As 'HSA': associated with cartridges made in Regina, Saskatchewan, Canada, by Hammerstrom's Small Arms Company Ltd. **2.** As 'HSa': applied to an experimental ★Mauser pistol. *See* 'HSc'.

'HSb', 'HSB', 'H.S.B. & Co.' – **1.** As 'HSB', 'HSB

& Co.': encountered in the headstamps of cartridges sold by ★Hibbard, Spencer, Bartlett & Company of Chicago. **2.** As 'HSb': applied to an experimental ★Mauser pistol. *See* 'HSc'.

'HSc'. A mark associated with a double-action 7.65mm or 9mm Short semi-automatic pistol made by ★Mauser-Werke AG of Oberndorf am Neckar, 1937–45, then for a few months under French supervision in 1945–46. It was distinguished by a streamlined web running forward from the trigger guard to the muzzle, and had a detachable box magazine in the butt. The designation represented *Hahn-Selbstspanner-Pistole, Modell 'c'* (Hammer self-cocking pistol, 'c' or third model); the HSa and HSb were experimental forerunners of the perfected design. Production of a modified HSc was begun in Italy by Renato ★Gamba in the early 1980s.

'HSH'. Found on US military firearms and accessories. *See* H.S. ★Hill.

Hsing-Ho. This Taiwanese arms factory has been responsible for ArmaLite-type rifles.

'HSL'. Found on US military firearms and accessories. *See* Homer S. ★Lathe.

HsP, HSP – 1. As 'HsP'. A designation associated with a recoil-operated pistol made by ★Mauser-Werke GmbH of Oberndorf/Neckar. Designed by Walter Ludwig, it was developed to compete with the Walther, SIG-Sauer and Heckler & Koch guns in the police trials of the mid-1970s, but was perfected too late to participate, and the project was abandoned in 1983 after only a handful of guns had been made. **2.** As 'HSP'. Applied to the handguns designed by Edgar Budischowsky and made by ★Korriphila-Präzisionsmechanik GmbH of Ulm. The unsuccessful HSP-70, which had a staggered-row magazine holding twenty 7.65 or 9mm Parabellum rounds, appeared in the mid-1970s; recoil operated, it was locked by a roller system. The HSP-701 of 1983 was similar, relying on a transverse locking roller in the frame behind the well, and had a nine-round box magazine. Offered in such chamberings as 7.65mm Parabellum, .38 Super, 9mm Police, 9mm Short, 9mm Steyr, 10mm Auto and .45 ACP, the double-action HSP-701 could be obtained in short-barrelled Compact form, or as a Competition pattern with a single-action trigger mechanism and adjustable sights.

'HT'. Found on US military firearms and accessories. *See* Henry ★Tracy.

'htg'. Used in 1941–45 by the Duderstadt factory of ★Polte Werke. The products included components for German military small-arms ammunition.

Hubbard – 1. C.C. Hubbard accepted US Army firearms and accessories c. 1906, marking them with a cartouche containing 'CCH'. **2.** George H. Hubbard was responsible for the acceptance of Federal Army firearms and accessories during the later stages of the American Civil War, marking them 'GHH'. **3.** Joseph H. Hubbard accepted firearms and accessories on behalf of the Federal Army in 1862–63, using a 'JHH' identifier. The guns can be distinguished by date and pattern from those marked by J.H. ★Howarth more than thirty years later. *See also* US arms inspectors' marks for the preceding three entries. **4.** Michael J. Hubbard. An English gunsmith, or possibly distributor, listed in 1874 at 174 Fenchurch Street, London.

Hubertus – 1. Often cursive. Attributed to Moll Sportwaffenfabrik, Lauenburg, prior to 1914. *See* Hubertus Metalwarenfabrik (below). **2.** Often cursive. A trademark used by Imman. ★Meffert of Suhl from about 1920 until the end of the Second World War. **3.** A push-barrel 4.5mm-calibre air pistol made by Meffert from c. 1927 until the mid-1930s. **4.** A single-barrel ★Krieghoff rifle: *see* panel, facing page. **5.** Hubertus Magnum. This steel-frame Krieghoff rifle chambers cartridges ranging from .270 Weatherby Magnum to .300 Winchester Magnum and may have a BreaK-O recoil reducer. **6.** Hubertus Metalwarenfabrik, also listed as the Hubertus Metal Works, Molln, Germany. Reportedly the maker of the Hubertus smoothbore push-in-barrel air pistol, but more probably confused with marks applied by Imman. ★Meffert of Suhl. However, there are two small villages named Molln in Germany –

one 25km south of Lübeck, another 18km west of Neubrandenburg – and information may yet be forthcoming from local archives. **7.** Hubertus S. Mechanically identical with the standard Krieghoff Hubertus rifle, this single-barrel break-open rifle is built on a steel ★box-lock action with side-plate extensions.

Hubing. Gustav Hubing, Zella-Mehlis in Thüringen, Germany. Listed in 1920 as a gunmaker and wholesaler. *See also* Mehliser Waffen- & Armaturenfabrik.

Hübner. Edgar Hübner, Suhl in Thüringen, Germany. Listed in the directories for 1930–39 as a *Waffenfabrik u. Spezialwerkstatt.*

Hudgins. Wescom Hudgins, a captain in the Army of the Confederate States of America, accepted ★Rigdon & Ansley revolvers in the early stages of the American Civil War. *See also* US arms inspectors' marks.

Hudson – 1. A 6.35mm Browning-inspired pocket pistol, probably made in Eibar, Guipuzcoa, Spain: hammer fired. **2.** Hudson Sporting Goods Company, New York. A retailer of sporting guns and ammunition active prior to the First World War.

Huger – 1. Benjamin Huger, then a major in the US Army, accepted firearms and accessories marked 'BH'. Dating from the period 1854–58, these pre-date by several years the guns accepted during the American Civil War by Benjamin ★Hannis. *See also* US arms inspectors' marks. **2.** James Huger, ranking as a captain in the US Army, designed the perfected, or 'fishtail', breech lever for the ★Hall carbines in the early 1840s.

Hughes – 1. John Hughes, Birmingham, Warwickshire. The name of this gun rifler and pistol maker, listed in Princip and Henry Streets in 1868–73, has been linked with a British Patent granted jointly in 1879 with W. ★McEntee to protect a drop-barrel action for sporting guns. **2.** Robert Hughes. This gunmaking business (also known as the Universal Fire Arms Works) traded in Moland Street, Birmingham, from 1855 onward. Hughes employed an agent named Edward Manser at 16 Laurence Pountney Lane, London E.C., in 1869. **3.** Hughes & Young, 7 Stone Buildings, Lincoln's Inn Fields, London, and also in New York. A British patent agency that was retained in the period 1895–1914 by, among others, John M. ★Browning.

Hulbert – 1. William Hulbert, Brooklyn, New York, USA. Designer of improvements in revolver design protected by US Patent 187,975 of March 1877, Hulbert was a partner in ★Merwin, Hulbert & Company of New York. **2.** Hulbert Brothers & Company. Successor to Merwin, Hulbert & Company; the business failed in 1896.

Hull – 1. F.F. Hull, a government inspector, accepted firearms and accessories for the US Army in 1905–06; they displayed 'FFH' in a cartouche. *See also* US arms inspectors' marks. **2.** Hull Cartridge Company, 58 De Grey Street, Hull, Yorkshire. This British gun- and ammunition-making business has loaded shotgun cartridges from a variety of components, including British and Italian cases. They have been sold under a wide range of brand- and retailers' names, including Standard and Three Crowns.

'Humber' [The]. A mark associated with shotgun cartridges loaded by R. ★Robinson of Hull from ★Eley-Kynoch components.

Humbert, 32 cours Fauriel, Saint-Étienne, France. Listed in 1951 as a gunmaker.

HUBERTUS

A single-barrel break-action rifle offered since 1996 by H. *Krieghoff GmbH of Ulm/Donau in chamberings ranging from .222 Remington to 8x75RS. The Hubertus is effectively a single-barrel variant of the *Classic Standard, built on the same *box lock and sharing both the Universal Trigger System and the Combi cocking mechanism.

Normally the guns are fitted with straight-comb butts with squared Bavarian-style cheek pieces and have slender fore-ends with elegant schnabel tips. A fixed back sight is set into the front of the quarter rib. Lightweight dural frames are popular, although the most powerful chamberings rely on forged steel.

The quality of Krieghoff Hubertus guns and their accessories, including the case shown here, is excellent.

Humphreys. George Humphreys. Co-designer with Rimmon *Fay of the perfected hammerless shotguns made by the *Remington Arms Company. Humphreys also received US Patent 732,187 of 30 June 1903, protecting an ejector mechanism.

Hunt – 1. C.H. Hunt accepted military stores, including firearms, during the American Civil War. His 'CHH' mark has been reported on breech-loading carbines (*Spencers?) dating from 1864. 2. H.W. Hunt, active c. 1899–1902, apparently accepted .38 *Colt revolvers and components on behalf of the US Army. *See also* US arms inspectors' marks. 3. Thomas Hunt. A gunmaker with premises in London at 32 & 33 Leman Street (1875–79), 66 Leman Street (1880–82) and Tenter Street East (1875–82). 4. Walter Hunt, New York City. *See* panel, p. 256.

Hunter, Hunter's... – 1. A name associated with a revolver made in Belgium prior to 1914 by A. *Bertrand. 2. A 4.5mm-calibre spring-and-piston air rifle, also known as the Model 61, made in China c. 1970–85 by the State Industry Factory in Shanghai. 3. A semi-automatic sporting rifle made in Poland: *see* Radom Hunter. 4. A Mauser-action sporting rifle made by Paul *Jaeger, which had a Bell & Carlson Kevlar-reinforced fibreglass stock with a wrinkle finish. It was chambered for cartridges ranging from .243 Winchester to .30-06. A laminated wood stock was an optional alternative. 5. A seventy-five-shot *BB Gun, also known as the No. 88, made in 1961–62 by the *Daisy Manufacturing Company. The butt bears a circle-and-crosshairs motif. 6. *See* Hy Hunter and American Weapons Corporation. 7. Hunter Arms Company, Syracuse, New York State (1888–90), and Fulton, New York State (1890 onward). 8. Hunter & Maddill, later Hunter & Son, Belfast, Northern Ireland. The name of this Irish gunmaking business, active from the 1880s until 1939 or later, has been found on shotgun cartridges sold under brandnames such as Favourite, Invictus and Long Shot. 9. Hunter One-Trigger. *See* Allan *Lard. 10. Hunter & Vaughan, Broad Street, Bristol, Gloucestershire. The name of this English provincial gunmaker has been found on shotgun cartridges dating prior to 1914. 11. Hunter's Model. A .44- or .45-70-calibre *Marlin-made *Ballard rifle, introduced in 1876 and subsequently known as the No. 1 Hunter's Model. There was also a No. 1½ Hunter's Model (.40-63 Ballard or .45-70) dating from 1879, which was a No. 1 with an extra-heavy frame and a double set trigger. 12. Hunter's Rifle. Made by E. *Remington & Sons from 1875 until c. 1882, this was a minor variant of the No. 1, with a round barrel generally chambering the .45-70 cartridge. *See also* Remington rifles, rolling-block action. 13. Hunter's Rifle. Usually built on the *Hepburn-Walker action, the Remington No. 3 Hunter's Rifle (1885–c. 1907) handled rim- and centerfire cartridges ranging from .25-20 to .50-70. Sights were generally plain *Rocky Mountain patterns. 14. Hunter's Rifle or Sharps' Hunter Rifle, 1874 pattern. Believed to have been a plain-finish sporting gun with a round barrel, this seems to have had a single trigger and a straight-wrist butt. It dates from c. 1875–77. 15. Hunter's Rifle, Sharps-Borchardt type. *See* New Model Hammerless Hunters' Rifle.

'Huntic' [The]. Found on shotgun ammunition handled in Britain by *Cogswell & Harrison of London.

Hunting, *Concorde Hunting or *Daytona Hunting. Known in Italy as Concorde Caccia or Daytona Caccia, these 12-bore over/under shotguns are the products of *Società Armi Bresciane of Gardone Val Trompia. They may be fitted with pistol- or straight-hand ('English') grips, *schnabel-tip fore-ends and single-trigger systems. The barrels are customarily 760 or 810mm long. The Hunting SL (Caccia SL in Italy) is identical, with the exception of side locks instead of a box-lock action.

WALTER HUNT

Born in Martinsburg on 29 July 1796, Hunt is remembered as the designer of the Volitional Repeater and the Volitional Ball, or rocket-ball cartridge. The projectile was patented on 10 August 1848, and the lever-action rifle was protected by US Patent 6663 of 21 August 1849. However, the application for the rifle had been made in September 1847, and it is evident that a period of experimentation must have preceded even this.

Hunt was a skilled, but very unlucky, mechanic who was almost always forced to sell his designs for a pittance. He assigned his Volition Repeater patent to a financier, George Arrowsmith, who sold it to the railroad magnate Courtlandt Palmer without Hunt seeing anything other than a paltry flat fee. Among Hunt's many inventions were a fountain pen, the safety pin, and the eye-pointed needle and double-lock stitch for sewing machines – developed by 1832, but never patented and subsequently appropriated by Elias Howe. Hunt died in straitened circumstances in New York on 8 June 1859.

The Jennings rifle of 1849, the refined successor to the original Hunt design, retained the curious self-contained Volition Ball ammunition.

Huntress. A name said to have been used on airguns and target equipment made by *Mayer & Grammelspacher. Authentication is lacking. *See also* 'Diana'.

Huntsman – 1. A brandname applied to a .22-calibre pistol-knife made by the *American Novelty Company in the 1920s. *See also* Defender. **2.** More than 100,000 of these *Colt-made pistols were produced in 1955–77, superseding the *Challenger. Built on a *Woodsman frame, the Huntsman lacked a hold-open, but had fixed sights and a magazine release on the heel of the butt. Its parallel-sided barrels could be 4.5in or 6.5in long. A few hundred specially-cased Huntsman Model S Master pistols were made in 1983, with slide stops and Elliason back sights; most guns had parallel-sided barrels, although the last few had the tapered design associated with the *Sportsman.

Hur, Saint-Étienne, France. Listed in 1933 as a gunmaker.

Hurricane – 1. A spring-and-piston air pistol introduced in 1977 by *Webley & Scott Ltd to replace the *Premier. Cocked by lifting the barrel from the rear, the Hurricane has always been available in .177 and .22 calibres. **2.** A barrel-cocking spring-and-piston airgun of *Gem type, made to the patent of Asa *Pettengill, first by *Haviland & Gunn, then by Henry *Quackenbush. **3.** Or Hurricane Air Gun. A spring-and-piston design made by Quackenbush in the 1880s, cocked by a pull-ring mechanism. Apparently also sold as the Excelsior.

Hurst. Charles Edward Hurst, West Street, Horsham, Sussex. Listed in 1861–75 as a gunmaker, Hurst was granted British Registered Design No. 4928 of 1860 for a muzzle protector. Sporting guns have also been reported with his marks.

'Hush Puppy'. A nickname given to the silenced Smith & Wesson pistol used by US Navy Special Forces.

Husqvarna Våpenfabriks, Huskvarna, Sweden. This long-established gunmaking business built a few 6.5x55 and 9.3x57 *Mauser-type sporting rifles on the basis of the 1896-pattern Swedish military action prior to 1940. The first 1898-type Mauser sporting rifles were produced in the late 1930s, but were followed in the late 1940s by sporters embodying actions purchased from *Fabrique Nationale. These were supplemented by the improved Model 1950, then by a Model 1951 with a modified safety catch. In 1955, however, the FN-Mauser action was replaced by the HVA pattern, with a stream-lined bolt shroud and a radial safety on the receiver behind the bolt handle. These guns have been offered under names such as *Crown Grade and *Imperial Custom Grade. Husqvarna-type rifles were sold in the USA by *Smith & Wesson. Eventually the company's operations were amalgamated with those of the *Carl Gustaf factory and marketed under the *FFV-Viking Sport Arms AB banner. *See* John Walter's *Rifles of the World* (second edition, Krause Publications, 1998), which gives a concise listing of the individual gun patterns.

'Hussa'. Found in the headstamps of German shotgun cartridges made by *Cramer & Buchholz, prior to 1914.

Hussey – 1. H.J. Hussey. A member of the gun trade listed at 81 New Bond Street, London W., in 1900. Probably the owner of the company in the following entry. **2.** H.J. Hussey Ltd, 81 New Bond Street, St James's, and 88 Jermyn Street, London S.W. The name of this gunmaker – trading from 1899 or 1900 – has been found on shotgun cartridges sold under the brand-name Times.

Huster & Hubing. *See* Mehliser Waffen- & Armaturenfabrik.

Hutchins. John Hutchins. First listed at 14 Bloomsbury

Street, London W.C., in 1861, this English gunmaker had moved to 44 Frith Street, Soho, by 1864. Trading ceased shortly afterward.

Hutchinson – **1.** Hutchinson & Company, Kendal, Westmorland. This English country gunmaking business is known to have marked sporting guns and ammunition, including pre-1914 shotgun cartridges made by *Nobel. **2.** Hutchinson, Roe & Company, Stone Street, Cranbrook, Kent. The mark of this English gunmaking business has been found on shotgun cartridges sold under the brandname Knockout.

Huzzey. Richard Huzzey. A member of the London gun trade listed in Upper East Smithfield in 1881–94, then at 17 Devonshire Square until 1897.

'H.V.' – **1.** Found on the barrels of British .303 *Lee-Enfield rifles sighted for <u>H</u>igh <u>V</u>elocity Mk VII ball ammunition. **2.** A trademark employed by *Hourat et Vie of Pau on 6.35mm automatic pistols, possibly purchased in Spain.

'HVA', often crowned. A trademark associated with the bolt-action sporting rifles made in Sweden from the mid-1950s onward by *Husqvarna Våpenfabriks Ab.

'HW', 'HWH', 'HWK'. Found on US military firearms and accessories. *See* Henry *Walker, H.W. *Hunt and Herbert W. *Kerr.

'HWM' – **1.** A trademark, occasionally in the form of a monogram, associated since 1950 with Hermann *Weihrauch of Mellrichstadt. *See also* 'HWZ'. **2.** A monogram correctly read as 'WHM', found on English sporting guns and shotgun ammunition. *See* William H. *Mark.

'HWW'. Found on US military firearms and accessories. *See* Henry W. *Wilcox.

'HWZ'. A mark found on the products of Hermann *Weihrauch of Zella-Mehlis prior to 1945. *See also* 'HWM'.

'Hy-Bird' [The]. Found on shotgun cartridges sold in Britain by *Francis & Dean of Stamford.

Hydran Products Ltd, Gresham Road, Staines, Middlesex. Makers of 'Mountings, Twin, Vickers .303 Machine-Gun, Motley Stork' during the Second World War. Code, 'S 54'. *See also* British military manufacturers' marks.

Hy Hunter. Henry 'Hy' Hunter was the original proprietor of the *American Weapons Corporation of Burbank, but his name was often used on products and is frequently regarded as a brandname.

Hyde – **1.** Andrew Hyde, Hatfield, Massachusetts, USA. Designer of the swinging-cylinder mechanism of the Model 1879 Iver *Johnson revolver, protected by US Patents 221,171 of 4 November 1879, and 273,282 of 6 March 1883. **2.** George Hyde, a talented American gun designer, is known for his work with submachine-guns and light automatic rifles, including a gas-operated gun submitted by Bendix to the US Army trials of 1941, which led to the adoption of the M1 Carbine. He also designed the abortive US .45 M2 submachine-gun, which proved to be too difficult to mass-produce to satisfy ever-increasing production demands. **3.** 'Hyde Park' [The]. Found on 12-bore shotgun cartridges sold in eastern England by Edward *Aldridge of Ipswich. **4.** Hyde & Shatuck, Hatfield, Massachusetts, USA. Makers of The *American single-barrel shotgun from 1876 until succeeded in 1880 by C.S. *Shatuck.

Hyderabad [Small Arms Factory]. This was established in India during the Second World War to make *Bren Guns, allowing *Ishapore to concentrate on the construction and refurbishment of *Lee-Enfield rifles and *Vickers Guns.

Hydra-Matic Division of General Motors, Ypsilanti, Michigan, USA. A maker of 5.56mm M16A1 rifles for the US armed forces from 1969 onward. They are clearly marked with the manufacturer's name on the magazine housing. *See* ArmaLite.

'Hymax' [The]. A British shotgun cartridge made by *Eley-Kynoch Ltd.

Hy-Score Arms Company, Brooklyn, New York City. Trading from premises in Tillery Street, this business appears to have been founded by Stephen E. *Laszlo about 1932. It made the spring-air pistol designed by Laszlo in association with Andrew *Lawrence. This was marketed as the Hy-Score models 800–804, two of which were repeaters. The business also distributed large numbers of air rifles and pistols of European origin – principally Mayer & Gammelspacher Dianas and Hämmerli types – using a wide variety of 800-series designations. It has also been known as the 'House of Imports', or even by Laszlo's name alone. Hy-Score was liquidated after Laszlo's death in 1981, rights to the pistol being acquired by Richard Marriott-Smith and assigned to the Phoenix Arms Company. Production began again in Britain in the late 1980s, but had ended within a few years.

I

'I'. Found on rifle and other military small-arms components made in 1940–45 by Elite-Diamantwerke of Siegmar-Schönau bei Chemnitz, Germany.

'IA'. A superimposition-type monogram, with neither letter dominant, customarily found on a shield. Encountered on the frames of break-open *Smith & Wesson-style revolvers made in Spain prior to 1914: significance unknown. On occasion, the mark has been interpreted as 'TA', and thus associated with *Trocaola, Aranzabal y Cia.

'IAS'. A superimposition-type monogram without dominant letters. Correctly 'SIA' (q.v.); used by *Security Industries of America, Inc.

Ibex. A *Mauser-pattern sporting rifle made in Austria in the 1960s by Karl *Dschulnigg of Salzburg. It was distinguished by a modernistic stock with an exaggerated pistol-grip cap and a beaver-tail fore-end.

I-Brand. See Industry Brand.

'ICI', 'I.C.I.', often in the form of an encircled trademark. Associated with ammunition made in Britain by the Metals Division of *Imperial Chemical Industries at the former *Kynoch factory in Birmingham. Headstamps including 'I.C.I.A.N.Z.' signified production by Imperial Chemical Industries of Australia and New Zealand in the 1936–56 era.

Ideal, Idéal – 1. Usually found as 'The Ideal' on shotgun cartridges sold in England by *Chaplin of Winchester, and in Ireland by *Kavanagh & Son of Dublin. 2. A brandname used on a small 6.35mm pistol made in the 1920s by *Dušek of Opočno. 3. As 'Idéal'. A double-barrelled 12- or 16-bore shotgun made by Manufacture Française d'Armes et Cycles of Saint-Étienne. Standard guns were made with a triple-lock action and two triggers, but a special quadruple-lock variant was made to handle high-power ammunition; an additional vertical cylinder rose to intercept the doll's head. An underlever, in the form of a spur at the rear of the separate trigger guard, was pressed upward to open the action, which included sliding strikers actuated by the coil spring that controlled the barrels. Automatic ejectors were optional, and a press-button safety catch was let into the right side of the stock above the front trigger. Guns were customarily engraved in 'English' or 'French' styles, essentially similar with the exception that only the former had borders to the scrolls and ribands. Some guns will be found with quickly-detachable fore-ends. See also Express-Idéal and Supra-Idéal. 4. Found on shotguns and spring-air guns of German origin, probably made in Suhl or the surrounding districts. Guns of this type were being advertised by A.L. *Frank in 1911, and Albrecht *Kind in the mid-1930s. 5. Reported on German-made air rifles dating from the 1930s. They are thought to have been made by *Mayer & Grammelspacher for an unidentified distributor (perhaps Albrecht Kind, above). 6. Idéal Canardier. A heavy 10-bore duck gun derived from the standard Idéal (q.v.). It had an 800mm barrel. 7. Ideal Extra. A name associated with the Modelo Ideal Extra, a barrel-cocking 4.5 or 5.5mm spring-and-piston air rifle made by Armas *Juaristi of Eibar, Spain, since the early 1970s. 8. Ideal Holster Company, Los Angeles, California. Assignees of the patents granted in the USA to Ross M.G. Phillips of Los Angeles, for the well-known stock-holster made for the Luger and some of the best-known US revolvers. See US Patent 762,862 of 14 June 1904, application for which had been made on 9 September 1901. 9. Idéal Junior. A lightweight 20- or 24-bore version of the MFAC Idéal shotgun, intended 'for women and young men' according to 1920s catalogues.

'I.G.', in fraktur. Found on the receivers of German military *Mauser-action rifles, usually as 'I.G. Mod. 71'. Often mistakenly read as 'J.G.', owing to the design of the initial letter; this simply signifies Infanterie-Gewehr (Infantry Rifle).

'I.G.A.' This cursive trademark should be read as 'J.G.A.' Used by J.G. *Anschütz of Zella-Mehlis.

'IGI', 'IgI'. See Italguns.

'IICO'. A floriated superimposition-type monogram: see 'JJCO.'

'IJCO'. A monogram, partly concentric and partly superimposed, with 'I', 'J' and 'C' equally dominant. Found on revolvers made in the late nineteenth century by Iver *Johnson & Company; the mark is often combined with the grip-screw, with the 'O' locating the screw head (and thus difficult to find).

'IK'. An encircled cursive linear monogram, with what appears to be 'I' slightly dominant. Probably interpreted more accurately as 'KJ' (q.v.); found on revolvers made in Spain prior to 1914.

Imbel, IMBEL. An abbreviated form of Industrias de Material Bélico de Brasil (Ordnance Industry of Brazil), associated with small-arms such as Mauser rifles and variations of the FN FAL. In addition, a few 9x19 MD-2 submachine-guns have been made. These incorporate a substantial number of FAL components, but are *blowbacks.

'I.M.I.' – 1. Found in the headstamps of cartridges made by *Imperial Metal Industries (Australia) Ltd of Melbourne. 2. On Israeli-made guns and ammunition. See Israeli Military Industries.

Imman-Meffert. See Meffert.

'Imp' [The]. Found on shotgun cartridges made in England by the *Midland Gun Company of Birmingham.

'Impax' [The]. A shotgun cartridge made in Britain by *Eley-Kynoch Ltd.

Imperator. Associated with a revolver sold in Belgium prior to c. 1914 by A. *Rongé.

Imperial – 1. Usually found as 'The Imperial'. British shotgun cartridges marked by George *Bate of Birmingham, *Blanton of Ringwood and E.J. *Churchill of London. 2. Applied to two different small 6.35mm Browning-type pistols made in Spain by Hijos de José

*Aldazabal of Eibar (some examples being marked 'Fabrique d'Armes de Précision'), or for Tómas de *Urizar of Barcelona. The Aldazabal guns usually have six-round magazines, whereas the Urizar patterns hold seven. **3.** *Suicide Special revolvers made in the USA in the 1880s by the *Lee Arms Company of Wilkes-Barre, Pennsylvania, and the *Hopkins & Allen Arms Company of Norwich, Connecticut. **4.** Imperial Arms Company. Operated in the USA during the 1950s by Edward Hoffschmidt. **5.** 'Imperial Champion' [The]. A name found on shotgun cartridges sold in southern England by *Lloyd & Sons of Lewes. **6.** Imperial Chemical Industries (ICI) – see Eley Bros. Ltd, Eley-Kynoch Ltd, Kynoch Ltd and Nobel Explosives Ltd. **7.** 'Imperial Crown' [The], accompanied by a large crown. This was associated with shotgun cartridges loaded from *Eley-Kynoch and possibly other components by T. *Page-Wood of Bristol. The headstamp usually bears Page-Wood's name alone. **8.** Imperial Custom Grade. These bolt-action sporting rifles were made in Sweden by *Husqvarna, c. 1968–71. They were based on the standard *Crown Grade patterns, but offered selected woodwork, fittings and additional decoration. An Imperial Custom Lightweight Rifle was also available. **9.** Imperial Metal Industries (Australia) Ltd, Melbourne, Victoria. A maker of ammunition bearing the headstamp 'I.M.I.' from 1970 onward.

Improved... – **1.** Improved Borchardt. A solitary pistol of this type, an intermediate stage between the German *Borchardt and the *Borchardt-Luger, was substituted for the Borchardt in the Swiss Army trials of October 1897. It was tried against a Bergmann and a Mannlicher, but subsequently was replaced by the Borchardt-Luger. Apparently the Improved Borchardt had the recoil spring in the grip – which was raked backward to improve handling characteristics – but retained the Borchardt-type toggle-breaking roller. **2.** Improved Britannia. A British .22-calibre spring-and-piston air rifle, cocked by lifting the barrel, made in Birmingham in 1908–10 in accordance with a patent granted to Christopher *Bonehill and Henry *Homer. Perhaps only 1,000 were manufactured in the *Belmont Firearms Works. **3.** Improved Bulldog. A name associated with diabolo-type airgun pellets made in Britain prior to 1939, presumably by *Lane Bros. **4.** Improved Buzz Barton Special. Also known as the No. 195 and No. 195 Model 36, this was a variant of the *Daisy No. 155 lever-action *BB Gun with a tube-type back sight, a hooded front sight and a distinctively branded stock. *See also* Buzz Barton. The Improved Buzz Barton Super Special was identical with the exception of a multi-coloured lariat-and-rider label on the butt. Production of both types was confined to 1936–42. **5.** Improved Challenger. Designed by George *Sage and made by *Markham in 1887–88, this underlever-cocking *BB Gun had a brass barrel liner inserted into a distinctive wooden body. **6.** Improved Creedmoor Rifle, also known as the No. 3 Improved Creedmoor. This was made by E. *Remington & Sons and the *Remington Arms Company from c. 1881 until 1891, chambering cartridges ranging from .38-40 to .45-90. Most guns had set triggers and vernier/wind-gauge sights; cheek-piece butts and Schützen-style butt plates were optional. **7.** Improved Daisy. A modification of the toplever-cocking *Hamilton Model, made by the *Plymouth Iron Windmill Company in 1890–1900. **8.** Improved Defender or Defender 89.

This single-action solid-frame revolver was made by Iver *Johnson from 1889 onward. **9.** Improved Lee. This term was applied by the British Army authorities, initially to the .43-calibre *Remington-made 1882-pattern rifle, with the bolt handle locking down behind a solid receiver bridge, then to the .45 Improved Lee Magazine Rifle made at the *Royal Small Arms Factory, Enfield, in 1886. It had a one-piece *Arbuthnot-style stock and a short hand guard running forward from the breech to the back sight.

'Imps' [The], or Improved Imps. A brandname associated with shotgun cartridges sold in southern England by *Lloyd & Sons of Lewes.

INDEP. An acronym of Industria Nacional de Defesa do Exército Português of Lisbon, the state-owned Portuguese manufacturer of licensed *Heckler & Koch-type rifles and 9x19 *Lusa submachine-guns.

India Rubber Air Gun. *See* John *Shaw.

Indian, Indian... – **1.** Found on shotgun ammunition made by the *Robin Hood Cartridge Company of Swanton, Vermont, prior to 1914. Unlike the other Robin Hood brands, the Indian was loaded with black powder. **2.** A .177-calibre barrel-cocking spring-and-piston air rifle made in the USA in 1965-71 by the *Noble Manufacturing Company. **3.** Indian Arms Corporation. US based makers of an automatic pistol based on the Walther Polizei-Pistole, dating from the early 1980s.

Indispensable. A name associated with a small double-action 5.5mm *Velo-Dog revolver with a crane-mounted cylinder and a folding trigger, made in Belgium by, or perhaps for, A. *Riga prior to 1914.

Industria, Industrias... – **1.** Industria Nacional de Defesa do Exército Português, Lisbon: *see* INDEP. **2.** Industria Peruana, Fábrica de Armas de Los Andes. Manufacturer of licensed *Ingram Model 6 submachine-guns for the Peruvian armed forces and gendarmerie, c. 1955–58. **3.** Industrias de Material Bélico do Brasil. Makers of FN *FAL-type rifles. *See* IMBEL. **4.** Industrias de Guerra de Cataluña. *See* Tarrassa. **5.** Industrias El Gamo SL: *see* El Gamo. **6.** Industrias Irus SL, Carretera de Ondarroa, Maquina, Vizcaya, Spain. A maker of spring-air guns – mostly break-barrel types – for sporting and target use. Details are lacking.

Industry Brand, or I-brand. These products emanate from the Shanghai factory of the Chinese Ministry of Light Industrial Products, based in Beijing. The marks will be found on products ranging from domestic kettles to spring-and-piston airguns. *See also* Arrow, Hunter, Lion and Super Hunter.

Inertia firing pin. *See* striker.

Infallible. This quirky .32 ACP semi-automatic pistol, marketed by the *Warner Arms Company and its successors, was based on patents granted in 1914–15 to Andrew *Fyrberg. The distinctive features included a barrel that could be tipped for cleaning and a fragile safety lever on the left side of the frame, behind the trigger. Production began in Norwich, Connecticut in 1915; in 1917, the manufacturer merged with N.R. Davis & Sons of Assonet to form the *Davis-Warner Arms Corporation. Work on the Infallible ceased in 1919, after no more than 1,500 had been made.

Inferno. A brandname associated with Karl von *Harys of Suhl.

Inglis. John Inglis Company, Toronto, Ontario. Inglis

was given an order for 5,000 *Bren Guns in October 1938, the first Canadian-made Mk I being test-fired in March 1940. Subsequently the company manufactured about 120,000 .303 Bren Guns for Canadian and British forces in 1938–43, and about 43,000 7.9mm-calibre guns for China in 1943–45. A handful of experimental .30-06 guns were also made. In addition, Inglis was responsible for 9mm Browning *High Power pistols, which were supplied in quantity to the British, Chinese and Canadian Armies. Work began in 1942, but no guns were delivered until February 1944; production totalled about 151,200 when assembly ceased in Canada in September 1945. Guns of this type were particularly popular with British Commandos and Special Forces, largely owing to the thirteen-round magazines. The Inglis-Browning was *sealed for limited British service in September 1944 as the 'Pistol, Browning, FN, 9mm, HP, No. 2 Mk 1*', but was declared obsolete in April 1945.

Ingram – 1. Found as 'The Ingram' on shotgun cartridges made by *Eley-Kynoch for Charles Ingram of Glasgow. **2.** Charles Ingram, 10 Waterloo Street, Glasgow, Lanarkshire. The marks of this gunmaker have been reported on sporting guns and ammunition, including shotgun cartridges. **3.** Gordon B. Ingram and the Ingram submachine-gun: *see* panel, below.

Inland Manufacturing Division [of the General Motors Corporation], Dayton, Ohio, USA. A maker of 2.35–2.65 million *M1, M1A1, M2 and M3 Carbines (estimates vary) in 1942–45.

Innova. A pneumatic rifle designed by Kensuke Chiba in 1975–77 and made by the *Sharp Rifle Company of Tokyo in 4.5 and 5.5mm calibres. It had a special semi-automatic loading system and a patented rod-type air valve. Charging was undertaken by swinging the fore-end handle.

'Instanter' [The]. Found on shotgun cartridges sold in Britain by *Grant & Lang of London.

INGRAM SUBMACHINE-GUN

The original guns, the conventional Model 6 (.45 ACP) and Model 7 (.38 Super) were made by the Police Ordnance Corporation of Los Angeles in 1950–52. Then Ingram left POC, producing the Model 8 (c. 1955) and the Model 9, which had a telescoping wire butt. Attractive enough to sell in small numbers in Cuba, Peru and Thailand, these weapons were mostly conventional blowbacks with a two-stage trigger mechanism doubling as a fire selector. Subsequently some guns were made under licence by *Industria Peruana.

Then Gordon Ingram developed the Model 10, persuading the short-lived Erquiaga Arms Company of Industry, California, to undertake production; the rapid collapse of Erquiaga led to a transfer of interest in 1966 to the Sionics Corporation

of Atlanta, Georgia. Sionics moved to Powder Springs in 1969, but was purchased in 1970 by the Military Armament Corporation almost as soon as series production of the Model 10 (9mm Parabellum .45 ACP) and Model 11 (.380 ACP/9mm Short) submachine-guns had begun. However, a dispute between inventor and manufacturer stopped production, and the liquidation of MAC in 1975 did nothing to help. Rights were transferred to SWD, Inc., of Atlanta, and the guns were marketed for a few years as the Cobray. SWD collapsed in turn, and – although attempts were still made to exploit the basic design – very little seems to have been done since the mid-1980s.

The perfected Ingrams were ultra-compact designs with an

'overhung' bolt and a detachable magazine, inspired by Czechoslovakian prototypes and the *Uzi, that ran up through the pistol grip. Normally barrels were threaded to receive sound suppressors. The Ingram was an efficient design; however, its chequered production history failed to exploit the potential that unquestionably lay in the basic design. The Ingram remains a design that, by attracting huge amounts of publicity as a result of film and television exposure, has a far higher public profile than its limited manufacturing success deserves.

This photograph shows the difference in size of the silencer-equipped .45 Ingram Model 10 (back) with the .38-calibre, but otherwise similar, Model 11 (front).

Instituto Nacional de Armas (INI), Spain. *See* CETME.

Interarmco, Interarms, Alexandria, Virginia, USA. The International Armament Corporation of Alexandria, Virginia, USA, was founded in the early 1950s by Samuel Cummings and acted as agent for the original ArmaLite AR-10 rifle in southern Africa and Central and South America, c. 1957–60. The company's marks will be found on a variety of sporting guns, including *Mauser-Parabellum and *Walther pistols, some of the latter being made in an Interarms factory in the USA. *Erma-made sub-calibre barrel inserts and *Mauser rifles produced by Zavodi Crvena *Zastava will also be encountered. A trademark consisting of an enrayed sun (sometimes described as a compass rose) is normally accompanied by 'INTERARMS'.

Intermount. A telescope-sight mount associated with *Sheridan Products of Racine, Wisconsin. Apparently the name dates from the 1970s.

International... – 1. A *Suicide Special revolver made in the USA by the *Hood Firearms Company of Norwich, Connecticut, in the late nineteenth century. **2.** International Business Machines Corporation, IBM, Poughkeepsie, New York, USA. A maker of 346,500 *M1 Carbines in 1943–44. **3.** International Free Rifle. A .22 rimfire target rifle made by the *Remington Arms Company on the basis of the 700-type action. It replaced the International Match Free Rifle (q.v.) in 1964. However, only 107 had been produced when work ceased ten years later. **4.** International (Giffard) Gun & Ordnance Company Ltd. This business was founded in London in 1892 to exploit the inventions of Paul *Giffard in Britain, but was liquidated voluntarily in 1894, re-emerging as the Giffard Gun & Ordnance Company. It had been listed in 1892 and 1893 at Copthall House, Copthall Avenue, London. **5.** International Harvester Corporation, USA. *See* Garand. **6.** International Match Free Rifle. Target rifles made in 1961–64 by the *Remington Arms Company. Chambered for .22LR rimfire ammunition, they had a thumbhole stock with hooked or rubber butt plates, a palm rest and a hand stop/swivel anchor. *See also* International Free Rifle. **7.** International Patent Office. A trading style, without official standing, used by the British patent agent William *Lake from c. 1865, and perpetuated by his successor *Haseltine, Lake & Company until 1910 or later. **8.** International Technology & Machines AG (ITM), Solothurn, Switzerland. This manufacturer of semi-automatic pistols, often based on Czechoslovakian or Hungarian prototypes, was formed in 1984 and became part of *Sphinx Industries in 1989.

Inter-State Arms Company. A brandname associated with shotguns made in the USA prior to the First World War by the *Crescent Arms Company of Norwich, Connecticut.

Intratec Inc., Miami, Florida, USA. Maker of the Intratec 22 and Intratec 25 automatic pistols, as well as a series of submachine-guns.

'Invicta' [The], beneath a prancing horse. Found on shotgun cartridges sold in southern England by W.R. *Leeson of Ashford, and *Sanders of Maidstone ('The Invicta Special'), but most probably manufactured by *Eley Bros. The White Horse of Kent was taken from the county arms.

'Invictus' [The]. A mark associated with shotgun ammunition handled in Ireland by *Hunter & Maddill of Belfast.

Invincible – 1. This mark, often as 'The Invincible', has been found on shotgun ammunition sold in Britain by *Bond & Sons of Thetford; Frank *Clarke of Thetford; *Helson of Exeter; *Knight of Nottingham; *Paragon Guns of Belfast; *Scotcher & Son of Bury St Edmunds; and C.H. *Smith & Sons of Birmingham. With the exception of the Helston examples, which were made in France, most of the cartridges have borne headstamps identifying *Nobel Industries or *Eley-Kynoch. Sometimes the name is linked with that of the first British battlecruiser, HMS *Invincible* (cf. Dreadnought), which would date most of them earlier than the First World War. **2.** A *Suicide Special revolver made by *Johnson, Bye & Company and/or *Iver Johnson of Worcester and Fitchburg, Massachusetts, in the late nineteenth century.

'I.P.' – 1. Applied to any British military store, including firearms, which were built in accordance with an India Pattern. These often differed from superficially similar designs adopted for Home Service. **2.** Beneath crossed pennants under a crown. A mark applied by an inspector working in the *Long Branch small-arms factory in Ontario, Canada. *See also* British military inspectors' marks.

'IR'. A mark found on US military firearms and accessories. *See* I. *Randell.

Irish Metal Industries Ltd, Dublin and Galway, Ireland (Eire). Marks applied by this ammunition manufacturer have been reported on shotgun cartridges sold under such brandnames as Alphamax, Maximum and Primax.

'Ironmonger' [The]. A mark associated with English shotgun cartridges distributed by *Scott & Sargeant of Horsham. They are believed to have been loaded from European-made components.

Iroquois. A seven-shot .22 rimfire revolver, made in Ilion, New York State, by E. *Remington & Sons c. 1875–86. It was similar to the *New Line No. 4, but weighed only 7½oz.

Irving. William Irving, a gunmaker plying his trade in New York City, was responsible for a range of fixed-barrel .22 and .32 rimfire revolvers made in 1862–63. A button in the tang released the recoil shield on the right side of the frame, which swung up and back to permit loading. Irving also made convertible .30 rimfire cartridge/.31 cap-lock solid-framed sheath-trigger revolvers to a patent granted to James *Reid in April 1863.

Irwin-Pedersen Arms Company, Grand Rapids, Michigan, USA. Recruited in 1942 to make *M1 Carbines; the contract and the manufacturing facilities were transferred to the *Saginaw Steering Gear Division of General Motors after only a few guns had been made.

'IS', above a number. A mark applied by an inspector working in the *Ishapore (Ishapur) small-arms factory in India after c. 1949. Apparently the abbreviation represents 'India Stores'. *See also* British military inspectors' marks.

'ISA'. A superimposition-type monogram without dominant letters. Correctly 'SIA' (q.v.); used by *Security Industries of America, Inc.

Ishapore, Ishapur [Small Arms Factory]. This arms manufactory was originally established by the East India Company in 1794 and produced gunpowder in mills on the Hooghli river until 1902. The rifle-making plant was built in 1903–05 to free the Indian Army from dependence on Britain, the first *Lee-Enfield rifles being completed in September 1907. Ishapore made substantial quantities of SMLE rifles – including more than 680,000 during the Second World War – while simultaneously manufacturing and refurbishing *Vickers Guns. Work continued after independence was gained from Britain in 1947, small quantities of .303 Rifle 1 (SMLE) being made until the late 1950s. Production of the 7.62mm Rifle 1A began in 1963, and about 250,000 of the 7.62mm Rifle 2A (an SMLE conversion) were remanufactured in 1963–70. The factory now makes the 5.56mm INSAS assault rifle.

'ISL'. A linear-type cursive monogram with 'S' dominant. A misreading of 'JSL' (q.v.).

Israeli Military Industries [IMI], Ramat ha-Sharon. The business was formed in 1950 to make *Mauser-action rifles for the armed forces. Operations were conducted briefly in the period 1993–96 as Ta'as Military Industries, but, as the change of name was unpopular, a return to the original trading style was soon made. *Galil and *Hadar rifles, military stores, and the *Desert Eagle and *Jericho pistols have been among IMI products, which often display a trademark of a sword, an olive branch and a cogwheel.

Itajuba. The Fábrica de Armas de Itajuba converted thousands of Brazilian .30-calibre M1 *Garand rifles to chamber 7.62x51 ammunition and accept the standard twenty-round *FAL box magazine. Apparently these date from the 1970s.

Italguns SpA, Via Leonardo da Vinci, Trezzano, Milano, Italy. The manufacturer of the IGI or Igi air pistols Model 202 and Model 203; the CU-400 single-stroke pneumatic introduced in 1980; and the Domino semi-automatic cartridge pistols. Italguns products have been distributed in Britain by *Nickerson and Norman *May, the latter agency being granted in early 1980 and ending in 1984.

'Italian Mannlicher', or Mannlicher-Carcano. A name given to the M1891 6.5mm bolt-action rifle, adopted by the Italian Army on 29 March 1892 and subsequently made also in short (*moschetto*) and carbine (*carabina*) forms. Essentially it was a hybrid of the *Reichsgewehr-type Mannlichers, with a new reversible six-round clip. Development is credited to Salvatore Carcano, although nominally it was a government commission. The guns were made until the early 1940s in the state-owned small-arms factories (*Fabbrica d'Armi) in Brescia, Terni, Torino and Torre Annunziata, a 7.35mm version being substituted for the 6.5mm design after 1938. Details of the individual models will be found in *Il 91*, by Gianfranco Simone, Ruggero Belogi and Allessio Grimaldi (Editrice Ravizza, 1971), and John

Walter's *Rifles of the World* (Krause Publications, second edition, 1998).

Ithaca Gun Company, Ithaca, New York State, USA. This gunmaking business was formed – possibly in 1883 – by William *Baker and Leroy *Smith, after Lyman *Smith had purchased W.H. *Baker & Sons Company in 1880. Baker left in 1887 (to create the *Syracuse Forging Company), but the Ithaca Gun Company, incorporated in 1904, continued to make boxlock shotguns in accordance with Baker's patents of 1880. Subsequently Ithaca purchased the assets of several other gunmaking businesses, including the *Lefever Arms Company, the *Union Firearms Company and the *Wilkes-Barre Gun Company, and is still making a range of shotguns, including the slide-action Model 37. Robert E. Gardner, writing in his book *Small Arms Makers*, also credits Itahaca with purchasing the *Syracuse Arms Company, but apparently this was a predecessor of the *Baker Gun & Forging Company. Among Ithaca products were .45 M1911A1 *Colt-Browning pistols, about 369,000 being made in 1943–45. Ithaca has made rimfire rifles and distributed a variety of guns made elsewhere, including *BSA cartridge rifles and airguns from c. 1972 to 1985. A move from the old factory in Ithaca to new premises in Kingferry, New York, occurred in 1988.

'ITM'. *See* International Technology & Machines.

'I.T.O.Z.' Found in Cyrillic, as 'И.Т.О.З.', and accompanied by a displayed-eagle motif. Associated with products of the Russian imperial small-arms factory in Tula – *Imperatorskiy Tulskiy Oruzheinyi Zavod.* It will be found on the grips of *Velo-Dog revolvers in addition to *Mosin-Nagant and other rifles. *See also* 'TOZ'.

'It's a Bear'. A slogan associated with *Reising, an illustration of a bear being the company's trademark.

Iver Johnson. *See* Iver *Johnson.

Iwashita. Koni Iwashita. A general in the Japanese army, Iwashita was the chairman of the commission that perfected the 7.62mm Type 64 service rifle, adopted in April 1964.

Izarra. *See* Bonifacio *Echeverria.

Izhevskii Oruzheinyi Zavod, Izhevsk, RSFSR. This Russian small-arms factory was founded in 1805, when Tsar Aleksandr I ordered the conversion of a small metalworking factory into a gunmaking centre. Production began in 1810. The factory has been involved with the Berdan, Dragunov, Kalashnikov, Mosin-Nagant, Simonov and Tokarev rifles (qq.v.), together with *Baikal/Vostok shotguns, air rifles and ammunition. The airguns have included a simple 4.5mm spring-and-piston rifle (apparently designated Izh-PCRM-2-55) sold in large quantities in Western Europe during the 1970s and 1980s. Firearms and munitions are still being made under the Izhmashzavod trading style.

J

'J'. Beneath a crown. Found on Dutch weapons: the mark of Queen Juliana (1948–80). *See also* Cyphers, imperial and royal.

'JA', 'JAB'. Encountered on US military firearms and accessories. *See* J. *Arnold, and John A. *Bell and John A. *Brooks.

Jack. A patent agent: *see* Martin, Jack & Company.

Jackal – 1. A British .22-calibre sidelever-cocking spring-and-piston air rifle designed by Richard Marriott Smith in 1976–77 and made for the *Sussex Armoury of Hailsham by NSP Engineering. The first guns, known subsequently as Jackal Parabellum, had an injection-moulded military-style ABS stock. They were followed by the short-barrelled Jackal AR-7 (1978), the Jackal Hi-Power (1979) and the Jackal Firepower (1980), with refined stock contours. The Firepower version also had a tube magazine above the loading tap. Woodstock versions – Jackal Parabellum Woodstock, Jackal Hi-Power Woodstock and Jackal Woodsman – were all made in small numbers, together with a .20-calibre version known as the Jackal Hi-Power 20-20. Production of the original guns ceased when Sussex Armoury collapsed in 1982, but formed the basis for the greatly improved range subsequently offered by *Air Arms. 2. Associated with .22-calibre diabolo airgun pellets made for the *Sussex Armoury by *Lanes Ltd.

Jack Rabbit. A brandname associated with shotgun cartridges made in the USA by the *American Ammunition Company.

Jackson – 1. H.G. Jackson, Bungay and Halesworth, Suffolk. The marks of this English ironmonger/gun dealer have been reported on shotgun cartridges. 2. John Low Jackson, Nottingham. This gunmaker, who styled himself 'Manufacturer to H.R.H. The Duke of Sussex', began trading in Low Pavement prior to 1821 and had moved to Church Gate by 1830. He had designed a self-priming *cap-lock prior to the move, receiving English Patent No. 4823 of 1823. 3. Richard Jackson began trading as a gunmaker in 1831, from 19 Princes Street, Portman Market, London. He moved to 30 Portman Place, Edgware Road, in 1847; to 185 Edgware Road in 1866; and lastly to 416 Edgware Road in 1869. Trading was continued as Richard & Elias Jackson at the same address, probably by Jackson's sons, then from 1873 as Richard Jackson (the Younger) from 15 Edgware Road until 1894, and finally 41 Upper Berkeley Street, London W., until work ceased in 1897. 4. Samuel Jackson, Church Gate, Nottingham. The marks of this English provincial gunmaker, successor to John L. Jackson (working at the same address between 1831 and 1868) have been reported on shotgun cartridges sold prior to 1914 under the brandname Nottingham. 5. Thomas Jackson. A gunsmith trading from 17 Upper George Street, Bryanston Square, London, in 1828–39, Jackson moved to 29 Edwards Street, Portman Square. There he stayed until 1869,

when the business moved to 89 Wigmore Street. The trading style became Thomas Jackson & Son in 1871, but work in the Wigmore Street premises continued only until the late 1870s. The last directory entries were made in 1879. 6. Thomas Jackson [Junior]. The son of Thomas Jackson (above), this gunsmith could be found at 4 Railway Place, Shoreditch, London N.E., in 1861–62. It is thought that subsequently he joined his father in Thomas Jackson & Son. 7. Jackson Arms Company. A brandname associated with shotguns made in the USA prior to 1920 by the *Crescent Arms Company of Norwich, Connecticut.

Jacobs. G.K. Jacobs, working on behalf of first the Federal Army, then the US Army in 1863–75, accepted a variety of firearms and accessories. Recognisable by their 'GKJ' marks, they included .58-calibre rifle-muskets made by *Amoskeag. *See also* US arms inspectors' marks.

Jacquemart – 1. C. Jacquemart, Liège, Belgium. A maker of sporting rifles and double-barrelled shotguns prior to 1914, usually based on the *Anson & Deeley action. 2. Jules Jacquemart et Cie, Liège. The Belgian maker of a small automatic pistol sold under the brandname *Le Monobloc.

Jacquet – 1. Saint-Étienne, France. Listed in 1933 as a gunmaker. 2. Jacquet aîné, rue Valbenoîte 16, Saint-Étienne, France. Listed in 1879 as a gunmaker.

Jacquith. *See* Jaquith.

Jaeger – 1. F. Jaeger & Co. GmbH, Suhl in Thüringen, Germany. Listed as a gunmaking business in 1914, and under the ownership of Franz Jaeger in 1919–39. 2. Paul Jaeger, Inc., Grand Junction, Tennessee, USA. This gunmaker introduced the Jaeger African, Alaskan and Hunter rifles in 1989, apparently built on *Santa Barbara Mauser actions. 3. W. Jaeger, Mehlis in Thüringen. Listed in the *Deutsches Reichs-Adressbuch* for 1914 as a gunmaker. 4. W. Jaeger, Suhl in Thüringen. Listed as a gunsmith in the 1920 edition of the *Deutsches Reichs-Adressbuch*. Perhaps the same as the previous entry, having moved in the intervening period. 5. Wilhelm Richard Jaeger, Mehlis, Zella-Mehlis and Suhl in Thüringen, Germany. Listed in the *Deutsches Reichs-Adressbuch* for 1914 as a gun-barrel maker in Mehlis; as a gunmaker and gun-barrel maker in Zella-Mehlis in 1919–20; and as gun-barrel maker in Zella-Mehlis, and gunmaker in Suhl by 1930. Jaeger was still being listed as a gun-barrel maker in Zella-Mehlis in 1939–45, and also in Wilhelm-Gustloff-Strasse, Suhl, in 1940–41. 6. *See also* Jäger.

Jaga. A compact 6.35mm *Browning-type pocket pistol made in Czechoslovakia by František Dušek of Opočno, c. 1925–38. The Duo and Perla were essentially similar.

Jagd-König. A brandname (German for 'Hunt King') associated with shotgun cartridges made prior to the First World War by *Pulverfabrik Hasloch.

Jäger, *see also* Jaeger – 1. A German-language term ('huntsman'), popular as a constituent of brandnames and also often used generically to signify sporting guns. **2.** Franz Jäger [& Co.], Suhl in Thüringen. The marks of this German gunmaking business will be found on sporting guns, as well as the 7.65mm Jäger-Pistole (below) introduced during the First World War. Jäger used the brandname *Herold. **3.** Gebr. Jäger, Benshausen in Thüringen, Germany. Listed in 1941 as a gunsmithing business. **4.** Jager-Armi di Armando Piscetta [Armi-Jager], Milan. This gunmaking business produced a few sporting rifles in the 1960s on the basis of refurbished military 1898-type Mauser actions. Chambered for cartridges ranging from .220 Swift to 8x57, they had half-stocks with Monte Carlo combs. The company has also made a wide range of .22 rimfire lookalikes of the *Galil, the *Kalashnikov, the FA MAS, the *Heckler & Koch G3, the Steyr *AUG and other modern rifles. **5.** Jäger-Pistole. This small 7.65mm-calibre *blowback semi-automatic personal-defence weapon was made during the First World War by Franz Jäger of Suhl. Produced in quantity in 1915–18, its quirky multi-piece construction gave it a uniquely streamlined appearance. The frame was assembled from two sturdy pressings, held apart by pinned straps that acted as spacers; the return spring was concentric with the barrel, and a detachable box magazine lay in the butt. Most guns of this type will be encountered with military proof and inspectors' markings.

Jaguar. A name associated with a simple British barrel-cocking .177-calibre spring-and-piston air rifle made by *Webley & Scott Ltd in 1947–76.

'JAH'. Found on US military firearms and accessories. *See* John A. *Howell.

Jallas. E. Jallas et Cie, Saint-Étienne, France. *See* Darne.

Jamar. Joseph Jamar-Smits, Liège. The name of this Belgian gunmaker will often be encountered on *Ghaye-pattern sporting rifles with the operating-lever pivot ahead of the trigger. Most of them date from the 1860s.

James – 1. Benjamin Franklin James accepted firearms and accessories on behalf of the US Army in 1904–06, marking them 'BFJ'. **2.** Enos James & Company. This Birmingham gunmaking business traded from 36 & 37 (later 36 & 38) Loveday Street in 1880–88, 14 St Mary's Row in 1888, and lastly Stamforth Street in 1889. **3.** M. James & Sons, Newcastle Emlyn, Carmarthenshire. The marks of this Welsh ironmongery and gun dealership have been reported on shotgun cartridges sold under the brandname Gwalia. **4.** James & Company, Great Western Mills, Hungerford, Berkshire, England. This company of millers made food for game birds. Its marks have also been found on shotgun ammunition sold under the brandname *Kennett.

Jane, Janes. W.H. Jane, or Janes, Bodmin, Cornwall. The marks of this English ironmonger/gun dealer have been found on shotgun cartridges sold under the brandname Bodmin.

Janeček. František Janeček. Had it not been for a series of patents granted to protect auto-loading rifles, munitions and artillery, Janeček would have been celebrated for his electrical engineering work. Born in Kláster on 23 January 1878, Janeček served in the Austro-Hungarian Army during 1914–18, transferred briefly to the Czechoslovakian Army in 1919, then left military service to start a small tool- and precision instrument-making business in Mnichovo Hradiště. This enterprise soon failed, but Janeček used the experience to build a new

factory in Prague to make arms, munitions and eventually motor vehicles. He continued work until his death on 4 June 1941. Most of Janeček's auto-loading rifles dated from the 1930s. Normally they were stocked similarly to the indigenous Mauser short rifles, but often had detachable box magazines. They relied on a pivoting strut, attached to the breech-block, to delay the opening of the breech until chamber pressure had declined.

Janisson, 26 cours Fauriel, Saint-Étienne, France. Listed in 1951 as a gunmaker.

Jansen. Adolphe Jansen, Brussels, Belgium. Active from 1830 until the 1860s or later, styling himself *Arquebusier du Roi* (Gunmaker to the King), Jansen often contented himself by purchasing guns in Liège. Caplock sporting rifles, pinfire shotguns, *Mariette pepperboxes and an assortment of revolvers have been found with his marks.

Janson. Stephen Kenneth Janson, Britain. *See* Stefan *Januszewski.

Janssen – 1. Joseph Janssen. Trading for many years in Liège, this Belgian gunmaker was sufficiently well-established to be a founder member of les *Fabricants d'armes réunis, 1886, and a founding shareholder in *Fabrique Nationale d'Armes de Guerre in 1889. Janssen also employed agents in London until the end of the nineteenth century. The directories list the premises successively as 45 and 8a Cross Street, Finsbury, in 1876; 8 & 13 Cross Street in 1877–78; 36 Basinghall Street in 1880–81; St Mary Chambers, St Mary Axe, in 1882–83; 3 & 6 Camomile Street, E.C., in 1884–86; and 4 Butler Street, E.C., from 1887 until 1891. An entry for Janssen, fils & Cie was made in 1896, apparently without an address. Janssen fils (below) continued to work in Liège until the beginning of the First World War. **2.** Janssen fils & Cie, Liège. Successors to Joseph Janssen (above). A founder-member of Le *Syndicat des Pièces interchangeables (1898), and also the maker of the *Jieffeco pistol. Work ceased shortly after the German invasion of Belgium in 1914.

Januszewski. Stefan Januszewski [Stephen Kenneth Janson]. The Polish-born British designer of the British .280 EM-2 rifle began work in the autumn of 1947 with hand-made prototypes, and patented the gun in August 1951. The gun was adopted as the 'Rifle 7mm No. 9 Mk 1', but the US and French Armies refused to accept the .280 cartridge as a NATO standard, and approval was rescinded in October 1951. Prototypes were made for the .30 T65 cartridge, .30-06 and 7x51, but eventually the entire project was abandoned in favour of the FAL.

Japanese... – 1. Japanese gun designations. Prior to 1930, service weapons were designated according to the reign-period (*nengo*) of each emperor reckoned from the restoration of 1868; 1890, therefore, was the 23rd Year of Meiji Emperor's reign. The system was maintained through the Taisho period (1912–26) and into the Showa era, before being replaced by a calendar based on the mythical foundation of Japan in 660 BC. After 1929, therefore, terms such as Type 94 were used, 2594 being 1934 when reckoned by the absolute calendar. The receivers of pre-1945 Japanese small-arms invariably displayed an imperial chrysanthemum and a mixture of pictographs derived from Chinese (*kanji*) and a phonetic alphabet used to assimilate foreign words into Japanese (*katakana*). **2.** Japanese serial numbers. By about 1932, when the serial numbers of Meiji

38th Year *Arisaka rifles had exceeded 2,000,000, a cyclical numbering system was adopted. Individual blocks (1–99999) were identified by small encircled *katakana* prefixes, the sequence being taken from the traditional poem *Iroha*. Numerical values can be given to these symbols, but it is better to regard them as letter groups.

Jaquith. Elijah Jaquith. Grantee of a US Patent on 12 July 1838, exploited by the *Springfield Arms Company to mislead Colt.

Jarmann. Named after its designer, this 10.15x51R bolt-action rifle, with an eight-round tube magazine beneath the barrel, was tested by a joint Swedish/Norwegian Army board in 1878–79. It was adopted only in Norway, as the Swedes retained their single-shot *Remingtons. About 500 trials guns were made in Eskilstuna in 1880–82 by the Royal Swedish gun factory (Carl Gustafs Stads Gevärsfaktori), followed by about 28,000 Jarmanns Repetergevær M/1884 and M/1884/87 – the latter with an additional magazine *cut-off – emanating from the principal Norwegian small-arms factory, Kongsberg Våpenfabrikk. The Jarmann was speedily replaced by the *Krag-Jørgensen.

Jarrett. Henry J. Jarrett & Company. This gunsmithing business was listed in London directories at 15 Tower Hill East and 15 King Street, Tower Hill, London E., during 1870–71.

Javelle – 1. A. Javelle, rue de la Vierge 13, Saint-Étienne, France. Listed in 1879 as a gunmaker. **2.** Javelle frères, rue Beaubrun 54, Saint-Étienne, France. Listed in 1879 as a gunmaker. **3.** Javelle-Magand, grande rue Saint-Roch 106, Saint-Étienne, France. A specialist gun-barrel maker working in the late 1870s.

'JAW'. A mark found on US military firearms and accessories. *See* J.A. *Wood and J.A. *Woodward.

Jay, place Villeboeuf 4, Saint-Étienne, France. Listed in 1892 as a gunmaker.

'JB', 'J.B.' – 1. A superimposition-type monogram, 'J' within 'B'. Found on pistols and possibly sporting guns made in Liège, Belgium, by Manufacture Générale d'Armes et Munitions Jules *Bertrand. **2.** In fraktur: found on the receivers of German military *Mauser-action rifles, usually as 'J.B. Mod. 71'. This identifies a *Jäger-Büchse* – the weapon of the rifle battalions. **3.** As 'The J.B.'; associated with shotgun cartridges sold in Ireland by James *Braddell & Son of Belfast.

'JBH', 'JBK, 'JBT'. Found on US military firearms and accessories. *See* Joseph B. *Hayes, John B. *Kirkham and J.B. *Tyler respectively.

'J.C.'. Found on components for the No. 4 *Lee-Enfield rifle made in Britain during the Second World War by John Curtis Ltd. This company was also allocated the area code 'N22', but often used its initials instead.

'JCA'. Associated with US military firearms and accessories. *See* John C. *Ayres.

J. Cesar. An otherwise unattributable Spanish 6.35mm Browning-style pocket pistol made (presumably in the Eibar district) for Tómas de *Urizar of Barcelona.

'JCH', J.C. Higgins. *See* Sears, Roebuck & Company.

'JCP'. A mark found on US military firearms and accessories. *See* J.C. *Parker.

'JCS', 'J.C. & S.' – 1. Found as 'JCS' on US military firearms and accessories. *See* John C. *Stebbins and John C. *Symmes. **2.** Found as J.C. & S. on British shotgun ammunition. *See* J. *Crockart & Son.

'JCZ'. A cursive superimposition-type monogram. Found on folding-trigger *Fox pistols made by *Jihočeská Zbrojovka of Prague, c. 1921–25. The gun was designed by Alois *Tomiška and made in his workshop in Pilsen in 1919–21. Subsequently the monogram may have become 'CZ' without otherwise changing its cursive design.

'JDM'. Found on US military firearms and accessories. *See* J.D. *McIntyre.

Jeffers. William N. Jeffers, active in the early 1860s, accepted signal pistols marked 'WNJ' on behalf of the Federal Navy. *See also* US arms inspectors' marks.

Jeffrey – 1. A.R. & H.V. Jeffrey, 100 Old Town Street, Plymouth, Devon. The marks of this English gunmaking partnership have been reported on shotgun cartridges made by *Eley-Kynoch. It is believed that A.R. and H.V. Jeffrey were grandsons of William Jeffrey (below). A branch was also maintained in Yeovil for a few years. **2.** C. Jeffrey & Sons, Dorchester, Dorset. The origins of this English country gunmaking business lay in William Jeffrey & Son, recorded in High Street East in 1866. Its marks have been reported on sporting guns and shotgun cartridges, including some marked 'Rabbit'. **3.** S.R. Jeffrey & Son, Guildford, Surrey. The marks of this English gunmaker, son of Richard Jeffrey (High Street, Guildford, 1850–66) have been reported on a variety of shotgun cartridges – mostly made by *Eley Bros. – sold prior to 1914 under such brandnames as Champion and Club. **4.** William Jeffrey & Son, 3 Russell Street, Plymouth, Devon. The business was begun sometime prior to 1849 by William Jeffrey, operating from 22 Briton Side and 10 Lockyer Terrace. The premises moved to 52 Union Terrace in the early 1850s, and 12 George Street in the mid-1860s, where it had been renamed W. Jeffrey & Son by 1869. This trading style lasted until at least 1914, being found on sporting guns and ammunition. These included shotgun cartridges marketed under names such as Eddystone, Rabbit and Sky High. **5.** W.J. Jeffrey, one of the best-known London gunmakers (renowned particularly for his sporting rifles and shotguns), began trading from 60 Queen Victoria Street in 1888. After trading briefly as Jeffrey & Davies, a style apparently confined to 1889–90, operations continued as W.J. Jeffrey & Company from 1891. Jeffrey offered sporting rifles chambered for a range of proprietary cartridges, including the .280 Rimless of c. 1913, the .333 Rimless Nitro Express (1911) and the .404 Rimless Nitro Express (c. 1909). Although these were often fired from the Double Rifles favoured in Britain prior to 1939, bolt-action magazine rifles were also offered. These guns were often based on *Mannlicher actions prior to 1914, but most of the post-1918 large-bore examples were Oberndorf *Mausers. In addition to firearms, Jeffrey sold *Gem-type airguns under the brandname Laballe. Marks have been reported on shotgun cartridges sold under brandnames such as Champion, Club Smokeless, High Velocity, Jeffrey Cartridge, Jeffrey XXX and Sharpshooter. Components were obtained from a variety of sources, including *Eley Bros. and *Utendörffer. Marks include a trademark of 'J' in a circle (or oval), and addresses such as 13 King Street or 26 Bury Street, St James's; 60 Queen Victoria Street, E.C.; and 9 Golden Square, Regent Street. **6.** Jeffrey Cartridge and Jeffrey XXX [The]. Associated with shotgun cartridges sold by W.J. *Jeffrey of London.

Jeffries – 1. George Jeffries, Norwich, Norfolk. This English country gunmaker began trading from Stepping Lane in 1841, moving to Golden Ball Street in 1849, and Orford Hill in 1865. Jeffries ceased trading in 1868, but was succeeded by his son George Lincoln Jeffries (q.v.) in Birmingham. The elder Jeffries is best known for his shotgun with side-swivelling barrels, patented in Britain in 1862. **2.** George Lincoln Jeffries: *see* panel, below. George Jeffries had four daughters and four sons, one of whom died in infancy. The other sons – Lincoln Parkes Jeffries, John Jeffries and Robert Jeffries – all became involved in their father's business until it ceased trading as a limited company. **3.** Lincoln Parkes Jeffries, Birmingham, Warwickshire. The son was known universally as Lincoln Jeffries Junior, as the father never used his forename outside family circles. He was granted a variety of British patents, including 181,640 and 180,641 of 15 and 22 June 1922, to protect improved latches, triggers and sears for the Lincoln air pistol. Patent 250,531 of 15 April 1926 described a complicated air rifle with the barrel placed above the air chamber; 254,640 of 8 July 1926 showed an essentially similar pistol. **4.** Lincoln Jeffries & Company Ltd, Birmingham. This was founded in the early 1900s, occupying 35 Whittall Street. The company may have been involved with the Hercules Welding Company of the same address, trading until it was liquidated in the spring of 1912. **5.** Lincoln Jeffries (Junior) & Company, 120 Steelhouse Lane, Birmingham. This was effectively a continuation of the business of G. Lincoln Jeffries (above) by Lincoln Jeffries Junior. It seems to have made the *Bisley and *Lincoln pistols, as well as a push-barrel spring-air pistol known as the *Scout. However, the rise of the German airgun industry during the inter-war years, typified by *Haenel and Mayer & Grammelspacher, persuaded the younger Lincoln Jeffries (by that time seriously ill) to cease operating c. 1935. He died in 1939 at the age of 64, but yet another Lincoln Jeffries business was started after the Second World War by L.G. and A.H. Jeffries, sons of the younger Lincoln. This traded into the 1980s, making the well-known *Marksman-brand diabolo pellets alongside slugs, lead shot, lead-wire tape and mouldings.

'JEH'. Found on US military firearms and accessories. *See* J.E. *Hitchcock and Jay E. *Hoffer.

Jelen – 1. Josef Jelen. The elder brother of the better-known Rudolf Jelen (q.v.), this gunsmith traded for some years in the Bohemian town of Weipert, where he made – among other things – parts for Mannlicher-type army rifles. **2.** Rudolf Jelen. Born on 27 January 1876 in Bolehost, near Nové Mesto nad Metují in Bohemia, Jelen was apprenticed to his gunsmithing brother, Josef, before receiving his army call-up papers in 1897. Jelen retired from military service in 1914, joining the police, but he returned to the colours for the duration of the First World War and did not formally leave the Czechoslovakian Army until 1920. Belated qualification as a mechanical engineer (1918–21) allowed Jelen to pursue a prolific, if largely unsuccessful, career as a designer. His output included fuzes, munitions, modified *Mauser rifles and *blow-forward and *blowback machine-guns. He died in Prague on 10 March 1938.

Jelly. A common misrepresentation of Telly (q.v.).

Jenks – 1. Alfred Jenks & Son, Philadelphia and Bridesburg, Pennsylvania, USA. Originally the Bridesburg Machine Works made machinery for wool and cotton mills, but began manufacturing firearms when the

GEORGE LINCOLN JEFFRIES

Jeffries (2)

Born in 1847, this English gunmaker, son of George Jeffries of Norwich, began trading from 31 Whittall Street in Birmingham in 1873. Premises at 48 Whittall Street were occupied from 1888 until a move to 121 Steelhouse Lane took place in 1898. By 1900, Lincoln Jeffries & Company (its principal never used his first initial) had established itself as a maker of *Lincoln-brand hammer and hammerless single- and double-barrelled sporting guns. In addition, the company modified Langenhan/Pulvermann *Millita rifles with sliding double-catch locking rather than a push-button.

Manufacture of the Lincoln Patent Air Rifle began c. 1902, and its success soon interested BSA, which subsequently exploited the Jefferies patents, made some improvements and produced great quantities of these guns until 1939/40. However, Jeffries gradually reduced his involvement in trading after 1912, apparently so that he could enjoy a lengthy retirement; he died at the age of 84 in 1932.

George Lincoln Jeffries' first British Patent, 20,246/03, accepted on 25 August 1904, protected an 'Improved Breech-fastening for Break-lock Guns'. Then came 8761/04, granted on 12 March 1904, to protect many variations of breech-block to minimise air loss; 10,426/05, accepted on 30 November 1905, to protect a simplified rod-cocking air rifle; 22,550/05, accepted on 17 May 1906, for a sliding loading port; 11,588/06 of 1906 to protect a rotary loading tap that was capable of compensating for wear; and 20,744/06 of 1906 (sought with George Frederick *Urry) for an improved 'Quick Release Breech plug Catch'.

Subsequently Jeffries & Urry also received British Patent 21,324/06 for a self-adjusting quick-release breech plug. British Patent 10,250/10, accepted on 27 April 1911, gave George Lincoln Jeffries protection for a spring-and-piston air pistol (the *Bisley) with a combination cocking lever/back strap; 25,783/10 was granted on 7 September 1911 to protect a supplementary sear or side-button catch that prevented the cocking lever from slipping as the mechanism was being set; and 30,338/10 followed in October 1911 for the 'Double Safety Sear'.

Other relevant patents included 1,405/11 of 1911 for the break-barrel *Lincoln pistol, with the piston and spring assembly in the butt; 9684/11 of 1911 for the grip safety fitted to the perfected Bisley pistol; 15,823/11 of 1911 for an improved pistol-cocking system; and 15,858/11 of 1911, which was a variant of 15,823/11 intended for air rifles.

Most of the Jeffries Pattern air rifles were made by the *Birmingham Small Arms Company Ltd and its 1919-vintage successor

American Civil War broke out in 1861. By 1865, the company had delivered 98,454 .58-calibre 1861-pattern *Springfield rifle-muskets against contracts amounting to 100,000. **2.** Barton H. Jenks, Bridesburg, Pennsylvania. Son of Alfred Jenks, this engineer submitted three experimental breech-loading carbines to the US Army trials of 1865. Protected by US Patent no. 74,760 of 25 February 1868, the multi-part breech was locked by a radial locking piece that bore against a shoulder in the rear of the receiver. **3.** William Jenks, Columbia, South Carolina, USA. Patentee in May 1838 (US 747) of a breech-loading carbine. The first flintlock musket was tried in 1838, to be followed by 100 .64 smoothbore carbines for the army and a few 1839-pattern .54 cap-lock muskets for the US Navy. The guns were recommended for adoption in 1845, but troop trials proved catastrophic. **4.** Jenks carbine. This was distinguished by its lateral 'mule ear' hammer. The breech was sealed by a plunger or piston sliding into the back of the chamber from the rear. This was locked by a toggle joint, and was opened simply by raising a lever running back from the breech above the stock wrist. Although the army rejected the Jenks after the disastrous field trials, the navy was well satisfied with its potential. More than 6,000 Jenks guns were ordered from Nathan *Ames and E. *Remington & Son in 1841–45, Remington's guns being the first martial arms to incorporate the Maynard Tape Primer and a cast-steel barrel. By 1860, most surviving guns had been transformed by James Merrill (q.v.) into conventional side-hammer cap-locks.

Jennie. Frederick Jennie, USA. *See* Weatherby.

Jennings – 1. Henry D. Jennings, active in 1862–63, during the American Civil War, accepted firearms and accessories marked 'HDJ'. *See also* US arms inspectors' marks. **2.** Lewis Jennings of Windsor, Vermont, is best known as the designer of the improved *Hunt Volition Ball rifle, protected by US Patent 6973 of 25 December 1849. Rights were assigned to George *Arrowsmith, who subsequently sold them to Courtlandt Palmer. About 5,000 Jennings-type rifles were made in 1851 by *Robbins & Lawrence; although comparatively unsuccessful, they laid the basis for the rimfire Smith & Wesson *Volcanic, then the *Henry rifle. **3.** Jennings Firearms Inc., Stateline, Nevada, and Irvine, California, USA. Manufacturer of compact .22- and .25-calibre automatic pistols.

Jericho. A recoil-operated semi-automatic pistol made by *Israeli Military Industries, on the basis of the *Tanfoglio-adapted CZ75. It is available in 9mm Parabellum and .41 Action Express (interchangeably) and, therefore, often known as the 'Model 941'.

Jervey. Thomas M. Jervey, a major in the US Army Ordnance Corps, accepted firearms made by *Colt's Patent Fire Arms Manufacturing Company. Dating from 1937–38, invariably they are marked 'TMJ'. *See also* US arms inspectors' marks.

Jet – 1. Or Silver Jet. A diabolo-type airgun projectile made since the 1970s by *Hausike Seiskusho, loosely based on Lane's *Triumph of 1929. It was still being made in 4.5 and 5.5mm versions in the 1990s. **2.** Jet King. A name sometimes associated with gas-powered rifles marketed by the *Benjamin Rifle Company, but restricted in practice to the propellant cylinders filled with carbon dioxide.

Jetfire. Also known as the M951 Jetfire, this small 6.35mm-calibre automatic pistol was made by Pietro *Beretta of Gardone Val Trompia, Brescia, Italy.

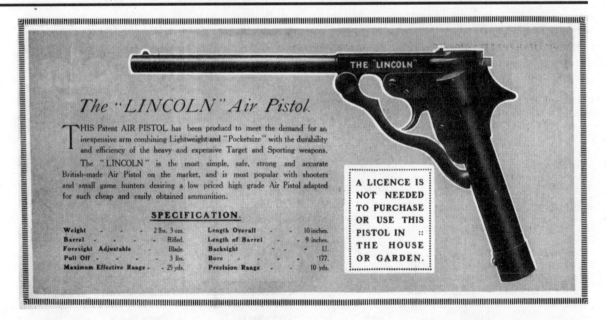

The "LINCOLN" Air Pistol.

THIS Patent AIR PISTOL has been produced to meet the demand for an inexpensive arm combining Lightweight and "Pocketsize" with the durability and efficiency of the heavy and expensive Target and Sporting weapons.

The "LINCOLN" is the most simple, safe, strong and accurate British-made Air Pistol on the market, and is most popular with shooters and small game hunters desiring a low priced high grade Air Pistol adapted for such cheap and easily obtained ammunition.

SPECIFICATION.

Weight	2 lbs. 3 ozs.	Length Overall	10 inches.
Barrel	Rifled.	Length of Barrel	9 inches.
Foresight Adjustable	Blade	Backsight	U.
Pull Off	3 lbs.	Bore	.177.
Maximum Effective Range	25 yds.	Precision Range	10 yds.

A LICENCE IS NOT NEEDED TO PURCHASE OR USE THIS PISTOL IN :: THE HOUSE OR GARDEN.

*BSA Guns Ltd, but Lincoln Jeffries also offered shooting accessories of his own design and shotgun cartridges loaded at the Steelhouse Lane premises.

The best source of information about some of the guns is John Knibbs's *The B.S.A. and Lincoln Jeffries Air Rifles* (published privately, 1986).

The .177 Jeffries Lincoln air pistol was made in small numbers after the First World War. This illustration was taken from a leaflet published c. 1921. The all-metal construction is most distinctive.

Jeury, 24 rue Badouillère, Saint-Étienne, France. Listed in 1951 as a gunmaker.

Jewel – 1. Or 'Jewel Gem'. Apparently this brandname has been found on German-made butt-cylinder spring-airguns sold by *Lane Bros. of London, prior to 1914. **2.** A *Suicide Special revolver made in the USA by the *Hood Firearms Company of Norwich, Connecticut, in the late nineteenth century.

Jewell. Thomas F. Jewell, a commander in the US Navy, accepted signal pistols in 1888–97, marking them 'TMJ'. See also US arms inspectors' marks.

Jewson. A.J. Jewson, 1 Westgate, Halifax, Yorkshire. The marks of this English gunmaker have been reported on sporting guns, as well as shotgun cartridges sold under the brandnames Champion, Crown and Westgate.

'JFC'. A mark found on US military firearms and accessories. See J.F. *Coyle.

'JF Co.', 'JF&CO'. An encircled monogram, with a dominant central 'J'. Found on Belgian *Jieffeco pistols made in Liège prior to the First World War by *Janssen, fils & Co.

'JFR', 'JFS'. Found on US military firearms and accessories. See J.F. *Riley and James F. *Sullivan.

'J.G.' – 1. In fraktur: found on German military rifles as 'J.G. Mod. 71'. A misreading of 'I.G.' (q.v.). **2.** Often underscored. A *headstamp applied by Joseph *Goldmark of New York City to rimfire cartridges made during the American Civil War.

'JGA', 'J.G.A.', often set vertically within a circle. A trademark associated with J.G. *Anschütz of Zella-Mehlis, Germany.

'JGB'. Found on US military firearms and accessories. See James G. *Benton and John G. *Butler.

J.G.R. Gunsport Ltd, Toronto, Ontario. This Canadian distributor of firearms, ammunition and sporting goods handled cartridges identified by the inclusion of 'J.G.R.' in their headstamps.

'JGS', 'J.G.S.', often in the form of a monogram. A mark used by Josef *Goessl of Suhl.

'JGW'. Found on US military firearms and accessories. See J.G. *Woodbury.

'JH', 'JHH', 'JHL' 'JHM'. Found on US military firearms and accessories. See Joseph *Hall, J. *Hannis, James *Harris, J. *Hawkins and Joseph *Harniss; J.H. *Howarth and Joseph H. *Hubbard; J.H. *Lyons; and Joseph H. *McGuire respectively.

'JHP'. An unidentified US inspector's mark, found on a 1928-pattern *Thompson submachine-gun.

'jhv'. Found on German military pistols, rifles and small-arms components made by the Hungarian state ordnance factory in Budapest (*Femaru Fégyver és Gépgyár, which was known to the Germans as Metallwaren-, Waffen- und Maschinenfabrik AG).

Jieffeco. Found on Belgian 6.35mm automatic pistols made in Liège by *Janssen, fils et Cie.

Jihočeská Zbrojovka s.s.r.o., South Bohemian Arms Company Ltd. Founded in Pilsen in 1919 by Karel Bubla and his backers, this Czechoslovakian gunmaking business began by manually fabricating 6.35mm *Fox pistols under the supervision of Alois *Tomiška. Production was mechanised in 1920, but the entire operation was moved to Strakonice in April 1921. In 1922, Jihočeská Zbrojovka was amalgamated with the *Hubertus company to form *Česká Zbrojovka.

'Jimpy'. A nickname bestowed by service personnel on the L7A1 General Purpose Machine Gun (GPMG), the standard rifle-calibre sustained-fire weapon of the British Army.

Jinsen arsenal, Korea. A manufacturer of 7.7mm Type 99 *Arisaka rifles under Japanese supervision, c. 1942–45. See also Heijo ordnance factory.

'JJB'. A mark found on US military firearms and accessories. See John J. *Breen.

'JJ Co.' – 1. A floriated superimposition-type monogram, often read as 'II', 'TT' or even 'FF'. Found on semi-automatic pistols made by Jules *Jacquemart & Co., Liège, prior to the First World War. **2.** Found on an assortment of surplus rifles – including British Short *Lee-Enfields – sold by the John Jovino Company of New York City.

'JJJ'. An unidentified US arms inspector's mark, found on *Joslyn carbines made in 1862 during the American Civil War.

'JJL', 'JJM'. Used on military firearms and accessories by J.J. *Lee and John J. *Lynch, and J.J. *Murphy.

'JK' – 1. An encircled cursive linear monogram, with 'J' slightly dominant. Probably interpreted more accurately as 'KJ' (q.v.); found on revolvers made in Spain prior to 1914. **2.** On US military firearms and accessories. See John *Kimbell.

'JKB'. A mark found on US military firearms and accessories. See James K. *Burbank.

'jkg'. Found on German small-arms components made under contract in 1941–44 by the Royal Hungarian iron, steel and machine-works, or Königliche ungarnische Staatliche Eisen-, Stahl- und Maschinenfabriken, Budapest.

'JL'. Associated with US military firearms and accessories. See Joseph *Lanman and J. *Lippold.

'JLH'. Found on US military firearms and accessories. See James L. *Hatcher and James L. *Henderson.

'jlj'. Used from 1941 on the products of the Heeres Zeugamt in Ingolstadt, Bavaria, Germany.

'JLS'. A mark found on US military firearms and accessories. See J.L. *Sticht and J.L. *Strong.

'JM' – 1. In an oval. A private proof mark used in the USA by *Marlin. **2.** Found on US military firearms and accessories. See John *Maggs, Julian *McAlister, J. *Mills and Justice *Murphy.

'jme'. A codemark associated with the products of the *Armee u. Marinehaus of Berlin, Germany, from September 1941 until the end of the Second World War.

'JMM', often encircled. A mark found on handguns made in the USA in the late nineteenth century by John M. *Marlin.

'JNB', 'JNH', 'JNJ', 'JNS'. Found on US military firearms and accessories. See J.N. *Boyer, James N. *Hemenway, John J. *Jordan and J.N. *Sollaceo respectively.

'JO'. Found on US military firearms and accessories. See J. *O'Malley.

Joanny frères, rue de l'Épreuve 2, Saint-Étienne, France. Listed in 1879 as a manufacturer of gun parts and accessories.

Joassart. Gustave Joassart. See Fabrique Nationale d'Armes de Guerre and Manufacture d'Armes de Paris.

Jobson. George Jobson, Milford, near Godalming, Surrey. The marks of this English country gunmaker have been reported on European-made shotgun cartridges sold in Britain under the brandname Milford.

Joha. Two typical Browning-inspired pocket pistols, made in Spain by an unknown gunmaker: (a) 6.35mm, six rounds, hammer fired; and (b) 7.65mm, seven rounds, hammer fired. These guns are believed to have been made for sale in Finland.

'John Brown Sharps'. Two hundred cap-lock *Sharps carbines were purchased in 1857 by the anti-slavery Massachusetts–Kansas Aid Committee for abolitionists in Kansas. They were impounded in Tabor, Iowa, in the summer of 1857, and subsequently retrieved by John Brown, who sold 100 to the Kansas abolitionists and retained the remainder for his own state. As a Sharps carbine was carried by John Brown, so the genre acquired the nickname 'John Brown Sharps'. They were also known as 'Beecher's Bibles', after the notorious Brooklyn preacher, Henry Ward Beecher. The 104 carbines that had been retrieved from Brown's supporters were stored in Harper's Ferry, where eventually they were seized by Confederate forces.

Johnson – **1.** Henry B. Johnson, active during the American Civil War, accepted *Remington-Beals revolvers on behalf of the Federal Army. Customarily marked 'HBJ', they date from 1862. *See also* US arms inspectors' marks. **2.** Iver Johnson was born in Norway and emigrated to North America during the Civil War. He began his gunsmithing work in a small workshop at 244 Main Street, Worcester, Massachusetts, c. 1867, then formed Johnson & Bye. **3.** Iver Johnson & Company. Formed from Johnson & Bye in 1883, this business had soon changed its trading style to Iver Johnson's Arms & Cycle Works. **4.** Iver Johnson's Arms & Cycle Works of Worcester and Fitchburg, Massachusetts, was an 1884-vintage successor to Iver Johnson & Company (above). This business continued to make at least some of the earlier Johnson & Bye revolvers, but these were joined by guns such as the *Boston Bull Dog, the *Improved Defender and the *Swift. An important addition to the range was the .38 Model 1879, introduced in 1884, which had a laterally-swinging cylinder patented in 1879–83 by Andrew *Hyde. The gun was too sophisticated for Johnson's markets, however, and did not sell in quantity prior to the move from Worcester to Fitchburg in 1891. Johnson also made single-barrel hammer and hammerless shotguns under the names *Side Snap and *Top Snap. **5.** Iver Johnson's Arms, Inc., Jacksonville, Arkansas, USA. Maker of a series of pocket automatics – copied from the *Walther TPH – under the designations TP22B and TP25B (.22 and .25 respectively). **6.** J.H. Johnson, Pittsburgh, Pennsylvania, USA. Owner of the *Great Western Gun Works. **7.** John Henry Johnson. This British patent agent, with chambers in 47 Lincoln's Inn Fields, London, and 166 Buchanan Street, Glasgow, was retained by inventors ranging from Paul *Mauser to Jacques *Daime. He entered into a partnership with a solicitor named Willcox c. 1893 to form Johnson & Willcox (below). **8.** Martin M. Johnson, a government employee, accepted firearms and accessories on behalf of the Federal Army during the American Civil War. Marked 'MMJ', they seem to have been confined to 1863. *See also* US arms inspectors' marks. **9.** Melvin M. Johnson (1909–70), a graduate lawyer and officer in the USMC Reserve, is better known for a career designing firearms, which began in the 1930s and ended only upon his death. In addition to the rifles and machine-guns described below,

Johnson – a notoriously vocal champion of his own designs – was responsible for the MMJ Spitfire, a variant of the *M1 Carbine introduced in the 1960s, together with a proprietary 5.7mm cartridge. **10.** R.S. Johnson accepted .45 M1911A1 pistols, and apparently also .30 *Browning machine-guns, made during 1940–41 by *Colt's Patent Fire Arms Manufacturing Company; they were marked 'RSJ'. *See also* US arms inspectors' marks. **11.** Thomas Johnson [later, & Son], Market Place, Swaffham, Norfolk. The marks of this English gunmaking business, said to have been founded in the 1860s, have been found on shotgun cartridges sold under the brandnames Johnson's Celebrated Ne Plus Ultra and Johnson's Reliable. **12.** Thomas Crossly Johnson: see panel, p. 270. **13.** Johnson Automatics, Inc., Providence, Rhode Island, USA. Promoters of the semi-automatic rifles and light machine-guns described below, operating during 1936–38. The guns were made by a subsidiary (*see* entry 15). It seems that the original incorporated business became – or was replaced by – a trust company c. 1938. **14.** Johnson Automatics Associates, Inc., Hope Valley, Rhode Island, USA. Promoters of a series of modified *M1 Carbines chambering the 5.7mm MMJ cartridge. Work ceased in the early 1960s. **15.** Johnson Automatics Manufacturing Company, Providence, Rhode Island, USA. This business, sharing the premises of the Universal Winding Company (believed to have been in partnership with Melvin Johnson), made and/or assembled Johnson rifles and sub-machine-guns. It is thought that many of the parts were sub-contracted, although their origins have yet to be identified. **16.** Johnson Automatics Trust, 84 State Street, Boston, Massachusetts. Said to have been formed in 1938 and working until 1953 or later, this organisation was responsible for the exploitation of the Johnson rifles and light machine-guns, although manufacturing was carried out elsewhere. Post-1945 work was confined to custom gunsmithing and, apparently, the conversion of military-style rifles to sporting guise. These are said to have been chambered only for .30-06 and .270 Winchester ammunition. **17.** Johnson & Bye, or Johnson, Bye & Company, Worcester, Massachusetts, USA. This gunmaking partnership was formed in 1871 by Iver Johnson and Martin *Bye, fellow Scandinavian émigrés, to make 'all kinds of firearms'. The earliest *Suicide Special revolvers were unmarked, or bore only brandnames; in 1879, however, Johnson & Bye began to use its own name. Among the identifiable brandnames were American Bull Dog, British Bull Dog, Defender, Eagle, Encore, Favorite, Favorite Navy, Old Hickory, Smoker and Tycoon (qq.v.). Bye sold his interest in the company in 1883, operations continuing as Iver Johnson & Company (above). The business marketed *Champion air pistols, protected by Johnson & Bye patents, but the guns were made by Quackenbush. **18.** Johnson automatic rifles and machine-guns: see panel, pp. 272/73. **19.** 'Johnson's Ne Plus Ultra' [The]. A brandname found on shotgun cartridges sold by *Johnson & Son of Swaffham, Norfolk, prior to 1914. Apparently the ammunition was made by *Nobel. **20.** 'Johnson's Reliable' [The]. On shotgun cartridges handled prior to 1914 in eastern England by *Johnson & Son. *See also* preceding entry. **21.** Johnson & Willcox, 47 Lincoln's Inn Fields, London. A patent agency, successor to John H. Johnson of London and Glasgow, which began operations c. 1893 and worked until the First World War

THOMAS CROSSLY JOHNSON

Johnson (12)

Born on 12 May 1862, Thomas Crossly Johnson served a gunmaking apprenticeship before joining the *Winchester Repeating Arms Company in 1885. A 'one-company man', he worked with Winchester until his death in 1934.

Understandably, therefore, most of the patents protecting Johnson's designs were assigned to his employer. Among his interests were 'guns' and 'firearms', beginning with US Patent 788,210 of 25 April 1905; 'magazine firearms', from US no. 597,908 of 25 January 1898 onward; and 'automatic firearms', the first being protected by 681,481 of 27 August 1901

However, he had other interests. For example, US Patent 719,808 (3 February 1903) was sought for a 'gravity charger for magazine guns'; 808,375 (26 December 1905) was granted for a 'wrought metal forearm

for tube-magazine guns'; and Patents 852,119 and 851,669 (both dating from 30 April 1907) protected a telescope-sight mount and a cartridge deflector for top-ejecting guns respectively. Robert E. Gardner, in *Small Arms Makers*, notes the grants of forty US patents between 1897 and 1908, and it is believed that ultimately the total exceeded 250; clearly Johnson is an inventor worthy of an authoritative biography.

Although responsible for improvements in tube magazines and lever actions, Thomas Johnson remains best known for the Winchester auto-loaders, beginning with the .22 rimfire M1903, which were hurriedly developed to compete with the *Browning-designed carbines promoted by *Fabrique Nationale d'Armes de Guerre.

Subsequently Johnson and Winchester's technicians refined the basic blowback action to handle centrefire ammunition, beginning

with the M1905 (.32 or .35 WSL). The most effective representative was the M1910, chambered for the .401 WSL cartridge, which was purchased in small numbers by the French for service in the First World War. Rifles of this class outlasted Johnson: the M1910 was discontinued in 1936, two years after its inventor's death, and a derivative of the M1903 (the M63) lasted until 1958.

Johnson was also responsible for the rimfire Model 52 bolt-action rifle, developed in 1919/20, which remained in production into the 1980s in an International Prone target-shooting guise. He also led the team that developed the Model 54 sporting rifle, introduced in 1925 on an action inspired by the M1903 *Springfield. It was chambered initially for the .270 Winchester and .30-06 cartridges only, but options such as 7x57 Mauser and .257 Roberts had been offered by the time the Model 54 was superseded by the Model 70 in 1936.

---

or later. *Lane Brothers provided Johnson & Willcox with notable clients. **22.** Johnson & Wright, Northampton. This English gunmaking business marked shotgun cartridges sold under the brandname County.

Johnstone. Douglas Vaughan Johnstone, Birmingham. Listed by Bailey and Nie in *English Gunmakers* at 81 Bath Street in 1891, Johnstone was involved in the formation of the abortive *Standard Small Arms Company during the First World War (by then described as an 'Engineer') and joined *Webley & Scott c. 1919. He was responsible for the development of the Webley air pistols in collaboration with John William *Fearn, under whose name the relevant patent legislation is listed.

Jo-Lo-Ar. A modified version of the *Sharp-Shooter, made in Eibar for a few years from c. 1923, this had a one-hand cocking lever (pivoted on the right side of the frame), which is said to have been the subject of Spanish patent no. 70,235, granted to José Lopez de Arnaíz. Most of the guns fitted with the cocking lever have slides marked 'PISTOLA JO-LO-AR EIBAR (ESPAÑA)' together with the two patent numbers, but often lack clues to their manufacturer. The grips are also marked 'JO.LO.AR.'; a few made, or perhaps simply sold, by *Ojanguren y Vidosa also display small white-metal 'OV' medallions.

Joker. *Suicide Special revolvers made in Connecticut, USA, in the late nineteenth century by the *Hopkins & Allen Arms Company of Norwich, and the *Marlin Fire Arms Company of New Haven.

Jones – 1. Buck Jones Special. A *Daisy BB Gun: *see* under 'B'. **2.** Charles Jones, 16 Whittall Street, Birmingham, Warwickshire. This gunmaker was granted two British Patents in the 1830s to protect a cap-lock mechanism with the hammer, tumbler and trigger made in a

single piece (no. 6394 of 1833) or, in an improved form, with the hammer and tumbler made in one unit (6436 of 1833). Guns were made until c. 1845, output is said to have included a few *pepperboxes. Jones also maintained premises in St James's Street, London, for a few years. **3.** Charles Frederick Jones, London. The marks of this English gunmaker have been reported on self-cocking pepperboxes dating from the middle of the nineteenth century. **4.** Edmund Jones, 6 Bath Street, Birmingham, Warwickshire. A gun rifler and pistol maker known to have been trading in the early 1860s, although operations may have dated back nearly thirty years. **5.** Edward Jones, Broomfield House, Perry Barr, Birmingham. This 'Engineer', employed by *Kynoch Ltd, was responsible for the breech seal of the *Swift air rifle. *See* British Patent 13,716/06 of 1906. **6.** Emanuel Jones, 3 Whittall Street and 22 Bath Street, Birmingham, Warwickshire (1860–65). This gun rifler was granted British Patent no. 3068 of 1860 to protect rifling that decreased in depth toward the breech. The patent was contested by John Bouch, and Jones was forced to file a disclaimer before his ideas could be exploited properly. **7.** Ernest W. Jones, Birmingham. A patent agent involved in the grant of British Patent 571,163 to *BSA Guns Ltd and Victor *Stohanzl. **8.** Harold Cyril Jones, Birmingham. An employee of *BSA Guns Ltd, and co-patentee of the *Scorpion air pistol. **9.** Henry Jones, Birmingham, Warwickshire. Another of the many gunmakers working in Birmingham in the middle of the nineteenth century, Jones could be found in Constitution Hill in 1855, trading from 174 Hockley Street in 1857–62, then in Key Hill until 1867 or later. He was granted at least four British Patents protecting break-open or 'drop-down barrel' guns: no. 2040 of 1859, no. 950 of 1861, no. 2395 of 1862 and no. 92 of 1870. **10.** Owen Jones, a Philadelphian 'mechanic', was responsible for some quirky revolvers (*Enfield) and a magazine-loading version of the *Martini action, tested and briefly approved in Britain. In 1885, after the magazine had been modified to eliminate the cartridge elevator, the Royal Navy ordered 5,000 Owen Jones rifles, although this total had been reduced to 2,000 long before the rifle was abandoned. **11.** Robert Jones, Liverpool, Lancashire. This English gunmaker traded successively from 27, then 32 Stanhope Street (1826–45); 9 Waterloo Road and 53 Oldhall Street (1847–54); and 32 Great Howard Street (1855–69). His marks have been reported on sporting guns, *pepperboxes and cap-lock revolvers. **12.** Samuel Jones, Birmingham. Listed variously as a gunmaker, a gun-stocker, or a gun rifler and pistol maker in 1845–61, trading first from Newtown Row, then from Bath Street. Sporting guns have been reported with his marks. **13.** Thomas W. Jones, Birmingham. Possibly the son of the gunsmith Thomas Jones of Aston Road, who traded until at least 1840, this man was recorded – often as a gun-stocker – in the 'Court of 6 Bath Street' until 1858. **14.** William Jones, Birmingham. There were two generations of these gunmakers, the son gaining control upon the retirement of his father in 1826. Premises were occupied at 2 Newton Street until 1834, then successively at 23 Lench Street (until 1852) and 75 Bath Street (until 1880). William Jones the Younger was succeeded by his son, William Palmer Jones (below). **15.** William Palmer Jones, Birmingham, Warwickshire. This gunmaker succeeded his father William Jones in 1880/81, continuing to trade from the Bath Street premises until a move to Whittall Street occurred in 1890. By 1914, the trading style had become W. Palmer Jones (Guns) Ltd. Sporting rifles were made in quantity, and shotgun cartridges were sold under such names as The Accuratus and The Priority; the components came from *Eley Bros. **16.** Jones & Sadler, Birmingham. A gunmaking partnership active in Spencer Street during the late 1860s. Nothing else is known.

Jopp. August Jopp, Albrechts bei Suhl in Thüringen, Kirchberg 29. Founded in 1850, this maker of guns, gun parts and optical-sight mounts was still being listed in 1941 as August Jopp (I).

Jordan – **1.** G. & H. Jordan, Birmingham, Warwickshire. Specialist gun-barrel makers trading from 26 Cecil Street in the mid-1850s. **2.** John L. Jordan, a lieutenant in the US Navy, accepted many of the .236 *Lee Straight Pull rifles made by the *Winchester Repeating Arms Company. Dating from the period 1896–97, usually they are marked 'JNJ'. *See also* US arms inspectors' marks.

Jørgensen. Erik Jørgensen, Denmark. *See* Krag-Jørgensen.

Joseph. Solomon Joseph & Company, a gunmakers' agent, was listed at 77 Wood Street, London E.C., in 1870–76.

Joslyn – **1.** Benjamin Franklin Joslyn, Worcester, Massachusetts, and Stonington, Connecticut. The first breech-loading rifle to be mass-produced in *Springfield Armory was a Joslyn conversion of the regulation M1863 rifle-musket, production of which began in 1865. **2.** Joslyn Fire Arms Company, Stonington, Connecticut. This gunmaking company employed a British agent –

E.H. Newby of 39a King William Street, London – while breech-loading rifles were being tested by the British Army in 1867–68. **3.** Joslyn revolvers. Benjamin Joslyn patented a 'spring clutch' and a ratchet mechanism to rotate revolver cylinders in May 1858. The first of about 1,100 .36-calibre Joslyn revolvers purchased by the Federal government during the Civil War were made by W.C. *Freeman of Worcester, but were rejected when Freeman failed to deliver them on time. Subsequently Joslyn made about 2,500 in Stonington, Connecticut, during 1861–62. They had iron trigger guards instead of the brass pattern used by Freeman. **4.** Joslyn rifles and carbines. The original, or 1855, pattern had a conventional side-hammer cap-lock. The breech lever ran back along the wrist of the stock, being lifted upward by means of a large finger ring to expose the chamber to receive a combustible paper cartridge. Steel rings in the face of the breech mechanism expanded momentarily on discharge to form a gas seal. Although the US Army was unimpressed, the US Navy ordered 500 .58 rifles from William *Freeman of New York in September 1858. Owing to problems with the sub-contractor, Asa *Waters & Company, delivery was delayed until the spring of 1861. An improved carbine, which appeared in 1861, had a laterally-hinged block, known as a 'cap', which opened to the left when the locking catch was released. A patent of addition, granted in 1862, added cam surfaces to improve cartridge seating and assure adequate primary extraction. The 1862-pattern Joslyn carbine chambered .56-52 Spencer rimfire ammunition and had brass furniture. There was a hook on the breech cap, and a single block hinge; 1864-model guns (chambered for .56-56 Spencer or special .54 Joslyn cartridges) had a chequered finger-piece beneath the breech hook, a cylindrical firing-pin shroud and iron furniture. Guns numbered above about 11000 had double-hinge breeches. The Federal ordnance purchased 860 carbines from *Bruff, Bros. & Seaver of New York City in 1861–62, but Joslyn acquired a much larger contract at the end of 1862 and began making the guns in his own Stonington factory. Total Federal purchases amounted to 11,261 carbines between 1 January 1861 until 30 June 1866.

Jourjon-Prat, rue de l'Épreuve 3, Saint-Étienne, France. Listed in 1879 as a gunmaker.

Jowett. William Jowett, an ironmonger of 3 Kingsbury, Aylesbury, Buckinghamshire, is known to have marked guns and ammunition. These included shotgun cartridges sold under the Kingsway brand.

Jox. Herbert Jox, Eisenach in Thüringen, Germany. Listed as a retailer of sporting guns and ammunition, in 1941.

Joyce – **1.** Frank Joyce, London. The co-patentee, with Newton and Rosewell, of ribbed and tapered airgun slugs made by Frederick Joyce & Company Ltd. Frank Joyce is presumed to have been the son of Frederick. *See* British Patent 24,314/01 of 1901. **2.** Frederick Joyce & Company Ltd, London. Joyce began his career in 1820 as an 'Operative Chemist', trading from 11 Old Compton Street in Soho. After perfecting a method of making non-corrosive caps, he entered a partnership with his brother, Edward, which lasted until 1834. Then he was listed alone at 55 Bartholomew Close during 1835–47, as a 'Percussion Cap & Wadding Manufacturer'; he moved to 57 Upper Thames Street, where he was listed as a car-

JOHNSON AUTOMATIC RIFLES AND MACHINE-GUNS

Johnson (18)

The prototype semi-automatic rifle appeared in 1936, about twenty guns being made by the *Marlin Firearms Company and Taft-Pierce Manufacturing Company. Some sporting-style guns had box magazines, but the military version had a detachable rotary drum that held eleven rounds. This could be loaded from standard US service-issue five-round chargers (stripper-clips).

Tests undertaken by the US Army and the USMC, often with old and well-worn Johnsons, continued until work stopped in February 1940. Johnson lacked the backing to be able to compete with the Garand on a level footing, but managed to sell a substantial quantity of .30-calibre M1941 rifles to the Netherlands Indies Army (*KNIL) in November 1940. The contract was cancelled after the Japanese invasion of the area in

1942, and the remaining guns were taken by the USMC.

Combat experience showed that the *recoil-operated Johnson was prone to jamming and barrel damage, but also that its rotary magazine was an improvement on the en-bloc clip used in the Garand. Many of the USMC guns were given to the Brazilian Army detachment sent to Europe in 1944, and a few hundred 7x57 guns were also supplied to Chile c. 1943.

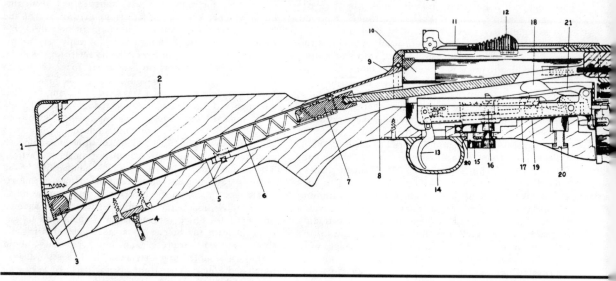

tridge manufacturer from 1852 onward. The trading style became Frederick Joyce & Company in 1864, and Frederick Joyce & Company Ltd in 1889. Additional premises were opened in Suffolk Lane, London E.C., in the 1890s. In 1907, however, the *Nobel Explosives Company took a major stake in Joyce & Company Ltd, and the business was formally integrated into its parent on 1 January 1910. Joyce's marks may be found on centrefire revolver cartridges and a variety of pin- and centrefire shotgun patterns, offered under such names as Bailey's Gas-Tight, Bonnaud, Improved Gas Tight, Joyce's D.B. Cartridge, Special Nitro and Waltham. Joyce's Solid Tapered Slugs, destined for airguns, were also made in quantity prior to 1910.

'JP', 'JPM', 'JPO'. Marks found on US military firearms and accessories. *See* John *Pope, J.P. *McGuinness, and J.P. *Oeller and James P. O'Neill respectively.

'J.P. & S.' Found in the headstamps of shotgun cartridges and blanks associated with J. *Pain & Son of Salisbury.

'JPW'. A mark found on US military firearms and accessories. *See* Joseph P. *Wells.

'JR'. An unidentified inspector's mark found on metallic-cartridge conversions of 1860-pattern Colt Army revolvers, dating from the early 1870s. *See also* J. *Reid.

'JRJR'. Associated with US military firearms and accessories. *See also* James *Rockwell, Jr.

'JRM'. Found on US military firearms and accessories. Usually identified with J.R. McGinness (*sic*); *see also* J.P. *McGuinness.

'JRMM'. A mark found on US military firearms and accessories. *See also* James R.M. *Mullaney.

'JSA', 'JSB'. Found on US military firearms and accessories. *See* James S. *Adams and J.S. *Burns.

'JSL'. A linear-type cursive monogram, with the central 'S' dominant. Found on the grips of *Spitfire pistols made in Britain in the 1990s by John Slough Ltd of Hereford.

'JT'. A mark encountered on US military firearms and accessories. *See also* John *Tatlor, Josiah *Tatnall and Jerome *Towne.

'JTB', 'JTT'. Associated with US military firearms and accessories. *See* James T. *Baden and John Taliaferro *Thompson.

'jua'. Found on small-arms and associated components made during 1941–45 by the Danube weapons and munitions factory in Budapest (Danuvia Waffen- und Munitionsfabriken AG), under contract to the German government.

Juaristi. Armas Juaristi, Eibar, Guipúzcoa, Spain. A manufacturer of spring-airguns for sporting and target use, Juaristi was making three rifles in 1980 – the *Ideal Extra and two patterns of the *Super-Especial.

Jubala. Another of the many 6.35mm-calibre

Derived from the semi-automatic rifle, the recoil-operated Johnson light machine-gun was developed in 1937–38, when at least one prototype was made by *Marlin, and tested extensively by the US Army at the end of 1941. As the specification had called for belt-feed and as the gun had only marginal reserves of power, the Johnson was rejected; similarly, trials undertaken in 1942 by the Infantry Board, Fort Benning, had little effect.

However, a few Johnson machine-guns were issued in Italy in 1942 to the First Special Service Force, and others were used in the Pacific by the Marines. The 1941-pattern Johnson weighed less than 13lb and had a twenty-round magazine, protruding laterally, which could accept single rounds or five-round chargers.

An altered M1944, with a monopod beneath the fore-end, was not perfected until the war in Europe had ended. Johnson Automatics Trust sold production rights to Israel in the late 1940s, allowing the *Dror to be made in small numbers.

The .30-calibre Johnson semi-automatic rifle was an interesting recoil-operated design with a rotary magazine that could be replenished from ordinary five-round stripper clips. However, although used in small numbers by Dutch colonial forces and the USMC, the Johnson failed to challenge the supremacy of the sturdier Garand.

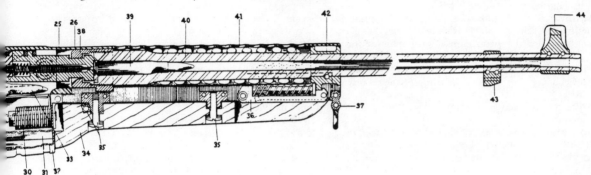

Browning-type pocket semi-automatics marked by Fabrique d'Armes de *Grande Précision of Eibar, Guipúzcoa, Spain. These particular guns have six-round box magazines and hammer-type firing mechanisms. They are said to have been made by *Larranaga y Elartza of Eibar.

'Jubilee' [The]. Associated with shotgun ammunition made by the *Midland Gun Company of Birmingham, Warwickshire, England. Also sometimes associated with cartridges (probably made by the Midland Gun Company) handled by John *Dickson of Edinburgh. The name is said to have commemorated the Silver Jubilee of George V and would, therefore, date from post-1935.

Judd. C.F. Judd, acting on behalf of the Federal Army, accepted firearms and accessories during the American Civil War. Distinguished by 'CFJ' marks, his work seems to have been confined to 1863. *See also* US arms inspectors' marks.

Judenflinte (Jewish Rifle). The *Judenflinten-Affäre* was a scandal affecting the German Army in the early 1890s, linking failures of *Reichsgewehre to manufacture by Jewish-owned companies. Rumours concerning breech explosions began to circulate almost as soon as the guns had entered service, and it was widely believed that Paul *Mauser had been spurned by the army authorities. Hermann Ahlwardt, a Berlin schoolmaster, asserted that Ludwig *Loewe & Cie had bribed government arms inspectors to accept inferior workmanship and was deliberately attempting to undermine the German Army. As the Loewe family and Max Duttenhofer (owner of the Rottweil propellant-making factory) were Jewish, the underlying motive was nothing more than anti-Semitism. Right-wing factions in the army and the business community all had reasons for backing the libel, and, as the story was gleefully exploited by the press, the Reichsgewehr gained the sobriquet *Judenflinte*.

Juhasz. Elek Juhasz made one of the few attempts to develop a self-defence sleeve gun, which was patented in the USA in August 1929. The barrel of the pistol, attached to the forearm by elasticated straps, unscrewed to load a single .30-calibre centrefire cartridge. The spring-loaded striker was cocked manually, then fired by a lanyard running from the trigger to a ring slipped around a finger. The firer only had to raise his hand to fire the gun.

Jülich – 1. A. Jülich, Zella-Mehlis in Thüringen, Germany. Listed in the 1930 edition of the *Deutsches Reichs-Adressbuch* as a retailer of guns and ammunition, but possibly also maintaining repair facilities. **2.** M. Jülich, Zella-Mehlis in Thüringen. Listed in Germany in 1920 as a weapon maker.

Jumbo. A small German 4.5mm-calibre spring-and-piston air pistol with concentric barrel/cylinder construction, cocked by pivoting the barrel unit up and forward. It was introduced in 1982 by Fritz *Barthelmes KG. The Jumbo Target of 1983 was identical apart from an adjustable back sight.

Jung – 1. Fr. Jung, Suhl in Thüringen, Germany. A weapon maker trading in 1930. **2.** Friedrich Jung & Söhne, Suhl in Thüringen. This German gunmaking business was owned in 1900 by Oskar Jung, and by Hugo Jung in 1914–30. The tradename Jungsohn was used. **3.** Fritz Jung, Suhl in Thüringen. This gunmaker advertised himself in the 1925 *Deutsches Reichs-Adressbuch* as a specialist maker of air pistols, although cartridge guns have also been reported with his marks. Perhaps the same as Fr. Jung (above), listed in Suhl in 1930. **4.** Richard Jung, Suhl in Thüringen. *See* Greifelt & Co.

Junghans & Kriegeskorte, Stuttgart-Hedelfingen. Sometimes identified only by the brandname Jungkort (which was also the partnership's telegraphic address), this gunmaking business also maintained branches in Stettin and Suhl between the world wars. Operations began again after 1945, under the name *Kriegeskorte & Co. (Krico).

Jungkort. A tradename used by *Junghans & Kriegeskorte.

Jung Roland. This mark is believed to have been used c. 1952–55 by Waffen-Jung of Stuttgart on spring-air guns. Made elsewhere, these had probably been in store since the end of the Second World War.

Jungsohn. A mark used on sporting guns made by Friedrich Jung & Söhne of Suhl.

Junior – 1. Applied to a compact 6.35mm semi-automatic pistol made in the Republic of South Africa by the *Pretoria Arms Factory. **2.** A simple .177-calibre barrel-cocking spring-and-piston air pistol, usually a smooth-bore, made in Britain by *Webley & Scott. The Mark 2 version was abandoned in 1977. **3.** Or Junior Colt. Offered by *Colt's Patent Fire Arms Manufacturing Company and the Firearms Division of *Colt Industries between 1958 and 1973, this was a .22 rimfire or .25 centrefire simplication of the original .25 *Hammerless Pocket Model with an exposed hammer; the original grip safety was omitted. The guns were made in Spain by *Astra–Unceta y Cia until 1968 and imported into the USA; guns dating from 1970–73, however, were made by *Firearms International. **4.** Or Junior Pump Gun. An

unsuccessful sixty-shot *BB Gun made by *Daisy in 1932–34, lacking mechanical advantage in the cocking mechanism and notoriously difficult to use. **5.** A lever-action repeating *BB Gun designed by Elmer E. *Bailey and made for a few years from c. 1893 by either the W.G. *Smith Company or *Heilprin.

'Juno' [The]. Found on a shotgun cartridge made by *Eley Bros. prior to the acquisition of the company by Explosives Trades Ltd in 1918.

Jupiter – 1. A name associated with a small seven-shot 5.5mm *Velo-Dog double-action revolver with a swinging ejector and a folding trigger, made in Belgium by Auguste *Francotte et Cie of Liège prior to 1914. **2.** This hammer-fired 6.35mm Browning-type pocket pistol is usually attributed to Fabrique d'Armes de *Grande Précision, of Eibar, Guipúzcoa, Spain, but may have been made elsewhere in Eibar. A seven-round box magazine was standard.

Just – 1. August Just, Suhl in Thüringen. Trading in Germany in 1939 as a gun-stocker. **2.** E. Just, Suhl in Thüringen. Listed as a barrel-blank maker in the *Deutsches Reichs-Adressbuch*, 1939. **3.** Hermann Just, Suhl in Thüringen. A specialist German gun-stocker, working in Suhl in 1939.

'jvb'. A mark found on German optical equipment made during the Second World War by Wessel & Müller of Lückenwalde.

'jve'. Found on telescope sights and associated components made during 1940–45 by Ernst Ludwig of Weixdorf in Sachsen, Germany.

'JW', 'JWA'. Found on US military firearms and accessories. *See* John *Wilder and John *Williamson, and J.W. *Alden respectively.

'J.W.G.' [The]. This mark is associated with shotgun cartridges loaded in Britain for *Clarke & Dyke.

'jwh'. Allocated in 1941 to the French government ordnance factory in *Châtellerault, this mark was applied to small-arms components made under German supervision until 1944.

'JWK', 'JWM', 'JWP', 'JWR'. Marks found on US military firearms and accessories. *See* John W. *Keene and John W. *Kelly; James W. *McCoy; J.W. *Porter; and James W. *Reilly and James W. *Ripley respectively.

'JY'. A mark found on US military firearms and accessories. *See* Jonathan *Young.

Jyväskylä arms factory. *See* Mosin-Nagant.

K

'k', 'K' – 1. Found as 'k' on small-arms components made in Germany during the Second World War by *Luck & Wagner of Suhl. **2.** Found as 'K', crowned. A mark found on Norwegian military firearms made by *Kongsberg Våpenfabrikk. **3.** Encircled. Found on miniature revolvers made in the USA prior to 1910 by Henry M. Kolb.

'Kaba', 'KaBa', 'Ka-Ba', 'KA-BA' – 1. Marks associated with Karl *Bauer of Berlin, a distributor of guns and ammunition. Bauer imported 6.35mm *Browning-type pocket pistols from Spain, and also sold Kaba patterns, which seem to have been the work of August *Menz. **2.** Kaba Spezial. A small Browning-type 6.35mm automatic pistol made in Spain by Francisco *Arizmendi of Eibar for Karl Bauer of Berlin: six rounds, striker fired.

Kabakov. Yevgeniy Kabakov. Co-designer with Irinarkh *Komaritskiy of the sight-hood bayonet issued with the perfected or 1930-pattern Soviet *Mosin-Nagant rifle.

Kadet, Kadet Army Gun. *See* King Kadet.

Kaduna arms factory. This is the principal Nigerian manufactory responsible for local adaptations to *Garand and FN *FAL rifles.

Kahl. Rob. Kahl, Suhl in Thüringen, Germany. Listed in the 1939 directories as a gunsmith. Perhaps a misprint for 'Karl' (*see below*).

Kalamazoo Air Pistol. A spring-air pistol patented by E.H. *Hawley and made by *Snowe & Cowe of New Haven, Connecticut, USA.

Kalashnikov – 1. Mikhail Timofeyevich Kalashnikov was born into a peasant family in the village of Kurya in 1919. After working as a clerk on the Turkestan-Siberia railway, he was drafted into the army in 1938 and sent to a tank regiment. There he showed his potential as a technician, but was severely wounded in combat near Bryansk in October 1941 and returned to Alma-Ata to convalesce. While recovering, he developed the ideas that led first to an unsuccessful submachine-gun, then to the eponymous *Avtomat. The success of the AK and its derivatives has not only brought Kalashnikov recognition in the form of countless state prizes, orders, medals and a doctorate of technical sciences, but also ensured that his name has entered common currency. However, quite how much of the Kalashnikov story is fact, how much is due to specialist advisers brought in to perfect ideas, and how much is due to the Soviet propaganda machine ('self-taught hero baffles arms experts.') remains unclear. Much of the biographical material has been accepted uncritically by Western writers, even by the late Ed Ezell in *The AK-47* (Stackpole Books, 1976), which nevertheless remains the best source of information. **2.** Kalashnikov assault rifle: *see* panel, pp. 276/77. **3.** Kalashnikov machine-guns. There are two basic patterns of these: the heavy assault rifle (RPK) derived directly from the *Avtomat Kalashnikova*, and the sustained-fire belt-fed weapons of the PK series.

Introduced in 1961 on the basis of the AKM, the RPK light machine-gun, or *Ruchnoi Pulemet Kalashnikova* has a long barrel, a drum magazine, a bipod and a deep-belly butt inspired by the *Degtyarev RPD. Comparable light support weapons have also been made in Hungary, Romania and the German Democratic Republic (the latter as the LMG-K). The RPKS, *Ruchnoi Pulemet Kalashnikova skladyvayushimsya prikladom* ('РПКС' in Cyrillic), had a butt that could be folded to the left. The original 7.62mm RPK was replaced in the mid-1970s by the 5.45mm RPK-74. The RPK-74N ('РПК-74Н' in Cyrillic) was similar, but had an additional sight rail on the receiver – now standardised – and the RPKS-74 had a folding butt; RPKS-74N ('РПКС-74Н' in Cyrillic) had a night-sight rail and a folding butt. Derivatives of the RPK have included the Finnish 7.62x39 and 7.62x51 *Valmet m/78, and a variety of Yugoslavian guns – M65A (fixed barrel) and M65B (detachable barrel) on the basis of the AK, followed by the M72, M72B1 (fixed butt), M72AB1 (folding butt) and the M77B1, based on an AKM-inspired stamped receiver. The Iraqui 'Al Quds light machine-gun was copied from the Yugoslavian M72B1, while North Korea once made a TUL-1 by combining the mechanism of the Type 58 (AK) assault rifle and the barrel, bipod and drum magazine of the RPD. The belt-fed PK, *Pulemet Kalashnikova*, was developed in the late 1950s to compete with the *Nikitin-Sokolov (NS) design. The operating system and rotating-bolt locking mechanism were based on the AK/RPK series, although the design of the receiver was very different. The 7.62x54R cartridges had to be withdrawn from the feed belt before they could be rammed into the chamber, but field trials showed that the PK prototypes performed better than the NS, and the Kalashnikov general-purpose machine-gun was adopted in 1961. It was issued with a bipod, as a light machine-gun (PK) or with a tripod as the *Stankoviy Pulemet Kalashnikova* (PKS). The original *Samozhenkov tripod was replaced in 1969 by the smaller *Stepanov pattern. The PKB, developed for use in vehicles, had distinctive spade grips; the PKT, destined for tanks (*tankoviy*) and armoured cars, had a solenoid firing mechanism instead of a mechanical trigger. The original guns were replaced in the late 1960s by modernised (*modernizirovanniy*) patterns: PKM, PKSM, and their vehicle (PKMB) and tank (PKMT) derivatives. All can be recognised by greater use of stamped components, and by their fluted barrels. **4.** Kalashnikov selector markings. Soviet and Russian guns display 'AB' above 'ОД'; Bulgarian guns are similar, with the exception of 'ЕД' in the lower position. German products are marked 'D' over 'E'; Hungarian examples display '∞' over '1'; Polish products have 'C' above 'P'; Romanian guns have 'S' above 'FA' above 'FF'; and Yugoslavian examples are usually marked 'U' above 'R' above 'J'. Chinese and North Korean Kalashnikovs will usually display ideo-

KALASHNIKOV ASSAULT RIFLE

Kalashnikov (2)

Adopted in 1949, after trials lasting several years, this has since become one of the world's best-known weapons. Chambered for a 7.62mm short-case intermediate cartridge inspired by the German 7.9mm Kurz type, the *gas-operated AK is locked by rotating lugs on the bolt head clockwise into the receiver walls; feed is from a detachable box magazine ahead of the trigger guard. The hammer-type firing system shows some *Garand features and usually allows single shots or automatic fire.

Marks on the selector lever (q.v.) often help to determine origin, as the Kalashnikov has been made in many countries. The *Avtomat Kalashnikova obr. 1947g* (AK or AK-47) has a slab-sided receiver, a separate butt and pistol grip, a gas tube above the barrel and a detachable magazine ahead of the trigger guard. Guns dating from the period 1948–51 were made largely of weldings, stampings and pressed-metal components, but later a change to receivers machined from forged-steel billets was made – possibly when production began in Izhevsk – and an extension, or 'shoe', was added to the receiver to accept the butt. On the perfected model, made from 1954 onward, the butt attaches directly with a tongue that enters the receiver body.

Derivatives of the standard fixed-butt Kalashnikov include the Bulgarian *Avtomaticheskiy Karabin Kalashnikova*, or AKK and AKK-M1 (with an additional grenade launcher); the Chinese Type 56; the MPi-K, or *Maschinenpistolen Kalashnikow*, made in the German Democratic Republic; the Hungarian AK-55 assault rifle, *or Automat Kalashnikov AK-55*; the North Korean Type 58; and the Polish PMK (*Pistolet Maszynowy*

Kalasznikow) and PMK-DGN (grenade-launching). The Romanian forces used an AK copy as the AI, whereas the Yugoslavians had the M64 and M64A (M70) rifles.

The AKS, *Avtomat Kalashnikova skladyvayushimsya prikladom obr. 1947g* ('AKC' or 'AKC-47' in Cyrillic), is essentially similar to the AK, but its pressed-steel butt folds down under the receiver. Folding-stock patterns include the Bulgarian AKKS, the Chinese Type 56-1, the GDR MPi-KS, the Polish PMK-S, and the Yugoslav M64B and M70A.

The AK was replaced in Soviet service in 1959 by the simplified AKM, *Avtomat Kalashnikova Modernizirovanniya*, with a pressed-steel receiver, a stamped bolt cover with reinforcing ribs and a rate-reducer in the trigger system. Fixed-butt AKM derivatives include the Bulgarian AKKM and AKKMS; post-1963 versions of the Chinese Type 56; the Egyptian Misr; the German Democratic Republic MPi-KM; the Hungarian AKM-63; the Iraqi Tabuk; the North Korean Type 68; the Polish PMKM; and the Romanian AIM. The Yugoslav M70B1 was inspired by the AKM, although details vary, and N-suffix guns can accept optical and electro-optical sights. *Zavodi Crvena Zastava has also made 7.62x51 M77B1 assault and M77 sniper-rifle Kalashnikovs, in addition to an M76 sniper rifle (*Poluautomatska puska vz. 76*) in 7.62x51 and 7.92x57.

The AKMS, *Avtomat Kalashnikova Modernizirovanniya, skladyvayushimsya prikladom* ('AKMC' in Cyrillic), is simply an AKM with a folding metal butt. Among other folding-butt guns are the Bulgarian AKKMS; post-1963 versions of the Chinese Types 56-1 (under-folding butt), 56-2 (side-folding butt with insert) and 56-C Compact (side-folding butt); the GDR MPi-KMS (under-folding

butt) and MPi-KMS 72 (side-folding butt); the Hungarian AMD-65 submachine-gun; the Polish PMKM-S; and the Yugoslav/Serbian M70AB2.

Both the Bulgarian Arsenal and the Polish factory in Radom make semi-automatic sporting/security versions of the Kalashnikov with one-piece wood stocks, the Polish gun being sold commercially as the *Radom Hunter. The Romanian factory in Cugir has made the 7.62x54R FPK, a sniper rifle with a *Dragunov-style skeleton butt and a modified AIM-type Kalashnikov action.

A desire to improve the performance of the AKM, particularly in comparison to the US 5.56x45 M16 (*ArmaLite) rifle, led to the introduction in 1973 of a 5.45x39 cartridge containing a bullet with a multi-part core. The AK-74 (*Avtomat Kalashnikova obr. 74*), instantly recognisable by a large cylindrical muzzle-brake/compensator, appeared in the mid-1970s to replace the AKM. Eventually butts, fore-ends and hand guards, once made of laminated wood or resin-impregnated wood fibres, became injection-moulded plastic. Longitudinal grooves cut into the butt enabled the calibre to be identified by touch. AK-74N ('AK-74H' in Cyrillic) have sight-mounting brackets on the left side.

The Russian *Izhmash factory has made a 7.62x39 version of the AK-74, designated AK-103. Fixed-butt AK-74 (5.45x39) derivatives include the Model 3, a bullpup version made in the Armenian Republic; the Bulgarian AKK-74; the Chinese Type 81; the Hungarian NGM-81; and the Romanian AI-74. Essentially similar are the fixed-butt AK-74 derivatives chambering the US 5.56x45 cartridge: the Chinese Type 81 and Type 86 bullpup; the Croatian APS-95; the Hungarian NGM; the Romanian AI-74; and the Yugoslav/Serbian M80.

---

graphs, although some Chinese export examples will be found marked 'L' over 'D'. Among Kalashnikov derivatives, the Finnish guns are customarily marked '•••' above '•', whereas Israeli Galils and their South African equivalents are marked 'S' over 'A' over 'R', with the marks repeated on the left side, above the pistol grip. **5.** Kalashnikov submachine-guns. The AKMS-U, or *Avtomat Kalashnikova Modificatsionniya skladyvayushimsya*

prikladom, ustankova obraztsa, was made in the Tula ordnance factory. Known as 'AKMC-У' in Cyrillic, it was the successful entrant in a competition to find a port-firing weapon for use in armoured personnel carriers (*samokhodnaya ustankova*); it has also been called AKR and 'Krinkov', apparently after the leader of the design team. It had a folding butt, a two-position back sight and a short wooden thumb-hole fore-end. The AKS-74U (*Avtomat*

Folding-butt derivatives of the 5.45mm AK-74 include the Soviet AKS-74, *Avtomat Kalashnikova skladyvayushimsya prikladom obr. 74* ('AKC-74' in Cyrillic), with a triangular skeleton butt folding to the left; and the AKS-74N ('AKC-74H' in Cyrillic), with an optical-sight mount and a folding butt.

The AK-74M (1987–92) had a modified receiver with an integral sight rail, a solid butt that swung to the left, plastic furniture and an improved muzzle-brake/compensator. It was entered in the ★Abakan competition, but the AN-94 ★Nikonov rifle was preferred.

Other folding-butt 5.45mm guns include the Bulgarian AKKS-74; the Chinese Type 81-1; the GDR MPi-K 74; the Polish KA-88 Tantal rifle; and the Romanian AIS-74. Essentially similar guns chambering the US 5.56x45 cartridge have been the Chinese Type 81-1; the Croatian APS-95; the Polish KA-90 Tantal and KA-96 Beryl; the Romanian AIS-74; the Russian AK-101; and the Yugoslav/Serbian M80A.

Kalashnikov-type rifles have emanated from many Soviet-bloc countries. Manufacturers have included the Soviet small-arms factories in ★Tula and ★Izhevsk (the latter now trading as Izhmash A/O); the Bulgarian Arsenal; several factories in the People's Republic of China; Factory No. 54 of ★Maadi Military & Civil Industries Company; VEB Fahrzeug- und Waffenfabik 'Ernst Thälmann' in Suhl, in the German Democratic Republic; ★Fegyver é Gázkészülékgyár (FÉG) in Budapest; the Iraqi Mosalsalasi ordnance factory; a state-owned factory in North Korea; ★Zaklady Metalowe Łucznik of Radom, Poland; the Romanian ordnance factory in Cugir; and the Yugoslav/Serbian state firearms factory in Kraguyevač – Zavodi ★Crvena Zastava (ZCZ).

Finnish ★Sako and ★Valmet assault rifles, and the Israeli ★Galil, even though they have developed along independent lines, all derive from the Kalashnikov.

Among the best sources of information about the Kalashnikov are *The AK-47* by Edward C. Ezell (Stackpole Books, 1976), and *The Kalashnikov* by John Walter (Greenhill Military Manual series, 1999).

Typical of the Kalashnikov clones is this Israeli 5.56mm Galil SAR, showing many of the accessories to be expected with a modern assault rifle: a bayonet, rifle grenades, an optical-sight mount and a whole range of magazines.

Kalashnikova skladyvayushimsya prikladom obr. 1974g ustanovka obratsza), made in ★Tula until 1997, was a short-barrelled AK-74 destined for commandos, communication teams, sappers, tank drivers, rocket-launcher crews and special police units. It has a special back sight and a folding open-triangle butt. The AKS-74UN ('AKC-74УH' in Cyrillic) could accept a passive infra-red sight, and the AKS-74UB had a semi-integral silencer attached to its shortened barrel. ★Izhmash now makes compact AK-74M derivatives as the 5.56mm AK-102, the 7.62mm AK-104 and the 5.45mm AK-105. The AKT was a short-lived experimental adaptation of the Kalashnikov entered by the Tula factory in the ★Abakan trials. Among other submachine-guns based on the Kalashnikov assault rifle are the Polish KA-91 Onyx and KbkA-96 ★Mini-Beryl patterns, and the Romanian AIR.

Kalinowski. An Oberst (colonel) in the Prussian Army, Wilhelm von Kalinowski chaired the committee responsible for the perfection of the 11mm centrefire Reichspatrone and the extractor of the 1871-type *Mauser rifle.

'kam'. Used by the Skarzysko-Kamienna (Poland) factory of Hugo Schneider AG (Hasag Eisen- und Metallwerke GmbH) on small-arms ammunition and components made under German control in 1942–45.

Kane. Henry Kane, a US government inspector, was responsible for the acceptance of firearms and ammunition in 1902. Kane's 'HK' identifier can be distinguished from that of Henry *Kirk by date. See also US arms inspectors' marks.

Kantany. Christo W. Kantany, a civilian in the pay of the US government, accepted *Colt-made 5.56mm M16 and M16A1 rifles in 1966–68. They were marked 'CWK'. See also US arms inspectors' marks.

Kapp. Alfred Kapp, Sisterdale, Texas, Confederate States of America. This farmer made about twenty copies of the *Remington-Beals revolvers during the American Civil War, entirely by hand.

Karcher. Arthur A. Karcher, often listed as Karchin, Chicago. The designer of the *Sterling lever-action BB Gun, protected by US Patent 1,101,698 of 30 June 1914.

'Kardax' [The]. A brandname associated with shotgun cartridges made in Britain by *Nobel Explosives Ltd of Glasgow. They date prior to 1918 and the purchase by Explosives Trades Ltd.

Karl, see also Carl – **1.** Rob. Karl, Suhl in Thüringen, Germany. Trading as a gunsmith, 1930. **2.** Karl Salvator. Born in Florence in April 1839, Erzherzog (Archduke) Karl Salvator was the younger brother of Emperor Franz Josef of Austria-Hungary. Entering the Austrian Army in 1858, he attained the rank of generalmajor in 1876 and generalfeldmarschall in 1886. An interest in small-arms design led to collaboration with Georg, Ritter von *Dormus in the design of an embryonic pistol and the *Škoda machine-gun. Karl Salvator died in Vienna in January 1892, before the Škoda gun had even completed its trials.

Kaspar & Kruger GmbH, Niederlassung Suhl. The marks of this German wholesaler, founded in 1875, will be encountered on guns, ammunition and accessories dating prior to 1939.

Kassnar Imports, Inc., Harrisburg, Pennsylvania, USA. This distributor of sporting guns, ammunition and accessories has handled *Sabatti bolt-action rifles under the Churchill brandname. The Churchill *Highlander and Churchill *Regent were the standard and deluxe versions of the Sabatti *Rover.

Kaufmann. Michael Kaufmann, Britain. See Webley.

Kautzky. Joseph Kautzky, Fort Dodge, Iowa. This Austrian-born gunsmith patented a single-trigger mechanism in the USA on 31 July 1906 (no. 827,242). A variation of this system was used after 1918 on some of the shotguns made by the A.H. *Fox Gun Company of Philadelphia.

Kavanagh. W. Kavanagh & Son, Dublin, Ireland (Eire). The name of this gunmaker has been reported on sporting guns and shotgun cartridges sold under the brandnames Ideal and Mirus.

Kawaguchiya Firearms Company, Tokyo and Osaka, Japan. A manufacturer of air rifles styled on the pre-war BSA patterns during the early 1950s, and of a modernised version thereafter under the designation SKB M53. The company still makes shotguns and cartridge rifles, but airgun production seems to have ceased. White Eagle pellets were also made. See also Asahi.

Kayaba Kogyo, Tokyo, Japan. Recruited as a maker of Type 99 *Arisaka rifles, c. 1940. Production lasted only until 1942.

'KB', 'K B', K...B'. These *headstamps were associated with the products of *Kynoch Ltd, Birmingham. They are customarily confined to shotgun and sporting-rifle ammunition. See also 'K'.

'K.C. [The]'. Encountered on shotgun cartridges loaded by *Coltman of Burton upon Trent, Nottinghamshire, England.

KDF, Inc. See Voere.

'kdj'. This mark will be found on small-arms ammunition made under contract to the German authorities by Ungarnische Metallplattenindustrie of Budapest during the Second World War.

Kedr. A compact Soviet 9x18 submachine-gun designed by the son of Evgeniy Dragunov and made by the Klin-Zlatoust engineering factory. It has a pressed-steel receiver, a projecting barrel and a twenty- or thirty-round box magazine running up through the pistol grip. The butt folds forward over the receiver.

Keegan. L. Keegan, 3 Inns Quay, Dublin, Ireland (Eire). The name of this gunmaker has been reported on sporting guns and shotgun cartridges sold prior to the First World War under the name Faugh-a-Ballagh.

Keeler. Samuel Keeler accepted *Dragoon-type revolvers made for the US Army in 1848–52 by *Colt's Patent Fire Arms Manufacturing Company, marking them 'SK'. This can be confused with a similar marking found on single-shot pistols made by *Aston, which allegedly was applied by an inspector named S. *Knows prior to 1848. See also US arms inspectors' marks.

Keen – 1. Job Keen. Listed in 1813 as a gun-stock maker and supplier of walnut blanks, Job had become a gunmaker by 1820. At the time, he was working from 61 Gloucester Street, Commercial Road, London E., but was succeeded (possibly upon his death) by Job Keen, Junior in 1849. The younger Keen continued trading under his own name until 1855, but then took his own son into partnership and continued as Job Keen & Son until about 1866. **2.** See Curry & Keen.

Keene – 1. James Keene, Newark, New Jersey. Patentee of the *Remington-Keene bolt-action rifle, 1874–77. **2.** John W. Keene, working on behalf of the Federal Army, accepted firearms and accessories during the American Civil War. His work – identified by 'JWK' marks – can be difficult to distinguish from that of John W. *Kelly, but seems to have been confined to 1862–64. See also US arms inspectors' marks.

Keeper, Keeper's – 1. Usually found as 'The Keeper' on shotgun ammunition made in England by the *Midland Gun Company of Birmingham. **2.** 'Keeper's Normal' [The]. A mark found on shotgun ammunition made, or perhaps simply assembled in Britain, by the *Normal Improved Ammunition Company of Hendon.

Kehl. F. Kehl, Zella-Mehlis in Thüringen, Germany. Listed in 1930 as a master gunsmith.

Keiner. Hugo Keiner, Heidersbach bei Suhl, Germany. Listed in 1925 as a gunmaker specialising in 'sporting and high-quality guns, *Drillinge and double-barrelled shotguns'. Trading ceased in 1929.

Kelber – 1. Gebr. Kelber, Suhl in Thüringen, Germany. This gun-barrel-making partnership of Rud., Louis & Wilhelm Kelber appeared in the directories for 1914–20. **2.** Louis Kelber, Suhl in Thüringen, Trübenbachstrasse 1. Listed in 1935–40 as a specialist gun-barrel maker. **3.** Wilh. Kelber, Suhl in Thüringen, Beiersgrund 3 (1940). A gun-barrel-making business owned in 1939, according to the *Deutsches Reichs-Adressbuch* by Wilhelm and Erich Kelber. Listed in 1940 as a specialist manufacturer of gun barrels and automatic barrel-blank drawing machinery.

Kell. Charles Aylett Kell, London. The marks of this gunmaker have been reported on self-cocking *pepperboxes dating from the middle of the nineteenth century.

Keller – 1. Edmund Keller, Zella-Mehlis in Thüringen, Germany. Listed in 1939 as a gun-barrel drawer. **2.** Heinrich Keller, Heidersbach bei Suhl in Thüringen. Listed as a gunmaker in German trade directories. **3.** P. Keller, a government inspector using a 'PK' mark, accepted guns and accessories for the US Army in the early 1900s. *See also* US arms inspectors' marks. **4.** Rudolf Keller, Suhl in Thüringen. A specialist gun-stocker active in Germany in 1939.

Kelly. John W. Kelly, a lieutenant in the US and Federal Navies, accepted a variety of firearms from the mid-1850s until the end of the American Civil War. They included *Remington and *Starr revolvers, although Kelly's 'JWK' may sometimes be difficult to distinguish from the similar mark applied to army-issue guns by John W. *Keene. *See also* US arms inspectors' marks.

'Kelor' [The]. This mark will be found on shotgun cartridges handled by *Cogswell & Harrison.

Kelsey. E.M. Kelsey accepted firearms and accessories on behalf of the US Army, marking them 'EMK'. Apparently his work was confined to 1904–06. *See also* US arms inspectors' marks.

Kemp – 1. Joseph Kemp. A gunmaker trading in London successively from Charlotte Street, 115 Jermyn Street and 31 Duke Street, Grosvenor Square. No entries seem to have been made in directories published after 1850, but it is possible that Joseph Kemp was a partner in Kemp Bros. (below). **2.** Kemp Bros. Listed as members of the English gun trade in 1859–60, trading from Iron Bridge Wharf, Barking Road, and 20½ King Street, Tower Hill, London E. **3.** Kemp, Leddall & Company. This gunsmithing business – listed at 41 London Wall, E.C., in 1860–62 – may have been a successor to Kemp Bros. (above).

Kempe. Adalbert Kempe, Olbernhau in Sachsen, Germany. The designer of an air rifle with a sliding barrel (1887/8), and an earlier gun of unknown form (c. 1885), Kempe's exploits were significant enough to be recorded in *Der Waffenschmied*.

'Kendal', 'Kendal Castle' [The]. Marks found on shotgun cartridges sold by T. *Atkinson & Sons of Kendal, Cumberland, England.

Kennedy. Samuel Kennedy, USA. *See* Burgess.

Kennett – 1. Sometimes listed as Kennet. A British barrel-cocking spring-air rifle designed in 1947 and apparently distributed by L. *Le Pesonne & Company Ltd. Advertised in 1948 in .177 (4.5mm), but nothing else is known. **2.** Usually encountered as 'The Kennett' on shotgun cartridges sold by *James & Company of Hungerford.

Kent – 1. Usually as 'The Kent': found on shotgun cartridges sold in northern England by T. *Atkinson & Sons of Kendal, Cumberland. **2.** Alfred Kent & Son, Wantage, Berkshire (Oxfordshire). This English 'Wholesale & Retail Furnishing & General Ironmonger, Lamp & Oil Merchant' handled 'Guns and Rook Rifles for Sale and Hire, and every Requisite for Shooting' – including *Kynoch and *Eley-Kynoch shotgun cartridges sold under the brandname Wantage.

Kentucky. Found on *Suicide Special revolvers made by *Johnson, Bye & Company and/or *Iver Johnson of Worcester and Fitchburg, Massachusetts, USA, in the late nineteenth century.

Kernan. E.J. Kernan, a government inspector, accepted firearms and accessories into the US Army; distinguished by 'EJK' marks, they all dated from the period 1909–10. *See also* US arms inspectors' marks.

Kerner – 1. Emil Kerner, Suhl in Thüringen, Germany. Listed as a gunmaker, 1914–20, and as a gunsmith in 1930 – perhaps Emil Kerner the Elder. **2.** Emil Kerner & Sohn, Suhl in Thüringen. Founded in 1890, this business was advertising in 1925 as a maker of 'first-class hunting and sporting guns...target rifles, automatic pistols, hunting accessories, and loading equipment for export to all parts of the globe'. By 1930, however, it was owned by A. Schlott and seems to have disappeared in the mid-1930s; no mention is made of Kerner in the 1939 *Deutsches Reichs-Adressbuch*. **3.** Ernst Kerner & Co., Suhl in Thüringen, Mauerstrasse 3 (1940). A gunmaking business founded in 1892 and still operating in Germany in 1930, by then under the ownership of J. Viereck; listed as Ernst Kerner KG, gunmaker, by 1939. Trading ceased at the end of the Second World War. **4.** Ernst Robert Kerner, Suhl in Thüringen. A gunmaking business active in Germany prior to 1920, possibly the precursor of Ernst Kerner & Co. (above). **5.** Gebrüder Kerner, Suhl in Thüringen. Listed as a gunsmith in 1920, when owned by Ernst & Karl Kerner. **6.** Rudolf Kerner & Co., Suhl in Thüringen. This metalware manufacturer also sold sporting guns and ammunition, probably made elsewhere. Active in 1941. **7.** Kerner & Funk, Suhl in Thüringen, Germany. Active as a gunmaking partnership in 1920 under the supervision of Ernst Kerner & Karl Funk.

Kerr – 1. Charles Kerr, Stranraer, Wigtownshire. This Scottish gunmaker handled sporting guns and shooting accessories, as well as shotgun cartridges sold under the brandname Royal. **2.** Herbert W. Kerr, a a US government employee, accepted pistols and other military firearms made in 1940 by *Colt's Patent Fire Arms Manufacturing Company. They bore 'HWK' identifiers. *See also* US arms inspectors' marks. **3.** James Kerr. Grantee of US Patent 17,044 of 14 April 1857, protecting a hinged rammer commonly encountered on *Beaumont-Adams revolvers. **4.** James Kerr & Company Ltd, also the London Armoury Company or L.A. Co. (Britain), London. Formed by James and John Kerr in 1854, and trading until about 1894. Maker of cap-lock revolvers, sporting guns and apparently air canes, at 54 King William Street, London Bridge. This business was founded by John Kerr and Robert & John Adams on the dissolution of *Deane, Adams & Deane, to make Beaumont-Adams and Kerr cap-lock revolvers. Kerr was listed separately in some London directories from 1870 until 1894, although premises were shared with the LAC.

Kerridge. Henry Edward Kerridge, Great Yarmouth, Norfolk. Marks applied by this English gunmaker have been found on sporting guns and shotgun cartridges sold under the brandname East Anglian.

Kesselring. Richard Kesselring, Suhl in Thüringen, Germany. Listed as a gunsmith in the *Deutsches Reichs-Adressbuch*, 1939.

Kessler, Keßler – 1. A. Kessler, Suhl in Thüringen, Germany. Trading in 1930 as a gunmaker; listed by 1939 as Albin Kessler, Nachf., gunsmith. **2.** Fritz A. Kessler, Suhl in Thüringen. A maker of guns and gun parts, and a wholesaler of gun-stock blanks, active in Germany during 1939–45. **3.** F.W. Kessler, also listed as Keßler and Keszler, Suhl in Thüringen, Kleine Backstrasse 1 (1940). Founded in Suhl in 1869, this gunmaker was still being listed in the *Deutsches Reichs-Adressbuch* in 1900; the 1914–20 directories give the proprietors as F. & B. Kessler, but these had become Bernh. Kessler & Erben by 1930. The listing F.W. Kessler KG, gunmaker, was being used by 1939 and lasted until operations ceased in 1945. Marks including 'F.W.K.' (sometimes in the form of a monogram) have been found on pistols and *Martini-action sporting rifles. **4.** Kurt Kessler, Suhl in Thüringen, Windeweg 7. Listed in 1940-vintage trade directories as a maker of hunting guns (*Jagdwaffen*). **5.** Otto Kessler, Zella-Mehlis in Thüringen, Germany. Listed in 1939 as a gun-stock maker. **6.** Kessler pistol. This *blowback semi-automatic gun, clearly inspired by the 1900-pattern *FN-Browning, was made in Germany c. 1907 by Friedrich Pickert of Zella St Blasii. It is assumed to have been designed by one of the Kessler brothers: see F.W. Kessler (above). Chambered for the 7.65mm Browning cartridge, the pistol had a hinged two-part frame and a reciprocating breech-block with grooved cocking spurs projecting forward outside the frame. The grips bear Pickert's *Arminius-head trademark, and there seems little doubt that it was made under sub-contract. **7.** Kessler Rifle Company, Buffalo, Rochester and Silver Creek, New York State. Maker of the Kessler pump-up pneumatic rifle, a 5.6mm-calibre copy of the Crosman patterns. Kessler seems to have been liquidated in 1956, and the guns had only been produced for about four years, 1949–53. The location of the offices and factory seem to have changed several times.

Keszler. An early automatic pistol, made in Germany by Friedrich *Pickert. See Kessler.

Ketley. See Forrester, Ketley & Company.

Kettner – 1. Eduard Kettner, Köln-Suhler Gewehr-fabrik, Köln and Niederlassung Suhl in Thüringen. A well-known gunmaking business, founded in Thüringen in the 1870s and owned by Julius Kettner during the period 1900–30. A 'KSG' mark may have been used until operations ceased at the end of the Second World War. **2.** Franz Kettner, Suhl in Thüringen (branch office). Listed in German trade directories for 1914–20 as a gunmaker, and in 1925 as a maker of hunting and sporting guns, with a depot in Köln (where trading continues). Kettner was still being listed as a weapons maker in directories for 1930–39. Trading ceased in 1945.

Key pistols. The true personal-defence weapon of this type is one in which the barrel forms the body of the key to fire forward, although a few examples had self-contained short-barrelled pistols built into the key grip. These usually fire backward, toward the holder. Most true key pistols date from the seventeenth or eighteenth centuries, when keys were large enough to conceal a gun-lock and barrel without exciting undue comment. They were much scarcer in the nineteenth century, owing to improvements in lock design. *See also* Disguised guns.

'kfa'. Found on small-arms components made in 1942–45 by the Yugoslavian state arsenal in Sarajevo under German control.

'kfk'. Allotted in 1942 to *Dansk Industri Syndikat AS 'Madsen' of Copenhagen, this mark will be found on military small-arms components made under German supervision during the Second World War.

'KH'. With the tail of 'K' superimposed on the stem of 'H'. A mark used by Kuno Helfricht on 6.35mm pocket pistols made in Germany in the 1920s.

Kharykin. Designer of a mount for the Soviet 12.7mm PKP machine-gun.

KI – 1. An encircled cursive linear monogram, with 'I' slightly dominant. Probably interpreted more accurately as 'KJ' (q.v.); found on revolvers made in Spain prior to 1914. **2.** Found on an Italian-made *IGI Model 202 air pistol dating from the 1970s. Significance unknown.

Kickspanner. A name given to a one-push-on/next-push-off cocking mechanism found on many German-made shotguns. Normally it is operated by a slide set into the top of the tang, behind the top lever. *See also* Handspanner.

Kick-Up. A single-shot tip-barrel pistol manufactured in the USA in the last quarter of the nineteenth century by the J. *Stevens Arms Company of Chicopee Falls, Massachusetts.

Kiess, Kieß – 1. Edg. Kiess, Berlin, Nürnberg and Suhl in Thüringen. A German weapons maker listed in 1930–45. **2.** Fritz Kiess u. Co. GmbH, Suhl in Thüringen. Listed in some of the German trade directories as either a gunmaker (1930) or a weapons maker ('Spez. Jagdwaffen', 1939). Trading in 1940 from Schleusinger Strasse 36, Suhl.

Kiley. P.J. Kiley accepted US Army firearms and accessories in the early 1900s, marking them 'PJK'. *See also* US arms inspectors' marks.

'Kilham' [The]. A brandname used by *Gallyon & Sons on shotgun cartridges sold in Britain.

Kill... – 1. Kill Deer Model. Associated with a *Peabody-Martini sporting rifle. Probably named after a rifle range. **2.** 'Kill Quick' [The]. Found on shotgun cartridges sold by *Stiles Brothers of Warminster, but apparently made by *Eley-Kynoch. *See also* 'Kilquick'. **3.** 'Kill Sure', 'Kill-Sure' [The]. Found on shotgun ammunition loaded for *Harrods of London, probably prior to 1939.

'Killer' [The]. Found on shotgun ammunition distributed in northern Scotland by John *MacPherson of Inverness. The cartridges usually prove to have been made by *Kynoch prior to 1914.

'Killwell' [The]. Associated with shotgun cartridges and ammunition made for William *Richards of Liverpool and Preston.

'Kilquick' [The]. Found on shotgun ammunition sold in Ireland by *Garnett of Dublin, apparently prior to the First World War. *See also* 'Kill Quick'.

Kilper. Max Kilper, Bockstedt. A retailer of sporting guns and ammunition active in Germany in 1941.

Kimball. W.W. Kimball, a lieutenant in the US Navy, accepted a variety of firearms made from 1878 until c. 1890. Marked 'WWK', they included *Remington-Lee rifles, *Colt revolvers and *Hotchkiss-type revolving cannon made by *Pratt & Whitney. *See also* US arms inspectors' marks.

Kimbell. J. Kimbell, active in the mid-1870s, accepted firearms and accessories on behalf of the US Army; they bore 'JK' marks. *See also* US arms inspectors' marks.

Kimber – 1. Kimber of America, Inc., Clackamas, Oregon, USA. Successor in 1991 to Kimber of Oregon, which had been rescued by the Warne family. However, due to wrangling over the change of ownership, production of the bolt-action rifles associated with the Kimber name did not begin again until 1994. The Models 82B and 84 were upgraded to 82C and 84C respectively, and a new K770 Custom Sporting Rifle replaced the Model 89 Big Game Rifle (BGR). **2.** Kimber of Oregon, Inc., Clackamas, Oregon, USA. This manufacturer of rim- and centrefire bolt-action rifles was founded in 1979, but failed in 1991. It was resurrected as Kimber of America (q.v.). Products included the Model 82 .22 rimfire sporting rifle (in 82A and 82B variants), the Model 84 Mini-Mauser and the Model 89 Big Game Rifle (BGR). Kimber products were marketed under a variety of names. These have included African, All-American Match, Big-Bore Sporter, Big-Game Rifle, Brownell Commemorative, Cascade, Centennial, Classic, Continental, Custom Match, Decennial, Government Model, Hunter, Mini-Classic, Mini-Mauser, Single-Shot Varmint, Super America, Super Continental, Super Grade, Ultra Varminter and Varminter. There were also grades identified as Deluxe, with AA-standard walnut half-stocks.

Kind. Albrecht Kind, Suhl in Thüringen, Germany. *See* panel, below.

King – 1. A single-shot break-open spring-air *BB Gun made in the USA by the Markham Rifle Company and its successor, the King Rifle Company, with a brass-tube barrel and a red-stained stock; probably dating from 1890–95. **2.** A similar version with a separate stamped trigger guard and a sheet-metal barrel, 1905–10, and a transitional frame. **3.** A 1910-vintage spring-air Markham/King BB Gun, with *Polley-patent frame and stepped barrel; also known as the Model D. **4.** Also known as the No. 21, a lever-action Markham/King BB Gun, 1916–23. **5.** A 1935-vintage single-shot lever-action Markham/King BB Gun, with distinct *Daisy influence. **6.** A.D. King, a government employee, accepted firearms on behalf of the US and Federal Armies from c. 1850 until the end of the American Civil War in 1865. Marked 'ADK', they included cap-lock revolvers made by *Colt and *Starr. *See also* US arms inspectors' marks. **7.** Benjamin T. King. This agent obtained British Patent 6373/07 for John Williams

ALBRECHT KIND

Founded in 1853, this distributor of hunting accessories was listed in the Suhl directories for 1930, when the business was owned by Albrecht Kind and Dr H. Knipping. Now based in Hunstig bei Dieringshausen, but with several subsidiaries. Kind, better known by its *Akah tradename, has warehouses in Nürnberg and Minden, and associated companies in Austria and France.

According to the company's letterheading, the business encompasses, 'Waffen, Munition, Jadgeräte, Herstellung, Handel, Export, Import...' ('Manufacture, Distribution, Import and Export of Munitions and Sporting Equipment...'). Sporting guns have been reported with the company's trademarks, but undoubtedly were made elsewhere.

Among the many sporting rifles offered since the Second World War have been the Mauser-pattern *Merkur and *Saturn rifles. Akah has also distributed airguns, large numbers being marketed under the *Gecado (or *Diana-Gecado) brandname; these were made by *Mayer & Gammelspacher of Rastatt. Other Akah marks have included an oak leaf and acorns; a bearskin, a rifle and shotgun in saltire, beneath a pistol and revolver (the whole enwreathed); and a fir tree. 'Eichel', 'Tanne', 'Schutzmann' and 'Hubertus' – formerly used by Imman. *Meffert of Suhl – may be found on sporting clothing. The last has been used since 1958/59, as Meffert had disappeared into the DDR state firearms industry.

Albrecht Kind AG (Akah) acts as a distributor for a wide range of firearms. This is a Japanese SKB Model 800 12-bore over/under shotgun.

and Edwin Lawrence from chambers at 165 Queen Victoria Street, London E.C. **8**. David M. King, a US Army lieutenant, accepted firearms made by *Colt's Patent Fire Arms Manufacturing Company. Dating from the period 1899–1905, they were marked 'DMK'. *See also* US arms inspectors' marks. **9**. King Breech Loader. A spring-air BB Gun designed by E.S. *Roe, but basically an all-metal *Chicago with external operating rods. Introduced in 1917. **10**. King Cobra. Dating from 1987, this stainless-steel derivative of the .357 Magnum *Colt Python featured a heavy solid-rib barrel with a full-length ejector-rod shroud, a short-fall hammer and Neoprene grips. A blued-steel version was introduced in 1988. **11**. King Cole, usually encountered as 'The King Cole'. Found on shotgun cartridges loaded for *Cole & Son of Devizes and Portsmouth. **12**. King Junior. A US break-open single-shot BB Gun designed by E.S. *Roe, and made by *Markham in three minor varieties: with a straight barrel and a spur trigger; with a stepped barrel and a spur trigger; and with a stepped barrel and a ring trigger. Manufactured from 1910 until 1935 or later. **13**. King Kadet Army Gun. A lever-action BB Gun, similar to the King Repeater No. 22, but with a military-type backsight, a rubber-tipped bayonet and sling swivels; 1917–18 only. **14**. King Leader. Otherwise known as the Model or No. 24, this was basically an all-metal version of the original *Challenger, made by *Markham from 1924. **15**. King Pin. This *Suicide Special revolver was made by the *Hopkins & Allen Arms Company of Norwich, Connecticut, USA, in the late nineteenth century. **16**. King Rifle Company, Chicago, Illinois, USA. This was the successor to the *Markham Rifle Company, which had been renamed in 1928. It continued to market a range of Markham-pattern BB Guns, which gradually became closer to the Daisies – scarcely surprising, as Daisy had purchased Markham in 1916. Most of the output was sold through mail-order channels by *Sears, Roebuck & Company, but the factory closed in 1931, and many of the employees and much of the equipment were assimilated by Daisy. The two ranges merged in 1934, and King finally disappeared in 1940. **17**. King Repeater. A name applied to several repeating BB Guns made by Markham and later King, the first being the Model E, with a Polley-patent frame and muzzle-lever repeating mechanism, 1905–10. **18**. King Repeater (Markham/King) No. 4, a lever-action 500-shot repeater with a half-octagon barrel, 1908–16. **19**. King Repeater: the Markham/King No. 5, as No. 4 but 1,000-shot, 1908–16. **20**. King Repeater. The Markham/King Model C, a break-open design with *Polley-patent frame, step-barrel and later-model gravity feed, 1910–16. **21**. King Repeater. The Markham/King No. 22, a 500-shot repeater similar to No. 4, 1916–22. **22**. King Repeater. Another Markham/King design: a 500-shot gun, made only in 1935, which resembled the Daisy No. 155. **23**. King Repeater. A 1,000-shot Markham/King design, 1935.

'Kingfisher' [The]. Found on 'foreign' shotgun cartridges, perhaps emanating from Belgium or Germany, made for James *Matthews of Ballymena. *See also* Hawk, Swift, Wizard.

Kingsbury. Edward A. Kingsbury, a government inspector using an 'EAK' mark, accepted firearms and accessories made for the US Army in 1905–06. *See also* US arms inspectors' marks.

Kingsland. A brandname associated with shotguns made by the *Crescent Arms Company of Norwich, Connecticut, USA.

King's Norton Metal Company Ltd, Birmingham, Warwickshire, and Abbey Wood, Kent. This cartridge-making business offered rim- and centrefire rifle ammunition under the tradename Palma, and a variety of shotgun cartridges. The commercial trademark was a 'KNM' monogram (q.v.), placed on a small cylinder or drum, although military ammunition was customarily marked 'KN' or 'K N'.

'Kingston' [The]. Often found as 'The Kingston Smokeless' on shotgun ammunition loaded from *Eley-Kynoch components by R. *Robinson of Hull. The name was provided by the original name of the city, Kingston-upon-Hull.

'Kingsway' [The]. A brandname associated with shotgun cartridges made in Britain by *Nobel Explosives Ltd of Glasgow, prior to 1918 and the purchase by Explosives Trades Ltd.

Kiralý. Pal D. Kiralý. A gun designer, employed at various times by *FÉG, *SIG and the Dominican Republic state arms factory in San Cristobal. He is best known for a two-part bolt design, patented in 1912, which was incorporated in the submachine-gun introduced in Hungary in the late 1930s for police and army use.

Kirchner – 1. Hugo Kirchner, Suhl in Thüringen. A specialist barrel-blank maker listed in the *Deutsches Reichs-Adressbuch* in 1939. **2.** Oscar Kirchner, Zella-Mehlis in Thüringen, Germany. Listed in 1939 as a weapon maker; possibly the same as Oskar Kirchner (below). **3.** Oskar Kirchner, Zella-Mehlis in Thüringen. Listed in 1920 as a gunmaker; in 1930 as a gun-stock shaper; and in 1941 as a maker of guns and gun-parts.

Kirikkale Tüfek Fb. Makers of the Turkish Kirikkale automatic pistol, a copy of the Walther *Polizei Pistole. *See also* MKE.

Kirk – 1. Henry Kirk, a government inspector, accepted firearms and accessories for the Federal Army in 1862–63, during the American Civil War. His 'HK' marks can be distinguished from those applied by Henry *Kane by gun date. *See also* US arms inspectors' marks. **2.** James Kirk of 36 Union Buildings, Ayr, Scotland, handled a variety of sporting guns and accessories, as well as shotgun cartridges sold under such brandnames as Land of Burns and Retriever.

Kirkham – 1. Albert H. Kirkham, active only in 1862–63, accepted firearms and accessories on behalf of the Federal Army. They were marked 'AHK'. **2.** John B. Kirkham (possibly the father of Albert H. Kirkham) accepted cap-locks for US Army firearms from c. 1823 until the early 1840s. They were marked 'JBK'. *See also* US arms inspectors' marks.

Kit Gun – 1. Also known as the M700 Kit Gun, this *Remington bolt-action rifle dated from 1987–89. It was simply a standard-barrelled action accompanied by an unfinished ADL-pattern hardwood stock. Chambering options were confined to .243 Winchester, .270 Winchester, 7mm Remington Magnum, .30-06 and .308 Winchester. **2.** Any of several swing-cylinder .22 rimfire revolvers made by *Smith & Wesson. Originally introduced in 1936, built on a round-butt J-type frame, the guns were intended to be carried as part of the 'kit' of hikers, hunters and fishermen. Production ceased for the duration of the Second World War, then began again c. 1947. An improved version with a rebound-slide hammer block appeared as the Model 1953 (Model 34 after 1957). The Model 63 was a stainless-steel version. *See also* Service Kit Gun and Target Kit Gun.

Kither. George Kither, Dartford, Kent. A gunsmith listed in High Street from the middle of the nineteenth century until 1870 or later. He is assumed to have succeeded John Kither, at the same address in 1823–47, who is presumed to have been his father.

Kittredge. Benjamin Kittredge & Company, Cincinnati, Ohio, USA. Established as Eaton & Kittredge in 1845, trading from 236 Main Street, this partnership made large numbers of *cap-lock sporting rifles and shotguns prior to the American Civil War. Eaton retired in 1859, leaving Kittredge to continue alone from a variety of addresses on Main Street (perhaps simply periodic renumberings) until the Kittredge Arms Company ceased trading in 1891. Single-shot rifles, including *Sharps breech-loaders, were ordered by the Federal government in November 1861 (presumably they were already in stock), and a metal cartridge box with a spring-loaded flap was patented on 27 January 1863. A second patent, 41,848 of 8 March 1864, was granted for a spring-loaded back-flash deflector embodied in the *Manhattan revolver. Kittredge became one of the leading gun dealers in the Midwest, and maintained a branch office at 55 St Charles Street, New Orleans, in the 1870s. Kittredge handled many of the earliest Remington cartridge revolvers. He was also responsible for many of the names popularly bestowed on the Colt revolvers (e.g. *Lightning and *Thunderer).

Kitu. A 6.35mm six-shot *Browning-type pocket pistol made in France prior to 1940, probably by *Manufacture d'Armes des Pyrénées. The slides usually display nothing but 'Fabrication Française'.

'KJ'. An encircled cursive linear monogram, with 'J' slightly dominant. Encountered on the frames of break-open *Smith & Wesson-style revolvers made in Spain prior to 1914; significance unknown. The mark has also been interpreted as 'IK', 'KI', 'KT' and 'TK', any one of which seems possible; and as 'TJC' (q.v.), which seems less plausible. It is also possible that the mark denotes a distributor – perhaps in the USA – despite the guns' obvious Spanish origins.

'kjj'. Apparently found on German military optical equipment made by Askania-Werke of Berlin-Friedenau during the Second World War. The attribution remains uncertain, as Askania has also been linked with the production of vehicle parts.

Kjobenhavn. *See* Copenhagen arms factory.

Klawitter, Herzberg in Harz. A maker of crank-operated Gallery Guns, or perhaps simply a retailer, operating about 1840–70; *see also* Nowotny. Sometimes Klawitter's name is linked with that of E.A. *Störmer in Herzberg.

Kleanbore. A mark associated with cartridges made by the *Remington Arms–Union Metallic Cartridge Company. It referred to the non-corrosive primer invented by James Burns, a chemist previously employed by the *United States Cartridge Company. Ammunition of this type was introduced commercially in the USA in 1926.

Klein – 1. August Klein, Suhl in Thüringen, Germany. Registered as a gunsmith prior to 1939. **2.** Klein's, Inc., Chicago. This well-known US department store adver-

tised the *Kessler pneumatic rifle in its 1949/50 catalogues under the name Rochester.

Kleinert. Karl Kleinert, Zella-Mehlis in Thüringen, Germany. Listed in 1930 as a gun-stock maker.

Kleingunther's, Inc. A distribution agency. *See* Voere.

Klett – 1. Aug. Heinr. Klett, Suhl in Thüringen, Germany. Listed in 1900 as a gunmaker. **2.** Emil Klett, Suhl in Thüringen, Gothaer Strasse 122b. Listed in German trade directories from c. 1927 as a maker of guns (1930) and gun barrels (1939–41), active until the end of the Second World War. **3.** F.A. Klett, Suhl in Thüringen. Listed in 1900 German directories as a maker of guns, gun barrels and tubes; owned in 1914 by Frau Hedwig and Alfred Hauche, the business was concentrating on gun barrels. Trading seems to have ceased c. 1923. **4.** Heinrich Chr. Klett & Söhne, Zella St Blasii and Zella-Mehlis in Thüringen, Germany. Listed in 1900–14 as a gunmaker and also, in 1912–14 only, as a gun-barrel maker. Listed in Zella-Mehlis in 1920 as a gunmaker and gun-barrel maker, as Heinrich Klett Söhne. Owned by Heinrich Louis Klett. Listed in 1930 as a gun-stocker (Heinrich Chr. Klett & Sohn). **5.** Johan Stephan Klett & Söhne, Suhl in Thüringen, Germany. Listed in 1900 as a gunmaking business, owned by Heinrich Klett. Trading seems to have ceased c.1911.

Klin-Zlatoust engineering factory, Zlatous-tovsk, Russia. *See* Kedr.

Kline. Richard M. Kline. Co-designer with Kenneth *Pitcher of the Healthways *Plainsman pistol, 1955–57. Kline is assumed to have been the president of Healthways, Inc.

'kls'. Used by the Warsaw factory of *Steyr-Daimler-Puch AG on small-arms components made during the Second World War.

'KM', 'K.M.' – 1. A mark applied to firearms and accessories used by the Royal Dutch Navy, or *Koninklijke Marine*. **2.** Found on US military firearms and accessories. *See* Kenneth *Morton.

'KN', 'K N'. Found in the headstamps of British military ammunition made by the King's Norton Metal Company Ltd of Birmingham.

Kneifel – 1. Bernh. Kneifel & Co., Berlin S59, Kottbuser Damm 95. Best known for producing an experimental zinc frame for the P.08 (Luger) pistol, Kneifel was recorded in 1925 as an agent for ammunition, hunting and shooting accessories, and sports goods of all types. The full extent of the company's manufacturing facilities is not known. **2.** Gebr. Kneifel, Mehlis in Thüringen, Germany. Listed in the directories of 1914 as a gunmaker. **3.** Waffenhaus Kneifel, Eisenach in Thüringen. This German gunmaking business, founded in 1890, was making 'first-class hunting and deluxe guns' by 1925, but does not seem to have survived into the Third Reich era.

Kneisel. Gebr. Kneisel, Mehlis in Thüringen, Germany. Listed in 1900 as a master gunsmith.

Knickerbocker. One of countless brandnames associated with shotguns made by the *Crescent Arms Company of Norwich, Connecticut.

Knife pistols. *See* panel, p. 284.

Knight – 1. P. Knight, Clinton Street, Nottingham. Marks applied by this English gunmaker have been seen on sporting guns and shotgun ammunition sold under such brandnames as Castle, *Invincible and Thurland. **2.**

KNIFE PISTOLS

These are customarily anonymous, obscuring their origins. Occasionally proof marks may identify nationality, but many knife pistols pre-date the establishment of mandatory proof. This is particularly true of pre-1891 German examples, as well as those manufactured in the USA (where there is still no national proof system).

Many attempts to provide multi-shot *combination weapons took knife-pistol form. Samuel *Colt even made a double-action Paterson-type revolver with a sturdy blade beneath the muzzle, and many pinfire examples emanated from Europe in a range of sizes.

Most of the pinfires will have been manufactured in Liège, but Spanish-made examples are known, and doubtless a few were produced in Birmingham. Normally knife pistols were single-shot firearms, which enabled them to be kept as compact as possible. However, a few double-barrelled examples survive, and a few European guns (generally Belgian) incorporate small-calibre pinfire revolvers. In general these date from the period 1870–1914.

The idea was resurrected by the British during the Second World War, when, in the spring of 1942, the staff of the Royal Small Arms Factory at Enfield Lock prepared the 'Pistol, Revolver, 9mm D.D.(E.) 3313' – Design Department, Enfield, drawing no. 3313. This was a refined Dolne *Apache with a six-chamber cylinder, folding three-ring knuckle-bow, a folding trigger, a swivelling blade on the left side of the frame and an internal hammer.

See also American Novelty Company, Bazar, Disguised guns, George *Elgin, Andrew *Peavey, L.H. *Polhemus Manufacturing Company, Joseph *Rodgers, Leo *Rogers, Self Protector and Unwin & Rodgers.

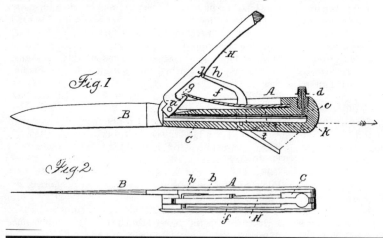

These drawings, taken from the relevant US patent, show the original cap-lock Peavey pistol-knife. When the latch 't' is pressed, pressure from the spring 'f' forces the hammer bar 'h' downward to strike the cap placed on nipple 'd'.

Knight's Armament Company, Vero Beach, Florida, USA. A specialist maker of military weapons, particularly on the basis of the *ArmaLite rifle, KAC was involved in the design of the Colt 2000 auto-loading pistol and has also made a wide variety of silencers.

'KNIL', 'K.N.I.L.'. The Netherlands Indies Army, or *Nederlandsch Indisch Leger*, was formed in the 1880s to protect the Dutch colonies in the Far East. Although equipped largely with regulation weapons, non-standard patterns of *Parabellum pistol and *Mannlicher carbine were developed specifically for colonial use. Guns of this type often bore distinctive unit marks (*see* Martens and de Vries, *The Dutch Luger*, Ironside International, 1994) or the marks of the *Centrale Werkplaatz/*Centrale Magazijn. The forces were granted the prefix 'Royal' (*Koninklijke*) in 1905, ordered *Johnson automatic rifles when threatened by the Japanese advance in the Second World War, and were disbanded when Indonesia gained independence in 1949.

'KNM', often in the form of a monogram: 'K' and 'N' with an elongated 'M' running through them horizontally. Marks associated with the King's Norton Metal Company Ltd, found on ammunition.

Knoble. William B. Knoble, Tacoma, Washington, USA. This inventor submitted a double-action semi-automatic pistol to the US Army in 1907, but the unfin-ished state of the model precluded firing trials, and it was summarily rejected.

Knock-About. A *Suicide Special revolver made by the *Crescent Arms Company of Norwich, Connecticut, USA, in the late nineteenth century.

Knockout – 1. Usually found as 'The Knock-Out' on shotgun cartridges sold in England by *Hutchinson, Roe & Company of Cranbrook, and William *Powell & Son of Birmingham, apparently loaded from components supplied by *Eley-Kynoch. **2.** As 'Knock Out' or 'Knock-Out'. Found on *Scheintod pistols of unknown make, but, presumably, German. The simplest consists of a bayonet-joint barrel attached to a frame embedded in an enveloping wooden handgrip; the best was a two-shot pattern with a tipping barrel block and a release button doubling as a safety catch. Knock-Out guns are usually marked 'GES. GESCH.' or 'GES. GESCHÜTZT' ('Protected Design').

Knoll – 1. Max Knoll, Berlin and Suhl. Founded in Suhl in 1887, this business was listed in pre-1914 directories as a maker of gun parts. By 1925, its headquarters were in Gustav-Müller-Platz in Berlin-Schöneberg; at the time, products included 'hunting rifles, automatic weapons, ammunition and hunting accessories for distribution and export'. Knoll used the brandname Emka and a trademark consisting of an 'MK' monogram, often on a shield supported by two lions. **2.** W. Knoll, Suhl in Thüringen. Listed as a gunmaker, 1920.

Knopf – **1.** Richard Knopf, Suhl in Thüringen, Germany. Trading in 1930–39 as a maker of deluxe sporting guns ('*Jagd- u. Luxuswaffen Fertigung*'). **2.** Wilhelm Knopf, Suhl in Thüringen. A specialist German gunstocker registered in Suhl some time prior to 1939.

Knous. Frederick Knous. Designer of a set-trigger system, used by *Remington.

Knows. S. Knows. Marks applied by this acceptor of US military firearms and accessories – including single-shot cap-lock pistols made by *Aston – have been dated to 1845–48, and have also been identified on *Dragoon revolvers made in 1848–52 by *Colt's Patent Fire Arms Manufacturing Company. However, it now seems that the revolvers were actually accepted by Samuel *Keeler. *See also* US arms inspectors' marks.

Knox, Knox-All, Knox Arms Company. Brandnames associated with shotguns manufactured prior to 1920 by the *Crescent Arms Company of Norwich, Connecticut, USA.

Knoxform. Usually refers to a prominent flat on the upper rear surface of a rifle barrel, which had originally been the hooked breech plug of a muzzle-loader. It is a corruption of the name of the London gunmaker, Henry Nock.

Knuckledusters – **1.** Knuckleduster pistols. The most popular form of striking weapon was based on the knuckleduster, known since the days of the Roman gladiators, although the name did not enter English (by way of American slang) until the middle of the nineteenth century. William and John *Rigby of Dublin made a large number of multi-barrel cap-locks with a rotating striker plate on the nose of the hammer and an all-metal grip. Four-barrel guns were most common, often made in matched pairs, although three- and six-barrel variants are said to have been made. They were designed specifically to serve as striking weapons after all the shots had been fired, and had a distinctive finger-hole through the grip. Reloading was achieved by unscrewing the barrels. The single-shot cartridge derringers made by *Moore's Patent Fire Arms Company, the *National Arms Company, then *Colt's Patent Firearms Manufacturing Company were conceived as dual-purpose shooting/striking weapons. *See also* Apache, Delhaxhe, Disguised guns, and My Friend. **2.** Found on tiny solid-frame double-action revolvers made in Belgium prior to 1914 by Manufacture Liégeoise d'Armes à Feu, whose crowned 'ML' will usually be found on the frames. The guns have vestigial bird's-head grips, folding triggers and short-spur or bobbed hammers.

Københavns Tøjhus. *See* Krag-Jørgensen.

Kober – **1.** Max Kober, Suhl in Thüringen, Germany. Listed as a maker of sporting guns ('*Jagdgewehr-Fabrikation*') in 1930. **2.** Wilh. Kober u. Co., Suhl in Thüringen. Listed in 1940 as a maker of metalware, and sometimes also associated with the production of gun parts. (But note that there was also F.W. Kober, a wholesaler of ironware, trading at the same time in the city from Lange Brucke 21.)

Kobold. The German equivalent of Cobold (q.v.).

Kobra. Found on a small 6.35mm pocket pistol, probably dating from the 1930s, with German proof and 'D.R.P.' patent marks; manufacturer unknown.

Koch – **1.** Albin Koch, Heidersbach bei Suhl in Thüringen. A maker of sporting guns and accessories active in Germany prior to 1939. **2.** Hermann Koch, Goldlauter bei Suhl in Thüringen. Listed in pre-1930 editions of the *Deutsches Reichs-Adressbuch* as a maker of hunting guns ('*Jagdwaffen-Fabrikation*').

Kodensha Company, Iwade-Cho, Tochigi, Japan. A maker of airguns in the early 1950s. Now part of Olin Kodenska Company, a joint venture with US Olin Chemical Corporation.

Kodiak, Kodiak... – **1.** A derivative of the M725 bolt-action rifle made by the *Remington Arms Company in 1961–62 as 'big-game' guns, chambered for the .375 H&H Magnum or .458 Winchester Magnum cartridges. The guns had muzzle brakes, recoil bolts through the stock beneath the chamber, and special ventilated rubber recoil pads. **2.** Kodiak Manufacturing Company, North Haven, Connecticut, USA. This gunmaking business built sporting rifles on the basis of refurbished 1898-pattern *Mauser actions from c. 1959 until 1973. Originally the guns were chambered for the .243 Winchester, .30-06 or .308 Winchester rounds, although subsequently other options were added. The standard pattern had a plain hardwood stock with a low *Monte Carlo comb, but deluxe versions were also made. *See also* Ultra and Varmint Ultra.

Koishikawa artillery arsenal, Tokyo, Japan. Founded in 1880 to make the first single-shot 13th Year Type *Murata rifles, subsequently this factory made Murata repeaters, *Arisaka rifles and *Hotchkiss-pattern machine-guns alongside a variety of military stores. Owing to the long-term effects of the 1923 Tokyo earthquake, production of small-arms was transferred to a new factory in *Kokura and work ceased in Tokyo in 1932. Koishikawa products can be identified by a mark of four interlocking circles signifying piled cannon-balls.

Kokura army arsenal. This Japanese ordnance factory, successor to the *Koishikawa plant in Tokyo, made 6.5mm-calibre 38th Year Type *Arisaka rifles in 1932–33, and 7.7mm Type 99 models in 1940–45. The interlocking four-circle mark was retained.

Kolesnikov. Ivan Nikolayevich Kolesnikov, the son of a peasant, was born near Ryazan in 1878. After rudimentary primary education, he was apprenticed to the workshop attached to the infantry officers' school in Oranienbaum and rose to become foreman of the experimental workshop at the Oranienbaum proving ground. Kolesnikov transferred to the Kovrov machine-gun factory in the 1920s, remaining there until his death in 1941. His name is associated with a mount for the Maxim machine-gun (PM), produced during the First World War, and a light MK, or Maxim Koleshnikov, machine-gun produced experimentally in the mid-1920s.

Kolibri. The smallest automatic pistol ever to be manufactured commercially, this 2.7mm-calibre gun was made by *Pfannl of Krems an der Donau.

Köln-Suhler Gewehrfabrik. *See* Eduard *Kettner.

'Ko-Ma', 'KOMA'. Marks associated with the products of Koma-Werke – now *Voetter & Co. (Voere). These included sporting firearms and spring-air pistols made c. 1950–55.

Komaritsky. Irinarkh Andreyevich Komaritsky, born in Tula in 1891, was educated in the local trade school before becoming a teacher at the Tula Military-Technical School. Transferring to the Tula arms factory after the

October Revolution, he was sent as a representative to the Military Industry Council and became involved in the design of new small-arms – in particular, the development with Evgeniy Kabakov of the sight-hood bayonet for the perfected, or 1930-type, Soviet *Mosin-Nagant rifle, and work with Boris *Shpitalniy on the *ShKAS aircraft machine-gun. Komaritsky was awarded a USSR State Prize for his participation in the ShKAS project, and another, after the Second World War, for the development of artifical limbs. He died in Tula in 1971.

Kombi, or Kombi-Handspanner. A proprietary cocking system associated with some of the shotguns, Double Rifles and combination guns made by H. *Krieghoff GmbH of Ulm/Donau since the 1980s.

Kommer – 1. Louis Kommer, Zella-Mehlis in Thüringen, Germany. Listed in 1939 as a master gunsmith. **2.** Theodor Kommer Waffenfabrik, Zella-Mehlis and possibly also Suhl in Thüringen, Germany. A manufacturer of sporting guns and Kommer-brand pistols (below). Normally the guns bore 'Th. K.' or a 'TK' monogram. The business was customarily listed in the *Deutsches Reichs-Adressbuch* for 1920–45 as a weapon maker. **3.** Kommer pistols. A series of semi-automatic pistols, derived from the FN-Browning blowbacks, made by Theodor Kommer of Zella-Mehlis in the early 1920s. The 6.35mm Modell 1 had an eight-round magazine; the Modell 2 was similar, with a short grip and a six-round magazine; the 6.35mm Modell 3 was little more than a Modell 1 with a knurled large-diameter muzzle crown to facilitate dismantling; and the 7.65mm Modell 4 was a copy of the 1910-pattern FN-Browning, lacking the grip safety mechanism of its prototype.

Kondakov. Mikhail Nikolayevich Kondakov, born in St Peterburg in 1898, volunteered to serve with the Red Army in 1918 and, by 1921, had risen to be the chief of staff of an artillery group. A period of study (1921–27) allowed him to serve the military scientific research bureau until his health failed in 1929. Kondakov returned to academic work, first as a designer, then as professor in the research department of the Artillery Academy. From 1932 until his death in 1954, Kondakov served as director of the Special Design Bureau. He is credited with an anti-aircraft mount for the *Maxim PM machine-gun, introduced in 1928, and a multi-barrelled 20mm cannon.

'Kondor'. A brandname used on shotgun cartridges, probably made in the Durlach factory of *Rheinisch-Westfälische Sprengstoff prior to 1914. *See also* Condor.

Kongsberg arms factory. *See* Heckler & Koch, Jarmann, Krag-Jørgensen, Krag-Petersson and Remington.

Konig, König – 1. Adolf König, Suhl in Thüringen. A maker of sporting-gun parts active in Germany in the 1920s. **2.** Albin König, Zella-Mehlis in Thüringen, Germany. Listed in the 1930 *Deutsches Reichs-Adressbuch* as a retailer of guns and ammunition, but possibly also maintaining repair facilities. **3.** Arth. König, Zella-Mehlis in Thüringen. Listed in 1930 as a master gunsmith. **4.** David Königs Söhne, Mehlis in Thüringen, Germany. Listed in 1900 as a gunmaker, and in 1914 as a gun- and weapon maker. **5.** D.H. König, Mehlis in Thüringen. Listed in 1900 as a weapon maker and wholesaler. **6.** Ferd. König, Mehlis in Thüringen. Listed in 1900–14 as a weapon maker and wholesaler. **7.** Heinrich [&] Adolf König, Zella-Mehlis in Thüringen. Listed in Germany in 1930–45 as a maker of guns and weapons. An 'HAK'

trademark has been attributed to this source, and it is possible that the name should be read simply as 'Hein. Adolf König'. **8.** H. Ferd. König, Zella-Mehlis in Thüringen. Listed in 1930 as a maker of guns and weapons. Sometimes listed as H. Ferd. S. König. **9.** S. Robert & Willi König, Zella-Mehlis in Thüringen. Listed in the 1939 edition of the *Deutsches Reichs-Adressbuch* as master gunsmiths. **10.** W. König, Zella-Mehlis in Thüringen, Germany. Listed in the 1930 edition of the *Deutsches Reichs-Adressbuch* as a maker of guns and weapons. **11.** Willi König, Zella-Mehlis in Thüringen, Germany. Listed in 1939 as a specialist gun-barrel drawer. **12.** König & Sohn, Benshausen in Thüringen, Germany. Listed in 1941 as makers of firearms.

Königlich... – 1. Königlich bayerische Gewehrfabrik, Bavaria. *See* Amberg. **2.** Königlich Gewehrfabrik, Prussia/Germany. *See* Danzig, Erfurt and Spandau.

'Konkor' [The]. A mark identifying shotgun ammunition handled in Britain by *Cogswell & Harrison. Also listed as 'Konor'.

Konstantinov. Designer of an experimental sniper rifle, made in small numbers in the 1960s to compete with the *SVD, or Dragunov.

Koon. Homer Koon. The designer of the *Alpha and Ranger rifles.

Kopřiva. Bedřich Kopřiva (Austria-Hungary, Czechoslovakia). This gunsmith, trading from the town of Nymburk, c. 1890–1925, made sporting guns in peacetime and rifle components during the First World War. Among Kopriva's apprentices was František *Myška, in 1913–17.

Kork-n-Seal Ltd, Anchor & Hope Lane, Charlton, London SE7. A maker of magazines for the British 9mm *Sten Gun during the Second World War. The regional code 'S 63' may have been used instead of the company name. [Note regional plant in Stirling, code 'N 93'.] *See also* British military manufacturers' marks.

Kornbusch & Co. *See* Oberspree.

Korovin. Sergey Aleksandrovich Korovin, born in Kharkov in 1884, the son of a clerk, took part in the abortive revolution of 1905 and was exiled from Russia. He moved first to Paris, then to Liège, where he worked until the outbreak of the First World War for *Manufacture de l'Armes de l'État. Returning to Russia, he was unable to gain an appointment in the Tula factory until 1920. Korovin is best known for the 6.35mm *TK or Tula-Korovin personal-defence pistol, which had its origins in patents granted in Britain (e.g. 25,744/12 of November 1912) and elsewhere prior to 1914. He also developed submachine-guns, automatic rifles and anti-tank weapons. Korovin remained in Tula, threatened by the German advance, even after the arms factory had been evacuated; subsequently he was able to design simple submachine-guns and mortars that were made from scrap material for the Tula Workers Regiment. Decorated with the Order of the Red Star and other honours, Sergey Korovin died in Tula in 1946.

Korriphila-Präzisionsmechanik GmbH, Ulm/Donau. This German engineering business has made handguns designed by Edgar Budischowsky, including the TP-70 pocket pistol and the roller-locked *HSP series.

Korth. W. Korth GmbH, Ratzeburg/Holstein, Germany. This gunmaking business produces some of the world's finest revolvers and also a recoil-operated semi-automatic pistol with a patented buffer to reduce the shock of firing. Offered in 9mm Parabellum and other chamberings, the gun has a slab-side frame and slide, an exposed ring-hammer and a double-action trigger.

Kotek. L. Kotek AS. Apparently this Czechoslovakian metalworking business was founded in Prague in 1931 to make *Stella airguns, most of which were barrel-cocking rifles. Series production began in 1933 with the assistance of František *Koucký, but is believed to have stopped in the early 1940s.

Koucký – 1. František Koucký. Born on 20 July 1907 in Krnsko, in the Mladá Boleslav district of Bohemia (then in Austria-Hungary, now Czechoslovakia), Kouckýjoined Československá Zbrojovka after graduating from the Prague technical college in 1926. There he worked on the vz. 26 light machine-gun and prepared a design for an auto-loading rifle that never went beyond the prototype stage. Moving in 1933 to L. Kotek AS, Koucký supervised series production of the *Stella airguns before returning to Zbrojovka Brno in 1943 to manage the rifle-making department. A semi-automatic rifle designed in collaboration with his brother, Josef (q.v.), was successful in trials in Italy and would have entered production in the Cremona arms factory had not the Second World War ended when it did. Most of Koucký's post-war work concentrated on guns such as the .22 rimfire ZKM-451 sporter, the .22 rimfire ZK-455 target rifle and the .22 Hornet ZKW-465. A selection of target pistols, submachine-guns and automatic rifles has also been made. František Koucký retired in the early 1970s and died c. 1981. 2. Josef Koucký. Born on 1 March 1904 in Krnksko, Bohemia, Koucký was apprenticed as a toolmaker. After graduating from the Prague technical college, he joined the arms factory established by František *Janeček before moving on to *Československá Zbrojovka to develop small-calibre automatic rifles. Often working in conjunction with his younger brother, František (q.v.), Josef Koucký produced a series of automatic rifles, submachine-guns, machine-guns and anti-tank rifles on the basis of more than 130 patents sought in Czechoslovakia and abroad. He retired in 1965.

'kov'. Found on German military optical sights and associated components made in Paris in 1942–44 by Barbier, Benard & Turenne.

Kovo AS, Prague, Czechoslovakia. Maker of a range of spring-air break-barrel rifles since the early 1950s, originally as the 519T, 521T and the 523T, but perhaps now as the *Slavia range. Originally the guns were marketed by *Omnipol, but now are handled by *Merkuria.

Kovrov arms factory. See Fedorov.

KPV. A Soviet 14.5mm-calibre heavy machine-gun, usually mounted in tanks and armoured personnel carriers. It was the work of Semen *Vladimirov.

Krack. Frank Krack, employed by *Rock Island Arsenal, was responsible for accepting .45 M1911A1 *Colt-Browning pistols refurbished and renumbered for the US Army in 1940–41; the guns are marked 'FK'. See also US arms inspectors' marks.

Krag – 1. Ole Hermann Johannes Krag, born in Gudbrandsdalen in 1837, was commissioned into the Norwegian artillery in 1857 and rapidly displayed an aptitude for mechanical engineering. Posted in 1870 to the government small-arms factory, *Kongsberg Våpenfabrikk, Krag eventually became director of the plant

(1880) and, later, master-general of ordnance (1895). He retired from the army in 1902, with the rank of colonel. Krag is best known for his rifle designs, produced initially in collaboration with Axel *Petersson, then with Erik *Jørgensen, but he was also responsible for enlarging the Kongsberg small-arms factory, and the ammunition and propellant-making factory in Raufoss. Continuing to work on small-arms after his retirement, including a semi-automatic pistol patented in 1909, Ole Krag died in Oslo in 1912. **2.** Krag-Jørgensen rifle: see panel, pp. 288/89. **3.** Krag-Petersson rifle. Apparently this quirky tube-magazine repeater, designed by Norwegian Army officer Ole Krag and Swedish engineer Axel Jakob Petersson, was inspired by the block-action *Lee rifle. Patented in Norway in 1874, it was confined largely to naval service, the 12.17mm rimfire Norwegian 1876-type navy rifle (*Marinen Repetergevær M/1876*) being made by Kongsberg Våpenfabrikk in 1876–77, and a Danish 11.35mm rimfire navy carbine (*Flådens magasin-karabin m/1877*) emanating from Geværfabrik Kjobenhavn in 1878–80. Krag-Petersson rifles had a hammer-like actuating lever above the breech, and a tube magazine beneath the barrel. Subsequently, however, a committee of Swedish and Norwegian officers rejected a Krag-Petersson army rifle in favour of the bolt-action *Jarmann.

Kraguyevač arms factory. See Crvena Zastava.

Kramer. See Schilling & Kramer.

Kraskov. The co-designer with *Serdyukov of the Soviet/Russian *ASS and *VSS silent firearms.

Kratochvil. Jan Kratochvil. This gun designer is best known for the 7.62x45 Model 52 semi-automatic rifle (*Samonabíjecki puška vz.52*) derived from the experimental ČZ 147, ČZ 475, ČZ 493 and ČZ 502, adopted on 20 March 1952 and made in quantity in the Uherský Brod factory of Československá Zbrojovka for the Czechoslovakian Army in 1952–57. Then a few vz. 52/57 guns chambered for the Soviet 7.62x39 cartridge were made, and original 1952-type guns were converted in the late 1950s.

Kraus. Irwin Rudolf Kraus. The co-designer with Edward R. Wackerhagen of the Sheridan pneumatic and gas-powered rifles.

Krauser. Alfred Krauser, Zella-Mehlis in Thüringen, Germany. This gunmaking business, perhaps simply a distributor, marked *Helfricht-patent *Helkra pistols sold in the 1920s. Nothing else is known.

Krausser – 1. Ernst Krausser, Zella-Mehlis in Thüringen, Germany. Listed in 1930 as a master gunsmith. **2.** Ernst, Otto & Udo Krausser, Zella-Mehlis in Thüringen. Listed in the *Deutsches Reichs-Adressbuch* for 1939 as master gunsmiths.

Krauss-Klein. Paul Krauss-Klein. Probably a merchant instead of a gunsmith, this member of the English gun trade was listed at 15 Tower Hill and 15 King Street, Tower Hill, London E., in 1870–72. Henry *Jarrett may have been a predecessor.

'krd'. Found on German small-arms ammunition made by *Lignose AG of Kriewald (subsequently renamed Sprengstoffwerke Oberschlesien GmbH) in 1942–45.

Kreinberger – 1. Aug. Kreinberger, Zella-Mehlis in Thüringen, Germany. Listed in 1939 as a master gunsmith. **2.** H. Kreinberger, Zella-Mehlis in Thüringen, Germany. Listed in 1930 as a master gunsmith.

Kreps. Marian T. Kreps, or 'Krepps', accepted guns and accessories on behalf of the Federal Army in 1862–63,

KRAG-JØRGENSEN RIFLE

Krag (2)

The first gun of this type to see military service was adopted in Denmark in 1889. Chambered for a rimmed 8x58 cartridge, the *Gevær m/89* (made from 1890 until 1921) was locked by a single lug on the bolt head, which engaged a recess in the receiver when the bolt handle was turned down, and by the bolt-guide rib abutting the receiver bridge; the pan magazine beneath the boltway held five rounds. There were no safety features other than a half-cock notch; the stock had a straight grip, and the barrel was jacketed in the manner of the *Reichsgewehr. Pointed-bullet ammunition was adopted in 1908, back sights were modified and, in 1910, a cocking-piece safety catch credited to C.C.G. Barry was added behind the bolt handle.

The Danes used a cavalry carbine, the *Ryttergevær* or *Rytterkarabin m/89* (1912–13), with a conventional wooden hand guard instead of a barrel jacket and a large stud in the left side of the stock-wrist. The engineer carbine, or *Ingeniørkarabin m/89* (1917–18), was similar, but accepted a sword bayonet. The *Rytterkarabin m/89/23* (1923–26) was basically an m/89 cavalry carbine capable of accepting a bayonet. The infantry carbine, or *Fodfolkskarabin m/89/24* (1923–40, 1944–45), lacking a barrel jacket, was originally converted from old m/89 infantry rifles, although production of new guns began in 1929. The earliest *Artillerikarabins m/89/24* (1925–30) were also conversions, retaining the original back sights. They had a triangular sling swivel on the second barrel band and a large stud on the left side of the straight stock-wrist.

The Danes also issued a few hundred marksmen's rifles, or *Finskydningsgevær*. Adopted in February 1928, Fsk m/28 had a large-diameter free-floating barrel, a hooded-blade or globe front sight and a micro-adjustable back sight on the left side of the receiver. Fsk m/28/31 chambered the rimless 6.5x55mm Norwegian rifle cartridge instead of the Danish 8x58 type. Krag-type *Salongevær* and *Salonkarabin m/89* were made for training, chambered for *Flobert primer-propelled ammunition. In addition, single-shot target rifles were made in several calibres, and unfinished actions were supplied directly to gunsmiths.

Most of the Danish rifles and carbines were made in Copenhagen by Geværfabriken Kjobenhavn and Københavns Tøjhus (1890–1915), by Hærens Tøjhus (1915–22), by Hærens Rustkammer (1922–32) and by Hærens Vaabenarsenal (1932 onward). The Germans seized at least 110,000 Danish Krag rifles and carbines during the Second World War, often adding their own inspectors' marks.

The Krag also became the service rifle of the US Army, after trials with more than fifty rifles had been concluded in August 1892. Krag-Jørgensen Rifle no. 5 was chosen instead of *Lee no. 3 and the Belgian-type *Mauser no. 5, simply because fresh cartridges could be inserted in the magazine when the bolt was shut on a loaded chamber. It was a .30-calibre gun with a Mauser-type safety and a downward-opening loading gate; the 'US Magazine Rifle, Caliber .30, Model of 1892' (made in quantity in 1894–97) was essentially similar.

The action was locked by a single lug on the bolt head, and the lateral pan magazine beneath the boltway held five rounds. The M1896 rifle (1896–99) was an improvement on the 1892 pattern, having a back sight with a stepless, or continuously curved, base. The M1896 cadet rifle was basically an 1896-type infantry rifle with a full-length cleaning rod and a barrel-band spring. A few hundred were made in 1896–97.

The perfected M1898 rifle (made between 1898 and 1904) had an improved bolt mechanism. The receiver and magazine loading-gate were simplified, and the bolt-handle seat was milled flush with the receiver. The M1898, or *Dickson-pattern, sight had a bullet-drift adjustment and a binding screw on the slider. Withdrawal of the high-velocity 1898-pattern cartridge, which had broken too many Krag locking lugs, heralded the 1901, or *Buffington-pattern, sight with a stepless base and an elongated leaf. However, this proved to be too fragile and was replaced by the 1902-type, or Dickson tangent sight, which was similar to the 1898 pattern, but had a single notch and a spring plunger in the slider.

The so-called Board of Ordnance and Fortification Rifle was made experimentally in 1902, with a short barrel and a special tangent-leaf sight. However, progress being made with modified Mauser-type *Springfield rifles was more encouraging, and the shortened Krag was soon abandoned.

Although carbines had been made for trials in 1893, the first regulation pattern was the M1896 (1896–99), which had a half-stock with a saddle-ring-and-bar assembly on the left side, above the trigger guard. The M1898 carbine was similar to the 1896 pattern, but incorporated the improved, or 1898-type, action. Unfortunately, the high-velocity cartridges proved troublesome, and M1898 carbines were soon recalled to Springfield Armory to receive 1899-type stocks and new sights. The fore-end of the M1899 carbine (1899–1904) was lengthened by 3in. All the guns had 1896-pattern back sights, but these were replaced by 1901-type Buffington examples.

Widespread issue of M1903 Springfield rifles allowed withdrawal of Krags. Some guns were exported, many to Cuba, while others were cut down for service in the Philippines.

Krags were sold to members of the *National Rifle Association of America; many were cut to carbine length and given rounded fore-ends (the NRA Carbine), but others were properly remodelled, as the smooth operating stroke and the renowned accuracy of .30-40 Krag rifles prompted gunsmiths, such as R.F. *Sedgley, Inc. of Philadelphia, to offer .25-35 WCF and even .250-3000 Savage variants.

US Krags are often difficult to identify; more than forty changes were made to the M1892 alone, and wholesale changes of sights were carried out on several occasions. Virtually all regulation-pattern rifles and carbines were made by the *National Armory in Springfield, Massachusetts, although most Philippine Constabulary Rifles were converted in Manila arsenal.

The last of the three major powers to adopt the Krag was Norway, where the 6.5x55 *Krag-Jørgensengevær M/1894* (made from 1895 until 1935) was approved in April 1894. Essentially similar mechanically to the US Krag, with a single locking lug on the bolt head, it had a five-round pan magazine and a loading gate that hinged downward. All Norwegian guns had pistol-grip stocks. The adoption of the M/1923 spitzer bullet led to a wholesale change of sights, although this was not completed until 1938. Norwegian marksmen's rifles, or *Skarpskyttegevær*, included the M/23 (1923–25) with an aperture sight, a full-length stock and a special heavy floating barrel; the M/25 (1926–27) was an 1894-type infantry rifle with the aperture sight and a front sight with eared protectors; and the perfected M/30 of 1931–34 had a half-stock held by a single band.

Some M/1894/43 rifles were modified to short-rifle length during the German occupation of Norway in the Second World War. Fitted with front sight protectors, the conversions displayed German ordnance marks.

After the war, 'new' 7.9x57 target rifles were assembled from M/1912

A typical Danish m/1889 infantry rifle (left), a popular and long-lived design. The principal difference between Krags lies in the loading gates, as the Norwegian and US types hinge downward and the Danish pattern (drawings, right) swings out.

short-rifle actions and surplus Colt machine-gun barrels. The M/48/51 pattern had an aperture sight in front of the chamber, whereas the M/48/53 had a folding open sight.

The standard cavalry carbine, or *Krag-Jørgensenkarabin for Kavaleriet M/1895* (1896–1912), had a half-stock with a tapering fore-end. The cadet carbine, *Krag-Jørgensenkarabin for Skoler M/1906* (1906–22), was identical with the M/95 cavalry carbine, but lacked a hand guard. Colloquially known as *Gutte karabin,* or 'boys' carbines', these guns were used for marksmanship training in Norwegian secondary schools. The mountain artillery and engineer carbine, the *Krag-Jørgensenkarabin for bergartilleriet og ingeniørvåpnet M/1897* (1897–1911), was practically identical to the cavalry carbine, with the exception of the rear swivel, which lay closer to the toe of the butt than the pistol grip. An engineer carbine, *Krag-Jørgensenkarabin for ingeniørvåpnet M/1904* (1904–15), otherwise similar to the 1897 pattern, was stocked virtually to the muzzle and accepted a bayonet. The field-artillery carbine, *Krag-Jørgensenkarabin for feltartilleriet M/1907* (1907–15), had one swivel on the left side of the rear barrel band and another on the under-edge of the butt.

Intended for universal issue, the *Krag-Jørgensenkarabin M/1912* (1912–35) was more of a short rifle than a carbine. A steel strengthening

collar was combined with the nose-cap in 1916, and the back sights were revised from 1925 onward for the M/1923 spitzer-bulletted cartridge.

Virtually all Norwegian military-pattern Krags were made by *Kongsberg Våpenfabrikk, the state small-arms factory, apart from a few thousand M/94 rifles produced in the 1890s by Österreichische Waffenfabriks-Gesellschaft in Steyr (OEWG), and a few hundred by Fabrique Nationale d'Armes de Guerre in Herstal-lèz-Liège. Army-type M/1894 sporters were made in Kongsberg and by Österreichische Waffenfabriks-Gesellschaft; Kongsberg also offered M/1912 short rifles and sniper rifles commercially, or for sale to members of the Norwegian rifle association. These guns lacked army-issue butt traps, and their bolts bore an axe-carrying rampant lion instead of the 'OII' or 'H7' monograms of Oscar II and Haakon VII.

The best sources of information about US Krag-Jørgensen rifles are *Krag Rifles* by Lieutenant-Colonel William S. Brophy (The Gun Room Press, 1980), and *The Krag Rifle Story* by Franklin B. Mallory and Ludwig E. Olson (Springfield Research Service, 1979); and, for Norwegian patterns, *Hærens håndvåpen. Geværer og karabiner 1814–1940* by O. Nielsen and F.C. Skaar (Haermuseet Akershus, c. 1970). Details of Danish weapons, however, are still comparatively difficult to find.

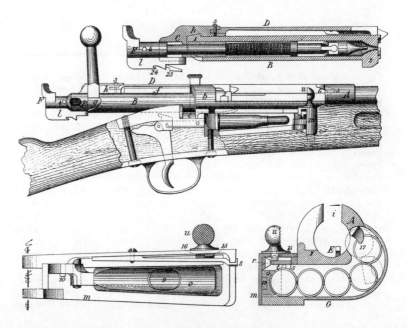

H. KRIEGHOFF GMBH & CO.

Krieghoff (2)

Immediately after the Second World War, this successor to the Suhl based Krieghoff company relocated to Ulm/Donau in western Germany. Today it makes a range of superb side-by-side and over/under shotguns, double rifles and combinations of smoothbore and rifled barrels (including three-barrel *Drillinge*). The quality of the metalwork and the fitting of wood to metal is exemplary; a range of decoration can be applied, from comparatively plain engraving to the finest high-relief inlay work.

Most of the current guns incorporate standard features, such as the Krieghoff Universal Trigger System and the Combi cocking device. The trigger has been designed specifically to preserve crisp operating characteristics, but prevent accidental doubling (firing a second shot inadvertently), which has often plagued double rifles chambering powerful ammunition. The Combi mechanism allows the rifles to be carried with the hammers down – the safest position – but they can be cocked simply by pushing forward on the slide on the tang. If the slide is locked forward, the action recocks automatically each time it is opened; alternatively, the hammers can be lowered safely (even if the chambers are loaded) simply by pushing the slide forward as far as it will go, then gently allowing it to move back to the rear, or uncocked, position.

In addition to the named guns considered separately, Krieghoff has also made the K-80 12-bore over/under shotgun and a single-barrelled derivative designated KS-5, in a variety of patterns suited to sporting use and clay-pigeon shooting. The K-80 was derived in the early 1950s from the Remington Model 32, designed by Crawford *Loomis and made in small quantities prior to 1942.

Krieghoff guns have fore-ends of different widths, and butts with a selection of combs and recoil pads. The K-80 RT is a special variant with a readily-detachable trigger mechanism ('Removable Trigger'). Krieghoff also offers sub-calibre inserts (*Einsteckläufe*) to convert shotgun barrels to rifles.

Krieghoff guns have been made in a variety of patterns, with decoration ranging from delicate English-style engraving to riotously baroque combinations of chiselling and encrustation. Butts may take standard, *Monte Carlo or *Bavarian form, and a wide range of accessories (single triggers, *Express sights, etc) has been offered. *See also* Bavaria, Classic, Crown Grade, Danube, Gold Target, Hubertus, Neptun, Parcours, Plus, Primus, Teck, Top Single, Trumpf, Ulm, Ultra and Unsingle.

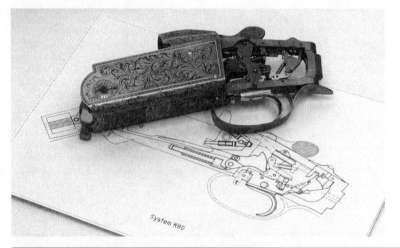

The action of the Krieghoff K-80 box-lock shotgun, with a drawing of the mechanism.

during the American Civil War; they bore 'MTK' marks. *See also* US arms inspectors' marks.

Krico. A tradename used by *Kriegeskorte & Co. of Stuttgart-Hedelfingen on spring-air guns made in 1948–55, and on firearms made since the mid-1950s.

Krider. John Krider & Company, Philadelphia, Pennsylvania, USA. Active from 1829 until 1876, this engineering company made revolvers for Jesse *Butterfield in the early years of the American Civil War.

Krieghoff – 1. Heinrich Krieghoff Waffenfabrik, Suhl. This gunmaking business was founded in 1916 by Heinrich Krieghoff (1889–1973), who had learned his trade as an apprentice in the factory of *Fabrique Nationale d'Armes de Guerre and had finally parted company with *Sempert & Krieghoff. Ludwig Krieghoff the Younger joined the firm in 1919, but the death of the elder Ludwig in 1924 effectively brought back the good-will of Sempert & Krieghoff – a name that seems to have been perpetuated on sporting guns and rifles until the late

1930s. These included an over/under shotgun without barrel lugs, since claimed as the first of its type to have been successful commercially; the *Trumpf *Drilling, with a separate rifle-cocking mechanism; and the *Neptun Drilling, with an automatic selector and an inertia-block safety system to prevent *doubling. Although the Krieghoff name will be found on a variety of guns that were bought-in from elsewhere (e.g. Walther pistols), the company is best known for involvement with the *Parabellum pistol, distributed in small numbers during the 1920s and 1930s, then made in quantity for the Luftwaffe in 1936–38; these airforce guns were made on machinery from the *Erfurt manu-factory, which had been passed on from the newly-liqui-dated *Simson & Sohn. Their history has been painstak-ingly documented in *The Krieghoff Parabellum* by Randall Gibson (Taylor Publishing, 1980). The company also developed a semi-automatic sporting rifle in the early 1930s, and was involved not only in the manufacture of machine-guns (MG. 15, MG. 81, MG. 131 and MG. 151) during the Second World War, but also in the development of the 1942-type paratroop rifle (FG. 42). The Erfurt-and-district telephone directories for 1940–41 list the 'Bau-Ansicht des RLM', in addition to factories in Suhl at Erffast Strasse 3 and Gothaer Strasse 155, and the drop-forge at Schmückestrasse 13. By 1945, Krieghoff was still operating four factories in Suhl, and four more in Thüringen at Schwarza, Kloster Vessra, Thema and Unterneubrünn. Anciens Établissements *Pieper had been acquired in the 1930s and operated as a Krieghoff 'feeder' after the German invasion of Belgium; a factory operated in Łodz in occupied Poland, another existed at Kufstein in the Austrian Tyrol, and there were three more in Sterzing, Mühlbach and Franzenfester in the Südtirol. The post-war partitioning of Germany gave Thüringen to the Russians, who subsequently demolished the Krieghoff factory; however, the owners and many of their employees, well aware of the consequences of staying, had already moved to the Ulm district. Guns handled by Krieghoff in the period 1916–30 usually bear the company name in full; those dating from 1930–40, however, customarily display 'H K' (q.v.) and a sword-and-anchor (*Schwertanker*) device. The code 'fzs' will be encountered on wartime products. **2.** H. Krieghoff GmbH, Ulm/Donau, Germany. *See* panel, facing page. **3.** Ludwig Krieghoff the Elder (c.1860–1924) was one of the founders of *Sempert & Krieghoff, which began trading in Suhl 1886. He is best remebered for his sporting-gun designs and particularly for a method of ensuring that gun-stocks fitted their owners – protected by German patent no. 123902, granted in 1900, when he was listed as a gunmaker in the *Deutsches Reichs-Adressbuch*. He also developed a sub cal ibre barrel insert, sold under the brandname Semper, and coined the slogan, 'the barrel shoots, the stock hits'.

Kriegskorte & Co. GmbH, also known as Krico-Werk, Stuttgart-Hedelfingen. This German weapons-making and distributing business, founded in Stuttgart in 1947 and now better known as Krico GmbH, began production of air rifles (the LG 1) in 1949. Work continued until c. 1965, by which time the LG 500 was being offered. Then production ceased. The first sporting rifles were made by refurbishing military-surplus *Mauser actions in the early 1950s. These were followed by a new short-action Miniature Mauser (1956–62) before more modern designs were developed.

Kriminalpolizei-Pistole, or PPK. A compact variant of the *Walther Polizei-Pistole (PP), introduced in 1931 and also known as the 'Polizei-Pistole, kurz' (short) or 'Polizei-Pistole, kleine' (small). The guns, offered in 6.35mm, 7.65mm and 9mm Short, were distinguished by a one-piece wrap-around grip, while their magazines held one less cartridge than the PP versions. The guns were numbered in a single series until 1939, when they were separated and began again at 100001P and 100001K for Polizei- and Kriminalpolizei-Pistolen respectively. The safety catch had changed from ninety-degree rotation to sixty degrees in 1938. Machining was simplified during the Second World War, but production of PPKs stopped in 1945, when the US Army reached Zella-Mehlis. Work began again in Ulm/Donau in the 1950s, although many of the post-war guns (indeed, all of those made prior to 1964) were assembled from parts made in France by *Manurhin.

Krinkov. *See* AKR and Kalashnikov.

'krl'. This mark was allocated in 1942 to the Krümmel factory of *Dynamit AG, for use on German military small-arms ammunition and components.

Krnka – 1. Karel Krnka. One of the best known, but by no means the most successful, of the pre-1918 Austro-Hungarian gun designers, Krnka's reputation rests more upon his abilities as a journalist and the textbook *Die prinzipiellen Eigenschaften der automatischen Feuerwaffen* ('*The principal characteristics of automatic firearms*', 1900) written under the pseudonym Kaisertreu. Karel Krnka was born in Velk´y Varadín on 6 April 1858, son of the gunmaker Sylvestr Krnka (below). After a period of apprenticeship, the younger Krnka was commissioned into an Austro-Hungarian infantry regiment for a short period of military service. During this time, he helped his father with the *Schnell-Lade-Gewehr* (rapid-loading rifle), developed an auto-ejecting version of the *Werndl and embarked on the first of his small-calibre military bolt-action rifles. This performed well in the trials of 1887–88, but was rejected in favour of the *Mannlicher, which was backed by a powerful syndicate headed by Waffenfabrik *Steyr. Krnka left the army in 1887 and moved to Britain to become chief engineer of the short-lived *Gatling Arms & Ammunition Company Ltd of Birmingham; he returned home in 1891 when the Gatling operation failed. After a spell in Prague as a patent agent (1891–98), Krnka became works manager of Patronenfabrik G. *Roth. There he continued to develop guns, although the patenting of his work in Roth's name has denied him much of the credit. The most important of the guns was the *Roth-Steyr, or Repetierpistole M 7, which was adopted by the Austro-Hungarian cavalry. Krnka left the Roth organisation when its founder died in 1909, working for the *Hirtenberg ammunition manufactory until 1922. He returned to Czechoslovakia in 1923, and was employed initially by Zbrojovka *Praga, then by *Československá Zbrojovka. He died in Prague on 25 February 1926. **2.** Sylvestr Krnka. Born on 31 December 1825 in Velk´y Bor, near Horazdvice in Bohemia (then a part of Austria-Hungary), Krnka was apprenticed in his youth to the Viennese gunmaker Nowotn´y before setting up on his own account in Volyn in 1848. A move to the Michl district of Prague occurred in 1871. Krnka is remembered largely for a series of single-shot rapid-loading rifles (*Schnell-Lade-Gewehre*) dating from the period 1849–76, and also for the successful conversion system applied in the late 1860s to hundreds of thousands of Russian rifle-muskets. His cartridge designs were also renowned in their day. However, despite collaborating with his better-known son, Karel (above), Sylvestr Krnka was never able to offer the Austro-Hungarian authorities a successful small-calibre repeater. He died in Prague on 4 January 1903.

Kromar. Konrad [Edeler von] Kromar, Austria-Hungary. *See* 'Mannlicher'.

'Krone', *see also* Crown **– 1.** A brandname found on shotgun cartridges loaded by *Cramer & Buchholz prior to 1914. **2.** Found on a top-lever-cocking spring-air pistol manufactured in the late 1930s by *Moritz & Gerstenberger. Basically it was a repeating version of the *Zenit.

Kropatschek – 1. Alfred [Ritter von] Kropatschek. This army officer was born in Bielitz in Schlesien on 30 January 1838, entering the Pest military academy in 1856.

KROPATSCHEK RIFLE

Kropatschek (2)

Prototypes of this bolt-action repeater were submitted to the Austro-Hungarian authorities on 24 September 1874. The action was based on the 1871-type German Mauser, using the bolt rib to lock against the receiver, and a *Vetterli-type tube magazine lay in the fore-end beneath the barrel. By 1876, the Kropatschek was being

declared as 'suitable for adoption', and a gendarmerie carbine was issued in 1881.

Leopold *Gasser of Vienna patented a spring-loaded loading gate in 1879, by adapting existing Winchester patterns, and added it to the Gasser-Kropatschek rifles tested in Austria-Hungary in the early 1880s. Some 11x58 M1881 Kropatschek rifles were issued for field trials with the Austro-Hungarian Army. They were conventional tube-magazine

patterns, locked by the bolt rib abutting the receiver ahead of the bridge. Made by Österreichische Waffenfabriks-Gesellschaft, Steyr, in 1880–82, the rifles were withdrawn after trials had been completed; apparently survivors were converted for naval use in the 1890s. The advent of the box magazine restricted distribution, although in France, the popularity of the Mle 1878 naval Kropatschek in Indo-China and Equatorial Africa eventually led to the creation of the *Lebel. Kropatschek rifles were also popular in Portugal, where a variant perfected by an army officer named Dechambès was adopted in July 1886 to replace the single-shot *Guedes pattern.

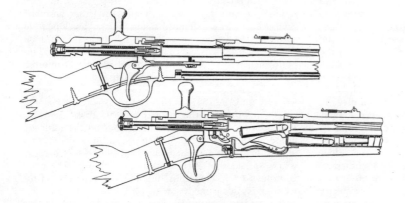

The drawings compare the single-shot French Gras rifle (top) with the magazine-feed Kropatschek (centre), illustrating the commonality of the bolt mechanism. The experimental 11mm French Mle 1885 infantry rifle (below) introduced the receiver/two-piece-stock design associated with the later 8mm Lebel.

After rapidly proving his abilities as an organiser, Kropatschek was appointed to the Austro-Hungarian artillery commission (subsequently the Militär-Technische-Kommitée) between 1866 and 1874. During this period, in addition to lecturing, he supervised the introduction of the *Gasser revolver and wrote textbooks, including the *Handbuch für die kais. kön. Artillerie* (1873). Knighted in 1870 for his work, Ritter von Kropatschek patented a bolt-action rifle on 2 November 1874. This tube-magazine weapon was very successful in France, forming the basis of the *Lebel, but it failed to enter Austro-Hungarian service in quantity. Promoted to the rank of general in 1890, Kropatschek became inspector-general of artillery in 1895. Much decorated and greatly respected for his administrative work, he died in retirement in Lovrana in 1911. **2.** Kropatschek rifle: *see* panel, above.

'krq'. Used by Emil Busch AG of Rathenow on optical equipment made for the German armed forces during the Second World War.

KS. An abbreviation associated with guns stocked in synthetic Kevlar, including the *Remington M700 and the *Winchester Model 70.

'ksb'. Found on small-arms ammunition components made in 1942–44, under German supervision, by Manufacture Nationale d'Armes de Levallois, Levallois-Perret, France.

'KSG'. Possibly found in the form of a monogram: associated with the products of Eduard *Kettner, Köln-Suhler Gewehrfabrik.

'KSM'. Found on US military firearms and accessories. *See* Kelley S. *Morse.

'KT' – 1. A superimposition-type monogram with neither letter prominent. Correctly interpreted as 'TK' (q.v.); associated with Theodor *Kommer of Zella-Mehlis, Germany. **2.** An encircled cursive linear monogram, with 'J' slightly dominant. Probably interpreted more accurately as 'KJ' (q.v.); found on revolvers made in Spain prior to 1914.

Kufsteiner Gerätebau [und Handelsgesellschaft mbH]. *See* Voere.

Kugler – 1. Adolphe Kugler, Kingston, New York State. This US gunsmith, the son, or possibly brother, of Albert Kugler (below), was listed in local directories for 1862–64. He is known to have made spring-air *Gallery Guns. **2.** Albert Kugler, Kingston, New York State. This maker of cap-lock firearms and spring-air Gallery Guns worked at 43 North Front Street from 1857 until 1860. *See also* Adolphe Kugler (above).

Kuhles. Gottlieb Kuhles Witwe, Albrechts bei Suhl in Thüringen. Founded in 1850, and still being listed in 1940 as a maker of gun parts and haberdashery items (*Kurzwaren*).

Kührt. Otto Kührt, Zella-Mehlis in Thüringen, Germany. Listed in 1930 as a master gunsmith.

Kulikov. Lev Leonidovich Kulikov was born in Tula in 1931, entering the S.I. Mosin Tula Mechanical-Technical College in 1946. After service with the Soviet Army (1952–57), Kulikov entered a design bureau and has contributed to a variety of firearms-related projects. These include the *PSM pistol and sporting guns.

Kummer. E. Kummer, Suhl in Thüringen, Germany. Listed as a gunsmith, 1920–32.

Kuralt. L.L. Kuralt, a government employee, accepted firearms and accessories for the US Army in 1905–10. They were identified by 'LLK' marks. *See also* US arms inspectors' marks.

Kurbelspanner. A German-language term applied to airguns, generally of *Gallery Gun form, which are cocked by winding back the piston with a crank (cf. *Bügelspanner). Popular in central Europe prior to 1914, they were still being made in small numbers in 1939.

Kurz. German for 'short'; used to identify short rifles (*Kurzgewehr*) or chamberings for the 9mm Kurz (9mm Short, .380 ACP) pistol cartridge.

'Kuvert' [The]. Associated with shotgun cartridges sold by Charles S. *Rosson of Norwich, this tradename is believed to be a corruption of Covert.

Kwantung arms factory. A maker of Model 21 *Mauser short rifles for the North China Army (Kuomintang), c. 1932–37.

'Kyblack' [The]. A shotgun cartridge, loaded with black powder, made in Britain by *Kynoch Ltd, prior to the acquisition of the company by Explosives Trades Ltd in 1918, and thereafter by *Eley-Kynoch Ltd. *See also* Kynoid.

Kynčl. Josef Kynčl, an engineer employed by *Janeček, was responsible for the experimental ZJ481 rifle or AK (*Automat Kynčl*) tested by the Czechoslovakian Army in 1949. One pattern had a conventional gas-piston system; another led gas directly back to act against the bolt.

Ultimately, however, the competing *Kratochvil ČZ 493 was preferred.

Kynoch Limited, Witton, Birmingham, Warwickshire. This company was founded in 1862, when George Kynoch bought out the existing businesses of Pursall & Phillips, percussion-cap makers of Witton (near Birmingham). A contempory advertisement identified 'Kynoch & Co. (Late W. Pursall & Co.), Contractors to the War Department and the Turkish Government, Patentees and Manufacturers of Percussion Caps, Military and Sporting Ammunition', trading from the Hampton Street premises. Kynoch & Company became 'G. Kynoch & Company Ltd' in 1884, but George Kynoch left the company in 1889 and died two years later. However, business prospered, and Kynoch Ltd was formed in 1897. Kynoch was a prolific producer of ammunition, including sporting-rifle and shotgun cartridges made under a variety of brandnames, including Bonax, C.B. or CB, Deep Shell, *Kyblack, *Kynoid, Nitro Ball, Nitrone, Opex, Paradox, Primax, Sallinoid, Swift, Tellax, Triumph and *Witton. Cartridges were also sold marked 'Patent 2090', referring to British Patent 2090/86 of 1886, which protected the cartridge construction. Kynoch's independence lasted until November 1918 when, together with Eley and many other interested parties, it became a part of Explosive Trades Ltd – which became Nobel Industries Ltd in 1920. In 1926, however, the business was sold to Imperial Chemical Industries, and thereafter ammunition production was concentrated at the Lion Works in Witton. The Eley factory in Edmonton was closed. Subsequently many of the pre-1918 Kynoch brandnames were perpetuated by *Eley-Kynoch Ltd, although the post-amalgamation origin (at least on cartridges made prior to c. 1963) can often be detected by the presence of the encircled ICI trademark in the headstamps. In addition to sporting-rifle ammunition and shotgun cartridges, Kynoch made the *Swift air rifle to the patents granted in 1906 to George *Hookham and Edward Jones, and also a number of projectiles. The Mitre was a slug for smoothbores, while the Lion, Match and Witton were diabolo pellets.

'Kynoid' [The]. A shotgun cartridge made by *Kynoch Ltd prior to the acquisition of the company by Explosives Trades Ltd in 1918. It contained smokeless propellant (cf. Kyblack).

L

'**L**' – **1.** Above a vertical arrow. A mark applied by an inspector working in the *Lithgow small-arms factory in New South Wales, Australia. *See also* British military inspectors' marks. **2.** Cursive, beneath a crown. Found on Bavarian weapons: the mark of Kings Ludwig II (1864–86) and Ludwig III (1913–18). *See also* Cyphers, imperial and royal. **3.** Often cursive, beneath a crown. Found on Belgian weapons: the mark of Kings Leopold II (1865–1909) and Leopold III (1934–50). *See also* Cyphers, imperial and royal. **4.** Stamped into the woodwork of 'Long' British military rifle butts, which were ¹/₂in longer than standard. **5.** Above crossed rifles and a pistol. A mark found on butt-cylinder airguns made by Friedrich *Langenhan of Zella St Blasii, Thüringen, Germany, from c. 1896 until 1914. **6.** As 'L' or 'L Iᵘ', beneath a crown. Found on Portuguese weapons: the mark of King Luis I (1861–89). *See also* Cyphers, imperial and royal.

La... – **1.** La Coruña, Fábrica Nacional de Armas. A maker of Spanish Mo.1916, Mo.1943 and other *Mauser-type short rifles. **2.** La France Specialties, San Diego, California, USA. A gunmaking business specialising in handgun silencers suited to such guns as the *Government Model Colt-Browning. **3.** La Fury: *see* LA Fury (below). **4.** La Industrial. A small Browning-type pocket pistol, usually attributed to *Orbea Hermanos of Eibar, Guipúzcoa, Spain, although on uncertain grounds: 6.35mm, six rounds. **5.** La Lira. This Spanish semi-automatic pistol, the work of *Garate, Anitua y Cia of Eibar, was essentially a 1901-pattern *Mannlicher in all but two respects: the chambering, for 7.65mm Auto cartridges, and the substitution of a detachable box magazine for the original integral charger-loaded design. A few thousand guns seem to have been made immediately prior to the First World War, but were superseded by simpler *Browning copies. **6.** La Mignonne. A folding .410 shotgun, with a revolver-type grip and a skeleton stock, made in the 1920s by, or perhaps for, Leopold *Ancion-Marx of Liège. **7.** La Reine, a small airgun: *see* Carabine la Reine. **8.** La Rosa. A Spanish gunmaker/patentee: *see* La *Rosa. **9.** La Rosa. A small Spanish-made revolver, customarily a six-shot chambered for the 7.65mm Auto cartridge, with a barrel/cylinder assembly that could be slid forward for loading. Essentially similar to the *Galand type.

'**LAB**'. Found on US military firearms and accessories. *See* Lester A. *Beardslee.

Laballe, La Balle. This mark is said to have been used by W. & J. *Jeffrey of London, England, on large *Gem-type butt-cylinder airguns sold in the early 1890s. It may signify French or Belgian origin – *La Balle* (The Bullet), perhaps indicating that the guns were capable of firing conventional cartridges when required, or that they were rifled to fire slugs instead of smoothbored for darts.

Labonte. H.J. Labonte, using an 'HBL' mark, accepted firearms and accessories made for the US armed forces by

*Colt's Patent Fire Arms Manufacturing Company. They date from 1939. *See also* US arms inspectors' marks.

'**L.A.C.**', '**L.A. Co.**' London Armoury Company (q.v.). *See also* James Kerr.

Lacey. Arthur Lacey, Bridge Street, Stratford-upon-Avon, Warwickshire, England. Lacey – who also traded as an ironmonger – handled sporting guns and ammunition prior to the First World War. Apparently some of the shotgun cartridges bore the name 'Welcome' or 'Welcome Smokeless'.

Lachat. Jules Lachat, rue de Vernay 50, Saint-Étienne, France. Listed in 1892 as a gunmaker.

Lacroix, Liège, Belgium. A maker of revolvers active in the 1870s.

Lacy – **1.** Lacy & Company, London. The marks of this English gunmaker have been reported on self-cocking *pepperboxes dating from the middle of the nineteenth century. A trading style of Lacy & Witton, perhaps? **2.** Lacy & Reynolds [& Company, after c. 1852]. Based in Birmingham, this English gunmaker and sword-cutler was listed in London in 1850–53, maintaining an office at 21 Great St Helen's.

Ladmore. Edwin Ladmore, Widemarsh Street, Hereford (1841–70). This English gunmaker is known to have marked sporting guns and self-cocking *pepperboxes dating from the mid-nineteenth century.

Lady, Lady's... – **1.** Lady Colt. A brandname applied unofficially in the early 1870s, by *Kittredge & Company of Cincinnati, Ohio, USA, to the .32 *New Line Colt revolver. **2.** Lady Model. Similar to the Fourth Model *Lord derringer, made by *Colt's Patent Fire Arms Manufacturing Company in 1959–63, this had gold plating on the frame and barrel, and pearlite grips. *See also* *Thuer derringer. **3.** Lady's Model. A tiny 6.35mm-calibre revolver made in Liège by Établissements A. Lebeaux, c. 1908–14.

'**lae**'. Allotted to Heinrich Zeiss (Union Zeiss KG), for use on sights and optical equipment made in a factory in Gostingen/Wartheland, Germany, during 1943–45.

LA Fury. A name associated with semi-automatic pistols made in Germany by *Reck of Lauf bei Nürnberg and distributed in the USA by Hawes Firearms Company of Los Angeles. The mark should be considered a corruption of L.A. Fury (L.A. being the abbreviation for Los Angeles).

Lahaye. Arnold Lahaye, Suhl in Thüringen, Germany. This gunmaking business was trading in 1900 under the proprietorship of Leonhard & Peter Lahaye.

Lahti – **1.** Aimo Johannes Lahti (1896–1970) is best known for the 9mm Lahti pistol adopted by the Finnish Army prior to the Second World War, then made in larger numbers in Sweden. He also developed submachineguns (*see* Suomi), the Lahti-Saloranta light machine-gun (below), the 20mm L-37 aircraft cannon and the 20mm L-39 anti-tank rifle. **2.** Lahti pistol: *see* panel, facing page. Comparatively little has been written about the Lahti in

English, although 'Simply Reliable: Finland's Lahti Pistol' in *Shooter's Bible*, no. 72 (1981), gives a summary of its history. **3.** Lahti-Saloranta. This 7.62x54R light machine-gun, designed by Aimo Lahti and Arvo Saloranta, was adopted by the Finnish Army in 1926, and made in small numbers prior to the Winter War of 1939–40; it remained in service until displaced by Soviet weapons in the late 1940s. However, the guns were held in reserve until sufficient quantities of the 7.62x39 m/62 – a derivative of the original LS-26 design – had been introduced. The action of the recoil-operated LS-26, locked by a tipping bolt, includes an ★accelerator to improve reliability. Firing is accomplished from an open bolt position, just before the parts reach the limit of their forward stroke. Detachable box and drum magazines can be used.

Laidley – 1. Theodore Thadeus Sobieski Laidley. Born in West Virginia in 1822, Laidley graduated from the US Military Academy, West Point, in 1842 and was posted immediately to the Ordnance Department. Author of the *Ordnance Manual of 1861*, commandant of Frankford Arsenal (1862–64), then Springfield Armory (1864–66), where he oversaw production of ★Joslyn and ★Allin metallic-cartridge rifle-musket conversions, Laidley is best known as the designer and co-patentee with C.A. ★Emery of the ★Laidley-Emery rotating-block action rifle (US no. 54,743 of 15 May 1866). Designer of 'Tompion for Fire Arms' (patented in 1868) and a centrefire cartridge (US no. 140,144 of 1871), Laidley resigned his commission in 1880 and died in Florida in 1886. His 'TTSL' marks will also be found on firearms and accessories accepted on behalf of the Federal and US Armies in the period 1864–66. *See also* US arms inspectors' marks. **2.** Laidley-Emery rifle. Similar externally to the Remington ★Rolling Block, but with an additional locking bar pivoted on the hammer axis-pin, this was patented in 1866 by Major Theodore T.S. Laidley and Charles A. Emery, respectively the commandant and a 'machinist' of ★Springfield Armory. The prototype carbine was submitted to trials in 1865 by 'M.Y. Chick of New York', camouflaging its origins, but it failed to impress. Although a few additional guns were made at Springfield, the ★Allin conversion system was preferred, owing to the ease with which existing rifle-muskets could be altered. ★Colt's Patent Fire Arms Manufacturing Company made a few Laidley-Emery rifles in the late 1860s, but rights were acquired by the ★Whitney Arms Company c.1871. Whitney made military-style rifles and carbines alongside sporting guns until 1882, when the lapse of patents granted to Joseph ★Rider allowed copies of the simpler Remington-type rolling block to be substituted.

Laird – 1. J.W. Laird & Company. Listed as a member of the London gun trade, operating during 1889–96 from '6 Bishopsgate Street, Without'. **2.** Laird-Metayne machine-gun. Some .303-calibre guns of this type, designed in France by Mentayne & Degaille and promoted by the ★Coventry Ordnance Works, were tested in Britain between 1908 and 1912. They were rejected on the grounds that they failed to meet the tactical doctrines of the time.

Lake – 1. Henry Harris Lake, London and New York.

LAHTI PISTOL

Lahti (2)

Developed from 1929 onward, this recoil-operated semi-automatic pistol was adopted by the Finnish Army in 1935. The *9mm Pistooli L-35* was made in small numbers by ★Valtions Kiväritehdas (VKT), the state-owned rifle factory, but only 9,000 had been produced – in several sub-varieties – when work stopped in 1954. With the exception of one batch of 200, which subsequently were converted, these guns all had ★accelerators to improve reliability in sub-zero conditions. They also had stock lugs on the butt heel and loaded-chamber indicators on top of the barrel extensions.

VKT made 1,250 additional guns in 1958, with plain-top barrel extensions. Finnish service pistols have plain serial numbers, but about 1,000 failed inspection and subsequently were sold commercially; these have 'VO' number prefixes.

Lahti pistols were used in large numbers in Sweden, nearly 84,000 being made by ★Husqvarna during 1942–46. Issued to the Swedish forces as the *Pistol M/40*, owing to the unavailability of the Walther P.38 and the FN-Browning GP-35 (the first and second choices), the Lahti was not as successful in Sweden as its Finnish prototype. It can be identified by its plain contours, especially in the shape of the barrel extension and the trigger guard, and by the crowned 'h' moulded into the grips.

A Swedish 9mm M/40 Lahti pistol made by Husqvarna; note the crowned 'h' moulded into the grips. These guns were not as successful as had been hoped, forcing the authorities to re-issue M/07 FN- and Husqvarna-Brownings that had been withrawn into store.

This British patent agent is believed to have been the son of William Robert Lake, and was active from 1884 to 1904 and later. His address is usually listed as 7 & 8 Southampton Buildings (that of the International Patent Office), and 60 Wall Street in New York. Lake acted for Elbert H. *Searle in 1910 (*see* British Patent 12,723/10). **2.** William Robert Lake began operating as a patent agent and consultant engineer in the middle of the nineteenth century, working from chambers in Chancery Lane, London. He formed the International Patent Office, 7 & 8 Southampton Buildings, London, in 1865, and entered into a partnership with Henry Haseltine four years later. Lake acted for, among other people, *Smith & Wesson, protection for the S&W Model No. 3 auto-ejecting revolver being granted in Britain on 17 May 1869. *See also* Charles A. *King. Eventually William Lake was succeeded by his son, Henry Harris Lake.

Lakeside. A brandname associated with shotguns made by the *Crescent Arms Company.

Lambin. Louis Lambin, Liège. A gunmaker working in Belgium in the second half of the nineteenth century. His marks have been reported on double-barrelled sporting rifles and on single-shot cutlass pistols, sharing the lines of the revolvers of the day and usually chambering pinfire ammunition. L. Lamblin & Company (*sic*) employed a British agent, Henry Haschke, from 1868 until 1893. The office stood at 60 Watling Street, London E.C., until 1871, then remained for eighteen years at 6 Love Lane, E.C. The trading style was changed in 1883 to Lamblin & Theak, and the agency was moved in 1890 to 5 London Wall Avenue. The last directory entries appeared in 1893, when the premises were listed as 15 George Street, London E.C. *See also* Lenders-Lambin.

Lamotte. Robert S. Lamotte, a captain in the US Army using an 'RSL' mark, accepted *Sharps breech-loading rifles and carbines in the period 1867–69, immediately after the American Civil War. *See also* US arms inspectors' marks.

Lampo. An Italian-made repeating pistol, designed by gunsmith Catello *Tribuzio and patented in Italy in 1890. Chambered for the 8mm Gaulois cartridge, the pistol was operated simply by pushing the ring trigger that projected from the lower front edge of the butt/magazine unit to open the breech, then pulling it back to load the chamber, close the breech and fire the gun.

Lamson – 1. E.G. Lamson [& Company], Windsor, Vermont. A US based gunmaking business active from 1850 to 1867; exhibitor at the Great Exhibition (London) in 1851, and maker of the breech-loading carbines patented by William *Palmer, 1,000 being sold to the Federal government in 1864–65. **2.** Lamson Engineering Company Ltd, Hythe Road, Willesden Junction, London. A maker of magazines for the British 9mm *Sten Gun during the Second World War. The code 'S 64' may have been used instead of the company name. *See also* British military manufacturers' marks. **3.** Lamson, Goodnow & Yale Company, Windsor, Vermont, Shelburn Falls, Massachusetts, and New York City. Active only during the American Civil War of 1861–65, this short-lived gunmaking business was granted one contract to make 25,000 .58 1861-pattern rifle-muskets for the Federal Army on 11 July 1861, and another on 7 October 1861. A total of 50,019 guns had been accepted by the summer of 1863, each marked 'L.G. & Y' beneath a displayed eagle.

Lamure. Lamure et Gidrol, rue d'Annonay 2, Saint-Étienne, France. Listed in 1892 as a gunmaker.

Lancaster – 1. Usually encountered as 'The Lancaster', this brandname can be found on shotgun cartridges handled by J. *Hodgson of Lancaster. **2.** Alfred Lancaster, an English gunmaker, traded first as a partner in Charles William & Alfred Lancaster – with his elder brother – but then began working independently, first at 27 South Audley Street, London (1862–85), and later at 50 Green Street, Grosvenor Square. Lancaster was the recipient of British Patents 2753/59 of 1859, protecting a breech-loading firearm and a cartridge-charger system, and 1525/65 of 1865 for an improved breech-loader. Alfred Lancaster died in 1890, and his executors subsequently transferred the business to Charles Lancaster & Company. **3.** Charles Lancaster. Founded in 1826, this gunmaking business occupied premises at 151 New Bond Street, London, where duelling pistols, shotguns, sporting rifles and pendant-ball reservoir airguns were made. Subsequently it was inherited by Charles William Lancaster, son of the founder, and became Charles Lancaster & Company in 1867. **4.** Charles William Lancaster. Son of the gun-barrel maker Charles Lancaster (above), Charles William worked from 151 New Bond Street from 1847 until he entered into a partnership with his brother Alfred in 1855. After the dissolution of this agreement in 1860, Charles William continued to trade from 151 New Bond Street and 2 Little Bruton Street, London, until his death in 1878. Then the business was sold to Henry A.A. *Thorn, its former manager, but continued to trade as Charles Lancaster & Company. C.W. Lancaster was renowned for his *oval-bore rifling, protected by English Patent no. 13,161 of 1850, and for the appropriate machinery (English Patent 13,454 of 1851). He also designed a pillar-breech rifle, in 1848, and a variety of guns and accessories protected by British Patents granted between 1853 and 1869. Lancaster was one of the major innovators in sporting-gun design in the middle of the nineteenth century, among his many designs being a shotshell with the primer concealed behind a thin brass 'cover-all' base. **5.** Charles Lancaster & Company. Formed by the sale of the business of Charles William Lancaster (above) to Henry *Thorn, in 1878, this firm continued to trade from the New Bond Street and Little Bruton Street premises into the twentieth century. Subsequently operations were undertaken in London from 11 Panton Street in 1904–25, 99 Mount Street (1925–32) and 151 New Bond Street from 1932 onward. In addition to guns and ammunition, Lancaster sold a variety of shotgun cartridges under such names as Generally Useful, Leicester, Norfolk and Twelve Twenty. Eventually Charles Lancaster & Company Ltd was absorbed by *Grant & Lang. **6.** Charles & William Lancaster. A partnership of the brothers Charles William and Alfred Lancaster – each listed separately – this traded from 151 New Bond Street and 2 Little Bruton Street, London, from 1856 until 1860. **7.** Lancaster's Pygmies. A shotgun cartridge made by *Eley Bros. prior to the acquisition of the company by Explosives Trades Ltd in 1918.

Lancer. A name given to the .22LR Star Modelo HK blowback semi-automatic pistol made by *Star–Bonifacio Echeverria SA between 1955 and 1968. It was essentially similar to the *Starfire, with the exception that it was chambered for rimfire ammunition.

Lanchester. The 'Machine Carbine, Lanchester, 9mm Mark I' (1941) was a British *submachine-gun, used largely by the Royal Air Force and the Royal Navy, as the army took priority on deliveries of the *Thompson. It was a copy of the German MP.28 (Bergmann) and accepted a sword bayonet. The Mark I had a selector ahead of the trigger lever and a tangent-leaf back sight; the Mark I* (1943) had a simple sight and was capable of automatic fire only. Mark I Lanchesters were usually converted to Mark I* standards after returning for repair. About 80,000 were made – 59,000 by the *Sterling Engineering Company Ltd, 17,000 assembled by *Greener, and 3,900 by *Boss & Company

Landes. Maschinenfabrik 'Landes', München, Bavaria. A maker of about 4,000 M/69 *Werder carbines for the Bavarian Army in 1869–70.

'Land of Burns' [The]. This name was associated with shotgun cartridges sold by *Kirk of Ayr. The name refers to the locality, as the Scottish poet Robert Burns was born nearby.

Lands. The raised portions of a gun-barrel bore between the grooves of the *rifling.

Lane – 1. Charles Lane. Best known as an ammunition maker, apparently Lane trained as a gunsmith. He is recorded in London directories of 1889–91 as trading on his own account from 60 Queen Victoria Street, but he formed *Lane Brothers soon after. He may be the son of the 25-year-old Charles Lane (below), identified by Howard Blackmore in *A Dictionary of London Gunmakers 1350–1850* (Phaidon-Christies, 1986), listed at Little George Street, St Pancras, by the census of 1841. **2.** Charles Lane, Ernest Lane: see Lane Brothers. **3.** George J. Lane. A gunsmith listed as trading from 4 Duck Lane, Edward Street, Soho, London W., in 1879. **4.** John Burr Lane. A principal of *Lane Brothers & Company, and patentee of an improved trigger mechanism for *Gem-type spring-air guns (British Patent 20,598/95 of 1895). He was also co-patentee of the Musketeer rifle with his brothers, Charles and Ernest, and inventor of several projectiles (see British Patents 297,612 of 1928 and 308,943 of 1929). British Patent 1827/04 of 1904 protected an airgun piston. **5.** Thomas Lane. Marks applied by this English gunmaker, trading from 1 Tavistock Street in Leamington, Warwickshire, in 1850–65, have been reported on self-cocking *pepperboxes. He was succeeded in the mid-1860s by his son John, who continued operating until 1870 or later. **6.** Lane Brothers, Faringdon, Berkshire (now Oxfordshire). This ironmongery and agricultural-supply business handled sporting guns and ammunition, including shotgun cartridges sold under the brandname *Eclipse. **7.** Lane Brothers & Company Ltd. Trading from 45a New Church Street in Bermondsey, London, from 1893 onward, Lane Brothers was the manufacturer and patentee of a large number of shot, airgun pellets and slugs. These were distributed under a variety of brandnames. Eventually the business moved to Footscray, Sidcup, Kent. British Patent 1560/02 of 1902 depicts a typical Lane projectile of the early twentieth century. Lane's Bango was an airgun slug with a charge of match composition in the rear, which exploded when the slug hit a hard surface. It dated from 1907, but was rapidly discontinued. Bully Bullets were diabolo pellets made from 1906. Lane's Cat was a lead airgun slug, with a short body, roughly 5mm long, and a rounded shallow head. Small ribs on the sides

were intended to adapt to different bore diameters. Lane's Expanded Bullet, or Expanded Number 1 Gem, an airgun slug similar to the Gem, was designed for use with the Patent Bullet Expander to expand airgun slugs into the rifling of any gun (assuming an approximate match of calibre). Lane's Heavyweight – developed prior to 1902 – was a short-bodied airgun slug, similar to the *Gem, specifically intended for use in air pistols. The Perfect Bullet was an airgun slug introduced prior to 1902, and the Perfect Number 1 Gem (c. 1900) was similar to the Cat, but had a longer body. Lane's Patent Shot Cartridge was basically an airgun projectile comprising several small ball shot in a paper body; it dated from 1900–02. The Rotary Bullet was a slug with soft lead wings, designed to effect rotation; it was patented in 1902. The Triumph was another of the proprietary airgun slugs, patented by John Burr Lane in 1929 and marketed by Lane Brothers from 1930/31 onward. It had a diabolo body, with a rounded head separated from the body by an additional flange; the Japanese *Jet and *Silver Jet are essentially similar. The Turbite projectile was little more than serrated lead shot. Lane Brothers made large numbers of pellets for other companies to market, including, for instance, the Sussex Armoury's Jackal and Magnum types. A spring-air rifle known as the *Musketeer, protected by British Patent 15,773/01 of 1901, was also marketed in small numbers – although the guns may have been made by the *Midland Gun Company.

Lang – 1. Aug. Lang, Mäbendorf bei Suhl in Thüringen. According to the *Deutsches Reichs-Adressbuch*, this metal-working business made gun parts and tools during the Second World War. **2.** Chr. Lang, Suhl in Thüringen, Germany. Registered as a gunsmith in 1919. **3.** Edward Lang. This English gunmaker began trading from 88 Wigmore Street, London W., in 1880. He is best known for sporting guns and rifles, although his marks have also been found on air canes and walking-stick guns. **4.** Hermann J. Lang. This Prussian gunmaker/sword-cutler, based in Solingen, employed *Heintzmann & Rochussen as his Britsh agent in 1867–69. **5.** James Lang. This gunsmith began his career in 1887, at 33 New Bond Street, London, but had moved to 18 Brook Street by 1888. The trading style became James Lang & Company Ltd in 1891, and a move to 102 New Bond Street was made in 1894. Lang & Hussey followed in 1896, then Lang & Hussey Ltd in 1897. By 1900, premises were being kept at Wells Mews, Wells Street, London, in addition to the New Bond Street shop. **6.** Joseph Lang [& Sons]. Lang opened a shop in Haymarket, London, in 1825, but moved to 22 Cockspur Street, Charing Cross, London, in 1853. The Turnover four- and six-shot revolving pistols (pepperboxes) were shown at the Great Exhibition in London in 1851. Joseph Lang is also noted as an inventor of a breech-loading gun with drop-down barrels (British Patent 1785/67 of 1867); he died in 1869. His business continued after 1874 as Joseph Lang & Sons, moving to 10 Pall Mall and 102 New Bond Street in 1890, but it amalgamated with Stephen *Grant & Sons c. 1899. Lang also handled shotgun ammunition sold under such brandnames as Lang's Special and Ventracta.

Langdon. John Langdon, 20 St Mary Street, Truro, Cornwall, England. This gunmaker marked sporting guns, accessories and shotgun ammunition, including cartridges sold as The Langdon.

Langenham. A popular mispelling of Langenhan (q.v.).

Langenhan – 1. Emil Langenhan, Zella-Mehlis in Thüringen, Germany. Listed in the 1930 *Deutsches Reichs-Adressbuch* as a retailer of guns and ammunition, but possibly also maintaining repair facilities. Langenhan was still listed in 1939 as a weapon maker. **2.** Friedrich Langenhan, Zella St Blasii and Zella-Mehlis in Thüringen, Germany. Valentin Friedrich Langenhan began operating in 1842 in Mehlis, moving to nearby Zella St. Blasii in 1855. Revolvers, sporting guns and bicycles were made during the 1890s – under the direction of Hermann Langenhan – and airgun production began about 1900. *See* British Patent 15,802/00 of 1900, granted to Friedr. Langenham (*sic*) of Zella St. Blasii, through Martin *Pulvermann, to protect a barrel catch for spring-air guns. An improved version was covered by British Patent 10,411/05 of 1905, both being used on *Millita guns made by Langenhan and imported into Britain by Pulvermann. The 1911 ALFA catalogue records the appearance of the new Modell 1909, or Original V, airgun, and various other patterns are known to have been made – including the post-war *FLZ spring-air pistol. In additional to sporting rifles, shotguns and airguns, Langenhan made semi-automatic pistols. These included the 7.65mm *FL-Selbstlader of 1915 and the 6.35mm FL Model 3. The business was listed in the *Deutsches Reichs-Adressbuch* during 1900–20 as a gunmaker and bicycle manufacturer. It was listed in 1930 simply as a gunmaker, owned by Fritz and Ernst Langenhan, and it traded until the end of the Second World War. Langenhan was unable to overcome competition from *Mayer & Gammelspacher, *Haenel and others during the 1930s and appears to have restricted airgun manufacture, although guns were marked with the previously unattributed brandname *Favorit. Normal marks included *Ace, *FL and *FLZ (the last sometimes in a three-segmented circle). **3.** Heinrich Langenhan, Mehlis in Thüringen, Germany. Listed in 1900–14 as a gunmaker. H. Langenhan was granted a British patent in May 1906 (apparently from Suhl) to protect a distinctive stick-gun. A small centrefire revolver with a folding trigger could be attached to a solid walking-stick shaft by a peg-and-catch retainer, or held to a rifled barrel extension that doubled as a stick. The revolver could be hidden inside a suitable cover until needed. **4.** R. Langenhan, Zella-Mehlis in Thüringen, Germany. Listed during 1930–39 as a master gunsmith.

Langguth. Gebr. Langguth, Suhl in Thüringen, Germany. A partnership of Julius and Paul Langguth, this business was listed in the 1900 *Deutsches Reichs-Adressbuch* as a gunmaker. By 1914, it was owned by Paul Langguth, but seems to have ceased trading in the late 1920s.

Langley – 1. Langley & Company, Hitchin, Hertfordshire, and (later?) Park Square, Luton, Bedfordshire. Marks applied by this English gunmaking business have been found on sporting guns and *Kynoch-made shotgun cartridges sold prior to 1914, under the brandnames Blue Roc (or Langley's Blue Roc) and Prize Winner. *See also* *Langley & Lewis. **2.** Langley & Lewis, Park Square, Luton, Bedfordshire, and Maldon, Essex. This partnership of Albert Langley and Aubrey *Lewis handled shotgun cartridges – apparently made in France – that were sold under the brandnames Blue Roc (or Langley's Blue Roc) and Prize Winner. *See also* Langley & Company.

Lanman. Joseph L. Lanman, a lieutenant in the US Navy, accepted firearms and edged weapons marked 'JL'.

They date earlier than 1845, distinguishing them from equipment accepted thirty years later by J. *Lippold. *See also* US arms inspectors' marks.

Lanston Monotype Company, Philadelphia, Pennsylvania. A contractor for 100,000 .45 M1911 *Colt-Browning pistols, recruited during the First World War. No guns are known to have been made, as the contract was cancelled immediately after the 1918 Armistice.

Laport, Liège. A gunmaking business working in Belgium during the last quarter of the nineteenth century. An associated dealership, Laport Irmaos, was formed in Rio de Janeiro, Brazil, in 1839. Marks of both businesses have been reported on firearms ranging from pepperboxes to double-barrelled shotguns.

LARC International. Based in Miami, Florida, this gunmaking business made, or perhaps simply marketed, the LARC Model 19 and Model 19A BB slug gun designed by its president, Russell *Clifford.

Lard. Allan Lard, St Joseph, Missouri. Lard was granted five US patents to protect single-trigger mechanisms: 630,061 of 1 August 1899, 636,050 of 31 October 1899, 668,526 of 19 February 1901, 674,508 of 21 May 1901, and 747,191 of 15 December 1903. The perfected design was used on shotguns made by L.C. *Smith as the 'Hunter One-Trigger' system.

Largo. Spanish for 'large'; used to identify chamberings for the 9mm Largo (9mm Bergmann-Bayard) pistol cartridge. *See also* Corto.

Laroche, rue de Paris 7, Saint-Étienne, France. Listed in 1879 as a distributor of, and agent for, arms and ammunition.

Larrosa. A brandname associated with pinfire sporting guns and rifles made in Spain by José Ramón la *Rosa.

Larsen. August Larsen of Liège patented a butt-magazine system in 1883. Similar to the *Schulhof type, the gravity-feed mechanism could be built into the 1871-pattern German Mauser, the Dutch Beaumont and other bolt-action rifles. Multi-chamber butt compartments could hold 7+5+3 rounds (and one in the feeder), but a simple single-chamber design had a mere five rounds in the butt plus three in the feed tube. An elevator bar transferred cartridges from the magazine to the chamber as the bolt was operated. The Larsen & Winteross rifle, patented in 1884, was a lever-action design with a locking bolt and a cartridge elevator operated by a rocking sector plate attached to a self-sprung shank.

'LAS'. Found on US military firearms and accessories. *See* Laurence A. *Stone.

Lasagabaster Hermanos, of Eibar, Guipúzcoa, Spain, made the *Douglas pistol.

Lashermès, 99 rue Antoine-Durafour, Saint-Étienne, France. Listed in 1951 as a gunmaker.

Lashnev. Tikhon Ivanovich Lashnev was born in Tula in 1919 and graduated from the local technical manufacturing school into a design bureau. He transferred to the Tula ordnance factory in 1940, shortly before the German invasion of Russia, and worked there until his retirement. In addition to a variety of sporting and hunting firearms, Lashnev was the co-designer, with Lev *Kulikov and Anatoliy *Simarin, of the Soviet *PSM pistol. He died in 1988.

Laspoussas, Driol et Cie, Saint-Étienne. Listed in 1933 as a gunmaking business, this French firm was still operating in 1951, from 8 place Villeboeuf.

Laszlo – **1.** Stephen Edwin Laszlo. Residing at 375 Riverside Drive, New York, Laszlo was the co-patentee with Andrew *Lawrence of the Hy-Score spring-air pistol and the co-founder of the *Hy-Score Arms Company. Laszlo was noted as the 'Old importee' of British-made *Warrior air pistols in an *American Rifleman* advertisement in 1934. **2.** S.E. Laszlo House of Imports: the trading name used by *Hy-Score in the 1970s.

Latger, Saint-Étienne, France. Listed in directories of 1933 as a gunmaker.

Lathe. Homer S. Lathe, using an 'HSL' mark during the American Civil War, accepted firearms and accessories on behalf of the Federal Army. Apparently his activities were confined to 1862. *See also* US arms inspectors' marks.

Lathrope. H.L. Lathrope accepted .44-calibre cap-lock revolvers made in 1862 on behalf of the Federal Army. Produced by *Colt's Patent Fire Arms Manufacturing Company, they were marked 'HLL'. *See also* US arms inspectors' marks.

Latimer Clark, Muirhead & Company Ltd, Millwall, London. This was a short-lived ammunition manufacturer, formed in 1885 to make .45 *Martini-Henry cartridges; it closed c. 1889. The headstamp was a distinctive 'L.C.M. & Co.', but little else is currently known about its history.

Lau. J.H. Lau & Company. A rarely-seen brandname associated with shotguns made in the USA by the *Crescent Arms Company.

Laudensack. Albert Laudensack, a gun designer associated with the *Winchester Repeating Arms Company, was a prominent member of the team led by Edwin *Pugsley that developed the highly successful Model 70 bolt-action rifle.

Laumann. Josef Laumann: *see* Mechanical repeating pistol and Schönberger.

Laurent. Trading in Liège, this Belgian gunsmith made breech-loading sporting rifles and shotguns during the 1860s. Essentially similar to the *Ghaye pattern, the barrel and fore-end were slid forward after a lever on the right side of the breech, ahead of the back-action lock, had been raised to release the locking collar from the interrupted-thread cut into the barrel. Then the barrel could be tipped downward to give access to the chamber.

Laute. J. Laute, Berlin. Marks applied by this Prussian entrepreneur have been found on a crank-wound *Gallery Gun dating from the 1850–80 period. Eldon Wolff (in *Air Guns*, 1958) assumes that Laute was its maker, but swords have also been examined, and it is concluded that Laute was merely a *Hoflieferant*, or purveyor to the royal household, active until c. 1920.

Lavaux, Liège, Belgium. *See* Levaux.

Lavigne. A. Lavigne, sometimes listed as 'Lavidne', was responsible for accepting US military stores marked 'AL'. They date from the period 1894–1909. *See also* US arms inspectors' marks.

Law. Thomas Law. Trading in the twentieth century in Castle Douglas, Kirkcudbrightshire, this Scottish gunmaker sold sporting guns, shooting requisites and shotgun ammunition. Some cartridges have been listed under the brandname Capercaillie, but this may have referred simply to the illustration on the case wall.

Law Enforcement – **1.** A name occasionally used during 1976–85 by *Valmet to describe semi-automatic versions of the Valmet-made *Kalashnikov assault rifles. **2.**

Law Enforcement Bulldog. A revolver made in the USA by *Charter Arms and its successor, Charco. The name applies specifically to a variant of the standard .357 or .44 Special *Bulldog with a spurless Pocket Hammer and a blued finish.

Lawman, or Lawman Mark III. Made by the Firearms Division of *Colt Industries between 1969 and 1983, this .357 Magnum revolver was customarily supplied with a 2 or 4in barrel, the shorter version having an integral ejector-rod shroud. Improvements on previous Colts included the use of stainless-steel springs and the adoption of surface hardening on all major parts. The Lawman Mark V (1984–85) had a more efficient trigger mechanism offering a significant reduction in *lock time.

Lawton. A. Lawton (Britain). Listed in the London directories of 1861–66 as a gunmaker, working from 27 Duke Street, Bloomsbury.

Lawrence – **1.** Andrew Lawrence of 6 Bay Avenue, Seacliff, New York State, USA, designed the Hy-Score spring-air pistol in collusion with Stephen *Laszlo. Smith claims that the gun was designed in 1938, but its British patents were not granted until the late 1940s. British Patent 621,417 was accepted on 8 April 1949 (suggesting also that the comparable US patent was issued on 28 February 1946) for the basic pistol action. Three part-patents each protected an individual feature: 621,461 for the spring-compressing mechanism, 621,462 for the breech construction, and 621,463 for the trigger and sear-train. **2.** Charles Lawrence & Son, London and Battle, Sussex. A gunpowder-making business operating in the early 1870s. **3.** George A. Lawrence, a government inspector, accepted rifle and carbine stocks made for the Federal Army between 1862 and 1863, during the American Civil War. They bore 'GAL' marks. *See also* US arms inspectors' marks. **4.** Richard Smith Lawrence. Born in 1817 in Chester, Vermont, Lawrence served an apprenticeship with Nicanor Kendall after leaving the US Army in 1838; by 1843, Lawrence and Kendall were in partnership. By 1847, however, Lawrence and an entrepreneur named Robbins had bought Kendall's share of the business, and what had been Robbins, Kendall & Lawrence became Robbins & Lawrence. The company grew in stature, particularly after a contract to equip the British *Royal Small Arms Factory in Enfield had been negotiated in 1851, and work on Sharps rifles had begun in 1852. In 1854, however, after a disastrous foray into the manufacture of railway rolling stock, Robbins & Lawrence collapsed. The Hartford factory was sold to the Sharps Rifle Company, Lawrence being retained initially as factory superintendent. Richard Lawrence is credited with the perfected gas-seal system embodied in the *Sharps breech mechanism, patented on 20 December 1859 (26,501), and rose to become co-owner of the *Sharps Rifle Company. He retired in 1872 and died in Hartford in 1892.

'LB' – **1.** Usually in monogram form. Found on No 4 *Lee-Enfield rifles made in the *Long Branch Arsenal, Canada. **2.** Plus an arrow and target. A trademark associated with the products of Louis *Bader, Valt. Sohn of Mehlis, Thüringen, Germany, 1905–14. **3.** Found as 'L B', 'L.B.', 'LBC', 'L B C', 'L.B.C.' or 'L.B. & C.' in the headstamps of cartridges made by Leon Beaux & Co. of Milan.

'LCA', 'LCB'. Found on US military firearms and accessories. *See* Lucius C. *Allen and Lucius C. *Brown respectively.

'L.C.M. & Co.' Found in the headstamps of .45 military rifle cartridges made by *Latimer Clark, Muirhead & Company, London.

Le… (or L'…), L.E. – 1. Usually found as 'L.E.': an abbreviated form of *Lee-Enfield, in designation marks on British-pattern rifles. **2.** 'L'Avengeur'. A mark found on a small six-shot double-action revolver made in Belgium prior to the First World War. Most guns have grips with a double-eagle motif, suggesting export to Russia. **3.** Le Brong. *See* Brong. **4.** 'Le Clairon'. A nickname ('The Bugle') applied to the 5.56mm FA MAS automatic rifle, owing to its unusual configuration of an elongated skeletal carrying handle above the receiver. **5.** Le Dragon. A small 6.35mm Browning-type automatic pistol made by *Aguirre, Zamacolas y Compañía of Eibar, Guipúzcoa, Spain: seven rounds. Identical to the *Basculant pattern, apart from markings. **6.** Le Dragon. A small Browning-type automatic pistol made in Eibar for a major distributor and wholesaler, Tómas de *Urizar of Barcelona: 6.35mm, six rounds. **7.** 'L'Éclair'. Found on solid-frame double-action revolvers, chambered for the 8mm Lebel cartridge, made in Spain prior to 1914 by *Garate, Anitua y Cia. The cocking spur of the enclosed hammer projects above the back of the grip. **8.** L'Explorateur-Mitraille, or Explorateur-Mitraille. This name was given to a large revolver, chambered for the 5.5mm *Velo-Dog cartridge, which was most probably made in Belgium (by Fabrique d'Armes 'HDH'?) prior to 1914. Its two barrels were placed side-by-side, and the twelve chambers in the cylinder were fired in pairs each time the trigger was pressed. Loading alternate chambers allowed the firer to economise on ammunition when necessary. Solid-frame guns had swinging ejector rods; break-open patterns were customarily auto-ejectors. **9.** Le Français. A brandname associated with 8mm revolvers made by M. *Berger et Cie of Saint-Étienne. **10.** Le Français. A series of *blowback semi-automatic pistols made c. 1925–69 by *Manufacture Française d'Armes et Cycles de Saint-Étienne in accordance with patents granted in 1913 to Étienne Mimard. The guns were distinguished by a tipping barrel and a double-action trigger mechanism that enabled the first round to be fired without retracting the slide. The recoil spring in the front of the grip was compressed by a pivoting lever as the slide ran back. Several variants of the basic *Pistolet à répétition automatique 'Le Français'* were offered by Manufacture Française d'Armes et Cycles. The standard 6.35mm gun, or *Modèle de Poche*, had a short barrel and a seven-round magazine, although an eighth could be inserted directly into the barrel; engraving could be applied to order, and highly decorative guns can still be found. The *Modèle Champion* was a long-barrelled 6.35mm gun, intended for unsophisticated target-shooting. The grip was elongated simply by fitting a deep base-unit to the otherwise standard seven-round magazine. The *Modèle de Gendarme* ('…de Police' or Policeman) was identical mechanically to the standard 6.35mm pistol, but originally had a 150mm barrel and weighed about 350gm. Later guns, however, were 7.65mm short-barrelled patterns. The *Modèle Militaire* (or *Type Armée*), the largest and least common of the series, chambered the 9mm Browning Long cartridge. **11.** Le Majestic. A 6.35mm six-shot *Browning-type pocket pistol made in France prior to 1940 by *Manufacture d'Armes des Pyrénées. The slides may display '*Pistolet Automatique à Double Sûreté*' and often (misleadingly) also '*Fabrique à St.*

Étienne' in addition to the tradename. **12.** Le Martiny. A compact 6.35mm Browning-inspired semi-automatic pistol, normally identified as Belgian, but more probably Spanish. Maker unknown. **13.** François Alexandre le Mat, New Orleans, Louisiana. This 'physician' was the grantee of US Patent 15,925 of 21 October 1856, which protected the substitution of an extra barrel for the cylinder-axis pin and a 'gun-cock with double hammer'. A metallic-cartridge version of the Le Mat *cap-lock revolver was protected by US Patent 97,780 of 14 December 1869. **14.** Le Mat revolvers. Patented in 1856 by François le Mat (above), these unique open-frame guns had a .67-calibre shot barrel acting as an axis pin for the nine-chamber .40-calibre cylinder. The guns seem to have been made by several manufacturers in Britain and France, although none has been positively identified and detail differences are common. An improved version handling pin- or centrefire cartridges was made in small numbers in Europe in the 1870s, probably in Liège. **15.** Le Monobloc. A 6.35mm semi-automatic pistol made in Liège c. 1911–14 by Jules *Jacquemart. The name referred to its one-piece frame, necessitating a separate reciprocating breech-block. **16.** Le Novo. A five-chamber 6.35mm pocket revolver, with a folding white-metal butt, invented by Dieudonné Oury of Mortier and made by Établissements Derkenne for F. *Dumoulin & Cie of Liège, c. 1927–30. **17.** Le Page, France. *See* Lepage. **18.** L. Le Personne & Company. Merchants and wholesalers listed in London from 1894 onward, first at 24 Great Winchester Street, E.C., then (from 1895) at 99 Cannon Street. Le Personne traded on into the twentieth century, handling, among other goods, *Kennett-brand airguns and the *Lepco automatic pistol from 7 Old Bailey, London E.C. Appropriate marks have also been found on shotgun cartridges sold under the brandnames Lepco and (possibly) Metalode. The ammunition was usually Belgian. The company also supplied Canadian-made Cooey rifles and shotguns to the British authorities in 1941. **19.** Le Petit Formidable, or Petit Formidable. A 6.35mm revolver with an enclosed hammer, a swing-out five-chamber cylinder and a folding trigger. Although generally believed to have been French, it may simply have been made in Spain by Francisco *Arizmendi – or *Arizmendi y Goenaga – for sale in France. **20.** Le Pistolet Automatique. A small Browning-type automatic pistol made by Francisco Arizmendi of Eibar: 6.35mm, six rounds, striker fired. **21.** Le Protecteur. *See* Protector. **22.** Le Rapide. A small 6.35mm semi-automatic pistol made in Liège c. 1910 by Manufacture Générale d'Armes et Munitions Jules *Bertrand. Possibly made in Spain. **23.** Le Sans Pareil. A 6.35mm six-shot *Browning-type pocket pistol made in France prior to 1940 by *Manufacture d'Armes des Pyrénées, apparently for Piot-Lepage of Paris. The slides usually display '*Fabrication Française*' in addition to the tradename. **24.** Le Secours. Another of the many pocket pistols, based on the FN-Browning of 1906, made in the Eibar district of Spain for the wholesaler Tómas de *Urizar of Barcelona: 7.65mm, seven rounds, hammer fired. **25.** Le Steph. A 6.35mm semi-automatic pocket pistol, manufactured in France shortly after the First World War. Perhaps a modernised Hermetic (q.v.), it may well have been the work of *Société Française d'Armes Automatiques de Saint-Étienne. A detachable plate on the left side of the frame facilitates identification. **26.** Le Vaux, Belgium: *see* Levaux.

Leader – 1. Usually found as 'The Leader' on shotgun cartridges marked by George *Bate of Birmingham, Warwickshire, England. **2.** *Suicide Special revolvers made either by the *Harrington & Richardson Arms Company of Worcester, Massachusetts, or the *Hopkins & Allen Arms Company of Norwich, Connecticut, USA. All date from the late nineteenth century. **3.** Leader Gun Company. A brandname associated with shotguns made in the USA by the *Crescent Arms Company. **4.** *See also* King Leader.

Lean. Clement Lean & Company. This British patent agency occupied chambers at Thanet House, Temple Bar, 231 & 232 The Strand, London WC2, in 1902, when it acted for Harold *Edenborough.

Leavitt. Daniel Leavitt invented a manually-rotated 'revolving firearm', protected by US Patent 182 of 29 April 1837, and subsequently made by the *Massachusetts Arms Company. An improved mechanically-rotated version was known as the *Wesson & Leavitt.

Lebeau – 1. Ernest Lebeau, Liège, Belgium. Owner of a gun-part polishing and ironmongery-making business, Lebeau entered into a partnership with Auguste Courally in the 1860s, creating Lebeau-Courally (below). **2.** Lebeau-Courally. Founded in 1865 and trading since 1896 as Société Anonyme Continentale pour la Fabrication des Armes à Feu Lebeau-Courally, this gun-making business is one of Belgium's leading manufacturers of high-quality sporting guns. *Mauser-action sporting rifles have been offered from time to time, although the product range currently concentrates on break-open patterns sold under names such as Ambassadeur, Ardennes, Battue, Big Five, Safari and Tyrol (qq.v.).

Lebel – 1. Nicolas Lebel, born in Paris in 1838, was commissioned into the French Army, rising to the rank of lieutenant-colonel when he was appointed to the infantry-weapon commission. Lebel became commandant of the marksmanship school at Châlons, where the first 8mm rifle was tested in 1886. His name was attached to the Mle 1886 rifle, largely because he was chairman of the trials board. Lebel himself protested vocally, but the name became inseparably linked with the 8mm tube-magazine repeater that served the French Army for many years. He was promoted to colonel in 1887, and died in Vitré in 1891. **2.** Lebel rifle: *see panel, p. 302.*

Leclair. N. Leclair, active in the early 1900s, accepted firearms and accessories on behalf of the US Army; they were marked 'NL'. *See also* US arms inspectors' marks.

Lecocq & Hoffmann. Based in Brussels, this gunmaking business offered Mauser-type sporting rifles prior to 1940, and again during 1955–70 on the basis of refurbished military-surplus actions. Chamberings ranged from 8x60 to 10.75x68. A big-game rifle in .375 H&H Magnum was also offered; pre-war guns had flat panels alongside the action, rounded pistol grips and schnabel-tip fore-ends, whereas post-war examples usually had ventilated rubber butt plates, capped pistol grips and rounded fore-ends.

Lee – 1. George Arthur Lee, 7 Hadley Road, Enfield, Middlesex, England. Co-patentee with *Millard Brothers and Charles Claude *Bater of a pump-up pneumatic airgun – British Patent 575,543 of 1946, although apparently the design dated from 1942/43. **2.** Herbert O. Lee, Bishop's Stortford, Herfordshire. This gunsmith and sporting-goods supplier handled shotgun cartridges marked 'The Sharpshooter'. They appear to have been made by the *Midland Gun Company. **3.** J.J. Lee, using a 'JJL' identifier, accepted firearms and accessories on behalf of the US Army in 1898. *See also* US arms inspectors' marks. **4.** James Paris Lee. Born in Hawick, Scotland, in 1831, Lee was raised in Canada. He was apprenticed to his clockmaker father, before starting out on his own account in 1850. He moved to Janesville, Wisconsin, in 1858 and thence to Stevens Point. His earliest activities in designing guns dated from this period, when a breech-loading conversion of the regulation *Springfield rifle-musket was produced. After a long and successful career, Lee died in Short Beach, Connecticut, in 1904. **5.** Lee rifles. James P. Lee is best known for his turning-bolt design, developed in the USA, then perfected in the USA and Britain. These guns were service issue not only in Britain and the British Empire, but also in many former colonies after independence had been gained (e.g. India and Pakistan). The earliest patent granted to James Lee was US no. 35,491, to protect a 'breechloading firearm', on 22 July 1862; the barrel swung sideways at the breech, and a manually-operated sliding ejector expelled the spent case. This was followed by US Patent 54,744 of 15 May 1866 (which protected a vertically-sliding breech-block operated by a lever that doubled as an extractor), then by three more patents for pivoting-block breech systems: US 114,951 of 16 May 1871, 166,068 of 20 June 1871 and 122,772 of 16 January 1872. The two 1871 patents were assigned to Philo *Remington. A prototype was tested by the army in 1872 (as the Lee no. 61) alongside an early straight-pull system (no. 53) and an alternative block-action gun (no. 54). Manufacture of 145 modified .45-70 no. 61-type rifles began at Springfield in 1874. They were operated by striking the hammer-lever above the receiver with the heel of the palm, to pivot the breech down and expose the chamber. After protecting a cartridge box (US Patent 162,481 of 27 April 1875), Lee produced another 'breechloading firearm' design, covered by Patent 193,821 of 7 August 1877, and a 'Primer for Cartridge' (193,524 of 24 July 1877). Then came the first of several grants to protect bolt-action rifles with detachable box magazines, US Patent 221,328 of 4 November 1879 (British Patent 2786/79 or 1879 was comparable), and the formation of the Lee Fire Arms Company of Bridgeport, Connecticut, to exploit the design. The bolt-handle of the original, or 1879-type, Lee rifle turned down in front of the split receiver bridge, but this was changed on the 1882 pattern so that it locked down behind the solid bridge. The action was locked by the base of the bolt-guide rib and a small diametrically-opposed lug engaging seats in the receiver, immediately behind the magazine. A US Navy contract was obtained in 1880 for 300 .45-70 1879-pattern rifles, but the collapse of Sharps forced Lee to license production to E. *Remington & Sons. Remington and its successor, the Remington Arms Company, continued to promote Lee-pattern rifles for many years. Two patents for turning-bolt magazine firearms followed – 295,563 of 25 March 1884 (with Louis P. *Diss), assigned to E. *Remington & Sons, and 383,363 of 22 May 1888. Lee was also granted British Patent 11,319/87 of 18 August 1887, for a bolt with a movable head, an improved extractor, a gas-venting sys-

LEBEL RIFLE

Lebel (2)

Developed from the 11mm
*Kropatschek, this 8x51R rifle was
adopted by the French Army on 22
April 1887. It had a two-piece
stock, separated by a massive
machine-steel receiver, and a bolt
handle that projected horizontally
ahead of the receiver bridge. A
tube magazine ran forward beneath
the barrel. Problems with the
earliest back sights were cured in
1892 by the substitution of an
improved design with claws that
extended around the barrel. An
improved *Mle 86/93* (or Mle 86
M. 93) had changes in the action
that included a lighter striker
retainer, a non-rotating obturator
on the bolt head to deflect gas in
the event of a case-head failure,
and a stacking hook on the nose-
cap. Changes were made after 1901
for the high-velocity Balle D,
necessitating sight leaves graduated

to 2,400m instead of the original
2,000m type.

The Lebel was the principal
French infantry rifle at the
beginning of the First World War,
the issue of the box-magazine
*Berthiers being confined largely to
cavalrymen and colonial forces. The
biggest drawbacks of the Lebel
were its box magazine, which
prevented the use of sharply-
pointed ammunition, and the
absence of satisfactory manual safety
features. However, although the
Mle 15 and Mle 16 Berthier rifles
were made in quantity during the
First World War, work on the Mle
86/93 continued in the government
small-arms factories in
Châtellerault, Tulle and Saint-
Étienne until 1919. Fitted with the
3x Mle 1916 telescope sight, the
Lebel was preferred by snipers to
the flimsier Berthiers. Use of V-B
grenade launchers was also
restricted to the Lebel.

A few Mle. 1886 M.93 Lebel
rifles were converted in 1927 for the

short-lived 7.5x58 Balle 1924 C.
These had internal Mauser-type
staggered-row magazines. Although
issued for field trials in 1928, they
were not deemed successful, and
progress with new *MAS rifles soon
rendered the converted Lebel
obsolete. However, large numbers of
surviving rifles were converted after
1935, apparently in the Châtellerault
factory, to provide a compact *Mle
86/93 R35* for cavalrymen and
motorised regiments pending the
introduction of the new MAS 36.
The principal changes concerned a
reduction in barrel length and,
consequently, a reduction in the
capacity of the tube magazine to just
three rounds (although a fourth
could be carried on the elevator, and
a fifth in the chamber). The
refurbishment programme had not
been completed when the Second
World War began, and it is believed
that most of the rifles had been sent
to Africa. Those that survived after
1945 were modified for the Balle
1932 N and placed in store.

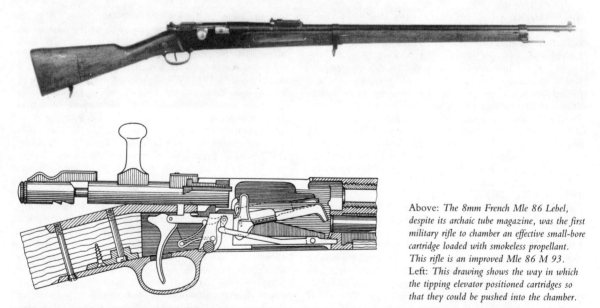

Above: *The 8mm French Mle 86 Lebel,
despite its archaic tube magazine, was the first
military rifle to chamber an effective small-bore
cartridge loaded with smokeless propellant.
This rifle is an improved Mle 86 M 93.*
Left: *This drawing shows the way in which
the tipping elevator positioned cartridges so
that they could be pushed into the chamber.*

tem and an improved magazine. Then he received
British Patent 8117/89 of 15 May 1889 for his perfected staggered-row magazine. Lee's next design was for a
'straight-pull bolt gun', US Patents 506,319–506,321 of
10 October 1893; ultimately these were exploited by
*Winchester in the form of the 1895-pattern .236 Lee
Straight Pull Rifle for the US Navy. US Patent 506,322
of 10 October 1893 protected a 'magazine gun', and
506,323 was for an integral box magazine. The last grant
to Lee was US Patent 547,583 of 8 October 1893 for

another 'magazine bolt gun'. *See also* Enfield-Lee,
Improved Lee, Lee-Enfield, Lee-Metford, Lee Straight
Pull, and Remington-Lee. **6.** Lee Arms Company,
Wilkes Barre, Pennsylvania, USA. This short-lived suc-
cessor to the Pittston Arms Company continued to make
*Imperial, *Red Jacket No. 1–4, *Royal and *Wm.
Tell *Suicide Special revolvers from 1880 until trading
ceased in 1889. The guns were offered in chamberings
ranging from .22 to .32 Long rimfire. Some were made
in accordance with a patent granted in 1881 to Roland

*Brewer, who apparently remained superintendent of the Lee Arms Company until its demise. The name came about because the president of the Pittson business was J. Frank Lee (there was no link with James P. Lee). **7.** Lee Arms Company, Bridgeport, Connecticut, USA. This promotional agency was formed in 1879 by the *Sharps Rifle Company and James P. Lee to promote the latter's bolt-action rifle. The factory and office premises in Clinton Avenue, Bridgeport, were shared with *Sharps until 1881. After the demise of Sharps, it is believed that the Lee Arms Company operated in Bridgeport until 1886. **8.** Lee Arms Company. Also known as the Lee Small Arms Company, apparently this promotional agency was formed in South Windham, Connecticut, USA, in 1886, to safeguard the interests of James P. Lee and control licensing of his patents after the demise of E. *Remington & Sons. An agency was also maintained in New York through the offices of Lee's attorney, Joseph W. Frazier. The Lee Arms Company survived until Lee's death in 1904. **9.** Lee Beilin Ltd, Alpine Works, Empire Way, Wembley. A maker of magazines for the British 9mm *Sten Gun during the Second World War. Used the brandname Lebel on commercial goods, but the code 'S 66' may have been used instead of the company name. *See also* British military manufacturers' marks. **10.** Lee-Enfield: *see* panel, pp. 304/05. **11.** Lee Fire Arms Company, also known as Lee's Fire Arms Company, 454 Canal Street, Milwaukee, Wisconsin, USA. A maker of rimfire carbines in accordance with US Patent 35,491 granted to James P. Lee in 1862, this gunmaking business was founded on 13 October 1864 and incorporated on 8 March 1865. The directors were James Kneeland (president), James P. Lee (superintendent of works), Charles Ilsley, Thomas Ogden, Lester Sexton, Solomon Tainter and Daniel Wells, Jr. The Federal government gave Lee an order for 1,000 guns in 1864, but none had been accepted by the time the American Civil War ended. Only 255 had been completed, with barrels supplied by *Remington. The contract was rescinded, apparently because the carbines had been chambered for the .44 rimfire cartridge instead of the .56-50 Spencer pattern. Work continued after the Civil War, until 1,250–1,300 guns had been made; however, although still trading in December 1866, the Lee Fire Arms Company disappeared early in 1867. **12.** Lee-Metford: *see* panel, pp. 304/05. **13.** Lee Small Arms Company. *See* Lee Arms Company, 1896. **14.** Lee Special. A brandname associated with shotguns made in Norwich, Connecticut, USA, by the *Crescent Arms Company. They date prior to the First World War. **15.** Lee Straight Pull. This unique rifle was made by the *Winchester Repeating Arms Company in accordance with patents granted to James Lee in 1893. Adopted by the US Navy in 1895, it was chambered for a .236 (6mm) high-velocity cartridge; its most unusual feature, however, lay in the design of the bolt. This could be unlocked by pulling back on the pivoted bolt handle, then slid back and slightly upward to give access to the breech. The magazine was a clip-loaded type. Unfortunately, the rifles performed so badly in service that they had been replaced by US Army-pattern .30 *Krag-Jørgensens by the early 1900s.

Leech – 1. Thomas Leech, Greensboro, Georgia, Confederate States of America. Assembler of about 100 Leech & Rigdon-type revolvers in 1864. **2.** Leech & Rigdon, Novelty Works, Columbus, Mississippi, Confederate States of America. Makers of a few .36 *Navy Colt-type revolvers with round barrels, before moving to Greensboro (Georgia) in 1863. Trading ceased in January 1864, each partner continuing alone; about 1,500 guns had been made. **3.** Leech & Sons, Chelmsford, Essex, England. This gunmaking business sold sporting guns and accessories, together with shotgun cartridges offered under such brandnames as Chelmsford, Essex County, Leech's Special Load and X.L.

Leek. Wayne Leek, a designer employed by *Remington and working in collusion with Charles Morse, is credited with the development of the simplified Model 788 bolt-action rifle of 1967.

Lees, Perth, Scotland. The marks of this gunmaker have been reported on self-cocking *pepperboxes dating from the middle of the nineteenth century.

Leeson – 1. William R. Leeson. A member of the English gun trade working at 29 Maddox Street, London, in 1899. **2.** W.R. Leeson Ltd, Ashford, Kent, England. The name of this gunmaker has been reported on sporting guns and shotgun cartridges sold under the brandname Invicta. Possibly the same as (or at least related to) William R. Leeson (above).

Leet – 1. C.D. Leet, Springfield, Massachusetts, USA. This ammunition maker was founded in 1864, acquiring *Hall & Hubbard in 1873. Many of its cartridges were distinguished by the inclusion in their *headstamps of 'CDL'. It is assumed that Charles S. Leet (below) was a relative, perhaps a son, of C.D. Leet. **2.** Charles S. Leet, Bridgeport, Connecticut, USA. This 'mechanic' was granted two US Patents in 1883: 282,997 to protect a spent shell extractor, and 288,459 for a 'gun wiper'.

Leetch – 1. James Leetch, sometimes wrongly listed as Leech or Leitch, began his working life as a gun-wadding maker. However, he is best known for his breech-loading long-arms protected by British Patents 2235/58 of 1858, 990/61 of 1861, 2907/64 of 1864 and 2279/66 of 1866. Directories published after 1858 list Leetch as a gunmaker, trading in London from 68 Margaret Street, Cavendish Square (1858); 29 Great Portland Street (1860); 315 Oxford Street (1864); and, finally, 19 New Church Street, Paddington (1866). **2.** Leetch carbine. Distinguished by a breech-chamber that hinged to the right, operated by a sidelever, this carbine was tested exhaustively by the Board of Ordnance during 1853–56. Eventually it was rejected, largely because a cartridge could jam across the joint between the chamber and the barrel. However, a few sporting guns were also made to the same general pattern prior to 1860.

Lefaucheux – 1. Casimir Lefaucheux was the inventor and first large-scale exploiter of the pinfire cartridge and associated drop-barrel sporting guns. He received his first French patent in 1827, and was offering a single-barrel drop-barrel rifle commercially by 1832. The earliest guns were *cap-locks that relied on the flash to penetrate paper-body cartridges with reinforced bases, which were unacceptable militarily and susceptible to damp. However, the advent of metallic-body pinfire cartridges in the mid-1830s improved efficiency greatly. Lefaucheux rifles and shotguns were locked when lugs on the spindle of a radial lever, beneath the breech, engaged recesses cut in blocks attached to the underside of the barrels. Guns of

LEE-METFORD AND LEE-ENFIELD RIFLES

Lee (10 & 12)

The Lee action appeared in Britain in the spring of 1880, when five .45 1879-pattern rifles and carbines were tried by the Small Arms Committee. By April 1883, a new Lee rifle, chambering the .45-70 US Army cartridge, was being tested, and a .402 Improved Lee was made in the Enfield factory in 1885; it had a one-piece *Arbuthnot-type stock. A .43 1885-type Remington-Lee rifle passed a stringent test in 1885, when 300 similar guns were ordered for trials against the Lee-*Burton.

However, development of an 8mm smokeless cartridge in France persuaded the British to abandon the short-lived .402 pattern. Sealed in 1888, the 'Rifle, Magazine, .303-inch (Mark I)', later known as the Mk I Lee-Metford, had a detachable box magazine holding eight cartridges in a single row, a cut-off and a long-range dial sight on the left side of the fore-end. Much of the developmental work is generally credited to Joseph *Speed, but the guns also had a distinctive nose-cap/bayonet retaining system patented by John *Rigby.

Omitting the original safety catch advanced the designation to Mark I* in 1890, and the Lee-Metford name was adopted in 1891 to honour the parts played in the design by James Paris *Lee and William Ellis *Metford. Extensive changes were made in the early 1890s, including the addition of the *Deeley & Penn bolt head and a staggered-row ten-round magazine; the Mark II rifle was formally sealed in 1893 but, although a Mark II* Lee-Metford rifle was approved with a new cocking-piece safety catch, the Lee-Enfield (q.v.) was substituted within two years. About 635,000 rifles were made, but subsequently many were converted.

A Charger-Loading Lee-Metford Mark II rifle was sealed in 1907, but most Lee-Metfords were altered by the substitution of *Enfield-rifled barrels (in addition to charger guides) and were reclassified as Lee-Enfields. A Mark I Lee-Metford carbine, with a flattened bolt handle and a six-round magazine contained almost entirely within the stock, was sealed for cavalry use in 1894.

Virtually all service-issue Lee-Metford rifles and carbines were made by the *Royal Small Arms Factory, Enfield Lock, or by the principal private contractors – the *Birmingham Small Arms & Munitions Company Ltd ('B.S.A. & M. CO.') or the *London Small Arms Company Ltd ('L.S.A. CO.'). Others were made for sale commercially, or for volunteer militia.

The Lee-Enfield was a modernised Lee-Metford rifle, the polygonal *Metford rifling, which wore too quickly when *Cordite-loaded ammunition was used, being replaced by a five-groove pattern. Lee-Enfield rifles had detachable box magazines, holding ten rounds in a staggered column, and, like their predecessors, the bolt handles were turned down behind the receiver bridge to bring the grasping ball

A sectional drawing of British .303 Marks I, I, Converted II and Converted II* rifles, from the fold-out plates accompanying* Instructions to Armourers, *1912.*

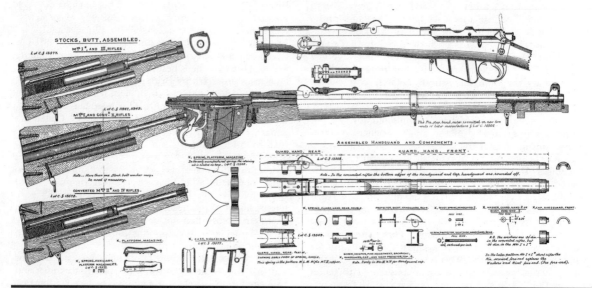

this type were made until the 1870s or later, by a variety of European gunsmiths. Eventually, however, the rise of chamber pressures highlighted a tendency of the barrels to pull away from the standing breech. **2.** Eugène Lefaucheux (1820–71), son of Casimir, is associated with the open-frame *double-action pinfire revolvers that originated in the 1850s and were still being made in their smallest chamberings when the First World War began. The 11mm revolver adopted by the French Navy in October 1847 (as the Modèle 1858) typifies the larger guns of this type, but minuscule 5mm folding-trigger guns were also made in quantity. The younger Lefaucheux was granted US Patent 31,809 of 26 March 1861, which protected a barrel opened by a rack-and-pinion mechanism and another opened by pivoting a radial lever on the right side of the breech upward.

Lefever – **1.** Charles Frederick Lefever, Toledo, Ohio, and Syracuse, New York State, USA. Son of Daniel M.

A 7.62x51 L39A1 target rifle, a conversion of the Rifle No. 4 (Lee-Enfield) dating from the 1960s.

closer to the trigger.

Full-length rifles – usually about 50in long – included the Mark I Lee-Enfield (1895), which otherwise was identical with the Mark II Lee-Metford. The Mark I★ rifle (1899) lacked a clearing rod and the associated rod-groove in the underside of the fore-end. Experience in the South African War of 1899–1902 led to the development of shortened universal rifles, usually about 45in long, which were designed to be issued to infantry and cavalry alike. Changes were made to the bayonet fitting and the sights, but the most important advance was the advent of a ★Watkin & Speed charger-loading system.

The experimental guns made in 1900–02 were followed by the 'Rifle, Short, Magazine, Lee-Enfield, .303-inch (Mark I)', or Mark I SMLE, originally sealed in December 1902. The Mark I★ SMLE of 1906 had a trap in the butt plate for the oiler and pull-through, a swivel on the butt and a modified magazine. The Mark III SMLE (1907) had improved monoblock charger guides instead of the older split pattern. Approved in 1916, the Mark III★ SMLE was a wartime expedient, lacking the long-range sights and sometimes the cut-off mechanism. Guns still in service after May 1926 were redesignated No. 1 Mark III (or III★), work finally

ending in 1943. About 907,000 Marks I and I★ rifles were made, and the output of SMLE rifles between 1 August 1914 and 31 December 1918 alone totalled 3.84 million.

Attempts made after the end of the First World War to simplify the SMLE design led to the experimental Marks V and VI of 1922–29. Subsequently the Mark VI was adopted as the 'Rifle No. 4 Mark 1' in 1939, but did not reach service until 1942. Guns of this type had a squared receiver and a simplified nose-cap that accepted a short spike bayonet. A modified No. 4 Mark I★ was approved in 1941, but made only in Canada and the USA. A sniper rifle known as the No. 4 Mark I (T) was approved in 1942, for issue with the No. 32 telescope sight. Most of these guns were set up by ★Holland & Holland (code 'S/51'). The No. 4 Mark 2 rifle was approved in 1947, with its trigger on the underside of the body instead of the trigger guard.

Conversions of .303 No. 4 Lee-Enfields for the 7.62x51 cartridge, the L8 series, were made in the 1960s. The most important was the L42A1 sniper rifle (1970), made on the basis of existing No. 4 Mark 1 (T) rifles. A commercial variant was sold as the Enfield ★Envoy, or L39A1.

Carbine-length Lee-Enfields (usually measuring 40in or less) included the Marks I and I★ carbines, approved in 1896 and 1899 respectively, the principal difference being the omission of the clearing rod from the Mark I★. Six-round magazines were retained, fitting all

but flush with the stock, and neither gun accepted a bayonet. The half-stocked Lee-Enfield Jungle Carbine, or Rifle No. 5, arose from a request in 1943 for a lighter weapon for use in the Far East. The No. 5 Mark I was approved in 1945, but was never successful and was declared obsolete in 1947.

Lee-Enfield rifles were made by a variety of contractors, particularly during the world wars. The principal manufacturers were the ★Royal Small Arms Factory, Enfield; the ★Royal Ordnance Factories in Fazakerley and Maltby; the Birmingham Small Arms & Munitions Company Ltd and ★BSA Guns Ltd; the Indian government factory in ★Ishapur; the Australian government factory in ★Lithgow; the ★London Small Arms Company Ltd; ★National Rifle Factory No. 1; the ★Savage Arms Company; ★Small Arms Ltd, Toronto; and ★Standard Small Arms Ltd. There were many lesser variants of the Lee-Enfield rifles, particularly the charger-loading conversions, ★Aiming Tube guns, and a selection of ★India Patterns.

The best source of information is *The British Service Lee* by Ian Skennerton (second edition, 1995), although *The Lee-Enfield Rifle* (Hubert Jenkins, 1960) by the late Major E.G.B. Reynolds presents more of a narrative approach. *Guns of the Empire* by George Markham (Arms & Armour Press, 1990), and the second edition of *Rifles of the World* by John Walter (Krause Publications, 1998) contain lists of individual models.

Lefever (below), this gunsmith was granted several firearms-related patents. These included US 732,420 of 30 June 1903 (half-assigned to Daniel Lefever) and 944,448 of 28 December 1908 for 'breechloading firearms'. US Patents 795,991 of 1 August 1905 and 810,987 of 23 January 1906 (the latter jointly with Daniel Lefever) were obtained for single-trigger mechanisms for double guns; and 865,310 of 3 September 1907 protected a gun-cocking system. Subsequently Lefever went to

work for ★Daisy. Smith (in *Gas, Air and Spring Guns*, 1957) credits Lefever with over sixty patents for spring-air and other guns, including one sought in 1912 (but not granted until 1915) for the elbow-pump, dismantling system and back sight of the Daisy No. 25, 20,000,000 of which were made between 1912 and 1977. US Patent 1,589,975 of June 1926 was granted for a threaded barrel-securing system; US Patent 1,686,702 of October 1928 protected a cocking system utilising a longer arm on the forward end of the trigger-guard lever; and US Patent 2,131,173 of October 1938 allowed claims for a slide-cocking pistol, subsequently marketed as the No. 118 *Targeteer. **2.** Daniel M. Lefever. This US gunsmith began his career in Canandaigua, New York State, where he operated from 1857 until c. 1862. Then he entered into a partnership with James A. Ellis, making cap-lock target rifles until 1867. Lefever reappeared in 1876 as a partner in *Nichols & Lefever, best known for shotguns, but began trading on his own account from 78 North Water Street in Syracuse until the Lefever Arms Company was formed in 1890. Lefever was a prodigious patentee. The first Lefever shotguns were patented on 25 June 1878 (205,193) and 29 June 1880 (229,429), but series production began only after US Patent 264,173 was granted to Daniel Lefever and Frederick R. *Smith on 12 September 1882, to protect what became known as the Lefever Ball Joint (below). Subsequent patents included four granted for 'breechloading firearms' – 329,397 of 27 October 1885, 343,040 of 1 June 1886, 372,684 of 8 November 1887 and 423,521 of 18 March 1890 (jointly with J.J. Brown). The 1890 patent was assigned to the Lefever Arms Company. Other protection included US Patent 385,360 of 3 July 1888, for a loading indicator (also assigned to the Lefever Arms Company), and two – 475,873 of 31 May 1892 and 536,636 of 2 April 1895 – for improved gunlock and ejector systems. Daniel Lefever's last patent, 810,871, obtained on 23 January 1906 jointly with his son, Charles F. Lefever, protected a single-trigger mechanism. He died shortly afterward. **3.** Lefever Ball Joint. Often associated with the shotguns made by the Lefever Arms Company, this consisted of a short hemispherical-tip bolt that acted in concert with the cupped face of the barrel under-lug to reduce the effects of wear. It was patented by Daniel M. Lefever and Frederick R. Smith in September 1882 (US no. 264,173). **4.** D.M. Lefever, Sons & Company, 107 North Franklin Street, Syracuse, New York, and Bowling Green, Ohio, USA. This business was formed by Daniel Lefever and his five sons in 1903. Apart from the patented self-compensating ball joint, the box-lock shotguns were very different from the side-locks being made by the Lefever Arms Company. Only 2,500 box-lock Bowling Green Lefevers were made, ranging from 0 Grade Excelsior to 'Uncle Dan'. Manufacture ceased when Daniel Lefever died in 1906, although the Syracuse office seems to have remained open until 1908. **5.** Lefever Arms Company, 213 Malthrie Street, Syracuse, New York State, USA (in 1892 and 1908). Lefever was offering his *Automatic Hammerless gun as early as January 1885. The guns had compensated actions, compensated cocking levers and other advanced features. A few double rifles and combination guns were also made on this action. Ejector guns were produced from 1891, but an improved top-lever shotgun was introduced in 1894, and a single-trigger mechanism was patented in 1898. Work continued even after the business had been sold to the Durston family in 1901, and then to the *Ithaca Gun Company in 1915. The last side-lock Lefever was made in 1919.

Legia – 1. A brandname used on a 6.35mm-calibre automatic pistol made in Belgium by N. *Pieper of Liège. **2.** A tradename used by *Fabrique Nationale d'Armes de Guerre on shotgun ammunition loaded with cube-shot, c. 1925–40. **3.** Legia Star. A tradename used by *Fabrique Nationale d'Armes de Guerre on shotgun ammunition, c. 1955–85. 'Star' refers to the design of the crimp.

Leicester. Usually encountered as 'The Leicester', this name was associated with shotgun cartridges sold by Charles *Lancaster & Company Ltd of London, England.

Leigh. John Leigh. This English gunmaker began working from 1 Duncan Street, Whitechapel, in 1844. The trading style became John Leigh & Son in 1856, but the elder Leigh died in 1859; the son's death occurred in 1862. Subsequently their executors continued operations until 1864.

Leipolds. Ch. Leipolds Witwe, Suhl in Thüringen, Germany. Registered as a gunmaker in 1919.

Leitch. James Leitch. An English gunmaker listed by H.J. Blanch, writing in *Arms & Explosives* in 1909, at 29 Great Portland Street. There is little doubt that actually this was James *Leetch.

Leman. Henry E. Leman, Lancaster, Pennsylvania, USA. Born in Pennsylvania in 1812, Leman served his apprenticeship with the gunmaker Melchior Fordney, before working for George Tryon in Philadelphia. A return to Lancaster, and the foundation of the Conestoga Rifle Works, persuaded the US government to order small batches of rifles annually from 1837 almost until the start of the Civil War in 1861. The original Conestoga Works were destroyed in 1860, but operations soon began again on a new site on the corner of East James and Christian Streets. Leman's output was considerable: during 1849–50, his factory made 5,000 gun barrels and 2,500 rifles; the census of 1860 indicated that not only was he employing a steam engine, but also that he had a workforce numbering 62. Leman died in Lancaster in 1887.

Lemille. Pierre-Joseph Lemille, Liège, Belgium. A leading gunmaker, active in the 1860s and 1880s. He made firearms ranging from double-barrelled sporting guns to *Lefaucheux-type pinfire cutlass revolvers.

Lemon Squeezer. A nickname conferred on the *Smith & Wesson .32 *Safety Hammerless, owing to the 'squeeze-in' safety lever set in the back strap.

Lenders – 1. Charles Lenders, Liège. This Belgian gunmaker was granted protection for a variety of firearms developed in the middle of the nineteenth century, including a seven-barrel breech-loading volley gun, which had its barrel cluster locked by a rotating collar. **2.** Lenders-Lambin rifle. A bolt-action pattern developed in Liège in the 1860s, this provided an inexpensive method of converting cap-lock rifle-muskets such as the British P/53 (Enfield) and French Mle 57. A cylindrical extension attached to the breech contained a bolt with a small handle on the right side. Most guns retained conventional side- or back-action locks and external hammers, but some were altered to fire a proprietary cartridge with an internal priming pellet in the base. However, ignition of this type was rapidly overtaken by rim- and centrefire metallic-case ammunition.

Lengerke – 1. [Von] Lengerke & Antoine, Chicago, Illinois., USA. This sporting-goods distributorship was founded in 1889, trading by 1900 from 277 & 279 Wabash Avenue and 35–39 Van Buren Street. Its trademarks included 'V.L. & A.' **2.** [Von] Lengerke & Detmold (USA), New York City. Undoubtedly related to Von Lengerke & Antoine of Chicago, this sporting-goods business was formed in 1897. Trading was being undertaken from 349 Fifth Avenue in 1928, when the business was purchased by *Abercrombie & Fitch, but Von Lengerke & Detmold retained independence until c. 1939. At that time, the premises were at the corner of Madison Avenue and 45th Street. The principal trademark consisted of a triangle containing a soaring duck and 'V.L. & D.'

Lenz. August Lenz, Zella St Blasii in Thüringen, Germany. Listed in the 1900 edition of the *Deutsches Reichs-Adressbuch* as a gun- and weapon maker.

Leo – 1. Heinrich Leo, Suhl in Thüringen, Germany. Listed in the directories for 1939 as a gunsmith. 2. Th. Leo, Suhl in Thüringen, Germany. A gunmaker trading in 1914 and 1920.

Leonard – 1. Charles S. Leonard, a government employee identified by 'CSL', accepted US military firearms and accessories in the mid-1870s. They can be distinguished by date from those accepted prior to the American Civil War by Charles S. *Lowell. *See also* US arms inspectors' marks. 2. D. Leonard & Son. Listed in London in 1880 at '15 & 18 Bishopsgate Street Without', this gunmaking business was trading from 90b Aston Street, Birmingham, by 1891. 3. Frederick S. Leonard, possibly the son of Charles Leonard (above), accepted firearms and accessories on behalf of the US Army in the period 1899–1902; they bore 'FSL'. *See also* US arms inspectors' marks. 4. George Leonard, Shrewsbury, Massachusetts. This US gunmaker, once employed by *Allen & Thurber, made *pepperboxes in accordance with US Patent 6723 of 18 September 1849 and 7493 ('Revolving hammer firearms') of 9 July 1850. Leonard also received 9922 of 9 August 1853 and 14,820 of 6 May 1856, each protecting a 'Repeating Firearm'. 5. Samuel Leonard, using the mark 'SL', accepted *Savage cap-lock and *Colt cartridge revolvers on behalf of the US Army during 1862–75. *See also* US arms inspectors' marks.

Leonhardt. A 7.65mm *Beholla-type semi-automatic pistol, made, or perhaps simply distributed, in the early 1920s by Hans *Gering of Arnstadt.

Lepage. This name includes a number of French and Belgian gunmakers, the most notable being Perin Le Page, *Arquebusier de l'Empereur* (later *Arquebusier du Roi*) active in Versailles between 1793 and 1813, then in Paris from 1816 until the 1840s. A Le Page breech-loading *cap-lock carbine, with a barrel that pivoted laterally to expose the breech, was tested unsuccessfully by the French Army in 1835. Lepage Mourtier, active in Paris c. 1840–65, exhibited firearms and edged weapons at the London Great Exhibition of 1851, and Lepage Faure, established in 1865 at 8 Rue Richelieu, Paris, continued to trade until the end of the nineteenth century.

Lepco, usually in a diamond. This trademark will be found on Langenhan-made *Millita spring-air guns, shotgun cartridges, and 6.35mm six-shot *Browning-type pocket pistols made in France prior to 1940 by *Manufacture d'Armes des Pyrénées. Customarily marked 'The Lepco Fire-Arms Company, London' (see *Le Personne), the slides of the pistols display 'Made in France' in addition to the distributor's name.

Lepersonne. *See* Le Personne.

Lepper – 1. Hugo Lepper, Zella-Mehlis in Thüringen, Germany. Listed in the 1920 edition of the *Deutsches Reichs-Adressbuch* as a weapon maker. 2. Max Lepper, Zella-Mehlis in Thüringen, Germany. Founded in 1888 and still listed in 1930 as a master gunsmith. Apparently his

operations ceased at the end of the Second World War.

'LES'. A mark found on the long-range dial sight plate of British Short *Lee-Enfield rifles Mks I, I*, II and II** – or, as 'LES III', on the Mk III and Converted Mk IV patterns. Guns modified to fire .303 Mk VII ball ammunition were marked 'LES 2'.

Leser. Ernst Leser, Suhl in Thüringen, Germany. Operating during 1930–39 as a gunsmith.

Lespinasse. This French Army officer, the director of the Châtellerault arms factory, has been credited with changes made (in collusion with arms inspector Close) in the design of the 1878-pattern bolt-action 11mm *Kropatschek navy rifle. These laid the basis for the 1885 pattern, with a two-piece stock, and ultimately for the small-calibre *Lebel.

Levaux. D.D. Levaux, Liège, Belgium. A patentee of revolvers in the early 1870s, including solid-frame guns with a yoke-mounted cylinder and a sliding ejector on the right side of the barrel/frame unit. Levaux was also responsible for a break-open simultaneous-ejecting design with a latching bar that protruded above the hammer. These guns were made in .32, .38 and possibly other chamberings by Établissements Levaux from the 1880s until overtaken by better designs at the end of the nineteenth century.

LeverBolt Rifle Company [The], New Haven, Connecticut, USA. This was formed to promote the last of the distinctive sporting guns designed by Charles *Newton, a straight-pull 'rocking-lever' bolt-action design patented in 1929. A batch of 500 guns was to be made by *Marlin if sufficient orders were forthcoming, but sales were poor and the project failed when Newton died in 1932.

Levin. Moses L. Levin. A merchant, or possibly gunmakers' agent, listed at 1 Bevis Marks, London E.C., between 1885 and 1888.

Levy. *See* Heilprin.

Lever action. A mechanism that relies on a lever or system of levers to open the breech, extract, eject, reload and then re-lock. The Winchester M1873 and Marlin M1895 are typical examples, but many different patterns have been made. Today the term is normally confined to magazine rifles (strictly, lever-action repeaters); otherwise, it could be applied to many single-shot block-action guns.

Lewes sights. Invented by Lieutenant-Colonel Lewes of the Northamptonshire Regiment, and eventually protected by British Patent 14,093/93 of 1 October 1893. Used on the *Martini-Metford rifle, they were also adopted for the *Lee-Metford, but were abandoned when a reversion to V-and-barleycorn sights was approved in July 1891. The essence of the design was a slit-in-post at the front and a broad square notch at the back.

Lewis – 1. A.H.G. Lewis. Active in 1906, this government employee accepted US Army firearms and accessories with 'AHGL' identifiers. *See also* US arms inspectors' marks. 2. Aubrey Lewis, 19 Church Street, Luton, Bedfordshire. This English gunmaker succeeded *Langley & Lewis after the Second World War and traded in Luton until 1969. His marks will be found on sporting guns and shotgun cartridges sold under such names as Blue Roc, Chelt and Severn. 3. C.F. Lewis accepted firearms and accessories on behalf of the Federal Army in 1863, during the American Civil War; they bore 'CFL' identifiers. *See also* US arms inspectors' marks. 4. Edward Lewis,

Basingstoke, Hampshire, England. The name of this gun-maker has been reported on sporting guns and shotgun cartridges made since 1945. **5.** George Edward Lewis, Birmingham, Warwickshire. This gun-rifler and pistol maker began trading from 32 & 33 Lower Loveday Street in 1859, making breech-loading rifles in addition to pumps for air canes. Lewis received British Patent 2100/63 of 25 August 1863 (jointly with H. Walker and J.B. Wayne) to protect the design of a drop-barrel breech-loader. Trading after c. 1905 as G.E. Lewis & Son, the business also handled shotgun cartridges. **6.** Isaac Newton Lewis. Born in 1858 in New Salem, Pennsylvania, Lewis was commissioned into the US Coast Artillery after graduating in 1880 from the West Point Military Academy. His inventive skills were embodied in a depression position finder, adopted in 1891, and eventually he became director of the Coast Artillery School in 1904. Subsequently he was approached by representatives of the ★Automatic Arms Company to perfect a machine-gun

designed by Samuel McLean, and, apparently after a disagreement with the Chief of Ordnance, retired from the US Army in 1911. Work on the gun was completed successfully in 1912/13. Lewis died in Hoboken, New York, in November 1931. **7.** Lewis Gun: *see* panel, below.

Leyh. G. Leyh, Suhl in Thüringen, Germany. Listed as a gunsmith, 1930.

'Lfb', 'LfB', 'lfb'. Abbreviations for *Lang für Buchse*, the German equivalent of 'Long Rifle', applied to the most popular of all .22 rimfire cartridges.

'lgp'. Found on machine-gun and small-arms components made during the Second World War by Veltener Maschinenbau GmbH of Velten/Mark, Germany.

Liberator. A simple .45 single-shot pistol made for use in occupied Europe during the Second World War by the ★Guide Lamp Division of General Motors.

Liberty – 1. A ★Suicide Special revolver made in the USA by the ★Hood Firearms Company of Norwich, Connecticut, in the late nineteenth century. **2.** A ★Suicide

LEWIS GUN

Lewis (7)

Developed by Isaac N. Lewis from patents granted to Samuel N. ★McLean, prototype guns of this type were demonstrated unsuccessfully to the US Army in 1911. Then Lewis went to Europe, where he accepted an offer of help from the ★Birmingham Small Arms Company Ltd (BSA) in 1913. The perfected gas-operated Lewis had a rotating pan magazine above the receiver and a large helical spring in a prominent housing beneath the receiver, ahead of the trigger, to return the piston and bolt assembly to battery.

The British Army remained as sceptical about the Lewis Gun as the US Army had been, but a 7.65mm version was supplied in quantity to the Belgian Army. These were marked by ★Armes

Automatiques Lewis, but made by BSA. The British government adopted the 'Gun, Machine, Lewis, .303-inch Mark I' in 1915. The Birmingham Small Arms Company Ltd alone made nearly 150,000 guns for the British, Belgians and Russians during the First World War. The Mark I★, introduced in November 1915, had a spade grip and a two-tier magazine, but lacked the forced-draught cooling system. The Mark II★ (converted) and Mark III (newly made) of 1918 were Mark I★ variants altered to give a higher rate of fire.

The Lewis Gun was the standard British light machine-gun until replaced by the ★Bren Gun in the 1930s. Guns were also made in the USA by the ★Savage Arms Company, and a few hundred .303 Savage-Lewis Guns were bought by the US Army in 1916, for use in the border wars with Mexico. A .30-calibre M1917 US Army Savage-

Lewis was unsuccessful, owing to the increased power of the .30-06 cartridge. However, the US Navy and Marine Corps took the .30 Savage-Lewis in quantity.

The M1918 air-service gun, with forty-seven- or ninety-seven-round pan magazine, was a great success: by the 1918 Armistice, 32,231 had been completed, followed by about 7,500 in 1919. Many obsolescent guns were altered in Britain during the 1920s and 1930s by the Soley Armament Company, seeking to improve their performance, and others were brought out of store in 1939–40 to serve the British merchant navy and home-defence forces.

A longitudinal section of a .303 Lewis Gun, the first true light machine-gun to be successful in combat in large numbers.

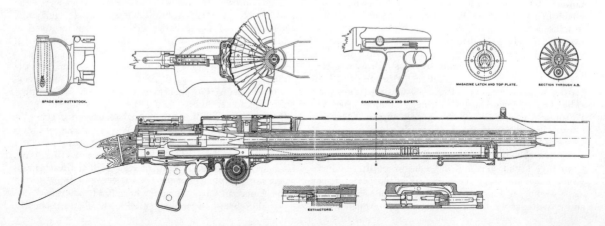

Special revolver made by Otis *Smith of Middlefield and Rock Fall, Connecticut, USA, in the late nineteenth century. **3.** A compact 6.35mm Browning-type pistol made by *Retolaza Hermanos of Eibar, Guipúzcoa, Spain: six rounds, striker fired. Sometimes these are marked by Fabrique d'Armes de Grande Précision (q.v.) and have been attributed to Gregorio Bolumburu.

Libia. A Spanish FN-Browning-type automatic pistol made in Eibar by *Beistegui Hermanos in two patterns: (a) 6.35mm Auto, and (b) 7.65mm; six rounds, striker fired. The guns were often marked by Fabrique d'Armes de *Grande Précision.

Lida. A brandname said to have been used by Libero *Daffini of Brescia, Italy.

Liddell & Sons, Haltwhistle, Northumberland, England. This gunmaker sold sporting guns, shooting accessories and shotgun cartridges. *See also* Liddle.

Liddle – 1. John Liddle was a patent agent, working from chambers at 154 St Vincent Street, Glasgow, Scotland, when he secured British Patent 26,329/12 of 1912 for Edgar P. *Cook. **2.** Robert Liddle, or Liddell, San Francisco, California. A maker of cap-lock rifles and shotguns, established by 1853, Liddle traded from Washington Street until shortly after the American Civil War. His operations were succeeded by Liddle & Kaeding (q.v.). **3.** Liddle Gun Company, San Francisco, California, USA. Successor to Liddle & Kaeding (below), this gunmaking business is assumed to have retained the Washington Street premises until work finally ceased upon the death of Robert Liddle in 1894. **4.** Liddle & Kaeding, Washington Street, San Francisco, California. Makers of sporting guns and rifles, this partnership succeeded to the business of Robert Liddle c. 1870 and traded until succeeded in turn by the Liddle Gun Company in 1889. **5.** *See also* Liddell.

Liebig, Baltimore, Maryland, USA. A maker, or perhaps simply a distributor, of spring-air *Gallery Guns of 'New York Secondary' pattern.

Liebmann. Helmut Liebmann. An employee of *Anschütz, this engineer received several German patents for recoilless airguns (e.g., 1,111,064 of 1958 – not accepted until 1966) for the LG220.

Liebtruth. F. Liebtruth & Company Ltd, Angel Road, Edmonton, Middlesex. A maker of magazines for the British 9mm *Sten Gun during the Second World War. The code 'S 304' may have been used instead of the company name. *See* British military manufacturers' marks.

Liège – 1. The centre of the Belgian gunmaking industry: *see* panel, pp. 310/11. **2.** Liege Arms Company. A brandname found on shotguns handled by the H. & D. *Folsom Arms Company, possibly made in Belgium by Manufacture Liégeoise d'Armes à Feu (but equally possibly an attempt to disguise low-grade US manufacture).

Liégeoise. *See* Manufacture Liégeoise d'Armes à Feu.

Life Long. A *Suicide Special revolver made by the *Hopkins & Allen Arms Company of Norwich, Connecticut, USA, in the late nineteenth century.

Light... – 1. Light Automatic Carbine. *See* Carabine Automatique Leger. **2.** Light Automatic Rifle. *See* Fusil Automatique Leger and Fusil Automatique Lourd. **3.** Light Blue [The]. A shotgun cartridge made, or perhaps simply assembled, in Britain by the *Normal Improved Ammunition Company of Hendon, London. **4.** Light Fifty. Made in the USA by *Barrett, this .50-calibre rifle,

also known as the Model 82A1, was designed to strike 'compressor sections of jet engines or the transmissions of helicopters' and to 'destroy multi-million dollar aircraft with a single hit delivered to a vital area'.

Lightfoot Refrigeration Company Ltd [The], Abbeydale Road, Wembley, Middlesex, England. A manufacturer of British rifle-type 'Dischargers, Grenade, 2½-inch, No. 2 Mk 1', 1941–43. Code: 'S 67'. *See also* British military manufacturers' marks.

Lightmode [The]. Associated with shotgun cartridges made by *Eley Bros. prior to the acquisition of the company by Explosives Trades Ltd in 1918.

Lightning, Lightning... – 1. Usually as 'The Lightning': found on 12-bore shotgun ammunition made, apparently by *Eley-Kynoch, for Thomas *Newton of Manchester. **2.** A compact Spanish 6.35mm-calibre Browning-type automatic pistol, made in Eibar during the 1920s by Echave y Arizmendi: six rounds, striker fired. **3.** A primitive rubber-band-powered spring-air gun made by *Quackenbush to his US Patent 302,283 of 22 July 1884 (British Patent 10,499/84 of 1884 is identical); 354 examples were manufactured in 1884, but thereafter production declined rapidly. **4.** A .38 Double Action Revolver announced by *Colt's Patent Fire Arms Manufacturing Company on 1 January 1877. The name was coined by Benjamin *Kittredge & Company. The guns typically had bird's-head butts, and ejectors were omitted if the barrels were less than 4½in long. About 167,000 .38-calibre Lightnings and .41 *Thunderers were made between 1877 and 1909. **5.** 'Lightning Killer' [The]. Usually accompanied by a flying grouse, this mark is associated with 12-bore shotgun ammunition made for *Smail & Sons of Morpeth by *Eley-Kynoch. **6.** Lightning Loader. The No. 108 *Daisy 1,000-shot lever-action rifle, with a quick-loading under-barrel magazine; apparently production was confined to 1939–41 and 1946–49. The Lightning Loader Military Model was a bayonet-equipped derivative, made in small numbers during 1940.

Lightweight Commander. *See* Commander.

Lightwood – 1. F.W. Lightwood, Brigg, Grimsby and Market Rasen, Lincolnshire. The name of this English gunmaker has been reported on sporting guns, shooting accessories and shotgun cartridges. **2.** Joseph Birks Lightwood, later Lightwood & Son, Birmingham, Warwickshire, England. This gunmaker began trading in Whittall Street in 1887, possibly succeeding Joseph Lightwood (a gun-stocker active in 1849), and traded under his own name until at least 1898. Pre-1914 *Eley-made shotgun cartridges have been reported with the mark of 'Lightwood & Son' and the brandname 'Ecel'.

Lignose AG, Theodor Bergmanns Erben, Berlin, Germany. The marks of this holding company will be found on the slide and grips of *Bergmann-type pocket pistols, including some one-hand-cocking variants, made in the former Bergmann Abteilung Waffenbau, Suhl (which had been renamed Lignose Sprengstoff Werke GmbH, Abteilung Suhl). Apparently Berlin based Lignose purchased the Bergmann gunmaking division in 1921, W. *Fahner of Suhl in 1922, and August *Menz of Suhl in 1937. Airgun pellets have been found in tins marked 'Lignose AG', with a distinctive blue design on a yellow lid.

L'il Champ. Also known as the L'il Champ Bolt 22 or the Model 2000, this was a simple single-shot .22 rimfire

LIÈGE

Liège (1)

The premier Belgian gunmaking centre, Liège, was renowned for large-scale firearms production, which began many years before independence was gained from France in 1830.

The census of 1856 revealed the existence of 9,675 men employed directly in the gunmaking trades, and ninety-seven 'manufacturers'. However, there were few – apart from the *Société des Anglais, and the *Petit and *Grand Syndicats (all co-operatives) – capable of fulfilling the large-scale contracts demanded by armies of ever-growing strength and sophistication. Yet by 1896, when the totals of men and manufacturers had risen to 11,402 and 180 respectively, much of the industry remained primitive. This has been ascribed by Claude Gaier,

in *Five Centuries of Liège Gunmaking*, to three principal factors: an over-reliance on piecework, the employment of vast numbers of homeworkers and an extraordinary multiplicity of manufacturing patterns.

The 1896 census had also shown that, although the largest businesses (such as *Fabrique Nationale d'Armes de Guerre and the *Manufacture d'Armes de l'État) could make guns by the thousand, three in every four of those who classed among the 'gunmakers' traded from their homes, and that mechanisation in those homes amounted to just forty horsepower! This was also true of ancillary trades; in 1894, for example, only four of nearly thirty gun-barrel manufacturers in the Vesdre valley owned steam engines. Virtually all the others relied on waterwheels.

The number of guns proved in Liège peaked in 1907, at about 1.58 million, and by 1914, the

apogee of local gunmaking, there were 118 private gunmaking businesses; 62 trading companies or partnerships; and a mere fourteen joint-stock companies. There were also about 150 makers of gun parts and accessories.

The German invasion in 1914 brought most of the work to an end, with the exception of that carried out by Anciens Établissements *Pieper (which had German origins). Although several small-scale manufacturers flourished during the twenty years that separated the world wars, and Fabrique Nationale d'Armes de Guerre recovered much of its previous glory, the trend was largely downward. This effect was magnified by the Second World War, when what remained of the Belgian gunmaking industry was mostly destroyed. A few thousand sporting guns were made each year, peaking in 1943 at 40,747, but a total of 114 gun manufacturers in

---

bolt-action rifle made first by Iver Johnson, then by the *American Military Arms Corporation of Jacksonville, Arkansas.

Liliput – 1. Alternatively known as the *Frommer Liliput, this compact 6.35mm pistol was made by *Fegyvergyár es Reszvenytársásg of Budapest, Hungary. **2.** Semi-automatic pistols made in Suhl, Germany, by August *Menz. The 6.35mm Model 1925 and Model 1926 differed in the milling of the slide, the former having fifteen fine retraction grooves, and the latter eight coarse grooves. The original 4.25mm gun may have had a half-length slide/breech-block unit, and the barrel and return-spring chambers bored directly into the slab frame, but this was replaced by the conventional Model 1927 with a full-length slide.

Limit. A tradename associated with the airguns and pellets marketed by Lincoln *Jeffries & Company Ltd of Birmingham. The highest known serial number of a Limit rifle is 2003, made c. 1929. *See also* Britannia and Scout.

Limited Classic. This name was applied to a variant of the *Remington Model 700BDL bolt-action sporting rifle, first offered in 1981 in 7x57, but then reintroduced annually in a single chambering until the LC pattern was combined with the standard Model 700 *Classic in 1992.

Limmex. S.J. Limmex & Company, Wood Street, Swindon, Wiltshire, England. Marks applied by this gunmaker have been encountered on sporting guns and shotgun ammunition.

Lincoln – 1. A name associated with a small rimfire revolver sold in Belgium prior to 1914 by H. *Ortmann. **2.** Found on .320, .380, .44 S&W Russian and .450 double-action revolvers of *Bulldog type, made in Belgium prior to 1914 by Manufacture Liégeoise d'Armes à Feu, whose crowned 'ML' will usually be found on the frames. A safety slider may lie behind the hammer. The Lincoln-Bossu was a five-shot 6.35mm *Browning-type revolver

with an enclosed hammer and a folding trigger. **3.** A mark found on shotgun cartridges and butt-cylinder spring-air *Gems 'made' by Lincoln *Jeffries & Company of Birmingham, Warwickshire, England, during 1900–05. Although the airguns were often sold as 'Improved', they undoubtedly came from Germany and were modified in Britain. **4.** A distinctive .22-calibre spring-and-piston pistol patented in 1911–21 and made in Britain after the end of the First World War by Lincoln *Jeffries of Birmingham. The air cylinder was combined with the butt, and the cocking lever doubled as the trigger guard.

Lindbergh. Charles Augustus Lindberg, Grand Rapids, Michigan, USA. A 'machinist' and co-patentee (with William Henry *Calkins, Matthew *Butts and Austin Kent *Wheeler) of a spring-air BB Gun made by the *Rapid Rifle Company. *See* US Patent 614,532 of 22 November 1898. Robert E. Gardner, in *Small Arms Makers* (Bonanza Books, 1963), lists Lindberg – or possibly his similarly-named father – as a maker of shotguns and combination weapons in the period 1875–78.

Lindner – 1. A.H. Lindner, Suhl in Thüringen, Germany. Founded in 1874 and trading in 1900 as a sporting gunmaker (*Jagdwaffenfabrik*); H.A. Lindner, a gunmaker listed in 1914, may prove to be the same. **2.** Edward N. Lindner, New York City. Grantee of several patents between 1854 and 1863, mostly for firearms, Lindner is best remembered for a breech-loading rifle patented on 29 March 1859. This gun existed in three versions, the most basic being an imported Austrian musket cut to carbine length. Later guns were made by the *Amoskeag Manufacturing Company, although they rarely bore anything other than an acknowledgement of Lindner's patent. The .58-calibre cap-lock carbine had a short grasping handle that rotated the breech cover to the left, allowing the pivoted breech-block to be lifted to

The Belgian gunmaking centre of Liège made guns in huge quantities. Although many were the products of individual artisans, the advent of mass-producers such as Fabrique Nationale d'Armes de Guerre and Anciens Établissements Pieper kept up momentum. This picture shows the proliferation of machinery and overhead shafting in the Fabrique Nationale cartridge factory in 1908.

1939 had dropped below fifty by 1945. Although a small-scale revival followed, there were still only about sixty manufacturers operating in the mid-1950s, and the creation of combines such as the Fabrique d'Armes Unies failed to reverse the trends.

Although Liégeois output grew steadily as a result of the success of Fabrique Nationale d'Armes de Guerre (557,623 guns were proved in 1969), only a handful of independent gunmakers, among them *Francotte, *Lebeau-Courally and *Raick, remained active in the 1990s. The finest source of information about the district is Claude Gaier's *Five Centuries of Liège Gunmaking* (Éditions du Perron, 1996).

---

receive a combustible cartridge. The Federal ordnance authorities ordered 400 on 6 November 1861; total purchases eventually amounted to 892, although apparently many others were acquired for units raised in individual states. Edward Lindner also patented an air pistol that was cocked by a butt-lever, protected by US Patent 37,173 of 16 December 1862. Similar guns, lacking the lever and possibly older, were made by Lindner & Molo (below). **3.** Lindner & Molo, often wrongly listed as Lindner & Mole, New York City. Manufacturers of a spring-air gallery-type pistol patented by Edward N. Lindner.

Lindsay – 1. John Parker Lindsay, New York City. Trained as a gunsmith in *Springfield Armory, Lindsay was granted US Patents protecting a cartridge (28,090 of 24 July 1860) and a distinctive gun-lock that allowed superimposed charges to be fired successively (29,287 of 9 October 1860). **2.** J.P. Lindsay Manufacturing Company, 208 Orange Street and 20 Howard Street, New Haven, Connecticut, USA. Active during 1864–69, this business made single-barrel two-shot firearms in accordance with John Lindsay's October 1860 patent. These included 1,000 .58-calibre rifle-muskets made for the Federal government during the Civil War, and the *Young America pistol. The long-arms are believed to have been produced in a factory owned by gunmaker Cyrus Manville, which shared the Orange Street address.

Lines Brothers Ltd, Tri-Ang Works, Modern Road, Merton, London SW19. Makers of about 880,000 Mark III *Sten submachine-guns during the Second World War. A manufacturer of box magazines for the British 9mm *Sten Gun, and drum magazines for the .303 *Bren Gun during the Second World War. The regional code 'S 68' may have been used instead of the company name. The company also renovated 4,500 ex-air-service *Lewis Guns for ground use (1940).

Ling. William Ling. An English gunmaker first listed in 1820 at 10 Macclesfield Street, Westminster, Ling plied his trade successively from 34 Dartmouth Street, Westminster (1829–32), 16 Church Street, Soho (1833–39) and 61 Jermyn Street (1840–63). Ling is known to have made pepperboxes and butt-reservoir tap-breech airguns in the mid-nineteenth century. He also worked for *Forsyth & Company for 22 years, according to Eldon Wolff in *Air Guns* (1958).

Linington. J.H. Linington, Newport, Isle of Wight, England. The name of this ironmonger/gun dealer has been reported on sporting guns and *Eley-made shotgun cartridges produced before 1914.

'LINLEY'. Found on *Lee-Enfield components made by Linley & Company Ltd of Birmingham.

Linsley Brothers, Lands Lane and 97 Albion Street, Leeds, Yorkshire; also in Bradford, Yorkshire. The name of this English gunmaking partnership has been reported on sporting guns and *Kynoch-made shotgun cartridges sold under the brandnames Nomis and Swift.

Linzel. Edward A. Linzel, St Louis, Missouri, USA. This maker of spring-air *Gallery Guns may be found in the St Louis directories for the period 1864–69, at 63 Walnut Street until 1866, and 822 North Fifth Street thereafter.

Lion – 1. A *Suicide Special revolver made in the USA by *Johnson, Bye & Company and/or *Iver Johnson of Worcester and Fitchburg, Massachusetts, in the late nineteenth century. **2.** Or Chinese Lion. An underlever-cocked fixed-barrel 4.5mm-calibre air rifle made by the State Industry Factory in Peking. Also known as the B-45-3 and possibly originally designed as a military trainer, as its size and balance resemble that of the SKS rifle. It has been imported into Britain by *Nickerson and others; *see also* Arrow, Pioneer and Hunter.

Lip-fire. Introduced by *Allen & Wheelock c. 1862,

these .32 and .44 cartridges had their priming compound in a lateral extension or 'lip' of the rims. Smith & Wesson objected to the use of a bored-through chamber to accommodate them, so production had ceased by the end of the American Civil War in 1865.

Lisle – **1.** Myron C. Lisle, Grand Rapids, Michigan. This firearms designer was granted US Patents 536,960 of April 1895 and 609,445 of August 1898, to protect magazine firearms; and 695,819 of March 1902, to protect a 'breech-loading firearm', a half-interest in the last being assigned to Frank A. *Simonds. Lisle was also the designer of a 'lubricated wire-wound bullet', patented in 1899, which was exploited by the *National Projectile Company. **2.** Robert Lisle, Queen's Hall Buildings, Derby. The name of this English gunmaker has been reported on sporting guns and shotgun cartridges sold under such names as Lisle's Field Cartridge, Tiger and Victa.

List. Wilhelm List & Co., Suhl in Thüringen. A maker of sporting guns active in Germany prior to the First World War.

Lithgow. Small Arms Factory, Lithgow, New South Wales. This, the principal Australian government small-arms factory, was built on a site purchased in 1908 and equipped with machinery from *Pratt & Whitney. It was opened in 1912, the principal product during the First World War being SMLE (*Lee-Enfield) rifles. Production peaked in 1918–19 at about 42,100. Substantial quantities of .22 rimfire rifles were made between the wars for *Slazengers, Pty., alongside .22 Hornet centrefire rifles and .410 shotguns built on Lee actions. The first *Vickers Guns were made in Lithgow in 1920, and the first *Bren Guns in 1941. Rifle production was largely concentrated in the *Orange subsidiary factories during the Second World War (when 136,200 SMLEs were made in 1942/43 alone), but work reverted to Lithgow when hostilities ceased, the last actions being made in 1956. The 7.62mm L1A1 rifle (FN *FAL) was made between 1958 and 1986, and the heavy-barrelled L2A1 during 1963–82, but today work is concentrated on an Australian version of the Steyr *AUG, known as the 5.56mm Rifle F88.

Little... – **1.** G. Little & Company. Gunsmiths listed at 63 Haymarket, London, in 1889–96. **2.** George D. Little, active in 1862–65, accepted .44-calibre cap-lock revolvers made for the Federal Navy by *Colt's Patent Fire Arms Manufacturing Company. They bore a 'GDL' identifier. See also US arms inspectors' marks. **3.** H.C. Little & Son, Yeovil, Somerset. This English gunmaking business handled sporting guns and accessories, including shotgun cartridges sold under the brandnames Blackmoor Vale and Sparkford Vale. **4.** Little All Right. A minuscule revolver patented by *Boardman & Peavey. **5.** Little Colt. A brandname applied unofficially in the early 1870s, by *Kittredge & Company of Cincinnati, to the .22 *New Line Colt revolver. **6.** Little Daisy. A break-open single-shot BB Gun made by the *Daisy Manufacturing Company as the No. 20, in three versions: the original, 1908–12; with an enlarged grip frame, 1912–15; and with a ring trigger, 1915–37. **7.** Little Dog. A name associated with a small six-shot 5.5mm *Velo-Dog double-action revolver featuring a swinging ejector, a ring-tip hammer and a folding trigger, made in Belgium (perhaps by *Francotte of Liège) prior to 1914. **8.** Little Giant. A *Suicide Special revolver made in the USA by the *Bacon Manufacturing Company of Norwich, Connecticut, in the late nineteenth century.

9. Little Pal. This name was applied to a pistol-grip clasp-knife pistol made by the L.G. *Polhemus Manufacturing Company. Apparently it was offered in different forms, chambered for the .22 Short or .25 ACP cartridges. Basically the Little Pal was a bolt-action pistol with additional knife blades beneath the muzzle. The guns generally had a simulated bone or staghorn fore-end, and chequered plastic grips that displayed an encircled 'S' mark. **10.** Little Pet. A *Suicide Special revolver made by the *Hopkins & Allen Arms Company of Norwich, Connecticut, USA, in the late nineteenth century. **11.** Little Scott (sic). A *Suicide Special revolver made in the USA by the *Hopkins & Allen Arms Company of Norwich, Connecticut, in the late nineteenth century. **12.** Little Tom. Designed by Alois *Tomiška, this was the first commercially successful small automatic pistol to incorporate a double-action trigger system. The first guns seem to have been made by *Wiener Waffenfabrik, perhaps as early as 1913, but series production did not begin until after the First World War. Then pistols were made simultaneously by Wiener Waffenfabrik and the Tomiška factory in Pilsen; 6.35mm and 7.65mm versions are comparatively common, but a few were also made in Vienna in 9mm Short.

Liversidge. Charles F. Liversidge, Gainsborough, Lincolnshire. The name of this English gunmaker has been reported on sporting guns and accessories, including shotgun cartridges made prior to 1918 by *Eley Bros.

Livingston. Joseph W. Livingston, Syracuse, New York State, USA. A gunmaker trading at the corner of Geddes and Fayette Streets in 1877–82, Livingston was the co-designer (with John A. *Nichols) of a 'gun-lock' and a 'hinge-joint breech-loading firearm' protected by US Patents 198,669 and 198,670 of 25 December 1877. He was also granted US Patent 227,907 of 25 May 1880 for a 'breech-loading firearm'.

'LJM', 'LJP'. Encountered on US military firearms and accessories. See L.J. *Megette and Laurence J. *Phelan respectively.

Ljungmann. Erik Ljungmann, a consulting mechanical engineer, was responsible for the basic design of the Swedish 6.5mm Ag.42 and Ag.42B automatic rifles. Adapted for production by Erik Eklund, guns of this type were made in quantity by *Husqvarna Våpenfabriks AB c. 1942–55. Others, differing in detail, were made in Denmark in the late 1940s by Dansk Industri Syndikat AS 'Madsen' – with the gas tube coiled around the barrel – and also in Egypt as the Hakim and Rashid.

Ljutic Industries, Inc., Yakima, Washington State, USA. This gunmaking business was responsible in the 1980s for the futuristic Space Rifle and a similarly quirky shotgun. Among the unusual features were thumb-button triggers, twist-off loading and recoil mechanisms built into the tubular butts.

'LJW'. A superimposition-type monogram, with 'L' and 'J' on the arms of the dominant 'W'. Found on the grips of semi-automatic pistols made in Belgium by L. & J. *Warnant Frères of Hognée prior to 1914.

'L&K'. Found on rimfire cartridges made by the Phoenix Cartridge Company for Liddell & Kaeding of San Francisco.

'lkm'. Associated with small-arms ammunition components made under German control during 1943–44 by Munitionsfabriken vorm. *Sellier & Bellot in the Prag-Veitsberg factory.

'LL'. Found on US military firearms and accessories. *See* Luther *Luge.

Llama – 1. Llama–Gabilondo SA. The successor to Gabilondo y Cia (q.v.); a move from Elgoeibar to Vitoria occurred in 1966, helping to date guns by a change in their markings. **2.** Llama pistols and revolvers: *see* panel, pp. 314/15.

'LLCo.' A linear monogram, with back-to-back letters 'L' sharing a common stem. Moulded into the grips of *Smith & Wesson-type *Russian Model revolvers made in Germany in the late 1870s by Ludwig *Loewe & Co., presumably for sale commercially in Russia.

'LLK'. Found on US military firearms and accessories. *See* L.L. *Kuralt.

Lloyd. James Lloyd, an English gunmaker, began trading from Priory Street, Southover, Lewes, Sussex, in 1831. A move to Station Street took place in 1851. By the beginning of the twentieth century, the trading style Lloyd & Sons had been adopted, and additional premises had been opened in Horsham. Appropriate marks have been found on sporting guns and ammunition, including shotgun cartridges sold under the names Imps (or Improved Imps) and Imperial Champion.

'LM'. Found on US military firearms and accessories. *See* L. *Menz.

'Imq'. This mark will be found on sights and optical equipment made during 1943–45 by Carl *Zeiss of Jena.

'LN'. Found on US military firearms and accessories. *See* L. *Newell.

Loaded-chamber indicator. A pin, blade or other device – sometimes combined with the extractor – which gives visual and tactile indication of the presence of a cartridge in the chamber.

Løbnitz. Nicolai Johan Løbnitz was born in the Danish town of Rendsburg in 1798 and died in Copenhagen in 1867. Well known for an assortment of chamber-loading rifles, he also developed a curious air machine-gun in 1834. The gun was tested a year later and found to be quite effective, but the two huge flywheels that operated its pump made the whole thing unwieldy, and nothing more came of the idea. *See also* Gustav Erik *Fleetwood.

Lochat. L. Lochat-Habran & Cie, Jupille-lèz-Liège. Founded in 1860, this metalworking business grew to become one of Belgium's leading gun-barrel makers. Trading ceased in 1914, never to resume.

Lock... – 1. C.H. Lock, Atherstone, Warwickshire, England. The name of this gunmaker has been reported on sporting guns, and on shotgun cartridges sold as Lock's Special. **2.** Lock-Fast. A term associated with a locking system patented in 1860 by James *Dougall, which moved the breech forward before the barrels could be dropped. It was used on double-barrelled break-open shotguns and rifles made between 1863 and 1875. **3.** Lock time is customarily defined as the period that elapses between pressing the trigger and the impact of the hammer, striker or firing-pin on the primer of a chambered cartridge. Alternatively, but much less commonly, lock time has been taken between pressing the trigger and the exit of the bullet from the muzzle, as the aim is susceptible to movement up to the latter point. The shortest possible lock time is desirable to reduce the chance of a shift in aim while the striker is falling. Lock times as short as two milliseconds (.002 sec) will be encountered in bolt-action sporting rifles, which usually have a short light

striker propelled very rapidly, while they may be as much as ten milliseconds (.01 sec) for some military rifles where heavy cocking pieces – and sometimes even the safety catch – are attached directly to the striker. The fastest lock time for a standard military rifle is generally attributed to the German Gew. 98, at about five milliseconds, closely followed by the 1905-pattern Japanese Arisaka. Among the slowest are those of the US Krag-Jørgensen and some of the early Mannlichers (about eight milliseconds), with the Gew. 88 at nine milliseconds or worse. **4.** Lock-work. An expression covering the whole of the mechanism necessary to fire a weapon, from the trigger through to the hammer or striker.

Locke. William Watts Locke & Company. This London gunmaking business, owner of the *Adams Small Arms Company Ltd, was listed at 391 Strand in 1882–92.

Locking rifle. A variant of the *Remington *Rolling Block system; 10,000 of these Model 1871 rifles were made at *Springfield Armory in 1872. Similar to the 1870-pattern US Navy rifles, they had an additional component to prevent accidents from occurring when the rolling-block rifles were being loaded at full-cock. The hammer of these guns automatically dropped to half-cock when the breech piece was closed, and had to be retracted manually before firing. Although Locking Bolt Remingtons were rejected by US Army trial boards, substantial numbers were purchased by the New York state militia.

Lockwood. J.E.S. Lockwood. With chambers in 3 New Street, Birmingham, Warwickshire, this British patent agent acted for Douglas Vaughan *Johnstone, John William *Fearn and Frank *Clarke. *See* British Patents 208,341 of 1922 and 231,557 of 1924.

Lockyer. Colonel William N. Lockyer of the Royal Artillery was the British Army's Chief Inspector of Small Arms (CISA) from 1894 to 1900. He is best remembered for the experimental Lockyer Carbines – shortened versions of the *Lee-Enfield rifle developed during the early stages of the South African War (1899–1900). They were not successful, but paved the way for the SMLE.

Loewe. Ludwig Loewe & Company, Berlin and Charlottenburg. Founded by the brothers Ludwig, Sigmund and Isidor Loewe in 1870, to make machine tools and sewing machines, this company was recruited in the early 1870s to make back sights for the single-shot Mauser service rifle, and subsequently tendered successfully for a contract to make 70,000 Smith & Wesson-type revolvers for the Russian government. By the late 1880s, Loewe had diversified so greatly that the company had become Germany's leading manufacturer of machine tools. The original factory had proved too cramped to accommodate the growing workforce, so a new one had been built alongside Hütten Strasse in Charlottenburg. In December 1887, Loewe gained control of Waffenfabrik *Mauser; by the end of the nineteenth century, a financial interest had also been taken in FGGY in Budapest. An agency for Loewe's products was even maintained in London by Henry F.L. Orcutt, trading from 145 Cannon Street during 1892–98. When Mauser gained a huge rifle order from Turkey in 1887, work was to be split between Oberndorf and Charlottenburg. Before it began, however, the German authorities offered a huge contract for the new 1888-pattern service rifle (*see* Reichsgewehr), but Mauser was not keen to promote a gun incorporating fea-

LLAMA PISTOLS AND REVOLVERS

Llama (2)

The first gun, the Llama Modelo IV, appeared commercially in 1931. Chambered for the 9mm Largo round, it lacked a grip safety and was replaced almost immediately by the Llama Model V (1931–40). The Modelo VI was a variant of the Model V chambered for the 9mm Short cartridge, but production seems to have been confined to 1931–32; the Modelo VII (1932–54) chambered the .38 ACP in addition to 9mm Largo; the Modelo VIII (1939 to date) was similar to the Modelo VII, but had a grip safety; the Modelo IX (1936–54) lacked the grip safety, and could be obtained only in 7.65mm Parabellum, 9mm Parabellum and .45 ACP.

The Modelo IX-A, introduced in 1950, was essentially the IX pattern with a grip safety set into the back strap. The Llama Modelo XI, or Llama Especial, of 1950 was a 9mm Parabellum variant with a ring hammer and a modified grip that had less rake and a more prominent toe-spur. The 7.65mm Llama Modelo I and 9mm Short Modelo II were blowbacks sharing the same general lines as the Modelo IV. Dating from 1933, they were soon replaced by the 7.65mm blowback Modelo X and the 9mm Short locked-breech Modelo III respectively, which lasted from 1935 to 1954. Introduced in 1950, the 7.65mm Modelo X-A and the 9mm Short Modelo III-A were modifications of the X and III patterns with a grip safety.

The Modelo XV-A was a .22-calibre variant of the X-A; the Modelo XVI was a deluxe version of the XV; and the Modelo XVII was a compact XV chambered only for the .22 Short rimfire cartridge. Designations prefixed 'B', 'C' and 'G' refer to blue, chrome and gold-plated finishes respectively, with a supplementary 'E' being added to denote engraved examples; the Modelo BE-III-A, therefore, is simply a blued III-A with engraving.

Although production of Colt-Browning adaptations continued into the 1990s, Gabilondo devoted much development work to the ★Omni, designed by the American Gary Wilhelm. This has been made in a variety of patterns without ever really encountering universal success. Consequently, a reversion to simplified Colt-Browning principles was made with the double-action Llama Modelo 82 (introduced in 1988) and Modelo 87 Competición (1989), which has an elongated ported barrel, an adjustable trigger and greatly refined sights.

The first revolvers seem to have been introduced soon after the end of the Second World War, the range comprising three Smith & Wesson-type swing-cylinder guns: the squared-butt Modelo XII (.38

---

tures developed by his arch-rival ★Mannlicher, so a compromise was arranged: the Turkish guns would be made in Oberndorf, and the Reichsgewehre would be made by Loewe. A suitable gunmaking factory was built in Kaiserin-Augusta-Allee in Charlottenburg to fulfil the German order. Loewe also supplied machine tools to many arms factories. A catalogue dating from c. 1910 noted that these included the Prussian arsenals in Spandau and Danzig; the Bavarian establishment in Amberg; the British Royal Small Arms Factory, Enfield Lock; Manufacture d'Armes de l'État, Liège; the Danish factory in Copenhagen; the Norwegian factory in Kongsberg; the Swedish factory in Eskilstuna; the Dutch small-arms factory in Hembrug; the Portuguese factory in Lisbon; the Toledo and Oviedo factories in Spain; the Izhevsk factory in Russia; the Turkish arsenal in Constantinople; the Serbian factory in Kragujevač; the Chinese factories in Hanyang, Canton, Changsha, Kiangnan, Tsinan-fu and Techow; the Japanese arsenal in Yokohama (*sic*); the Brazilian arsenal in Rio de Janeiro; the Mexican factory in Mexico City; the Argentine factory in Buenos Aires; and the Chilean factory in Valparaiso. Private clients had included DWM, Waffenfabrik Mauser; OEWG; FGGY; Fabrique Nationale d'Armes de Guerre; Vickers, Sons & Maxim Ltd; the Maxim-Nordenfelt Guns & Ammunition Company Ltd; BSA&M Company Ltd; Cogswell & Harrison Ltd; and Eskilstuna Jernmanufactur AB.

'LOH'. Found on US military firearms and accessories. *See* Linus O. ★Hale.

Lohmeyer, Tait & Company. Listed as a member of the English gun trade at 3 Wilson Street, London E.C., in 1889, but possibly little more than a manufacturers' agent.

Lomax. M.P. Lomax, a major in the US Army, accepted firearms and accessories during 1837–45. Distinguished by 'MPL' marks, they included single-shot cap-lock pistols and ★Hall breech-loading carbines. *See also* US arms inspectors' marks.

Lombard. B.B. Lombard, using the identifier 'BBL', accepted US military firearms and accessories in the late 1890s. *See also* US arms inspectors' marks.

London, London… – 1. A double-barrelled side-lock shotgun made by ★Società Armi Bresciane to the designs of Renato ★Gamba. Essentially it is a plainer version of the ★Ambassador Executive, with less ostentatious decoration and a conventional double-trigger system. The standard 12-bore barrels can be replaced with 20-bore versions on request. **2.** Edward London. This gunmaker began trading from 50 London Wall in 1826, and was still operating from 51 London Wall when he died in 1866. Executors perpetuated the business until 1872. Sporting guns and pump-up pneumatic air canes are known with London's marks. **3.** London Armoury Company Ltd [The]. One of the best known of the nineteenth-century British series- or mass-production gunsmithing businesses, this was listed for the first time in 1857. At that time, premises were being occupied in Railway Arches, Henry Street, Bermondsey Street, London E., where they stayed until 1863. Then a move was made to Victoria Park Mills, Old Ford Road, London E., and offices were opened in 36 King William Street and 27 Leman Street in 1868. The King William Street office moved to no. 54 in 1875, then to 118 Queen Victoria Street in 1884. This seems to have been renumbered 114 in 1888, and the office was still there in 1900. **4.** London, Birmingham & Foreign Armour Agency [The]. This business was listed as a gunmaker in London in 1864–68, at 38 Lime Street. Operations are believed to have been concerned more with the promotion of composite ships' armour than

A typical short-barrelled Llama revolver, chambered for the .38 Special cartridge.

Long), with a 100mm barrel; the round-butt Modelo XIII (.38 Special), with 100 or 150mm ventilated-rib barrel; and the Modelo XIV (.22LR rimfire or .32 S&W), which came with adjustable target-type sights and a variety of barrel lengths. All three of these guns could be marked 'RUBY EXTRA', generally with less attention to finish than the Llama examples. They seem to have been made in Elgoeibar, whereas the pistols came from the new factory in Vittoria.

New guns appeared in the 1960s, doubtless inspired by the Astra–Unceta patterns, although the conventional swing-cylinder design was retained. Post-1960 guns have been sold under such names as Comanche, Martial, Olimpico, Piccolo, Scorpio and Super

Comanche, and are all listed individually. The Llama XXVI is a simplified variant of the Olimpico, with standard grips and a half-length ejector-rod shroud; the .32 Long

Llama XXVII, similar mechanically to the XXVI, had a 50mm barrel and fixed sights; the .22LR rimfire Llama XXVIII had a 150mm barrel and adjustable sights.

---

infantry weapons, but the agency history remains unclear. **5.** London Breech-Loading Firearms Company [The]. Operating briefly from an office at 447 West Strand in 1882–84, the affairs of this promotional agency are also uncertain. **6.** London Firearms Company. This promotional agency was listed at 431 Strand in 1886–87, and may have been a successor to, or continuation of, the London Breech-Loading Firearms Company (above). Its goals remain unknown. **7.** London Gun Company. A gunsmithing business, or possibly only a merchant, trading from 42 Wool Exchange, London E.C., from 1882 until 1900 or later. **8.** London Pistol Company: *see* Manhattan Fire Arms Company. **9.** London Small Arms Company Ltd [The], Victoria Mills, Old Ford Road (1866–1921) and Albion Works, Ossary Road (1921–25), London. Listed in the directories from 1867, this gunmaking business was formed, like the ★Birmingham Small Arms Company Ltd, to make military rifles with interchangeable parts. ★Snider, ★Martini-Henry and ★Lee-Metford rifles (Mks I, I★ and II), Lee-Enfield rifles Mks I and I★, and SMLE rifles Mks III and III★ will all be found with appropriate 'L.S.A. Co.' marks, which were still being used when trading ceased in the early 1920s. The company was liquidated in 1925. **10.** 'London Sporting Park, London, England'. Marks of this type have been found on shotgun ammunition made by ★Eley Brothers prior to the First World War. It is assumed that the 'Park' was a shooting ground maintained by commercial interests, possibly within the gun trade, but no other details are known.

Lone Star. A ★Suicide Special revolver made in the USA by Otis ★Smith of Middlefield and Rock Fall, Connecticut, in the late nineteenth century.

Loneux. André & Charles de Loneux. This Liège based

Belgian gunmaking partnership employed the London agents ★Heintzmann & Rochussen in 1865–66.

Long, Long... – 1. J. Long, Glasgow, Lanarkshire. The marks of this Scottish gunmaker have been reported on self-cocking ★pepperboxes dating from the middle of the nineteenth century. **2.** Richard Long & Company. Based at 31 Threadneedle Street, London, this merchanting business represented the Belgian gunmaker A. Bourchez in 1867. **3.** Long Branch Small Arms Factory, Long Branch, Ontario. Approval to build gunmaking facilities was granted by the Canadian government in June 1940 to the Dominion Small Arms Factory Corporation (renamed Small Arms Ltd in August 1940). The first guns were made in 1941 and, by the end of the Second World War, production had amounted to about 911,000 .303 ★Lee-Enfield No. 4 Mk I★ and 5,200 .22 rimfire No. 7 rifles; 128,200 9mm ★Sten Guns; 59,000 .30 and .303 ★Browning machine-guns; and some 20mm Polsten cannon. About 330,000 of the No. 4 Mk I★ rifles had been made for the British government. The Long Branch factory was taken over officially on 1 January 1946 by the Small Arms Division of Canadian Arsenals Ltd, making ★Lee-Enfield, then FN ★FAL derivatives (C1, C1A1, C2, etc) until closed in June 1976. Today Canadian service rifles are made by ★Diemaco. **4.** Long Range Military Creedmoor Rifle. Built on the ★Remington-Hepburn action, chambered exclusively for the .44-75-520 cartridge, the No. 3 Long Range Military Creedmoor Rifle appeared in 1882. It had a vernier back sight on the tang, a steel ramrod and a full-length fore-end retained by two bands **5.** Long-Range Model. This name was applied to a series of ★Ballard rifles. The original .45-100 No. 7 Long-Range model (1876–82) had a half-octagon barrel and a 1,300-yard vernier back sight. The wind-gauge front sight was supplied with bead and aperture discs, plus a spirit level. The butt had a chequered pistol grip, and the fore-end had a *schnabel tip. The No. 8 Long-Range also had a pistol-grip butt, although it was much plainer; No. 9 was simply No. 8 with a straight-wrist butt. Dating from 1877–80, the No. 7 A.1 rifle was a deluxe variant of the No. 7, with Rigby barrels, English walnut stocks, rubber shoulder plates and vernier sights of the finest pattern. Special No. 7 A.1 Extra rifles were made in 1879 and finally, in 1885–86, a few No. 7 Creedmoor Model guns were assembled. **6.** Long Range Rifle, later known as the Sharps Long Range Creedmoor Rifle. This .44-77 or .44-90 gun appeared in 1873, before the *Creedmoor name became fashionable. Made by the *Sharps Rifle Manufacturing Company and the *Sharps Rifle Company, it had an octagon barrel, a chequered pistol-grip butt, a vernier back sight on the tang behind the breech and a globe-pattern front sight (with wind gauge and spirit level) at the muzzle. There were four versions: the No. 1 rifle had a half- or full-octagon barrel, a chequered pistol-grip butt, a chequered fore-end and vernier/spirit level sights; No. 2 was similar to No. 1, but had a plain straight-wrist butt and lacked chequering on the fore-end; No. 3 had a straight-wrist butt and a plain aperture-type sight on the tang; and No. 4 was little more than a No. 3 stocked in poorer wood. These guns were superseded in 1876 by the second pattern (below). **7.** Long Range Rifle. Introduced by the *Sharps Rifle Company in 1876, this was a Mid-Range Rifle (q.v.) with a longer half- or full-octagon barrel chambered for cartridges ranging from .44-90 to .45-100. The No. 1 pattern had a vernier back sight that could be mounted on the tang or on the comb of the butt, near the heel; the globe-type front sight had both wind gauge and spirit level. The chequered woodwork had a silver escutcheon let into the fore-end. The No. 2 pattern had a plain fore-end and lacked the spirit level on the front sight; No. 3, similar to No. 2, had a straight-wrist butt. **8.** Long Range Rifle (Sharps): *see also* New Model Hammerless Long Range Rifle. **9.** Long recoil: *see* recoil operation. **10.** Long Rifle. A name applied to the *Daisy No. 80 1,000-shot lever-action BB Gun, dating from 1955/56, with plastic furniture. A kneeling rifleman firing a 'long rifle' is stamped into the butt and traced with gold paint. **11.** Long Rifle. Applied to the most popular of the .22 *rimfire rounds, also known as *Lang für Buchsen*. **12.** Long Shot [The]. Associated with 12-bore shotgun cartridges loaded by *Eley-Kynoch for H.E. *Pollard & Company of Worcester, *Fuller of Dorking and *Hunter & Maddil of Belfast. **13.** Long Spur, Longspur. A name associated with a cap-lock revolver made in the middle of the nineteenth century by P. *Webley & Son. **14.** 'Long Tom' [The]. Found on shotgun ammunition sold by *Sanders of Maidstone, made, or at least loaded, from components supplied by *Eley Brothers. The name was derived from a long-barrelled cannon at nearby Rochester Castle.

Longford. This brandname was associated with a Mauser-pattern sporting rifle, built on an *FN action by *Cogswell & Harrison of London. Introduced in the early 1960s in .30-06 and .308 Winchester.

Looking Glass. A small Browning-type automatic pistol made in Spain by *Acha Hermanos y Compañía of Ermua: 6.35mm, six rounds, hammer fired. Some examples may also bear the marks of Fabrique d'Armes de *Grande Précision.

Loomis – **1.** Crawford C. Loomis, Ilion, New York State. Loomis worked for the *Remington Arms Company, designing many cartridge weapons and the Model 26 pump-action BB Gun. The patents for the latter, including 1,760,652 of 27 May 1930 and 1,830,763 of 10 November 1931, were granted after the Depression had stopped production. **2.** Oliver Loomis: *see* Pedersen Device.

Lopez. José Lopez de Arnaiz. Designer of the one-hand cocking system applied to the Jo-Lo-Ar pistol (q.v.).

Lorcin Engineering Company Inc., Mira Loma, California, USA. Manufacturer of the Lorcin-25 pocket automatic.

Lord – **1.** Horace Lord. Inventor of an improved cylinder retainer, patented in the USA on 5 August 1884 and subsequently exploited by *Colt. **2.** Lord Model. This was a variant of the Fourth Model .22 Short RF derringer manufactured by *Colt's Patent Fire Arms Manufacturing Company between 1959 and 1963. A gold-plated frame, a blued barrel and wood grips distinguished it from the *Lady Model. *See also* Thuer derringer.

'Lorne' [The]. Found on *Eley-Kynoch shotgun ammunition sold by Duncan *McDougall of Oban. The brandname is usually accompanied by an illustration of a longship, taken from the Arms of Macleod of Dunvegan, Lords of the Isles.

Loron. Henri Loron, rue Saint-Denis 13, Saint-Étienne, France. Listed in 1879 as a gunmaker, Loron made the otherwise-mysterious rifle offered to the British trials by Charles *de Grelle.

Loughran. Benjamin Franklin Loughran, often listed as 'Lougharan', accepted firearms and accessories on behalf of the US Army during 1905–06. He used a 'BFL' identifier. *See also* US arms inspectors' marks.

Lovell – **1.** John P. Lovell [& Sons], Boston, Massachusetts. This US gunmaker, a partner in Grover & Lovell prior to 1844, made cap-lock pistols and revolvers on his own account until John P. Lovell & Sons was formed c. 1866. The business is said to have been acquired by Iver *Johnson in 1868, but the Lovells continued to operate from 27 Dock Square, Boston, until 1873 or later. Revolvers were exhibited in Philadelphia in 1876, and in Paris in 1878, when premises were being occupied in Boston at 145 Washington Street. By 1890, the John P. Lovell Arms Company (below) was being listed at 147 Wade Street. **2.** John P. Lovell Arms Company, Boston, Massachusetts, USA. This gunmaking business may have been a successor to John Lovell & Sons (above), although the lineage remains unclear. It made single-barrel shotguns under the name The *Champion from c. 1887 until shortly before the death of John Lovell in 1897.

Loveridge & Company. Trading from 172 King's Street in Reading, Berkshire, this English ironmongery business also sold sporting guns and ammunition, including *Kynoch-made shotgun cartridges marked 'Royal County'.

Lovering. E.M. Lovering accepted firearms and accessories on behalf of the US Army, marking them 'EAL'. Apparently his activities were confined to 1909. *See also* US arms inspectors' marks.

Lovett. T.J. Lovett, in the employ of the US government, accepted military firearms and accessories. Marked 'TJL', they dated from the early 1900s. *See also* US arms inspectors' marks.

Lowell – **1.** Charles S. Lowell, a major in the US Army, accepted firearms and accessories in the period 1858–63. His 'CSL' marks – distinguishable from those of C.S. *Leonard by date – will be found on *Colt and *Starr cap-lock revolvers. **2.** Lowell Arms Company, Lowell, Massachusetts. Working in 1865–68, this US gunmaking business was a successor to the Rollin *White Arms Company, although White no longer had a financial interest, so *Smith & Wesson regarded guns made after the reorganisation as patent infringements. **3.** Lowell Manufacturing Company, Lowell, Massachusetts. This agency was formed to promote the Lowell machine-gun (below), but does not seem to have had direct links with the Lowell Arms Company (above). Its operations seem to have been confined to 1876–80. **4.** Lowell machine-gun. Invented by De Witt Farrington, and promoted (but probably not actually made) by the Lowell Manufacturing Company of Lowell, Massachusetts, a gun of this type was tested most successfully in October 1876 in the Annapolis Navy Yard, firing 10,000 rounds with only one misfire. Only the upper of the two barrels fired, as the lower one was simply rotated into place when its companion overheated. In July 1877, a modified gun fired 55,000 rounds with only two stoppages – a staggering performance for its day. However, although a few guns went to the US Navy, twenty went to Russia, and a few were issued to Californian state militiamen, Lowell soon disappeared into history.

Lower. Gunsmith John P. Lower was born in Philadelphia in 1833, establishing his first shop in the town in the early 1850s. There he made Indian Guns until the outbreak of the Civil War. A move to 281 Blake Street, Denver, Colorado occurred in 1872. A variety of sporting guns, rifles and revolvers has been reported with Lower marks, although many were made by manufacturers such as *Colt and *Remington. Trading continued until John Lower died in 1915, and thereafter was perpetuated for a few years as J.P. Lower's Sons Company, from 1729 Champa Street, Denver.

'Lowrecoil' [The]. Apparently written as one word, this mark is found on shotgun cartridges distributed in East Anglia by Charles S. *Rosson of Norwich.

'LP'. Found on US military firearms and accessories. *See* L. *Papanti.

'L' and 'P', with crossed pennants. A military proof mark used during the reigns of George V (1910–36) and George VI (1936–52). *See also* British military proof marks.

'lpk'. Allotted in 1943, this code will be found on small-arms ammunition made by Servotechna AG of Prague during the German occupation of Czechoslovakia.

'LSA', 'L.S.A. Co.', 'LSA Co.', 'L.S.A.Co.Ld.' Marks employed by The London Small Arms Company Ltd from c. 1864 until 1925.

'L.S.P.', 'LSP'. Marks encountered on shotgun ammunition used exclusively by the London Sporting Park. *See also* 'SPL'.

LSS. Laminated, Stainless-Steel. A variant of the *Remington M700 bolt-action rifle, introduced in 1996.

'LT', 'L T', 'L.T.' Stencilled on the butts of guns adapted for line throwing, many of which prove by the presence of other identifiable marks to be Canadian.

Luca. A brandname associated with the products of Ludwig *Catterfeld of Zella-Mehlis.

Lucas. Joseph Lucas Ltd, Birmingham. A maker of magazines for the British 9mm *Sten Gun during the Second

World War. The regional code 'M 158' may have been used instead of the company name. *See also* British military manufacturers' marks.

Luck – 1. Gebr. Luck, Suhl in Thüringen. Founded in 1879, this German gunmaking business was being operated in 1900 by Franz Aug. Luck. By 1914, however, the proprietors were Richard, Ernestine, Elsa, Hedwig and Aga Luck. At that time, guns were being made alongside bicycles ('*Waffen u. Fahrradfabrik*'). After the First World War, operations were re-registered in the names of Richard Luck and Ludwig Wagner, and continued until c.1933, when they were succeeded by Luck & Wagner. Individual guns may be identified by 'GL' or 'G.L' marks, sometimes in the form of monograms. **2.** Luck & Wagner, 'vorm. Gebr. Luck', Suhl in Thüringen. Listed in 1938–41 as a maker of gun and bicycle parts.

Luckes. S. Luckes, Bridge Street, Castle Green and St James Foundry, Taunton, Somerset. This English gun and ammunition distributor had depots in Langport, Washford and Wiveliscombe. His name has been found on sporting guns and accessories, including shotgun cartridges sold under the brandname Taunton Demon.

Lucking. John Lucking. This patent agent, or possibly mechanical engineer, obtained British Patent 14,447/07 of 1907 for Gustav *Pabst, acting in conjunction with G.F. *Redfern & Company. Lucking's address was listed as 102 & 104 Leonard Street, Finsbury, London.

Łucznik, *see also* Zaklady Metałowe Łucznik. Airguns made in Poland by a company of uncertain trading style, imported into Britain by the *Viking Arms Company. They included the Model 170 spring-air pistol, copied from the Walther LP53, and the Model 188 break-barrel rifle – both in 4.5mm.

'Luda' [The]. A brandname found on shotgun cartridges handled by *Hodgson of Louth.

Ludwig. Walter Ludwig. An engineer employed by *Mauser-Werke GmbH of Oberndorf/Neckar, responsible for the development of the unsuccessful recoil-operated 9x19 *HsP pistol.

Luge. Luther Luge, a US government employee, accepted military firearms and accessories during 1841–45, marking them 'LL'. *See also* US arms inspectors' marks.

Luger – 1. Georg Luger: *see* panel, p. 318. **2.** Luger Pistol: *see* Borchardt-Luger and Parabellum (2); *see also* American Luger, Borchardt and Improved Borchardt. **3.** Luger Sales Company, 828 George Street, Chicago, Illinois, USA. This short-lived promotional agency – which may have concealed the activities of Hugo *Panzer – was formed immediately after the First World War to handle war-surplus firearms, but had ceased trading by 1929. Its trademark comprised two flying geese (cf. *Stoeger).

Lugerlike. A term coined for its similarity to lookalike, describing any pistol based deliberately on the external lines of the *Parabellum (Luger) – even though they may be simple blowbacks made by *Erma-Werke, *Echave y Arizmendi or *Stoeger Industries.

Luna – 1. Associated with Ernst Frederich Büchel of Zella-Mehlis; found on sporting guns and target pistols, but also, doubtfully, reported on an air pistol. **2.** Luna Park. These gas-powered rifles were made during the 1960s by Stefano *Marocchi e Figli of Gardone Val Trompia. *See also* 'Artemis'.

Lunch. *See* Harry F. *Lynch.

Lund conversion. The first Norwegian breech-loader

GEORG LUGER

Luger (1)

The son of a doctor, Georg Luger was born in 1849 in Steinach in the Austrian Tyrol. After military service in the Austrian Landwehr, Luger worked as a railway engineer. His work brought him into contact with Ferdinand von *Mannlicher, and in 1875 they collaborated in the design of a gravity-feed magazine for the *Werndl rifle. Luger joined Ludwig *Loewe & Co. in 1891, continuing to design rifles. A 6mm-calibre bolt-action pattern was submitted to the US Navy trials in 1894, but was not successful.

After transferring to the newly-formed *Deutsche Waffen- & Munitionsfabriken in 1897, Georg Luger was entrusted with the task of transforming the *Borchardt pistol into an acceptable weapon. This he did with great success, millions of the resulting *Borchardt-Luger, or *Parabellum, being made prior to 1945.

Luger's German patents included 78,406 of 26 September 1893 and 90,433 of 1896, protecting gas-ported strikers for 'bolt guns'; and 109,481 of 30 September 1898 for a selection of safety devices applicable to the *Improved Borchardt pistol.

British Patent 9040/99 of 1899 and US Patent 639,414 of 19 December 1899 were both comparable with DRP 109,481. A selection of patents was sought in Germany in May 1900, being granted as 129,842 for the basic action of the perfected *Borchardt-Luger; 130,377 for the sliding barrel action and the dismantling system; 130,847 for the magazine-actuated hold-open system; 130,911 for the safety arrangements; 131,451 for the toggle-train; 132,031 for the trigger system; and 134,003 for the means of breaking the toggle by ramps on the frame. These individual grants were consolidated in British Patent 4399/00 of 7 March 1900, and US Patent 753,414 of 1 March 1904.

German Patent 164,853 of 22 May 1904 was granted for combination extractors and loaded-chamber indicators; British Patent 13,147/04 of 14 July 1904, and US Patent 808,463 of 1904 were broadly comparable. US Patent 851,538 of 23 April 1907 protected a unique toggle-breaking mechanism with cam shoulders on the frame and an extended toggle grip. German Patent 213,698 of 7 November 1907 was granted for an improved hold-open mechanism; 237,192 of 16 February 1910 protected a chambering system

Georg Luger (1849–1923), designer of the eponymous pistol. Apparently this picture was taken during the First World War. Courtesy of Reinhard Kommayter.

with the cartridge case locating on its mouth; and 312,919 of 1 April 1916 allowed the Parabellum pistol to be loaded even if the safety catch was applied. Luger died in Berlin in 1923.

---

was the so-called Chamber-loading Rifle, or *Kammerladningsgevær*, an underhammer cap-lock design adopted in 1842. The breech-block, containing the chamber, was pivoted at the rear; a sidelever, mounted on an eccentric, opened the action. After the Norwegian Army had adopted the *Remington Rolling Block in 1867, many old chamber-loaders were altered to fire the same rimfire cartridge. Conversions, depending on pattern, were known as Landmark's and Lund's. They included the M1855–67 infantry rifle, the M1860–67 rifle-musket, the M1860–67 short rifle, the M1866–69 foot artillery carbine and the M1865–69 cavalry carbine.

Lüneschloss. John D. Lüneschloss. Listed as a member of the London gun trade in 1867–68, with an office at 90 Newgate Street, presumably Johann D. Lüneschloss was a member of the Solingen based sword-cutlery business P.D. Lüneschloss. No firearms have ever been identified from this particular source.

'Lunesdale' [The]. Found on shotgun cartridges sold by *Fawcett of Kirkby Lonsdale.

Lunsmann. Franz or Francis Lunsmann, St Louis, Missouri, USA. Working between 1848 and 1870 from premises in South 22nd Street; these are believed to have been numbered 103 until c. 1867, and 410 thereafter, although Gardner, writing in *Small Arms Makers*, lists the address as 105, and the 1864 directory gives 153.

Lunsmann is known to have made spring-air *Gallery Guns and breech-loading sporting guns.

Lurch – 1. David Lurch, New York City. A maker of spring-air *Gallery Guns between about 1863 and 1875, Lurch is listed in the city directories as a gunsmith and maker of mechanical targets, airgun darts and springs until the late 1870s. Then he became a sporting goods wholesaler. Lurch traded from 142 Grand Street, New York City, during 1863–66, and thereafter from 157 Grand Street. Operations ceased c. 1896. **2.** Joseph Lurch, New York City. Maker of spring-air *Gallery Guns (rifles and at least one pistol) during the 1860s and 1870s; possibly a brother of David Lurch.

Lur-Panzer. A name associated with a .22LR rimfire *Lugerlike pistol copied from the *Erma EP-22 by *Echave y Arizmendi of Eibar. Dating from c. 1968 to 1973, it had a ten-round detachable box magazine and a horizontal toggle-return spring in the frame. Medallions set into the grips customarily bore 'PANZER' in a diamond or an encircled 'EYA', with 'E' and 'A' separated by three short radial arms approximating to 'Y'.

Lusa. These 9x19 submachine-guns were made in Portugal by *INDEP, the Lusa A1 dating from 1986 and the improved A2 pattern from 1994. The basic design relies on an overhung bolt, but there are differences in the design of the sliding steel-rod butt and the barrel-detaching mechanism. The Lusa A2 may be found with an optional three-round burst capability and an integral silencer.

Lutkovskiy. Nikolai Lutkovskiy, a Russian Army officer, is best known for developing a detachable quick-loader for the ★Berdan rifle. Apparently this was issued in small numbers to the Tsarist Army, until the advent of the magazine-fed ★Mosin-Nagant in the 1890s made it obsolete. Lutkovskiy also designed magazine rifles, but none proceeded beyond the prototype stage.

Luukkonen. Viotto A. Luukkonen, a government inspector, accepted US Army .45 M1911A1 pistols made in 1940–41 by ★Colt's Patent Fire Arms Manufacturing Company. *See also* US arms inspectors' marks.

Lux – 1. Found in the headstamps of shotgun cartridges advertised in 1911 by A.L. ★Frank, possibly the products of ★Rheinisch- Westfälische Sprengstoff. **2.** Lux-Metallwarenfabrik: associated with parts made during 1943–45 for the German MP.43. Possibly 'lux', a code used by Schlieper & Baum AG of Wuppertal-Elberfeld.

Luzier et Martin, rue Villeboeuf 28, Saint-Étienne, France. Listed in 1892 as a gunmaker.

'LW'. An unidentified government inspector's mark found on some of the earliest M1892 US Army ★Colt revolvers.

'lwg'. Found on German military optical equipment made during 1943–45 by Optische Werke Osterode GmbH of Freiheit bei Osterode im Harz.

'LWS'. Associated with semi-automatic pistols made in the USA by L.W. ★Seecamp.

'lxr'. Found on rifle and other small-arms components made in Germany during 1943–45 by Dianawerk ★Mayer & Grammelspacher of Rastatt in Baden.

Lyle. David A. Lyle, a lieutenant in the US Army, accepted ★Single Action Army Model ★Colt and Smith & Wesson ★Schofield revolvers for US Army service in the period 1876–80. They customarily bore 'DAL' marks. *See also* US arms inspectors' marks.

Lyman – 1. William Lyman (1854–96) received US Patent 211,753 of 28 January 1879, to protect an improved aperture-type 'No. 1 Tang Sight' made by the Lyman Gun Sight Company. This was followed by a variety of US Patents: 298,305 of 6 May 1884; 327,957 of 6 October 1885 for an ivory-bead target sight; 341,426 of 4 May 1886 for an ivory-bead shotgun sight; 348,224 of 31 August 1886; 366,121 of 5 July 1887; 368,598 of 23 August 1887 for a tang sight that was adjustable for windage as well as elevation; 396,043 of 8 January 1889 for a method of clamping the base screws of a target sight; 447,886 of 10 March 1891 for a shotgun sight with a centre in the form of a vertically-adjustable ivory cylinder; 454,015 of 14 July 1891 for a folding leaf sight; 455,911 of 22 September 1891; 541,558 of 25 June 1895 for a receiver-sight suitable for top-ejecting lever-action rifles; 558,402 for a peep sight adapted to the bolt-action Mannlicher sporting rifle; and 558,403 of 14 April 1896 for revolver back sights. He was also responsible for US Patents 629,670 and 629,671, granted on 25 July 1899 to his executor George Durrenberger. **2.** Lyman Gun Sight Company, Middlefield, Connecticut, USA. This renowned maker of iron and optical sights for firearms was founded in 1878 by William Lyman (above), who

also sold rifles equipped with his sights – including Ballard, Marlin, Maynard, Merwin & Hulbert, Quackenbush, Winchester, and Double English Express patterns. The company passed into the hands of Lyman Mills, a cousin of William Lyman, and was incorporated in 1901. A younger brother of the founder, Charles E. Lyman, gained control in 1917, and the business remained in the hands of the Lyman family until it was sold in 1969 to The Leisure Group, Inc., of Los Angeles. Improved sights continued to appear, many being the work of James Windridge, and the Ideal Reloading Tool Company was acquired in 1925. The first telescope sights followed in 1929, after Lyman had purchased the optical-sight businesses of both the ★Winchester Repeating Arms Company and J. ★Stevens Arms & Tool Company. A series of famous brandnames followed, including the Lyman Alaskan sight, which was developed in 1937 and introduced commercially in 1939. ★Cutts Compensators were also made in large numbers from c. 1932 until recent times. The company's centenary history, *Lyman Centennial 1878–1978*, is an invaluable source of additional information.

Lynch – 1. Harry F. Lynch (sometimes listed as 'Lunch'), using an 'HFL' mark, accepted military firearms made for the US armed forces by ★Colt's Patent Fire Arms Manufacturing Company. They date from the period 1940–41. **2.** John J. Lynch accepted .45 M1911A1 semi-automatic pistols made by ★Colt's Patent Fire Arms Manufacturing Company. Bearing 'JJL' identifiers, they date from 1940 and thus can be distinguished from guns accepted many years earlier by J.H. ★Lyons. *See also* US arms inspectors' marks for both entries.

Lyndon. W.M. Lyndon, using the identifier 'WML', accepted firearms on behalf of the US Army in 1898. *See also* US arms inspectors' marks.

Lynn. C.P. Lynn, a government employee using the identifier 'CPL', accepted US military firearms and accessories in 1905. *See also* US arms inspectors' marks.

'Lynton' [The]. Found on 12-bore and other shotgun cartridges sold in Britain by ★Gallyon & Sons.

Lyon. Benjamin Lyon, a government employee, accepted US Army firearms and accessories marked 'BL'. They date from the mid-1870s. *See also* US arms inspectors' marks.

Lyons. J.H. Lyons accepted firearms and accessories on behalf of the US Army, marking them 'JHL'. His activities were confined to 1898–99, distinguishing them from those of John J. ★Lynch. *See also* US arms inspectors' marks.

Lyttleton Engineering Works Pty, Ltd, Pretoria, Republic of South Africa. This manufacturing business has been responsible for the R 4, R 5 and R 6 rifles. Issued to the South African armed forces, these are minor derivatives of the 5.56mm Israeli ★Galil, distinguished principally by their marks and long butts. The business became Vektor Engineering in the 1980s.

'L Z'. A mark applied prior to 1919 by ★Langenhan of Zella St Blasii, most commonly encountered on butt-cylinder ★Gems.

'lza'. Allotted in 1943 to identify machine-gun and other small-arms components made in the ★Mauser-Werke KG factory in Karlsruhe/Baden.

M

'm' – 1. Found on rifle and other small-arms components made in Germany in 1940 by Limbacher Maschinenfabrik Bach & Winter of Limbach/Sachsen. **2.** With a number. Found on components of British military stores (including firearms) made during the Second World War, this indicates a company operating in the Midlands (of Britain). The numbers identified individual companies. Among the many examples associated with small-arms are 'M 1', *Accles & Pollock; 'M 8', *Anstey & Wilson; 'M 13', the *Austin Motor Company. Ltd; 'M 47', *BSA Guns Ltd ('A', Small Heath; 'B', Redditch; 'C', Shirley); 'M 78', *Elkington & Company Ltd; 'M 91', *Godins Ltd; 'M 94', W.W. *Greener Ltd; 'M 109', *Harrison Bros. Ltd; 'M 111', Frank *Hawker Ltd; 'M 117', the *Hercules Cycle & Motor Company Ltd; 'M 136', *Willen, Jones & Sons Ltd; 'M 158', Joseph *Lucas Ltd; 'M 170', the *Midland Gun Company; 'M 183', *Parker-Hale Ltd; 'M 224', *Skimmin & Wood; 'M 233', *Standard Sporting Guns; 'M 260', *Walls Ltd; 'M 264', *Webley & Scott Ltd, Birmingham; 'M 265', *Webley & Scott Ltd, Stourbridge; 'M 268', Westley *Richards & Company Ltd; 'M 292', the *Morris Motor Company; 'M 601', I.L. *Berridge & Company; 'M 602', Alfred *Bray & Son; 'M 615', BSA Guns Ltd, Leicester; 'M 616', BSA Guns Ltd, Mansfield; and 'M 634', *Mettoy Ltd. *See also* British military manufacturers' marks. **3.** As 'M2', beneath a crown. Found on Portuguese weapons: the mark of King Manuel II (1908–10). *See also* Cyphers, imperial and royal.

M1 Carbine. Developed in 1941 in answer to a requirement formulated by the US Army as early as 1937, the prototype of this .30-calibre light automatic rifle reached Aberdeen Proving Ground on 9 August 1941 and immediately showed more promise than either the *Springfield Light Rifle or the *Hyde/Bendix pattern, which had survived previous trials. On 30 September 1941, the perfected Winchester Carbine was recommended for immediate adoption, and the 'Carbine, Caliber .30, M1' was standardised on 22 October 1941. Subsequently a wide range of manufacturers was entrusted with production, including, in addition to Winchester, the *Inland Manufacturing and *Saginaw Steering Gear Divisions of General Motors, *International Business Machine (IBM), *Irwin-Pedersen, *National Postal Meter, *Quality Hardware, *Rock-Ola, *Standard Products and *Underwood-Elliott-Fisher. The M2 Carbine was a selective-fire version of the semi-automatic M1, adopted on 23 October 1944. The guns were outstandingly successful, more than 6,000,000 M1, M2 and M3 Carbines being made for the US armed forces prior to 1946. The M1 Carbine is customarily credited to David M. *Williams, but was really an amalgamation of a rotating-bolt-action developed by Jonathan *Browning and the Williams short-stroke piston gas system.

'ma', 'MA' – 1. Found as 'MA' on Australian *Lee-Enfield rifles and other small-arms made by the *Lithgow Small Arms Factory in New South Wales. **2.** A superimposition-type monogram with both letters equally prominent. Correctly interpreted as 'MA'; used by August *Menz of Suhl. **3.** A superimposition-type monogram, usually encircled or enwreathed, with 'M' splayed to accommodate 'A' and (sometimes) an accompanying ring target. Correctly read as 'AM' (q.v.); associated with August *Menz of Suhl. **4.** A superimposition-type monogram, usually encircled, with 'A' formed by extending the medial strokes of 'M'. Effectively formed of two opposed right-angle triangles, overlapping at the foot, this actually reads 'MANN', with one 'N' reversed; it will be found on the grips of pocket pistols made in Germany by Fritz *Mann of Suhl. **5.** Found as 'ma' on German small-arms ammunition and components made by F.A. Lange Metallwerke AG of Aue/Sachsen during the Second World War.

Maadi Military & Civil Industries Company, Port Said. This firearms manufactory, operated by the Egyptian government, was built with Soviet aid in the early 1960s to make a copy of the *Kalashnikov AKM, known as the *Misr. *See also* Ljungmann.

'MAB'. *See* Manufacture d'Arms de Bayonne.

'MAC'. *See* Châtellerault.

Mac..., Mc... This Scottish name prefix, meaning 'son of', may be written in several ways. Owing to potential confusion, the permutations (which can include the widespread pre-1900 preference for M'...) are treated here in a single alphabetical sequence. – **1.** McAllister; a US arms inspector. *See* McCallister. **2.** Albert H. McAllister, Cotton Plant and New Albany, Mississippi, USA. Patentee of 'machine-guns' (US 201,810 of 26 March 1878 and 674,811 of 21 May 1901, rights in the latter being assigned to the McAllister Machine Gun Company). **3.** McAllister Machine Gun Company, Memphis, Tennessee, USA. Assignee of rights to the machine-gun patented in 1901 by Albert McAllister. Production seems to have been meagre. **4.** Isaac E. McAvoy, Huntingdon, West Virginia, USA. Designer of an 'automatic rapid-fire gun' protected by US Patent 566,214 of 18 August 1896. **5.** James McAlpine, New Haven, Connecticut, USA. Patentee of a breech-loading firearm (US no. 204,675 of 11 June 1878). **6.** McAusland Brothers, Deadwood, Dakota Territory, and Miles City, Montana, USA. The marks of this gunmaking business, a partnership of brothers Alexander, John and William McAusland, will be found on sporting guns and ammunition. Most of the breech-loaders were purchased from major manufacturers, such as *Colt's Patent Fire Arms Manufacturing Company, E. *Remington & Sons and the *Winchester Repeating Arms Company. The move from Dakota Territory to Montana occurred in 1880, and may have affected only Alexander. **7.** James E. McBeth, New Orleans, Louisiana. Designer of a 'safety gun-lock for firearms' (US Patent 58,443 of 2 October 1866) and two breech-loaders, with enclosed locks contained in a block that pivoted laterally to expose the breech, which were protected by 73,357 of 14 January 1868 and 80,985 of 11 August 1868. Rights to the earlier of these were part-assigned to Sheldon Sturgeon. **8.** William McCall [& Company]. This business, subsequently William McCall & Sons, based in the Scottish town of Dumfries, handled sporting guns and ammunition. These included shotgun cartridges marked 'The Border' and 'The Tally-Ho!'. **9.** G.J. McCallin, working on behalf of the US Army, accepted firearms and accessories c. 1902. They bore a 'GJM' identifier. *See also* US arms inspectors' marks. **10.** Julian McCallister, a major in the Federal Army Ordnance Department, active during the American Civil War, accepted firearms and accessories marked 'JM'. Dated '1865', they can be difficult to distinguish from equipment attributed to John *Maggs, J. *Mills and *Justice *Murphy. *See also* US arms inspectors' marks. **11.** McCarthy, Buck & Company. A member of the London gun trade, perhaps a merchant, listed at 40 St Andrew's Hill, E.C., in 1899–1900. Possibly still trading in 1914. **12.** Samuel N. McClean of Washington, Iowa, and Cleveland, Ohio, USA, was a surprisingly prolific patentee, among the relevant US grants being several for 'magazine firearms' (575,265 of 12 January 1897 and 601,838–601,844 of 5 April 1898). US Patent 723,706 of 24 March 1903 protected a 'magazine bolt gun', whereas 735,131 and 783,453 of 4 August 1903 and 28 February 1905 were granted for 'gas-operated firearms'. McClean developed a series of recoil buffers, a 'one-pounder machine-gun' (858,745 of 2 July 1907), and a gun carriage (862,502 of 6 August 1907). He was also responsible for the unsuccessful prototypes of the *Lewis Gun, protected by US Patent 922,098 of 7 September 1908. Most patents granted after 1906 were assigned to the McClean Arms & Ordnance Company (below). **13.** McClean Arms & Ordnance Company, Cleveland, Ohio, USA. This business was the assignee of patents granted to Samuel McLean, but failed in 1909. Subsequently rights were acquired by the *Automatic Arms Company of Buffalo, New York State. **14.** Reuben McChesney of Ilion, New York State, was granted US Patent 58,444 on 2 October 1866 to protect a rifle with a breech-block that travelled radially down and back as the hammer was moved to half-cock. An improvement of this mechanism was patented on 28 May 1867 (US no. 65,103). **15.** McColl & Fraser, Dunfermline, Fifeshire, Scotland. The name of this gunsmithing partnership has been reported on sporting guns and shotgun ammunition made in the 1950s by *Eley-Kynoch. **16.** James W. McCoy, a government inspector working c. 1927–40, accepted firearms and accessories on behalf of the US Army, marking them 'JWM'. Most seem to have been .38-calibre revolvers made by *Colt's Patent Fire Arms Manufacturing Company. *See also* US arms inspectors' marks. **17.** McCririck & Sons. A gunmaking business trading from 38 John Finnie Street, Kilmarnock, Ayrshire, Scotland. Its marks have been seen on sporting guns and ammunition, including shotgun cartridges made by *Eley-Kynoch. **18.** Edward McCue, a Federal government employee using the identifier 'EM', accepted guns and accessories destined for the Federal Army. His activities seem to have been confined to 1863–64, although they may be difficult

to distinguish from those of Edwin *Martin. *See also* US arms inspectors' marks. **19.** John L. McCullough, Brooklyn, New York City. This inventor was responsible for several magazine-rifle designs, including some that were operated electrically: *see* US Patents 509,091 of 21 November 1893, 509,548 of 28 November 1893, 557,863 of 7 April 1896 and 626,501 of 6 June 1899. **20.** Duncan McDougall. Trading in Oban, Argyllshire, this Scottish gunsmith sold sporting guns and ammunition. Among the shotgun cartridges were some post-war *Eley-Kynoch examples marked 'The Lorne'. **21.** W.C. McEntee, Birmingham. Co-recipient, with J. *Hughes, of British Patent 8314 of 1885 to protect a drop-barrel action for sporting guns. The patent notes that McEntee was trading as J. *Reeves & Company at this time. **22.** McEntee & Company. An English gunsmithing business listed at 17 Great St Helen's, London E.C., in 1885. Possibly a sales office maintained by W.C. McEntee (above). **23.** Albert C. McFarland of Upper Lisle, New York State, patented a 'gun-lock for firearms' on 4 October 1887 (US no. 370,966). **24.** Henry McGee, Norwich, Connecticut, USA. Designer of a 'cylinder stop for revolving firearms', proetcted by US Patent 239,821 of 5 April 1881 and assigned to Freeman *Hood. **25.** Macglashan Air Machine Gun Corporation, also listed as Mcglashan, Long Beach, California, USA. This business was the developer and manufacturer of the air- or gas-powered machine-gun that bears its name, marketed in 1942 as a training device (Trainer, Aerial, Gunnery, Type E3) for air gunners. The gun had an electromagnetic feed mechanism containing up to 2,000 BB shot, and could be powered by a tankful of compressed air, carbon dioxide or similar gas. Several hundred were made: no. 1453 and others survive. **26.** John McGovern of New York City received US Patent 88,890 of 13 April 1869 to protect a simple tip-barrel action suitable for single-shot rifles and pistols. **27.** Charles MacGregor. Trading in Kirkwall in the Orkney Islands, this gunsmith/ironmonger handled sporting guns and ammunition. Kynoch-made shotgun cartridges loaded with *E.C. powder have been reported with his marks. **28.** George A. MacGuder, sometimes listed as MacGruder or Magruder, holding the rank of captain in the US Navy, accepted small-arms and accessories prior to the American Civil War. Marked 'GAM', apparently they date from the period 1855–57. *See also* US arms inspectors' marks. **29.** J.P. McGuinness, a lieutenant in the US Navy, accepted *Colt and *Smith & Wesson revolvers in the early 1900s, marking them 'JPW'. *See also* US arms inspectors' marks. **30.** J.R. McGuinness, or McGinness, a captain in the US Army, accepted guns and accessories in the late 1860s; they bore the identifier 'JRM'. It seems likely that the two McGuinnesses were father and son. *See also* US arms inspectors' marks. **31.** James H. McGuire, working on behalf of the Federal Army in 1862, during the American Civil War, accepted firearms and accessories marked 'JHM'. *See also* US arms inspectors' marks. **32.** John MacGuire. A member of the English gun trade, operating during 1865–87 from 7 Chambers Street, London, E. **33.** William McIlwraith & Company, Elgin, Morayshire. This Scottish gunsmithing and ironmongery business sold sporting guns and ammunition, including shotgun cartridges bearing its own name. These appear to have been loaded prior to 1914 by *Kynoch. **34.** J.D. McIntyre, a captain in the US Army, accepted firearms and accessories marked 'JDM'. Customarily made by *Colt's Patent Fire Arms Manufacturing Company, they date from the mid-1920s. *See also* US arms inspectors' marks. **35.** Alexander MacKay & Son, trading in the small Scottish town of Tarbert in Argyllshire, distributed sporting guns and shotgun ammunition marked 'The Argyll'. **36.** George W. McKee, a captain in the US Army, accepted firearms and accessories in the mid-1870s. His 'GWM' marks have been confused with those said to have been applied prior to the American Civil War by George W. *Morse. *See also* US arms inspectors' marks. **37.** William McKee, Detroit, Michigan. Patentee (US 868,616 of 15 October 1907) of a 'firearm', part-assigned to A.N. Ericsson of Detroit. **38.** Emroe A. McKeen of Boston, Massachusetts, received protection on 26 December 1905 for a 'magazine gun'. *See* US Patent 808,107. **39.** Henry H. McKenney, Biddeford, Maine, USA. Active from 1855 until c. 1867, then a partner in McKenney & Bean, this gunsmith was co-patentee with Fredrick Goth of a 'repeating firearm': US Patent 22,969 of 15 February 1859. **40.** McKenney & Bean, Biddeford, Maine, USA. A gunmaking partnership of Henry McKenney (above) and Joseph Bean, active only in 1867–69. **41.** MacKenzie Brothers. A gunmaking business listed at 84 Mark Lane, London E.C., in 1881–92, then at 132 Queen Victoria Street in 1893–94. **42.** Mackenzie & Duncan. This Scottish gunsmithing business in Brechin, Angus, possibly doubling as an ironmonger and distributor of sporting goods, handled shotgun ammunition marked 'The Dunmax'. This may have been loaded on the premises, using *Eley or *Eley-Kynoch components. **43.** James Mackie. A gunmaker registered at 42 Cambridge Street, Pimlico, London, from 1879 until 1883. **44.** Mackintosh & Sons. The marks of this British gunsmithing business, trading in Cambridge, have been reported on shotgun ammunition loaded by *Eley with Schultze powder prior to 1900. **45.** James Henry McLean, St Louis, Missouri, USA, 1829–c. 1890. This Scottish-born 'physician' and purveyor of patent medicines was also the promoter of gimcrack schemes that ranged from an 'impregnable floating fortress' to the 'Hercules Gun', a large-bore repeating cannon. Among them were several small-bore machine-guns patented by Myron *Coloney in 1880. McLean and Coloney jointly received US Patent 282,548 of 7 August 1883 for a 'breech-loading composite gun', and 282,549 for a machine-gun on 7 August 1883. On the same day, McLean alone was granted US Patents 282,552 and 282,553 for a machine-gun, together with 282,551 and 282,554 for a magazine gun. His last US patent, 290,905, was granted on 25 December 1883 to protect a 'breech-loading firearm'. Few of McLean's schemes came to much, although it is believed that prototype machine-guns made the transition from outlandish claim to reality. **46.** McMillan Gunworks, Inc., Phoenix, Arizona. A maker from 1987 of *Mauser-type bolt-action rifles under such names as Signature and Talon. Short-action guns were chambered for cartridges ranging from .22-250 to .308 Winchester; long-action guns for .25-06 to .375 H&H Magnum. A Talon Safari Super Magnum rifle has been chambered for cartridges as powerful as .416 Remington Magnum; a series of sniper rifles (M86, M89) has also been made, and there have been .50 bolt-action anti-matériel rifles. Most of the guns made after 1995

seem to have been marketed under the Harris Gun Works banner. **47.** James MacNaughton & Sons. This gunmaking business traded from 1865 until 1947. The principal workshop was always maintained in Edinburgh, but a branch office was kept for many years in Perth. In addition to sporting guns, MacNaughton also sold *Eley-made shotgun cartridges marked with its own name. **48.** Robert W. McNeely accepted military firearms on behalf of the US Army, applying his 'RWM' marks. They date from the early 1890s, distinguishing them from guns accepted in an earlier era by Commander Richard W. *Meade. *See also* US arms inspectors' marks. **49.** John MacPherson [& Sons]. Based in Inverness from 1887, MacPherson handled fishing tackle, sporting guns and ammunition under a variety of brandnames: The Angler, The Bargate, The Barrage, The Clach, The Killer and The Royal. Sometimes a mark of a standing grouse was also used. **50.** Robert MacPherson. Trading from Kingussie in Inverness-shire, Scotland, this distributor of sporting goods sold shotgun ammunition marked 'The Badenoch'. **51.** J.T. McWilliam. This member of the London gun trade – perhaps a gunmakers' or patent agent – was recorded at 16 East India Chambers in 1871. Practically nothing else is known of him.

Mäckinen. Eino Mäckinen, Finland. A gun designer employed by *Sako.

Macher. F.W. Macher, a government employee, accepted firearms and accessories marked 'FWM' on behalf of the US Army. They date from c. 1906. *See also* US arms inspectors' marks.

Madden. H.E. Madden, active in 1902 on behalf of the US Army, accepted firearms and accessories marked 'HEM'. *See also* US arms inspectors' marks.

Mädel. E. Mädel, Suhl in Thüringen, Germany. Listed in the 1930 and other pre-1939 editions of the *Deutsches Reichs-Adressbuch* as a gunsmith.

Madsen. This interesting *recoil-operated machine-gun used a pivoting breech-block instead of a reciprocating bolt, and was fed from a box magazine mounted on top of the receiver. Despite its apparent complexity, the Madsen soon attained a reputation for reliability that persisted as late as the Second World War and enabled it to be chambered for a variety of rimmed and rimless cartridges. Trials undertaken successfully prior to 1914 persuaded many of the combatants to acquire guns for use in the First World War. The Austro-Hungarians obtained more than 600 6.5x55mm examples from *Dansk Rekyriffel Syndikat in 1915, altering them in Vienna arsenal for the 7.9x57mm cartridge (known as 7.92mm in Austria-Hungary). The German Madsens first saw service in the Champagne district of France in September 1915, but they were withdrawn after the Somme battles. The Russians also used the Madsen in large quantities, making 7.62x54 weapons at a Danish-financed factory in Kovrov. Subsequently many were captured by the Germans, adapted for the rimless 7.9x57 cartridge and issued to mountain troops (*Gebirgsjäger-Maschinengewehr-Abteilungen*, GMGA). The light weight and box-magazine feed of the Madsen were particularly advantageous in highland areas.

'MAFCO'. A superimposition-type monogram, with 'M', 'F' and 'A' prominent. Correctly 'MFACO' (q.v.); found on revolvers made by the *Meriden Fire Arms Company.

Magazine – 1. The container in which cartridges are held to permit repetitive fire with only occasional reloading. Magazines take many different forms. Among the earliest were tubes, usually contained in the fore-end beneath the barrel (e.g. Henry, Vetterli and Winchester) or, more rarely, in the butt (Chaffee-Reece and Hotchkiss). These were superseded by box patterns, credited – although not without dispute – to James *Lee. Some boxes were detachable, others have been fixed. Fixed magazines are customarily described as 'internal' if they are carried entirely inside the stock (introduced on the Spanish Mauser of 1893), and 'fixed' or 'integral' if they project externally, but are part of the receiver or frame (e.g. most Mannlichers and Mosin-Nagant). Some of the earlier Mausers, such as the Argentine gun of 1891, have semi-integral magazines, which can be removed with the aid of a tool, but are not genuinely readily detachable. Magazines described as 'blind' are carried internally and are not visible from the outside of the gun, owing to the lack of a floor plate. Other patterns that have reached service status include a pan (lateral) magazine, featured on guns such as the Krag-Jørgensen, and the spool (rotary) mechanism embodied in Mannlicher-Schönauer and similar guns. Military magazines may be loaded from chargers or with clips (qq.v.). **2.** Magazine Repeating Pistol, USA. *See* Remington pistols. **3.** Magazine safety. This ensures that the firing mechanism cannot function, the objective being to prevent accidental discharge if a live round remains in the chamber after the magazine has been removed. However, magazine safeties are unpopular on military weapons precisely because they prevent the firing of single shots when the magazine is absent. On guns destined for commercial sale, however, safety systems of this type have enjoyed renewed popularity in recent years.

Maggs. John Maggs, active in 1862, during the American Civil War, accepted firearms and accessories on behalf of the Federal Army. They were marked 'JM', date alone distinguishing them from guns attributed to Julian *McCallister, J. *Mills and Justice *Murphy. *See also* US arms inspectors' marks.

Magna, or Magna Classic. Brandnames associated with variants of the Model 629 *Smith & Wesson *Magnum revolver.

'Magnet' [The]. A mark found on shotgun cartridges loaded by R. *Robinson of Hull from *Eley-Kynoch components.

Magnum, Magnum… – 1. Used generically for any ammunition developing high power (or the guns chambering it). It owes its origin to the introduction of the .357 Magnum cartridge by Smith & Wesson. **2.** Or 357 Magnum. Mechanically identical to the *Trooper, but fitted with a heavy frame, extended grips and adjustable Accro target sights, this gun was made from 1953 until 1961 by *Colt's Patent Fire Arms Manufacturing Company. Then the distinction between Magnum and Trooper was abandoned, use of the latter name being extended to cover both patterns. **3.** A name originally associated with a large-frame .357 revolver introduced in the 1930s by *Smith & Wesson, but now generally associated with any gun chambering Magnum Power cartridges; *see* panel, p. 324. **4.** Magnum Military & Police. A name applied to the Model 58 *Smith & Wesson swing-cylinder revolver; *see* Military & Police.

Magnus. Moritz Magnus der Jüngere, of Hamburg, was one of the leading large-scale wholesalers of weapons and equipment in Germany in 1925. Operations seem to have ceased in the early 1930s.

Maguin-Berthéas, place Dorian 1, Saint-Étienne, France. Listed in 1879 as a gunmaker.

Mahely Compania y Industria, Buenos Aires, Argentina. Little is known about this business, apparently active between 1949 and 1965, with the exception that *Webley-style air pistols were made from about 1953 onward. The company seems to have disappeared, no further information having been obtained.

Mahillon, Brussels, Belgium. Styled as *Arquebusier du Roi* (Gunmaker to the King), this man seems to have bought many of the firearms in Liège. He was active in 1937.

Mahrholdt. Richard Mahrholdt & Sohn, also known as the Tiroler Waffenfabrik Peterlongo, Innsbrück, Austria. This company was founded as Tiroler Waffenfabrik in 1854, and became Mahrholdt & Sohn in 1939; today it trades from Saturnerstrasse in Innsbruck. It was responsible for the simple barrel-cocking spring-air rifles noted by Smith (in *Gas, Air and Spring Guns*, 1957) as the products of the Tirol Arms Company in the early 1950s. Similar weapons were still being made in the 1970s. The company also seems to have made gas-powered guns alongside cartridge rifles.

Main spring, mainspring. The spring that propels the hammer or striker into the primer of a chambered cartridge.

Maisonnial, Saint-Étienne, France. Listed in 1933 as a gunmaker; still trading in 1951, from 13 rue Clément-Forissier.

Makarov. Nikolay Federovich Makarov, born in Sasovo in 1914, was the son of a railway engineer. After serving an apprenticeship on the railway, he graduated from the Tula Mechanical Insitute just as the Germans invaded the Soviet Union in the summer of 1941. Makarov began working at a factory producing the Shpagin (*PPSh) submachine-gun, and was transferred after the war to a design bureau. He is best known for the 9mm *PM semi-automatic pistol and the AM-23 aircraft cannon, but also worked on rocketry before retiring in 1974 with a host of decorations. He died in 1988.

Makína ve Kímya Endüstrísí. *See* MKE.

Maleham. Charles H. Maleham. Trading in Sheffield c. 1868, from 5 West Bar, in succession to his father George, this gunmaker was also a member of the London gun trade – listed at 20 Regent Street in 1878–82, and again from 1884 until 1900 or later. The trading style changed to Maleham & Company in the early 1900s, but the business was sold to Arthur Turner shortly after the First World War and ceased operating under it own name. In addition to sporting guns and rifles, a variety of *Eley-made shotgun cartridges has been reported. Brandnames include The Clay Bird, The Double Wing, The Regent, The Steeltown and The Wing. A trademark was also popular, comprising six shot-holes around a central seventh, with a heraldic pinion or 'wing' extending from each side.

Malherbe – 1. E. Malherbe, Liège, Belgium. A gunmaker involved in the 1870s with le *Grand Syndicat. **2.** P.J. Malherbe & Cie, Liège. One of Belgium's leading manufacturers of firearms, edged weapons and accessories, working c. 1830–57, Philip-Joseph Malherbe retained the agent Frederick L. *Homer of London in the mid-1850s. **3.** Prosper Malherbe & Company. Probably a successor to Philip-Joseph Malherbe (above) this gunmaking business was also based in Liège. A British agent – *Rochussen &

MAGNUM

Magnum (3)

A name originally associated with a large-frame .357 revolver introduced in the 1930s by *Smith & Wesson. The project was initiated by the writer Philip B. Sharpe, who had developed ammunition for the .38/44 *Heavy Duty N-frame revolver that produced far greater power than *Smith & Wesson's normal loads.

The Model .357 Magnum revolver appeared in 1935, with adjustable sights, a ribbed barrel and a choice of grips. Production continued until the end of 1941, although the original scheme of separately registering each gun for a lifetime warranty had ended in 1938. Work began again in 1948, when an improved version with S-prefix

numbers appeared in a selection of barrel lengths, and the .357 Magnum became the Model 27 in 1957. Changes have been made on several occasions, but, in 1975, the revolver gained a target-style hammer, trigger and grip.

The .44 Magnum, introduced in 1955 for the powerful .44 Magnum cartridge and renamed Model 29 in 1957, owed its existence to the handgunner Elmer Keith and the participation of the ammunition-making division of the *Remington Arms Company. Sales received a great boost from the film *Dirty Harry*, and continue day. A Model 629 stainless-steel version appeared in the 1970s, followed in 1990 by the Model 29 Classic and Model 29 Magna Classic; the Classic had Hogue combat grips, a squared butt and provision for a telescope sight,

whereas the Magna version had a 7¹/₂in ported barrel with a full-length ejector-rod shroud. The Model 629 Classic DX, introduced in 1992 in stainless steel, gave a choice of square-heel Hogue or round-heel Morado wood butts; and the Model 29 Silhouette, dating from 1992, offered a 10⁵/₈in barrel, adjustable sights and Goncalo Alves target grips.

The Smith & Wesson Model 53 Magnum revolver was a convertible pattern capable of firing either the standard .22 Long Rifle rimfire or the .22 Remington Jet. Only about 15,000 guns were manufactured between 1961 and 1974. The Model 57, which was chambered for the .41 Magnum cartridge, appeared in 1963, but has never achieved the popularity of the .44 version. *See also* Highway Patrolman.

The introduction of the .357 Magnum cartridge and an accompanying revolver, in 1935, inspired modern trends toward high-power designs. This Smith & Wesson is a commemorative model issued to celebrate the half-centenary.

Company of London – was retained during 1858–61.

'Mallard' [The]. A mark used on shotgun ammunition loaded by the *Chamberlain Cartridge Company of Cleveland, Ohio, USA.

Malloch. Gunmaker P.D. Malloch, trading from 24 Scott Street, Perth, Scotland, sold sporting guns and shotgun ammunition under such brandnames as The Matchless, The Red Grouse, The Standard and The Triumph.

Maloney. James A. Maloney, Washington D.C., USA. Recipient of US Patent 271,645 of 6 February 1883, protecting an extractor mechanism for drop-barrel guns.

Maltby – 1. Royal Ordnance Factory [ROF], Maltby, Yorkshire, England. Work on this site began in May 1940, the first guns being completed in the summer of 1941. About 737,000 *Lee-Enfield No. 4 Mk 1 rifles were made during the Second World War. The guns

were marked 'ROF[M]'. **2.** Maltby, Curtis & Company, New York City. This US distributor of sporting goods also handled double-action five-shot revolvers made in accordance with the patents of John *Smith (1889), which had a distinctive rifled barrel liner. Like virtually all Maltby guns, these were made by the *Norwich Pistol Company. Maltby, Curtis & Company, and its 1889 successor (Maltby, Henley & Company), also sold revolvers made by *Otis Smith; guns offered under the Metropolitan Police brandname were protected by patents granted to William *Bliss during 1878–85, but also made elsewhere.

Manby. Frederick Manby & Brother, trading in Skipton, Yorkshire, England, distributed sporting guns and ammunition. The latter included shotgun cartridges marked 'Manby's Special'.

Manchester... – 1. Manchester Airguns, Manchester, England. Originators of the Mercury Magnum, a variant of the BSA *Mercury air rifle offered in .25 (6.35mm) in the 1980s. **2.** Manchester Ordnance & Rifle Company [The]. Listed in London in 1865, at 28 Pall Mall, but registered in Manchester. Possibly associated with Sir Joseph Whitworth.

Mandall Shooting Supplies, Inc., Scottsdale, Arizona. A distrubutor of *Krico bolt-action rifles in the USA from 1990 onward.

Manente. Giuseppe Manente, Brescia, Italy. Apparently this gun and airgun maker – trading from Via Trento in 1979 – made spring-air barrel-cockers.

Manganese Bronze Holdings Ltd. *See* BSA Guns Ltd.

Mangeot. Henri Mangeot, Brussels, Belgium. A gunmaker trading in the middle of the nineteenth century, styling himself *Arquebusier du Roi* (Gunmaker to the King). His marks have been found on a variety of sporting rifles, shotguns and revolvers.

Manhattan – 1. A *Suicide Special revolver made in the USA by *Johnson, Bye & Company and/or *Iver Johnson of Worcester and Fitchburg, Massachusetts. It dates from the late nineteenth century. **2.** Manhattan Fire Arms Company, Newark, New Jersey. This US gunmaking business produced .31 pocket and .36 Navy-type *Colt copies in accordance with a patent granted to *Gruler and Rebety in December 1859 to protect the inclusion of safety notches on the cylinder. Colt managed to stop production in 1864, but not before 5,000 .31 and 80,000 .36 guns had been made. Some bore the marks of the spurious London Pistol Company. Subsequently Manhattan turned to close copies of the Smith & Wesson Model No.1 in .22 and .32 rimfire, with seven and six chambers respectively, until *Smith & Wesson successfully removed the guns from the market. The Manhattan Fire Arms Company was succeeded in 1870 by the *American Standard Tool Company, although the relationship between the two businesses is not known.

Manila Ordnance Depot. A converter of US *Krag-Jørgensen rifles to carbine or 'constabulary' length, 1910–14.

Mann – 1. Fritz Mann, Suhl, Thüringen, Germany. Designer of the Mann pistols (below). **2.** Otto Mann, Suhl in Thüringen. A sales agency operating in Germany in 1930. **3.** Mann pistols. Designed by Fritz Mann of Suhl, this series of small semi-automatic pistols began with an extraordinary-looking 6.35mm Model 1920, with a short centrally-placed grip, the slide reciprocating on internal rails, and the return spring above the barrel. The larger 7.65mm and 9mm Short Model 1921 patterns had more conventional Browning-type construction. **4.** Mann-Werke AG, Suhl-Neundorf, Thüringen. This business was founded shortly after the end of the First World War (probably in 1921) to exploit patents granted to Fritz Mann. Most directory entries describe the business as '*Feinmaschinen-, Waffen- und Werkzeug-Fabrik*' ('Precision Machinery, Weapons and Tool Makers'). In 1925, the Mann pistols were described as the 'smallest, lightest and longest-lasting automatic pistols of any calibre', but apparently the gunmaking side of the business had failed by 1929/30. A distinctive encircled 'MA' monogram will often be encountered.

Manning. Alfred C. Manning accepted firearms and accessories on behalf of the Federal Army, marking them 'ACM'. His activities were confined to 1863, during the American Civil War. *See also* US arms inspectors' marks.

Mannlicher – 1. Ferdinand [Ritter von] Mannlicher. Born on 30 January 1848 in Most, a small town in Bohemia, Mannlicher was educated in the Vienna technical college, then retained as an engineer by the state-run Austrian railway system. Visiting the World Exhibition in Philadelphia in 1876, primarily to inspect developments in railway technology, he was intrigued by rifles exhibited by *Winchester and *Hotchkiss. Deciding to produce repeating firearms of his own, Mannlicher embarked on a new career as a gun designer, although he maintained his interests in railways until his premature death in Vienna on 20 January 1904. In addition to a knighthood, conferred in 1887, he gained a Gold Medal from the 1900 International Exposition in Paris. Ferdinand von Mannlicher was granted more than 100 patents in Austria-Hungary and other countries, some of the last bearing the name of his widow, Cäcilie, but whether he truly deserves his place in the Pantheon of gun designers is arguable: many of his designs were failures, and even the first to be adopted officially by Austria-Hungary had serious weaknesses. Although the 1886, 1888, 1890 and 1895-pattern straight-pull bolt-action rifles were made in huge quantities, they were not as robust or efficient as the 'Mannlichers' made by *Österreichische Waffenfabriks-Gesellschaft on the basis of the *Reichsgewehr action. Comparatively little information concerning Mannlicher firearms is available in English, although Konrad Edeler von Kromar's *Repetier- und Automatische Handfeuerwaffen der systeme Ferdinand Ritter von Mannlicher* (1900) was reprinted in 1976. A summary may be found in John Walter, *Rifles of the World* (Krause Publications, second edition, 1998) and *Central Powers' Small Arms of World War One* (Crowood Press, 1999); Walter H.B. Smith's book, *Mauser, Walther and Mannlicher Firearms* (combined edition, Stackpole Books, 1962), is also useful, although basically a translation of Kromar's work. *See also* *Austro-Hungarian firearms and Waffenfabrik *Mauser AG. **2.** Mannlicher pistols. The first design, protected by a German patent granted in December 1894, was a 6.5mm or 7.6mm *blow-forward pattern with a return spring between the barrel and the front of the breech housing. The case-magazine in the frame, above the grip, could be loaded with a clip. Very few M. 1894 pistols were made, the majority being produced by Waffenfabrik *Neuhausen (SIG) in Switzerland. A *blowback design was patented in 1896, with a box magazine ahead of the trigger and a special elongated cocking lever protruding at the rear of the frame. It was not successful, but another patent granted in the same year was for a much more effective design. Now customarily known as the M. 1896, few guns of this pattern had been made by the time the basic design had been revived as the Model 1903. Superficially resembling the *Mauser C/96 externally, the 1896/1903 pattern Mannlicher was locked by a flimsy strut between the bolt and the rear of the receiver. Subsequently blowback pistols, protected by a German patent granted in October 1898, were marketed as the models of 1900, 1901 and 1905. The earliest examples were made by Waffenfabrik von *Dreyse in Sömmerda, but later guns emanated from *Österreichische Waffenfabriks-Gesellschaft in Steyr (1902–11). They could be identified by their slender appearance and a

MANNLICHER BOLT-ACTION RIFLES

Mannlicher (4)

The original *Repetir-Gewehr mit Rohrbündel-Magazin in Kolben* (1880) had a triple tube magazine in the butt and a *Kropatschek-like bolt. It was followed by the *Repetir-Gewehr mit anhangbarem Magazin M1881*, with a box magazine, then by the *Repetir-Gewehr mit Vorderschaft-Magazin M1882* with a tube magazine under the barrel. The *Repetir-Gewehr mit aufsteckbarem Magazin M1882* had a gravity-feed magazine on the right side of the receiver.

However, the rifles most commonly associated with Mannlicher were the straight-pull patterns (*Geradzug-Verschluss*), originally made with a gravity magazine offset on the left side of the receiver, but replaced in 1885 by the 11mm *Repetier-Gewehr 'Österreichische Vorlage'* made by *Österreichische Waffenfabriks-Gesellschaft of Steyr. A bar beneath the back of the bolt pivoted down into the bolt-way floor as the bolt was closed, and the projecting case-type magazine was loaded with a clip. The *Infanterie-Repetier-Gewehr M1886*, chambering 11mm *Werndl cartridges, soon recognised as ineffective, was hastily revised to become the 8mm M1888, which could be distinguished by the shallowness of its magazine case.

An improved straight-pull mechanism was patented in 1889. Cam-tracks on the bolt acted with lugs inside the bolt sleeve to rotate external lugs into engagement with the receiver, a much stronger lock than the pivoting bar of older guns. Both 1890-pattern 8mm short rifles and carbines were soon accepted for service, but trials with infantry rifles dragged on until the perfected *Repetiergewehr M1895* was approved in 1896. The straight-pull action remained in service in Austria-Hungary until the end of the First World War, but guns of this type were never popular on the export market; only Bulgaria purchased them in quantity. The Germans made limited use of straight-pull Mannlichers in the First World War, although the circumstances are still unknown.

Turn-bolt Mannlichers, with the exception of pre-1885 prototypes,

---

charger-loaded box magazine in the frame, above the grip. Small quantities were used by the Argentinian Army, but only about 10,000 had been sold by 1914. **3.** Mannlicher rifles, automatic/semi-automatic. Locked by struts or 'tongs' that dropped into a frame-well, the recoil-operated *Handmitrailleuse* (1885) had a ten-round gravity magazine above the left side of the breech. An improved version (1891) was locked by a transverse lug on the top rear of the tongs engaging a recess on the underside of the bolt; it had a fixed clip-loaded magazine. A delayed-blowback mechanism, patented in 1893, relied either on steeply-pitched lugs on the bolt head rotating in seats in the receiver, or on straight-pull systems relying on cam-lugs moving in helical grooves to rotate the bolt head in relation to the bolt body. The 1895-patent gas-operated rifle had a two-piece stock and a five-round magazine within the receiver. Gas tapped from the bore forced the cocking slide back, pivoting the breech-block laterally to disengage the locking lug. This was replaced by a better design, introduced in 1900 and perfected posthumously during 1905–08. Gas forced an operating rod backward to rotate the bolt-handle base from its seat in the receiver. Most of the guns had a spool magazine in a detachable housing. **4.** Mannlicher bolt-action rifles: *see* panel, above. **5.** Mannlicher-Carcano. *See* Italian Mannlicher. **6.** Mannlicher-Schönauer rifle. The 1887/88-pattern rifle, the first Mannlicher to embody a spool magazine patented by Otto *Schönauer, had a straight-pull bolt system with the locking lugs on the connecting-piece between the bolt head and the body. The magazine could be loaded from a stripper clip or *Patronen-Packet*, but military trials were unsuccessful. A modified 1900-pattern gun was tested in Portugal, losing to the *Mauser-Vergueiro, but it fared better in Greece. The Greek Army adopted the Mannlicher-Schönauer in 1903, many thousands being supplied by Österreichische Waffenfabriks-Gesellschaft prior to the First World War. Subsequently others were refurbished by Società Ernesto Breda. In addition, the Mannlicher-Schönauer proved popular with sportsmen; many thousands were stocked and finished by gunsmiths

in *Ferlach, and Steyr-Mannlicher GmbH continued to make them until the 1980s.

Mansfield. William Mansfield, Wolverhampton, Staffordshire. This gun-lock maker began trading in Cornhill in 1875, moving to Lord Street West in 1878. The business of Joseph Brazier was purchased shortly afterward, as a British patent granted to Mansfield in 1887, to protect a game counter (10,343/87) and developed in collusion with Sir Ralph Payne-Gallwey, notes that he was 'trading as J. Brazier & Sons'. Mansfield also received British Patent 9450 of 1893, protecting a safety system for hammerless sporting guns, and 11,068 of 1896 (sought jointly with H.W. *Holland) for a single-trigger mechanism for double-barrelled guns.

Mansvelt. P. Mansvelt & Zoon, 's-Gravenhage, Dennenweg 10b, the Netherlands. A distributor of sporting guns and ammunition active during 1912–14.

Manteuffel. Reinhold Manteuffel & Companie, Zella-Mehlis in Thüringen, Suhler Strasse 9a (1941). Founded in 1911, listed as a gunmaker in 1920 (owned by Reinhold Manteuffel, Hugo Manteuffel, Moritz Roth and W. Roth), and in 1930 – when the owners also included A. Schmidt and M. Heyer. By 1941, the business was being described as a maker of firearms and accessories.

Manton – **1.** George Henry Manton. Son of the gunmaker John Manton, and the proprietor of John Manton & Company from 1834 until his death in 1854, George Manton was granted several English patents. These included 7965 of 1839 for a percussion-cap magazine, and 12,543 of 1849 – in collusion with J. Harrington – for a 'magazine lock'. **2.** Manton & Company, London and Calcutta. Gunsmiths and distributors of sporting guns and ammunition, including pre-1914 shotgun ammunition offered under such brandnames as Contractile and Standard Smokeless. **3.** J. Manton & Company. A name found on shotguns handled in the USA by the H. & D. *Folsom Arms Company, possibly imported from Europe. **4.** John Manton & Son. One of the most famous of all the London gunmakers, John Manton (1752–1834), was superseded by his son, George Henry Manton (1789–1854). Trading ini-

were normally built on the basis of the *Reichsgewehr. This had arisen from a patent-infringement lawsuit brought against the German government by Österreichische Waffenfabriks-Gesellschaft. Rifles of this pattern enjoyed success in Romania and the Netherlands, and also, fitted with Schönauer rotary magazines, in Greece. However, they were not 'Mannlichers' in the truest sense.

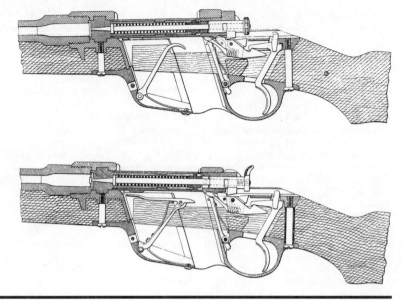

These drawings show the actions of the semi-experimental 1890 (top) and perfected 1895 (bottom) straight-pull Mannlicher actions adopted by the Austro-Hungarian Army. The 1895 pattern, in particular, was made in huge numbers.

tially as John & George [Henry] Manton, the business became George & Gildon Manton in the 1840s. However, George died in 1854 and his son, Gildon, followed in 1856; the business was carried on by Gildon Manton's widow and Charles Coe until 1867, being listed alternatively as John Manton, Son & Coe and John Manton & Company. Subsequently Charles Coe traded on alone until liquidation occurred in 1878. Premises had been occupied at 6 Dover Street since 1815. An alternative address – 4 South Street, Grosvenor Square – given by H.J. Blanch, writing in *Arms & Explosives* in 1909, is now known to have been Mrs Gildon Manton's home.

Manufacture [d'Armes...], *see also* Châtellerault, Saint-Étienne and Tulle – **1.** Manufacture d'Armes Automatiques, Saint-Étienne, France. This business is believed to have been responsible for 6.35mm-calibre automatic pistols marked *Le Steph and *Securitas. **2.** Manufacture d'Armes de Bayonne, also known as MAB, Bayonne, France. Founded shortly after the First World War, this gunmaking business was best known for its *Browning-type blowback pistols. Most of the individual variants were identified by letters: the 6.35mm MAB Modèle A and the 6.35mm MAB Mle B pocket pistols were similar to the *FN-Browning of 1906 and the *Walther Model 9 respectively; the 7.65mm MAB Mle B was essentially an exposed-hammer derivative of the *FN-Browning Mle 10/22; the 7.65mm or 9mm Short MAB Mle C of 1933 was smaller, with a safety lever set in the back strap and a detachable muzzle bush; and the 1935-vintage MAB Mle D, in 7.65 or 9mm, was basically an enlarged C. The MAB Mle E was a 6.35mm version of the Mle C with a nine-round magazine. Most of the guns made since c. 1965 had their slide-retraction grooves milled diagonally and a streamlined trigger-guard/frame fillet. The MAB Mle R (1951) was offered in .22 LR rimfire and four centrefire chamberings: 7.65mm Auto, 7.65mm Longue, 9mm Short and 9mm Parabellum. The 7.65mm Longue and 9mm Parabellum (R-Para) versions incorporated a rotating-barrel delay adapted from the *Searle-patent Savage, the others being

*blowbacks. The Mle G and Mle GZ, in .22 LR rimfire and 7.65mm Auto, were made for MAB by *Echave y Arizmendi and were identical to the Echasa Fast patterns. The MAB PA-8, introduced in 1966, was a derivative of the R-Para with the same delayed-blowback breech system. A hold-open was added, the slide stop was modified and the contours of the frame were refined. The PA-15 was similar, but its magazine held fifteen rounds instead of eight, and the PAP F-1 (*Pistolet Automatique Précision F-1*) was a target-shooting derivative with an elongated barrel and adjustable sights. Handgun production finally ceased in 1985. *See also* Defender. **3.** Manufacture d'Armes de Chasse, Belgium. *See* Masquelier. **4.** Manufacture d'Armes de Paris, Paris, France. This maker of small-arms components was founded as Manufacture Parisienne d'Armes in 1915 by a group of French industrialists together with Gustave Joassart and Alexander Galopin, two directors of *Fabrique Nationale d'Armes de Guerre who had escaped from Belgium to France following the German invasion. Part of the stockholding was purchased by Fabrique Nationale in 1921; thereafter, MAP made typewriters alongside FN-type motorcycles. **5.** Manufacture d'Armes des Pyrénées, also known as MAP, Manufacture d'Armes des Pyrénées Françaises (MAPF) or Unique, Hendaye, France. Founded shortly after the end of the First World War by Basques with strong family links in Spain, this gunmaking business specialised in sturdy blowback pistols derived from the *Ruby patterns supplied in great numbers to the French Army during the First World War. In addition to its own Unique guns, MAP promoted a range of 6.35mm *Browning-type pocket pistols. They were essentially similar to guns made in Eibar, and it seems likely that either complete guns or their unfinished components were simply brought over the Franco-Spanish border. Among the names associated with these pistols are Audax, Furor, Gallia, Helepco, Kitu, Le Majestic, Lepco, Le Sans Pareil, Société d'Armes Paris and Triomphe Français (qq.v.); others were listed as the Unique Mle 10. Some guns had extended butts, often to chamber the larger 7.65mm Auto cartridge, while a second Audax and the Unique Model 18 were based on the streamlined 1910-type FN-Browning instead of the earlier pocket pistol. French-made, or assembled, guns are often marked *Fabrication Française*, or bear *Le Veritable Pistolet Français "Unique"* on the slide. Today rifles are also being made alongside the 6.35mm and 7.65mm ★Mikros pistols. *See also* Unique. **6.** Manufacture de l'Armes de l'État, Faubourg Saint-Léonard, Liège. This, the Belgian government-owned small-arms factory, was founded in 1838 and entirely re-equipped in the late 1880s with machine tools supplied by Ludwig ★Loewe & Co. This enabled the manufactory to produce a range of weapons, including rifles and machine-guns, until the German invasion of Belgium in 1914. Maker of many Belgian Mle 1889 Mauser rifles, short rifles and carbines, c. 1895–1914. **7.** Manufacture de Machines du Haut-Rhin (Manurhin), Mulhouse, Alsace. This engineering company became involved in the production of firearms in the 1950s, when a licence to make ★Walther pistols was negotiated. Manurhin made the Walther PP and PPK until work began in the Walther factory in Ulm/Donau in the mid-1960s. A few P-38 (P1) models will also be found with Manurhin marks; these were made in Ulm, shipped to France and specially marked so that they could be supplied to the police in West Berlin without breaking the terms of a treaty agreed with the Russians. Subsequently Manurhin contracted with ★SIG to make the Swiss-designed 5.56x45 SG540-series assault rifles in France. The MR73 revolvers have also been made in quantity. **8.** Manufacture Française d'Armes et Cycles (MFAC) – also known simply as Manufacture d'Armes et Cycles or Manufrance SA – was once the largest privately-owned gunmaking business in France. A catalogue dating from the mid-1920s reveals the existence of two enormous factories in Saint-Étienne, as well as impressive retail and administrative premises at 42 rue du Louvre in Paris. Sales offices were also maintained at 125 cours d'Alsace-Lorraine in Bordeaux; at 122 rue Nationale in Lille; at 25 rue Childebert in Lyon; at 36 rue de la République in Marseilles; at 54 rue Saint-Jean in Nancy; at 3 rue du Feltre in Nantes; at 19 rue Thiers in Rouen; and at 45 rue de Metz in Toulouse. The factories made goods ranging from canoes and bicycles (the latter under the name Hirondelle) to agricultural machinery (Coq), cameras (Luminor), fishing rods, sewing machines (Omnia), sports equipment, tools (Grenade) and typewriters (Typo). They also produced large quantities of guns and ammunition. Trademarks included an enwreathed 'MF' monogram and 'M' and 'F' accompanied by a target, two cannons and an arrow. MFAC is best known for the ★Le Français pistols, but also made a variety of rifles and shotguns. *See also* Buffalo, Étoile, Express, Idéal, Populaire, Reine, Rival, Robust, Simplex and Supra-Simplex. **9.** Manufacture Générale d'Armes et Munitions de Jules Bertrand, Liège, Belgium. Maker of the 6.35mm ★Le Rapide pistol. **10.** Manufacture Générale de Munitions, Bourges les Valence, France. A manufacturer of military and sporting ammunition, identified by the headstamp 'M.G.M.' **11.** Manufacture Liégeoise d'Armes à Feu, Robar & Companie. This Liège-based Belgian gunmaking business maintained representation in London between 1867 and 1880 (through ★Heintzmann & Rochussen), then on its own account –

as Société Anonyme – from 8 Coleman Street during 1882–84. A founding shareholder in ★Fabrique Nationale d'Armes de Guerre in 1889, when the relevant documents were signed on the company's behalf by Léon Collinet as *Administrateur délégué*, Manufacture Liégeoise was unsuccessful in promoting the ★Engh rifles in the late 1880s. Firearms made by this source can often be recognised only by the crowned 'ML' trademark. A series of 6.35mm, 7.65mm and 9mm automatic pistols were marked 'Melior' or ★'M.L.' **12.** Manufacture Nationale d'Armes, Saint-Étienne, Loire. This, one of the French government's small-arms factories, was established during the reign of Louis XV in 1718 and operated as the Manufacture Royale until the Revolution of 1789, after which its name changed to Manufacture Impériale (1815–71), before reverting to Manufacture Nationale. Finally it was referred to simply as MAS. The factory is better known for its pistols, rifles and machine-guns, but it also made a spring-air training pistol, the Modèle 50, in the early 1950s. The bulk of this was similar to that of the cartridge pistol sharing the designation. **13.** Manufacture Parisienne d'Armes: *see* Manufacture d'Armes de Paris.

Manufrance SA, formerly known as ★Manufacture Française d'Armes et Cycles, Saint-Étienne. This world-renowned gunmaking business was offering refurbished ★Mauser-action sporting rifles as late as 1965. They were sold under the brandname ★Rival.

Manurhin. *See* Manufacture de Machines du Haut-Rhin.

Manville. Cyrus Manville, a gunmaker of 208 Orange Street, New Haven, Connecticut (1864–67), is believed to have made the two-shot rifle-muskets sold to the Federal government during the Civil War by John P. ★Lindsay.

MAO. Found on rifles and small-arms components made in the Australian government small-arms factory in Orange, New South Wales.

'MAP', 'MAPF'. *See* Manufacture d'Armes des Pyrénées.

Mappin & Webb. Makers of the holster and carrying straps for the ★Welrod pistol, but better known as the Crown Jewellers.

MAR. A short-barrelled or compact version of the Israeli ★Galil, otherwise known as the Micro Assault Rifle.

Marathon Products, Inc., Wethersfield, Connecticut, USA. This distributor of guns, ammunition and accessories introduced the Sportsman Bush & Field ★Mauser-type sporter in 1984.

Marcaido. *See* Ojanguren y Marcaido.

Marck, Liège, Belgium. A maker of revolvers active during the 1870s.

'Marco'. This mark was employed on ★Will/ ★Venuswaffenwerke latch-lever lock spring-air guns made prior to c. 1925, then on ★Haenels sold in Britain by the ★Modern Arms Company of London from 1925 until 1939.

Marcy. Samuel Marcy, a lieutenant representing the US Navy Board of Ordnance, accepted firearms and accessories in the period 1852–61. They were marked 'SM', making them difficult to distinguish from the US Army guns attributed to Stillman ★Moore. *See also* US arms inspectors' marks.

Marengoni. Tullio Marengoni designed many autoloading weapons for ★Beretta prior to the 1950s, including the Mo. 31 and Mo. 37 rifles, and the Mo. 38 sub-machine-gun.

Marga. Uldarique Marga, a Belgian Army officer, was responsible for a range of bolt- and auto-loading rifles designed between 1885 and 1907. The earliest bolt-action rifles were made in accordance with a series of patents granted in 1889–92. The so-called Model 1888 had a very simple striker system with a V-spring contained in the bulbous bolt handle, while a sliding safety catch lay on the back of the bolt where the cocking piece would normally be found. Patents of addition, granted in 1891 and 1892, protected a clip-fed magazine and an improved extractor respectively. All Marga rifles had an interrupted-thread lock on the rear of the bolt body and a magazine case formed as an integral part of the trigger guard. Most of them were the work of Auguste *Francotte & Cie of Liège; the most popular chambering seems to have been 7.65x53. About 2,500 of the M1894, with an internal five-round box magazine, were made by Francotte prior to c. 1902. Possibly destined for trials in Brazil, rifles of this type were still being exhibited by Francotte at the Paris Exposition Universelle of 1900.

Mariette – 1. Mariette, Cheratte. A Belgian gunsmith, patentee of a 'revolver', 1839. In fact, this was a ring-trigger pepperbox. The *Hermann version seems to have been essentially similar. Mariette is also credited with the introduction of the *fist revolver, a modification of the pepperbox. **2.** A generic name for any ring-trigger pepperbox.

Marina. A Spanish 6.35mm-calibre Browning-type automatic pistol made in Eibar by Gregorio *Bolumburu: six rounds, hammer fired.

Marine Corps Model, or M1905. Fewer than a thousand of these .38 revolvers were made during 1905–07 for the USMC, by *Colt's Patent Fire Arms Manufacturing Company. Mechanically identical to the *New Army Model, they had characteristically small round-base butts.

Marion & Sanner. French, or possibly Belgian, these makers of a volute-spring crank-wound air pistol signed themselves as 'Charles Marion & Ch. Sanner', but nothing else is known. The gun probably dates from 1850–65.

'Mark Down' [The]. Found on shotgun cartridges distributed in England by William *Richards of Liverpool and Preston.

Markham – 1. William F. Markham, Plymouth, Michigan, USA. Recipient of several US Patents granted to protect the design of air- and spring-air guns. They included 372,161 of 25 October 1887; 473,633 of 26 April 1892; 483,159 of 27 September 1892; 553,716 of 28 January 1896; 557,849 of 7 April 1896; 651,634 of 12 June 1900; 655,170 of 31 July 1900; 696,461 of 1 April 1902; 718,646 of 20 January 1903; and 842,324 of 29 January 1907, assigned to the Markham Air Rifle Company. His last patent, 911,056 of 2 February 1908, sought jointly with E.S. *Roe, was also assigned to the company. In addition to guns, William Markham patented improvements in manufacturing technology. Typical of these was US Patent 698,502, granted on 1 April 1902 to protect a method of making rifled barrels. **2.** Markham Air Rifle Company [The], Plymouth, Michigan, USA. Markham made the *Challenger wood-pattern BB Gun in 1885/86, then graduated to improved guns designed by George W. *Sage, David F. *Polley, Ernest S. *Roe and William B. *Greenleaf. The *Challenger of 1886 was followed by the Improved Challenger of 1887, the *Chicago of 1888, a series of *Kings (from 1890 onward),

the *Prince of 1900, the *Sentinal of 1908, and others. Markham's strengths never lay in advertising, and eventually Daisy's competition proved too strong. He sold out to Edgar Hough and Charles Bennett in 1916, and eventually the business was renamed the *King Rifle Company in 1928.

'Markor' [The]. This mark is associated with shotgun cartridges handled by the English gunmakers *Cogswell & Harrison.

'Markoroid' [The]. Another of the marks to be found on shotgun ammunition handled by *Cogswell & Harrison of London.

'Mark Over' [The]. A brandname found on shotgun cartridges loaded by William *Evans of London.

Marks & Clerk. This British patent agency occupied various chambers at 18 Southampton Buildings, London, as well as in Birmingham and Manchester prior to 1914; a new address at 57 & 58 Lincoln's Inn Fields, London, appeared after 1920. Marks & Clerk worked for a number of inventors, including Walter Rogers *Benjamin (in the applications for what became British Patent 22,554/02 of 1902); George *Hookham (11,557/06 of 1906); Edward *Jones and *Kynoch Ltd (13,716/06 of 1906); Arthur Vane *Dickey (122,854); William *Baker and Arthur Herbert *Marsh (160,057 and 162,923); William Filmore *Markham (191,291); Eugene Edwin *Miles (202,106); and Etore *Caretta (219,261).

Marksman Products, Torrance, California. Manufacturer of the US Marksman repeating pistol and other guns, the former having been developed by the *Harris Company during 1955–57. Break-barrel spring-air rifles are also made, and limited numbers of British *Milbro Diana rifles have been distributed. The Marksman 746, for example, was the Milbro Diana G79.

Mark X. A brandname associated with *Interarms sporting rifles, introduced in 1972 and based on Zavodi *Crvena Zastava *Mauser actions, in chamberings ranging from .22-250 Remington to .300 Winchester Magnum. The stock had a Monte Carlo comb. The Mark X Cavalier of 1974 was similar, but had a roll-over comb. Mark X Viscount rifles had a plain stock with a low Monte Carlo comb and a plain round-tipped fore-end. Mark X Continental Carbines had full-length 'Mannlicher' stocks with a straight comb. The Mark X Marquis was similar to the Continental Carbine, but had a Monte Carlo comb and a steel fore-end cap. The Mark X Alaskan of 1976, in .375 H&H Magnum and .458 Winchester Magnum, had a recoil bolt through the stock beneath the chamber.

'Marlboro' [The]. Found on shotgun ammunition loaded by William *Evans of London.

Marlin – 1. John Mahlon Marlin, Rock Falls, New York. A gunmaker and patentee, responsible for *Plant revolvers in 1866–67, and *Ballard rifles in the 1870s. **2.** Marlin Fire Arms Company, New Haven, Connecticut, USA: *see panel, pp. 330/31.* **3.** Marlin machine-guns. The Marlin Machine Gun M1915 was a minor variant of the old *Colt 'Potato Digger' (M1895) with cooling fins on the barrel and a lightened tripod. This had been licensed to Marlin earlier in 1915 to enable ground guns to be supplied to Russia. The Canadian Army used some guns of this type with success on the Western Front until they were replaced by *Vickers patterns. In 1916, at the request of the US Navy, Marlin replaced the original radial actuating lever with a straight-line piston and pro-duced the M1916 aircraft machine-gun. Although most of the parts remained interchangeable with the M1915, modifications were required to slow the opening of the breech, minimise case-head separations and reduce the number of extractors broken by the violence of the revised action. However, no sooner had these changes been proven than a change was made from mechanical to hydro-pneumatic propeller synchronisers, and the M1916 was replaced by the modified M1917 in July 1917. Purchases of M1915 (ground) machine-guns during the First World War amounted to 4,805. More than 13,000 M1917 aircraft guns had been delivered by the 1918 Armistice, 428 being converted into M1918 tank guns by the addition of large aluminium radiators and pistol grips. **4. Marlin shotguns.** The company produced a variety of exposed-hammer slide-action shotguns, beginning with the 12-bore Model 1898 Take Down. Made until 1905, this was followed by the 16-bore Model 16 (1904–10), the Take Down Model 19 of 1906–07 and the solid-frame Model 17 (1906–08). The Model 21 was a Model 19 with a straight-wrist stock, and the Model 24 (1908–15) had a recoil safety lock. The Model 26 was a solid-frame variant of the Model 24, while the Model 30 of 1910 was a 16- or 20-bore version of the Model 16 with a recoil safety lock. The hammerless 12-bore slide-action Model 28 appeared in 1913, in Take Down form, and the Model 31 (16- or

20-bore) followed in 1915. Both guns were made until 1922, but a variety of designs followed over the succeeding forty years.

Marmey et Tétafort, rue des Jardins 19, Saint-Étienne, France. Listed in 1892 as a distributor of, and agent for, arms and ammunition.

Marnas, 13 rue du Rozier, Saint-Étienne, France. Listed in 1951 as a gunmaker.

Marnes – 1. John Marnes. An English gunmaker listed at 31 Cumberland Road, Walworth Road, London, from 1844 until 1852, Marnes moved successively to 14 Cross Street, Newington Butts (1853), 7 Kennington Row (1854–65), 190 Kennington Park Road (1866–8) and 2 Windmill Row, Kennington, until 1874. *See also* William Marnes (below). **2.** William Marnes. A gunmaker listed at 2 Windmill Row, Upper Kennington Lane, Kennington, London, from 1875 until 1881; the son of John Marnes (above).

Marnette. Joseph Marnette, Herstal-lèz-Liège, Belgium. Best known as a maker of double-barrelled sporting guns, Marnette patented a sliding-barrel system in the mid-1870s. Pulling down on a ring-tipped lever beneath the front of the trigger guard moved the barrel-block away from the standing breech. Surviving guns are usually found with back-action locks and external hammers.

Marocchi. Stefano Marocchi e Figli, Gardone Val Trompia, Brescia, Italy. This well-known shotgun manufacturer was founded in 1922, and marketed a line of gas-

MARLIN FIRE ARMS COMPANY

Marlin (2)

Based in New Haven, Connecticut, this gunmaking business had its origins in the affairs of John Mahlon Marlin (1836–1901), a one-time apprentice with Philos Tyler's *American Machine Works, who was listed as a 'Manufacturer of Fire Arms' in Hartford, Connecticut, directories from 1871. Marlin had produced a lever-action rifle by 1879 (US Patent no. 222,064), but was also a prolific handgun patentee, receiving ten patents for pistols and revolvers between February 1870 (US no. 99,690) and October 1889 (no. 413,197),

The Marlin Fire Arms Company was incorporated in 1881 to succeed Marlin's own operations, its first president being Charles Daly of *Schoverling, Daly & Gales. Among the earliest products were about 40,000 *Ballard rifles (c. 1875–90), single-shot 1863-type pistols improved by an 1870-patent ejector, and a few small XXX Standard tip-barrel revolvers chambering .30, .32 and .38 rimfire cartridges. Marlin also manufactured Smith & Wesson-

style break-open .32 and .38 centrefire double-action revolvers during the 1880s, but production of handguns had ceased by 1898. The company is now much better known for its rifles.

The M1881 lever-action rifle was made in accordance with patents granted to Henry *Wheeler, Andrew *Burgess, Adolf Toepperweim and John Marlin. It was followed by the M1888, with a short action suited to the .32-20, .38-40 and .44-40 WCF cartridges; by the M1889, the first of the side ejectors; by the .22 rimfire/.32 centrefire M1891 and M1892; by the centrefire M1893 and M1894 (short receiver); by the long receiver M1895; and by the take-down .22 rimfire M1897. Much of the development work on these guns was entrusted to Lewis *Hepburn.

A slide- or pump-action .22 rimfire rifle (the Model 18) appeared in 1906, the first of many such guns made until the Model 47 was abandoned in the early 1930s.

In 1910, Marlin purchased the Ideal Manufacturing Company of New Haven, Connecticut, but sold it to Phineas Talcott in 1916;

Talcott sold it to the Lyman Gun Sight Company in 1925.

The advent of the First World War in Europe led to Marlin being asked to quote for 100,000 *Mauser-type rifles; apparently the order was to be placed by Britain on behalf of the Belgian government in exile. Subsequently a few thousand of these 7.65x53 1889-pattern guns were made by Hopkins & Allen, a company that became the Norwich Division of Marlin Rockwell in 1917. Marlin also made *Colt-type machine-guns, beginning with a contract placed in 1914 by Russia; these (and the shotguns) are listed separately.

The Marlin Arms Corporation was incorporated on 8 December 1915, but was superseded by the Marlin-Rockwell Corporation in 1916. Among the wartime products were the M1918 *Browning aircraft machine-gun and the *Browning Automatic Rifle.

The post-war collapse of the arms industry hit Marlin-Rockwell hard, and a sale of assets ensued. The Marlin Firearms Corporation was incorporated in Delaware in July 1921, but had failed by 1924. It was replaced by a new Marlin Firearms Company, incorporated in

powered rifles and shotguns during the 1960s, under the brandnames *Artemis, *Luna Park and *Competizione.

Maroney. T.P. Maroney accepted guns and accessories on behalf of the US Army, marking them 'TPM'; they dated from the last few years of the nineteenth century. *See also* US arms inspectors' marks.

Marquis – 1. *See* Mark X. **2.** Marquis of Lorne. A *Suicide Special revolver made by the *Ryan Pistol Company of Norwich, Connecticut, USA, in the late nineteenth century.

Marr – 1. Friedrich Marr, Zella-Mehlis in Thüringen. A maker of guns and accessories active in Germany between the world wars. **2.** Fritz Marr, Zella St Blasii and Zella-Mehlis in Thüringen, Germany. Listed in 1914 as a gunmaker, and in 1920 with the qualification '(Elektr.)' – guns with electric ignition, perhaps? Still listed as a master gunsmith in 1930. **3.** Richard Marr, Zella-Mehlis in Thüringen. Listed in 1939 as a master gunsmith.

Marres. Joseph Marres. A member of the London gun trade listed at 110 Cannon Street (1878–83) and 24 Great Winchester Street (1889–93). Marres is believed to have been the principal promoter of the *Martini-Marres-Braendlin *Mitrailleuse pistol, made by the *Braendlin Armoury of Birmingham in the 1880s.

Marrison. Samuel Marrison, Norwich, Norfolk, England. The marks of this gunmaker have been reported on self-cocking *pepperboxes. Marrison operated from St Benedict's between 1821 and 1842, then from 50 Great

Orford Street until 1853. He may have been succeeded by Benjamin Marrison, listed in nearby Stalham in 1857.

Marrow & Company. Sometimes listed as Morrow, this business was trading from 25 Corporation Street in the Yorkshire town of Halifax as early as 1864. The business was owned by gunsmith John Marrow, but had adopted the style '...& Company' by the time shotgun cartridges marked *'Challenge' were being sold in the twentieth century. A shop was also kept in Harrogate for some years.

Mars – 1. A powerful British pistol, operated by long recoil, locked by a rotating multi-lug breech-block, and incorporating an elevator to raise cartridges from the magazine to the feed position. Designed by Hugh W. *Gabbett Fairfax, apparently the Mars was made under contract c. 1899–1905 by the *Webley & Scott Revolver & Arms Company Ltd. Chambered for a variety of 8.5mm, .36 or .45 high-velocity cartridges, the Mars was a failure; Gabbett Fairfax was bankrupted in 1902, and the Mars Automatic Pistol Syndicate, formed to exploit his patents, eventually entered liquidation in 1907. Some guns will be found with the marks of a French agent, A. *Guinard. **2.** Usually found as 'The Mars' on a shotgun cartridge made by *Eley Bros., prior to the acquisition of the company by Explosives Trades Ltd in 1918. **3.** A series of 6.35mm and 7.65mm semi-automatic pistols, based on the *Browning blowbacks, made in the early 1920s in the Czechoslovakian town of Kdyně, firstly by

Connecticut in January 1926, which prospered under the presidency of Frank Kenna (1874–1947), even though its most talented designer – Carl Swebilius – had left to form *High Standard.

The Marlin Firearms Company continued to make lever-action sporting guns, such as the M1936, M36 and M336, until the Second World War. A return to war work brought production of the UDM42 (Swebilius) and M2 (Hyde) submachine-guns alongside parts for the *Garand and the *M1 Carbine – work that resumed during the Korean War of 1950–53.

Modern sporting guns have been based on a variety of inexpensive lever-action patterns, including the M62 Levermatic. There have been .22 rimfire auto-loaders ranging from the Model 50 (introduced in 1931) to the Model 70 Papoose

(1986); bolt-action rifles from the Model 65 to the 880 series of 1988; two rimfire sporters made on *Sako actions between 1954 and 1958, the M322 and M422; and a few .30-06 and .308 centrefire rifles built on *FN-Mauser actions in 1955–59.

These have been sold alongside well-proven lever-action patterns such as the Model 444, introduced in 1965 for the .444 Winchester cartridge; the New Model 94 of 1969; and the Model 375 (1980–83), also chambering proprietary Winchester ammunition.

In addition to guns bearing the Marlin name, the company has offered a range of plain budget-price versions under the *Glenfield banner. It has also manufactured 'private brand' guns for such distributors as Cotter & Company of Chicago (West Point); Montgomery *Ward & Company (Western Field);

This .22 Model 39A lever-action rifle is typical of the products of the Marlin Firearms Company. Although the guns are often mistaken for Winchesters, they have lateral ejection and a prominent bolster for the lever pivot beneath the frame, ahead of the trigger.

the Oklahoma Tire & Supply Company (Otasco); J.C. Penney (Formost); *Sears, Roebuck & Company (Ranger, J.C. Higgins); United Merchandising Inc. (Big Five); and the Western Auto Supply Company (Revelation).

By far the best source of information about all these guns is the amazingly comprehensive *Marlin Firearms. A History of the Guns and the Company that made them*, by Lieutenant-Colonel William S. Brophy (The Stackpole Company, 1989).

*Kohout & Spol, then by *Pošumavská Zbrojovka. Later guns, therefore, will bear 'PZK' marks. **4.** A German-made semi-automatic pistol, with a detachable box magazine ahead of the trigger. *See* Bergmann-Mars. **5.** Found on bolt-action ball firers made in Germany by *Venuswaffenwerke of Zella-Mehlis from 1935 until c. 1940, and possibly also in the late 1940s under Russian control. **6.** Mars Equipment Corporation, Chicago, Illinois. The US distributor of *CETME sporting rifles.

Marsh, *see also* March – **1.** John Marsh, 30 Drapery, Northampton. This English gunsmith, known to have been trading independently in 1869, marked sporting guns and ammunition. Subsequently his business passed to Alfred *Rutt. **2.** M.R. Marsh, using an 'MRM' mark, accepted revolvers made by *Colt's Patent Fire Arms Manufacturing Company, apparently dating from the early 1900s, although confirmation is lacking. *See also* US arms inspectors' marks. **3.** Samuel W. Marsh of Washington D.C., USA, received US Patent 26,362 of 6 December 1859 to protect a tip-barrel rifle with a 'detachable headed breech-pin' obturator. Guns of this type were marketed by the Marsh Breech & Muzzle-Loading Arms Company (q.v.). A later patent, 33,655 of 5 November 1861, protected a rifle with a breech-block that turned up and forward around a transverse pivot. **4.** Marsh & Baker, Birmingham, England. *See* Midland Gun Company. **5.** Marsh Breech & Muzzle-Loading Arms Company, Wahsington D.C., USA. This gunmaking business was formed in 1859, under the presidency of R.H. Gallagher, to exploit the patent granted to Samuel W. Marsh. Its failure in 1862, even though the Civil War had begun, testifies to its inability to translate the prototype tip-barrel breech-loading carbines into series production.

Marshall – **1.** Made in Hartford, Connecticut, by *Colt's Patent Fire Arms Manufacturing Company, this was a version of the .38 *Official Police revolver with barrels of 2 or 4in. Only 2,500 were made during 1954–55. **2.** Joseph C. Marshall, Springfield, Massachusetts. Co-patentee with G.L.*Holt of a breech-loading pistol with the hammer and trigger made in one piece (US no. 138,157 of 22 April 1873, which was assigned to E.H. & A.A. Buckland). Marshall also collaborated with Dexter *Smith in the design of a firearm with a breech-block that swung down and back (US 141,603 of 5 August 1873), and in the development of a 'revolving firearm' (162,863 of 4 May 1875). **3.** J. Plympton Marshall of Millbury, Massachusetts, designed the breech-loading firearms protected by US Patents 25,661 of 4 October 1859, and 35,107 of 29 April 1862. The former was an underhammer rifle with a breech that broke up and forward; the latter was a crude form of straight-pull bolt opened by raising, then pulling a ring-handle. **4.** Simeon Marshall, Philadelphia, Pennsylvania, USA. Co-patentee with Jesse *Butterfield of a 'cartridge opener' (US 14,850 of 13 May 1856) and a self-priming gun-lock (24,372 of 14 June 1859).

Marshwood. A brandname associated with shotguns made in the USA by the *Crescent Arms Company.

Marson. Samuel Marson. An English gunmaker, apparently specialising in pistols, trading in Birmingham, Warwickshire, between 1872 and 1878, then as Samuel Marson & Company from 1879 until the period of the First World War. The directories list the premises as 37 & 40, or sometimes 39–40, Livery Street

Marston – **1.** Stanhope W. Marston, New York City. Listed in the directories as a gun and pistol maker, trading from 197 Allen Street, then 348 Houston Street, Marston received US Patent 7887 on 7 January 1851 to protect the lock of a double-action pepperbox ('fly-tumbler lock for firearms'); it was reissued in 1859 and assigned to James M. *Cooper. Stanhope Marston also sought protection for a 'revolving trigger-opeated firearm', US Patent 45,712 of 4 January 1865. **2.** William W. Marston, Phoenix Armory, Second Avenue & 22nd Street, New York City. A successor to Marston & Knox (Jane and Washington Streets, 1850–54), Marston made a single-shot pistol patented in the USA on 18 June 1850 (no. 7443) and the break-open .22 or .32 derringer protected by US Patent 17,386 of 26 May 1857. The pistol breech-block slid vertically in the frame, whereas the derringer had a three-barrel monoblock and a striker that fired the barrels from the bottom upward. Marston also made *Whitney-type cap-lock revolvers and *Gibbs-patent breech-loading carbines until the Phoenix Armory was destroyed during the New York Draft Riots of June 1863.

Marte. A compact Spanish 6.35mm-calibre automatic pistol of Browning type, made in Eibar by *Erquiaga, Muguruzu y Compañía: six rounds, hammer fired.

Marthourey, cours Saint-Paul, Saint-Étienne, France. Listed in 1892 as a distributor of, and agent for arms and ammunition.

Martial. A *Smith & Wesson-type revolver made in Spain between 1969 and 1976 by *Llama–Gabilondo SA. A double-action pattern with a conventional swing-out cylinder mounted on a yoke, it could be obtained in .22 LR and .38 Special. Adjustable sights and chequered wooden grips were standard, although the finish could be blue, chrome or gold plate.

Martian. A 6.35mm Browning-type pocket pistol made in Eibar, Spain, by Martin A. *Bascaran: six rounds, striker fired.

Martin – **1.** Rue Badouillère 38, Saint-Étienne, France. Listed in 1892 as a gunmaker. **2.** Alexander Martin & Company. Founded in the 1830s, this well-known Scottish gunmaker eventually opened a number of workshops: 20 Exchange Square, Glasgow; 25 Bridge Street, Aberdeen; and 2 Friars Street, Stirling. Premises at 22 Frederick Street and (possibly) 12 Andrew Street, Edinburgh, were inherited with the goodwill of the business of Alex. *Henry. Martin was known for sporting guns and ammunition, but assembled a few hundred .22 No. 2 *Lee-Enfield training rifles and 420 .303 Rifles No. 3 Mk 1* (T) A in the early days of the Second World War. Substantial quantities of 12-bore shotguns were also handed to the British military authorities in 1942. Martin's shotgun ammunition included *Eley-Kynoch cartridges marked with brandnames such as 'The AGE' (an abbreviated form of 'Aberdeen-Glasgow-Edinburgh'), 'The Caledonia', 'The Scotia', 'The Stirling', 'The Thistle' and 'The Velm'. An 'AGE' trademark was also used, sometimes in the form of a monogram. **3.** Arthur Martin. A gunsmith or gunmaker operating from 11 Princeton Street, Red Lion Square, London W.C., from 1886 until 1890. **4.** Edwin Martin, using an 'EM' identifier, accepted firearms and accessories on behalf of the Federal Army during the American Civil War. Apparently his activities were confined to 1862, which may enable them to be separated from those of *Edward McCue. *See also* US arms inspectors' marks. **5.** J.E. Martin, Glasgow. This Scottish gunsmith, associated with Alex Martin & Company (above), was granted British Patent 23,423/1914 for a 'luminous fore sight for the Lee-Enfield rifle'. **6.** Martin, Jack & Company. Operating from chambers at 88 Chancery Lane, London WC2, this patent agency helped to obtain British Patent 607,444 for Leslie Wesley.

Martini – 1. Alexander Martini, son of Friedrich von Martini, this Swiss-born engineer was granted British Patent 1531/80 of 14 April 1880 to protect a multi-barrelled self-cocking pistol. Subsequently this was made in Britain by the ★Braendlin Armoury Company Ltd and promoted as the ★Mitrailleuse. **2.** Friedrich von Martini is best known for his breech-loading rifle, developed in the 1860s from the ★Peabody, but was also active in the production of steam engines, then gas engines in his factory in Frauenfeld, Switzerland. The rifle was protected by British Patents 2305/68 of 22 July 1868 and 603/70 of 1 March 1870, and roughly comparable US Patent 90,614 of 25 May 1869. Martini was granted US Patents for improvements to his basic design: 115,546 of 30 May 1871 (with a leaf instead of spiral striker-spring), 120,800 of 7 November 1871, and 132,222 of 15 October 1872. The rifle was very successful, in both its British Martini-Henry guise and American ★Peabody-Martini version. **3.** Martini-Enfield rifles: *see* panel, pp. 334/35. **4.** Martini-Francotte. The British-pattern ★Martini rifle was copied extensively in sporting guns made in Liège during 1880–1910, principally by Auguste Francotte. Many guns incorporated Francotte's patented cocking indicator in the right receiver wall. Belgian-made guns can usually be identified by their proof marks, but may be misleadingly marked as a product of the ★Braendlin Armoury Company Ltd of Birmingham. **5.** Martini-Henry Breech-Loading Rifle Company [The]. Formed to protect the rights of the inventor, Friedrich von ★Martini, and collect the royalties due to him, this agency maintained an office at 65 Gracechurch Street, London E.C., from 1877 to 1890. It was known for part of the post-1887 period as the 'Martini-Henry & Martini-Enfield Breech-Loading Rifle Company'. At least one directory lists an additional address at 2 Chatham Buildings, London E.C., in 1878–79, which may have been a private residence. A move of office to 31 Queen Victoria Street, E.C., occurred in 1891, thence to 140 Leadenhall Street in 1894. Operations seem to have continued until c. 1912. **6.** Martini-Henry rifles: *see* panel, pp. 334/35. **7.** Martini-Marres-Braendlin: *see* Mitrailleuse pistol. **8.** Martini-Metford rifles: *see* panel, pp. 334/35.

Martinier – 1. Charles Martinier et fils jeune, place Chavanelle 6, Saint-Étienne, France. Listed in 1879 as a gunmaker. **2.** Denis Martinier, rue de la Charité 11 (later 7), Saint-Étienne, France. Listed in 1879–92 as a gunmaker. **3.** Martinier-Collin, rue Badouillère 21, Saint-Étienne. Listed in 1879 as a gunmaker.

Martouret et Boisson, cours Saint-Paul 8, Saint-Étienne, France. Listed in 1879 as a distributor of, and agent for, arms and ammunition.

Martz – 1. John V. Martz, Lincoln, California, USA. Renowned for his innovative work, particularly on ★Parabellum pistols, this gunsmith was granted US Patent 3,956,967 of 1976 to protect the Martz Safe Toggle Release (below). **2.** Martz Safe Toggle Release (MSTR).

Patented by John V. Martz (above), this allows the toggle of a suitably modified ★Parabellum, or Luger, pistol to close safely over an empty magazine; alternatively, simply rotating the safety lever to its rear (safe) position automatically shuts the open action once a new magazine has been inserted in the feedway.

'Marvel' [The]. This mark was applied to shotgun ammunition loaded by, or for, ★Curtis's & Harvey of London, prior to 1918.

MAS. *See* Manufacture d'Armes de ★Saint-Étienne.

Maschinen- und Apparätebau 'Wagria' GmbH, Ascheberg/Holstein. This German airgun maker was active from 1953 until 1961 or later, although it is assumed that the business was liquidated in the early 1960s. A limited range of barrel-cocking spring-air rifles included the Wagria-★Aerosport, Wagria-★Scout, Wagria-Standard and Wagria-★Rapid.

Maschinenbau-Gesellschaft Nürnberg. Based in Nürnberg, Bavaria, this metalworking business made 70,000 actions for the ★Podewils-Lindner-Braunmühl rifle during 1867–68. The guns were assembled in the ★Amberg manufactory. The business was amalgamated with ★Maschinenfabrik Augsburg in 1899, to form Maschinenfabrik Augsburg-Nürnberg (MAN).

Maschinenfabrik... – 1. Maschinenfabrik Augsburg, Augsburg, Bavaria. A maker of 10,000 actions for the ★Podewils-Lindner-Braunmühl rifle during 1867–68. The guns were assembled in the ★Amberg manufactory. The business also made about 25,000 new ★Werder actions in the mid-1870s. It was amalgamated in 1899 with ★Maschinenbau-Gesellschaft Nürnberg to form Maschinenfabrik Augsburg-Nürnberg (MAN). **2.** Maschinenfabrik 'Landes', München, Bavaria. A maker of about 4,000 M/69 ★Werder carbines for the Bavarian Army in 1869–70.

Mason – 1. James M. Mason, Washington D.C., USA. Designer of the breech-loading firearms protected by US Patents 112,523 and 117,908 of 7 March and 8 August 1871 respectively. The earlier bolt-action design seated the cartridge by cam action; the later one was a variant of the rolling-block mechanism popularised in the early 1870s by Remington. **2.** Joseph Mason, New Haven, Connecticut, USA. Patentee on 5 November 1889 of a 'breech-loading firearm' (US no. 414,651). **3.** Robert Mason. A gunsmith listed at 47 Tenter Street South, London E., from 1855 until 1861. **4.** William Mason, Taunton, Massachusetts, USA. Designer of an improved ejector rod for the first cartridge conversions of cap-lock ★Colts, protected by US Patent 128,644 of 2 July 1872. *See also* Richards-Mason Transformation. Mason was also responsible for the cylinder-locking bolt and loading gate of the ★New Line revolvers made by ★Colt, which were part of a patent issued in September 1874, and for additional improvements in revolver design allowed by US Patent 158,957 of 19 January 1875. Elements of all these were included in the ★Single Action Army Model Colt revolver. In addition, William Mason was credited with the trigger system of the double-action Colt revolvers – Double Action Army & Frontier, Lightning and Thunderer (qq.v.) – embodied in parts of US Patents 247,374, 247,379, 247,938 and 248,190, granted on 20 September, and on 4 and 11 October 1881. Mason obtained US Patent 250,375 of 6 December 1881 to protect a solid-frame revolver with a cylinder that swung out laterally. This was also exploited

MARTINI-HENRY, MARTINI-METFORD AND MARTINI-ENFIELD RIFLES

Martini (3, 6 & 8)

The Martini was submitted in prototype form to Swiss government trials in 1866, then appeared in Britain in 1867 – where it faced stiff competition from a rifle submitted by Alexander *Henry. Eventually, with the trials all but tied, the committee recommended amalgamating the compact Martini tilting-block breech mechanism, which was simpler than Henry's, with the Henry barrel. The Martini-Henry resulted, the first of the perfected long-action rifles being made in Enfield in 1869.

They were followed by a shortened action, consequent on the development of a bottleneck cartridge that was substantially shorter than the previous elongated straight-case design. This allowed the .450 Mark I Martini-Henry rifle to be approved for service on 3 June 1871, although problems delayed final acceptance until July 1874. It was followed by the improved Mark II rifle (sealed in April 1877) and Mark III rifle (August 1879), and also by a series of carbines. The Mark I Martini-Henry Cavalry Carbine was sealed in September 1877, followed by a Garrison Artillery Carbine in April 1878; a Mark I Artillery Carbine in July 1878; a Mark II Artillery Carbine in June 1892; and a Mark III Artillery Carbine (never made in quantity) in 1894. The guns were made by the Royal Small Arms Factory in Enfield, the Birmingham Small Arms & Metal Company Ltd (B.S.A.& M. Co.), and the London Small Arms Company Ltd (L.S.A.Co.).

The .450-calibre Martini-Henry was followed in British service by an abortive .40 version, about fifty P/1882 rifles being made in Enfield during 1882–84. They had a combless butt, and the body was cut away behind the block axis pin to facilitate grip. Subsequently all but two of the earlier rifles were upgraded to P/1883 standards. These experiments led to the .402 *Enfield Martini. Introduction of the original .450 Mark IV rifle was abandoned in 1882, but the designation was re-used in September 1887 to allow Enfield-Martini rifles to be converted from .402 to .450. These

were made in three patterns (A, B and C).

The introduction of the .303 *Lee-Metford magazine rifle persuaded the British authorities to convert hundreds of thousands of sturdy Martini-breech rifles and carbines for small-bore ammunition. This produced the Martini-Metford, then the Martini-Enfield, the differences being almost exclusively in the style of rifling: Metford-type barrels had seven-groove polygonal rifling, whereas Enfield types had five-groove concentric rifling, which was less susceptible to erosion. Many Martini-Metfords, however, were soon converted to Martini-Enfield pattern simply by substituting barrels; their classification can be difficult to determine!

The Mark I Martini-Metford rifle was adopted on 30 July 1889, followed by the Mark II on 10 January 1890. These were converted from Mark III and Mark II Martini-Henry rifles respectively. The .303 Marks I* and II* rifles of February 1903 had front sights that could be adjusted laterally. The Mark I Martini-Metford Cavalry Carbine (May 1892) was a conversion of the Mark II Martini-Henry rifle; the Mark II Cavalry Carbine (1892) and Mark II* (1893) had been Martini-Henry artillery carbines; and the Mark III Cavalry Carbine (1892) had been a Mark II .450 rifle. The Mark I Artillery Carbine (June 1893) was a conversion of the Mark I .450 Martini-Henry artillery carbine; the Mark II Artillery Carbine (October 1893) had been a Mark II .450 rifle; and the Mark III Artillery Carbine (March 1894) had been a .450 Mark III rifle. Most of the conversions were the work of the Royal Small Arms Factory in Enfield and the Birmingham Small Arms & Metal Company Ltd (B.S.A.& M. Co.), but some emanated from the Henry Rifled Barrel Company (H.R.B.).

Guns of the Martini-Enfield series were essentially similar to their predecessors, with the exception of rifling, and were often created simply by substituting barrels. The Mark I Martini-Enfield rifle (sealed in October 1895) and the Mark II rifle (February 1896) were converted from .450 Mark III Martini-Henry

rifles. The Marks I* and II* rifles, with laterally adjustable front sights, were approved in January 1903. Martini-Enfield carbines included the Mark I Cavalry Carbine (August 1896), converted from a Mark II .450 Martini-Henry rifle; the Mark I Artillery Carbine (November 1895), orginally a .450 Mark III rifle; the Mark II Artillery Carbine (December 1897), formerly a Mark I or Mark III .450 Martini-Henry artillery carbine; and the Mark III Artillery Carbine (July 1899), which had been a .450 Mark II rifle. Most of the guns were converted in Enfield, but a few were the work of the Henry Rifled Barrel Company, and others emanated from the Beardmore Engineering Company and bore 'BECO' marks.

Many sporting rifles were made in Britain, Belgium, Switzerland and elsewhere in Europe on the basis of military-surplus or purpose-built Martini actions (sometimes in Peabody-Martini form). These were chambered for a variety of black-powder sporting ammunition. In addition, small-calibre .297/210 and .310 Cadet Rifles were made prior to 1914 by such firms as the *Birmingham Small Arms Company Ltd, C.G. *Bonehill, Auguste *Francotte and W.W. *Greener, while a variety of rimfire target rifles were produced by *BSA Guns, *Vickers Ltd and others after 1920. Indeed, the BSA-Martini International Mark V ISU and Mark V Match rifles were still being made in 1986.

The best source of information about British military rifles is the first two volumes of *A Treatise on the British Military Martini*, by B.A. Temple and I.D. Skennerton (privately published, 1983–93); John Walter's *Rifles of the World* (Krause Publications, second edition, 1998) gives brief details of both military and commercial patterns; and George Markham's *Guns of the Empire* (Arms & Armour Press, 1990) lists the British military patterns.

A Westley Richards advertisement for small-bore derivations of the British service rifle. Both of these guns have round-backed 'commercial' receivers and Francotte-patent cocking indicators, but otherwise are essentially the same as government-issue guns.

Westley Richards' Martini Miniature Rifle.

The "SHERWOOD" ·300 Mid-range Rifle
for English Deer Parks and Target Shooting.

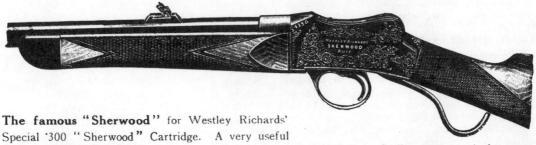

The famous "Sherwood" for Westley Richards'
Special ·300 "Sherwood" Cartridge.   A very useful
weapon in English Deer Parks, where the high power Highland Deer Stalkers' weapon is dangerous.
The target has proved it to be the best mid-range weapon made.   Muzzle velocity, 1,450 feet
per second, with 140 grs. bullet, solid or expanding.

Prices: With Ratchet Sight, **£8.8.0**   With Folding Sights as illustrated, **£9.0.0**
Engraved and Superior Finish as illustrated, **£10.10.0**

SMALL BORE RIFLES WITH DETACHABLE TELESCOPES.

·22, ·297/·250, ·300 "Sherwood."

Telescope Sight for Miniature Rifles.   Lightly built. Compact.   Magnification × 3½ sliding
focus arrangement, with milled drum and wheel elevating screw **A**.   Screw **B** is for finely correcting
adjustment—high and low; and screw **C** is for lateral correction—right or left.

Total length, 9 inches.   Weight, with solid attachment, 8¾ ozs.

A most desirable instrument for picking off Rabbits and similar objects at long distances.   This kind
of shooting with a small and accurate rifle affords enjoyable sport, and with the accuracy of sighting
and aiming obtainable by the use of the telescope sight, the enjoyment and interest are considerably
enhanced.   With its adequate magnification, this telescope sight has also a wide field of view.

Price of Rifles, as illustration, fitted with Telescope, **£18.18.0**.

Weight of Rifles approximately 6½ lbs.

by *Colt. Then he patented a simplified hammer and spring mechanism, on 29 August 1882; the perfected Colt swing-cylinder system was protected by a patent granted on 6 November 1888.

Masquelier. Manufacture d'Armes de Chasse Masquelier, Liège. This Belgian gunmaker handled *Mauser-type sporting rifles as AMD-1, AMD-2 (both in 8x68S) and AMD-3 (7x64). The actions seem to have been *FN-Mausers, although it has been suggested that the rifles were actually purchased in a finished state from *Raick Frères.

Massachusetts Arms Company – 1. Chicopee Falls, Massachusetts. This gunmaking business, incorporated on 5 March 1850, was an outgrowth of the *Wesson Rifle Company. The principal shareholders included Daniel *Leavitt, William *Miller, Horace *Smith, Joshua *Stevens, Benjamin Warner and Daniel *Wesson; Thomas *Warner was the factory superintendent. The Massachusetts Arms Company made the *Wesson & Leavitt cap-lock revolvers, which were efficient enough to attract the attention of Colt, who was successful in suing for infringement of his patents. Production of *Wesson & Leavitts ceased in favour of .28 Pocket and .31 Belt Model guns with manually-rotated cylinders. Almost all were fitted with Maynard Tape Primers, while a few .31 examples made after 1853 had a rammer patented by Joshua *Stevens. Stevens was also responsible for two trigger systems developed in an attempt to outwit Colt. No more than 3,500–4,000 revolvers of all types had been made when Colt's master patent expired in 1857, allowing the Massachusetts Arms Company to revert to hammer-rotated cylinders. A manufacturing licence was obtained to make the *Beaumont-Adams revolver, but only about 6,000 .31 five-shot and .36 six-shot guns had been made by 1861. In addition to manufacturing *Maynard carbines during the American Civil War, the company produced a selection of 20- and 28-bore 1865- and 1873-pattern tipping-barrel shotguns on the same basic action. A few single-barrel shotguns with box-locks and exposed central hammers were also made. **2.** A brandname associated with shotguns made prior to 1920 by the *Crescent Arms Company of Norwich, Connecticut, USA.

Massey – 1. D.W. Massey, using the identifier 'DWM', accepted military firearms on behalf of the US Army in 1909. **2.** F.A. Massey – possibly the brother of D.W. Massey (above) – accepted guns and accessories destined for the US Army in the period 1903–06, applying 'FAM' marks. See also US arms inspectors' marks for both entries.

Master, or Model 52 Master. This *Smith & Wesson pistol was a special target-shooting derivative of the Model 39, introduced in 1961 to fire .38 Wadcutter ammunition. The lockwork was initially that of the double-action Model 39, locked into a single-action mode, and the barrel was *swamped at the muzzle to engage a hand-finished bush. In 1963, a purpose-built single-action trigger mechanism was substituted on the Model 52-1, and a coil-spring extractor was fitted from 1971 (Model 52-2).

Masterpiece – 1. Or K-22 Masterpiece. Built on a medium or K-frame, this .22 rimfire *Smith & Wesson swing-cylinder revolver superseded the *Outdoorsman in 1940. When work began again after the Second World War, improvements were made in the sights and the trig-

ger mechanism, and three new guns appeared: the K-22, K-32 and K-38, known also (after 1957) as the Models 17, 16 and 14 respectively. The Model 14 was discontinued in 1981, and the Model 16 was reintroduced in 1990, being chambered to fire the .32 H&R Magnum cartridge interchangeably with the .32 S&W Special. See also Combat Masterpiece. **2.** Masterpiece Magnum, or K-22 Masterpiece Magnum. A name given to a swing-cylinder revolver, also known as the Model 48, made by *Smith & Wesson until 1986. It was essentially similar to the K-22 Masterpiece (q.v.), but chambered the .22 Winchester Magnum rimfire cartridge. Several variants were made, some with barrels as long as 8³/₈in. See also Magnum.

Mâsu. Gustave Mâsu, and Mâsu Bros. This gunmaking business, perhaps originating in Liège, was listed as a member of the London gun trade from 1864 until 1892. It specialised in importing Belgian-made sporting guns, including sliding-barrel shotguns made on the *Bastin system. Directories list operations variously as Gustave Mâsu, Gustavus Mâsu, Mâsu Bros. and Mâsu Bros. & Company, at 3a Wigmore Street (1864–69), then 10 Wigmore Street (1870–92).

'Mat', 'MAT'. See François Alexandre *Le Mat and Manufacture d'Armes de *Tulle.

Mata. Onofre Mata, a Spanish Army officer, patented a magazine rifle in 1883. Based on the Remington rolling-block, it relied on an operating lever on the right side of the breech to transfer cartridges from the case magazine in the butt to the chamber by way of an elevator tube.

'Matchless' [The]. Associated with shotgun cartridges and possibly also accessories sold by P.D. *Malloch of Perth, Scotland. The ammunition usually proves to have been made by *Eley-Kynoch.

Matchmaster. The half-stocked .22 LR rimfire Remington Model 513TR Matchmaster (1941, 1945–69) had a heavy semi-floating barrel, a patented trigger mechanism with an adjustable stop and Redfield competition sights.

Match Rifle. A single-shot *Remington-Hepburn target rifle made by E. *Remington & Sons and the *Remington Arms Company from 1883 until 1907, this was chambered for cartridges ranging from .25-20 Single Shot to .40-65. A vernier sight lay on the tang behind the hammer.

Mather. J. Mather & Company. Trading in Newark and Southwell, Nottinghamshire, England, this ironmongery business also sold sporting guns and ammunition. Shotgun cartridges marked 'The Britannia' have been seen with Mather's markings, although apparently they were made by James R. *Watson & Company.

Mathieu, 25 rue Badouillère, Saint-Étienne, France. Listed in 1951 as a gunmaker.

Matthews – 1. James Matthews. Best known as a dealer in ironmongery and sporting guns – the business was founded in 1906 in Ballymena, County Antrim, Ireland – Matthews sold shotgun ammunition with such brandnames as Hawk, Kingfisher, Swift and Wizard. Its origins are unclear. **2.** R. Matthews, using a simple 'RM' identifier, accepted firearms and accessories on behalf of the US Army. They date from the early 1900s. See also US arms inspectors' marks. **3.** W.J. Matthews. A gunmaker of Aston-in-Birmingham, Warwickshire, England, this man was the co-recipient with Walter *Scott of US Patent 144,870 of 25 November 1873.

Maumey, 35 rue Mulatière, Saint-Étienne, France. Listed in 1951 as a gunmaker.

Mäurer. Ernst Mäurer, Suhl in Thüringen, Germany. Registered as a gunsmith during the 1920s, and still trading in 1939.

Mauser – 1. Alfons Mauser. Brother of *Paul and *Wilhelm Mauser, this gunsmith was the recipient of US Patent 496,691, granted on 2 May 1893 to protect a 'breech-bolt for guns'. **2.** [Peter-] Paul Mauser. Born in Oberndorf, Württemberg, on 27 June 1838, Mauser was the son of a gunsmith employed by the state firearms factory, serving his time as an apprentice, then as a journeyman gunsmith. He designed an auto-cocking version of the *Dreyse needle gun in the mid-1860s, followed by an improved gun chambered for metalllic-case ammunition. Mauser's subsequent reputation as a designer, however, is obscured by the patenting of everything in his name, particularly after the formation of Waffenfabrik Mauser AG in 1884, and it is possible that the work of many anonymous employees laid the basis of his success. He died in Oberndorf on 29 May 1914. Too many patents were granted to Mauser to list individually in any detail, although the most important are summarised in the relevant sections below. The best source of details is R.H. Korn's *Mauser-Gewehre und Mauser-Patente* (Eckstein, 1908), which lists every patent granted prior to 1908...virtually in full! **3.** Wilhelm Mauser. Born on 2 May 1834, an elder brother of the better-known [Peter-]Paul Mauser, Wilhelm also underwent a traditional gunmaking apprenticeship in the state firearms factory in Oberndorf, then worked there as a journeyman gunmaker until 1867. After participating in the design of the first single-shot rifles, he undertook sales and promotional activities after the withdrawal of Samuel *Norris. The part played by Wilhelm Mauser in the success of Gebrüder Mauser & Cie is difficult to assess, although he may have been more inventive than supposed. His death, on 13 January 1882, robbed the company of a guiding hand. **4.** Gebrüder Mauser [& Companie], Oberndorf am Neckar, Württemberg. This great arms-making business was founded on 23 December 1872 by [Peter-] Paul and Wilhelm Mauser, to make parts for the 1871-pattern *Mauser rifle. Initially the workshop employed about fifty men, but the workforce had doubled by mid-1873, and a new factory – subsequently known as the Oberes Werk – began operating in October 1873. Then the Württemberg state government sold the Mausers the state-owned firearms factory in Oberndorf, which had been set up in 1811 in an old Augustine friary, and Gebrüder Mauser & Cie was the result. Financial aid was provided by the Württembergische Vereinsbank of Stuttgart, and rifles were made in large numbers. The death of Wilhelm Mauser (1882), however, was followed by the formation of Waffenfabrik Mauser AG (q.v.). **5.** Waffenfabrik Mauser AG, Oberndorf am Neckar. This public company was formed in 1884 from Gebrüder Mauser & Cie, the assistant director of the Württembergische Vereinsbank, Alfred Kaulla, joining the Mauser board as financial director. The company's fortunes dipped in the late 1880s, largely due to the adoption of the *Reichsgewehr in Germany, but the advent of the Belgian (1889) and Spanish (1893) Mausers heralded a runaway success that lasted until the end of the First World War. The Württembergische Vereinsbank was purchased by Ludwig

*Loewe & Cie in the 1880s, allowing the Berlin based engineering company to take a substantial stake in Mauser. When a large contract for the *Reichsgewehr was gained in 1889, Loewe fulfilled the order in Berlin, allowing the Mauser rifles ordered by Turkey to be made exclusively in Oberndorf. So many contracts were shared that, with effect from 1 January 1897, a cartel was formed of Waffenfabrik Mauser, *Deutsche Waffen- und Munitionsfabriken of Berlin (an amalgamation of Loewe's gunmaking business and Deutsche Metallpatronen- fabriken), *Fabrique Nationale d'Armes de Guerre and *Österreichische Waffenfabriks-Gesellschaft. Waffenfabrik Mauser continued to make rifles and semi-automatic pistols until 1918, but the Armistice and the ensuing collapse of the German economy led to Waffenfabrik Mauser AG being superseded by *Mauser-Werke AG in 1922. **6.** Mauser-IWK. The post-war controlling group of Mauser-Werke Oberndorf GmbH, best known for its highly successful aircraft-cannon designs. **7.** Mauser- Jagdwaffen GmbH, Oberndorf/Neckar. The sporting-gun division of Mauser-IWK/Mauser-Werke Oberndorf, responsible for the *Mauser-Parabellums, a modernised *HSc and a variety of bolt-action sporting rifles that includes the Model 66 pattern credited to Walter *Gehmann. *See also* Heym. **8.** Mauser pistols and revolvers: *see* panel, pp. 338/39. **9.** Mauser automatic and semi-automatic rifles: *see* panel, p. 340. **10.** Mauser bolt-action rifles: *see* panel, pp. 341–43. **11.** Mauser-Dovitiis rifle. This was a conversion of the 1871-pattern Mauser rifle, undertaken in France to chamber the 6.5x53.5 No. 12 Daudetau cartridge. The work was supervised by an engineer named Dovitiis, and the gun is said to have been used in Uruguay for some years. **12.** Mauser-Vergueiro rifle. Adopted in Portugal in 1904, after trials that initially had favoured the *Mannlicher-Schönauer, this 6.5mm rifle combined the internal magazine of the Gew. 98 with a simplifed bolt system credited to a Portuguese Army commission led by Colonel Vergueiro. The bolt handle turned down ahead of the 'split' receiver bridge. The guns were made in Berlin by *Deutsche Waffen- & Munitionsfabriken prior to the First World War. Subsequently a few M. 904/37 rifles were rechambered for the 7.9x57 cartridge to serve alongside Kar. 98k-type short rifles supplied from Oberndorf in the late 1930s. **13.** Mauser-Werke AG, Oberndorf am Neckar, Berlin, and elsewhere in 'Greater Germany'. This was the lineal successor to Waffenfabrik Mauser AG, formed during the financial crisis of the early 1920s. Work began again on bolt-action sporting rifles and automatic pistols in 1923, although owing to the enormity of Mauser's contribution to the pre-1918 war effort, work refurbishing military weapons was given to *Simson & Company in Suhl. In 1930, owing to a reorganisation of the holding company that owned both Mauser-Werke and Berlin-Karlsruher Industrie Werke (the post-1922 version of DWM), work on the *Parabellum, or Luger, pistol was transferred from the BKIW factory in Berlin-Wittenau to Oberndorf as part of a programme of rationalisation. Ironically, this led to Parabellums being assembled virtually alongside the Mauser C/96 pistol, which had been an important rival in both commercial and military markets prior to 1914. Mauser also made substantial quantities of 6.35mm and 7.65mm auto-loading pistols in this period, including tiny *Westentaschenpistolen. However, much of the rifle mar-

MAUSER REVOLVERS AND PISTOLS

Mauser (8)

German Patent no. 1192 was granted to Paul Mauser on 7 August 1877, protecting a single-shot C/77 pistol with a tipping-block breech. Only prototypes of this gun were made. It was followed by the so-called *Zig-Zag revolver, patented in 1878, then by a mechanical repeater known as the *Repetierpistole C/86*, which was protected by DRP 38007 of 24 July 1886. However, although the revolver was made in small quantities, none of these guns could be classed as successful.

Next came the recoil-operated *Selbstladepistole C/96*, locked by a pivoting block beneath the bolt. The mechanism was protected by German Patent 90430 of 11 December 1895, British Patent 959/96 of 14 January 1896, and US Patent 584,479 of 15 June 1897. Other elements of the design were protected by DRGM 59732 of June 1896 and DRGM 75915 of May 1897, for the wood-body holster stock and the tangent sight; DRP 142359 of 3 May 1902 protected an improved hammer safety.

Although patented in Mauser's name, the pistol is said to have been the work of the Feederle brothers. It was powerful, clumsy and badly balanced, and chambered a controversial adaptation of the *Borchardt cartridge. Waffenfabrik Mauser was owned at that time by Ludwig *Loewe & Cie, the original promoters of the Borchardt pistol.

The earliest Mausers jammed with distressing frequency, and the competing *Borchardt-Luger pistol was much more successful militarily. However, the C/96 was very popular commercially and remained in production until the beginning of the Second World War; the 100,000th example had been sold in 1910. It is now widely known as the Bolo, owing to extensive service in Russia.

British Patent 2917/08 was sought on 10 February 1908 for the ejector and hold-open system of the C/06-08 pistol. Derived from the auto-loading rifle of the same designation, the handgun relied on pivoting flaps to lock its breech. Small quantities were made for trials, but had no lasting effects, other than to inspire development of the M12/14 (below). British Patent 28,707/09 of 8 December 1909 showed the *Selbstladepistole M/09*, a blowback design with the return spring in a chamber beneath the barrel, with 'Improvements in and relating to Firing Mechanism for Automatic Pistols' (protecting the sear and trigger system) following in 10,596/10. British Patent 18,363/10, sought on 17 March 1910, allowed claims for a delayed-blowback fixed-barrel pistol adapted from the 1909 pattern, whereas 20,221/10 of 3 August 1910 and 18,423/12 of 10 August 1912 protected improved lockwork.

A 'Recoil-Loading Pistol' with flaps beneath the fixed barrel was protected by British Patent 21,105/12, sought on 16 September 1912; 22,556/12 was granted for a magazine safety/hold-open plate; 24,246/12 of 23 October 1912 allowed claims for a disconnector; and 25,172/13 of 4 November 1913 protected the construction of a box magazine. Guns of this type are known as the *Selbstladepistole M/12* and *Selbstladepistole M12/14*.

Introduced commercially in Germany c. 1910, 6.35mm and 7.65mm *blowbacks sold in small numbers despite their expense. The hump-backed slide of the earliest guns had been replaced by a straight-top design before war began. Many post-1915 examples ket had been lost to Belgium and Czechoslovakia, where Fabrique Nationale d'Armes de Guerre and Česko-slovenská Zbrojovka respectively had been able to fill gaps forcibly vacated by the German gunmaking businesses. Although the Oberndorf factory was able to honour a few small export orders in the 1930s, from countries as diverse as Abyssinia and China, most Kar. 98k (short rifles) were delivered to the Wehrmacht. Great strides were also made in the design and manufacture of machine-guns, automatic cannon and associated munitions – often for airborne use – and Mauser-Werke once again rose to a position of eminence. The Second World War brought another short-lived boost in profitability and, when the fighting ceased in 1945, Mauser-Werke was operating factories in Berlin (letter code, 'ar'), Karlsruhe ('lza'), Köln ('auc'), Neuwied ('amn'), Oberndorf ('byf', 'svw') and Waldeck bei Kassel ('amo'). *See also* Karl *Westinger. **14.** Mauser-Werke Oberndorf GmbH, Oberndorf am Neckar. *See* Mauser-IWK (above) and CETME.

Max-1, Max-2. Names applied to 5.56mm-calibre *Daewoo automatic rifles sold in the USA during the late 1980s by *Stoeger Industries of Hackensack, New Jersey.

Maxim – 1. A double-barrelled side-lock big-game rifle made by Società Armi Bresciane to the designs of Renato *Gamba. Chambered only for .375 H&H Magnum, .458 Winchester Magnum or .470 Nitro Express, the guns have 630mm barrels and weigh 4.65kg. An *Express back sight with a standing block and three folding leaves is set into the quarter-rib. **2.** Hiram Percy Maxim, the son of Hiram S. Maxim (below), was born on 2 September 1869 in Brooklyn, New York. By no means an inventive genius, Hiram P. Maxim was granted British Patent 14,310/03 of 1903 for 'Improvements in Devices for Lessening the Sound of Discharge of Guns', followed by 6845/08 and 25,269/08 of 1908, and one relevant US patent, 916,885 of 30 March 1908. The British specifications record his domicile as 550 Prospect Avenue, Hartford, Connecticut, USA. Maxim died in La Junta, Colorado, on 17 February 1936. **3.** Hiram Stevens Maxim. Born on 5 February 1840 at Brockway's Mills, Sangerville, Maine, USA, Hiram Maxim is one of the world's best-known firearms inventors. However, this naturally talented engineer's association with machine-guns arose only after he had visited Europe in 1881 to attend the Paris Exhibition – at the time his interests lay in electrical equipment. Maxim stayed over in London, where he was persuaded to open a workshop at 57D Hatton Garden to pursue the design of weapons that would function automatically. This marked the foundation of the Maxim Gun Company Ltd (q.v.), which subsequently merged with *Nordenfelt and eventually became *Vickers, Sons & Maxim. Maxim's machine-guns were protected by a selection of patents, beginning with British Patent 606/84 of 1884 for a gas-operated design.

This 7.63mm Mauser Modell 712 Schnellfeuerpistole, made in accordance with patents granted in the 1930s to Karl Westinger, reveals a selector lever on the left side of the frame. The wooden stock-holster was an essential shooting accessory, as lightweight guns of this type are notoriously difficult to control when firing automatically. Courtesy of Weller & Dufty, Birmingham.

will be found with military inspectors' marks, and it is likely that virtually all of them were diverted to the armed forces.

Work resumed after the First World War. Production of C/96-type pistols began again on a small scale in the early 1920s, and the ★Westentaschenpistolen (WTP) made their appearance later in the same decade. Eventually, after an amalgamation of the handgun-making operations of Mauser-Werke and BKIW, formerly ★Deutsche Waffen- & Munitionsfabriken, production of the ★Parabellum (Luger) pistol began in Oberndorf in 1930; output rose greatly during the late 1930s as the German armed forces began to re-equip for war.

Mauser introduced an improved pocket pistol in 1934, based on the guns that were being made before the First World War, but not until the advent of the ★HSc in the late 1930s was there an effective rival for the Walther ★PP/PPK series. Military production of the Parabellum ceased in 1942, the last

guns being sent to Portugal, although small-scale assembly continued until 1945, then on into 1946 under French supervision. Toward the end of the Second World War, Mauser took part in the ★Volkspistole programmes, but the fighting ceased before work could be completed.

More influential was the design described in British Patent 3493/84 of 1884 and its US equivalent, no. 297,278, granted on 22 April 1884 to protect a 'Mechanism for operating gun-locks by recoil'. Maxim received additional British Patents in 1884 (3844/84, 9407/84 and 13,113/84), followed by 1307/85, 8281/85 and 14,047/85 in the following year, in the main protecting 'Improvements in and relating to Machine Guns and other firearms…' At the same time, patents were granted in the USA in 1885 to protect machine-guns: 317,161 of 5 May, 319,596 of 9 June, 321,513 and 321,514 of 7 July, then 329,471 of 3 November for a 'Machine-gun support'. A 'recoil mechanism for guns' was patented on 24 August 1886 (US 347,945), a 'machine gun' followed on 9 August 1887 (367,825), and a 'method of manufacturing guns' was accepted on 24 January 1888 (376,990). With few exceptions, the patents granted to Maxim in the USA after 1888 protected machine-guns: 395,791 of 8 January 1889, 424,119 of 25 March 1890, 430,210 and 430,211 of 17 June 1890, 436,899 of 23 September 1890, 439,248 of 28 October 1890, 447,524 and 447,525 of 3 March 1891, 447,836 and 447,837 of 10 March 1891, 459,828 of 22 September 1891, 577,485 of 23 February 1897 (gas-operated), 579,401 of 23 March 1897, 583,362 of 13 July 1897 (gas-operated) and 593,228 of 9 November 1897. Hiram Maxim received a number of patents jointly with his long-time assistant, Louis

Silverman. These included British Patents 7156/92 of 1892 (for a gun) and 16,260/94 of 1894 (for a tripod), which were duplicated by US Patents 551,779 of 24 December 1895 and 544,364 of 13 August 1895 respectively. The British Patents also record Hiram Maxim's progression from a small workshop in Hatton Garden to Crayford Works, Kent, then to Baldwyn's Park, Bexley, Kent, before he ended his days in Thurlow Lodge, West Norwood. In addition to the eponymous machine-gun, Maxim also developed an immense steam-powered 'flying machine'. He became a British subject, was knighted by Queen Victoria in 1901 and died on 24 November 1916. **4.** Hudson S. Maxim was the younger brother of Hiram Maxim, born in Orneville, Maine, on 3 February 1855. A short stay in Britain (1886–88) ended when he returned to the USA as North American representative of the ★Maxim-Nordenfelt Guns & Ammunition Company Ltd, but this lasted only until he moved to the short-lived Columbia Powder Manufacturing Company in 1891. Most of his patents were concerned with explosives, and the sale of the assets of the Columbia company to E.I. Du Pont de Nemours & Company made him a fortune. Hudson Maxim continued his work, however, inventing propellant, explosives and a torpedo prior to his death on 6 May 1927. **5.** Maxim Gun Company Ltd [The]. This was formed in London, in October 1884, to promote the first patents granted to Hiram S. ★Maxim, the offices

MAUSER AUTOMATIC AND SEMI-AUTOMATIC RIFLES

Mauser (9)

Patented in 1898/99, the long-recoil-operated *Selbstladegewehr C/98* was locked by struts in the front of the receiver. The patent drawings show a magazine case formed integrally with the elongated trigger guard, although a rifle pictured in R.H. Korn's *Mauser-Gewehre und Mauser-Patente* has an internal magazine and a small oval trigger guard.

A modification of the C/98, with a sliding barrel, was the subject of a group of patents granted on 20 February 1898: DRP 105,618 protected the magazine and lockwork; 105,619 allowed claims for the locking system; 105,620 protected the barrel-return spring; 105,621 covered the trigger mechanism; 105,622 protected the striker safety; and 105,623 protected the fastening of the trigger and lockwork in the receiver. Two patents of addition, 107,213 and 109,454 (December and May 1898 respectively) improved on the striker-safety mechanism.

US Patent 639,421, granted on 19 December 1899, also protected the C/98 auto-loader. A variety of lesser German patents followed in quick succession, among them DRP 147,490 (14 November 1902) – and its British equivalent, British Patent 12,398/03 of 3 September 1903 – protecting a large auxiliary magazine with two coil springs bent in U-shape around the body. German Patents 151,940 and 152,454 (6 November 1902 and 20 August 1903) protected methods of manually operating auto-loading guns, while 154,453 of 17 January 1902 protected a recoil booster that allowed sliding-barrel guns to operate with blank ammunition; its British equivalent was 16,252/04, granted in August 1904 for

'Improvements in Automatic Fire Arms'. DRP 155,771 of 6 November 1902 protected the construction of the receiver of auto-loading rifles.

The clumsy *Selbstladegewehr C/02*, which relied on a rapid-pitch thread in the multi-piece bolt to rotate locking lugs out of engagement, was protected by DRP 159,157 of 6 November 1902 and DRP 169,233 of 8 July 1905. DRP 169,234 protected an improved manual cocking system; 164,860 of 25 March 1903 improved the trigger system; and 174,456 of 4 December 1904 described a nose-cap that isolated the bayonet from the barrel. British Patent 27,257/05 of 30 December 1905, 'Improvements in Recoil-operated Small Arms', protected a bolt-cocking system and the coupling of the striker to the cocking piece, but the C/02 was abandoned shortly afterward. The original German patents show a projecting magazine case, but in the main the few guns that survive have internal magazines.

The C/02 was replaced by the short-recoil *Selbstladegewehr C/06-08*, also offered as a handgun. The barrel and receiver slid back in the frame just far enough to release the bolt, which was locked either by lateral struts, protected by DRP 199,544 (25 October 1906), or a saddle-type lock, described in DRP 199,576 of 30 June 1906; British Patent 3496/07 of 12 February 1907 protected the flap-lock, the saddle pattern being part of 4803/07 (below).

Sought on 27 February 1907, British Patent 4803/07 was split into seven parts. 4803/07, 'Improvements in Recoil-loading Fire Arms with Sliding Barrels', protected the single-loading mechanism, the barrel arrester and the safety system; 4803A/07

protected the buffer to reduce the sensation of recoil; 4803B/07 protected the firing-pin arrester/safety unit; 4803C/07 protected the mechanical safety provided by the trigger and the sear; 4803D/07 was 'An Ejector for Fire Arms, especially Recoil-loaders'; 4803E/07 depicted a detachable large-capacity magazine; and 4803F/07 claimed novelty in a saddle-type locking mechanism.

The *Selbstladegewehr C/10-13*, an unsuccessful delayed-blowback, relied on an inertia block on top of the breech to pivot locking flaps outward into the receiver walls, but the slender locking bars were particularly prone to breakage.

The *Flieger-Gewehr*, or M1915, a development of the C/06-08, was made in small quantities during the First World War. Fully-stocked rifles with military-pattern nose-caps and bayonet lugs were tested in the trenches of the Western Front, while half-stock patterns were issued initially for air service. Experience soon showed the ★Mondragon to be preferable.

Experiments undertaken during the 1930s led to the recoil-operated Model 1935, then to the gas-operated Gew. 41 (M), which used a ★Bang-type muzzle cup. Toward the end of the Second World War, Mauser developed the Gerät 06 on the basis of a gas-operated roller-locked breech system originated by Wilhelm ★Stähle. This led to the Gerät 06 (H) of 1944, which had a delayed-blowback action.

Although better known for bolt-action rifles, Mauser also experimented prior to 1918 with a range of auto-loaders. This is a 7.9x57mm Flieger-Selbstladekarabiner, used in small numbers during the First World War. Courtesy of Joseph J. Schroeder.

MAUSER BOLT-ACTION RIFLES

Mauser (10)

The first gun, which remained experimental, was a self-cocking adaptation of the *Dreyse needle gun dating from 1866. It was followed by a promising rifle that chambered a self-contained metallic-case cartridge, rejected in Württemberg and Prussia in 1867, but at least given a trial in Austria. This led to an association with Samuel *Norris, the European sales agent of Eliphalet Remington & Sons, and secret negotiations leading to manufacture in France. In the summer of 1867, therefore, Norris and the Mausers had moved to Liège.

US Patent no. 78,603, granted on 2 September 1868 to the Mauser brothers and Samuel Norris, protected the single-shot C/67-69 rifle, or Mauser-Norris, rights being assigned to 'Samuel Norris of Springfield, Massachusetts'. The patent drawings show an adaptation of the *Chassepot, and a gun with the striker driven by a leaf-spring attached to the rear of the bolt handle. Two patents granted in Austria-Hungary (XIX/9 and XIX/26 of 24 December 1867 and 15 January 1868) improved the basic design, but Remington & Sons learned of Norris's duplicitous dealings, and the French government lost interest. Rights to the patents reverted to the Mauser brothers in 1870.

An improved C/70 rifle, tested in Spandau during 1870–71, showed that the Mauser was far superior not only to the original Dreyse needle guns, but also to the *Beck Transformation. Consequently, the Prussian government arsenal in Spandau made 2,500 *Interims-Modell* rifles to facilitate field trials, and the *Infanterie-Gewehr Modell 1871* was adopted officially on 22 March 1872. Series production was undertaken in *Danzig, *Erfurt and *Spandau; by the Bavarian state rifle factory in *Amberg; by *Österreichische Waffenfabrik-Gesellschaft in Steyr (Waffenfabrik Steyr); by Gebr. Mauser & Cie in Oberndorf am Neckar; and by a cartel of *Spangenberg & Sauer, V.C. *Schilling and C.G. *Haenel in Suhl, Thüringen. The British *National Arms & Ammunition Company Ltd made 6,000 rifles, and

some guns even went to China.

The 1871-pattern rifle provided the basis for the M78/80, or Mauser-*Koká, adopted by Serbia. Protected by DRP 15,204 of 23 1880, this embodied a modified action with a rail behind the receiver to support the open bolt. By 1880, however, the first magazine rifles had appeared (cf. Kropatschek and Vetterli), and among the many conversions applied to the Mauser were those of Carl *Holub, whose tubular design dated from 1878; Franz von *Dreyse, son of the inventor of the needle rifle and patentee of a tube magazine in 1879, and a conventional box pattern in 1882; Louis *Schmeisser, who developed a drum unit in 1881–82; Ludwig *Loewe & Co., whose saddle unit dated from the early 1880s; and Edward *Lindner, who contributed a gravity-feed box in 1883.

Patented in March 1881, the prototype *Mauser-Probegewehr C/81* was adapted from the M78/80 Serbian infantry rifle and protected by DRP 15,202 of 16 March 1881. A tube magazine lay beneath the barrel, and a cartridge elevator was contained in a new receiver. Another German patent, 20,738 filed on 7 May 1882, described refinements to the breech mechanism. The experimental C/82 rifle performed well enough in the field to become the *Infanteriegewehr M1871/84* (later known simply as the Gew. 71/84). The first series-made guns appeared in 1886. US Patents 249,967 and 270,599 (22 November 1881 and 16 January 1883) are broadly comparable to DRP 15,202 and 20,738 respectively.

A modified extractor/ejector mechanism was patented in Germany in November 1883 (DRP 28,109) and protected in the USA by Patent 289,113 of November 1883. DRP 30,035 of 30 March 1884 protected improvements to the bolt and cocking piece of the experimental C/82 rifle, but tube magazines were ineffective and Mauser began work on box patterns. Gravity-feed baskets or boxes, offset on the left side of the breech, were the subject of DRP 41,375 and 43,073 of 1 May and 18 October

1887; US Patent 383,895 (granted on 5 June 1888) protected a 'Detachable Magazine for Firearms'.

The advent of smokeless propellant in France, accompanied by the *Lebel rifle, showed that the action of the 1871 and 1871/84 Mausers was not strong enough. Austro-Hungarian Privilegium 37/1692 of 14 September 1887 protected an additional locking lug (*Mauser-Kammer mit doppeltem Widerstand*) incorporated in the 9.5mm Turkish Mauser rifle of 1887. Assigned to Waffenfabrik Mauser AG, US Patent 370,964 of 4 October 1887 was essentially similar to the Austro-Hungarian Privilegium, and DRP 44,393 of 29 February 1888 protected a bolt-mounted ejector pin driven by a small coil spring.

The adoption of the Gew. 88, or *Reichsgewehr, is usually seen as a snub by the German authorities to Paul Mauser. However, the first of the small-calibre Mauser rifles, the C/88, was an ungainly design, protected principally by DRP 44,323 of 2 March 1888 (for the combination of bolt-stop and ejector) and by DRP 45,561 of 18 April 1888 for the construction of the magazine; the layout of the C/88 breech was extremely awkward.

Although DRP 45,792 of 29 February 1888 improved the bolt, the cocking piece and the bolt stop, the C/88 was superseded almost immediately by the first *charger-loaded Mauser. This, the 7.65mm M1889 infantry rifle adopted in Belgium, had a compact bolt and a single-column magazine protruding beneath the stock, ahead of the trigger. The first guns were made by *Fabrique Nationale d'Armes de Guerre; later examples, including a variety of carbines and short rifles (*mousquetons*), were made by Fabrique Nationale and by Manufacture de l'Armes de l'État. Most could be identifed by the combination of jacketed barrels and protruding single-row magazines.

Austro-Hungarian Privilegium 39/609 of 8 October 1888 protected an improved magazine and charger, while DRP 50,306 of 30 June 1889 protected the distinctive combination charger-guide/bolt stop encountered on the 7.65mm M1890 Turkish rifles. US Patent 431,668 of

MAUSER BOLT-ACTION RIFLES CONT.

8 July 1890 ('Bolt-stop with cartridge-shell ejector for breech-loading guns') is comparable with German Patent 50,306. Guns with protruding single-row box magazines were supplied to several South American countries during the early 1890s, most notably Argentina (Mo. 1891), and also in limited quantities to Spain.

The principal recognition features are the chamber crests, described in greater detail in the section devoted to *National markings. Mauser, meanwhile, continued to improve the rifle, receiving a large number of relevant patents. These included DRP 53,073 of 4 July 1889, and US Patents

431,669 and 431,670 of 8 July 1890, protecting improved bolt-mounted extractors. German Patents 51,241 and 56,499 (15 September 1889 and 19 November 1890) protected the under-cut bolt heads that prevented double loading; 56,497 of 4 November 1890 protected a single-row magazine with an interruptor; and 59,299 of 29 March 1891 claimed novelty in an improved bolt-mounted 'collar' extractor.

US Patent 449,352 of 31 March 1891 was granted to protect a 'Safety Lock for Breech Bolts', whereas 451,768 of 5 May 1891 protected a 'Gun Barrel'. Work continued throughout 1892. DRP 65,644 of 28 April 1892 protected a

These two Mauser rifles present a contrast in styles. The wartime Kar. 98k (top), shown with a 1.5x Zf.42 sight, embodies a classic 1898-type action; the highly decorative Model 66 (above) incorporates the ultra-short action developed by Walter Gehmann during the early 1960s.

*charger; DRP 65,255 of 16 February 1892 (and its US equivalent, 477,671 of June 1892) protected bolt-mounted extractors; DRP 67,325 of 31 July 1892 described a cut-off mechanism; and DRP 67,343 of 1 April 1892 – together with US Patent 488,694 of 27 December 1892 – protected a

being listed at 57 Hatton Garden until 1888. The first chairman of the Maxim Gun Company was Albert Vickers, representing the Sheffield manufacturers of heavy ordnance, *Vickers, Sons & Company. A factory was built in Crayford, Kent, in 1885–87, but then the business was amalgamated with the *Nordenfelt Guns & Ammunition Company, to form the *Maxim-Nordenfelt Guns & Ammunition Company Ltd. **6.** Maxim Gun: *see* panel, pp. 344/45. **7.** Maxim-Kolesnikov. The MK was a lightweight machine-gun developed in the USSR by Ivan *Kolesnikov. It was produced in small numbers in the mid-1920s to compete with the Maxim-Tokarev, or MT. **8.** Maxim-Nadashkevich. Also known as the *PV or PV-1, this was a lightweight air-cooled derivative of the Soviet Maxim, with a spring-buffer in the back of the receiver to increase the rate of fire. Adopted in 1928 for

air service, it was made in quantity for about ten years. It was replaced by the UB, or *Berezin, 12.7mm design. **9.** Maxim-Nordenfelt Guns & Ammunition Company Ltd [The]. This was formed in 1888 by amalgamating the machine-gun manufacturing businesses of *Maxim and *Nordenfelt, whose factories in Crayford and Erith respectively were only a few miles apart. The first managing director was Sigmund Loewe, younger brother of Ludwig *Loewe; in 1897, however, the business was renamed Vickers, Sons & Maxim. **10.** Maxim Silent Firearms Company, 38 Park Row, New York. This company was formed in 1907 in anticipation of a patent-grant to Hiram P. Maxim (q.v.), which followed on 30 March 1908. The first silencers were made in 1909, and an associated business was organised to explore the application of silencing to internal-combustion engines. The Maxim

trigger-safety that prevented the striker from being released until the bolt was locked.

Work continued with single-row magazines, DRP 67,861 of June 1892 and US Patent 490,029 of January 1893 being typical, but the introduction of a double-row magazine was a great improvement. Described in DRP 74,162 of 12 July 1893, the first of these was incorporated in the 7x57 M1893 Spanish Army rifle together with a detachable magazine floor plate protected by DRP 74,163.

The 'Spanish Mauser', one of the greatest of nineteenth-century weapons, provided the basis for guns used throughout South America, in the Balkans, by Turkey, in Asia, by the Orange Free State and in the South African Republic. Mauser continued to patent improvements to the *charger-loaded bolt-action rifles, US Patent 547,932 ('Cartridge Pack for Magazine Guns') being granted on 15 October 1895 to protect the C/94 charger. German Patent 127,291 of 23 February 1900 and US Patent 661,743 of 13 November 1900 ('Cartridge Holder for charging Magazine Firearms') protected another *charger variant.

One of the most important of all Mauser patents was DRP 90,305, granted on 30 October 1895 to protect an improved bolt with an extra safety lug. Gradually, German Army interest in the new weapons increased, greatly helped by encouraging field trials undertaken during 1895–96. These led to the approval of the *Gewehr 88/97* on 11 March 1897, with the 1895-patent 'safety' locking lug; a cocking-piece

housing with integral gas deflector lugs; a special two-band nose-cap/bayonet mounting system, protected by DRP 86,365 of 30 October 1895; the left side of the receiver cut away (in accordance with DRGM 56,068 of 9 August 1895) to allow the thumb to press cartridges from the charger into the magazine; and gas-escape ports cut into the underside of the bolt body, in accordance with Belgian Patent 120,477 of 12 March 1896.

However, the Gew. 88/97 encountered so many problems that it was replaced by the *Gewehr 98* (Gew. 98) in April 1898. Few mechanical changes were made to the Gew. 98 between 1914 and 1918, although, late in 1915, the markings disc attached to the right side of the butt was replaced by two washers connected by a short hollow tube, and a finger groove was added in the fore-end. Stocks were made of walnut until 1916, when substitutes such as birch and European maple were permitted.

However, the advent of the British Rifle, Short, Magazine *Lee-Enfield, or SMLE, forced the Germans to experiment with *Einheitswaffen* (short rifles for universal issue). The first experimental carbine had appeared in April 1900, and about 3,000 *Kavallerie- und Artillerie-Karabiner 98* were made in Erfurt during 1900–01. These were superseded on 26 February 1902 by the *Karabiner 98 mit Aufplanzvorrichtung für das Seitengewehr 98* (1898 model carbine with attachment for the 1898 model bayonet, or Kar 98A). Production of the 98A carbine ceased in 1905, and the *Karabiner 98 AZ* (1908) was

developed instead. Subsequently surviving Karabiner 98 and 98A were converted to *Zielkarabiner.

After the First World War, surviving Gew. 98s were converted to *Karabiner 98b* (they remained full-length rifles), and Karabiner 98 AZ were retained for mounted troops and ancillary units. With Mauser in disgrace, the work was entrusted to *Simson & Companie of Suhl. However, Mauser-Werke began work again in the mid-1930s once Simson (Jewish owned) had been appropriated by the state to form the basis of *Berlin-Suhler-Werke.

The Wehrmacht had almost entirely re-equipped with the *Karabiner 98k*, a short (*kurz*) rifle derived from the Gew. 98. Millions of these guns were made by a variety of contractors, but quality declined noticeably as the end of the war approached. Mauser actions also provided the basis for a variety of *Volkskarabiner (VK-98) developed during 1944–45.

Among the best sources of information about the Mauser rifle are R.H. Korn, *Mauser-Gewehre und Mauser-Patente* (Ecksteins biographischem Verlag, Berlin, 1908; reprinted by Akademische Druck- und Verlagsanstalkt, Graz, c. 1971); Ludwig E. Olson, *Mauser Bolt Action Rifle* (F. Brownell & Sons, third edition, 1976); John Walter, *Rifles of the World* (Krause Publications, second edition, 1998); and Robert W. Ball, *Mauser Military Rifles of the World* (Krause Publications, 1996). *Backbone of the Wehrmacht: The German K98k Rifle, 1934–1945*, by Richard D. Law, (Collector Grade Publications, 1993) is a more specifically targeted source.

---

factory made grenades and gun parts during the First World War, but apparently stopped making silencers in 1925. **11. Maxim-Tokarev.** A lightweight gun credited to Fedor *Tokarev, also known as the MT, this was produced in the USSR in small numbers during the mid-1920s to compete with the Maxim-Kolesnikov (MK).

'Maximum' [The]. A mark associated with shotgun ammunition made by *Irish Metal Industries Ltd.

May. Norman May & Company, Bridlington, Yorkshire. This British distributor handled a range of products in the 1970s, including *BSF airguns and *Bimoco pellets. The business collapsed in the early 1980s, owing large sums of money to its creditors, and contributed greatly to the demise of its principal partners, Bimoco and BSF (qq.v.). *See also* Vixen.

Mayall. A revolver cannon, or *Battery Gun, patented

in the USA in 1860 and tested unsuccessfully during the American Civil War. The combustible cartridges were ignited electrically, but trials revealed a rate of fire of just 12rds/min. Since the Federal Army regarded it as a menace to its crew, the Mayall gun was abandoned.

Maybury. C. Maybury, Birmingham, Warwickshire. The marks of this English gunmaker have been reported on self-cocking *pepperboxes dating from the middle of the nineteenth century.

Mayer – **1.** Erwin & Rudolf Mayer: *see* Mayer & Grammelspacher. **2.** Mayer & Grammelspacher: *see* panel, pp. 346/47.

Maynadier. William Maynadier, sometimes listed as 'Maynardier', was a lieutenant-colonel in the US Army Ordnance Department. He accepted a variety of military firearms and accessories from c. 1838 until the beginning

MAXIM GUN

Maxim (6)

This owed its origins to a patent granted in 1884 to American-born Hiram S. *Maxim. The earliest Maxims comprised two basic assemblies: the fixed part was mounted on trunnions; the aiming handles and the trigger lever were attached to the breech-casing. The recoiling assembly slid inside the breech casing, moving back by about an inch. The recoil force was absorbed largely by the spiral main spring, although a small portion rotated and cocked the hammer.

Even the prototypes were very efficient, passing their trials with ease. Many outstanding demonstrations were given in Europe, one of the most impressive being a 13,500-round endurance trial held in Austria in July 1888. The Austro-Hungarian authorities purchased 160 8mm-calibre Maxim machine-guns from Britain in 1889; apparently most were intended for fortress use, but a few were given to the navy. The Maxims worked extremely well, but political pressure was brought to bear on the authorities in Austria-Hungary to adopt the rival *Škoda.

The British Army was another of the early purchasers of Maxims: the .45 Mark I and the .303 'Mark I Magazine Rifle Chamber'. Subsequently, large-calibre guns

were rechambered under the designation .303 Converted, Mark I. Normally they were accompanied by cumbersome wheeled carriages, but a selection of tripod mounts was also available. However, despite the impressive testimony to the efficacy of the Maxim provided by the Russo-Japanese War, and the worrying evidence of increasing enthusiasm in Germany (where a production licence had been granted to *Deutsche Waffen- und Munitionsfabriken), the British had acquired only 108 guns from Vickers, Sons & Maxim and its successor, Vickers Ltd, by the time the First World War began in the summer of 1914.

A British-made Maxim Gun was demonstrated successfully in Germany in 1889, and, in 1895, Ludwig *Loewe & Cie imported a gun from the Maxim-Nordenfelt Guns & Ammunition Company Ltd. Loewe also acquired a licence permitting Maxim-type guns to be made and sold throughout much of Europe, with the exception of Greece, Portugal and Spain. Formation of *Deutsche Waffen- und Munitionsfabriken (1897) encouraged work on Maxims to continue in the former Loewe factory in Hollmannstrasse, Berlin. The first guns, featuring many bronze parts, were supplied to the navy in 1897–98.

Army-issue MG. 01 Maxims were much the same as their navy

predecessors, but the transverse hole for the tripod-cradle retaining pin was replaced with lugs on the rear of the brass water jacket. Guns of this type were issued originally with a wheeled sled mount known as the *Schlitten 01*, soon replaced by the more robust *Schlitten 03*. A lightened Maxim Gun was adopted in 1908 as the *Maschinengewehr Modell 1908* (MG. 08), together with the *Schlitten 08* and a special panoramic optical sight – the *Zielfernrohr für Maschinengewehr* (ZfM) – developed by C.P. Goerz. This gun provided most of the small-calibre support fire available to German forces during the First World War. It had a steady, efficient action, but its cyclic rate was not much more than 300 rds/min. During the First World War, therefore, a recoil booster (*Rückstossverstärker S*) was added to increase fire rate to about 450 rds/min.

Although the Maxim-pattern MG. 08 was sturdy and reliable, it was not suited to close-range infantry-support roles. *Madsen guns were acquired from *Dansk Rekylriffel Syndikat of Copenhagen, but these fed from detachable box magazines and could not sustain fire for long periods. An answer was provided by the *Maschinengewehr 08/15* (MG. 08/15), developed by a team of army technicians led by Oberst von Merkatz, even though it was little more than a lightened MG. 08 with a wooden shoulder stock, and a pistol-grip and trigger

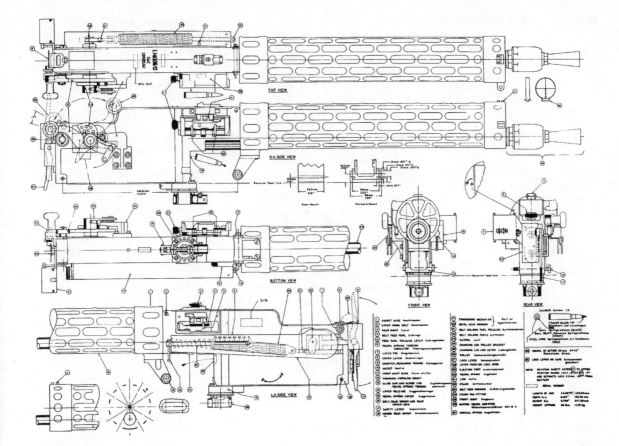

A German 7.9x57 LMG 08/15 aircraft gun, introduced during the First World War.

Facing page: *The first machine-guns were usually seen by the untutored military mind as a form of light artillery. This 'Carriage, Field, Machine Gun, Cavalry, 0.303-inch Maxim, Mk I' of the 1890s typifies the clumsy carriages issued until the virtues of mobility were appreciated after the Russo-Japanese War of 1904–05.*

mechanism beneath the receiver. A 100-round belt could be carried in a drum-like box, or *Patronenkasten*, attached to a bracket on the right side of the receiver, beneath the feed-way.

German Maxims were made in the government factory in Erfurt; by ★Rheinische Metallwaaren- und Maschinenfabrik (Rh.M.& M.F.) in Sömmerda; by Siemens & Halske (S.& H.) in Berlin; and also by ★Maschinenfabrik Augsburg-Nürnberg (M.A.N.). The ★Parabellum machine-gun was a lightweight derivative.

The first US Army trial of a .45-calibre 1889-pattern Maxim Automatic Machine Gun ocurred in 1890, when the testing board recommended that additional guns be acquired for troop trials. However, money was short and the army authorities were satisfied with the hundreds of service ★Gatlings. After the Spanish-American War had shown the potential of the machine-gun, the US Army tested a British-pattern Maxim, an M1895 ★Colt and a strip-feed ★Hotchkiss. The water-cooled Maxim was preferred owing to the ease with which fire could be sustained.

The US Army bought 282 examples of the 'Maxim Automatic Machine Gun, Caliber .30, Model of 1904' from ★Vickers, Sons & Maxim in Britain. Rechambered for the .30 M1906 cartridge, they proved to be sturdy and dependable. The increasing number of German Maxim guns captured by the AEF, particularly after the great German Spring Offensive in early 1918, inspired the Ordnance Department

to develop a .30 M1906 conversion kit. The MG.08 was, after all, little more than a minor variant of the US .30 M1904 Maxim. By substituting the barrel, changing the feed-block and using M1906 cartridges in the German feed belt, the guns could be put back into action. However, before mass conversion could be attempted, hostilities ended and the project was abandoned.

The Maxim was outstandingly successful, remaining in service in Russia, China and many other countries until the end of the Second World War. Indeed, the Soviet 1910-pattern *Pulemet Maxima* remained in production until 1944, and the British Vickers Gun, a comparatively straightforward adaptation of the original Maxim design with the locking mechanism inverted, was not declared obsolete until the 1960s. The best source of information on the Maxim Gun is *The Devil's Paintbrush – Sir Hiram Maxim's Gun*, by Dolph L. Goldsmith (Collector Grade Publications, revised and expanded edition, 1993).

MAYER & GRAMMELSPACHER

This partnership was founded in 1890 in Rastatt, Baden, by Jacob Mayer and a financier named Grammelspacher. Household goods were made until the first simple MGR air pistols, cocked by pressing the barrel inward, were produced in the mid-1890s. Mayer patented a method of latching an airgun breech, the subject of British Patent 20,559/01 of 1901, but soon had developed the Mayer Detent – a spring-loaded sliding bolt, protected by British Patent 7218/05 of 1905, which is still used on barrel-cockers.

Mayer & Grammelspacher prospered, using the *Diana name from c 1905; children's cork- and dart-firing toys were made under the Eureka brand. Catalogues dating from 1914 reveal the company to be making a Junior rifle, some *Gems, good-quality barrel-cocking rifles (nos. 26–28), and a pair of bolt-action trainers (known generically as *Mauser Verschluss*, or Mauser-type lock).

By 1923, the range had shrunk to the break-action Junior rifle, the simple No. 20, and the No. 27 and No. 27E barrel-cockers. More sophisticated designs appeared in the mid-1920s, with sporting-style half-stocks instead of the butt-only

pattern that previously had been universal across the range. The Model 25 was followed by the Model 35 (large) and Model 22 (small), and was accompanied by a pair of 'hinge-bolt' guns – No. 15 and No. 16 – patented in Germany in February 1930. A barrel-cocking pistol, the LP5, was patented in Germany on 13 December 1931 (DRP 524,329), and fixed-barrel underlever-cocking rifles were sold as the Models 48, 48E and 58. These were based on the *Jeffries Pattern BSA rifles that had been popular in Germany prior to 1914

The production of airguns ceased c. 1942; wartime M&G products (which often bore the letter code 'lkp') included butts and associated parts for the Gew. 43 and MP 43. Work stopped when the war ended and, in circumstances that have yet to be explained satisfactorily, the airgun machinery was sold to *Millard Brothers (Milbro) and installed in a newly-built factory in Carfin-by-Motherwell, Scotland. This created an anomalous situation, in which the Millards controlled the use of the Diana trademark in Britain, forcing Mayer & Grammelspacher to use the brand Original in British territory.

This situation lasted until the collapse of Milbro in the late 1980s.

Cork-firing toys were made in Rastatt in 1950, and gradually the airguns were put back into production; first was the LG15, in July 1951, but the LP5 did not reappear until August 1958. The first new gun was the Model 50 (May 1952), which offered the well-known Ball Sear for the first time. The greatest advance made in this period, however, was the perfection of a recoilless airgun patented in Germany in March 1956 by Kurt Giss (*see also* British Patent 803,028 of 15 October 1958). The first gun to incorporate the Giss contra-piston system was the LP6, introduced in April 1960. This barrel-cocking pistol was followed by the first barrel-cocking rifle, the LG 60 (February 1963), then by the LG65 (August 1968) and LG66 (March 1974); the LP10 competition pistol appeared in August 1974. A fixed-barrel sidelever-cocking LG 75 was introduced commercially in 1977. All of these guns are easily identified by the short transverse capped cylinder through the receiver.

Giss-system guns were successful throughout the 1970s and 1980s, but were expensive, complicated and difficult to make. The success at the highest competition levels of

---

of the American Civil War in 1861, marking them 'WM'. *See also* US arms inspectors' marks.

Maynard – 1. Edward P. Maynard, Washington, D.C., USA. Maynard's experiments with metallic-case cartridges began with US Patent 15,141 of June 1856, in which the base of a metal tube was closed by a waxed paper disc. Eventually he settled on a closed iron (later brass) tube brazed to a sturdy perforated base, combining excellent sealing properties with a rim that offered good purchase for an extractor. The earliest Maynard carbine did not succeed, but its replacement received excellent testimonials and was adopted by the US Treasury for service on revenue cutters. **2.** Maynard carbine. The perfected gun was an unconventional dropping-barrel design locked by a trigger-guard lever, which could tip the barrel to allow a new cartridge to be inserted directly into the chamber. Made by the *Massachusetts Arms Company, the guns fired a .35 or .50 copper-case cartridge, ignited by the flash from a cap struck by a centrally-hung hammer. Although its straight-comb wristless butt looked ungainly, the Maynard was light and handy. The earliest guns were made with tape primers and a folding back sight on the tang, behind the central hammer. Later government guns, produced exclusively in .50 calibre, lacked the tape primer and patch box, and had a conventional back sight on the barrel, above the frame hinge.

Federal purchases of Maynard carbines amounted to about 20,000 between 1 January 1861 and 30 June 1866. **3.** Maynard Arms Company, Chicopee Falls, Massachusetts, USA. Formed in 1857, reorganised c. 1873 and sold to Stevens in 1890. **4.** Maynard Tape Primer. Patented by Edward *Maynard, this was a mechanical feeder fitted to a number of guns, beginning with the *Jenks breech-loading carbines made by E. *Remington & Sons in the mid-1840s. The primer was also fitted to *Springfield rifle-muskets, *Sharps rifles and *Massachusetts Arms Company revolvers. It contained priming caps sandwiched between waterproofed paper strips, one being fed over the nipple every time the hammer was cocked.

Mayor. Ernest & François Mayor, Lausanne, Switzerland. Makers of the 6.35mm *Arquebusier pocket pistol.

'MB', 'M.B.' – 1. A floriated monogram, often superimposed on a sunburst motif. Correctly read as 'BM' (q.v.); used by *Bernardon-Martin et Cie of Saint-Étienne. **2.** Found on components for British No. 4 *Lee-Enfield rifles made during the Second World War by the Metal Box Company. This company was also allocated the area codes 'S66' and 'S67', but often used its initials instead.

'MBT' in a rectangular cartouche. Found on the grips of Brixia pistols produced by Metallurgica Bresciana gia Temprini. *See also* Glisenti.

'M.C.'. Found on shotgun cartridges loaded with explo-

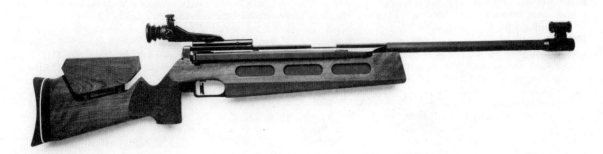

gas-powered guns and the single-stroke or pre-charged pneumatics offered by *Anschütz, *Feinwerkbau and *Walther forced Mayer & Grammelspacher to abandon all but a junior Giss-type gun in the 1990s; only the LP6 survives today. A similar fate befell a range of .22 rimfire target rifles, the 820 series, even though they offered some very good features at a highly competitive price.

There followed a period of trying, unsuccessfully, to be all things to all people, during which the company experimented with gaudily painted stocks and introduced the new Models 24, 26 and 34 (in 1984). The Model 36 and Model 38 followed in 1986. Today Mayer & Grammelspacher concentrates on barrel-cocking

spring-piston guns, in addition to the Model 48 and Model 52 (1987) sidelever-cocking sporting guns; the Model 54 Air King (1994), a sidelever-cocking sporter with a sliding-action recoil-suppressing system; and the Model 46 (1996), a modern underlever-cocking rival for the *Weihrauch HW77. Interestingly, the Model 46 retains the proven ball-sear mechanism. A solitary gas-powered revolver, the R357, was announced in 1997.

Little has been written in English about this company. Some details will be found in W.H.B. Smith, *Gas, Air & Spring Guns of the World* (1958 and various reprints), but a more reliable history is presented by John Walter, 'Diana Airguns. The Story of Mayer & Grammelspacher, Rastatt' in the

Mayer & Grammelspacher is best known for the Diana-brand airguns, although .22 rimfire target rifles have been made in small numbers in recent years. This is a 4.5mm Model 75 HV (Hohere Visierlinie, 'High-mounted Sight Line') sidelever-cocking recoilless spring-and-piston target rifle.

British magazine *Guns Review* (September/October 1983, March 1984). M&G products will also be found bearing marks applied by the principal distributors: Albrecht Kind (Akah) and Dynamit Nobel (RWS, Geco) in Germany; Frank *Dyke & Company (Sharmrock) and *Millard Brothers (Milbro) in Britain; *Hy-Score, *Stoeger, *Winchester and others in the USA.

---

sives supplied by Muller & Co.; *see* Clermont Explosives Company Ltd.

'MCCO'. A superimposition-type monogram with 'M', 'C' and 'C' equally prominent. Found moulded into the rubber grips of revolvers marketed by *Maltby, Curtis & Company.

Meade. Richard W. Meade, a commander in the US Navy, accepted revolvers made during 1861–68 by *Colt's Patent Fire Arms Manufacturing Company. Marked 'RWM', they included cap-lock patterns and, apparently, some of the earliest metallic-cartridge conversions. Date and pattern distinguish them from the guns accepted in later years by Robert W. *McNeely. *See also* US arms inspectors' marks.

Mears Brothers. A British gunsmithing business trading from 4 Tachbrooke Street, Pimlico, London S.W., between 1886 and 1892.

Mechanical... – 1. Mechanical repeating pistol. Although strenuous attempts were made to perfect the mechanical repeater in the last quarter of the nineteenth century – mainly in Bohemia – few had any lasting effect on technology. It is thought that the *Bittner pistol achieved the widest distribution, but it was never successful militarily. However, the mechanical repeaters developed by Josef *Laumann in the early 1890s led directly to the Schönberger auto-loader. *See also* Passler & Seidl and Weipert. **2.** Mechanical safety. This term is applied to any

method of ensuring that the action does not fire before the breech is closed properly. A mechanical safety is obligatory in an auto-loader, but is also present in most manually-operated rifles to ensure that the striker cannot reach the primer of a chambered round until the locking mechanism is engaged.

Medallion Grade. A term used by the *Browning Arms Company from 1961 onward, to distinguish Mauser-action sporting rifles with scroll engraving on the receiver and barrel and a select walnut stock. *See also* Olympian and Safari grades.

'Medicus'. A *headstamp found on some .41 rimfire cartridges made shortly after 1945 by the *Union Metallic Cartridge Company.

Medved. Also known as the Bear, this sporting rifle was made in the Izhevsk ordnance factory during 1965–73. It was chambered for the 8.2x53R and 9.2x53R sporting-rifle cartridges, both derived from the original Russian 7.62x54R service-rifle round. The rifle shared the gas system and rotating-bolt lock of the SVD, or *Dragunov, sniper rifle, although the receiver was refined and a conventional straight-comb butt was fitted. Military-style open sights and an under-barrel cleaning rod were standard fittings, while a stubby 4x optical sight was carried in a trapezoidal mount attached to the lower left side of the receiver.

'Medway' [The]. A mark found on shotgun cartridges,

probably made by *Eley Bros. (or at least from Eley components) for *Sanders of Maidstone. The name was that of the principal local river.

Meffert – 1. Imman. Meffert, Hubertus-Jagdgewehrfabrik, Suhl in Thüringen, Steinweg 22 (1940). This well-known German metalsmithing business, specialising in hunting and sporting guns, was founded by Immanuel Meffert in 1839. It was listed in 1900 as a gunmaker, under the stewardship of Friedrich Justin and Ernst Richard Meffert; in 1914, it operated under the ownership of Ernst Richard and Bruno Meffert; and, during 1920–45, was under the proprietorship of Bruno Meffert. Trading ceased when the Russians overran eastern Germany in 1945. A few air pistols seem to have been made under the *Hubertus brandname, and possibly also *Titan, 1928–33. Meffert's operations continued under DDR state control, but the company finally disappeared into the Ernst *Thälmann organisation in 1958/9. Today the Hubertus mark is associated with Albrecht *Kind. **2.** Paul Meffert, Suhl in Thüringen, Amtmannsweg 9 (1941). This gunmaker was active until the end of the Second World War, making sporting rifles and gun parts.

Megastar. A variant of the M45 *Firestar, made since 1992 by *Star–Bonifacio Echeverria SA. Chambered for the .45 ACP round, it has a full-length barrel and a large-capacity magazine.

Megette. L.J. Megette, identified by an 'LJM' mark, accepted US military firearms and accessories during 1898–1900. *See also* US arms inspectors' marks.

Méhier – 1. Méhier frères, rue de la Loire 3, Saint-Étienne, France. Listed in 1892 as a maker, distributor and agency for guns and ammunition. Possibly the successor to Méhier-Cédier et Cie (below). **2.** Méhier-Cédier et Cie, rue de Foy 11, Saint-Étienne, France. Listed in 1879 as a distributor of, and agent for, arms and ammunition.

Mehliser Waffen- & Armaturenfabrik, Huster & Hubing, Mehlis in Thüringen, Germany. Listed between 1900 and 1914 as a gunmaker and wholesaler, credited in the early twentieth century with the production of 100,000 'Handwaffen' annually. This seems unbelievable, owing to the low survival rate of guns marked by this particular business, unless they bore no special marks. Owned by Gustav *Hubing from c. 1912.

Meldrum. H.J. Meldrum, sometimes listed as 'Meldrun', accepted firearms and accessories made for the US Army by *Colt's Patent Fire Arms Manufacturing Company. Dating from c. 1898, they are customarily identified by 'HJM'. *See also* US arms inspectors' marks.

Melior. A mark found on a selection of 6.35mm-, 7.65mm- and 9mm-calibre automatic pistols made by *Manufacture Liégeoise d'Armes à Feu.

Melland. George S. Melland. A member of the London gun trade listed at 9 St Benet's Place, E.C., in 1861–63, then 38 Lime Street until the 1870s. According to W.W. Greener, writing in 1871 in *Modern Breech Loaders*, 'Mr Melland of Lime Street' entered a *Lancaster-patent breech-loading 12-bore shotgun in the trials undertaken by *The Field* in 1866.

Mendibe. *See* Garate & Mendibe SA.

Mendoza. Productos Mendoza SA, Mexico City. The manufacturer of a lever-operated Daisy-type spring-air gun designed by Rafael Mendoza, and also of a wide range of cartridge weapons.

Menta. Made by August *Menz of Suhl, apparently in the early 1920s, this *blowback semi-automatic pistol was a variant of the pre-1918 *Beholla. The 7.65mm Menta had a seven-round detachable box magazine in the butt, whereas the cartridge capacity of the short-grip 6.35mm pattern was just six. *See also* Leonhardt and Stenda.

Menz – 1. Albert Menz, Albrechts bei Suhl in Thüringen. A maker of gun parts active in Germany prior to 1939. Few other details are known. **2.** August Menz Waffenfabrik, Suhl in Thüringen, Germany. Founded in 1904. Listed in the 1914 edition of the *Deutsches Reichs-Adressbuch* as a gunmaker, in the 1920 edition as a gunsmith/gunmaker (owned by Alfred Menz), and between 1930 and 1939 as a gun-part maker/weapons maker, Menz produced a range of good-quality sporting guns. However, he is renowned for 6.35mm and 7.65mm *Beholla-type pistols manufactured in the early 1920s, and a range of 4.25mm and 6.35mm vest-pocket pistols (*Westentaschenpistole*) made in the late 1920s under the tradename *Liliput. Guns dating later than 1937 may be found with the marks of the company's successor, AG *Lignose of Berlin. The 1941 edition of the *Deutsches Reichs-Adressbuch* still listed 'Aug. Menz' operating at Schleusinger Strasse 122, Suhl, under the direction of Karl Menz, and it is assumed that trading did not cease until the end of the Second World War. **3.** Hugo Menz, Suhl in Thüringen, Germany. Trading as a gunmaker in 1914 and 1920. **4.** Karl Menz, Suhl in Thüringen. *See* Waffen-Versand-Haus. **5.** L. Menz, a government employee identified by an 'LM' mark, accepted US military firearms and accessories in 1907. *See also* US arms inspectors' marks. **6.** Menz & Co., Suhl in Thüringen, Germany. Listed in the 1939 *Deutsches Reichs-Adressbuch* as a gunmaker. Possibly the same as Waffenfabrik August Menz (above). **7.** Menz pistols. The *Beholla variants were replaced by an enlarged Liliput, known as the Modell II, chambered for the 6.35mm or 7.65mm cartridges. A 'new model' appeared in the 1930s, with the front underside of the frame cut away to give a streamlined effect. The P&B Modell III (external ring hammer) and P&B Modell IIIa (enclosed hammer), available in 6.35mm and 7.65mm versions, was a modernised design inspired by the Walther *Polizei-Pistole. The 'P&B' mark represented 'Polizei und Behörde' – 'Police and Authorities [model]'. The PB-Special of 1935 was a derivative of the P&B pattern with an exposed ring hammer and a double-action trigger mechanism; it will be encountered with 'Theodor *Bergmann Erben' or 'AG Lignose' marks instead of the Menz name.

'MER'. Found on US military firearms and accessories. *See* Mark E. *Reynolds.

Mercenier. Gunsmith Henri Mercenier of Liège, Belgium, is best known for a solid-frame revolver operated by pressing a ball-like catch ahead of the trigger guard to the left. This pivoted the cylinder out of the frame to the right, allowing the ball to be pushed forward to extract all six spent cases simultaneously. Made in .320, .380 and possibly also .44, apparently the design dates from the early 1880s.

Mercié. Henri Mercié. An engineer employed by *Hotchkiss, co-designer with Laurence V. *Benét of the Benét-Mercié Machine Rifle.

'Merco'. A mark used by Oskar *Merkel & Companie of Suhl.

Mercury. A barrel-cocking spring-and-piston air rifle

made in Britain by ★BSA Guns Ltd and its successors from 1971 until the 1990s, combining the appearance of the ★Airsporter with the 1959-patent barrel-block system of the ★Meteor. Made in .177 and .22, the Mercury progressed through several patterns: the Mark I of 1971–73 (serial numbers prefixed 'W' in .177, and 'Z' in .22); the Mark 2 of 1974–78 ('WB', 'ZB'); the Mark 3 of 1978–83 ('WC', 'ZC') with a bluff-contoured stock; and the Mark 4 of 1983–94 ('WC', 'ZC') with a slim rounded fore-end. The Mercury Target was a short-lived (1974–75) variant with aperture sights, and the Mercury S (1980–83; 'WH' in .177, 'ZH' in .22) had a walnut stock and a one-piece extruded cylinder. The Mercury S Mark 2 (1983–95; 'WH', 'ZH') introduced a stock with a slender round-tipped fore-end. A few guns have also been made in .20 and .25, but were often sold under different names (e.g. the .25-calibre Manchester Magnum, sold in the 1980s by Manchester Air Guns).

Meriden – **1.** A ★Suicide Special revolver made by the Meriden Fire Arms Company (below) of Meriden, Connecticut, USA, in the late nineteenth century. **2.** Meriden Fire Arms Company, 508 North Colony Street, Meriden, Connecticut (in 1908). This gunmaking business was created by ★Sears, Roebuck & Company c. 1893. Among its products were ★Fyrberg-type auto-ejecting revolvers and shotguns, sold under the A.J. Aubrey brand (named after the first factory superintendent) and ammunition marked 'M.F.A. Co.' in the headstamps. Then the company turned to five-shot .32 and .38 break-open guns, made c. 1905–14 in hammer or hammerless forms. **3.** Meriden Manufacturing Company, West Meriden, Connecticut, USA. This gunmaking business – probably founded c. 1863 – is best known for Triplett & Scott carbines, patented by Louis Triplett in 1864, but the company also offered the rifle-musket conversions and double-barrelled hammer shotguns designed by William H. and George W. ★Miller. Its president was Charles Parker, who subsequently allowed his sons not only to form ★Parker Brothers & Company, but also to take rights to the Miller shotguns with them.

Mérigneux, grande rue Saint-Roch 39, Saint-Étienne, France. Listed in 1879 as a gunmaker.

Merke. A compact Spanish 6.35mm-calibre Browning-type pistol made by F. ★Ormachea of Eibar, Guipúzcoa: six rounds, hammer fired.

Merkel – **1.** Bernh. Merkel, Suhl in Thüringen, Wolfsgrube 16 (1940). Listed in German trade directories for 1914–41 as a gunmaker. **2.** Ernst Merkel. Co-owner with Adolf Schade of Suhler Waffenwerke Gebr. Merkel (below). **3.** E.A. Merkel, Suhl in Thüringen, Rimbachstrasse 17 (1940). A gunmaker trading in Thuringia during the twentieth century. Listed in the Suhl district during 1900–20, under the ownership of Marie Merkel, and in 1930–39 as a weapons maker (proprietors, Ferd. and R. Merkel). **4.** Franz Merkel, Zella-Mehlis in Thüringen. This gunmaking business seems to have succeeded Udo ★Anschütz in the 1930s, then traded until the end of the Second World War. **5.** Gebhardt Merkel, Suhl in Thüringen. This man was listed in the 1930 *Deutsches Reichs-Adressbuch* as a gunmaker. **6.** Gebrüder Merkel, Suhl in Thüringen. This gunmaking business (claiming eighteenth-century pedigree, but in reality founded in 1898) rose to become one of Germany's leading manufacturers of sporting guns. Trade directories dating from 1900 usually

list the owners as Oskar, Gebhardt and Paul Merkel, changed to Gebhardt and Paul Merkel by 1914. By 1920, Suhler-Waffenwerk Gebr. Merkel, gunmaker, was still being operated by Gebhardt and Paul Merkel. By 1939, however, the proprietor was listed as Adolf Schade. In 1941, Gebr. Merkel, Suhler Waffenwerke was listed under the ownership of Ernst Merkel and Adolf Schade. Offices were maintained in Strasse der Stumabteilung, Suhl, with a factory at Rimbachstrasse 51. Although best known for shotguns, double rifles and combination guns of impeccable quality, Merkel also made ★Mauser-type sporting rifles prior to 1939. The actions were purchased from the Mauser factory in Obendorf and could be supplied in any of the standard Mauser chamberings. Most had long half-octagonal barrels and were stocked almost to the muzzle, the fore-end customarily being made in two pieces. Set triggers were common, although individual details were left to the whims of the purchaser. Ssometimes all that distinguished them was a 'GM' or 'G.M.' mark. Trading ceased in 1945, but the name was resurrected by the post-war nationalised DDR firearms industry The group containing Gebr. Merkel regained independence after the reunification of Germany, but worked only until 1997. *See* Haenel. **7.** Oskar Merkel & Co., Suhl in Thüringen, Schlageterstrasse 60 (1941). The owners of this German gunmaking business, founded in 1908, were listed in 1914 as Albert Oskar and Frau Merkel. This had changed to Albert Oscar, Paul and Frau Merkel by 1920, and to Albert Oskar, Paul and Franz Merkel by 1930. Paul Merkel had become sole proprietor by 1939, but trading ceased at the end of the Second World War. Sometimes the guns were marked 'MERCO'.

Merkur – **1.** This name was associated with a ★Mauser-type bolt-action sporting rifle sold by Albrecht ★Kind c. 1959–68. Built on refurbished military actions, possibly by ★Kriegeskorte, the guns had double set triggers, and half-stocks with hog's-back combs and small oval cheek pieces. They were chambered for cartridges ranging from .243 Winchester to 8x57. **2.** Merkur-Super. Sold by Albrecht ★Kind in 1968–77 or later, this ★Mauser-pattern sporting rifle replaced the ★Merkur and the ★Saturn. The walnut stock had a ★Monte Carlo comb.

Merkuria. A Czechoslovakian export agency, working from Argentinská 38 in Prague-7, distributor of firearms, and Czech-made ★Slavia and other airguns. It replaced ★Omnipol.

Merlett. John Merlett of Bound Book, New Jersey, USA, patented a 'breech-loading firearm' on 18 August 1868 (no. 81,283), assigned in part to John Smalley.

Merlin – **1.** Usually encountered as 'The Merlin'; a brandname used on shotgun cartridges sold by Charles ★Hellis & Sons of London. **2.** A small underlever-cocking air rifle made in the 1960s by ★BSA Guns Ltd in accordance with British Patent 978,502, granted in 1959 to Josef ★Veselý and Roger ★Wackrow. It was distinguished by a loading block that rose automatically as the action was cocked. The first version of 1962–64, made in .177 (K-prefix numbers) and .22 ('L' numbers), was replaced by a modified Mk 2 pattern ('KA', 'LA') with an automatic safety mechanism and a separate back sight. This variant lasted until the end of 1968, but only about 20,000 Merlins were made. **3.** Saint-Étienne, France. Listed in 1933 as a gunmaker.

Mermier et Cie, Saint-Étienne, France. Listed in 1879

(at rue Beaubrun 21) and 1892 (at rue Désirée 48) as a distributor of, and agent for, arms and ammunition.

Merriam. Lincoln A. Merriam, New York City, USA. This gunmaker was granted protection for breech-loading firearms on 19 January 1869 (US Patent 86,091) and 16 February 1869 (87,058). Magazine rifles followed on 11 February and 1 July 1879 (212,105 and 217,134 respectively).

Merrill – 1. George Merrill, East Orange, New Jersey, USA. Grantee of US Patents 119,939 and 119,940 of 17 October 1871, to protect breech-loading firearms. **2.** Ira M. Merrill, Springfield, Massachusetts, USA. Designer of 'hook attachments for bands of firearms' (US Patent 137,786 of 15 April 1873) and 'implements for firearms' (174,634 of 14 March 1876). **3.** James H. Merrill, Baltimore, Ohio, USA. This gunmaker was responsible for the so-called Merrill, Latrobe & Thomas carbine (below). The first Merrill gun to be issued officially, in the US Navy, was an Ames-made *Jenks adapted to handle combustible paper cartridges. The conversion was duly approved on 26 January 1861, guns of this general pattern being protected successively by US Patents 20,954 of 20 July 1858; 32,032 and 32,033 of 9 April 1861; 32,450 and 32,451 of 28 May 1861; 33,536 of 22 October 1861; and 40,884 of 8 December 1863. The major internal difference between the Jenks and Merrill actions was the annular copper disc on the latter's piston head. This was crushed momentarily by the pressure of firing, expanding outward to provide an effective gas seal. The carbines had a modified actuating lever, locking on the back sight base, and a conventional side-hammer lock; 5,000 were ordered on Christmas Eve, 1861. The earliest examples had an actuating lever with a flat knurled locking catch, and brass furniture. Later guns had the modified locking catch on the breech lever, and the patch box was eliminated. The .54-calibre Merrill rifles accepted sabre bayonets. The first guns had flat knurled breech latches, but these were superseded by a rounded pattern embodying a sprung plunger. The Federal authorities bought 14,495 carbines and 769 rifles prior to 30 June 1866; some guns were made for Merrill by the *Brown Manufacturing Company and, therefore, may be listed under 'Brown-Merrille'. **4.** Samuel Merrill. Co-founder with Joseph C. White of the *White-Merrill Arms Company of Boston. **5.** Merrill, Latrobe & Thomas. This carbine was designed by James Merrill in partnership with Latrobe and Thomas, embodying a rotary tap or 'faucet' breech protected by US Patent 14,077 of 8 January 1856. The guns were made under contract by E. *Remington & Sons, but were too complicated and soon failed. **6.** Merrill, Thomas & Company. A successor to *Merrill, Latrobe & Thomas, this gunmaking business was responsible for the earliest Merrill-type conversion of the *Jenks carbines. **7.** Merrill Patent Fire-Arm Manufact-uring Company, Baltimore, Maryland, USA. Active during 1860–69, this business promoted (but did not actually make) the plunger-breech rifles and carbines designed by James H. Merrill.

Merrimack Arms & Manufacturing Company, Newburyport, Massachusetts. Maker of *Ballard rifles, *Southerner cartridge derringers and an assortment of Martin and Beach sights during 1867–69, then succeeded by the *Brown Manufacturing Company.

Merveilleux. A name found on a repeating pistol produced by Manufacture Française d'Armes et Cycles of Saint-Étienne.

Merwin – 1. Joseph Merwin, New York City. Co-designer with Edward Bray of an auxiliary cap-lock ignition system used on the *Ballard rifle: US Patent 41,166 of January 1864. **2.** Merwin & Bray Fire Arms Company, New York City and Worcester, Massachusetts, USA. Active during 1863–68, this distributor of arms and equipment handled *Plant revolvers immediately after the American Civil War. Merwin & Bray was succeeded in 1868 by Merwin & Simkins, then by Merwin, Taylor & Simpkins (c. 1869–71), and finally by Merwin Hulbert & Company (below). **3.** Merwin, Hulbert & Company. The only military-pattern revolver to be offered by this wholesaler – trading from c. 1871 until superseded by *Hulbert Bros. & Company in 1891 – was the M1877, made by *Hopkins & Allen in accordance with patents granted to Benjamin *Williams, Daniel *Moore and William *Hulbert in 1874–77. The barrel was held to the standing breech only by the cylinder-axis pin and a lock on the frame ahead of the trigger guard, and could be swung laterally and drawn forward until a star-plate extractor, attached to the breech, pulled spent cases (but not unfired rounds) out of the cylinder. The open-frame design was weak, however, and soon was replaced by sturdier top-strap patterns. *See also* Double Action Army, Double Action Pocket Army, Pocket Army and Triumph.

Merz-Werke Gebrüder Merz GmbH, Frankfurt am Main. A metal-stamping agency and sub-contractor to *Haenel on the first German assault rifles, using the letter code 'cos'.

Metallwaren-, Waffen- & Maschinenfabrik. The German name for Fémaru Fegyver és Gépgyár (q.v.).

Metal Box Company. A maker of magazines for the British 9mm *Sten Gun during the Second World War. The company had several factories, and it is not clear which made the magazines. Most probably it was the Machine Section at Kendal Avenue, Acton, London W3, which used the code 'S 77'. *See also* British military manufacturers' marks.

Metallique, or Metallique-FN. *See* FN-Metallique.

'Metalode' [The]. This mark has been associated with Belgian-made alloy-case shotgun cartridges sold by *Le Personne of London.

Metcalf, Metcalfe – 1. William Metcalf. A supplier of sporting guns and ammunition to British military personnel, Metcalf maintained premises at the corner of Richmond and Shute Roads in the Catterick army camp. Shotgun cartridges made by *Eley-Kynoch have been reported with his marks. **2.** Henry Metcalfe, a lieutenant in the US Army Ordnance Department, accepted martial Smith & Wesson revolvers (1873–74), although his 'HM' identifier may be difficult to distinguish from a similar mark used in the mid-1870s by H. *Murdock. Metcalfe is also renowned for the quick-loading device that bears his name (below). *See also* US arms inspectors' marks. **3.** Metcalfe Quick Loader. Two prototypes were made in 1874, and about 1,000 single-shot M1873 Trapdoor Springfield rifles were produced in Springfield Armory in 1876, with a special detachable block containing eight cartridges, carried head-upward, on the right side of the stock.

METEOR

Meteor (2)

A barrel-cocking spring-and-piston air rifle made by *BSA Guns Ltd, incorporating a barrel-block designed by Josef *Veselý and Roger *Wackrow (British Patent 941,711 of 1959), a buffered pistol (937,658 of 19 May 1959) and an air cylinder made from a single piece of steel formed around a mandrel, then welded along the seam.

Several variants have been made: the Mark 1 of 1959–62 (serial numbers prefixed 'N' in .177 and 'T' in .22), with three flutes on each side of the fore-end; the Mark

2 of 1962–68 ('NA' and 'TA', 'NB' and 'TB' numbers) with a simpler back sight, a plain stock and a spring-loaded ball barrel-lock; the Mark 3 of 1969–73 ('NE', 'TE') with an O-ring seal on the piston and a reversion to the bolt detent; the Mark 4 of 1974–78 ('NG', 'TG') with improved sights; the Mark 5 of 1979–83 ('NH', 'TH') with an articulated cocking lever, a Power Seal piston and blunt-tipped fore-end; and the Mark 6 of 1983–95 ('NH', 'TH') with a slim round-tip fore-end.

Super Meteors have also been made, Mark 3 examples initially being numbered in a separate series (1968–69 – ND', 'TD'), then

intermixed with the standard Mark 3 (1969–73). These were followed by Marks 4, 5 and 6, numbered in the same series as ordinary guns. Their stocks customarily have Monte Carlo combs, ventilated rubber butt plates and deeper fore-ends than the standard version.

The .177 and .22 BSA Super Meteor Mk 5, distinguished by an articulated cocking lever and an angular fore-end with a rounded tip, dated from the period 1978–83. Note the rubber recoil pad on the butt and the distinctive shape of the cheek piece.

Meteor – 1. A knife pistol made by Joseph *Rodgers. **2.** A British airgun: *see* panel, above.

Metford. William Ellis Metford, born in 1824, was educated as an engineer, finding his first employment on the railway. His experiments into the accuracy of rifles began prior to 1850, arising from an interest in competitive shooting, and he has been credited not only with the bullets commonly ascribed to Richard E. *Pritchett, but also with the mechanically fitting projectiles credited to Joseph *Whitworth. Metford is best remembered for the distinctive polygonal rifling incorporated in rifles ranging from cap-lock match patterns to the .303 *Lee-Metford. He died in 1899, after several years of failing health.

Metropolitan – 1. A *Suicide Special revolver made by the *Crescent Arms Company of Norwich, Connecticut, USA, in the late nineteenth century. **2.** A brandname associated with shotguns made by the *Crescent Arms Company of Norwich, Connecticut, USA. **3.** Or Metropolitan Mark III. Made in 1969–72 by the Firearms Division of *Colt Industries, this was a variant of the Lawman, chambered specifically for .38 Special ammunition. It had a heavy 4in barrel. **4.** Metropolitan Fire Arms Company, New York City. This business began trading in 1864, capitalising on the fire that had destroyed Colt's Hartford factory. Its products included copies of the six-shot Navy Model, six-shot New Model Navy and five-shot .36 New Model Police Colts, identified by simple pivoting rammers. Many guns were unmarked, although some were produced for H.E. *Dimick & Company. **5.** Metropolitan Police. *Suicide Special revolvers made by the *Hopkins & Allen Arms Company of Norwich, Connecticut, *Maltby, Curtis &

Company and *Maltby, Henley & Company in the late nineteenth century.

'Mettax' [The]. Found on shotgun cartridges made by *Eley-Kynoch Ltd.

Mettoy Company Ltd [The], Northampton. A maker of magazines for the British 9mm *Sten Gun during the Second World War. The code 'M 634' may have been used instead of the company name. *See also* British military manufacturers' marks.

Metzner. Albin Metzner, Thüringer Waffenhaus, Zella St Blasii in Thüringen, Germany. Listed in pre-1914 directories as a gun and weapon maker. At that time, the business was owned by Albin, Georg and Max Metzner (although some entries suggest that this was one person).

Meunier – 1. A French Army officer, responsible for the 7mm Fusil A6 briefly adopted by the French Army prior to the First World War. **2.** A French gunmaker, listed in 1951 at 7 rue Jean-Baptiste David, Saint-Étienne.

Mewburn – 1. J.C. Mewburn was a patent agent, responsible for the affairs of Paul *Giffard, acting during the grants of British Patents 2077/86 of 1886, 11,050/89 of 1889 and 10,308/90 of 1890. The first notes Mewburn's address as 169 Fleet Street, the other two as 55 & 56 Chancery Lane. **2.** O.R. Mewburn & Company. Listed as gunmakers' agents in the London directories for 1874, with offices at 1 & 2 Fenchurch Street.

'Mexican Model' – 1. Found on small solid-frame .320 and .380 double-action revolvers made in Belgium prior to 1914 by Lepage et Cie of Liège. Normally they have vestigial round-butt grips and distinctive ring triggers. **2.** A nickname given by Smith & Wesson to 2,000 .38 Hand Ejector Target Model revolvers assembled immediately after the Second World War from *Military & Police Model components. They had Patridge front and micro-adjustable back sights.

Mexico City arms factory. The principal Mexican arms factory, maker of *Mauser and hybrid Mauser-Springfield rifles.

Meyer – 1. Place Villeboeuf 12, Saint-Étienne, France. Listed in 1892 as a gunmaker. **2.** Gustav Meyer, Zella-Mehlis in Thüringen, Germany. Listed in 1939 as a gun-stock maker. **3.** Gustav Meyer & Sohn, Zella-Mehlis. A maker of guns, gun parts and accessories, often identified simply by a Starrkrampf brandname. **4.** Michel Meyer, impasse Saint-Honoré 7, Saint-Étienne, France. Listed in 1879 as a gunmaker. **5.** Meyer Veuve, rue Gambetta 41, Saint-Étienne, France. Listed in 1892 as a gunmaker.

Meyers. Albert J. Meyers, or Myers, a major in the Federal Army, accepted signal pistols during the American Civil War, marking them 'AJM'. *See also* US arms inspectors' marks.

'MF', 'M.F.' – 1. In a rectangular cartouche, sometimes placed above the date of manufacture or reconstruction. Found on Chilean military weapons, usually confined to woodwork. Significance unknown. **2.** A monogram (encircled, enwreathed and/or two cannons in saltire) with the tail of 'M' forming the vertical of 'F'. Used on a range of guns and accessories made by *Manufacture Française d'Armes et Cycles de Saint-Étienne, also known as MFAC or Manufrance. These included the *Le Français pistol and a range of sporting rifles marketed under the *Bufalo brand.

MFAC. *See* Manufrance.

'MFACO', 'M.F.A. Co.' – 1. In a banner or cartouche, black-letter or sans-serif lettering. A mark used by the *Marlin Fire Arms Company. **2.** A headstamp associated with the *Meriden Fire Arms Manufacturing Company. It is assumed that the cartridges were made elsewhere. **3.** A superimposition-type monogram with 'M', 'F' and 'A' prominent. Used on revolvers made in the USA by the *Meriden Fire Arms Company. The style of the lettering can vary from cursive to angular.

'MG', 'M. & G.' These marks have been associated with *Mayer & Grammelspacher of Rastatt/Baden.

'MGB', 'MG B', 'MG' and 'B'. *Headstamps associated with the *Midland Gun Company of Birmingham, customarily restricted to shotgun cartridges.

'MGC', normally in a diamond. Correctly 'GMC' (q.v.); used by Garbi, Moretti y Cia of Mar del Plata.

'MGCB', 'MGC B', 'MGC' and 'B'. *Headstamps associated with the *Midland Gun Company of Birmingham, Warwickshire. They usually appear on shotgun ammunition.

'M.G.M.' A mark found in the headstamps of cartridges made by Manufacture Générale de Munitions of Bourges les Valence.

'MGR', on a target. This was used by *Mayer & Grammelspacher of Rastatt/Baden from c. 1895 until replaced by 'Diana' early in the twentieth century. A variant accompanied by two rubber-tipped darts in saltire was registered for use on children's guns in 1905. *See also* Eureka.

'MH&CO'. A superimposition-type monogram with 'M' and 'H' equally prominent. Found moulded into the rubber grips of revolvers marketed by *Maltby, Henley & Company.

'MHW'. A monogram, correctly read as 'WHM', found on sporting guns and shotgun ammunition. *See* William H. *Mark.

Micheels. Marius Micheels of Maastricht in the Netherlands was a distributor of sporting guns and ammunition active in 1911. He specialised in 'launch, yacht and ships' weapons'.

Micheloni. A burst of enthusiasm for combination weapons occurred in Britain in the mid-nineteenth century, owing to a rise in colonial wars. A patent protecting a cap-lock revolver-sabre was granted in 1864 to Isaiah Williams, acting for this Italian designer.

Michie. George M. Michie & Company. Trading in the Scottish city of Stirling, this gunsmith/ironmonger handled shotgun cartridges branded 'Michie's Unequalled', made from *Eley, or possibly Belgian, components prior to 1914.

Michigan Armament, Inc., Detroit, Michigan, USA. Maker of the *Guardian 27C (or 270) compact automatic pistol.

'Midget' [The]. A shotgun cartridge made by *Eley Bros. prior to the acquisition of the company by Explosives Trades Ltd in 1918. Also sometimes associated with ammunition handled by *Cogswell & Harrison.

Midland – 1. 'Midland' [The]. Found on shotgun ammunition loaded for H. *Clarke & Sons of Leicester, possibly by the *Midland Gun Company. **2.** A brand-name used by the US based *Gibbs Rifle Company on guns that were based on components acquired from *Parker-Hale. They have included the Midland 2100, built on an 1898-type *Mauser action in chamberings ranging from .22-250 to .308 Winchester. The Midland 2600 and Midland 2800 were similar, but had plain hardwood or laminated birch stocks instead of walnut. A Midland 2700 Lightweight was introduced in 1992. **3.** Midland Gun Company, Bath Street, Birmingham 4. This was a partnership of William *Baker and Arthur Herbert *Marsh, operating from the Bath Street Works (sometimes known as the Demon Gun & Gun Barrel Works). The business was founded at 77 Bath Street in 1888, but was listed in the Birmingham directories for 1890–1901 at 81 Bath Street, before moving to Vesey Street in 1902. Trading continued until the business was absorbed in 1956 by *Parker-Hale Ltd. The Midland Gun Company seems to have been a distributor of some guns while making others under the sub-contract. *See* *Lane Brothers, whose airguns appear to have been among the latter group. Baker and Marsh are thought to have produced a copy of the Langenhan *Millita as the *Bull's Eye, in addition to the *Demon and its variations, and air canes were still being sold in 1924. The Midland Gun Company was allotted the code 'M 170' during the Second World War, supplying the authorities with 1,450 12-bore shotguns in 1942. In addition to sporting rifles, shotguns and accessories, there was a bewildering selection of shotgun cartridges. Among the brandnames thus far identified are Best of All, Demon, Double Demon, Edward, Imp, Jubilee, Keeper, Rabbit, Record and Sudden Death. *See also* British military manufacturers' marks. **4.** Midland Gun Company. This trading name was used by *Parker-Hale on the Midland Model 2100 rifle, built on an 1893-type Spanish *Mauser action. *See also* Gibbs Rifle Company.

Mid-Range... – 1. Mid-Range Model. Dating from the

period 1878–85, the ★Ballard No. 4¹/₂ rifle had a pistol-grip butt, a half-length fore-end, and a peep-and-globe sight system. Chamberings ranged from .38-50 Ballard to .50-70 Government. The No. 4 A.1 of 1879–83 had an English walnut half-stock, Marlin's improved 800yd vernier back sight, and a wind-gauge front sight with bead and aperture discs. **2.** Mid-Range Rifle, No. 1 Pattern. Introduced by the ★Sharps Rifle Company early in 1876, this .40-70 gun had a half- or full-octagon barrel, a chequered pistol-grip butt, a nickelled rifle-type butt plate and vernier/spirit-level sights. The No. 2 was similar, with a plain finish and a straight-wrist butt; and the No. 3 was a No. 2 chambered for the .40-50 cartridge. **3.** Mid Range Target Rifle. Built during 1875–90 by E. ★Remington & Sons and the ★Remington Arms Company, on the basis of the No. 1 ★rolling-block action, this had a half-octagon barrel chambered for rounds ranging from .40-50 Sharps to .50-70 Government. A pistol-grip butt was usually fitted, together with globe and vernier aperture sights. *See also* Remington rifles, rolling-block action.

Mieg. Armand Mieg of Leipzig and Heidelberg, Germany, has been credited with at least part of the design of the 8mm ★Reichsgewehr. He was granted US Patent 400,472 of 2 April 1889 (jointly with H. Bischoff of Berlin) for a magazine rifle, and 533,911 of 12 February 1895 for a 'recoil-operated firearm'.

Mikros. Made in France by ★Manufacture d'Armes Pyrénées of Hendaye, the first six-shot 6.35mm and 7.65mm pocket pistols of this name were based – very closely – on the striker-fired ★Walther Modell 9 and FN-Browning respectively. They could be distinguished by their markings, which often included '*Fabrication Française*' ('French Make'). Post-1958 examples, the Unique Mikros (Mle 5, Mle 58 and Mle K), had squared contours, an enlarged trigger guard, a cross-bolt magazine release and an external hammer.

Milanović. Koká Milanović, Serbia. *See* Mauser.

Milbank – 1. Isaac M. Milbank, Greenfield Hill, Connecticut, USA. Milbank was granted a wide range of patents during the period 1862–77, but few of his designs encountered tangible success. The earliest patent, US 37,048 of 2 December 1862, protected a gun with a detachable powder chamber locked by a radial wedge in the back of the breech. The gun shown in the papers accompanying US Patent 46,125 of 31 January 1865 had a breech-block that could be swung laterally on a longitudinal pin once a wedge-plate lock had been swung clear. US Patent 52,734 of 20 February 1866 was granted for a lifting-block breech locked by a wedging bar that slid down into the floor of the receiver to take the shock of firing; US Patent 55,520 was granted on 12 June 1866 to protect a variation of this locking system with a locking lever that swung laterally. US Patent 61,082 (granted on 8 January 1867) protected a rotary breech plug that lifted up and forward, whereas 61,751 of 5 February 1867 showed a block that swung sideways. Comparable in general terms to the ★Needham system, the side-swinging-block Milbank was tested by the US Army in 1867 on a converted .58-calibre Springfield rifle-musket. Subsequently Milbank received US Patent 65,585, on 11 June 1867, to protect a breech-block that swung upward at the rear when a rotary lateral locking-bar had been released. US Patent

84,566 of 1 December 1868 protected an improved version of the side-swinging breech (61,751, above) with an internal striker instead of an external side hammer. The rifle shown in drawings accompanying US Patent 125,829 of 16 April 1872 was a bolt-action pattern with a trigger safety system and a separate inertia striker; the mechanism was locked by pivoting the breech-lever base plate so that it abutted the receiver. US Patent 136,850 of 18 March 1873 allowed claims for an improved bolt-action rifle, based on 125,829, with the locking latch set in the under-edge of the operating handle. Milbank's last patent, 147,567 of 17 August 1874, protected yet another improvement of his bolt-action design. Although Isaac Milbank was never able to convince the US authorities of the merits of his rifles, a modified form was adopted in Switzerland once improvements had been made to the design by Rudolf Amsler. **2.** Milbank-Amsler rifle. Patented in the USA by Isaac Milbank in 1866, then adapted by Rudolf Amsler of Schaffhausen, this swinging-block mechanism was adopted in Switzerland on 22 December 1866. The block hinged laterally once the hammer had been retracted to half-cock; a spring-loaded striker ran slightly diagonally through it. Several conversions were made, including the M1851–67 short rifle, the M1856–67 short rifle, the M1863–67 infantry rifle, the M1864–67 short rifle (all 10.4mm) and a selection of 18mm-calibre ex-French Mle 1840 T.59 and Mle 1842 T.59 infantry rifles.

'Milbro' – 1. Found on ★Mayer & Grammelspacher Diana spring-air guns sold by Millard Bros. of London, prior to 1945. **2.** Found on copies and derivatives of the ★Mayer & Grammelspacher Diana spring-air guns made by ★Millard Bros. Ltd of London, and ★Milbro Ltd of Carfin by Motherwell, 1949–82.

Milburn – 1. Usually found as 'The Milburn'. A shotgun cartridge loaded by ★Milburn & Son of Brampton, using components supplied by ★Eley-Kynoch. **2.** Milburn & Son. The name of this English gunmaking business has been reported on shotgun cartridges sold under such brandnames as Don, Milburn, M.S.B., Noxall and Rex. Trading was undertaken from 5–7 Cross Street, Brampton, Cumberland.

'Milford' [The]. A mark associated with shotgun cartridges sold by ★Jobson of Milford.

Militär-Pistole (Military Pistol). A term associated with an enclosed-hammer predecessor of the P. 38, better known as the Armee-Pistole (q.v.), and also with a prototype of the P. 38 made by Carl ★Walther Waffenfabrik c. 1938.

Military, Military... – 1. Found on a Spanish 6.35mm Browning-type automatic made by ★Retolaza Hermanos of Eibar: six rounds, hammer fired. **2.** Military Armament Corporation, Powder Springs, Georgia, USA. Promoter of the ★Ingram submachine-gun, c. 1966–75. **3.** Military Creedmoor Rifle. *See* Long Range Military Creedmoor Rifle. **4.** Military Model. An alternative name for the Model 4S ★Remington rifle (rolling-block action), also known as the Boy Scout's Rifle, made by the Remington Arms Company between 1913 and 1933. **5.** Military Model. Often used as a generic term, but specifically associated with a variant of the 1902-pattern ★Browning locked-breech pistol made by Colt's Patent Fire Arms Manufacturing Company. It had diced panels on the front

MILITARY & POLICE MODEL

Military (6)

This Smith & Wesson handgun was known originally as the Hand Ejector Military & Police. A .38 six-chamber swing-cylinder revolver, now built on the medium or K-Frame, it was introduced commercially in 1899 and has progressed through several patterns since. The original, or First Model, gave way to the Second Model in 1902, then to the Third Model, or Model of 1905, after nearly 62,500 guns had been made.

The Model 1905 underwent a series of changes until work finally stopped in 1942, after about 927,500 had been made with a variety of barrel lengths. The total included more than 568,000 guns produced for the British forces during 1940–45, chambered for the British .38/200 (.38 S&W) cartridge instead of the .38 S&W Special version. Guns made after 10 April 1942 had plain wood grips and a Parkerised finish. When the serial numbers reached 1000000, they began again at V1 (*see* Victory Model).

Production was resumed after the Second World War, using a simple S-prefix to distinguish the guns from the last of the 'VS'-marked Victory Models. A new short-hammer-throw version appeared in 1948, at S990184, and a new C-prefix series began when the million had been reached again. The C-prefix series reached C999999 in November 1967, when D-numbers were employed.

When numerical designations were introduced, the standard .38 Special Military & Police revolver became the Model 10; the Model 11 (c. 1948–63) was a variant that chambered the British .38/200 cartridge; the Model 12 was the *Airweight pattern; the Model 13 was a .357 Magnum variant, introduced in 1974 to satisfy the New York State Police; the Model 64 (c. 1970–83) was the .38 S&W Special Stainless Steel Military & Police, and the Model 65, developed for the Oklahoma Highway Patrol in 1974, was a .357 Magnum version of the Model 64. A heavy-barrel option was introduced in 1959, these guns being distinguished by barrels that had parallel sides instead of the customary tapered shape.

The Model 58 Magnum Military & Police revolver of c. 1964–85, chambered for the .41 Magnum cartridge, had a 4in barrel and fixed sights. It did not prove popular, and only a few thousand were made. The Model 547 Military & Police was a short-lived variant chambered for the 9mm Parabellum (9mm Luger) round, with a snubbed hammer and a sharply-curved grip to improve control; it was abandoned in 1985.

The Smith & Wesson Model 64 Stainless was a variant of the original Model 10 Military & Police Revolver.

---

of the slide, a slide-lock and a hold-open catch, and a lanyard ring on the butt. The magazine held eight rounds instead of seven. **6.** Military & Police Model. A revolver made by *Smith & Wesson: *see* panel, above.

Millard Brothers Ltd, London and Carfin by Motherwell. This company was founded in 1887 by Oliver L. and Samuel E. Millard, with premises in Stockwell Road, London S.W. Incorporation occurred in 1900, and Millard Brothers Ltd moved to Caledonian Road, London N7, in 1926. Millard Brothers supplied *Savage rifles to the British authorities in 1941. Shortly after the Second World War, the company purchased the entire movable contents of the *Mayer & Gammelspacher factory in Rastatt from Allied occupation authorities, and the Carfin Works, Wishaw, Motherwell, Scotland, opened in 1949. Many *Diana rifles were assembled from existing pre-1939 components, and production of several pre-war models began on ex-German machinery. Millard Brothers joined the Grampian Group (Grampian Holdings Ltd) in 1961, and by the 1970s had developed a new line of Diana rifles to replace the old Mayer & Grammelspacher patterns. Pistols were also made, including push-in barrel designs and the G4 series based on the pre-1939 Moritz & Gertensberger *Zenit, which suggests that Millard Brothers also acquired equipment from elsewhere. In addition to making Diana rifles, the company also imported Daisy products and Russian *Baikal shotguns. These were customarily sold under a new G-prefix designation. The G5 *Cougar pistol and G85/1 *Bobcat rifle were often sold under the brandname Caledonian, but Milbro collapsed in the mid-1980s and was liquidated. A successor company, Milbro Caledonian Pellets Ltd, was salvaged to continue the well-established production of airgun ammunition.

Miller – 1. Arthur Miller. An engineer employed by *ArmaLite, Inc., credited with transforming the unsuccessful AR-16 rifle into the AR-18 in 1964–65. **2.** Calvin Miller, Canadia, New York State. A US gunmaker active from 1837 to 1861. **3.** G.E. Miller, a government employee, accepted firearms and accessories on behalf of the US Army during 1905–06, using a 'GEM' identifier. *See also* US arms inspectors' marks. **4.** James Miller, Brighton and Rochester, New York State. A gunmaker active until 1843, then succeeded by John Miller (below). **5.** John Miller, Rochester, New York State. Successor to James Miller, trading from 1843 onward. **6.** William H. Miller, West Meriden, Connecticut, USA. This gunmaker was granted a number of firearms-related patents, beginning with 47,902 of 23 May 1865. Granted jointly with George W. Miller, this rifle-musket conversion system (with a lifting breech-block) was assigned to Edmund Parker and the ★Meriden Manufacturing Company. US Patent 51,739 of 26 December 1865 protected a 'breechloading firearm' with a radial breech-block, and 59,723 of 13 November 1866 protected a breech-loading shotgun with a spring-loaded locking bar in the top of the breech. This bar was pushed out of engagement by a vertically sliding latch ahead of the trigger guard, guns of this type being made by the Meriden Manufacturing Company, then by ★Parker Bros. & Company. Miller's last patents were US 64,786 of 14 May 1867 and 68,099 of 27 August 1867 (both jointly with G.H. Miller), protecting a radial-breech firearm and an ejector respectively. **7.** William R. Miller, Baltimore, Maryland, USA. Believed to have been the son of William H. Miller (above), this mechanic received three US Patents protecting loading indicators for magazines: 394,872 of 13 December 1888, 387,531 of 7 August 1888 and 393,653 of 27 November 1888. He was also granted US Patent 395,913 of 8 January 1889 ('hammer for firearms') and 404,921 of 11 June 1889 for a method of changing the balance of sporting guns at will.

'Millita'. This mark is associated with spring-air guns made by Friedrich ★Langenhan for Martin ★Pulvermann & Company of London, prior to 1914.

Mills – **1.** J. Mills, active in the mid-1870s, accepted firearms and accessories on behalf of the US Army. Marked simply 'JM', they can be difficult to distinguish from equipment attributed to John ★Maggs, Julian ★McCallister and Justice ★Murphy. **2.** W.M. Mills, a US government inspector using a 'WMM' identifier, accepted military firearms and accessories in the mid-1890s. *See also* US arms inspectors' marks for both entries.

Mimard – **1.** Étienne Mimard, also listed erroneously as 'Mimort', 'Minard' and 'Minort', Saint-Étienne, France. A director of ★Manufacture Française d'Armes et Cycles; designer of the ★Le Français pistol patented in France in 1913. **2.** Mimard et Blachon, cours Fauriel, Saint-Étienne, France. Listed in 1892 as a gunmaker. Étienne Mimard and Pierre Blachon were the founders of ★Manufacture Française des Armes et Cycles.

Minerva. A Browning-type pocket automatic made in Eibar, Spain, by Fabrique d'Armes de ★Grande Précision: 6.35mm, seven rounds, hammer fired.

Miniature Pattern Rifle. A term applied to the ★Martini cadet rifles used by several individual Australian states, and also by the Commonwealth of Australia after its formation in 1900.

Mini-Beryl. A short-barrelled version of the Polish Beryl assault rifle, a variant of the ★Kalashnikov.

MiniMax. Made in Hungary in recent years, this squeeze-grip repeating pistol may be chambered for 9mm Short, 9mm Makarov or 9mm Parabellum cartridges. Among its advantages are one-handed operation and compact dimensions: the 9mm Short/9mm Makarov version is 96mm long, 68mm deep and 24mm thick.

Ministry of Light Industrial Production, Peking (Beijing), People's Republic of China. This agency has been responsible for the development of the PRC airgun industry, based on the Ministry's factories in Peking, Shanghai (I-Brand and Industry Brand) and Tientsin (Tianjin). The guns have been made under such names as Arrow (Shanghai), Deer (Tientsin), Lion (Peking), Hunter (Shanghai), Super Hunter (Shanghai), Mao (Tientsin) and Pioneer (Shanghai).

Minneapolis Fire-Arms Company, Minneapolis, Minnesota, USA. This distributor promoted the seven-shot .32 Short rimfire Protector turret pistol, patented by Jacques ★Turbiaux. The guns were made by the ★Ames Sword Company and usually have a manual safety lever. Subsequently distribution was switched to the ★Chicago Firearms Company.

Minnesota Arms Company. A brandname associated with shotguns made by the ★Crescent Arms Company.

Minories, or The Minories. A name given to a small district of London, close to the Tower of London (later known as EC3), once the centre of the city's gunmaking industry. The name derived from a 'minor' abbey of the nuns of St Clare, replaced in the sixteenth century by storehouses for arms and armour, then by the gunsmiths. However, with the rise of mass-production in the middle of the nineteenth century, the Minories lost ground to the ★London Armoury Company and to 'Best' makers (e.g. ★Purdey) clustered in St James's. By 1891, one observer recorded that the district was a place of 'general trade, without a gunsmith from end to end'.

Minx. A .22-calibre pocket automatic pistol made by Pietro ★Beretta of Gardone Val Trompia, Brescia, Italy.

Miroku Firearms Manufacturing Company, or Miroku Taiyo Zuki, Japan. A maker of handguns, bolt-action rifles and shotguns.

'Mirus' [The]. A brandname reportedly found on shotgun cartridges sold by ★Kavanagh & Son of Dublin, Ireland.

Misr. An AKM-type ★Kalashnikov copy made by Factory No. 54 of Maadi Military & Civil Industries Company. Guns of this type were sold in the USA during the 1970s by Steyr-Daimler-Puch of America, Inc., under a variety of names and designations, including ARM. Intended for sporting and security use, invariably these guns were restricted to semi-automatic fire.

Mississippi Valley Arms Company. A brandname associated with shotguns manufactured by the ★Crescent Arms Company.

Mitraille. *See* Buffalo-Mitraille.

Mitrailleuse ('Grape Shooter') – **1.** *See* panel, p. 356. **2.** Mitrailleuse Pistol. A few of these interesting four-barrel repeaters were made during the 1880s by the ★Braendlin Armoury Company Ltd of Birmingham, and marketed by Joseph ★Marres of London as the Martini-Marres-Braendlin Mitrailleuse. The self-cocking trigger mechanism was protected by British Patent 1531/80, granted to A. ★Martini in April 1880. **3.** Mitrailleuse à Poche. The original name for the French Gaulois pistol.

Mixte. *See* Express-Mixte.

MITRAILLEUSE

Mitrailleuse (1)

This sophisticated volley-gun, an early competitor of mechanically-operated guns, such as the *Gatling, was the work of a Belgian artillery officer named Fafschamps. Developed in the early 1850s, it was patented in 1867 by Joseph

Montigny and Louis Christophe. A few guns were made in Belgium by *Montigny & Mangeot, but the basic design attained greater notoriety during the Franco-Prussian War.

The French Mitrailleuse was an improved 25-barrel form of the Belgian prototype. Credited to de *Reffye and Pothier, 190 were made in the Atelier de Meudon

during 1866–68. In general, the weapon was not employed to tactical advantage during the Franco-Prussian War, although when deployed properly as an infantry-support weapon (at St Privat for example), it was effective. Consequently, the volley guns failed to have the decisive effect predicted by promoters. Their day had passed by 1875.

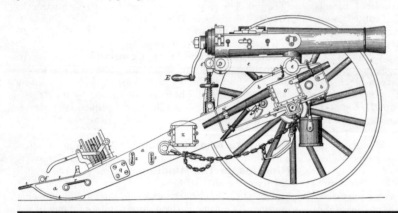

A drawing of the French 11mm De Reffye Mitrailleuse, or 'Grape Shooter', used with promise, but no distinction in the Franco-Prussian War of 1870–71.

MK. *See* Maxim-Kolesnikov.

MKE. Makína Kímya ve Endüstrísí, the principal Turkish small-arms manufacturer.

'ML', 'M.L.', sometimes in monogram form. A trademark associated with *Manufacture Liègeoise d'Armes à Feu, found on a range of revolvers, in addition to automatic pistols in 6.35mm, 7.65mm and 9mm calibre.

'MM'. Found on US military firearms and accessories. *See* M. *Moulton.

'MMJ' – 1. Found on US military firearms and accessories. *See* Martin M. *Johnson. **2.** Associated with the designs of Melvin M. *Johnson, including the 5.7mm MMJ Spitfire cartridge and a variant of the *M1 Carbine.

'MMMM', in the form of a cross, each limb being crowned. Found on Romanian weapons: the mark of King Míhaí I (1927–30, 1940–47). *See also* Cyphers, imperial and royal.

'MO'. A superimposition-type monogram, sometimes encircled, with neither letter prominent. Correctly 'OM'; used by *Ojanguren y Marcaido.

Mock. August Mock, New York City. Mock was primarily a surgical-instrument maker, according to directories prior to 1867, but, after being listed as a machinist and toolmaker, had become a gunsmith by 1875. His gunmaking operations ended shortly after 1880. Premises were listed successively at 59 Lewis Street, 89 Thompson Street and 211 Spring Street in New York. Mock is best known for spring-air *Gallery Guns.

Moddite. This was a modified form of *Cordite, introduced in 1908 by *Eley Bros. Ltd and loaded in all types of 'express and military cartridges of .475 bore and under'.

Modèle de Poche. A generic term ('Pocket Model') for any small revolver or automatic pistol, but specifically associated with the products of *Fabrique Nationale, *Manufacture Française d'Armes et Cycles and Nicolas *Pieper.

Model Four. An auto-loading sporting rifle introduced by the *Remington Arms Company in 1981 to replace the Model 742, chambered for cartridges ranging from 6mm Remington to .308 Winchester. The chequered woodwork had a high-gloss polyurethane finish. The Model Four *Peerless (4D) was a variant of the standard rifle with an engraved receiver; the Model Four *Premier rifle (4F) had game scenes inlaid in gold. The Model 7400 was essentially similar to the Model Four, but – at least until the mid-1980s – had a much plainer finish. A short-barrelled carbine variant was offered briefly in .30-06.

Modern Arms Company, Marco House, 28 Marshalsea Road, Southwark, London SE1, in 1930–34. This company is known to have distributed *Haenel air-guns from about 1928 until the outbreak of the Second World War.

Moeller & Kellner, Zella St Blasii in Thüringen, Germany. Listed in 1900 as a gunmaker.

Moggridge. John James Moggridge, or 'Muggridge'. An English gunmaker operating during 1849–50 from 23 Bath Place, New Road, London. Probably the son of James Moggridge, an itinerant gunmaker listed in London in the census of 1841, he was born c. 1826.

Mohawk – 1. *Suicide Special revolvers made by the *Crescent Arms Company of Norwich, Connecticut, or the Rome Revolver & Novelty Works of Rome, New York State. All date from the late nineteenth century. **2.** A name found on shotguns made by the *Crescent Arms Company of Norwich, Connecticut. **3.** Or Mohawk 600: a name applied to 660-series bolt-action rifles made by the *Remington Arms Company prior to 1972, but still being distributed in the mid-1970s. **4.** Mohawk Arms Company. A *Suicide Special revolver made by Otis *Smith of Middlefield and Rock Fall, Connecticut, in the late nineteenth century. **5.** Mohawk Brown. A name applied to a version of the *Remington *Nylon 66 auto-loading rifle with brown synthetic butt and fore-end. *See also* Apache Black and Seneca Green. **6.** 'Mohawk Mfg. Co.' A mark found on shotguns made in the USA by the *Crescent Arms Company.

Mohegan. A *Suicide Special revolver made by Otis *Smith of Middlefield and Rock Fall, Connecticut, in the late nineteenth century.

Molgora. Modesto Molgora. The Italian manufacturer of *Oklahoma and other break-barrel spring-air pistols dating from the 1960s, and also of 5.6mm (.22) starting pistols. Sometimes they were marked 'Mondiale'.

Moll Sportwaffenfabrik, Lauenberg an der Elbe, Schleswig-Holstein, Germany. This airgun manufacturer – or perhaps retailer – was linked by Dr J.S.E. Gilbart (in an article in *Guns Review* in 1981) with the brandname *Hubertus and the production of push-in-barrel pistols during 1895–1910. However, Gilbart lists the company as Sportwaffen Fabrik, Moll Lauenberg, but it seems clear that 'Moll' is part of the name rather than a location. *See also* Imman. *Meffert, Suhl.

Möller – 1. E. Möller, Zella-Mehlis in Thüringen, Germany. Listed in 1930 as a master gunsmith. **2.** Max Möller, Zella-Mehlis in Thüringen. Listed during 1930–39 as a gun-barrel maker.

Molo. *See* Lindner & Molo.

'Molto' [The]. Found on British shotgun cartridges loaded by the *Cogschultze Ammunition & Powder Company Ltd, in 1911–14.

'Molton' [The]. Associated with shotgun ammunition made for T.H. *Moor of South Molton and Exford; source unknown.

Mommer. *See* Bildstein, Mommer & Co.

Monarch – 1. *Suicide Special revolvers made by the *Hopkins & Allen Arms Company of Norwich, Connecticut; *Johnson, Bye & Company and/or *Iver Johnson of Worcester and Fitchburg, Massachusetts. All date from the nineteenth century. **2.** A tradename associated with ammunition made by the *Federal Cartridge Company of Minneapolis.

'Mondial'. Found on Spanish 6.35mm pocket pistols made by Gaspar *Arizaga of Eibar, Guipúzcoa.

Mondiale. *See* Molgora.

Mondragon – 1. Manuel Mondragon (1858–1922) was a Mexican gun designer/patentee, best known for his straight-pull bolt-action rifle and the semi-automatic weapon adopted by the Mexican Army in 1908. **2.** Mondragon automatic rifle. This gas-operated design originated in the 1890s, although progress was slow; its US Patent was not sought until August 1904, and adoption by the Mexican Army (as the *Fusil Automatico de 7mm 'Porfirio Diaz'*) was delayed until 1908. The perfected guns were made in Switzerland by *SIG. Four hundred reached Mexico prior to the 1911 revolution, but the remainder were stored until sold to Germany as *Flieger-Selbstlade-Karabiner Modell 1915*. Adopted in December 1915, the German Mondragons proved to be prone to jamming and unable to endure rigorous front-line service. Most were passed to the navy; Kiel dockyard still had nearly 500 when the war ended. **3.** Mondragon bolt-action rifle. This interesting straight-pull design, developed in 1891/92, was tested successfully by the Mexican Army in 1893/94. A sliding handle on the right side of the receiver operated a separate bolt (doubtless inspired by

the Swiss *Schmidt-Rubin), but a unique selector system allowed the gun to be fired automatically, and in perfect safety, as the breech closed. This feature was intended to give 'fire on the march', allowing soldiers to fire from the hip as they advanced toward the enemy. Guns made prior to 1893 chambered 6.5mm rimless cartridges, but the 1894 pattern fired unique high-pressure 5.2x68 ammunition loaded with 'piston bullets'. With the exception of a prototype or two, all the guns were made by *Schweizeische Industrie-Gesellschaft. They had locking lugs in two widely separated rows.

Monitor – 1. A *Suicide Special revolver made by the *Whitney Arms Company of Whitneyville, Connecticut, USA, in the late nineteenth century. **2.** A brandname associated with shotguns manufactured by the *Crescent Arms Company.

Monk – 1. Henry Monk was the successor to W.H. Monk (below), trading in Chester, England, until the 1950s. His marks have been found on shotgun cartridges supplied by *Eley-Kynoch. **2.** William Henry Monk, or Monks. Established by 1868 at 65 Foregate Street, Chester, Cheshire, this English gunmaker handled sporting guns and ammunition, including shotgun cartridges made by *Eley prior to 1914. Business had passed to W.H. Monk's son, Henry, by the early 1920s. Monk customarily used a trademark in the form of a 'WHM' monogram and a rabbit disappearing into a corn-stook.

Monobloc. *See* Le Monobloc.

'Monocle' [The]. A mark found on 12-bore shotgun ammunition made by *Eley-Kynoch for *Stanbury & Stevens of Exeter.

Monograms. *See* panel, p. 358.

Mono Trap, or *Daytona Mono Trap. A single-barrel 12-bore shotgun made by *Società Armi Bresciane on the basis of the standard over/under action. It has a pistol-grip butt with a Monte Carlo comb, a beavertail fore-end, a ventilated top rib and a single trigger. Normally barrels are 810 or 860mm long.

Monotype – 1. Monotype Corporation Ltd [The], Salfords, Redhill, Surrey. A major part of the *Monotype Scheme, this British typefounding business made a variety of components for the *Bren Gun during the Second World War. Often marked with the code 'S 81', they ranged from springs and pins to Mk III bodies and bipods. Assembly of guns was also undertaken in the Salfords factory. **2.** Monotype Scheme [The]. Promoted enthusiastically by Monotype & May Ltd, this was a method of making *Bren Guns by combining 'syndicated' components, minimising disruption if any individual factory was disabled by an air raid. The principal participants were the *British Tabulating Machine Company Ltd, *Climax Rock Drill & Engineering Ltd, the *Daimler Motor Company Ltd, the *Hercules Cycle & Motor Company Ltd, the *Monotype Corporation Ltd, F. *Tibbenham Ltd and *Sigmund Pumps Ltd. Individual components were assembled in the Monotype factory in Salfords, 83,438 guns being made during 1940–45.

Montagnon, rue Saint-Jean-Baptiste 6, Saint-Étienne, France. Listed in 1892 as a gunmaker.

Montagny – 1. Montagny aîné, rue Saint-Roch 20, Saint-Étienne, France, in the 1890s. Listed in 1892 as a gunmaker. Still trading in 1933, and in 1951 at 48 rue Gambetta. **2.** Régis Montagny, place Villeboeuf 9, Saint-Étienne, France. Listed in 1892 as a gunmaker.

MONOGRAMS

The penchant for this method of marking dates back to the nineteenth century, the origins perhaps lying in the successful development of methods of moulding grips and rubber fittings. These were particularly popular on pre-1914 revolvers, the first perhaps dating from the 1880s. The mould makers were keen to show their skills in handling the tiniest of design details, and the results could be very impressive technically, but often almost totally illegible. This is particularly true of concentric and superimposed lettering, although linear designs are frequently significantly easier to read.

There are three basic types of monogram: superimposed, with the letters on top of each other or intercutting; concentric, where they take a circle-within-circle form; and linear, where the letters, while conjoined, are in a sequence that can be read as a continuous string. However, the characteristics can be blurred by superimposing only a few of the letters. This makes it difficult to decipher monograms – letter forms may be too distorted, or the dominant letter difficult to

determine – and they have been listed in the directory under each of the most obvious permutations.

A mark that apparently reads 'ABC', therefore, could be listed under 'ACB', 'BAC', 'BCA', 'CAB' or 'CBA', and it may be necessary to try several possible sequences before an answer can be found. A monogram containing five different letters of equal significance has 120 possible permutations, so attempts have been made – helped by the subordination of 'CO.' or 'Co.', for 'Company' – to assess dominant letter(s) in each trademark in an effort to keep entries to a minimum.

1. *Accuracy International.* 2. *American Arms Company.* 3. *Chartered Industries of Singapore.* 4. *Davis-Warner Arms Corporation.* 5. *Deutsche Waffen- & Munitionsfabriken (DWM).* 6. *G.C. Dornheim (Gecado).* 7. *Fabrique Nationale d'Armes de Guerre/FN Herstal SA.* 8. *Andrew Fyrberg & Co.* 9. *Heckler & Koch GmbH.* 10. *Hopkins & Allen.* 11. *Lebeau-Courally & Cie.* 12. *Manufacture Française d'Armes et Cycles (Manufrance).* 13. *Maltby, Curtis & Co.* 14. *Maltby, Henley & Co.* 15. *Heinrich Ortgies.* 16. *Pacific Arms Co.* 17. *Rheinische Metallwaaren- & Maschinenfabrik (RMF).* 18. *Sears, Roebuck & Co.* 19. *Sellier & Bellot.* 20. *Smith & Wesson.* 21. *Venuswaffenwerke.* 22. *Warner Arms Co.*

1.   2.   3.

4.   5.   6.

7.   8.   9.   10.   11.   12.   13.   14.

15.   16.   17.   18.   19.   20.   21.   22.

Montana... – 1. Montana Armory, Inc., Big Timber, Montana, USA. A maker of re-creations of the single-shot 1885-type Winchester dropping-block rifle. **2.** Montana Model. Made only during 1882–83, the *Ballard No. 5½ rifle usually had a ring-tip breech lever and chambered the .45 Sharps cartridge.

Montcoudiol, Saint-Étienne, France. Listed in 1933 as a gunmaker.

Montenegrin Model, or Type Monténégrin. A name used, often generically, to describe the largest of the *Gasser revolvers. Popular in the Balkans and South America, where physical size was often of greater appeal than mechanical efficiency, Montenegrin revolvers had open-top or solid frames; an ejector rod attached to the right side of the barrel could be used in conjunction with a pivoting loading gate on the right side of the frame,

behind the cylinder. Some later Belgian-made guns had ejectors on swing-out cranes.

Monteremart, Saint-Étienne, France. Listed in 1933 as a gunmaker.

Montgomery Ward & Company. *See* *Ward.

Montigny – 1. Joseph Montigny, a Paris-trained gunmaker, began trading from Passage des Princes, Brussels, in 1848; the guns were made in a factory in the Fontaine l'Évêque district of Liège. Montigny made *Bastin-system shotguns and a needle-fire rifle, which had a breech-block that was lifted and then slid backward. John Henry Walsh ('Stonehenge'), writing in the 1880s in *The Field*, credited this needle gun to the Comte de Châteauvillier, even though others saw a link with Samuel *Pauly. **2.** Montigny & Fusnot. This Belgian gunmaking partnership, active in Brussels c.1850–61, exhibited military rifles at the Great Exhibition in London in 1851. **3.** Montigny & Mangeot, Gallerie de la Reine, Brussels. Successor to Montigny & Fusnot (above), this business traded from 1861 until Montigny died c. 1868. Subsequently his widow married Henri ★Christophe. *See also* Mitrailleuse.

Mont Storm – **1.** William Mont Storm: see Storm. **2.** Mont Storm Gun Works Company. This business was formed in Birmingham in 1863 by Charles ★Phelps, trading from 33 Constitution Hill. The goal was to promote the breech-loading conversion system patented by William Mont ★Storm in 1857–60, with improvements made by the Mont Storm Gun Works' manager, Francis ★Braendlin in 1863–65. However, large-scale orders failed to materialise, and the separate listing of the business in Birmingham ceased after 1865. However, Phelps continued to represent Mont Storm from 3 Rood Lane, London E.C., until 1871.

'Monvill' [The]. A mark associated with English shotgun ammunition, sold by Charles ★Rosson of Derby.

Moody – **1.** Charles Moody, Church Street, Romsey, Hampshire. This English gunmaker is listed in local directories for 1854–59, but is believed to have worked until the end of the nineteenth century before being superseded by his son, William Frederick Moody (below). **2.** William Frederick Moody. The name of this cutler and gunmaker, trading from 13 Church Street, Romsey, Hampshire, has been recorded on shotgun ammunition made by Kynoch prior to the First World War, and ★Eley-Kynoch thereafter. He was the son of Charles Moody (above).

Moon. A. Moon: a possible misinterpretation of A. ★Mock.

'Moonraker' [The]. A mark associated with shotgun cartridges assembled by ★Nightingale & Son of Salisbury from components originating outside Britain. The cases are customarily marked 'FOREIGN-MADE CASE' and (appreciably larger) 'BRITISH HAND LOADED'.

Moor. Thomas H. Moor, an ironmonger trading in South Street, South Molton, Devon, sold shotgun ammunition under such brandnames as The Molton and Special Rabbit. Moor may have succeeded William Huxtable, a gun dealer and watchmaker listed in South Street in 1869; he also maintained premises in the Somerset village of Exford for some years.

Moore – **1.** Daniel Moore & Company, Brooklyn, New York. This gunmaking business produced .32, .38 and .44 rimfire revolvers based on a patent granted on 18 September 1860 ('revolving firearms', 30,079). The open-frame guns had a spring-loaded ejector rod and a barrel/cylinder group that rotated laterally to facilitate loading, but their bored-through chambers infringed the Rollin ★White patent. A single-shot knuckle-duster derringer with a laterally-swinging barrel was patented on 19 February 1861 ('firearms', 31,473), and was followed in 1863 by a .32 six-chamber teat-fire cartridge revolver. This had a hinged loading gate ahead of the cylinder, but, as Moore had not claimed novelty in the ammunition, he was forced to pay royalties to David ★Williamson. Most of the revolvers acknowledge patents granted to Williamson in 1864 to protect the combination extractor/cartridge retainer. Guns of this type were also briefly marked under the ★National brand during 1866–68. An 1866-patent Williamson sliding-barrel single-shot derringer was made during 1866–67, capable of handling rimfire cartridges or powder and ball. The adaptor was an iron tube, not unlike an empty cartridge case, with a nipple to accept a conventional percussion cap. In December 1874, Moore was granted US Patent 157,860 to protect improvements in revolver design. The patent was assigned to ★Merwin, Hulbert & Company. **2.** Robert Moore. Patentee of a silencer prior to the First World War, which was made in small numbers by the Moore Silencer Company; 100 were purchased by the US Army in 1914. **3.** Stillman Moore, acting on behalf of the US Army during 1846–52, accepted single-shot cap-lock and other military firearms. They bore the identifier 'SM', making them difficult to distinguish from guns accepted for the navy prior to the American Civil War by Samuel ★Marcy. *See also* US arms inspectors' marks. **4.** William Moore & Company. This English gunmaking business succeeded William Moore & William Grey in 1854, operating from 43 Old Bond Street in London. The trading style became William Moore & Grey in 1873. Moore & Grey marks have been reported on a wide variety of sporting guns and ammunition, including pinfire shotgun cartridges. **5.** 'William Moore & Company'. A name found on shotguns handled by the H. & D. ★Folsom Arms Company, possibly imported from Europe. They may have been made in Britain; *see* William Moore & Company, London (above). **6.** William Moore & Grey. This was a successor to William Moore & Company, trading from 43 Old Bond Street, London, from 1873 onward. The trading style became William Moore & Grey Ltd in 1879, and a move to 165 Piccadilly was made in 1896. (This gunmaking business must not be confused with William Moore & William Grey, trading from Edgware Road, London, in 1848–53.) **7.** Moore's Patent Fire Arms Company, Brooklyn, New York. Maker of the ★Moore and ★Williamson cartridge derringers. Succeeded by the ★National Arms Company c. 1868. **8.** Moore & Woodward: *see* James ★Woodward & Sons.

Moorey, Moorey's. This distributor of ironmongery and sporting guns, trading in Holmes Chapel, Cheshire, offered shotgun cartridges of unknown origins marked 'Moorey's Special'.

'Moray' [The]. A mark found on shotgun cartridges handled by Francis ★Davie of Elgin, Morayshire, Scotland.

Mordant. Gustave Mordant, Liège. A Belgian gunmaker, one of many to take part in the late 1860s in the manufacture of French ★Chassepot needle rifles under sub-contract from ★Cahen-Lyon & Cie. Double-barrelled sporting guns have also been reported with Mordant's marks. He was involved in the 1870s with le ★Grand Syndicat.

More Light. Distinguished by a contrasting line on the back edge of the front-sight blade and an additional aperture in the back-sight leaf beneath the notch, this combination was the subject of US Patent 189,721 of 17 April 1877, granted to Frank W. ★Freud, and improved by US Patent 229,245 granted to Frank and George ★Freund on 29 June 1880. *See also* Wyoming Saddle Gun.

Morgan – **1.** William Morgan & Company. An English gunmaking business listed at 30 Budge Row, London E.C., Morgan's activities seem to have been confined to 1868–69. **2.** Morgan & Clapp. American manufacturers of a sheath-trigger .32 cartridge derringer with a laterally-swinging barrel, not unlike the ★Southerner. Location unknown.

Morgenstern. Wenzel Morgenstern, one of the leading

gunmakers established in *Weipert, Bohemia (then part of Austria-Hungary), was one of the principal members of a co-operative formed in 1887 to produce components for the straight-pull *Mannlicher service rifle that had been adopted for the Austro-Hungarian Army.

Moritz – **1.** Heinrich Moritz, Zella St Blasii and Zella-Mehlis in Thüringen, Germany. Listed in 1914 as a wholesaler, Moritz was granted the trademark Hei-Mo on 8 January 1917 (no. 214,981), when air- and sporting guns were being handled. Work continued after the First World War, a range of sporting rifles and shotguns being made alongside airguns and the *He-Mo semi-automatic pistol. Moritz was listed in the *Deutsches Reichs-Adressbuch* as a wholesaler (1920) and a gunmaker (1930). Operations are believed to have ceased in 1945, although directory listings dating later than 1939 have proved difficult to find. **2.** Max W. Moritz, Zella-Mehlis in Thüringen. A gunsmith active in Germany in 1941. **3.** Wilhelm Moritz, Zella St Blasii and Zella-Mehlis, Thüringen. Founded in 1869, this gunmaking business was advertising itself in 1925 as a manufacturer of precision weapons and gun components. Some of these bore a trademark of a cartouche containing 'W', 'M' and a bishop above a shield bearing crossed hammers. Wilhelm Moritz himself was listed in 1920 as a gunmaker, and in 1930 as a master gunsmith. **4.** Moritz & Gerstenberger, Zella-Mehlis in Thüringen. This German gunmaking partnership is believed to have been founded in 1922 or 1923, and was granted a patent protecting a signal pistol in June 1926; the patentees were Franz *Möller and Martin Moritz of Zella-Mehlis, and Albin Gerstenberger of Chemnitz. The business was listed in 1930 as a maker and wholesaler of guns and weapons, when owned by Albin Emanuel Gerstenberger, Hermann Martin Moritz and Franz Möller; it was listed in 1939 as a weapon maker. An assortment of air pistols and rifles was made prior to 1940, including the *Herkules, *Krone and *Zenit pistols, and several *Em-Ge rifles. The company was allocated the code letters 'ghk' in 1941, although its wartime products have not yet been identified. Trading ceased in 1945, but *Gertensberger & Eberwein was re-established in Gussenstadt c. 1950, and use of the 'Em-Ge' mark continues.

Morley – **1.** M.W. Morley, acting on behalf of the Federal Army, accepted 'bought-in' firearms and accessories during the American Civil War; they were marked 'MWM'. **2.** W.H. Morley, sometimes listed as 'Morely', accepted firearms and accessories destined for the US Army during 1899–1905, marking them 'WHM'. *See also* US arms inspectors' marks.

Morris – **1.** P. Morris & Son. Trading in Hereford, this English ironmongery and gunsmithing business sold sporting guns and a range of *Kynoch-made shotgun ammunition, including cartridges marked 'The Hereford'. **2.** Richard Morris is best remembered as the inventor of the first British sub-calibre barrel-insert system, although his earliest patents protected conventional box magazines. A patent granted in 1886 protected a 'conveyor', or carrier mechanism, and 5786/87 of 20 April 1887 allowed a claim for a box magazine with an external depressor. Morris continued to improve his designs, including 'magazines for rifles' protected by British Patents 2306/90 and 4522/90 of 1890. *See also* Morris's Aiming & Sighting Apparatus Company, The Morris Tube Ammunition &

Safety Range Company Ltd, and Sub-calibre adaptor. **3.** Samuel Morris: *see* Louis *Rodier. **4.** William H. Morris, New York City. Co-patentee with Charles L. *Brown of a distinctive repeating rifle. **5.** Morris & Brown, New York City. Manufacturer of the multi-chamber cone-throat Conical Repeater rifles patented in 1860 by Charles L. *Brown and William H. Morris. The business failed in the early days of the American Civil War. **6.** Morris Motors Ltd, Cowley Works, Oxford. A maker of magazines for the British 9mm *Sten Gun during the Second World War. The code 'M 292' may have been used instead of the company name, although it has been suggested that actually the magazines were made by Caberton Works, the Radiators Branch factory in Oxford, which was allotted 'S 82'. *See also* British military manufacturers' marks. **7.** Morris's Aiming & Sighting Apparatus Company. Formed in 1883 to exploit the patents granted to Richard Morris, initially this traded from 63 Haymarket. By 1887, the style had become '...& Co. Ltd', and a move had been made to 7 & 9 St Bride's Street. In 1888, however, the company was reorganised as the Morris Tube Ammunition & Safety Range Company Ltd. **8.** Morris Tube. This was the first successful sub-calibre training system to be used by the British Army, being approved for the *Lee-Metford rifle in 1891 in conjunction with a .297/230 centrefire cartridge. Morris Tubes had the advantage of allowing the rifle to revert to .303 ammunition if necessary, but were not particularly accurate and were replaced after 1908 – first by the permanently fitted .22 rimfire Aiming Tube (which required a modified bolt) and eventually by purpose-built .22 rifles. *See also* Richard Morris and Sub-calibre adaptor. **9.** Morris Tube Ammunition & Safety Range Company Ltd [The]. This was formed in 1888 by reorganising Morris's Aiming & Sighting Apparatus Company Ltd, trading from 7 & 9 St Bride's Street, London, until a move was made to 11 Haymarket in 1889.

Morrison – **1.** Charles C. Morrison, a lieutenant in the US Army, accepted firearms made during 1878–92 by *Colt's Patent Fire Arms Manufacturing Company; they were marked 'CCM'. **2.** George F. Morrison, a lieutenant in the US Navy, accepted *Starr cap-lock revolvers during the American Civil War. Identified by their 'GFM' marks, apparently all the .44-calibre guns were made in 1864. *See also* US arms inspectors' marks for both entries.

Morrone. Joseph A. Morrone, Providence, Rhode Island. Inventor of the Morrone hammerless over/under shotgun, US Patent 2,568,556 of 18 September 1951 being granted to protect the single-trigger mechanism and a tapered locking bolt that compensated automatically for wear. The guns were made by the *Rhode Island Arms Company.

Morrow & Company. *See* Marrow & Company.

Morse – **1.** Writing in his book, *Air Guns*, in 1958, Eldon Wolff notes that boxes for Quackenbush darts list a Morse pistol among the suitable guns. It has not been identified, although the inventor may have been George W. Morse. **2.** Charles Morse, USA. *See* Remington. **3.** George S. Morse. The name of this inspector, allegedly active in 1862, during the American Civil War, has been linked with the acceptance of *Starr cap-lock revolvers marked 'GSM'. *See also* 'George W. Morse' (below) and US arms inspectors' marks. **4.** George W. Morse. One of the first steps toward the modern military weapon was taken by this gunmaker, who presented a breech-loading carbine to the US Army in 1857. Morse's cartridge developed no real power, but it had an internal primer and was genuinely self-contained. The conversion of 2,000 muskets to the Morse system (q.v.) was authorised in September 1858, but only sixty had been completed by the end of 1859, and work was still under way when Confederate forces seized Harper's Ferry Armory in April 1861. The few completed Morse-system conversions spent their time in the Federal stores, apparently without seeing service. Ten thousand Morse conversions of .69 Model 1842 muskets were ordered in 1860 from the *Muzzy Rifle & Gun Manufacturing Company of Worcester, Massachusetts, but few – if any – were completed. George W. Morse may have been responsible for inspecting guns made in accordance with his patents, perhaps applying a 'GWM' identifier, although this has also been linked with George W. *McKee. *See also* George S. Morse (above) and US arms inspectors' marks. **5.** Kelley S. Morse, possibly a grandson of George W. Morse, accepted a variety of military firearms for service with the US Army. They included *Gatling Guns, M1892 revolvers and M1911 pistols made by *Colt's Patent Fire Arms Manufacturing Company; M1899 revolvers made by *Smith & Wesson; and *Winchester M1895 rifles. Morse's activities, dating from 1893 to c. 1916, were identified by 'KSW' marks. *See also* US arms inspectors' marks.

Mortimer & Son, Edinburgh. Claiming origins as early as 1720, this Scottish gunmaking business began life at 78 Princes Street in 1835 – originally as a branch of Mortimers of Ludgate Hill, London. Thomas Edward Mortimer moved to 97 George Street (1839–54), then to 86 George Street from 1854, until the business was acquired in 1938 by John *Dickson & Son. It had become Mortimer & Son in 1861, and had taken over Joseph *Harkom & Son in 1922. Mortimer's name has been reported on many types of sporting gun and ammunition.

Morton – 1. Kenneth Morton, a major in the US Army Ordnance Department, accepted .45 *Colt semi-automatic pistols during 1907–08. They bore the identifier 'KM'. *See also* US arms inspectors' marks. **2.** William Morton. An English gunsmith listed between 1876 and 1887 at 8 Railway Approach, London Bridge, and at 2 Railway Approach in 1888.

Mosalsalasi arms factory. The principal Iranian small-arms factory. It has made, among other things, Mauser, Kalashnikov and Heckler & Koch rifles.

Mosin – 1. Sergey Ivanovich Mosin, the son of a clerk, was born near Voronezh in 1849. Entering a military elementary school in 1861, eventually he graduated from the Mikhailovskoye artillery academy in 1875 with the rank of lieutenant. After working in the Tula ordnance factory for nearly twenty years, he was appointed director of the *Sestroretsk factory when production of the Mosin-Nagant rifle began there in 1894. Mosin died unexpectedly in 1902, his great contribution to Russian small-arms design acknowledged only after the 1917 revolution, and in the eventual creation of the S.I. Mosin Prize. **2.** Mosin-Nagant rifle: *see* panel, pp. 362/63.

Mosman. Dexter F. Mosman accepted firearms and accessories on behalf of the Federal Army. Dating from 1862, the early stages of the American Civil War, they were marked 'DFM'. *See also* US arms inspectors' marks.

Mossberg – 1. Oscar Mossberg, Chicopee Falls, Massachusetts. Inventor of the *Shatuck Unique pistol, patented on 4 December 1906 (no. 837,867). **2.** O.F. Mossberg & Sons, North Haven, Connecticut, USA: *see* panel pp. 364/65.

Moston. J. Moston. Supplier of 12-bore shotguns to the British military authorities, 1942.

Moulin – 1. Moulin aîné, rue Villeboeuf 34, Saint-Étienne, France. Listed in 1879 as a maker of gun parts and accessories. **2.** Jean-Baptiste Moulin [veuve], rue de la Charité 7, Saint-Étienne, France. Listed in 1879 as a maker of gun parts and accessories.

Moulton. M. Moulton, acting on behalf of the Federal Army during the American Civil War, accepted cap-lock revolvers made by *Savage and *Colt, in addition to some of the *Palmer breech-loading carbines. Dating from the period 1861–65, the guns bear an 'MM' identifier. *See also* US arms inspectors' marks.

Mountain... – 1. Mountain Eagle. A *Suicide Special revolver made by the *Hopkins & Allen Arms Company of Norwich, Connecticut, USA, in the late nineteenth century. **2.** Mountain Rifle. Also known as the M700 MTR or BLR Mountain Rifle, this *Remington bolt-action sporter was offered from 1986 until 1995. It combined a tapered lightweight barrel with a straight-comb half-stock and an ebony fore-end tip. Offered initially only in .270 Winchester and .30-06, the range was broadened to include .243 Winchester, 7mm-08 and .308 Winchester options (all from 1988), 7x57 (1990), .257 Roberts (1991) and .25-06 (1992). Variants have included the M700 MTR Custom KS, made from 1986 in right- and left-hand actions with a Kevlar-reinforced stock featuring plain or (from 1992) wood-grain finish. Initially chamberings were .270 Winchester, .280 Remington, 7mm Remington Magnum, .300 Winchester Magnum, .30-06 and .375 H&H Magnum, but 8mm Remington Magnum and .338 Winchester Magnum options were added in 1988, followed by .300 Weatherby Magnum and .35 Whelen in 1989. The M700 MTR DM (introduced in 1995) is distinguished by its detachable four-round magazine and a half-stock with an oil-rubbed finish. At first, chamberings were .243 Winchester, .25-06, .270 Winchester, 7mm-08, .280 Remington and .30-06. The M700 MTR SS, announced in 1993, has a lightweight tapered stainless-steel barrel in a textured synthetic half-stock. For chamberings were offered initially, ranging from .25-06 to .30-06.

'Mount Vernon Arms Company'. A name found on shotguns handled in the USA by the H. & D. *Folsom Arms Company, possibly imported from Europe.

'Mousetrap'. *See* Theophilus *Murcott.

'mow'. A codemark found on German telescope sights and associated components said to have been made during 1944–45 (although not confirmed) by Seidenweberei Berga C.W. Crous & Co. of Berga in Elster.

Mowry. James D. Mowry, Norwich, Connecticut. A gunmaker active in the USA during the American Civil War.

'MP'. An abbreviation for *Militärisches Pistole* or *Militär-Pistole* ('Military Pistol'), found as 'Mod. HP' on the slides of the 9x19 adaptation of the *Walther *Polizei-Pistole, and also on a prototype of the Walther P. 38.

'MPB'. Found on US military firearms and accessories. *See* M.P. *Benjamin.

MOSIN-NAGANT

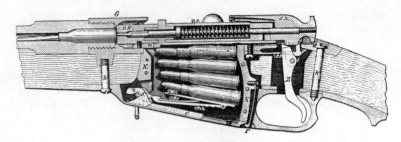

Mosin (2)

The first Russian small-bore rifle trials, undertaken in 1888, resolved in favour of single-shot submissions from Nikolay Lutkovskiy and Sergey Mosin. However, a five-shot .30 Mosin rifle and a .35 Nagant appeared in 1890 and, as neither design was ideal, the testing commission amalgamated them. The Mosin bolt, somewhat like the French Lebel, was amalgamated with the magazine system and feed-interruptor mechanism of the Nagant, allowing the obr. 1891g, or Three Line Rifle, to be adopted in April 1891. This had a distinctive protruding magazine case, curving up into the stock; it was loaded from a charger and could accept a socket bayonet, which the Russians were apt to carry in its fixed position.

The *Tula factory was equipped with machines purchased from Greenwood & Batley of Leeds, which then were copied to enable *Izhevsk and *Sestroretsk to begin work. Although production began in Tula in 1892, only 1,439 rifles had been made by the end of the year, and even these were classed as trainers. Half a million rifles were ordered from the French government early in 1892, 503,539 being delivered from Châtellerault

by the end of 1895. By the spring of 1893, Tula was ready to begin series production, and tooling in Izhevsk and Sestroretsk was well under way. During the first phase of rearmament (1892–96), the Russian arsenals made 1,470,000 combat rifles and more than 30,000 trainers.

Dragoon and cossack rifles were also produced, each a few inches shorter than the infantry rifle; cossack rifles, with elongated handguards and spring-retained bands, had Cyrillic 'КАЗ' serial-number suffixes. Mosin-Nagant cavalry carbines were made in comparatively small nmbers between 1907 and 1914.

Rifle sights were altered after 1908 for ammunition loaded with new lightweight spitzer-type 'L'-bullets, which increased the muzzle velocity; the original flat sight leaf was replaced with a larger curved pattern.

The Mosin-Nagant rifle performed reasonably well during the Russo-Japanese War of 1904–05, but was found to be poorly sighted

and very inaccurate when fired with the socket bayonet in place.

Rifles were in such short supply in December 1914 that virtually any weapon could be pressed into service. Large numbers of 6.5mm Japanese Arisakas and a collection of obsolete French guns were purchased, while substantial quantities of Mosin-Nagants were ordered in the USA.

Immediately after the October Revolution, the supply of rifles was problematical, owing to the destruction of some facilities and the loss of many key workers, although at least 1,272,751 new guns were completed during 1918–20, and about a million assorted rifles were refurbished. In October 1922, the Revolutionary Military Council proposed the standardisation of the obr. 1891g dragoon rifle, which was several inches shorter than the infantry pattern, and that no full-length obr.1891g rifles should be made once existing stocks of components had been exhausted.

MPi-K. An abbreviation of *Maschinenpistole Kalashnikow*, the indigenous designation for the *Kalashnikov assault rifle. Made by VEB Fahrzeug- u. Gerätewerke 'Ernst Thalmann' in Suhl, the guns have been offered in differing forms: 'M' suffix versions (e.g. MPi-KM) are based on the AKM instead of the AK, and 'S' patterns (MPi-KMS) have folding butts.

'MPL' – 1. With 'P' dominant: a monogram associated with Martin *Pulvermann Ltd of London. **2.** Found on US military firearms and accessories. *See* M.P. *Lomax.

'mpu'. A code associated with German cartridge clips and chargers made by the Wlaschim factory of Wlaschimer Maschinenfabrik GmbH during 1944–45.

MR. A linear monogram with the tail of the black-letter 'M' forming the vertical of the 'R'. Used in recent times by *Manurhin, particularly on post-1973 revolvers.

'MRF'. A part-linear part-superimposition monogram, with 'M' dominant. Correctly interpreted as 'RMF' (q.v.); used by Rheinische Metallwaaren- u. Maschinenfabrik of Sömmerda.

'MRM'. Found on US military firearms and accessories. *See* M.R. *Marsh.

'MS' – 1. Often in monogram form. Associated with the

pre-1918 products of *Munitionswerke Schönebeck. **2.** A small Spanish 6.35mm-calibre Browning-type pocket pistol made in Eibar by Modesto *Santos: six rounds, hammer fired. **3.** Found on US military firearms and accessories. *See* Maurice *Sherman.

'MSB', 'M.S.B.' [The]. Brandnames used by *Milburn & Son, Brampton, on sporting guns and ammunition. Shotgun cartridges of this type were made from *Eley-Kynoch components.

MSTR. *See* Martz Safe Toggle Release.

'MT', 'M.T.' – 1. Normally as 'M.T.'; found on British rifles (usually *Lee-Enfields) chambered for .22 rimfire *Morris Tube ammunition. **2.** *See* Maxim-Tokarev.

'MTK'. Found on US military firearms and accessories. *See* Marian T. *Kreps.

MTN. An abbreviation of 'Mountain'; sometimes applied mistakenly to the Remington M700 MTR bolt-action rifle. *See* Mountain Rifle.

MTR, MTR DM. *See* Mountain Rifle.

Mugica. José-Cruz Mugica, Eibar. A maker of shotguns and sporting rifles, Mugica also distributed handguns – not only in Europe, but as far afield as China and Siam. Invariably the pistols were the work of *Gabilondo y Cia;

The Russian/Soviet Mosin-Nagant rifle owed something in the design of its bolt to the French Lebel, but had a charger-loaded box magazine and an interruptor to improve the feed of the cumbersome 7.62x54R cartridges. The drawing depicts the original 1891-pattern infantry rifle, with a finger spur on the lower tang, behind the trigger guard; the photograph shows the 1944-pattern Soviet carbine, which has an integral folding bayonet mounted on the right side of the muzzle.

Production of the new dragoon-pattern infantry rifles did not begin at Izhevsk until mid-1923.

Experiments to simplify the basic design continued until a suitably modified obr. 1891/30g. rifle was accepted on 28 April 1930. It had a plain cylindrical receiver and a tangent-pattern back sight. The advent of war accelerated production so greatly that about 17,500,000 Mosin-Nagants of all types were made between 1930 and 1945. Sniper rifles were issued with PU, PE, VT or PT telescope sights.

A carbine was adopted in 1939, as the obr. 1938g., and an obr. 1944g. carbine, with an integral folding bayonet, was approved on 17 January 1944. Mosin-Nagants were also popular in Finland, where much-modified rifles built (and in many cases rebuilt) on original pre-1917 actions served until the introduction of Kalashnikov-type assault rifles in the 1960s. The Finnish guns are shorter than their Russian prototypes and (with the exception of the army m/24 and m/27) can usually be identified by pistol-grip stocks; all but the m/24 accept knife bayonets. The m/27 was a short-barrelled army rifle, the m/28 and m/28-30 were issued to the Protective Corps (*Suojeluskunta Ylieskunnen*, or Sk.Y), and the m/39 was a universal-issue version with a two-piece stock and a two-piece interruptor copied from the Soviet 1930 pattern. Long-barrelled sniper rifles will also be encountered in small numbers.

Mosin-Nagants have served in many Soviet satellite states; have been made in quantity in Hungary (44.M carbines and 48.M sniper rifles), Czechoslovakia (vz. 54 sniper rifle) and the People's Republic of China (Type 53 carbine, copied from the Soviet obr. 1944g.); and have formed the basis for a variety of sporting and target rifles. However, there is no particularly good guide to their history, with the exception of parts of Ed Ezell's *The AK47 Story* (Stackpole Books, 1986) and an article or two in gun magazines. Russian/Soviet guns have been made by the small-arms factories in Izhevsk, Sestroretsk and Tula; by the French government factory in Châtellerault (1893–96 only); by the New England Westinghouse Company (1915–17) and by the Remington Arms–Union Metallic Cartridge Company (1915–17).

they included the Llama models III, III-A, VII, VIII, X, X-A and XI. Sometimes listed as Mugica Sucesor, José Cruz.

Muir. William Muir & Company, Windsor Locks, Connecticut. A US gunmaker active during 1861–63.

Mukden arsenal. This Manchurian factory made 7.9mm *Mauser-type rifles c. 1933–39, apparently during the period of the Japanese-inspired Manchukuo state, but then concentrated on *Arisaka rifles and carbines until 1944 or later.

'Mule Ear'. A nickname applied to the *Jenks carbine.

Mulholland. James Mulholland [& Company], Reading, Pennsylvania, USA. This engineering firm made a few guns for the Federal Army during 1861–63.

Mullaney. J.R.M. Mullaney, a lieutenant in the US Navy Bureau of Ordnance, accepted .36-calibre *Colt revolvers bearing 'JRMM' prior to the American Civil War. *See also* US arms inspectors' marks.

Muller, Müller – 1. Muller. Associated with British spring-airguns and sporting equipment. *See* Relum Ltd. **2.** A. Müller, a German Army officer, was responsible for Major Müller's Fire Control, protected by British Patents 6358/07 of 23 March 1907; 9252/08 of 25 April 1908; and 21,340/10 of 6 October 1910. Tested by Germany, Britain and the USA – among many other nations – the control mechanism in the rifle butt was intended to allow the gun to fire when a pre-set inclination was achieved. The idea was to simplify volley fire, but was much too complicated to gain favour and had been abandoned by the time the First World War began. **3.** Carl Müller & Sohn, also listed as 'Karl', Benshausen bei Suhl in Thüringen. Described in pre-1939 German trade directories as a maker of tools and gun parts. Still active in 1941. **4.** H. Müller, Zella-Mehlis in Thüringen, Germany. Listed in 1930 as a master gunsmith. **5.** Muller & Company. This agency was founded in 1901, perhaps to replace the Clermont Explosives Company (q.v.). Initially trading was undertaken from Horseshoe Yard, Mount Street, London. German-made shotgun cartridges loaded with Clermonite and Mullerite propellant were sold in Britain for a few years. However, despite a move to Winchmore Hill in Middlesex in 1903, Muller & Company ceased trading in 1905. The cartridge agency passed to Martin *Pulvermann, who may well have been one of the original backers. Cartridges were distinguished by brandnames such as Clermonite, Mullerite and Negro. **6.** Müller & Greiss, München. This gunmaking business

O.F. MOSSBERG & SONS

Mossberg (2)

Oskar F Mossberg (c. 1870–1937) opened his workshop in Hatfield, Massachusetts, in 1892, remaining there until he moved first to Chicopee Falls, then to Fitchburg in 1902/3. A factory was opened in New Haven, Connecticut, on the formation of O.F. Mossberg & Sons in 1919 and – finally – the business relocated to nearby North Haven in 1966.

Mossberg's first products included simple rifles, small pistols, and gun sights. He was granted a number of patents, but the assignment of many to well-known gunmakers suggests that his own manufacturing capacity was small. For example, US Patent 754,080 of 8 March 1904 ('Hinge-pin for Break down Guns') and 818,461 of 24 April 1906 ('Breech-loading Firearm') were both assigned to Marie Johnson, executrix of Iver *Johnson, whereas two breech-loading firearms patents – 765,039 of 29 March 1904, and 840,507 of 8 January 1907 – went to the J. *Stevens Arms & Tool Company.

In 1915, Mossberg began to market a four-shot palm pistol, which he called 'Novelty', but the project was sold to Charles S. *Shatuck after no more than 600 had been produced; Shatuck, who was probably already manufacturing the guns for Mossberg, renamed them *Unique.

Mossberg is now best known as a maker of shotguns, but was also responsible for a variety of rifles. Beginning in 1922 with the Model K hammerless tube-magazine design, these included the Model 26B (1938), which was the first Mossberg with the bolt handle at the extreme rear of the receiver. Made during the Second World War, the Model 42MB was a bolt-action trainer purchased in quantity by the US and British Armies; about 50,000 were made during 1942–43, before the design was superseded by the Model 44US (53,000 during 1943–45).

Modified designs appeared after the Second World War, often signified by adding 100 to the pre-war designations. The Model 340B of the 1950s was the first to feature a new action with the bolt handle placed well forward of the trigger. Among other notable rimfire rifles, the auto-loading Model 377 Plinkster (1977–79) had a distinctive thumb-hole stock.

Mossberg has also manufactured a variety of centrefire sporters, including the lever-action Model 472 (introduced in 1972) and Model 479 (1985), mostly chambered for .30-30 WCF ammunition. Designers Louis Seecamp and Carl Benson began work on what became the Model 800 in 1963, to provide Montgomery *Ward & Company with a suitable bolt-action rifle to sell under the Western Field banner. Production lasted from 1967 until 1978, encompassing a variety of patterns – 800V (Varmint), 800M (Mannlicher stock) and 800D (Deluxe). Chamberings ranged from .222 Remington to .308 Winchester.

---

built *Mauser-action rifles in Germany prior to 1914, chambering a special 9.5x73 cartridge created by necking the British .404 Rimless Nitro Express.

Mullerite – 1. Usually encountered as 'The Mullerite'. A brandname associated with shotgun cartridges, generally loaded by *Eley Bros., referring specifically to their propellant loading. Mullerite was supplied by the *Clermonite Explosives Company Ltd and *Muller & Company. **2.** Mullerite Cartridge Works [The]. Established in Birmingham, Warwickshire, in 1922, trading from 59 Bath Street and St Mary's Row, this venture may have involved Martin *Pulvermann, whose 'MPL' monogram sometimes appears on the shotgun cartridges. Although loaded in Britain, the ammunition incorporated Clermonite and Mullerite propellant imported from Germany. Brandnames included The Ace and The Ace Long-Range, The British Champion, The Champion, Clay King, Fourtenner, General Service, Green Seal, Grey Seal, Heyman(n) Smokeless, Red Seal, Silver Ray and Yellow Seal.

Munck. C.H. Munck, Washington County, Ohio, USA. A maker of spring Gallery Guns during the period 1865–75. Sometimes wrongly listed in Washington D.C.

Munitionswerke Schönebeck, Schönebeck an der Elbe. Owned by *Sellier & Bellot, this cartridge-making business was responsible for shotgun ammunition sold with 'MS' and 'MWS' monograms, and under such brandnames as Füllhorn (possibly), Halali, Saxonia, Teutonia and Waldheil.

Munroe. G.H. Munroe, also listed as 'Munro' and 'Monroe', accepted US Army firearms and accessories identified by 'GHM'; they date from the period 1899–1902. *See also* US arms inspectors' marks.

Munts. Joh. Munts, Amsterdam. A distributor of guns and ammunition, operating in 1932 and still in existence. Used a trademark of a white 'Dutch' lion, often holding a bayonetted rifle and superimposed on a ring target.

Murat – 1. Saint-Étienne, France. Listed in 1933 as a gunmaker. **2.** Louis-Édouard Murat, rue des Creuses 4, Saint-Étienne, France. Listed in 1879 as a gunmaker.

Murata – 1. Tsuneyoshi Murata, a Japanese Army officer, was the head of the commission entrusted with developing the first Japanese infantry weapons, a series of single-shot and magazine guns being introduced during 1880–94 (below). **2.** Murata rifle. A combination of features adapted from the French *Gras and German *Mauser, this Japanese rifle was developed immediately after the Satsuma rebellion of 1877, by a committee chaired by Tsuneyoshi Murata. It was made in three single-shot patterns – Meiji 13th Year type rifle, 16th Year carbine and 18th Year Type rifle – then as a tube-magazine repeater, known as the Meiji 22nd Year Type (1889). The Meiji 27th Year Type of 1894 was a short-barrelled cavalry carbine.

Murat-Cizeron, rue Badouillère 40, Saint-Étienne, France. Listed in 1892 as a gunmaker.

Murcott. Theophilus Murcott, a gunmaker trading in London from 68 Haymarket during 1861–78, is best remembered as the designer and sole manufacturer of the first hammerless shotgun to be marketed successfully in Britain. Patented in Britain in 1871 (no. 1003/71) and known universally as 'The Mousetrap', owing to its unfamiliar shape and somewhat complicated mechanism, the gun was made in substantial numbers. However, although serial numbers as high as 6400 have been reported, it is

The Model 800 was replaced by the refined Model 810 (1972–78), another multi-lug bolt pattern handling cartridges from .270 Winchester to .338 Winchester Magnum. The RM-7 (1978–84) was the last of the range, with squared contours instead of the rounded shapes that had characterised its predecessors. Then efforts were made to sell *Howa-made Model 1500, 1550 and 1700 rifles acquired from *Smith & Wesson, but the last of these had disappeared by 1987, and thereafter Mossberg concentrated on producing shotguns.

The first 12-bore shotguns dated from 1940, but almost immediately work was interrupted by the Second World War. The best known of the post-war slide-action guns are the Model 200 (1955–59) and the Model 500, which has been made since 1962 in a huge variety of models. These have included guns with such names as Bantam, Camper, Mariner, Persuader and Slugster. Current products also include the semi-automatic Models 5500 and 9200.

Mossberg has also made plain-finish guns under the New Haven name, as well as a few deluxe Pedersen-series rifles and shotguns dating from 1973–75.

Oscar Mossberg was the son of a Swedish immigrant, and the company continues to reflect this heritage in its logo: a yellow cross on a yellow edged oval blue ground, with the *Tre Kronor* (Three

Mossberg has made a wide range of sporting guns, including pump-action shotguns and bolt-action rifles. This is a .22 rimfire Model 144 target rifle, with a heavy barrel and aperture sights. The finger grips on the front surface of the pistol grip, made integrally with the tang of the trigger guard, are typical of many Mossberg products.

Crowns) of the Swedish Arms. *See* National Markings.

The best source of information is *Mossberg: More Gun for the Money*, by V. and C. Havlin (Investment Rarities, 1995), although a list of the rifles will be found in John Walter, *Rifles of the World* (Krause Publications, second edition, 1998).

thought that this particular sequence included all guns made or sold by Murcott.

Murderer. A name associated with a revolver made in Belgium prior to 1914 by A. *Bertrand.

Murdock. H. Murdock accepted firearms and accessories on behalf of the US Army in 1875, using an 'HM' identifier. This can be difficult to distinguish from marks used at the same time by Henry *Metcalfe. *See also* US arms inspectors' marks.

Murgues fils, cours Saint-André 23, Saint-Étienne, France. Listed in 1879 as a gunmaker.

Murigneux, grand rue Saint-Roch 49, Saint-Étienne, France. Listed in 1892 as a gunmaker.

Murphy – 1. John Murphy, Norwich, Connecticut, USA. Designer of the *Triple Action Safety Lock, protected by US Patent 829,082 of 21 August 1906 and used by the *Hopkins & Allen Arms Company on its *Safety Police revolver. **2.** John J. Murphy, an inspector retained by the US government, accepted military firearms and accessories in 1898. They were marked 'JJM'. It is possible that J.J. Murphy and John Murphy (above) were one and the same. **3.** Justice Murphy, also listed as 'Justin Murphy', accepted a variety of US military firearms from 1813 to 1841 and probably later. However, his 'JM' mark is easily confused with similar identifiers used by John *Maggs, Julian *McCallister and J. *Mills. *See also* US arms inspectors' marks for this and the previous entry.

Murray. T.W. Murray & Company (Britain prior to 1922, Eire thereafter). Trading in the southern Irish city of Cork, this gunsmithing and gun-dealing business handled a variety of sporting guns and ammunition. These included shotgun cartridges sold as The Speedwell and The Wildfowler. Some of these appear to have been loaded by *Kynoch prior to the First World War; later examples often embody *Eley-Kynoch components.

Murry. Michael W. Murry was a partner of the Harts, father and two sons, in *Hart & Company during 1896–98 only.

Museum of Firearms, Museum Works. *See* George Gibson *Bussey.

Musketeer. This brandname was used during 1963–72 to distinguish sporting rifles offered by *Firearms International Corp. on the basis of *FN-Mauser actions, in chamberings ranging from .243 Winchester to .300 Winchester Magnum.

Musketoon. A short-barrelled firearm, usually capable of accepting a bayonet (cf. carbine).

Mustang – 1. A single-barrelled *Holland & Holland-type side-lock rifle with a Purdey/Greener Triple Lock action, made by *Società Armi Bresciane to the designs of Renato *Gamba. The 620mm or 650mm barrel can be chambered for cartridges ranging from .243 Winchester to .30-06. Normally a set-trigger mechanism is fitted, and a standing back sight is let into the front of the quarter-rib. **2.** Or 380 Mustang. Announced in 1983 by the Firearms Division of *Colt Industries, but not made in quantity for several years, this was a compact *Government Model fitted with a 2.75in barrel chambering the .380 (9mm Short) cartridge. Finished in blue or nickel, or made of stainless steel (from 1990), guns of this pattern have magazines that hold five rounds (six from 1992). The Mustang Plus II of 1988 mates the short Mustang-length slide with a full-grip frame, raising the magazine capacity to seven – the standard five 'plus two'.

The Mustang Pocketlite (1987) has a blued aluminium-alloy frame, reducing weight to 12.5oz. A stainless Pocketlite variant appeared in 1991.

Mustow. R.J. Mustow. An English gunmaker listed in 1854 at 18 St Mary's Axe, London E.C., Mustow could be the same man as R. Muston, a gun-stock maker recorded in the 1841 census at Sugar Loaf Court, Goodman's Fields (Blackmore, *A Dictionary of London Gunmakers 1350–1850*).

Muzzle brake. An attachment similar to a *compensator, intended to turn the emerging gases and drive them rearward. This counteracts the recoil sensation by thrusting the muzzle forward. The effectiveness of muzzle brakes varies, as utility has to be balanced against the unpleasant consequences of directing the gas blast sideways.

Muzzy Rifle & Gun Manufacturing Company, Worcester, Massachusetts, USA. This gunmaking business received a Federal government contract for 10,000 *Morse breech-loading transformations of .69 M1842 muskets in 1860, but few, if any, were completed before the company failed at the beginning of the Civil War.

'MW' – 1. A superimposition-type monogram with both letters equally prominent, usually on a shield. Correctly 'WM' (q.v.); associated with Waffenfabrik *Mauser AG. **2.** A monogram said to have been associated with the products of *Patronen-Hülsen-Fabriken Bitschweiler. Its significance is still uncertain; possibly to be read 'WM'. **3.** Found on US military firearms and accessories. *See* M. *Witkop. **4.** Often encircled, superimposed or in monogram form. A trademark associated with Montgomery *Ward & Company, found on sporting guns and ammunition.

'MWH'. A monogram correctly read as 'WHM', found on sporting guns and shotgun ammunition. *See* William H. *Mark.

'MWM'. Found on US military firearms and accessories. *See* M.W. *Morley.

'MWS', often in the form of a monogram. Associated with the pre-1918 products of *Munitionswerke Schönebeck.

My... – 1. My Chick: *see* M.Y. *Chick and Theodore T.S. *Laidley. **2.** My Companion. A *Suicide Special revolver made by the *Hopkins & Allen Arms Company of Norwich, Connecticut, in the 1880s. **3.** My Friend. Patented in the USA in 1865 by James *Reid, basically this was a solid-frame barrelless revolver with an all-metal frame extended to contain a ring-grip for the smallest or fourth finger of the firer's hand. The guns also had a sliding safety catch beneath the frame, which could lock the cylinder when the hammer was mid-way between nipples. Consequently, My Friends always had an odd number of chambers (usually five). Reloading was simply a matter of releasing the axis pin and removing the cylinder. The guns were available in seven-shot .22, five-shot .32 and five-shot .41 versions, usually chambered for rimfire ammunition. About 20,000 Reid revolvers were made during 1866–80, when they were superseded by the *New Model My Friend, although only about 500 .41-calibre examples were included.

Myers. *See* Albert J. *Meyers.

Mylady. Found on small .320-calibre double-action revolvers made in Belgium prior to 1914 by Manufacture Liégeoise d'Armes à Feu, whose crowned 'ML' will usually be found somewhere on the frame. A safety slider may lie on the left side of the frame.

Mylona[s]. An unsuccessful dropping-block-action rifle, unique to Greece. It was replaced by the Gras (q.v.).

'Myrddin'. Found on shotgun ammunition handled by *Bowen of Carmarthen, Wales.

Myška. František Myška was born on 17 September 1899 in the provincial Bohemian town of Dvory (then in Austria-Hungary, now in the Czech Republic). He began an apprenticeship with gunmaker Bedřich *Kopřiva in 1913. Completing his practical studies in 1917, he worked briefly for Škoda and others before the First World War ended. Myška attended the Prague technical college in 1919–21, then joined the staff of Zbrojovka *Praga at the beginning of 1922. His responsibilities included work transforming the Nickl pistol into the vz. 24 service pistol, and the subsequent transformation (during 1926–27) of this recoil-operated gun into the blowback vz. 27. Patent no. 2814 of 1928 protected a double-action trigger system adapted in 1934 for what became the 6.53mm ČZ 36 pocket pistol; an alternative design, patented in 1936 (no. 65,556) was embodied in the vz. 38 army pistol. Among Myška's other products were a signal pistol known as the vz. 30, the vz. 35 airgun (with a gravity-feed magazine protected by Czechoslovakian patent no. 72,901 of 1937), the ČZ 241 auto-loading shotgun and the vz. 38 submachine-gun.

N

'n', 'N' – 1. Found as 'N' under the wrist of 'normal-length' British *Lee-Enfield rifle butts. *See also* 'B', 'L' and 'S'. **2.** Associated (as 'N') with stores, including firearms, issued to the British Royal Navy. Usually the mark is found on the left side of the *Lee-Enfield receiver. **3.** As 'N', with crossed pennants. A British naval proof mark. *See also* British military proof marks. **4.** As 'N', with a number. Found on components of military firearms made in Britain during the Second World War, indicating a company operating in the 'North' (of Britain). The numbers identified individual companies. Typical of those found on small-arms are 'N 1' (*Albion Motors), 'N 29' (V. & H. *Hardey), 'N 65' (*Sigmund Pumps Ltd), 'N 67' (*Singer Manufacturing Company) and 'N 90' (*Wilson & Mathieson Ltd). *See also* British military manufacturers' marks. **5.** Found as 'n' on rifle and other small-arms components made in Germany during the Second World War by Elsterwerdaer Fahrradfabrik E.W. Reichenbach GmbH of Elsterwerda-Biehla. **6.** A *headstamp associated with the *National Cartridge Company of St Louis.

'na'. Found on military ammunition components made in Germany during 1940–45 by Westfalische Kupfer- und Messingwerke AG of Ludenscheid in Westfalen.

'N A A CO.', 'N.A.A.Co.', 'N.A. & A.Co.' Marks found on the products of the *National Arms & Ammunition Company Ltd of Birmingham, Warwickshire, England, ranging from guns to ammunition.

'NAC', 'N.A.C.', often in a diamond. Found on a break-barrel spring-air rifle made by the *Norica Arms Company of Eibar, Guipúzcoa, Spain. This was imported into Britain by *Sussex Armoury of Hailsham. The marks may be found in the form of an arrow superimposed on a target background.

'N.A.C.Co.' Found in the headstamps of ammunition manufactured in Canada by the *North American Cartridge Company.

Nadir. A singularly unfortunate mark applied to two break-barrel *Mayer & Grammelspacher-type air rifles made in Italy by Fabbrica Armi Valle Susa di Guglielminotti (*see* FAVS).

Nagant. Emile & Leon Nagant, or E. & L. Nagant frères, Liège. A Belgian gunsmithing company active prior to the First World War. Founder member of les *Fabricants d'armes reunis, 1886, and founding shareholder (somewhat reluctantly) in *Fabrique Nationale d'Armes de Guerre in 1889; Leon Nagant (1833–1900) signed the FN agreement on the brothers' behalf. Best known as a maker of revolvers, including the well-known *gas-seal pattern adopted in Russia, Nagant was also the principal European licensee of the Remington rolling-block breech system; countless thousands of rifles, short rifles and carbines were made prior to the 1890s to satisfy military contracts and commercial demand. Nagant Remingtons included double-barrelled constabulary pistols and quirky side-by-side shotguns embodying a modified Belgian-patent breech. Nagant also made a few hundred bolt-action rifles, precursors of the *Mosin-Nagant, for trials held in Belgium and Russia during the late 1880s.

Nagoya army arsenal. Identifying its products with a distinctive mark of two stylised fighting fish, which appears to be two circles within a circle, the Nagoya factory made *Arisaka rifles and carbines (including Type 2 paratroop examples) between 1933 and 1944. Other guns were made in the Toriimatsu sub-plant during 1940–45. These were identified by an additional mark.

Nagy-Willoughby. According to Eldon Wolff, quoting *The Scientific American* in his book *Air Guns* (1958), this name was applied to a pump-up pneumatic gun that could fire a wide range of projectiles through a series of interchangeable barrel liners. Nothing else is known.

'Nailer' [The]. A mark found on shotgun ammunition associated with J.C. *Paterson of Lisburn. It is assumed that it was purchased from *Irish Metal Industries.

Naismith. J.W. Naismith; *see* Nasmith.

Nakulski. Fabryka Nakulski, Gneizno, Poland. Maker of the 6.35mm *Smok automatic pistol.

Nambu – 1. Kijiro Nambu (1867–1943) was a Japanese Army officer, who retired in 1924 with the rank of lieutenant-general. He is renowned for perfecting the Japanese derivation of the *Hotchkiss machine-gun and for an eponymous semi-automatic pistol, designed by combining the best practice observed on a government-sponsored tour of Europe shortly before the Russo-Japanese War began in 1904. **2.** Nambu pistol: *see* panel, p. 368.

Nanking arsenal. A manufacturer of *Arisaka rifles in China under Japanese supervision, c. 1944. The guns seem to have been assembled from largely sub-contracted parts.

Napoleon. A *Suicide Special revolver made by the *Ryan Pistol Company of Norwich, Connecticut, USA, in the late nineteenth century.

'Narodni Podnik'. Found on a variety of pistols, rifles, machine-guns and even airguns made in Czechoslovakia by *Československá Zbojovka and others. Applied for a short while after the 1948 revolution, it simply means 'State Product'.

Naseby. Børge Naseby. A Danish engineer, designer of *Pallet diabolos and special pellet-making machinery, sold to *Barberblade-Fabrik in 1979.

National, National... *see also* National markings – **1.** A cartridge derringer designed by Daniel *Moore and made successively in the USA by the *Brooklyn Arms Company, the *National Arms Company and *Colt's Patent Fire Arms Manufacturing Company. **2.** A breech-loading carbine made in the USA c. 1867/68 by the National Arms Company in accordance with US Patent 33,847, granted to Daniel Moore in December 1861 for the two-part breech-block, then improved by the grant of

NAMBU PISTOL

Nambu (2)

Elements of many European designs have been seen – or perhaps simply imagined – in the design of this recoil-operated pistol, credited to Kijoro Nambu. This may reflect the influence of a European tour made by the inventor early in the twentieth century, at a time when the *Mauser and *Borchardt-Luger pistols were vying for supremacy in Germany, and the first examples of blowback *FN-Brownings had appeared in Belgium.

The earliest Nambu is said to date from 1904. Its distinctive features include a raked grip containing a detachable box magazine, and a return spring in a separate chamber made as an integral part of the receiver. The spring chamber is offset to the left to allow a pivoting strut to lock the frame and receiver together at the instant of firing.

Guns of this type were sold to Siam (perhaps 2,000) and also to officers of the Japanese Army, apparently through a private-purchase scheme. Once minor changes had been incorporated, including enlarging the original cramped trigger guard to acceptable proportions, Nambu pistols were made in two sizes (the 8mm Model A and the 7mm Model B) in the Koishikawa ordnance factory until, in September 1909, the Imperial Navy adopted the A-pattern for marines and landing parties. No additional production capacity existed in Koishikawa, so a contract was placed with the Tokyo Gas &

Electric Company (TGE) in 1910. Both contractors continued work until 1923, when the Tokyo earthquake interrupted production. TGE seems to have continued as the only participant until 1927 or later, although the basic Nambu pistol had been superseded in military service by the simplified Taisho 14th Year Type Pistol of 1925. The principal change lay in the introduction of two return springs and a straight-sided grip.

Guns of this modified type were made in quantity by Nambu-Seisakusho (renamed Chuo Kogyo KK in 1936), and the government factories in Koishikawa, Nagoya and Kokura until the end of the Second World War. The best source of information remains Harry Darby, *The Hand Cannons of Imperial Japan* (Taylor Publishing, 1993).

The large 8mm 'Papa', or Otsu-Gata' Nambu pistol bore a resemblance to the Parabellum, although the affinities were superficial.

---

no. 45,202 to Alfred Bergen and David Williamson (November 1864), and 46,977 to Williamson alone (March 1865). The National was a dropping-block design, externally resembling a leaner version of the *Peabody, but it had an integral box-lock instead of a separate back-action side-lock. Only a few hundred were made for Government .50-70 ammunition. **3.** Usually encountered as 'The National' on shotgun cartridges made in Britain by *Nobel Explosives Ltd of Glasgow prior to 1918 and the purchase by Explosives Trades Ltd. **4.** National Armory, USA. *See* Springfield Armory. **5.** National Arms & Ammunition Company Ltd [The]. This British gunmaking business was formed in 1872, principally by Westley *Richards and Major-General William *Dixon. The initial goal was to make ammunition, substantial quantities being produced in accordance with an order for 11mm cartridges received from Germany in 1873. The company also made 1871-pattern *Mauser

rifles in this period, although only a fraction of the 75,000 guns ordered was completed. Small numbers of *Snider and *Martini-Henry rifles were manufactured for the British government, but, despite the most strenuous efforts (which even involved litigation), NA&ACo. was never able to compete effectively with the *Birmingham Small Arms Company Ltd or the *London Small Arms Company Ltd. *Martini and Westley *Richards-pattern single-shot rifles were made in quantity, but work dropped away steadily in the 1880s; the Holford Mills were sold to the *Gatling Gun Company Ltd in 1888, and the Montgomery Street factory in the Sparkbrook district of Birmingham was taken over by the government when NA&ACo. eventually failed in 1896. In addition to rifles and rifle cartridges, the business also made 12-, 14- and 16-bore shotgun ammunition with distinctive thin-walled brass cases. These were sold under the generic names Ejector and Express, the headstamps incorporating

'N.A.A. Co.' **6.** National Arms Company, Brooklyn, New York. This US gunmaking business is said to have been founded c. 1864; although sometimes claimed as the successor to *Moore's Patent Fire Arms Company, originally it may have been run concurrently. Gardner, in *Small Arms Makers*, records the National Arms Company on 'Kent Avenue, corner of Hewes' in 1867. Products included single-shot breech-loading pistols, teat-fire cartridge revolvers and carbines protected by patents granted in the USA to Alfred *Bergen, Daniel *Moore and David *Williamson. National continued to make the .41 Models No. 1 and No. 2 Knuckle Duster cartridge derringers until the operations were acquired by *Colt's Patent Fire Arms Manufacturing Company in 1870. **7.** National Arms Company. A brandname associated with shotguns made in the USA by the *Crescent Arms Company of Norwich, Connecticut, prior to 1917. **8.** National Cart Company, Pasadena, California, USA. Makers of the short-lived *Apache pump-up pneumatic rifle in the early 1950s. The design was plagued by leaking valves and proved unable to compete with the rival *Crosman designs. (It has been suggested that the name should be interpreted as 'National Cartridge Company', although there is no proven connection with the succeeding entry.) **9.** National Cartridge Company, St Louis, Missouri. A short-lived ammunition-making business operating in the USA in the 1870s and 1880s. The usual *headstamp was 'N'. **10.** National Cash Register Company, Dayton, Ohio. A contractor for 500,000 .45 M1911 *Colt-Browning pistols, recruited during the First World War. No guns are known to have been made, as the order was cancelled immediately after the 1918 Armistice. A British subsidiary – the National Cash Register Company Ltd of Marylebone Road, London NW1 – produced magazines for the 9mm *Sten Gun during the Second World War. The code 'S 88' may have been used instead of the company name. *See also* British military manufacturers' marks. **11.** National Lead Company. Partner (from 1910) and eventual owner (1919) of the *United States Cartridge Company. **12.** National Match, or National Match Model. Produced from 1933 until 1941, this was a version of the Colt-made *Government Model prepared for target shooting. Each gun was assembled and finished by hand, although the components were standard military pattern. Sights could be fixed or adjustable. **13.** National Match Rifle. A name applied to the .308 Winchester Model 40XC, made by the *Remington Arms Company from 1974 until 1989. It had charger guides on the front of the receiver bridge, a half-stock with a vertical thumb-groove pistol grip and an unusually deep fore-end. The Model 40XR KS National Match Rifle had a Kevlar stock. **14.** National Ordnance, Inc., USA. *See* Springfield. **15.** National Postal Meter Company, Rochester, New York. A maker of 413,020 *M1 Carbines during 1943–44. **16.** National Projectile Works, Grand Rapids, Michigan, and Napa, California. Formed to exploit a patent protecting a 'lubriicated wire wound bullet' granted to Myron Lisle (in 1899), this US ammunition-making business began work c. 1897 and traded in Lyon Street, Grand Rapids, before moving to California in 1906. The business is believed to have closed c. 1913, but confirmation is lacking. **17.** 'National Rifle Association of America'. Found on commemorative guns produced by Daisy (Model 179 Six-Gun, Model 3894 rifle) to cele-brate the association's centenary. *See also* Krag-Jørgensen. **18.** National Rifle Factory No. 1, 8 Lench Street, Birmingham, Warwickshire, England. Formerly operated by the *Standard Small Arms Company Ltd, this factory was purchased by the Ministry of Munitions in June 1918 and made SMLE (*Lee-Enfield) rifle components marked 'NRF' for a few months. The guns were assembled in the *Royal Small Arms Factory, Enfield. National Rifle Factory No. 2 was a Greener-built plant specialising in gun barrels. **19.** National Stock Number (NSN). *See* Nato Standard Number. **20.** National Volcanic Corporation, Seoul. Manufacturer of the *Swift pneumatic shotgun, designed c. 1974 in Korea. Very few were made (perhaps only 100) before production was discontinued.

National markings. The absence of countries or states from this list indicates that either they applied no marks that could be classified as national, or that no reliable information has been obtained. Arms have often been changed when crowns have been assumed by new monarchs, when republics have superseded monarchies, and when provinces or colonies have been won or lost; consequently, the notes that follow should be regarded as guides only. In addition, restrictions of space have often forced die engravers to simplify or even omit details. *See also* Cyphers, imperial and royal. **1.** Argentina. Found on stores ranging from *Maxim machine-guns and *Mauser rifles to Ballester-Molina pistols, bayonets and accoutrements, the national arms consisted of an oval shield containing two hands clasping a Phrygian, or 'Liberty', Cap on a pole within a laurel wreath, generally surmounted by a sunburst (*Sol de Mayo*). Inscriptions will be in Spanish and may be accompanied by 'E-A' or 'EJERCITO ARGENTINO' ('Argentinian Army'). **2.** Australia. No readily identifiable national marks have been used, other than 'D' or 'DD' ('Department of Defence') and the marks applied by individual states (e.g. 'W.A.' for Western Australia and 'TAS.' for Tasmania). Many state marks were applied before the 1900 confederation. **3.** Austria. Some post-1945 guns will bear a displayed eagle mark, often accompanied by 'BH' (*Bundesheer*, 'State Army'). The Austrian eagle has a single head topped by a mural (or 'civic') crown, and a breast shield charged with a single horizontal bar. One talon holds a hammer, while the other clasps a sickle; broken shackles signify release from oppression. **4.** Austria-Hungary. No national marks were applied, although the double-headed Habsburg eagle was used as a military proof mark. **5.** Bavaria. Few national markings were ever used on small-arms, although the shield of the state arms – a distinctive lozenge-like pattern – has been perpetuated in the mark applied by the Munchen proof house. *See also* Cyphers, imperial and royal. **6.** Belgium. No specific national marks have been identified. *See also* 'ABL', 'GB' and Cyphers, imperial and royal. **7.** Bolivia. The arms consist of a shield bearing a depiction of Potosi mountain in a landscape, with a breadfruit tree, a llama and a wheat-sheaf, within a circlet containing the name of the country and nine stars. The arms are customarily surmounted by an enwreathed condor and backed by a trophy of two crossed cannon, four bayonetted rifles and three pairs of national flags. One cannon-mouth holds a Phrygian Cap; the other contains an axe. The marks may be found beneath 'EJERCITO DE BOLIVIA' ('Bolivian Army'); inscriptions will be in Spanish. **8.** Brazil. Customarily accompanied prior to 1968 by 'ESTADOS UNIDOS DO BRASIL' (or simply, 'E.U. do Brasil'), the crest consists of a large five-pointed prismatic star impaled on a sword, point uppermost. A constellation of five stars – the Southern Cross – lies within a circlet of small stars on the centre of the prismatic star; the circlet originally contained twenty stars to represent the original provinces, but the total was increased to twenty-one in 1960, to twenty-two in 1962, to twenty-three in 1977, to twenty-four in 1981, and finally to twenty-seven in 1989. Marks found on weapons ranging from ★Mauser rifles to ★Madsen submachine-guns and FN FAL rifles customarily have twenty-star circlets. In general, the device is contained within a wreath of laurel and coffee leaves, and may be placed on a stylised sunburst, particularly on post-1930 guns. The legend 'ESTADOS UNIDOS DO BRASIL' and '15 DO NOVEMBRE DE 1889' (the date of the formation of the Brazilian republic) may be found on a scroll. Property marks may take the form of the letter 'B', for 'Brazil', within a circle or an encircled six-pointed star. Inscriptions will be in Portuguese, highlighted by a preference for 'Berlim' ('Berlin'); 'EXERCITO BRASILEIRO' ('Brazilian Army') has also been used. **9.** Britain. No national marks, although the 'WD' and broad arrow of the War Department will be found. *See also* Cyphers, imperial and royal. **10.** Bulgaria. The arms comprised a lion rampant on a shield, sometimes, especially on older guns, superimposed on a pavilion and supported by two lance-bearing lions. This was replaced early in the twentieth century by a rampant lion on a shield, beneath a crown supported on two batons, which can be found on ★Parabellum pistols and ★Maxim machine-guns supplied shortly before the First Balkan War. From 1947 onward, the lion appeared on a demi-cogwheel within a wreath of wheat ears separated at their tips by a five-pointed star. A small version of the Bulgarian lion has been used as a military proof or property mark. **11.** Canada. Small-arms used during the period of British domination, including ★Ross rifles, bore a broad arrow within 'C'. Modern military stores may bear a stylised maple leaf instead. **12.** Chile. Encountered above the chambers of 7mm ★Mauser rifles or on the slides of 9mm ★Steyr-Hahn pistols, the Chilean arms consist of a five-pointed prismatic star on a shield halved horizontally, with a crest of three rhea feathers, supported by a crowned huemal (Andean deer) and a crowned condor. Usually they will be found on a mound strewn with laurel, particularly when impressed into butts; stock marks may be accompanied by 'M.F.' in a rectangular cartouche, sometimes placed above the date of manufacture or reconstruction. Some guns display a chamber mark consisting of crossed slung Mauser carbines, 'CHILE' and 'ORDEN Y PATRIA'; others have an unidentified stock roundel that seems to consist of 'C', 'I', 'A' and 'E', with the first and last letters dominant. Inscriptions will be in Spanish. **13.** China. Marks in Chinese characters are usually distinctive, but can easily be confused with Japanese. Guns made in the principal Chinese arsenal in Hanyang will be marked with a double interlocking diamond logo, which, particularly on guns made in the 1930s, may be combined into a flattened octagonal border enclosing the designation. Others may have a stylised cogwheel enclosing a bow-and-arrow, the significance of which is still not known; some may display a stylised disc-like sun with twelve short pointed rays,

adopted in 1928, but customarily used simply as a property or proof mark on military stores. **14.** Colombia. Customarily surmounted by a condor with shackles in its beak and a scroll bearing 'LIBERTAD Y ORDEN', the arms consist of a pomegranate and two cornucopiae above a Phrygian Cap on a spear-head, and a representation of the Isthmus of Panama separating a sailing ship on the Caribbean Sea from a similar ship on the Pacific Ocean. The shield was customarily placed on two pairs of flags and backed by a sunburst within an oval border, although guns supplied by ★Československá Zbrojovka after c. 1930 lacked the sunburst and border, and had 'REPÚBLICA DE COLOMBIA' added beneath the arms. Others displayed 'EJERCITO DE COLOMBIA' ('Colombian Army'), whereas ★Mauser rifles supplied in the 1950s by ★Fabrique Nationale d'Armes de Guerre often used 'COLOMBIA' and 'FUERZAS MILITARES' ('Military Forces'). Inscriptions will be in Spanish. **15.** Costa Rica. The arms consist of a shield bearing seven stars above three volcanoes (representing the Isthmus of Panama) separating sailing ships on the Pacific Ocean and Caribbean Sea, the latter being accompanied by a sun rising over the horizon. Marks will be in Spanish. **16.** Croatia. Marks applied during the German occupation in the Second World War featured the traditional chequered shield beneath the letter 'U' within an eight-looped rope border. This denoted the *Ustaže*, a right-wing Catholic militia raised by Ante Pavelič. **17.** Cuba. Found on firearms ranging from ★Remington-Lee rifles to the ★FN FAL, the arms used from 1902 until 1958 consisted of a shield divided into three. The top bears a key superimposed on land- and seascape representing the Gulf of Mexico; the lower portions contain five diagonal bars and a Royal Palm in a stylised pastoral scene. A single supporter in the form of a *fasces* topped with a Phrygian Cap lies behind the shield, which may be enreathed in oak and laurel. Inscriptions will be in Spanish. **18.** Czechoslovakia. Guns will sometimes bear the crowned two-tailed Lion of Bohemia, charged prior to 1960 with a breast shield (for Slovakia) bearing a double-armed cross on a base of three mountains. They may also be marked 'CSK' for *Ceskoslovenska* (Czechoslovakia). **19.** Denmark. No national markings were used. *See also* Cyphers, imperial and royal. **20.** Dominican Republic. The arms consist of a plain cross on a shield, charged with six national flags, a Cross of Christ and an open Bible. The shield may be enwreathed in palm and laurel leaves. Marks will be in Spanish. **21.** Ecuador. The arms consist of an oval shield or cartouche displaying a landscape (featuring the volcano Chimborazo) rising beneath a shining sun set on a band bearing the March–June zodiacal signs. A steamer rides off the mouth of the Rio Guyas. Surmounted by a condor, the device is backed by two paired flags and a wreath of palm and laurel, and usually will also feature a *fasces* at its base. Marks will be in Spanish. **22.** Egypt. A country with a troubled history, this has rarely applied distinctive marks to its guns. However, the Eagle of Saladin was used during 1952–58 and from 1984 to date, and a stylised Hawk of Quraish during the Federation of Arab Republics (1972–77). The Egyptian Army eagles customarily had breast shields divided vertically into three. Marks will be in Arabic. **23.** El Salvador. Rifles will bear a triangular seascape with five volcanoes beneath a rainbow and a staff supporting an enrayed Phrygian Cap, which may be encircled by the date of independence: '15 DE SET DE 1821'. Usually this is backed by five national flags and may be enwreathed in laurel. **24.** Estonia. The arms comprised three lions *passant guardant* on a plain shield. It is not known to have been used on small-arms. **25.** Ethiopia. Guns used in Ethiopia may bear the Lion of Judah, apparently a property mark, and a mark consisting of the imperial crown above an Amharic inscription and a stylised lion's-head mask within a wreath of laurel. Others are said to bear the cypher of Haile Selassie within a wreath of a grapevine and a wheat ear. **26.** Finland. Small-arms used in Finland rarely bear national markings, although 'S.A.' and 'Sk.Y' marks (qq.v.) are common. A few guns have been reported bearing a *fylfot*, or swastika, with its arms pointing to the left (cf. marks used in Germany during the Third Reich, which pointed to the right), but so have some modern Chinese firearms and the attribution is unclear. **27.** France. National insignia has rarely, if ever appeared on military small-arms. However, 'R.F.', for *République Française* ('French Republic'), has been reported on the grips of *Unique and other handguns. **28.** Germany. Although imperial cyphers and displayed-eagle military proof marks were used prior to 1918, no national marks were applied with the exception of 'DEUTSCHES REICH' ('German Empire') on captured guns, or *Beutegewehre. Guns made during the Third Reich may bear an assortment of marks based on the displayed-eagle state emblem, but these were customarily used simply as proof and inspectors' marks. The swastika, or *Hakenkreuz*, was rarely used, although it did appear in marks applied by some of the paramilitary formations. **29.** Greece. Firearms may bear the national arms, comprising a cross on a horizontally-barred shield enwreathed in laurel. Marks will be in Greek lettering. **30.** Guatemala. Guns often bore a quetzal bird perched on a scroll reading 'LIBERTAD DE 15 DE SET. DE 1821' ('Liberation Day, 15 September 1821'), with two bayonetted rifles crossed above two crossed sabres, within a wreath of laurel tied with a riband recording the national motto. Marks will be in Spanish. **31.** Haiti. The national arms consisted of a trophy of anchors, swords, flags, drums, rifles, cannon and cannon-balls in front of an Emperor Palm, superimposed on (or topped by) a Phrygian Cap on a vertical staff. Marks will be in Spanish. **32.** Honduras. Last revised in 1935, the national arms consist of a triangle with five flames (now often shown as a sun), flanked by two towers, in front of a Mayan pyramid rising from the sea. Topped by a quiver of arrows and two cornucopiae, this was set inside a border bearing the date of independence (15 September 1821). Marks will be in Spanish. **33.** Hungary. Part of Austria-Hungary (q.v.) until 1918. Hungarian firearms made between 1918 and 1943 will occasionally bear a shield, halved vertically. One half contains seven bars; the other has a double-armed cross, encircled by a coronet, on a triple-step base or (particularly in later examples) a grassed mound. The mark is customarily surmounted by St Stephen's Crown, which is topped by a distinctive bent cross. Hungarian small-arms produced since the Communists came to power in 1948 (e.g. *Tokarev 48M pistols) may display a crest of a crossed hammer and sword within a circlet of wheat ears. **34.** India. Part of the British Empire until 1947. The Indian authorities applied marks in the form of 'I' beneath a broad arrow to their military stores. Post

independence weapons will display the cap of the Pillar of Sarnath, created by the Buddhist emperor Asoka (by whose name it is often known). Only three of the pillar-cap lions are visible. **35.** Indonesia. The national emblem, the Garuda, a mythical half-human bird, may be found on Beretta-made *Garand rifles and a range of machineguns. Other firearms will bear a large five-pointed star, taken from the presidential flag. *See also* 'TNI'. **36.** Iran. Some guns will bear the mark of the imperial dynasty, which consisted of a scimitar-wielding lion backed by a rising sun. This customarily appears beneath a Pahlavi crown within a wreath of oak and laurel leaves. **37.** Iraq. Some guns – *Lee-Enfield rifles, for example – will bear a mark comprising an Arabic character (appearing as a reversed angular 'S') within a triangle. More modern weapons may display what appears to be a monogram comprising 'A' and an inverted '2', which is said to be an Arabic abbreviation used by the Republican Guard. **38.** Ireland (Eire). No national markings. **39.** Israel. The six-pointed *Magen David* (Star of David) appears in the Defence Force badge, accompanied by a sword, an olive branch and a scroll bearing the national motto. Marks will be in Hebrew. **40.** Italy. The Arms of Savoy were used by the Kingdom of Italy until 1946, but rarely, if ever, appeared on weapons. They consisted of a shield bearing a St George's Cross within a plain border. A bundled *fasces*, however, may be found on firearms made during the supremacy of Benito Mussolini (1922–43). **41.** Japan. An imperial *Mon* in the form of a stylised chrysanthemum was used on small-arms. **42.** Korea. The emblem of a circular yin-yang and four *Kwae* trigrams representing the four seasons (or the elements of creation) may have been used. **43.** Laos. Guns may be marked with an emblem depicting three elephants beneath a parasol. **44.** Latvia. The arms consisted of a shield charged with a rising half-sun above a lion and a griffin in separate quarters. **45.** Liberia. A shield bearing a star above eleven vertical bars may have been used. Marks will be in English. **46.** Lithuania. The Shield of Arms consisted of a sword-wielding knight mounted on a rearing horse, his own shield being charged with a Patriarchal Cross. However, a highly stylised crown may be found on small-arms. **47.** Luxembourg. The arms consisted of a crowned lion rampant on a horizontally-barred shield, originally with an inescutcheon in the form of a small shield bearing the Netherlands lion (q.v.) on a billeted ground. The term 'Letzebourg' may be used instead of 'Luxembourg'. **48.** Manchuria (Manchukuo). This short-lived republic, formed in the 1930s under Japanese control, does not seem to have used any identifiable national marks other than the cross-and-concentric-circles attributed to *Mukden arsenal. **49.** Mexico. A distinctive mark of an eagle with a snake in its beak, perched on a cactus on an island in a lake, has been used on military firearms for many years. Usually the device is enwreathed in oak and laurel. Marks on guns imported into Mexico generally take the form of a heraldic displayed eagle, and often also bear 'REPÚBLICA MEXICANA'; indigenous products have a less formal mark, more traditionally Aztec, accompanied by 'FÁBRICA NACIONAL DE ARMAS – MEXICO D.F.' Weapons used by Mexican insurgents may bear a Phrygian Cap on a sunburst, accompanied by 'R' and 'M' or 'R de M'. Inscriptions will be in Spanish. **50.** Netherlands. Rarely encountered on firearms, the national arms bear a rampant lion (clutching a sword and a sheaf of arrows) on a plain ground strewn with gold billets. *See also* Cyphers, imperial and royal. **51.** New Zealand. Part of the British Empire and Commonwealth. The New Zealand authorities often marked their service weapons with 'N' and 'Z', separated by a broad arrow. **52.** Nicaragua. The national arms comprised five volcanoes and an enrayed Phrygian Cap on a staff rising out of a seascape, beneath a rainbow. **53.** Norway. A mark of a crowned lion bearing the Axe of St Olav has been widely used. *See also* Cyphers, imperial and royal. **54.** Orange Free State. This short-lived republic simply used 'O.V.S.' on its small-arms. **55.** Paraguay. The principal mark – found on *Mauser rifles and *FN-Browning pistols – consisted of a five-pointed prismatic star (*Estrella de Mayo*) on a stylised sunburst, generally within a wreath of palm and olive leaves, although laurel alone seems to have been used on most guns. An oval border, and also sometimes 'REPÚBLICA DEL PARAGUAY' will often appear. Inscriptions will be in Spanish. **56.** Persia. *See* Iran. **57.** Peru. The national arms consisted of a shield divided into three, with a llama and a chichona tree (each in an upper compartment) above a cornucopia. Usually the shield was placed on two pairs of national flags, surmounted by a sunburst and/or a wreath of laurel, surrounded by a wreath of palm and olive leaves. Guns may also be marked 'REPÚBLICA PERUANA' or 'REPÚBLICA DEL PERU'. **58.** Philippines. Guns may be marked 'R.O.P.' ('Republic of the Philippines'). **59.** Poland. Part of Russia until 1917. Guns may bear a crowned single-headed displayed eagle, often accompanied by 'R' and 'P' for *Reszpublika Polska* (Polish Republic), or 'F.B.', 'RADOM' (q.v.) and the date; 'FB' within a triangle may also be found. **60.** Portugal. Small-arms may bear a version of the national arms, which comprised a shield within a shield, containing five small shields each charged with five discs; seven castles (the Bordure of Castile) lay around the outer edge of the large shield, the whole being placed on an Armillary Sphere and surrounded by an unusually naturalistic spray-wreath of laurel leaves. *See also* Cyphers, imperial and royal. **61.** Prussia. The displayed-eagle national mark was customarily confined to proof marks. *See also* Cyphers, imperial and royal. **62.** Romania. A large crown was used on many pre-1918 small-arms, customarily above the designation (e.g. 'ARMA MD. 1892'). *See also* Cyphers, imperial and royal. **63.** Russia (Tsarist, pre-1917). The double-headed imperial eagle was widely used in proof and property marks. It can be distinguished by its double crowned heads, beneath a single large crown symbolising the unity of the many provinces. It should bear a breast shield showing St George slaying the Dragon (taken from the Arms of Moscow), an encircling collar of the Order of St Andrew, and four small shields on each wing bearing the arms of major cities and provinces of the Empire. However, most small-arms marks are too small to show these in detail. Inscriptions will be in Cyrillic (shared only by Bulgaria, Serbia and Yugoslavia prior to 1948). **64.** Saudi Arabia. The national arms consist of crossed scimitars beneath a palm tree, although the current flag bears only a single Sword of Abd al-Aziz (straight-bladed since 1981) beneath the *shahada* – an expression of the creed of Islam in Arabic script. **65.** Saxony. No national markings. *See also* Cyphers, imperial and royal. **66.** Serbia. Found on *Mauser rifles, among

other guns, the pre-1918 arms consisted of a pavilion containing a double-headed eagle on a shield, with a quartered inescutcheon, or breast shield, bearing two lions and two crosses with fire-stones alongside them. **67.** Siam. The *chakra* mark was widely used on Siamese military stores. Originally an Indian term to describe a spinning wheel, *chakra* came to signify a war quoit with a series of flame-like blades issuing from a circle. The largest examples, particularly those used prior to the 1920s, sometimes contained lines radiating from the top centre of the inner ring; later examples usually have concentric-circle interiors. **68.** Slovakian Republic. Formed by the German authorities during the Second World War. The armed forces of this short-lived territory marked small-arms with a Patriarchal Cross atop three mounds. **69.** South Africa. Part of the British Empire and Commonwealth until 1960. South African weapons of this period were marked 'U' (for 'Union of South Africa'), often containing a broad arrow. **70.** Spain. The national arms have been revised many times, but, owing to the need for compact marks, those used on small-arms have almost always taken a standard simplified form. The marks found on stores ranging from *Mauser rifles to *Astra pistols comprise a crowned shield quartered with a castle (for Castile), a lion (León), vertical bars (Aragón) and a wheel of chains (Navarra). An inescutcheon bore three fleurs-de-lis for the House of Bourbon on a plain ground, but a small compartment at the shield-tip, which should have contained the pomegranate of Granada, was customarily empty owing to lack of space. Spanish-made Mausers often omitted the arms, bearing instead a crown over 'FÁBRICA DE ARMAS, OVIEDO' and the date. The so-called Falangist guns, made during the Spanish Civil War of 1936–39, often by Industrias de Guerra de Cataluña, were marked with a crossed *fasces* and a sword. Modern small-arms may bear revised arms, lacking the inescutcheon, placed on the displayed Black Eagle of the Holy Roman Empire with a Nimbus and a scroll charged with 'UNA GRANDE LIBRE' around its head. Badges of a ribanded yoke and a sheaf of arrows are placed to the right and left of the eagle's tail respectively. Some guns may be marked 'LA CORUÑA'; others will bear the modern Spanish air force mark, an encircled displayed eagle beneath a crown, superimposed on stylised wings. **71.** Sweden. Many older small-arms – *Mauser rifles, for example – bear a crowned black-letter 'C', the mark of *Carl Gustavs Stads Gevarsfaktori, the state-owned gunmaking plant. Modern weapons may display property marks in the form of three ultra-simple stylised crowns. **72.** Switzerland. Swiss *Schmidt-Rubin rifles, *Schmidt revolvers and *Parabellum pistols may display a cross (*Schweizerkreuz* or *Croix Helvétique*) on a sunburst or, usually post-1909, on a vertically-barred shield. Small crosses may serve as proof or inspectors' marks; the latter customarily include an identifying letter. **73.** Syria. Small-arms issued since the 1960s may bear the Hawk of Quraish with a breast shield divided vertically into three. Virtually identical with the marks used by Egypt (above) in the days of the Federation of Arab States (1972–77), Syrian examples were distinguished by two small five-pointed stars on the centre bar of the shield. Inscriptions will be in Arabic. **74.** Thailand. *See* Siam. **75.** Transvaal. This short-lived republic marked its military stores with 'Z.A.R.', for *Zuid Afrikaansche Republiek* (South African

Republic). **76.** Turkey. Some Turkish guns will bear a *Toughra* – normally placed above the chamber of ★Mauser rifles – which is basically a calligraphic version of the sultan's cypher. Others may be marked with a star-and-crescent, with a 'TC' monogram, for *Turkíye Cümhuríyeti* (Republic of Turkey), or with an 'AS.FA' mark representing the military factory, or *Askerí Fabríka*, in Ankara. Marks will be in Arabic prior to 1926, then customarily in Roman lettering. **77.** Uruguay, also known as *República Oriental del Uruguay* ('R. O.U.') or simply as *República Oriental* ('R.O.'). The arms consist of a laurel-enwreathed quartered oval beneath a rising sun, bearing the Scales of Justice, the Cerro citadel of Montevideo, a horse and a bull. Normally the marks are accompanied by a date, and, on later examples, by 'R.O.U. EJERCITO NACIONAL' ('National Army of the Oriental Republic of Uruguay'). Inscriptions will be in Spanish. **78.** United States of America. Military stores are simply marked 'U.S.', or 'US PROPERTY'. A few guns – the ★American Luger, for example – may bear marks in the form of a displayed bald eagle with arrows and thunderbolts in its talons. **79.** USSR. Small-arms made prior to the fragmentation of the Soviet Union in 1991 will bear a hammer-and-sickle mark. *See also* 'C.C.C.P.' **80.** Venezuela. The arms consist of a shield divided into three, with a wheatsheaf and a trophy of flags and sabres above a white horse. The mark is surmounted by two cornucopiae and may be surrounded by a wreath of coffee and sugar-cane leaves. A riband bearing the dates of independence and federation of the *Estados Unidos de Venezuela* ('EE.UU. Venezuela'), 19 April 1816 and 20 February 1889 respectively, binds the limbs of the wreath. Some modern firearms will also be marked 'FUERZAS ARMADAS DE VENEZUELA' ('Venezuelan Armed Forces'). **81.** Yugoslavia. The Kingdom of Serbs, Croats and Slovenes, formed after the First World War, initially used marks based on those of Serbia (q.v.). The shield bore a crowned double-headed eagle with an inescutcheon, or breast shield, divided with two compartments above a third. Used on ★ZB machine-guns, ★Mauser rifles and ★FN–Browning pistols, these are believed to have held arms representing the three principal constituents of the federation. Post-1948 guns may bear the state emblem of six torches forming a single flame within a circlet of wheat ears; some may also be marked 'S.F.R.J.' ('Socialist Federal Republic of Jugoslavia'). Pre-revolutionary marks will often be in Cyrillic; later examples are in Roman lettering. Guns may be marked 'BTZ' for *Voino Tekhniki Zavod*, the state ordnance factory in ★Kraguyevač; others may display 'PRE-DUZEČE' (q.v.) in Cyrillic or Roman.

Nato Standard Number, or NSN. This system was based on the US Federal Stock Numbers (FSN), introduced as part of an Act of Congress in 1952 to assist governmental stock control, which extended to virtually any article of military value. A typical FSN consisted of a four-digit prefix, the Federal Supply Code (FSC) and a seven-digit serial number. In September 1974, a two-digit National Codification Bureau (NCB) component was added to identify the originating country, and the NSN was formed. All NSNs have thirteen digits, customarily separated into groups of four, two and seven. In addition to a general '11', which simply refers to NATO itself, identifiers for individual NATO members include '00', '01' and '06' for the USA; '12', Germany; '13', Belgium;

'14', France; '15', Italy; '17', Netherlands; '21', Canada; '22', Denmark; '23', Greece; '24', Iceland; '25', Norway; '26', Portugal; '27', Turkey; '28', Luxembourg; '33', Spain; and '99', Britain. The system has been expanded intermittently to include non-NATO members, '30' signifying Japan for example, and '66' representing Australia. Sometimes the marks will be found on small-arms. For example, a British 7.62mm L8A1 armoured-vehicle machine-gun, an indigenous variant of the FN ★MAG, will be marked on the left side of the receiver with the designation 'MACHINE GUN 7.62MM TK L8A1' over the manufacturer's code (RSAF ★Enfield), the date (1965) and serial number – 'UE 65 A282' – above the NSN. The group contains the '1005' prefix common to all guns and small-arms of 30mm calibre and below; the code for Britain, '99'; and an arbitrary stock number '960-6851'. The codes will also be found on much more mundane items: the 'Cloth coated bayonet frog, polyurethane on textured nylon, IRR' bears '8465-99-011-2306'. Although most of the marks may be read without difficulty, some will include the country of manufacture instead of the country of use. Consequently, the Belgian-made ★MAG machine-guns used by the British Army (7.62mm L7A1) exhibit '13' in the NSN instead of '99'.

Naughton. T. Naughton. A dealer of sporting goods trading in Galway, Eire, Naughton handled sporting guns and ammunition. The cartridges may bear such trade-names as The Blazer and The Connaught.

Navarro. Manuel and Everado Navarro, Celaya, Guanajuarto, Mexico. These 'mechanics' obtained US Patent 1,113,239 of 13 October 1914 to protect a conversion of the ★Parabellum pistol, which could fire automatically if required. A spring, retained by a distinctive sliding thumb-screw, was added to the sear bar.

Navy... – 1. Navy Arms Company, Ridgefield, New Jersey, USA. Renowned for its reproduction black-powder firearms, made in Italy and the USA, this distributor promoted .45-70 rifle- and carbine-length conversions of the military Siamese (Thai) Mauser rifles in the mid-1970s. *See also* Classic Arms. **2.** Navy-Hudson machine-gun. Prior to the Second World War, the US Navy had adopted a 1.1in machine-gun designed by Robert F. Hudson of the Naval Gun Factory in Washington. This complicated box-feed combination of gas and recoil operation was fitted on many of the navy's warships until ultimately replaced by the appreciably simpler Oerlikon and Bofors guns during 1942–44. A few experimental .30- and .50-calibre Hudsons were produced for trials in the late 1930s, but they were unable to challenge the Brownings. **3.** Navy Model Revolver. Made by ★Colt's Patent Fire Arms Manufacturing Company, and also known as the Old Model Belt Pistol of Navy Caliber, this was basically a .36-calibre enlargement of the .31 ★Pocket Model. Made in great numbers – 215,000 in Hartford (1850–73) plus 40,000 in London – its 'navy' connotation arose from the calibre and the naval scene rolled into the cylinder periphery. *See also* New Navy Model. **4.** Navy Model Revolver. The first revolver made by ★Colt's Patent Fire Arms Manufacturing Company to offer a cylinder that could be swung out of the frame on a yoke, the Model 1889 was purchased in .38 calibre by the US Navy (1889–90) and marketed commercially in .38 and .41; the plain-surfaced cylinder turned anti-clockwise when viewed from the rear. It was soon succeeded by the ★New Navy Model, which had recesses in the cylinder periphery.

Naylor – **1.** Charles Naylor, Sheffield, Yorkshire. The marks of this English gunmaker and sporting-goods supplier (perhaps a successor to Thomas Naylor, active 1847–68) have been found on shotguns and shotgun ammunition, the origins of the latter being unknown. Some cartridges will be found marked 'CANNOT BE BEATEN' or 'NAYLOR'S CANNOT BE BEATEN'. **2.** Thomas Naylor, Sheffield, Yorkshire. This gunmaker was active in England from 1847 until 1868, trading successively from 66 Snig Hill (1847 only), 37 Church Street (1861) and 38 West Bar (1863–68). Naylor's marks appear on ★pepperboxes and cap-lock revolvers.

'nbe'. This code was granted to Hasag Eisen- und Metallwerke GmbH, for use on German military small-arms ammunition components made in the Tschenstochau factory during 1944–45.

'NCA'. Possibly a Spanish version of ★Norica Compañía de Armas. *See also* 'NAC'.

'NCT'. Found on US military firearms and accessories. *See* Nathan C. ★Twining.

'ndn'. Used by Heinrich Blucher of Spremberg on small-arms ammunition made in Germany during 1944–45.

'nea'. Associated with small-arms and ammunition components made during 1944–45 in Suhl, Thüringen, Germany by Walter Steiner.

'nec'. Found on small-arms components made under German supervision in the Guerin factory of Waffenwerke Brunn AG in 1944.

Necaš. Augustin Necaš. Born in the Moravian town of Vilemov on 22 May 1918 and trained in the Brno technical college as a precision machinist, Necaš joined Zbrojovka Brno in 1941. Beginning in 1949, he established himself as a designer of handguns – including the .22 ZKP 493S and 4mm ZKP 504 target pistols (also known as the Champion), and the interchangeable-barrel ★Universal auto-loader. He has also been involved in the development of revolvers.

'N.E.C. Ld'. A monogram-type trademark associated with the products of the ★New Explosives Company Ltd of London.

'Neco' [The]. A mark identifying shotgun ammunition loaded in Britain by the ★New Explosives Company Ltd, 1907–19.

Nederlandsch Wapen- en Munitiefabriek 'de Kruithoorn' was an outgrowth of the Dutch state-owned manufactory in ★Hembrug and ★Artillerie-Inrichtingen. However, although NWM acquired a licence to make ★CETME rifles in 1956 and became involved with a number of small-arms projects during the 1960s and 1970s (in particular the ★Stoner series), profitability declined. The struggling business was acquired by ★Rheinmetall, but finally was closed in 1998 owing to a lack of orders.

Needham – **1.** Henry Needham, Birmingham, Warwickshire, and London. Possibly the brother of William Needham (below), this gunmaker traded from Little Cannon Street from 1834 until moving to 5 Meard's Court, Little Wardour Street, London, where he remained until 1856. Needham received English Patent no. 12,432 of 1849, protecting safety catches and a self-priming system with a tubular cap magazine in the stock. He was awarded a prize medal at the Great Exhibition in 1851, and was the grantee of British Patent 2184 of 1853 for a cap-lock revolver. **2.** Joseph Needham [& Company]. Trading in London, from 26 Piccadilly, this gunmaking business succeeded William & Joseph Needham in 1853, and traded until succeeded by Joseph & Henry Needham in 1870. Needle-fire sporting guns were made by Joseph Needham during the 1850s. US Patent 64,999 was granted on 21 May 1867 to 'Joseph & George Henry Needham of London' to protect the design of a rifle with a laterally-opening breech-block, but it is not certain if, as Robert Gardner claimed in *Small Arms Makers*, this refers specifically to Joseph Vernon Needham. London directories record subsequent moves to 53 Piccadilly in 1853; 1a Wilton Place, Knightsbridge, in 1879; and 6 Park Side, Knightsbridge, in 1880. The Knightsbridge addresses were probably Henry Needham's residences. **3.** Joseph Vernon Needham, Birmingham, Warwickshire. Needham, perhaps the son of William Needham (q.v.), traded from 108 New Street from 1861 until moving to Damascus Works, Loveday Street, in 1887. Operations continued until the First World War. Needham was granted protection for a variety of firearms, including British Patent no. 31/73 of 1873 for a lever-action magazine rifle; 1205/74 of 1874 for a sporting gun with a dropping barrel that also moved laterally; 2793/75 of 1875 for a drop-barrel action; 706/79 of 1879 (sought jointly with George Hinton) for a drop-barrel action and associated safety catches; 716/81 of 1881 (with J.T. Atkinson) for a magazine rifle with a revolving- or hinged-chamber; and 7995/84 of 1884 (with T.H.S. Hawker) for a hinged breech-block. He also patented a special dagger handle in 1872, and marked 12-bore Uneedem shotgun cartridges. US Patent 225,994, granted to Needham & Hinton on 30 March 1880, is comparable with British Patent 706/79; the papers reveal that it was assigned to W.M. and J.C. ★Scott. Similarly, J.V. Needham's US Patent 248,339 of 18 October 1881 (protecting a 'breech loader') was assigned to W.W. ★Greener. **4.** William Needham, Birmingham and London. This gunmaker traded from Royal Hotel Yard, Temple Row, Birmingham from the early 1840s until moving to 26 Piccadilly, London, in 1844. Trading continued until 1854 or later. William Needham, perhaps a brother of Henry (above), was granted English Patent 9801 of 1843 to protect a priming system with a vertical tube and an automatic capping mechanism in the stock.

'Negro' [The]. Associated with the ★Mullerite Cartridge Works of Birmingham, Warwickshire, England. It is thought that the shotgun cartridges, which were made before the First World War, were loaded with a charge of black powder.

Nelson. Francis Nelson, Sligo. The marks of this Irish gunsmith and ironmonger have been found on shotgun ammunition made prior to the First World War by ★Nobel's Explosives Company Ltd. In general, they are accompanied by 'The Reliable'.

Nemrod. A brandname associated with self-cocking shotguns made by M. ★Berger et Cie of Saint-Étienne.

'Neoflak' [The]. Found on shotgun cartridges made in Britain by ★Eley-Kynoch Ltd.

'N.E. Powder' [The]. Found on shotgun cartridges introduced in Britain by the ★New Explosives Company Ltd, 1913.

Nepperhan Fire Arms Company, Yonkers, New York, USA. A maker of .31-calibre detachable side-plate *Colt-type open-frame revolvers during the American Civil War. Their brass trigger guards were dovetailed into the frame.

Neptun – 1. Originating prior to 1939, essentially this is a side-lock variant of the *Krieghoff *Trumpf *Drilling* and can be obtained in the same chamberings and the same basic options: as a side-by-side shotgun above a central rifle barrel, or as a side-by-side double rifle above a single central smoothbore. The original patterns incorporated leaf springs, but those made after production recommenced in 1954 are fitted with coil springs on shortened readily-detachable lock plates. **2.** Neptun Primus. The deluxe variant of the standard *Krieghoff Neptun combination gun, this offers extensive engraving, gold plating on many of the internal components and select European walnut woodwork.

'Neptune' [The]. A shotgun cartridge made in Britain by *Eley Bros. prior to the acquisition of the company by Explosives Trades Ltd in 1918.

Nercke. Oswald Nercke, Erfurt, Lange Brücke 51. A retailer of sporting guns and ammunition active in Germany during 1941.

Nero. Two types of *Suicide Special revolver made in the USA by the *Hopkins & Allen Arms Company of Norwich, Connecticut, or the J. *Rupertus Patent Pistol Manufacturing Company of Philadelphia, Pennsylvania; they date from the late nineteenth century.

Nestor. A. Nestor, Limerick. An Irish gunsmith and sporting-goods supplier known to have handled shotguns and shotgun ammunition. No tradenames have been reliably linked with this particular source, most pre-1914 cartridges proving to have been standard Kynoch or Eley patterns.

Nettleton. Henry Nettleton, active c. 1875–83, accepted a variety of firearms for service with the US Army. Identified by their 'HN' markings, they included *Remington-Lee and *Winchester Hotchkiss rifles; .45-calibre *Colt, *Remington and Smith & Wesson *Schofield revolvers; and even Colt-made *Gatling Guns. *See also* US arms inspectors' marks.

Neue Spitz. A brandname associated with an airgun pellet made in Germany by *Bimoco.

Neuhausen – 1. A range of machine- and submachine-guns was made under this name by *SIG. Most of them dated from the period 1925–35. **2.** Neuhausen rifle. Designed in 1887/88, but not patented in Switzerland until July 1889, this rifle had a bolt with an annular actuator collar rather than the separate side-mounted pattern of the competing *Schmidt rifle; however, its twin lugs still locked into the receiver behind the magazine well. The first Neuhausens were converted from Vetterli actions, but ninety 7.5mm-calibre guns were ordered from *Schweizerische Industrie-Gesellschaft for trials. The basic rifle had a solid-bridge receiver with a straight-pull bolt and a stubby bolt handle.

Neumann – 1. Franz Neumann, Suhl in Thüringen, Roschstrasse 7 (1941). Founded in Suhl in 1906, this gun-making business remained active in Germany until the end of the Second World War. *Aydt-action sporting guns are known with Neumann's marks, but the company's best-known product was the *Zentrum pistol. **2.** Neumann frères, Liège, Belgium. This gunmaking business was a partner in the *Syndicat des Pièces interchangeables (1898), and bought the ailing *Clément organisation c. 1912.

Never Miss. A *Suicide Special revolver made by the *Hopkins & Allen Arms Company of Norwich, Connecticut, in the late nineteenth century.

New... – 1. New Army Model Revolver, or New Model Double Action Army Revolver. The first of these .38 M1892 guns, made by *Colt's Patent Fire Arms Manufacturing Company, was ordered by the US Army in the summer of 1892. Their cylinders had two sets of locking notches, preventing rotation when the gun was holstered. Original guns acknowledged patents granted in 1884–88, but subsequently also those of 1895 and 1901. This can assist dating. **2.** New Cadix, or Astra New Cadix (NC). Changes introduced to conform with the US Gun Control Act of 1968, particularly those that influenced safety, forced Astra–Unceta to improve the basic *Cadix design by the addition of a *transfer-bar mechanism. The New Cadix, or NC-6, of 1973 is otherwise much the same as its predecessor. **3.** 'New Chicago', or 'New Chicago Model'. Found on spring-air guns made in the USA by the *Markham Air Rifle Company. *See also* King New Chicago. **4.** New Departure. An alternative name for the *Smith & Wesson .32 *Safety Hammerless revolver. **5.** 'New Dictator'. A mark found on a US-made *Suicide Special revolver. Attribution unknown. **6.** New England Westinghouse Company [The], USA. *See* Mosin-Nagant. **7.** New Explosives Company Ltd, 62 London Wall, London E.C., and Stowmarket, Suffolk. This propellant manufacturer, formed in Britain in, or shortly before, 1907, made smokeless powders under the names Felixite, Neonite, Red Star and Shotgun Neonite. Second-grade brands included Primrose Smokeless and Stowmarket Smokeless. All of these had been introduced by the summer of 1908. The New Explosives Company Ltd also loaded shotgun cartridges under such brandnames as Fourten, Green Rival, Neco, N.E. Powder, Premier, Primrose and Red Rival. A trademark of an 'N.E.C. Ld' monogram was also used. The company was incorporated in *Explosives Trades Ltd in 1918, and had soon lost its separate identity. However, a couple of its brandnames were perpetuated by *Eley-Kynoch. **8.** New Frontier. Introduced by *Colt's Patent Fire Arms Manufacturing Company in 1961, capitalising on a campaign slogan attributed to President John F. Kennedy, this was simply a variant of the original *Flat Top Target Model chambered for the .357 Magnum, .38 Special, .44 Special or .45 Colt cartridges. About 4,200 guns were made between 1961 and 1975, followed by a few Third Model examples during 1978–81. Distinguished by a highly-polished finish and medallions set into the grips, the New Frontier was also offered as a New Frontier *Buntline Special, with a 12in barrel, but fewer than 100 were made during 1962–67 and 1980–81. **9.** New Frontier. A modernised version of the *Frontier Scout, with a flat-top receiver and adjustable sights, this was made in .22 LR and .22 WMR by the Firearms Division of Colt Industries (1970–77, 1982–86). Post-1982 guns lacked exchangeable cylinders, but had an additional crossbolt safety catch. A few examples with 7.5in barrels were classified as the *Buntline. *See also* Peacemaker. **10.** New Haven Arms Company (1), New Haven, Connecticut, USA. Run initially by a syndicate of prominent local businessmen, led by a shirt maker named Oliver *Winchester, this gunmaking business succeeded the *Volcanic Arms Company in 1857. It is now best known for the lever-action rifle protected by US Patent 30,446 granted to Benjamin Tyler *Henry on 16 October 1860. Henry rifles were made in quantity during the American Civil War (1861–65), but their fortunes declined rapidly after the fighting had ceased. Improved by the addition of a loading gate credited to Nelson King, the Henry rifle soon became the Winchester Model 1866. Meanwhile the New Haven Arms Company had been dissolved and its assets were acquired by the Winchester Repeating Arms Company (q.v.). **11.** New Haven Arms Company (2), New Haven, Connecticut. Related to the preceding business in name only, this twentieth-century gunmaker was responsible for the .22 semi-automatic target pistols designed by Eugene *Reising. **12.** New House Pistol. This five-shot .38 and .41 centrefire revolver, an adaptation of the *New Line series, was introduced by *Colt's Patent Fire Arms Manufacturing Company in 1880. The most distinctive feature was the squared butt heel. About 4,000 were made during 1880–86. **13.** New King. Dating from the period 1895–1900, this was identical to the first US *Markham-made King BB Gun, except that it had a sheet-metal barrel. **14.** New King Chicago. A spring-air-gun made in the USA by the *Markham Air Rifle Company. **15.** New King Repeater. This was a repeating version of the break-open New King BB Gun (above), with a 150-shot magazine and a muzzle-cap loading lever. It was made in the USA by *Markham between 1895 and 1900. **16.** New Line Revolver. Often inappropriately classed among the *Suicide Specials, this name applied to *Colt's sheath-trigger solid-frame New Breech-Loading

Revolver, intoduced in 1873 and made until c. 1884 in five calibres: .22, .30, .32, .38 and .41. With the exception of the .22, which had a seven-chamber cylinder, the guns were all five-shot models. A major improvement in the action was made in 1876, when the locking slots were moved to the back of the cylinder. **17.** New Line Revolver. A series of solid-frame sheath-trigger revolvers introduced during the 1870s by E. *Remington & Sons to compete with the similarly-named Colts (above). About 100,000 guns were made between 1873 and 1886, more than half the total being .22 rimfire *Iroquois. Based on a trigger system patented by William *Smoot in October 1873, the New Line range consisted of the .30 No. 1 of 1873, the .32 No. 2, the .38 No. 3 of 1875, and the .38 No. 4 of 1877. **18.** New Model Army Revolver. Sometimes known as the Model of 1860, this exceptionally streamlined .44 six-chamber design was introduced commercially in 1861 by *Colt's Patent Fire Arms Manufacturing Company. Nearly 130,000 were purchased by the Federal government alone during the American Civil War. **19.** New Army Revolver. A term applied to the first newly-made .44 rimfire revolver to be offered by *Colt. It had an open-top frame, a Navy Model grip and a cylindrical barrel with a *Mason ejector. Production is believed to have been about 7,500. **20.** New Army Revolver. Used to describe the perfected .44-calibre six-shot cap-lock 'of army caliber' introduced in 1863. It was fitted with the rammer patented by Samuel *Remington and had safety notches between the nipples. E. *Remington & Son supplied the Federal government with more than 120,000 of these weapons prior to mid-summer 1866. **21.** New Model Belt Revolver. Eight thousand of these .36 six-shot cap-lock revolvers were

NEW MODEL DOUBLE ACTION REVOLVER

New… (23)

Introduced in the late 1870s by *Colt's Fire Arms Manufacturing Company, this handgun featured lockwork patented by William

*Mason. It had a bird's-head butt and, in the short-barrelled patterns, lacked the ejector rod and its casing. Although characterised by weaknesses in the action, these revolvers were surprisingly

successful: 166,000 were made between 1877 and 1909. The .38 and .41 versions were known as the Lightning and the Thunderer respectively, the names being conferred by the distributor Benjamin *Kittredge & Company of Cincinnati.

The Colt New Model Double Action Revolver, better known by its Kittredge-bestowed sobriquets – Lightning (.38) and Thunderer (.41) – marked Colt's first foray into the self-cocking field. The gun was renowned for the delicacy of its lockwork, which often failed, but was praised for the rapidity with which a first shot could be fired. This is a deluxe version of the Thunderer, with gold-plated cylinder and hammer, exhibited at the St Louis Exposition of 1877.

made by E. ★Remington & Sons, with 6¹/₂in octagonal barrels, and single- or double-action trigger systems. Many will now be found with ornate decoration. **22.** New Model Hammerless Business Rifle. Made only during 1879–81, this ★Sharps-Borchardt chambered .40-70 Sharps or .40-90 Sharps rounds. It had a blued octagonal barrel, an oil-finished straight-wrist butt and a plain half-length fore-end. **23.** New Model Double Action Revolver: *see* panel, facing page. **24.** New Model Hammerless Express Rifle. Chambered for the .45-100 or .45-120 Sharps cartridges, this ★Sharps-Borchardt was made in small numbers during 1880–81 for the African market. It had an octagonal barrel, a multi-leaf Express back sight, a shotgun-type butt and chequered woodwork. Sling bars were driven through the woodwork. **25.** New Model Hammerless Hunters' Rifle. Dating from the period 1879–81 and made only for .40-50 or .40-70 cartridges, this ★Sharps-Borchardt had a round barrel, a plain fore-end and a straight-wrist butt with a rifle-type butt plate. **26.** New Model Hammerless Long Range Rifle, or Hammerless Long-Range Rifle. Chambered for the .45-90 Sharps round, this gun had a 34in round barrel, chequering on the fore-end and pistol-grip butt, a long-range vernier sight on the tang, and a globe-type front sight with a wind gauge and a spirit level. The standard barrel-mounted back sight was usually omitted. **27.** New Model Hammerless Military Rifle. Chambered for the .45-70 Government or .45-75 Sharps cartridges, this ★Sharps-Borchardt had a straight-comb butt, a full-length fore-end and two barrel bands. Apparently it was purchased by National Guardsmen in Michigan and North Carolina. **28.** New Model Hammerless Military Carbine. A half-stock version of the ★Sharps-Borchardt military rifle, made only in small numbers. **29.** New Model Hammerless Officer's Rifle. This variant of the standard ★Sharps-Borchardt had chequering on the butt wrist and diced rubber inserts in the receiver-side. **30.** New Model Hammerless Sporting Rifle. A version of the ★Sharps-Borchardt rifle, with an octagonal barrel chambered for the .45-70 Government or .45-120 Sharps cartridges. It had a half-stock and a shotgun-style butt. Double triggers and engraving were among the options. **31.** New Model Hammerless Short & Mid-Range Rifle. Chambering .40-70 cartridges, this ★Sharps-Borchardt was similar to the Short Range Target Rifle, but had a 30in barrel and a back sight graduated to 1,200yd instead of 800yd. **32.** New Model Hammerless Short Range Rifle. Made during 1878–81, this .40-50 gun had a 28in barrel, vernier back sight and globe-pattern wind-gauge front sight. The pistol-grip butt and fore-end were chequered. A rubber shotgun-style butt plate was fitted. **33.** New Model Holster Revolver, USA. *See* New Model Army (Colt). **34.** New Model Light Rifle. An alternative name for the No. 2 Sporting Rifle, made by E. ★Remington & Sons and the ★Remington Arms Company prior to 1910. **35.** New Model My Friend. A derivative of the barrelless ★My Friend revolver patented by James ★Reid and introduced in 1880, this was distinguished by its short barrel and markings. Work lasted only until 1884. The changes may have been due to accidents arising from the absence of a barrel on the original gun. **36.** New Model Navy Revolver. A .36-calibre version of the New Model Army ★Colt, with the same sinuous barrel shroud and creeping rammer. Production amounted to 38,800 between 1861

and 1874, 17,000 of which had gone to the Federal government during the Civil War. **37.** New Model Navy Revolver. Only about 23,000 examples of this .36-calibre cap-lock were made by E. ★Remington & Sons. Apart from calibre and smaller overall dimensions, they were comparable with the ★Remington New Model Army pattern. **38.** New Model Pocket Revolver. Also known as the New Model Pocket Pistol of Navy Caliber, this .36 five-shot ★Colt revolver appeared in 1861, although now it is generally known as the Model 1862. About 22,000 were made prior to 1874, with a plain cylinder and a hinged rammer. **39.** New Model Pocket Revolver. The smallest of the cap-locks made in the USA by E. ★Remington & Son with the 1863-patent rammer, this was a .31 five-shot gun with a sheath trigger. About 27,500 were made in a variety of finishes. **40.** New Model Police Revolver. This streamlined cap-lock revolver was a .36-calibre five-chamber design, introduced by ★Colt's Patent Fire Arms Manufacturing Company in 1861 – although customarily known as the Model 1862. About 25,000 were made during 1862–74, with fluted cylinders and creeping rammers. **41.** New Model Police Revolver. A .36 five-shot cap-lock revolver made by E. ★Remington & Son, this was basically a short-barrel New Model Belt pattern. About 18,000 were made during 1863–70, the last being sold in the 1880s. **42.** New Model Russian Revolver. An improved form of the ★Smith & Wesson ★Russian Model, incorporating an extraction mechanism patented by Daniel B. ★Wesson in 1875. **43.** New Model Single Action Revolver. A modification of the .38 ★Baby Russian, introduced in the USA by ★Smith & Wesson in 1877 and made until 1891, during which time about 108,000 guns were assembled. The extractor mechanism was improved; the new cylinder retainer was patented by Daniel ★Wesson and James ★Bullard in February 1877; and an improved extractor-cam actuator dated from 1880. The so-called New New Model Single Action .38, also known as the Model of 1891, superseded the New Model. A trigger guard replaced the sheath trigger, but only about 28,000 had been made by 1911. **44.** New Navy Model Revolver, or New Model Double Action Navy Revolver. The original ★Navy Model revolver introduced by ★Colt's Patent Fire Arms Manufacturing Company in 1889, which had shown weaknesses in its design, was succeeded in 1892 by this gun. Recesses in the cylinder periphery are an obvious identification feature. **45.** New Normal Ammunition Company Ltd, Hendon, London NW4. Although its name was calculated to suggest otherwise, this business was more of an importer of propellant and ammunition components than a manufacturer, purchasing its raw materials in Europe, then assembling cartridges in Britain. New Normal shotgun cartridges included The Gas-Tight, The Hendon, The Normalis and the Special Twenty. The New Normal business succeeded the ★Normal Powder Company, perhaps when the latter failed, but itself seems to have been superseded by the ★Normal Improved Ammunition Company. **46.** New Pocket Model Revolver. This, the first of the ★Colt's Patent Fire Arms Manufacturing Company double-action pocket revolvers, appeared in 1893. Made in a selection of .32 chamberings, the New Pocket Model shared many of its features with the .38 ★New Army Model, but had a clockwise-turning cylinder; 31,000 had been made by 1905. **47.** New Police

NEW SERVICE MODEL REVOLVER

New... (51)

This .45 Colt or .476 Eley pattern was introduced in the USA by *Colt's Patent Fire Arms Manufacturing Company in 1897. Little more than an improved *New Model Army pattern, its name was registered with the US Patent Office in 1899. It is said to have been derived from the chambering of the original 1899-vintage guns for the new [British

military] service cartridge – the .455 Cordite Mk I pattern. The cylinder rotated clockwise and the *Positive Safety was added after 1905. Standard frames had sighting channels cut in the strap above the cylinder, but the Target Model had

a flat-topped frame and an adjustable back sight. Production ended in 1943. In addition to guns purchased prior to the First World War, 150,700 .45 examples were bought by the US government during 1917–18. Known as M1917, these needed *Half-Moon Clips to fire .45 ACP cartridges.

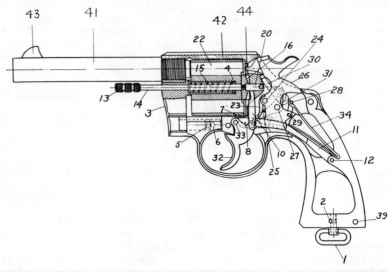

A longitudinal section of the action.

Model Revolver. This .32-calibre *Colt revolver is said to have been developed in 1896 for the New York Police Department. It was little more than a New Pocket Model (q.v.) with a longer grip; almost 50,000 were made between 1896 and 1907. About 5,000 .32-calibre New Police Target Model guns were made during 1897–1905. They were identical mechanically with the standard New Police, but had flat-top frames, 6in barrels and adjustable sights. **48.** New Police Pistol. Introduced in 1882, this .32-, .38- or .41-calibre *Colt's Patent Fire Arms Manufacturing Company *New Line revolver was made with barrels up to 6in long. Unlike the short-barrel patterns, these had ejector cases on the right side. New Police Pistols had gutta-percha 'Cop-and-Thug' grips. About 4,000 guns had been made when work ceased in 1886. **49.** New Rapid. A spring-air rifle made by the *Rapid Rifle Company of Grand Rapids, Michigan, USA. The original design was patented in 1898 by Calkins, Lindberg, Butts & Wheeler, and a modification followed in 1901 by Simmonds, Ross & Fisher. *See also* Cycloid, Cyclone and Rapid. **50.** New Rival. A version of the Markham *Prince BB Gun, made in the USA in the early 1900s for *Sears, Roebuck & Company. **51.** New Service Model Revolver: *see* panel, above. **52.** New Service Rifle. An alternative name for the British *Webley & Scott Mark 2 Service air rifle of the 1933–40 era. **53.** New York Arms. A *Suicide Special revolver made by the *Crescent Arms Company of Norwich, Connecticut, USA, in the late nineteenth century. **54.** New York Arms Company. A brandname associated with shotguns made in the USA prior to 1920 by the *Crescent Arms Company of Norwich, Connecticut. **55.**

New York Cartridge Company, New York City. A maker of ammunition identifiable by the inclusion of 'N.Y.C.' or 'N.Y.C. Co.' in the headstamps. **56.** New York Metallic Cartridge Company, New York City. Founded toward the end of the American Civil War, this short-lived cartridge-making business may have supplied ammunition to William *Irving. **57.** 'New York Pistol Company'. A mark found on small rimfire *single-action revolvers made in the USA in the 1870s. It is believed to have been a tradename, but identification is still lacking.

Newark, Newark... – 1. John Newark, 28 Bailey Lane, Coventry, Warwickshire. The marks of this English machinist and loom maker (active 1853–70) have been found on self-cocking *pepperboxes. The guns were clearly bought elsewhere. **2.** 'Newark Cartridge' [The]. Found on 12-bore shotgun ammunition loaded by Charles *Smith & Sons of Newark.

Newby. Edwin Henry Newby. A gunmakers' agent listed in London at 39a King William Street (1867–75); Chatham Buildings, New Bridge Street, E.C. (1876–79); and 8 Bucklersbury and John Street, Wandsworth, from 1880 until 1900 or later.

Newell. L. Newell, a government inspector active c. 1876–86, accepted firearms and accessories on behalf of the US Army. They included *Sharps and *Springfield-Allin rifles identified by their 'LN' stamps. *See also* US arms inspectors' marks.

Newham. George Newham [& Company]. A gunmaking business trading from 29 Commercial Road, Lamport, Portsmouth, Hampshire. Shotgun ammunition has been reported with Newham's marks, although most was standard *Eley Bros., *Eley-Kynoch or *Kynoch fare (e.g.

The Keeper's Cartridge and Pegamoid). However, some 12-bore cartridges carried 'THE SPECIAL GAME' and a drawing of a cock pheasant; they are also customarily marked 'Specially loaded by the Newham Company', although the components were supplied by *Eley-Kynoch (usually headstamped 'ICI').

'Newport' [The]. A brandname associated with shotgun ammunition handled by *Edmonds of Newport.

Newton – 1. The co-patentee with Rosewell and Frank *Joyce of a ribbed and tapered airgun slug; see British Patent 24,314/01 of December 1901. **2.** Charles Newton, Birmingham, Warwickshire. The marks of this English gunmaker, successor to George *Rooke (Birmingham, 1810–57) have been reported on sporting rifles and shotguns, premises being occupied at 15 Bath Street from 1857 until 1888. He noted in an advertisement that he was a 'Manufacturer of Guns, Pistols, and Rifles...Needle, Saloon, and every description of Breech-loading Rifles, and Fowling Pieces on the newest and best principles, Air Guns and Canes'. **3.** Charles Newton, Boston, Massachusetts, USA. Trained as a lawyer, Newton is best known as the designer of the first commercially successful high-power bolt-action sporting rifle to be manufactured in the USA – although, ironically, his fame is due more to cartridge designs, such as the .250-3000 Savage, that have stood the test of time far better than the rifles. Newton began by importing Oberndorf-made German *Mauser actions and fitting them with barrels chambered for his own cartridges. These were replaced by the Newton Sporting Rifle, built on a patented multi-lug turning-bolt action notable for its slender contours. Production under the Newton Arms Company banner began in 1916, but the advent of the First World War (and the traditional reluctance of American purchasers to favour bolt actions) forced the manufacturer into liquidation in April 1918. Only a few thousand guns had been completed, in chamberings ranging from .256 Newton to .35 Newton. Then the inventor formed the Charles Newton Rifle Corporation, which lasted until 1922. This made a few rifles to an improved 1921 design with an interrupted-thread locking system instead of lugs. Meanwhile a few hundred guns marked by the spurious 'Newton Arms Corporation' had been assembled from parts sold by the liquidators of the original Newton Arms Company to a machine-tool refurbisher. The Buffalo Newton Rifle Company was formed to exploit the 1921 design, trading in Buffalo, New York State, until 1924, then in New Haven, Connecticut, until 1930; however, the guns were not as well made as those dating from 1916–18 and could not compete with the products of established businesses such as *Marlin, *Remington and *Winchester. Newton had already left Buffalo Newton to start the LeverBolt Rifle Company (q.v.), but his death in 1932 brought even this venture to a premature end. **4.** James Newton, Bath Street, St Mary's Row and Ludgate Hill, Birmingham, Warwickshire. This English gun- and (latterly) gun-barrel maker is known to have traded from 1838 until c. 1870. **5.** Thomas Newton, 48 King Street West, Manchester, Lancashire. This gunmaker started trading from 56 Lower King Street in 1860, receiving British Patent no. 132/62 of 1862 for adjustable rifle sights, and no. 297/64 of 1864 for a drop-barrel breech-loading sporting gun. As his name has also been reported on 12-bore shotgun cartridges marked 'The Lightning' or 'Newton's G.P.', it is clear that operations continued into the twentieth century. **6.** Newton Arms Company, Buffalo, New York State, USA. The maker of bolt-action sporting rifles to the designs of Charles Newton (above). **7.** 'Newton Arms Corporation', Buffalo, New York State. Active in 1919–20 only; see Charles Newton (above). **8.** Newton Rifle Corporation, USA. See Charles Newton. **9.** 'Newton's G.P.' A mark found on 12-bore shotgun ammunition, made by *Eley-Kynoch ('ICI' headstamps) and sold by Thomas *Newton of Manchester. It is assumed that 'G.P.' signifies 'Grand Prix'.

'NF'. A superimposition-type monogram, usually within an oval. Correctly 'FN' (q.v.); associated with the products of *Fabrique Nationale d'Armes de Guerre.

'nfix'. This code was used by the Warsaw-Praga factory of RWS Munitionsfabrik GmbH on small-arms ammunition components made during the German occupation of Poland in 1944.

'Ng', 'Ng.' Marks found on Polish-made *Nagant gas-seal revolvers, usually accompanied by a date (e.g. '31' for 1931). See also 'FB' and 'Radom'.

NGM. A designation applied to the current 5.45mm and 5.56mm Hungarian adaptations of the *Kalashnikov.

Nickerson. David Nickerson (Tathwell) Ltd. Trading from 1966 onward in the village of Tathwell, Louth, Lincolnshire, England, this company distributed Chinese and Italian airguns under such names as Arrow, Igi and York. It also distributed Swedish *Stiga and own-brand airgun ammunition made by *Lanes or in Italy.

'N.I.' – 1. Found in the designations or on the components of British military weapons classed as non-interchangeable. **2.** Found in the headstamps of ammunition made in Britain by *Nobel Industries during the 1920s. Additional marks will determine whether the cartridges were made in the London (*Eley) or Birmingham (*Kynoch) factory.

Niblo. Urban Niblo, a lieutenant in the US Navy using the identifier 'UN', accepted .38-calibre *Colt revolvers during 1928–29. See also US arms inspectors' marks.

Nichols – 1. John A Nichols of Syracuse, New York State, was the co-designer, with Joseph W *Livingston, of a 'gun-lock' and a 'hinge-joint for breech-loading firearms' protected by US Patents 198,669 and 198,670 of 25 December 1877. He traded briefly in partnership with Daniel *Lefever (1876–78), then continued to make the Nichols & Lefever shotguns on his own account. Still trading in Syracuse in 1879, where he had moved to Geddes Street by 1882, Nichols had ceased working by 1885. **2.** Nichols & Lefever. A partnership of John A. *Nichols and Daniel *Lefever, this business was renowned for double-barrelled break-action shotguns. Operations were confined to 1876–78, after which the partners continued trading separately.

Nicholson. William D Nicholson accepted 1866-pattern *Remington rolling-block pistols for US Navy service, identifying them with 'WDN' stamps. See also US arms inspectors' marks.

Nico. This *Scheintod pistol had a three-barrel block that tipped down to load. Undoubtedly it was made in Suhl by August *Menz for Adolf *Niemeyer, as it duplicated Menz's Regnum four-barrel cartridge pistol. Most examples have a 'NICO'-and-star medallion set into the grips. They were introduced some time prior to 1911 and were still being offered in the Glaser catalogue of 1933. A simplified pattern was made in small numbers during the early 1920s, entirely of aluminium, with a two- (rare) or three-barrel block, which could be lifted up and out of the frame when the catch on the left side of the frame was pressed downward. One pattern had a conventional trigger guard, while another was a short-frame guardless design.

Nicoll. J.O. & R.W. Nicoll, Aberfeldy, Perthshire. Also sometimes listed as 'Nicholl'. A gunmaking and ironmongery business operating in Scotland prior to the First World War, Nicoll's marks have been reported on 12-bore shotgun cartridges made by *Nobel's Explosives Ltd. These may also be marked 'Shooter's Best Hand-Made Water-Tight'.

Niemeyer. Adolf Niemeyer, a Suhl based gunmaker, seems to have been the largest distributor of *Scheintod guns, often using the brandnames *Diki-Diki, *Nico and Scheintod. Trademarks of a dancing skeleton and an elephant will also be found, while many barrels will bear such marks as '*nur für Leuchtpatrone*' ('for flare cartridges only') or '*für Gaspatronen*' ('for tear-gas cartridges'). German-made guns are usually identifiable by their proof marks (particularly 'crown/crown/U') and by *'D.R.G.M.' or *'D.R.W.Z.' The best of Niemeyer's guns were pocket revolvers, usually purchased in Belgium from manufacturers such as *Rongé, *Henrion, Dassy & Heuschen and *Manufacture d'Armes 'HDH'. Normally these are recognisable by Belgian proof marks.

Nightingale & Son, Salisbury, Wiltshire. The marks of this English provincial gunmaking business have been found on shotgun cartridges marked 'The Avon' and 'The Moonraker'.

Nikitin – 1. Grigory Nikitin, USSR. Co-designer with Yuri *Sokolov of the 7.62mm *Nikitin-Sokolov or NS universal machine-gun, and with Sokolov and *Volkov of the 12.7mm *NSV pattern. 2. Nikitin-Sokolov machine-gun. Also known as the NS, this Soviet gas-operated 7.62x54R *universal machine-gun design relied on a slot in the carrier to rotate the bolt, and a stud on the bolt to operate the belt-feed pawl. The first prototypes dated from 1952/53, and some field-trials guns were made in 1958. Testing suggested that the rival *Kalashnikov machine-gun was simpler to make, easier to handle and more reliable in wet conditions, when the efficiency of the NS feed system declined. Consequently, the Nikitin-Sokolov design was abandoned in 1961.

Nikko Firearms Manufacturing Company, Tochigi, Japan. Maker of bolt-action rifles for Golden Eagle Rifles, Inc., of Houston, Texas (1976–82).

Nikonov. Gennadiy Nikonov. Designer of the Russian *NSM assault rifle. See also Abakan.

'NIL', 'N.I.L.' See 'KNIL'.

'Nile' [The]. A brandname associated with shotgun cartridges made by *Nobel Explosives Ltd of Glasgow prior to 1918 and the purchase by Explosives Trades Ltd.

Nimrod – 1. Found, usually as 'The Nimrod', on shotgun ammunition made, or perhaps simply assembled, by the *Normal Powder Company of Hendon, London. *See also* Super Nimrod. 2. Nimrod-Gewehrfabrik, Suhl in Thüringen, Germany. See Thieme & Schlegelmilch.

Nitro... – 1. 'Nitro-Ball' [The]. A shotgun cartridge made in Britain by *Kynoch Ltd prior to the acquisition of the company by Explosives Trades Ltd in 1918. 2. Nitro-Bird, Nitro-Hunter. Brandnames associated with shotguns made in the USA prior to the First World War

by the *Crescent Arms Company of Norwich, Connecticut. 3. 'Nitro Club'. Encountered on shotgun ammunition made in the factory of the *Remington Arms–Union Metallic Cartridge Company at Bromsdown, Middlesex, England. 4. 'Nitro Paradox' [The]. Found on British shotgun cartridges loaded for *Holland & Holland of London.

Nitrokol Powder Company, London. This short-lived assembler, or perhaps simply distributor, of shotgun ammunition bought components in France. Customarily marked 'The Best British Loading', they were sold under such names as The Redskin and The Rover.

'Nitrone' [The]. A shotgun cartridge made in Britain by *Kynoch Ltd prior to the acquisition of the company by Explosives Trades Ltd in 1918, then by *Eley-Kynoch Ltd.

Nixon – 1. David Nixon, Newark, Nottinghamshire. The marks of this English gunmaker have been reported on self-cocking *pepperboxes dating from the middle of the nineteenth century. Nixon was trading from Stodman Street in 1829, Middlegate in 1834, and Market Place in 1840–64. 2. William Millington Nixon, 9 Duddleston Row, Birmingham, Warwickshire. The marks of this English gun- and pistol maker – active from 1845 until 1853 or later – have been reported on *pepperboxes. 3. Nixon & Naughton, Newark, Nottinghamshire. The marks of this gunmaking partnership, perhaps a successor to David Nixon (above), have been recorded on sporting guns and ammunition.

'NL', 'NLB'. Found on US military firearms and accessories. See N. *LeClair and Nathan L. *Benoit respectively.

Nobel. Nobel Explosives Ltd, Glasgow, Scotland. Founded in 1871, as the British Dynamite Company, this business was famed originally for its blasting explosives. When the first *smokeless propellant was developed in the 1880s, the company, by then known as Nobel Explosives Ltd, developed a form of *ballistite suited to ammunition. This was introduced commercially in 1889. Nobel seems to have bought in many of its cartridge and shotgun-shell cases until 1907, when the business of F. *Joyce & Company Ltd was purchased. Trading continued until the end of the First World War, whereupon Nobel became a part of Explosives Trades Ltd. Among the brandnames associated with Nobel's shotgun ammunition were Ajax, Clyde, Ejector, Empire, Eureka, Kardax, Kingsway, National, Nile, Noneka, Orion, Parvo, Regent, Special Primrose, Sporting Ballistite' Target and Valeka. See also Dynamit Nobel AG.

Noble Manufacturing Company. Trading from the small Massachusetts town of Haydenville (1965–71), Noble is best known for a range of inexpensive sporting rifles and shotguns. However, the company was also one of the few manufacturers of break-barrel spring-air rifles to have operated in North America in the twentieth century. The barrel-cocking Model 300 Indian air rifle was the principal product.

Nock. Samuel Nock, gunmaking nephew of the legendary Henry Nock (1741–1804), worked at 43 Regent Circus, London – where he had been since a move from Fleet Street in 1823 – until his death in 1851. His executors continued to trade until 1858, transferring to 116 Jermyn Street in 1852, and business continued until 1862 under the proprietorship of 'John Wallis trading as

Samuel Nock'. Nock's marks have been reported on self-cocking *pepperboxes dating from the late 1840s. *See also* Knoxform.

'Nomis' [The]. A brandname ('no miss') found on *Kynoch-made shotgun cartridges sold in England by *Linsley Brothers of Leeds prior to 1914.

Non-ejecting, non-ejector. A class of gun unable to eject spent cartridges, generally confined to double rifles, although many early military rifles lacked ejectors and some dropping-block patterns can be set to extract only partially. The feature is useful for those who do not want to lose spent cases or to have them damaged during ejection.

Noël, Saint-Étienne, France. Listed in 1933 as a gunmaker.

'Noneka' [The]. A brandname associated with shotgun cartridges made in Britain first by *Nobel Explosives Ltd of Glasgow, prior to 1918, when Nobel was purchased by Explosives Trades Ltd, and subsequently by *Eley-Kynoch Ltd.

Non-XL. A *Suicide Special revolver made by the *Hopkins & Allen Arms Company of Norwich, Connecticut, USA, in the late nineteenth century.

Nordenfelt – 1. Thorsten Wilhelm Nordenfelt. Born in 1842 in Orby, Sweden, this Nordenfelt made his fortune during the 1860s in hardware and ironmongery. In 1872, however, he was approached by Heldge Palmcrantz to finance a machine-gun operated by a reciprocating lever instead of the crank associated with the *Gatling Gun. This was protected by a variety of patents, including British no. 1739/73 of 1873 and 3678/78 of 1878 ('Battery Guns'). Both of these were granted in Nordenfelt's name, although the earlier was accompanied by a 'Disclaimer and Memorandum of Alteration' stating that it was a 'Communication from abroad by H. Palmcrantz, civil engineer, and J.T. Winborg, manufacturer, both of Stockholm; and E. Unge of Motala, Sweden'. The Nordenfelt Gun & Ammunition Company (below) was registered in Britain in the 1870s, although much of the work was undertaken initially in a factory in Carlsvik. The advent of the *Maxim automatic machine-gun and the pooling of common interests (1897) to create the *Maxim-Nordenfelt Guns & Ammunition Company Ltd forced Thorsten Nordenfelt to relinquish his holdings. Subsequently he founded a workshop in Paris, hoping to promote a machine-gun designed by the Swedish engineer O.W. Bergmann, which was seen as a

NORDENFELT GUN

Nordenfelt (2)

Designed by Heldge Palmcrantz, these guns were made originally in a factory owned by Thorsten *Nordenfelt in Carlsvik, near Stockholm; many of the later examples, however, were produced in Britain. Chamberings ranged from .303 to 1in. A reciprocating operating handle beneath the back of the receiver moved the action block laterally, then withdrew the breech-pieces. Replacing the lever pushed cartridges forward into the chambers and returned the action block to lock the mechanism; and the barrels were fired sequentially. An experimental three-barrel Nordenfelt was offered to the British authorities in 1875 by *Temple & Company of London. The 'Gun, Nordenfelt, 0.45-inch, 3-barrel, Martini-Henry Chamber (Mark I)' and Mark II were adopted by the Royal Navy on 22 July 1880. By 1912, although the advent of automatic weapons had reduced them to instructional trainers, four different Nordenfelts remained in British service: two- and four-barrel 1in guns; a three-barrel .303 version, converted from .45; and .45 five-barrel Marks I and II.

A typical ten-barrelled, rifle-calibre Nordenfelt machine-gun, from the British periodical Engineering, *1883.*

Maxim rival, but work ceased c. 1905. Nordenfelt retired, eventually dying in 1920. **2.** Nordenfelt Gun: *see* panel, p. 381. **3.** Nordenfelt Guns & Ammunition Company Ltd [The]. This firm was formed in London in 1886 to promote the manually-operated Nordenfelt machine-gun (above). No sooner had a factory in Erith, Kent, been completed than the business was amalgamated with the *Maxim company to form the *Maxim-Nordenfelt Guns & Ammunition Company Ltd (1888).

[von] Nordheim – **1.** Edmund von Nordheim, Zella-Mehlis in Thüringen, Germany. Listed in the *Deutsches Reichs-Adressbuch* for 1939 as a gun-stock maker. **2.** Emil von Nordheim. Trading from Mehlis, then Zella-Mehlis in Thüringen, Germany, this gunmaker was listed in trade directories of the period 1914–30 and used the trademark Vono prior to the Second World War. This has been reported on *Parabellum pistols and sporting rifles. **3.** Gotthilf von Nordheim, Mehlis and Zella-Mehlis in Thüringen. Listed during 1914–20 as a gun- and weapon maker. **4.** Willi von Nordheim, Zella-Mehlis in Thüringen, Germany. Listed in 1939 as a distributor of guns and ammunition.

Norfolk, Norfolk... – **1.** 'Norfolk' [The]. A mark found on shotgun ammunition sold by Charles *Lancaster & Company Ltd of London. **2.** 'Norfolk High Velocity Load' [The]. Associated with shotgun ammunition sold by *Plumbers of Great Yarmouth.

'Norica'. This mark, used in Spain by Norberto *Arizmendi SA of Eibar, may often be found in the form of an arrow on a target background.

Norinco. *See* China North Industries Corporation.

Noris. A trademark used in Germany by Wilhelm *Meyer of Nürnberg from 1927 until the early 1940s. It is said to have appeared on spring-air guns, particularly those which were effectively children's toys.

Normal – **1.** Usually found as 'The Normal' on shotgun cartridges made, or perhaps simply assembled, by the Normal Improved Ammunition Company of Hendon, London. **2.** Normal Improved Ammunition Company, Hendon, London NW4. Assumed to be the last of the businesses begun by the Normal Powder Company, this firm produced a variety of shotgun cartridges distinguished by such marks as 'The Hendon', 'Keeper's Normal', 'Light Blue', 'Normal', 'Normal Midget', 'Pegamoid', 'Pigeon Case' and 'Super Nimrod'. **3.** 'Normal Midget' [The]. Encountered on shotgun ammunition made, or perhaps simply assembled, by the Normal Improved Ammunition Company of Hendon, this may signify a short-case round. **4.** Normal Powder Company, Hendon, London NW4. Predecessor of the *New Normal Ammunition Company Ltd, the activities of this company are no longer clear. Shotgun cartridges have been reported with such tradenames as 'Nimrod' and 'Wasters', together with such marks as 'Ejector' and 'Water Proof'. Some of the components were purchased elsewhere, as some cases bear the 'W.R.A. Co.' head-stamp of the *Winchester Repeating Arms Company. It is assumed that the business soon failed, being superseded by the New Normal Ammunition Company Ltd and the Normal Improved Ammunition Company (although the progression is unclear).

'Normalis' [The]. A brandname used by the *New Normal Ammunition Company Ltd of Hendon, London, on .410 shotgun ammunition made from components

purchased in Europe. The propellant appears to have been German *Walsrode Jagdpulver.

Norman – **1.** Benjamin Norman. Listed as a member of the London gun trade, working at 43 Markham Street, Chelsea, in 1869–71. **2.** George Norman, a 'Mechanical Engineer' employed by the *Birmingham Small Arms Company Ltd and *BSA Guns Ltd, was responsible for much of the development work on the pre-1939 Lincoln Jeffries BSA rifles. His patents included 14,558/05 of 1905 and 22,681/05 of 1905, with Augustus Henry Murray *Driver and the *Birmingham Small Arms Company Ltd, for back-sight assemblies; 8246/06 of 1906, with *Driver and BSA, for an improved rotary loading plug; 9262/06 of 1906, with Driver and BSA, for a sight hood; and 3306/08 of 1908, with Driver and BSA, for a fulcrum cocking lever and a safety device (although this was never exploited). Other protection included 12,692/11 of 1911, with Driver and BSA, for a fulcrum cocking lever and safety device (which never seems to have been used) and 5283/12 of 1912, with BSA, for an improved means of cocking the pistol patented in 1911. Sought jointly with BSA, British Patent 5564/13 of 1913 described an improved cocking lever that worked on the forward and return strokes; 502/14 of 1914 protected an improved trigger mechanism; and 1988/14 of 1914 illustrated a simplified rifle with a push-in barrel. Also known for his firearms designs, George Norman died in 1943, after attending a party held in BSA's Small Heath factory to celebrate the end of production of the No. 1 *Lee-Enfield rifle. **3.** Joseph Norman, Springfield, Massachusetts. An engineer employed by *Smith & Wesson, credited with the development of the first of the company's very successful semi-automatic pistols. **4.** Norman & Sons, Woodbridge and Framlingham, Suffolk. A long-established firm of English provincial gunmakers, claiming origins dating back to 1870, Normans of Framlingham is now probably best known for the manufacture and distribution of black-powder replicas. However, a variety of shotgun cartridges has also been found with such marks as 'The Service', 'The Special' and 'The Standard'.

Normay. *See* Norman *May & Company.

Norris – **1.** John Norris, Springfield, Ohio, USA. The designer of a double-ring finger guard for the *Protector turret-pistol c 1900. **2.** Samuel Norris, Springfield, Massachusetts. Best known for financing the *Mauser-Norris bolt-action rifle, Norris and his partner, William T. *Clement, contracted to make 3,000 1861-pattern rifled muskets for the State of Massachusetts during the American Civil War. Delivered in 1863/64, these were marked 'S.N. & W.T.C. FOR MASS.' on the lock-plates. Norris continued trading alone between 1865 and 1869, representing not only the Mausers, but also E. *Remington & Sons, although whether his claim to be a salesman for Remington indicated a formal employer/employee relationship is still subject to doubt. However, whatever it may have been, the agreement ended acrimoniously.

North – **1.** A.H. North, working on behalf of the Federal government, accepted military firearms and accessories during the American Civil War. The guns, which bore the identifier 'AHN', dated from 1862–63. **2.** F.S. North accepted guns and accessories destined for the Federal Army in 1862–63, marking them 'FSN'. *See also* US arms inspectors' marks for previous two entries. **3.**

Henry North. On 17 June 1856, Henry North received US Patent 15,144 to protect a 'revolving firearm'. This was made by Edward *Savage, then by *Savage & North of Middletown, Connecticut, until an improved version was patented jointly by North & Savage on 18 January 1859 (US no. 22,566) and 15 May 1860 (28,331). A particularly interesting claim concerned the gas seal made by camming the cylinder forward at the moment of discharge. Both patents were assigned to the Savage Revolving Fire-Arms Company. *See also* Game Shooter. **4.** John H.B. North & Sons, Stamford, Lincolnshire, and Peterborough, Northamptonshire. The marks of this gunmaking and ironmongery business, including 'North's Universal', will be found on shotgun ammunition made by *Eley-Kynoch. **5.** Simeon North, Middletown, Connecticut. Maker of *Hall breech-loading rifles during 1833–36, and the improved *Hall–North carbine during 1842–50. He was also co-patentee with Savage of the breech-lever for the *Hall–North carbine, protected by US Patent 3686 of July 1844. **6.** Walter North, active from c. 1830 until the beginning of the American Civil War in 1861, accepted a variety of firearms for service in the US Army. They included single-shot cap-lock pistols and .36-calibre Colt Navy revolvers marked 'WN'. *See also* US arms inspectors' marks. **7.** North American Arms Company, Dominion Rifle Factory, Quebec. This Canadian gunmaking business was formed to make 50,000 .45 M1911 Colt-Browning pistols for the US government and purchased the former *Ross Rifle Company factory from the Canadian authorities in 1918. Unfortunately, the pistol contract was cancelled when the First World War ended, and the North American Arms Company went into liquidation in 1919. No more than 100 pistols are believed to have been made, readily identifiable by the markings on their slides. **8.** North American Arms Company. A modern US based maker of Mini-Revolvers. **9.** North American Cartridge Company. A Canadian maker of ammunition, identified by the inclusion of 'N.A.C.Co.' in *headstamps. **10.** North China Industries Corporation (Norinco): *see* China North Industries Corporation. **11.** North & Savage, Middletown, Connecticut, USA. Maker of revolvers, revolver-rifles and shotguns from 1856 until succeeded in 1860 by the *Savage Revolving Fire Arms Company.

'Northern'. Found on shotgun cartridges: *see* Hardy.

Northfield Knife Company. Rather oddly associated with a *Suicide Special revolver made by the Rome Revolver & Novelty Works of Rome, New York State, in the late nineteenth century.

Norwich – **1.** Norwich Arms Company. A brandname associated with shotguns made in the USA by the *Crescent Arms Company of Norwich, Connecticut. **2.** Norwich Falls Pistol Company, Norwich, Connecticut, USA. This was the successor to the original *Norwich Pistol Company, formed in 1881, but trading ceased in 1887. Revolvers were made in the intervening period for *Maltby, Curtis & Company. **3.** Norwich Pistol Company, Norwich, Connecticut, USA. Formed in 1875, this company had failed by 1881. However, the assets were bought by *Maltby, Curtis & Company, and production began again under the Norwich Falls Pistol Company banner.

Nosecap, nose-cap. The band or fitting nearest the muzzle. The term is usually applied to a military rifle, musketoon or carbine, where the nose-cap will often carry a lug for the bayonet, double as an anchor for the cleaning rod, and support a sling swivel or piling rod. The design of individual nose-caps can vary from the simplest of encircling bands to a complicated multi-part machining, often (e.g. the German Gew.98/Kar. 98 patterns) designed to relieve the strain arising from attaching a bayonet directly to the muzzle.

Not-Nac Manufacturing Company. A brandname associated with shotguns made in the USA by the *Crescent Arms Company of Norwich, Connecticut.

'Nottingham' [The]. A brandname found on shotgun cartridges sold in England by S. *Jackson of Nottingham.

Nouvelle. Arthur Nouvelle et Companie, Paris. A maker of small-calibre training rifles similar externally to the *Gras and *Lebel, but reduced in scale. They date prior to the First World War.

Novelty Works. *See* Leech & Rigdon.

Nowotny. J.M. Nowotny, Leitmeritz an der Elbe, Prussia; often listed as Polish. A maker of a crank-operated Gallery Gun in the middle of the nineteenth century – or perhaps simply a retailer, as it also bears the marks of *Klawitter. Støckel, in *Haandskydevaabens Bedømmelse* (1964), lists Nowotny as active as a gunsmith c. 1840.

'Noxall' [The]. A name found on shotgun cartridges sold by *Milburn & Son of Southampton. They were made after the First World War by *Eley-Kynoch, the name being derived from 'Knocks All' (i.e. 'knocks all out of the sky').

'NP'. A superimposition-type monogram, with 'P' dominant. Found on the grips of semi-automatic pistols made in Belgium by Nicholas *Pieper of Liège prior to 1914.

NRA – **1.** An abbreviation for the *National Rifle Association of America. **2.** NRA Commemorative Model. This was a variant of the *Daisy M1894 Spittin' Image BB Gun, the Model 5894, made in 1971 to celebrate the anniversary of the *National Rifle Association. It has an antique bronze finish and an NRA medallion set into the butt.

'NRF', 'N.R.F.' Marks found on British SMLE (*Lee-Enfield) rifle components produced during 1918–19 by the government-owned *National Rifle Factory No. 1, Birmingham.

NRS. Applied to a combination knife pistol, correctly designated NRS-2, issued in the Soviet/Russian Army. The gun chambers a special noiseless cartridge.

'N.S.', 'NS'. Found on British small-arms components to indicate that they are non-standard.

NSM. An abbreviation applied to the perfected assault rifles designed by the Russian engineer Gennadiy *Nikonov.

NSN. *See* Nato Standard Number.

NSV. The Soviet 12.7mm-calibre heavy machine-gun designed by *Nikonov, *Sokolov and *Volkov. The NSVT was a variant adapted for vehicle use.

'Nulli Secundus' [The]. A brandname found on shotgun cartridges handled in England by J. *Collis.

Number 1 Gem. An airgun pellet made by *Lane Brothers of Bermondsey prior to the First World War, correctly known as the Perfect No. 1 Gem. *See also* Gem.

Núñez de Castro. This 11mm centrefire block-action *Fusil de Retrocarga Núñez de Castro*, made by *Euscalduna of Placencia, was one of the leading competitors of the Remington in the Spanish Army's breech-loading rifle trials of 1870. Heavy and cumbersome, it was rejected by

NYLON SERIES

This name is associated with a range of modernistic rifles made by the *Remington Arms Company. The earliest was the .22 rimfire blowback Nylon 66 of 1959–87, with a tube magazine in its synthetic DuPont Zytel butt. Originally the butts and fore-end were made only in 'Mohawk Brown', but were supplemented by 'Apache Black' (1962–84), complemented by chromed metalwork, and the short-lived 'Seneca Green' of the mid-1960s. The Nylon 77 (1970–78) – known after 1971 as the Model 10C – was a Nylon 66 auto-loader with a detachable five-round box magazine. The Nylon 77 *Apache was a

variant sold by the K-Mart retail chain. The first of the bolt-action .22 rimfire rifles, introduced in 1962, had a split-bridge receiver set in a one-piece nylon stock. The Nylon 10 was restricted to single shots, the Nylon 11 had a box magazine protruding ahead of the trigger guard, and the Nylon 12 had a tube magazine beneath the barrel. The guns did not sell especially well, and production ceased in 1966. Subsequently, however, remaining actions were completed as *Sesquicentennial and *Bicentennial rifles. Rights and the production machinery were sold to *CBC in Brazil, where production continues.

The Nylon 76 Trail Rider was a modification of the Nylon 66 auto-

loader, with a short-throw closed-loop lever behind the trigger. The action was locked by wedging the bolt behind the chamber. A tube magazine lay beneath the barrel, and the DuPont Zytel stock was usually brown. However, owing to teething troubles, the Nylon 76 was soon abandoned.

The Nylon Series of .22 rimfire auto-loading rifles were made by the Remington Arms Company (1959–87) in a variety of finishes. This example has a butt and fore-end of DuPont Xytel in 'Mohawk Brown'; metalwork was blacked.

the army after protracted testing. The design of the massive receiver was unmistakable, with a straight hammer spur and an underlever.

'NW'. Found on US military firearms and accessories. *See* Nathaniel *Whiting.

NWM. *See* Nederlandsch Wapen- en Munitiefabriek.

'NWP'. Found on US military firearms and accessories. *See* Nahum W. *Patch.

'N.Y.C.', 'N.Y.C. Co.'. Found in the *headstamps of

ammunition made in the USA by the *New York Cartridge Company.

Nylon Series. *See* panel, above.

'nyw'. Found on German military small-arms components made by the Meiningen factory of *Gustloff-Werke during 1944–45.

'N.Z.' Found in the headstamps of cartridges made between 1938 and 1945 by the *Colonial Ammunition Company of Auckland, New Zealand.

O

'o', 'O' – **1.** As 'O', above a vertical arrow. A mark applied by an inspector working in the *Orange small-arms factory in New South Wales, Australia. *See also* British military inspectors' marks. **2.** As 'O', beneath a crown. Found on Bavarian weapons: the mark of King Otto (1886–1913). *See also* Cyphers, imperial and royal. **3.** As 'o': found on German rifle- and other small-arms components made during the Second World War by Madix Nähmaschinenteilefabrik Alfred Keller & Co. KG of Dresden. **4.** As 'O', often found in conjunction with 'AR' (q.v.). Associated with the Spanish arms factory in *Oviedo.

'oa' 'OA' – **1.** As 'OA': a mark found on *Lee-Enfield rifles and small-arms components made by the Australian government factory in *Orange. **2.** As 'oa': on small-arms ammunition made during the Second World War by Eduard Hueck of Lüdenscheid, Westfalen, Germany.

'OAC'. Found on cartridges, sometimes in the form of a monogram. Correctly read as 'COA' (Cartucheria Orbea, Argentina).

'Oakment' [The]. A brand of shotgun ammunition associated with John *Cornish of Okehampton, Devon, England.

'OAS', in a cartouche. Used by Otis A. *Smith on revolvers made in the USA in the late nineteenth century.

'OAT'. Found on US military firearms and accessories. *See* O.A. *Thornton.

Ober. W.J. Ober was a US Army inspector, responsible for accepting firearms and equipment marked 'WJO' during 1904–06. *See also* US arms inspectors' marks.

Oberspree. Waffenwerk Oberspree, Kornbusch & Co. A gunmaking business purchased by Waffenfabrik *Mauser in 1915, and put to making Gewehre 98.

Occidental Arms Company. A brandname associated with shotguns made in the USA by the *Crescent Arms Company of Norwich, Connecticut.

Ochnev. Known as the co-designer with *Paramanov and *Upirov of the Soviet/Russian TP-82 survival pistol issued with the *SONAZ kit.

'O D'. An abbreviation of 'oil dressed', found on British ammunition boxes made for service abroad of something other than regulation teak.

Odd Fellow. A *Suicide Special revolver made in the USA by Otis *Smith of Middlefield and Rock Fall, Connecticut, in the late nineteenth century.

Ode. Jacques Ode, rue Villeboeuf 14 (later no. 10), Saint-Étienne, France. Listed in 1879–92 as a gunmaker.

Odell. Warren C. Odell accepted US Army .45 M1911A1 pistols made in 1939 by *Colt's Patent Fire Arms Manufacturing Company, marking them 'WCO'. *See also* US arms inspectors' marks.

Odin, Saint-Étienne, France. Listed in 1933 as a gunmaker.

Odkolek – 1. Adolf [Freiherr von] Odkolek 'von Augezd' was born in Prague on 1 December 1854 and, after studying law, entered the Austro-Hungarian Army. He resigned his commission in 1896, but was recalled in 1914 and served until his death in Stockerau on 2 January 1917. Odkolek was the inventor of the *Hotchkiss gas-operated machine-gun, but also he experimented with manually-operated and auto-loading rifles from 1882 onward. A trench mortar of his design was tested successfully in 1915. Domiciled in Vienna, Odkolek was granted three US patents to protect his machine-gun: no. 726,187 for a 'gun locking device' on 21 April 1903; and 799,884 of 19 September 1905 and 831,923 of 25 September 1906 for 'automatic firearms'. **2.** Odkolek machine-gun: *see* Hotchkiss machine-gun.

Oehring – 1. August Oehring, Zella-Mehlis in Thüringen, Germany. Listed in 1939 as a master gunsmith. **2.** Otto Oehring, Zella-Mehlis in Thüringen. Listed in trade directories published prior to 1939 as a maker and supplier of gun stocks, specialising in animal-horn work. **3.** Otto & Rob. Oehring, Zella-Mehlis in Thüringen. Listed in the 1939 as a gun-stock maker.

Oeller. James P. Oeller, a lieutenant attached to the US Navy Bureau of Ordnance, accepted a variety of cap-lock firearms during a career that ran from 1809 to 1848. His 'JPO' markings are readily distinguishable from similar stamps found on guns accepted early in the twentieth century by J.P. *O'Neill. *See also* US arms inspectors' marks.

'OEWG', 'OE' above 'WG'. Marks associated with the products of *Österreichische Waffenfabriks-Gesellschaft of Steyr, commonly encountered on *Mannlicher rifles. The 'OE' may be found in the form of a diphthong.

Off Hand Model. Also known as the No. 6½ Rigby, the *Ballard No. 6½ rifle appeared in 1876. Made by *Marlin, it was similar to the No. 6, but had a modified 'German'-pattern walnut butt with a chequered pistol grip and a *Farrow shoulder plate. The barrels were bought from John *Rigby & Company of London, and vernier-adjustable Marlin mid-range sights were standard.

Officer's... – 1. Officer's ACP. Made by the Firearms Division of *Colt Industries during 1985–90, and thereafter by *Colt Manufacturing Company, Inc., this is a commercial equivalent of the US Army *General Officer's Model. Chambered for the .45 ACP cartridge, it has a 3.5in barrel and a six-round magazine. Stainless-steel and lightweight alloy-frame versions were introduced in 1986. **2.** Officer's Model. This revolver, made by *Colt's Patent Fire Arms Manufacturing Company only in .38 Special, appeared in 1904 with a cylinder that rotated anti-clockwise. In 1908, however, clockwise rotation was substituted and the Positive Safety was added in the trigger system. Officer's Models offered excellent finish and were often sold with *Peard-patent sights. Other versions included the Target Model (1908–72), offered in nine centrefire chamberings and .22 LR rimfire (1930 only), with barrels as long as 7.5in, adjustable sights and, after 1908, cylinders that rotated clockwise. Made only in .22 LR rimfire and .38 centrefire, the Special Model (1949–52) was a minor variant of the Target Model with a parallel-sided barrel, a modified hammer and a ★Coltmaster back sight. The Match Model (OMM, 1952–72), in .22 LR, .22 WMR or .38 Special, replaced the Special, and had a tapered heavy barrel, over-size grips and Accro sights. **3.** Officer's Rifle (Sharps-Borchardt). *See* New Model Hammerless Officer's Rifle.

Official Police Model. Nominally introduced in 1927, succeeding the ★Army Special Model, this six-shot ★Colt revolver was popular with military and police forces alike. Most guns chambered .38 cartridges, although a few were made in .32 centrefire and .22 rimfire. Production ceased in 1969, the last guns being marked as products of the Firearms Division of Colt Industries.

Officina Costruzione d'Artiglieria, Rome. This federal government ordnance factory is claimed to have made M1870 ★Vetterli rifles, short rifles and carbines for the Italian Army, c. 1870–85, but none have been traced.

Offrey-Crozet fils et Cie, rue du Chambon 12, Saint-Étienne, France. Listed in 1879 as a gunmaker.

'OH' – 1. A superimposition-type monogram with the axis of the letters set diagonally, usually encircled. Correctly read as 'HO' (q.v.); associated with Heinrich ★Ortgies of Erfurt, Germany. **2.** A superimposition-type monogram, sometimes encircled, with neither letter prominent. Found on ★Smith & Wesson-type swinging-cylinder revolvers made in Eibar, Spain, by ★Orbea Hermanos.

Öhring. *See* Oehring.

Ojanguren – 1. Ojanguren y Marcaido SA, Dos de Mayo, Eibar, Guipúzcoa, Spain. Maker of ★Colt- and ★Smith & Wesson-type revolvers, as well as spring-air guns for target use. **2.** Ojanguren y Vidosa, Eibar, Guipúzcoa, Spain. This company made semi-automatic pistols under the brandnames ★Apache, ★Puppel, ★Salvaje and ★Tanque (mostly 6.35mm copies of the ★FN-Browning of 1906).

'OK', 'O.K.' – 1. Found on a single-shot US cartridge derringer, based on the ★Thuer-patent Colt No. 3, made by John ★Marlin of New Haven. **2.** Associated with a ★Suicide Special revolver made by the ★Marlin Fire Arms Company of New Haven, Connecticut, USA, in the late nineteenth century.

Oklahoma – 1. A brandname associated with break-barrel spring-air pistols made in Italy by ★Molgora during the 1960s. **2.** Oklahoma Tire & Supply Company (Otasco): *see* Marlin.

Olby's, Ashford, Canterbury, Folkestone, Margate and Ramsgate, Kent. This sporting-goods business sold guns and ammunition. Apparently the shotgun cartridges bearing its name, which included the brandname Cantium, were made by the ★Midland Gun Company and others.

O&L Guns, Inc., Seminole, Texas. US distributor of Model 700 ★Krico bolt actions under the name Wolverine.

Olagnier, Saint-Étienne, France. Listed during 1933 as a gunmaker.

Old... – 1. Old Hickory. A ★Suicide Special revolver made by the ★Hopkins & Allen Arms Company of Norwich, Connecticut, in the late nineteenth century. **2.** Old Hickory. A brandname associated with revolvers made in the USA by ★Johnson & Bye, beginning in 1877. These included .22 and .32 double-action guns with trigger guards, and .32 sheath-trigger versions. **3.** Old Reliable. Associated with single-shot dropping-block rifles and a few double-barrelled hammer shotguns handled in the USA by the ★Sharps Rifle Company, from 1874 until 1881. **4.** Old Reliable. Used in the USA c. 1897 by ★Sears, Roebuck & Company to describe the Markham ★Chicago BB Gun.

O'Leary. Herbert O'Leary, a major in the US Army, accepted guns made by ★Colt's Patent Fire Arms Manufacturing Company; marked 'HO', they dated from 1926–29. *See also* US arms inspectors' marks.

Olimpic, *see also* Olympic. Found on a break-barrel spring-air pistol made in Italy by ★Molgora in the 1960s.

Olimpico. Llama Olimpico or Llama XXIII. A six-shot .38-calibre target revolver made by ★Llama–Gabilondo SA on the basis of Smith & Wesson swing-cylinder practice, this gun has an anatomical grip, micro-adjustable sights and a web joining the muzzle to the ejector-rod housing beneath the 140mm heavyweight barrel. The Llama XXIX Olimpico is essentially similar, but chambers the .22 LR rimfire cartridge and, as a result, is somewhat heavier.

Olin – 1. Olin Corporation: *see* Winchester. **2.** Olin Kodensha Company Ltd: *see* Kodensha.

Oliver, Oliver... – 1. A ★Suicide Special revolver made by the ★Hopkins & Allen Arms Company of Norwich, Connecticut, USA, in the late nineteenth century. **2.** Oliver & Company, Hull, Yorkshire. A gunmaker known to have handled shotgun ammunition marked 'The Estate'.

Olympia – 1. A bolt-action ball-firing spring-air rifle made in Germany by August ★Menz of Suhl, c. 1937. **2.** An unattributable Spanish Browning-type semi-automatic pistol, probably made in the Eibar district: 6.35mm, six rounds.

Olympian Grade. This term was used by the ★Browning Arms Company of Utah, USA, to identify its best Mauser-action sporting rifles, which had extensive engraving, gold inlay on the pistol-grip cap and specially selected stocks. *See also* Medallion and Safari.

Olympic – 1. *See* Olimpic and Armigas-Comega. **2.** Olympic Wadcutter. A flat-headed 4.5mm diabolo airgun pellet made in Britain by L.J. ★Cammell Ltd.

'OM'. A superimposition-type monogram, sometimes encircled, with neither letter prominent. Found on ★Colt- and ★Smith & Wesson-type swinging-cylinder revolvers made in Eibar, Spain, by ★Ojanguren y Marcaido.

'oma'. Used from 1944 by Ernst Mahla of Prag-Michl on military small-arms ammunition components made during the German occupation of Czechoslovakia.

O'Malley. J. O'Malley, a US government employee, accepted military firearms and accessories in 1896–1902, marking them 'JO'. *See also* US arms inspectors' marks.

OMC, Inc., El Monte, California. Manufacturer of the ★Back Up 380 automatic pistol, chambered for the 9mm Short cartridge.

Omega – 1. A small Browning-type pocket pistol made by Armero Especíalistas of Eibar, Guipúzcoa, Spain, in two basic patterns: (a) 6.35mm, six rounds, hammer fired; (b) 7.65mm, six rounds, usually striker fired. **2.** A brandname used on revolvers made in Germany by ★Gerstenberger & Eberwein. **3.** A modern British Webley spring-and-piston air rifle. It was introduced in .177 and .22 in 1985.

'OMM'. *See* Officer's Model Match.

Omni. A double-action semi-automatic pistol made in Spain by ★Llama–Gabilondo SA. Designed largely by an American engineer, Gary Wilhelm, the Omni had a roller-bearing slide, a double-action trigger and other unique features, even though it operated on the basis of a modified ★Colt-Browning dropping-barrel lock. The Omni I chambered the .45 ACP round, and had a seven-round single-column magazine; the Omni II was a lighter 9mm Parabellum version with a capacity of nine rounds; and the 9mm Parabellum Omni III had a thirteen-round

ONE-HAND COCKING

The German for this term is *Einhandspannung*. The inability to retract the slide of a semi-automatic pistol was seen by most users to be a serious weakness compared with a double-action revolver. Consequently, several attempts have been made to provide suitable cocking systems based on slides or pivoting levers. Among the first was the .45 *White-Merrill pistol submitted to US Army trials in 1907, which had a spur beneath the trigger guard. The Spanish *Jo-Lo-Ar pistol, dating from the early 1920s, had a bar pivoted on the right side of the frame, but the most successful seems to have been the *Chylewski-patent gun made as the Einhand series by Theodor *Bergmann Erben and AG *Lignose of Berlin between the world wars. A Chinese-made derivation of this gun has recently been offered commercially by *Norinco as the Type 77.

Top: *an advertisement extolling the virtues of the Lignose Einhand pistol, from the 1932 catalogue of Waffen-Glaser.*
Right: *Bergmann-marked Modell 3A Einhand. Lignose purchased Bergmann in the period between the world wars, explaining the presence of the otherwise unfamiliar markings.*

---

staggered-column magazine. It was superseded by the Llama Modelo 82.

Omnipol, Prague, Washington 11. This government-run export agency, ultimately replaced by *Merkuria, was responsible for the distribution of *Slavia and other Czechoslovakian guns.

'Omnipotent'. A nickname applied unofficially, apparently by *Kittredge of Cincinnati, to the Colt *Double Action Army & Frontier Model revolver.

One-hand cocking. *See* panel, above.

O'Neill. J.P. O'Neill accepted firearms for the US Army during 1904–10, marking them 'JPO'. Date distinguishes the guns from those accepted many years earlier by James P. *Oeller. *See also* US arms inspectors' marks.

'One of...' – 1. One of One Hundred. Found on a few select-grade lever-action rifles made by the *Winchester Repeating Arms Company. They were 'second best' to One of One Thousand examples (q.v.). **2.** One of One

Thousand. *Mauser-pattern sporting rifles, incorporating bolt actions made by Zavodi *Crvena Zastava, sold in Britain in 1973 to celebrate the twentieth anniversary of *Interarms. Chamberings ranged from .270 Winchester to .458 Winchester Magnum. **3.** 'One of One Thousand'. A mark found on select quality lever-action rifles made in the USA in the late nineteenth century by *Winchester.

'ONP'. Found on US military firearms and accessories. *See* O.N. *Perkins.

Onyks, Onyx. Names applied (the latter incorrectly) to a short-barrelled version of the Polish *Tantal assault rifle, a minor variant of the *Radom-made *Kalashnikov.

Open Top – **1.** Applied generically to virtually any revolver without a top strap above the cylinder, but more specifically associated with the pre-1873 *Colts (e.g., Open Top Frontier). **2.** Open Top Army Model, or Open Top Frontier: a *Colt-made revolver. *See* New Model Army. **3.** Open Top Pocket Model. Made by Colt's Patent Fire Arms

Manufacturing Company, in Hartford, Connecticut (114,200 c. 1871–8), this seven-shot .22 rimfire handgun had a sheath trigger and a bird's-head butt. It was distinguished by the lack of a top strap above the cylinder; guns made prior to 1874 had an ejector rod on the right side of the barrel, but post-1874 cylinders had to be removed to reload. It was superseded by the *New Line Colt.

Operating cycle. This is simply the complete routine required for the satisfactory functioning of an automatic weapon: firing, unlocking the breech, extracting, ejecting, cocking, feeding, chambering and breech-locking. (Note: not all functions may be present; some may overlap, and the order of their occurrence may vary.)

'Opex' [The]. A shotgun cartridge made in Britain by *Kynoch Ltd prior to the acquisition of the company by Explosives Trades Ltd in 1918.

'Optimus'. A brandname used on the highest grade of *Automatic Hammerless shotgun made by the *Lefever Arms Company of Syracuse, New York State, USA.

Orange. Rifle Factory No. 3, Edward Street, Orange, New South Wales, Australia. This factory was established in 1942 to assemble SMLE (*Lee-Enfield) rifles, freeing the *Lithgow facilities to concentrate on *Bren and *Vickers Guns. Orange products were normally marked 'OA'.

Orban. Rudolf Orban, Suhl in Thüringen. Listed as a gunmaker prior to 1914.

Orbea – 1. A hammer-fired Spanish 6.35mm-calibre semi-automatic pistol made by Orbea y Compañía of Eibar, Guipúzcoa, based on the 1905-pattern Browning: six rounds, hammer fired. **2.** Orbea y Compañía, Eibar, Guipúzcoa, Spain. Maker of the 6.35mm Orbea pistol and a variety of Smith & Wesson-type revolvers. **3.** Orbea Hermanos, Eibar, Guipúzcoa, Spain. Manufacturer of cap-lock rifle-muskets and short rifles during the mid-nineteenth century, many of which subsequently provided the basis for *Berdan transformations. Possibly also the source of a pocket pistol marked 'La Industrial' (q.v.).

'Orford' [The]. Associated with shotgun ammunition loaded by W. *Darlow from components supplied by *Kynoch or *Eley-Kynoch.

'ORH'. Found on US military firearms and accessories. *See* Orvin R. *Hayden.

ÖSTERREICHISCHE WAFFENFABRIKS-GESELLSCHAFT (OEWG)

Österreichische… (2)

This great arms-making business owed its origins to Josef *Werndl, who succeeded to his father's gunsmithing operation in Steyr in 1853. The first major success came with an Austro-Hungarian order for 100,000 *Werndl-Holub rifles, followed by conversion work on rifle-muskets from Bavaria, France, Greece and Switzerland. Werndl was soon forced to open a subsidiary in Pest to supply guns to the Honvéd.

The spectacular growth of business required appropriate finance, so Österreichische Waffenfabriks-Gesellschaft was founded on 1 August 1869 with a capital of 6,000,000 gulden. Josef Werndl became managing director, overseeing a workforce of about 3,000 men. Purchases in 1870 included the *Fruwirth gunmaking business in Vienna, and Bentz of Freiland, both operations being closed to allow their machinery to be transferred to Steyr. By 1872, production had reached 622,000 rifles and 8,500 carbines (mostly Werndls), together with 2,600 Fruwirth repeating rifles, 1,800 sporting guns, and 114 multi-barrel machine-guns.

The adoption of the improved Werndl-Holub-Spitálsk´y rifle in 1873 brought more Austro-Hungarian orders, and a request for 500,000 1871-type *Mauser rifles, placed by Prussia in 1875, was fulfilled within eighteen months. By then the factory was employing 5,500 and making 8,000 guns a week. By 31 December 1877, 474,622 1871-type Mauser rifles, 60,000 carbines, 150,000 bolts, 55,963 receivers and 52,000 barrels had been delivered to the governments of Prussia and Saxony. Orders followed from Romania, then from France, where *Kropatschek repeating rifles were particularly popular.

The great success of the *Mannlicher rifles had a beneficial effect on the prosperity of the Steyr factory which, by the early 1890s, had become one of the most important small-arms manufacturing centres in Europe. The annual report for 1889/90 recorded that 469,070 of the 760,631 rifles on the order books had been delivered during the financial year, and that the receipt of additional orders promised full employment in 1890/91. Weekly output was rated as 8,000–11,000 rifles.

The 1890s represented the high point of the Austro-Hungarian small-arms industry. OEWG had sold substantial quantities of *Reichsgewehr-type rifles and carbines to Peru and Brazil, while Mannlichers derived from the Reichsgewehr were adopted by Romania in 1893.

Disappointment followed, however. Chile took a Spanish-type Mauser instead of a Mannlicher, possibly due to the aggressive support given to Waffenfabrik Mauser by the German government. And although Mannlicher-Schönauer rifles were acquired for field trials in 1900–01, the Portuguese elected to develop the *Verguiero-Mauser instead. In January 1897, therefore, Österreichische Waffenfabriks-Gesellschaft was forced to join a German-controlled cartel to assure a share of production of Mausers.

Work on Mannlicher rifles was declining, as the initial Romanian orders had been fulfilled, the Dutch were making guns under licence, and the Austro-Hungarian government orders were not sufficient to keep the workforce fully occupied. Acquiring a licence to make the *Schwarzlose machine-gun, adopted by the Austro-Hungarian Army in 1907, proved to be an astute move, while Belgian *Pieper-patent semi-automatic pistols were made in quantity under the designation Model 1909.

A new factory was built in Steyr in 1913/14, but the Austro-Hungarian government still placed nothing other than token orders. The shortage of serviceable rifles became evident as soon as mobilisation began. However, nearly 67,000 Mauser-system Mo. 1912 rifles being made for Mexico were issued to Austro-Hungarian units, together with the remnants of large orders for 6.5x54 Greek *Mannlicher-Schönauer rifles and 1893-pattern Romanian

Orient. Found on *Suicide Special revolvers made by the *Hopkins & Allen Arms Company of Norwich, Connecticut, USA, in the late nineteenth century.

Original – 1. Used by many manufacturers to distinguish their products from copies or imitations, this should rarely be regarded as a brandname. **2.** Often cursive. Associated with spring-airguns made in Germany prior to c. 1922 by Oscar *Will of Zella St Blasii and Zella-Mehlis (as 'Original Will'). **3.** Associated with some pre-1914 *Millita-type spring-airguns made in Germany by Friedrich *Langenhan. **4.** Applied by the wholesaler *Gustav Genschow to some *Langenhan spring-airguns sold in the mid-1920s. **5.** Often cursive. A trademark used in Britain since 1951 by *Mayer & Grammelspacher of Rastatt/Baden, owing to the loss of the *Diana brand to *Millard Bros. **6.** 'Original J.W.G.' [The]. Found on shotgun cartridges distributed in southern England by Charles *Clarke of Salisbury. **7.** 'Original Norfolk' [The]. Found on shotgun cartridges attributed to *Plumbers of Great Yarmouth, but probably made elsewhere.

Oriol – 1. 22 rue Rouget-de-l'Isle, Saint-Étienne, France. Listed in 1951 as a gun-barrel maker. **2.** Oriol Père et Fils, 58 boulevard Valbenoîte, Saint-Étienne, France. Listed in 1951 as a gunmaker.

'Orion' [The]. Associated with shotgun cartridges made by *Nobel Explosives Ltd of Glasgow prior to 1918 and the purchase by Explosives Trades Ltd.

Ormachea. F. Ormachea, Eibar, Guipúzcoa, Spain. A manufacturer of compact semi-automatic pistols under the brandnames *Duan and *Merke.

Ortega. D.F. Ortega de Seija, Madrid. This Spanish gunmaking business has been credited with the *Benemerita pistol, although sometimes this is disputed.

Ortgies – 1. Heinrich Ortgies, Erfurt, Thüringen, Germany. Patentee in 1916–18 of a semi-automatic pistol, made in quantity after the First World War. **2.** Ortgies & Co., Erfurt. Manufacturer, or perhaps merely the distributor, of the semi-automatic pistols designed by Heinrich Ortgies during the First World War. Post-1922 guns are marked by *Deutsche-Werke AG, but it is not known whether this business (the remnants of the Prussian small-arms factory in Erfurt) had simply acquired the Ortgies

---

Mannlichers ordered in 1913. The Romanian guns were converted for the standard 8x50 rimmed cartridge instead of the rimless 6.5x53 type.

A decision to replace the 1895-pattern Mannlicher was taken in the spring of 1915, but work on the new gun – not a Mauser, but a 7.9x57mm Mannlicher-Schönauer with a rotary magazine – was stopped by the entry of Italy into the war. One result was an immediate acceleration of production of Mannlicher rifles and Schwarzlose machine-guns in the Steyr (OEWG) and Budapest (FGGY) factories. Five thousand ex-Colombian Mauser rifles were acquired from Steyr in May 1915, being distinguished from the otherwise similar Mexican guns by the chamber mark.

When the First World War began, Österreichische Waffenfabriks-Gesellschaft had made the staggering total of 6,065,234 military rifles and carbines, 284,447 pistols, 9,215 machine-guns and about 20,000 sporting guns. By 1 November 1918, these figures, boosted by war production, had reached 9,065,559 rifles, 519,366 pistols and 49,739 machine-guns; in addition, many aircraft engines had been built.

Like many great arms-making businesses, OEWG suffered greatly in the immediate post-war period. Despite attempts to diversify into the production of motor vehicles, profitability declined and many thousands of workers were laid off. The formation of *Steyr-Werke AG

Among the many firearms made in the Steyr factory of Österreichische Waffenfabriks-Gesellschaft was this Belgian-designed 7.65mm Pieper pistol.

in 1922 brought a change in structure and, in 1934, Steyr-Daimler-Puch was formed by amalgamating Steyr-Werke and Austro-Daimler-Puch.

The rise of militarism in Germany brought a renewed interest in the production of weapons, allowing Steyr-Daimler-Puch to make rifles, submachine-guns and machine-guns in modest numbers until the German annexation (*Anschluss*) of Austria in 1938. The Steyr business was enveloped in Reichswerke Hermann Göring and embarked on the production of war matériel in earnest. This included not only guns but also a wide range of vehicles.

A brief period of Soviet occupation in 1945 was followed by

US control. The factory was entirely demilitarised and all the appropriate machinery distributed by the Allies as reparations. Tools to make motorcycles, tractors and associated components were supplied in the late 1940s by the USA, and production of Mannlicher-Schönauer sporting rifles began again in 1950. Steyr-Mannlicher GmbH has since made pistols, submachine-guns, assault rifles (*see* AUG), sporting guns, machine-guns, armoured vehicles and artillery.

operation or had always been making the guns under sub-contract. **3.** Ortgies pistol. A *blowback 7.65mm or 9mm Short semi-automatic pistol designed by Heinrich Ortgies (above) and made for about twelve years, first by Ortgies & Companie, then by *Deutsche-Werke AG of Erfurt. Externally similar to the 1910-pattern FN-Browning, the guns were distinguished by a pivoting safety lever, set into the backstrap, which could be unlocked only by pressing up on a button on the left side of the frame, above the grip; pressing the button in allowed the slide to be removed.

Ortloff. Hermann Ortloff, Suhl in Thüringen, Germany. Listed as a sales agency in 1939. *See also* Dianahaus.

Ortmann. Henri Ortmann, Liège. Sometimes this Belgian 'merchant', listed by H.J. Blanch in *Arms & Explosives* in 1909, is mistakenly said to have been part of the English gun trade. However, an agency was maintained at 4 Falcon Street, London E.C., between 1888 and 1890. Ortmann marketed revolvers prior to 1914 under such names as Defender ('American Model of 1878'), Lincoln (rimfire) and Thunderer.

Osborn. J.P. Osborn, occasionally listed as Osborne, The Golden Padlock, Daventry, Northamptonshire. A supplier of ammunition, Osborn marketed smokeless 12- and 16-bore shotgun cartridges under the tradename *Danatre. The components seem to have been imported, although their origins have yet to be determined.

Osborne. Charles Osborne [& Company], Birmingham, Warwickshire. Specialising in exports to South America and the Indian colonial trade, this English gunmaking business began operating from 1 Lichfield Street in 1845, before moving to 12 & 13 Steelhouse Lane in 1855. The trading style became '…& Company' in 1877, when Osborne is believed to have relinquished control to a partnership of C.O. Ellis and E.W. Wilkinson. Business continued in this way until a limited-liability company was formed in 1899 (some sources suggest 1895 or 1896), when trading from 14 Steelhouse Lane and 16 & 17 Sand Street, Birmingham. Ellis and Wilkinson ('trading as C. Osborne') were granted British Patents 8402/84 of 1884 and 7222/87 of 1887 for drop-down-barrel actions; 11,970/88 of 1888 for a sliding-breech mechanism for punt guns; plus 12,050/98 and 26,493/98 of 1898 (the latter with W. Jerman) for single-trigger mechanisms for double-barrel guns. Sales offices were maintained at 3 Broad Street Buildings, London E.C., in 1881–84; at 7 Whitehall Place, London S.W., in 1885–92; and at 2 Great Scotland Yard from 1893 to 1900 and later.

Osprey. A sidelever-cocking fixed-barrel .177 or .22 spring-air rifle introduced by *Webley & Scott Ltd of Birmingham, in June 1975. The Osprey Supertarget, made in .177 only, was a variant of the standard Osprey with a match stock and target aperture sight. It was announced in 1976.

Österreichische… – **1.** Österreichische Waffenfabriks-Anstalt, Vienna. Maker of the *ÖWA pistol. **2.** Österreichische Waffenfabriks-Gesellschaft (OEWG): see panel, pp. 388/89.

Ost-Schweizerische Büchsenmacher (East Swiss Gunmakers), St Gallen. This gunsmiths' union was formed to make M1869 *Vetterli infantry rifles for the Swiss government during 1869–74.

Otasco. A brandname associated in the USA with the products of the *Oklahoma Tire & Supply Company.

'Ottervale' [The]. A mark associated with shotgun ammunition distributed in the west of England by *Roberts & Company of Ottery St Mary.

Otto – **1.** Fritz Otto, Zella St Blasii and Zella-Mehlis in Thüringen, Germany. Listed in 1914–20 as a gunmaker. **2.** Paul Otto, Zella St Blasii and Zella-Mehlis in Thüringen, Germany. Listed during 1914–30 as a gunmaker. **3.** Richard Otto, Zella St Blasii and Zella-Mehlis in Thüringen, Germany. Listed during 1914–20 as a gunmaker, when the business was being operated by Friedrich and Paul Otto. Still being listed as a gunmaker in 1930.

Our… – **1.** 'Our Game'. Found on shotgun cartridges loaded by *Eley-Kynoch for H.E. *Pollard & Company of Worcester. **2.** Our Jake. A *Suicide Special revolver made by *E.L. Dickinson of Springfield, Massachusetts, USA, in the late nineteenth century.

Oury. Dieudonné Oury, Mortier, Belgium. Inventor of the 6.35mm *Le Novo pocket revolver.

'OV' – **1.** Usually as 'V' within 'O', beneath a crown. Found on Norwegian weapons: the mark of King Olaf V (1957 to date). *See also* Cyphers, imperial and royal. **2.** A mark associated with *Ojanguren y Vidosa of Eirbar.

Oviedo arms factory, Real Fábrica de Armas Portatiles de Oviedo, a Fábrica Nacional de Armas. The principal Spanish arms factory known for *Mauser and *CETME rifles, and the *Campo-Giro pistol. 'FAO' and 'FNA' marks have been used.

'OWA', 'ÖWA' – **1.** Found on the grips of 6.35mm *Clément-type pocket pistols made under licence by Österreichische Werke Anstalt of Vienna. Some marks may have the 'dots' (diaeresis or umlaut) within the body of the letter 'O'; this usually indicates post-1920 origins. **2.** A mark found on US military firearms and accessories. *See* O.W. *Ainsworth.

'ÖWG'. A vertical superimposition-type monogram, with 'W' dominant, accompanied by 'STEYR' in a banner. Found on the grips of *Pieper-type pistols made by Österreichische Waffenfabriks-Gesellschaft prior to the First World War. 'OE' and 'Ö' are synonymous in written German.

Oxford – **1.** Oxford 90. A deluxe double-barrelled *Holland & Holland-style side-lock shotgun made in 12- and 20-bore by Società Armi Bresciane to the designs of Renato *Gamba. The guns customarily have gold-plated triggers and delicate floral scrolls on the side-plates. **2.** Oxford Extra. This is a deluxe variant of the 20-bore Oxford 90 (above), with a single selective trigger mechanism and better-quality 'English-style' decoration. The barrels are usually only 660mm long compared with the standard 680mm (20-bore) or 700mm (12-bore) patterns. **3.** Oxford Arms Company. A name associated with shotguns made in the USA prior to the First World War by the *Crescent Arms Company of Norwich, Connecticut.

'oxo'. This code was allotted in Germany during 1944 to Teuto Metallwerke GmbH of Osnabrück, for use on small-arms ammunition components.

'oyj'. Allocated in 1944, this code identified small-arms ammunition components made in France, under German supervision, by Ateliers de Construction de Tarbes.

Ozieh. This mark, together with a 1910 date, has been found on a copy of the *Crescent BB Gun. Arni Dunathan speculated in *The American BB Gun* that the Crescent was made in the Orient, and it is possible that the defunct Bartlett company's machines could have gone to Japan in 1908/09.

P

'**P'** – **1.** In a heart. On the left side of the *knoxform of parallel-bored British .303 *Lee-Enfield rifle barrels. **2.** Sometimes as 'P 2'. Found on British rifle butts that have been pre-compressed ('P') after saturating in paraffin wax and benzole ('P 2'). The 'P' mark may be found in conjunction with 'B', 'L' or 'S', signifying the butt length. **3.** Used on German small-arms ammunition made by *Polte Armaturen- und Maschinenfabrik AG (later Polte-Werke) of Magdeburg during 1940–45. **4.** Within a circle, often decorative. A mark applied to US service rifles and other stores to indicate that they had successfully passed a proof-firing. It is usually found behind the trigger guard on *Krag-Jørgensen and *Springfield rifle stocks. **5.** Encircled. A private proof mark used in the USA by O.F. *Mossberg & Sons. **6.** Encircled, accompanied by a crowned lion holding a target. Encountered on handgun grips made in the USA by Pachmayr. **7.** A *headstamp associated with the *Peters Cartridge Company of Cincinnati. **8.** Impressed or encircled. A *headstamp found on rimfire ammunition made by the *Phoenix Cartridge Company of Coventry, Connecticut.

Paatz. Bernhard Paatz, Mehlis and Zella-Mehlis in Thüringen, Germany. Established in 1890, Paatz was known by the mid-1920s for 'all types of *Flobert pistols, revolvers, *Teschings, and single-barrel shotguns'. A typical shotgun of this period had an exposed hammer ahead of a top-lever, and a pistol-grip butt. The owners in 1919 were Theodor and Heinrich Paatz, and P. Kühlig. Listed in 1930–39 as a gun- and weapon maker, and in 1941 as a weapons maker (*Waffenfabrik*).

PA Baby. See Baby.

Pabst. Gustav Pabst, 25 Besenbinderhof, Hamburg. This German inventor obtained British Patent 14,447/07 of 1907 to protect a gas-powered gun or cane.

Pacific Model. The 1876-vintage *Ballard No. 5 Pacific Model rifle had an extra-heavy iron frame, a heavy octagonal barrel, double set triggers and a cleaning rod beneath the muzzle. Rocky Mountain sights were standard. Chamberings customarily ranged from .40-85 to .45-100 Ballard.

Packham. Frank James Wilson Packham, Puckeridge, Hertfordshire, England. A 'Doctor of Medicine', Packham obtained British Patent 960/55 of 1855 to protect an airgun and a design for airgun projectiles.

'**PAF', 'P.A.F.'** See Pretoria Arms Factory.

Page. William Page accepted firearms and military equipment on behalf of the Federal Army in 1863, during the American Civil War. Marked simply 'WP', the items can be distinguished by date from those accepted several years later by William *Prince. See also US arms inspectors' marks.

Page-Wood. T. Page-Wood, Bristol, Somerset. This gunmaker specialised in loading his own cartridges, although the components were acquired from *Eley-Kynoch. Among the tradenames were Anti-Recoil Cartridge, The Bristol, The Climax Cartridge, The Double Crimp, The Imperial Crown, The Page-Wood DS, Page-Wood's Shield Cartridge, The Park Row and The Wildfowler. Some examples exhibit a proprietary roll-crimp, said to have been the subject of a patent.

Pain, Paine – **1.** James Pain & Sons, Salisbury, Wiltshire, and London. Best known as a maker of pyrotechnics (Pains-Wessex), Pain also made the Bird Scaring Cartridge (q.v.) and distributed shotgun cartridges bearing the headstamp mark 'J.P. & S.' **2.** James Paine. A member of the London gun trade, listed in the census of 1841 at High Holborn, in partnership with Robert Braggs, then alone at 8 Gray's Inn Lane in 1851–52. **3.** Richard Paine, a civilian inspector retained in the mid-1840s by the US Navy Board of Ordnance, accepted a variety of firearms and accessories marked 'RP'. They included single-shot cap-lock pistols and *Jenks carbines made by *Ames and *Remington. Navy marks distinguish the guns from those accepted for the army in the same era by Richard *Perher. See also US arms inspectors' marks.

Pal. This brandname is associated with the Model 105 Pal, a lever-action *BB Gun made by *Daisy in the 1950s. The gun was produced for many years, although the name had been dropped long before production ended.

Paliard-Vialletou frères, rue des Gaux, Saint-Étienne, France. A maker of *Lefaucheux pinfire breech-loaders between 1838 and 1845.

Palix et Ravel, rue Beaubrun 21, Saint-Étienne, France. Listed in 1879 as a distributor of, and agent for, arms and ammunition.

Pallad. A name bestowed on a 40mm bolt-action grenade launcher made in Poland; often encountered on the Polish version of the *Kalashnikov assault rifle.

'**Pallet'.** A brandname found on the packaging of diabolo-pattern airgun pellets made in Denmark by *Barberbladefabrik and sold in Britain by the *Abbey Supply Company. See also Black Box.

'**Pall Mall' [The].** This mark will be found on shotgun cartridges loaded by William *Evans of London.

'**Palma' [The].** Associated with rifle ammunition made by the *King's Norton Metal Company Ltd, often specifically for target-shooting (cf. the Palma Match competition).

Palmcrantz. Heldge Palmcrantz, Sweden. Designer of the *Nordenfelt mechanically-operated machine-gun.

Palmer – **1.** Courtlandt Palmer. Bought the rights to the *Hunt/Jennings rifle and the self-contained rocket ball ammunition, acquired from George Arrowsmith in 1850. Five thousand guns were ordered from *Robbins & Lawrence, Horace Smith being hired by Palmer to oversee the work. Smith's 1851 patent was assigned subsequently to Palmer. Eventually Palmer funded the first Smith & Wesson partnership, withdrawing when returns on his investment did not reach expectations. **2.**

G. Palmer, 29 High Street, Sittingbourne, Kent. A gun-smith known to have sold 12-bore shotgun cartridges marked 'The Champion'. **3.** George Palmer, active in 1862, during the American Civil War, accepted firearms and accessories on behalf of the Federal Army. However, his 'GP' mark may be difficult to distinguish from a similar mark employed in the same era by Giles *Porter. *See also* US arms inspectors' marks. **4.** William Palmer, New York City. E.G. *Lamson made carbines patented by William Palmer in December 1863 (41,017), the first bolt-action pattern firing metallic-case ammunition to be adopted by the US Army. The external-hammer Palmer had a collar-type extractor and a spring-loaded ejector. A thousand .56-50 guns were ordered in June 1864, but they were delivered too late to see action in the American Civil War. **5.** Palmer Chemical & Equipment Company, Douglasville, Georgia. The manufacturers of the *Cap-Chur tranquiliser system. **6.** Palmer, Sons & Company, Barnet, Hertfordshire. Marks applied by this gunsmithing and ironmongery business have been reported on The Rocketer 12-bore shotgun ammunition.

'Panem Labore'. A mark found on the barrels of toy-like guns, usually firing only paper caps, made in Belgium during the First World War to raise funds for the *Panem Labore* ('Bread through Work') charitable organisation devoted – in part at least – to alleviating distress caused to gunsmiths' dependents by the German-imposed prohibition of arms production.

Panstwowna Fabryka Karabinow, Warsaw. The principal Polish small-arms factory made 1898-type *Mauser rifles in 1923–29.

Panther – **1.** A *Suicide Special revolver made by *Ely & Wray of Springfield, Massachusetts, USA, in the late nineteenth century. **2.** Panther Standard. A break-barrel spring-air pistol made in Italy by *Gun Toys, as the RO71, the Panther was distributed in Britain by *Sussex Armoury. The Panther de Luxe was the marginally more sophisticated Gun Toys RO72. **3.** The M418 Panther was a 6.35mm-calibre pocket pistol made by Pietro *Beretta of Gardone Val Trompia, Brescia, Italy.

'PANZER', often in a diamond. A mark associated with the *Lur-Panzer pistol made in Spain by *Echave y Arizmendi.

Papanti. L. Papanti, using an 'LP' mark, accepted firearms and accessories on behalf of the US Army; most

PARABELLUM PISTOL

Parabellum (3)

This term is popularly applied to the *Borchardt-Luger pistol, particularly in Europe, although 'Luger' persists in most English-speaking countries. The adoption of the Borchardt-Luger by the Swiss Army, in 1900, was success enough to persuade many other authorities to try it. By 1905, the Parabellum had been tested extensively in the USA (*see* *American Eagle), and had been adopted in Bulgaria.

The Parabellum of this era – known as the Old Model after the introduction of the New Model in 1906 – had a grip safety, a rebound lock and toggle grips that were partly cut away. The first 9mm-calibre guns, introduced by 1903, were built on existing components until special short-frame versions appeared c. 1904. A change from four- to six-groove rifling also dates from this period.

Parabellum pistols were ordered in quantity by the German Navy in December 1904, although the pattern of delivery and issue is still disputed. Naval guns had 150mm barrels and two-position back sights on the toggle mechanism. The perfected New Model Parabellum (made in quantity from 1906) had a coil-pattern return spring, said to

have originated in 1904.

New Model Parabellums were service issue in Brazil, Bulgaria, Portugal, Switzerland and perhaps even Russia. The greatest success, however, was the adoption of the *9mm Pistole 1908* (P. 08) by the German Army on 22 August 1908. This was essentially a New Model, but the grip-safety mechanism was replaced with a manually-operated lever. Very few mechanical changes were made to the 1908-type pistol, although a mechanical hold-open was added in May 1913, and a long-barrelled derivative (LP. 08) was adopted on 3 June 1913 for the field artillerymen. This gun also had a tangent-leaf back sight and a detachable butt, the butt-lug being added subsequently to standard short-barrel guns.

Parabellum pistols were made exclusively by *Deutsche Waffen-& Munitionsfabriken prior to 1911, when a duplicate production line was installed in the Prussian government small-arms factory in *Erfurt. DWM and Erfurt delivered about 1,300,000 P. 08 pistols prior to November 1918. A few are said to have been assembled in the *Spandau factory in 1918, but the claim remains controversial. A new production line was created in the *Eidgenössische Waffenfabrik in this period, and the distinctive Swiss-style pistols – culminating in

the 7.65mm 06/29 W+F pattern – were made in Bern until 1947.

After the First World War, the situation changed: DWM (then trading as Berlin-Karlsruher Industrie-Werke, or BKIW) was not permitted to recommence work on the Parabellum until 1922/23, and the Erfurt factory had been demilitarised. However, the Allies permitted *Simson & Co. of Suhl to supply the needs of the Reichswehr during the 1920s; *Mauser-Werke AG of Oberndorf took over BKIW's production in 1930; and even *Vickers Ltd became involved in the supply of Parabellums to the Netherlands Indies in the early 1920s.

Virtually no manufacturing changes were made to the basic design, although German police guns of the 1930s will often be found with the Schiwy sear and Walther magazine safeties. Mauser made Parabellums for export during the 1930s (e.g. for the Netherlands, Persia, Sweden and Siam), but the quantities were never large. In 1934, however, production began again for the German armed forces, and had reached six-figure numbers annually by 1940.

Parabellums were also made by Heinrich *Krieghoff of Suhl from 1936 onward, although the total involved was less than 15,000. Military procurement of P. 08 pistols ceased in 1942, unwanted

items seem to date from the end of the nineteenth century. *See also* US arms inspectors' marks.

Pape. Gunsmith William Rochester Pape traded from 44 Westgate Street, Newcastle upon Tyne, from 1857 until 1870, receiving British Patent no. 1501/66 of 1866 to protect a drop-barrel breech-loading sporting gun with choked muzzles. Pape entered 12- and 16-bore *Lefaucheux-type pinfire breech-loaders in *The Field* shotgun trials of 1866. Subsequently operations were moved to 21 Collingwood Street, and a variety of shotgun cartridges were promoted under names such as The Beryl, The Heather, The Ranger and The Setter. Apparently Pape's business continued after the First World War, but he died in 1923, suggesting that there may have been two generations of W.R. Pape.

Parabellum – 1. Taken from the Latin phrase *Si vis pacem para bellum* ('If you seek peace, prepare for war'), trademark no. 43353 was granted to *Deutsche Waffen- & Munitionsfabriken of Berlin on 21 April 1900. Although used surprisingly widely, especially as a telegraphic codename, Parabellum is associated specifically with the *Borchardt-Luger pistol and the *Heinemann-Maxim machine-gun. **2.** A name applied to a light machine-gun, adapted from the *Maxim by Karl Heinemann in 1911/12. Made by *Deutsche Waffen- & Munitionsfabriken of Berlin during 1914–18, in water- and air-cooled variants, the *Parabellum-Maschinengewehr* was particularly popular for airborne use, as it was substantially lighter than the standard Maxim MG. 08, and its water-cooling system suited the needs of the Zeppelin service. The principal improvement over the Maxim was the inversion of the toggle-lock to give a more compact receiver (cf. *Vickers Gun) and an improved belt feed. The MG. 14 was the standard pattern, customarily cooled with water, whereas the air-cooled MG. 14/17 had a slotted barrel jacket. **3.** Parabellum pistol: *see* panel, below.

'Paradox' [The]. A British shotgun cartridge made by *Kynoch Ltd prior to the acquisition of the company by Explosives Trades Ltd in 1918.

Paragon – 1. Usually found as 'The Paragon'. A mark used by W.W. *Greener of Birmingham, England, on shotgun cartridges. Also found on ammunition (Greener's?) sold in India prior to the First World War by *Rodda & Company. The manufacturer was probably *Kynoch. **2.** *Suicide Special revolvers made by the *Hopkins & Allen Arms Company of Norwich,

The Parabellum pistol was popular in many European countries, this particular gun being a 7.65mm Finnish m/23 with a replacement 9mm barrel made by Oy Tikkakoski. The mark of an infantry-regiment machine-gun company appears on the grip-disc.

guns being sent to Bulgaria and Portugal, but assembly in the Mauser and Krieghoff factories did not cease until April 1945. French occupation forces continued to make guns from spare and cannibalised parts in the Oberndorf factory until 1946. Others were refurbished in the German Democratic Republic into the mid-1950s for the *Volkspolizei* (People's Police). Many of these ended their days in the Far East.

Blowback .22 rimfire 'Lugerlikes' appeared in the form of the *Erma EP-22 (1964), the Spanish *Lur-Panzer (c. 1968) and the Stoeger Luger of 1976. The success of these rimfires encouraged the development of the 7.65 and

9mm Mauser-Parabellums (1968–87). The most recent development has been the *Mitchell Arms American Eagle P. 08, announced in 1992, and the comparable *Stoeger Luger of 1996. One of the leading enthusiasts, gunsmith John *Martz, has even been reponsible for one of the few worthwhile mechanical improvements in the Luger since the 1930s. *See* MSTR.

The special status of the Parabellum, or Luger, pistol among collectors has led to the publication of many books and countless articles. Among the best are: *The Luger Pistol (Pistole Parabellum),* by Fred A. Datig, (Fadco, 1955, but since reprinted on several occasions); *The*

Krieghoff Parabellum, by Randall Gibson, (published by the author, 1980); *Die Pistole 08,* by Joachim Görtz (Stocker-Schmid, Zürich-Dietikon, Switzerland, 1985); *Lugers at Random,* by Charles Kenyon, Jr (new edition, Handgun Press, Glenview, Illinois, 1990); *The Dutch Luger (Parabellum),* by Bas Martens & Guus de Vries (Ironside International, 1994); *Imperial Lugers and Their Accessories,* by Jan Still (published by the author, Douglas, Alaska, 1991); *Third Reich Lugers and Their Accessories,* by Jan Still (published by the author, Douglas, Alaska, 1988); *Weimar and Early Nazi Lugers and Their Accessories,* by Jan Still (published by the author, Douglas, Alaska, 1993); *The Luger Book,* by John Walter (Arms & Armour Press, London, 1986); and *The Luger Story,* by John Walter (Greenhill Books, London, and Stackpole Books, Harrisburg, 1995).

Connecticut, USA, and the *Prescott Pistol Company of Hatfield, Connecticut. They date from the late nineteenth century. **3.** Paragon Guns, 43 Ann Street, Belfast. The name of this Irish gunsmithing business has been reported on shotgun ammunition, possibly supplied by *Eley-Kynoch. The cartridges were sold under such names as The Crown, The Invincible and Paragon Special.

Paramanov. Co-designer with Ochnev and Upirov of the Soviet TP-82 pistol, issued with the *SONAZ kit.

Paramount. A small Spanish 6.35mm Browning-type pocket automatic made by *Apaolozo Hermanos of Eibar, Guipuzcoa: six rounds, hammer fired.

Paratrooper. A brandname used by *ASI on the break-barrel Gamo-68 air rifle, made in Spain by *El Gamo. The Paratrooper Repeater (alias *Gamatic) had a magazine tube above the air cylinder.

Parcours – 1. A term applied by H. *Krieghoff GmbH to an engraved pattern on the K-80 over/under shotgun. Introduced in the early 1990s, it consists of dog and game-bird scenes in an oval panel within a plain incised line border. *See also* Bavaria, Bavaria-Suhl, Crown Grade, Danube and Gold Target. **2.** Parcours Special. A better version of Parcours engraving, this has the illustrations engraved in relief, better detailing and a light acanthus-leaf border.

Parent & Leroy, Paris. Successors to David, Vouzelle & Francou in the 1890s, this distributor had a warehouse 'Aux Buttes Chaumont' and a sales office at 10 rue Bertin-Poirée 'à la Tour Saint-Jacques'. Its catalogues described it as a source of 'hunting weapons; sporting [lead] bullets; hardened and nickelled bullets; balls and buckshot; hunting requisites; guns; cases; covers; whips; collars; mirrors; hunting horns; whistles; etc.' The business was also 'Agent-General for France and the Colonies' for Browning automatic firearms (*Armes automatiques Browning*). Trading is believed to have ended shortly after the First World War.

Paris arms factory [Manufacture d'Armes de Paris], Saint-Denis. Maker of Lebel rifles, 1915–18.

Parker – 1. A.G. Parker & Company Ltd, Birmingham, Warwickshire. This English gunmaking business was founded in 1890 by Alfred Gray Parker (d. 1975), and subsequently became A.G. Parker & Company (1900), then A.G. Parker & Company Ltd in 1904, with shares held by the Parker and Hale families. Bailey and Nie, in *English Gunmakers*, record premises at 69 Icknield Field Street in 1894–1900. Parker & Company made the air pistol designed by Alfred Thomas Corbyn *Hale and Ernest Edwin Harris, as well as *Lee-Enfield sporters. Most of these guns were refurbished SMLE Mk III/Rifle No. 1 actions, although a few new items may have been purchased from BSA. Ultimately the company was renamed *Parker-Hale Ltd in 1936, when the Bisley works in Whittall Street were still being used. **2.** 'C. Parker & Company'. A name found on shotguns handled in the USA by the H. & D. *Folsom Arms Company, possibly imported from Europe. **3.** C.H. Parker, a civilian employee of the US Ordnance Department using a 'CHP' identifier, accepted military firearms and accessories early in the twentieth century. **4.** J.C. Parker, using the identifier 'JCP', accepted firearms and accessories on behalf of the US Army; they date from c. 1905. *See also* US arms inspectors' marks for the preceding two entries. **5.** Parker Brothers & Company. Trading in West

Meriden, Connecticut, successors to *Parker, Snow, Brooks & Company, this business was formed by the brothers Charles, Dexter and Wilbur Parker to make 10- and 12-bore shotguns in accordance with the patents of William H. *Miller. It is believed that the assets of the Meriden Manufacturing Company had been purchased, bringing with them rights to Miller's inventions. An 1878-vintage gun acknowledges patents dated 11 April 1870, 3 September 1872 and 16 March 1875. The perfected, or 1882-pattern, double-barrelled Parker hammer gun had a top-lever with a doll's-head bolt, although the earlier rocking-bar mechanism was made into the 1890s. The first Parker hammerless box-lock double-barrelled shotguns appeared about 1890. The company was acquired by the *Remington Arms Company in 1934, although guns marked 'Parker' were made until 1941. **6.** Parker, Field & Sons was formed in 1841 upon the death of gunmaker William Parker, of 233 High Holborn, London. Subsequently the business was run by John Field – Parker's son-in-law – then, after Field died in 1850, by his sons, John W.P. Field and William S. Field. Some directories note the trading style in these particular periods as John Field & Sons and J. & W. Field, but most of the sporting guns, rifles and pepperboxes were simply marked 'Parker, Field & Co., 233 High Holborn', even though premises at 58 Mansell Street, London E., were listed in 1851–70, and others at 62 Tenter Street South in 1871–75. A move to 59 Leman Street occurred in 1877. A subsequent relocation was to 122 Leman Street in 1879, then to 22 Tavistock Street, W.C., in 1882. Trading ceased in 1886. **7.** Parker-Hale Ltd: *see* panel, facing page. **8.** Parker Revolver Company: *see* Otis *Smith. **9.** Parker's Patent Precision Pistol. A spring-air pistol made by A.G. *Parker & Company, this incorporated a rack-and-pinion cocking mechanism designed by Alfred *Hale and Ernest Harris in 1920. Several hundred guns were made, but they were much too cumbersome, expensive and complicated to compete with the first Webleys. **10.** Parker, Snow, Brooks & Company: *see* Parker Brothers & Company.

Parkhouse. Joseph Parkhouse, High Street, Taunton, Somerset. The marks of this English gunmaker, active from 1821 until 1866, have been reported on sporting guns, *pepperboxes and cap-lock revolvers.

Parkhurst – 1. Edward Parkhurst, Hartford, Connecticut. This US inventor and patentee (c. 1830–1902) was retained first by *Pratt & Whitney, then by the *Lee Fire Arms Company of Connecticut. Among his US patents were several connected with machine-guns: 277,648 of 18 May 1880 (tripod), 228,777 of 15 June 1880 (gun), 229,007 of 22 June 1880 (cartridge feeder), 231,607 of 24 August 1880 (gun), 235,627 of 21 December (cartridge feeder, jointly with William *Gardner) and 341,499 of 11 May 1886 (carriage); all were assigned in whole or part to Pratt & Whitney. These concerned the Gardner machine-gun, which Pratt & Whitney made. Parkhurst's rifle patents were 599,287 of 15 February 1898 and 604,904 of 31 May 1898 (assigned to Lee), and 679,908 of 6 August 1901 and 719,254 of 27 January 1903 (posthumously); both were part-assigned to L.E. Warren of New York City. **2.** Parkhurst-Lee. A few fully-stocked rifles and even fewer half-stocked carbines were made under this system during 1899–1900 by the *Remington Arms Company. Protected by patents granted to Edward

PARKER-HALE LTD

Parker (7)

This British gunmaking business was formed in 1936 from what had previously been A.G. *Parker & Company Ltd. Large numbers of cartridges were produced during the Second World War, when a subsidiary company, the Parker-Hale Arms Company, formed for the duration of the hostilities, refurbished about 21,250 .303 No. 3 *Enfield rifles to Weedon Repair Standards (WRS) during the summer of 1939.

Parker-Hale also assembled about 2,100 .22 No. 2 *Lee-Enfield training rifles during 1940–45; supplied *Winchester rifles to the British authorities in 1941–43; and renovated more than 6,000 *Lewis Guns (1940–41) so that they could be fired from the shoulder. Parker-Hale was allotted the code 'M 183' in the early stages of the Second World War, the 'P.H. Arms

Company, Birmingham' receiving 'M 192'. *See also* British military manufacturers' marks.

Normal operations were re-established after 1945, and the company finally moved from the Bisley Works to new premises in Golden Hillock Road in 1967. The first of the company's *Lee-action sporters were converted from military-surplus No. 1 Mark III* service rifles in the early 1950s. Subsequently the *Supreme No. 1 (1958), *Custom No. 1 and Custom No. 4 (1965) were introduced to satisfy an increasingly discerning clientele.

Mauser-action rifles were built from the 1960s onward, based on actions purchased in Spain. Work continued alongside the distribution of a wide range of accessories and equipment until 1990, when the business passed to the *Gibbs Rifle Company. With the exception of the Model 2100 Midland pattern, discussed separately, Parker-Hale Mausers featured a classic 1898

Mauser action. The Model 85 sniper rifle was judged to be fit for service by the British Army, and was sold to many police and paramilitary organisations.

Many derivatives were made for target shooting, being chambered for cartridges ranging from .243 Winchester and 6.5x55 to .300 Winchester Magnum and 7.62x51mm. *See also* African and African Magnum; Bisley; Canberra; Classic; Clip and Clip Magnum; Safari and Safari Magnum; and Super, Super Magnum and Super Safari.

Prior to a transfer of work to the USA in the mid-1990s, Parker-Hale Ltd of Birmingham made a selection of bolt-action rifles on the basis of Spanish 'Santa Barbara' actions. This is a 7.62x51 Model 85 sniper rifle, approved by the British Army as fit for service, although the competing Accuracy International rifle was adopted.

Parkhurst in February and May 1898 as an improvement on the M1895 *Lee straight-pull navy rifle, the guns had two opposed lugs on the front of the bolt and a combination bolt-stop/ejector patented by William *Larraway in 1897. **3.** Parkhurst & Warren. Patented by Edward Parkhurst (but possibly co-designed by L.E. Warren), this rapid-loader was applied experimentally to about 100 M1898 *Krag-Jørgensen rifles and 100 M1898 carbines; charger guides were machined in the receiver at the rear of the loading gate. However, the Krag was notoriously difficult to adapt to this type of loading system and the experiments were abandoned once progress had been made with the then-experimental Mauser (Springfield) rifle.

Parkin. Elizabeth Parkin was listed by H.J. Blanch, in his 1909 survey of the London gun trade, at 3 Marylebone Street, Piccadilly, in 1857–60. He also sug-

gests that a Thomas Parkin was at the same address in 1861, but gives no additional information.

'Park Row' [The]. Found on the case-bodies of shotgun cartridges loaded from *Eley-Kynoch components by T. *Page-Wood of Bristol.

Parks. Joseph M. Parks, Birmingham, Warwickshire, England. A gun-rifler and pistol maker trading from 26 Price Street during 1861–63, then at 53 Lancaster Street until 1866.

Parkes – 1. Benjamin Parkes, Birmingham, Warwickshire, England. A gun- and pistol maker listed at 67, then 22 Weaman Street in 1829–52. Succeeded by his son, Isaiah (below). **2.** Isaiah Parkes, Birmingham, Warwickshire. This gunmaker traded in England from 1853, when he succeeded his father Benjamin (above), until the beginning of the First World War. The premises at 22

Weaman Street were retained. **3.** Parkes & Company, Birmingham, Warwickshire, England. Listed in 1871 as a maker of 'Cartridge Closers, Powder Measures, Pocket Cleaners and Re-cappers, and every description of Breech-Loading Implements…' The premises were at 49 Princip Street.

Parlor Gun, Parlour Gun. *See* Saloon Gun.

Parole. A small *Suicide Special revolver made by the *Bacon Manufacturing Company of Norwich, Connecticut, USA, in the late nineteenth century.

Parsons – 1. Charles Parsons, Nuneaton and Coventry, Warwickshire, and Hinkley, Leicestershire. Best known as an agricultural-supply and hardware merchant, Parsons handled shotgun ammunition prior to the First World War. Most of it seems to have been loaded in the Nuneaton premises from components supplied by *Kynoch. The business was renamed Parsons, Sherwin & Company (below) c. 1910. **2.** Edward Henry Parsons, Bourneville, near Birmingham, Warwickshire. Parsons was co-designer with Leslie Bown *Taylor of an SMLE-type airgun trainer protected by British Patent 5495/06 of 1906. Taylor worked for Westley *Richards, and it is presumed that Parsons, a 'sight maker', also did so. **3.** Parsons, Sherwin & Company, Nuneaton, Coventry and Hinkley. This partnership was an outgrowth of the business of Charles Parsons (above), continuing to trade in the same goods. Cartridges continued to be marked 'Special Loading', although most surviving examples display a drawing of a cock pheasant instead of a bounding rabbit.

'Parva'. A brandname used on sporting guns distributed in the period between the world wars by *Thieme & Schlegelmilch of Suhl. *See also* Feldmann.

'Parvo' [The]. A brandname associated with shotgun cartridges made by *Nobel Explosives Ltd of Glasgow and *Eley Bros. prior to the acquisition of the companies by Explosives Trades Ltd in 1918. Subsequently ammunition of this type was made by *Eley-Kynoch Ltd.

Pascal, Saint-Étienne, France. Listed in 1933 as a gunmaker. Still operating in 1951, from 7 rue Pierre-Blachon.

Passler & Seidl. These Bohemian (Austro-Hungarian) gunmakers patented a mechanically-operated repeating pistol in 1887. Guns of this type were made in small numbers before the advent of the semi-automatic pistol made them obsolete: pushing the ring-tipped lever forward opened the breech; pulling it back closed the breech and fired the gun. Most examples chambered a special 7.7mm cartridge and had a clip-loaded magazine. Cartridges were lifted by a spring-loaded arm pivoted beneath the gun barrel.

'PAT', 'PAT.' – 1. Used generally: 'Patent'. **2.** Found on US military firearms and accessories. *See* P.A. *Teham.

Patch – 1. George W. Patch. An inspector of US military firearms, active during 1847–58, Patch's 'GWP' marks will be found on cap-lock Colt *Dragoon revolvers. **2.** Nahum W. Patch. This Ordnance Department inspector, active during 1830–49, accepted a variety of US military firearms. His 'NWP' marks will be found on single-shot cap-lock pistols and muskets; cap-lock Colt *Walker and *Dragoon-pattern revolvers; Starr rifles; and, in particular, some of the *Hall carbines made by Simeon *North. Patch designed the folding-elbow, or L-shape, operating lever for the 1840-pattern Hall breech-loaders. *See also* US arms inspectors' marks' for both entries.

Patchett. George V. Patchett designed what has since become known as the British *Sterling submachine-gun.

Patent… – 1. Many changes have been made over the years to national and international patent law, and the original English intention of petitioning the King by way of the Lord Chancellor soon gave way to a system by which applications were made directly to officials appointed by the Crown to receive, assess and grant protection. Grants have even inhibited progress, even though the patents ran only for their full term. This was true of US Patent 9430X, granted to Samuel Colt on 25 February 1836 and reissued on 24 October 1848 (no. 124), which prevented any revolver being made with a mechanically-rotated cylinder until the mid-1850s. It was also true of a patent granted in the 1850s to Rollin White, subsequently the designer of the White Steam Car, which allowed the little-known partnership of Horace Smith and Daniel Wesson to prevent the manufacture of any revolver with chambers bored through its cylinder. Each nation has practices of its own, some of which are described individually in the appropriate sections. Practically all European countries, with the exception of Britain and Austria-Hungary (which issued Privilegium numbered in annual-cycle sequences), relied on simple cumulative numbering series from which the earliest date of an item may be deduced with comparatively little difficulty. However, Spain, had a more flexible 'patent' system, which could incorporate the registry of trademarks, and knowledge of the progression of patents in consecutively numbered sequences is an extremely useful identification tool. Unfortunately, the French and Belgians often neglected to include patent numbers, relying simply on 'BREVETÉ' and 'DEPOSÉ'. A problem can arise from Communicated patents, which often bear the name of a patent agent working on behalf of an inventor domiciled overseas. Prior to 1859, in Britain at least, the identity of the inventor was seldom revealed; thereafter, it was a statutory requirement. Yet many spelling mistakes were made in British records – particularly where foreign names were concerned – and there have been unaccountable lapses of geography. **2.** Patent Arms Manufacturing Company, Paterson, New Jersey. This gunmaking business was founded in 1835 by Samuel *Colt, to make revolver-rifles and the first *Paterson Revolvers. Unfortunately, the enterprise was not successful, and was liquidated in 1842. **3.** Patent Breech Loading Rifle Company Ltd [The]. This British promotional agency, listed in 1864–67 at 34 Southampton Buildings, London W.C., was formed to exploit a breech-loading rifle patented by McKenzie & Wentworth. **4.** Patent, British. Prior to the last day of September 1852, English and Scottish patents were numbered in separate series. With effect from 1 October 1852, however, the implementation of the Patent Law Amendment Act combined the disparate series; numbers were reduced to '1' and a simple progression occurred until, on 1 January 1853, the series began again at '1'. A trademark registry was created in 1875, applying marks from 1 January 1877 onward, and an Act of Parliament passed in 1902 ensured that investigation (albeit limited) was made into claims of novelty before patents were granted; by 1907, all British patents had been abridged and assessed in 146 classes occupying more than 1,000 volumes. Pre-1852 English patents were granted, with some significant exceptions, to run for fourteen years from the application of the seal of the Lord Chancellor's office; the 1852 Act, while retaining the fourteen-year maximum, backdated protection to the date of application to ensure that unwarranted infringement could not occur between the first submission and the final grant. Additional provisions included fee-supported renewal of patents after three, then seven years, and the submission of a Provisional Specification with the patent application. Thus items made in the few months between initial submission and the final grant will display such marks as 'P.P.', 'P.PT.', 'P.PAT.' and 'PROV. PAT.' The 1852-type British patent grant system continued until the end of December 1915; from 1 January 1916, however, a new series began at '100001' and ran on, supposedly ad infinitum, without regard to calendar year. The Patent Act 1977 made an important change, as applications made after 1 July 1978 were numbered from 2000000 upward. However, processing the claims made on, or prior to, 30 June 1978, often slowed by investigation (and litigation), has ensured that the old numbering system is still being used in the twenty-first century. Numbers that had stood at about 1525000 on 1 July 1978 were approaching only 1610000 by 1 September 2000. **5.** Patent, German. The German system, which was implemented in 1877, also runs sequentially; patents granted by the German Federal Republic (1945–91) followed on from those granted during the Kaiserzeit (1871–1918), the Weimar Republic (1919–33) and the Third Reich (1933–45). The sequence has been continued since the reunification of Germany, although the individual year-date/patent number correlation is not yet available. However, a few examples will illustrate the progression: 1192 (7 August 1877), 28109 (4 November 1883), 65225 (16 February 1892), 105620 (20 December 1898), 256606 (22 November 1911), 578765 (7 November 1930), 824160 (4 July 1950) and 1553964 (July 1966). **6.** Patent House Pistol. A .41 rimfire four-chamber solid-frame revolver made by ★Colt during 1871–75 in accordance with a patent granted to Charles B. ★Richards in September 1871. Also known as the Cloverleaf, owing to the shape of the cylinder, the design was notable for its counter-bored chambers. **7.** Patent identifiers. English-speaking countries have customarily used 'PATENT'. Franco-phone countries, notably France and Belgium, marked patented items with 'BREVET' ('Patent') or 'BREVETÉ' ('Patented'), often accompanied by 'S.G.D.G.' for *Sans Garantie du Gouvernement* ('Without Governmental [statutory] Guarantee'). Marks of this type may also be accompanied by 'DEPOSE' or 'DEPOSÉ', indicating that the marks had been 'deposited', or registered, with the authorities. However, 'DEPOSE' alone does not necessarily indicate a patent; it could just as easily refer to a registered design or a trademark. Marks 'BREVETTO' and 'BREVETTATO' are Italian; 'DRP', 'D.R.P.' and 'D.R.Pa.' are German (*Deutsches Reichs-Patente*) and represent the highest category of protection a design may be granted. Care must be taken to distinguish 'D.R.Pa.' and 'D.R.P.A.', as the latter, more commonly 'D.R.P. Ang.' or 'D.R.P. Angem.', signifies *Deutsches Reichs-Patent Angemeldet* (i.e. that the patent had been sought, but not yet granted). 'D.R.P. Ang.' marks were customarily used only for a short time before being replaced with 'D.R.P.', and can be a dating aid. The use of blanket identifiers, including 'FOREIGN', can hide origins, and attempts have been made to capitalise on better-known locations – 'MADE IN GOTHA' was widely used in Britain prior to 1900 on goods made in the Thüringen district of Sachsen-Coburg-Gotha, a principality that, although incorporated in the German Empire in 1871, had provided the British Royal Family. Few Britons had heard of Thüringen, and even fewer knew the names of the principal metalworking centres, Mehlis, Suhl and Zella St Blasii. Occasionally patents and registered trademarks are confused, although British applications are usually identified by 'REGISTERED TRADE MARK', 'TRADE MARK' or simply 'T.M' (now often written as ™), whereas 'DRWZ' or 'D.R.W.Z.' (*Deutsches Reichs Waren-Zeichen*, 'Imperial German trademark') was used in Germany. Spanish-speaking countries applied 'MARCA REGISTRADA', often abbreviated simply to 'MCA. RDA'. **8.** Patent India Rubber Air Gun: *see* John ★Shaw. **9.** Patent Masonic Institution Gun: *see* Demoulin Brothers. **10.** Patent Oxonite Company Ltd. This company was formed in 1886 to promote Oxonite explosive – doubtless deemed suitable for small-arms cartridges – but lasted at 12 Buckingham Street, London W.C., for little more than a year. **11.** Patent Shot Cartridge: *see* Lane Brothers. **12.** Patent, USA. This system owed its inception to an Act, signed on 1 April 1790, that recognised the rights of inventors to profit from their inventions. In 1793, however, the Patent Board was abolished in favour of a straightforward fee-based registration system based not on novelty or utility, but on the raising of revenue. Finally, on Independence Day, 1836, a new Patent Act repaired much of the damage that had been done by the ineffective grant system, and a system of investigating claims against 'prior art' appeared. The continuous nature of US patents, even though they began again at '1' after the implementation of the new Patent Act on 13 July 1836, ensured that numbers had reached 6981 by 1 January 1850; 640167 by 1 January 1900; 2492944 by 1 January 1950; and 6009555 by 1 January 2000. The US Patent Office has also sparingly re-issued patents, numbering them separately from 1838 onward. Occasionally numbers representing this sequence will be found, and, unless accompanied by proper identification, can be perplexing. Marks such as 'REISSUE' or simply 'RED' can be helpful. Reissue numbers stood at a mere 158 on 1 January 1850; at 11798 on 1 January 1900; at 23186 on 1 January 1950; and at 36479 on the first day of 2000.

Paterson Colt. This name was given to the first Colt revolvers made by the ★Patent Arms Manufacturing Company of Paterson, New Jersey. Offered in several sizes ranging from a tiny .28 pocket version to the No. 5 Holster Pistol, they had triggers that sprang down out of the frame when the hammer was thumbed back.

Pathfinder – **1.** A semi-automatic pistol made in Spain by ★Echave y Arizmendi of Eibar, prior to the Spanish Civil War (1936–39). **2.** A ★Suicide Special revolver manufactured by the ★Hopkins & Allen Arms Company of Norwich, Connecticut, in the late nineteenth century.

Paton. Edward Paton & Sons. Listed as a gunmaking business active in London at 3 Mount Pleasant Street, Grosvenor Square (1871–73), and 99 Mount Street in 1884–85.

Patrick. Jeremiah Patrick, Liverpool, Lancashire. The

marks of this gunmaker have been reported on self-cocking *pepperboxes, dating from the 1850s. However, Patrick's working life – according to Bailey and Nie in *English Gunmakers* – was confined to 1795–1832. It seems more likely that the guns were handled by his successors, Williams & Powell, who may have been trading as 'late Patrick' (i.e. 'formerly Patrick') in this period. Thomas Williams and Samuel Powell began trading from 10 Pool Lane in 1833, moved to South Castle Street in 1834, and worked until 1870 or later.

Patronen-Hülsen-Fabrik Bitschweiler, Bitschweiler in Elsass. Little is known about this propellant and ammunition manufacturer, working in Alsace prior to 1918, except that its marks – which included 'P.H.F.B.' and a 'WM' monogram – have been found on a variety of shotgun cartridges. The primers often display the 'GG' monogram and 'SFM' marks of *Société Française des Munitions.

Patstone – 1. Patstone & Son, 28 High Street, Southampton; also in Winchester, Hampshire. This gunsmithing business was established some time prior to 1878, when a medal was gained at the Paris Exhibition. In addition to rifles and shotguns, Patstone handled shotgun ammunition (apparently assembled largely from foreign-made components). Among the brandnames identified with this particular agency were The Precision, The Reliable and The Renown. Subsequently the business became Patstone & Cox (below). **2.** Patstone & Cox, Southampton and Winchester, Hampshire. Successor to Patstone & Company (above), this gunmaking business continued to offer shotgun cartridges under some, perhaps all, of the original names. Ammunition marked 'The Pheasant' has also been reported.

Patterson. J.C. Patterson, Lisburn, County Down. The name of this Irish gunsmith/ironmonger has been reported on shotgun cartridges marked 'The Nailer'.

Pattison. Robert Pattison, or 'Patterson', Nottingham. The marks of this gunmaker have been found on sporting guns made in England during the mid-nineteenth century. Directories record his premises in Parliament Street (1834–42) and Bunker's Hill (1843–64).

Paubel. C. Paubel, Suhl in Thüringen, Germany. This man was listed as a gunmaker in the 1900 edition of the *Deutsches Reichs-Adressbuch*.

Paul. William Paul, Beecher, Illinois, USA. This engineer designed a .410 pump-action air shotgun patented in the USA in March 1923 and February 1924: nos. 1,481,526 and 1,506,995 respectively.

Pauler. Th. Pauler, Sondershausen, Lange Strasse 1. A retailer of sporting guns and ammunition listed as active in Germany in 1941.

Payne. Oscar Payne. Chief draughtsman of the *Auto-Ordnance Corporation, responsible with Theodore *Eickhoff for perfecting the *Thompson submachine-gun.

Payre. P. Payre, grande rue des Capucins, Saint-Étienne, France. Listed in 1879 as a distributor of, and agent for, arms and ammunition.

'PB', 'P.B.' – 1. Found on US military firearms and accessories. *See* Peter *Barrett and Pomeroy *Booth. **2.** Applied to a special silenced version of the 9mm *PM or Makarov pistol. **3.** Often floriated and usually encircled. A mark associated with Pietro *Beretta of Gardone Val Trompia, Italy, commonly moulded into the grips of pistols. **4.** PB Special. A pistol made by Pietro *Beretta or August *Menz.

'PBBH'. Found on US military firearms and accessories. *See* P.B.B. *Havens.

'P.C.C.', 'P.C.Co.' Found in the headstamps of ammunition made by the *Peters Cartridge Company of Cincinnati, Ohio, USA.

'P', 'D' and 'C', with crossed pennants. A military proof mark – Dominion of Canada Proof. *See also* British military proof marks.

Peabody – 1. Henry O. Peabody, Boston, Massachusetts, USA. This gunmaker is best known for the single-shot swinging-block breech-loading rifle patented in the USA on 22 July 1862 (no. 35,947), which, but for ill fortune, could have become standard throughout the US Army. External-hammer rifles and carbines of this type sold in large numbers in the decade following the American Civil War, but were superseded in the mid-1870s by the Peabody-Martini. Essentially this was a copy of the British *Martini-Henry; bad feeling ensued, and threats were made by both parties. Peabody always maintained that Martini had copied his 1862 patent, and thus that he had every entitlement to copy Martini's improvement to the original design. The extraordinary success of both rifles, however, ensured that a mutually beneficial settlement was reached. Henry Peabody also received US Patent 72,076 of 10 December 1867, protecting a variant of his 1862 design operated by lifting a lever formed as the tail of the breech-block, and no. 76,805 of 14 April 1868 for a firing pin suitable for rim- and centrefire ammunition alike. **2.** Peabody Breech Loader Agency [The]. Formed in 1869 as a successor to the *Providence Tool Company's Armoury, this business was little more than an office in George Yard, London E.C., controlling rights to the patents obtained by Henry *Peabody. Moving to 65 Gracechurch Street in 1872, it was superseded c. 1877/78 by the Peabody-Martini Breech Loader Agency. This appeared for the first time in directories published for 1880.

Peace. Joseph Peace, Darlington, County Durham. A gunsmith and sports-equipment supplier, Peace is known to have handled shotguns and shotgun ammunition. Most of the cartridges prove to have been made by *Eley Bros. and *Eley-Kynoch.

Peacekeeper. A replacement for the *Lawman Mk V, dating from 1985–87, this revolver was made by the Firearms Division of *Colt Industries. Mechanically similar to the *King Cobra, produced only in .357 Magnum chambering, the Peacekeeper was of blued steel, had a half-length ejector shroud and an adjustable back sight, and was fitted with rubber grips.

Peacemaker – 1. *See* Single Action Army Revolver. **2.** A name applied by the Firearms Division of Colt Industries to an improved form of the rimfire *Frontier Scout, about 190,000 being made between 1970 and 1977. The guns could be obtained with exchangeable .22 LR/.22 WMR cylinders, those with 7.5in barrels often being marked *'BUNTLINE'. **3.** A twelve-shot spring-powered *Daisy Model 179 revolver, introduced in 1959. An *NRA commemorative version, the M5179, was made in 1971. **4.** Peacemaker 44. A carbon-dioxide-powered revolver made by the *Crosman Arms Company. *See also* Frontier.

Peaks. Edgar A. Peaks. Supplier of 12-bore shotguns to the British military authorities, 1942.

Peard. James J. Peard, Hartford, Connecticut, USA. An

employee of ★Colt's Patent Fire Arms Manufacturing Company, serving by 1910 as the Hartford factory superintendent, Peard invented an adjustable back sight protected by US Patents 671,609 of April 1901 and 761,706 of June 1904. Sights of this type were often fitted to Colt ★Officer's Model revolvers. He was also responsible for the loaded-chamber indicator described in US Patent no. 891,438 of 23 June 1908.

Pearson. E.H. Pearson, an employee of the Ordnance Department using an 'EHP' identifier, accepted guns made for the US armed forces by ★Colt's Patent Fire Arms Manufacturing Company; apparently they date from the period 1898–1901, distinguishing them from similar marks applied by Edwin H. ★Perry during the American Civil War. *See also* US arms inspectors' marks.

Peavey – 1. Andrew J. Peavey. This inventor, of South Montville, Maine, USA, patented a cap-lock knife pistol on 5 September 1865 (49,784), and a rimfire adaptation on 27 March 1866 (53,473). *See* Peavey knife pistol (below). Also co-patentee with Edward P. ★Boardman of the ★Little All Right revolver. **2.** Peavey knife pistol. Among the most heavily disguised of all the guns of this type were the pen- or clasp-knife patterns, which gave few clues to their additional function. The Peavey design was made in cap-lock and cartridge-firing patterns, with a single folding blade offset to one side to allow a barrel to run the length of the grip, beneath an elongated bar-hammer. Pulling the rear of the hammer upward against the pressure of the leaf spring allowed it to be held by a serpentine catch, which doubled as the trigger lever.

Pecare & Smith, New York City. This partnership of Jacob Pecare and Josiah M. Smith made a variety of ★caplock ★pepperboxes, c. 1847–53, displaying them at the Great Exhibition in London during 1851. The partners were jointly granted US Patent 6925 of 4 December 1849 to protect a concealed trigger mechanism.

Peck. E.B. Peck, a civilian employee of the Ordnance Department, accepted military firearms made by ★Colt's Patent Fire Arms Manufacturing Company. Dating from 1898–1913, they bear 'EBP' identifiers. *See also* US arms inspectors' marks.

Peddled Rifle Scheme. This name was applied to a system of accelerated production based on the supply of ★Lee-Enfield rifle components – by contractors such as the ★Standard Small Arms Company Ltd – for assembly in the ★Royal Small Arms Factory, Enfield. The scheme was never entirely successful, and only about 250,000–275,000 of the several million rifles made in Britain during the First World War were created in this way.

Pedersen – 1. John Douglas Pedersen, Denver, Colorado, and Jackson, Wyoming, USA. Best known for the ★Pedersen Device of the First World War and his toggle-lock rifle, which was tested extensively by the US Army in the 1920s, Pedersen was a brilliant engineer who often designed all the gauges, fixtures and production machinery for his own guns. He also developed a highly successful slide-action shotgun for the ★Remington Arms

PEDERSEN DEVICE

Pedersen (3)

Developed in 1916 by John Pedersen with the assistance of Oliver Loomis of ★Remington-UMC, this was intended to deliver withering fire during an advance across 'no-man's land'. Working prototypes for the French Lebel, Russian Mosin and US Springfield rifles were produced in 1917.

Few changes were required in the M1903, apart from a minor alteration in the cut-off to lock the Pedersen Device in place. An auxiliary sear was added to the trigger mechanism, and an ejection port was cut through the left side of the receiver. The firer only needed to replace the standard bolt with the Pedersen Device and insert the magazine to transform an M1903 Mark 1 ★Springfield rifle into a low-powered semi-automatic. The device was little more than a blowback pistol, with a 'slide' behind the receiver bridge and a short barrel extending forward into the chamber.

Fitted with the Pedersen Device and a magazine for forty .30 M1918 cartridges, the rifle weighed only a little more than 10lb. Tests showed that the Pedersen Device – officially the '.30 Automatic Pistol, Model of 1918' – worked surprisingly well. An order for 100,000 was given to Remington, to be made in the Bridgeport factory, and almost immediately was extended to 500,000. However, the war ended before any could be delivered; about 65,000 Pedersen Devices had been completed before work ceased in 1919, and 101,780 rifles were converted in Springfield Armory during 1919–20. Most of the devices were scrapped in the 1920s, although the rifles remained in service until they wore out.

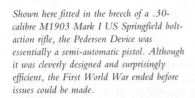

Shown here fitted in the breech of a .30-calibre M1903 Mark I US Springfield bolt-action rifle, the Pedersen Device was essentially a semi-automatic pistol. Although it was cleverly designed and surprisingly efficient, the First World War ended before issues could be made.

Company. Pedersen's US patents included three granted prior to 1910 for magazine firearms: 719,955 of 3 February 1903, and 789,932 and 789,933 of 16 May 1905. The two 1905 patents were assigned to Remington. Patent 789,755 of 16 May 1905 protected a 'firearm recoil lock'; 908,883 of 5 January 1908 was granted for a 'firearm'; and 936,806 of 12 October 1908 protected the construction of a combination firing pin/ejector. **2.** Pedersen Custom Guns: *see* Mossberg. **3.** Pedersen Device: *see* panel, p. 399. **4.** Pedersen military rifles. The first delayed-blowback toggle-lock military rifle was submitted to the US Army in 1925 and led to the .276 T1 of 1928. This was tried during 1928–31 against primer-actuated and gas-operated .276 and .30 ★Garands, a ★Thompson Automatic Rifle and an improved .256 ★Bang. Unfortunately, the toggle-lock was difficult to machine accurately, and the waxed cartridge case was unacceptable; as the action was prone to jamming, and the rising toggle was apt to strike the firer's helmet, work in the USA ceased. In the late 1920s, Pedersen went to Britain to assist ★Vickers-Armstrongs to tool for his rifle. The first two Vickers-made guns were submitted to the Small Arms Committee in 1929, passing their trials successfully enough for additional experiments to be undertaken during 1931–33, but after that the project was abandoned.

Peerless – 1. A ★Suicide Special revolver made by the ★Hood Firearms Company of Norwich, Connecticut, USA, in the late nineteenth century. **2.** A brandname associated with shotguns made by the ★Crescent Arms Company prior to 1920. **3.** A brandname used by A.F. ★Stoeger & Company of New York on ★Mayer & Grammelspacher Diana spring-airguns sold in the USA between 1930 and 1960. **4.** A name given to virtually any of the guns made by the ★Remington Arms Company that were distinguished by good-quality woodwork and light scroll engraving on the action. They have included the bolt-action Model 700D Peerless (1965–89), the slide-action Model 760D Peerless (1961–81) and the Model Six Peerless (1981–83). *See also* Custom Grade and Premier. **5.** Peerless Manufacturing Company. Trading in Greenville, Pennyslvania, this manufacturer of sewing machines, needles and accessories was also a distributor of ★premium airguns. The ★Bijou and ★Magic seem to have been favoured.

'Pegamoid' [The]. A mark said to have been found on shotgun ammunition made, or perhaps simply assembled, by the ★Normal Improved Ammunition Company of Hendon. Subsequently it was made by ★Eley-Kynoch. The name is believed to have indicated use of waterproof paper (cf. Aquoid).

Pegler. Samuel Pegler & Son, Blandford, Dorset. The marks of this English gunmaking business, founded by Samuel Pegler in Salisbury Street during the 1820s, have been reported on sporting guns and ★pepperboxes. These date from the period after the change in trading style, '...& Son' being adopted about 1847, when a move to Market Place occurred.

Pell-Clip. A magazine-loading system encountered on the Model 622 Pell-Clip rifle made by the ★Crosman Arms Company.

Pelletier Veuve, 35 rue Mulatière, Saint-Étienne, France. Listed in 1951 as a gunmaker.

'Pell-Gun'. Applied as a brandname to some airguns manufactured by the ★Crosman Arms Company.

Pelo. Carl Pelo, Finland. This army officer designed a distinctive recoil-operated auto-loading rifle in the 1930s. This was tested extensively in several countries – including Sweden and Britain – but was not successful.

Pelzer & Companie. *See* Vereinigte Automaten-Fabriken.

Pen- and pencil-guns. Guns of this type have a pedigree dating back to disguised cap-locks made in the second quarter of the nineteenth century. A surprising number of survivors will encountered, although many chamber only blank or gas cartridges instead of ball ammunition. Pen-guns are usually fired by retracting a striker until it is held against the pressure of a spring by pivoting bars, sliding catches or button triggers. External appearance has ranged from extremely unconvincing to plausible facsimiles of the pen styles of the day. *See also* Enpen, Stinger, Stop and Welpen; Lewis Winant, *Firearms Curiosa* (Greenberg, 1955); and John Walter, *Secret Firearms* (Arms & Armour Press, 1997)

Penfield. Walter G. Penfield, a major attached to the US Ordnance Department, accepted .45 M1911 ★Government Model pistols made for the armed forces by ★Colt's Patent Fire Arms Manufacturing Company. Dating from the period 1911–14, they displayed 'WGP'. *See also* US arms inspectors' marks.

Penn – 1. F.J. Penn, Britain: *see* John ★Deeley. **2.** John Penn. Listed as a member of the English gun trade at 69 Middleton Street, Clerkenwell, London, in 1867–80. **3.** William John Penn. A gunmaker listed in 1873 at 46 Wynyatt Street, Goswell Road, London. Later directories have William J. Penn at 1 & 2 Chiswell Street, London E.C., in 1887–92, then at 46 Wilson Street, Finsbury, E.C., until 1899. It is thought that all refer to one gunmaker, although they may have been father and son.

J.C. Penney Company. *See* Marlin.

Pepperbox. *See* panel, facing page.

Pequeño Police Positive Model, also listed as 'Pequano'. This was a second-grade version of the Police Positive, made in 1933–35 by ★Colt's Patent Fire Arms Manufacturing Company. Most of the revolvers were sold to police forces in South America, Puerto Rico and the Philippine Islands, but some survived to be acquired by the British Purchasing Commission in 1940.

Percival. Orville B. Percival, East Haddam and Moodus, Connecticut. The designer, jointly with Asa ★Smith, of a magazine pistol, protected by a US Patent granted on 9 July 1850 ('chargers attached to firearms'). Made by Horace ★Smith, the pistol had three magazines – one each for powder, balls and primers – which were fed into position automatically simply by rotating the barrel through 180 degrees.

Percorso caccia. *See* Caccia.

Perfect – 1. Perfect Number 1 Gem. *See* Lane Brothers. **2.** Found, often as 'The Perfect', on English-made shotgun ammunition, the work of the ★Midland Gun Company of Birmingham. **3.** Another of the many 6.35mm Browning-type pistols made in Spain by ★Gabilondo y Urresti of Elgoeibar. Apparently distributed by José ★Mugica of Eibar. **4.** A revolver made in the USA by the ★Foehl & Weeks Manufacturing Company during the early 1890s.

Perfecta. A brandname associated with spring-air rifles made in the early 1920s by Oscar ★Will of Zella-Mehlis for the ★Midland Gun Company of Birmingham.

PEPPERBOX

A term applied to *cap-lock and other pistols with multiple barrels grouped in a rotating cluster, although often excluding designs in which the barrel cluster is supported at the muzzle in addition to the breech (these are often classed as Fist Revolvers). The barrels of the first pepperboxes were rotated manually and fired by single-acting triggers. The guns were simple and easy to make, but accurate only at short range.

Among the many British pepperbox makers were *Brooks & Son, John R. *Cooper & Company, Joseph *Lang (marketed as the Turnover), Charles *Osborne of Birmingham, Westley *Richards & Son, William & John *Rigby, *Tipping & Lawden, and Edward *Trulock & Son.

Charles Smith of Whittall Street, Birmingham (active 1845–52) obtained an English Patent in 1845 to protect priming magazines and a double-action pepperbox pistol, and, as late as 1860, Robert Hughes of Birmingham was advertising himself as a manufacturer.

Although cap-lock pepperboxes were made in France and Belgium, notably in the Liège district, they were soon overhauled by pinfires. Among the best-known is the *Mariette, allegedly developed in the 1830s by a Belgian gunmaker of the same name, which had a double-action ring trigger.

Cap-lock pepperboxes were also made in the USA. The first American designs were rotated

Marked – perhaps misleadingly – 'Jos. Manton/London', this eighteen-shot pepperbox has three concentric rows of barrels and the nipples clustered in threes. It may have originated in Belgium about 1840, but bears London proof marks.

manually, but the introduction of the *Paterson Colt revolvers persuaded enterprising gunsmiths to revolve the cylinders mechanically. The guns made by Barton & Benjamin *Darling, initially in Shrewsbury, Massachusetts, are generally regarded as the earliest self-rotating pepperboxes. However, production of Darling pepperboxes was never large, and the grant of the relevant patent in April 1836 – after Colt's – undermines their claim to fame. Much more successful than the single-action Darling was the double-action, or self-cocking, pepperbox patented by Ethan *Allen in November 1837.

This double-action bar-hammer gun was made by Allen & Thurber in Grafton, Norwich and Worcester. Later guns were produced by Allen & Wheelock, successors to Allen & Thurber in the mid-1850s. Other US manufacturers included *Bacon

& Company, *Blunt & Syms, George *Leonard, the *Manhattan Fire Arms Company, William *Marston, *Pecare & Smith, *Robbins & Lawrence, *Stocking & Company, the *Union Arms Company, and the *Washington Arms Company of Washington, D.C. However, the marks of retailers, sporting-goods promoters and other agencies will often be found; Taylerson, Andrews and Frith alone listed more than 130 British examples in *The Revolver, 1818–1865* (Barrie & Jenkins, London, 1968).

Perfected Model. This .38 double-action *Smith & Wesson, designed by Joseph H. *Wesson, was introduced commercially in 1909. Essentially it was a top-break version of the .32 *Hand Ejector. About 60,000 had been made when production ended in 1920.

Perfection – 1. Found, often as 'The Perfection', on shotgun ammunition made in England by the *Midland Gun Company of Birmingham. **2.** A brandname associated with shotguns made by the *Crescent Arms Company of Norwich, Connecticut, USA. **3.** Perfection Model. The No. 4 *Ballard hunting rifle of 1876–89 was made in chamberings from .38 to .50. Normally it had open Rocky Mountain sights and an octagonal barrel.

Perforator. A name associated with a revolver sold in Belgium prior to 1914 by A. *Riga.

Perher. Richard Perher, a lieutenant attached to the US Ordnance Department, accepted military firearms and accessories during 1838–45. Marked 'RP', they can be

distinguished from guns accepted by Richard *Paine in the same era by the absence of navy marks. *See also* US arms inspectors' marks.

Periscopic Prism Company, 23 Prince of Wales Crescent, Kentish Town, London. This business was responsible for some of the telescope sights used during the First World War on the *Lee-Enfield rifle. The standard pattern had range drums graduated for 100–600yd; male dovetails on the sight rings fitted into a bar brazed to the left side of the SMLE action, in accordance with a patent granted to A.B. *Rolfe-Martin in 1915. The company, which had become notorious for slow deliveries, was taken over by the Ministry of Munitions in 1917.

Perkes. Thomas Perkes, a member of the English gun trade, was recorded at 70 Osnaburgh Street, London N.W., in 1882–89; at 14a Castle Street, London W., in 1890–94; at 119 Jermyn Street in 1892–94; and at 18 Cork Street, Bond Street, London W., in 1895. After that, the trading style changed to Perkes, Adams & Company, which continued to work from 15 Swallow Street, London W., until 1896.

Perkins – 1. Anson G. Perkins accepted firearms and accessories on behalf of the Federal Army immediately before, then during, the American Civil War, marking them 'AGP'; most items date from 1859–63. **2.** Dwight A. Perkins, working on behalf of the Federal Army in 1862, during the American Civil War, accepted the firearms and equipment marked 'DAP'. *See also* US arms inspectors' marks for the previous two entries. **3.** Jacob Perkins, a talented engineer, was born in the USA in 1766 and died in Britain in 1849. He is best known for the Perkins Steam Gun, but had far greater success with inventions as diverse as banknote printing presses, nail-making machinery and high-pressure steam engines. His son, Angier March Perkins (1800–81), continued development work after his father's death. Several arms inspectors named Perkins were employed by the US Ordnance Department in the early years of the nineteenth century – for example, the 'JP' identifier of Jacob Perkins has been reported on Waters flintlock muskets dating from 1819–21 – but no links have been proved between these and the inventor. **4.** O.N. Perkins, retained by the US Ordnance Department in the late 1890s, accepted the military firearms and accessories identified with 'ONP'. *See also* US arms inspectors' marks. **5.** Perkins Steam Gun. Dating from 1843, this was an attempt to use high-pressure steam to propel ball ammunition. Trials undertaken in Britain revealed that the gun was not only surprisingly powerful, but also capable of firing at a prodigious rate. However, the necessity to accompany it with a steam-raising facility – even in the form of Jacob Perkins' flash boiler – made it extremely unpractical in the field. Subsequently a large-calibre cannon version was offered to the French Navy, but without success.

Perla. A compact 6.35mm *Browning-type pocket pistol made in Czechoslovakia by František Dušek of Opočno, c. 1925–38. The Duo and Jaga were essentially similar.

Perplex. This *Scheintod pistol was made by Bernhard *Paatz of Zella-Mehlis, being identified by the brand-name and a 'BP' monogram. The Perplex Model 1 had an external hammer and a single tipping barrel, locked by a push-button on the left side of the frame, above the sheath trigger. The Model 2 had two superimposed barrels, an automatic ejector actuated by a spur projecting from the frame, a folding trigger and enclosed-hammer lockwork. A push-button catch inspired by the Model 1 was soon replaced by a slider.

Perrin – 1. A.C. Perrin, a captain in the US Army, accepted firearms and equipment made by *Colt's Patent Fire Arms Manufacturing Company; marked 'ACP', they date from the mid-1930s. Note, however, that the mark should not be confused with the similar abbreviation for 'Automatic Colt Pistol'. *See also* US arms inspectors' marks. **2.** Perrin et Maisonneuve, Saint-Étienne, France. Listed in 1933 as a gunmaker. **3.** Perrin revolver. This double-action design, patented in France in 1859 by Perrin & Delmas, was inspired by the British *Adams. The earliest guns had open frames, decoratively-spurred trigger guards, hammers without spurs, and small sprung rammers carried on collars around the barrel. Later guns had simpler fittings and often had straps carried back over the cylinder to improve strength. All chambered centrefire thick-rim cartridges with the priming carried internally.

Perrins. John Perrins, sometimes listed as 'Perkins', Worcester. This gunsmithing business began trading from New Street in 1827, moving successively to College Street (1834) and St Swithin's Lane (1852). Operations were being conducted from premises in Mealcheapen Street by the time the title changed to John Perrins & Son in 1868, and continued until the First World War or later. 'Perrins & Son' marks have been found on shotgun ammunition loaded by *Eley Brothers prior to 1914.

Perry – 1. Alonzo D. Perry of Newark, New Jersey, USA, received a variety of US Patents protecting firearms. These included 6945 of 11 December 1849 for a breech mechanism based on a horizontal plug, or 'faucet'; 12,001 of 28 November 1854 for a radial-block breech; and 12,244 of 16 January 1855 for a breech-block swinging on trunnions, equivalent protection being granted in Britain as early as 1853. Guns were made by, or perhaps for, the Perry Patent Fire Arms Company (below). **2.** Claude Alfred Perry, an engineer employed by *BSA Guns Ltd, has been credited with much of the design of the early post-war airguns, including the *Airsporter. **3.** Edward C. Perry accepted firearms and accessories made for the US armed forces by *Colt's Patent Fire Arms Manufacturing Company. Dating from 1936–41, they display 'ECP'. **4.** Edward L. Perry of Paterson, New Jersey, received US Patent 210,626 on 10 December 1878 to protect a 'breech-loading firearm'. **5.** Edwin H. Perry, active during the early part of the American Civil War, accepted firearms and accessories on behalf of the Federal Army. Marked 'EHP', they can be distinguished by date from guns bearing a similar mark employed at the end of the nineteenth century by E.H. *Pearson. *See also* US arms inspectors' marks for the preceding two entries. **6.** H.V. Perry, Fredonia, Pomfret, Ellicott and Jamestown, New York State. A gunmaker active from c. 1858 until 1891 or later, Perry made *cap-lock target rifles and (in later days) tip-barrel shotguns. *Sharps and *Remington rifles have also been found with his marks. **7.** Samuel M. Perry, Brooklyn, New York. Patentee of a breech-loading pistol (no. 43,259 and 43,260 of 21 June 1864), part-assigned to Edward S. Renwick. Perry's Perpetual Pistol had a chamber at each end of a barrel that could rotate around a vertical spindle at its mid-point. **8.** William Perry. A gunmaker listed in 1866 at 11 Great May's Buildings, St Martin's Lane, London W.C. **9.** Perry Patent Fire Arms Company, Newark, New Jersey. Maker, or perhaps simply the promoter, of guns made in accordance with patents granted to Alonzo Perry. These included 200 'tap-breech' carbines ordered by the US Army in 1855, and a six-barrel rifle. Work appears to have been confined to 1856–59.

Personne. *See* L. *Le Personne.

'Perth' [The]. A mark found on shotgun ammunition handled by D.B. *Crockart of Perth, Scotland.

Pet – 1. A *Suicide Special revolver made by the *Hopkins & Allen Arms Company of Norwich, Connecticut, in the late nineteenth century. **2.** Pet Colt. A brandname applied unofficially in the early 1870s, by *Kittredge & Company of Cincinnati, to the .38 *New Line Colt revolver.

Peter. Friedrich Peter, Suhl in Thüringen, Germany. Trading in 1939 as a gunsmith.

Peterlongo. *See* Richard ★Mahrholdt & Sohn.

Peters Cartridge Company, King's Mills and Cincinnati, Ohio. One of the leading North American ammunition manufacturers prior to its acquisition by the ★Remington Arms Company on 15 May 1934, this was founded by George M. Peters – president of the King Powder Company – in January 1887. The first machine-loaded shotgun cartridges to be produced in North America bore Peters' marks, which included 'P', 'P.C.C.', 'P.C.Co.' and, in later days, 'Peters HV' in the ★headstamps.

Petersson. Axel Jakob Petersson. This Swedish engineer was the co-designer with Ole H.J. ★Krag of the ★Krag-Petersson rifle.

Petit... – 1. Petit Formidable. *See* Le Petit Formidable. **2.** [Le] Petit Syndicat, Herstal-lèz-Liège. An association of the Belgian gunmakers ★Ancion & Cie, ★Dresse-Laloux & Cie, Auguste ★Francotte and ★Pirlot-Frésart to make ★Comblain rifles ordered by the government on behalf of the Garde Civique. *See also* Grand Syndicat.

Petra. Made during 1982–86 by ★Valmet Oy of Jyväskylä, in .243 and .308 Winchester, this sporting rifle was a semi-automatic adaptation of the ★Kalashnikov. Developed from what was basically a Valmet M78 light machine-gun action, Petra rifles had good-quality wood butts and chequered open-top fore-ends; the receiver was fitted with an optical-sight mount.

Petrel. A ★Suicide Special revolver made by the ★Hopkins & Allen Arms Company of Norwich, Connecticut, USA, in the late nineteenth century.

Pettengill – 1. Asa Pettengill, Keene, New Hampshire, USA. Possibly the son of the revolver inventor Charles S. Pettengill (below), this man designed a spring-airgun in the 1870s (*see* US Patent no. 204,167 of 28 May 1878). Initially his gun was made by ★Haviland & Gunn, then by ★Quackenbush. Most of the credit for its design is customarily, if mistakenly, given to Haviland & Gunn. **2.** Charles S. Pettengill, New Haven, Connecticut, USA. The first Pettengill revolver patent dated from July 1856. It featured a top-mounted cam to revolve the cylinder, place the mainspring under tension, disengage the sear from the hammer and fire the gun. The revolvers were made by ★Rogers & Spencer.

Pevee, Pevey. Joseph Pevee, also known as 'Pevey' and 'Peavey'. A member of the London gun trade, perhaps simply a merchant or gunmakers' agent, listed in 1878 at 40 Fore Street.

Peynaud, Saint-Étienne, France. Listed during 1933 as a gunmaker.

Peyron – 1. Rue Michelet 46, Saint-Étienne, France. Listed in 1892 as a gunmaker. **2.** G. Peyron, rue Michelet 53, Saint-Étienne, France. Listed in 1892 as a gunmaker. **3.** Peyron fils aîné, rue Badouillère 9, Saint-Étienne, France. Listed in 1879 as a maker of gun parts and accessories. **4.** Peyron père et fils, rue des Creuses 10, Saint-Étienne, France. Listed in 1879 as a gunmaker.

'PF' – 1. Found on military-style firearms used by the Argentinian federal police (*Policia Federal*). **2.** A superimposition-type monogram, with both letters equally prominent and often placed diagonally. Correctly 'FP' (q.v.); used in Austria by Franz ★Pfannl. **3.** A superimposition-type monogram, often encircled, with 'F' domi-

nant and the tail of the 'P' projecting laterally. Correctly 'FP' (q.v.); associated with Friedrich ★Pickert of Zella St Blasii and Zella-Mehlis, Germany.

Pfannl. Franz Pfannl, Krems an der Donau. This Austrian gunsmith is best known for the ★Erika and ★Kolibri pistóls.

'Pfeil'. Sometimes mistakenly associated with spring-airguns made by ★Haenel, this mark is believed to distinguish some of the guns made by ★Langenhan in the mid-1920s. This attribution is still uncertain, however.

Pfefstorf. Karl Pfefstorf, Zella-Mehlis in Thüringen, Germany. Listed during 1930–39 as a master gunsmith and gun- and weapon maker, and in 1941 simply as a 'weapons maker' (*Waffenfabrik*). His products included sporting guns and accessories.

Pfeiffer. Robert Pfeiffer, Suhl in Thüringen. Trading in Germany in 1930 as a sales agency; and in 1939 and 1941 as a 'weapons maker' (*Waffenfabrik*). Pfeiffer's products included sporting guns and accessories.

Pfenninger. Rudolf Pfenninger, Stäfa, Switzerland. The marks of this gunmaking business will be found on M1871 ★Vetterli carbines made under contract to the Swiss federal government during 1872–74.

'PH', P-H', 'P.-H.' Found on rimfire conversions of .303 No. 4 rifles made during 1950–56 by Parker-Hale Ltd of Birmingham.

Pheasant – 1. Usually as 'The Pheasant'. Associated with shotgun cartridges sold in England by E.J. ★Churchill of London, and ★Patstone & Son or ★Patstone & Cox of Southampton. Apparently the principal components were supplied from Europe. **2.** A mark – usually 'The Pheasant Smokeless' – associated with shotgun ammunition attributed to ★Phillips & Powis of Reading; usually the cartridge cases are also marked 'Hand Loaded'.

Phelen. Laurence J. Phelen (also listed as 'Laurance'), working on behalf of the Ordnance Department in 1939–40, accepted US military firearms marked 'LJP'. Most seem to have been made by ★Colt's Patent Fire Arms Manufacturing Company. *See also* US arms inspectors' marks.

Phénix. A brandname associated with hammerless shotguns made by M. ★Berger et Cie of Saint-Étienne, France.

'P.H.F.B.' A mark found on shotgun cartridges made prior to 1918 in Alsace, then a part of Germany, by ★Patronen-Hülsen-Fabriken Bitschweiler.

Philadelphia Arms Company, Philadelphia, Pennsylvania. This US gunsmithing business made hammerless top-lever box-lock shotguns in accordance with patents granted to Ansley ★Fox. The company began operating in 1902, succeeding the ★Baltimore Arms Company, but the assets were sold in 1905 to the A.H. Fox Gun Company.

Philibert, rue Pélissier, Saint-Étienne, France. Listed in 1879 as a gunmaker.

Philippon, Saint-Étienne, France. Listed in 1933 as a gunmaker. Still trading in 1951 from 17 rue Pierre-Termier.

Phillips – 1. H. Phillips, or 'Phillipps', a gunmaker listed in 1885–56 at 31 Chapel Street, London W., is believed to have been Horatio Phillips (1847–1922) – better known as the aviation pioneer responsible for a unique series of flying machines with 'Venetian Blind' wings. He also patented drop-barrel sporting guns. **2.** Phillips & Powis, 34 & 37 West Street, Reading, Berkshire. Suppliers of bicycles, accessories and sporting goods, which included guns and ammunition, Phillips & Powis handled shotgun ammunition marked 'The Pheasant'. It is thought that this was purchased in component form from the *Midland Gun Company. Apparently the partnership was absorbed into Miles Aircraft in the 1950s.

'PHMB'. Found on US military firearms and accessories. *See* Peter H.N. *Brooks.

Phoenix – 1. A Spanish Browning-type pocket automatic pistol made for Tómas de *Urizar of Barcelona, although often marked simply 'Victoria Arms Co.': 6.35mm, six rounds, hammer fired. **2.** A *Suicide Special revolver made by the *Hopkins & Allen Arms Company of Norwich, Connecticut, USA, in the late nineteenth century. **3.** A block-action rifle made by *Whitney as a fully-stocked military rifle, a half-stocked sporter or a shotgun. Patented by Eli Whitney III in 1874, the Phoenix had a breech that opened laterally. The hammer was mounted centrally and a mechanical extractor was included, but the guns were neither well made nor particularly successful. Production had ceased by the time Winchester purchased Whitney in 1888. Chamberings ranged from .38 Long to .50-70 Government. **4.** Phoenix Armory, New York City. A factory operated by W.W. *Marston during the American Civil War, destroyed during the Draft Riots of 1863. **5.** Phoenix Arms Company, Ontario, Canada. Maker of small-calibre pocket pistols in .22 rimfire (HP-22) and 6.35mm centrefire (HP-25). **6.** Phoenix Arms Company, Lowell, Massachusetts. The marks of this gunmaking business have been found on compact automatic pistols, chambered for the .25 ACP cartridge. It has been suggested that they were made in Spain, or at least copied from Spanish prototypes, but information is lacking. **7.** Phoenix Cartridge Company, Coventry, Connecticut. Founded in 1872, this ammunition-making business was short-lived. The customary *headstamp was an encircled 'P'. *See also* Liddell & Kaeding.

Piat, rue Tarentaise 42, Saint-Étienne. Listed in 1879 as a distributor of, and agent for, arms and ammunition. Listed as a gunmaker in 1933 (possibly two different businesses); still trading in 1951 from 22 cours Gustave-Nadaud.

'PIC', 'P.I.C.' Marks associated with the *Precise Imports Corporation of Suffren, New York State, and Decatur, Georgia, USA. They will be found on a variety of guns and accessories, including 6.35mm SM-11 pistols purchased from *Reck in Germany.

Picard-Fayolle, Saint-Étienne, France. Listed in 1933 as a gunmaker. Trading in 1951 from 42 rue du Vernay.

Piccolo. Chambered for the .38 Special cartridge, this compact six-shot *Llama–Gabilondo personal-defence revolver copies Smith & Wesson swing-cylinder construction with an additional *transfer-bar safety system. Customarily supplied with a 50mm barrel, it can be identified by double squared projections on the trigger guard and by its smooth walnut grips. *See also* Scorpio.

Pichon – 1. 31 rue César-Bertholon, Saint-Étienne, France. Listed in 1951 as a gunmaker. **2.** Pichon-Sauvinet, Saint-Étienne, France. Listed in 1933 as a gunmaker.

'Pickaxe' [The]. British shotgun ammunition loaded by the *Schultze Gunpowder Company of London, apparently using cases and caps supplied by *Eley Bros.

Picken. James Picken, Port William, Wigtonshire. This Scottish enthusiast developed a double-piston 'recoilless' air rifle, protected by British Patent 19,303/02 of 1902. It anticipated in principle, if not in detail, the *Giss Contra-Piston employed sixty years later by *Mayer & Grammelspacher.

Pickert – 1. Friedrich Pickert, Zella St Blasii and Zella-Mehlis in Thüringen, Germany. Founded in 1869, Pickert rose shortly after 1900 to become Germany's most prolific revolver maker, producing a wide range of comparatively inexpensive designs prior to 1939. Many of these were distinguished by the brandname Arminius, although Pickert also used an encircled 'FP' monogram. The business was owned between 1919 and 1930 by Wilhelm Pickert. Advertisements published in the 1920s record the specialities as 'Arminius revolvers and target pistols. Best German products!' Trading ceased after the Second World War. **2.** W. Pickert, Zella St Blasii in Thüringen, Germany. Listed in the *Deutsches Reichs-Adressbuch* of 1914–39 as a gun- and weapon maker.

Picot Frères, 10 rue Jean-Baptiste David, Saint-Étienne, France. Listed in 1951 as a gunmaker.

Piedmont Gun Company. A brandname associated with shotguns manufactured in the USA by the *Crescent Arms Company.

Pieper – 1. Friedrich Pieper, Zella St Blasii and Zella-Mehlis in Thüringen, Germany. Listed in 1914 as a gun-and weapon maker, and in 1920 (when owned by H.M. Meffert) as a shooting-target maker. **2.** Henri Pieper, Liège. A Belgian gunsmith active prior to the First World War, Pieper began trading in 1866 and was one of the European pioneers of mass-produced sporting guns. Among these were guns with a distinctive sidelever-cocking system patented in Belgium in 1881 and a top-lever dating from c. 1884. Henri Pieper was recruited to the ranks of les *Fabricants d'armes réunis in January 1887, and was a founding shareholder in *Fabrique Nationale d'Armes de Guerre in 1889. He patented a distinctive gas-seal rifle in Belgium in 1885. This relied on an underlever combined with the trigger guard to pull the barrel forward to break the seal formed with the mouth of the cartridge case, index the cylinder, cock the hammer and move the barrel back to its closed position. Incapable of handling the powerful cartridges demanded for military service, the gas-seal rifle was abandoned. Pieper also made gas-seal revolving carbines in the early 1890s; most seem to have been supplied to Mexico, where they were used by the rural gendarmerie. A bolt-action rifle patented in Belgium in February 1888 competed unsuccessfully in the Belgian Army trials of 1888–89. It had an interrupted-screw locking thread on the rear of the bolt, an external hammer in the stock-wrist behind the bolt-handle base and a six-round rotary magazine. An improved design with a box magazine and two locking lugs on the rear of the bolt appeared in the early 1890s; tested in Brazil during 1893–94, it was rejected in favour of the Spanish-pattern *Mauser. *See also* Anciens Établissements *Pieper. **3.** Nicolas Pieper & Cie, Liège. This gunmaking business made .22 rimfire sporting guns (unrelated to the *Bayard series), many of which were single-shot auto-ejecting 'half-automatics' operated by blowback. The Piepers had simple cylindrical receivers, with charging handles on the right side of their reciprocating bolts. Production seems to have been confined to 1909–13, but included a junior pattern (.22 Short), an enlarged standard pattern handling three rimfire chamberings interchangeably, and a military

ANCIENS ÉTABLISSEMENTS PIEPER

Pieper (4)

Often known simply as AÉP, this business succeeded Établissements Pieper, itself a successor to Henri Pieper & Companie, in 1905. At the time, premises were being occupied at 24 rue des Bayards in Liège, with a barrel-making factory in nearby Nessonvaux. In 1907, however, a new factory was opened in Herstal-lèz-Liège and the operations were consolidated. Pieper was renowned for the breadth of its range of shotguns – single- or double-barrelled, hammer or hammerless – and the Belgian-made version of the *Bergmann-Mars pistol.

Pieper also made Mle 1889 *Mauser rifles for the Belgian government prior to the First World War, the contracts having been placed, apparently, in 1905/06. Blowback .22 Short and Long rimfire auto-loading carbines were marketed under the Bayard brandname, c. 1908–13. Made in ordinary and deluxe patterns, these guns had cylindrical receivers with spring-leaf ejectors on the left side of the breech; some had tube magazines in the butt, but most appear to have been 'half-automatic' (q.v.).

Owing to the Pieper family's ties with Germany, AÉP was recruited to make components for the Parabellum pistol during the First World War. Hold-opens, strikers, magazine followers, safety catches, triggers, trigger-plates and other items were supplied directly to the *Erfurt ordnance factory.

Conversion of old German *Bergmann submachine-guns for the Belgian Army began in 1934, followed in 1936 by the transformation of Mle 1889 rifles to Mle 35 standards. The resulting rifles combined the action and shortened stock of the Mle 89 with the barrel, sight, fore-end and hinged nose-cap of the Mle 35, but the German invasion of Belgium brought operations to a halt in 1940, after only a few thousand rifles had been transformed.

Operations resumed after the Second World War, when a unique 'actionless' shotgun was made in small numbers c. 1950. This had barrels that hinged laterally and triggers set completely into the stock. Pieper used the brandnames *Bayard and *Diana, together with a trademark of 'A.E.P.' and a mounted knight.

Anciens Établissements Pieper of Herstal took over production of the Bergmann-Mars military pistol c. 1907, renaming it Bergmann-Bayard. This is a Pieper-made Danish 9mm m/1910–21 variant.

---

trainer with an extended fore-end. A variety of automatic pistols appeared from 1909 onward, including the Models C (*Demontant), P (*Basculant) and D. Later designs included the 6.35mm *Legia and Modèle de Poche. Apparently trading ceased in the early 1930s. **4.** Anciens Établissements Pieper [often known simply as AÉP]: *see* panel, above.

Pieri. Giacomo Pieri, Italy. This gunmaker is best known for his thumb-trigger system, developed in the 1860s and patented in several countries during 1874–75. US Patent no. 166,138 of 27 July 1875 is typical. Interestingly, this patent records Pieri as 'Jacques' and his residence as Ghisoni, Corsica, which would make him French originally instead of Italian. Also strange is the fact that the patent was assigned to William *Smith of London, although the prototype rifles seem to have been made in the *Glisenti factory at Brescia. At least one Swiss *Vetterli rifle was made with a thumb trigger of this type on the upper tang behind the bolt, and many other experiments were undertaken elsewhere. Pieri was granted

another US Patent on 13 April 1886 (no. 340,002) to protect a breech-loading rifle with a magazine.

'Pigeon Case' [The]. Associated with British shotgun ammunition manufactured, or perhaps simply assembled, by the *Normal Improved Ammunition Company of Hendon, London.

Pigou & Wilks, London and Dartford, Kent. A gunpowder-making business active in Britain in 1871.

Pillivant. Raymond A. Pillivant, a lieutenant in the US Army, accepted a variety of firearms during the period 1938–42. Marked 'RAP', they included .45 M1911A1 *Government Model pistols made by *Colt's Patent Fire Arms Manufacturing Company and .22 rimfire training rifles produced by *Harrington & Richardson. *See also* US arms inspectors' marks.

'PIMLICO'. Found in the roundels of British rifle and carbine stocks, identifying the ex-*Colt Thames Bank factory in Pimlico, London. The British government made use of this as an overflow plant for some years in the 1860s.

Pinckney. Cyrus A. Pinckney, Plymouth, Michigan, USA. Pinckney, in collusion with Clarence J. ★Hamilton, obtained US Patent 390,311 of 2 October 1888 to protect a ★Daisy spring-airgun.

Pinder. C. Pinder, or 'Pinders', Basingstoke, Hampshire. The name of this gunsmithing/ironmongery business has been found on shotgun ammunition loaded prior to 1914. It is possible that operations expanded soon after the First World War, as the mark of 'Pinders & Company' of Market Place, Salisbury, Wiltshire, has been reported on The Deadshot cartridges made by Frank ★Dyke & Company Ltd of London.

Pinfire. See Cartridge.

Pinkerton. A small Spanish 6.35mm-calibre Browning-type automatic pistol made in Eibar by Gaspar ★Arizaga: five or six rounds, striker fired. May be misleadingly marked 'Société d'Armes'.

'Pintail' [The]. Found on shotgun cartridges loaded by the ★Chamberlain Cartridge Company of Cleveland, Ohio.

Pioneer – 1. Normally found as 'The Pioneer'. A mark used on shotgun cartridges loaded for ★Harrods of London, probably prior to 1939. See also British Pioneer. **2.** A break-barrel spring-air rifle made in the People's Republic of China by the ★State Industry Factory in Shanghai, apparently also known as the ★Hunter. **3.** A ★Suicide Special revolver made by the ★Forehand & Wadsworth Arms Company of Worcester, Massachusetts, USA, in the late nineteenth century. **4.** Pioneer Arms Company. A brandname associated with shotguns made in the early 1900s by the ★Crescent Arms Company of Norwich, Connecticut.

Pipe pistols. The shape of a smoker's pipe lends itself naturally to the concealment of a small handgun, although most surviving examples seem to have been made on a one-off basis. A typical .22 Short rimfire example contains a spring-loaded striker travelling in a short L-slot in the pipe body. It is cocked simply by retracting the striker arm and turning it through ninety degrees to enter the shorter slot-arm. Firing is simply a matter of easing the striker arm over until it flies down the long slot arm under spring pressure to hit the rim of the cartridge. More sophisticated designs incorporated a retractable straight-line striker and a rocking bar or button trigger. The principle was revived during the Second World War, as apparently the OSS used a few Welwyn-made .22 pipe pistols locked by a bayonet-catch mechanism. See also Lewis Winant's Firearms Curiosa (Greenberg, 1955), and John Walter's Secret Firearms (Arms & Armour Press, 1997).

Piper. Charles Piper, 7 Benet Street, Cambridge (1849–55). The marks of this English gunmaker have been reported on self-cocking ★pepperboxes.

Pire. J. Pire & fils, Anvers, Avenue de Keyser 41. A retailer of guns and ammunition active in France prior to 1914.

Pirkö. Carl Pirkö, a Viennese gunmaker, perhaps originally working with the Malzac brothers, was active from 1847 until 1867.

Pirlot – 1. Pirlot frères, Liège. Belgian gunmakers, working in 1830; members of the ★Société des Anglais in the mid-1850s. **2.** Pirlot-Frésart, or Pirlot et Frésart, Liège. A member of the ★Petit Syndicat, formed in Herstal in 1870. Founder member of les ★Fabricants d'armes réunis, 1886, and founding shareholder in ★Fabrique Nationale d'Armes de Guerre in 1889, when

Gustave Pirlot acted as signatory. Ceased trading in 1914.

Pirotte. Établissements Pirotte, Liège, Belgium. A maker of revolvers active in the 1870s; still making sporting guns in 1970.

Piscetta. Armando Piscetta, Italy. See Jager-Armi.

Pistol cane. This should not be confused with a cane gun (q.v.), which is generally a single-shot design having a full-length barrel that is an integral part of the cane body. A pistol cane, conversely, is a combination of a short-barrelled handgun – a single-shot pistol or sometimes a small-calibre revolver – and a solid-body cane. The gun must be detached before use.

Pistor & Kost, Schmalkalden in Thüringen. Claiming origins in 1745, the oldest of the Thüringian gunmaking businesses, this partnership does not seem to have survived into the twentieth century. The Pistor family, however, was related directly to Carl ★Walther.

Pitcher. Kenneth Pitcher was the co-designer, with Richard ★Kline, of the Healthways ★Plainsman pistol.

Pittston Arms Company. Founded in 1877 in Exeter, Pennsylvania, USA, by local subscription, this gunmaking business specialised in ★Suicide Special revolvers made in accordance with a design patented by the factory superintendent, Roland ★Brewer, in 1881. The Pittston business was renamed ★Lee Arms Company in 1880, when J. Frank Lee became its president, and had moved to Wilkes-Barre, Pennsylvania, by the early 1880s. It is not known which of the various Lee-era gun patterns were made under the Pittston name, and it is possible that the Exeter-made examples bore no marks other than the brandnames.

'pjj'. This code was used to identify small-arms ammunition made by the Royal Danish munitions factory in Copenhagen, operating under German supervision during 1944–45.

'PJK'. Found on US military firearms and accessories. See P.J. ★Kiley.

PK – 1. The Pulemet Kalashnikova, the original belt-feed machine-gun version of the Soviet ★Kalashnikov system in its bipod-mount configuration. **2.** Found on US military firearms and accessories. See P. ★Keller.

PKM, PKM... A modernised variant of the original Soviet/Russian ★Kalashnikov, or PK, machine-gun. The PKMS is a heavy infantry-support version, customarily encountered on the ★Samozhenkov tripod mount; the PMKT is mounted in battle tanks and armoured vehicles.

PKP. A 14.5mm heavy infantry-support machine-gun based on the KPV, designed by Semen ★Vladimirov.

PKT. The original tank and vehicle version of the 7.62x54 Soviet ★Kalashnikov PK machine-gun.

Plainsman – 1. A brandname found on ★Challenger pump-up pneumatic rifles distributed in the 1950s by the ★Goodenow Manufacturing Corporation. Subsequently Goodenow made another line of Plainsman gas-powered guns after the Challengers had been discontinued. **2.** Associated with a series of gas-powered pistols marketed in the USA by ★Healthways, Inc. See also Plainsmaster.

Plainsmaster. This carbon-dioxide-powered pistol, also known as the M9405 and M9406, was marketed by ★Healthways, Inc., in the USA. See also Plainsman.

Plant's Manufacturing Company, Southington, New Haven, then Plantsville and Southington, Connecticut, USA. Founded by Ebenezer Plant in 1860, this gunmaking business produced .42-calibre revolvers in accordance with patents granted to Willard *Ellis & John White during 1859–63. These fired self-contained metallic-case *cup-primer cartridges loaded from the front of the cylinder. The guns were made originally with a tipping frame, but post-1863 examples were generally solid and eventually embodied an improved ejector patented by Henry *Reynolds in 1864. Plant, like James *Reid, also made convertible cap-lock/cartridge revolvers. The factory was destroyed by fire in 1866, whereupon production was undertaken by Marlin until Plant's operations failed a year later. Plant revolvers may be marked by, among others, the *Eagle Arms Company, J.M. *Marlin, *Merwin & Bray Fire Arms Company, and *Reynolds, Plant & Hotchkiss.

Plate. A.J. Plate & Company, San Francisco, California, USA. A gunsmithing business active from 1855 until 1878, best known for its derringer copies.

Playtime Products, Inc., Honeoye, New York State. This company, active between 1968 and 1975, marketed a gas-powered rifle and pistol under the brand-name *Ampell. The factory was sited at 24 East Main Street in Honeoye until 1974, but it is believed that operations ceased in the late 1970s.

'Plink-n-Whiz'. A slogan associated with the pistol and accessories marketed by *Playtime Products Inc.

Ploton et Baret, 31 rue Antoine-Durafour, Saint-Étienne, France. Listed in 1951 as a gunmaker.

Plotton frères, rue des Francs-Maçons 21, Saint-Étienne, France. Listed in 1879 as a gunmaker.

Plumbers, Great Yarmouth, Norfolk. The marks of this gunsmithing business have been reported on shotgun ammunition sold as The Norfolk High Velocity Load and The Original Norfolk. The source of the components is not known.

Plume. A French-language term applied generically to any French or Belgian ultra-light, or 'featherweight', shotgun, but specifically to the fixed-barrel *Darne.

Plus. This *Drilling was introduced in 1985 by H. *Krieghoff GmbH. Its two 12-bore shotgun barrels are mounted above a single rifle barrel chambered for cartridges ranging from .22 Hornet to 9.3x74R. Two hammers are used, a manual *Kickspanner* cocking slide appearing on top of the tang, and a selector button to the rear right side of the top-lever allows the right shotgun barrel or the rifle barrel to be fired. The standard Plus is lightly engraved, but deluxe verions can be obtained to order. The pistol-gripped butt customarily has a cheek piece and a low hog's-back comb.

'Pluto' [The]. Found on shotgun cartridges made by *Eley Bros. prior to the acquisition of the company by Explosives Trades Ltd in 1918.

'Pluvoid' [The]. Associated with shotgun cartridges loaded by the *Cogschultze Ammunition & Powder Company Ltd during 1911–14.

Plymouth – 1. Plymouth Air Rifle Manufacturing Company, Plymouth, Michigan, USA. This company made the *Magic BB Gun, possibly designed by Merrit *Stanley and/or George *Decker. (It is tempting to speculate that the Plymouth Manufacturing Company and Anderson Brothers were one and the same, which would explain the links with Stanley. Confirmation is lacking, however.) **2.** Plymouth Iron Windmill Company, Plymouth, Michigan, USA. Founded in 1882, this business traded under its own name until 1895, when it

became the *Daisy Manufacturing Company – and rapidly went on to greater things. **3.** Plymouth naval ordnance depot: *see* Lee-Enfield.

PM. This designation is applied to the Soviet 9mm *Pistolet Makarova*, designed by *Makarov in the late 1940s and accepted officially in 1951.

PMK... These designations apply to a range of *Kalashnikov assault rifles made by Zakłady Metalowe in Radom, Poland. The PMK-DGN pattern is adapted for grenade launching; the PMKM guns are based on the AKM instead of the AK; and S-suffix patterns (PMK-S, PMKM-S) have folding butts.

'PN'. A superimposition-type monogram, with 'P' dominant. Correctly 'NP' (q.v.); associated with Nicholas *Pieper of Liège.

'Pneuma' [The]. The subject of British Registered Trademark 290283, this distinguishes the products of the *Pneumatic Cartridge Company of Edinburgh, Scotland.

Pneumatic – 1. Pneumatic Cartridge Company, 61–67 Albert Street and 96–98 Holyrood Road, Edinburgh, Midlothian, and Bristol. The name of this business will be encountered on the cases of shotgun ammunition made from c. 1906 until 1968; 12-, 16- and 20-bore, and .410 examples have been found. It seems that the components were made by *Eley Bros., and that the affairs of the Pneumatic business were concerned more with cartridge-loading machinery than the manufacture of the cases themselves. The claims to novelty involved the use of Bathgate's Patent (the use of 'pneumatic cork wadding'), suitably protected by legislation granted during 1904–10. Ammunition was distinguished by the marks 'Pneumatic' and 'Pneuma'. Operations in Edinburgh ceased in 1954, but the sale of its machinery and goodwill allowed work to begin again in Bristol. **2.** Usually found as 'The Pneumatic'. Registered Trademark 288783, this was associated with the products of the Pneumatic Cartridge Company of Edinburgh (above). Different loads were signified either by supplementary numbers (e.g. 'Pneumatic No. 1') or by suffixes: 'Pneumatic Pegamoid', 'Pneumatic Trap-Shooting Cartridge', 'Pneumatic Twenty Gauge'.

Pochert. Otto Pochert, Suhl in Thüringen, Germany. Trading as a gunsmith, 1939.

Pocket... – 1. Pocket Army. Produced from c. 1879 by *Hopkins & Allen, for *Merwin, Hulbert & Company, this US-made five-shot .38 revolver had a sheath trigger and a top strap. **2.** Pocket Army, or Pocket Army Model. Introduced by *Merwin, Hulbert & Company in 1881, this short-barrelled .44 revolver had a conventional trigger guard and (except on the earliest examples) a top strap above the cylinder. **3.** Pocket Bulldog. A name applied to the shortest variant of the *Bulldog revolver made in the USA by the *Charter Arms Corporation and its successor, Charco. **4.** Pocket Colt. The *Baby Dragoon was replaced in 1850 by this .31-calibre cap-lock revolver, made by *Colt's Patent Fire Arms Manufacturing Company of Hartford, Connecticut, USA. Fitted with a rammer and now often misleadingly labelled Model 1849, at least 314,000 had been made by 1862; the last 1850-type Pocket revolver was not sold until 1873. A few thousand guns had even been made in London. **5.** Pocket Model. Often applied as a generic term to almost any short-barrelled or unusually compact handgun, although the smallest may be classified alternatively as *vest-pocket pistols. **6.** 'Pocket Model'. Found on 6.35mm semi-automatic pistols made by *Webley & Scott Ltd of Birmingham. Also made in *Hammerless Pocket Model form. **7.** Pocket Model. Applied specifically by Colt, as the .38 Pocket Model of 1903, to a short-barrelled version of the *Browning-type .38 *Sporting Model introduced in 1902. It was available ex-factory stock until 1929. **8.** Pocket Nine. A compact automatic pistol made in the USA by *Detonics. **9.** Pocket Positive Model. This .32 *Colt revolver superseded the *New Pocket Model, embodying the Colt Positive Safety Lock. About 130,000 had been made when work ceased in 1943. **10.** Pocket Rifle: *see* Franklin *Wesson. **11.** Pocket-watch pistol: *see* Leonard *Woods.

Podewils-Lindner-Braunmühl-Gewehr. This rifle embodied a modification of the *Lindner breech credited to the commandant of the Amberg manufactory, Freiherr von Podewils, and Adolf von Braunmühl. Converted from the 1858-pattern rifle-musket, the gun had a cylindrical bolt-housing protruding behind the external hammer of the side-lock, and was stocked with two bands and a nose-cap. Its back sight was graduated only to 600 schritt. The *Schützen-Gewehr*, or Marksman's rifle, had a special 1,200-pace back sight, and the *Jägerbüchse*, issued to men of the rifle battalions, had a short barrel and a double-trigger system incorporating a setting lever. By February 1869, 113,277 rifle-muskets had been altered in the *Amberg manufactory from parts made by sub-contractors such as *Maschinenfabrik Augsburg, *Maschinenbau-Gesellschaft Nürnberg and Werkstätte L.A. *Riedinger. When eventually these guns were displaced by *Weder and *Mauser patterns, they were either recalled into store or sold to military-surplus dealers such as Benny *Spiro and A.L. *Frank.

'P.O.F.' Found on British-type *Lee-Enfield rifles, *Bren Guns and other small-arms refurbished in the 1950s by the Pakistan government ordnance factory in Wah.

Poilvache. L. Poilvache, Liège, Belgium. A gunmaker renowned for the production of sporting guns on the *Snider system; most date from the period 1868–75.

Pointer – 1. Usually as 'The Pointer'. Found on shotgun cartridges sold by Bagnall & Kirkwood of Newcastle upon Tyne, England. **2.** 'Pointer Brand': a mark found on ammunition associated with the *Meriden Firearms Company, Meriden, Connecticut, USA.

'Point Shooting'. A name used on shotgun cartridges loaded in the USA by the *Chamberlain Cartridge Company of Cleveland, Ohio.

Polain, Liège, Belgium. This Belgian gunmaker designed a revolver, patented in the USA, with a pierced disc in which chamber-lining tubes were secured (cf. *Pond) to allow the tubes to be inserted or removed simultaneously. Operations continued into the 1870s and probably later.

Polanka. Václav Polanka, a Czechoslovakian engineer, was responsible (with Jan Kratochvíl) for the design of the ČZ 38 semi-automatic rifle. This was adopted provisionally in 1939, as the 7.92mm samočinna puška vz. 39, but the German invasion put an end to work.

Polhemus. L.G. Polhemus Manufacturing Company. Trading from Miami in Arizona, this metalworking company was responsible for the *Little Pal knife pistol.

Police… – 1. Police [Mark III], also known as Official Police Mark III. Offered by the Firearms Division of *Colt Industries (1969–75), in .38 Special with standard-weight barrels of 4–6in, this replacement for the original *Official Police revolver was a minor variant of the *Lawman Mark III. **2.** Police Automatic Model. This was essentially similar to the *Automatic Ejecting Model revolver made by *Harrington & Richardson. It had a special concealed-hammer cocking system patented in October 1887 by Homer *Caldwell. **3.** Police Bicycle Model. This was simply a variant of the *Harrington & Richardson *Bicycle Revolver with a spurless hammer. **4.** Police Bulldog. A variant of the *Bulldog revolver made by the *Charter Arms Corporation and its successor, Charco. A five-shot swing-cylinder design, it is chambered specifically for .38 Special ammunition instead of .357 Magnum. Some guns have spurless Pocket Hammers, some have heavy barels, and others are made of stainless steel. **5.** 'Police Gun' [The]. Found on 12-bore cartridges sold by W.W. *Greener of Birmingham, specifically intended for use in the company's *Martini-action shotgun. **6.** Police Model. A *blowback semi-automatic pistol made in Britain by *Webley & Scott Ltd of Birmingham, c. 1906–39. Chambered for the 7.65mm or 9mm Short cartridges, the guns had cylindrical barrels projecting from short slides, external hammers and near-vertical grips. The name was coined after adoption by the Metropolitan Police (London) in 1911. **7.** Police Ordnance Corporation, Los Angeles, California, USA. Promoter of *Ingram submachine-guns, 1950–52. **8.** Police Positive Model. This .32-calibre revolver, made by *Colt's Patent Fire Arms Manufacturing Company of Hartford, was introduced in 1905. It was distinguished from the *New Police Model largely by the inclusion of the *Positive Safety Lock; about 200,000 guns had been made by the time the pattern was discontinued in 1943, post-1925 examples having a larger frame than their predecessors. A target version, known as the Model G, was offered in .22 rimfire from 1911. **9.** Police Positive Special Model. Dating from 1907, this was an enlargement of the *Colt .32 Police Positive Model (above) to chamber .38 Special ammunition; .32-20 WCF was an unpopular option. A short-barrel (2in) version appeared in 1926. **10.** Police Premier. Essentially similar to the *Harrington & Richardson *Premier, this had a Safety Hammer without a spur.

Polizei… – 1. Polizei-Pistole, or PP: *see* panel, facing page. **2.** Polizei-Selbstladepistole [PSP]. This name was used originally for the *Heckler & Koch P7.

Pollard – 1. H.E. Pollard & Company, Broad Street, Worcester. The marks of this gunmaking business have been reported on a variety of shotgun cartridges, bearing such names as 'The Long Shot' and 'Our Game'. Most of them seem to have been supplied by *Eley-Kynoch. **2.** William H. Pollard. A London gunmaker, with premises at 42 Fish Street Hill, E.C., from 1877 until 1884, then at 63 King William Street until 1900 or later.

Polley. David Frank Polley, Plymouth, Michigan, USA. A designer employed by the *Markham Air Rifle Company and responsible for several BB Guns. On 23 October 1903, he was granted US Patent 742,734 to protect a gun with an integral stamped frame and a trigger guard, a barrel that was screwed into the breech frame, and a double-wall barrel housing. US Patent 808,680 of 23 January 1906 protected a stepped barrel housing, and 878,560 of 11 February 1908 allowed claims for a muzzle cap retained by a hinged front-sight latch.

POLIZEI-PISTOLE

Polizei (1)

A brandname associated with the streamlined double-action personal-defence pistol patented in Germany during 1929 by Fritz *Walther, and introduced commercially in 1930. Highly successful, it spawned a vast range of copies – as well as the *Kriminalpolizei-Pistole (PPK) and PP Super.

The earliest guns had safety catches with a ninety-degree rotation, but later this was changed to sixty degrees. Initial 7.65mm Auto and 9mm Short chamberings were supplemented in the early 1930s by .22 and 6.35mm, but neither of these was popular.

Production continued throughout the Second World War – although quality declined appreciably in 1943–45 – and began again in 1954. However, the earliest post-war guns were made in France by *Manurhin until the Walther factory in Ulm began to produce guns of its own.

A post-war 9mm Polizei-Pistole, initially made for Carl Walther in the Manurhin factory in Mulhouse before production was switched to the Ulm/Donau facility.

Polte-Werke AG. One of the leading German ammunition manufacturers, this business was formed in 1887 in Sudenburg, then an outlying district of Magdeburg, as Polte Armaturen- & Maschinenfabrik. Involvement with research, development and manufacture of cartridges seems to have been confined to 1922–45, when factories were operated in Arnstadt (post-1941 code, 'auz'), Duderstadt ('htg'), Grüneberg/Nordbahn ('auy') and Magdeburg ('aux').

Pomeroy – 1. C.M. Pomeroy & Company, Fargo, Dakota Territory. The marks of this US gunsmithing business have been reported on sporting guns sold in the 1870s. **2.** Edward S. Pomeroy, Springfield, Massachusetts. The factory superintendent of *Smith & Wesson, Pomeroy is credited with the redesign of the *Clément-pattern pistol to become the .32 Automatic of 1924, and with the development of the abortive 9mm *Light Rifle. The latter was patented in the USA on 3 September 1940.

Pond. Lucius W. Pond, Worcester, Massachusetts, USA. This gunmaker built six-shot .32 and .44 rimfire revolvers in accordance with a patent granted to Abram *Gibson in July 1860. They had a Smith & Wesson-style barrel/cylinder assembly, locked by a distinctive lever. The stop-slots lay toward the front of the cylinder, and the cylinder-face was recessed in a recoil shield when the guns were closed. Pond also made revolvers in accordance with a patent granted in 1862 to John *Vickers. Separate lining tubes, or 'thimbles', containing rimfire cartridges were inserted into the chambers from the front of the cylinder. The seven-shot .22 and six-shot .32 guns had brass frames and sheath triggers. An improved revolver, introduced in 1864, had a pivoting ejector, or 'discharger', patented by Freeman *Hood.

Pondevaux, place de l'Hôtel-de-Ville 8, Saint-Étienne, France. Listed in 1879 as a gunmaker.

Ponel fils, petite rue Neuve 6, Saint-Étienne, France. Listed in 1879 as a maker of gun parts and accessories.

Pony Colt. A brandname applied unofficially in the early 1870s, by *Kittredge & Company of Cincinnati, to the .30 *New Line Colt revolver.

Pope – 1. Albert A. Pope, Boston, Massachusetts, USA. Pope's part in the history of airgun development is not particularly clear, although it is believed he sold *Quackenbush pistols under his own name. The Herkimer inventor assigned his pistol patent of 17 November 1874 (US no. 156,890) to Pope, who, according to Eldon Wolff in *Air Guns* (1958), was a bicycle maker of some renown. Pope may even have made the pistols in Boston. Albert Pope invented an airgun with a revolving magazine in the mid-1870s (British Patent 1381/76 of 1876), which was communicated by A.C. *Carey of Malden, but he seems to have died in the same year and his operations passed to Augustus *Bedford. Bedford continued air pistol production after the improvements credited to George A. *Walker had been incorporated. *See also* A.G. *Gifford. **2.** Harry Pope. The legendary US gun-barrel maker was born in 1861 in Walpole, New Hampshire. Pope graduated from the Massachusetts Institute of Technology in 1881, made his first rifle in 1884 in a workshop on Morris Street, Jersey City, and received US Patent 384,277 of 12 June 1888 for a 'breech-loading firearm'. He died in Jersey City in 1950. *See also* Stevens. **3.** John Pope, a lieutenant in the US Army, accepted caplock firearms on behalf of the Ordnance Department in 1843–47. They bore 'JP' identifiers. *See also* US arms inspectors' marks. **4.** Pope Brothers & Company, later Pope Manufacturing Company, 45 High Street, Boston, Massachusetts, USA. A maker of air pistols and such items as cigarette rollers. *See* Albert A. Pope (above).

Populaire – 1. Made by *Manufacture Française d'Armes et Cycles de Saint-Étienne, these guns were simple single-shot patterns locked by the base of the bolt-handle rib turning down ahead of the receiver bridge. A spring-loaded extractor slid in the base of the feed-way. The basic pattern had a straight-wrist hardwood half-stock, although chequering was offered on an optional walnut stock, and engraved deluxe patterns could be obtained to order. **2.** Populaire-Pistolet. The handgun derivative had a slight saw-handle grip, a plain trigger guard and a bolt handle that turned down against the stock; the back sight was fixed. Chambering was restricted to .22 rimfire, overall length was about 440mm and weight averaged 900gm. **3.** Populaire-Scolaire. Chambered only for .22 Extra Short and 6mm 'Type Française' rimfire ammunition, this gun was destined for cadets and the members of the Sociétés de Tir. It had a straight-wrist stock extending almost to the muzzle, swivels, two bands (one doubling as a nose-cap) and a grasping groove in the fore-end. **4.** Populaire-Sport. Confined to .22 Extra Short rimfire cartridges, this could only be obtained with a plain straight-wrist half-stock. The back sight was usually a spring-leaf type.

'Popular' [The]. Found on shotgun cartridges sold in England by *Gold of Bristol.

Portadyne Radio Company, Portadyne Works, Gorst Road, London NW10. Makers of .303 *Vickers machine-gun tripods during the Second World War (code, 'S 254'). Possibly made in a subsidiary factory in Bath.

Portafaix. J. Portafaix, Saint-Étienne, France. A gunmaker listed in 1933.

Porter – 1. Giles Porter accepted firearms and accessories on behalf of the Federal Army during the American Civil War. His 'GP' mark will be found on cap-lock *Remington and *Pettengill revolvers, dating from 1863–65, but can be difficult to distinguish from a similar (but apparently slightly earlier) mark used by George *Palmer. **2.** J.W. Porter accepted guns and accessories on behalf of the US Ordnance Department, apparently during the mid-1870s. Details of the employment of his 'JWP' identifier are lacking. **3.** Patrick W. 'Parry' Porter, Memphis, Tennessee, and New York City. Porter received US Patent 8210 of 18 July 1851 to protect a pill-lock repeating rifle with a vertical disc containing eight or nine chambers in its periphery. He is said to have died as a result of injuries sustained during a demonstration of the system in 1855, but conformation is lacking. **4.** Samuel W. Porter. A 'machinist' and, ultimately, master armorer at *Springfield Armory, Porter accepted a variety of military equipment from c. 1859 until his death in 1894. Identified by their 'SWP' marks, the guns included 1892-type Krag-Jørgensen rifles. *See also* US arms inspectors' marks for all preceding entries apart from no. 3.

Port Firing Weapon. This term is applied to an assortment of weapons – modified submachine-guns and cut-down assault rifles – adapted to fire from mounts within armoured vehicles. They include a CETME-like design made for the Spanish Army by *Santa Barbara, and a variant of the Steyr MPi-69 submachine-gun. The US Army M231, standardised in 1979, is an adaptation of the CAR-15 (*see* ArmaLite). Capable only of automatic fire, it lacks sights and a butt; a rapid-pitch screw thread on the front of the barrel casing mates with a suitable ball mount in the US Army M2 Bradley Fighting Vehicle.

Portlock. John Portlock, a London gunmaker, was listed at 56a South Molton Street in 1870–72; at 2 Globe Yard, South Molton Street, in 1873–75; and at 3 St George's Row, Pimlico, in 1876–78. The trading style changed to Portlock & Godfrey, but had reverted to J. Portlock by 1880. Work ceased in the early 1880s.

Portsmouth naval ordnance depot. Converter of long *Lee-Enfield rifles to charger-loading, c. 1908–10. These were naval service guns.

Poser. Karl Poser, Zella-Mehlis in Thüringen, Germany. Listed in 1930 as a maker of guns and weapons.

Positive Safety Lock. Patented in the USA in 1905, this was embodied in virtually all the revolvers made by *Colt's Patent Fire Arms Manufacturing Company after that date. A solid bar was placed between the hammer and the cartridge-head until the trigger was pressed.

Pošumavská Zbrojovka, Kdyně, Czechoslovakia. Formerly trading as Kohout & Spol., this gunmaking business was responsible for the *Mars and *PZK pistols.

'Potato Digger'. *See* Colt machine-gun.

Potter – 1. R. & E. Potter, Thame, Oxfordshire. Gunsmiths and ironmongers, known to have marked sporting guns and shotgun ammunition. **2.** S.E. Potter & Company, 16–20 High Street, Whitchurch. A gunsmith and sporting-goods supplier whose marks have been found on sporting guns and ammunition. **3.** Potter & Company, 1 Cornmarket, High Wycombe, Buckinghamshire. The marks of this gunsmithing business have been reported on sporting guns and *Eley-made ammunition dating prior to 1914.

Potts. Thomas Henry Potts worked in London successively at Haydon Square, 32 & 33 Leman Street and 27 Tenter Grounds from 1848 until he emigrated to New Zealand in 1854. The business was continued as Potts & Hunt until 1874, the Tenter Grounds address changing to 27 Tenter Street East c. 1868.

Poulson. Gunnegard Poulson, designer of the *Madsen assault rifle (LAR) in the late 1950s.

Poultney & Trimble, Baltimore, Maryland, USA. Assignees of the breech-loading firearm patent granted to Gilbert *Smith. Although work on the Smith carbines was sub-contracted, initially to the *Massachusetts Arms Company, subsequently Poultney & Trimble made metallic-case ammunition patented in 1863 by Thomas *Rodman and Silas *Crispin.

Powell – 1. C.T. Powell & Company. This Birmingham based patent agent helped William Blake to obtain British Patents 5045/15 of 1915 and 101,562 (1916). **2.** Palemon Powell, Cincinnati, Ohio, USA. Founded in Walnut Street in 1835, this gunsmithing business traded as Powell & Brown in 1855–58, and became P. Powell & Son in 1870, shortly after which small numbers of spring-air Gallery Guns were produced in a factory at 238 Main Street. The trading style became Powell & Clement in 1891, and operations continued until 1908 or later. Eldon Wolff, in *Air Guns* (1958), has suggested that Powell was a retailer and distributor of the airguns, but this has not been proved. **3.** Thomas Powell & Company; said to have worked in Salisbury, Wiltshire. The marks of this English sporting-goods supplier and gunsmithing business have been reported on 12-bore shotgun cartridges made by *Eley Bros. prior to the First World War. **4.** William Powell, Birmingham, Warwick-shire. This gunmaker began operating from 3 Bartholomew Row in 1822, moving to 49 High Street in the late 1820s, then to Carrs Lane by 1832. The trading style became '...& Son' in 1847. Powell was granted British Patent no. 1163/64 of

1864 to protect a drop-barrel sporting gun with a top-lever, made in some numbers in pin- and centrefire variants; British Patent 2287/66 of 1866 (sought jointly with W.P. ★Bardell) featured an improved gun-lock; 1055/69 of 1869 and 493/76 of 1876 protected drop-barrel breech-loaders. Work continued for many years, Powell's name appearing on a wide variety of shotgun cartridges – hand-loaded in premises at '35 Carrs Lane, Birmingham 4', from components supplied by ★Eley-Kynoch. Powell & Son supplied substantial quantities of 12-bore shotguns to the British military authorities in 1942. Among the tradenames found on shotgun ammunition are 'Admiral', 'Clay Bird', 'General', 'Knockout' and 'Super Velocity'. **5.** William Powell, Birmingham. Listed as a 'Gun-lock Maker' at Haslock's Bridge, Bagot Street, in 1859–60, then at Park Lane, Aston New Town, until 1868. Although the local directories describe the business as William Powell & Son from 1860 onward, there is no evidence that it was connected directly with William Powell (4). **6.** Powell & Clement: *see* Palemon Powell.

Power... – **1.** 'Power King'. A brandname used by ★Daisy. **2.** 'Powerlet'. A brandname found on carbon-dioxide cylinders sold in the USA by the ★Crosman Arms Company for use in its gas-powered rifles. **3.** Powerline. This name has been applied to several guns made by ★Daisy from 1976 onward – specifically the Models 63, 65, 770, 880, 881, 882, 917, 922, 1770, 1880 and 1881. **4.** Powermaster, or Powermaster XL. A name associated with pump-up pneumatic rifles made by the ★Crosman Arms Company of Fairport, New York, as the Model 760 Powermaster and Model 761 Powermaster XL. **5.** Powermatic. Applied to two carbon-dioxide-powered guns made by the ★Crosman Arms Company of Fairport, New York: the Model 500 rifle and the Model 1600 semi-automatic pistol.

'PP'. Usually encountered as 'Mod. PP' on the slides of double-action ★Polizei-Pistolen made in Germany by Carl ★Walther Waffenfabrik and its successors. The PP Super was a modernised version, made by Carl Walther Sportwaffenfabrik of Ulm/Donau during 1975–81.

PPD. Applied to the 7.62mm ★Degtyarev submachine-guns, made in several versions from 1934 until the early 1940s. They were replaced by the PPSh (q.v.).

'PPK'. Usually encountered as 'Mod. PPK' on the slides of double-action ★Kriminalpolizei-Pistolen made in Germany by Carl ★Walther Waffenfabrik and its successors.

PPS. This abbreviation signified the 7.62mm *Pistole-Pulemet Sudaeva*, submachine-guns designed by Aleksey ★Sudaev, also known as the PPS-42 (semi-experimental) and PPS-43 (perfected). The PPS largely replaced the PPSh in Soviet service toward the end of the Second World War.

PPSh. An abbreviation applied to the 7.62mm submachine-guns designed by Georgiy ★Shpagin, also known as the PPSh-41. They replaced the ★PPD, but in turn were largely superseded by the ★PPS.

'PR'. A monogram, encircled. A private proof mark used in the USA by ★Sturm, Ruger & Company.

Praga – **1.** A name associated with ★blowback pistols made during 1920–26 in Prague, Czechoslovakia, by ★Zbrojovka Praga. The 7.65mm model was conventional, resembling the 1910-pattern ★FN-Browning, but the 6.35mm pocket pistol had a folding trigger and a finger-grip in the slide-front to facilitate one-hand cocking. **2.** A light machine-gun designed in the early 1920s by Václav ★Holek for ★Zbrojovka Praga, progressing through the Praga 1, Praga 2a and I-23 to the perfected 7.9mm M-24 'Hand-held Machine Gun'. No sooner had this been adopted by the Czechoslovakian Army, however, than the Praga company failed and production was switched to ★Československá Zbrojovka in Brno. **3.** A small Spanish-made Browning-type automatic pistol, the work of Sociedad Española de Armas y Municiones (★SEAM) in Eibar, Guipúzcoa: 7.65mm, seven rounds, hammer fired.

Prairie... – **1.** 'Prairie Chicken' [The]. A brandname associated with shotgun ammunition loaded by the ★Chamberlain Cartridge Company of Cleveland, Ohio, USA. **2.** Prairie King. A ★Suicide Special revolver made in the USA by the ★Bacon Manufacturing Company of Norwich, Connecticut. It dates from the late nineteenth century.

Prasch. An Austrian-designed breech-loading rifle submitted to the Austro-Hungarian rifle trials of 1866. The ★Wänzl design was preferred.

Pratt – **1.** Albert Pratt, Knaresborough, Yorkshire. The marks of this English gunsmithing and ironmongery business have been reported on shotgun cartridges bearing the brandname 'The Fysche'. **2.** Albert Pratt. An eccentric engineer of Lyndon, Vermont, USA, patentee of a series of 'hat guns' in the early twentieth century. Ranging from modified service revolvers to auto-loading pistols and even a small cannon, in general these were fired by blow-tubes and, at least in the case of the US patent granted in May 1916, could be fitted into a helmet that doubled as a cooking pot! **3.** John Pratt. This Edinburgh based gun-maker was active in Scotland from 1825 until 1861. **4.** Pratt & Whitney, Hartford, Connecticut. Renowned as one of the USA's leading manufacturers of machine tools, and eventually of jet engines, this precision-engineering business was founded in 1860. Among the many firearms made during the nineteenth century was the ★Gardner machine-gun (c. 1872–85) and the ★Hotchkiss revolver cannon, but Pratt & Whitney was better known as a supplier of gunmaking plant and machinery. *See also* Spencer Arms Company.

Präzisions-Rundkugel. This German-language term ('Precision Round Ball') has been used by most of the major German manufacturers of ball-shot suitable for sporting guns and airguns (e.g. ★Bimoco, ★Dynamit Nobel and ★Haendler & Natermann).

Prealle. C. Prealle. This gunmaker (possibly Belgian) was represented in London in 1868 by T. ★Christy of 155 Fenchurch Street.

Precise... – **1.** Precise Imports Corporation, 3 Chestnut, Suffern, New York State. Trading from c. 1962 until the mid-1970s, this airgun distributor handled Spanish ★El Gamo break-barrel spring-air rifles (as the Tournament and Carbine), in addition to the ★Bobcat rifle and ★Roger BB pistol of uncertain origin. A move to Decatur, Georgia, took place in the 1970s, when a variety of guns and accessories was being imported from Europe, including 6.35mm ★Reck SM-11 pistols. **2.** Precise Minuteman. A name given to Lanes' ★Beatall when sold in the USA by Precise Imports.

Precision, Précision – **1.** Usually found as 'The Precision' on shotgun cartridges sold in southern England by ★Patstone & Son and ★Patstone & Cox. The components came from Europe. **2.** Found on spring-air guns sold in Britain; this may simply be an anglicisation of the 'Präzisions-Luftgewehr' mark associated with the Oscar *Will-made Original series. A 'Precision Junior' mark is also known. **3.** Or Universal Precision: *see* Universal. **4.** A compact Spanish-made automatic pistol, based on the *FN-Browning of 1906, attributed to Fabrique d'Armes de *Grande Précision of Eibar: 7.65mm, six rounds, hammer fired. **5.** Precision Ball: *see* Präzisions-Rundkugel. **6.** 'Precision Junior': *see* Precision. **7.** Précision Liégeoise SA [La], Herstal-lèz-Liège, Belgium. Makers of the 9mm Vigneron submachine-gun in the 1950s.

Predom. *See* Łucznik Predom.

Premier – 1. A barrel-cocking .177 or .22 spring-air pistol made in Birmingham, Warwickshire, England, by *Webley & Scott from c. 1970 until 1977. It replaced the Senior Mark 2. **2.** Usually found as 'The Premier'. A mark used by the *New Explosives Company Ltd on shotgun ammunition made in Britain between 1907 and 1919. **3.** Usually as 'The Premier'. Found on shotgun cartridges loaded by, or perhaps for, E.J. *Churchill of London. **4.** This Spanish Browning-pattern automatic pistol was made for the distributor/wholesaler Tómas de *Urizar of Barcelona: 6.35mm, six rounds, hammer fired. The slides may be marked 'Model 1913'. **5.** A *Suicide Special revolver made by the *Ryan Pistol Company of Norwich, Connecticut, USA, in the late nineteenth century. **6.** Premier Model. A .22 or .32 double-action break-open revolver made in the USA by *Harrington & Richardson of Worcester, Massachusetts, in the 1880s. **7.** A name given to a virtually any of the guns made by the *Remington Arms Company distinguished by game scenes inlaid on the action in gold and woodwork offering excellent figuring. They have included the bolt-action Model 700F Premier (1965–89), and the slide-action Model 760F Premier (1961–81) and Model Six Premier (1981–83). *See also* Custom Grade and Peerless.

Premium – 1. Any firearm or airgun distributed free as a sales inducement. *See* Adams & Westlake. **2.** A *Suicide Special revolver made by the *Ryan Pistol Company of Norwich, Connecticut, in the late nineteenth century.

Prentice. G.L. Prentice, using the identifier 'GLP', accepted firearms and accessories on behalf of the US Army in the mid-1870s. *See also* US arms inspectors' marks.

Prescott – 1. Edwin A. Prescott, Worcester, Massachusetts, USA. A partner with Edwin Wesson in Wesson & Prescott (1847–50), Prescott subsequently made a close copy of the *Smith & Wesson Model No. 2, with an iron frame. Guns made from 1862 onward had an additional cylinder latch protected by Prescott's US Patent 30,245 of 2 October 1860. A later US Patent, 159,609 of 9 February 1875, was granted to protect a 'magazine firearm', which does not seem to have been made in quantity. **2.** Prescott Pistol Company, Worcester and later Hatfield, Massachusetts, USA. Active during 1853–75 or later, this business was owned by inventor Edwin Prescott (above). It made the 1860-patent revolvers for *Merwin & Bray until litigation pursued by *Smith & Wesson brought production to an end in 1863. Guns of this type included seven-shot .22 and six-shot .32 sheath-trigger pocket models, and a .38 'Navy-pattern' with a conventional trigger guard. Sporting guns and rifles seem to have been made into the 1870s.

Prešne Strojírentsví, Uherský Brod, Czechoslovakia. This engineering company has made a variety of firearms

and airguns, including the *Tex barrel-cocking spring-air pistol sold in Britain by *Edgar Brothers.

Pretoria Arms Factory, Pretoria, Republic of South Africa. Maker of the .25-calibre Junior, or P.A.F., pocket automatic pistols.

'Preussen'. A brandname ('Prussia') used on shotgun cartridges thought to have been made in the Durlach (Karlsruhe) factory of *Rheinisch-Westfälische Sprengstoff prior to 1914.

Preynat – 1. Saint-Étienne, France. Listed in 1933 as a gunmaker, and in 1951 as a gun-browner trading from 21 rue des Armuriers. **2.** Preynat et Clavier, rue de l'Épreuve 12 , Saint-Étienne, France. Listed in 1892 as a gunmaker.

Pridie. Henry Stephen Pridie. The marks of this gunmaker, a member of the London gun trade, have been reported on self-cocking *pepperboxes dating from the middle of the nineteenth century. Listed as 'Henry Prudie' by H.J. Blanch in *Arms & Explosives* (1909), he occupied premises at 28 Fleet Street, E.C., in 1888.

Priestley. S. Priestley, acting on behalf of the Ordnance Department, accepted firearms and accessories for the US Army. Identified by 'SP' stampings, apparently his work was confined to 1906–07. *See also* US arms inspectors' marks.

Prilutskiy. Sergey Prilutskiy designed a 7.65mm recoil-operated semi-automatic pistol in the 1920s. Prototypes were made in Tula in 1928, but failed to impress their Red Army testers. The design, which could be identified by an exposed barrel and a wedge-shaped hammer spur, was abandoned in favour of the Tula-Tokarev. It is possible that only ten were ever made.

Primax – 1. Usually found as 'The Primax' on shotgun cartridges made in Britain by *Kynoch Ltd prior to the acquisition of the company by Explosives Trades Ltd in 1918, and subsequently by *Eley-Kynoch Ltd. **2.** A name found on shotgun cartridges made in Eire (Irish Free State) by *Irish Metal Industries Ltd.

'Primo' [The]. A name associated with shotgun cartridges sold in Scotland by *Graham of Inverness.

'Primrose' [The]. A mark found on shotgun ammunition loaded by the *New Explosives Company Ltd during the period 1907–19.

Primus. Associated with 'best-quality' German sporting guns made in Ulm/Donau by H. *Krieghoff GmbH, renowned for the quality of their materials, construction and decoration.

Prince – 1. An airgun pellet made by *Lane Brothers. *See also* King and Queen. **2.** Frederick Prince. Listed at 138 New Bond Street, London, in 1859, Prince is best remembered for the design of a breech-loading carbine tested by the British Army in the mid-1850s. **3.** Or 'Model 624'. A plain double-barrelled *Anson & Deeley-style box-lock shotgun made by Società Armi Bresciane to the designs of Renato *Gamba. Available only in 12- and 20-bore, it will be found with double triggers and barrels measuring 635–700mm. The action body is sparingly engraved in 'English' style. **4.** William Prince, a captain in the Ordnance Department, accepted firearms and military equipment on behalf of the US Army in 1875–77. Marked simply 'WP' and including breech-loading rifles made by *Whitney, they can be distinguished by date from those accepted during the American Civil War by William *Page. *See also* US arms inspectors' marks.

Princeps – 1. A Spanish Browning-type pocket automatic made in Eibar by, or more probably for, Fabrique d'Armes de *Grande Précision: 7.65mm, six rounds, hammer fired. Near-identical guns were made for *Thieme y Edeler. 2. Another Spanish Browning-type pocket automatic pistol distributed by Tómas de *Urizar of Barcelona, this 6.35mm-calibre hammer-fired gun may bear the alternative marks of Fabrique d'Armes de *Grande Précision of Eibar. The magazine almost always holds six rounds, although some seven-round examples have been reported.

Princess. A *Suicide Special revolver made in the USA by the *Hood Firearms Company of Norwich, Connecticut. It dates from the late nineteenth century.

Principe. A Browning-type pocket automatic distributed by Tómas de *Urizar of Barcelona, Spain: 6.35mm, six rounds, striker fired. The slides may be marked by Fabrique d'Armes de *Grande Précision.

'Priority' [The]. This mark will be found on shotgun cartridges marketed in England prior to 1914 by W.P. *Jones of Birmingham.

Pritchard. William Pritchard [& Son], Birmingham, Warwickshire, England. Pritchard began trading from the Bull Ring in 1828, but had moved to New Street by 1837, 9 Union Street by 1845, 135 New Street by 1847, and 76 Worcester Street by 1850. The trading style changed to William Pritchard & Son in 1853, and new premises were taken at 97 New Street. A final move to 108½ New Street was made in 1859, but trading ceased soon afterward. Pritchard's marks have been reported on a variety of sporting guns, *pepperboxes and cap-lock revolvers.

Pritchett – 1. Richard Ellis Pritchett (1781–1866) began his gunmaking operations in Prescott Street, London, in 1813. Trading from 59 Chamber Street, London E., began in 1832, and the trading style became '...& Son' in 1851. Directories for the 1850s present a confusing account of additional business premises, listing 7 Poultry (1853–55), 18 St Mary Axe (1855–56 only), 86 St James's Street (1856–63), 4 St James's Street (1864 only) and 24 Great Prescot Street (1857–64). The confusion is probably due to the presence of two Richard Ellis Pritchetts, father and son, and Robert Taylor *Pritchett. 2. Robert Taylor Pritchett (1828–1907). Younger son of, and successor to, R.E. *Pritchett the Elder, this gunmaker is credited with designing the Pritchett expanding bullet in collusion with William *Metford. He continued in business until 1865, then retired to follow a career in art.

'Prize Winner' [The]. Found on Kynoch-made shotgun cartridges sold in England by *Langley & Company (prior to 1914), then *Langley & Lewis in the 1920s.

Probin. John Probin, a survivor from an earlier era, was first listed as a gunmaker in London in 1826, at 29 Lisle Street, Leicester Square. After trading in and around the Strand, he was still listed at 115 St Martin's Lane during 1850–51.

Proctor – 1. C. Proctor, Handsworth, Staffordshire. Co-designer with William M. *Scott of a drop-barrel gun protected by British Patent 3859/83 of 1883, and US Patent 288,670 of 20 November 1883. 2. William Proctor. A member of the London gun trade listed at 82 Leman Street in 1854–59.

'Prodigy' [The]. This mark has been found on shotgun ammunition associated with E.J. *Churchill of London.

Productos Mendoza SA, Wömlein ¶ Zellhofer. Sub-contractor to Haenel, making parts for the MP.43 coded 'kqf'.

Progress-Werke. See Haenel.

Prometheus – 1. A special airgun pellet with a concave synthetic body and a steel head, developed by Hugh Earl and *Prometheus Pellets Ltd. It was marketed originally by Millard Brothers as the Prometheus Double-Two (.22). A selection of .177 and .22 designs have been made since, including flathead target pellets and heavy-core patterns. 2. Prometheus Pellets Ltd, Archway Road, London. The developer of the *Prometheus airgun pellets, designed by Hugh Earl in the late 1970s.

Proof mark. Applied by an official body (proof house) to certify that a gun is strong enough to withstand the rigours of continual use. Details will be found in Gerhard Wirnsberger's *The Standard Directory of Proof Marks* (Jolex, 1975).

Prost et Fraisse, Saint-Étienne, France. Listed in 1933 as a gunmaker.

Protecter (*sic*). A semi-automatic pistol made by *Echave y Arizmendi of Eibar prior to the Spanish Civil War (1936–39).

Protector – 1. A brandname associated with a turret pistol patented in 1883 by Jacques *Turbiaux. It had a disc-like magazine with a short barrel, which protruded between spurs to retain the firer's fingers. A spring-loaded trigger was pressed against the base of the firer's palm to fire the gun and index the disc. The gun was made by the *Ames Sword Company, first for the *Minneapolis Fire-Arms Company, then for the *Chicago Firearms Company. 2. A Spanish automatic pistol of Browning type, made by Echave y Arizmendi of Eibar: 6.35mm, six rounds, striker fired. 3. A Spanish 6.35mm Browning-type pocket pistol made by Santiago *Salaberrin of Eibar, although sometimes identified as a product of *Echave y Arizmendi: six rounds, hammer fired. 4. Protector Arms Company. A *Suicide Special revolver made by J. *Rupertus Patent Pistol Manufacturing Company of Philadelphia, Pennsylvania, USA, in the late nineteenth century.

Providence Tool Company, Providence, Rhode Island. *See* panel, p. 414.

Prudie. Henry Prudie, Britain: see Pridie.

Pryse – 1. Charles Pryse the Elder, Birmingham, Warwickshire. Listed in St Mary's Row from 1838 onward, often as '...& Co.' in later years, Pryse was the co-patentee with Paul *Cashmore of a cap-lock revolver (British Patent 2018/55 of 1855) distributed by George H. *Daw of London. The business was succeeded by *Pryse & Redman (below) in 1842. 2. Charles Pryse the Younger, Birmingham, Warwickshire. The son succeeded his father, the elder Charles (above) in 1873, trading from 84 Aston Street until 1888. He was the recipient of British Patent 4421/76 of 1876, protecting an improved trigger mechanism for revolvers. 3. Charles Pryse & Company. An English gunmaking business trading from 5 Great Titchfield Street, London W., in 1884–85, and 285 Oxford Street in 1886–88. It was owned by Charles Pryse the Younger (above). 4. John Pryse & Company. A gunmaker listed at 9 Great Castle Street, West London, in 1874; succeeded by Charles Pryse & Company. 5. Thomas & Lewis Pryse. Listed at 90 Bath Street, Birmingham, Warwickshire, in 1888–90, but also at 5 Hills Place, Oxford Street, London, in 1890–93. 6. Pryse

PROVIDENCE TOOL COMPANY

Best known for *Peabody and *Peabody-Martini rifles, this gunmaking business was founded in 1850 to manufacture machine tools. The acquisition of several lucrative contracts during the American Civil War, to make 82,000 1861-pattern rifle-muskets (70,000 had been delivered by the end of 1864), was followed by involvement with not only Peabody, but also Benjamin *Roberts, whose breech-loading rifles were produced in small numbers in 1869–72.

A contract placed in 1873 by the Turkish government, for a staggering total of 650,000 Peabody-Martini rifles, was followed by many others, and success was assured. Interests were maintained in guns and ordnance until ultimately the business failed in 1917.

London directories for 1867–69 list the presence at 3 St George's Yard, E.C., of the Providence Tool Company's Armoury European Agency ('Henry Grelgud, Agent' [*sic*]) at a time when the *Peabody rifle was being tested extensively by many armies.

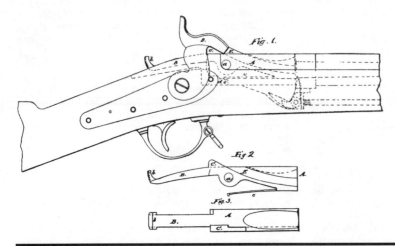

*The Providence Tool Company made rifles in accordance with the patents granted to Henry Peabody, including US no. 72,076 of 1867. Later guns were essentially the same as the British *Martini-Henry.*

& Redman, sometimes listed as 'Redmond', Birmingham, Warwickshire. A partnership of Charles Pryse the Elder and Richard Redman, trading as gun- and pistol makers from 84 Aston Street. They were associated with British Patent 635/52 of 1852, granted to Pryse & Redman to protect a breech-loading saloon rifle; British Patent 750/63 of 1863, to Pryse and D. Kirkwood for a cap-lock breech-loader; and 1367/67 of 1867, granted to Pryse & Redman for a drop-barrel breech-loading sporting gun. In addition, British Registered Design 4864 of 1867 was granted to the partners to protect a loaded-chamber indicator.

'PS', on a target, accompanied by an illustration of a primitive air pistol. A trademark associated with Paul *Schwenke of Berlin.

PSM. The designation of the 5.45mm-calibre automatic pistol introduced to replace the *Makarov. Designed by Lev *Kulikov, Tikhon *Lashnev and Anatoliy *Simarin.

PSP, Polizei-Selbstlade-Pistole. This was the original designation for the *Heckler & Koch P7.

PSS. A designation applied to the special Soviet silent pistol designed by *Levchenko.

PTR... A designation applied to Soviet anti-tank rifles, or *protitotankovoye ruzhe*, designed by Vasiliy *Degtyarev (PTRD), Nikolay *Rukavishnikov (PTRR) and Sergey *Simonov (PTRS).

'PTS'. Found on US military firearms and accessories. *See* P.T. *Safford.

Pugsley. Edwin Pugsley, USA. A designer/engineer employed by *Winchester, best known for the original Model 70 bolt-action rifle.

Pulcifer. W.P. Pulcifer, an Ordnance Department inspector using a 'WPP' identifier, accepted US military firearms and accessories in the mid-1890s. *See also* US arms inspectors' marks.

Pulverfabrik Hasloch GmbH, Hasloch am Main. One of the leading manufacturers of sporting-rifle and shotgun ammunition active in Germany prior to 1914, this company is known to have used the brandnames Fasan, Hasloch, Jagd-König, Specht and Steinbok.

Pulvermann. Martin Pulvermann. A merchant listed at 26 *Minories (later 31 Minories), London E.C., from 1896 onward. Pulvermann's marks have been reported on sporting guns, as well as the spring-airguns popularly known as *Millita. Large numbers of these break-barrel spring-airguns were made in Germany by Frederich *Langenhan. Several types of gun were advertised, including the Millita Models 1, 2 and 3, the Model D Club and the Original Model V. Pulvermann also filed for protection on Langenhan's behalf, including British Patent 15,802/00 of 1900, for the early Millita barrel-locking catch (a press-in button), and British Patent 10,411/05 of 1905. Both were sought with the assistance of the agent G.F. *Redfern & Company, Pulverman's address being quoted as 'Lancaster Buildings, 26 Minories, London EC'. In addition to handling sporting guns, airguns and associated ammunition from c. 1905 onward, Pulvermann had a controlling interest in the Mullerite Cartridge Works (q.v.). The connection arose from an agreement to import and distribute Clermonite and Mullerite propellant in Britain. Apparently the business continued until 1928.

Puma – 1. This compact Spanish automatic pistol, derived from the *FN-Browning of 1905, was made in Eibar for distribution by Tómas de *Urizar of Barcelona: 6.35mm, six rounds, hammer fired. **2.** A sidelever-cocking spring-air rifle made by the *Hammerli factory in Tiengen/Hochrhein.

Pump – 1. A repeating *BB Gun, with an elbow-pump action, designed by Charles *Lefever in 1912. By 1980, more than 20,000,000 guns had been made by the ★Daisy Manufacturing Company in several patterns. The original 1914–24 model had a straight-wrist butt and an adjustable front sight. The guns made between 1925 and 1935 were similar, but had a fixed sight. The third type (1936–41 and 1946–53) had a pistol-grip butt and stamped 'engraving'. The fourth version, confined to 1954–55, had plainer 'engraving' and a simplified back sight. The fifth version had stencilled paint decoration and, more often than not, a synthetic butt. It was introduced in 1956. **2.** Pump action: *see* Slide action. **3.** Pump Gun. A generic term applied to any shotgun or (less frequently) rifle, operated by a slide mechanism. The handle is customarily combined with the fore-end.

Punktkugel. *See* Rundkugel. A term for ball ammunition, generally associated with ★RWS-brand ammunition.

Pupil, rue Chapelon 12, Saint-Étienne, France. Listed in 1892 as a gunmaker.

Puppel. A 7.65mm-calibre Browning-type pistol made in Spain by ★Ojanguren y Vidosa, Eibar: seven rounds, hammer fired.

Puppy – 1. Found on solid-frame double-action revolvers made in Belgium prior to 1914 by Manufacture Liégeoise d'Armes à Feu, whose crowned 'ML' will usually be found on the frames. They included a sixteen-shot .22 rimfire version, and personal-protection guns (in 8mm Lebel and .38 Long) with six-chamber cylinders and bobbed or round-spur hammers. The 8mm Puppy-Municipal generally had a five-shot cylinder and a squared butt with a lanyard ring. The Puppy-Lincoln was a short-barrelled seven-shot .320 gun with a folding trigger and a blocking lever on the

right side of the hammer. **2.** A term used generically for virtually any ultra-compact pocket revolver emanating from Belgium and Spain prior to 1920. Possibly introduced by ★Ojanguren y Vidosa, it was also used by such manufacturers as ★Manufacture Liégeoise d'Armes à Feu (using a crowned 'ML' mark), ★Henrion, Dassy et Heuschen ('HDH'), J.B. ★Rongé fils, Felix ★Raick ('FR'), ★Ojanguren y Marcaido ('OM') and Francisco ★Arizmendi ('FA').

Purdey. James Purdey [& Sons]. This world-famous gunmaking business was formed in 1813 at 15 New Grey Coat Place, Tothill Fields, London. Previously James Purdey (1784–1863) had worked for Joseph Manton and the Forsyth Patent Gun Company. A move to 4 Princes Street, Leicester Fields, took place in 1816, then to 314½ Oxford Street in 1827. His business was managed from 1857 onward by his son, James Purdey II, the trading style '…& Sons' being adopted in 1877. A move to South Audley Street was made in 1881, possibly via temporary premises at 279 and 289 Oxford Street. The business still trades in South Audley Street, London W1. James Purdey II (1828–1909) received several British Patents. These included 302/61 of 1861 for a cartridge-loading device; 1104/63 of 1863 for a snap-action breech-loader chambering pinfire ammunition; 424/65 of 1865 for a breech mechanism; 1464/66 of 1866 for the loaded-chamber or cocking indicator; 2319/68 for a back sight mounted on the upper tang; 3118/70 of 1870 for a 'snap action safety'; 2952/71 of 1871 for a rifled muzzle extension for smoothbore guns; and 397/78 for a top-lever locking system for drop-barrel breech-loaders. Large number of sporting guns were

PYTHON

Introduced by ★Colt's Patent Fire Arms Manufacturing Company in 1955, with the ★Trooper, these double-action revolvers had heavy 2.5–8in ventilated-rib barrels with ejector-rod shrouds. The back sight was adjustable, and an inertia firing-pin, set into the frame, was struck by a flat-face hammer. Most guns chambered the .357 Magnum cartridge, although a .38 Special variant was also made in small quantities. A stainless-steel version appeared in 1983, and a cased Python Hunter – with an 8in barrel and a 2x Leupold telescope sight – has also been made in small quantities.

The .357 Magnum Colt Python revolver, offering exceptional quality for a series-made product, was often sold as part of a pistol pack. Note the small-magnification optical sight, which also had the long eye relief obligatory for handgun shooting.

made for many years. James Purdey & Sons modified about 35,300 .303 No. 3 *Enfield rifles to Weedon Repair Standards (WRS) in the summer of 1939. The business was allotted the code 'S 388' during the Second World War. *See also* British military manufacturers' marks. Purdey has also made a few *Mauser-type sporters, using Oberndorf-made actions prior to 1939, and *Fabrique Nationale patterns since the 1950s (although a few have been built around refurbished military-surplus components). Chamberings have ranged from 7x57 Mauser to .404 Nitro Express; stocks took the classical English form, with a straight comb and a plain rounded fore-end tip; and *Express sights were common. In addition to guns, Purdey also handled ammunition. Shotgun cartridges, made by *Eley Bros., then *Eley-Kynoch, bore such marks as 'Purdey's Large Cap', a trademark composed of four cartridges forming a saltire often accompanying the Purdey name.

Pursall. William Pursall & Company, Hampton Street, Birmingham, Warwickshire. This gun-rifling and pistol-making business, first listed in 1862, was purchased by George *Kynoch in 1864.

Purse pistols. As handguns became smaller, it became easier to build them into purses, cigarette cases and wallets. Among the best was the Combination Pocket-Book & Revolver, or 'Revolver Purse', patented in 1877 by Otto *Frankenau of Magdeburg, Germany. *See* A.W.F. Taylerson, *The Revolver 1865–88* (Herbert Jenkins, 1966).

Pusan arsenal. *See* Daewoo.

Push-lever lock, or *Hebelscheiber Verschluss.* Applied to *airguns in which a detachable barrel may be used as a T-grip to allow paired rods or levers, sliding longitudinally, to push the piston back to the cocking position. Patented in Germany in 1896, apparently by Oscar *Will, the system was superseded within a few years by sturdier barrel-cocking patterns.

Puteaux – **1.** Puteaux machine-gun. This 'improvement' of the strip-feed *Hotchkiss machine-gun was adopted by the French Army in 1905. The Mle. 05 was particularly troublesome, soon being relegated to fortifications and static use, where its drawbacks were not so obvious. It was replaced by the *Saint-Étienne pattern, which was little better. **2.** Puteaux automatic rifle: *see* APX. **3.** *See also* Berthier.

PV – **1.** Officially known as the PV-1, this was a lightened 7.62mm Soviet-made *Maxim machine-gun developed for air service. *See also* Maxim-Nadashkevich. **2.** Found on US military firearms and accessories. *See* P. *Valentine.

'pvf'. Found on German military optical equipment made toward the end of the Second World War by C. Reichert of Wien.

'PW', 'P.W.' – **1.** Associated with guns that had been refurbished in the Weedon factory, but reissued with 'Parts Worn' – a much less radical overhaul than *Factory Thorough Repair. **2.** As a monogram: *see* 'WP'. **3.** An unidentified inspector's mark found on *Joslyn carbines made in 1862–63, during the American Civil War. **4.** Found on barrels and small-arms components made by the *Winchester Repeating Arms Company.

Pylarm – **1.** A brandname used by *BSA Guns Ltd. **2.** Associated specifically with .177- and .22-calibre diabolo airgun pellets made for *BSA Guns Ltd by the *Eley Division of Imperial Metal Industries. *See also* Wasp.

Python. *See* panel, p. 415.

'PZK', often with 'P' and 'K' set into the voids of a dominant 'Z'. A trademark used by *Pošumavská Zbrojovka of Kdyně, Czechoslovakia, on 6.35mm Browning-type pocket pistols made prior to the Second World War.

Q

'q'. Found on small-arms components made in Germany in 1940–45 by Julius Köhler of Limbach in Sachsen.

'qa'. Used on German military small-arms ammunition components made in 1940–45 by William Prym of Stollberg/Rheinland.

'qrb'. Found on small-arms ammunition and other military stores made under German supervision in 1944 by the Italian state munitions factory in Bologna.

Quackenbush – 1. Henry Marcus Quackenbush, Herkimer, New York State. Born in 1847, Quackenbush worked for E. ★Remington & Sons in the 1860s, but patented an extending ladder in 1867 and used the proceeds to open his own workshop in 1872. He filed several patents to protect improved airgun designs during 1871–96, and undertook an appreciable amount of production. However, his original facilities seem to have been too small, and one design was assigned to Albert A. ★Pope; these pistols were made in Boston by Pope and his successor, Augustus ★Bedford, until the rights reverted to Quackenbush. The latter also produced the distinctive spring-airgun with its air cylinder in the butt wrist, widely credited to ★Haviland & Gunn (thanks to Smith, who dated it too early in *Gas, Air and Spring Guns*), but actually patented by Asa ★Pettengill in 1878. Quackenbush also patented airgun darts and slugs, and his cheap rifles rapidly supplanted the popular Gallery Guns. The Herkimer factory produced eight major variations of the rifles, numbered 1 to 10, omitting 6 and 8 (which were .22 rimfires). Most of these were variations of the push-in-barrel type, but No. 5 was a combination airgun/firearm, and No. 7 was a sheet-metal ★BB Gun designed by Paul ★Quackenbush to compete with the Daisy. Quackenbush also pioneered the use of spiral springs and rubber-band power, incorporated in the short-lived ★Lightning, patented in 1884. Although the company was pre-eminent among its contemporaries, production was never large; Wolff, in *Air Guns* (1958), states that only 40,677 guns were made between 1893 and 1922, even though 157,295 darts and 3,970,000 slugs were made in 1884 alone. Quackenbush lost interest in guns after the turn of the century, and the business deteriorated. Sales during 1923–43 never exceeded 500 guns annually. Protection granted to Quackenbush included US Patent 115,638 of 6 June 1871, for a push-in-barrel spring-air pistol. US Patent 156,890 of 17 November 1874 protected a modified push-in cocking system (using a fixed barrel) of the type normally associated with A.A. ★Pope, to whom this patent was assigned. US Patent 165,425 of 2 February 1875, and its British equivalent, 3448/75 of 1875, protected an airgun dart; 188,028 of 7 March 1876 was basically a reissue of 156,890. Granted on 6 June 1876, US Patent 178,327 protected the push-in-barrel No. 1 airgun. British Patent 756/76 of 1876 allowed claims for the design and manufacture of airgun slugs, and US Patent 244,484 of 19 July 1881 protected a push-in-barrel airgun. US Patent 303,283 of 22 July 1884, and its British equivalent, 499/84 of 1884, cov-

ered the Lightning gun, powered by a rubber band. US Patent 336,586 of 23 February 1886 protected a breech-loading airgun, whereas 370,817 of 4 October 1887 protected the No. 5 combination gun. US Patent 436,977 of 23 September 1890 and 562,487 of 23 June 1896 protected skeleton stocks. Quackenbush also made a .22 rimfire rifle with a breech-block that pivoted laterally to give access to the chamber. **2.** Paul Quackenbush, Herkimer, New York State. Son of Henry Quackenbush, this man designed the spring-air ★BB Gun protected by US Patent 841,815 of 22 January 1907. The patent was assigned to his father's business and formed the basis for the Quackenbush No. 7.

Quail – 1. A brandname associated with shotguns made in the USA by the ★Crescent Gun Company of Norwich, Connecticut. **2.** Usually encountered as 'The Quail': a name used by the ★Chamberlain Cartridge Company of Cleveland, Ohio, USA, on shotgun cartridges.

Quality Hardware & Machine Company, Chicago, Illinois. Maker of about 360,000 ★M1 carbines, 1942–44.

Queen – 1. An airgun slug made by ★Lane Brothers of Bermondsey, London, England. *See also* King and Prince. **2.** Queen City Arms Company. A brandname associated with shotguns made in the USA prior to the First World War by the ★Crescent Arms Company of Norwich, Connecticut.

Quick... – 1. 'Quick Fire' [The]. A brand of shotgun cartridge sold in Britain by ★Corden of Warminster. **2.** 'Quick Kill' [The]. Associated with shotgun ammunition made for ★Strickland of Gillingham by ★Kynoch Ltd prior to 1914. **3.** Quick Kill. Applied to a lever-action forced-feed ★BB Gun made in the USA by the ★Daisy Manufacturing Company from 1967. Thirty thousand were purchased by the US Army to help train recruits to shoot instinctively. Little more than a lightened version of the No. 96, without the sights and fore-end, the Quick Kill (or Model 2299) was renamed Quick Skill for the civilian market. **4.** Quick-loader. A method of holding cartridges so that they are readily available for insertion in the chamber. The term is associated with single-shot rifles, although a charger and even a clip are quick-loaders of a particular form. A typical loader may take the form of a spring-clip attached to the breech, or a wooden block screwed to the fore-end. **5.** Quick Skill. *See* Quick Kill.

Quimby. Benjamin Franklin Quimby, employed by the Federal Ordnance Department during the American Civil War, accepted the firearms and accessories marked 'BFQ'. Apparently his activities were confined to 1863. *See also* US arms inspectors' marks.

Quitaud, Saint-Étienne, France. Listed during 1933 as a gunmaker.

'Quorn' [The]. This mark was applied to shotgun cartridges handled in England by J.E. ★Whitehouse of Oakham, in whose district the Quorn Hunt rode.

'qve'. Associated with 1945-vintage products of Carl ★Walther of Zella-Mehlis, Thüringen, Germany, which included small-arms components.

R

'r', 'R' – 1. Transfixed by a vertical sword, hilt upper-most. A mark found on the grips of pistols made in Suhl by *Römerwerke AG. 2. Found as 'r' in the *headstamps of small-arms ammunition made in Germany after 1940 by Westfälisch-Anhaltische Sprengstoff AG of Rheindorf. 3. 'R' encircled, often in black-letter form. Used by the *Remington Arms Company on revolvers, rifles and shotguns made in the USA from c. 1888 to the beginning of the First World War. 4. A *headstamp associated with ammunition made in the USA by the *Robin Hood Cartridge Company. The letters are usually small. 5. An abbreviation of 'Revelation': a *headstamp found on cartridges sold by the *Western Auto Stores. The letter is usually large and cursive.

'ra', 'RA', 'R.A.' – 1. Found as 'ra' on small-arms ammunition components made during 1940–45 by Deutsche Messingwerke, Carl Eveking AG, of Berlin-Niederschönweide, Germany. 2. As 'RA' or 'R.A.': found in the headstamps of cartridges made in the USA by the Bridgeport factory of the *Remington Arms Company.

Rabbit – 1. Usually as 'The Rabbit'. Found on shotgun cartridges said to have been made by Frank *Dyke & Company of London. It will also be found on shotgun cartridges sold by C. *Jeffrey of Dorchester and W. *Jeffrey of Plymouth, which presumably were also loaded by Dyke. 2. Rabbit Special. Associated with shotgun cartridges made by the *Midland Gun Company of Birmingham, Warwickshire, England. 3. 'Rabbit Brand' [The]. A brandname found on shotgun cartridges handled in Britain by *Harding Bros. of Hereford, probably prior to 1914.

'R.A.C.' Found on US military firearms and accessories. See Rinaldo A. *Carr.

'RACO'. A superimposition-type monogram with 'R' and 'A' equally dominant. Used by the *Remington Arms Company, often moulded into the grips of revolvers.

Racquet – 1. Christian Racquet, 428 Main Street, Cincinnati, Ohio, USA. Successor to *Racquet & Bandle, and a maker of spring-air *Gallery Guns. Trading in 1868 and possibly later. 2. Racquet & Bandle, Cincinnati, Ohio, USA. This gunmaking partnership of Christian *Racquet and Jacob *Bandle was active between 1862 and 1866.

Radcliffe. K.D. Radcliffe, 150 High Street, Colchester, Essex. This gunsmithing and ironmongery business succeeded J.S. Boreham in 1899. Sporting guns and shotgun ammunition have been found with Radcliffe's marks, which included 'A True Fit' (q.v.) and 'Warranted Gas Tight', accompanied by an encircled partridge.

Radium. Two patterns of Spanish Browning-type pocket pistols, one made in Elgoeibar by *Gabilondo y Urresti (6.35mm, six rounds) and the other by an unidentified contractor.

Radom – 1. Established after the First World War, largely with confiscated German machinery, this Polish arms factory is best known for the Radom, or *VIS, pistol. It has also made *Mauser and *Kalashnikov-type rifles. See also Zakłady Metalowe Łucznik. 2. Radom Hunter. This is a semi-automatic derivative of the 7.62mm Polish AKM-type *Kalashnikov assault rifle, or PMKM, made by Zakłady Metalowe Łucznik.

Radovanovič. Andreas Radovanovič, Austria-Hungary. See Škoda machine-gun.

Raffat, Saint-Étienne, France. Listed during 1933 as a gunmaker.

Rahn Gun Works, Grand Rapids, then Hastings, Michigan, USA. Rahn has built sporting rifles around *Santa Barbara Mauser actions. See Deer, Elk, Himalayan and Safari series.

Raick frères, Liège. This long-established gunmaking business was founded by Mathieu Raick (1784–1865) c. 1842 as M. Raick et fils; subsequently it was taken over by his sons – Félix (1814–71) and Mathieu Jeune – as Raick frères. Sporting guns were made during the nineteenth century, beginning with cap-locks and progressing to pinfire cartridge guns in the 1850s. A sales office was even maintained in London for a few years, beginning in 1898. Its address was 12 St Mary Axe. Trading ceased during the First World War, but the business was rebuilt after the 1918 Armistice, and again after the liberation of Belgium in 1944; it continues today. Raick has made substantial quantities of *Mauser-type sporting rifles, initially built around refurbished wartime actions, then on new examples purchased from Fabrique Nationale. The Mle 155, the basic pattern available in 1965, was built on an FN action and offered in chamberings ranging from .243 Winchester to 9.3x62. The Mle 156 was a four-shot Magnum version, chambered for the 7mm Remington Magnum, .300 Winchester Magnum and .375 H&H Magnum rounds; the Mle 160 had a short barrel and a full-length *Mannlicher stock; and the Mle 161 was a version of the 160 offered in the same Magnum chamberings as the Model 156. The Mle 165 Big Game Rifle had a ventilated rubber butt pad and a folding-leaf *Express sight on a quarter-rib.

Raine – 1. Robert Raine, Carlisle, Cumberland. The marks of this English gunmaker have been reported on shotgun ammunition loaded from *Eley-made components prior to the First World War. This was sold under names such as The Border Cartridge and Raine's Special. 2. Raine Brothers, Carlisle, Cumberland. Successors to Robert Raine (above) and believed to be his sons, these gunsmiths continued to trade until the Second World War or later. Their marks have been reported on shotgun cartridges made by *Eley-Kynoch.

'Rainproof' [The]. A British-made shotgun cartridge, loaded by the *Schultze Gunpowder Company Ltd, introduced prior to 1908.

Rakov. Ivan Ivanovich Rakov designed a 7.62mm semi-automatic pistol in 1938/39, at a time when the

Soviet authorities were considering replacing the Tokarev with a gun that was better suited to firing through the slits of tanks and other armoured vehicles. All the competitors had slender barrels made integrally with the receivers, which had reciprocating bolts. The Rakov had not been perfected when the Germans invaded Russia in the summer of 1941, and the trials were abandoned, although a modified version is believed to have been tested in the late 1940s.

Ram. An Austrian *Mauser-pattern sporting rifle, made by Karl *Dschulnigg of Salzburg in the 1960s, with a roll-over comb and carved oak leaves instead of chequering on the pistol grip and fore-end.

Ramsbottom & Company, Manchester, Lancashire. A retailer of sporting goods, active in England in the early twentieth century, Ramsbottom's name has been encountered on German-made barrel-cocking spring-airguns marked 'Sure Shot', on *Britannia patterns marked 'Anglo Sure Shot Mark 1', on sporting guns and on 12-bore shotgun ammunition. These cartridges were made by *Eley Brothers, loaded with *Schultze Powder and customarily bore the early trademark of a shield and 'EBL'.

Ramses. This was a barrel-cocking 4.5mm spring-air rifle made in the mid-1960s by the Egyptian state firearms factory in Port Said, probably for military training.

Ramsey – 1. Francis M. Ramsey, a commander in the US Navy, accepted firearms and equipment during 1867–70. Among individual items bearing his 'FMR' marks were components for 1866-pattern *Remington single-shot pistols and 1861-pattern signal pistols. **2.** George D. Ramsey, Jr, a captain in the Federal Army, accepted guns and equipment during the American Civil War, applying a distinctive 'GDR' identifier in 1863–65. *See also* US arms inspectors' marks for both entries.

Randall. I. Randall accepted firearms and accessories on behalf of the US Ordnance Department c. 1905, marking them 'IR'. *See also* US arms inspectors' marks.

Randell – 1. F.E. Randell, using an 'FER' mark, accepted US military firearms and equipment during 1905–06. *See also* US arms inspectors' marks. **2.** Myron Randell, Waupaca, Wisconsin. This US gunmaker (1895–1944) is said to have made muzzle-loading rifles and reservoir-type airguns.

Rangemaster. Guns made by the *Remington Arms Company. **– 1.** Model 37 Rangemaster. A .22 rimfire target rifle, dating from the period 1937–54, made in accordance with patents granted to *Loomis & Lowe, this was basically an improved 1934-type bolt action with a heavy barrel, a high straight-comb half-stock and a beavertail fore-end. The guns had detachable box magazines, although a single-shot adapter could be used. An improved version appeared in 1940, with a Miracle trigger system and a high-comb Randle stock. **2.** Model 40XB Rangemaster. This single-shot .22 LR bolt-action target rifle replaced the rimfire version of the Model 40X in 1964. Distinguished by a straight-comb butt, rising at the heel, it could be fitted with a special extra-heavy barrel and was made until 1974. A version with a detachable five-round box magazine was also produced in small numbers.

Ranger – 1. Usually encountered as 'The Ranger' on shotgun cartridges loaded in Britain by the *Cogschultze Ammunition & Powder Company Ltd prior to 1911, and possibly by *Eley Brothers thereafter; *see* next entry. **2.** 'The Ranger Smokeless'. This mark is encountered on

shotgun ammunition made by *Eley Bros. for W.R. *Pape of Newcastle upon Tyne. Owing to the differences in name style, it is thought that there was an original black-powder version. **3.** A brandname applied to a small number of *Erma ELG10 lever-action air rifles sold in Britain in the 1980s by *Webley & Scott Ltd. **4.** Small *Suicide Special revolvers made by *E.L. Dickinson of Springfield, Massachusetts; the *Hopkins & Allen Arms Company of Norwich, Connecticut; and the J. *Rupertus Patent Pistol Manufacturing Company of Philadelphia, Pennsylvania. Although they differ in detail, virtually all date from the 1880s. **5.** A repeating lever-action *BB Gun made in 1928/29 for *Sears, Roebuck & Company by the *All-Metal Products Company of Wyandotte, Michigan, USA. It was identical to the *Upton Model 40. **6.** A pump-action *BB Gun made in the USA during 1932–34 by *Daisy, under contract to *Sears, Roebuck & Company; it was a longer-butt version of the Junior Pump Gun No. 105, and subsequently became the *Buck Jones Special. **7.** 'Ranger Arms Company, USA.' A 'manufacturer's name' found on single-barrel shotguns made by the *Crescent Arms Company prior to the First World War.

Ransom. George M. Ransom, a captain attached to the US Navy Bureau of Ordnance, accepted firearms and items of equipment between 1854 and 1877. These included .36 cap-lock *Colt revolvers marked 'GMR'. *See also* US arms inspectors' marks.

'RAP'. Found on US military firearms and accessories. *See* Ray A. *Pillivant.

Raphael – 1. A French gunsmith, best known for a distinctive pattern of revolver. **2.** Raphael Gun. A .50-calibre, slide-fed, side-loading Battery Gun tested by the Federal ordnance authorities during the American Civil War. Inaccurate and unreliable, it had been abandoned by 1862.

Rapid – 1. A barrel-cocking repeating air-rifle made in Germany in the 1960s by Maschinen und Apparätebau *Wagria. It fired 4.4mm ball ammunition. **2.** A spring-air *BB Gun made by the *Rapid Rifle Company, but little other than the *Cyclone/Cycloid under a different name. **3.** Rapid Rifle Company, Grand Rapids, Michigan, USA. A partnership between William Mathews *Butts and Austin Kent *Wheeler, this business was founded c. 1898 to exploit the airgun design of *Calkins and Lindberg, protected by US Patent 614,532 and British Patent 24,688/98 of 1898. These guns were made as the Cyclone, Cycloid and Rapid until 1900, when the business collapsed. **4.** Rapid Rifle Company, Grand Rapids, Michigan, USA. Reconstituted in 1901, this business, sometimes known as the New Rapid Rifle Company, made the *New Rapid *BB Gun in accordance with a US Patent granted on 13 December 1901 to *Simonds, Ross and Fisher, which was assigned to the company. Apparently it ceased trading c. 1905.

Rapide – 1. A name given to a shotgun invented in Belgium c. 1880 by Père D.-J. *Roland, characterised by barrels that slid forward when the trigger guard was rotated horizontally to the right. Some guns also featured Roland's Double Adjustable Sound Absorber and Shot Concentrator, a combination of primitive muzzle brake and adjustable choke. They were made in very small numbers in Liège, but had no lasting effect on the local firearms industry. **2.** Associated with the Hungarian-made

Artex/*Telly rifle imported into Britain by *Relum Ltd. (Alternatively listed as the LG522.). **3.** *See also* 'Le Rapide'

'Rapido' [The]. A brandname encountered on shotgun cartridges handled in northern England by *Hodgson of Ripon.

RASAF, Royal Australian Small Arms Factory. *See* Lithgow.

Rasch. Otto Rasch, Zella-Mehlis. Listed in pre-1900 directories as a gunmaker (*büchsenmacherei*) and gun repairer.

Rashid. A 7.62x39 semi-automatic carbine, derived from the Hakim, made in Egypt by the *Maadi factory.

Rasmussen – 1. Julius Rasmussen, Denmark. The designer of polygonal rifling and the Madsen-Rasmussen rifle; *see also* Krag-Jørgensen. **2.** Peder Rasmussen, Rundkoping, Denmark. Better known for his revolving rifles and other firearms, Rasmussen is said to have developed an 'air' gun c. 1834. Eldon Wolff, writing in *Air Guns* (1958), suggested that it was powered by carbon dioxide, which Arne Hoff disputes in *Airguns and Other Pneumatic Arms* (1972). Apparently the gun had a single barrel and an iron butt reservoir.

Rassmann – 1. Friedrich Rassmann, Zella-Mehlis in Thüringen, Germany. Listed in 1930–39 as a maker of guns and weapons. **2.** Luise Rassmann, Ohrdruf in Thüringen, Germany. Listed in 1941 as a retailer of sporting guns and ammunition. **3.** Rud. Rassmann, Zella-Mehlis in Thüringen, Germany. Listed in 1939–41 as a weapons maker, specialising in sporting guns.

Rational Stock. *See* Stock.

Rätzel. Gustav Rätzel, vorm. J.A. Frank & Co., Zella-Mehlis in Thüringen. Successor to the business of Frank, which had been based in Berlin, this gunmaker seems to have been active only until the end of the First World War.

Rau. Arthur Rau, Westerstetten and Ulm/Donau, Germany. An employee of J.G. *Anschütz, responsible for the recoilless LG 380 air rifle protected by German Patent 2,329,425, sought in 1973, but not granted until 1979.

Raub. William Raub, or Raubs, New York City. Listed by Robert L. Gardner, in Small Arms Makers (1963), as active between 1862 and 1877, this gunsmith made spring-air *Gallery Guns in addition to firearms.

Ravel, rue des Jardins 29, Saint-Étienne, France. Listed in 1879 as a distributor of, and agent for, arms and ammunition.

Raven Arms Inc., Bixby Drive, Industry, California. Maker of the 6.35mm Auto/.25 ACP Raven P-25 and MP-25 semi-automatic pistol in the 1980s. The deluxe version will be found with nickel- or chrome-plating and grips of ivorine.

Ray. M. Ray, Dartford, Kent. This English gunsmithing business is known to have marked sporting guns and shotgun cartridges manufactured in Birmingham by *Kynoch.

Raymond. Edward Raymond. Co-patentee with Charles *Robitaille of a simplification of the *Pettengill revolver made by *Rogers & Spencer, protected by US Patent granted in July 1858.

Rayon. Another of the many unidentifiable Browning-type pocket automatics made in the Eibar district of Spain, this 6.35mm example has a six-round box magazine and a hammer-type firing mechanism.

Raznoeport V/O, Kaliaevskaia 5, Moscow. This Soviet government-run export agency distributed *Baikal and *Vostok sporting guns during the 1960s and 1970s, including break-barrel airguns made in *Izhevsk.

'RB'. Found on US military firearms and accessories. *See* Robert *Beals and Roger *Birnie.

'RC', 'R.C.' – 1. And arrowheads. A mark denoting the sale of surplus or obsolete British service weapons to county cadet corps. **2.** Found on components for the No. 4 *Lee-Enfield rifle made in Britain during the Second World War by Raleigh Cycles Ltd.

'RCO'. A mark consisting of 'R' within a large 'C' containing a small 'O' in its jaws. Associated with pistols, sporting guns and associated products of *Robar & Co., Liège (formerly Manufacture Liégeoise d'Armes à Feu). *See also* 'TR' monogram.

'RCS'. A superimposition-type monogram with 'R'

RECOIL, LONG AND SHORT

Recoil (5)

Diagram 1 shows a basic long-recoil system. As the gun fires, the bolt is locked to the barrel extension by the locking arm 'b'. The barrel and bolt begin to move back, still securely linked, until the tail of the unlocking bar 'd' rides over the bolt latch 'f'. Then the return spring 'a', concentric with the barrel, begins to pull the parts back to battery. However, the unlocking bar 'd' is held by the projecting tail of the bolt latch 'f', and this in turn pivots the bolt lock, 'g', to release the barrel and bolt.

The barrel runs forward by itself, allowing the extractor in the now-static breech-block to withdraw the spent case 'h' from the chamber. As the barrel reaches battery, it forces the bolt latch 'f' downward, and the bolt return spring 'e' pushes the bolt forward. When the bolt finally catches up with the barrel, the bolt lock 'b' re-engages with the barrel extension and the gun is locked ready to fire again.

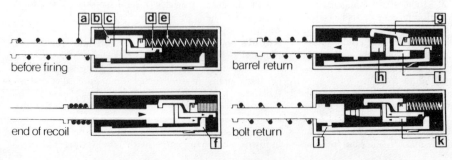

before firing

end of recoil

barrel return

bolt return

Left: *Long recoil.*

Right: *Short recoil.*

dominant. Correctly 'SRC' (q.v.); associated with ★Sears, Roebuck & Company.

'RCW'. Found on US military firearms and accessories. *See* Russel C. ★Wilson.

'R. de M.' A mark associated with Mexican firearms: República de Mexico. It may also be found as 'R.M.' (q.v.).

'R E', often encircled. A mark associated with the Italian Royal Army, or *Regio Esercito*, found on ★Mannlicher-Carcano rifles, ★Beretta pistols and other stores.

Read. William Read & Sons, Faneuil Hall Square, Boston, Massachusetts, USA. This wholesaler advertised itself in 1871 as 'Dealers in Fine Sporting Guns of all the Best Makers. Always in stock, a large assortment of Muzzle & Breech-Loading Guns of Every Size and Pattern'. Read also handled flasks, pouches and loading equipment made in Britain by James ★Dixon & Sons, and cartridges made by ★Eley Bros.

Reams. Joseph M. Reams, Meriden, Connecticut. Co-designer with William L. ★Horne of the magazine firearm protected by US Patent 406,667 of 9 July 1889.

Rebaud-Peyron, grande rue Saint-Roch 2, Saint-Étienne, France. Listed in 1879 as a gunmaker.

Rebety. August Rebety, sometimes mistakenly listed as 'Reberty'. Co-grantee with Joseph ★Gruler of US Patent 25,259 of 27 December 1859, protecting the inclusion of safety notches on a revolver cylinder. *See also* ★Manhattan Fire Arms Company.

Rebounding... – 1. Rebounding hammer/striker. Applied to a safety feature in the form of a spring-cushioned hammer or striker that can bounce back from the primer or a chambered cartridge (or, theoretically, from the nipple of a ★cap-lock) immediately after ignition has occurred. **2.** Rebounding lock. Any gun-lock that incorporates a rebounding hammer or striker system.

Receiver. A term often applied to the frame of a rifle, especially if it 'receives' the bolt or breech-block. The sides of a solid-bridge receiver are connected above the bolt or breech-block, while a split-bridge receiver allows the bolt or operating handle to pass through.

Reck. Karl Arndt Reck GmbH, Lauf bei Nürnberg. Germany's leading maker of inexpensive handguns, Reck concentrates on small semi-automatic pistols and blank-firers. Cartridge-firing guns – including the P-8 and SM-11 – have been marketed in the USA in quantity, and will be encountered under a variety of brandnames applied by ★Hawes Firearms, ★Precise Imports Corporation, ★Spesco and others since the early 1960s.

Recknagel – 1. E. Recknagel, Suhl in Thüringen. Listed in the 1939 edition of the *Deutsches Reichs-Adressbuch* as a gun-part maker. **2.** Erich Recknagel, Albrechts bei Suhl in Thüringen. A maker of gun parts and tools, trading in 1941 from Zellaer Strasse 37; Recknagel's operations ceased at the end of the Second World War. **3.** Franz Wilh. Recknagel Sohn, Albrechts bei Suhl in Thüringen, Rüssenstrasse 16 (1941). Listed as a maker of gun parts and metalware in pre-1945 German trade directories. **4.** Rud. Recknagel, Albrechts bei Suhl in Thüringen, Goldbachstrasse 5. This German metal-working business, active prior to 1945, included gun parts among its products. **5.** Recknagel & Zimmermann, Albrechts bei Suhl in Thüringen. Listed as a maker of gun parts and accessories prior to the First World War.

Reckweg. H.H. Reckweg (*sic*). The designer of shot charges for airguns, Reckweg was granted British Patent 502,893 of 1938. The idea was scarcely new, as Benjamin ★Banks had pre-empted Reckweg by more than forty years.

Recoil, recoil... – 1. A force generated by firing, opposite to the forward motion of the projectile. **2.** Recoil bolt. A transverse bolt through the stock, acting in concert with the recoil lug (below) to spread the force that otherwise may split or damage the woodwork. **3.** Recoil lug. A projection on the underside of the breech designed to spread the recoil force to a greater area of the stock than a bolt running up through the trigger guard, tang or magazine floor plate into the receiver. **4.** Recoil operation. Most of the first successful automatic machine-guns worked by allowing the parts to move backward –

A short-recoil system is essentially similar to a long-recoil design, but may be more complex (Diagram 2). At the instant the gun fires, the bolt is held to the barrel extension by the locking bar 'd'. After the parts have moved a short distance backward, a cam-surface inside the top plate of the receiver tips the locking bar 'd' to break the link between the bolt and the barrel.

The barrel is halted by a buffer 'e' and held in place by the latch 'g'. The accelerator 'e', meanwhile, gives additional rearward impetus to the bolt, which continues back alone to extract the spent case.

When the bolt has reached the limit of its backward movement, the bolt return spring 'g' reasserts itself and drives the bolt forward once again. As the tail of the bolt passes

the projection on the tail of the latch 'f', it pivots the latch to release the barrel. Then the barrel return spring 'a' forces the barrel back to battery, followed by the bolt. A new cartridge is stripped into the chamber and, often before the components have reached the limit of their forward travel, the bolt lock 'b' re-engages to allow the gun to fire again.

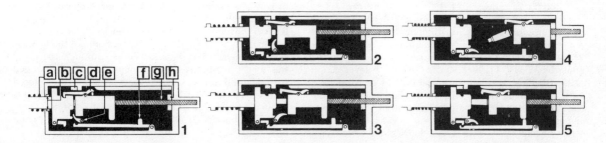

or recoil – to open the breech. They included the *Maxim and the *Vickers Gun, which relied on a toggle lock (not unlike the human knee-joint) to form the rigid strut that kept the breech closed until the residual pressure within the cartridge case dropped to a point where the brass walls of the case were no longer being pressed tightly against surface of the chamber. This ensured that the spent case would extract satisfactorily as the breech opened. Other guns relied on flap-locks or rotating bolts. Recoil systems are customarily classified according to the distance travelled by the locked parts in relation to the length of the cartridge case. Long recoil often involves distances of 75–80mm or more, whereas the locked-breech movement in short-recoil designs is rarely more than 15mm. *See also* blowback, delayed blowback, gas operation, locked breech and operating systems. **5.** Recoil, long and short: *see* panel, pp. 420/21. **6.** Recoil spring: *see* return spring.

'Recoilite' [The]. A name used by *Holland & Holland of London on shotgun ammunition.

Record – 1. Associated with a wide range of shotguns advertised in 1911 by A.L. *Frank of Hamburg, Germany, as 'made in Suhl'. Some of the engravings are quite clearly marked with 'S. & D.' above crossed cannon on a shield. Unfortunately, the manufacturer has not yet been identified. **2.** A gas-powered 4.5mm rifle made by *Armigas-Comega in Italy c. 1959–66; an eighty-shot BB repeater, it could also fire diabolo pellets singly. **3.** Record Cartridge. *See* John *Rigby & Company. **4.** 'Record Special'. Marks of this type will be encountered on shotgun cartridges made in England by the *Midland Gun Company of Birmingham. **5.** *See also* FB Record.

Red... – 1. Red Banner Factories, Yugoslavia/Serbia. *See* Zavodi *Crvena Zastava. **2.** Red Cloud. A *Suicide Special revolver made by the *Ryan Pistol Company of Norwich, Connecticut, USA, in the late nineteenth century. **3.** 'Red Devil'. This brandname will be found on shotgun cartridges made in the USA by the *American Ammunition Company. **4.** 'Red Flash' [The]. Found on shotgun cartridges made for *Stanbury & Stevens of Exeter by *Eley-Kynoch. **5.** 'Red Grouse' [The]. A shotgun cartridge marketed by P.D. *Malloch of Perth, made by Eley-Kynoch. **6.** 'Red Head' [The]. Found on shotgun cartridges loaded by the *Chamberlain Cartridge Company of Cleveland, Ohio, USA. **7.** Red Hot. *Suicide Special revolvers made by the *Hopkins & Allen Arms Company of Norwich, Connecticut; *Johnson, Bye & Company and/or *Iver Johnson of Worcester and Fitchburg, Massachusetts, USA. Although differing in style, all date from the late nineteenth century. **8.** Red Jacket. A *Suicide Special revolver made by the *Lee Arms Company of Wilkes-Barre, Pennsylvania, USA, in the late nineteenth century. **9.** 'Red Rival' [The]. Used on shotgun cartridges loaded in Britain by the *New Explosives Company Ltd during 1907–19. **10.** Red Ryder. Inspired by a fictional comic-strip cowboy, this brandname was associated with the old-pattern Model 94 lever-action spring-air *BB Gun made in the USA in the 1950s by *Daisy. **11.** Red Ryder Carbine. A lever-action Daisy BB Gun, also known as the No. 11 or Model 40, with a Lightning Loader magazine, a saddle ring on the left side of the receiver, a pistol-grip stock and a horse-and-rider brand. It was made in several variants: in 1940–41 and 1946, with a wood stock and a cast-iron

lever; in 1947, with an aluminium lever; in 1952, with a plastic stock and fore-end; and in 1956–58 with a straight-wrist butt, the back sight at the extreme rear, a dummy hammer and a longhorn-cattle motif on the butt. **12.** Red Ryder Commemorative. Also known as the Model 1938, this lever-action spring-air *BB Gun, made by *Daisy Manufacturing Company, was also named after the comic-strip cowboy hero. **13.** 'Red Seal'. Found on shotgun cartridges made in Birmingham, England, at the *Mullerite Cartridge Works. The name refers to the colour of the case-crimp disc. *See also* 'Green Seal', 'Grey Seal' and 'Yellow Seal'. **14.** Red Willow Tool & Armory, Inc., Stevensville, Montana, USA. This gunmaking business introduced a replica of the *Ballard single-shot lever-action rifle in 1992, chambering a range of cartridges from .32-40 Winchester to .45-70. The Red Willow No. 1$\frac{1}{2}$ had an S-type lever and a single trigger; the No. 5 Pacific Rifle had an octagonal barrel, a double trigger and a ring-pattern operating lever; Red Willow No. 8 had a half-octagonal barrel, a double set trigger mechanism and a nickel-plated Off Hand shoulder plate.

Redfern. G.F. Redfern & Company. This British patent agency, with chambers at 4 South Street, Finsbury, London E.C., in 1900–05, and at 21 Southampton Buildings, London W.C., in 1907, acted for Martin *Pulvermann (i.e. for Frederich *Langenhan) and Gustav *Pabst. *See* British Patents 15,802/00 of 1900, 10,411/05 of 1905 and 14,447/07 of 1907.

Redman. Richard Redman, a gunmaker listed in 1887–88 at 170 Edmund Street, Birmingham, was also included in H.J. Blanch's 1909 *Arms & Explosives* list of the members of the London gun trade.

Redmayne & Todd, Nottingham. The marks of this gunmaking partnership have been reported on sporting guns and ammunition. Apparently shotgun cartridges marked 'The Champion' were assembled and loaded from components imported from Europe.

'Redskin' [The]. Found on shotgun ammunition assembled in Britain from French-made components by the *Nitrokol Powder Company.

Reece. General James N. Reece of the US Army was the co-designer with Reuben Chaffee of the *Chaffee-Reece bolt-action rifle.

Reed – 1. Archibald Reed, a London gunmaker, was listed in 1832–34 at 14 Commercial Place, City Road; at 3, then 5 Fountain Place, City Road, in 1835–58; and at 11 Hackney Road Crescent in 1853–56. **2.** Charles S. Reed, a major in the Army Ordnance Department, accepted US military firearms made by *Colt's Patent Fire Arms Manufacturing Company. Dating from 1937–40 and marked 'CSR', apparently they included .45 M1911A1 pistols. *See also* US arms inspectors' marks.

Reeves – 1. Charles Reeves [& Company], Birmingham, Warwickshire. First listed in Canal Street in 1854, as a sword-cutler and maker of guns, rifles and pistols, Reeves moved to Charlotte Street in 1855, George Street in 1863 and St Mary's Row in 1870. Some of the premises were described as Toledo Works, although the name was used sporadically. Best known as a maker of edged weapons and tools, Charles Reeves also manufactured revolvers. These were protected by British Patents 2690/57 and 3156/57 of 1857, and 1623/58 of 1858; British Patent 2852/59 of 1859 protected a bolt-action breech-loader; 3069/60 of 1860 was granted to protect a screw-plug breech-loading rifle; 256/61 of 1861 allowed the conversion of rifle-muskets to breech-loading; 2951/64 of 1864 described a breech-loading gun chambering a cartridge with the cap set laterally; 3337/65 of 1865 protected a breech-loading rifle with a lifting-block mechanism; and 2272/66 of 1866 was granted for a cartridge extractor. Charles Reeves also maintained premises at 8 Air Street, West London. This seems to have been confined to 1860–62, possibly at the time of the second Great Exhibition. **2.** John Reeves [& Company], Weaman Row, Birmingham. Believed to have been the son of Charles Reeves (above), this gunsmith was listed from 1877 and received British Patent 2147/79 of 1879 for a drop-barrel sporting-gun action. He may have died or retired in 1885, when the business was acquired by W. ★McEntee. Later directories also list offices in London, at 17 Great St Helen's in 1885; 35 Coleman Street in 1886–87; 29 Coleman Street in 1888; and 11 Queen Victoria Street, E.C., from 1889 until at least 1892.

'Referee' [The]. A mark used by A.W. ★Gamage of London on sporting goods, including shotgun ammunition dating prior to 1920.

Reffye [de]. Verchère de Reffye (1821–81), a French artilleryman, was director of the Atelier de Meudon from 1862. Assisted by his subordinate, Pothier, de Reyffe refined the French ★Mitrailleuse in the mid-1860s. He also designed breech-loading cannon and, after the Franco-Prussian War, reorganised the equipment of the artillery. De Reyffe retired from military service with the rank of general.

Reform. A 6.35mm repeating pistol patented in 1905 (German no. 177023) and made during 1907–14 by August ★Schüler of Suhl. The most distinctive feature was a four-barrel block that moved vertically upward each time a shot was fired. The first three spent cases were ejected by residual gas pressure in the breech, but the fourth had to be punched out manually before the gun could be reloaded and the action reset in its lowest position.

Regent – 1. Usually as 'The Regent' on a 12-bore shotgun cartridge made by ★Eley Bros. prior to 1919 and distributed by Charles ★Maleham of Sheffield and London. **2.** Browning-type semi-automatic pistols made in the 1920s by Gregorio ★Bolumburu in Eibar: 6.35mm Auto or 7.65mm, six rounds, hammer fired. Some guns will also bear the markings of Sociedad Española de Armas y Municiones (see S.E.A.M.). **3.** Or Churchill Regent. A name associated with the ★Sabatti Mauser-pattern sporting rifles sold in the USA during the 1970s and 1980s by ★Kassnar Imports of Harrisburg.

Regina. A compact Spanish semi-automatic pistol, based on Browning principles, made by Gregorio ★Bolumburu of Eibar. The hammer-fired 6.35mm pattern, sometimes marked 'Model 1912', had a seven-round magazine; the magazine of the larger 7.65mm version held six or seven rounds.

Regnum. This 6.35mm repeating pistol, with four fixed barrels (cf. Reform), was made by August ★Menz of Suhl prior to the First World War. The breech contained a rotating multi-hammer device that struck each of the four firing pins in turn. Spent cases were extracted automatically as the breech was broken open.

Regulation Police. A name applied to a small swing-cylinder revolver made by ★Smith & Wesson from 1917 onward, little more than a ★Hand Ejector (with an enlarged square-heel butt) chambered for the .32 S&W Long cartridge. The guns were built on the small or I-frame until 1960, when the J-pattern was substituted. Guns made after 1957 were known as Model 31. The advent of guns chambering .38 Special and .357 Magnum ammunition caused the .32 versions to lose popularity, and production stopped in 1991. A few .38 guns were also built on the I-frame (.38/32).

Reich – 1. Adolf Reich, sometimes listed as 'Adolph Reich', Albrechts bei Suhl in Thüringen, Ziegenhügel 6 (1941). Listed in German trade directories as a maker of gun parts (Waffenteile), specialising in optical-sight mounts. **2.** Emil Reich, Zella-Mehlis in Thüringen, Germany. Listed in 1930 as a maker of guns and weapons.

Reichmuth. G. Reichmuth, Erfurt, Marktstrasse 15. A retailer of sporting guns and ammunition active in Germany in 1941.

Reichsgewehr. See panel, pp. 424/25.

Reid – 1. J. Reid, an inspector employed by the Ordnance Department, using the marking 'JR', accepted US military firearms and equipment during 1904–10. See also US arms inspectors' marks. **2.** James Reid, Catskill, New York State. This US gunmaker-inventor was granted US Patent 38,336 of 28 April 1863 to protect a 'revolving firearm' exploited by William ★Irving. Reid was also responsible for ★My Friend, a knuckleduster revolver protected by US Patent 51,572 of 26 December 1865. The guns had a flat frame with a prominent finger-hole and an extra-long cylinder. See also New Model My Friend.

Reif. Albert Reif, Albrechts bei Suhl in Thüringen, Aschenhofer Weg 1. A specialist manufacturer of optical-sight mounts and associated accessories, active in Germany until 1945.

Reilly – 1. Edward Michael Reilly, London. This gunsmith made cap-lock pistols, duelling pistols, ★pepperboxes and air canes from about 1835 until he was succeeded by his son, Edward Michael Reilly Junior, in 1848. Some of the air canes were marked 'Staudenmayer's Patent'. **2.** Edward M. Reilly, son of Joseph Charles Reilly, was listed in London as an airgun maker at 502 Oxford Street from 1848 until 1860. He also obtained British patent 1259/69 of 1869 for an explosive bullet. The business became E.M. Reilly & Company in 1861 and traded until 1917, latterly occupying premises at 295 Oxford Street. Its marks have been reported on self-cocking pepperboxes dating from the middle of the nineteenth century and on bolt-action rifles, sporting guns and ammunition. These included a selection of pinfire patterns, and 12-, 16- and 20-bore shotgun cartridges marked 'The Harewood'. See also Comblain. **3.** James W. Reilly, a major attached to the Federal Ordnance Department, accepted military firearms and ammunition. These included some of the .44 cap-lock ★Remington revolvers issued during the American Civil War; they can be recognised by Reilly's 'JWR' markings, which, however, must be distinguished from those applied prior to the war by James W. ★Ripley. See also US arms inspectors' marks. **4.** Joseph Charles Reilly, father of Edward M. Reilly, began his career as a jeweller in High Holborn, London. First listed as a gunmaker at 316 High Holborn in 1835, he had moved to 502 Oxford Street – which he shared with his son – by 1848. The business was re-established as Reilly & Company at 315 (later 277) Oxford Street in 1859, but

REICHSGEWEHR

This bolt-action magazine rifle was developed in Germany during 1887/88 to counter the introduction in France of the Mle 1886 *Lebel rifle and smokeless-propellant ammunition. Most of the development work has been credited to Louis *Schlegelmilch, a workshop foreman in the Spandau small-arms factory. The rifling profile was copied from the Lebel. Trials with pre-production guns continued until calibre had been resolved in favour of 8mm.

Encouraging field-trial reports persuaded the GPK, the military rifle testing agency, to recommend immediate adoption of the experimental rifle, and the orders were signed by Wilhelm II on 12 November 1888; the first issues of the new Gewehr 88 were made in Alsace-Lorraine in the spring of 1889. However, the Reichsgewehr was not without its problems (*see* Judenflinte). The clip-loaded magazine was clearly based on Mannlicher's, and no arrangements had been made to compensate Mieg for a barrel jacket he had patented in 1887. Eventually the Prussian government recognised Mieg's contribution, and argument over infringement of Mannlicher patents was solved by allowing *Österreichische Waffenfabriks-Gesellschaft to offer 'Mannlicher' rifles commercially on the basis of Reichsgewehr actions.

Most Reichsgewehre were made either by Ludwig *Loewe & Cie in Berlin or by the Prussian government arsenals; however, many of the carbines (Kar. 88) and short rifles (Gew. 91) were made in Suhl by C.G. *Haenel and V.C. *Schilling. Thousands of sporting rifles were also made on the basis of new or converted 1888-type actions. The Reichsgewehr provided the basis for the *Haenel military rifle of 1907, and also for the Chinese *Hanyang pattern.

Undoubtedly the Gewehr 88 was introduced too quickly, and lack of experience with the chemistry of smokeless propellant was a great handicap. Many changes were made during its service life, including deepening the rifling grooves – betrayed by 'Z' for *Züge* ('Grooves'), above the chamber and often also on the right side of the butt – yet not until the approval of an *Einheitshülse* ('universal cartridge case') in 1901 were the problems finally solved. Intended for use in rifles and machine-guns interchangeably, cartridges of this type included an additional 'E' in their headstamps.

Subsequently most Gew. 88 were altered for the pointed-nose S-Patrone, and bear 'S' above the chamber and often also on the side of the butt. The Gew. 88/05 of 1905–07 and the Gew. 88/14 of 1914–15 were *charger-loading alterations of the perfected Gew. 88/S, with appropriate guides on the bridge, cuts in the left wall of the receiver and grooves milled vertically

---

was absorbed by E.M. Reilly & Company in 1899. **5.** *See also* Riley.

Reims. A Spanish pocket automatic pistol, based on the 6.35mm *FN-Browning, made in Eibar by Azanza y Arrizabalaga in two patterns: (a) 6.35mm, six rounds, hammer fired; (b) 7.65mm, six rounds, hammer fired. The guns are customarily marked 'Model 1914'.

Reine, or Carabine Reine. Introduced commercially in the early 1950s and used in quantity by the French prison service until 1971, this .22 LR rimfire blowback semi-automatic *Unique rifle was fed from a detachable eight- or fifteen-round box magazine. Designed by an engineer named Sidna, it had a one-piece half-stock with a pistol grip and a Monte Carlo comb on the butt, while a grasping groove lay beneath the back sight. The cylindrical receiver was most distinctive. *See also* Carabine *La Reine.

Reinhardt. Gustav Reinhardt, Dietzhausen bei Suhl in Thüringen. Listed in Germany prior to 1939 as a maker of gun parts and accessories.

Reising. Eugene G. Reising was born in 1885 in Port Jervis, New York State. After serving as an assistant to John M. *Browning, Reising successfully designed target pistols, submachine-guns and sporting rifles for a variety of gun-makers – including Harrington & Richardson, Marlin, Mossberg and Savage – in addition to his own companies. These included the Reising Manufacturing Corporation, the Reising Arms Company and the *New Haven Arms Company. The precise chronology and interrelationship of these is not clear. **2.** Reising Arms Company, Waterbury and Hartford, Connecticut. The manufacturer of .22 semi-automatic target pistols in accordance with patents granted to Eugene Reising. Work seems to have begun in Waterbury in 1916, then moved to Hartford until c. 1924. **3.** Reising Manufacturing Corporation, New York City.

This is believed to have been the parent organisation of the Reising Arms Company, operating c. 1922–24.

Reitz – 1. Friedrich Reitz, Albrechts bei Suhl in Thüringen. Listed in the 1940 edition of the *Deutsches Reichs-Adressbuch* as a manufacturer of gun parts, a grindery (*Fräserei*) and metal-drawer (*Metallzieherei*). **2.** Rudolf Reitz, Suhl in Thüringen, Germany. Recorded in pre-1914 directories as a wholesaler of gun parts and hunting accessories (*Gewehrteile u. Jagdutensilien*). The entries had changed to 'sales agency' by 1920, under the proprietorship of A. Günzel. Trading seems to have ceased in 1935. **3.** Reitz & Recknagel, Albrechts bei Suhl in Thüringen, Hauptstrasse. Founded in 1867 and active until the end of the Second World War, this German metalworking business specialised in sporting guns, gun parts and accessories.

Rekord. *See* Record.

'Reliable' – 1. Usually as 'The Reliable'. Often found on British shotgun cartridges loaded for Francis *Nelson of Sligo prior to 1914, accompanied by a drawing of a swooping game bird (probably a snipe); or loaded by *Patstone & Son from components from Europe. *See also* Johnson's Reliable. **2.** Found on *Suicide Special revolvers made by the *Bacon Manufacturing Company and the Hopkins & Allen Arms Company of Norwich, Connecticut, USA, in the late nineteenth century.

Reliance – 1. Usually found as 'The Reliance' on shotgun cartridges sold in southern England by *Hammond Bros. of Winchester. *See also* Hardy's Reliance. **2.** A *Suicide Special revolver made by the *Hopkins & Allen Arms Company of Norwich, Connecticut, in the late nineteenth century.

Relum Limited. This company, now part of the SER Group, was formed in London in 1954 by George Muller,

across the face of the chamber to accept S-Patronen. The open base of the magazine was blocked by a sheet-steel cover. The Gew. 88/14 conversions, of comparatively poor quality, usually display 'n' on the chamber and the barrel.

Reichsgewehre also served the Austro-Hungarian Army during the First World War, when about 70,000 obsolete Gewehre 88 were supplied in 1915–16. With the exception of their sling swivels, these *Repetiergewehr M. 13* were still in their original condition. Most were issued to the k.k. Landwehr, then sent to Turkey later in the war.

These German Landwehr soldiers, pictured in the winter of 1915, during the First World War, are armed with 8mm Gewehre 88 – the so-called Reichsgewehr.

who intended simply to distribute Hungarian-style football boots. However, his company soon graduated to track suits, tents, sports bags, and airguns. Most of the guns were Artex/*Telly patterns marketed under a variety of distinctive names and designations, such as 322, 522 and 527. The range in 1980 was confined to the Hungarian-made *Rapide, *Taurus and *Super Tornado rifles, and the Chinese-made G.6235 pistol. The company name is a reversal of Muller.

Remington – **1.** E. Remington & Sons, Herkimer and Ilion, New York State, USA. Maker of 1,000 *Jenks carbines during 1841–45. They were the first martial arms to incorporate the *Maynard Tape Primer and a cast-steel barrel. These were followed by the *Remington-Geiger and *Remington-Rider breech-loaders, the latter establishing the *Rolling Block as one of firearms history's classic systems. Although the business had established a reputation as a maker of sporting rifles and shotguns, Remington also enjoyed a long-term relationship with James *Lee, beginning with the assignation of two patents to Philo Remington in 1871 and culminating in the series production of the *Remington-Lee bolt-action rifle after the failure of the *Sharps Rifle Company. E. Remington & Sons also briefly employed representatives in London, the office being at 50 (later 50 & 52) Queen Victoria Street in 1876–79. However, the business failed in 1886 and eventually was reconstituted as the Remington Arms Company (q.v.). **2.** Samuel Remington was the patentee of the rammer fitted to the perfected *Remington caplock revolvers. The patent was granted in March 1863. **3.** Remington airguns. Eldon Wolff, in *Air Guns* (1958), described Remington as a 'maker of a recent BB gun', while Haviland & Gunn are believed to have worked for the company in the early 1870s. Their prototypes may well have been made in the Remington factory. **4.** Remington Arms Company. This was formed in 1888, after the liquidation of E. Remington & Sons. Work continued on the Rolling Block and the Remington-Lee bolt-action rifle, which was offered in a selection of military and sporting forms until about 1906. **5.** Remington Arms of Delaware Company, USA. *See* Enfield. **6.** Remington Arms–Union Metallic Cartridge Company, Bridgeport, Connecticut, USA. Formed by amalgamating the ammunition-making facilities of the Remington Arms Company with those owned by the *Union Metallic Cartridge Company, this combine identified its products by including 'REM–UMC' in headstamps. Remington–UMC was given an order for 150,000 .45 M1911 *Colt-Browning pistols during the First World War. The contract was cancelled immediately after the November 1918 Armistice, but assembly continued into 1919. Production is said to have amounted to 21,265 guns, although the precise total is disputed. Remington–UMC also maintained the UMC Works in Brimsdown, Enfield, Middlesex, operating for a short period in England close to the site of the Royal Small Arms Factory at *Enfield Lock. Output included a selection of 12-, 16- and 20-bore shotgun cartridges sold under such names as Arrow, Economy, *Kleanbore and Nitro Club, with additional markings such as 'Loaded in Britain–Case made in the U.S.A.' Most examples can be recognised by the inclusion of 'Remington–UMC' (prior to 1925) or simply 'Remington' (post-1926) on the case body or within the headstamp. **7.** Remington-Beals revolver: *see* Fordyce *Beals and Remington revolvers. **8.** Remington-Elliott derringer (sometimes listed as Elliot or Eliot). This was a repeating pistol designed by William *Elliott, patented in 1860/61, and made by E. Remington & Sons. It had a

REMINGTON BOLT-ACTION RIFLES

Remington (19)

The early history of these guns will be found under Enfield, Remington-Keene and Remington-Lee. Such vast numbers of P/1914 and M1917 ★Enfield rifles had been made during the First World War that huge quantities of parts remained when peace returned. The Model 30 rifle was conceived to make use of them, more than 20,000 being made between 1920 and 1940. Credited to Crawford ★Loomis and Charles Barnes, the M30 shared the M1917 Enfield (★Mauser-type) action, but the barrel was shortened and had a commercially acceptable finish. Guns were offered in 1920 in .30-06, with a pistol-grip half-stock, a schnabel-tip fore-end and an adjustable tangent-slide back sight graduated to 550yd on the receiver bridge; proprietary Remington chamberings appeared about 1923.

The Model 30A (1932–40), with a new free-floating barrel, could be obtained from 1933 in 7x57, 7.65x53 and 8x57, replacing the proprietary Remington options. The Model 30 carbine (c. 1924–32) was simply a short version of the standard sporter, and the Model 30 Express rifle (c. 1926–31) cocked on opening instead of closing. The stock was improved and a recoil bolt appeared through the stock beneath the chamber. The modified Model 30R carbine of 1932–40 had the free-floating barrel. The Model 30S (1930–40) had an improved straight-comb stock, a shotgun-style butt plate and a Lyman No. 48R sight on the receiver.

The Model 30S Special rifle (1932–40) had improvements in the stock and barrel bedding, and the benefit of additional chamberings. The Model 30SL (1938–40) had a Lyman back sight, whereas the contemporary 30SR had a Redfield pattern. The Model 30SX lacked fixed sights.

Designed by Crawford ★Loomis, the .22 rimfire Model 33 of 1932–35 was a simple take-down gun with a plain pistol-grip stock. The Model 33 NRA rifle had Lyman (back) and Patridge (front) sights, and was fitted with swivels. The Model 34 (1932–36) was an improved Model 33 with a tube magazine beneath the barrel, and the Model 34 NRA had the same sights as the Model 33 NRA pattern.

Derived from the Model 41A ★Targetmaster of 1936, the Model 41AS chambered .22 Remington Special rimfire ammunition; the Model 41P had a micrometer aperture sight on the receiver and bases for optical-sight mounts on the barrel; the Model 41SB (1937–38) was a rarely-seen smoothbore version. The Model 341P of 1937 was based on the Model 341A Sportsmaster, with a micrometer-adjustable aperture sight and bases for optical-sight mounts on the barrel-top; the Model 341SB was a smoothbore derivative. The Model 411 (1937–39) was made for shooting-gallery use, chambering CB Cap or .22 Short rimfire ammunition, and had a screw-eye for a retaining chain beneath the breech.

Similar mechanically to the Model 510A ★Targetmaster, the Model 510P (1939–41) had an aperture back sight on the receiver, a Patridge sight at the muzzle, and blocks for optical-sight mounts on the barrel. The Model 510SB (1939) was a smoothbore. A version of the Model 511A ★Scoremaster, the Model 511P rifle (1940–41) had an aperture back sight on the receiver and blocks for telescope-sight mounts on the barrel. Essentially similar to the Model 512A ★Scoremaster, the Model 512P (1940–41, c. 1945–59) had a peep sight on the receiver and, on some guns, blocks for optical-sight mounts on the barrel. The Model 513S (1941, 1945–56), based on the 511 design, had a detachable box magazine and a chequered walnut half-stock. The M513TR ★Matchmaster was similar.

The Model 720 Sporting Rifle, developed in 1941 by the Loomis brothers and Aubrey Lowe in 1941, was the first Remington to embody the proprietary variation on the ★Mauser action – now regarded as a classic of its type – with twin opposed locking lugs, additional security provided by the bolt handle turning down into its seat, the extractor and ejector mounted in the bolt head, and the bolt-face recessed in a counter-bore in the barrel.

However, only about 2,430 guns had been made before the Japanese attack on Pearl Harbor pushed the USA into the Second World War.

The Model 720A of 1941–47 could be obtained with Lyman (720AL), Marble-Goss (720AM) or Redfield (720AR) back sights. The short-barrelled Model 720R and the long-barrelled Model 720S could also be obtained with the same range of sights.

Work began again after the Second World War, the first new gun being the Model 521TL. Dating from the period 1947–69, this was a junior version of the Model 513TR, with a half-stock and a micro-adjustable ★Lyman aperture back sight. A short-butt version may have been made in small quantities as the 521TL-JR. The Model 514 (1948–70) was a simplified lightweight gun lacking a safety catch. It had a 24in barrel and weighed only 4.7lb; the Model 514BC Boy's Carbine (1961–71) was a short-butt junior version. The Model 514P (c. 1948–71) could be distinguished by the peep sight on the receiver and a ramped hooded blade at the muzzle.

Introduced commercially in 1949, the Model 721A, developed by a team led by Michael ★Walker, embodied patents granted to John Howell for the extractor (1949) and Michael Walker and Phillip Haskell (1950) for the safety and trigger mechanism. Chamberings were confined to .270 Winchester, .30-06 and .280 Remington; about 125,000 guns had been made when production ended in 1962. A high-power Model 721A Magnum was made only for .300 H&H Magnum and .264 Winchester Magnum ammunition between 1951 and 1962. Minor variants included the Model 721AC of 1953–55, with chequered woodwork, and the Model 721B rifle with a detachable magazine floor plate. The Model 721BDL (1955–62) had a de luxe stock with a low Monte Carlo comb.

The Model 722A (1949–62) was a short-action version of the Model 721, available in chamberings ranging from .222 Remington to .308 Winchester. The Model 722AC of 1953–55 had chequering on the pistol grip and fore-end, and the Model 722B had a detachable magazine floor plate. The Model

722BDL (1955–62) had a stock with a Monte Carlo comb.

The Model 725ADL, announced in 1958, accepted cartridges ranging from .222 Remington to .30-06. It resembled its predecessors, but had a detachable magazine floor plate and a modified safety system that duplicated the original Model 30 pattern. Only about 10,000 guns had been made by 1961 and, as a decision to replace the 725-type rifle had already been taken, many actions were completed as *Kodiak big-game rifles.

A few rimfire 510X, 511X and 512X rifles were assembled in 1964–66, after production of the 510 series had finished. The back sight was a sturdy spring-leaf pattern with a slider instead of an elevator.

Introduced in 1961, the Model 40X target rifle was an immediate success, being offered until replaced by the Model 40XB in 1964. Built on a single-shot 721- or 722-type action, with a solid-floor receiver, its chamberings ranged from .222 Remington to .30-06. The half-stock had a straight comb and a plain pistol grip. Mounting blocks for optical sights and rails for aperture sights were standard, and an adjustable hand-stop track lay beneath the fore-end.

The Model 40XB replaced the Model 40X in 1964. Distinguished by a straight-comb butt, rising at the heel, it could be fitted with a special extra-heavy barrel; chamberings have ranged from .220 Swift and .222 Remington to .30-338 and 300 Winchester Magnum. The basic gun was also offered with a five-round magazine, and in *International

Match Free Rifle and *International Free Rifle forms. The heavy-barrel half-stock Model 40XBBR (Bench Rest) rifle, introduced in 1969, was available in a variety of chamberings: .22 Remington BR to .308 Winchester. Production ceased c. 1990, although work continues on a 1987-vintage variant with a Kevlar stock (M40XBBR KS).

Kevlar-stocked versions of the Model 40XB (Model 40XB KS), made only in .220 Swift, and the M40XC National Match Rifle (M40NM KS) were introduced in 1987–88. The Model 40XR was a heavy-barrelled single-shot action bedded in a half-stock with an adjustable butt plate and an elevating comb; the Model 40XR KS (announced in 1988) was a Kevlar-stocked variant of the 40XR; and the Model 40XR Custom Sporter, introduced in 1986, was a .22 LR rimfire pattern supplied with an assortment of decoration. A centrefire *National Match rifle was also made in small batches between 1974 and 1989.

The Model 40X Target Rifle of 1955–74 was a single-shot .22 LR rimfire with a heavy barrel and Redfield Olympic sights. The Model 40X SB (1957–74) was a lightweight 40X Target, whereas the Model 40X Sporter (1969–80) combined a heavy barrel with an adaptation of the 700ADL half-stock.

The Model 700 was introduced in 1962 to replace the 720 series. A one-piece sear was fitted from 1968, when the bolt plug was lengthened to enclose the cocking-piece head, and a special bolt guide-rib system was introduced in 1974. Originally

Among the many bolt-action rifles produced by the Remington Arms Company have been the centrefire Model 700 BDL Varmint Special (top) and the .22 rimfire Model 581 (above).

the standard 700ADL had a half-stock with a low Monte Carlo comb, a 'blind' magazine and a short nylon or alloy trigger guard; chamberings have ranged from .222 Remington Magnum to .30-06. The 700ADL LS is a laminated-stock variant, introduced in 1988; the 700ADL S (Synthetic) version of 1996 has a straight-comb fibreglass-reinforced stock.

The Model 700BDL rifle has been made since 1962 on the basis of short and long actions, in chamberings ranging from .17 Remington to .35 Whelen. Essentially it is an ADL with a better stock and a detachable magazine floor plate. A stainless-steel barrel was offered until the early 1970s in .264 Winchester, 7mm Remington and .300 Winchester Magnum only. A left-hand version appeared in 1973, although production has been restricted only to the most popular chamberings; other variants include the 700BDL DM (Detachable Magazine), made from 1995 to date with a Monte Carlo-style half-stock; the 700BDL European of 1993–95, with an oil-finish stock; and the 700BDL Limited Classic rifle, introduced in 1991, but merged with the Model 700 Classic from 1992 onward.

The Model 700BDL SS rifle (1993 to date), in chamberings

REMINGTON BOLT-ACTION RIFLES CONT.

ranging from .270 Winchester to .300 Winchester Magnum, has an action of matt-finish stainless steel and a synthetic stock with a straight comb; the 700BDL SS-DM, announced in 1995, is identical with the exception of its detachable magazine. A Model 700BDL SS-DM-B variant, offered from 1996 in magnum chamberings, has an additional muzzle brake. The Model 700C (Custom Grade) rifle, made from 1965 until 1989, was a deluxe version of the BDL offered in four grades of stock quality and finish.

Dating from the same era, the Model 700D *Peerless and Model 700F *Premier rifles had engraved actions and high-quality stocks. The Model 700 AS, offered between 1989 and 1991 in chamberings ranging from .22-250 to .300 Weatherby Magnum, had a synthetic matt-black Arylon stock and matt-finish metalwork.

The Model 700 FS (Fiberglass Stock) rifle, made only in 1987–88, had a straight-comb butt made of Kevlar and fibreglass, finished in black or a black-base camouflage. It was chambered for the .243 Winchester, .270 Winchester, 7mm

Remington Magnum, .30-06 or .308 Winchester rounds. The Model 700 LSS (Laminated, Stainless Steel) rifle, introduced in 1996, has a stainless-steel-barrelled action in a greyed wood-laminate *Monte Carlo half-stock. Chamberings are restricted to 7mm Remington Magnum and .300 Winchester Magnum. The Model 700 RS (Rynite Stock) rifle, offered only in 1987–88, was stocked in synthetic Du Pont Rynite, with a grey or grey-camouflage finish; chamberings were confined to .270 Winchester, .280 Remington and .30-06. The M700 SS (Stainless Synthetic) rifle, dating from 1992, has a matt-finish stainless-steel barrel/action set in a black-textured composite stock. Standard BDL-type SS guns have been offered in chamberings ranging from .25-06 to .338 Winchester.

Other versions of the M700 are listed separately. They include the African Plains Rifle (introduced in 1995), Alaskan Wilderness Rifle (1994), Camo Synthetic (1992), Classic, Classic Magnum (1981), European (1993), Kit Gun (1987), Mountain Rifle (1986), Safari (1962), Sendero (1994) and the

Varmint Special (1967). There were also several bolt-action patterns in the *Nylon Series.

Made between 1964 and 1971 in chamberings ranging from .222 Remington to .35 Remington, the Model 600 was introduced to compete in the market for inexpensive Brush Guns. The bolt handle was cranked forward above the wedge-shaped synthetic trigger guard, a detachable box magazine was fitted, and the pistol-grip half-stock of the earliest guns was accompanied by a tapering fore-end. The M600 was distinguished by the prominent ventilated barrel rib. A short-lived Model 600 Magnum was made in 1965–67 for the 6.5mm Remington Magnum and .350 Remington Magnum cartridges, with an integral recoil stop for the sight mounts and a walnut/beech-laminate stock with swivel eyes beneath the butt and fore-end. Improved Model 660 and 660 Magnum rifles appeared in 1968. The barrel rib disappeared, but a contrasting fore-end tip and spacer were added. Guns were still being sold as *Mohawks long after production ended in 1972.

The Model 788 Sporting Rifle of 1967–84 was designed by Charles Morse and Wayne *Leek. Offered in

tipping barrel cluster and a revolving striker mechanism operated by a ring trigger. About 50,000 five-shot .22 and four-shot .32 examples were made between 1863 and 1888. **9.** Remington-Geiger. Many of the breech-loaders purchased from Remington by the Federal authorities during the Civil War incorporated the split-breech action, designed by Leonard *Geiger and perfected by Joseph Rider. The essence of the action lay in a high-wall receiver and a radial breech-block containing the hammer. The nose of the hammer struck the rimfire cartridge through a slot in the top surface of the block. Although the Remington-Geiger action was neither as strong nor as efficient as the succeeding Rolling Block (see Joseph H. *Rider), the Federal government ordered 15,000 carbines chambering .56-50 Spencer rimfire carbine cartridges on 24 October 1864, during the American Civil War. They were followed by 5,000 small-frame guns chambering a weaker .46 rimfire cartridge, which put less strain on the comparatively weak action. These were ordered in January 1865, but few had been delivered before hostilities ended. **10.** Remington-Hepburn rifle. A name given to a modification of the *Rolling Block system, designed by Lewis L. *Hepburn. Most of the guns made prior to 1886 were marked as the product of E. Remington & Sons, but those dating later than 1888 were marked by the Remington Arms Company. The No. 3 Sporting Rifle (1880–92) was offered in chamberings ranging from .22 rimfire to .45 centerfire. Compared with the standard

Rolling Blocks, the Remington-Hepburn had a receiver with squared contours, a serpentine operating lever on the right side of the breech and a rebounding hammer. Most guns had half- or full-octagon barrels, pistol-grip butts and short tapering fore-ends. Strengthened to accept ammunition loaded with smokeless powder, the New Model No. 3, introduced in 1893, lasted until c. 1912. Chamberings ranged from .30-30 to .38-72 Winchester; the barrels were usually octagonal. Included among the other guns built on the No. 3 system were the *Improved Creedmoor Rifle, the *Hunter's Rifle, the *Long Range Military Creedmoor Rifle, the *Match Rifle and the *Schuetzen Match Rifle. **11.** Remington-Keene rifle. Locked by the bolt-guide rib abutting the front of the receiver bridge as the bolt handle was turned down, this gun was made by E. *Remington & Sons to the designs of James W. *Keene, about 5,000 examples being produced during 1877–80. A loading port lay on the underside of the stock, ahead of the trigger, although the magazine could also be loaded through the open action. As the cartridges were retained securely in the elevator during the loading stroke, the Remington-Keene could be operated upside-down. The US Navy acquired 250 .45-70 rifles in 1880, probably with 30in barrels, and the US Army purchased a similar number in 1881 for trials against the *Hotchkiss and *Remington-Lee; army guns are said to have had 32.5in barrels and nine-round tube magazines. They also had a full-length stock, two bands, a

chamberings from .222 Remington to .44 Magnum, it had a tubular receiver, a bolt with nine small lugs in three rows of three, and a very plain pistol-grip half-stock; a left-hand 788L action appeared in 1969.

The .22 LR rimfire Model 540X target rifle, made from 1968 until 1974, was built on a new action that lacked the split bridge of its predecessors. The heavyweight barrel was set in a massive half-stock with an anatomical pistol grip, the butt plate could move vertically in its channel-block, and an accessory rail was let into the underside of the squared fore-end. The Model 540XR (1974–83), intended for three-position shooting, had an extra-deep fore-end; and the Model 540XR Junior, or JR, of the same era had a short, or 'junior', butt.

The Model 541S Custom Sporter (1972–84) had a scroll-engraved 540-series action, a detachable five-round box magazine, and a straight-comb walnut half-stock with a rosewood fore-end tip and pistol-grip cap. The Model 541T was similar to the 541S, but had plain metalwork and a stock with an ebonite tip. Its barrel was drilled and tapped for optical-sight mounting bases.

The single-shot .22 rimfire Model 580 of 1967 had rails for an optical-sight mount on top of the tubular solid-bridge receiver, a plain ambidextrous ★Monte Carlo half-stock and a large stamped-strip trigger guard. Production ended in 1978, but a range of derivatives has been offered. The Model 580BR Boy's Rifle (1971–78) was a short-butt version of the standard gun; the Model 580SB (1967–78) was a smoothbore; the Model 581 (1967–83) had a detachable six-round box magazine; the Model 581-S (1987–92) had a five-round magazine and a walnut-finish hardwood stock with a tapering fore-end; and the Model 582 (1967–83) had a tube magazine beneath its barrel. The Model 591 of 1970–74 chambered the 5mm Remington Magnum rimfire cartridge, and the otherwise similar Model 592 had an under-barrel tube magazine.

Sharing the action of the Model 721, the Model Seven (1983 to date) is a short-barrelled Brush Gun chambered for cartridges ranging from .222 Remington to .308 Winchester. It has a silent side-mounted safety and a largely free-floating barrel. The KS version,

introduced in 1987 and available in chamberings as powerful as .350 Remington Magnum, has a Kevlar-reinforced stock; MS guns, introduced in 1993, have wood-laminate straight-comb stocks; an FS version, made in 1987–90, had a fibreglass stock with Kevlar inserts; and the SS pattern, announced in 1994, has a stainless-steel action set in a black synthetic half-stock. The Model Seven Youth Rifle (1993 to date), restricted to .243 Winchester and 7mm–08, has a short-butt hardwood stock.

Also known as the M78 Sportsman, the Model 78 Sporting Rifle, made in 1988–91 in chamberings from .223 Remington to .308 Winchester, combined a 700-type action and a plain hardwood stock.

The Model 24 Sniper Rifle of 1988, part of the M24 Sniping System, was developed to compete in US Army trials. Essentially it is an improved M40A1, a militarised Model 700 with a heavy barrel and a special trigger adapted from the M40 Match Rifle pattern. The composite Kevlar/graphite half-stock has an aluminium bedding-block, and an accessory rail lies beneath the fore-end.

---

cleaning rod set in a channel on the left side of the fore-end and a magazine cut-off on the left side of the breech. A few .45-70 half-stocked carbines were made with 20.5in barrels and seven-round magazines. About 250 half-stocked .45-70 rifles, with 24in barrels and full-length magazines, were purchased on behalf of the US Indian Bureau in 1884, and a few thousand sporting guns were made in .40-70 Remington, .43 Spanish and .45-70. Remington-Keenes had butts with a notably 'bellied' under-surface and a prominent spur on the manually-retracted cocking piece. **12. Remington-Lee rifle.** The failure of the ★Sharps Rifle Company in 1881 allowed E. Remington & Sons to acquire the uncompleted US Navy contract for the 1879-pattern ★Lee magazine rifle, and an improved Model 1882 appeared with the bolt handle locking down behind the bridge. More than 30,000 of these were made (1882–84) in .43 Spanish and .45-70. Three .45-70 Lee rifles were among those tested by the US Army in the summer of 1882, two with the 1879-patent action, while the third was the 1882-type Gun No. 36. The Lee No. 36 was preferred to the ★Chaffee-Reece and the ★Hotchkiss, as it had a detachable box magazine and an additional locking lug. Subsequently Remington delivered 750 1882-pattern Lee rifles for trials against Chaffee-Reece and Hotchkiss guns made by ★Springfield Armory and the ★Winchester Repeaating Arms Company respectively. The Lee rifles had new magazines protected by patents granted in 1884 to Louis ★Diss, with two

prominent cartridge-guide grooves in the sheet-metal bodies. The 1882-pattern Lee rifles, and a few carbines, were also sold to China, Haiti and Peru. The Model 1885, or Improved Magazine Rifle, made by E. Remington & Sons and the Remington Arms Company (1885–96) featured a non-rotating extractor, an enlarged cocking-piece and a separate bolt head patented in March 1885 by Louis Diss. Guns made after 1888 were custom-arily marked 'REMINGTON ARMS COMPANY'. More than 500 guns were sold to Denmark, 350 .43-cal-ibre examples went to Britain, and 500 were sold to New Zealand; by far the largest quantity, however, went to the US Navy, which accepted nearly 4,000 .45-70 examples. The earliest were acquired by way of the ★Lee Arms Company, which sub-contracted work to Remington. A few carbines were also made during 1889–93, with 24in barrels and half-length fore-ends. The Bolt Action Big Game Rifle (q.v.) was a sporting version. The M1899, or Small-Bore Magazine Rifle, of 1898–1906 chambered cartridges ranging from 6mm Lee to the rimmed British .303. Louis Diss had moved the lugs on to a separate bolt head (although this was little more than an adaptation of the bolt developed for the side-magazine ★Lee-Cook rifle of 1893) and provided an improved magazine with three guide grooves. A wooden hand guard lay above the bar-rel. Fewer than 6,000 rifles were made, most going to the Michigan National Guard at the time of the Spanish-American War (1898) and to Cuba early in the twentieth

REMINGTON ROLLING BLOCK

Remington (21)

Although the US Army viewed this system unenthusiastically, Denmark ordered large numbers of guns in 1867, and other states soon followed; by 1873, Remington had sold them to the US Army, to the US Navy, to a variety of US militia units, to Spain (for use in Cuba) and to Sweden. Guns were being offered in the 1870s under such names as *Civil Guard Model, *Egyptian Model, *French Model and *Spanish Model, alongside adaptations of Springfield rifle-muskets accepting the rolling-block breech.

Ten thousand .50-70 M1870 Navy Rifles were ordered from *Springfield Armory in February 1870, but after they had been accepted into store in the summer, the back sights were seen to be wrongly positioned. The guns were hastily sold to *Poultney & Trimble, then sold on to France during the Franco-Prussian War while replacements were sought.

The Remington was also tested extensively by the US Army, trials undertaken in 1870 recommending (in declining order of preference) the Remington, the *Springfield-Allin, the *Sharps, the *Morgenstern, the *Martini-Henry and the *Ward-Burton.

About 1,000 .50-70 M1871 army rifles were made in Springfield Armory in 1870–71 to compete against 1870-pattern Springfield and *Sharps conversions. They accepted socket bayonets instead of the sword pattern associated with the earlier naval rifles. Concurrently, the cavalry tested about 300 .50-70 Remington carbines. Trials suggested that they performed best, but as ejection was poor and dust jammed the mechanism, the rolling-block breech was rejected in favour of the Trapdoor Springfield-Allin pattern.

The simplicity, legendary strength and ready availability of the rolling-block action allowed individual gunsmiths – and Remington, indeed – to build guns to individual order. Great variety will be found in chambering, stocks and sights. In 1888, however, the manufacturer's marks changed from the old 'E. REMINGTON & SONS, ILION, N.Y.' to the new 'REMINGTON ARMS CO.' after the failure of the original family business.

The first commercially-successful Rolling Block, the No. 1 Sporting Rifle, was made from 1867 until c. 1890, in a variety of chamberings from .32-20 Winchester to .50-70 Government, with round, or half- or fully-octagonal barrels. Some guns had pistol-grip butts; others had vernier-adjustable peep-and-globe sights. The No. 1½ Sporting Rifle (1888–97) was a lightened No. 1, customarily with an octagonal barrel chambering cartridges ranging from .22 rimfire to .38 centrefire. The No. 2 Sporting Rifle (1872–1910), also known as the Gem or New Model Light Rifle, had an ultra-lightweight action chambered for cartridges ranging from .25-20 Single Shot to .44-40 Winchester.

Light Model, or Baby, Sporting Carbines were completed in 1888–1908 from actions that had remained in store after the collapse of E. Remington & Sons in 1886. Finished in nickel or blue, the guns had round barrels and traditional military-style sights. A sling ring could often be found on the left side of the receiver.

The No. 5 Military/Sporting Rifle provided another means of using obsolete actions. Introduced in 1897, apparently for sale to Mexico, it was strengthened for smokeless ammunition and had a 30in barrel.

century; the majority of the 3,000 carbines produced by 1907 had also gone to Cuba. About 1,500 sporting rifles were built on the 1899-pattern action during 1899–1909, chambered for cartridges ranging from 6mm Lee to .405 Winchester. They had pistol-grip half-stocks with slender *schnabel-tip fore-ends. There was also an associated *Special Grade Rifle, and a few full-stock military and half-stock sporting target rifles with micro-adjustable sights. **13.** Remington pistols. The .22 rimfire six-shot *Zig-Zag derringer was made in accordance with patents granted to William *Elliott in 1858 and 1860. This was followed by the tipping-barrel Remington-Elliott derringer, patented in 1860/61, then the .22, .32 and .41 rimfire *Vest Pocket Pistol of 1865, which had a *Rolling Block breech and a saw-handle grip. The single-shot .41 rimfire Deringer Pistol, with a hammer doubling as a breech-block, was patented by William Elliott in 1867. The Double Repeating Deringer Pistol was another Elliott design, patented in December 1865 and marketed commercially from 1866 until the 1930s. The superimposed barrels could be swung upward after a latch had been pressed. Guns made after 1887 were marked by the Remington Arms Company and eventually bore 'Remington Arms–UMC Co.' The Magazine Repeating Pistol was patented by Joseph *Rider in 1871. It had a tube magazine beneath the barrel for .32 Extra Short rimfire cartridges, and was locked by a variation of the Rolling Block action. Production continued until 1888. **14.** Remington-Rand, Inc., Syracuse, New York State. A contractor for .45 M1911A1 *Colt-Browning pistols, recruited during the Second World War; about 1,086,000 guns were made during 1943–45. **15.** Remington

Many 7x57 guns were supplied to France in 1914, while work began on a large order for an 8x51 version. A few 7.62x54mm guns were also supplied to Russia before assembly finally ceased in 1917.

Military-style carbines usually had short barrels, straight-wrist butts and short fore-ends held by a single band; Sporting Pattern rifles (1898–1905) were offered in chamberings ranging from 7x57 Mauser to .38-55 Remington High Powered. They had straight-wrist butts and rounded *schnabel-tip fore-ends.

The No. 4 Sporting Rifle of 1890–1933 was offered in solid-frame or take-down versions, the latter with a 1902-patent radial locking lever on the right side of the frame. Chambering options ranged from .22 Short to .32 Long rimfire. The standard butt had a straight wrist (a pistol-grip type could be obtained to order), and the fore-end had a rounded tip. The Model 4S Military Model of 1913–33, sometimes advertised as the Boy Scout's Rifle, was confined to .22 Short and .22 Long Rifle. It featured a full-length stock, sling swivels and military-style sights. The 4S rifle could also

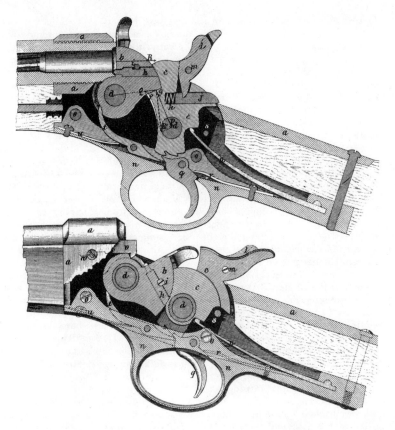

be accompanied by an all-metal knife bayonet.

Built on the standard pistol action, the No. 7 Sporting Rifle of 1903–11 chambered .22 Short, .22 Long Rifle or .25 Stevens rimfire cartridges. It had a straight-comb butt with a full pistol grip and sometimes also a *Schuetzen-style shoulder plate. A *Lyman aperture sight was carried on a spur on the frame tip behind the hammer.

Among other rolling-block rifles

introduced during 1874–77 were the Buffalo Rifle, the Business Rifle, the Black Hills Rifle, the Creedmoor Target Rifle, the Hunter's Rifle, the Mid Range Target Rifle and the Short Range Target Rifle. All are listed separately. The No. 6 Sporting Rifle (1901–33), often wrongly classified as a rolling-block design, embodied a simplified action chambering cartridges from .22 Short to .32 Long. It could be recognised by its elongated receiver.

Repeating Double Deringer. *See* Remington pistols. **16. Remington revolvers.** The earliest foray into this market had been a five-shot .31 pocket revolver patented in 1856/57 by Fordyce *Beals, but only a few thousand had been made when the project was abandoned in favour of a .31 five-shot gun designed by Joseph *Rider. This had an instantly recognisable 'mushroom' cylinder. About 100,000 were made, remaining in stock into the 1880s. Production of .36-calibre Navy- and .44 Army-type revolvers with Beals' Patent Rammer began in 1858 and lasted until superseded by improved models with the *Elliott rammer in 1861, and the perfected Samuel *Remington rammer in 1863 (*see* New Model Army). Subsequently, nearly 5,000 .44 army revolvers were converted for a .46 rimfire cartridge by substituting a new five-cartridge cylinder for the original six-chamber cap-

lock type. A royalty was paid to Smith & Wesson on each gun. Remington also made cartridge-firing versions of the cap-lock revolvers, a .38 centrefire version of the old .36 New Model Navy lasting until 1888. Then Remington produced about 25,000 M1875 revolvers in .44 Remington, .44-40 WCF and .45 Colt, but the US Army retained the Colt. The first cartridge revolver to be offered was the M1890, differing principally from the M1875 in the removal of the under-barrel web. Assembly ceased in 1894, after only about 2,000 had been made. **17. Remington-Rider.** A term usually applied to a cap-lock revolver made by E. Remington & Sons; *see* Remington revolvers. **18. Remington rifles, auto-loading.** The Remington Arms Company also made a variety of auto-loading sporting rifles, including the Model 8 Sporting Rifle, subsequently known as the Model 8A, which dated from the period 1906–36. The first center-fire auto-loader to be made in North America, it was the work of John *Browning. The use of a barrel that slid back within a sleeve to unlock the breech – two lugs on the bolt engaged the barrel extension – had been patented in 1900–02, although post-1918 guns listed additional patents granted in 1907 and 1911. Chambered for proprietary cartridges ranging from .25 to .35, the guns had detachable five-round box magazines. They were offered in several grades, but were superseded in 1936 by the Model 81A *Woodsmaster. The Model 16 Sporting Rifle (1914–28), subsequently known as the Model 16A, could be chambered for a variety of .22 rimfire cartridges, including the Short, Long Rifle, Winchester and Remington Automatic patterns. It was designed by Charles *Barnes to compete with the Johnson-pattern Winchesters, but was not particularly successful. It had a squared slab-sided receiver and a concealed hammer, and often had extensive decoration. Made in accordance with Belgian patents granted to John *Browning in 1913–14, the .22 rimfire Model 24 Sporting Rifle (1922–35, later known as the Model 24A) was essentially similar to the *FN-Browning rifle introduced prior to the First World War, with a tube magazine in the butt. It was superseded by the Model 241A *Speedmaster. About 220,000 Model 550A Sporting Rifles were made by Remington in 1941, and between 1945 and 1971. A tube magazine lay beneath the barrel, but the most interesting feature was a floating chamber, or Power Piston, adapting the action to fire three different rimfire cartridges (.22 Short, Long and Long Rifle). The basic 550A, with a plain hardwood pistol-grip half-stock and open sights, was joined by the peep-sighted 550P and the 550G (alias 550-2G or 550-GS), intended for use in shooting galleries, which had an eye for a retaining chain and a spent-case deflector on the right side of the receiver. The later M740A *Woodsmaster (1952 to date), M552A *Speedmaster (1957 to date), M742A *Woodsmaster (1960–80), *Model Four (1981 to date), M522 *Viper (1993 to date) and the Nylon Series are described separately. **19.** Remington rifles, bolt-action: see panel, pp. 426–29. **20.** Remington rifles, lever-action. Few of these have been made, as the North American market has always been dominated by the products of *Winchester and *Marlin. However, the Remington Arms Company did make small quantities of the Model 76 Trail Rider rifle in 1962–64. One of the *Nylon series, it is listed separately. **21.** Remington rifles, rolling-block action: see panel, pp. 430/31. **22.** Remington rifles, slide-action. The Remington Arms Company made a range of these, based on patents granted during 1909–12 to John D. *Pedersen. Introduced commercially in 1909 and made until 1936 in a variety of 'Grades', the .22 rimfire Model 12 was a hammerless take-down pattern locked by displacing the bolt lug into the top of the receiver. The magazine tube ended well short of the muzzle. Early guns had Remington–UMC marks; later examples, however, also known as the Model 12A, bore Remington marks only. A Gallery Gun, the Model 12B, was chambered specifically for the .22 Short rimfire cartridge; an NRA Target Grade version, the Model 12C, had an octagonal barrel, a semi-pistol-grip butt and better sights; and the Model 12CS chambered the .22 Remington Special cartridge. The Model 14 (1912–36), eventually redesignated Model 14A, was an

enlarged Model 12 chambered for .30 Remington centre-fire ammunition. A special spiral magazine was used to prevent cartridge noses from igniting the primer ahead of them. Standard guns had straight-wrist butts and ribbed slide handles. A short-barrelled Model 14R carbine was made between 1912 and 1934, while short-action Model 14¹/₂ rifles and Model 14¹/₂R carbines (1915–25) handled .38-40 or .44-40 Winchester cartridges. The Model 121A *Fieldmaster and Model 141A *Gamemaster replaced the Models 12A and 14A in 1936, but are listed separately. These were followed by the Model 572 *Fieldmaster (1959) and the Model 760 *Gamemaster (1952). Last in the series was the Model Six, introduced in 1981 to replace the 760 series. Although a few Model Six rifles were made in *Peerless and *Premier grades, the distinctions were lost when the Models Six and 7600 merged in the mid-1980s under the 7600 designation; the Model 7600 was originally a plain-finished Model Six. Chamberings have ranged from 6mm Remington to .35 Whelen, and a short-barrelled M7600 carbine (.30-06 only) has also been made in small numbers. **23.** Remington Rolling Block. This name was applied to any single-shot rifle, made by E. Remington & Sons and the Remington Arms Company, that incorporated a radial-block breech locking mechanism to the patents of Joseph *Rider. See panel, pp. 430/31. **24.** Remington shotguns, auto-loading action. The Model 11 (in 12-, 16- and 20-bore) was the first commercially successful auto-loading shotgun made in North America. Based on patents granted to John M. *Browning in 1900–03, it had a tube magazine beneath the barrel and ejected laterally. Huge quantities were sold before the Model 11 was discontinued in 1948. Many other guns have been made since, including the Model 11-48 (1949–60), Sportsman 48 (1949–60) and Sportsman 58 (1956–64). **25.** Remington shotguns, break-open action. Several types of double-barrelled hammer shotguns were made, beginning with the 10-, 12- or 16-bore Model 1874 patented by Andrew *Whitmore. Faults in the action led to the abandonment of the Model 1874 only four years after its introduction. It was replaced by the New Model 1882 (1882–1910), which had a top-lever lock, low 'Circular Hammers' and rebounding locks; 10-bore New Model Heavy guns, discontinued in 1895, had an additional top rib and could weigh 10lb or more. The Model 1889, made until 1908 in 10-, 12- and 16-bore, was an improved version of the Model 1882 with recurved hammer shanks. The Remington No. 3 of 1893–1902, made in a variety of chamberings from 10- to 28-bore, was a single-barrel semi-hammerless top-lever shotgun with a cocking lever on the left side of the frame. Based on patents granted to Rimmon *Fay in 1894–1902, it was superseded by the No. 9 (1902–10). This had a distinctive spurred trigger guard and acknowledged an additional Fay patent of 28 June 1904. The box-lock Remington Hammerless Double Barrel Shot Gun, or Model 1894, a top-lever pattern, was made until 1910 in 10-, 12- and 16-bore. The Model 1900 (10-, 12-, 16- and 20-bore) was an improved version based on patents granted to Rimmon Fay and George *Humphreys; a Trap Gun derivative followed in 1902. **26.** Remington shotguns, rolling-block action. From 1867 until about 1892, Remington advertised the Remington Rolling Block Shotgun No. 1, in 16- and 20-bore. The Shotgun No. 2 was a 'juvenile' 30-bore built on a smaller action. **27.** Remington shotguns, slide-action. The exposed-hammer Model 10 shotgun was protected by patents granted to John *Pedersen on 3 February 1903 (719,955) and 18 May 1905 (789,755). Introduced commercially in 1907 in 12-bore only, it was made until 1929 in several versions. It was the first of many Remington guns of this type, culminating in the Model 17 (1921–33), the Model 29 (1929–33) and the Model 31 (1931–41, 1946–49), made in accordance with patents granted to Crawford Loomis, and the Model 870 Wingmaster introduced in 1950.

Remo-Gewehrfabrik, Suhl, Germany. *See* Rempt.

Rempt. Gebrüder Rempt, Remo-Gewehrfabrik, Suhl in Thüringen, Rimbachstrasse 37 (1941). Listed in the 1900 *Deutsches Reichs-Adressbuch* as a gunmaking business, this producer of hunting and sporting guns was being operated by Walter Rempt by 1914. Rempt owned the business until the end of the Second World War, although usually it was listed after c.1937 as 'Remo Gewehrfabrik, Gebr. Rempt'. Maker of two-shot 12-, 16- and 20-bore *Remo shotguns from war-surplus Gew. 98, c. 1932/33. Operations ceased at the end of the Second World War.

'REM–UMC'. Associated with the products of the *Remington Arms–Union Metallic Cartridge Company, this mark is commonly encountered in headstamps and on packaging.

Renaissance – 1. A three-barrel sporting rifle, or *Drilling*, made in Belgium during the 1970s by Armes Ernest *Dumoulin SPRL. It is distinguished by a triple trigger system, and – most unusually – it has two small-calibre rifled barrels flanking a central smoothbore. The quality is excellent. **2.** A term associated with an engraved pattern applied in recent years to firearms (including pistols) made by *Fabrique Nationale of Herstal.

Renard – 1. This pocket-size Spanish semi-automatic pistol, based on the *FN-Browning, was made by Echave y Arizmendi of Eibar, Guipúzcoa: 6.35mm, six rounds, hammer fired. **2.** Renard-Aron, rue des Jardins 38, Saint-Étienne. Listed in French directories of 1879 as a gunmaker.

Renault. Henri Renault, Liège. A Belgian gunmaker; succeeded by *Rolland & Renault.

Renkin frères, Liège. This gunmaking business was founded by Jean Renkin (d. 1839) and continued by his son, J.H. Renkin l'Aîné. A member of La *Société des Anglais in the mid-1850s, the business also made stirrups, spurs and harness parts. Subsequently involved in the 1870s with le *Grand Syndicat. The factory was closed by order of the German occupation forces on 1 October 1914.

Renodier pére et fils, rue Beaubrun 39, Saint-Étienne, France. Listed in 1879 as a distributor of, and agent for, arms and ammunition.

'Renown' [The]. Found on shotgun cartridges distributed in southern England by *Patstone & Son. Apparently they were loaded using European-made components.

Réocreux et Bessy, rue de la Loire 27, Saint-Étienne, France. Listed in 1879–92 as a distributor of, and agent for, arms and ammunition. The address in 1892 was rue de la Loire 23, which may simply have been the original premises renumbered.

'R.E.P.', 'REP', in an oval, generally on the barrel near the breech. Found on rifles made by the Remington Arms Company; used as an in-house proof mark.

Retolaza – 1. Another of the many small Browning-type pistols made in Spain during the 1920s by *Retolaza Hermanos of Eibar: 6.35mm, six rounds, hammer fired. **2.** Retolaza Hermanos, Eibar, Guipúzcoa. This Spanish gunmaking partnership manufactured *Ruby-pattern semi-automatic pistols for the French Army during the First World War. It was also responsible for the *Gallus, *Liberty, *Military, *Retolaza, *Stosel, *Titan and *Titanic. (Some examples of the Liberty were marked by Fabrique d'Armes de *Grande Précision, and the gun has been attributed elsewhere to Gregorio Bolumburu.)

Retriever – 1. Usually encountered as 'The Retriever': associated with shotgun ammunition handled in south-western Scotland during the 1920s by *Kirk of Ayr. **2.** A *Suicide Special revolver made by the *Ryan Pistol Company of Norwich, Connecticut, USA, in the late nineteenth century.

Return spring. The spring in an auto-loader that returns the bolt or breech-block after firing; sometimes less accurately called the recoil spring.

Reuben. Alexander Reuben, working on behalf of the Federal ordnance authorities, accepted military equipment during the American Civil War. The guns, which date from 1863, customarily bear 'AR', but can be distinguished by date from those accepted some years earlier by Adam *Ruhlman. *See also* US arms inspectors' marks.

Réunies. *See* Fabrique d'Armes Réunies.

Reuss – 1. Ferd. Reuss, Mehlis and Zella-Mehlis in Thüringen. Listed in 1900/20 German directories as a gunmaker. Owned in 1900 by Max Reuss. **2.** K. Reuss, Zella-Mehlis in Thüringen, Germany. Listed in 1939 as a master gunsmith.

Revaud – 1. Barthélemy Revaud, rue Badouillère 24, Saint-Étienne. Listed in France in 1879 as a gunmaker. **2.** Revaud cadet, grande rue Saint-Jacques 29, Saint-Étienne, France. Listed in 1879 as a maker of gun parts and accessories.

'Revelation'. A brandname associated in North America with the *Western Auto Supply Company. It is found on guns bought from *Marlin and others in recent years.

'Revenge' [The]. Associated with shotgun ammunition loaded in southern England by Russell *Hillsdon.

Revol. J.B. Revol, New Orleans, Louisiana. A maker of cap-lock saloon rifles, Revol has also been (mistakenly?) identified as a manufacturer of spring-air Gallery Guns. Robert Gardner (in *Small Arms Makers*) lists him at 346 Royal Street, New Orleans, in 1853–76.

Revolver. *See* panel, p. 434.

Rev-o-Noc. A brandname associated with shotguns made prior to the First World War by the *Crescent Arms Company of Norwich, Connecticut, USA.

Rex – 1. Usually found as 'The Rex' on shotgun cartridges distributed in England by *Milburn & Son of Southampton. Most of the examples recorded seem to have been made by *Eley-Kynoch, dating them later than 1920. **2.** A pocket pistol made in Eibar, Guipúzcoa, Spain, by Gregorio *Bolumburu, based on the 1910-pattern *FN-Browning: (a) 7.65mm Auto, seven rounds, striker fired; (b) 9mm Short, six rounds, striker fired.

Rexer Arms Company Ltd, 20 Cockspur Street, London. This promotional agency was formed c. 1902 by an entrepreneur named Snell to promote a recoil-operated automatic rifle and light machine-gun, which had been developed in Denmark. The Rexer rifle was tested in Britain in 1904, winning a prize at Bisley in competition

REVOLVER

A name used to describe virtually any handgun (and also a particular type of rifle) with cartridges held in a rotating cylinder. The guns are customarily single-barrel, but there have been exceptions, such as the *Le Mat revolver/shotgun and twin-barrelled volley revolvers briefly fashionable in Europe at the end of the nineteenth century.

Although manually-operated revolvers have been made for virtually as long as there have been firearms, the introduction of a cylinder that rotated as the action was cocked is generally believed to have been due to Elisha Collier. However, most surviving Collier revolvers have a simpler manual system, and thus the credit for the first truly commercially-successful self-rotating cylinder (notwithstanding the existence of the *Darling pepperbox) is given to Samuel *Colt.

The Paterson Colt was little more than a qualified success, but in time it led to the *Walker and the *Dragoon Colts of the late 1840s. Many people attempted to produce rival designs, but Colt resorted successfully to litigation; not until the master patent expired in 1857 did the floodgates open, although the monopoly Colt enjoyed in the USA did not extend to Britain, where the *Adams revolver introduced the first successful double-action lock mechanism.

Other landmarks in the history of the revolver include the advent of efficient rimfire ammunition, developed by *Smith & Wesson, and the bored-through cylinder (Rollin *White patent), which led to the creation of another monopoly; the widespread acceptance of *cap-lock and metallic-cartridge revolvers during the American Civil War of 1861–65; the introduction of efficient auto-ejecting systems in the 1870s, by companies such as Smith & Wesson and P. *Webley & Sons; the perfection of a swing-out cylinder in the 1890s, usually attributed to *Colt's Patent Fire Arms Manufacturing Company, although the idea was much older; and the eventual introduction during the 1930s of the first *Magnum cartridge.

There have been far too many individual novelties to summarise here, but information can be found in the many books devoted to the subject. Particularly useful is the The Revolver... trilogy, written by Anthony W.F. Taylerson, initially with the assistance of R.A.N. Andrews and J.N. Frith; and the recent encyclopaedic study by Rolf H. Müller, Die Revolver-Lexicon. (Journal-Verlag Schwend, two volumes, 1996). Many excellent studies of individual gunmakers and gun patterns – especially the Colt Peacemaker – have also been made in recent years. See also Pepperbox.

An elaborately-engraved 54-bore patented double-action revolver made by William Tranter of Birmingham. Dating from the period of the American Civil War, it bears the marks of Isaac Hollis on the top strap of the frame, above the cylinder.

with the Hallé pattern, but then was the subject of a lengthy patent-infringement suit bought by the promoter of the Danish *Madsen guns. The Rexer Arms Company Ltd was finally liquidated in 1908.

Rey, 7 cours Fauriel, Saint-Étienne, France. Listed in 1951 as a gunmaker.

Reymond, 40 rue Désiré-Claude, Saint-Étienne, France. Listed in 1951 as a gunmaker.

Reynaud-Meunier, place Villeboeuf 10, Saint-Étienne, France. Listed in 1892 as a gunmaker.

Reynolds – 1. Henry Reynolds, Springfield, Massachusetts. Designer of the extractor used on the *Plant revolvers after 1864, protected by US Patent 42,688 of 10 May 1864 ('revolving firearm') and 45,176 of 22 November 1864 ('cartridge extractor'). **2.** Mark E. Reynolds, a civilian inspector employed by the Ordnance Department, using 'MER' marks, accepted firearms and accessories made by *Colt's Patent Fire Arms Manufacturing Company. His activities date from c. 1937. See also US arms inspectors' marks. **3.** W. Cook Reynolds, a member of the English gun trade, was listed at 48 Devonshire Street, London S.W., from 1897 until the First World War. **4.** Reynolds, Plant & Hotchkiss, New Haven, Connecticut, USA. Distributor of *Plant revolvers immediately after the American Civil War in 1865.

'R.F.' A superimposition-type monogram, sometimes enwreathed. Found on the grips of *Unique and other French handguns: *République Française* ('French Republic').

'RFI', 'R.F.I.' Marks used on small-arms and stores

made by the Royal Indian Small Arms Factory in Ishapore (now the Indian Government Rifle Factory, Ishapur).

'RG', 'rG', 'rg' – 1. Often encircled, cursive or (more recently) squared. Used by *Röhm-Gesellschaft on an assortment of cartridge- and blank-firing pistols. **2.** 'RG', stylised, beneath a displayed eagle. A mark associated with Armi Renato *Gamba SpA of Gardone Val Trompia, Italy. Found on handguns, including Mauser-*Parabellums, and a wide variety of sporting guns. *See also* 'Gr rG'.

'RH', 'R.H.', 'R-H', 'R&H' – 1. A superimposition-type monogram with both letters equally dominant. Correctly 'H&R' (q.v.); associated with *Harrington & Richardson. **2.** As 'RH' or 'R-H'; a mark used by *Vereinigte Köln-Rottweiler Pulverfabriken on propellant and shotgun cartridges made in Germany.

'R.H.A. Co.' A *headstamp said to have been associated with the products of the *Robin Hood Ammunition Company of Swanton, Vermont, USA. *See also* 'RHCC'.

'RHB'. Found on US military firearms and accessories. *See* Robert H. *Bailey.

'RHCC', 'RHCCo.' *Headstamps said to have been used by the *Robin Hood Cartridge Company of Swanton, Vermont.

Rheinische... – 1. Rheinische Metallwa[a]ren- und Maschinenfabrik (RM&M), Sömmerda, Thüringen, Germany. Founded in April 1889 to exploit patents granted to Heinrich Ehrhardt of Düsseldorf, an inventor of artillery and gun carriages, this company also made 6.35mm, 7.65mm and 9mm *Dreyse semi-automatic pistols prior to 1914; the name was used after the purchase of the moribund Dreyse gunmaking business in 1901. By 1918, RM&M had risen to become second only to Krupp among German munitions makers, and had made *Dreyse and *Maxim machine-guns alongside field guns and naval artillery. Restricted by the Treaty of Versailles to the manufacture of guns with calibres no greater than 17cm, RM&M changed its trading style to Rheinmetall AG in 1926, then amalgamated in 1935 with A. Borsig Maschinenbau AG of Berlin, a leading steam-locomotive and vehicle manufacturer. This resulted in Rheinmetall Borsig, a conglomerate that lasted until the end of the Second World War. **2.** Rheinische Waffen- und Munitionsfabriken (RWM), Köln, Germany. The marks of this business have been reported on 6.35mm *Continental pistols, which undoubtedly were made in Spain. **3.** Rheinisch-Westfälische Sprengstoff AG (RWS), Köln, Durlach bei Karlsruhe, Stadeln bei Fürth and elsewhere. This German munitions maker was founded in Köln in 1886 by Emil Müller, who built a factory in Troisdorf shortly afterward. The ammunition-making business of Heinrich Utendörffer of Nürnberg was acquired in 1889, although it continued to trade autonomously until the 1920s. A new factory was erected in 1897 in Stadeln bei Fürth (Nürnberg). A controlling interest in RWS was acquired by IG Farben of Frankfurt in 1926, and the business was amalgamated with *Dynamit Nobel in 1931. The companies traded independently until 1945, but now RWS is simply a trademark used by Dynamit Nobel Troisdorf AG. RWS-made ammunition can be recognised by the presence of the 'RWS' mark; by 'N' or 'U' (often in shields), inherited from Utendörffer; by 'Sinoxid', which was a registered trademark for the non-corrosive primers; and by the wartime codes *'dnf', *'dnh' and *'nfx'.

Rheinmetall – 1. And Rheinmetall-Borsig AG. *See* Rheinische Metallwa[a]ren- & Maschinenfabrik. **2.** Rheinmetall Handelsgesellschaft mbH, Berlin W8, Friedrichstrasse 56/57, Germany. Listed in directories dating from the 1920s as a sales and promotion agency for weapons (including automatic rifles designed by Karl *Heinemann) produced by the *Rheinmetall organisation. **3.** Rheinmetall pistol. A simple 7.65mm *blowback semi-automatic, made in small numbers c. 1921–26 as a replacement for the *Dreyse. Superficially similar to the 1910-pattern FN-Browning, the Rheinmetall pistol had a fixed barrel and a slide that could be detached merely by unscrewing the rear section as the trigger was pressed.

'RHKW'. Found on US military firearms and accessories. *See* Robert H.K. *Whiteley.

Rhode Island Arms Company, Hope Valley, Rhode Island, USA. This gunmaking business was incorporated in April 1949 to make the over/under shotgun designed by Joseph A. *Morrone. Only about 475 guns had been made (including 100 built to New Model specification) when the company was liquidated in December 1953: 420 in 12-bore, fifty in 20-bore and a handful of samples in other chamberings.

Rhodes. Richard Rhodes, Hartford, Connecticut. This mechanic is believed to have worked for the Spencer Arms Company, the assignee of his patents. These were 299,264 of 27 May 1884, 299,282 of 27 May 1884, and 308,702 (jointly with C.M. *Spencer) of 2 September 1884.

Rhöner Sportwaffenfabrik GmbH, Obereisbach-Weisbach, Germany. Best known for a series of inexpensive single-shot bolt-action rifles and a range of interesting break-open rifles made in accordance with a patent granted to Ralph Krawczyc. Most of the guns are chambered for rimfire ammunition, although the break-open examples may be obtained in .222 Remington or 5.2x50R Vierling. An encircled 'SM' mark (Sport & Munition) is associated with Rhöner products. It has also been reported on the blank-firers and .22 rimfire pistols once sold by Rhöner, but made by *Röhm.

Rhulman. *See* Adam *Ruhlman.

'RIA', 'R.I.A.' Applied to US military stores, including .45 M1911A1 *Government Model pistols, refurbished by *Rock Island Arsenal.

Ribbed barrel. *See* Barrel rib.

Ribe, 104 rue Antoine-Durafour, Saint-Étienne, France. Listed in 1951 as a gunmaker.

Ribeyre, Saint-Étienne, France. Listed in 1933 as a gunmaker. Still trading during the early 1950s from 60 rue Mulatière.

Ribeyrolle(s). Co-designer of the *Chauchat machine-rifle with Chauchat and Sutter. *See also* Gladiator.

'RIC', 'R.I.C.' An abbreviation of 'Royal Irish Constabulary', found on British-made firearms, such as *Webley revolvers and *Martini-pattern carbines.

Rice. David Rice, an Ordnance Department inspector, accepted a variety of gun stocks. Usually marked 'DR', they date from the period c. 1835–63. *See also* US arms inspectors' marks.

Richard. Frank Richard, sometimes listed as Richards (apparently incorrectly), accepted single-shot .50-70 *Springfield-Allin rifles on behalf of the US Army. Dating from the early 1870s, they are identified by an 'FR' mark, which may be confused with those applied in the same era by Frederick ★Rodgers and Franklin ★Root. *See also* US arms inspectors' marks.

Richards – **1.** Charles Brinkerhoff Richards (1833–1919), a consulting engineer retained by ★Colt's Patent Fire Arms Manufacturing Company, of Hartford, Connecticut, was responsible for the Richards Conversion, protected by US Patent 117,461 of 25 July 1871 and applied during 1870–71 to a few thousand cap-lock Colt revolvers. On 19 September 1871, Richards was granted US Patent 119,048 to protect, among other things, the design of a revolver with counter-bored chambers to envelope the cartridge-case head. This feature was first seen on the ★Colt ★Patent House Pistol, but parts of the patent were also incorporated in the ★Single Action Army Model Colt. Subsequently Richards became Professor of Engineering at the Sheffield Scientific School, Yale University (1884–1909), and a renowned authority on ventilation. **2.** Harold Richards, an inspector employed by the Ordnance Department, accepted US military firearms made by ★Colt's Patent Fire Arms Manufacturing Company. Dating from the period 1940–41, they bore 'HR' marks. *See also* US arms inspectors' marks. **3.** 'W. Richards'. A name found on shotguns handled by the H. & D. ★Folsom Arms Company, possibly imported from Westley ★Richards & Company prior to the First World War. **4.** Westley Richards & Company Ltd. This company was formed in 1874, and a move to 178 Bond Street occurred in 1878. London directories also list other premises – probably offices – at 27 Laurence Pountney Lane, E.C., in the mid-1850s (sometimes listed as Laurence Pountney Street); 14 Ironmonger Lane, E.C., in 1876; 19 Gracechurch Street, E.C., in 1877–78; and Leadenhall Buildings, E.C., in 1884–89. Richards made self-cocking ★pepperboxes in the middle of the nineteenth century, and a wide variety of proprietary dropping-block and drop-barrel sporting guns. By 1900, the company was offering BSA-made ★Lee-Enfield rifles, even chambering a few sporting rifles of this pattern for the proprietary .303/375 Axite cartridge introduced about 1906. Considerably more powerful than the service .303, Axite ammunition tested the Lee-Enfield action to its limit. Then Westley Richards changed to the ★Mauser action, making large numbers of sporting rifles – from c. 1909 onward – for proprietary cartridges such as .318 Nitro Express and .425 Rimless Magnum. As the Second World War approached, Westley Richards modified 36,200 .303 No 3 ★Enfield rifles to Weedon Repair Standards (WRS) in the Bournbrook factory in the summer of 1939. Some Mark III★ and Mark IV ★Lewis Guns were created in 1940/41 from old parts, and Drill Purpose (D.P.) guns were returned to serviceable condition. Richards also reconditioned 4,170 .303 ★Hotchkiss Mark I and Mark I★ machine-guns in 1940. These may have borne the code 'M 268' instead of the company name. *See also* British military inspectors' marks and John ★Deeley. **5.** William Richards, Liverpool and Preston, Lancashire. The marks of this English provincial gunsmith have been reported on shotgun cartridges supplied by ★Eley Bros. and ★Kynoch Ltd prior to the First World War. These have borne brandnames such as 'The Castle', 'The Express', 'Grand Prix', 'The Killwell' and 'The Mark Down'. Richards is listed at 152, then 144 Dale Street, Liverpool, from 1851 until 1864 or later, but it is clear that he (or perhaps his son) was still working in the early

1900s. **6.** William Westley Richards, having begun his gunmaking operation in Birmingham, Warwickshire, in 1812, opened a shop at 170 New Bond Street, London, in 1826. His agent was William ★Bishop. Trading continued after the death of W.W. Richards in 1865, under the supervision of his son, Westley Richards, until the trading style '…& Co.' was adopted in 1872 on the retirement of 'Billy' Bishop. **7.** Richards and Richards-Mason Transfor-mations. The first of these was patented by C.B. Richards in 1871 and applied to cap-lock ★Colt revolvers. The conversion allowed the guns be loaded from the rear with rimmed cartridges. A fixed non-rotating disc, or Conversion Plate, containing a firing pin and a hinged loading gate, lay behind a short cylinder. An ejector rod was attached to the right side of the barrel. About 9,000 revolvers were converted, including nearly 1,200 for the US Army and a few hundred for the US Navy. The Richards-Mason Transformation was basically the Richards type fitted with an improved ejector patented by William ★Mason in 1872.

Richardson – **1.** George Richardson, Philadelphia, Pennsylvania. A partner in Richardson & Overman, maker of ★Gallager-patent carbines during the American Civil War, Richardson was responsible for two firearms tested by the US Army in 1865, one based on the 1855-pattern ★Springfield rifle-musket, and the other on the Gallager carbine. Made in accordance with US Patent 43,929 of August 1864, Gun No. 49 had a pivoting breech-block that moved up and forward; Gun No. 50 was a break-open pattern adapted to fire metallic-case ammunition. The principal claim to novelty was the use of a slot-and-double-pin system to lock the breech. **2.** George B. Richardson, Maidstone, Kent, England. A gunmaker known to have been working at 44 King Street in 1869. **3.** George M. Richardson, Dumfries. The marks of this Scottish gun dealer have been reported on shotgun cartridges bearing the tradenames 'Buccleuch' and 'Ideal'. These seem to have been the work of ★Eley-Kynoch. **4.** William A. Richardson (1833–98), Worcester, Massachusetts. The partner of Gilbert Harrington in ★Harrington & Richardson. **5.** William G. Richardson, Barnard Castle, County Durham. The marks of this gunsmithing business, also known for the supply of sporting goods and fishing tackle, have been reported on sporting guns and ammunition. These have included a variety of shotgun cartridges labelled 'The Baliol', 'The Barnite' and 'The Barnoid'. Most cases also bear a trademark in the form of the arms of Barnard Castle: a splayed-arm 'cross formy' with a crescent and an *estoile* (star of heaven) in its upper quarters. **6.** Richardson & Company, Dunfermline, Fifeshire, Scotland. A gunsmithing and ironmongery business known to have distributed 12-bore shotgun cartridges marked 'Crieffel'. It is assumed that they were British-made, perhaps by ★Eley Bros. or ★Eley-Kynoch, but dating is uncertain and nothing else is known. **7.** Richardson & Overman, Philadelphia, Pennsylvania, USA. This gunmaker was active during the American Civil War, being best known for the ★Gallager breech-loading carbine (1861–65). **8.** *See also* Fifield & Richardson.

Richter. Found as 'Charles Richter' on shotguns made in the USA by the ★Crescent Arms Company; possibly a distributor's name.

Rickard Arms Company. A brandname associated

with shotguns manufactured prior to the First World War by the *Crescent Arms Company of Norwich, Connecticut, USA.

Rider. Joseph Rider, Newark, Ohio. Rider is best known for the *Rolling Block breech, successfully promoted in the 1860s and 1870s by E. *Remington & Sons of Ilion. An experimental external-hammer version of the radial-block breech system, known as Gun No. 57, was tested by the US Army in 1865/66. Gun No. 67 was essentially similar, but its hammer was mounted centrally. Protected by US Patent no. 45,797 of January 1865, the rolling-block design was far superior to the *Split-breech Geiger pattern. Patentee of 'revolving firearms' on 17 August 1858 (21,215) and 3 May 1859 (23,861), Rider was also responsible for a magazine pistol protected by US Patent 118,152 of 15 August 1871, exploited by E. Remington & Sons as the 'Magazine Repeating Pistol'. *See* Remington pistols.

Ridley. Thomas Ridley, a gunmaker, was trading from 45 Long Acre, London, in 1841, and 22 Russell Court, Drury Lane, in 1861–62.

Riedinger. Werkstätte L.A. Riedinger, Nürnberg, Bavaria. A maker of 6,000 actions for the *Podewils-Lindner-Braunmühl rifle in 1867–68. The guns were assembled in the *Amberg manufactory.

Rifling. *See* panel, below.

Riga. A. Riga, Liège, Belgium. A gunsmith, or possibly simply a distributor, and a promoter of the Executioner, Indispensable, Perforator and Rivalless revolvers prior to 1914.

Rigarmi. *See* Rino *Galesi.

Rigby – 1. John Rigby was a gunmaker/engineer and partner in John Rigby & Company. Originally hailing from Dublin, where his grandfather, father and uncles had worked since 1770, Rigby moved to London in 1867 and established a shop at 72 St James's Street. Additional premises at 1 & 2 Ham Yard were used from 1894. John Rigby is best remembered for his controversial tenure of the superintendency of the *Royal Small Arms Factory, Enfield, between 1889 and 1895, and for improvements in the *Lee-Metford and *Lee-Enfield rifles patented in his own name. He obtained British

RIFLING

This provides the means by which spin is imparted to a bullet before it emerges from the muzzle. In general, rifling comprises grooves separated by lands, although the details vary appreciably; some early guns (e.g. the US .45 M1873 Springfield) have three grooves, while others (such as modern Marlins) may have twenty or more.

Concentric rifling has its grooves and lands cut on the basis of concentric circles. Polygonal rifling is formed of several equal sides and has no obvious grooves. British Metford-type polygonal rifling was seven-sided (heptagonal), although the British Whitworth and Danish

Rasmussen patterns were six-sided (hexagonal). Some modern forms of 'squared-circle' rifling (e.g. Heckler & Koch's) are also classifiable as polygonal. Ratchet rifling is little more than a series of stepped arcs, being known as reverse ratchet if it opposes the direction of twist. Patterns that fit none of these categories are often classed as composite rifling, although the term covers a multitude of different styles.

The direction of twist, when viewed from the breech to the muzzle, may be left (anti- or counter-clockwise) or right (clockwise). Pitch describes the rate at which the rifling turns about the axis of the bore: fast pitch turns very rapidly, while slow-pitch

barrels have rifling that turns so gradually that, in extreme cases, it may appear to be straight. Progressive rifling (often known simply as gain-twist) starts with a slow spiral, then quickens toward the muzzle; progressive-depth rifling is usually deeper at the breech than at the muzzle.

A comparison between Metford (left) and Enfield (right) rifling, as used in British .303 rifles. The angular Enfield pattern replaced the polygonal Metford type, which proved to wear too rapidly when used with smokeless propellant.

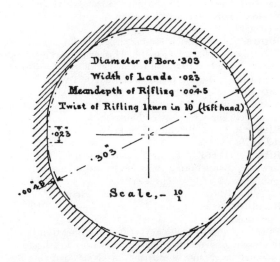

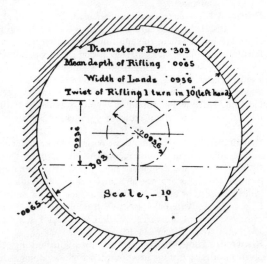

Patent 16,321/88 of 10 November 1888, protecting the nose-cap and bayonet-bar assembly of the Lee-Metford rifle. Rigby proved to be a fine teacher and an excellent organiser, but his lack of military experience dogged his time as superintendant of the Enfield factory. John Rigby & Company offered *Mauser-action rifles chambered for cartridges ranging from the .275 Rimless of 1907 to the .416 Rigby pattern of 1911. Pre-1914 guns usually incorporated actions bought directly from the Mauser factory in Oberndorf, but later examples showed greater diversity. Working from 43 Sackville Street, London W1, and 32 King Street, St James's, London SW1, in the period between the wars, Rigby handled shotgun ammunition made by *Eley-Kynoch. Some cases displayed 'Rigby's Record Cartridge', but few other tradenames seem to have been used. Rigby also reconditioned 150 .303 *Hotchkiss Mark I and Mark I* machine-guns for service in Britain in 1940. After the fighting had ceased, the company re-established itself with *Mauser-action sporting rifles built either on refurbished military-surplus or on new actions purchased from *Fabrique Nationale and others. English-style stocks remained popular, with *Express sights and a swivel eye carried on a collar around the barrel. 2. William & John Rigby, 24 Suffolk Street, Dublin, Ireland. These gunmakers exhibited self-cocking *pepperboxes at the Great Exhibition held in London in 1851. 3. Rigby Model, or No. 6½ Rigby: a US *Ballard rifle. See Off Hand Model. 4. Rigby Model. A bolt-action rifle made in the USA by *Dakota Arms. Introduced in 1990, it had an enlarged action to handle cartridges ranging from .404 Jeffrey to .450 Dakota, while the stock had been deepened to accept a four-round magazine. Weight could reach 10lb with the standard 24in heavyweight barrel.

Rigdon & Ansley, Augusta, Georgia, Confederate States of America. The maker of *Leech & Rigdon-type revolvers during 1864–65.

Riggs. Charles Riggs & Company. The marks of this gunmaking business, trading from 107 Bishopsgate, London E.C., have been reported on 12-bore shotgun cartridges made by *Eley Bros. prior to 1914 and sold as The Bishop among other names. The address was often rendered as 'Ye Bishop's Gate', which has also been listed as a tradename.

Riker. A *Suicide Special revolver made by J. *Rupertus Patent Pistol Manufacturing Company of Philadelphia, Pennsylvania, USA, in the late nineteenth century.

Riley – 1. A gunmaker's mark reported on an English self-cocking *pepperbox dating from the middle of the nineteenth century. 2. J.F. Riley, active c. 1897–1910, accepted guns and accessories on behalf of the US armed forces. His 'JFR' mark will be found on revolvers made by *Colt's Patent Fire Arms Manufacturing Company. See also US arms inspectors' marks. 3. Robert Riley, Green Lane, Walsall, Staffordshire. This 'Boot & Shoe Maker', according to the specifications accompanying British Patent 17,731/04 of 1904, designed a bell target that automatically displayed the scores for all scoring rings. 4. William S. Riley. A member of the London gun trade operating from Eagle Works, Vauxhall Street, Birmingham (1874), and from 63 Bishopsgate Street Within, London E.C., from 1878 until 1887. 5. See also Reilly.

Rimfire. These *cartridges are distinguished by the position of the priming compound, which occupies a thin annulus formed inside the case-rim. Introduced commercially in the USA early in 1858, by *Smith & Wesson, the original .22 (subsequently known as the .22 Short) was soon joined by a wide variety of rimfire rounds as large as .58. However, the method of priming restricted the size and power, so the rimfire was speedily replaced by *centre-fire patterns for all but .22 applications.

Rimington-Wilson. R.M.R. Rimington-Wilson designed a special folding-butt mechanism for the *Lee-Enfield rifle, protected by British Patent 25,483/99 of 23 December 1899.

Rimless, or rimmed, case. See Cartridge case.

Ringold. Cadwalder Ringold, or 'Ringgold', a captain in the US Navy, accepted firearms and equipment on behalf of the Navy Bureau of Ordnance between 1828 and 1862. The guns were marked 'CR'. See also US arms inspectors' marks.

Ringwood. Arthur E. Ringwood, a gunmaker of Banbury, Oxfordshire, England, marked sporting guns and ammunition, including shotgun cartridges made by *Eley-Kynoch for distribution under such names as The Dreadnought, The Ideal and The Special.

Ripley – 1. Ezra Ripley, Troy, New York State. Patentee of the multi-barrel Battery Gun that bore his name: US no. 33,544 of October 1861. 2. James Wolfe Ripley. Best known as an ultra-conservative Chief of Ordnance, Ripley was born in Connecticut in 1794 and was commissioned into the artillery in 1814. Commandant of the National Armory, *Springfield, between 1841 and 1854, he oversaw the introduction of the rifle-musket into the US Army and was serving as Inspector of Arsenals when the American Civil War began. Blinkered by prejudice against breech-loading, 'Old Fogey' Ripley's tenure as Chief of Ordnance ended in 1863; he retired in 1869, as a brigadier-general, and died a year later. His 'JWR' marks will be found on equipment dating from the period 1833–54, and can be distinguished by date from a similar identifier used by Major James W. *Reilly. See also US arms inspectors' marks. 3. Ripley Battery Gun. Made in very small quantities during the opening months of the American Civil War (1861–65), this bore a considerable external resemblance to the Gatling, although its barrels were fixed. The detachable breech-block was loaded with standard .58-calibre combustible cartridges, which could be fired singly or as a volley by turning the crank-handle attached to the cascabel.

Ripperger. Friedrich Ripperger, Albrechts bei Suhl in Thüringen, Zellaer Strasse 14. This metalworking business was listed in 1940–41 as a maker of gun parts; trading ceased at the end of the Second World War.

Rip Rap. Associated with a *Suicide Special revolver made in the USA in the 1880s by the *Bacon Manufacturing Company of Norwich, Connecticut.

Rissack, Liège, Belgium. A maker of revolvers active in the 1870s.

Ritz – 1. Hugo Ritz, Zella-Mehlis in Thüringen, Germany. Listed during 1920–39 as a master gunsmith and gunmaker. 2. Otto Ritz, Zella-Mehlis in Thüringen. Listed in 1930 as a maker of guns and weapons.

Rivailler, Saint-Étienne, France. Listed during 1933 as a gunmaker.

Rival – 1. Also known as Carabine à Répétition Rival, this was based on the *Daudetau action and made by Manufacture Française d'Armes et Cycles de Saint-Étienne between the world wars. Most guns retained the standard military-style action, with the bolt handle turned downward ahead of the receiver bridge and a projecting flat-sided magazine case formed integrally with the trigger-guard bow. The one-piece stock had chequering on the shallow pistol grip and elongated fore-end; sights varied from a conventional folding three-leaf design sharing a common pivot to *Express patterns with separate pivots for each leaf. **2.** A sporting rifle built by Manufacture Française d'Armes et Cycles on the basis of refurbished wartime German Mauser actions, the charger guides being removed and the cut-away in the receiver-side filled. Chamberings included 10.75x68 and .375 H&H Magnum. The guns were about 1115mm overall and weighed 3.6kg. The half-stocks usually had straight-comb butts and rounded fore-ends; *Express sights were common. **3.** A compact Browning-type semi-automatic pistol made in Spain by Fábrica de Armas *'Union' of Eibar: 6.35mm, six rounds. **4.** *See also* New Rival.

Rivalless. A name associated with a revolver sold in Belgium prior to 1914 by A. *Riga.

Riviere. Henry Riviere. London directories suggest that this member of the gun trade (1833–93), son of the con-cealed-gun-lock patentee Isaac Riviere (1781–1851), began work from 2 Davies Street, Berkeley Square, short-ly after his father's death. He moved to 8 Queen's Road, Bayswater, in 1860; to 19 Queen's Road in 1862; and to 41 Queen's Road in 1866. Riviere's marks have been found on self-cocking *pepperboxes dating from the mid-dle of the nineteenth century. He was also the co-paten-tee with F.T. *Baker of a cartridge loader, protected by British Patent 1865/69 of 1869.

Rivoire jeune, place Villeboeuf 2, Saint-Étienne, France. Listed in 1879 as a gunmaker.

Rivollier et Blanc, rue Villedieu 9, Saint-Étienne, France. Listed in 1879 as a gunmaker, and in 1892 and 1933 as Rivollier père et fils. Usually recorded as 'Rivolier' in post-1900 directories. Still trading in 1951, from 21 rue César-Bertholon. This business made *Giffard gas-powered rifles until about 1887, when pro-duction was switched to *Manufacture Française d'Armes et Cycles. Shotguns were made between 1928 and 1939.

'rln'. Reportedly used in 1945 by Carl *Zeiss of Jena on optical equipment made for the German armed forces.

'RM', 'R.M.' – 1. A mark used during the Second World War by the British Royal Ordnance factory in *Maltby. **2.** With an anchor, often encircled. A mark associated with the Italian Royal Navy (*Regia Marina*), found on the grips of *Beretta pistols and other stores. **3.** Found on Mexican military firearms. An abbreviated form of *República Mexicana*; alternatively, 'R. de. M.' (q.v.). **4.** Found on US military firearms and accessories. *See* R. *Matthews.

'R.M.C.' A mark found on cartridges made in the Union of South Africa by the Roden Manufacturing Company.

'RMF'. A part-linear part-superimposition monogram, with 'M' dominant. Found on *Dreyse pistols, rifles and machine-guns made in Sömmerda prior to 1918 by *Rheinische Metallwaaren- u. Maschinenfabrik.

'RMH'. Found on US military firearms and accessories. *See* R.M. *Hill.

'RM&M', 'R.M. & M.' *See* Rheinische Metallwaaren- u. Maschinenfabrik.

'RNS'. Found on US military firearms and accessories. *See* R.N. *Stannard.

Robar et Cie. *See* Manufacture Liégeoise d'Armes à Feu.

Robbins – 1. Robbins & Lawrence, Windsor, Vermont, USA. Successors in 1848 to Robbins, Kendall & Lawrence, this gunmaking business continued to make 1841-pattern cap-lock rifles for the US government. The partners were also responsible for the *Jennings magazine rifle and *Leonard pepperboxes, but the business col-lapsed in 1854 after a disastrous foray into railway stock-car building. Richard *Lawrence had already left (in 1852) to become 'Master Armorer' of the *Sharps Rifle Manufacturing Company. **2.** Robbins, Kendall & Lawrence, Windsor, Vermont. A partnership of Samuel E. Robbins, Nicanor Kendall (1807–61) and Richard S. Lawrence, this gunmaking business was formed in 1844. A contract was signed with the US government for the manufacture of 10,000 1841-pattern *cap-lock rifles, but Kendall withdrew in 1848, and Robbins & Lawrence (above) was formed.

Robert – 1. Rue Roanelle 12, Saint-Étienne, France. Listed in 1892 as a gunmaker. **2.** Auguste Robert. Frenchman Auguste Robert designed one of the earliest breech-loading rifles to chamber a metallic-case cartridge, although the quirky 16mm-calibre tube-fire pattern was unsuccessful. The rifle was based on the Pauly of 1812, with a breech-block that opened on trunnions alongside the chamber as its handle was lifted. This automatically extracted the remnants of the cartridge and cocked the internal hammer. Tested unenthusiastically by the French Army in 1833, Robert guns were made thereafter only in sporting guise; work had come to an end by 1840.

Roberts – 1. Benjamin Roberts and the Roberts Breech-Loading Rifle Company, New York City. A breech-loading conversion of a Springfield rifle-musket, patented in February 1866 by Brevet Brigadier-General Benjamin Roberts, was tested by the US Army in 1867. The breech-block swung upward around a pivot above the chamber once a catch that locked into the floor plate had been released by pulling up on a small eared latch on top of the breech, behind the external hammer. The rifle was rejected by the US Army and the US Navy, but Roberts had powerful friends, and a .50-70 rifle was still being tried in 1872. A few guns were acquired by the New York State militia, but only Serbia used Roberts conver-sions in quantity. Most of the guns were made by the *Providence Tool Company. **2.** Edgar Roberts. The marks of this English gunmaker, based in Birmingham, have been reported on breech-loading shotguns and spring-airguns, including *Millita-type Langenhans. Trade directories record Roberts at 5 Steelhouse Lane in 1897, but it is evident from the airguns that trading continued into the twentieth century. **3.** George Roberts, the Younger. A gunmaker listed in London at 17 Great Chapel Street, Oxford Street, in 1856–58. Subsequently he moved to 6 Crown Street, Soho, remaining there as a 'gun-barrel browner' until 1875. Probably the nephew of John Roberts (below). **4.** John Roberts, a gunmaker, was listed during 1852–68 at 6 Little Chapel Street, Soho. Probably the uncle of George Roberts (above). **5.** William Henry Roberts was employed by the Federal government during the American Civil War. His 'WHR' marks have been found on .44-calibre *Colt army revolvers dating from 1863, which distinguishes them from contempory stampings applied to equipment by William H. *Russell. *See also* US arms inspectors' marks. **6.** Roberts & Company, Ottery St Mary, Devon, England. The marks of this business, believed to be an ironmonger, have been reported on shotgun cartridges distributed as The Ottervale. Their origins and date are uncertain.

Robertson – **1.** Alexander Robertson & Son, Wick, Caithness. The marks of this gunsmithing and ironmongery business, operating at the northern tip of Scotland, have been found on cartridges supplied by *Eley Bros. prior to the First World War. **2.** John Robertson, Haddington, Scotland. An exhibitor at the Great Exhibition held in London in 1851, Robertson displayed an assortment of firearms 'fitted with Captain Davidson's Patented Telescopic Sights'. Possibly the same person as the next entry. **3.** John Robertson, a member of the London gun trade, occupied premises at 101 Great Titchfield Street during 1874–79. Then he moved to 4 Dansey Yard, Wardour Street (1887–89), and was at 1 & 2 Ham Yard, West London, by 1900. The Ham Yard address suggests that Robertson may have been working for John Rigby & Company. A 'John Robertson, London, England' received US Patents 582,094 of 4 May 1897 and 756,896 of 12 April 1904 for drop-barrel sporting guns. **4.** William Robertson, New London, Connecticut. Co-patentee with George *Simpson of a breech-loading carbine tested by the US Army in 1866. **5.** Robertson & Simpson carbine. Patented in the USA in March 1866 (no. 53,187) by William Robertson and George Simpson, apparently this gun was made in *Springfield Armory and incorporated several original Sharps components. Internally, however, it was locked by a radial block mechanism controlled by an underlever. A sling ring and bar assembly was fixed to the left side of the butt, above the trigger and underlever catch. At least one gun was made for the US Army trials of 1865/66, and others may have been tried elsewhere.

Robin Hood... – **1.** Robin Hood Ammunition Company, Swanton, Vermont, USA. Possibly a short-lived successor to the Robin Hood Cartridge Company (below), marking its products with 'R.H.A. Co.', this business traded independently until purchased in 1916 by the *Remington Arms Company. Work then ceased. **2.** Robin Hood Cartridge Company, Swanton, Vermont. Active immediately prior to the First World War, this ammunition maker was responsible for a variety of shotgun cartridges sold under the brandnames Autocrat, Capital, Clipper, Comet, Crescent, Eclipse, Indian and Robin Hood; .22 rimfire, and .32 and .38 centrefire rounds were also made. The *headstamp was customarily 'R', although 'RHCC' has been reported.

Robinson – **1.** Edward Robinson, New York City. Best known for 30,000 1861-pattern Springfield rifle-muskets produced under contract to the Federal government in 1863–65, during the American Civil War, this gunmaker also promoted the breech-loading rifle patented in 1864 by William Cleveland *Hicks. **2.** H. Robinson, Bridlington, Yorkshire. The marks of this gunsmith or ironmonger, trading from 102 High Street, have been found on *Eley-Kynoch shotgun cartridges overprinted 'Burlington Cartridge' and 'Burlington Express'. **3.** H. Robinson, Bridgnorth, Shropshire. Gunsmith, ironmonger and bicycle maker, often listed as H. Robinson & Company, this business distributed 'The Castle' shotgun

cartridges. These were made by *Eley-Kynoch between the world wars. Most seem to have borne an illustration of a pheasant, but others may have featured the distinctive Leaning Tower of Bridgnorth Castle. **4.** M.W. Robinson & Company. A leading distributor of guns and ammunition in the post-American Civil War period. **5.** Orvil Robinson, Upper Jay, New York State. Patentee of magazine rifles made in accordance with US Patent 103,504, granted in May 1870. An improved design was patented in 1872. **6.** R. Robinson, Hull, Yorkshire. This gunmaker marked shotgun ammunition loaded in the Queen Street premises from components supplied by *Eley-Kynoch. Individual examples may be marked 'The Humber', 'The Kingston', 'The Kingston Smokeless' or 'The Magnet'. **7.** Robinson rifles. A few hundred of these were made to the designs of Orvil Robinson (above) by A.S. *Babbitt and the *Adirondack Fire Arms Company of Plattsburgh, New York State, in 1870–74. The 1870-patent breech was opened by pressing inward on the prominent ears above the hammer and pulling them backward. This pivoted the rear face of the locking strut out of the receiver floor and retracted the breech-bolt to eject a spent case. Then a new cartridge rose on the carrier-block, to be pushed forward into the chamber as the breech was closed. The rifle had a brass frame, an octagonal barrel, a half-length magazine tube and a spurred trigger guard. The action was very rapid, although a lack of primary extraction may have proved troublesome with poor ammunition. An improved, or 1872-patent, rifle relied on toggle-like construction with a 'breech-bolt brace' and a linking strut to open the breech-bolt. Undoubtedly a few prototypes were made, but series production by the Adirondack Fire Arms Company had only just begun when rights were sold to Winchester in 1874.

Robitaille. Charles Robitaille was the co-patentee with Edward *Raymond of a simplification of the *Pettengill revolver made by *Rogers & Spencer. This was protected by US Patent 21,054 granted in July 1858.

Rob Roy. A *Suicide Special revolver made in the USA by the *Hood Firearms Company of Norwich, Connecticut, in the 1880s.

Robust. A double-barrelled hammerless side-by-side shotgun made in 12- and 16-bore by *Manufacture Française d'Armes et Cycles. It had a simple box-lock, which was locked by a rotary spur on the top-lever entering a slot in the semi-doll's-head forged integrally with the barrel-block. There was a sliding safety catch on top of the tang; the internal hammers were cocked automatically, although ejectors were optional. The choice of engraving was left to the purchaser, but ranged from simple scrolls to high-relief chiselling. *See also* Supra-Robust.

Rochester – **1.** A brandname found on pneumatic rifles made by the *Kessler Company between 1948 and 1955, and sold by Klein's of Chicago. **2.** Rochester Defense Corporation, Rochester, New York. Formed by *National Postal Meter and others in 1942 to make *M1 Carbines. Eventually these were produced under the NPM name.

Rochetin jeune, Saint-Étienne, France. Listed in 1879 as a maker, distributor and agent for gun parts and accessories. Listed in 1892 simply as 'Rochetin', at rue d'Annonay 32.

Rochussen & Company. This wholesaler acted as a gunmakers' agent, being retained in 1858–61 by Prosper

*Malherbe of Liège. London directories record the premises as 13 Great St Thomas Apostle and 75 Cannon Street in 1858–60, and 114 Fenchurch Street in 1861. The company was succeeded by *Heintzmann & Rochussen in the early 1860s.

Rock, Rock… – **1.** Denis T. Rock & Company. Listed in London in 1871–72 at 46 Leadenhall Street, this business was probably a merchant of some type. **2.** Rock Island Arsenal, Rock Island, Illinois. Founded in 1843 to make gun carriages and limbers, this ordnance factory, occupying 896 acres in 1939, had diversified by the early 1900s into small-arms, then eventually into tanks and armoured vehicles. Its products included a variety of *Springfield rifles prior to 1920, identified by the inclusion of 'R.I.A.' in their markings. **3.** Rock-Ola Company, Chicago, Illinois. A maker of about 229,000 *M1 Carbines (and a huge quantity of barrels), 1942–44.

Rocket – **1.** Or Super Rocket. This name was applied by the *Benjamin Rifle Company of St. Louis, Missouri, USA, to a gas-powered pistol. **2.** Rocket Balls. A name given to the self-propelled Volition Ball patented in 1847 by Walter *Hunt for use in his tube-magazine repeating rifle.

'Rocketer' [The]. A mark associated with shotgun ammunition said to have incorporated a trace element to allow aim to be corrected. It will be found with a variety of dealers' names, including *Grant & Lang of London, and *Palmer, Sons & Company of Barnet. The cartridges were headstamped 'KB' (*Kynoch, Birmingham) and date immediately prior to the First World War.

Rockwell. James Rockwell, Jr, a lieutenant in the US Army, accepted military firearms and accessories in the mid-1870s. They included the .44 Smith & Wesson *Schofield-pattern revolvers marked 'JRJR'. *See also* US arms inspectors' marks.

Rocky Mountain Sight. *See* Sights.

Rocroy. Fernand Rocroy, Roanne, Département Loire, France. This engineer designed a pneumatic rifle, protected by British Patent 254,976 of 1925.

Rodda. R.B. Rodda, Birmingham, Warwickshire, and Calcutta. Best known for its exploits in India, this gun-making/distributing business marked a variety of cartridges, including shotgun ammunition usually made in Birmingham by *Kynoch. Examples marked 'Paragon', 'Rotax Ball Cartridge' and 'The Wellesley' have all been found.

Rodgers – **1.** Frederick Rodgers, a commander in the US Navy, is said to have accepted 1875-pattern *Remington cartridge revolvers in the mid-1870s. Identified by an 'FR' mark, the guns may be confused with those approved in the same era by Frank *Richard and Franklin *Root. **2.** George W. Rodgers, a commander in the US Navy, accepted firearms and accessories during 1839–58. They included the .36-calibre cap-lock revolvers, made by *Colt's Patent Fire Arms Manufacturing Company, that bore 'GWR' identifiers. *See also* US arms inspectors' marks for this and the previous entry. **3.** Joseph Rodgers [& Sons]. Successor to *Unwin & Rodgers, possibly in 1867, this cutlery manufacturer continued to make knife pistols. These were often marked simply with a distinctive trademark in the form of a six-pointed linear star and a cross *patée*. Joseph Rodgers also sometimes simply used 'Acme', 'Meteor', 'Star and Cross' (or the German-language version,

'Sternenkreuz'), the misleading 'U★S', or '6 Norfolk Street, Sheffield' instead of his name. The trading style became '…& Sons' about 1888. **4.** *See also* Rogers.

Rodier. Louis Rodier, Springfield, Massachusetts, USA. Recipient on 11 July 1865 of US Patent 48,775, protecting a ratchet that was integral with the extractor for rotating the cylinder. Initially assigned to Samuel Morris (*sic*), rights were acquired subsequently by *Smith & Wesson.

Rodman. Thomas Rodman. Co-designer, with Silas *Crispin, of a metallic-case cartridge patented in December 1863. This was assigned to *Poultney & Trimble, and subsequently made during the American Civil War as Poultney's Patent Metallic Cartridge.

Roe – **1.** Ernest S. Roe of Plymouth, Michigan, was employed by the *Markham Air Rifle Company, for whom he designed several *BB Guns. His US Patents included 911,056 of 2 February 1909, granted jointly with William Filmore *Markham, for an improved hinged-butt-cocking airgun. US Patent 1,062,855 of 27 May 1913 protected a lever-action design; 1,250,304 of 18 December 1917 (with William B. *Greenleaf) protected a break-open BB Gun; and 1,268,238 of 4 June 1918 (also with Greenleaf) allowed claims for improvements in BB Gun design. **2.** Francis A. Roe, a lieutenant in the US Navy, accepted cap-lock .44 Army-type revolvers made by *Colt's Patent Fire Arms Manufacturing Company. Dating from the American Civil War (1861–65), they were identified by 'FAR' in a cartouche. *See also* US arms inspectors' marks.

Roebuck – **1.** An Austrian *Mauser-pattern sporting rifle, the work of Karl *Dschulnigg of Salzburg in the 1960s. Essentially similar to the *Ram, it had a spatulate bolt handle. **2.** A brandname used in the USA by *Sears, Roebuck & Company.

Roedich. A registered trademark associated with shotgun cartridges sold by Charles *Rosson of Derby and Charles S. *Rosson of Norwich.

'ROF', 'R.O.F.' *See* Royal Ordnance Factories.

Rofe. Henry James Rofe, 'Sportsmans' Outfitter' of 93 Piccadilly, Manchester, was granted British Patent 109,309 in 1916. This protected a breech-loading air rifle that shared the lines of the *SMLE.

'ROF [F]', 'ROF[M]'. Used during the Second World War by the British Royal Ordnance factories in Fazakerley and Maltby.

Roger. This name has been reported on a gas-powered pistol distributed in the USA during the early 1970s by *Precise Imports Corporation. It is believed to have been made in Italy by Modesto *Molgora (Mondial) as the Roger 007.

Rogers – **1.** Charles F. Rogers, a civilian employee of the US Ordnance Department using the identifier 'CFR', accepted .45 M1911A1 Colt-*Browning pistols and other military firearms made by *Colt's Patent Fire Arms Manufacturing Company during the First World War. *See also* US arms inspectors' marks. **2.** Francis Heron Rogers, an agent with chambers in Bridge House, 181 Queen Victoria Street, London E.C.4, obtained British Patent 380,036 for Ulrich *Boecker. **3.** J.F. Rogers, a member of the London gun trade, was listed at 20 High Holborn, W.C., in 1887–88. **4.** Leo Rogers. Patentee of the Rogers knife pistol (below). **5.** T.H. Rogers, a civilian inspector attached to the Ordnance Department and using the identifier 'THR', accepted firearms and equipment on behalf of the US Army. His activities seem to have been confined to 1896–1905. *See also* US arms inspectors' marks. **6.** William Rogers. A gunsmith listed in 1891 at 3 Waterloo Road, London S.E. Possibly the 14-year-old apprentice listed in the 1841 census in Doris Street, Lambeth. **7.** Rogers knife pistol. Patented in the USA in February 1916 by Leo Rogers, this was basically a penknife, divided longitudinally into two compartments. One contained a brace of folding blades; the other held the striker, its spring, the trigger mechanism and a minuscule barrel containing a single .22 Short rimfire cartridge, which was fired by a latch in the right grip. The barrel-block could be pivoted to load and eject. **8.** Rogers & Spencer, Willowvale, New York State. This US gunmaking business made the *Pettengill revolver, as improved in 1858 by Thomas *Austin and *Raymond & Robitaille. A Federal contract for 5,000 .44 Pettengills was gained in December 1861, the design being a simple enlargement of the .34-calibre Navy model, but the first deliveries were rejected. A trigger patented by Henry Rogers in November 1862 had soon been substituted for the original cam type, and 2,000 guns had been accepted by January 1863. Then acquisition of the contract previously placed for *Freeman revolvers allowed Rogers & Spencer to design a .36-calibre revolver of its own – albeit using many old Pettengill parts. It had a characteristic shoulderless butt. Interestingly, a replica of this odd-looking revolver has been made in Germany in recent years by *Feinwerkbau Westinger & Altenburger of Oberndorf. **9.** *See also* Rodgers.

Rogerson & Andrews, Eton, Berkshire. The marks of this gunmaking business have been reported on English self-cocking *pepperboxes dating from the 1850s.

Röhm – **1.** Röhm-Gesellschaft, Zella-Mehlis in Thüringen, Germany. Listed in 1920 as an engineering workshop. However, the production of semi-automatic pistols began shortly afterward and soon became the principal business. Trading ceased in 1945. **2.** Röhm GmbH, Sontheim an der Brenz, Germany. A reconstitution of the pre-war business in western Germany, Röhm now makes inexpensive revolvers and starting pistols. Most have been given RG designators (e.g. RG-14, RG-66 Western-Revolver). The guns range from simple solid-frame swing-cylinder patterns to sturdy Peacemaker lookalikes chambering cartridges as powerful as .44 Magnum, .44 Special and .45 Long Colt. **3.** Röhm-Waffenhandels GmbH, Hermannsplatz, Berndorf, Niederösterreich. An Austrian wholesaler and distributor of many types of sporting guns, airguns and ammunition.

Röhmer – **1.** Röhmer & Companie, Suhler mech. Büchsenmacherei, Suhl in Thüringen, Germany. Listed as a gunmaking business operating in 1900, under the ownership of Jacob Röhmer. **2.** Röhmerwerk Waffenteilefabrik mbH, Suhl in Thüringen, Germany. Listed in the 1914–20 editions of the *Deutsches Reichs-Adressbuch* as a gun-part maker.

Röhner. Alfred Röhner, Suhl in Thüringen, Germany. Listed in directories for 1939 as a specialist gun-stocker.

Roland – **1.** A brandname associated with the airguns and special self-registering targets promoted by Friedrich Carl Tilgenkamp of Köln, c. 1909–28. *See also* Jung Roland. **2.** A 7.65mm-calibre Browning-type semi-automatic pistol made in Spain by Francisco *Arizmendi of Eibar, Guipúzcoa: six rounds, striker fired. **3.** D.-J. Roland, a self-promotional parish priest of Tournai in

Belgium, is credited with the design of the *Rapide shotgun and an assortment of accessories. Guns of this pattern were made in prototype form in Liège during the early 1880s, but never in the quantities Roland anticipated.

Rolfe-Martin. A.B. Rolfe-Martin. Inventor of the telescope-sight mounting system protected by a British Patent granted in February 1915 and assigned to the *Periscopic Prism Company of London.

Röll. Ernst Röll, Suhl in Thüringen. A German gunstocker, trading in Suhl in 1939.

Rolland & Renault, Liège. A Belgian gunmaking business, best known for a selection of *Lefaucheux-type pinfire, rimfire and centrefire revolvers made in the last quarter of the nineteenth century. It is believed to have superseded Henri Renault, active c. 1845–65.

Rolling-block breech. Copied by Whitney and others, this was developed from the Split-breech (q.v.) pattern credited to Leonard *Geiger and perfected largely by Joseph *Rider. Rolling blocks were opened by thumbing back the hammer to full-cock and pulling back on the finger spur of the breech-piece to give access to the chamber, partially extracting a spent case. After the gun had been reloaded and the breech-piece rotated forward to its closed position, a pull on the trigger dropped the hammer. As the hammer fell, shoulders ran forward under the breech-piece to direct the thrust generated back through the case-base (as the gun fired) so that the mechanism was locked in its closed position. *See also* Remington rifles, rolling-block action.

Rollins & Son. Suppliers of *Stevens and *Savage rifles and shotguns to the British authorities, 1941.

Rolls Razor Company Ltd, Cricklewood Broadway, London NW2. Maker of magazines for the British 9mm *Sten Gun during the Second World War. The regional code 'S 102' may have been used instead of the company name.

'Rome'. Found on a *Suicide Special revolver made by the Rome Revolver & Novelty Works of Rome, New York State, in the late nineteenth century.

Römer – **1.** Hans Römer, Suhl in Thüringen, Germany. Patentee of the Römer semi-automatic pistol. **2.** Römer pistol. Made in Suhl c. 1925–31 by Römerwerke, this blowback was the work of Hans Römer. It was distinguished by the ease with which the long barrel, chambered for .22 LR rimfire ammunition, could be switched for a short 6.35mm barrel, the change of barrel and magazine allowing an inexpensive target pistol to double as a personal-defence weapon. The guns are easily recognisable by the separate reciprocating breech-block/half-slide unit, and by the 'back-heavy' appearance owing to the slenderness of the frame and barrel shroud ahead of the grip. **3.** Römerwerke AG, Suhl, Thüringen, Germany. Manufacturer of the Römer pistols, believed to have been active until the great Depression of the early 1930s put paid to the need for cheap firearms.

Ronchard jeune, rue de l'Épreuve 2, Saint-Étienne, France. Listed in 1892 as a gunmaker.

Rongé. A. Rongé frères, Liège. A gunsmith working in Belgium between 1844 and 1914, renowned for sporting rifles and shotguns. Among the names applied to pre-1914 revolvers were 'Centennial', 'Centennial USA', 'Champion of the World', 'Imperator' and 'Simplex'.

Ronnebeck. Heinrich Richard Ronnebeck of 260 Marton Road, Middlesbrough, Yorkshire, was granted

British Patent 203,076 in 1922. This described a means of controlled dieselling in airguns. See also Barakuda.

Rooke. George Rooke succeeded an earlier gunsmithing business, William & Samuel Rooke, which had been founded in 1810 and had traded in Whittall Street, Birmingham, before moving to 15 Bath Street in 1821. Rooke operated alone from 1839 or 1840, until being superseded by Charles *Newton. Sporting guns, airguns and possibly air canes were among his products.

Rook Rifle. A generic term for any small-calibre rifle used for birding, although associated specifically with *Martini-action guns introduced in the 1880s.

Root – 1. Elisha King Root (1808–65) was the superintendent of the Hartford factory of *Colt's Patent Fire Arms Manufacturing Company, and patentee of the side-hammer Root Colt revolving rifles and revolvers. He was also a very talented engineer, responsible for the efficient way in which the Hartford factory made firearms. **2.** Franklin Root – believed to have been a son of Elisha K. Root – accepted firearms on behalf of the Federal Army during the American Civil War. Dating from c. 1862–63, they can be identified by 'FR' marks, although these can be confused with those applied in the same era by Frank *Richard and Frederick *Rodgers. See also US arms inspectors' marks. **3.** R.L. Root, Plymouth, Michigan, USA. A store owner in Plymouth from c. 1873 onward, Root and others founded the *Plymouth Iron Windmill Company in 1882. Later this became the *Daisy organisation. **4.** Root Colt, or Root Model. The perfected Model 1855 revolver-rifle and the .28- or .31-calibre five-chamber Model 1855 pocket revolver were developed by Elisha Root. The guns had solid frames, sheath triggers and cranked side hammers, which allowed the axis pin to enter the cylinder through the back of the frame.

Roper – 1. Francis Roper, 2 Silver Street, Halifax, Yorkshire. The marks of this English gunmaker have been reported on self-cocking *pepperboxes. These must date from about 1850, as the trading style became Roper & Edmunds in 1853. **2.** R. Roper [Son & Company], Sheffield, Yorkshire. The marks of this gunmaking business have been reported on a variety of ammunition made by *Eley Bros., *Kynoch Ltd and *Eley-Kynoch, including some shotgun cartridges marked 'The Hallamshire'. Premises were being occupied at 8 South Street and 9 Exchange Street in the 1930s. **3.** Sylvester H. Roper of Roxbury, Massachusetts, was a talented engineer whose interests encompassed sewing machines and hot-air engines in addition to firearms. He was granted US Patent 53,881 of 10 April 1866 to protect a shotgun with an unusual 'slam fire' bolt system and a revolving cylinder-type magazine. These were made by the *Roper Repeating Rifle Company, then by the Roper Sporting Arms Company. Most of the shotguns had a detachable choke protected by US Patent 79,861 of July 1868. Roper was also co-patentee with Christopher M. *Spencer of a slide-action shotgun, protected by US Patent 255,894 of 4 April 1882. Subsequently he produced an improved design, protected by US Patent 316,401 of 21 April 1885, and received two patents to protect 'magazine firearms' (409,429 of 20 August 1889 and 413,734 of 29 October 1889). **4.** Roper Repeating Rifle Company [The], Amherst and Roxbury, Massachusetts. This was formed in 1867 under the presidency of Henry Hills, whose Hills Palm Leaf Works undoubtedly made many of the components. The 'Agent'

of the new company was none other than Christopher Spencer, a close friend of Sylvester Roper. Initial production concentrated on shotguns; although it is thought that a few rifles were made in this period, exploitation was delayed until the Roper Sporting Arms Company had been formed in March 1869. **5.** Roper rifles. Only about 500 sporting rifles were made by the *Roper Sporting Arms Company during 1872–76. When the combination hammer/operating lever was thumbed back, the breech bolt was withdrawn from the cylinder chamber, extracting the spent case and replacing it in the magazine. As the backward bolt-stroke was nearing its end, the cylinder, revolving within a shroud, brought the next chamber into line with the breech. At that point, the bolt was held back at full-cock. Pressing the trigger released the bolt to fly forward, pushing a self-primed .40-calibre cartridge out of the cylinder into the barrel, then firing it in a single movement. Alternatively, the bolt could be run forward under control, then retracted to either a safety notch or a half-cock position, from which sufficient power could be generated to fire the gun. Firing from the half-cock position minimised the shock of the full 'slam fire' stroke. Most guns had small round trigger guards with a rearward spur. The fore-end and barrel assembly were easily detached from the butt and standing breech, allowing convertible rifle/shotgun combinations to be made. See also Cloverleaf rifle. **6.** Roper Sporting Arms Company [The], Amherst, Massachusetts, and Hartford, Connecticut. Formed in March 1869, succeeding the Roper Repeating Rifle Company (q.v.), this partnership of Christopher *Spencer and Charles *Billings made Roper-patent .40 rifles and four-shot 12-bore shotguns, adding what an 1872-vintage broadsheet called 'The Roper Six-Shooting Rifle'. Trading continued until 1874.

Rosa – 1. José Ramón la Rosa. This Spanish gunmaker, apparently based in Madrid, is now best known for pinfire long-arms (below). **2.** [La] Rosa rifle. Probably dating from the early 1860s, this pinfire breech-loading rifle had a barrel that could pivot axially when a small catch on the receiver was pressed forward. Sporting guns were made by the inventor under the name Larrosa, but the experimental military patterns were probably made in the *Fábrica de Trubia.

Rosch, Steyer & Co., Suhl in Thüringen, Germany. Listed in 1900 as a gunmaking business (Büchsenmacherei). The proprietor was Emil Schilling.

Rosewell. The co-patentee with Frank *Joyce and Newton of a ribbed and tapered airgun slug: British Patent 24,314/01 of 1901.

Roshchepey. Yakov Roshchepey (1879–1958), a one-time regimental blacksmith, spent more than twenty years in a Kiev gunmaking factory (1907–28), trying to perfect a semi-automatic rifle – initially on the basis of a *Mosin-Nagant conversion. His contribution to the development process that led first to the *Simonov, then the *Tokarev rifles was vital, but now commonly is overlooked.

Ross – 1. Charles Henry Ross of 70 Barrows Street, West Bromwich, Staffordshire, a 'Spring Maker', was the designer of a bell target relying on a plunger-operated lever to ring the bell. Protected by British Patent 3,510/08 of 1908, it was the first practical device of its type. **2.** Charles Henry Augustus Frederick Lockhart Ross, the ninth Baronet of Balnagown, was born in Scotland, but achieved his greatest successes in Canada and died in the USA. In addition to the straight-pull rifles that achieved great success on the target ranges and seduced the Canadian authorities into adopting them officially, Ross invented a toggle-locked pistol and a controlled-platform magazine protected by British Patent 20,644/01 of 15 October 1901. *See also* Edwards and Harris. The best source of details is *The Ross Rifle Story*, by Chadwick, Dupuis and Phillips (published privately, 1985), but John Walter, *Rifles of the World* (Krause Publications, second edition, 1998), contains a useful list of individual models. **3.** Daniel Ross first appears in the Edinburgh directories in 1815, listed as a gunmaker at 64 Pleasance. In 1819, he moved to 9 South St Andrew Street, and by 1838 was listed as Daniel Ross & Company; he disappeared a year later, however. Airguns are known with his markings. **4.** John Ross was a gunmaker to be found at 3 Wells Mews, Wells Street, London W., in 1896–98. **5.** L.C. Ross, Grand Rapids, Michigan. Co-designer with Frank *Simonds and Chauncey *Fisher of a spring-air BB Gun protected by US Patent 689,923 of 13 December 1901. The patent was assigned to the *Rapid Rifle Company. **6.** Ross Rifle Company, Montreal, Quebec. This Canadian rifle-making business was established in 1903 to make guns in accordance with the designs of Sir Charles Ross for the Canadian armed forces, who were anxious to free themselves from dependence on Lee-Enfield rifles supplied from Britain. However, although the subject of constant modification, the rifles performed very poorly. Ultimately, after a disastrous showing in the mud of the Western Front during the First World War, they were replaced by *Lee-Enfields and relegated to sniping and training roles. The Canadian government took over the assets of the Ross Rifle Company in March 1917 and eventually sold the factory to the *North American Arms Company.

Rossi. Amadeo Rossi SA, Metalúrgica e Munições, São Leopoldo-RS, Brazil. This company, founded in 1922, was formed by Italian gunmakers who arrived in Brazil from Brescia in 1881. A move to São Leopoldo occurred in 1937, the present trading style being adopted in 1968. Rossi has made a range of *Smith & Wesson-style revolvers in chamberings ranging from .22 rimfire to .38 Special/.357 Magnum, identified by such names as Champion and Sportsman, although often also classified numerically; in addition, a variety of rifles (including a Winchester clone sold as the Puma) and shotguns have also been made. The business was purchased by Forjas *Taurus in 1998, and the current status is uncertain. A list of individual models will be found in John Walter, *The Pistol Book* (Arms & Armour Press, first edition, 1983).

Rossler. Adolf Rossler: *see* Erste Nordböhmische Waffenfabrik.

Rössner. Hugo Rössner, Suhl in Thüringen, Germany. Trading in 1939 as a sales agency, handling sporting guns and ammunition alongside sporting goods.

Rosson – **1.** Charles Rosson, Derby, Derbyshire. This English gunmaker began trading in the late nineteenth century, being listed initially at 4 Market Head before moving to 12 Market Place; the trading style had become Charles Rosson & Son by 1910. In addition to sporting guns, Rosson marked a variety of shotgun cartridges loaded from components supplied by *Kynoch of Birmingham. These included The Eclipse, The Monvill, The Roedich and The Vipax. **2.** Charles S. Rosson, Rampant Horse Street, Norwich, Norfolk. Assumed to have been the son and probable successor of Charles

Rosson (above), this gunmaker operated in the East Anglia district of England. His marks have been found on shotgun ammunition made by *Eley-Kynoch and distributed under such names as The Crown, The Ektor, The Kuvert, The Lowrecoil, The Roedich, The Sixteen Cartridge, The Star, The Twenty Cartridge and The Vipax.

Rost. Max Rost, Apolda. A German retailer of sporting guns and ammunition, active in 1941.

Rota-Clip. A clip-loading magazine system developed by *Daisy in the early 1970s and applied to several guns in the 450 series.

Rotary Bullet. An airgun projectile developed and manufactured by *Lane Brothers of Bermondsey, London, prior to the First World War.

'Rotax' [The]. Generally found as 'Rotax Ball Cartridge' on shotgun ammunition distributed by *Rodda & Company of Calcutta.

Roth – **1.** Franz Roth, Ritschershausen in Thüringen. Listed in German trade directories as a maker of gun parts, 1941. **2.** Georg Roth, Vienna, Austria-Hungary. Best known as an ammunition manufacturer, Roth was also instrumental in assisting Karel *Krnka. Consequently, his name is customarily attached not only to the Krnka-Roth long-recoil firearms, but also the Roth-Sauer and Roth-Steyr pistols (below). Among the patents for 'automatic firearms' granted to Roth in the USA were 616,260 and 616,261 of 20 December 1898; 634,913 of 17 October 1899 (with Karel Krnka); 683,072 of 24 September 1901 (with Krnka); and 681,737 of 3 September 1901. Roth died in Vienna in 1935. **3.** Karl Roth, Zella-Mehlis in Thüringen, Germany. Listed in 1939 as a master gunsmith. **4.** Otto Roth, Zella-Mehlis in Thüringen. Listed in the early 1920s as the proprietor of a gunmaking and gun-repair workshop. **5.** Wilhelm Roth, Benshausen bei Suhl in Thüringen, Germany. A maker of gun parts and accessories prior to 1914. **6.** Roth-Sauer pistol. This small long-recoil semi-automatic 7.65mm design, based on patents granted to Georg Roth and Karel Krnka, was made in Gemany by J.P *Sauer & Sohn of Suhl c. 1907–12. Many guns were supplied to German colonial police units in German South-West Africa. **7.** Roth-Steyr pistol: *see* panel, facing page.

Rottweil. A brandname originally associated with the products of *Vereinigte Köln-Rottweiler Pulverfabriken, which included propellant and shotgun cartridges. The name is now owned by *Dynamit Nobel Troisdorf AG.

Rouchouse. J. Rouchouse et Cie, 'succ. de Manufacture d'Armes Escoffier', rue Villeboeuf, Saint-Étienne, France. Listed in 1892 as a gunmaker, succeeding the long-established Escoffier business, this company is best known for a 'squeezer' pistol, but also made a wide range of sporting guns and rifles. It was still operating in 1933.

Rouillier – **1.** Roullier-Beaume, Saint-Étienne, France. Listed in 1933 as a gunmaker. Trading in 1951 from 4-bis, rue Badouillère. **2.** Roullier et Colomb, rue Martin-Bernard 23, Saint-Étienne, France. Listed in 1892 as a distributor of, and agent for, arms and ammunition.

Roundhead. A generic term for any round-headed or 'English'-style diabolo airgun pellet.

Roux – **1.** Rue Boulevard-Valbenoîte, Saint-Étienne, France. Listed in 1892 as a gunmaker. **2.** Louis Roux, 8 rue du Vernay, Saint-Étienne. Listed in 1951 as a gunmaker.

Rover – **1.** Usually found as 'The Rover', associated

ROTH-STEYR PISTOL

Roth (7)

The *Repetierpistole M. 7* was adopted in 1907 for the Austro-Hungarian cavalry regiments. Some of its features originated in a patent granted in 1895 to Wasa Theodorovič, but the basic recoil-operated locking mechanism is usually attributed to Karel ★Krnka. Krnka-★Roth pistols were tested throughout Europe from 1898 onward, until the perfected version was issued for field trials with the Common Army in 1905–06.

The resulting M. 7 pistol was claimed to embody important advantages as a cavalry weapon, particularly in the isolation of the trigger system from the auto-loading action to reduce the possibility of accidental firing. However, the guns were complicated and expensive. Although substantial quantities were made prior to the First World War, in Steyr (marked 'STEYR') and Budapest ('FGGY'), they were superseded by the ★Steyr-Hahn.

Based on patents granted to Georg Roth and Karel Krnka, the 8mm long-recoil Roth-Steyr pistol was adopted by the Austro-Hungarian cavalry in 1907. The photograph shows a Hungarian-made FGGY example, with the marks of the 42nd Infantry Regiment on the grip disc.

---

with shotgun cartridges assembled in Britain from French-made components by the ★Nitrokol Powder Company. **2.** Or Carabine Rover. This name has been associated with the ★Mauser bolt-action sporting rifle made in Italy by ★Sabatti, in classic straight-comb or ★Monte Carlo-stock form. The chamberings have ranged from .243 Winchester to .30-06.

Rowden Manufacturing Company, Cape Town, Republic of South Africa. A post-1960 manufacturer of ammunition distinguished by the inclusion of 'R.M.C.' in the headstamps. Now part of Swartklip Pty.

Rowe. A.H. Rowe, Hartford, Connecticut. Two guns tested by the US Army in 1865 were made in accordance with US Patent 42,227, granted in April 1864 to this designer. The patent illustrations bore too great a resemblance to the 1862 design of William Johnson (q.v.) to be coincidental; it has been suggested (by Robert E. Gardner, in *Small Arms Makers*) that Rowe was forced to hand over his guns to ★Robbins & Lawrence in 1864 –

for infringing Richard S. ★Lawrence's US Patent 8637 of January 1852 – but nothing at all has been said about the links between Johnson and Rowe. The guns were operated by twisting the barrel unit to the right after a catch on the top of the receiver had been depressed.

Rowell & Son, Chipping Norton, Oxfordshire. Believed to have been an ironmonger and supplier of agricultural equipment, this business distributed shotgun cartridges marked 'The Surekiller'.

Rowen. Stephen C. Rowen, or 'Rowan', a commander in the US Navy, accepted a variety of firearms and accessories in the decade prior to the American Civil War. They included the .36 ★Colt Navy-pattern revolvers marked 'SCR'. *See also* US arms inspectors' marks.

Rowland. Garland T. Rowland, a captain in the US Army, accepted firearms and accessories marked 'GTR', made in 1932–34 by ★Colt's Patent Fire Arms Manufacturing Company. *See also* US arms inspectors' marks.

Royal, Royal... – 1. Usually found as 'The Royal' on

shotgun cartridges loaded by *Eley-Kynoch for *Holland & Holland of London. The marks are usually accompanied by the British Patent no. 494,264, dating them to the late 1930s. The name has also been found on shotgun cartridges sold by Charles *Kerr of Stranraer and John *MacPherson of Inverness. **2.** A Browning-type pocket semi-automatic pistol made in Spain for M. Zulaica y Compañía of Eibar, Guipúzcoa. The 6.35mm version had a six-round magazine; the 7.65mm gun customarily contained seven rounds. Both were hammer fired. **3.** A tradename found on handguns made in Spain by *Beistegui Hermanos of Eibar, based on the Mauser C/96. The first of these semi-automatic Royals was made in 1926, with a simplified cylindrical bolt and minor changes made in the locking mechanism; it was followed in 1927 by the first of the selective-fire guns. All had integral ten- or twenty-round magazines. The improved Royal *Modelo Militares 1931* (MM31) followed the external lines of its Mauser prototype far better than the 1926 pattern had done; it could be obtained with integral magazines holding ten or twenty rounds, or with detachable magazines holding ten to thirty cartridges. One gun could even handle Beistegui and Mauser-Schnellfeuerpistole magazines interchangeably. A few MM31 pistols were made in 1934 with a rate-reducing mechanism in the grip, but work ceased soon afterward. Total production of Mauser-type Royals is believed to have reached about 33,000. Undoubtedly their introduction inspired development of the *Astra 900. The Super Azul was simply an MM31 distributed by Eulogio Arrostegui of Eibar. **4.** *Suicide Special revolvers made by the *Hopkins & Allen Arms Company of Norwich, Connecticut; the *Lee Arms Company of Wilkes-Barre, Pennsylvania; and by Otis *Smith of Middlefield and Rock Fall, Connecticut, USA. Although differing in design, almost all of them date from the 1880s. **5.** Royal Australian Small Arms Factory: *see* Lithgow. **6.** 'Royal County' [The]. A brandname found on British *Kynoch-made shotgun cartridges sold by *Loveridge & Company of Reading prior to 1914. **7.** Royal cyphers: *see* Cyphers, imperial and royal. **8.** Royal Gun Company, Wheeling, West Virginia, USA. This short-lived gunmaking business, successor to the *Three Barrel Gun Company c. 1908, was itself succeeded by the *Hollenbeck Gun Company in 1910. **9.** Royal Irish Constabulary (RIC). Associated with a revolver made by P. *Webley & Sons. **10.** Royal Netherlands Indies Army (KNIL): *see* Koninklijke Nederlanse Indisch Leger. **11.** Royal Ordnance Factories, Britain: *see* Fazakerley, Maltby and Theale. **12.** Royal Ordnance plc. This British arms-making business was created when all the former state-owned factories (Birtley, Blackburn, Cardonald, Chorley, Enfield, Glascoed, Leeds, Nottingham, Powfoot and Radway Green) were transferred to private ownership. The site of the former Royal Small Arms Factory in Enfield was sold after operations had been transferred in 1988 to the existing factory in King's Meadow, Nottingham. The standard British infantry rifle and light support weapon, the 5.56mm L85A1 and L86A1, are currently being made in Nottingham alongside the 7.62mm L7 series GPMG and a selection of large-calibre weapons. The company is now owned by British Aerospace (BAe). **13.** Royal Service. A brandname associated with some of the shotguns made in Norwich, Connecticut, USA, by the *Crescent Arms Company. Apparently they pre-date 1910. **14.** Royal Small Arms Factory (widely listed simply as RSAF), Enfield Lock, Middlesex: *see* Enfield.

15. Royal Small Arms Factory (RSAF), Montgomery Street, Sparkbrook, Birmingham: *see* Sparkbrook. **16.** Royal Small Arms Repair Factory (RSARF), Bagot Street, Birmingham. Known locally as The Tower, this site was used from the beginning of the nineteenth century until sold in 1894 to W.W. *Greener. Government work was transferred to the *Royal Small Arms Factory in the nearby Sparkbrook district of Birmingham. The Bagot Street inspectors' mark was a crown above 'BR' ('Birmingham Repair'). **17.** Royal Typewriters, Inc., USA. A principal sub-contractor for folding-butt *M1 Carbines (M1A1), active in 1944. **18.** Royal-Vincitor, or SA Royal-Vincitor, Eibar, Spain. A maker of *Ruby-pattern semi-automatic pistols for the French Army during the First World War.

Royet, Saint-Étienne, France. Listed in 1879 as a gunmaker, trading from rue Badouillère 30, and in 1892 from place Chavanelle 15.

'RP', 'R.P.' – **1.** Usually encountered as 'The R.P.' on shotgun cartridges sold by Stephen *Grant of London. **2.** As a monogram: *see* 'PR' monogram. **3.** Found on US military firearms and accessories. *See also* Richard *Paine and Richard *Perher.

'RPB'. Found on US military firearms and accessories. *See* R.P. *Barry and Robert P. Beales.

RPD. An abbreviated form of *Ruchnoi Pulemet Degtyareva* (Light Machine-gun, Degtyarev) a bipod-mounted 7.62x39 weapon derived from the RP-46 and introduced in the early 1950s. The feed belt was often concealed in a carrying drum. *See also* Degtyarev. It was replaced by the *RPK. The RPDM was a modernised form of the RPD, introduced in the late 1950s.

RPK. The original version of the 7.62mm *Kalashnikov light machine-gun, on a bipod mount. The RPKS was a folding-butt version.

'RR', back-to-back (addorsed). Usually struck on the *knoxform, the receiver, the butt and the fore-end of British military rifles condemned as unsafe to fire.

'RS' – **1.** Found on US military firearms and accessories. *See* Robert *Sears. **2.** Applied to *Remington M700 bolt-action rifles fitted with DuPont Rynite synthetic stocks.

RSA – **1.** An abbreviated form of *Revolver Stechkina-Avramova*, this designation refers to a Soviet double-action revolver designed by *Stechkin and *Avramov in the 1970s. The cylinder is mounted on a swinging yoke inspired by US practice. **2.** A property mark found on *Galil-type rifles and the *Vektor machine-gun ('Republic of South Africa').

RSAF (Royal Small Arms Factory). *See* Enfield.

RSC – **1.** Associated with two auto-loading rifles (Mle. 17 and Mle. 18) introduced to the French Army during the First World War. The designation was taken from the initials of the designers: Ribeyrolles, Sutter and Chauchat. **2.** A superimposition-type monogram with 'R' dominant. Correctly 'SRC' (q.v.); associated with *Sears, Roebuck & Company.

'RSJ', 'RSL'. Encountered on US military firearms and accessories. *See* R.S. *Johnson and Robert S. *Lamotte respectively.

'RSM'. Found on a horizontal band within a circle. A trademark associated with Karl Arndt *Reck of Lauf bei Nürnberg ('Reck Sport-Modell').

'RT'. A monogram, 'T' within 'R', usually encircled. Correctly 'TR' (q.v.); used by T. Robar.

'**RTS'.** Found on US military firearms and accessories. Allegedly used by R.T. Safford, but *see also* 'PTS'.

Rubin. Eduard Rubin (1846–1922), one-time director of the Swiss military laboratory in Thun, is best known as a ballistician. His greatest contribution was the development of a copper-coated bullet to combat the tendency of lead bullets to fail if muzzle velocity rose too highly – a problem made worse by the introduction of efficient smokeless propellant. Rubin also collaborated with Rudolf ★Schmidt in the design of the Schmidt-Rubin rifle, which, in an improved pattern, remained the Swiss service rifle until the 1950s. Rubin's patents included US 338,191 and 338,192 of 16 March 1886 for a jacketed bullet and a 'firearm barrel'.

Ruby – 1. A mark found on shotgun ammunition made by ★Eley for ★Thompson Brothers of Bridgwater, prior to 1914. **2.** *See* panel, below. **3.** A copy of the 1910-pattern FN-Browning pistol, made in the early 1920s by ★Gabilondo y Urresti of Guernica. *See* 'Ruby Arms Co.' (below). **4.** Usually enountered as 'The Ruby' on shotgun cartridges loaded by, or for, ★Curtis's & Harvey of London, prior to 1918. **5.** 'Ruby Arms Co.' or 'Ruby Arms Company'. A mark found on 7.65mm Auto and 9mm Short ★Eibar-type blowback pistols made by ★Gabilondo y Cia in the late 1920s, but abandoned on the introduction of the ★Llama name. Some guns were marked 'Eibar'; others apparently bore 'Guernica'. The 6.35mm pattern had a six-round magazine, was generally striker fired and often had a grip safety. The 7.65mm design, based on the 1910-type ★FN-Browning, was striker fired and had a seven-round magazine. **6.** Ruby Extra. A brandname associated with a range of swing-cylinder ★Smith & Wesson-type revolvers made by ★Llama–Gabilondo. *See also* Llama revolvers.

Rudd. A.J. Rudd, Norwich and Great Yarmouth, Norfolk. The marks of this English provincial gunsmith, trading in East Anglia, have been reported on sporting guns and ammunition. These included shotgun cartridges, made by ★Eley Brothers or ★Eley-Kynoch, marked 'The Standard', 'The Star' and 'Rudd's X.L. Cartridge'. Operations are believed to have begun in the 1880s, but details are lacking.

'**Ruffed Grouse' [The].** A mark used on shotgun ammunition made in the USA by the ★Chamberlain Cartridge Company of Cleveland, Ohio.

'**Rufford' [The].** Associated with shotgun ammunition loaded by Charles ★Smith & Sons of Newark, possibly adapted from the name of a local hunt.

'**Rufus' [The].** A shotgun cartridge introduced into Britain by the ★Schultze Gunpowder Company Ltd, 1912.

Ruger. William B. Ruger, USA: *see* Sturm, Ruger & Company, Inc.

Ruhlman. Adam Ruhlman, also listed as Rhulman or 'Ruhlmann', accepted firearms and military equipment on behalf of the US Army. Active in ★Harper's Ferry Armory during 1836–57, he applied 'AR' marks that can be distinguished by date from those employed in the early 1860s by Alexander ★Reuben. *See also* US arms inspectors' marks.

Rukavishnikov. Nikolay Rukavishnikov, a Soviet gun designer, was responsible in 1938–40 for an experimental 'straight-line' auto-loading rifle and the 14.5mm-calibre PTRR anti-tank rifle. However, none of his designs reached service status and, perhaps owing to official bias in favour of Fedor ★Tokarev, he is rarely given the credit that he may deserve. It is thought that Rukavishnikov may have died shortly after the German invasion of the Soviet Union in the Summer of 1941.

'**Rummel'.** A mark associated with shotguns made in the USA by the ★Crescent Arms Company of Norwich, Connecticut; possibly a distributor's name.

Rundkugel. A generic German-language term ('Round-

RUBY PISTOL

Ruby (2)

A name given to a simple Browning-type 7.65mm semi-automatic pistol made in Spain for the French and Italian Armies during the First World War, then offered commercially in large numbers under a variety of names during the 1920s. The pistol originated with ★Gabilondo y Urresti of Guernica, being introduced shortly before the First World War.

The major participants included Domingo ★Acha y Cia, Vizcaya; ★Azanza y Arrizabalaga, Eibar; Francisco ★Arizmendi y Goenaga, Eibar; Vincenzo ★Bernedo, Eibar; Bonifacio ★Echeverria, Eibar; ★Erquiaga y Cia, Eibar; Antonio ★Errasti, Eibar; ★Esperanza y Unceta, Guernica; Isidro ★Gaztañaga, Eibar; Modesto ★Santos, Eibar (by way of Les Ouvriers Reunis); ★Retolaza Hermanos, Eibar; ★Urrejola y Cia, Eibar; SA ★Royal-Vincitor, Eibar; and M. ★Zulaica y Cia, Eibar.

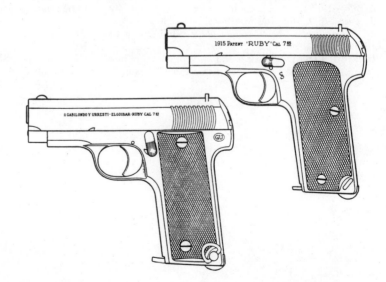

Typical Ruby-style pistols, from The Illustrated Encyclopedia of Handguns, *by A.B. Zhuk (1995).*

ball') for ball-type airgun projectiles and shotgun loads.

Rupertus – **1.** Jacob Rupertus of Philadelphia, Pennsylvania, USA, was granted several US Patents to protect his 'revolving firearms': 23,711 of 19 April 1859; 37,059 of 2 December 1862; 43,606 of 19 July 1864; 121,199 of 21 November 1871; and 165,369 of 6 July 1875. Rupertus also obtained US Patent 23,852 for an automatic cap-priming mechanism; 25,142 of 16 August 1859 for a percussion pellet; 209,925 of 12 November 1878 for a 'breechloading firearm'; and 633,734 of 26 September 1899 for a 'firearm lock'. *See* next entry. **2.** Rupertus Patented Pistol Manufacturing Company, Philadelphia, Pennsylvania. Founded in 1858 by Jacob Rupertus (above), this gunmaking business was responsible for cartridge derringers, pistols, pepperboxes, revolvers, rifles and shotguns. Trading continued until 1900.

Russell – **1.** A.J. Russell, High Street, Maidstone, Kent, England. A gunsmith known to have distributed shotgun cartridges marked 'Russell's Special' and 'Russell's Special Loading'. **2.** Thomas W. Russell, a Federal Ordnance inspector, was active c. 1862–63 during the American Civil War. He used a 'TWR' mark. **3.** Samuel Russell. Patentee of an electric-ignition system. *See* American Electric Arms & Ammunition Company. **4.** William H. Russell, a civilian inspector employed by the Federal government, accepted firearms and equipment during the American Civil War. Operating in 1862 only, he used the identifier 'WHR'; this can be difficult to distinguish from the similar mark used in the same era by William H. *Roberts. *See also* US arms inspectors' marks.

Russian Model – **1.** A name originally applied specifically to the .44 revolvers made by *Smith & Wesson of Springfield, Massachusetts, USA, for the Russian government, in three patterns, but subsequently applied commercially by many rival makers. **2.** A large six-shot single-action .44-calibre *Forehand & Wadsworth revolver, with a spring-loaded ejector rod beneath the barrel, made in 1877–79. **3.** A .32-calibre revolver made by *Forehand & Wadsworth, possibly about 1880 and basically a small-calibre sheath-trigger F&W *Bull Dog with a rounded butt.

'Rutland' [The]. A mark found on shotgun ammunition sold in England by J.E. *Whitehouse of Oakham.

Rutt. Alfred H. Rutt, Northampton. The marks of this English provincial gunmaker, trading in the Cattle Market, have been reported on shotgun cartridges made prior to the First World War by *Eley Bros. Rutt succeeded John Marsh (q.v.), apparently in the 1890s.

Rutte. Wilh. Rutte, Böhmische Lieppa (Česká Lipa, Czechoslovakia). A maker of large numbers of crank-wound volute-spring pistols and rifles, the forerunners of the *Gallery Guns. Most date from the 1820–33 era, although some may be as late as 1860.

Rutter. William Rutter began trading as a gunmaker from 24 Boston Place, Dorset Square, London, in 1836. From there, he moved to Somerstown, first at 12 Wellesley Street (1839–41), then 48 Aldenham Street until 1857.

RWM – **1.** Found on US military firearms and accessories. *See* Robert W. *McNeely and Richard W. *Meade. **2.** An abbreviation associated with *Rheinische Waffen- & Munitionsfabriken of Köln.

'RWS', 'R.W.S.' – **1.** Used as a trademark or headstamp prior to 1945 by *Rheinisch-Westfälische Sprengstoff AG. **2.** Found on shotguns and sporting rifles distributed by *Dynamit Nobel of Troisdorf/Oberlar. Most of the centrefire bolt-action cartridge rifles have been made by *Kriegeskorte, but some *Mausers (perhaps Spanish) have also been offered. *See also* Hobby, Hornet, Meisterkugel and Superpoint. **3.** A superimposition-type monogram with 'S' dominant. Found on pistols made in Suhl by *Römerwerke AG.

Ryan – **1.** Thomas J. Ryan Pistol Manufacturing Company, Franklin Street, New York City, USA. This gunmaking business, active for a few years from 1874 onward, made a variety of inexpensive *Suicide Special revolvers under the name Napoleon (q.v.) among others. **2.** William Ryan & Son, Birmingham, Warwickshire. A maker of fowling pieces, rifles, airguns and pistols, possibly a successor to Ryan & Watson of Whittall Street (listed in directories during 1799–1818), William Ryan was to be found in Whittall Street (1820–33) and thereafter at 110 New Street until 1835 or later.

Rychner & Keller. *See* Vetterli.

Ryder. *See* Red Ryder.

Rynnakkokivääri, or RK. The Finnish-language term for 'Assault rifle'. *See also* Kalashnikov, Sako and Valmet.

S

'S' – 1. Beneath a crown, above a number. A mark applied by an Australian government arms inspector working in the Sydney depot in New South Wales. *See also* British military inspectors' marks. 2. Found stamped into the heel of British Lee-Enfield 'Short' rifle butts, which were ¹/₂in shorter than the standard pattern. 3. Stamped under the butt, near the socket, of British *Lee-Enfield rifles made for India Service with a spring washer on the stock-retaining bolt. 4. With a number. Found on components of British military firearms made during the Second World War, indicating a company operating in the south (of Britain). The numbers identified individual companies. Typical examples associated with small-arms include 'S 3', *Adams Bros. & Burnley; 'S 7', *Auto Engineering (Croydon) Ltd; 'S 30', *Dashwood Engineering Ltd; 'S 51', *Holland & Holland Ltd; 'S 54', *Hydran Products Ltd; 'S 63', *Kork-n-Seal Ltd; 'S 64', the *Lamson Engineering Company Ltd; 'S 66', *Lee Beilin Ltd; 'S 67', the *Lightfoot Refrigeration Company Ltd; 'S 68', *Lines Bros. Ltd; 'S 77', the *Metal Box Company; 'S 88', the *National Cash Register Company Ltd; 'S 102', the *Rolls Razor Company Ltd; 'S 103', *Scoffin & Wilmot; 'S 109', the *Sterling Engineering Company; 'S 114', *Trevor Stampings Ltd; 'S 121', *Vickers-Armstrongs Ltd, Bath; 'S 123', Howard *Wall Ltd; 'S 125', A. *Wells & Company; 'S 135', *Air Ducts Ltd; 'S 136', the *Aircraft & General Engineering Company; 'S 144', H. *Atkin; 'S 156', J. *Boss & Company; 'S 159', *Bratt Colbran Ltd; 'S 171', *Cogswell & Harrison; 'S 173', the *Cooden Engineering Company; 'S 202', Stephen *Grant & Lang Ltd; 'S 223', *E.S.S. (Signs) Ltd; 'S 254', the *Portadyne Radio Company; 'S 292', *Waygood Otis Ltd; 'S 304', F. *Liebtruth & Company; 'S 309', *Shannon Ltd; 'S 311', the *Art Metal Construction Company Ltd; 'S 355', *Sharpe & Wright; 'S 365', *Unity Heating Ltd; and 'S 388', James *Purdey & Sons. 5. With two arrowheads. A sale mark used on surplus or obsolete British military equipment. 6. Encircled, often in outline black-letter form. Associated with the products of the *Sterling Engineering Company Ltd of Dagenham, England. 7. Associated with small-arms ammunition components made in Germany after 1940 by Dynamit AG of St Lambrecht. 8. Encircled. Found on miniature revolvers made in the USA by R.F. Sedgley, Inc., between 1910 and 1938. 9. Squared, often in a box border. Found on No. 4 Lee-Enfield rifles made in the former Stevens Arms Company (by then Stevens-Savage) factory in Chicopee Falls, Massachusetts, USA. 10. Within a lozenge, generally taking a squared italic form. A mark associated with firearms, airguns and gas-powered guns made in the USA by Sheridan Products, Inc.

'SA', 'S.A.' – 1. Usually within a square or oval border. *Suomen armija* ('Finnish army'), used as a property mark. *See also* 'Sk. Y.' 2. A superimposition-type monogram, sometimes encircled, with neither letter prominent. Found on

*Smith & Wesson-type swinging-cylinder revolvers made in Eibar, Spain, by *Suinaga y Aramperri. 3. Applied as 'SA' or 'S.A.' to US military stores – including .45 M1911A1 *Government Model pistols – refurbished by the National Armory, *Springfield, Massachusetts.

'SAA'. *See* Single Action Army Revolver.

SAB – 1. *See* Società Armi Bresciane SRL. 2. Applied to the SAB G90 Super Auto pistol, a modified form of the Czech ČZ 75 chambering 9mm Parabellum or 9x21 IMI ammunition. Most guns are intended for Practical Pistol competitions and have adjustable sights.

Sabatti – 1. Fabbrica Italiana Armi Sabatti SpA (FIAS), Gardone Val Trompia, Brescia, Italy. FIAS has made Carabina *Rover sporting rifles on the basis of a modified *Mauser action. A range of shotguns and combination guns has also been offered. 2. Sabatti & Tanfoglio, Gardone Val Trompia, Brescia, Italy. In addition to rifles and shotguns, this gunmaking business has offered 6.35mm-calibre automatic pistols under the brandname *Sata.

Sabot – 1. F. Sabot, 67 rue César-Betholon, Saint-Étienne, France. Listed in 1951 as a gun-barrel maker. 2. J. Sabot, 14 rue des Francs-Maçons, Saint-Étienne, France. Listed in 1951 as a gunmaker.

'SACM'. *See* Société Alsacienne de Constructions Mecaniques.

Saco Systems, Inc. *See* panel, p. 450.

Sadler. Arthur Sadler & Goold, Birmingham, Warwickshire, England. This patent agency was a partnership of Arthur Sadler and Lewis William Goold, with chambers at 44 Waterloo Street. It acted for John William *Fearn and Douglas Vaughan *Johnstone. *See* British Patents 229,851 and 231,270 of 1924.

Saez. Cosmé Garcia Saez of Madrid patented a rifle in the mid-1860s (US no. 45,801 of 3 January 1865), an ineffectual breech-loader, converted from 1859-pattern short rifles (*Carabina de Cazadores M. 1857–59*) and tested extensively by the Spanish Army. Its most distinctive feature was the disc-like breech-block, which rotated inside a two-piece housing. Pressing a latch to the right released the clamp, allowing a small button projecting from the top of the breech housing to retract the disc until the chamber-mouth was exposed.

Safari – 1. Made by Société Anonyme Continentale pour la Fabrication des Armes à Feu *Lebeau-Courally only in .470 Nitro Express, this Big Game rifle has double back-action side-locks, double triggers and a specially strengthened frame. High-relief matted-ground Renaissance tracery is cut into the action, barrels, rib and pistol-grip cap, with finely detailed trophy heads in panels. An Express-type sight lies on the quarter-rib. 2. This brandname was given to a British *Mauser-type sporting rifle introduced c. 1965 by *Parker-Hale Ltd on the basis of a *Santa Barbara action. Several versions have been made, including a box-magazine type (1000C). Chamberings ranged from .243 Winchester to .30-06. An

SACO SYSTEMS, INC.

This company is based in Saco, Maine, USA. The failure of the heavy-barrel *Garand derivatives, the M15 and M14A2, was counterbalanced by the standardisation of the M60 light machine-gun in 1956. This had a gas system originating in the *Lewis Gun, by way of Ruger's T10 and T23, and a belt-feed mechanism provided by the MG.42/T24.

Service showed that the M60 had severe faults of its own, however, including a bipod fitted on to the barrel rather than the gas-tube, and poor zeroing. The M60E1 received some of the obvious changes – the bipod on the gas-tube and a repositioned carrying handle – but the gun is still regarded as being inferior to the MAG and the Russian PK.

Recently, Saco has produced a much-lightened M60E3, with a fore-pistol grip, in an attempt to improve the M60 for the light-support role. The M60C is a stripped-down M60 with an electric trigger and a hydraulic charger, widely used as a fixed gun on helicopters, while the spade-gripped M60D is commonly employed on pintle mounts in helicopter doorways.

Saco also makes .50-calibre *Browning machine-guns, including improved patterns, and has dabbled with submachine-guns.

The 7.62x51 M60E3 is a Saco Systems modification of the basic M60 general-purpose machine-gun, which has been service issue in the US Army for many years.

improved Model 1100 appeared in 1968, with a safety catch on the right side of the receiver and the bolt handle swept downward. **3.** A series of *Mauser-pattern sporting rifles made in the USA by *Rahn Gun Works, with the choice of an elephant, a rhinoceros or a Cape buffalo head on the magazine floor plate. Chamberings ranged from .308 Norma Magnum to 9.3x64. **4.** Or BDL Safari. A big-game version of the *Remington M700 bolt-action rifle, introduced in 1962. Guns of this type have been offered in chamberings ranging from 8mm Remington Magnum to .458 Winchester Magnum; they have heavy barrels and stocks reinforced with two recoil bolts. Most guns made since 1981 have straight-comb butts instead of the earlier *Monte Carlo type. A variant with a synthetic *Kevlar stock (M700 Safari KS) was introduced in 1989. **5.** Safari Grade (1). A term applied by the *Browning Arms Company to the plainest of the three grades of Mauser-action sporting rifles made in the USA. *See also* *Medallion and *Olympian grades. **6.** Safari Grade (2). A bolt-action rifle announced by the *Dakota Arms Company in 1989. Built on a slightly modified *Mauser/Winchester Model 70 action, chambered for cartridges ranging from .300 Winchester Magnum to .458 Winchester Magnum, it had a gloss-finish walnut stock. However, the original Monte Carlo comb was replaced by a straight version within a year of introduction. **7.** Safari Magnum. This was a version of the *Parker-Hale Safari rifle, made only in .375 H&H Magnum with an addition-al recoil bolt through the stock beneath the chamber. **8.** Safari Mark I. Otherwise known as the Model 86/70 Safari Mk 1, this was a lever-action *Daisy BB gun, derived from the No. 102 *Cub, with a concealed lever in the wrist and pistol grip. It was introduced in 1970.

Safety... – 1. Safety Action. A brandname associated with Anciens Établissements *Pieper of Herstal, near Liège. It is usually found on a shotgun introduced c. 1909. **2.** Safety Automatic. A brandname associated with a revolver made in the USA by Iver Johnson's Arms & Cycle Works from 1892 onward. It was replaced by the Automatic Safety, or Hammer-the-Hammer, design (q.v.), although the differences were minimal. **3.** 'Safety Hammer'. This mark will be found on revolvers made in the USA by *Harrington & Richardson of Worcester, Massachusetts, with a spurless no-snag hammer. It was applied specifically to the *American and *Young America patterns, but *see also* Police Bicycle Model and Police Premier. **4.** Safety Hammerless. Developed largely through the efforts of Joseph H. *Wesson, these revolvers had their hammers within the frames, a spring-loaded safety plate in the back strap and an inertia firing pin. The first .38-calibre guns were made in 1886. About 260,000 had been made (in five versions) when the last batches were shipped in 1940, but it is unlikely that much production had been carried out since 1920. Also known as the New Departure or Lemon Squeezer, the .32 Safety Hammerless was introduced in 1888. By the time the last guns were sold in 1937, 243,000 had been made in the three major sub-varieties. **5.** Safety Hammerless Model. This was a concealed-hammer version of the Iver *Johnson .32 and .38 Safety Model revolver, dating from 1894. **6.** Safety Model. Subsequently known as the Safety Hammer Model. Introduced c. 1893, this double-action .32 or .38 revolver was the first of the Iver Johnson products to embody what (after 1904) became known as the *Hammer-the-Hammer system. **7.** Safety Police. Made in Norwich, Connecticut, USA, by the *Hopkins & Allen Arms Company (c. 1907–14), these revolvers were chambered for .22, .32 and .38 rim- and centrefire ammunition. They were based on the *Automatic Model, but introduced the *Triple Action Safety Lock patented in 1906 by John *Murphy.

Safford. P.T. Safford, sometimes listed as 'R.T. Safford' or identified individually (the marks can be difficult to read), working on behalf of the US government, inspected firearms and equipment marked 'PTS'; the items date from the Civil War and the early 1870s. See also US arms inspectors' marks.

SAFN. See FN-Saive rifle.

Saft. Max Saft, Zella-Mehlis in Thüringen, Germany. Listed during 1930–39 as a master gunsmith.

Sage – 1. George W. Sage, Plymouth, Michigan, USA. The designer of the *Improved Challenger BB gun for the *Markham Air Rifle Company. See US Patent 477,385 of 21 June 1892, sought in 1891. **2.** Thomas C. Sage, Middletown, Connecticut. The marks of this cartridge maker, founded in 1862 and subsequently known as the Sage Ammunition Works, will often be found on rimfire ammunition dating from the American Civil War. They include 'TCS' and 'SAW'.

SAGEM. See Société d'Applications Générales, Électriques et Mecaniques.

Saginaw Steering Gear. A division of *General Motors, maker of M1 Carbines, machine-guns and components during the Second World War. See also Winchester.

'SAI'. A superimposition-type monogram without dominant letters. Correctly 'SIA' (q.v.); used by *Security Industries of America, Inc.

Saiga. See Sayga.

Saint, St. – 1. Gaston de Saint-Aubyn. Listed as a member of the London gun trade in 1894, this gunsmith – or more probably gunmakers' agent – could be found at 7 St Martin's Lane, E.C. **2.** Saint Chamond. Compagnie des Forges et Acieries de la Marine, Saint Chamond, France. See Daudetau. **3.** Saint-Étienne, or Manufacture d'Armes de Saint-Étienne (MAS). One of the principal French government arsenals, founded in 1718, MAS made arms and equipment ranging from the Saint-Étienne machine-gun (below) to 11mm *Chassepot, 11mm *Gras, 8mm *Lebel, 8mm *Berthier and 7.5mm MAS rifles. Among the handguns made in Saint-Étienne have been Mle. 1873, Mle 1874 and Mle 1892 revolvers; a series of experimental blowback pistols produced between the wars (the 7.65mm MAS 1925 M No. 1 and 1932 A No. 4 for example); and the Modèle 1935S service pistol of 1940, based on the SACM-Petter Mle 35. A few MAC-50 pistols were assembled in the factory in 1963. Among the semi-automatic rifles have been the 7.5mm MAS 49, 7.62mm MAS 62 and the 5.56mm FAMAS. See also Châtellerault and Tulle. **4.** Saint-Étienne machine-gun. Accepted by the French Army as the Mle. 1907, this was an improved form of the French *Puteaux design, with a reversed action.

Although issued in substantial quantities, it was not entirely successful. **5.** 'St. George's'. Usually accompanied by 'W', 'G' and a knight-and-dragon mark, this slogan identifies guns made prior to the First World War by W. *Grah of Liège. **6.** 'St Louis Arms Company'. A brand-name found on shotguns handled by the H. & D. *Folsom Arms Company, possibly imported from Europe. Some guns have been reported bearing Belgian proof marks. **7.** Saint Nicholas gun. See Fusil Saint-Nicolas.

Saive. Dieudonné J. Saive (1888–1970). Designer of the *Fabrique Nationale *FAL rifles. See also FN-Saive.

Sakaba. See SKB Firearms Company.

Sako. See panel, pp. 452/53.

Salamon, 21 chemins des Acacias, Saint-Étienne, France. Listed in 1951 as a gunmaker.

Salter & Varge Ltd. Supplier of *Winchester rifles and shotguns to the British authorities, 1941–42.

Salvator-Dormus. An early Austro-Hungarian pistol, designed in 1892 by Archduke *Karl Salvator and Georg, Ritter von Dormus. A blowback chambering a special 8mm cartridge, it had a cocking lever beneath the barrel and an exposed hammer; the magazine, contained within the butt, accepted a five-round clip that fell out of the gun after the last round had been chambered. A few prototype Salvator-Dormus pistols were made c. 1894/95, perhaps by Škoda, but found no lasting success.

Salvaje. A 6.35mm Browning-type automatic made in Spain by *Ojanguren y Vidosa of Eibar: seven rounds, hammer fired.

Salaberrin. Santiago Salaberrin, Eibar, Guipúzcoa, Spain. The *Etna, *Protector and *Tisan pistols are usually attributed to this gunmaking business, although sometimes the Protector is also identified as a product of *Echave y Arzimendi.

Salaverria. Iraola Salaverria y Compañia, Eibar, Guipúzcoa, Spain. Maker of the *Destructor pistol.

Salle system. Incorporated in a few Belgian-made shotguns, this relied on a dropping-block mechanism (undoubtedly inspired by the *Martini), which was actuated by a spur-like cocking lever protruding from the top of the action body. Pressing the spur forward dropped the block and often also ejected spent cases; pulling it backward raised the block and cocked the striker.

Saloon Gun. Also known as a Parlour Gun, or *Zimmerstutzen* in German, invariably this was a low-power firearm chambered for *Flobert or primer-propelled ammunition. Quiet and surprisingly accurate, cartridges of this type were ideally suited to ultra-short-range target shooting and were extremely popular in Europe prior to the First World War. The low power enabled the guns to be of simple construction, often with breech-blocks locked by nothing other than the fall of the hammer, but manufacturing quality could be surprisingly good. See also Gallery Gun.

Samozhenkov. The designer of the original 7.2kg tripod mount for the *Kalashnikov PKS machine-gun. It was replaced in 1969 by the lightweight *Stepanov pattern.

San Cristobal arms factory, Dominican Republic. Created with Italian and Hungarian assistance, this gunmaking plant made the distinctive .30 M1 Cristobal Carbine and 7.62x51 Model 62 assault rifles in small numbers. Its current status is uncertain. See Fábrica de Armas Dominicana.

Sanders – 1. A. Sanders, Maidstone, Kent. A gunmaker, successor to John *Swinfen, whose marks have been

SAKO

The Civil Guard of newly-independent Finland created its first workshop in 1919, in the old Bastmann brewery in Helsinki, to repair and refurbish ex-Russian small-arms. The name *Suojeluskuntain Ase- ja Konepaya Osakeyhtio* (SAKO, 'Arms and Engineering Workshop of the Civil Guard') was adopted when a move to Riihimaki occurred in December 1927. However, the date of foundation was accepted as 1 April 1921. The facilities in Helsinki and later Riihimaki initially made m/24, m/28 and m/28-30 *Mosin-Nagant rifles for the Protective Corps (*Suojeluskuntain Ylieskunnen*, Sk.Y.) until a Sako-developed m/39 rifle was adopted for universal service. About 71,000 m/39 rifles had been made by the time the Continuation War between Finland and the USSR ended in 1944. Bizarrely Sako was sold to the Finnish Red Cross, and the military arms-making facilities were speedily demolished.

Sako engineer Niilo Talvenheimo began developing the L42 sporting rifle when the Winter War with the USSR ended in 1941, but the sale of Sako brought work to an end. However, the success of the improved post-war L46 sporter – particularly in the USA – subsequently allowed the firearms business to be rebuilt. The perfected bolt-action rifles, customarily credited to Eino Mäckinen, have been made on three much-modified actions: the short Vixen (L461, introduced in 1961), the medium Forester (L579 of 1959, reintroduced in 1962) and the long Finnbear (L61, 1961). There are two variants of the L461, a solid-floor single-shot pattern and a magazine-feed type; there are also two L579 actions, the Super Match version being pierced only by the ejection port. The L61 has been made in right- and left-hand versions. Chamberings have ranged from .17 Remington to 6mm PPC (L461); from .22-250 to .308 Winchester (L579); and from .25-06 Remington to .375 H&H Magnum (L61).

The names applied to the rifles have usually reflected their design instead of the difference in action lengths. The Carbine, Deluxe, Hunter, Super Deluxe and Target variants have been offered in all three guises: L461, L579 and L61. The Handy (L579, L61) is a short rifle with a half-length fore-end; the Laminated variant (L461, L579, L61) has a multi-layer warp-resistant stock; the Super Match (L579) is a sophisticated target rifle; and the Varmint rifle (L461) is essentially a Hunter with a heavy barrel. The Fiberclass is an L61 action in a charcoal-grey synthetic stock, and the Handy Fiber is a similar gun with a short barrel and a half-length stock. The Safari (L61 only) is a big-game rifle with a straight-comb butt, transverse recoil bolts through the stock and an *Express-type back sight.

The L61 replaced the high-power Sako rifles that had been made on the basis of refurbished 1898-type *Mauser actions in 1950–61. Actions have been supplied to gunmaking businesses such as the Browning Arms Company, Colt's Patent Fire Arms Manufacturing Company, Harrington & Richardson and others. Consequently, Sako-type guns may be listed under a variety of distributors' names. The latest designs include the .22 rimfire Finnfire series (1994), based on a bolt with a fifty-degree throw, and the TRG sporting-rifle series (1995) with a three-lug sixty-degree bolt. The TRG is manufactured in sport and magnum forms, in chamberings from .243 Winchester to .30-06, and also as the TRG-21 (7.62x51) and

---

found on sporting guns and pin-, rim- and centrefire ammunition sold prior to the First World War. Among the shotgun cartridges were The Allington, The Invicta, The Long Tom and The Medway. **2.** Sanders Small Arms Ltd, London. Maker of auto-loading shotguns in accordance with patents granted to *Chevallier & Sanders. One gun – the Coronation Model No. 1 – was made for exhibition at the Coronation of King George VI in 1937, but the Second World War put an end to development. An 'SSA' monogram trademark was used.

Sanderson. F.W. Sanderson, a government arms inspector working from the period of the American Civil War into the early 1880s, accepted gun stocks and other military stores marked 'FWS'. *See also* US arms inspectors' marks.

'Sandringham' [The]. A mark applied by *Gallyon & Sons to shotgun cartridges.

Sanner. Ch. Sanner. *See* Marion & Sanner.

Santa… – 1. Santa Barbara. Empresa Nacional de Industrias Militares 'Santa Barbara' SA, La Coruña, Spain. This state-owned small-arms factory makes a variety of firearms, including the *CETME series and other military-orientated products. It also makes Santa Barbara *Mauser actions, with a radial safety on the receiver behind the bolt handle. These have been supplied to *Fajen, *Golden State, *Parker-Hale and many other gunmaking businesses. **2.** Santa Fé Arms Company, Pasadena, California, USA. Importer in the mid-1960s of 1903-type *Springfield receivers made in Japan. These investment castings lacked charger guides and did not offer the durability of the machined-steel originals.

Santos – 1. Casimir Santos, Eibar, Guipúzcoa, Spain. This business was responsible for the pocket pistols bearing the brandnames *El Cid and *Venzedor. **2.** Modesto Santos, Eibar, Guipúzcoa, Spain. The compact automatic pistols made under the names *Action and MS have been attributed to this manufacturer. By way of Les Ouvriers Reunis, Santos made *Ruby-pattern semi-automatic pistols for the French Army during the First World War.

Sanvinet, 31 rue César-Bertholon, Saint-Étienne, France. Listed in 1951 as a gunmaker.

'SAR', 'S.A.R.' – 1. A designation applied to a short-barrelled, but otherwise standard Israeli *Galil automatic rifle. It represents 'Short Automatic Rifle'. **2.** Found on 5.6mm-calibre Japanese break-barrel spring-air rifles, the manufacturers of which remain untraced. The mark may simply have been a misreading of *SKB.

Sarda et Gonon, or Sarda-Gonon, Saint-Étienne, France. Listed in 1933 as a gunmaker.

Sarson & Roberts, New York City. Gunmakers operating in 1861–63.

Sata. A compact 6.35mm automatic pistol made by *Sabatti & Tanfoglio.

Saturn. Associated with *Mauser-type sporting rifles sold by Albrecht *Kind c. 1959–68. It was identical to the *Merkur, but usually had a single trigger.

Sauer – 1. Hans Sauer. Co-owner of J.P. Sauer & Sohn

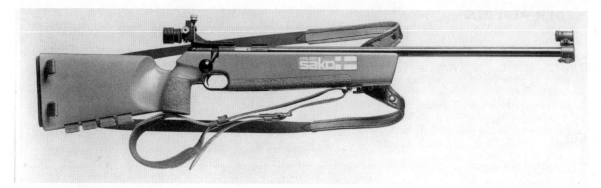

Sako is best known for its bolt-action rifles, made in a wide range of rim- and centrefire patterns. This is a .22 Finnbiathlon 78, built on the Finnscout action for specialist shoot-and-ski competitions.

TRG-41 (.338 Lapua Magnum) sniper rifles.

The M72 and M78 Finnscout series of .22 rimfire rifles (1973–84), which included HB, Magnum, Hornet and Biathlon variants, replaced guns built on the P46 and P54 actions. A solitary lever-action rifle design, the VL-63 Finnwolf, was made in small numbers in .243 Winchester and .308 Winchester options from c. 1964 until replaced by the VL-73 (1973–75), with its magazine flush with the stock. Sako also made a few *Kalashnikov-type m/60 (1960–61) and m/62 (1963–66) assault rifles for the Finnish Army, but the *Valmet variant was preferred. Then Sako made parts for Valmet,

until the two businesses became Sako-Valmet Oy on 1 January 1987. Work on assault rifles finally ceased in 1997, and it is assumed that the Finns will now simply buy-in weapons when necessary.

Sako has also made target pistols. The 22/32 (1971–80) and the Triace (1982–87) were distinguished by the ease with which they could be altered to chamber .22 Short rimfire, .22 Long Rifle rimfire or .32 S&W wadcutter rimfire ammunition. Conversion simply entailed changing the receiver/breech-block unit and the magazine.

Comparatively little has been written about Sako, the best source of information being the company's

commemorative booklet, *Sako 1921–1971*, which is written in Finnish with an English summary. A few details will also be gleaned from John Walter's 'David and Goliath: Sako and the Winter War' in *Shooter's Bible* no. 74, 1983; the same author's *Rifles of the World* (Krause Publications, second edition, 1998) contains a concise, but useful, listing of individual rifle models.

(q.v.), prior to 1945. **2.** Hans Sauer, Nürnberg, Germany. This inventor received British Patent 17,150/14 of 1914 for 'safety projectiles': rubber balls with a wooden insert to retain the flights. **3.** J.P. Sauer & Sohn, Suhl, Thüringen. Claiming origins in 1751, Sauer & Sohn was one of the first gunmakers to favour the *Mauser action, making sporting rifles from c. 1901 until the beginning of the First World War. The rifles often had slim fore-ends held to the barrel by a transverse key, horn trigger guards and 'flats' in the woodwork beneath the receiver. The *Deutsches Reichs-Adressbuch* for 1900 lists the proprietor as Franz Sauer, but by 1914 he had been joined by his sons, Hans and Rolf. The brothers were still running the company in 1939. In addition to the Suhl factory, a smithy (*schmeidewerk*) was to be found in nearby Steinsfeld, and an office was being maintained in Meiningen in 1941. Trading ceased at the end of the Second World War, but a new business of the same name began operating in 1948 in Eckenförde/Holstein. **4.** J.P. Sauer & Son GmbH & Companie, founded in 1948 in Eckenförde/Holstein, Germany, is the post-war successor to J.P. *Sauer & Sohn of Suhl. Now a division of SIG, it is best known for the *SIG-Sauer pistols, but also once made revolvers. Dating from the 1970s, these included SR3 target, TR6 personal-defence and VR4 sporting patterns, all with Smith & Wesson-style swing-out cylinders, and a sturdy Peacemaker-style gun known as the Western Six Shooter. **5.** Rolf Sauer, co-owner of J.P. Sauer & Sohn (q.v.), prior to 1945. **6.** Sauer pistol: *see panel, p. 454.*

Sauerbrey – 1. Aug. Sauerbrey, Suhl in Thüringen, Germany. Listed in the *Deutsches Reichs-Adressbuch* as a gunsmith, 1930–39. **2.** Erich Sauerbrey, Zella-Mehlis in Thüringen, Germany. Listed in 1939 as a gun-stock maker. **3.** Valentin Sauerbrey, Basel, Switzerland. Better known for sporting guns, Sauerbrey also made 7,000 Swiss M1869 *Vetterli rifles (1869–73).

Saunders – 1. George E. Saunders. This Federal government arms inspector, working in the early 1860s during the American Civil War, accepted cap-lock revolvers marked 'GES'. **2.** G.G. Saunders. Operating in the period immediately before the Civil War, this government arms inspector accepted *Colt Dragoon revolvers marked 'GGS'. **3.** H. Saunders, a US government arms inspector operating in the mid-1870s, accepted guns and equipment marked 'HS'. Care is necessary to distinguish his work from that of Horace *Scott, Harrison *Shaler, Harris *Smith, Howard *Stockton and H. *Syrett; although the periods differ, overlaps are to be expected. *See also* US arms inspectors' marks for this and the previous two entries.

Saunier, 3 rue Jules-Vallès, Saint-Étienne, France. Listed in 1951 as a gunmaker.

Sauvageon, rue de Lyon 47, Saint-Étienne, France. Listed in 1892 as a gunmaker.

Savage – 1. A.J. Savage Munitions Company, San Diego, California. A contractor for 100,000 .45 M1911 *Colt-Browning pistols, recruited during the First World War. No complete guns are known to have been made,

SAUER PISTOLS

Sauer (6)

These included the ★Bär and the ★Roth-Sauer, but by 1910, Sauer had decided to make guns of its own. Inspired by the ★Roth-Sauer pistol, the Old, or 1913-pattern, Sauer was designed by Heinz ★Zehner and patented in 1912. Chambered for the 6.35mm or 7.65mm Browning cartridge, it had a distinctive tubular-top frame and a separate reciprocating breech-block. The return spring was concentric with the barrel, and a striker-type firing mechanism was used. Minor variants differed in safety arrangements and dismantling systems: the first guns, for example, had a separate magazine safety system.

At least 85,000 Sauers had been made by 1918, and production of 1913-pattern pistols continued until the 7.65mm ★Behörden-Modell appeared in 1930. Unfortunately for Sauer, the improvements were not enough to allow the archaic-looking Behörden-Modell to compete with the Walther Polizei-Pistole; in 1939, therefore, a new enclosed-hammer design appeared.

Chambered for the 7.65mm

A typical 7.65mm Old Model Sauer & Sohn pistol, designed by Heinz Zehner and introduced commercially shortly before the First World War.

Browning or 9mm Short cartridge, the Modell 38-H (for *Hahn*, 'hammer') offered a sophisticated double-action trigger and a de-cocking system. It was made in large numbers during the Second World War, proving popular with military and paramilitary formations alike.

Sauer also made compact 6.35mm vest-pocket pistols (*westentaschenpistolen*) in the 1920s. The Model 1925 and Model 1928

were essentially similar, although the slide of the earlier gun was less streamlined and had additional three-quarter-depth retraction grooves at the muzzle.

although slides were produced; these bore a large 'S' within a flaming bomb centrally on the left side, directly behind the patent acknowledgements. The remainder of the contract was cancelled immediately after the Armistice of November 1918. **2.** Arthur William Savage. The first patent obtained by this gun designer was granted in July 1887 to protect a tube-magazine variant of the ★Peabody-Martini, but hinged-block actions were unsuited to magazine feed. By 1889, however, Savage had developed an improved lever-action mechanism and, in February 1893, received a patent protecting a magazine in which each cartridge was carried in a separate cradle. **3.** Edward N. Savage. Co-patentee with Henry ★North of a 'revolving firearm' protected by US Patents 22,566 of 18 January 1859 and 28,331 of 15 May 1860. Both were assigned to the Savage Revolving Fire-Arms Company. Savage also patented a shoulder stock for the revolver, protected by US Patent 32,003 of April 1861. **4.** Savage Arms Company, Utica, New York State, USA. The Savage Repeating Arms Company was organised in Utica in 1893 to exploit the ideas of Arthur W. Savage. The Savage Arms Company followed in 1899; the business was acquired in 1915 by the Driggs-Seabury Ordnance Company, and incorporation (forming the Savage Arms Corporation) occurred in 1917. The company is best known for its automatic pistols and the thousands of Lewis machine-guns made during the First World War, but was also given an order for 300,000 .45 M1911 ★Colt-Browning pistols

in 1917. No guns are known to have been made, as the contract was cancelled immediately after the 1918 Armistice. Savage made Lee-Enfield (q.v.) No. 4 Mark I★ rifles during the Second World War, the first being test fired in July 1941. By 22 June 1944, when work ceased, at least 1,000,000 guns had been assembled in the former ★Stevens Arms & Tool factory. It has been suggested that as many as 1,240,000 were made, the discrepancy arising apparently from the inclusion of many thousands of guns supplied to China under Lend-Lease arrangements. In the 1970s, by then trading from Westfield in Massachusetts, the company was distributing the products of J.G. ★Anschütz in the USA. **5.** Savage rifles, bolt-action: *see* panel, facing page. **6.** Savage rifles, lever-action: *see* panel, pp. 456/57. **7.** Savage rifles, slide-action. The centrefire 1903-pattern rifle lasted until 1921. It was a take-down design with a round-back receiver, a pistol-grip butt and a ribbed slide handle. Barrels could measure as long as 30in, and a decorative Gold Medal Model could be obtained. The 1909-pattern rifle, made until 1915, had an angular receiver and a plain cylindrical slide handle that lacked decoration. The 1914 pattern, a take-down design, was a derivative of the basic action designed to chamber Short, Long and Long Rifle .22 rimfire rounds interchangeably, but was made only in comparatively small numbers until 1924. It had a tube magazine beneath the barrel, a round-backed receiver, a ribbed slide handle and an octagonal barrel. The Model 25 of 1925–29 and the Model 29

(1929–57, with a gap for the war years) were similar, but had minor changes in the action. Pre-war guns had octagonal barrels; post-war examples usually had round barrels, while a safety catch was added in the rear web of the trigger guard. The last slide-action Savage was the Model 170, made in Westfield between 1970 and 1981 in .30-30 Winchester and .35 Remington. Locked by rotating lugs on the bolt into the receiver walls, it had a three-round tube magazine beneath the barrel and a *Monte Carlo butt with an impressed chequered panel on the pistol grip. The safety catch lay on the upper tang behind the receiver. A short-barrel .30-30 carbine version, with a straight-comb butt, appeared in 1974. **8.** Savage-Stevens. This company made 1,196,700 *Lee-Enfield .303 No. 4 Mark 1* rifles for the British government during the Second World War, together with about 40,000 supplied to China under Lend-Lease. **9.** Savage Revolving Fire-Arms Company, Middletown, Connecticut, USA. The assignee of the 'revolving firearm' patents granted to Henry Savage and Edward *North in 1859–60, this gunmaking business succeeded Savage & North in 1861. The trigger guard of the improved .36-calibre Navy, or heart guard, revolver extended back to the base of the butt. The first sales of the new .36-calibre Navy gun were made to the Federal government in August 1861, and 11,284 had been acquired by the end of the American Civil War. A few guns were made

---

SAVAGE BOLT-ACTION RIFLES

Savage (5)

Renowned for the Model 99 lever-action rifle, the Savage Arms Company – in a variety of guises! – has also made large numbers of bolt-action rifles, including No. 4 Mark I and I* Lee-Enfield (q.v.) rifles for the British and Canadian governments during the Second World War.

Although a selection of .22 rimfire patterns had been made prior to the First World War, Savage, like Remington, began work on centrefire bolt-action rifles only after hostilities had ceased. The Model 40 (1928–40) arrived hard on the heels of an unsuccessful adaptation of a classic 1898-type Mauser action. It relied on two lugs on a sleeve around the bolt to lock the breech, but was strong enough to chamber cartridges ranging from .250 Savage to .30-06. The Model 45 was a deluxe version, but the Savages were unable to compete with the Winchester M54 and M70.

The Model 340 (1957–85) originated in 1947 as the ultra-plain Stevens 320 series, Savage having purchased the J. *Stevens Arms Company in 1920. The Savage-brand guns, chambered for cartridges ranging from .22 Hornet to .30-30 Winchester, were locked by a single lug on the bolt head and another on

the back of the bolt body.

The most interesting of the post-war designs is undoubtedly the Model 110, made in accordance with patents granted in the 1950s to Nicholas Brewer. This gun has never been regarded in the same way as the legendary US designs, the *Remington Model 700 and the *Winchester Model 70; however, as these are both essentially slightly modified Mausers, the Savage is much more interesting mechanically than either. The barrel is retained by a collar, the tip of the sear/bolt-stop doubles as an indicator, protruding from the right side of the stock alongside the receiver bridge when the trigger is cocked, and a sliding safety lies on the tang behind the bolt. The most obvious feature, however, is the unusually short cocking-piece shroud.

Introduced commercially in 1958, the M110 has been made in a stupefying variety, partly due to the changing fortunes of its manufacturer. The initial chamberings were .243, .270 and .308 Winchester, plus .30-06. Medium and long actions were made in right- and left-hand versions, at a time when left-handers were often ignored; a Magnum action appeared c. 1963; and detachable box magazines were offered for the first time in 1966.

A renaissance has led to the Model 111 Classic Hunter (introduced in 1994), the Model 112 (1994), the Model 114 (1996, but retrospectively applied to an existing Classic Ultra pattern), the Model 116 (1992) and the Model 118 (1999), although all of these embody the same action. While guns are often given names (e.g. Weather Warrior), Savage habitually designates them alpha-numerically, ranging, in the case of the basic rifle, from the Model 100B (originally with a select *Monte Carlo stock) to the 110XP3 shooting-outfit guns (introduced in 1991) with 3–9x optical sights and Kwik Site mounts.

Savage rifles were made in Chicopee Falls, Massachusetts, until a move to Westfield occurred in 1959. Then the original Savage Arms Company was superseded by Savage Arms, Inc., a name that has been retained to this day.

A list of pre-1998 variants will be found in John Walter's *Rifles of the World* (Krause Publications, second edition, 1998); surprisingly, as yet there is no authoritative history of Savage.

Most of the centrefire Savage bolt-action rifles have been based on an underrated design credited to Nicholas Brewer. This is a Model 111 FCXP3, introduced in 1994 and sold as part of a shooting kit.

SAVAGE LEVER-ACTION RIFLES

Savage (6)

Made by ★Marlin, the original 1895-pattern military musket chambered .30-40 Krag cartridges and had an eight-round magazine; the carbine was similar, with the exception of its short barrel and half-stock. These guns were also made in sporting guise.

The perfected 1899-pattern musket, made until 1908 in Utica by the Savage Arms Company, was offered in .303 Savage and .30-30 Winchester. There was also a half-stocked carbine and a sporting rifle, made until 1917, which could be chambered for cartridges ranging from .22 High Velocity to .38-55 Winchester. Magazine capacity was reduced to five rounds (a sixth round could be carried in the breech if required), and changes were made in the action: a cocking indicator was set into the top surface of the bolt, and a firing-pin retractor was added. Barrels were round, half-octagonal or fully octagonal.

Simple and sturdy, the basic Savage action could handle most of the cartridges available prior to 1917, although, as the Savage breech-block compressed fractionally on firing, ultra-high-power rounds were unsuitable. The standard chambering was .303 Savage, known in Britain and the British Empire as .301 Savage to avoid confusion with the standard service cartridge.

The 1899-pattern rifle laid the basis for the sporting guns that lasted until the 1980s. These included the Model 99A (1920–42), with a straight-wrist butt and a schnabel-tip fore-end; the take-down Model 99B (1920–36); the carbine-length Model 99E (1920–36); the Featherweight Model 99F (1920–42); the Model 99G (1920–42), with chequered woodwork; the Model 99H (1931–42), a military-style solid-frame carbine with a straight-wrist butt; and the Model 99K (1931–42), a deluxe variant offered with an engraved receiver.

The Model 99EG of 1936 was an improved solid-frame gun designed to replace all of its predecessors. Other guns in this group included the Model 99R, with chequering on the pistol-grip butt and round-tip fore-end; the Model 99RS, identical to the 99R with the exception of an additional Lyman peep sight on the upper tang; and the Model 99T, a lightweight solid-frame gun. Work on all three ceased in 1942 to allow Savage to concentrate on war work.

Production of the Models 99EG (1946–60), 99R (1946–60) and 99RS (Redfield tang sight, 1946–57) began again after the Second World War, a few minor changes having been made. Work moved from Chicopee Falls to Westfield,

---

for shoulder stocks patented by Charles Alsop in May 1860 (28,433) or Edward Savage in April 1861 (32,003). Operations ceased in 1867. **10.** Savage & North, Middletown, Connecticut, USA. This business made the .36-calibre '8-Guard' revolvers patented by Henry ★North in June 1856. The US Navy ordered 300 in July 1858, and the army took 500, but neither order was completed until 1860. Total production of all the 8-Guard Savages scarcely exceeded 2,000 when work finished in 1861.

Savin-Norov, also known as the SN, this was a Soviet aircraft machine-gun designed by ★Savin and ★Norov.

Savoye. P. Savoye, rue d'Annonay 28, Saint-Étienne, France. Listed in 1879 as a distributor of, and agent for, arms and ammunition.

'SAW', 'S.A.W.', 'S...A...W' ★Headstamps found on rimfire ammunition made by the Sage Ammunition Works of Middletown, Connecticut. *See* T.C. ★Sage.

Sayga. A semi-automatic shotgun (*Samozaryadnyi gladkostvolnyi karabin Sayga*), based on the ★Kalashnikov assault rifle, was introduced by ★Izhmash A/O in 1994 in .410 and 20-bore. The Sayga-20 was not particularly successful and was replaced in 1996 by a more effective 12-bore Sayga-12 variant. The standard guns have conventional wooden butts and fore-ends, although pistol grips can be fitted instead of the butt when appropriate. The K- and S-suffix versions have assault-rifle-type pistol grips and folding butts, and short and long barrels respectively.

'Saxonia'. A brandname found on shotgun cartridges made by ★Munitionswerke Schönebeck prior to 1914.

'SB', 'S B', 'S. & B.' Marks associated with the products of ★Sellier & Bellot of Prague, often found on Austro-Hungarian (pre-1918) and Czechoslovakian (post-1918) ammunition.

'S.C.' Found on the barrels of British ★Lee-Enfield rifles with a Small Cone, an abbreviated lead from the chamber to the rifling suited to Mark VII ball ammunition.

'S.C.A.T.S.' Possibly used as a headstamp on British shotgun ammunition. *See* Southern Counties Agricultural Trading Society.

'S.C.C.', 'S.C.Co.' – **1.** Marks used in the headstamps of ammunition made by the ★Strong Cartridge Company of New Haven, prior to 1900. **2.** Found in the headstamps of cartridges made by the Standard Cartridge Company of Pasadena, California.

Schafer – **1.** George F. Schafer, Batavia, New York. Patentee (US no. 858,674 of 2 July 1907) of an ejector mechanism for shotguns. This was assigned to the ★Baker Gun & Forging Company. **2.** Th. Schäfer, Erfurt, Regierungstrasse 13, Germany. Listed in 1941 as a retailer of sporting guns and ammunition.

Schaller. H. Schaller, Suhl in Thüringen, Germany. A gunsmith known to have been trading in 1920.

Schamal. Franz Schamal, Prague, Bohemia. An air pistol made by this gunsmith was displayed at the Great Exhibition in London in 1851. Gardner, in *Small Arms Makers* (1963), dates his activities as 1847–51, but trading continued into the 1870s, possibly under the supervision of a son of the same name.

Scharf & Son, St Louis, Missouri, USA. Little is known about this business, which may only have been a retailer of spring-air Gallery Guns. One surviving example is known to have been made in St Louis by ★Basler & Denk.

Scharfenberg. Heinrich Scharfenberg, Zella-Mehlis in Thüringen, Germany. Listed in 1939 as a master gunsmith.

Schaum. Hans Schaum, Suhl in Thüringen, Germany. *See* Franken & Lünenschloss.

Schedetal. Zieh- und Stanzwerk Schedetal AG, Hannover-Munden, Germany. Founded in the 1880s, this company made ball-shot and diabolo-pattern airgun pellets. It was acquired by ★Haendler & Natermann in 1927,

Massachusetts, in 1959, and the millionth Model 99 was presented to the National Rifle Association in March 1960. Post-war patterns include the Model 99F (Featherweight, 1955–73), with a solid frame; the 99DL (1960–73), basically a 99F with a *Monte Carlo butt; the short-barrelled carbine-style Model 99E (1960–85) with skip-line chequering on the woodwork; and the Model 99C (1965 to date), with a detachable box magazine holding three .284 Winchester cartridges, or four .243 or .308 Winchester rounds.

The Model 99CD (1965–81) was a deluxe form of the 99C, but the high-qualty Models 99DE Citation Grade and 99PE Presentation Grade, introduced in 1968, sold so badly that they were abandoned within two years. A special Model 1895 commemorative was made in 1970 to mark the rifle's 75th anniversary, but it was little more than a perfected Model 99.

The modernised Model 99A of 1971, abandoned in 1982, had a sliding safety catch on the tang and could be obtained in chamberings ranging from .243 Winchester, to

The Savage Model 99C, with a detachable box magazine, is the last representative of a lever-action breech mechanism that has celebrated its centenary – although the original spool magazine, regrettably, has been discontinued.

.300 Savage. The short-lived Model 99-358 (1977–81), with a straight-comb butt and a ventilated recoil pad, was made only for the .358 Winchester round. Abandoning these guns left only the Model 99C to celebrate the design's centenary.

and finally ceased trading as a separate entity on 12 March 1974. The distinctive 'Z & S' mark has been retained by the present owners for use on export lines.

Scheintod guns. *See* panel, p. 458.

Schemann, USA: *see* Wirsing & Schemann.

Schenk. C. (or possibly G.) Schenk, Berne, Switzerland. Maker of a crank-wound volute-spring gallery pistol, probably about 1875–80.

Schenkl. John Schenkl of Boston, Massachusetts, patented a needle rifle in June 1857 and offered it commercially prior to the Civil War without success. It had a half-octagonal barrel and a case-hardened receiver. The trigger guard could be turned to the right to move the barrel away from the standing breech, tip it forward and expose the chamber.

Scheufler. Bernhard Scheufler, Berlin, Germany. This man was granted a German patent on 10 August 1881, protecting a push-in barrel airgun very similar to the contemporary *Quackenbush.

Schieler. Oskar Schieler & Sohn, Suhl in Thüringen, Germany. A gunmaking business trading in the 1920s.

Schiesse mit Luft. A brandname ('Shooting with Air') registered by *Mayer & Grammelspacher of Rastatt/Baden in 1904.

Schilling – 1. A. Schilling, Zella-Mehlis in Thüringen, Germany. Listed in 1930 as a master gunsmith. 2. Bernhard Schilling, Suhl in Thüringen, Hügel 1, in 1940. Listed as a gunmaker (*büchsenmacher*) in the *Deutsches Reichs-Adressbuch* and other German trade directories of 1930–45. 3. Charles Schilling, St Louis, Missouri, USA. Son of Frederick Schilling (below), working until the late 1870s. 4. Ed. Schilling, Suhl in Thüringen. Listed in the 1920 edition of the *Deutsches Reichs-Adressbuch* as a gunsmith, 1920. 5. Ernst Friedr. Schilling, Suhler Waffen- u. Fahrrad-schmiede, Suhl in Thüringen, Schneid 11. Listed in 1914 as a gun-

maker, and again in 1939–41 as a maker of sporting guns and accessories under the proprietorship of Friedrich Paul Schilling. 6. F. Schilling, Suhl in Thüringen, Germany. Trading in 1939 as a specialist gun-part maker. 7. Frederick Schilling, St Louis, Missouri, USA. Schilling may have come originally from Lancaster, Pennsylvania, where a gunsmith of the same name was active in the 1850s. He joined *Blickensdorfer in 1865, becoming a partner in the business in 1869. Gallery Guns were being made by 1870, but by 1873 Schilling was operating alone. The 1875 city directory lists Charles F. *Schilling at 12 Third Street in St Louis, and Frederick Schilling apparently in Columbus, Ohio. (NB: Robert E. Gardner, in *Small Arms Makers* confusing listed the proprietor of Blickensdorfer & Schilling as J. Schilling.) 8. Friedr. Paul Schilling, Suhl in Thüringen. The owner of Ernst Friedr. Schilling (above) from c. 1930 until the end of the Second World War. 9. G. Schilling, Zella-Mehlis in Thüringen, Germany. Listed in 1939 as a master gunsmith. 10. Gottlieb Schilling, Suhl in Thüringen, Germany. Listed during 1920–39 as a gunsmith. 11. H. Schilling, Suhl in Thüringen, Germany. A specialist gun-barrel maker trading in 1930. 12. Hugo Schilling, Suhl in Thüringen, Germany. Listed in 1930 and 1939 as a gunsmith. 13. Paul Schilling, Suhl in Thüringen. Proprietor of Schilling & Kramer (below) prior to 1945. 14. Rob. L. Schilling, Suhl in Thüringen, Germany. A 'weapons maker' operating in 1939. 15. Str. Schilling, Suhl in Thüringen, Germany. Listed as a specialist barrel-blank maker in the *Deutsches Reichs-Adressbuch* for 1939. 16. Val. Chris. Schilling, Suhl in Thüringen, Germany. Founded in 1816, this business became one of Germany's leading nineteenth-century gunmakers. Schilling made revolvers as part of a combine with *Haenel and *Sauer in the late nineteenth century, and may have made airguns for *Bergmann or Eisenwerke Gaggenau. Schilling made semi-automatic pis-

SCHEINTOD GUNS

Among the most popular non-lethal 'disabling guns' have been the *Scheintod* (simulated-death) patterns, often originating in Germany – Adolf *Niemeyer of Suhl was one of the most prominent makers – at the end of the nineteenth century, accompanying the rise of bicycling. Cyclists in urban and rural areas alike soon realised that they needed some protection against dogs and wolves. One result was the development of the small-calibre *Puppy and *Velo-Dog revolvers, but the use of firearms of this type came under increasing restriction.

Scheintod guns were an alternative, firing blanks, flares, tear-gas, pepper or even sand. The calibre was customarily 12mm prior to the First World War, although 10mm versions were also made; post-1918 guns may chamber cartridges as small as 6mm. At their crudest, Scheintod pistols consisted of a barrel that was either screwed into the breech face or attached by a bayonet joint. More sophisticated designs could have sliding barrels locked by radial levers, but almost all had simple single-

action lockwork and sheath triggers.

Fare pistols, marked '*Entlarvt*' ('Flash') are generally comparable. The earliest examples, usually made prior to the First World War, had steel barrels and gutta-percha grips; post-war guns often had zinc barrels and Bakelite grips. Additional details will be found in Lewis Winant's

A three-barrel Menz Scheintod pistol, clearly derived from the same manufacturer's cartridge-firing Regnum, made in Germany prior to the First World War.

Firearms Curiosa (Greenberg, 1955), and John Walter's *Secret Firearms* (Arms & Armour Press, 1995).

---

tols for Bergmann, until allegedly the facilities were acquired in 1904 by Henrich Krieghoff. However, the *Deutsches Reichs-Adressbuch* lists the owners in 1900 as Albert and Moritz Schilling, who had been joined by 1914 by Walter Schilling. Fortunes declined considerably in the immediate post-1918 period, and the 1920 directories record the sole proprietor as Ludwig Bornhöft. Schilling completed 1898-pattern *Mauser rifle actions in half-stocked sporting guise, offering them in chamberings ranging from 6x58 Förster to 8x75. Most will bear a discreet 'V.C.S.' mark. In a trade directory entry dating from the mid-1920s, the company offered 'hunting and practice weapons of all types, optical sights, ammunition and the ability to offer catalogues and handle correspondence…in all languages'. The *Deutsches Reichs-Adressbuch* continued to list Schilling as a 'weapons maker and sales agency' in 1930, and a 'weapons maker' (*waffenfabrik*) in 1939. Premises were occupied in Suhl at Strasse de Sturm-Abteilung 10 (1938–41), but the once-renowned business had lost much of its impetus by the time the Second World War began, and had regained very little when work finally ceased in 1945. It used 'VCS' and 'V.C.S.' as trademarks. **17.** Schilling & Kramer, Suhl in Thüringen, Strasse der Sturm-Abteilung 21. A maker of guns and gun parts listed in the *Deutsches Reichs-Adressbuch* for 1940.
Schimel Arms Company. This business was formed in 1952 to make the Schimel gas-operated pistol, known as the GP 22. The fixtures were acquired by the *American Weapons Corporation in 1955, and manufacture continued as the *American Luger (later Carbo-Jet).

Schindler. Christian Ludwig Schindler Sohn, Zella St Blasii, Thüringen, Germany. Listed in 1900 as a gunmaker.
Schleenstein. Ernst Schleenstein, Suhl in Thüringen, Germany. Listed in 1939 as a gunsmith.
Schlegelmilch – 1. Caspar Schlegelmilch, Suhl in Thüringen, Germany. Trading in 1914–20 as a specialist gun-barrel maker, under the ownership of Ernst Wilhelm Schlegelmilch. **2.** Franz Schlegelmilch, Suhl in Thüringen, Germany. A barrel-blank maker listed in the 1939 edition of the *Deutsches Reichs-Adressbuch*. **3.** H. Schlegelmilch, Zella-Mehlis in Thüringen, Germany. Listed in 1939 as a master gunsmith. **4.** Hermann Schlegelmilch, Suhl in Thüringen, Germany. Registered as a gun-stocker shortly before 1939. **5.** Hermann Schlegelmilch, Zella-Mehlis in Thüringen, Germany. Listed in 1939 as a gun-barrel drawer. **6.** H. & K. Schlegelmilch, Suhl in Thüringen, Germany. Listed in 1900 as a gunmaker. **7.** Louis Schlegelmilch. A gunmaker associated with the German *Reichsgewehr, and also with a primitive semi-automatic pistol. **8.** Reinhard Schlegelmilch, Suhl in Thüringen, Germany. This gun-stocker was listed in the 1939 directories, but had ceased operations by 1945. **9.** Robert Schlegelmilch, Meiningen an der Ower. Listed in pre-1914 directories as a maker of sporting guns.
Schlesinger. Joseph Schlesinger. An English based gunmaker listed in 1856 at Albion Place, London Wall.
Schlütter – 1. Alfred Schlütter, Zella-Mehlis in Thüringen. Listed in 1920 as a wholesaler of guns, accessories and ammunition. Listed in the *Deutsches Reichs-Adressbuch* for 1930 (as Alfred Schlüter) as a retailer of

guns and ammunition, but possibly also maintaining repair facilities. **2.** Herbert Schlütter, Zella-Mehlis in Thüringen, Germany. Listed in 1930 as a gunmaker. **3.** Robert Schlütter, Zella-Mehlis in Thüringen, Germany. Listed in 1939 as a gun-stock maker.

Schmaltzern, New York City. Recorded by Eldon Wolff, in *Air Guns* (1958), as a maker of volute-spring *Gallery Guns, operating in the 1870s. On occasion the name has been listed as 'Schmalzlar'.

Schmalz & Decker, Zella St Blasii in Thüringen, Germany. Listed in 1900 as a gun- and weapon maker.

Schmeisser, Schmeißer – 1. Hans Schmeisser, Suhl, Thüringen, Germany. The co-patentee with his father, Hugo, of the pan magazine for the *Haenel air rifle: British Patent 302,279. **2.** Hugo Schmeisser, Suhl. The son of the gunmaker Louis Schmeisser (below), Hugo Schmeisser is best remembered for the submachine-guns and assault rifles designed for C.G. *Haenel, but he also patented the *Sportmodell bolt-action airgun. Most patents granted to Schmeisser list his address as 5 Philosophenwerg, Suhl. British Patent 277,265, accepted on 15 September 1927, protected the cocking mechanism of the Haenel Models 26 and 28 air pistols. The action resembles the *Improved Britannia rifle. British Patent 302,279 (with Hans Schmeisser) was accepted on 30 January 1930 to protect an automatic pan magazine used on the Haenel IVR and VR rifles. British Patent 391,695 of 4 May 1933 allowed claims for a means of latching cheap children's-type airguns, using a spring-steel bar above the receiver. British Patents 422,231 of 1934 (for the detachable box magazine) and 422,638 of 1934 protected the perfected *Sportmodell bolt-action. British Patent 472,854, accepted on 1 October 1937, was a combination of the two German patents (21 May 1935 and 8 October 1936) granted for a revised version of the *Sportmodell with a multiple spring assembly to provide greater power. There was also an automatic loading port for diabolo pellets. British Patent 499,543 allowed improvements to 472,854. Schmeisser's name is also attached mistakenly to the German MP. 38 and MP. 40 submachine-guns, and, with a little more justification, to the Mkb. 42 (H) that developed into the MP. 43/Stg. 44 series. **3.** Louis Schmeisser (1848–1917), father of Hugo Schmeisser (above), worked first for *Bergmann, then with *Rheinische Metallwaaren- & Maschinenfabrik. He is remembered as the designer of the *Dreyse pistols and machine-gun.

Schmidl. Eduard Schmidl, one of the leading gunmakers established in *Weipert, Bohemia (part of Austria-Hungary prior to 1918), was a principal member of a co-operative formed in 1887 to produce components for the straight-pull *Mannlicher service rifle that had been adopted for the Austro-Hungarian Army.

Schmidt, Schmidt… – 1. Franz Schmidt, Zella-Mehlis and Suhl, Thüringen, Germany. Listed in 1930 as a gunmaker; in 1939 as a gunsmith; and in 1941 as a maker of weapons (*waffenfabrik*). **2.** Franz & Herbert Schmidt, Zella-Mehlis in Thüringen. Founded in 1919, this partnership made sporting guns and accessories, often marked 'FHS', before moving to Suhl in the 1920s. *See also* Franz Schmidt. **3.** Herbert Schmidt, Ostheim an der Rhön, Germany. In addition to good-quality revolvers and an array of blank-firers, made since 1963, Schmidt produces a small 6.35mm Model 5 semi-automatic pistol with a six-round box magazine in the butt. Guns may be marked simply 'HS'. **4.**

Moritz Schmidt, Zella-Mehlis in Thüringen, Germany. Listed in 1930–39 as a master gunsmith. **5.** Paul Schmidt, Zella-Mehlis in Thüringen, Germany. Listed in 1939 as a maker of guns and weapons. **6.** Rob. Schmidt, Suhl in Thüringen, Germany. Trading in 1930 as a gunsmith. **7.** Rudolf Schmidt was born in Basel in June 1832, the son of a water-colourist. Joining the army in 1853, he obtained a commission two years later, was eventually promoted to the rank of colonel (*oberst*) in 1887, retired in 1894 and died in 1898. He is remembered principally for a series of revolvers, culminating in the 1882-pattern 7.5mm army model, and the Schmidt-Rubin rifle of 1889. However, he was also responsible for the modernisation of the Swiss arms industry and the foundation of the *Eidgenössische Waffenfabrik in Bern. **8.** Theodor Schmidt, Zella-Mehlis in Thüringen, Germany. Listed in 1930 as a maker of guns and weapons. **9.** E. Schmidt & Habermann, Suhl in Thüringen, Roschstrasse 1 (in 1940–41). Founded in 1886, this gun-making business was listed in 1900 and 1914 as being owned by Richard, Franz and Paul Stadelmann; in 1920–30 by Franz and Paul Stadelmann; and in 1939 by Paul Stadelmann alone. Schmidt & Habermann was responsible for a unique short-action *Mauser-pattern rifle known as the Model 21. Offered only in 6.5x54, 8x51 and .250-3000 Savage chamberings, it had a special knurled cocking-piece knob and a simplified safety system. The company also offered Mauser-pattern sporting rifles, often identified only by a small 'S & H' mark (cf. 'S & K'). **10.** Schmidt-Rubin. Designed by Rudolf Schmidt (above), this military rifle chambered a 7.5x53.5mm semi-rimless cartridge designed by Eduard *Rubin. First tested in 1885, although not patented until September 1889, the straight-pull action was remarkable chiefly for its excessive length and for the cammed rod-like actuator in a chamber on the right side of the receiver. The *Infanterie-Repetier-Gewehr* was adopted in Switzerland on 26 June 1889 after trials against the *Neuhausen (SIG) design, rifles and carbines subsequently being made in quantity by the *Eidgenössische Waffenfabrik. Experience showed the action to be weak, and the improved M89/96 of 27 September 1897 embodied a shortened action credited to Vogelsang & Rebholz. This was followed on 10 January 1913 by the strengthened M1911 and a new long-mouth 7.5x55mm cartridge, then on 16 June 1933 by the Kar.31 and a perfected compact action, 70mm shorter than the M1889. By far the best source of details is Sallaz and Am Rhyn, *Handfeuerwaffen Gradzug-Systeme* (Stocker-Schmid, 1978), but a brief listing of individual patterns will be found in the second edition of John Walter's *Rifles of the World* (Krause Publications, 1998).

Schmitt – 1. Listed in 1892 at rue Gambette 32, Saint-Étienne, France, this gunmaker was one half of Schmitt et Freyssinet (below). Still trading in 1933 as Schmitt frères. **2.** Schmitt et Freyssinet, place de l'Hôtel-de-Ville 5 and rue du Treuil 9, Saint-Étienne, France. Listed in 1879 as a gunmaker.

Schnabel tip. A distinctive swelling of the tip of a *fore-end. Occasionally rendered colloquially as 'snobble'.

Schneider – 1. Alfred Schneider, Zella-Mehlis in Thüringen, Germany. Listed in 1939 as a master gunsmith. **2.** Edmund Schneider, Zella-Mehlis in Thüringen, Germany. Listed during 1920–30 as a gunmaker. **3.** Eduard Schneider, Zella St Blasii in Thüringen, Germany. Listed in 1900 as a gunmaker. **4.** Ernst Hugo Schneider, Zella-Mehlis in Thüringen, Germany. Listed during 1920–30 as a gunmaker, and in 1939 as a distributor of guns and ammunition. **5.** François Eugène Schneider, France. *See* Snider. **6.** Gustav Schneider, Zella St Blasii and Zella-Mehlis in Thüringen, Germany. Listed during 1900–20 as a gunmaker and engineering workshop, when owned by Rudolf Schneider. Listed as a gunmaker until 1945. **7.** Hermann Schneider, Zella St Blasii and Zella-Mehlis in Thüringen, Germany. This gunmaker was listed between 1914 and 1939, but ceased trading at the end of the Second World War. **8.** Max Schneider, Zella-Mehlis in Thüringen, Germany. Listed in 1930 as a gunmaker. **9.** M. & R. Schneider, Zella-Mehlis in Thüringen, Germany. Listed in 1930 as a master gunsmith. **10.** R. Schneider, Zella-Mehlis in Thüringen, Germany. Listed in 1930 as a gun-stock maker. **11.** Rudolf Schneider, Zella-Mehlis in Thüringen, Germany. Listed in 1930–32 as a maker of guns and weapons. Possibly the same as R. Schneider (above). **12.** Rudolf Schneider, Zella-Mehlis in Thüringen, Germany. Listed in 1939 as a gun-stock maker.

Schnell. George C. Schnell, sometimes listed as Snell, was a US government arms inspector. Working in the first decade of the twentieth century, he accepted equipment marked 'GCS'. *See also* US arms inspectors' marks.

Schnellfeuerpistole (rapid-fire pistol). This term was applied to two selective-fire pistols made in the 1930s by Mauser-Werke AG, largely as a result of the introduction of similar *Astra, *Azul and *Royal patterns in Spain. The original Mauser pattern was credited to Josef Nickl (1933), but the perfected version was the work of Karl Westinger (1936); the former had a plain bar selector, whereas the latter had an oval plate on the left side of the frame, above the trigger aperture. Production was comparatively small, as the modified Model 712 C/96-type pistols were inaccurate when the selector was set to fire automatically. However they were popular in China and the Far East.

Schnorrenberg. Wilh. Schnorrenberg, Suhl in Thüringen. A wholesaler of guns and ammunition active in Suhl in the 1890s.

Schobbert. Henry Albert Charles Schobbert. Listed as a 'merchant', and possibly an importer of European-made guns, this patentee (British Patent 20,578/07 of 1907) developed a repeating airgun. His address was listed as 59 Darenth Hill, Stamford Hill, London N.

Schoch. Edward J. Schoch. A US government arms inspector, working early in the twentieth century, Schoch accepted weapons and equipment marked 'EJS'. *See also* US arms inspectors' marks.

Schoettlin. Anna Barbara Belzner Schoettlin, 121 Richardson Avenue, Jefferson, Alabama, USA. This 'Gentlewoman' was the co-patentee of an airgun with her brother, Nathan *Price.

Schofield – **1.** Frank H. Schofield, a lieutenant in the US Navy working c. 1895–1905, accepted *Gatling Guns, and *Colt and *Smith & Wesson revolvers marked 'FHS'. *See also* US arms inspectors' marks. **2.** George W. Schofield. A major in the US Army, Schofield obtained US Patents 116,225 of 20 June 1871 and 138,047 of 22 April 1873 to protect improvements in revolver design. The guns were made in substantial numbers by Smith & Wesson as the 'Schofield Model'. Schofield committed suicide with one of his own revolvers in 1882. **3.** Schofield Model. Made by *Smith & Wesson in accordance with patents obtained by Major George Schofield of the US Army, this revolver had a simplified extractor

and a latch on the standing frame instead of the barrel extension. The US Army had purchased more than 8,000 Schofield Smith & Wessons by the end of 1879, but these were unable to challenge the Colt *Single Action Army revolvers and nothing more was done.

Schön. A. Schön, Suhl in Thüringen, Germany. Listed in 1920 as a gunsmith, and in 1930 as a gunmaker.

Schönauer. Otto Schönauer. Born in 1844 in Reichraming, in Austria-Hungary, Schönauer underwent a gunsmithing apprenticeship before working for *Vetterli in Switzerland. In 1868, he was invited by Josef *Werndl to join Waffenfabrik Steyr; his subsequent career included promotion to head of the inspectorate (1889) and factory manager (1896). Although renowned for his skills as an administrator, Otto Schönauer also designed bolt-action rifles and the rotary, or spool, magazine associated with the perfected *Mannlicher-Schönauer. He died in Steyr on 17 September 1913.

Schönberger. Among the earliest auto-loading handguns, although still the subject of controversy, this was tested by the Austro-Hungarian military authorities c. 1895. The name appears to have been provided by the promoters, the Schönberger brothers of Vienna, but the design was due to Josef Laumann. The operating system has been debated on many occasions, as some writers have identified it as a delayed blowback, while others have claimed it to be an example of primer actuation. In addition, the date of introduction is contested vigorously. Although the Austro-Hungarian authorities were happy to test handguns such as the Schönberger, the *Kromar and the *Salvator-Dormus, few were efficient enough. Better designs prevailed eventually, including the *Borchardt, the *Mauser-Feederle and the *Mannlichers.

Schorn. Josef Schorn, Koblenz-Lützel, Germany. This gunsmith (1909–69) was granted German Patent 763,786 of March 1943 to protect a selective-fire modification of the *Parabellum pistol. Alterations were made to the sear bar, and a pivoting selector lever was added in the trigger plate.

Schoverling & Daly, subsequently Schoverling, Daly & Gales, New York City. A distributor of guns and ammunition, active in the second half of the nineteenth century. In 1888 the partnership, which then included Gales, purchased the gunsmithing and distribution business of John P. Moore of Broadway, New York (established in 1823). *See also* Marlin.

Schroeder, Salewski & Schmidt. Grantees of US patent 16,288 (23 December 1856) protecting a needle gun. Immigrant German gunmakers Herman Schroeder, Louis Salewski and William Schmidt are credited as the designers, the guns being made in Schmidt's workshop in New York. Turning a lever on the right side of the fore-end simultaneously down and back allowed a rack-and-pinion mechanism to move the barrel away from the breech and cocked the needle mechanism. Prototypes tested by the US Army performed as badly as the few that were sold as sporting guns. Schroeder patented an improved version in June 1861, but the project was overtaken by better designs.

Schubarth. Caspar D. Schubarth, or 'Schuberth', Providence, Rhode Island, USA. A gunsmith active during 1855–68.

Schuch. Paul Schuch, Suhl in Thüringen, Germany. A gunsmith trading in 1939.

Schuetzen, Schützen – **1.** This term, which means

'marksmen' in German, is applied to a particular type of target shooting (and, by extension, target rifle) originating in central Europe and popularised in the USA during the nineteenth century. The rifles usually have elaborate set triggers, palm rests beneath the fore-ends, exaggerated cheek pieces and combs, hooked butt plates and fully adjustable sights. **2.** Schuetzen Junior Model. Offered only for the .32-40 and .38-55 Ballard cartridges, the 1884-vintage No. 10 *Ballard target rifle was essentially the same as the No. 8 *Union Hill pattern, but had a heavy octagonal barrel and an 800yd vernier back sight. **3.** Schuetzen Model. Known as the Off-Hand Model when it was introduced in the USA in 1876, the heavyweight No. 6 *Ballard rifle was intended for *Schuetzen-style target shooting. Most guns had a double set trigger system, Marlin's short- or mid-range vernier peep back sights, and hand-made straight-wrist 'German'-style butts with a nickel-plated hook-pattern shoulder plate. Chamberings ranged from .32-40 Ballard to .44-75 Ballard. **4.** Schuetzen Match Rifle. Built on the *Remington-Hepburn or *Hepburn-Walker action, the No. 3 Schuetzen Match Rifle (1904–07) had a scrolled trigger guard, a vernier wind-gauge peep sight on the tang and a straight-wrist butt with a shallow cheek-piece. It chambered cartridges ranging from .32-40 Ballard to .40-65 Remington.

Schüler – **1.** August Schüler, Suhl in Thüringen, Germany. Listed in the 1900 edition of the *Deutsches Reichs-Adressbuch* as a gunmaking business, owned by Friedrich Schüler and his son, Oskar. Friedrich retired in 1912, to be succeeded by Oscar and grandson Richard. Some products will be found marked 'ASS'. **2.** August Gottlieb Schüler, Suhl in Thüringen. A gunmaking business claiming a foundation date of 1850. **3.** Friedrich Wilhelm Schüler, Suhl in Thüringen. A gunmaking business claiming to have begun operations in 1835. **4.** Oscar Schüler & Sohn, Suhl in Thüringen, Germany. Trading in 1930 as a gunmaker and sales agency. **5.** Oscar & August Schüler, Suhl in Thüringen. Founded in 1880; usually listed as a weapon maker (*waffenfabrik*). It was superseded c. 1900 by August Schuler (above). **6.** Oscar & Richard Schüler, Suhl in Thüringen, Germany. This gunmaking partnership, perhaps only active in 1912/13, offered *Mauser-action sporting rifles made by *Sempert & Krieghoff. Richard Schüler (below) succeeded his father, although the original trading name may have been retained until the end of the First World War. **7.** O. & F. Schüler Söhne, Suhl in Thüringen, Germany. Listed as a gunmaker in 1900. **8.** Richard Schüler, Suhl in Thüringen, Schillingstrasse 1 (1941). Claiming to have been founded in 1913, succeeding Oscar & Richard Schüler (q.v.), this mechanised weapon- and ammunition-making business, at Roschstrasse 13, continued until the end of the Second World War. Richard Schüler specialised in *Mauser-action rifles chambering a variety of proprietary cartridges, beginning with an 11.2x60 dating from 1913 and progressing to a huge 12.7x70 in the early 1920s. Made for Schüler by Sempert & Krieghoff, these rifles were large and heavy, with the magazine box protruding from the fore-end, ahead of the trigger. The last Schüler round, 6.5x68, appeared in the early 1930s.

Schulhof. Josef Schulhof: *see panel, below.*

Schüller – **1.** A. Schüller, Zella-Mehlis in Thüringen, Germany. Listed in 1930 as a gun-stock maker. **2.** Otto Schüller, Zella-Mehlis in Thüringen, Germany. Founded in 1884; listed in 1920 as a gun-stock maker, and during 1930–39 as a master gunsmith and gun-stocker.

Schulte – **1.** Al. Schulte, Herbrüggen-Gewehrfabrik, Zella St Blasii and Zella-Mehlis in Thüringen. The Zella manufactory also acted as a gun distributor, based in the Ruhr in a small town close to Essen. The business was listed in the 1914 edition of the *Deutsches Reichs-Adressbuch* as a gunmaker and lasted until the end of the Second World War. **2.** Charles Schulte. A member of the London gun trade, operating from 25 Moorgate Street in 1871/72.

Schultze... – **1.** Schultze Gunpowder Company, 28 Gresham Street and 254a Gray's Inn Road, London, and

JOSEF SCHULHOF

Born in Dolní Kalná in 1824, Josef Schulhof had an interesting career. The son of a tenant farmer on the Esterhazy estates in Hungary, Schulhof exhibited considerable skills in repairing agricultural equipment. This encouraged him to relinquish his farming tenancy in 1870 and move to Vienna. Schulhof is remembered for a series of extraordinary repeating rifles with magazines in their butts, originally adapted from *Vetterli actions, but later specially built in Austria and Belgium.

The 1882-pattern rifle had a thumb trigger on the stock wrist and a multiple tandem-column magazine encased in the butt. This was improved in 1883, retaining the basic principles of its predecessor, but with a simpler '5+4+1' magazine, an interrupted-thread locking system and a conventional trigger.

The failure of the butt-magazine system discouraged Schulhof sufficiently to substitute a five-round rotary design adapted from Spitalsky's. The 1887-pattern gun was made in Liège – possibly by *Pieper – and had a turning-bolt action with two locking lugs. Tested several times in Austria-Hungary, but rejected each time of grounds of needless complexity and expense, the guns were never successful; a target pistol, however, was good enough to sell in quantity. Schulhof died in Heitzing on 11 June 1890.

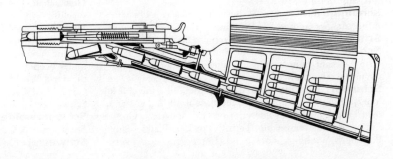

A drawing of the aberrant Schulhof magazine rifle, showing how the cartridge capacity was increased by using the butt as a magazine.

Eyeworth Lodge, Hampshire. This business was registered in July 1868 at 3 Bucklersbury, London, to perfect a semi-smokeless wood-based propellant invented by a Prussian Army officer, Hauptmann (Captain) Johannes Eduard Schultze. The directors were C. Dale, R.W.S. Griffith, V.T. Mitchell and H.T. Withers. Schultze had visited Britain in 1864, at the suggestion of the gunmaker James D. *Dougall the Elder, but it took some years for the project to become a commercial reality. Even then, it required many years of research and the substitution of wood fibres for cubes before the propellant was stable enough to be used in small-arms ammunition. From 1880, however, business grew steadily. Improved forms of the propellant were introduced in the early 1900s: Imperial in 1902 and Cube in 1908. Prior to 1909, Schultze seems to have relied greatly on cases provided by *Eley Bros., but the short-lived *Cogschultze Ammunition & Powder Company Ltd (active c. 1909–11) changed the source of components, until Schultze was acquired by *Eley Bros. c. 1912. However, a vestige of independence was retained by the formation of the Schultze Company Ltd (below). Among the many shotgun cartridges loaded under the Schultze banner from 1899 onward were The Albion, The Bomo, The Captain, The Caro, The Conqueror, The Eyeworth, Grand Prix, The Pickaxe, The Torro, The Westminster and The Yeoman. Most also bore a registered trademark in the form of a clenched fist holding a bolt of lightning. Although these often bore 'S.G. Co.' in the headstamps, most had been made with components supplied by *Eley Bros. **2.** Schultze Company Ltd [The], 28 Gresham Street, London, and Eyeworth, Hampshire. This was the post-1912 incarnation of the Schultze Gunpowder Company (above), owned by *Eley Bros. Among the new products introduced in the post-Eley period were the Popular and Lightning propellants, dating from 1912 and 1913 respectively. Trading continued independently throughout the First World War – a change of name to The Schultze Gunpowder Company Ltd occurred in 1916 to emphasise British origins – until the formation of *Explosive Trades Ltd and *Nobel Industries. It has been claimed that Schultze-branded cartridges were being made as late as 1923, and some of the names were perpetuated by *Eley-Kynoch, increasing the confusion.

Schultz & Larsen, Otterup, Denmark. This gunsmithing business, specialising in custom-made sporting rifles (often built on wartime Czechoslvakian M24 or German Kar. 98k *Mauser actions), also supplied 8x58R bolt-action carbines, or *Rigspolitikarabiner m/42*, to the Danish state police during the German occupation of Denmark in the Second World War. These had tubular receivers with large oval ejection ports, and one-piece stocks that extended to the muzzle. Some post-war sporting and target rifles were built on an improved form of this same action.

Schuman(n). George W. Schuman(n) was a US arms inspector. *See* George W. *Sherman.

Schütt. Hans Schütt oHG: *see* Bayerische Sportwaffenfabrik.

Schutzmann. A brandname and trademark associated with Albrecht *Kind, often accompanied by a three-quarter perspective view of a moustachioed pistoleer.

Schuyler, Hartley & Graham, Maiden Lane, New York, USA. This wholesaler advertised itself in 1871 as a distributor of 'Every description of Sporting Guns, imported on Reasonable Terms; Powder Flasks, Shot Pouches, Washing Rods, and Implements of every description requisite for the Sporting Field; Agents for Caps, Wads, Metallic Cartridges, &c., manufactured by the Union Metallic Cartridge Company, Bridgeport, Connecticut…' Schuyler, Hartley & Graham was sole US agent for several British and European gunmakers, including W.W. *Greener of Birmingham, and sold large numbers of Smith & Wesson *Russian Model revolvers in the 1870s. It was succeeded by *Hartley & Graham c. 1877.

Schwab. Elias Schwab, one of the leading gunmakers established in *Weipert in Bohemia (then part of Austria-Hungary), was a principal member of a co-operative formed in 1887 to produce components for the straight-pull *Mannlicher service rifle that had been adopted for the Austro-Hungarian Army. Little else is known of his operations.

Schwarte & Hammer. This gunmaking partnership traded from 6 Lime Street, London, from 1885 until 1900 or later.

Schwarzlose – 1. Andreas Wilhelm Schwarzlose, born in Altmärkisches Wust on 31 July 1867, is one of the more interesting of the pre-1914 German firearms inventors. Unlike contemporaries such as *Mannlicher and *Mauser, whose reputation depended largely on the perfection of a single design – often with the help of others – Schwarzlose was always prepared to try something different. The son of a farmer, he served in the Austro-Hungarian artillery during the 1890s, graduating from the army ordnance school, then, after leaving military service, from the technical college in Suhl. Testimony to the fertility of Schwarzlose's mind is provided by a range of pistols produced in the 1890s, culminating in a military, or 1898, pattern that was very nearly a great success. He also developed the only blow-forward design to find commercial favour, selling several thousand in Europe before rights were hawked to North American interests prior to the First World War. The inventor died on 18 April 1936. **2.** A.W. Schwarzlose GmbH. Formed in Berlin early in the twentieth century, this gunmaking business made the blow-forward pistols patented by Andreas Schwarzlose in 1908. It is also believed to have made the prototype Schwarzlose machine-guns, although volume production was licensed to *Österreichische Waffenfabriks-Gesellschaft. The factory was closed soon after the First World War, although machine-guns and machine-gun parts were still being made in Sweden and Czechoslovakia as late as 1930. **3.** Schwarzlose machine-gun. This had been perfected by 1902. Compared with the recoil-operated *Maxim, the delayed-blowback mechanism was extremely simple. It was easy to make and proved reliable once the rapid opening of the breech had been delayed sufficiently. The experimental 1905-type gun was superseded by the perfected short-barrelled *Maschinengewehr M. 07*. Made under licence in Austria by *Österreichische Waffenfabriks-Gesellschaft, the 8mm Schwarzlose M. 07 and M. 07/12 machine-guns not only survived with the Austro-Hungarians until the end of the First World War, but also equipped the post-war Austrian, Hungarian, Czechoslovakian and Yugoslav Armies. Large numbers had been made under licence in Sweden and the Netherlands even before the First World War began, and a few M1912 guns in 6.5x54 had been supplied to Greece prior to 1914. **4.** Schwarzlose pistols: *see* panel, facing page.

Schwarzwalder Jagd- und Sportwaffenfabrik. *See* Voetter & Co.

Schweizer. Karl August Schweizer, Stuttgart, Germany.

SCHWARZLOSE PISTOLS

Schwarzlose (4)

Andreas Schwarzlose obtained a variety of patents to protect his earliest handgun designs, including British Patents 23,881/92 of 27 December 1892 and 9490/95 of 1895. The former protected what has been described as an automatic form of the Remington *Rolling Block, with the cartridges contained in the frame, whereas the latter was a more conventional long-recoil design locked by a rotating bolt.

The first Schwarzlose to encounter success was the Standart or Military Model, patented in Britain on 25 January 1898 (no. 1934/98), which chambered the 7.63mm Mauser cartridge and apparently was made in Suhl c. 1898–1900 (perhaps by Waffenfabrik von *Dreyse). Locking lugs on the bolt were disengaged when the barrel recoiled, allowing the bolt and its tubular housing to reciprocate alone. The principle was efficient, but sales were poor; remaining stocks are said to have been sold to Russian revolutionaries in 1905.

An unsuccessful toggle-locked gun patented in 1900 was followed by the 7.65mm Schwarzlose of 1908, the only *blow-forward pistol ever to achieve commercial success. Several thousand were made by A.W. Schwarzlose GmbH in Berlin, before the project was transferred to the *Warner Arms Corporation in 1911 to allow the Berlin facilities to concentrate on machine-guns. The earliest guns have grooved-breech barrel-blocks and a grip-safety

The 7.65mm Schwarzlose Standard pistol of 1898 was offered commercially in small numbers, but failed to challenge the supremacy of the Mauser C/96 and the Borchardt–Luger. The remaining inventory is said to have been sold to Russian revolutionaries in 1905. Courtesy of Joseph J. Schroeder.

mechanism; later examples, often bearing the patent dates (13 April and 24 August 1908), have diced barrel-blocks and radial safety levers.

Trading from Werrastrasse 81 in 1925, Schweizer advertised his services as a wholesaler of guns and ammunition, particularly the products of *Simson & Co. of Suhl, offering to supply 'all kinds of guns and accessories'.

Schweizerische Industrie-Gesellschaft, Neuhausen am Rheinfalls. *See panel, pp. 464/65.*

Schweinsruckenschaft. *See* Stock.

Schwertanker (sword-anchor). A description of the central component of a trademark granted in 1928 to Heinrich *Krieghoff Waffenfabrik of Suhl. *See* 'HK'.

Scoffin & Wilmot, Ironcrete Works, Barking By-Pass. A maker of magazines for the British 9mm *Sten Gun during the Second World War. The regional code 'S 103' may have been used instead of the company name. *See also* British military manufacturers' marks.

Scolaire. *See* Buffalo-Scolaire, Gras-Scolaire and Populaire-Scolaire.

Scope Gun. A lever-action *Daisy BB gun, introduced in 1961. Basically a No. 102 with a 'lightning loader', it also had a permanently attached 2x telescope sight.

Scoremaster – 1. Or Model 511A Scoremaster. Made by the *Remington Arms Company during 1940–41 and 1945–62, this was a repeating version of the Model 510 with a detachable five-round box magazine. **2.** Usually as Score Master: a variant of the *Government Model Colt-Browning M1911A1 pistol made by *Detonics. Inc., of Bellevue. Washington. Essentially a standard gun, it features an extended grip safety, adjustable sights, a refined trigger and stainless-steel construction. *See also* Service Master.

Scorpio. A six-shot .38-calibre personal-defence revolver made in Spain by *Llama–Gabilondo SA. It is simply a heavier version of the *Piccolo with chequered grips and a rounded trigger guard.

Scorpion. A break-barrel .177 or .22 spring-air pistol made in Britain by *BSA Guns Ltd. Designed during 1973–75, it was introduced commercially in 1977.

Scotcher. John A. Scotcher & Son, Bury St Edmunds, Suffolk. The marks of this gunsmithing business, claiming origins as early as 1803, have been reported on shotgun ammunition made by *Eley Bros. prior to the First World War, including 'The *Invincible'. John Adam Scotcher was listed at 17 Meat Market from 1863, expanding the business to include his son by 1885, but work ceased when the stock and goodwill was acquired by Henry *Hodgson in 1913.

'Scotia' [The]. A mark found on shotgun ammunition sold by Alex *Martin of Glasgow; the manufacturer seems to have been *Eley-Kynoch, dating the products later than 1920.

Scott – 1. A *Suicide Special revolver made in the USA by the *Hopkins & Allen Arms Company of Norwich, Connecticut, in the late nineteenth century. **2.** Alfred Scott, London. The marks of this English gunmaker have been reported on self-cocking *pepperboxes dating from the middle of the nineteenth century. **3.** Gustavus H. Scott, a commander in the US Navy, accepted *Colt caplock revolvers marked 'GHS'. His work seems to have lasted from 1858 until the 1870s, date and navy connotations distinguishing it from that of Gilbert H. *Steward. *See also* US arms inspectors' marks. **4.** Horace Scott, a gov-

SCHWEIZERISCHE INDUSTRIE-GESELLSCHAFT (SIG)

This Swiss company was founded in Neuhausen am Rheinfalls in 1853, to make railway rolling stock and signalling equipment. The first guns were single-shot *cap-lock muzzle-loaders, but these were soon followed by bolt-action *Vetterli M1869 rifles, M1870 cadet rifles and M1871 short rifles for the Swiss Federal Army, production of the 1869-pattern Vetterli alone totalling nearly 60,000. A Neuhausen

The picturesquely-sited SIG factory, renowned for pistols (particularly since a liaison was forged with J.P. Sauer & Sohn), has also made assault rifles.

straight-pull bolt-action rifle was developed to compete with the Schmidt-Rubin in the late 1880s, but failed to convince the authorities of its merits. Subsequently, however, SIG made components for the Schmidt-Rubin rifles and *Parabellum (Luger) 06/29 W+F pistols, although these guns were assembled by the *Eidgenossische Waffenfabrik in Bern.

SIG has been involved in the development of many weapons, including the *Mondragon bolt-action and semi-automatic rifles designed prior to the First World War, and has also made Fürrer-type submachine-guns. Among the most successful of co-operative ventures

was that undertaken with Charles Petter, best known for an adaptation of the *Browning dropping-barrel lock (patented in France and Switzerland in 1934–37). The experimental SP44/8 and SP44/16 were refined into the SP47/8, adopted as the Swiss *Ordonnanzpistole 49 SIG* in 1949. Sold commercially as the SP210, in a variety of guises, this pistol was a great success. However, it was so expensive to make that SIG progressed to the P220 – the Swiss *Ordonnanzpistole 75* – in 1975. Developed in collusion with J.P. *Sauer & Sohn, to evade strict Swiss arms export laws, this gun has evolved into a series of improved models: the compact 9mm P225; the P226 of 1980, made for trials in the USA, with ambidextrous controls; the ultra-compact 9mm P228 (1988); the .40 S&W P229; and the deep-framed P239, available in .357 SIG, 9mm Parabellum and .40 S&W. The P230 (and a modernised substitute known as the P232) is a blowback personal-defence pistol inspired by the Walther PP. Although available now only in 7.65mm Auto and 9mm Short, originally the guns could also be obtained in .22 LR rimfire and 6.35mm Auto. The P240, developed with Hämmerli (which SIG now

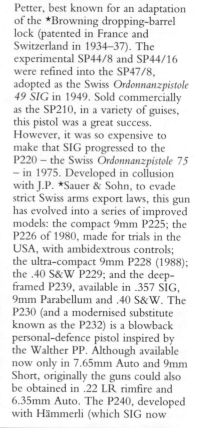

ernment arms inspector operating c. 1879–90, accepted guns and equipment marked 'HS'. Care is necessary to distinguish his work from that of H. *Saunders, Harrison *Shaler, Harris *Smith, Howard *Stockton and H. *Syrett; although the periods differ, overlaps are to be expected. *See also* US arms inspectors' marks. **5.** Walter Scott, or W.W. Scott. Trading from 47a Princip Street, Birmingham, Warwickshire, during 1871–80, where he was best known as a merchant of *Smith & Wesson and de Mouncie revolvers, Scott was a licensee of the *Carter & Edwards bolt-action breech-loader. He received British Patent 1691/71 of 28 June 1871 for a hinged breech-block and a proprietary recoil pad for shotguns; and was also the co-designer, with W.J. Matthews, of a breech system protected by British Patent 138/73 of 13 January 1873 and US Patent 144,870 of 25 November 1873. This consisted of a screwed plug that could move laterally to expose the chamber. A later patent (British no. 3079/73 of 1873, jointly with A.E. Bruno) protected a rifle sight. **6.** William Scott. This English gunmaker was listed in the census of 1841 at Henry Street, Stepney, London. He traded from 27 Leman Street, London E., between 1843 and 1849, then from 33 Leman Street (probably the same premises renumbered by the postal authorities) from 1851 until 1853. It is thought that then he moved to Birmingham, where a 'William Scott' was listed at 14 Whittall Street

from 1855. This business became William Scott & Son in 1859, when a move to 47 Princip Street took place, then William Scott & Sons in 1869. Trading ceased in 1875. **7.** William Middleditch Scott, a partner in W. & C Scott (below) of Birmingham, was granted patents protecting a broad range of improvements in firearms. They included British Patent 2752/65 of 25 October 1865, protecting cocking indicators and a locking mechanism for drop-barrel breech-loaders; 452/70 of 1870 for a drop-barrel action; and 1268/70 of 1870 for drop-down-barrel and gun-stock construction; 2052/74 and 3424/74 of 1874 for drop-barrel actions; 186/75 and 1902/75 of 1875 for drop-barrel actions; and 3223/75 of 1875 for loaded-chamber indicators. British Patent 615/76 of 1876 was granted to W.M. and M. Scott for a drop-barrel action, and 761/78 of 1878, to W.M. Scott and T. *Baker, was similar. Patent 617/82 of 1882 (also with Baker) allowed claims for vent design; 3859/83 of 1883, granted in partnership with C. Proctor, and 5564/84 of 1884 (sought alone) also protected drop-barrel actions. Among the protection granted in the USA were US Patent 108,942 of 1 November 1870, for a drop-barrel gun; 157,699 of 15 December 1874 for a fore-end attachment system; 161,559 of 30 March 1875 for a drop-barrel gun; 264,773 of 19 September 1882 (with T. Baker) and 288,670 of 20 November 1883 (with C. Proctor), also for drop-barrel

owns) was a short-lived target-shooting adaptation of the P220, chambered for .32 S&W Wadcutter and .38 Special ammunition.

SIG has also made large numbers of automatic rifles, including the SG 46, a gas-operated adaptation of the Schmidt-Rubin, and the extraordinary *blow-forward AK 53. Success awaited the perfection of the AM-55, customarily credited to Rudolf Amsler and now better known as the *Sturmgewehr Modell 57* (Stgw. 57 to give it its Swiss Army designation) or SG510. The SG510 series included the 510-1, a commercial variant of the Stgw. 57 chambered for the Swiss 7.5x55 cartridge; the 510-2, a lightened variant of the 510-1; the 510-3, chambered for the Soviet 7.62x39 round; and the perfected 510-4, introduced in 1963/64 in 7.62x51 NATO. A semi-automatic sporting version of the SG 510-4, the AMT, was also made in small numbers.

An attempt to adapt the basic mechanism to become a gas-operated locked-breech chambering the 5.56x45 cartridge, the SG530 (1967–71), proved to be a failure. Far more effective was the SG540 series (1972), offered in 5.56mm and 7.62mm, which incorporated a rotating bolt. The SG543 was licensed to *Manurhin of Mulhouse,

the first guns being made for the French Special Forces and export to French colonies in 1978.

After several years of trials, including competitions against a rival design promoted by the Eidgenössische Waffenfabrik, the SG550 (1984) was accepted for service as the 5.56mm *Sturmgewehr 90*, re-equipment spanning 1986 to 1995. This gun has since been offered in a variety of guises, including the PSG550 sniper rifle, the SG551 carbine and the ultra-compact SG552 Commando.

Bolt-action sniper rifles have been offered on the basis of the *Sauer Model 80 wedge-lug and Model 200 turning-lug actions, as the SSG2000 and SSG3000 respectively; these have been chambered exclusively for the

7.62x51 NATO round and its commercial .308 Winchester equivalent.

The basic flap or roller-locking system has also been incorporated in a variety of machine-guns, beginning with the MG55 and culminating in the MG710. However, production of these has ceased.

SIG continues to prosper, making a variety of packaging machinery and rolling stock. The company has controlling interests in both Hämmerli and Sauer. However, comparatively little has been written yet about its affairs.

The 5.56mm StG 90 is currently being issued throughout the Swiss Army.

guns. **8.** William & Charles Scott. Based in Birmingham, this gunmaking concern was eventually absorbed into *Webley & Scott. It began trading from 11 Lench Street in 1840, then moved successively to 33 Lench Street and 21 Loveday Street (1842–48), 4 Shadwell Street (1849–54), 94 Bath Street (1855–63) and Bagot Street (1864–97). From 1873, an office was also maintained for some years at 10 Great Castle Street, London. W. & C. Scott was best known for good-quality shotguns, many being exported in the second half of the nineteenth century. They often incorporated features designed by William M. Scott (q.v.). In 1897, however, the business was acquired by P. Webley & Son to form the *Webley & Scott Revolver & Arms Company Ltd, and lost its autonomy. **9.** Scott & Sargeant, East Street, Horsham, Sussex, England. The marks of this ironmongery business have been reported on sporting guns and shotgun ammunition marketed shortly after the Second World War as The Horsham Special and The Ironmonger.
Scotti. Alfredo Scotti (son of Luigi Scotti [Douglas], Conte della Scala di San Giorgio, once chief technician in the Pirotecnico di Bologna) built a number of experimental rifles in a small factory in Brescia, Italy, relying on a short-stroke-piston gas system to operate a rotating bolt. They included a range of auto-loading rifles, of which the Modelo X of 1931 was the most successful. It was made as

a rifle, stocked in the fashion of the clip-loading Mo. 1891 Mannlicher-Carcano; as a carbine with a separate pistol grip behind the trigger; and as a naval anti-aircraft rifle, with a detachable box magazine and a pistol grip on the fore-end.
'Scottie' [The]. A mark found on shotgun cartridges distributed by J.S. *Sharpe of Aberdeen, usually accompanied by an illustration of a Scots Terrier.
Scout – 1. A British push-in-barrel air pistol, marketed by Lincoln *Jeffries & Company Ltd early in the twentieth century. **2.** An airgun pellet made in Britain by *Eley Bros., introduced prior to 1910. **3.** A push-in-barrel spring-air pistol made by *Millard Brothers of Motherwell, Scotland. **4.** A break-barrel spring-air rifle in 4.5mm calibre, made by Maschinen- und Apparatebau *'Wagria' of Ascheberg in Holstein, Germany. **5.** A *Suicide Special revolver made in the USA by the *Hood Firearms Company of Norwich, Connecticut, in the late nineteenth century. **6.** An airgun made by the *Crosman Arms Company of Fairport, New York State, USA, as the Model 788 BB Scout. **7.** The old-type Model 75 *Daisy spring-air BB Gun, a lever-action design made in the 1950s. **8.** A 500-shot lever-action Daisy BB Gun made during 1955–61, basically a No. 102 *Cub fitted with sling swivels, and a plastic butt and fore-end. **9.** The Model 1300C Scout was a *Parker-Hale-type Mauser rifle introduced by the *Gibbs Rifle Company in 1992.

Offered only in .243 and .308 Winchester, it had a short barrel, a laminated stock and a detachable box magazine.

'SCR' – **1.** A superimposition-type monogram with the 'R' dominant. Correctly 'SRC' (q.v.); associated with *Sears, Roebuck & Company. **2.** Found on US military firearms and accessories. *See* Stephen C. *Rowen.

'SCS'. A superimposition-type monogram with 'S' dominant. *See* 'CSS'; used by C.S. *Shatuck.

'S. & D.' Found on a range of *Record-brand shotguns promoted in 1911 by A.L. *Frank, these initials have yet to be identified.

'SE'. A superimposition-type monogram, 'S' slightly dominant. *See* 'ES'; found on a Belgian or Spanish-made revolver.

Sealed Pattern. *See* panel, below.

SEAM, S.E.A.M. A Browning-type pistol made by, or more probably for, *Sociedad Española de Armas y Municiones of Eibar: 6.35mm or 7.65mm, six rounds, hammer fired.

Sear. An intermediate component or series of components (sear train) linking the trigger with the hammer or firing pin, holding the latter back until released by trigger pressure.

Searle – **1.** Elbert Hamilton Searle, Springfield, Massachusetts, USA. Searle is best known as the designer of the Savage semi-automatic pistol, but he was also responsible for the *Bull's Eye Pistol, an airgun with a special ratchet-cocking system. *See* US Patent 959,889 and British Patent 12,723/10, both of 1910. **2.** Thomas Searle. This member of the London gun trade was listed at 23 Jermyn Street in 1869–71.

Sears, Sears... – **1.** Henry Sears & Company, 88 Lake Street, Chicago, Illinois, USA. A dealer in sporting guns and ammunition, Sears also loaded shotgun cartridges for a few years in the late nineteenth century. **2.** Robert Sears, a colonel in the US Army Ordnance Corps, accepted a variety of .22 and .45 *Colt-made pistols during the Second World War. They bore 'RS' marks. *See also* US arms inspectors' marks. **3.** Sears Ranger: *see* Ranger. **4.** Sears, Roebuck & Company, Chicago, Illinois. This retailing business had its origins in the Sears Watch Company, formed in 1886 in Minneapolis, Minnesota, by Richard Warren Sears (1863–1914). A move to Chicago occurred in 1887, when Alvah Roebuck was hired as a watch repairer. A mail-order catalogue promoting watches and jewellery soon followed. Sears sold out to Roebuck in 1889, intending to farm land purchased in Iowa, but then entered a partnership with Roebuck, forming Sears, Roebuck & Company in 1893; Julius Rosenwald and Aaron Nusbaum bought Roebuck's shares in 1895, and Rosenwald assumed control when Sears left the business in 1909. General Robert E. Wood was elected to the board in 1924, marking a move towards retail operations that, by the 1970s, had grown to more than 800 stores. Sears Roebuck has handled a wide variety of guns and ammunition. Brandnames have included A.J. *Aubrey, J.C. Higgins and Ted Williams; 'X-R' has been found in *headstamps, and 'Sta-Clean' has been reported on cartridge boxes.

'SEB'. Found on US military firearms and accessories. *See* Stanhope English *Blunt.

Section Technique de l'Artillerie. *See* STA.

Securitas. This strange little 6.35mm *blowback pistol, made in France prior to 1914, had a finger rest instead of

---

SEALED PATTERN

Unique to the British armed forces and their colonial counterparts, this term denotes government acceptance. It has been used since 1631 to describe military stores deposited in the Tower of London and subsequently the Royal Small Arms Factory, Enfield, to ensure that equipment was manufactured to a standard pattern.

A method of regulating a chaotic system that allowed individual gunmakers to supply weapons of their own design, instead of complying with government demands, took the form of a wax seal – duplicating the Royal Arms – applied to guns and other stores approved, or 'sealed', to guide manufacture. As a Sealed Pattern gun was deemed to be dimensionally correct, all manufacturing patterns and gauges had to comply with it.

The wax seals were often set into gun butts, which could also bear additional information stamped into the woodwork; after the 1870s, however, the seals were customarily attached to wax-and-calico tags. No deviations were allowed from the Sealed Pattern unless agreed by the Board of Ordnance or the War Department, and the British inspectorate ensured that the rules were applied with unbending strictness.

This Garate, Anitua y Cia .455 Pistol, Revolver, Ordnance Pattern, Mk 1 No. 2, adopted for service in the British Army during the First World War, has a Sealed Pattern tag dangling from the trigger guard.

a trigger guard. Fired by a lever set into the back strap, it is believed to have been made by *Société Française d'Armes Automatiques de Saint-Étienne. *See also* Hermetic and Wegria-Charlier.

Sedgley. Reginald F. Sedgley, Inc., Philadelphia, Pennsylvania, USA. A manufacturer and patentee of compact revolvers; converter of thousands of Krag-Jørgensen rifles to sporting use; and maker of flare pistols.

Seeber. August Seeber, Suhl in Thüringen, Germany. Listed in directories for 1930–39 as a gunmaker.

Seecamp – 1. Louis Seecamp: *see* Mossberg. **2.** L.W. Seecamp & Company Inc., New Haven, Connecticut, USA. Makers of a range of automatic pistols, including the LWS-32 (7.65mm).

Seelig. Georg Seelig, Weimar. A minor retailer of sporting guns and ammunition, active in Germany in 1941.

Seidenzahl. Richard Seidenzahl, Suhl in Thüringen, Germany. Listed in the *Deutsches Reichs-Adressbuch* as a gunsmith, 1930 and 1939.

Seitzinger. Robert Seitzinger, Suhl, Thüringen, Germany. A gunsmith known to have been operating in 1939.

Selecta. Made by Echave y Arizmendi of Eibar, this Browning-type pocket pistol had a seven-round box magazine and was hammer fired. The slide may be marked 'Model 1918', and sometimes a grip safety mechanism is present.

Select-Armes, 3 rue de Roubaix, Saint-Étienne, France. Listed in 1951 as a gunmaker.

Selecter (*sic*). A semi-automatic pistol made by *Echave y Arizmendi of Eibar prior to the Spanish Civil War (1936–39). *See also* Selecta.

Selective fire. Applied to any gun that may, when required, be set (with the selector) to fire single shots, multi-shot bursts or fully automatically. The selector is often combined with the manual safety catch.

Selector. *See* Selective fire.

Self... – 1. Self-cocking. A firing mechanism in which the action of cocking the hammer or firing pin is performed automatically, either by the breech mechanism or by pulling back the trigger (cf. double action). Note that it is not released automatically, requiring an additional action on the part of the firer. **2.** Self-loading. *See* Autoloading. **3.** Self-Protector [The]. A double-barrelled knife pistol made by *Unwin & Rodgers of Sheffield, Yorkshire, England, with as many as four blades. These generally had twin triggers. A few guns had a distinctive false breech, which had to be lifted before the extractor could be activated.

Sellier & Bellot, Prague (Austria-Hungary prior to 1918, Czechoslovakia thereafter). This partnership of emigrant Parisian chemist Jean Bellot and merchant Louis Sellier began making percussion caps in Prague in 1825. By the 1860s, Sellier & Bellot was producing metallic-case cartridges, and by 1914 had risen to become one of Austria-Hungary's most powerful munitions makers. Cartridges were customarily distinguished by 'S.B.' or 'S. & B.' in their headstamps. Work continued until 1945, small-arms ammunition being made during the Second World War in factories in Vlasim (coded 'ak'), Schönebeck an der Elbe ('ad'), and the Veitsberg district of Prague ('lkm').

Semi-automatic. This term is customarily applied to a gun that fires once for each pull on the trigger and reloads automatically, but requires the firer to release the trigger lever before another shot can be fired (cf. Automatic).

Semin. Co-designer with *Elizarov of the Soviet 7.62x39 intermediate, or M43, cartridge chambered in the *Simonov carbine (SKS), *Kalashnikov assault rifle (AK) and light automatic weapons such as the *RPD and *RPK.

Semi-rimmed case. *See* Cartridge case.

Sempert – 1. This German engineer was a partner in Sempert & Krieghoff (below). **2.** Sempert & Krieghoff began trading in Suhl in 1886, intending to make firearms and electrical components. The founders were Ludwig Krieghoff the Elder (q.v.) and an otherwise obscure Germano-American who had worked with Thomas Edison. Listed in the *Deutsches Reichs-Adressbuch* for 1900 as a gunmaking business, owned by Ludwig Krieghoff alone. Sempert & Krieghoff acquired V.C. *Schilling & Co. of Suhl in 1904, gaining an interest in the production of German Mauser service rifles, but Heinrich Krieghoff left the business in 1916 to begin working on his own. Sempert & Krieghoff traded independently until 1924, when the death of Ludwig Krieghoff brought work to an end. However, Heinrich Krieghoff (q.v.) perpetuated the use of the 'S.u.K.' and 'S & K' marks on sporting rifles and shotguns. *Mauser-action sporting rifles were stocked for general sale, and also for supply to August *Schüler of Suhl. An 'S. & K.' mark customarily identified them (cf. 'S. & H.'). Sempert & Krieghoff was still being listed in 1941 at Rimbachstrasse 37 in Suhl, but ceased trading at the end of the Second World War.

Senator. A *Suicide Special revolver made by the *Meriden Arms Company of Meriden, Connecticut, in the late nineteenth century.

Sendero. A version of the *Remington M700 bolt-action rifle, introduced in 1994, with a heavy 26in barrel and a straight-comb composite half-stock having a grey/black mottled finish. Chamberings have included .25-06, .270 Winchester, 7mm Remington Magnum and .300 Winchester Magnum. Introduced in 1996, the Sendero SF has a non-reflecting Satin Finish on its fluted barrel and stainless-steel action.

Seneca Green. A name applied to a short-lived version of the *Remington *Nylon 66 auto-loading rifle with leaf-green synthetic butts and fore-ends. *See also* Apache Black and Mohawk Brown.

Senior. A barrel-cocking spring-air pistol made (in two Marks) by *Webley & Scott in .177 and .22; the former dates only from c. 1964. An essentially similar pistol was made by *Mahely Industria y Compania in Buenos Aires, c. 1953–65.

Senn. Heinrich Senn (1871–1958), Bern, Switzerland. This government arms inspector was granted German Patent 310,499 of 31 October 1916 to protect a modification of the *Parabellum pistol, which could fire automatically when required. A bipod, a water-cooled barrel sleeve and a large-capacity box magazine were among the optional features.

Sentinel. A break-open BB Gun made in the USA in 1909–15 by the *Markham Air Rifle Company, with a *Polley-type frame and a sheet-metal trigger guard. The Sentinel Repeater was similar, but had a repeating device controlled by the muzzle cap.

Serdyukov. Co-designer with *Kraskov of the silenced submachine-gun and rifle, often known as the *ASS and *VSS respectively.

Serre, Saint-Étienne, France. Listed during 1933 as a gunmaker.

Service – 1. Usually found as 'The Service' on shotgun ammunition handled by Charles *Hellis & Sons of London, and *Norman & Sons of Woodbridge and Framlingham. Made by *Eley-Kynoch, they will bear 'ICI' headstamps. 2. Service Kit Gun, or Model 650. Dating from 1982–87, this *Smith & Wesson swing-cylinder revolver was derived from the standard *Kit Gun, but chambered .22 Magnum rimfire ammunition instead of the Long Rifle pattern. A heavy 3in barrel, fixed sights and a round-heel butt were standard. *See also* Target Kit Gun. 3. Service Mark 2. Associated with a lifting-barrel spring-air rifle made by *Webley & Scott Ltd of Birmingham between 1929 and 1940 (although a few were assembled from pre-war parts in 1945–46). It was marketed in .177, .22 and .25, often as a cased set with interchangeable barrels. 4. Service Master. A variant of the *Government Model Colt-Browning M1911A1 pistol made by *Detonics. Inc., of Bellevue, Washington. It has an extended grip safety and a refined trigger; construction is usually in stainless steel. *See also* Score Master. 5. Service Model Ace. Chambered for .22 rimfire ammunition, this gun served as a trainer for the .45 M1911A1 *Government Model pistol. It was made from 1937 by *Colt's Patent Fire Arms Manufacturing Company, work ceasing in 1945. The minimal recoil of the .22 cartridge was magnified by a floating chamber to approximate that of the .45 ACP round.

Sesquicentennial. Guns made by the *Remington Arms Company in 1966 to celebrate the 150th anniversary of the founding of Eliphalet Remington's business. 1. Model 552 Sesquicentennial. A version of the auto-loading M552 *Speedmaster with an appropriate logo on the left side of the receiver. 2. Model 572 Sesquicentennial. A *Fieldmaster slide-action rifle with an inscription on the left side of the receiver. 3. Model 760 Sesquicentennial. This was a variant of the centrefire Model 760 *Gamemaster, made in small numbers in .30-06 only. The guns had engraved receivers. 4. Nylon 66 Sesquicentennial. A variant of the standard .22 rimfire *Nylon 66 auto-loader, with an appropriate inscription on the left side of the receiver. *See also* Bicentennial.

Sestroretsk arms factory, Russia/USSR. Although small-scale facilities had existed on this particular site for many years, Sestroretsk did not participate in the mass-production of military weapons until a production line installed to make *Mosin-Nagant rifles began operating in 1894, under the supervision of Sergey Mosin himself. Thereafter the factory made millions of weapons, including the pre-Revolutionary *Fedorov Avtomaty. Its importance declined under Bolshevik control.

Setra. A pneumatic rifle similar to the US-made *Sheridan, but produced in Spain. It was brought into Britain in small numbers by *Salter & Varge and may be found with appropriate marks.

Setter – 1. Usually found as 'The Setter' on 12-bore shotgun cartridges sold by W.R. *Pape of Newcastle upon Tyne and supplied by *Eley Bros. or *Kynoch Ltd prior to the First World War. 2. A 28-bore pneumatic shotgun made by Armibrescia in the late 1930s. A pneumatic rifle of the same type may also exist.

Set trigger. A mechanism, commonly used on target guns, in which a lever or button 'sets' the trigger by taking up all the slack in the system; thereafter, a very slight pressure on the trigger is sufficient to fire. Set triggers come in many designs, some of which combine the function of the setting and trigger levers in a single component.

Sevart. Lambert Sevart, 16 rue Grandgagnage, Liège. A gunmaker working in Belgium from the 1880s until the First World War.

'Severn' [The]. A mark associated with shotgun cartridges handled by Aubrey *Lewis of Luton.

Seydel & Company. Probably a merchant and gunmakers' agent, this business was recorded at 7¹/₂ St Mary's Row, Birmingham, in 1877–79.

Seyffarth. Fritz Seyffarth, Zella-Mehlis in Thüringen. A gun- and gun-barrel making business (*Gewehrlaufzieherei*) operating in Germany in 1920–45.

Seytre – 1. M. Seytre, Saint-Étienne, France. Listed in 1933, this gunmaker was basically a distributor of sporting guns, including the 6.35mm *Union, or Union-France, automatic pistols purchased in Spain. 2. Seytre-Montagny, or Seytre et Montagny, Saint-Étienne, France. Listed in 1933 as a gunmaker; still trading in the early 1950s from 68 rue Mulatière.

SFAP (Société Française des Armes Portatives). *See* Hotchkiss.

'SFB'. Found on US military firearms and accessories. *See* S.F. *Bugbee.

'SFM', 'S F M', 'S.F.M.' – 1. These marks will be found in the headstamps of cartridges made by *Société Française des Munitions. 2. A mark found on the grips of a 7.65mm five-shot revolver with a folding trigger and a swing-out cylinder, credited to *Société Française des Munitions, but probably made in Liège or Saint-Étienne.

'S.F.R.J.', usually accompanied by a five-pointed star. 'Socialist Federal Republic of Jugoslavia', found on the grips of M48 *Tokarev pistols made for export to English-speaking countries.

SG, or SG-43. An abbreviation of *Stankoviy Goryunova* (Heavy Goryunov). This identified the 7.62mm SG machine-gun designed by Petr *Goryunov and his associates during the Second World War, and used in large numbers by the Soviet armed forces. *See also* SGM.

'S.G. Co.' A mark found on shotgun cartridges loaded with propellant supplied by the *Schultze Gunpowder Company.

SGM, SGM... An improved, or modernised, form of the *Goryunov machine-gun (SG or SG-43), this appeared in the 1950s. It was sturdy and reliable, but eventually was replaced by the PK. The SGMB was a flexibly-mounted vehicle gun derived from the SGM, with spade grips, and the SGMT was a fixed-mount tank variant.

'sgx'. This code is said to have been used by E. & F. Hörster of Solingen on bayonets and small-arms components made in Germany in 1945.

'SH' – 1. A superimposition-type monogram, with neither of the letters dominant. Correctly 'HS' (q.v.); used by C.G. *Haenel of Suhl. 2. Sometimes in the form of a superimposition-type monogram. Correctly 'HS' (q.v.); used by Herbert *Schmidt of Ostheim an der Rhön, Germany. 3. Usually in a diamond. A trademark associated with *Schuyler, Hartley & Graham of New York City. 4. Found on US military firearms and accessories. *See* Samuel *Hawkins.

'S&H', 'S. & H.' Trademarks associated with *Schmidt & Habermann of Suhl, but readily confused with 'S&K' (q.v.).

Shaler. Harrison Shaler, a US government arms inspector, accepted .45 M1911A1 *Colt-Browning pistols made at the end of the Second World War by *Remington Rand. The guns were marked 'HS', but are easily distinguished by their date from those accepted by H. *Saunders, Horace *Scott, Harris *Smith, Howard *Stockton and H. *Syrett. *See also* US arms inspectors' marks.

'Shamrock'. This mark was used on shotgun cartridges and *Mayer & Grammelspacher Diana spring-air rifles handled by Frank *Dyke & Company Ltd of London in the mid-1920s.

Shannon Ltd, Shannon Corner, New Malden, Surrey. A maker of magazines for the British 9mm *Sten Gun during the Second World War. The regional code 'S 309' may have been used instead of the company name. *See also* British military manufacturers' marks.

Sharp – 1. Frank A. Sharp & Son, Poole, Dorset. This ironmongery business sold shotgun cartridges as Sharp's Express. Their origins are unknown. **2.** William Lacy Sharp. An English gunmaker listed in East London at 7 Little Alie Street in 1839–50. Subsequent directory entries list Mrs H. Sharp at the same address until 1856, suggesting that her husband had died in 1850 or 1851. **3.** Sharp Rifle Company, Tokyo, Japan. Maker of a modified *Crosman-pattern pneumatic rifle known as the Sharp Innova. The loading system, consisting of an automatic plunger, or bolt, and a side-mounted operating catch, differs radically from its prototype. Sharp has been owned by SKB (q.v.) since the 1980s. **4.** Sharp's Express. See Frank A. *Sharp & Son. **5.** *See also* Sharpe and Sharps.

Sharpe, Sharpe... – 1. James S. Sharpe, Belmont Street, Aberdeen. The marks of this gun- and fishing-tackle maker have been found on sporting guns and shotgun ammunition, made by *Eley-Kynoch, which was distributed under the tradename The *Scottie. **2.** Sharpe & Wright, Diamond Buildings, Coombe Road, Brighton 7, Sussex. A maker of British rifle-type 'Projectors, Grenade, No. 5 Mk 1/L', 1944, allotted the code 'S 355'. *See also* British military manufacturers' marks. **3.** *See also* Sharp and Sharps.

Sharps – 1. C. Sharps Rifle Company, Big Timber, Montana. This manufacturer offered a range of Sharps-type rifles from 1987 onward. Since 1992, they have been distributed under the Montana Armory name. The Model 1874 has been offered in calibres from .40 to .45, in the guise of Military Rifles, Military Carbines, Business Rifles, Sporting Rifles No. 1, and No. 1 or Long Range Express Sporting Rifles. Announced in 1986, the Model 1875, patterned on the improved Sharps rifle, had a greatly simplified slab-sided receiver and a shorter operating lever. Chambered for cartridges ranging from .22 Stevens to .45-90, it had a case-hardened receiver, a round or octagonal barrel and a straight-wrist butt with a shotgun-style shoulder plate. Individual patterns included a Sporting Rifle, with a 30in octagonal barrel; a Saddle Gun with a 26in octagon barrel; a Carbine with a 24in round barrel and a half-length fore-end retained by a single barrel band; a Business Rifle with a 28in round barrel; and a 1991-vintage Target & Long Range Model with a long-range vernier sight on the tang, an oval cheek-piece and a chequered steel shoulder plate. **2.** Christian Sharps. Patentee of a dropping-block mechanism reliant on a breech-block that slid downward within a sturdy frame, protected by US Patent no. 5763 of 12 September 1848 ('gun with sliding breech-pin and self capping'); and combustible cartridges that fired with a side-hammer *cap-lock. The rifles attained undying fame in the hands

of the United States Sharpshooters, who were issued with 2,000 double-trigger guns in 1862. **3.** John Brown Sharps: *see under* 'J'. **4.** Sharps Arms Company. Formed in 1967 to promote a much-modernised *Sharps-Borchardt action, then acquired by *Colt. Unfortunately, the project was abandoned in the mid-1970s, after fewer than 500 actions had been made by *Bellmore-Johnson. These were used to make presentation-grade guns in chamberings ranging from .17 Remington to .458 Winchester. **4.** Sharps-Borchardt. A sophisticated hammerless dropping-block breech-loader, this was derived from the familiar Sharps system of 1848 by Hugo *Borchardt. It was protected by US Patents 185,721 of September 1876 and 206,217 of 23 July 1878, both being assigned to the Sharps Rifle Company. The action was designed to cock the striker automatically as the breech-block descended. A safety lever behind the trigger was applied as the breech was opened; when the action had been reloaded and closed, the firer could override the safety by pressing the projecting catch. Sharps made about 23,000 rifles, beginning in 1878, but the failure of the manufacturer in September 1881 brought work to an end. The guns were sold as the New Model Hammerless Business Rifle, Express Rifle, Military Rifle and Carbine, Hunter's Rifle, Long Range Rifle, Officer's Rifle, Short & Mid Range Rifle, Short Range Rifle and Sporting Rifle (qq.v.). **5.** Sharps & Hankins, Philadelphia, Pennsylvania. Relations between Christian Sharps and Richard *Lawrence were never particularly cordial and, eventually, the inventor sold his shares in the Sharps Rifle Manufacturing Company, entering into a partnership with William *Hankins. The new business intended to make sliding-barrel rifles and four-barrel .22, .30 and .32 rimfire sheath-trigger derringers, work continuing in Philadelphia until Sharps died in 1874. The carbine was protected by US Patent 32,790, granted in July 1861 for a firearm loaded by sliding the barrel forward when the trigger-guard lever was pressed. Production began in 1862, shortly before receipt of a US Navy order for 500 fully-stocked rifles chambering the .52 Sharps & Hankins No. 56 rimfire cartridge and accompanied by sword bayonets. These were followed by the army, or Old Model, carbine, chambering the same ammunition, but with a short barrel and a half-length fore-end. The firing pin was fixed in the hammer face. Post-1863 New Model carbines had a floating pin in the standing breech, and a safety slider on the rear of the frame. Guns of this type were used by the army and the navy, the latter being issued with a leather barrel-sleeve to prevent corrosion. Federal government acquisitions during the Civil War eventually amounted to 7,804 Sharps & Hankins carbines – 1,468 for the army and 6,336 for the navy – but many others were sold privately. **6.** Sharps rifles and carbines: *see panel, pp. 470/71.* **7.** Sharps Rifle Company, Hartford (1874–76) and Bridgeport (1876–81), Connecticut, USA. In addition to the better-known dropping-block rifles, Sharps made a few smoothbore shotguns on the same basic action. A number of Old Reliable double-barrelled hammer shotguns were sold from 1879 until the business collapsed in 1881. Most of them seem to have been purchased from P. *Webley & Sons. **8.** Sharps Rifle Manufacturing Company [The], Hartford, Connecticut. The success of the first Sharps firearms led to the formation of a manufacturing company in the autumn of 1851,

SHARPS RIFLES AND CARBINES

Sharps (6)

The earliest designs, made to the 1848 patent by Daniel Nippes of Mill Creek, Pennsylvania, had a breech-block that moved obliquely and a primer-wheel in the frame, ahead of the breech-block, which could be removed once the cover had been opened. The guns had *back-action locks and breech-levers forged separately from the trigger guard. Octagonal barrels were retained by a lateral key, and a brass patch box was incorporated in the butt.

Later guns, made by *Robbins & Lawrence from 1850 onward, substituted the *Maynard Tape Primer. Most had iron mounts, an adjustable chamber bushing and a special platinum-alloy sealing ring in the breech-block face to prevent gas leaks. Next came the 1851-pattern rifle, the first to have the breech lever combined with the trigger guard and the hammer inside the lock plate. The Maynard Tape Primer was retained, but the receiver was rounded.

The 1852-pattern, made in rifle and carbine forms (sporting and military) in 1853–54, was essentially similar to the contemporary military issue, with the Sharps-patent disc-primer system, a tube of priming discs being held in a hole bored vertically in the lock plate. The guns incorporated the platinum-ring gas-check and adjustable chamber bushing, but had an angular receiver and a conventional outside hammer. Production, though meagre, included a few large-bore shotguns.

The 1853-pattern rifle was also scarce, but may be found with barrels ranging from a mere 14in to a stupendous 39in. Made by *Robbins & Lawrence prior to 1855, then by the Sharps Rifle Company, the M1853 carbine had an improved breech-lever pivot-pin retainer. Production in Windsor and Hartford amounted to about 13,000 1853-type guns. Two hundred rifles of this type were purchased by the US Navy and the Marine Corps with half-stocks, brass furniture, a single barrel band and a bayonet-fitting tenon beneath the muzzle.

The 1855-type carbine was made in answer to a request from Britain, although several hundred .52-calibre examples were delivered to the US Army. They had the *Maynard-patent tape-priming mechanism on the right side of the receiver and straight-necked hammers.

Other guns of this type were the 1855 Army Rifle, with full-length stock, three bands and provision for a socket bayonet, and the essentially similar, but half-stocked, Navy Rifle. Fifty of the latter had an unsuccessful self-cocking system designed by Rollin *White, linking the hammer with the breech-lever.

Trials had often showed that they leaked gas too badly to be acceptable. Although the problems had been eased when Sharps inserted a platinum ring in the breech-block face, the first solution was provided by an expandable gas-check ring patented on 1 April 1856 by Hezekiah *Conant of Hartford, Connecticut; the final solution was an improved seal patented by Richard *Lawrence in December 1859.

The perfected 1859-pattern, or New Model, Sharps rifle had the improved Lawrence-type obturator, changes in the lockwork and a breech-block that moved vertically. The US Navy ordered the first of its .56-calibre rifles in 1859, with a full-length stock, two barrel bands and a bayonet-fitting tenon. Ordered by the Federal Army from C.C. *Bean of New York in June 1861, Sharps 'Long Range Rifle with bayonet' was similar, but had three bands and customarily accepted a socket bayonet locking around the base of the front sight. There was also an essentially similar *Sharpshooters' Rifle and a short-barrelled carbine with a tapering half-length fore-end, held to the barrel by a single band.

Revised New Model guns, marked 'MODEL 1863' on the barrel, can be identified by the sturdy bed of the back sight, which replaced the flimsy spring bed of their predecessors. The patch box was abandoned in 1864, the remaining furniture being iron. The American Civil War (1861–65) prevented Sharps from making sporting rifles in quantity, although more than 80,000 carbines and 9,000 rifles were purchased by the Federal government. The army inventory was nearly 50,000 by the end of 1866, many being converted for metallic-case ammunition in the late 1860s.

A few full-length rifles were converted to fire metallic-case ammunition, and others were remodelled to half-stock design, but the Improved Breech-loading Sporting Rifle was the first purpose-built metallic-cartridge gun to be offered by the Sharps Rifle

---

production being sub-contracted to *Robbins & Lawrence. Trading continued until 1874, when the original company was superseded by the Sharps Rifle Company (above). **9.** *See also* Sharp and Sharpe.

Sharpshooter – **1.** Usually as 'The Sharpshooter'. A brandname found on shotgun cartridges sold by W.J. *Jeffrey of London, and Herbert *Lee of Bishop's Stortford, normally made by the Midland Gun Company (head-stamped 'MG' and 'B'). **2.** Sharpshooter or Sharp-Shooter. A name applied to a semi-automatic pistol made by Hijos de Calixto *Arrizabalaga. Protected by Spanish patent 68,027 (1917), the gun originally had an unprotected trigger and a barrel that could be tipped at the breech when the safety lever was rotated past the 'safe' position. This allowed the bore to be inspected, or single rounds to be loaded. The

first Sharp-Shooter lacked an extractor, spent cases being expelled by residual gas pressure; however, as this prevented the expulsion of unfired rounds, a conventional extractor was added in 1919. *See also* Jo-Lo-Ar. **3.** A spring-powered pistol, subsequently known as *Topscore, made in the USA for *Healthways, Inc. The Sharpshooter name was retained in Britain during the mid-1970s, when *Parker-Hale was still distributing the gun. **4.** Sharpshooter Cadet Rifle. A name associated with the small-calibre *Martini-action training rifles supplied to Australia prior to 1914. **5.** Sharpshooter's rifle. A variant of the 1859-pattern rifle made by the *Sharps Rifle Manufacturing Company, this was issued to the regiments of United States Sharpshooters raised in 1861 by Colonel Hiram *Berdan. They had distinctive double triggers, and all bore the 'JT'-in-cartouche

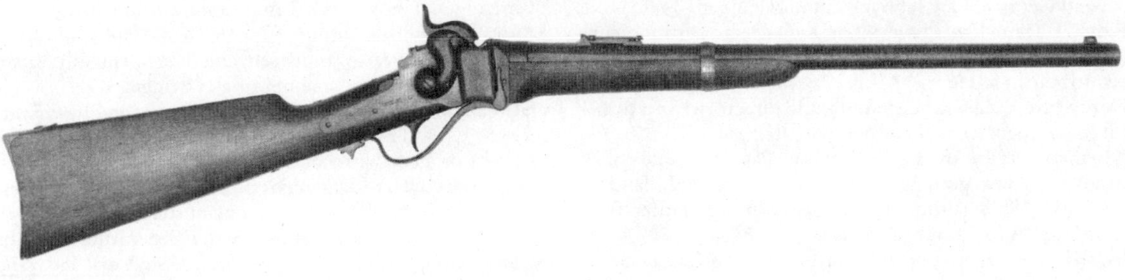

This .52-calibre 1863-pattern Sharps carbine was made during the American Civil War. The omission of a patch box from the butt and iron mounts instead of brass distinguishes it from the earlier 1859 New Model. Courtesy of Wallis & Wallis, Lewes.

Manufacturing Company. Guns of this type, dating from the period 1866–71, were based on the 1863-type cap-lock. An improved half-stock gun appeared in 1869, featuring a cranked firing pin that allowed the side-mounted hammer to ignite a centrefire cartridge, and a new extractor that shared the axis pin of the operating lever. Chamberings ranged from .44 Berdan Short to .52-70.

The US Army trials of 1865 included two dropping-block Sharps carbines with an auxiliary reciprocating extractor bolt protected by a patent granted in February 1867. In the autumn of 1867, therefore, the US authorities signed a contract with Sharps to convert cap-lock guns to take the standard .50-70 centrefire cartridge. Some guns had already been altered to accept a special rimfire round, based on the .56-50 Spencer pattern, but problems were solved only when Richard Lawrence perfected an S-shaped striker that could be fitted within the existing breech-block.

The Model 1870 rifles, used in US Army field trials, mated the barrels of 1863-type *cap-lock rifle-muskets, lined down from .58, with New Model (1863-type) Sharps actions taken from existing carbines. The work was done in *Springfield Armory in 1870–71. Most of the guns had fore-ends held by two bands, although a few three-band examples were made, and there were also a few short-barrelled .56-50 carbines with half-length fore-ends held by single bands.

Essentially similar Military Model rifles and carbines were offered by the Sharps Rifle Manufacturing Company (1870–74) and the Sharps Rifle Company, Hartford (1874–76 in Hartford, 1876–78 in Bridgeport). They could be based on the original (1869) or perfected (1871) sporting rifles.

The 1871-pattern New Model Sporting Rifle could handle the most powerful sporting cartridges. The receiver was lengthened to form a loading tray, the firing-pin assembly was modified, the hammer nose was straightened to strike the head of a firing pin set into the breech-block, and the breech-lever spring assembly was revised. About 25,000 were made by the Sharps Rifle Manufacturing Company (1871–74). Chamberings ranged from .40 Berdan Short to .50-90 Big Fifty.

The Model 1874 Sporting Rifle was identical to its predecessor, with the exception of the new 'Sharps Rifle Company' name. Barrels could be round, half-octagonal or fully octagonal; double set triggers were common; vernier sights could be supplied on request; and pewter fore-end tips were characteristic. Production continued until 1881, many post-1875 examples chambering new straight-case cartridges designed specifically to help reloading. Rifles leaving the Bridgeport factory from 1876 onward had barrels marked 'OLD RELIABLE'.

Perfected sporting rifles were made in a variety of styles: the Business Rifle, the English Model, the Hunter Rifle, the Long Range Rifle and the Mid Range Rifle. The standard Sharps-action guns were superseded by the hammerless Sharps-Borchardt (q.v.), but the original exposed-hammer patterns have proved very popular in recent years with manufacturers such as Pedersoli, the *Sharps Arms Company and the *Shiloh Manufacturing Company.

---

mark of government arms inspector John Taylor.

Sharpsooter. *See* Sharpshooter.

Shatuck, Shattuck – 1. Charles S. Shatuck, Hatfield, Massachusetts, USA. This gunmaker received US Patent 210,677 of 4 November 1879 to protect a revolver with a cylinder that swung out horizontally, then slid forward on its axis pin to eject spent cartridges. The name is often wrongly listed as Shattuck. **2.** C.S. Shatuck [& Company], Hatfield, Massachusetts. This gunmaking and engineering business made Shatuck-patent revolvers (above) and single-barrel 'The American' shotguns from 1880 – in succession to *Hyde & Shatuck – until about 1908. It also produced the multi-barrel *Unique pistol, patented in 1906 by Oscar *Mossberg. **3.** George D. Shattuck. A Federal government arms inspector working during the American Civil War, Shattuck accepted cap-lock *Colt revolvers marked 'GDS'. *See also* US arms inspectors' marks.

Shatterer. A brandname associated with a revolver made in Belgium prior to 1914 by A. *Bertrand.

Shaul. William Shaul. This English gunsmithing business was listed at 3 King Street, Tower Hill, London E., from 1890 to 1900 and possibly later.

Shaw – 1. George Shaw & Company. Working from chambers at 35 Temple Row, Birmingham, Warwickshire, this British patent agent acted for inventors including Charles *Gardner, Arthur Henry *Hill, Edward Henry *Parsons, Leslie Bown *Taylor and Frederick *Williams (*see* British Patents 5495/06 and 2863/06 of 1906, 19,519/07 of 1907 and 19,445/08 of 1908). **2.** George Shaw, Bowker & Folkes. This patent agency succeeded George Shaw (above) and moved from 35 Temple Row, Birmingham, to 8 Waterloo Street, Birmingham, in 1935. *See* British Patents 425,555 and 425,755, granted to Arthur Henry *Hill. **3.** John Shaw, Glossop, Derbyshire, England. Listed in trade directories as a musical instrument maker, Shaw patented an elastic-band-powered airgun in 1849 (English Patent 12728 of 1 August). A few guns were made by Henry *Holland in the early 1850s, although they used springs rather than elastic bands to compress the air.

'SHB'. Found on US military firearms and accessories. *See* S.H. *Broughton.

Shearing. F. Shearing & Company. This business, a member of the English gun trade, was listed at 21 Water Lane, London E.C., in 1899–1900.

Sheldon. Henry Newton Sheldon, Boston, Massachussetts, USA. An inventor and/or patent agent, this man was involved in British Patent 23/76 of 1876, granted to Augustus *Bedford with the collusion of Allison Owen *Swett and James Rollin Marble *Squire.

Shelvoke. George Edward Shelvoke, Britain. *See* Accles and Shelvoke.

Shepherd. Reginald V. Shepherd [Major]. Co-designer with Harold Turpin of the British *Sten Gun.

Sheridan – 1. A pneumatic rifle, designed by Edward *Wackerhagen and Irwin *Krause, and made by *Sheridan Products, Inc., from 1949 onward. *See also* *Bimoco-Sheridan-Torpedo, *Blue Streak and *Silver Streak. **2.** Sheridan Products, Inc., Racine, Wisconsin, USA. This company was formed by Edward R. Wackerhagen, in 1947, to exploit a high-quality pump-up airgun designed in 1946 in collusion with Irwin R. Krause. The business was named after a prominent street in Racine. A large range of 5mm- (0.2in-) calibre rifles (pneumatic and gas-powered) has been marketed under the brandnames *Blue Streak and *Silver Streak. Super Grade and Sporter rifles have also been made, as has the Knocabout cartridge pistol. A solitary carbon-dioxide-powered pistol, designated EB, has also appeared in recent years.

Sheriff's Model – 1. Used generically for almost any short-barrelled 'Western-style' revolver, but particularly for a short-barrel version of the Colt *Single Action Army revolver, lacking an ejector, which was introduced about 1880. **2.** Based on the *Single Action Army Model, about 1,000 of these .45-calibre guns were made in 1961 by *Colt's Patent Fire Arms Manufacturing Company, with SM-suffix numbers and 3in barrels lacking ejector-rod cases. They were followed by 4,560 Third Model examples, produced by the Firearms Division of *Colt Industries in 1980–85 for the .44-40 WCF and .45 Long Colt cartridges.

Sherman – 1. Charles E. Sherman. This government arms inspector, working during 1842–47 and possibly later, accepted military equipment marked 'CES'. A similar mark was used by Clarence *Simpson, but in a much later era. **2.** George W. Sherman, sometimes listed as 'Schuman(n)', accepted *Colt Dragoon revolvers for the US Army shortly before the Civil War began in 1861. They were marked 'GWS'. **3.** Maurice Sherman, a government arms inspector working in the early 1940s, accepted .45 M1911A1 *Colt-Browning pistols marked 'MS'. *See also* US arms inspectors' marks for this and the previous two entries.

'Shield Cartridge' [The], or 'Page-Wood's Shield Cartridge'. Found on shotgun ammunition loaded from *Eley-Kynoch components by T. *Page-Wood of Bristol. The mark was accompanied by a shield containing the name and a drawing of a cartridge.

Shilen. Edward 'Ed' Shilen and Shilen Rifles, Inc., Ennis, Texas, USA. This business was formed in 1961 to make gun barrels, progressing to rifles in the mid-1970s. Built on the proprietary DGA ('Damn' Good Action') turn-bolt system, these have been offered in a variety of styles, such as Bench-Rest, Silhouette, Single Shot, Sporter and Varminter. More than seventy chamberings were being listed in 1988, ranging from .17 Remington to .458 Winchester.

Shiloh Sharps. Originally known as Shiloh Products, trading in Farmingdale, New York, from 1976, this division of the Drovel Tool Company expanded to become the Shiloh Rifle Manufacturing Company, Inc., and moved to Big Timber, Montana, in 1983. It is now renowned for high-quality reproductions of *Sharps-pattern dropping-block rifles. These range from a re-creation of the *Business Rifle to a .45-70 Montana Model introduced in 1989 to commemorate the state centennial. A brief summary of the individual guns will be found in John Walter, *Rifles of the World* (Krause Publications, second edition, 1998).

ShKAS. This was an aircraft machine-gun with an unusually high rate of fire, designed by Boris *Shpitalny and Irnakhr *Komaritsky in the early 1930s. It was accepted for service in 1933 and rapidly improved; most authorities now recognise several separate variants of the basic design. The 20mm *ShVAK was essentially an enlarged version of the ShKAS, developed by *Voronkov from the basic design.

'SHT.L.E.' An abbreviated form of *Short Lee-Enfield, encountered in designation marks.

Shillito. Thomas R. Shillito. This British patent agency, which occupied chambers at 89 Chancery Lane, London, acted for Theodor *Hornhauer; *see* British Patents 7,932/95 and 23,188/95.

Shipley. W.R. Shipley, a government arms inspector, working in the 1890s, accepted weapons and equipment marked 'WRS'. *See also* US arms inspectors' marks.

Short... – 1. Short & Mid-Range Rifle (Sharps). *See* New Model Hammerless Short & Mid-Range Rifle. **2.** Short Range Rifle (Sharps). *See* New Model Hammerless Short Range Rifle. **3.** Short Range Target Rifle (c. 1876–90). This Remington was similar to the Mid-Range pattern, but had a short barrel chambered for cartridges ranging from 38 Extra Long to 46 Rimfire. An aperture sight was normally mounted on the barrel. *See also* Remington rifles, rolling-block action. **4.** Short recoil. *See* Recoil operation.

Shorty. Also known as the Model 9404 *Plainsman Shorty, this was a gas-powered pistol marketed by *Healthways, Inc.

Shotgun. *See* panel, pp. 474/75.

Shot sizes. The complexity of the system applied to *bore sizes (gauge) is matched by the quirky method of classifying the diameters of shot, which apparently originated in the mesh sizes of the grading sieves. The standard sizes range from No. 12 Shot (with a diameter of a mere .05in) up to No. 1 (.16), then to B (.17), Air Rifle (.175), BB (.18) and BBB (.19). The next series extends from T (.20) to TTTT (.23), followed by No. 4 Buck (.24) to No. 00 Buck (.33). TTT and TTTT sizes have also been known as F and FF respectively, and the most commonly encountered numbered sizes are 2, 4–6, 7¹/2, 8 and 9.

Shpagin. Georgiy Shpagin is best remembered as the designer of the Soviet PPSh, or Shpagin, submachine-gun, which was made in huge quantities after replacing the ★Degtyarev-designed PPD in 1941.

Shpitalny. Boris Gabrielovich Shpitalniy is best known for his contributions to the ShKAS high-speed aircraft machine-gun, developed in collaboration with Irnakhr ★Komartiskiy; Shpitalniy also experimented with submachine-guns.

Shue – 1. Earl V. Shue, Milwaukee, Wisconsin, USA. Patentee of a spring-air break-open BB Gun on 30 June 1914 (US Patent 1,102,904), very similar to the ★Daisy of 1892. **2.** Shue Air Rifle [Manufacturing] Company, Milwaukee and Neceeda, Wisconsin, USA. This business was formed in 1914 to exploit the BB Gun designed by Earl Shue, although few (if any) survive. It reappeared in Neceeda in the early 1920s, claiming to have developed a powerful airgun and to have perfected a BB shot-making machine, but disappeared for good in 1923. **3.** Shue's Special. A brandname associated with shotguns made by the ★Crescent Arms Company.

Shuffreys Ltd, Wallsall, Staffordshire. The marks of this gun and fishing-tackle distributor have been found on shotgun ammunition loaded by ★Kynoch Ltd of Birmingham prior to 1914, and have included 'The Beacon'.

Shuttleworth. S. Shuttleworth. A London gunmaker recorded at 51 Bishopsgate Street Within, E.C., in 1877.

'SHW'. Found on US military firearms and accessories. *See* Sheffield H. ★Wright.

'SIA'. A superimposition-type monogram without dominant letters. Found on revolvers made (or perhaps simply distributed) in the USA by ★Security Industries of America, Inc.

'S.I.C.Co.' This mark is found in the headstamps of ammunition made by, or perhaps for, the ★Sportsman's International Cartridge Company of Kansas City.

Sickels Arms Company. A name found on shotguns handled by the H. & D. ★Folsom Arms Company, possibly imported from Europe.

Side-lock. This term refers to a method of construction – originating in snaphance and flintlock days – where the main spring lay on the attachment, or lock, plate ahead of the cock. This system was perpetuated on the first generation of military metallic-cartridge guns, but found greatest favour on double-barrelled shotguns, even though the external hammers were soon replaced with enclosed hammers or internal strikers. Side-locks remain popular on side-by-side doubles, particularly the best grades, because they give the engraver an ideal platform to display his skills. On over/under shotguns, however, the side-lock has been almost universally superseded by the ★box-lock – although on high-quality over/unders, a false side plate is often used as a base for engraving.

Sidem International SA. This Brussels based agent for the original ArmaLite AR-10 rifle was responsible for sales made in Europe and North Africa, c. 1957–60.

Side-plate lock. *See* Side lock.

Side Snap. A name applied to a single-barrel box-lock central-hammer shotgun made in the USA by Iver ★Johnson from c. 1885 until the early 1900s.

Sidorenko. Co-designer with ★Malinovsky of the Sidorenko-Malinovsky tripod mount for the ★SGM machine-gun.

Siebelist – 1. A. Siebelist & Co., Goldlauter and Heidersbach bei Suhl in Thüringen. Said to have been listed in German trade directories as a wholesaler of sporting guns and ammunition, probably in the 1920s. **2.** Christian Siebelist, Suhl in Thüringen. A gunmaker trading in Germany in the early twentieth century.

Siebert. Anton Siebert, Carlsbad, Bohemia (Austria-Hungary prior to 1918, Czechoslovakia thereafter). Maker of a crank-wound volute-spring airgun with a set-trigger, c.1850.

SIG... – 1. An abbreviated form of ★Schweizerische Industrie-Gesellschaft. **2.** SIG-Hämmerli. Schweizerische Industrie-Gesellschaft acquired the shareholding of the ★Hämmerli gunmaking business in 1971, but the latter has continued trading under its own name. **3.** SIG-Sauer. A name denoting the products of co-operative ventures between Schweizerische Industrie-Gesellschaft and J.P. ★Sauer & Sohn GmbH.

Sigaud, Saint-Étienne, France. Listed in 1933 as a gunmaker. Listed in 1951 as Sigaud Fils, with premises at 56 cours Fauriel.

Sights – 1. Sights, fixed (iron): *see* panel, p. 476. **2.** Sights, optical. Coarse adjustment, poor regulation and the excessive width of the front-sight blade/back-sight notch combination were highlighted when engagement distance stretched to 1,000yd or more. Initial attempts to satisfy long-range requirements with pendulum, folding-bar and elongated-ladder sights characterised a period when complexity could be mistaken as a mark of technological advance. A better solution was provided by the telescope, which had appeared early in the seventeenth century and had become commonplace within 100 years. Exactly when the first practicable telescope rifle sight was introduced is not known with certainty, although a London gunsmith, Isaac Riviere, was offering them in the early 1830s, and optically-sighted target rifles had attained limited popularity in the USA by the time of the American Civil War (1861–65). Major Davidson patented his optical sight in Britain in 1862, persuading the British Army to undertake a trial in conjunction with a .451 Whitworth cap-lock rifle in 1865. Not until the 1880s, however, were trials undertaken with vigour, but the sights were mounted far too high to be successful, and their eye relief was poor. The modern optical sight is usually a seamless tube, with a diameter of 25 or 30mm, drawn from aluminium or sheet steel. It can be anodised, blacked, nickelled, chromed or clad in rubberised armour. The barrel of the sight contains a series of lenses, a graticle and a method of adjusting focus. Most modern lenses consist of several individual elements. The lens farthest from the shooter's eye, called the objective, forms the primary image – which, but for the inclusion of a separate erector lens, would be inverted. The image passes out through the eyepiece to enter the pupil of the firer's eye. Optical sights normally magnify the image, but the final size may vary between a modest fifty-per-cent gain (1.5x) and a twentyfold increase (20x). Although problems that can occur with optical sights are potentially serious, manufacturing standards are surprisingly high, and even the cheapest sights offer acceptable performance. A discussion of the many problems that can be associated with optical sights, from chromatic aberration to poor image brightness, may be found in *The Rifle Book*, by John Walter (Arms & Armour Press, 1987). Sights are usually supplied with detachable lens caps, the translucent patterns doubling

SHOTGUN

This term has been used to describe any long-arm – customarily smoothbored – used to fire a charge of shot instead of a single heavyweight projectile. By the 1840s, the development of rudimentary self-contained cartridges and the earliest breech-loaders (e.g. the pinfire *Lefaucheux) allowed the first real steps to be taken toward the modern shotgun. However, although the origins of their cartridges lay in France, most of the early advances toward the guns were made in Britain.

The top-lever is said to have been invented c. 1857 by Samuel *Matthews of Birmingham, who received a British Patent in October 1863. However, credit is usually given to Westley *Richards, whose British patent (2149/58 of 24 September 1858) pre-dated Matthews' by some years.

There was considerable variety among the earliest double-barrelled guns. Some had barrels that slid forward (*Bastin system); others tipped downward (*Lefaucheux); a few moved laterally at the breech (*Jeffries); and guns such as the *Bacon relied on fixed barrels and sliding bolts. The biggest problem with the first moving-barrel guns lay in the weak 'single-bite' methods of locking the breech. The locking components were usually placed in the bar, or forward extension, of the action, ahead of the standing breech (or 'action face'). When the gun was fired, however, elasticity in the material allowed the breech to spring briefly and open very slightly. This problem grew steadily worse as the gun aged, even though gunmakers often incorporated self-adjusting systems to reduce the effects of wear.

Many methods were tried in an attempt to improve the locking system, including rotary underlevers and barrels, which could be moved forward away from supporting discs on the action face before they were dropped (e.g. Dougall *Lock-Fast breech). Eventually, in September 1862, Westley Richards patented the Doll's Head, a small round-headed tenon projecting back from the top of the barrel block, or lump. When the action was closed, the doll's head was locked in a recess in the standing breech to provide additional support for the bites in the action bar.

The classic under-bolt locking mechanism was added by James Purdey in 1863, while the Wedge Fast system was perfected by William Greener in 1873 (British Patent 3084/73). Hundreds of proprietary variations had been patented by 1900, and treble-, quadruple- and even quintuple-bite locking systems were being touted by 1914. The *Greener Cross-bolt was favoured particularly.

The earliest double-barrelled shotguns were fired by external hammers inspired by their cap-lock predecessors, and often retained – in a debased form – the fences that had once enveloped the nipples. Some hammers rebounded, others hit spring-loaded inertia strikers set in the action face, and a few retracted

as filters for use on particularly bright days. Others will be encountered with range-finding graticles. The British Army currently accepts 4x sights as the best compromise of magnification and field-of-view, but the Austrian AUG has a fixed-focus 1.5x pattern, and the German H&K G36 has a 3x sight. Many leading gunmakers offer own-brand telescope sights, although virtually all are made by the same little group of manufacturers in Japan, and the differences between the sights are often simply restricted to their markings and external finish. Zeiss and Schmidt & Bender in Germany, and Kahles and Swarovski-Optik in Austria are among the leading European manufacturers; Bushnell, Bausch & Lomb and Weaver still make their own lenses in the USA, but no British manufacturers survive. Among the terms associated with optical sights are 'anastigmatic', indicating that an attempt has been made to correct astigma-

tism; 'achromatic', corrected for chromatic aberration (inability to focus light rays at a point); 'orthoscopic', where image distortion has been minimised; and 'aplanatic', referring to a correction for spherical aberration. A Relative Brightness value may be obtained by dividing the effective diameter of the objective lens by the sight aperture and squaring the result; if a 6x telescope sight has an objective lens diameter of 40mm and a sight aperture of 5mm, therefore, its relative brightness is 64 (40 ÷ 5 = 8; 8 x 8 = 64). The human eye adjusts automatically to ambient light, but its iris diameter rarely exceeds 3mm in daylight, and relative brightness greater than 9–10 is wasted: at dusk, the iris can expand to a little over 5mm for an optimal relative brightness of 25–30. Some large-objective sights may provide relative brightnesses as great as 100, allowing the eye to see detail in conditions where ambient light is insuf-

Shotguns have been made in a vast profusion of sizes and styles. These photographs show a double-barrelled 12-bore 'bar in wood' hammer gun by Westley Richards (facing page), dating from the 1870s, and a traditional (but expertly engraved) side-by-side side-lock Gamba Ambassador Executive Double (right).

automatically to half-cock when the barrels were dropped. Attempts were soon made to eliminate the hammers in favour of modernised hammerless locks, although these are often properly described as enclosed-hammer designs.

The first successful hammerless shotgun, patented in 1871 by London gunmaker Theophilus *Murcott, was made in considerable numbers prior to about 1876; by 1900, the hammerless gun had largely overhauled hammer patterns.

The earliest hammer guns were usually *back-locks. Although a few *side-lock examples had been made in cap-lock days, locks of this type became popular only when the hammerless shotguns were introduced and barrel-locking systems had been greatly refined.

The advent of the *Anson & Deeley gun, patented in 1875, introduced the Body Action, or *box-lock, with the mechanism mounted directly into the breech housing instead of being carried on separate detachable plates.

The earliest shotguns were inert, or passive, requiring the firer to hold the components of the breech closed while he activated the locking mechanism. This wasted effort inspired gunmakers to produce *snap-action systems with breeches

that shut automatically as the barrels were returned to battery. Shotguns of this type may also be assisted-opening or self-opening.

Some guns (ejectors) expel spent cases automatically, and others can be set to do so when required, although many (non-ejectors) leave the firer to remove spent cases and unfired shells. Efficient single-trigger systems (capable of firing barrels sequentially or selectively), safety devices and cocking/loading indicators have all been patented in large numbers.

Most of the shotguns made prior to 1914 were drop-barrel designs, with their barrels placed side-by-side. There were exceptions, however, such as the fixed-barrel French *Darne, which had a sliding breech. The development of multi-shot *combination weapons encouraged the introduction of the over/under (or superposed) style. Although the majority of over/under guns are

drop-barrel designs, exceptions have been made, such as the side-opening *Britte and the sliding-barrel *Bretton. Single-barrel guns have taken drop-barrel forms (hammer or hammerless, ejector or non-ejector) or have followed the sturdy fixed-barrel bolt-action pattern that has found particular favour in North America since the First World War. The multi-shot pump- or *slide-action design was established by the Spencer-Roper guns, patented in the USA in 1882, and led to the first truly successful auto-loading shotgun patented by John Browning in 1900–04.

Among the finest sources of information about shotguns are W.W. Greener's *The Gun and Its Development* (particularly the ninth edition of 1910); *The Modern Shotgun*, by Major Sir Gerald Burrard (1931); and *The British Shotgun*, in two volumes, by David Baker and Ian Crudgington (1981).

ficient to satisfy even the fully-opened iris. **3.** Sights, electro-optical. The first attempts to improve weapons sights relied on straightforward optical means, magnifying the image so that the target could be seen more clearly, but the gains were limited by the performance of the human eye – which receives electromagnetic radiation in the form of 'light', but can only resolve a tiny part of the spectrum. The visible band occupies an almost infinitesimal part of a total electromagnetic spectrum, ranging from radio waves at one extreme to gamma rays at the other, and thoughts soon turned to extending human sight by concentrating on the portion of the infra-red spectrum nearest the visible band. The German vehicle-control system known as Fahrzeug-Gerät 1229, developed during the Second World War by the Forchungsanstalt der Deutschen Reichspost in collusion with Leitz of Wetzlar, presented the human eye

with an otherwise unseen image by 'converting' radiation with wavelengths in the near-infra-red part of the spectrum. Resolution was very poor initially, until an infra-red lamp was added to flood the target area. However, this active system allowed an adversary equipped with a passive detector to see the infra-red lamp without being seen. FG 1229 was soon adapted to become the Zielgerät 1229 Vampir, which was tested on the Kar. 98k, Gew. 43 and MP. 43/Stg. 44. A 130mm-diameter transmitting lamp accompanied a converter with a magnifying eye-piece lens in a telescope-like tube, but a separate battery-pack electrical supply was necessary. Vampir inspired the USA to develop the SniperScope, which was the first entirely self-contained passive viewer to be successful. The greatest single advance made since the Second World War concerns the converter, which, aided by advances in technology and

SIGHTS, FIXED (IRON)

Sights (1)

An appreciation of the curved trajectory of projectiles created multi-setting sights, often in the form of standing plates pierced with several sighting holes. Folding-leaf sights made an early appearance, and tube sights had become popular by the end of the sixteenth century. A sprung sight-block sliding along a stepped elevator had also been tried long before it attained great prominence in the USA during the nineteenth century.

Attempts were made early in the eighteenth century to provide back sights that could be adjusted by screws either vertically (elevation) or laterally (drift or windage). In general these were made by instrument makers, however, and did not become common until improvements in machine-tool design were made early in the nineteenth century.

Back sight design remained surprisingly static for many years, largely because the performance of guns remained unchanged. The first real improvement came with the adoption of the self-expanding ammunition that, virtually at a stroke, increased maximum effective range many times over and emphasised the need for more efficient sights. Thereafter fixed standing-block sights were confined to short-range weapons such as handguns and carbines; on infantry rifles, however, the leaf sight – usually combining a stepped-base and a pivoting leaf or 'ladder' – became popular for more than a hundred years.

Commonly found in central Europe, particularly in Switzerland and southern Germany, the tangent sight had an arm that could be elevated either by turning a knob or by sliding a control block horizontally along its bed.

Tangent and leaf-type back sights were comparatively delicate and expensive to make. The rise of close-range trench warfare in the twentieth century suggested that refinement was unnecessary, and 'battle sights' appeared. These were normally set for only one or two ranges, but were sturdy and dependable.

This simplification process may be seen in some late twentieth-

Back sights come in a variety of designs. These photographs depict a military-style rocking 'L' sight on an FN FNC (left), an Élite Model 101 aperture sight (above) and an Anschütz 6697 tangent-leaf on an air rifle (below).

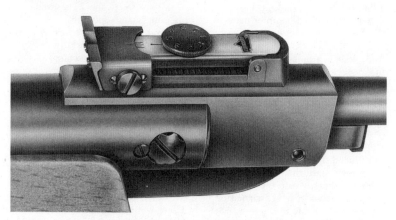

century designs, but a compromise is usually accepted; the drum sight favoured by Heckler & Koch and the rocking 'L' of the FNC typify the balance that must be sought between ease of use and accuracy of setting.

The open sights of the 1990s include standing notched blocks, vertically-sliding plates controlled by finger-wheels, multiple leaves pivoted on a single block, and the so-called Express sights, which have a rank of several separately-pivoting folding leaves.

The Cape [of Good Hope] sight – a useful, but apparently artificial designation – was a variant of the Express pattern with several small folding leaves and a large leaf-and-slider for longer ranges. The semi-buckhorn sight, with a sprung leaf and a notched elevator, remains popular in North America. A flat spring bent into an open notch may

be elevated by a sliding stepped plate; alternatively, a screw may raise the leaf. Sights of this type were once known as 'Rocky Mountain' Sights when fitted with a buck-horn sighting notch.

Tangent-leaf sights of different forms are still used in large numbers, alongside aperture, or peep, sights ranging from the simplest battle pattern to micro-adjustable competition diopter sights with integral filters and adjustable irises.

The finest target sights are made in Europe by Anschütz, Feinwerkbau, Grünel & Elmiger (Elite brand), Tanner, Walther and others. Front sights still generally consist of a simple ramp-mounted blade or barleycorn (an inverted 'V'), often protected by a sheet-steel cover, but luminous dots, coloured inserts and white beads may be added to improve contrast.

progressive miniaturisation, can enhance the image electronically. Most intensifier sights are essentially a television tube inserted in a telescope sight between the objective and eye-piece lenses. Light from the target – natural or boosted by a floodlight – enters through the objective lens and is focussed on to the front element of the converter. Photons provided by the energy entering from the target image cause electrons to be emitted from the converter's photo-cathode and focused on to a phosphorescing screen which, in turn, emits the photons that reconstruct the image. The key to success was the degree of amplification, releasing as many electrons as possible for each initial photon strike. Although the cascade tubes of the first-generation sights were very bulky, the inclusion of additional intermediate amplification stages gave surprisingly good performance, and 60,000-fold gains were not uncommon. The major drawbacks of these early intensifier sights were expense, excessive size and the delicacy of the converter unit. Improvements in converters, which in general have changed from cascade-type photo-cathodes to fibre-optic micro-channel plates, have allowed intensifier sights to be reduced to surprisingly compact dimensions. Their performance remains much the same as their predecessors (perhaps limited by maximum attainable image-gain) and the optical components remain largely unchanged, but a considerable reduction in manufacturing costs has been reflected in price. Powered by two 1.5-volt AA batteries, the Pilkington Optronics Kite Night Sight typically offers 4x magnification. It is a mere 255mm long, has a 73mm-diameter objective lens and weighs about 1.2kg with its batteries. Intensifiers operate at their best in conditions ranging from overcast starlight to full moonlight with light cloud cover. Full moonlight may bring excessive brightness and the beginning of black-out, whereas overcast starlight or unbroken cloud cover may reduce even a third-generation intensifier to impotence in woodland. **4.** Sights, thermal imaging. Similar to intensifiers in many respects, these rely on a different operating system: they reconstruct images from tiny differences in thermal emissions. Although normally these emissions have been absorbed or scattered by the atmosphere by the time they reach the firer, there are two principal 'windows' where they penetrate the atmosphere efficiently enough to allow good images to be reconstructed. Unfortunately, thermal-imaging sensors need to be cooled continuously (often relying on liquid nitrogen) and are usually bulky. Officine Galileo offered a thermal-imaging/image-intensifying sight in the 1980s, which had the ability to superimpose the infra-red and thermal-emission images to improve performance, and development potential may still lie in multi-system sights of this type. **5.** Sights, target designating. The basis of many modern targeting systems is a laser beam, although the details vary greatly from manufacturer to manufacturer. The principle of the laser (an acronym of 'Light Amplified by Stimulated Emission of Radiation') has been known for many years, but the first commercially practicable system was not perfected until the early 1960s. Individual atoms are excited with a beam of light to generate additional radiation in phase with the light beam, which thus is reinforced. The results can be magnified to produce a beam of coherent (single-frequency) light of great power. This system has been widely touted as the 'death ray', but a more immediate benefit has been the development of continuous-line projectors to assist in medicine or surveying tasks. Lasers of

this type, usually gas-discharge patterns, inspired the development of laser designators, or aiming projectors. Some designators operate in the visible spectrum, projecting a beam that can be seen by the firer and the target at all times, while others operate in the infra-red bands and require a headset equipped with monocular intensifier-type detector tubes. Designator systems undoubtedly improve shooting skills, particularly snap shooting, but the designator unit must be activated to obtain a sighting mark, and proceeding in too leisurely a fashion can encourage counter-sniping. Restrictions are also placed on peripheral vision by headset construction. **6.** Sights, collimating. Although image-intensifying sights have made tremendous progress in recent years, they are still expensive compared with optical sights. Beginning with Singlepoint, introduced in the 1970s, attempts have been made to enhance snap shooting with sighting equipment that relies on an optical illusion. Collimator sights combine an aiming mark within the sight body, illuminated either by ambient light or by electrical batteries, with the ability of the firer's binocular eyesight to accommodate the reflected aiming mark and a view of the target simultaneously. Singlepoint appeared to be projecting a red dot on to the target and undoubtedly facilitated rapid fire, but few of these sights – even those with powered graticles – have proved to be of much use in darkness. Ambient-light reflectors are also generally ineffective under dark-to-light conditions. Collimator sights lost favour for much of the early 1990s, even though the South African Armson OES (Occluded Eye Sight) and the Swedish AimPoint have been touted with vigour. However, FN Herstal is currently promoting a powered sight of this general class on its P-90 Individual Weapon.

Sigmund Pumps Ltd, based in Gateshead-on-Tyne, Northumberland, England, made drum magazines for the British .303 ★Bren Gun during the Second World War, often marking them with the code 'N 65' instead of the company name. *See also* British military manufacturers' marks.

Signature – 1. Usually as 'The Signature': associated with shotgun ammunition loaded for ★Cole & Son of Devizes and Portsmouth. **2.** A brandname associated with rifles made from 1987 by ★McMillan Gunworks, Inc., of Phoenix, Arizona. The Signature Classic Sporter (introduced in 1987), built on a ★Mauser-type bolt action, chambered cartridges ranging from .22-250 to .375 H&H Magnum. The Signature Alaskan (1989) had a folding-leaf back sight and nickel-plated metalwork; the Signature Mountain Rifle (1989), in chamberings from .270 Winchester to .300 Winchester Magnum, had a titanium-alloy receiver and a black fibreglass stock; and the Signature Super Varminter (1989), offered in options ranging from .220 Swift to .308 Winchester, had a heavy barrel in a specially-bedded synthetic stock.

Silber & Fleming Ltd. This merchant and gunmakers' agent was listed at 56½, 62 and 71 Wood Street, and 7 and 10 Fell Street, London E.C., in 1886–90, and in Wood Street and London Wall in 1891–97.

Silencer. This device is attached to the muzzle of a gun – or incorporated in its construction – and traps the gases emerging from the barrel, circulating them in expansion chambers to allow their temperature and pressure to drop before releasing them to the atmosphere. This prevents the usual noise of the muzzle blast. Silencers are rarely encountered on rifles, as the excessive muzzle velocity of most cartridges necessitates the use of special low-power subsonic ammunition. The first practicable silencer was patented by Hiram Percy *Maxim in 1909 and made in large numbers by the Maxim Patent Silencer Company.

'Silesia'. Found in the headstamps of shotgun cartridges advertised in 1911 by A.L. *Frank; possibly made by *Munitionswerke Schönebeck.

Silhouette, or Model 29 Silhouette. A .44 *Magnum revolver made in Springfield, Massachusetts, by *Smith & Wesson.

Silin. Vladimir Silin. This Soviet inventor was responsible for a universal, or general-purpose, machine-gun based on the *Goryunov, but his prototypes were not acceptable.

'Silvanus'. This brandname was found on shotgun cartridges made in Germany prior to 1914, probably by *Cramer & Buchholz.

Silver, Silver... – 1. S.W. Silver & Company, London and Manchester. Silver distributed guns, ammunition, sporting goods and camping equipment. An insert in W.W. Greener's *Modern Breech-Loaders* (1871) advertised The Explorer's Room, 66 & 67 Cornhill, London, as vital to 'Officers departing on Foreign Service, Explorers, Missionaries and Emigrants, [who] may, without the expenditure of valuable time, obtain every article of equipment required to meet the exigencies of Camp Life, Travel or Exploration'. Among the items offered were 'The Settler's Double Gun, Muzzle Loading, 11-bore..., shoots with either shot or ball, Rifles, Revolvers, Kives, &c.' Premises were listed at 2–4 Bishopsgate Within (the principal warehouse), and 100 Market Street, Manchester. An address in Sun Court, Cornhill, London, was first listed in 1882. Additional premises in Old Bond Street were opened in 1890, and the directories for 1892–94 record Silver not only at Sun Court and Old Bond Street, but also at 11 Leadenhall Street and 15 Bury Street, St Mary Axe. By 1895, however, only 67 Cornhill was being used, where the business remained when the trading style became 'S.W. Silver & Co. & B. Edgington Ltd' in 1899. Silver's marks will be found on shotgun and sporting-rifle ammunition, usually loaded by *Eley Bros. **2.** Silver Jet. An airgun pellet similar to the obsolete British *Lane's Triumph, made by *Hasuike Seisakusho of Osaka, Japan. *See also* Jet. **3.** 'Silver Ray' [The]. A mark reported on shotgun ammunition made in Birmingham by the *Mullerite Cartridge Works.

Simarin. Anatoly Simarin (1936–91). Co-designer of the Soviet 5.45mm *PSM automatic pistol with *Lev Kulikov and Tikhon *Lashnev.

Simco. A short-lived pneumatic rifle made in the USA by the *Sims Rifle Company until the early 1950s.

Simon. Gebrüder Simon, Schmalkalden in Thüringen, Germany. This gunmaking business, active between the world wars, specialised in target and hunting rifles. It is often linked mistakenly with the *Simson family of Suhl.

Simonds. Frank A. Simonds, Grand Rapids, Michigan, USA. Co-patentee of a spring-air BB Gun with Chauncey H. *Fisher and Hugh C. *Ross (US 689,923 of 13 December 1901). Subsequently this was exploited by the *Rapid Rifle Company.

Simonis. Albert Simonis, Liège. A Belgian gunsmith active prior to the First World War; a founder member of les *Fabricants d'armes réunis, 1886 and of *Fabrique Nationale d'Armes de Guerre in 1889. Simonis made revolvers from the 1870s onward.

Simonov – 1. Sergey Gavrilovich Simonov (1894–1986) was apprenticed to a blacksmith at the age of sixteen. After working for a small engineering business, he moved to the Kovrov machine-gun factory in 1918. By 1929, he had become senior master gunsmith, and his talents as a designer were recognised. Among his more successful creations were the AVS of 1936, the first automatic rifle to be adopted in the Red Army since the Fedorov Avtomat, and the PTRS (anti-tank rifle) of 1941. Sergey Simonov worked throughout the Second World War to perfect his 1941-pattern semi-automatic rifle, eventually transforming it for the 7.62x39 intermediate cartridge. The resulting SKS was adopted in 1949 as a safeguard against the failure of the *Kalashnikov assault rifle. Decorated with the Hero of Socialist Labour award, among others, Simonov retired in 1950. **2.** Vladimir Vasilyevich Simonov, nephew of Sergey Gavrilovich, was born in Kovrov in 1935. After completing a mine-engineering course in the Poldolsk Industrial-Technical College in 1955, he began work at the Central Scientific Research Institute for Precision Engineering. In addition to research work in other subjects, V.V. Simonov has been responsible for the APS (a silenced version of the Stechkin pistol) and SPP-1 underwater pistol. **3.** Simonov anti-tank rifle (*Protitotankovoye Ruzhe Simonova*, PTRS). Developed in haste immediately after the Germans invaded the Soviet Union in the summer of 1941, and ordered into production 'off the drawing board' together with the simpler bolt-action *Degtyarev competitor (PTRD), this giant auto-loading rifle chambered a powerful 14.5x114 cartridge. The PTRS incorporated a conventional gas system with an adjustable regulator, and had a box magazine loaded with a five-round clip. Although more than 100,000 were made, the gun was too large and too sophisticated to be cost efficient in machine time; the simpler PTRD, therefore, was made in far larger numbers. **4.** Simonov automatic rifle (AVS). Sergey Simonov began his design work in the Kovrov factory in 1922, but ten years of comparative testing elapsed before the 1931-type rifle was approved for service trials. These showed that improvements were needed, but finally, on 22 March 1934, the Simonov rifle was adopted for service. Series production of the AVS (or AVS36) began in Izhevsk in 1937, but combat experience showed its weaknesses. Construction was too light to withstand prolonged automatic fire (the guns weighed only 4.5kg empty), and the vertically-moving locking block jammed too easily. Changes were made as production progressed, removing the advantage of parts interchangeabiliy, but work stopped in favour of the *Tokarev in 1939, after about 66,000 1936-type guns had been made. Simonov had prepared a revised design, but by then had fallen out of favour. The improved gun became the 7.62x54R Model 1941, which in turn became the 7.62x39 *Samozariadniya Karabina Simonova* (SKS) in 1949. The SKS was made in quantity in the Soviet Union, but the *Kalashnikov assault rifle was preferred. However, copies of the Simonov design were made in huge numbers elsewhere, particularly in the People's Republic of China, where output may have exceeded 20,000,000. Others were made in the German Democratic Republic and Yugoslavia. Additional details will be found in John Walter's *Rifles of the World* (Krause Publications, second edition, 1998) and *Soviet Small-Arms and Ammunition*, by David N. Bolotin (Finnish Arms Museum Foundation/Handgun Press, 1995). **5.** Simonov underwater pistol, SPP-1. Apparently dating from the late 1960s, this four-barrel design fires 4.5mm darts inserted in modified 7.62x39 cases. These are loaded as four-round clips simply by breaking open the action. The double-action self-cocking striker fires each barrel sequentially, novelty lying more in the ammunition than the gun itself.

Simple Rifles. These guns were made in China, for the Japanese occupation forces, at the end of the Second World War. A crude, but otherwise conventional, emergency weapon, the first single-shot Simple Rifle fired the 7.7mm Type 99 round. This proved much too powerful and was speedily replaced by the 8mm pistol cartridge. Simple Rifles had slab-pattern butts and split-bridge receivers. Locking relied on the base of the bolt handle, while the trigger system often consisted simply of a spring and lever engaging directly in the cocking piece. The only contractors thus far identified are Toa Ironworks, Shanghai; Nanking arsenal; the Sixth Army repair depot, Tung-Shan; and the Chi-Fo, Wang-Shih and Shu-Chow workshops in Tung-Shan.

Simplex – 1. A name associated with a revolver sold in Belgium prior to c. 1914 by A. *Rongé. **2.** A self-cocking single-barrel shotgun made in 12- and 16-bore by *Manufacture Française d'Armes et Cycles. This simple design could have an internal or external hammer, the action being opened by an underlever that doubled as the trigger guard and was locked by a horizontal slide entering a recess in the barrel-block. An automatic ejector was fitted. Some guns will be found with decoration ranging from simple scroll panels to overall engraving. *See also* Supra-Simplex. **3.** A mark found on the grips of *Bergmann-Simplex pistols, made in Germany and possibly also Belgium or France in the early twentieth century. **4.** Simplex-Canardier. An 800mm-barrelled 10-bore variant of the Simplex (above), intended for duck hunting. A large standing-block back sight could be found on top of the breech. **5.** Simplex-Junior. A lightweight variant of the Simplex (above) in 20- and 24-bore. **6.** A very low-powered US-made BB Gun, cocked by a thumb hammer and made of two pieces of sheet metal by the *Chicago Rifle Manufacturing Company, 1898–1900.

Simpson – 1. Piccadilly, London. The name of this gentlemen's outfitter has been reported on 12-bore shotgun cartridges of unknown provenance. **2.** Clarence E. Simpson. This government arms inspector, working shortly before the Second World War, accepted .45 M1911A1 *Colt-Browning pistols marked 'CES'. A similar mark was used prior to the American Civil War by Charles E. *Sherman. *See also* US arms inspectors' marks. **3.** George Simpson, Hartford, Connecticut. Co-patentee with William *Robertson of a breech-loading carbine tested by the US Army in 1866.

Sims – 1. John G. Sims: *see* John G. *Syms. **2.** Sims Rifle Company, California, USA. This short-lived business made the unsuccessful *Simco pump-up pneumatic rifle, introduced in 1948/9 as a potential rival for the *Benjamin and *Crosman types. The Sims company was liquidated in 1953.

Simson & Companie, Suhl in Thüringen, Germany. One of Thüringia's best-known gunmaking businesses prior to the First World War, Simson & Co. was being operated in 1900 by Gerson and Julius Simson. Ownership had passed to Leonhard, Julius, Max and Witwe Jeanette Simson by 1914. The 1925 *Deutsches Reichs-Adressbuch* records the products of Simson & Co. as 'hunting and sporting guns, small-calibre guns, automatic pistols, cars and bicycles', and lists a branch office in Berlin NW7, Unter den Linden 75–76. The customary trademark consisted of 'S' superimposed on the central of three pyramids, although the brandname 'Astora' will be encountered on shotguns. The company was still listed in 1930 – directed by Leonhard Simson, Arthur Simson, Dr Julius Simson and Julius Simson senior – as a maker of vehicles, bicycles, sporting guns, precision machinery and instruments. Simson became the German Army's major supplier of *Mauser-action rifles in 1920, completing many others in sporting form. The company became Berlin-Suhler Waffen- und Fahrzeugwerke GmbH in 1932, but was nationalised forcibly in the mid-1930s; by 1940, it had become a division of Gustloff-Werke. In addition to sporting guns, Mauser rifles and Luger pistols, the company made 6.35mm vest-pocket pistols (*Westentaschenpistolen*). The Models 1922 and 1927 were essentially similar, although the latter had an entirely slab-sided slide instead of the semi-tubular form exhibited on the older gun.

Simulated-death guns. *See* Scheintod.

Singer – 1. A small Browning-type automatic pistol marked by Francisco *Arizmendi of Eibar in two patterns: (a) 6.35mm, six rounds, striker fired; (b) 7.65mm, seven rounds, striker fired. The gun may have been made by *Arizmendi y Goenaga. **2.** Singer Manufacturing Company, Elizabethville, New Jersey. Best known for its sewing machines, Singer obtained a contract to make .45 M1911A1 *Colt-Browning pistols when the USA entered the Second World War in December 1941. However, only about 500 guns had been made in 1942 before production was suspended in favour of artillery range-finders. Gun slides were marked 'S. MFG. CO.' above the address. A British subsidiary, The Singer Manufacturing Company Ltd, made more than 300,000 *Sten Mark I and Mark I* submachine-guns in its Clydebank (Scotland) factory during the Second World War. Large quantities of components for the *Lee-Enfield No. 4 rifle also date from this period. Many of them bore 'N 67' instead of the company name, although other factories in Coventry used M-prefix identifiers. *See also* British military manufacturers' marks.

Single action – 1. Applied generically to any trigger system embodying a hammer (or striker) that must be cocked manually before it can be released by the trigger. *See also* Double Action. **2.** An alternative name for the Model 422 carbon-dioxide-powered pistol made by the *Benjamin Rifle Company of St Louis, USA. **3.** Single Action Army Model Revolver, SAA, Peacemaker, Model P or M1873. This single-action gun was introduced in 1873 by *Colt's Patent Fire Arms Manufacturing Company, of Hartford, Connecticut, USA, to succeed the open-frame *New Model Army pattern. The Peacemaker appears to have been the work of William *Mason, who combined the traditional Colt layout with a solid-top frame, but also acknowledged a series of patents granted to Mason and Charles *Richards in 1872–75. The US Army purchased more than 37,000 .45-calibre Single Action Army Colts between 1873 and 1891, mostly with 7½-inch barrels, although many survivors had their barrels shortened in the 1890s for issue to artillerymen (the so-called Artillery Model, q.v.). The Colt was also popular commercially; about 357,000 guns were made between 1873 and 1940, plus an additional 850 assembled immediately after the Second World War. They had been offered in chamberings ranging from .22 Short rimfire to .476 Eley centrefire (but .45 Long Colt and .44-40 WCF accounted for sixty per cent of sales) and also often on the basis of a Smokeless Powder frame. Barrels varied between 4¹/₂in and 16in; grips were wood, gutta-percha, ivory or mother-of-pearl. Virtually the only major change concerned the cylinder pin, which from 1893 onward became a transverse bolt locked by a spring. This improvement had been patented by William Mason in September 1874. Production began again in 1956, when the first batch of about 80,000 Second Model guns was made prior to the advent in 1976 of the Third, or New, model. They were chambered for the .357 Magnum, .38 Special, .44 Special and .45 Colt cartridges. The Third Model (1976–85), sharing numbers containing 'SA' with its predecessor, contained internal refinements; some guns were made on the Smokeless Powder frame, and others on the original Black Powder pattern. Fourth Model guns (1985 to date) have been offered on the Black Powder frame only, in .44-40 WCF and .45 Colt.

Single Six. A .22 rimfire *Peacemaker lookalike introduced by *Sturm Ruger in 1953 and improved by a *transfer-bar safety system in 1973.

Sionics, Inc., Atlanta and Powder Springs, Georgia, USA. Best known for sound suppressors (silencers), this business was also responsible for promoting the *Ingram submachine-gun in 1966–70. Subsequently, the operation was purchased by the *American Military Aarmament Corporation (AMAC).

Sirocco. A gas-ram air rifle patented in 1981 by H.F *Taylor and D.R. *Theobald. The guns were made originally in Britain by *Theoben Engineering of St. Ives, Cambridgeshire, but have been licensed since to many leading manufacturers (e.g. Hermann *Weihrauch).

Sitting Bull. A *Suicide Special revolver made in the USA by the *Ryan Pistol Company of Norwich, Connecticut, in the late nineteenth century.

Sivispacem – 1. A small Spanish automatic pistol of Browning type, made in Eibar by Sociedad Española de Armas y Municiones (*SEAM): 7.65mm, six rounds, hammer fired. Possibly also made in 6.35mm. **2.** Sivispacem Parabellum. A Browning-type pocket pistol made in Spain by, or perhaps for, *Thieme y Edeler of Eibar: 6.35mm, six or seven rounds.

Six-Gun – 1. A colloquial name for virtually any revolver, although technically restricted to those with six-chamber cylinders. **2.** The Daisy-made Model 179 spring-powered revolver.

'Sixteen Cartridge' [The]. A mark found on 16-bore shotgun cartridges sold by Charles S. *Rosson of Norwich, Norfolk. *See also* 'Twenty Cartridge'.

'SJ&D', sometimes in the form of a monogram, and often within an oval cartouche. Found on revolvers made in Belgium prior to 1914 by *Simonis, Janssen & Dumoulin of Liège.

'SK' – 1. Beneath a crown, above a number. A mark applied by inspectors working in the *Royal Small Arms Factory in the Sparkbrook district of Birmingham. *See also* 'B' and British military inspectors' marks. **2.** Found on US military firearms and accessories. *See* Samuel *Keller and S. *Knows.

'S&K', 'S. & K.' Trademarks associated with *Sempert & Krieghoff of Suhl, but readily confused with 'S&H' (q.v.).

SKB Arms Company. This gunmaking business was founded by the Sakaba family in 1855, and was sited originally in what is now Mito City; matchlocks were made for the Tokuguwa shogunate, until the advent of the Meiji era in 1868 and the development of foreign trade, which led to the production of cartridge firearms. Hunting and sporting rifles have been made continuously since the late 1870s. The plant facilities, now located in Cho-ku, Tokyo, were modernised after the Second World War, and gun production began again in 1947. SKB has made a small range of airguns, including the M53 and M3 of the 1950s, and also owns the Sharp Rifle Company. The SKB trademark derives from the Sakaba name, which in Japanese consists of three ideographs (sa-ka-ba). (NB: Walter Smith, in *Gas, Air & Spring Guns of the World*, confused the products of SKB with those of *Kawaguchiya.)

Skeet, *Concorde Skeet or *Daytona Skeet. 12-bore over/under shotguns made by *Società Armi Bresciane of Gardone Val Trompia, with an anatomical pistol grip, a special fore-end and a single selective trigger. Barrels are customarily 680 or 710mm long. The Skeet SL is similar, but has side-locks instead of a box-lock action.

Skerrett. Henry Skerrett. This patent agency, with chambers at 24 Temple Road, Birmingham, assisted several well-known inventors. Included in the protection sought with Skerrett's aid were British Patents 14,588/05 and 22,681/05 of 1905, and 8246/06 of 1906, granted to the *Birmingham Small Arms Company Ltd, Augustus *Driver and George *Norman; British Patents 11,817/05 of 1905 and 25,830/06 of 1906 to Driver and Norman alone; and 15,712/02 of 1902 and 9153/04 of 1904 to Frederick S. *Cox. Lincoln *Jeffries (Senior) was assisted in applications for what became British Patents 20,246/03 of 1903; 10,426/05 and 22,550/05 of 1905; 11,588/06 of 1906; 10,250/10, 25,783/10 and 30,338/10 of 1910; 1405/11 and 9684/11 of 1911. The younger Lincoln Jeffries was helped in relation to British Patent 181,277 (1921). Other Skerrett clients included George F. *Urry, who obtained British Patent 20,744/06 of 1906 in collaboration with Lincoln Jeffries (Senior), and W.J. 'Bill' *Whiting in connection with British Patent 4213/10 of 1910. Skerrett appears to have died or retired shortly after the First World War, to be suceeded by his sons, Henry N. and William S. Skerrett.

Skimmin & Wood, sometimes listed as 'Skimin & Wood', Birmingham. This agency modified about 41,330 .303 No. 3 *Enfield rifles to Weedon Repair Standards (WRS) in the summer of 1939. The code 'M 224' may have appeared on guns instead of the partnership's name. *See also* British military manufacturers' marks.

Skinner & Company, Haywood Street, Leek, Staffordshire. This English gun, fishing-tackle and sporting-goods retailer is known to have marked shotgun cartridges supplied prior to 1914 by *Kynoch Ltd of Birmingham.

'SKN.' A mark found on many British firearms that have been 'skeletonised' (i.e. cut away) for educational use. Some of the examples dating from the early stages of the Second World War will prove to be the work of H. *Atkin.

Škoda – 1. Emil Škoda, born in 1839, was deported from Germany to his native Austria at the time of the Seven Weeks War (1866). Then he became works superintendent of an arms-making workshop, which had been founded in 1859 in Valdštejn by Graf Arnošt. Purchasing the facilities only three years later, in 1869, Skoda began to put his knowledge of steel making, gained in the Weser shipyard in Bremen, to good use. A steelworks was opened in 1884 and, by 1890, the company was advertising a range of guns, gun carriages, ammunition, cast-steel armour plate and the Patent Mitrailleuse. Škoda died in 1900. **2.** Škoda machine-gun: *see* panel, p. 482.

SKS. An abbreviated form of *Samozariadniya Karabina Simonova*, this was applied to a 7.62x39 auto-loading carbine designed by Sergey *Simonov during the Second World War and ordered into series production in 1949.

'Sk. Y.' Found on Finnish military firearms, ranging from *Maxim machine-guns and *Mosin-Nagant rifles to *Suomi submachine-guns and *Lahti pistols. Applied by the headquarters units of the Protective Corps (*Suojeluskuntain Ylieskunnen*). The remainder of the units used a mark comprising an 'S' and a fir leaf.

'Sky High' [The]. This mark will be found on British shotgun cartridges, associated with William *Evans of London, and also with *Jeffrey & Son of Plymouth.

'Skyrack' [The]. Found on shotgun cartridges made by *Greenwood & Batley.

'SL', 'S.L.' – **1.** Found on Single Loading guns – usually special .303 *Lee-Enfields – destined for Indian troops whose loyalty or proficiency was uncertain. **2.** Found on components for the No. 4 Lee-Enfield rifle made during the Second World War by William Sykes Ltd. This company was also allocated the area code 'N74', but often used its initials instead. **3.** Found on US military firearms and accessories. *See* Samuel *Leonard.

Sladden, Brothers & Company. Describing itself as an agency, but also a member of the English gun trade, this business appeared in the London directories for 1873 at Albert Buildings, Queen Victoria Street; 4 King Street, Cheapside; and 29 Ironmonger Lane.

Slant-breech [Sharps], also known as the Model of 1851. This was characterised by the oblique movement of the breech, a combined operating lever and trigger guard, and a tape primer ahead of the hammer. The hammer was carried inside the back-action lock plate, and the receiver had distinctly rounded contours. Sporting guns usually chambered .36, .44 or .52 linen-case combustible ball cartridges, although .52 shot loads were made in small quantities, and .56-calibre carbines were produced for trials in Britain. The Model 1853 was generally made as a .52-calibre carbine with brass furniture. The lock plate contained Sharps' patented pellet magazine, with a slender brass tube of waterproofed priming discs. The Model 1853 was supplemented by the Model 1855, 400 carbines with *Maynard Tape Primers being ordered by the US Army in April 1855, and 200 .52-calibre rifles by the US Navy between March and September 1856. The 1859 and subsequent patterns had a new breech-block that moved vertically.

Slave. *See* Buffalo-Slave.

Slavia – **1.** A 6.35mm Browning-type pocket pistol made in the 1920s in Kdyne, Czechoslovakia, by A. Vilimeč. **2.** Associated with a range of break-barrel spring-air rifles, from the simplest junior type upward, made in Czechoslovakia, possibly by Kovo AS. The guns have been distributed in Britain by *Edgar Brothers.

'SLAZ.' A mark associated with the products of Slazengers (Australia) Pty Ltd of Sydney, New South Wales. A branch of the British sporting-goods manufacturer, Slazengers Pty marketed as many as 350,000 .22 rimfire rifles made between the world wars by the government small arms factory in *Lithgow. Stocks, handguards and wooden furni-

ture for the SMLE and other guns were made in huge quantities during the Second World War.

Sleeve pistol. *See* Elek *Juhasz.

SLEM. This automatic rifle was an experimental forerunner of the *SAFN, made in the *Enfield small-arms factory during the Second World War. It was designed by Dieudonné *Saive with the assistance of British technicians.

Slide action. An operating system relying on the reciprocal motion of a forward hand grip to unlock the breech, extract and eject the cartridge case, cock the firing mechanism, then reload and relock. The first slide-action design was the Haveness (q.v.) patented in 1878/79 by Andrew *Burgess, but it was not exploited for some years – and a lawsuit brought by *Winchester against *Bannerman in the 1890s cited ideas going back to the 1840s. The first slide-action design to be successful commercially, however, was patented by Christopher *Spencer and Sylvester *Roper in 1882–85. The basic system became popular by 1900, and many similar guns have been made since. Most are shotguns, but a substantial number of shotgun-like rifles have also been produced.

Slidemaster. A brandname customarily applied to the 4.5mm/BB Model 3500 slide-action pneumatic rifle made by *Crosman.

Slingsby Guns, Boston and Sleaford, Lincolnshire. The name of this provincial English gunmaker has been reported on a variety of shotgun cartridges made by *Eley-Kynoch. Among the tradenames are Slingsby's Champion, Slingsby's Fen, Slingsby's Special and Slingsby's Stump, the last being named after a prominent church tower in Boston, known locally as the 'Boston Stump'.

Slocum. Frank Slocum invented the sliding-sleeve loading system patented on 27 January and 14 April 1863 (US nos. 37,551 and 38,204). Rights to these were assigned to the *Brooklyn Firearms Company.

Slotter & Company, Philadelphia, Pennsylvania, and San Francisco, California. A gunmaking and distributing business, best known for *cap-lock sporting/target rifles and the .41-calibre *Deringer-type pistols popular at the time of the California Gold Rush (1849).

SLR. A generic term, self-loading rifle (q.v.), often used in the designation of light automatic weapons.

'SLT'. Found on US military firearms and accessories. *See* S.L. *Tuttle.

Slugs Limited. A maker of airgun ammunition operating in Bromley, Kent, from 1933 until acquired by *Lane Brothers in 1953 or 1954; thereafter *Eagle slugs were 'made' by Lanes until 1955/56, although this may have been simply a way of disposing of existing stock.

'SLW'. Found on US military firearms and accessories. *See* Samuel L. *Worsley.

'SM', 'S.M.', 'S.M.C.' – **1.** Marks found on components for the No. 4 *Lee-Enfield rifle made in Britain during the Second World War by the Singer Manufacturing Company Ltd of Clydebank, Scotland. This company was also allocated the area code 'N67', but often used its initials instead. **2.** Or Sport-Modell: used generically to describe a variety of sporting guns marketed in Germany. **3.** An abbreviated form of 'Sport & Munition'. A trademark associated with *Rhöner. **4.** Found on a horizontal band within a circle. A trademark used by Karl Arndt *Reck of Lauf bei Nürnberg. **5.** Found on US military firearms and accessories. *See* Samuel *Marcy and Stillman *Moore.

ŠKODA MACHINE-GUN

Škoda (2)

Promoted by the renowned arms-making company of the same name, the Škoda machine-gun was the work of two soldiers with influence at the highest level: Archduke *Karl Salvator and Georg, Ritter von *Dormus. Designed in 1885, only a year after *Maxim had been granted his first patent, the Salvator-Dormus gun was seen as a cornerstone of the business formed by Emil *Škoda.

Experiments had been made with the Salvator-Dormus prototypes as early as 1886, after an agreement had been reached with the inventors. By 1889, the basic design had been finalised with the assistance of technicians led by Andreas Radovanovič, and a patent was sought in Škoda's name. In October 1893, the Škoda was accepted for service instead of the *Maxim. The manufacturer endeavoured to obtain export orders, exhibiting guns in 6.5mm, 7mm and 8mm at the Paris Exposition in 1900, but only 210 had been made by 1901. It is assumed that most of these were being used by Austria-Hungary, but the actual total is not known.

An improved design appeared in 1901. Although the gravity-feed magazine and the pendulous rate reducer were greatly refined, the changes could not disguise the fact

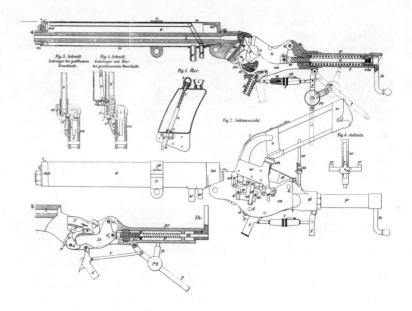

that the weapon was obsolete. The Model 1903 was a long-barrelled derivative of the M. 1901, mounted on a light tripod intended for cavalrymen, but only six were made.

By 1907, the pendulum-type rate reducer had been abandoned and a belt-feed system had replaced the unsatisfactory gravity-feed box. Škoda advertised the M. 09 in 6.5mm, 7mm, 7.65mm, 7.9mm and 8mm (8x50R), and trials were undertaken for Bulgaria, China, the Netherlands, Peru, Romania and Turkey prior to 1914. Only the Chinese purchased the guns in any numbers.

The original M93 Skoda machine-gun was a curious design, with a rate regulator in the form of a swinging pendant weight.

The M. 09 was superseded by the M. 13 and M. 14, which were identical apart from the date of manufacture. These guns had longer barrels, improved belt-feed systems and more efficient lubricators. They were mounted on the compact M. 13 tripod, with steel links connecting the legs to prevent collapse in the firing position.

Smail. John Smail & Sons, Morpeth, Northumberland. The name of this ironmongery business has been found on 12-bore shotgun cartridges made by *Eley-Kynoch and distributed under the brandname The Lightning Killer.

Small Arms... – 1. Small Arms Group, Britain. See FN-Saive. **2.** Small Arms Ltd, Long Branch, Toronto, Ontario, Canada. Maker of No.4 *Lee-Enfield rifles for Britain, Canada and China, 1942–45. Also produced more than 128,000 Mark II *Sten submachine-guns for the Canadian armed forces during the Second World War.

Smallwood – 1. Shrewsbury, Shropshire. The marks of this gunsmithing business have been found on shotgun ammunition distributed as Smallwood's Challenge; the cartridge headstamps show that they were acquired from James R. *Watson & Company of London, but apparently had been made in Belgium. **2.** Horace Will[iam] Smallwood, an employee of *Webley & Scott, was granted two patents in 1941 (as co-beneficiary with the company) for a simplified trigger mechanism with an inbuilt safety catch; the latter was not a new idea, but protection on a previous pattern had ceased.

'Smasher' [The]. A brandname found on shotgun ammunition handled by Henry *Elliott of Dartford, Kent, England.

'Smeaton' [The]. Associated with British shotgun cartridges handled by C.G. *Edwards & Son of Plymouth, Devon. Named after a famous engineer.

'S. MFG. CO.' A mark found on the slides of .45 M1911A1 *Government Model pistols made for the US armed forces during the Second World War by the *Singer Manufacturing Company.

S.M.F.M., Saint-Étienne, France. Maker of electric-ignition shotguns in the post-1945 era, relying on dry batteries in the butt heel to excite special igniters in the cartridges when pressure on the trigger completed the circuit.

'SMI', 'S.M.I.' Abbreviations found in the headstamps of cartridges made by Società Metallurgica Italiana of Brescia, Italy. Now known as La Metalli Industriale SpA, but still using the original marks.

Smith – 1. A.F. Smith, Hailsham, Sussex. The marks of this gunsmith and ironmonger have been found on shotgun cartridges sold in southern England as The Hailsham Special. **2.** Alfred Smith. Trading at 27 & 28 Whittall Street in Birmingham, Warwickshire, England, from about 1866 until 1900 or later, Smith is believed to have succeeded Smith & Townsend; the trading style became '...& Son' in 1883 or 1884. **3.** Asa Smith. Co-patentee with Orville B. *Percival of a unique three-magazine repeating pistol, made briefly in Norwich, Connecticut, by Horace Smith. **4.** C.H. Smith & Sons, Birmingham, Warwickshire. The marks of this gunmaking business, probably a successor to Charles Smith (below), have been found on shotgun cartridges sold under the tradenames The Abbey and The *Invincible. Most of them date from the 1920s. **5.** Charles Smith, Birmingham, Warwickshire. The marks of this English gun-rifler and pistol maker, trading from 86, then 25, Weaman Street from 1861 onward, have been reported on shotgun ammunition, but it seems more likely that these were the work of C.H. Smith & Sons (below). **6.** *See* Samuel & Charles *Smith. **7.** Charles Smith & Sons, Market Place, Newark, Nottinghamshire. The marks of this gunsmithing business have been found on sporting guns and a variety of shotgun cartridges, most of which apparently were loaded in Newark into cases supplied from Europe. Among the identifiable tradenames are All-British Extra Special, The Castle, The Clinton, The Newark Cartridge, The Rufford and The Universal. **8.** Charles James Smith first appears in 1839 as a partner with his brother, Michael, in M. & C.J. Smith, at 79 Steelhouse Lane, Birmingham, Warwickshire, England. Subsequently he traded on his own account from 27 & 28 Whittall Street, Birmingham, making 'Magazine Self-Priming Guns, Rifles and Pistols of Every Description' protected by English Patent 10,667 of 14 May 1845. He was also a member of the Gunmakers Company, being listed at 61 King William Street, London E.C., in 1846–47, and at 24 King William Street in 1850. Smith may have been succeeded by his son, Charles (above), in 1852. **9.** Dexter Smith, Springfield, Massachusetts, USA. Son of Horace Smith, born in 1833, this gunmaker produced single-shot 12- and 16-bore radial-breech-block shotguns in accordance with US Patent 111,814 of 14 February 1871 (sought jointly with Martin *Chamberlain). Patents 129,433 of 16 July 1872, 138,207 of 22 April 1873 and 141,603 of 5 August 1873 (jointly with Joseph C. *Marshall) were granted for variations on the basic theme. Production was confined to 1872–75. Smith also received US Patents 60,074 of 27 November 1866 for a cartridge-loading machine; 230,582 of 27 July 1880 to protect a 'firearm'; and 176,412 of 18 April 1876 (with C.C. and Joseph C. Marshall) for 'an extractor for revolving firearms'. After the commercial failure of his shotguns, Dexter Smith turned his attention to revolvers. His many relevant US Patents (in chronological order) were: 160,551 of 9 March 1875; 162,863 of 4 May 1875 (with Joseph C. Marshall); 163,032 of 11 May 1875; 171,059 of 14 December 1875; 176,448 of 25 April 1876 (with Marshall); 193,836 of 7 August 1877 (assigned to D.B. *Wesson); 196,491 of 23 October 1877; 221,000 of 28 October 1879; 247,217 and 247,218 of 30 September 1881; 248,223 of 11 October 1881; 250,591 of 6 December 1881; 315,352 of 7 April 1885; and 318,315 of 19 May 1885. In view of this commitment to revolver design, it is likely that Otis A. Smith was Dexter Smith's son. **10.** Edwin Smith. An English gunmaker, trading in 1870 from 34 Castle Street East, West London. **11.** Frederick Smith was joint patentee, with Daniel M. *Lefever, of a compensating joint to reduce the effects of

wear in shotgun actions (US Patent 264,173 of 12 September 1882). **12.** George Smith. This peripatetic gunmaker – perhaps the thirty-year-old George Smith listed in the 1841 census in Upper King Street, London – was listed from 1859 until 1866 at 40 Davies Street, West London; he was at 16 Davies Street in 1867, at 104 New Bond Street in 1868–69, and at 82 New Bond Street in 1870. A move back to Davies Street (to no. 10) took place in 1871, then to 253 Oxford Street in 1872. The 1874 directories place him at 3 Park Lane, and those of 1885 at 110 Mount Street. Then Smith transferred to 3 Angel Court, King Street, West London, in 1888, but was at 4 Stafford Street by 1891. The trading style became George Smith & Company in 1897, with premises at 153 Piccadilly, and business continued at least until the First World War. **13.** George Smith & Company (active 1862–64 and probably into the 1870s), New York City. Smith made cap-lock pistols and spring-air gallery rifles, some of which had double set triggers. **14.** Gilbert Smith, Buttermilk Falls, New York State, USA. Smith was responsible for a break-action carbine, patented in 1856, which originally fired cartridges with a gutta-percha case. The breech was locked by a sturdy spring-steel bar that projected back from the top of the barrel over a stud on the standing breech. A small locking catch ahead of the trigger lever was pressed upward to release the bar, allowing the barrel to open. Three hundred .50-calibre Smiths were purchased for field trials shortly before the outbreak of the American Civil War. They were made by *Poultney & Trimble, assignees of the original patents, but manufacture was sub-contracted to the Massachusetts Arms Company. In August 1863, however, the Massachusetts Arms Company passed part of the work on the Smith carbine to the *American Machine Works to free facilities for the *Maynard gun, and soon the entire contract was shifted to the latter company. A new promoter, the *American Arms Company, was formed to oversee the work. Although Smith carbines had originally fired rubber-case ammunition, Poultney's Patent Metallic Cartridge transformed the carbine into a better design. Federal purchases between 1 January 1861 and 30 June 1866 totalled 30,062 carbines. **15.** Harris Smith, working for the Federal and US governments, accepted firearms and equipment from the Civil War period on into the late 1870s. Marked 'HS', the items may be difficult to distinguish from those accepted by H. *Saunders, Horace *Scott, Harrison *Shaler, Howard *Stockton and H. *Syrett. *See also* US arms inspectors' marks. **16.** Horace Smith. Born in Cheshire, Massachusetts, on 28 October 1808, Smith was apprenticed in the National Armory, *Springfield, where he remained until 1842. A move to New Haven, Connecticut, allowed him to make tools for Eli *Whitney, and it is believed that subsequently he was employed by *Allen & Thurber during 1845–48. Operating on his own account in Norwich until 1852, producing magazine pistols to the patent of *Percival & Smith, then whaling guns and explosive harpoons, Horace Smith began working for *Allen, Brown & Luther of Worcester, Massachusetts. During the early 1850s, Smith had been employed by the financier Courtlandt *Palmer, helping to perfect the *Jennings Rifle and the *Volition Ball. He had been granted US Patent 8317 of 26 August 1851 to protect an improved breech-loading rifle, but Palmer withdrew his support shortly afterward and development of the Jennings/Smith rifle ceased. The project was resurrected when Smith entered into a partnership with Daniel B. *Wesson, beginning in 1853. Smith and Wesson jointly received several US Patents: 10,535 of 14 February 1854, to protect a lever-action magazine pistol that cocked automatically as the breech opened; 11,496 of 8 August 1854 for a cartridge loaded with fulminate propellant; 14,147 of 22 January 1856 protecting 'primers for cartridge of firearms'; and 27,933 of 17 April 1860 describing a method of priming cartridges by spinning fulminate centrifugally into the rims. There were also two patents for 'revolving firearms' (30,990 of 18 December 1860 and 51,092 of 21 November 1865). Smith and Wesson's plans also failed to prosper, and rights were sold in 1855 to the *Volcanic Arms Company. Smith retired to run a livery stable, but Wesson doggedly continued development of a metallic-case rimfire cartridge. In 1857, armed with both a perfected cartridge and an effective revolver (made in accordance with a patent granted to Rollin *White), Smith & Wesson once again entered business together. Horace Smith retired from Smith & Wesson on 1 July 1873, selling his stake in the company to Daniel Wesson, and lived out a long and prosperous life that ended in Springfield on 15 January 1893. **17.** John Smith invented a revolver with a one-piece frame and barrel shroud, and a rifled steel liner. This was protected by US Patent 376,922 of 24 January 1889 and 413,975 of 28 October 1889. **18.** John Smith & Son, Britain. See Henry *Adkins. **19.** L.C. Smith & Company, New York. After acquiring the assets of W.H. *Baker & Sons Company in 1880, Lyman Cornelius Smith continued to make *Baker-pattern side-by-side hammer doubles for some years. In 1883, however, Smith stopped making Baker-patent side-locks in favour of the improved pattern developed by Alexander *Brown. The first hammerless shotgun appeared in 1886, but Smith sold the business to John Hunter in 1888, and operations were transferred to Fulton, New York, in 1890. By 1906, Smith guns could be obtained with the Hunter One-Trigger, made to the designs of Allan *Lard. The perfected Lard mechanism was guaranteed never to 'double' or jam. **20.** L.C. Smith & Corona Typewriters, Inc.: see Springfield. **21.** Leroy H. Smith. Patentee, inventor and co-founder with W.H. *Baker of the *Ithaca Gun Company. **22.** Lyman Cornelius Smith, USA: see L.C. Smith & Company. **23.** Morris F. Smith, Philadelphia, Pennsylvania, USA. This gun designer was granted US Patents 548,096 of 15 October 1895, 784,966 of 14 March 1905, 812,242 of 6 March 1906, 817,134 of 3 April 1906, and 817,197 and 817,198 of 10 April 1906, to protect a variety of gas-operated machine-guns and automatic rifles. With the exception of the earliest, all of these were part- or wholly assigned to financier W.D. Condit of Des Moines, Iowa. Several of Smith's patents were embodied in the auto-loading rifles made in the USA by *Standard Arms Company. **24.** Orlando Smith, 14 London Street, Derby. The marks of this English provincial gunsmith – active from 1856 to 1863 or later – have been reported on sporting guns and self-cocking *pepperboxes. Smith may have moved to Uttoxeter, where a similarly-named gunmaker was listed in 1867. **25.** Otis A. Smith, Middlefield and Rock Fall, Connecticut, USA. Smith made solid-frame sheath-trigger revolvers incorporating a quick-release cylinder catch protected by his US Patent 137,968 of 15

April 1873. These guns were superseded by a break-open auto-ejecting sheath-trigger Model 83 Shell Ejector patented on 20 December 1881 in collusion with his brother, John (US no. 251,306). Next came a solid-frame hammerless five-chamber .38 rim- or centrefire M1892 gate-loader. This gun had a double-action trigger system and an exposed cylinder stop, which, when pressed, allowed the cylinder to rotate freely. Smith revolvers were handled by *Maltby, Curtis & Company, and may be encountered under several misleading manufacturer's names (e.g. Columbia Armory, Spencer Revolver Company and Parker Revolver Company). **26.** Patrick Smith, Main Street, Buffalo, New York State. A gunmaker active in the USA between 1848 and 1882, producing *cap-lock sporting guns before progressing to metallic-cartridge breech-loaders; eventually he became a dealer. Smith was the assignee of two US Patents granted to Jarvis Davis: 103,154 of 27 May 1870, to protect an extractor for a drop-barrel gun, and 112,127 of 28 February 1871 for a revolver-rifle with a spring-and-chain drive auxiliary magazine tube in the butt. **27.** R. Smith, Carlisle, Cumberland. The marks of this English gunmaker have been reported on self-cocking *pepperboxes dating from the middle of the nineteenth century. **28.** Samuel Smith the Younger. A partner with his brother, Charles, in Samuel & Charles Smith (below), and designer of a breech-loader protected by British Patent 1075/67 of 1867. He emigrated to Australia c. 1876. **29.** Samuel & Charles Smith. A gunmaking partnership found at 64 Princes Street, Soho, London, between 1834 and 1869, then at 18 Oxendon Street, Haymarket, in 1870–75. Samuel Smith died in 1855, the business being perpetuated by his sons, Samuel and Charles. It ceased trading when the younger Samuel emigrated. **30.** Steven Smith, High Friar Street, Ashton under Lyme, Staffordshire. The marks of this gun and sporting-goods retailer have been reported on shotgun ammunition sold under the name 'Trap and Game'. **31.** Thomas Smith was a London gunmaker, recorded at 10 Ray Street, Clerkenwell, and 15 Great Portland Street in 1829, when he was in partnership with Robert Alden. He began trading on his own account from 55 Parliament Street in 1835, then moved to 3 Bridge Street, Westminster (1842), 288 High Holborn (1845) and finally 13 Little Compton Street, Soho, (1849/50 until 1860). He may have died then, as the entries changed to 'Mrs E. Smith' until 1862. **32.** T.J. Smith, a colonel in the US Army, accepted .45 M1911A1 pistols made by *Colt's Patent Fire Arms Manufacturing Company. Dating from the mid-1930s, they were marked 'TJS'. See also T.J. *Stevenson and US arms inspectors' marks. **33.** W.G. Smith, Philadelphia, Pennsylvania. The assignee of an air-gun patent granted in the USA in 1893 to Elmer E. *Bailey. **34.** Smith Arms Company, New York City. This gunmaking business produced the revolver patented in 1865 by Silas *Crispin. Distinguished by a two-part cylinder and cartridges with annular priming bands, the .32 Crispin was never successful. **35.** Smith & Townsend was a partnership of Alfred Smith and James *Townsend, apparently dating from 1852 or 1853 and operating at various combinations of 27, 28, 28a and 29 Whittall Street, Birmingham, Warwickshire, England, between 1853 and 1862. The partnership was succeeded in 1865 by Alfred Smith & Son. **36.** Smith, Hall & Buckland, Mill Street, Springfield, Massachusetts. A successor to Smith, Hall &

Farmer (q.v.), formed in June 1866 when the factory superintendent of Smith & Wesson, Cyrus Buckland, replaced the original partner, Charles Farmer. Operations continued until 1869, when, after the expiry of Smith & Wesson's cartridge-making patent, the business was sold to Joseph Hall and a new partner named Hubbard. *See also* Hall & Hubbard. **37.** Smith, Hall & Farmer, Mill Street, Springfield, Massachusetts. This business was formed in 1863 to acquire the ammunition-making operations of Smith & Wesson. The partners were Dexter Smith, son of the senior partner in Smith & Wesson; Charles K. Farmer, a local businessman related to the Wessons by marriage; and Joseph Hall, Smith & Wesson's bookkeeper. It lasted in its original form until June 1866, when Hall was replaced by Buckland. *See* Smith, Hall & Buckland. **38.** Smith, Midgley & Company, Bradford, Yorkshire. The marks of this gunsmithing and ironmongery business have been reported on 12-bore Pegamoid shotgun cartridges made by *Eley immediately after the First World War. **39.** Smith & Wesson, Springfield, Massachusetts. The second partnership of Horace Smith and Daniel B. *Wesson was formed in 1857, working from a small workshop in Market Street, Springfield. By 1858, demand for their products had grown to a point where expansion was necessary, and a large new factory fronting on to Stockbridge Street opened in March 1860. Best known for their firearms, the partners also made the first successfully mass-produced *rimfire cartridges, beginning in 1859. Revolvers produced before that date had been sold with CB Caps. By 1862, however, more than 6,400,000 rimfire cartridges were being made annually. Then Horace Smith and Daniel Wesson decided to separate the ammunition-making business from the firearms, resulting in Smith, Hall & Farmer. Manufacture of the cartridges was also licensed to C.D. *Leet and *Crittenden & Tibballs, in 1864, then to the *Union Metallic Cartridge Company in 1866. Operations were very succcessful, despite ill-advised forays into the sporting-gun market (Wesson Firearms Company, q.v.); on 1 July 1873, however, Horace Smith sold his interests to Wesson and retired to a life of leisure. Gradually Daniel Wesson involved his sons in the business; Walter H. Wesson (1850–1921) became a partner in 1882, followed by Joseph H. Wesson (1859–1920) in 1887. Daniel Wesson lived until 1906, but his death removed a necessary guiding hand from the company; neither of his sons was forceful enough to succeed him, although each held the presidency prior to the First World War. Joseph and Walter Wesson died within the space of eighteen months, leaving the company's affairs in the hands of Harold Wesson (1878–1946), the son of a third brother who had died young in 1888. After negotiating the Depression with great difficulty, Smith & Wesson returned to prosperity during the Second World War, thanks to the guidance of Carl Hellstrom (1895–1963), a consulting engineer hired in 1940 to solve the *Light Rifle crisis. Changes made by Hellstrom's successor, William Gunn, raised Smith & Wesson to profitability in the 1960s and ultimately attracted a predatory bid from Bangor Punta, Inc., in 1973. Semi-automatic Smith & Wesson pistols have been acquired by the US Navy and the Special Forces, but the business has never broken the hold that first Colt, then Beretta have had on the US Army. However, sales of handguns since Smith & Wesson's beginnings prior to the American Civil War were

approaching 20,000,000 by 1990. The conduct of the JSSAP trials that had standardised the Beretta M9 persuaded S&W to file suit in the State of Massachusetts, accusing the US Army of 'illegal, improper and suspect actions' but while a Congressional investigation revealed serious flaws in the trial process, the result was not rescinded. Smith & Wesson's profitability waned until it became clear that the parent Lear-Siegler Group (which had taken over Bangor Punta in 1983) was keen to sell. In May 1987, therefore, the gunmaking business was acquired by the British organisation, F.H. Tompkins Holdings. In addition to handguns, Smith & Wesson made about 6,000 Model 76 9mm blowback submachine-guns in 1968–74, which were tested extensively by many agencies, but adopted by none of them. The project was abandoned to allow production facilities to concentrate on the semi-automatic pistols. The company also distributed *Husqvarna-made bolt-action sporting rifles in 1969–72. They were designated 'A' to 'E', but did not sell in large numbers. A series of shotguns manufactured by *Howa fared better, but was discontinued in 1984. **40.** Smith & Wesson airguns. The company's contribution to airgun development scarcely approaches the level of the better-known revolvers. However, a small range of gas-powered and spring-airguns was marketed from the early 1960s, including the 77A and 80G rifles, and 78G and 79G pistols. G-suffix guns were powered by carbon-dioxide cylinders. **41.** Smith & Wesson handguns: *see* panel, pp. 486/87.

'S.M.L.E.' An abbreviated form of the official British name for the [Rifle] Short, Magazine, *Lee-Enfield, encountered in designation marks.

Smok. A brandname used on a 6.35mm pistol made by *Nakulski of Gneizno.

Smokeless... – 1. Smokeless Diamond. *See* Diamond. **2.** Smokeless Powder & Ammunition Company Ltd, London. The 'S.P. & A. CO.' mark of this short-lived business (c. 1898–1907) has been reported in the headstamps of 12-bore shotgun cartridges.

Smoker. Introduced in 1875, this .22, .32, .38 and .41 *Johnson & Bye revolver had a fluted cylinder and a squared grip with a humped backstrap (Russian Handle).

Smoky City. A *Suicide Special revolver made in the USA by the *Harrington & Richardson Arms Company of Worcester, Massachusetts. It dates from the late nineteenth century.

Smoot. William Smoot, a gunsmith employed by E. *Remington & Sons, was granted US Patent 143,855 of 21 October 1873 to protect improvements in revolver design exploited in the Remington *New Line series.

Smooth. A general term for smoothbored 'rifles'.

Smythe – 1. Joseph F. Smythe, an 'outside' member of the London gun trade, was established at 13 Blackwell Gate, Darlington, in 1895. He moved to 12 Horse Market in 1896, but the London directories include no entries thereafter; additional premises were opened subsequently in Stockton-on-Tees. Smythe's marks have been found on a variety of shotgun cartridges, including Durham Ranger, The Field, Smythe's Champion and Smythe's Special Load. **2.** *See also* Smith.

SN. An abbreviated form of the name of the Soviet *Savin-*Norov aircraft machine-gun, made in small numbers in the 1930s.

Sneezum. H. & R. Sneezum, 14–20 Fore Street, Ipswich, Suffolk, England. The marks of this East Anglian

SMITH & WESSON HANDGUNS

Smith (41)

This company is best known for exploiting the patent granted to Rollin ★White for a revolver with the chambers bored through the cylinder. The seven-shot .22 rimfire Model No. 1 appeared in January 1858; although production was slow, the American Civil War gave Smith & Wesson a huge boost. Smith & Wesson and Rollin White successfully fought many suits for patent infringement, but ★Moore, ★Warner, ★Pond and ★Bacon were able to complete guns 'in the course of manufacture', provided that royalties were paid and the controlling patent was acknowledged.

When the licence agreed with Rollin White lapsed in April 1869, more than 270,000 revolvers had been made. Although the weak .22 rimfire cartridge was a great handicap, problems had been overcome by 1861, and a .32 version appeared. Six-shot .32 Model No. 2 revolvers were joined in 1864 by the five-shot Model No. 1½. These lasted in production until 1870. However, the failure of the .41 rimfire Model No. 3 left S&W without a large-calibre gun to challenge the cap-lock ★Colts.

The first top-break design appeared in 1868, with the hinge at the bottom front of the frame and an ejecting mechanism that worked automatically as the barrel was dropped. The .44 New Model No. 3, or Model No. 3 Army Revolver, was very successful, the US Army agreeing to take 1,000 in December 1870, while commercial sales were also encouraging. It was renamed No. 3 ★American Model after the introduction of the No. 3 ★Russian Model in 1871. Production continued for some years, in two basic patterns. Most were .44 centrefires, although 3,500 rimfire guns were also made. The Russian Model was produced in large numbers until the late 1870s, but it prevented Smith & Wesson from establishing a hold on the US domestic market for large-calibre revolvers (much to the benefit of the Colt ★Peacemaker).

The first double-action guns, designed largely by James ★Bullard, were completed in 1879 in .32 and .38. The .32 ★Double Action revolvers were produced in five variants between 1880 and 1919, total production approaching 330,000. The five-shot .38 was also introduced commercially in 1880; when production ceased in 1911, more than 550,000 had been made in five major sub-varieties. In addition, about 55,000 .44 Double Action revolvers

were made between 1881 and 1913.

The break-open revolvers were replaced by the first of the ★Hand Ejector series, introduced in 1896. These guns found it difficult to overcome the competition from the essentially similar ★Colts, and no real headway was made until the first .38 Military & Police pattern appeared early in the twentieth century. Guns of this general pattern are still being produced in large numbers; most of the differences are in the size and frame, and in the trend toward target-grade sights and full-length ejector-rod shrouds.

Although designated numerically since 1957, many S&W revolvers are still better known by such names as Aircrewman, Airweight, Bodyguard, Chief's Special, Centennial, Distinguished Combat Magnum, Distinguished Service Magnum, Hand Ejector, Kit Gun, Magnum, Masterpiece, Regulation Police, Service Kit Gun, Target Kit Gun and Target Stainless (qq.v.).

Smith & Wesson attempted to market semi-automatic pistols prior to the First World War, purchasing the rights to the Belgian ★Clément in 1910; modifications were made to this design by Joseph H. ★Wesson in 1910–12. The gun was introduced commercially in 1913, chambering a unique .35 S&W Automatic cartridge loaded with a half-mantle bullet to minimise bore wear. The magazine catch was changed from lateral to longitudinal in 1914, in the quest for simplicity, but work was suspended between 1916 and 1919, and abandoned in 1922 when sales dropped below economic limits.

The replacement was the .32 Automatic, developed by Edward ★Pomeroy, which amalgamated the old frame with a new streamlined slide. However, fewer than 1,000 pistols were sold between 1924 and 1937. Success awaited the end of the Second World War, when the development of a double-action pistol inspired by the ★Walther P. 38 was entrusted to Joseph ★Norman. The first prototype was completed in the autumn of 1948, amalgamating a

A cased .38-calibre Top Break double-action revolver of the so-called Third Model, made c. 1886 and subsequently sold in Britain by Hooton & Jones of Liverpool.

double-action trigger mechanism with the basic *Colt-Browning tipping-barrel breech. However, the US Army requested a single-action trigger, and a handful of guns of this type were made in 1953.

Limited production of the 9mm double-action pistol began in 1954, but work was very slow. The pistols were designated Model 39 (double-action) and Model 44 (single-action) in 1957, but the latter had been discontinued by 1959. Small-scale production of the Model 39 increased gradually, some being chambered in 1960–61 for the .38 AMU cartridge developed by the US Army Marksmanship Training Unit. These alloy-framed pistols were known originally as the Model 39-1, subsequently changed to Model 52, and then altered to Model 52-A. A narrow-bar extractor driven by a coil spring replaced a broad spring-steel bar in 1971, but few other changes were made to a popular and successful design.

Introduced in 1971 and abandoned in 1981, the Model 59 was basically an improved double-action Model 39 with a fourteen-round magazine in a straight-back butt. Derivatives have included the Model 439 (discontinued in 1988), an alloy-framed variant of the Model 39 with prominent back-sight protectors; the Model 459, with an alloy frame and a staggered-row magazine; the Model 539, a steel-framed 439; and the Model 559, a steel-framed 459. Work on the Models 539 and 559 stopped in 1983.

The Models 469 (blued, 1983–88) and 669 (stainless-steel, 1986–88) were compact versions of the double-action M459 with bobbed hammers, synthetic grips and recurved trigger guards. The Models 639 and 659, introduced in 1982 and abandoned in 1988, were stainless-steel versions of the 439 and 459 respectively. The Model 645 (1985–88) was an enlargement of the basic double-action design to chamber the .45 ACP cartridge, with a single-column box magazine in an elongated butt. The Model 745 (1987–90) had a single-action trigger, a ball-ended barrel and a fixed barrel bushing; magazine-release catches and safety levers were enlarged to satisfy 'practical-pistol' shooters.

A new designation system appeared in 1990. The first two digits

A .38 Model 36 Chiefs Special revolver. With the exception of the engraved frame, the latter is typical of the many revolvers that have been made for close-quarters defence in virtually every part of the world.

of any four-digit designation represent the basic model (e.g. Model 10, Model 39), now cutomarily based on calibre; the third digit signifies an individual model; and the fourth digit identifies the manufacturing material. Third-digit identifiers include '0' for a standard pattern; '1' for the compact version; '2' for a gun fitted with a de-cocking lever; '3' for a compact pistol with a de-cocking system; '4' for a standard gun with its trigger mechanism restricted to double-action; '5' for a compact double-action-only gun; '6' for any gun with a non-standard barrel; '7' for pistols with non-standard barrels and de-cocking systems; and '8' for guns with non-standard barrels and double-action-only triggers. Fourth-digit identifiers are '3' for a combination of an alloy frame and a stainless-steel slide; '4' for an alloy frame allied with a steel slide; '5' for a steel frame and slide; '6' for guns with a stainless-steel frame and slide; and '7' for those combining a stainless-steel frame with a standard carbon-steel slide.

The basic designs currently encompass the 1000 series chambered for the 10mm Auto cartridge; the 2200 series in .22 rimfire; the 3900, 5900 and 6900 series in 9mm Parabellum; the 4000 series in S&W .40 Auto; and the 4500 series in .45 ACP. The Model 4546, for example, is a .45-calibre pistol with a double-action-only trigger ('4') and a non-standard barrel ('6'). Few of these guns have been named, with the exception of the *Sportsman and the LadySmith patterns.

In addition to their locked-breech military-style automatic pistols, and the .22 M-41 series target guns (below), Smith & Wesson marked a tiny 6.35mm pocket pistol known as the *Escort.

Introduced in 1957 after a development period lasting ten years, the Model 41 pistol was a .22 rimfire blowback destined for target shooting. Guns of this type have been made with long barrels, often fitted with muzzle brakes or extendable front sights. The Model 41-1 of 1960 was intended for rapid-fire competitions and chambered the .22 Short rimfire cartridge instead of the Long Rifle pattern. The Model 46 (1959–68) was a simplified Model 41, developed for the USAF and also touted briefly as a 'field gun'. Next came the Model 422 of 1987, an unusual internal-hammer blowback design offered as the *Field Model and *Target Model.

No attempt has been made to catalogue minor manufacturing variations of Smith & Wesson handguns, and the distinctions between the Models 10, 10-1, 10-5, etc, have been ignored. Details should be sought from the standard book on the subject, notably *History of Smith & Wesson*, by Roy Jinks (Beinfeld, 1977 and subsequent editions).

gunmaker have been recorded on shotgun cartridges sold under such names as Sneezum's Anglia (accompanied by a bounding rabbit) and Sneezum's Special High Velocity Load. They seem to have been supplied by *Eley-Kynoch.

Sneider. C. Edward Sneider, Baltimore, Maryland, USA. In March 1862, Sneider was granted US Patent 34,703 to protect an 'Improvement in Revolving Fire-Arms'. The Sneider revolver had a two-row cylinder and an extended hammer-nose. When seven shots had been fired, the action was opened and the cylinder was reversed so that another seven rounds could be fired. The inventor received many other firearms-related patents in 1860–90.

Snell. George C. Snell: *see* George C. *Schnell.

Snider – 1. Jacob Snider was an American, but is best remembered for the success of his lifting-block conversion system adopted by the British government in 1867. Snider conversions were applied to a range of British service weapons, such as the P/1853 (Enfield) rifle-musket, the P/1855 (Lancaster) engineer carbine and the P/1858 naval short rifle. The system was also used in Denmark, on the M1848–65 short rifle and the M1853–66 navy rifle, while the French Tabatière conversion was essentially similar – although the French cited the existence of earlier patents (notably Clairville's of 1853) to avoid paying licensing fees. A few 11mm-calibre Snider-type rifles were also made in Spain during the Carlist Wars of 1873–75, probably for one of the feuding factions. They are marked 'La Azpeitiana'. The breeches swung to the right, while the back sights were similar to those of the 1871-model Spanish Remington rifle. **2.** Snider Rifles & Cartridges [Company]. Presumably this business was established to protect the rights of Jacob *Snider's executors; it maintained an office at Chatham Buildings, London E.C., in 1878–79.

'Snipe' [The]. Found on shotgun cartridges loaded by the *Chamberlain Cartridge Company of Cleveland, Ohio.

Sniper – 1. Usually found as 'The Sniper' on shotgun cartridges loaded, or perhaps simply sold, by *Emslie of Elgin since the Second World War. **2.** A break-barrel spring-air rifle made in Spain by *El Gamo and sold in Britain by *ASI. The Sniper Repeater had an additional tubular pellet magazine above the air-chamber. **3.** Sniper rifles: *see* panel, facing page.

Snook. Charles W. Snook. Operating in the 1870s, this government arms inspector accepted *Colt revolvers marked 'CWS'. *See also* US arms inspectors' marks.

Snow. Charles H. Snow, New Haven, Connecticut, and later Stockton, California, USA. A partner in *Snow & Cowe and co-patentee of an air pistol with Edward H. *Hawley. *See* US Patent 112,886 of September 1871. Made by Snow & Cowe, the gun was marketed commercially as the *Kalamazoo. A second patent (752,932) was granted on 23 February 1904 to Charles H. Snow to protect the design of a magazine gun.

SNT. *Snayperskaya* [*vintovka*] *Tokareva*, applied to specially-selected *Tokarev auto-loading rifles fitted with optical sights on a mount curving forward from the back of the receiver. *See also* SVT.

'SO.C.CO.' An abbreviation used in the headstamps of cartridges made by the *Southern Cartridge Company of Houston, Texas, USA.

Sociedad Española de Armas y Municiones, or SEAM, Eibar, Guipúzcoa, Spain. The affairs of this gun-making business are still shrouded in mystery, and it is by no means certain how great a part SEAM played in the construction of the automatic pistols marked *Diana, *Praga, *S.E.A.M., *Sivispacem and *Waco. The Diana is also often attributed to *Erquiaga, Muguruzu y Compañía, while the Waco was made for the dealer Tómas de *Urizar.

Società… – 1. Società Armi Bresciane SRL (SAB), Via Artigiani 93, Gardone Val Trompia. This Italian gunmaking business is best known for rifles and sporting guns, often made under the name of Renato *Gamba, but has also made handguns and a *Mauser-action sporting rifle in conventional or *Battue form for snap shooting at driven game. The shotguns are often superbly decorated with delicate English-style bouquets, scrolls and animals, and can be inlaid with precious metals on request. *See also* Ambassador, Concorde, Daytona, London, Maxim, Mustang, Oxford, Prince and Trident. **2.** Società Metallurgica Italiana. This Italian cartridge-making company headstamped cartridges with the initials 'SMI'.

Société… – 1. Société Alsacienne de Constructions Mécaniques, also known as SACM, Cholet, Alsace. This metalworking company made substantial quantities of the French 7.65mm Mle 35 service pistol during 1937–40 and on into the period of German occupation. Although basically dropping-barrel recoil-operated *Brownings, the guns were made in accordance with patents granted to Charles *Petter in the early 1930s and incorporated improvements in the trigger/hammer mechanism. **2.** Société Anonyme Commerciale Belge. This Liège based promotional agency was regarded as a member of the London gun trade in 1884, when an office was maintained at 12 Lime Street, London E.C. **3.** Société Anonyme Établissements Hotchkiss. Based in Saint-Denis, this gunmaking business was responsible for the well-known strip-feed *Hotchkiss machine-gun prior to 1918. **4.** Société Belge d'Optique et d'Instruments de Précision. A Belgian telescope-sight maker; *see* Saive. **5.** [La] Société d'Applications Générales, Électriques et Mecaniques, also known as SAGEM. A manufacturer of French 7.65mm Mle 35S and Mle 35SM1 service pistols, 1946–51. *See also* SACM and Saint-Étienne. **6.** Société d'Armes, Paris. A 6.35mm six-shot *Browning-type pocket pistol said to have been made in France prior to 1940 by *Manufacture d'Armes des Pyrénées. The slides may be marked 'FABRICATION FRANÇAISE. ST. ÉTIENNE'. Some guns have a grip safety; others do not. **7.** Société d'Armes 'HDH' (once Henrion, Dassy & Heuschen), Liège, Belgium. Maker of a small 6.35mm-calibre automatic pistol known as the *H&D, prior to 1914. **8.** Société des Anglais [La]. Also known as 'La Société pour les Armes de Guerre Ancion & Cie, Renkin frères, Pirlot frères et Auguste Francotte', this association of Liège gunmakers was formed to make 150,000 .577 'interchangeable' *Enfield rifle-muskets for the British Board of Ordnance during the Crimean War. It installed US-made production machinery, but disbanded in 1863 when the work had been completed. **9.** Société Française d'Armes Automatiques de Saint-Étienne. The French manufacturer of the last few *Hermetic pistols immediately after the First World War, in succession to *Établissements Bernardon-Martin et Cie, and possibly also of the *Le Steph and *Securitas guns. **10.** Société Française d'Armes Portatives (SFAP), Saint-Denis, France. The manufacturer of *Hotchkiss machine-guns, and also the promoter of the *Daudetau rifles prior to the First World War.

SNIPER RIFLES

Sniper (3)

The unexpected rise of trench warfare in 1914–15 renewed interest in sniping that had lain dormant since the American Civil War. The first move, by virtually every participant, was to requisition hunting rifles.

The British acquired a variety of Mausers, Mannlichers and Lee-type sporting guns, fitting them with ★Galilean and conventional optical sights. The German *Jagdgewehre* were mostly Mausers fitted with commercial Gérard, Goerz and Zeiss telescope sights, but a few Gewehre 98 with 4x Goerz Certar Kurz were soon being tested on the Western Front. One major problem concerned the supply of ammunition, particularly as some of the British rifles chambered cartridges other than the regulation .303, while the German sporting rifles customarily chambered the Patrone 88 instead of S-Munition.

The first purpose-built sniper rifles included 15,000 German *Zielfernrohr-Gewehre 98* – subsequently known as *Scharfschützen-Gewehre* – although

these were little more than specially selected and finished infantry rifles with Goerz or Zeiss 4x telescope sights fitted in two ring mounts offset to the left to allow the magazine charger to be used. British marksmen preferred Long Lee-Enfields until first the P/1914, then the Canadian Ross rifle displaced the SMLE from service. These were fitted with a variety of sights, although the Periscopic Prism Company and Aldis Brothers patterns eventually prevailed.

Initially the US Army used ineffective Warner & Swazey Telescopic Musket Sights, while the French fitted the 3x Mle 1916 to selected Lebels.

The need for sniping disappeared between the wars, only to reappear after 1939. The Germans had maintained their interest, fitting a variety of conventional and low-magnification long-eye-relief sights to the Kar. 98k; the Russians had always regarded sniping as an integral part of infantry attacks. Consequently, the ★Mosin-Nagant sniper rifle, *Snayperskaya vintovka obr. 1891/30*, was distributed in very large numbers. An attempt was also made to issue semi-automatic Tokarevs in quantity, but the

resulting SNT did not prove to be as accurate as the Mosin-Nagant. The British made do initially with refurbished P/1914 rifles, but then developed the Lee-action Rifle No. 4 (T); the US armed forces had a variety of M1903A4 bolt-action ★Springfields and optically-sighted M1C and M1D ★Garands.

As sniping has been accorded specialist studies of its own in recent years, a variety of modern equipment has appeared. Many of these guns are accompanied by sophisticated electro-optical and thermal-imaging ★sights, and more details may be found in such books as *The World's Sniping Rifles* (Greenhill/Stackpole Military Manual series, 1998). The historical aspects of sniping may be learned from such works as L. Hesketh-Pritchard's *Sniping in France* (Lancer Militaria, 1993) and *British Sniper* by Ian Skennerton (published privately, 1983).

Sniper rifles, highly specialised tools, often have unusual features. This British Accuracy International .338 Lapua Magnum AWM, for example, has stock sides bolted to a central frame. Guns of this type are service issue in several countries, including Britain and Sweden.

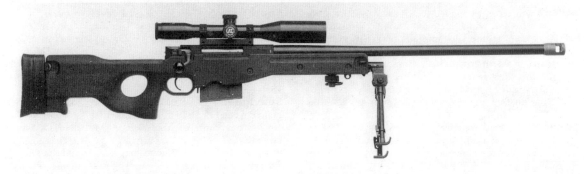

11. Société Française des Munitions de Chasse et de Guerre (SFM). This French ammunition-making business was formed in 1884, when ★Gevelot & Gaupillat changed its name, and traded until renamed Gevelot SA in 1950. Substantial quantities of ammunition were made, usually distinguished by the headstamps 'SFM' and 'GG', the latter often being reserved for rimfire cartridges and primers. 12. Société Générale de Mécanique, 6 cours Fauriel, Saint-Étienne, France. Listed in 1951 as a gunmaker, responsible for a variety of sporting firearms, including the ★Bretton shotgun. 13. Société Industrielle Suisse: *see* SIG. 14. Société Liègeoise [La], Liège, Belgium. A gunmaker involved in the 1870s with le ★Grand Syndicat. 15. Société Moderne de Fabrications Mécaniques (SMFM), 56 rue Tarentaize,

Saint-Étienne, France. Listed among the gunmakers operating in the district in 1951. 16. Société Stéphanoise d'Armes, rue de la République 14, Saint-Étienne. Listed in 1892, this French gunmaking business had been formed in the 1880s to make high-quality sporting guns and revolvers of all types. It was also advertised as 'sole agent for France and the colonies for the patents of M Paul [★]Giffard for the manufacture and sale of guns of the new ballistic of liquefied gas'. The Giffard guns, previously made by ★Rivolier, gained Société Stéphanoise a gold medal at the Saint-Étienne industrial exhibition in 1891. 17. Société Manufacturière d'Armes (SMA), rue Tréfilière, Saint-Étienne, France. Listed in 1892 as a gunmaker.

Soderholm. W.H. Soderholm, a major in the US

Army, accepted M1911A1 pistols made by *Colt's Patent Fire Arms Manufacturing Company. Dating from the mid-1930s, the guns will be marked 'WHS'. *See also* US arms inspectors' marks.

Sodia. Franz Sodia, Ferlach, Kärnten, Austria. Sodia was best known in the 1950s for good-quality sporting rifles built on the Mannlicher-Schönauer action, but turned his attention to the *Mauser in the 1960s. The guns often had a Bavarian-style cheek-piece and an oddly humped comb. Chamberings ranged from .220 Swift to 9.3x64mm. *See also* Super Express.

Sokolov – 1. A name applied to a wheeled mount for the Russian Maxim (PM) machine-gun, honouring the designer Ya. M. *Sokolov. The original mounts had two additional folding legs, which converted into a tripod, but these were abandoned during the First World War. **2.** Yuri Sokolov. Co-designer with Grigory *Nikitin of the Soviet Nikitin-Sokolov, or NS, universal machine-gun.

Soleilhac. François Soleilhac, Saint-Étienne, France. Listed during 1933 as a gunmaker, and in 1951 at 12 rue des Armuriers.

Sollaceo. J.N. Sollaceo, a government arms inspector working prior to 1850, accepted firearms and equipment marked 'JNS'. *See also* US arms inspectors' marks.

Solothurn. Waffenfabrik Solothurn, Switzerland: *see* Steyr-Solothurn.

Somers & Sworder, Bishops Stortford, Hertfordshire. The marks of this English gunmaking partnership have been reported on self-cocking *pepperboxes dating from the middle of the nineteenth century.

Sommerville. A. Sommerville, a partner in *Braendlin & Sommerville, may have been Belgian or French. He was the co-designer with Charles F. *Galand of a series of ejector levers for revolvers. *See* British Patent 3039/68 of 5 October 1868.

SONAZ. An acronym applied to Soviet/Russian cosmonauts' support kit, which included the TP-82 multi-barrel pistol and appropriate ammunition. The gun was designed by *Paramonov, Upirov and Ochnev.

'Sonnen', 'Sonnenmarke'. Brandnames found on shotgun cartridges made by *Wolff & Co. of Walsrode, Germany, prior to 1911. They were usually accompanied by a sun-face, the rays being partly composed of the letter 'W'.

Soper – 1. Richard Soper, later R. & W. Soper, 138 Friar Street, Reading, Berkshire. This English gunmaking business was founded sometime prior to 1850, but had become R. & W. Soper by 1862. Sporting guns, pepperboxes and cap-lock revolvers are known from this period. By 1868, however, the partnership had been dissolved and operations were being continued by William Soper (below) alone. **2.** William Soper, 138 Friar Street, Reading, Berkshire. This gunmaker, previously a partner in R. & W. Soper (*see* Richard Soper), is best known for a single-shot rifle with a laterally-pivoting breech-block. This was the subject of British Patent 2151/65 of 19 August 1865, which protected an underlever-cocker, and a side-lever adaptation protected by British Patent 3637/67 of 30 November 1867.

'Sora' [The]. A mark found on shotgun ammunition loaded by the *Chamberlain Cartridge Company of Cleveland, Ohio.

Soulier, 83 rue Antoine-Durafour, Saint-Étienne, France. Listed in 1951 as a gunmaker.

South African Model. A large *blowback semi-auto-

matic pistol made in Britain by *Webley & Scott Ltd of Birmingham, c. 1920–30. Little more than the original 9mm Short Webley & Scott pistol with a radial safety lever high on the left side of the slide, chambered for the 9mm Browning Long cartridges, the South African gun had a cylindrical barrel projecting from a short slide, an external hammer and near-vertical grip. The name was applied in recognition of an important colonial export market.

'Southampton' [The]. This brandname will be found on shotgun cartridges handled by Cox & Clarke of Southampton. *See* John *Cox.

Southern... – 1. Southern Armoury, Britain. *See* B. *Webster & Company and *Collins Brothers. **2.** Southern Counties Agricultural Trading Society (SCATS), Winchester, Hampshire. The marks of this co-operative, accompanied by an illustration of a hen pheasant, have been found on shotgun ammunition distributed as 'The Challenge Smokeless'. Although the cases were of European origin, the source of the cartridges remains uncertain. **3.** Southern Arms Company. A brandname associated with shotguns made by the *Crescent Arms Company. **4.** Southern Cartridge Company, Houston, Texas, USA. A small independent ammunition maker, this business marked its products with 'SO.C.CO.'

Southerner. This single-barrel cartridge derringer, loaded by swinging the barrel away from the frame, was made by the *Merrimack Arms & Manufacturing Company and the *Brown Manufacturing Company in during 1867–73. It has been re-created more recently by Classic Arms.

Southgate – 1. Thomas Southgate. A gunmaker recorded at 6 Burton Crescent, London W.C., from 1896 until 1900 or later. Patentee of the Southgate *Ejector. **2.** Southgate & Mears. This gunmaking partnership was at 4 George Yard, Wardour Street, London, in 1884.

Southron. A *Suicide Special revolver made in the USA by *Johnson, Bye & Company and/or *Iver Johnson of Worcester and Fitchburg, Massachusetts, in the late nineteenth century.

Southwell. William Samuel Southwell. An English gunmaker listed in Old Ford Road, East London, from 1856 until 1870.

Souvignet – 1. Rue Saint-Roch 29, Saint-Étienne, France. Listed in 1879 as a gunmaker, and possibly also in 1892 at rue Saint-Roch 23. **2.** Rue Mulatière 23, Saint-Étienne. Listed in 1892 as a gunmaker. It seems possible that these two establishments may be one and the same.

Souzy jeune, place Dorian 1, Saint-Étienne, France. Listed in 1879 as a distributor of, and agent for, arms and ammunition.

Sowman. J.W. & E. Sowman, Olney, Buckinghamshire. This English ironmongery business sold shotgun ammunition marked 'The Sureshot Smokeless'.

'SP' – 1. Often encircled. A private proof mark used by the *Savage Arms Company. **2.** Found on US military firearms and accessories. *See* S. *Priestley.

Spack. *See* Benjamin Rifle Company.

Space Rifle. A single-shot bolt-action pattern made by *Ljutic Industries.

'S.P. & A. CO.' Found in the *headstamps of shotgun cartridges made in Britain by the short-lived *Smokeless Powder & Ammunition Company.

Spandau arms factory. *See* Königlich Gewehrfabrik, Spandau. This Prussian arms factory was purchased by the government in 1851 and moved from Potsdam to Spandau in 1855. It is usually associated with *Mauser rifles, but also occasionally with the *Parabellum pistol.

Spandauer-Selbstladepistole. Also known as the M1896, this gun was tested in Germany in the 1890s. It was not successful enough to challenge even the earliest semi-automatic pistols (i.e. the *Borchardt) and was speedily abandoned.

Spanish Model, or Spanish Model Remington. A name given in the 1870s by E. *Remington & Sons to a version of the standard military *rolling-block rifle chambering the .43 centrefire cartridge; it accepted a socket bayonet. *See also* Civil Guard Model, Egyptian Model and French Model.

Sparkbrook. Royal Small Arms Factory (RSAF), Montgomery Street, Sparkbrook, Birmingham. This factory was purchased by the British Government in 1886 from the liquidators of the *National Arms & Ammunition Company Ltd, having stood idle since 1883. Production of *Lee-Metford rifles began in 1889, followed by *Lee-Enfield and Mark I SMLE rifles made until the factory was sold to the *Birmingham Small Arms Company Ltd in 1906. Although BSA assembled a few Mark I SMLE rifles, marked 'B.S.A.-SPARKBROOK' or 'B.S.A. Co' over 'SPARKBROOK' in 1906–07, subsequently work was concentrated in the Small Heath factory, and firearms-related operations at Sparkbrook ceased. The Sparkbrook inspectors' mark was a crown above a Roman (upright) letter 'B'.

'Sparkford Vale' [The]. This mark will be encountered on shotgun ammunition sold by H.C. *Little & Son of Yeovil, Somerset, England.

Spaulding. Sidney P. Spaulding, a lieutenant-colonel in the US Army, accepted .45 M1911A1 pistols made in 1939–40 by *Colt's Patent Fire Arms Manufacturing Company. They bore 'SPS' identifiers. *See also* US arms inspectors' marks.

'SPB'. Found on US military firearms and accessories. *See* Samuel P. *Baird.

Spearman. J. Spearman, a London gunsmith (but originally also a gun-stock maker), was first recorded in Swallow Gardens in 1833. Subsequently he moved to Prescot Street in 1839; to 25 & 26 Chamber Street, London E., in 1845; and to 73 Great Prescot Street in 1863. Trading appears to have ceased in the mid-1860s.

Specht. A brandname associated with shotgun cartridges made by *Pulverfabrik Hasloch prior to the First World War.

Special... – 1. 'Special' [The]. A mark reported on a 12-bore shotgun cartridge made by *Eley Bros. prior to the First World War for W. *Metcalf of Catterick. 2. 'Special Brown' [The]. Associated with shotgun cartridges sold by *Garden of Aberdeen. 3. 'Special Clay King'. Found on English shotgun cartridges. *See* 'Clay King'. 4. Special Commando Knife. A name given to a Soviet/Russian combination knife-bayonet. 5. 'Special Game' [The]. On British shotgun ammunition. *See* George *Newham & Company. 6. Special Grade Rifle. This was a version of the 1899-pattern *Remington-Lee sporting rifle, with a sturdier stock of selected walnut. 7. 'Special I.X.L'. [The]. A brandname found on shotgun cartridges sold by George *Hinton of Taunton, England, after 1918. 8. Special Model. Associated with a Mauser-pattern sporting rifle, built on an *FN action by *Cogswell & Harrison, in

chamberings ranging from 7x57mm Mauser to .404 Nitro Express and .458 Winchester. It had a better-quality stock and finish than the *Longford. The Take Down model was similar, but had an interrupted-screw joint between the action and the barrel. The De Luxe Model was a Special Model with a select walnut stock and a *Cape or *Express back sight. 9. Special Navy Rifle. Made in Japan in 1945, by Yokosuka navy arsenal, this was basically a crude cast-iron training rifle receiver with a barrel modified to receive the locking lugs directly in the enlarged chamber. This allowed ball ammunition to be fired without blowing the gun apart. 10. 'Special Rabbit' [The]. Found on shotgun ammunition distributed by T.H. *Moor of South Molton and Exford. Origins unknown. 11. Special Service. A brandname associated with shotguns made by the *Crescent Arms Company. 12. 'Special Skeet', or 'FN-Special Skeet'. A tradename used by *Fabrique Nationale d'Armes de Guerre on shotgun ammunition, c. 1932–40. 13. 'Special Twenty' [The]. This was associated with 20-bore shotgun ammunition created by the *New Normal Ammunition Company Ltd of Hendon (London), from parts purchased in Germany. Apparently the propellant was *Walsrode Jagdpulver.

Speed. Joseph J. Speed joined the staff of the *Royal Small Arms Factory at the age of 25, rising to become assistant manager, then manager (1891–1909). He received several British Patents, including 6335/87 of 30 April 1887, for a magazine cut-off mechanism; 13,335/87 of 1 October 1887, for an improved magazine, long-range sights and a dust cover for the bolt; 17,944/87 of 30 December 1887 for a magazine spring; and 15,786/88 of 1 November 1888 to protect the construction of a magazine, a hand guard and safety catch. Elements of these were all incorporated in the *Lee-Metford rifle, guns being made commercially by the *Birmingham Small Arms & Metals Company Ltd and the *London Small Arms Company Ltd, being marked 'LEE-SPEED PATENTS'. Patenting designs in his own name while in government employment attracted much adverse comment at the time. Subsequently, however, Speed was granted three patents jointly with the superintendent of the Enfield factory, Colonel Henry *Watkin.

Speedmaster. Rifles made by the *Remington-UMC and the *Remington Arms Company. 1. Model 241A Speedmaster. This .22 rimfire auto-loading rifle, produced in 1935–41 and 1945–51, was a modernised Model 24 adapted for high-speed ammunition. It had a 24in barrel, and could be obtained in B (Special), D (*Peerless), E (Expert) and F (*Premium) grades. 2. Model 552A Speedmaster. Introduced in 1957, this was a modernised 550A. Lacking the floating-chamber system and its predecessor's ability to handle different cartridges interchangeably, the 552A had a round-backed slab-sided receiver. The deluxe 550BDL (1966 to date) had chequered woodwork and, particularly on later guns, distinctive fleur-de-lys strapwork. The 552C carbine (1961–77) had a short barrel; and the 552GS (1957–77) chambered the low-power .22 Short rimfire cartridge, being sold with retaining-chain eyes and spent-case deflectors for use in shooting galleries. *See also* Sesquicentennial.

'Speedwell' [The]. Associated with shotgun ammunition bearing the marks of T.W. *Murray & Company of Cork; origins unknown.

Speedy. Associated with *Mayer & Grammelspacher

Diana spring-air rifles – particularly the junior patterns – sold during the 1920s by *Clyde's Game & Gun Mart of Glasgow.

Spencer – **1.** Alfred L. Spencer, Richmond, Yorkshire. The name and address of this English gunmaker have been reported on shotgun ammunition, hand loaded in Richmond from components supplied by *Eley-Kynoch. **2.** Christopher Miner Spencer, South Manchester, Hartford and Windsor, Connecticut, and Boston, Massachusetts, USA. This inventor (1841–1922), renowned for his brilliance in several fields, patented his tube-magazine repeating rifle on 6 March 1860 (US no. 27,393). Large quantities of rifles and carbines were made for the Federal government during the American Civil War. In addition to the master patent, reissued in April 1864 and assigned to the Spencer Repeating Rifle Company, Christopher Spencer was granted US Patents 34,319 of 4 February 1862 for a laterally-swinging breech-block with an attached hammer; 38,702 of 26 May 1863 (ante-dated to 3 January) for an oscillating breech-block containing a cartridge tube; 45,952 of 17 January 1865 for an improved magazine tube; and 58,737 and 58,738 of 9 October 1866 for improvements to the basic radial breech design. After concentrating his energies elsewhere, Spencer returned to gunmaking to develop a slide-action shotgun. Patented jointly with Sylvester H. *Roper on 4 April 1882 (no. 255,894), the guns were made first by the *Spencer Arms Company, then under the control of Francis *Bannerman & Son. Spencer's last firearm patent was 299,282 of 27 May 1884, granted jointly with Richard *Rhodes. However, he had also been granted 36,062 of 29 July 1862 for a cartridge retractor (assigned to Charles Cheney) and subsequently obtained 386,614 of 24 July 1888 for a safety-lock mechanism. **3.** F.P. Spencer, Lugley Street, Newport, Isle of Wight. The marks of this gunsmithing and ironmongery business have been seen on a variety of shotgun cartridges (date and origins unknown) distributed as Spencer's Vectis Bunnie and Vectis Special Loading. Some may also include 'F.P.S.' in the marking, or a coat-of-arms customarily identified as that of the Isle of Wight, but more plausibly of Newport. **4.** Matthew Spencer. This English gunsmithing business traded from Lynn Regis (now King's Lynn), Norfolk, successively occupying premises in Red Cow Street in 1804–22 and High Street in 1829–53. Spencer made sporting guns, reservoir airguns, revolvers, etc. **5.** M.S. Spencer, Lyme Regis, Dorset, England. The marks of this gunmaker have been reported on self-cocking *pepperboxes dating from the middle of the nineteenth century. However, the identification may arise from misreading Lynn Regis as Lyme Regis; see Matthew Spencer (above). **6.** Spencer Arms Company, Hartford, Connecticut, USA. This gunmaking business produced the first commercially successful slide-action shotgun, patented by Christopher *Spencer and Sylvester *Roper in 1882–85. A stubby fore-grip was used to pivot the breech-block, cartridges being fed from an under-barrel tube. A few rifles were made for US Army trials, but the 12-bore shotgun was more successful. The business failed in 1889, its assets passing to *Pratt & Whitney, then to Francis *Bannerman & Sons. **7.** Spencer Gun Company. A brand-name associated with shotguns made in the twentieth century by the *Crescent Arms Company, used long after the original business had disappeared. **8.** Spencer Repeating Rifle Company, established in 1862 in Boston, Massachusetts, USA, made the breech-loading magazine

guns designed by Christopher Spencer (above) in the Chickering Piano Company building in Tremont Street. The business was absorbed by the *Winchester Repeating Arms Company in 1870. **9.** Spencer Revolver Company: see Otis *Smith. **10.** Spencer-Roper rifle. Designed in the late 1870s and made in accordance with US Patent 255,894 granted to Christopher Spencer and Sylvester *Roper on 4 April 1882, these slide-action guns were tested by several armies in .45-70 and 11mm chamberings. The earliest examples ejected vertically, but later short-action examples ejected laterally to the right. The rifles were unsuccessful, but subsequently 20,000 shotgun derivatives were made by the Spencer Repeating Arms Company (c. 1886–90) and Francis Bannerman & Sons (c. 1893–1902).

'Spesco' – **1.** A mark associated with the Spesco Corporation of Atlanta, Georgia, USA. It will be found on a variety of guns and accessories, including SM-11 pistols purchased from *Reck in Germany. **2.** Spesco Corporation [The], Atlanta, Georgia. A US importer of a variety of guns and accessories from Europe, including 6.35mm *Reck SM-11 pistols.

SPI. See Syndicat des Pièces interchangeables.

Spiller & Burr, Atlanta, Georgia. Maker of 800 brass-frame .36-calibre copies of the *Whitney Navy revolver in 1863. The government of the Confederate States of America purchased the business in January 1864, moving the factory to Macon, Georgia, where 750 guns were produced before work ceased in November.

Spirlet. Gunmaker A. Spirlet of 5 Quai de la Boverie, Liège, Belgium, was granted British Patent 2107/70 of 1870 (communicated by way of agent John Piddington) to protect a break-open revolver with a simultaneous-ejection system in the form of a manually-operated star plate set into the rear face of the cylinder.

Spiro. Benny Spiro, Hamburg, Germany. Established in 1864, Spiro was one of the principal dealers of 'war weapons and munitions', which were exported and imported in vast quantities. The business failed to survive the depression of the early 1930s and the rise to power of the NSDAP.

Spitalsky. Antonin Spitalsky, after collaborating in the redesign of the *Werndl rifle in the mid-1870s, produced a series of drum-magazine bolt-action guns between 1879 and 1884 on the basis of the German Mauser M1871. Konrad *Kromar improved the ruggedness of the system in 1885, but the Kromar-Spitalsky rifle was too late to challenge the *Mannlicher.

Spitfire – **1.** A semi-automatic pistol made in Britain by John Slough Ltd of Hereford, chambered for 9mm Parabellum or .40 S&W cartridges. Dating from the early 1990s, the guns were derived from the Czechoslovakian ČZ 75. **2.** A *Suicide Special revolver made by the *Hopkins & Allen Arms Company of Norwich, Connecticut, in the late nineteenth century.

Spittin' Image. Applied by the *Daisy Manufacturing Company to several of its products, particularly those based on the Winchester lever-action rifle (e.g. Models 1894, 3994 and 3030).

SPIW, Special Purpose Infantry Weapon. This US development project was seen as a replacement for the conventional *ArmaLite rifle, firing high-velocity flechette ammunition, but the project was a costly failure.

'S.P.L.', 'SPL'. Marks found on shotgun ammunition used exclusively by the London Sporting Park. See also 'LSP'.

Split-breech. A term used to describe the action of carbines purchased by the Federal authorities during the American Civil War, designed by Leonard *Geiger and perfected by Joseph *Rider. Patented in the names of Rider and Remington in 1865, the high-wall receiver contained a radial breech-block. The nose of the hammer struck the rimfire cartridge through a slot in the top surface of the block. Fifteen thousand .56-50 Remington-Geiger carbines were made by E. Remington & Sons of Ilion, to fill an order of 24 October 1864, followed by 5,000 smaller guns ordered in January 1865 for a .46 rimfire cartridge, which put less strain on the action. Their frames were notably smaller than the .56-50 pattern. The walnut butt of the Remington-Geiger carbine had a straight wrist; the half-length fore-end was held by a single band; and a sling ring was anchored on the left side of the case-hardened receiver.

Spooner. G.A. Spooner. This government arms inspector, working from c. 1900 until the beginning of the First World War, accepted items marked 'GAS'. *See also* US arms inspectors' marks.

Spörer – **1.** Albin Spörer, Zella St Blasii in Thüringen, Germany. Listed in the *Deutsches Reichs-Adressbuch* for 1914 as a gunmaker. Later Albin Spörers Sohn, owned by Otto E. Spörer (below). **2.** Oskar Spörer, Zella-Mehlis in Thüringen, Germany. Listed during 1920–30 as a weapon maker. **3.** Oskar & W. Spörer, Zella-Mehlis in Thüringen, Germany. Listed in 1939 as a master gunsmith. **4.** Otto E. Spörer, Zella-Mehlis in Thüringen, Germany. Listed in 1920 as a gunmaker. **5.** Spörer & Harl, employees of the Bavarian government arms factory in *Amberg, patented a bolt-action rifle in 1882. The basic mechanism was adapted from the 1871-type Mauser, but a gravity-feed case magazine in the butt fed the breech by a *Hotchkiss-like feed-way and elevator system.

Sport – **1.** Sport 'French': *see* Buffalo-Sport and Populaire-Sport. **2.** Also known as Universal Sport, Czechoslovakia: *see* Universal. **3.** A *Suicide Special revolver made in the USA by the *Ryan Pistol Company of Norwich, Connecticut, in the late nineteenth century. **4.** 'Sport & Munition': *see* 'SM'.

Sporting... – **1.** Sporting Clays, *Concorde Sporting Clays or *Daytona Sporting Clays. These 12-bore over/under shotguns are made by *Società Armi Bresciane of Gardone Val Trompia. They have anatomical pistol grips, *schnabel-tip fore-ends and a single selective trigger mechanism. Barrels are 710–810mm long. **2.** 'Sporting Life' [The]. Associated with the shotgun cartridges sold by W.W. *Greener of Birmingham. **3.** Sporting Model. Applied to octagonal-barrelled No. 2 *Ballard rifles, made between 1876 and 1889 for rim- and centrefire cartridges ranging from .32 to .44. **4.** Sporting Model. A name applied by *Colt's Patent Fire Arms Manufacturing Company, of Hartford, Connecticut, to semi-automatic pistols made to the patents of John M. *Browning. The .38 Model 1902 (1902–08) had moulded rubber grips and an inertia firing pin.

Sportmodell. This term applies specifically to the bolt-action air rifles produced under the patents of Hugo *Schmeisser by C.G. *Haenel of Suhl, prior to 1945 – as the Sportmodell 33 – and, during the early post-war era, by VEB Fahrzeug- und Gerätewerk 'Ernst *Thalmann' of Suhl, as the Sportmodell 49 (or *Blitz). The *Wehrsport-Luftgewehr Model 33 was a military trainer variant; all the guns fire 4.5mm ball ammunition.

Sportsman – **1.** Usually found as 'The Sportsman' on shotgun cartridges sold in Britain by, among others, *Garrick of Sunderland, and *Tickner of Bishops Waltham. **2.** A brandname associated with shotguns made by the *Crescent Arms Company. **3.** Found on a revolver made in recent years by *Smith & Wesson. **4.** Sportsman Bush & Field. This name was applied to a *Mauser-action sporting rifle offered in the USA in 1984–88 by *Marathon Products, Inc. Built on a *Santa Barbara action in chamberings ranging from .243 Winchester to .30-06, the rifle could be obtained in kit form. It had a walnut stock with a low *Monte Carlo comb and a heavy squared-tip fore-end. **5.** Sportsman's International Cartridge Company, Kansas City, Missouri, USA. This short-lived ammunition maker, or possibly distributor, trading for a few years prior to the entry of the USA into the First World War in 1917, was responsible for cartridges headstamped 'S.I.C. Co.'

Sportsmaster. Guns made by the *Remington Arms Company. **1.** Model 341A Sportsmaster (1936–39). This .22 bolt-action rifle had a bigger stock than the others in the 341 series and a tube magazine beneath the barrel. **2.** Model 512A Sportsmaster. Made in 1940–41 and 1945–62, this was an M341 with a radial-lever safety catch behind the bolt, open sights and a plain pistol-grip half-stock.

Sport Waffenfabrik 'Moll'. *See* Moll Sportwaffenfabrik, Lauenberg an der Elbe.

'Sportsmatch'. Found on telescope-sight mounts made in England by J. & J. Ford.

'Spotfinder' [The]. A mark associated with shotgun cartridges handled by D.B. *Crockart of Perth, Scotland.

SPP, or SPP-1. A silenced underwater pistol designed in what was the Soviet Union by Vladmir *Simonov.

'Springer'. A mark found on Bazar (q.v.) knife pistols, indicating that the knife components, if nothing else, had been provided by Wilhelm *Weltersbach of Solingen.

Springfield – **1.** Springfield-Allin or Trapdoor Springfield rifle. The prototype designed by Erskine *Allin appeared in the summer of 1865, performing well enough for large quantities to be ordered for field trials. About 5,000 .58 rimfire rifles were made in the Springfield factory in 1865–66. They were adapted 1863-pattern cap-lock rifle-muskets with a new breech-block hinged laterally at the front of the action. The block could be swung up to reveal the chamber, but the alteration was much too complicated; the ratchet-pattern extractor was weak and the cartridge performed poorly. As soon as the first M1865 Allin-type conversions were being issued for trials, a search began to find a better weapon. The M1865 was soon replaced by the M1866, with its barrel lined to reduce it from .58 to .50, and a simplified extractor. Trials still favoured the *Berdan as the best conversion and the *Peabody as the best new rifle, but controversially the .50 Allin was selected for production. An improved .45 version was approved on 5 May 1873. As the Allin breech had cost the US Treasury more than $124,000 to settle patent-infringement claims, the government was reluctant to make wholesale changes. Virtually all Allin-type guns were made by the National Armory in *Springfield, Massachusetts. Many different models were introduced prior to 1889 (see Bibliography for sources of information). Many obsolete .50-70 Model 1865 and Model 1866 *Trapdoor Springfields were converted in the 1880s to make inexpensive 12- and 16-bore shotguns. They are normally recognisable by their short fore-ends. **2.** Springfield (or National) Armory. Founded in the small Massachusetts town of Springfield in 1782, although no guns were made until 1794, this facility grew to become the principal government-owned small-arms factory – making M1903 bolt-action rifles at the rate of 1,500 daily by November 1918. The site extended in 1933 to 297 acres, but this was enlarged even further during the Second World War. The factory has made a wide range of firearms, including *Burton, *Chaffee-Reece, *Enfield, *Garand, *Hotchkiss, *Krag-Jørgensen, *Remington, *Sharps and *Springfield (Allin and Mauser types) rifles. *Colt-Browning pistols have also been produced, but operations were scaled down until eventually the factory closed in the 1980s, by which time it was little more than a glorified repair shop. **3.** Springfield Armory, Inc., Geneseo, Illinois, USA. A current manufacturer of .45-calibre pistols based on the Colt M1911A1 and rifles based on the M14. **4.** Springfield Arms Company. Based in Springfield, Massachussets, this gun-making business manufactured revolvers designed by its superintendent, James *Warner. The .40-calibre six-shot Dragoon Pistol was followed by the .31 Jaquith Patent Belt Model, although the relevant patent had very little to do with the gun. Next came the Warner Patent Belt Model, with a modified Jaquith-pattern cylinder-rotating hand, and (from 1852) a two-trigger mechanism and Warner's patent rammer. A few .36-calibre six-shot Warner Patent Navy Model revolvers were made in the mid-1850s, mostly with the twin-trigger mechanism, together with the .28 six-shot Warner Patent Pocket Models, with cylinders rotated by the hammer, a ring trigger or the perfected two-trigger system. The company failed about 1863, allowing James *Warner to continue operations under his own name. **5.** Springfield Arms Company. A brandname associated with shotguns made by the *Crescent Arms Company. **6.** Springfield (-Mauser) bolt-action rifle: *see* panel, below.

Spring & Western. A spring-air revolver marketed by *Healthways, Inc.

Sprinter. A Spanish 6.35mm-calibre pocket pistol, based on the *FN-Browning of 1905, made in Eibar by *Garate, Anitua y Compañía: six rounds, striker fired.

'Sproxton' [The]. Found on shotgun cartridges sold by J.H. *Gill of London.

'SPS'. Found on US military firearms and accessories. *See* Sidney P. *Spaulding.

'Sp. & Sr.', in fraktur. Found on rifles and handguns made for the German authorities by Spangenberger & Sauer of Suhl. They included 1871-pattern *Mauser carbines and *Reichsrevolvers.

'S.Q.' An abbreviation of 'Super Quality', used on cartridges manufactured by the *Winchester Repeating Arms Company.

Square Deal. A brandname associated with shotguns made by the *Crescent Arms Company.

SPRINGFIELD BOLT-ACTION RIFLE

Springfield (6)

This bolt-action rifle, a replacement for the *Krag-Jørgensen in US Army service, was the culmination of experiments with Mauser-type actions that dated back to 1900. The original full-length rifle had been superseded by an improved short-barrel version as soon as the US authorities realised that the British were working on the short *Lee-Enfield.

The original M1903 rifle was approved for service on 19 June 1903, but work was suspended in January 1905 to allow details of the design to be reconsidered. The Chief of Staff of the US Army soon reported that the reduction in barrel length was acceptable, but that the rod bayonet should be replaced immediately with a sword pattern. The back sight was changed in May 1905; a pointed spitzer bullet was adopted in October 1906 (changing the sight graduations); and a solid tubular back-sight mount replaced the skeletal pattern in 1910.

The first guns were made exclusively by *Springfield Armory (S.A.), although work had soon begun in Rock Island Arsenal (R.I.A.). When the First World War began, however, only Springfield was making rifles, so the machinery in Rock Island, which had lain inactive since 1913, was put back into commission immediately.

The M1903 Marksman's Rifle, the result of experiments undertaken in the early 1900s, was fitted with a 6x M1908 or 5.2x M1913 Warner & Swazey optical sight, but was neither popular nor successful.

Work continued throughout the First World War: a parkerised finish was adopted, a second recoil bolt was added through the stock, and the bolt handle was bent slightly backward. The M1903 Mark 1 was an adaptation for the *Pedersen Device, with an auxiliary sear in the trigger system and an ejection port in the left side of the receiver. Although the Pedersen Devices were scrapped immediately hostilities ended, the rifles remained in service until they wore out.

Increasing reports of receiver failures in 1917/18 were traced to poor heat treatment during manufacture, and a new double-treated receiver was approved. The first Springfield-made guns of this type were assembled in February 1918, shortly before the serial number reached 800000, and the first Rock Island example, no. 285507, was completed in May 1918. Work continued in Rock Island Armory only until June 1918, but military production at Springfield Armory lasted until 1927. Thereafter, the only guns to be made were destined for National Match target shooting and the National Rifle Association. The M1903 NRA rifle was approved on 30 March 1915, to be sold to NRA members by the National Board for the Promotion of Rifle Practise; the M1903 NRA Sporter (1924–38) was a post-war equivalent, although enterprising gunsmiths (such as R.F. Sedgley of Philadelphia) made many similar guns from military-surplus actions. The first rimfire Springfields, the M1922, M1922M1 (1925) and M2 (1933), also dated from this era.

Approved on 15 March 1929, the M1903A1 had a modified Style C pistol-grip stock instead of the straight-wrist Style S. The change in designation was authorised on 5 December, but few guns of this type were ever made; S-types were still being used in 1939. A 'scant pistol grip' was approved in 1942 to enable under-size or flawed stock blanks to

Squire, Squires – **1.** James Rollin Marble Squire, Boston, Massachusetts, USA. Co-agent, with Allison Owen Swett and Henry Newton Sheldon, involved in the specification submitted on behalf of Augustus Bedford (British Patent 23/76 of 1876). **2.** James Squire, or Squires. A gunmaker first listed in Mile End Old Town in 1847, then at 14 Newcastle Street, London E., in 1860–67; additionally at 72 Kingsland Road in 1868–73; then at Newcastle Street alone until 1892. Then the business was continued until 1895 by John Squires, presumably James Squires' son.

'Squirrel' [The]. This brandname was used by the *Chamberlain Cartridge Company of Cleveland, Ohio, on shotgun cartridges.

'SR'. A linear monogram with neither letter dominant, usually placed on the breast of a stylised eagle. Associated with the products of *Sturm, Ruger & Company, Inc.

'SRC'. A superimposition-type monogram with 'R' dominant. A mark used by *Sears, Roebuck & Company, often found moulded into the rubber grips of bought-in revolvers or on shotgun butt plates.

'SRW'. A superimposition-type monogram with 'S' dominant. Correctly 'RWS' (q.v.); used by *Römerwerke AG of Suhl.

'SS', 'S&S', 'S u. S' – **1.** 'SS', 'stainless steel'; used generically. **2.** As 'SS': a vertical superimposition-type monogram, with letters of equal dominance. Found on the grips of semi-automatic pistols made in Germany after the end of the First World War by J.P. *Sauer & Sohn of Suhl. **3.** 'SS', often set into three overlapping triangles. A mark associated with *Simson & Companie of Suhl, found on the slides of semi-automatic pistols, on the receivers of bolt-action rifles, and on the butt plates of shotguns. **4.** An 'S&S' or 'S u. S.' mark may be found on the grips of semi-automatic pistols made prior to 1919 by J.P. *Sauer & Sohn of Suhl. **5.** 'SS', 'Stainless Synthetic'. Applied to a version of the *Remington M700 bolt-action rifle with a stainless-steel-barrelled action set in a composite half-stock.

'SSA', 'S.S.A.' – **1.** Found on *Lee-Enfield rifles and rifle parts made by the *Standard Small Arms Company of Birmingham, Warwickshire, England, in 1916–18. SSA was succeeded by the *National Rifle Factory No. 1 (N.R.F.). **2.** As a monogram: a trademark associated with Sanders Small Arms Ltd (q.v.).

'SSC'. A superimposition-type monogram with 'S' dominant. *See* 'CSS'; used by C.S. *Shatuck.

'SSS'. A monogram in triangular form, customarily encircled, each attenuated sans-serif letter sharing a common base. Used on handguns, shotguns and sporting rifles made in Germany since the late 1960s by J.P. *Sauer & Sohn GmbH of Eckenförde.

'SS' within 'U'. A mark found on the slides of .45 M1911A1 *Government Model pistols made for the US armed forces by the *Union Switch & Signal Company.

'SSW'. A superimposition-type monogram with 'W'

---

be used. The simplified M1903A3 rifle, incorporating many stamped and fabricated parts, was approved in May 1942. The guns were made by Springfield, Remington, and L.C. Smith & Corona, Inc. The straight-wrist stock lacked a grasping groove, and an aperture sight lay on top of the receiver bridge. The stamped trigger guard was deepened ahead of the trigger lever in 1943, allowing a gloved finger access to the trigger, but progress with the M1 *Garand and the *M1 Carbine led to production contracts being cancelled in February 1944.

Extensive use was made of sub-contractors, including *Johnson Automatics, Inc., of Providence; R.F. Sedgley, Inc., of Philadelphia; and the *Savage Arms Company of Utica, New York. These three made barrels marked respectively with 'JA', an encircled 'S', and an angular 'S' within a square.

Standardised on 14 January 1943, the M1903A4 sniper rifle was made exclusively by the *Remington Arms Company. The first guns had two-groove cut rifling, but subsequently this was changed to a four-groove draw-formed pattern. The bolt handle was bent downward to clear the 2.5x Telescope M73B1, made by the

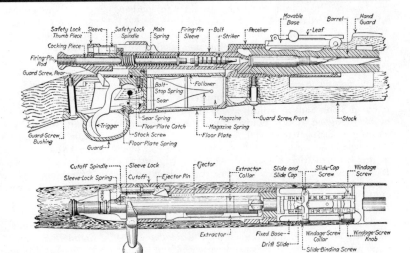

W.R. Weaver Company and carried in a Redfield mount. The final batches of M1903A4 rifles were delivered in June 1944, as the M1C and M1D *Garand rifles were being developed as replacements. Total military Springfield 03 production has been estimated at 1,970,000.

The history of the Springfield rifle has been covered in detail by Colonel William S. Brophy, in *The Springfield 1903 Rifles* (Stackpole Books, 1985), and Clark S.

These longitudinal sections of the .30 US M1903 Springfield rifle show that it is essentially a slightly modified Mauser. The US government was forced to pay for patent infringement before the First World War began.

Campbell, in *The '03 Era – When Smokeless Revolutionized U.S. Riflery* (Collector Grade Publications, 1994). A useful listing of the individual patterns will be found in John Walter's *Rifles of the World* (Krause Publications, second edition, 1998).

placed centrally on two overlapping letters 'S', usually within a diamond placed on concentric circles. Found on the grips of *Pieper-type pistols made in the 1920s by *Steyr-Solothurn Waffen AG.

'STA'. This designation (*Section Technique d'Artillerie*) covered a variety of auto-loaders developed between 1894 and 1916. Fusil STA No. 4 (later reclassified Fusil A1) was a Pralon-Meunier design dating from 1897. It was gas operated and locked by rotating interrupted-thread-type lugs into seats in the receiver. It was also the precursor of a series of improved rifles, No. 5 to No. 7 (Fusils A2, A3 and A5), culminating in the 7mm-calibre STA No. 6. This was adopted officially as the 7mm Fusil A6, or *Meunier.

Stacey. Benjamin J. Stacey, an English gunsmith, was recorded in 1887–94 at 17 & 19 Settles Street, London E., and thereafter as Stacey & Company until 1900 or later.

Sta-Clean. A tradename associated with *Sears, Roebuck & Company, a corrupted form of 'Stay Clean', indicating cartridges loaded with non-corrosive priming (cf. Kleanbore and Sinoxid).

Stadelmann. Paul Stadelmann, Suhl in Thüringen. A gunmaker working in the period 1920–45, with a manufactory at Schlageterstrasse 61 in 1941.

'Stafford' [The], or 'The Stafford Deep Shell'. A name found on shotgun ammunition sold by *Harrison & Hussey of London.

Stahl – **1.** B. Stahl, Suhl in Thüringen. Listed in German trade directories of the 1890s as a maker of 'weapons and cartridge cases' (*waffen- u. patronenhülsenfabrik*), this business was run by Babette Stahl, the daughter (or perhaps widow) of Richard Stahl, until sold in 1901 to G.C. *Dornheim of Suhl. **2.** John Stahl, a government arms inspector, accepted military equipment in the years immediately after the American Civil War. They were marked 'JS', but can be difficult to distinguish from others accepted in an earlier era by James *Stillman and John *Symington. *See also* US arms inspectors' marks. **3.** Richard Stahl, Suhl in Thüringen, Germany. Two types of rifle designed by this gunmaker may be encountered. The rarer, dating from 1869, embodied a self-cocking pivoting-block action operated by a bulky two-part lever in the enlarged trigger guard ahead of the trigger. The 1873 pattern was operated by a breech-block extension lever running down the right side of the stock wrist. By 1880, Richard Stahl had turned to true Martini-action rifles at the expense of his own designs. He was succeeded by Babette Stahl (above).

Stähle. Wilhelm Stähle designed the roller-locking system embodied in the Mauser Gerät 06 series, and later in the *CETME rifle.

Stainless, Stainless… – **1.** Stainless Steel Bodyguard. This swing-cylinder *Smith & Wesson revolver was introduced in 1986 as the Model 649. *See* Airweight and Bodyguard. **2.** Stainless Steel Chief's Special. A swing-cylinder revolver made by *Smith & Wesson. *See* Airweight and Chief's Special. **3.** Stainless Steel Combat Magnum. Also known as the Model 66, this .357 swing-cylinder revolver was the work of *Smith & Wesson. *See* Combat Magnum. **4.** Stainless Steel Combat Masterpiece. A swing-cylinder revolver made by *Smith & Wesson, also known as the Model 67. *See* Combat Masterpiece. **5.** Stainless Steel Distinguished Combat Magnum. A swing-cylinder revolver made by *Smith & Wesson, also known as the Model 686. *See* Distinguished

Combat Magnum. **6.** Stainless Steel Distinguished Service Magnum. A swing-cylinder revolver made by *Smith & Wesson, also known as the Model 681. *See* Distinguished Service Magnum. **7.** Stainless Steel Kit Gun. A *Smith & Wesson swing-cylinder revolver, also known as the Model 63. *See* Kit Gun. **8.** Stainless Steel Magnum. The first of these, known as the Model 629, was a .44-calibre swing-cylinder *Smith & Wesson introduced c. 1980. A .41 version followed in 1982 (Model 657). *See* Magnum. **9.** Stainless Steel Military & Police. A swing-cylinder revolver made by *Smith & Wesson. *See* Military & Police Model. **10.** Stainless Steel Service Kit Gun. A revolver made by *Smith & Wesson. *See* Service Kit Gun. **11.** Stainless Steel Target. A blowback semi-automatic pistol made by *Smith & Wesson. *See* Target Stainless. **12.** Stainless Steel Target Kit Gun. A revolver made by *Smith & Wesson. *See* Target Kit Gun.

'Stalham' [The], or 'The Stalham Superior'. Marks associated with shotgun ammunition sold by *Edmonds of Stalham, Norfolk, England.

'Stamford Champion' [The]. Found on shotgun cartridges sold by *Grimes of Stamford, Lincolnshire, England.

Stanbury & Stevens, Alphington Street, Exeter, Devon. The marks of this gunmaking business have been found on a variety of shotgun cartridges, sold under such names as The Devonia, The Game, The Monocle, The Red Flash, The *Stanby and The Swift. Most of them seem to have been made by *Eley-Kynoch.

'Stanby' [The]. Reportedly found on a 12-bore shotgun cartridge made by *Eley-Kynoch for *Stanbury & Stevens of Exeter, this is believed to have been a contraction of the 'Stanbury' name.

Stand. *See* Buffalo-Stand.

Standard, Standard… – **1.** Usually found as 'The Standard' on shotgun cartridges handled by Charles *Hellis & Sons of London; by George *Hinton of Taunton prior to 1918; by P.D. *Malloch of Perth; *Rudd of Norwich and Great Yarmouth (made by *Eley-Kynoch); and by the *Hull Cartridge Company in recent years. **2.** A *Suicide Special revolver made in the USA by the *Meriden Arms Company of Meriden, Connecticut. It dates from the late nineteenth century. **3.** Standard Arms Company, Wilmington, Delaware. Maker of auto-loading rifles patented in the USA prior to 1906 by Morris F. *Smith. Apparently production of the gas-operated Model G was confined to 1910–12, although a manually-operated derivative (Model M) lasted until 1914. **4.** Standard Products Company, Port Clinton, Ohio. Maker of *M1 Carbines for the US government during the Second World War. The contract was granted in August 1942, requiring the delivery of an unprecedented 45,000 guns monthly; it was cancelled on 30 April 1944, after 247,160 carbines had been delivered. Their receivers were usually marked 'STD. PRO.' **5.** Standard Small Arms Company Ltd [The], 8 Lench Street, Birmingham, Warwickshire, England. This business was formed in November 1914 by Douglas V. *Johnstone, a partner named Peterson and a London financier named Waring, eager to take advantage of a government grant. A contract to make SMLE rifles was agreed with the Ministry of Munitions in January 1915, but such great problems ensued that production (and then only of a few key components) did not begin in earnest until 1917. The rifles were assembled in the *Enfield factory under the

*Peddled Rifle Scheme. The Ministry of Munitions, having lost patience with bad management and erratic deliveries, bought the Standard Small Arms Company in June 1918 and renamed it *National Rifle Factory No. 1. Rifle components from this particular source were marked 'SSA' and later 'NRF'. **6.** 'Standard Smokeless'. A mark found on 12-bore shotgun cartridges distributed by *Manton & Company, 'London & Calcutta', prior to the First World War; manufacturer unknown. **7.** Standard Sporting Guns, Birmingham. Allotted the code 'M 233', this wholesaling business supplied 12-bore shotguns to the British military authorities in 1942. *See also* British military manufacturers' marks.

Standing breech. The fixed part of the frame that abuts the base of the cartridge in the firing position, carrying the firing pin or the firing-pin bush. The term is usually applied to single-shot dropping-block rifles.

Stange. Louis Stange, working for *Rheinmetall, has been credited with the design of the German FG. 42 automatic rifle.

Stanley – 1. Merrit F. Stanley, Plymouth, Michigan, until 1890/91, and Northville, Michigan, thereafter. Stanley was granted several airgun patents and is best remembered for the *Globe and *Warrior BB guns. Among his patents were US Patent 420,316 of 28 January 1890, protecting the hinged-stock cocking system of the Globe. US Patent 461,224 of 13 October 1891 protected an airgun with a sliding barrel; 454,081 of 16 June 1891 allowed claims for a modification of the Globe, assigned to the manufacturer prior to production. US Patents 627,764 of 27 June 1889 and 767,968 of 16 August 1904 protected spring-air guns. **2.** 'Stanley Arms Company'. A name found on shotguns handled by the H. & D. *Folsom Arms Company, possibly imported from Europe.

Stannard. R.N. Stannard, a government arms inspector working in 1905, accepted revolver components and firearms accessories marked 'RNS'. *See also* US arms inspectors' marks.

Stanton. John Stanton [& Son], Wolverhampton, Staffordshire. Listed as a gun-lock maker from 1855, Stanton traded from Clifton Street, Chapel Ash, until the early 1880s. Then the trading style became Stanton & Son, and a move to 17 Merriedale Road occurred in 1886/87. Stanton was the recipient of several British Patents protecting the design of *rebounding locks: 367 of 1867, 3774 of 1869, and 928 of 1877. Work seems to have ceased shortly after the First World War.

Stapp. Richard Stapp. This British metalsmith was listed originally as a gun-barrel maker in Wheeler Street, Spitalfields, London, in 1816. By the census of 1841, however, he had become a gunmaker in St John Street, Clerkenwell. Later directory entries put him at 2 Goldsmith's Place, Hackney Road (1846–48), then finally at 16 Road Side, Mile End, from 1852 until 1858. It is assumed that then he died or retired.

Star – 1. A mark, usually as 'The Star', associated with shotgun cartridges sold by *Rudd of Norwich and Great Yarmouth, possibly acquired from Charles S. Rosson (q.v.), and also with .410-calibre examples (often marked 'The Star 410') sold in East Anglia by Charles S. *Rosson of Norwich. **2.** An underlever-cocking air pistol made by E. *Anson & Company of Birmingham, England, from 1922 until c. 1929. **3.** A *Suicide Special revolver made by the *Prescott Pistol Company of Hatfield,

Connecticut, USA, in the late nineteenth century. **4.** Star and Cross. A brandname and trademark associated with Joseph *Rodgers. **5.** Star–Bonifacio Echeverria SA. Known for much of the inter-war period as Fábrica de Armas 'Star'–Continuadora de B. Echeverria, the business was renamed Star–Bonifacio Echeverria SA in 1939, and continues to trade. **6.** Star Model DK: *see* Starfire. **7.** Star Modelo CU: *see* Starlet. **8.** Star Modelo BKS: *see* Starlight. **9.** Star pistols: *see* panel, pp. 498/99.

Starfire, or Star Modelo DK. A small semi-automatic pistol made by Star–Bonifacio Echeverria SA, from 1957 to the present day. It chambers the 9mm Short (.380 ACP) cartridge and can be obtained in a variety of finishes. *See also* Starlet.

Starlet, or Star Modelo CU. A replacement for the Star Modelo CO pocket pistol, this small blowback semi-automatic pattern appeared in 1957. Chambered for the .25 ACP cartridge, it has been offered with a blue or chrome-plated steel slide, and aluminium-alloy frames anodised black, blue, gold, green or grey. *See also* Starfire.

Starlight, or Star Modelo BKS. A compact Colt-Browning-type semi-automatic pistol made by Star–Bonifacio Echeverria SA in 1970–81. It was chambered for the 9mm Parabellum cartridge and had a 4.25in barrel.

Staron, Saint-Étienne, France. Listed during 1933 as a gunmaker.

Starr – 1. Ebenezer Townsend Starr, Yonkers, New York State, USA. Starr was a prolific designer, among his firearms patents being US no. 14,118 of 15 January 1856 for a 'revolving firearm'. He received additional protection in December 1860, when US Patent 30,843 was granted to protect an improved trigger system; a bar-type safety mechanism followed on 20 December 1864 in US Patent 45,532. The distinctive cap-lock revolver was built in considerable quantity prior to 1864 by the Starr Arms Company. The Starr breech-loading carbine, patented in September 1858 (21,523), was tested favourably at Washington Arsenal in January 1858. Somewhat like the *Sharps externally, it was made in large numbers during the American Civil War. **2.** Starr Arms Company, Binghamton and Yonkers, New York State. This US gunmaking business (active 1858–67) made large quantities of cap-lock revolvers in accordance with US patents granted to Ebenezer Starr (above) in 1856. These were .36- and .44-calibre self-cockers embodying an early *double-action trigger mechanism with an additional 'hesitation element', possibly inspired by the two-trigger *Tranter or *North & Savage designs. The first Starr revolvers to see military service were acquired by the US Navy in 1858, but a single-action .44 version was introduced in 1864 to facilitate production. The single-action trigger system was based on patents granted to Starr in December 1860 (US no. 30,843) and Thomas Gibson in April 1864 (42,435), and a few even had a bar-type safety on the side of the hammer, patented by Starr at the end of December 1864 (45,532). Much of the production work was sub-contracted to the *Savage Revolving Fire-Arms Company; by the middle of 1866, nearly 48,000 Starr handguns had been purchased by the Federal government. The .54-calibre Starr carbine resembled the Sharps carbine externally, but was rather more angular and had a longer receiver. Its two-piece radial breech-block was locked by a wedge as the actuating lever was closed. A conventional side-hammer cap-lock provided satisfactory ignition. Three thousand guns were ordered in February 1865, chambered for the .56-52 Spencer rim-fire cartridge. They had a new breech-block, fitted with an ejector, and a modified hammer with a short straight shank. Newly-made rimfire guns had iron furniture instead of brass. Federal purchases amounted to 25,603 Starr carbines prior to the end of June 1866.

State... – 1. State Arms Company. A brandname associated with shotguns made by the *Crescent Arms Company. **2.** State Industry Factory, Shanghai, People's Republic of China. This unit, part of the nationalised Chinese engineering industry, makes airguns under a number of different names and model designations, the first of which appeared in Britain in 1973. The guns appear to be the Models 45-3 (*Lion), 55 (*Super Hunter), 61 (*Hunter), 62 (*Pioneer) and *Arrow, plus a pistol designated Model 1. **3.** State Industry and Munitions Factory, Port Said, Egypt. Believed to have been the maker of the *Ramses 4.5mm air rifle, in addition to Rashid rifles and the Port Said submachine-gun.

Statham. Albert Edward Statham, an employee of *Webley & Scott (in whose name his patents were also filed), was responsible for some of the features of the Mark 2 rifle, otherwise known as the *Service or New

Service. The three patents were: 371,548 of 1932 for the method by which the barrel is cammed back into its seat to prevent air leakage; 388,547 of 1933 for the secondary sear, preventing premature release of the piston; and 388,548 of 1933 for the quickly-detachable barrel.

Statical. This fixed-barrel recoilless 5.6mm rifle was made by *El Gamo and distributed in Britain by *ASI.

'STB'. Found on US military firearms and accessories. *See* Samuel T. *Bugbee.

Stebbins. John C. Stebbins, a government arms inspector, accepted *cap-lock firearms made by Henry *Deringer, Henry *North and Asa *Waters in the 1830s. They were marked 'JCS' and can be distinguished from the guns marked by John C. *Symmes by type. *See also* US arms inspectors' marks.

Stechkin. Igor Yakovlevich Stechkin, son of a doctor, was born near Tula in 1922 and graduated from the Tula Mechanical Institute shortly after the end of the Second World War. He designed the 9mm *APS, a selective-fire 9x18 pistol used in small numbers in the 1950s. However, the gun was much too light to function effectively in automatic fire, even when attached to its holster-stock, and was made only in comparatively small numbers. The APB

STAR PISTOLS

Star (9)

The earliest guns associated with this name were 6.35mm Mannlicher-style Modelo 1908 and Modelo 1914 blowbacks made in Eibar by the *Echeverria brothers (until 1910), then by Bonifacio Echeverria alone. The Modelo Militar 1, or 'Model 1 Military', was an enlarged version of the pocket pistols, chambered for the 7.65mm cartridge. The last guns of this type were not sold until 1929, although they had probably been in stock for some years. Commercial examples sometimes chambered the 6.35mm or 9mm Short rounds instead of the much more popular 7.65mm type.

After the First World War, the Echeverria management decided that the locked-breech *Colt-Browning pistol had more to commend it than an experimental locked-breech adaptation of the Military Model 1 that had been offered to the French. The Modelo Militar 1920 embodied a conventional Browning dropping-link barrel depressor, although some of its constructional details – especially the radial safety drum mounted in the slide – mirrored the Echeverria-modified Mannlichers.

The failure of the M1920 to interest the army – it was taken only in small numbers by the Guardia Civil – led to the Modelo 1921.

This embodied a grip-safety mechanism, but it was rapidly superseded by the perfected Modelo 1922 with a plain backstrap. The 9mm Largo M1922 was adopted by the Guardia Civil on 5 October 1922, and many examples have been found with an enrayed coronet mark on the left side of the slide. It is essentially a 1911-type Colt-Browning, with a coil-type main spring, changes in the trigger and the omission of a grip-safety lever.

Known commercially as the Modelo A, chambered for the 7.63mm Mauser, 9mm Largo, .38 ACP and .45 ACP cartridges, the M1922 formed the basis for a range of locked-breech Star pistols. The Modelo AD was a selective-fire variant of the Modelo A, with a selector on the right side of the slide; this was protected by a Spanish patent granted to Bonifacio Echeverria in February 1930 (no. 116,773).

The A-type guns were replaced in 1931 by the more robust M-patterns: semi-automatic Modelo M, selective-fire Modelo MD, and a rarely-encountered variant of the MD incorporating a rate reducer patented in Spain in February 1934 (no. 133,526).

Rate-reducing pistols would have been adopted in Siam as the 80th Year Type, production machinery having been delivered from Greenwood & Batley of Leeds, but the advent of the Second World

War prevented series production. Military Model MD pistols usually have tangent-leaf back sights and combination shoulder stock/holsters.

The Super Star series appeared after the Second World War. This consisted of adaptations of the A, B, M and P pistols with a loaded-chamber indicator and a magazine safety system, while dismantling had been made easier. Introduced in 1941, the Star Modelo S was a small version of the Modelo A, lacking the grip safety; it was chambered for the 7.65mm Auto cartridge. The contemporary Modelo SI was similar, but adapted for the 9mm Short round. Both patterns were discontinued in 1965. The Super S and Super SI (1946–72) had loaded-chamber indicators and magazine-safety systems. They were replaced by the Star Super SM, discontinued in 1982, which had an adjustable back sight.

Other guns included the Star Modelo CO Pocket, made from 1941 until 1957, and its replacement, the CU *Starlet. The Modelo DK and HK, known as the *Starfire and the *Lancer respectively, were essentially similar to the Starlet.

A range of .22-calibre pistols has been offered in the F-series: the Star Modelo F had a 100mm barrel and fixed sights; the Modelo FS had a 150mm barrel and adjustable sights; and the Modelo F Olimpico, supplied only in .22 Short, had a

was a silenced version credited to Vladimir *Simonov.

Steel... – **1.** Steel City Arms, Inc., Pittsburgh, Pennsylvania, USA. Makers of the .22 *Double Deuce and .25 *Two Bit Special pistols. **2.** Steeltown. Found on shotgun cartridges sold by Charles *Maleham of Sheffield and London, 'Steeltown' being Sheffield's nickname. They were made prior to the First World War by *Eley Bros.

Steiger. W. von Steiger (Thun, Switzerland). This gunsmith made 15,200 M1869 *Vetterli rifles for the Swiss government in 1869–74.

Steigleder – **1.** Ernst Steigleder, Suhl in Thüringen, Germany. Listed in 1914 and 1920 as a gunmaker, and in 1930 as a maker of weapons and ammunition, Steigleder was best known in the Suhl district as a wholesaler. Premises were clearly maintained elsewhere, as the 1930 Suhl directory entry is qualified as '(Zwgn.)', for *Zweigniederlassung* ('branch office'). The business has been accorded some modern glory – perhaps misleadingly – by W.H.B. Smith, in *Gas, Air & Spring Guns of the World* (1957), who claimed that Steigleder was one of Germany's major airgun distributors. It is possible that Steigleder's wares were distinguished by the unattributed brandname *Precision, but nothing else is proven. **2.** Franz Steigleder, Suhl in Thüringen. Operating, according to the *Deutsches Reichs-Adressbuch* of 1939, as a gunsmith.

Stein – **1.** William Stein, Camden, New Jersey, USA. This gunmaker was trading from 215 Market Street from 1860 until 1869, and thereafter at 309 Federal Street. In 1874, the company became William Stein & Son, then William Stein Jr & Bros. – well known locally as a sporting-goods store – and was still trading under the management of Hermann Engel in the early 1960s as the William Stein Company (a style adopted in 1914/15). **2.** Stein & Hunter, Cape Town, Cape Province. A distributor of *Guedes rifles in southern Africa in the early 1890s.

'Steinbok'. A brandname found on shotgun cartridges probably made by *Pulverfabrik Hasloch prior to the First World War.

Steinecke. E. Th. Steinecke, Suhl in Thüringen, Germany. Listed in 1900 as a gunmaker (*büchsenmacherei*).

'Steiner'. A name of unknown significance found on a spring-air gallery pistol made by *Wirsing & Schemann of Cincinatti, Ohio, USA.

Stella. A series of airguns, mainly barrel-cocking rifles, made by L. *Kotek AS of Prague c. 1933–43. Also associated with *Kovo AS.

185mm barrel with adjustable counterweights. All three patterns were introduced in 1942 and discontinued in 1967, when the modernised Star Modelo FR appeared. This was made for a few years only, although the Modelo FM (with a heavy frame and a trigger-guard web) and Modelo FRS (with a 150mm barrel) lasted into the 1990s.

The Modelo BKS, or *Starlight, was a compact 9mm Parabellum derivative of the standard Colt-Browning guns; the Modelo BM and Modelo BKM were similar, but had steel and aluminium-alloy frames respectively; and the Modelo PD (1975 to date) was a short-barrelled .45 ACP variant with adjustable sights.

The traditional Star pistols were supplemented by a range of pistols based on the tipping-barrel *Colt-Brownings, but with their lockwork mounted on a readily detachable sub-assembly. The slide of the 9mm Parabellum Modelo 28 DA (1983–84) ran on rails inside the frame, a radial safety lever lay high on the slide, and a fifteen-round staggered-column magazine was used. The barrel was 110mm long. The retraction grooves were badly placed, however, being extended forward on the compact Model 28 PDA, introduced in 1984, which had a 98mm barrel; the Model 28 PKDA was similar, but had an aluminium-alloy frame.

The perfected Modelo 30 (1985 to date) is a 9mm double-action gun. The 30M has a steel frame, whereas the 30PK has an alloy version. Introduced in 1990 in 9mm Parabellum and .40 S&W, the Star Modelo 31 is a compact short-barrelled version with ambidextrous controls. PK versions of the Models 30 and 31 were offered with aluminium-alloy frames, but

A group of Star pistols: top to bottom: Model 28DA, Model PD, Model BK and Model SS.

apparently had been discontinued by 1991. Other derivatives of the new double-action guns include the M40, M43 and M45 *Firestar (introduced during 1990–92), and the *Megastar of 1992.

Stenda – **1.** Stenda pistol. A 7.65mm *Beholla-type semi-automatic, made in Suhl in the early 1920s by Stenda-Werke GmbH. **2.** Stenda-Werke GmbH, Abteilung Waffen, Suhl in Thüringen and Gemünden am Main, Germany. This gunmaking business appears to have been formed immediately after the end of the First World War, possibly in 1919, and was listed in the *Deutsches Reichs-Adressbuch* for 1920. An advertisement dating from 1925 notes that Stenda made 'hunting and best-quality guns, specialising in the Stenda self-loading pistol', but trading seems to have ceased in the late 1920s. Stenda-Werke may have acquired the business of *Becker & Hollander after the First World War, inheriting sufficient components to enable assembly of handguns to be continued for several years.

Stendebach – **1.** Fr. Stendebach, Suhl in Thüringen, Germany. A gunmaker operating in 1914. **2.** Karl F.P. Stendebach of Leipzig-Gohls, Germany, received US Patent 804,349 of 14 November 1905, to protect a 'firearm with drop-down barrel'.

Sten Gun. *See* panel, facing page.

Stensby – **1.** Robert Stensby, Manchester, Lancashire. This gunsmith traded from 11 Hanging Ditch in 1837, but died c. 1853. The business was listed until 1869 as Mrs M. Stensby & Son, and it is assumed that eventually the son – possibly named Thomas – traded independently. *See* T. Stensby & Company (below). **2.** T. Stensby & Company, Manchester, Lancashire. Possibly the successor to Robert Stensby (above), by way of his widow, this gunmaking business traded for many years from Withy Grove, Manchester. Among its products were shotgun cartridges, one of the tradenames being The All British.

Stepanov. Co-designer with Konstantin *Baryshev of the tripod mount for the 12.7mm *NSV machine-gun and, by himself, of a perfected 4.5kg tripod mount for the *Kalashnikov PKS machine-gun, which superseded the Samozhenkov type from 1969 onward. A special bracket on the tripod allowed a cartridge-belt box to be attached.

Stephanoise [Société d'Armes]. *See* Société Stephanoise d'Armes.

Stephens – **1.** Stephens, Smith & Company. Agent for the Swedish *AGA sub-calibre trainer, six being acquired by the British authorities for experiments in 1939. **2.** *See also* Stevens.

Sterling – **1.** A *Suicide Special revolver made by *E.L. Dickinson of Springfield, Massachusetts, USA, in the late nineteenth century. **2.** A brandname associated with shotguns made in the USA by the *Crescent Arms Company. **3.** A single-shot break-action BB Gun made by the American Tool Works, 1891–1911. Designer unknown. *See also* Sterling Special. **4.** A single-shot lever-action BB Gun, designed by Arthur *Karcher and made by the *American Tool Works in 1911–12. *See also* Sterling Lever Action. **5.** Sterling Armament & Company Ltd, Dagenham, Essex, England. Maker of 7.62mm conversion units for the L8-series Lee-Enfield rifles, marked with the code letters 'US'. However, the *Enfield factory brought pressure to bear on Sterling over patent rights, and the propects of export success (e.g. in India) were greatly handicapped. *ArmaLite AR-18 rifles were produced in 1976–78, but Sterling is best known for its submachine-guns. The HR81 and HR83 air rifles were made briefly in the 1980s, but then the assets were sold to a Canadian consortium. In addition to guns, Sterling marketed shotgun ammunition under its own name. Apparently this was loaded elsewhere in Britain, although its origins are not clear. **6.** Sterling Arms Corporation, Lockport and Gasport, New York State. Sterling made a variety of auto-loading pistols, including the .25-calibre Model 300 and the .22 Model 302. **7.** Sterling Automatic Rifle. This was developed by Frank Waters for the *Sterling Engineering Company Ltd of Dagenham, but was little more than a modified *ArmaLite AR-18. Subsequently it was refined by *Chartered Industries of Singapore to become the SAR-80 and SR-88. **8.** Sterling Engineering Company, Dagenham, Essex, England. This metalworking business made about 59,000 *Lanchester submachine-guns during the Second World War, then progressed to the *Patchett design, which ultimately became known as the Sterling. A few De Lisle carbines were also produced, beginning in 1944. The Dagenham plant was allotted the code 'S 109', but according to British official records, the Sterling Armaments Company, Northampton used 'M 619'. *See also* British military manufacturers' marks. **9.** Sterling Lever Action Repeater. A 500- or 1,000-shot version of the 1911-pattern Sterling lever-action BB Gun, made by the *Upton Machine Company and *All-Metal Products Company between 1917 and 1929. The guns are usually marked 'American Tool Works, St Joseph'. **10.** Sterling Special. The break-open Sterling BB Gun made by the Upton Machine Company between 1917 and 1927, and the All-Metal Products Company from 1927 to 1929. The guns are marked 'American Tool Works, St Joseph'. **11.** Sterling (Patchett) submachine-gun. Designed by George V. Patchett, twenty guns of this type were made by the Sterling Engineering Company Ltd in January 1944, and others were used during the D-Day landings in June. The Patchett defeated rival designs in post-war testing and, after troop trials held in 1949, was approved in 1951 as the 'Submachine-gun, 9mm L2A1'. Ribs on the bolt minimised the accumulation of fouling. The L2A2 followed in 1953: the folding butt was strengthened, the back sight was improved and a plunger was added to the bolt. The perfected L2A3 (1954) had a simpler butt and lacked the back-sight change lever. A Sterling with a large-diameter integral silencer is currently issued for special service as the L34A1, replacing the Stens IIS and Mk 6. More information about these guns can be obtained from *The Guns of Dagenham*, by Peter Laidler and David Howroyd (Collector Grade Publications, 1995).

'Stern' – **1.** A trademark found on 6.35mm-calibre blowback pistols made in Germany in the early 1920s by Albin *Wahl of Zella-Mehlis. Most of them had a ten-round magazine, housed in an extended grip; however, although marked 'WAHL'S D.R.G.M.' on the left side of the slide, they are unremarkable mechanically. **2.** This mark, which appears in Gustav Genschow catalogues, is believed to identify spring-airguns made by Friedrich *Langenhan in the mid-1920s.

Sternenkreuz. *See* Joseph *Rodgers.

Stevens – **1.** Edgar M. Stevens, Medford, Massachusetts. Co-designer with Francis J. Vittum of a rifle with a laterally-sliding breech-block, protected by US Patent 33,560 of 22 October 1861. This was assigned to Alfred B. *Ely. **2.** Joshua Stevens, Chicopee Falls, Massachusetts, USA. Born in 1814, this gunmaker is best

STEN GUN

Designed by Reginald V. Shepherd and Harold Turpin of the Royal Small Arms Factory, Enfield, this *blowback 9x19 submachine-gun was designed to be made by inexperienced sub-contractors. Approved in 1940, the 'Machine Carbine, Sten, 9mm Mark I' was made by the Singer Manufacturing Company Ltd from 1941 onward. It had a folding hand grip, a wooden butt insert and a flash-hider/compensator on the muzzle. The simplified Mark I* had a skeletal butt, and lacked the fore-end and flash-hider assembly. Singer made over 300,000 Mark I and I* guns.

The Sten Mark II had a simple tube butt and a short cylindrical barrel casing. The magazine housing could be rotated to seal the feed aperture when required, but variations in fitting and construction depended on the origins of the parts. Guns were assembled by *BSA Guns Ltd (404,383 in Tyseley from September 1941); by the Royal Ordnance Factories in Fazakerley and Theale; and in Canada.

The Mark III was made exclusively by *Lines Bros. Ltd from 1942 onward, production eventually totalling about 880,000. Its one-piece receiver/barrel jacket, made from sheet-steel tubing, had a prominent weld seam along the top of the gun. The Mark 4A Sten was an experimental short-barrel paratroop weapon with a pressed-steel shoulder-piece pivoted on the underside of the pistol grip; the Mark 4B was similar, but its pistol grip/butt arrangements differed. The Mark 5 was an improved Mark II, made in Fazakerley and Theale, with a wooden butt and pistol grip.

Produced for commandos and Special Forces, the Sten Mark IIS (Theale and Fazakerley, 1944) had a shortened barrel and a silencer threaded on to the receiver. The Mark 6 (Enfield and Theale, 1944–46) was a silenced Mark 5, distinguished from the Mark IIS by its wooden butt. Production amounted to 4,184,237 Stens by March 1945, more than half the guns emanating from the Royal Ordnance Factory in Fazakerley, where 2,350,000 assorted Marks II, IIS and 5 had been produced in 1941–45. *Small Arms Ltd of Long Branch, Ontario, manufactured 128,238 Mark II Stens for the Canadian armed forces.

The 9mm Mark 1 Sten Gun was better made than its successors, with a folding hand grip, a short wooden fore-end and a compensator attached to the muzzle. All these features were soon abandoned, partly to cut costs, but also to accelerate production.

known for his inexpensive single-shot pistols and target rifles. Although these guns were made in large numbers, Stevens was not a great patentee. Beginning with a 'locking device for firearms', US Patent 7802 of 26 November 1850, he obtained 8412 of 7 October 1851 for a 'revolving firearm' (assigned to the *Massachusetts Arms Company); 9929 of 9 August 1853, protecting a trigger mechanism that relied on thumb-cocking the hammer to operate the *Maynard primer and a pull on the trigger lever to rotate the cylinder; and 12,189 of 2 January 1855 for 'magazine firearms' (also assigned to the Massachusetts Arms Company) for an improved mechanism that rotated the cylinder before the hammer was cocked. US Patent 44,123 of 6 September 1864 protected a single-shot pistol with a barrel that tipped upward at the breech. A combination rifle-shotgun, protected by US Patent 211,642 of 28 January 1879, relied on a 'locking trigger' in an auxiliary guard to lock a sliding under-bolt mechanism. **3.** J. Stevens Arms & Tool Company, Chicopee Falls, Masschusetts. Stevens began trading on his account in 1864, making single-shot cartridge pistols. He soon turned his attention to rifles, and made 12-, 14- and 16-bore shotguns on the basis of his *Pocket Rifle (although the barrels could be as long as 32in). A 10- or 12-bore Stevens-patent double-barrelled hammer gun was introduced in 1877, to be followed c. 1880 by a rifle-shotgun made in accordance with Stevens' patent of January 1879. The Stevens Arms & Tool Company was incorporated in 1886, and eventually was absorbed by the *Savage Arms Company. A list of its many products will be found in John Walter, *Rifles of the World* (Krause Publications, second edition, 1998). **4.** Stevens-Savage: *see* Savage Arms Company. **5.** *See also* Stephens.

Stevenson. T.J. Stevenson, an arms inspector working for the US government in the 1870s, accepted *Springfield breech-loading-rifle components marked 'TJS'. *See also* T.J. *Smith and US arms inspectors' marks.

Steward. Gilbert H. Steward, a colonel in the US Army, accepted *Colt and *Smith & Wesson handguns immediately before the USA entered the First World War in 1917. They were marked 'GHS', date and pattern distinguishing them from guns accepted more than fifty years earlier by Gustavus H. *Scott. *See also* US arms inspectors' marks.

Stewart. P. Stewart. An English gunmaker listed in 1861–70 at 25 Denmark Street, Soho, London, then at 16 Denmark Street in 1871.

Steyr... – **1.** *See also* Österreichische Waffenfabriks-Gesellschaft'. **2.** Found as 'STEYR' within concentric circles, some broken into arcs: a mark associated with *Österreichische Waffenfabriks-Gesellschaft and its successor, Steyr-Mannlicher GmbH. **3.** Steyr-Daimler-Puch AG, Steyr, Kärnten, Upper Austria. This combine continued to make *Mannlicher-action sporting rifles and submachine-guns alongside modified Model 1934 *Pieper-type automatic pistols. Guns may be encountered with the marks of Steyr-Solothurn AG, but usually prove to have been made in the Steyr factory. **4.** Steyr-Hahn. The Austro-Hungarian *Repetierpistole M. 12* derived from the same basic recoil-operated rotating-barrel action as the *Roth-Steyr, but had been refined greatly by Steyr technicians as a commercial venture. When the First World War began, the Austro-Hungarians were so short of combat-worthy handguns that the Steyr-Hahn was ordered into series production. By 1918, more than 250,000 pistols had been made. Many survived to serve German police and paramilitary formations during the Second World War, converted to chamber the 9x19 (9mm Parabellum) cartridge. These are usually stamped '08' for *Pistolenpatrone 08* to identify the change. **5.** Steyr-Mannlicher GmbH. The current title of the small-arms and sporting-gun division of Steyr-Daimler-Puch, formed in 1990. Current products include *Mannlicher-style sporting, target and sniper rifles, submachine-guns and the *AUG assault-rifle series, but pistols have also been made in small numbers. **6.** Steyr-Solothurn AG, Austria/Switzerland. This co-operative venture originated in 1929 when *Rheinmetall absorbed Solothurn, a small Swiss engineering company, so that German-designed weapons could be field-tested. The guns, including machine-guns and small-calibre automatic cannon, were made by *Steyr-Daimler-Puch and marketed by Steyr-Solothurn AG (apparently from 1933/34 onward). Work ceased in Switzerland upon the outbreak of the Second World War, although Solothurn continued to trade in a revised form.

Sticht. J.L. Sticht, Jr, a lieutenant in the US Navy at the beginning of the twentieth century, accepted *Colt and *Smith & Wesson .38 revolvers marked 'JLS'. Pattern and naval marks distinguish them from army stores accepted at the same time by J.L. *Strong. *See also* US arms inspectors' marks.

Sticknet. Curtis R. Sticknet, or 'Sticknett'. This government arms inspector, working in the 1870s, accepted single-shot *Springfield, *Sharps and *Remington rifles, and Remington *rolling-block pistols marked 'CRS'. *See also* US arms inspectors' marks.

Stiegle. Carl Stiegle, Berlin, Germany. Best known as a maker, or distributor, of *Heeren-action sporting guns prior to 1914.

Stiga. This brandname is associated with the products of 'Stiga'–Stig Hjelmqvist AB of Trånas, a maker and distributor of firearms, sporting goods, 'Stiga Dogg' airgun pellets and accessories. Stiga AB made rifles based on refurbished M1896 military actions in .270 Winchester, .30-06 and 8x57mm. Single-trigger systems were standard, although a double set pattern was optional.

Stiles Brothers, Warminster, Wiltshire, England. The marks of this gunsmithing and ironmongery business have been reported on shotgun ammunition sold as The Kill Quick.

Stillman. James Stillman, working on behalf of the US government c. 1830–50, accepted guns and equipment marked 'JS'. *See also* John *Stahl, John *Symington and US arms inspectors' marks.

Stinger. The US Office of Strategic Services (OSS) made limited use during the Second World War of this single-shot .22 pen-pistol, which was comparable with the *Enpen, with the exception that the .22 Short cartridge was integral with the fabric of the weapon. The Stinger was fired by raising a short lever set into the body, which armed the striker. Replacing the lever released the striker and fired the cartridge. Then the gun, which was only about 3½in long and weighed less than half an ounce, was simply thrown away.

Stingray, or RSM Stingray. Associated with a 6.35mm pocket pistol made in Germany by *Reck, probably for one of its North American distributors.

Stirrup pistols. A matched pair of these sold at an auction in Toronto in 1935, but there is nothing to suggest that they were unique. Apparently they had been made in France in the 1860s and found in Bordeaux in 1917. One of the two-shot stirrups faced backward, discouraging pursuit, while the other pointed forward to assist an attack. They were fired by means of lanyards.

St Louis Air-Rifle Company, Inc. See Benjamin Air Rifle Company.

Stobbe. Albert Stobbe, Suhl in Thüringen, Germany. Founded in 1865, and still being listed in 1914 as a gunmaker. By 1930, however, the business was being run by Witwe Emilie and Rudolf Stobbe.

Stock – **1.** *See* panel, facing page. **2.** Franz Stock & Companie, Berlin. A member of the family controlling Richard Stock & Co., one of Germany's leading tool makers, Franz Stock diversified between the wars to make substantial numbers of an inexpensive target pistol. **3.** Stock pistol. This was a simple blowback semi-automatic pistol, with a combination of slab-sided slide and a tubular barrel shroud, somewhat reminiscent of the Römer pattern. It could be chambered for .22 LR rimfire, 6.35mm or 7.65mm centrefire cartridges. Guns made in the 1930s, numbered above about 10000, had a faired transition from the frame to the barrel shroud, without the step that characterised their predecessors.

Stocker – **1.** A.J. Stocker & Son, Chulmleigh, Devon. An ironmongery business known to have promoted shotgun cartridges under the tradename The Chulmleigh. **2.** C. & E. Stocker, Chulmleigh, Devon. Believed to have succeeded A.J. Stocker & Son in the 1950s; presumably the principals were A.J.'s sons. Details are lacking.

Stocking & Company, Worcester, Massachusetts, USA. Active in 1849–52, this gunmaking business was best known for pepperboxes.

Stockton. Howard Stockton, a lieutenant in the US Army, accepted guns and equipment marked 'HS'. Apparently his inspection duties were confined to 1868/69, but it can be difficult to distinguish his work from that of H. *Saunders, Horace *Scott, Harris *Smith and Howard *Stockton – all of whom used the same marks. *See also* US arms inspectors' marks.

Stoeger – **1.** A.F. Stoeger & Company, New York, Long Island City and South Hackensack, New Jersey, USA. This company was founded by Austrian-born Adolf Stoeger c. 1922, trading from 606 West 49th Street in New York City. A move to 224 East 42nd Street took place in 1924, then to 509 Fifth Avenue (1928–60); a

STOCK

Stock (1)

The stock of a gun contains, or supports, the barrel and action. It comprises the butt, grip and fore-end, but may be made in one piece or two. Originally wood, military stocks are now generally synthetic. Wood remains pre-eminent among the sporting patterns, despite an ever-increasing challenge from fibreglass, Kevlar and other synthetics, which offer durability and warp resistance.

A one-piece sporting stock extending to the muzzle is normally called a Mannlicher pattern, on no defensible authority; full-length stocks have been used almost since the dawn of gunsmithing. The Rational stock, proposed by W.W. ★Greener shortly before the First World War, was basically similar to the German *Schweinsruckenschaft* (below). The butt had a pistol grip and a high rounded comb, which turned down as it approached the wrist. The cheek support was moved back toward the heel to reduce the blow to the cheek arising from recoil, the result being an essentially primitive form of the Monte Carlo stock.

Popular in southern Germany and some parts of central Europe, the Hog's Back stock, or *Schweinsruckenschaft*, had a distinctive

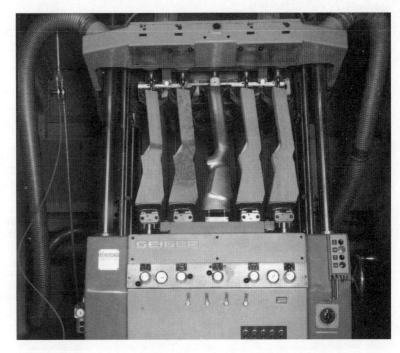

curved comb, dropping at the wrist and the heel. It was often combined with a squared cheek-piece angled to direct recoil away from the firer's cheek. The Tyrolean stock, or *Tirolerschaft*, popular in southern Germany, Switzerland and Austria, has an extraordinarily high comb and a deeply-dished cheek-piece, which must be shaped to deflect recoil back and away from the firer's cheek.

Modern gun stocks are made on computer-controlled copying machines, allowing several to be produced simultaneously simply by following a master pattern. These are Mayer & Grammelspacher Diana airgun stocks, made of fine-grained beech.

---

storehouse in Long Island City finally opened in 1948, but all of Stoeger's operations finally moved in 1962 to purpose-built premises in South Hackensack. The firm is best known for its association with the ★Parabellum pistol (registering the name 'Luger' in the USA in 1929), but it also imported bolt-action sporting rifles built on Oberndorf- and FN-Mauser actions prior to 1939. Many ★Mayer & Grammelspacher ★Diana airguns were handled in the 1933–59 period, often under the ★Peerless brand-name and an assortment of model designations. Stoeger's original trademark consisted of flying geese, although two seated bald eagles were used at a later date. **2.** Stoeger Industries, Hackensack, New Jersey, USA. The modern successor to A.F. Stoeger & Company (above), renowned for the distribution of Daewoo, Husqvarna and other firearms. Stoeger also guards its ownership of the Luger trademark in the USA, and has been sponsoring blowback and recoil-operated Stoeger Luger and American Luger derivatives since the 1970s.

Stogos. A trademark associated with ★Stotz u. Goessl of Suhl.

Stohanzl. Victor Johann Stohanzl, Birmingham, Warwickshire, England. This Austrian-born employee of ★BSA was the co-patentee of a piston-valve for pneumatic

guns (British Patent 571,163, accepted on 9 August 1945).

Stokes. John Stokes. An American-born co-patentee, with Daniel ★Wesson and John Blaze, of the ★Wesson shotgun. *See* US Patents 72,434 of 17 December 1867 and 84,314 ('gun lock') of 24 November 1868.

Stoll – 1. E. Stoll, Suhl in Thüringen, Germany. Listed in the *Deutsches Reichs-Adressbuch* for 1900, this gunmaking business was owned at that time by E. Lieber. **2.** Ernst Stoll, Suhl in Thüringen, Döllstrasse 4–6 (1940–41). Listed in directories published between 1914 and 1941 as a maker of gun barrels (*Gewehrlauffabrik*), owned by Max Heinrich Stoll.

Stone. Laurence A. Stone, an army lieutenant, accepted .45 M1911A1 pistols made by ★Colt shortly before the USA entered the Second World War. They were marked 'LAS'. *See also* US arms inspectors' marks.

Stoner – 1. Eugene Morrison 'Gene' Stoner was born in Gasport, Indiana, in November 1922. Graduating from technical high school, he worked for Vega Air Craft (subsequently part of Lockheed), then served with the US Marine Corps during the Second World War. Stoner joined the Fairchild Airplane Company in 1954, intending to develop lightweight infantry weapons that could be marketed by the new Fairchild-inspired ★ArmaLite

Company, and the chequered development of the AR-3, AR-7, AR-10 and AR-15 has been related many times. Eventually Fairchild sold the rights to Artillerie-Inrichtingen in the Netherlands, but subsequently they were retrieved by *Colt's Patent Fire Arms Manufacturing Company. The introduction of the M16 and M16A1 rifles to the US armed forces remains not only controversial, but also the focus of more than one Congressional enquiry. However, by then, Stoner had moved on to the Cadillac Gage Company, designing the Stoner 63 weapons system and becoming involved in projects ranging from the Colt Model 2000 pistol to a 25mm aircraft cannon. He died in Palm Beach in April 1997. **2.** Stoner weapons system. The adoption of the 5.56x45 'intermediate' cartridge inspired development of systems in which basic components could be assembled to provide a range of weapons, from a sub-machine-gun to a tripod-mounted belt-fed infantry-support weapon. The Stoner M63 and M63A1 attempted to challenge the supremacy of the M16 *ArmaLite rifle in the late 1960s. Made initially by the Cadillac Gage Company, then licensed to *NWM, the Stoner system was based on a standard pistol-gripped receiver that could be assembled to form an assault rifle, a carbine, a light machine-gun with top-mounted box feed, a similar gun with belt feed, a belt-fed infantry-support machine-gun mounted on a tripod, and even a stripped-down vehicle gun. All relied on a simple gas-operated rotating bolt lock. The system encountered limited success when a few XM22 rifles and XM207 light machine-guns were purchased for the US Special Forces, but combat experience showed the Stoners to be delicate and prone to jamming. Although the faults could have been overcome had funding been available, the weapons-system concept was abandoned.

Stop – 1. A single-shot .320 blank/gas-cartridge pistol resembling the mechanical propelling pencils popular in the inter-war period. It is believed to have been made by *Moritz & Gerstenberger of Zella-Mehlis. **2.** A Hungarian pistol; see Frommer-Stop.

Storekeeper's Model. A black-powder .45-calibre version of the Third Model *Single Action Army Model, offered by the Firearms Division of *Colt Industries in 1984–85, this had a 4in barrel lacking an ejector-rod case. Only a few hundred were made.

Storer. David Storer. Listed in 1852–53 at 10 Craven Buildings, Drury Lane, London, this man was regarded as a member of the English gun trade.

Storm – 1. William Mont Storm, or Mont-Storm (USA), New York City. The affairs of this inventor-patentee remain mysterious, and his name is sometimes regularly, but possibly mistakenly, rendered as Montgomery Storm. Among his US Patents were three for 'breech-loading firearms' (15,307 of 8 July 1856, 24,414 of 14 June 1859 and 132,740 of 5 November 1872) and one for 'revolving firearms', US Patent 14,420 of 11 March 1856. He also patented a bullet mould (10,834 of 25 April 1854), a charging system (10,846 of 2 May 1854), and a combustible cartridge 'of intestines, coated with gutta percha' protected by 33,611 of 29 October 1861. The breech-loader was tested by the Ordnance Department prior to the American Civil War. The weapon had sufficient potential for the conversion of 2,000 Model 1842 muskets to be authorised in September 1858, although little was ever achieved. The Storm breech-block, which swung up and forward over the barrel, was locked by a

sliding bolt as the hammer fell. A pattern to guide production of a similar breech-loading rifle-musket conversion was *sealed in Britain in September 1865. The paper-cartridge guns were to be made in Birmingham by the *Mont Storm Gun Works Company, but were rapidly overhauled by the metallic-cartridge *Snider. **2.** Storm's Breech-Loading Arms Depot. Formed in Britain to promote the breech-loading rifle-musket conversion patented by William Mont *Storm, this firm occupied premises at 121 Pall Mall, London, in 1864–65.

Störmer – 1. Albert Störmer, Suhl in Thüringen, Germany. Listed in 1939 as a gunsmith. **2.** E.A. Störmer, Herzberg in Harz, Germany. A maker of crank-wound volute-spring breech-loading gallery pistols, probably during 1840–65, Störmer had produced Girandoni-system reservoir guns in the 1820s.

Storrs. J.W. Storrs. A leading distributor of guns and ammunition in the 1860s and 1870s.

Stosel. A compact Spanish-made Browning-type automatic pistol made by *Retolaza Hermanos of Eibar: (a) 6.35mm, six rounds, hammer fired, sometimes marked 'No. 1' or 'Model 1912'; (b) 7.65mm 'Model 1912', six rounds, striker fired; and (c) 7.65mm 'Model 1913', seven rounds, hammer fired. Named after a famous Russian soldier.

Stotz & Goessl, Suhl in Thüringen, Erffastrasse 16. A weapons-making partnership active in 1930–39 under the ownership of Leopold Stotz. Listed during the Second World War as a gunmaker, using the trademark Stogos.

Stötzer. Hilmar Stötzer, Zella-Mehlis in Thüringen. A master gunmaker founded in 1905 and active in Germany until the end of the Second World War. Erroneously listed in the 1939 edition of the *Deutsches Reichs-Adressbuch* as Stötzner.

Straube – 1. Dieter Straube, Ulm am Donau, Germany. An employee of J.G. *Anschütz and patentee of a loading port for an airgun (German no. 2,555,973). **2.** Johann Straube, Berlin. The patentee of a spring-loaded barrel-locking system for airguns, briefly mentioned in *Die Waffenschmiede* in 1887.

Streak. See Blue Streak and Silver Streak.

Streels. J. Streels, Liège, Belgium. This gunmaker was famed for highly-decorative single-shot cap-lock and pin-fire pistols, including one, engraved in gothic style, shown at the Great Exhibition held in London in 1851.

Street. W.W. Street, working on behalf of the US government, accepted gun parts and equipment marked 'WWS'. His activities seem to have been confined to the mid-1870s. See also US arms inspectors' marks.

Streitberger. Karl Streitberger, Rudolfstadt. A supplier of sporting guns and ammunition active in the Thüringen district of Germany during 1940–45.

Strempel – 1. Edgar Strempel, Suhl in Thüringen, Germany. Trading in Suhl in 1930 as a gunmaker, and in 1939 as a gunsmith. **2.** Franz Strempel, Suhl in Thüringen, Germany. A gunmaker trading prior to 1930, often using the trademark 'Stresu' on sporting guns and accessories.

Stresu. A trademark associated with Franz *Strempel of Suhl.

Strickland. E.R. Strickland & Son, Gillingham, Dorsetshire. The marks of this gunmaking, or possibly ironmongery, business have been found on sporting guns and shotgun ammunition sold as The Gillingham Cartridge and The Quick Fire.

Striker – 1. A *Suicide Special revolver made by the *Hopkins & Allen Arms Company of Norwich, Connecticut, USA, in the late nineteenth century. **2.** Also known as the firing pin, this is driven by a spring so that it gains sufficient energy to fire the cartridge primer. There is confusion over the terms 'striker' and 'firing pin', which are interchangeable. Strictly speaking, the term 'inertia firing pin' should be applied only to a floating pin that is driven forward by the hammer to reach the primer of a chambered round, then forced or cammed back to allow the breech to open; now, however, the term is also used to describe the spring-opposed, or rebounding, pattern. The rebounding (or flying) firing pin is shorter than the distance between the hammer and the primer of a chambered cartridge, being driven forward when required, then pushed back into the breech-block or bolt by a small coil spring.

Stringer. William Stringer. This English gunmaker was first recorded in London in Queen's Head Court, Giltspur Street, in 1826, but had made several moves by the time he reached 104 White Lion Street, Pentonville, a decade later. The directories of 1849–63 record him at 86 High Street, Camden Town.

Strong – 1. Daniel P. Strong. This Federal government arms inspector, working during the American Civil War, accepted military equipment marked 'DPS'. **2.** Frederick S. Strong. A Federal arms inspector, working during the American Civil War, Strong accepted firearms marked 'FSS'. **3.** J. Strong & Son, Castle Street and Warwick Road, Carlisle, Cumberland. The marks of this dealership have been recorded on shotgun cartridges bearing a distinctive illustration of six feeding pheasants in woodland. The cases and caps were made by *Eley-Kynoch, although the cartridges may have been loaded in the Carlisle premises. **4.** J.L. Strong, a government arms inspector operating at the beginning of the twentieth century, accepted firearms and military equipment marked 'JLS'. Their army origins distinguish them from navy stores accepted during the same period by Lieutenant J.L. *Sticht. **5.** Urial P. Strong, a Federal government arms inspector working during the Civil War, accepted military equipment marked 'UPS'. **6.** W.E. Strong, a US government arms inspector, accepted .45 M1911 pistols marked 'WES' shortly before the USA entered the First World War in 1917. *See also* US arms inspectors' marks for all previous entries except no. 3. **7.** Strong Cartridge Company, New Haven, Connecticut, USA. A maker of ammunition identifiable by the inclusion of 'S.C.C.' or 'S.C.Co.' in the headstamps.

Ströver. A. Ströver, Nordhausen. A retailer of guns and ammunition active in Germany in 1941.

'Stump' [The]. See Slingsby Guns.

Sturm – 1. Alexander Sturm: *see* Sturm, Ruger & Company. **2.** Christian Sturm, Suhl in Thüringen, Germany. Listed in 1900 as a gunmaker. By 1914, the business had passed to Heinrich & Marie Sturm, but was being run in 1920 by Witwe Marie Sturm alone. **3.** Heinrich Sturm, Benshausen bei Suhl in Thüringen. Listed prior to 1914 as a gunmaker, specalising (unusually in Germany) in the manufacture of revolvers. **4.** Max Sturm & Söhne, Suhl in Thüringen, Germany. A gunmaking business operated by Max, Leo and Curt Sturm during 1920–39. **5.** Sturm, Ruger & Company, Inc.: *see* panel, pp. 506/07.

Sturman – 1. Benjamin Sturman. This English gunmaker was recorded at 17 Union Street, London, in 1832–34, then at 42 (perhaps later 45) Kingsland Road, London, in 1835–56. Premises were listed at 72 Kingsland Road in 1857 only. **2.** George Sturman. A gunmaker listed at 197 Kingsland Road, London, in 1827. The directories reveal successive moves to 27 Gloucester Street, Hoxton (1830–35); 29, then 25 (29 renumbered?) East Road, City Road (1836–48); and to 1 or possibly 2 West Place, Islington (1849–51). A move to 2 Church Row, Islington, occurred in 1852, then to 4a Church Row in 1858. The last directory entries appeared in 1870.

Sturtevant. Foster E. Sturtevant, an engineer employed by *Colt, designed the plunger breech-closing system fitted to the *ArmaLite-type 5.56mm M16A1 rifle.

Stutzen. A name, often used generically, applied to a short-barrelled rifle – often (but not exclusively) stocked to the muzzle.

'St.W.', 'ST W'. Marks associated with *Stenda-Werke GmbH of Suhl, found on the grips of Stenda pistols.

'SU'. A monogram, taking the general form '$'. Used in the *headstamps of ammunition made by the *United States Cartridge Company.

Sub-calibre adaptor, also known as a liner. This may be inserted permanently into a barrel to alter the calibre or serve as an adaptor when required – usually to permit training with low-cost rimfire ammunition. The adaptor was generically known as an *Aiming Tube in Britain, but then became a *Morris Tube after a particularly notable patentee.

Sudaev. Aleksey I. Sudaev (1912–46) is renowned for the design of the PPS submachine-gun, developed in Leningrad during the German siege (1941–44). However, he also contributed two 1945-model Sudaev rifles (a heavy blowback and a folding-butt rotating-bolt pattern) to Avtomat trials undertaken toward the end of the war. A few hundred guns were made for troop trials in 1945, but Sudaev's death brought development to an end.

'Sudden Death' [The]. A shotgun cartridge made by the *Midland Gun Company in Birmingham, England.

Suhler... – 1. Suhler Waffengesellschaft: *see* Wittwer, Schemmer & Mahrholdt GmbH. **2.** Suhler Waffenwerk: *see* Gebr. *Merkel. **3.** Suhler-Werke AG: *see* Berlin-Suhler-Werke.

Sühn – 1. Albert Sühn, Albrechts bei Suhl in Thüringen, Meininger Strasse 11. Listed in 1940–45 as a maker of guns, gun parts and metalware. **2.** Wilhelm Sühn, Albrechts bei Suhl in Thüringen. A maker of gun parts, active prior to c. 1920.

Suicide Special. This term was first applied in 1948 by Duncan McConnell, writing in the *American Rifleman*, to define single-action revolvers that were distinguished by poor quality and, if not by the identity of the manufacturer, at least a wide variety of brandnames. The name achieved broader acceptance after the publication of *Suicide Special Revolvers*, by Donald B. Webster, Jr (1956). Revolvers of this class began to appear as soon as the Rollin *White patent expired in 1869. A typical Suicide Special was a seven-shot .22 or five-shot .32, usually (but not exclusively) chambering rimfire ammunition. The one-piece frame normally had a detachable plate on the left side that gave access to the simple single-action lockwork. Sheath triggers were customary, butts were squared or bird's heads, and the barrels were generally shorter than 3in. The cylinders were loaded

STURM, RUGER & COMPANY

Sturm (5)

This gunmaking business was founded in January 1949 by Alexander Sturm and William B. Ruger, in Southport, Connecticut, to exploit a semi-automatic pistol designed by the latter – a one-time US Ordnance officer. The production facilities moved to a new purpose-built factory in Manchester, New Hampshire, in 1969.

The .22-calibre Mark 1 pistol was protected eventually by US Patent 2,655,839, granted in October 1953, almost seven years after the application had been made. Although a blowback, its name and general outline recalled the German *Luger (no mere coincidence!), and sales were pleasingly brisk. A target-shooting variant was introduced in 1951, and 150,000 pistols of all types had been made by 1957. The Mark 1 was upgraded to the Mark 2 in January 1982, with better magazine and safety arrangements. Blued-steel standard, target and Bull Barrel versions are still being made, alongside guns with stainless-steel metalwork. The Government Target Model (1985) is simply a Mark 2 Bull Barrel Ruger with a barrel length of 6.9in.

Ruger also makes locked-breech pistols on the basis of a much-modified Browning tilting-barrel action. The series began in 1987 with the 9mm Parabellum P-85 and has since progressed to the 9mm P89

(1992) and the .40 S&W P94 (1996). In addition, guns have been made in small numbers chambering the .45 ACP round.

The first cartridge revolvers appeared in the 1950s, beginning a line that has expanded over the years to include the .22 rimfire Bearcat, made between 1958 and 1973 in its original form, then as the New Model until the late 1970s; the Bisley (1980s to date), inspired by the Colt *Peacemaker variant of the same name, which is little more than a variant of the Single Six, or Blackhawk, with a modified grip and a low hammer-spur; the Blackhawk (.30 M1 Carbine, .357 Magnum, 9mm Parabellum, .41 Magnum, .45 Colt, .45 ACP; 1955–73, 1973 to date); and the Old Army (introduced in 1977), a .44-calibre cap-lock. The Police Service Six is a fixed-sight variant of the Security Six in .357 Magnum and .38 Special; the Redhawk, dating from 1980, chambered the .44 Magnum cartridge; the Security Six (1968–87), a general-purpose police/personal-defence revolver chambered the .357 Magnum round and had adjustable sights; the Speed Six was a short-barrelled Security Six with fixed sights; the Single Six, made in old (1953–73) and new (1973 to date) models, is Ruger's interpretation of the Colt *Peacemaker; and the Super Blackhawk (1960–73, 1973 to date) and Super Redhawk (1987 to date)

are essentially long-barrelled versions of the Blackhawk and Redhawk chambering the .44 Magnum round. The MR F-1 Special Police was a simplified version of the Security Six made in France by *Manurhin.

The original Security Six and its variants were replaced in 1987 by the GP series, the GP-100 introducing a stronger frame, a double-latch cylinder lock and cushioned grips. The guns have a full-length under-barrel ejector-rod shroud.

The Hawkeye (1963–67), chambered exclusively for the .256 Remington Magnum round, looked like a revolver, but was effectively a single-shot design with a laterally-tipping block where the cylinder would normally lie.

Ruger has also acquired a fine reputation as a manufacturer of rifles, beginning with the .44 Magnum 44 Carbine (1959–85) and the rimfire 10/22 Carbine (1964 to date). Then came the .223/5.56mm Mini-14 and the 7.62x39 Mini-Thirty (introduced in 1975 and 1987 respectively); the AC-556 was a militarised variant of the Mini-14, and the Ranch Rifle (1982 onward) offered improvements in safety. Folding-stock versions also appeared in the early 1980s.

A fascinating single-shot dropping-block Number One rifle, inspired by the British *Farquharson, appeared in 1966. This particular series has included a Number One Standard Rifle, chambering a variety of cartridges from .220 Swift to .338 Winchester Magnum, and a Number

---

through a hinged gate on the right side of the frame, but could be removed simply by detaching the axis pin. The guns were blued or nickel-plated, and often had poor-quality 'engraving' rolled into the surface of the cylinder. Grips were usually wood or gutta-percha, although sometimes mother-of-pearl was used on the gaudier nickelled examples. Guns of this genre were made in very large numbers, particularly in the 1880s. Production is believed to have exceeded 500,000 annually by 1885, but then went into a steady decline, until few were being made by 1900. An incredible profusion of wholesalers', distributors' and spurious manufacturers' marks will be found. Typical of these are 'Aetna Arms Co.' (Harrington & Richardson), 'Chicago Arms Co.', 'Enterprise Gun Works' (Philadelphia), 'Great Western Gun Works' (J.H. Johnson of Pittsburgh), 'Mohawk Mfg. Co.' (Otis Smith), 'New York Pistol Co.', 'United States Arms Co.' and the 'Western Arms Co.' However, successful names were so often simply copied that interpretation may be hotly disputed; there are said to be

more than thirty different revolvers marked 'Defender', made by a dozen agencies.

SUIT. An abbreviation used in the British Army for the 4x optical 'Sight, Unit, Infantry, Trilux' issued with the 7.62mm SLR and the 5.56mm SA-80. Now known as *SUSAT.

'suk'. This codemark is said to have been allocated to the Karlsruhe-Durlach (Germany) factory of *Deutsche Waffen- und Munitionsfabriken, where it was used on small-arms ammunition components made in 1945.

Sullivan – **1.** J.F. Sullivan, a US government arms inspector working at the beginning of the twentieth century, accepted *Colt revolvers and other military stores marked 'JFS'. *See also* US arms inspectors' marks. **2.** James L. Sullivan, an engineer employed by the *ArmaLite Division of the Fairchild Engine & Airplane Corporation, was responsible for improvements in the ArmaLite AR-15 rifle (with Robert *Fremont) in 1957/58. **3.** Sullivan Arms Company. A brandname associated with shotguns made in the USA by the *Crescent Arms Company.

One International Rifle with a short barrel and a full-length Mannlicher-style stock. Special Varminter (.22-250, .220 Swift, .223, 6mm Remington and .25-06) and heavyweight Tropical Rifle versions have also been manufactured, the latter in chamberings as powerful as .458 Winchester Magnum. The Number Three (1972–87) was a simplified version most commonly chambering .22 Hornet, .30-40 Krag or the .45-70-405 Government black-powder cartridge.

The Model 77 bolt-action rifle, basically a refined 1898-type Mauser, has also been very successful. The Mark 1 was made from 1968 until 1990, being discontinued shortly after the improved Mark 2 had been

introduced. A variety of individual patterns have been made, including African (.458 Winchester Magnum), All-Weather Stainless, Express, International (full-stocked, short-barrelled), Magnum, Police, Special Top and Varmint models. Two action lengths exist, and a left-hand option is available.

The M77/22 (.22 rimfire) and M77/44 (.44 Magnum), inspired by the Model 77, have also been made in several sub-varieties. Introduced in 1984, the M77/22 has a ten-round spool magazine, whereas the

M77/44 (1997) has a four-round box. The M96/44 and M96/22, dating from 1996, are essentially lever-action derivatives of the auto-loading M44 and M10/22 carbines.

Comparatively little has yet been written about Ruger's products, apart from a detailed study of the pistols and the original auto-loading carbines. In addition to the many directories common in North America, *Rifles of the World*, by John Walter (Krause Publications, second edition, 1998), contains concise listings of Ruger products.

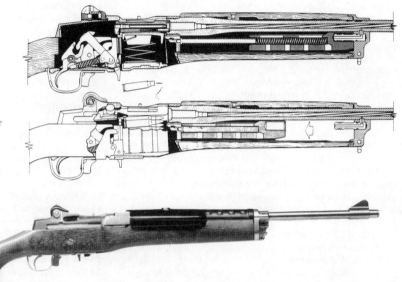

The .223 Mini-14, a semi-automatic amalgamating design elements taken from the Garand and the M1 Carbine, has not only been sold in large numbers, but has also provided the basis for a series of .223 and 7.62mm-calibre derivatives.

Sundance Industries, North Hollywood, California, USA. Maker of the .25-calibre A-23 automatic pistol.

Suojeluskuntain Ase- ja Konepaja Osakeyhtiö. *See* Sako.

Suomi. This submachine-gun, designed by Aimo ★Lahti, was developed in the early 1920s and made in quantity in Finland in 1927–44 by Oy Tikkakoski. The box-magazine m/26 chambered the 7.63mm Mauser pistol cartridge, but was superseded by the 9x19mm m/31, which could accept a box or high-capacity drum magazine interchangeably. Sturdy, accurate and reliable, the Suomi had a profound effect on the Russians during the Winter War of 1940–41.

Super, Super... – 1. Found in cartridge headstamps, this signifies that the ammunition had been made by the Super Cartridge Company. (NB: The mark should not be confused with '.38 Super' chambering.) **2.** This ★Parker-Hale sporting rifle, also known as the 1200 Super or 1200S, built on a ★Santa Barbara Mauser action, was introduced in 1984. Its half-stock had a roll-over Monte Carlo comb and a rosewood fore-end tip. Super Magnum

(1200SM) rifles were similar, but chambered 7mm Remington, .300 Winchester or .308 Norma Magnum cartridges. **3.** Super Azul: *see* Royal. **4.** Super Carbine. Another name for the ★Benjamin Model 352 pneumatic pump-up rifle. **5.** Super Cartridge Company [The]. A short-lived Australian manufacturer of ammunition identified by the inclusion of 'SUPER' in the headstamps. **6.** Super-Champion: *see* Buffalo Super-Champion. **7.** Super Comanche. A ★Llama revolver made in Spain since the early 1980s, built on the proven ★Comanche action – swing-cylinder construction based on ★Smith & Wesson practice. The Super Comanche IV chambers the .44 Magnum cartridge; the Super Comanche V handles the .357 Magnum. The barrels have ventilated ribs, frames are blued steel and the sights are adjustable. **8.** Super-Especial. A Spanish break-action air rifle made by Armas ★Juaristi of Eibar, 4.5 or 5.5mm-calibre, rifled or smooth-bore. **9.** Super Express. Also known as the Model 1964, this ★Mauser-action sporting rifle was made by Franz ★Sodia of Ferlach (Austria) in chamberings ranging from

5.6x61mm to 8x68mm. **10.** Super Grade. Found on a pneumatic pump-up rifle made by *Sheridan Products Inc. of Racine, Wisconsin, USA. **11.** Super-Hunter. A break-barrel 5.5mm-calibre spring-air rifle, also known as the Model 55, made by the *State Industry Factory in Shanghai, People's Republic of China. *See also* Hunter. **12.** Super Match Model. A target-shooting version of the .38 Super Model, this semi-automatic pistol dated from 1935–41; only a few thousand were ever made by *Colt's Patent Fire Arms Manufacturing Company, distinguished by their matted-top slides and adjustable sights. **13.** Super Meteor: *see* Meteor. **14.** Super Model, or .38 Super Model. Introduced by *Colt's Patent Fire Arms Manufacturing Company, made in quantity during 1928–42 and 1946–70, this was little more than a small-calibre version of the .45 *Government Model with a nine-round magazine. About 35,000 guns were made prior to the Second World War. *See also* Super Match Model. **15.** 'Super Nimrod' [The]. A mark found on shotgun ammunition made, or perhaps simply assembled, in England by the *Normal Improved Ammunition Company of Hendon, London. *See also* 'Nimrod'. **16.** Super Rapid or Universal Super Rapid (Czechoslovakia): *see* Universal. **17.** Super Rocket, Super CO$_2$ Rocket. A carbon-dioxide-powered pistol made by *Benjamin of St Louis, Missouri, USA. **18.** Super Safari. A Mauser-action sporting rifle introduced by *Parker-Hale Ltd in two versions: one with a hinged floor plate (Model 1200) and the other (1200C) with a detachable box magazine. Made in chamberings from .243 Winchester to .30-06, 1200-series guns were also offered for 7mm Remington and .308 Norma Magnum ammunition (1200M). The 1200 TX was a .308 target rifle, fitted with a PH5 aperture sight and a straight-comb butt. Presentation (1200P) and Varmint (1200V) models were made from 1969. **19.** Supertarget. A special adaptation of the *Webley & Scott Mark 3 fixed-barrel underlever-cocking air rifle, 1964–75. It was superseded by the *Osprey Supertarget. **20.** Super Target. A name associated with the M160 gas-powered pistol made by the *Benjamin Rifle Company of St Louis, Missouri. **21.** Super Thirty. Also known as .300 Holland's Super Thirty, but more popularly as the .300 H&H Magnum, this sporting-rifle cartridge was introduced by *Holland & Holland of London in 1925. **22.** Super Tornado. Applied by *Relum Ltd to the Hungarian *Telly LP15 underlever-cocking air rifle. **23.** 'Super Velocity' [The]. Encountered on the cases of shotgun ammunition distributed by William *Powell & Son of Birmingham. Most, if not all, of the components were acquired from *Eley-Kynoch.

Superbritte. A name given to a distinctive over/under shotgun with barrels that pivoted to the left instead of downward, a curved locking lever being fitted on the right side of the breech. It was patented in Belgium in 1931 by Theophile *Britte, but only about 250 actions were made in 1932/33 by Établissements Britte of Vivegnis before the project was overtaken by the Depression. The components were supplied to gunmakers in the Liège district, who completed 12-, 16- and 20-bore guns c. 1935–41 in a profusion of styles. Apparently the last few were completed after the German occupation of Belgium in 1940.

Superposed. This brandname, sometimes used generically for any over-and-under shotgun, was associated specifically with the Browning design manufactured by *Fabrique Nationale d'Armes de Guerre and its successor, *FN Herstal SA.

Supra – 1. Supra-Idéal. Derived from the *Manufacture Française d'Armes et Cycles double-barrelled shotgun, this had a rifled right-hand barrel for ball ammunition. Quadruple-lock actions were preferred. **2.** Supra-Robust. A 12- or 16-bore bore side-by-side double-barrelled *Robust shotgun made by MFAC. The right-hand barrel was rifled, and automatic ejectors were often fitted. **3.** Supra-Simplex. This was a version of the 12-bore MFAC *Simplex shotgun with the barrel rifled for ball ammunition. Ejectors were optional.

Supreme – 1. Supreme, or FN Supreme. This was an improved form of the standard Belgian *Fabrique Nationale *Mauser action, with the safety catch on the receiver behind the bolt handle. **2.** Supreme No. 1. This .303 Lee-action sporting rifle, made by *Parker-Hale Ltd, was introduced in 1958. Although retaining the original military-pattern action, complete with charger guides, it had a new pistol-grip butt with a Monte Carlo comb, and a half-length fore-end.

'Suredeath' [The]. A mark associated with shotgun cartridges sold by *Garnett of Dublin, Ireland.

'Surekiller' [The]. Encountered on shotgun cartridges distributed by *Rowell & Son of Chipping Norton. They are believed to have been made prior to 1914 by *Eley Bros.

Sureshot, Sureshot… – 1. Usually encountered as 'Sure-Shot' on a Langenhan-made *Millita spring-air rifle sold by *Ramsbottom & Company of Manchester, prior to 1905. *See also* Anglo Sure Shot. **2.** 'Sureshot Smokeless' [The]. Associated with a shotgun cartridge made in England by *King's Norton for sale by *Sowman of Olney prior to the First World War. The charge was E.C No. 5 propellant.

Susa [di Guglielminotti]. *See* Valle Susa.

SUSAT. An abbreviation for the British 4x optical 'Sight, Unit, Small Arms, Trliux' issued with the SA-80 rifle. The term replaced SUIT (q.v.) in the 1980s.

Sussex – 1. Sussex Armoury, Sturton Place, Hailsham, East Sussex, and Shambles Square, Manchester. This British metalworking company began life in the 1960s as a retail outlet for airguns and accessories, in addition to reproduction daggers and similar impedimenta, but then produced a few guns of its own – notably the *Jackal series. Airgun pellets were also marked with the Sussex Armoury brand, although they were made elsewhere (e.g. by *Lane Brothers or in Italy). **2.** 'Sussex Champion' [The]. Used by Russell *Hillsdon on shotgun ammunition. **3.** 'Sussex Express' [The]. A brandname found on shotgun cartridges loaded by Russell *Hillsdon.

Sutherland Sight Company. *See* Ross Rifle Company.

Sutter. A gun designer, responsible for the *RSC rifles and the *CSRG machine-rifle with his colleagues Chauchat and Ribeyrolles.

Suttie. *See* Grant-Suttie.

SVD. An abbreviated form of *Samozaridniya Vintovka Dragunova*, applied to the Soviet/Russian 7.62x54R *Dragunov sniper rifle.

SVT. An abbreviated form of *Samozaridniya Vintovka Tokareva*, applied to the 7.62x54R *Tokarev auto-loading rifles of the 1930s. *See also* AVT and SNT.

'svw'. A mark associated with small-arms components

made in Germany in 1945 by *Mauser-Werke KG of Oberndorf am Neckar.

'SW', 'S&W' – 1. A superimposition-type monogram, with neither letter dominant. Correctly 'WS' (q.v.); associated with *Charlier et Cie of Liège. *See also* Wegria-Charlier. **2.** A superimposition-type 'S&W' monogram, often encircled, either with both letters equally dominant or slight prominence given to 'S'. Associated with the products of *Smith & Wesson. **3.** Popularly used to identify a specific chambering (e.g. .32 S&W), originating with Smith & Wesson of Springfield, Massachusetts.

Swallow. Clark Swallow. This government arms inspector, working during the American Civil War, accepted cap-lock revolvers and other stores marked 'CS'. *See also* US arms inspectors' marks.

Swamp Angel. A brandname associated with a .38 single-action *Bull Dog-type revolver made by *Forehand & Wadsworth, c. 1880.

Swamped. Applied to any gun barrel that is greater in diameter at the muzzle than the breech. (Also known as 'reverse taper'.)

Swanson. A.C. Swanson Company, Sun Valley, California, USA. Manufacturer of the *Schimel, or *Carbo-Jet, gas pistol, initially for the Schimel company and latterly for the American Weapon Corporation.

Swartz. William Swartz. Grantee of a US Patent to protect the grip safety and concealed hammer system of the 1915-type Savage pistol.

SWD, Inc., Atlanta, Georgia, USA. Promoters of the *Ingram submachine-gun, c. 1977–81.

Swebilius. Carl Gustaf Swebilius was born in Sweden in 1879 and emigrated to America in 1896. There he started as a barrel driller with the *Marlin Fire Arms Company, but his talents were soon recognised and he embarked on a highly successful career as a designer. His work included shotguns, rifles and the adaptation of the *Colt 'Potato Digger' machine-gun for use in tanks and aircraft during the First World War. When the Marlin Firearms Corporation failed in the early 1920s, Swebilius worked first as a consultant to Winchester, then formed the *High Standard Manufacturing Company. He re-entered the firearms business when High Standard bought the assets of the defunct Hartford Arms Company in 1931. Subsequently he designed the UD-42 submachine-gun for the United Defence Corporation. Swebilius died in October 1948. His many patents used by Marlin ranged from US no. 1,083,708, granted on 6 January 1914 for a pump-action rifle, to 1,702,063 of 12 February 1929 for the Model 38 rifle. A list is given by Lieutenant-Colonel William S. Brophy in *Marlin Firearms* (Stackpole Books, 1989).

Sweeney. Joseph L. Sweeney, New Haven, Connecticut, USA. An employee of Winchester, Sweeney was a co-patentee of two 'magazine firearms' with William M. *Wetmore.

Swett. Allison Owen Swett, Boston, Massachusetts. Co-agent with James Rollin Marble *Squire and Henry Newton Sheldon in the application for Augustus Bedford's British Patent 23/76 of 1876.

'S.W.F.' Used in the headstamps of Italian *Fiocchi-made cartridges sold by *Smith & Wesson.

Swift – 1. Encountered on foreign-made shotgun cartridges sold by James *Matthews of Ballymena. Origins unknown. *See also* Hawk, Kingfisher and Wizard. **2.** Found on shotgun ammunition made by *Eley-Kynoch for *Stanbury & Stevens of Exeter. **3.** A British break-barrel .22 spring-and-piston air rifle made by *Kynoch Ltd prior to 1914, in accordance with a patent granted in 1906 to George *Hookham. Its most distinctive feature were the sprung locking arms on the side of the breech. **4.** Usually found as 'The Swift' on *Kynoch-made shotgun ammunition handled in Britain by *Linsley Brothers of Leeds prior to the First World War. **5.** Introduced in 1890, this .38 double-action Iver *Johnson revolver was made in exposed- and concealed-hammer patterns. **6.** Swift Rifle Company, London. Patentee of a training-rifle system that relied on a spring-loaded needle in the muzzle of a wooden 'rifle' imprinting a reduced-scale target. Many thousands of British soldiers were trained on this system during the Second World War.

'Swiftsure' [The]. This mark will be found on shotgun cartridges handled by *Cogswell & Harrison of London, prior to 1914.

Swinburn. *See* panel, p. 510.

Swinfen. John Swinfen, Maidstone, Kent. This English gunsmith, engraver and cutler traded successively from 5 Week Street (1831–39), Sandling Road (1846) and 73 Bank Street (1858–70). The business was acquired soon afterward by A. *Sanders, but Swinfen's marks will be found on shotgun ammunition made prior to 1899 by *Eley Bros.

Swinging-yoke cylinder. A form of revolver construction popularised in the 1890s by *Colt and *Smith & Wesson, and since perpetuated by vast numbers of gunmakers. The idea appears to date back at least as far as the Belgian *Levaux pattern of the 1870s.

Sword pistols. The pistol component of these combination weapons is easily detected if the direction of fire is toward the blade tip, but less so if the pistol barrel forms the hilt. Many of the latter are designed to fire backward, away from the blade tip; triggers were often hidden. Cap-locks were easier to disguise than flintlocks, particularly if enclosed locks and bar hammers were fitted. Most of those made during the second half of the nineteenth century incorporated revolvers. *See also* Robert *Colvin, Walter *Davis, R. *Howard, Knife pistols and Micheloni.

'SWP'. Found on US military firearms and accessories. *See* Samuel W. *Porter.

Sykes Brothers, Ossett, Yorkshire. The marks of this gunsmithing/ironmongery business have been found on shotgun cartridges made by *Eley Bros. prior to the First World War.

Syllaba. Tomas Syllaba, Schlau (*sic*) Bohemia, Austria. A maker of a crank-wound volute-spring airgun, with a tip-up breech and set triggers. Probably active in the mid-nineteenth century.

Sylven. Thomas Sylven. A London gunsmith, Sylven could be found at 33 Leicester Square and 10 Panton Street, Haymarket, in 1864. A move to 44 Bedford Square, London W.C., occurred in 1865, that address being listed until 1879/80.

Symington. John Symington, a colonel in the US Army working during the American Civil War, accepted *Springfield rifle-muskets marked 'JS'. Care should be taken to distinguish them from guns bearing the similar marks of John *Stahl and James *Stillman. *See also* US arms inspectors' marks.

Syms, Symmes – 1. John C. Syms, also listed as 'Symes' or 'Symmes', New York City. A carbine made to

JOHN FIELD SWINBURN

Trading from 16 & 17 Russell Street, Birmingham, Warwickshire, John Swinburn, son of gunsmith Charles Philips Swinburn (died or retired, 1850), continued to make sporting guns and rifles until 1883 or later. He was granted British Patents 1881/53 of 12 August 1853 (jointly with Thomas Turner) for a back sight;

2625/57 of 14 October 1857 (a communication from Thomas Bailey of New Orleans) for a gun-lock mechanism; 2269/58 of 12 October 1858 for a barrel band; and a group protecting a single-shot dropping-block rifle: 110/72 and 1895/72 of 1872; 3635/75 of 1875; 3689/76 of 1876; and 2206/77 of 1877. US Patent 134,014 of 17 December 1872 also protected a block-action rifle.

These pivoting-block guns, although clearly inspired by the success in Britain of the *Martini-Henry service rifle, were made commercially in some numbers during the 1870s and 1880s. Typical of the colonial orders was one for 300 rifles placed on 15 July 1875 on behalf of the Crown Agents for Natal. They were hammer fired and had straight-wrist butts attached to tangs so that the trigger mechanism could be accommodated.

Among Swinburn's other British Patents was 2711/80 of 1880 (for cocking and firing systems), while 4291/80 of 1880, 525/83 and 1145/83 of 1883, 6624/84 of 1884 and 17,088/85 of 1885 all protected shotguns and sporting rifles with drop-barrel actions.

The Swinburn rifles and carbines, carried here by men of the 90th Perthshire Light Infantry during the Second Zulu War (1879), were similar externally to the Martini-Henry. However, the trigger system included a hammer, and the shape of the operating lever was noticeably different.

the patent of John Symmes, then a captain in the US Army stationed in Watertown Arsenal, Massachusetts (US no. 22,094 of November 1858), was approved on 21 April 1856, although only twenty had been made by March 1857. The rotating breech-block had an 'elastic lip' gas-seal around the chamber. When the action was opened, a hole through the block gave access to the chamber. John Symmes accepted firearms and accessories in the decade immediately preceding the American Civil War. The items were marked 'JCS', but care is needed to distinguish them from similarly-marked guns accepted in an earlier era by John C. *Stebbins. *See also* US arms inspectors' marks. **2.** The name 'John Syms' has been reported on a spring-air Gallery Gun and is associated with the 44 Chatham Street address of Blunt & Syms (*sic*); as the Gallery Gun probably dates from about 1870, he may have continued the business alone.

Syndicat... – **1.** Syndicat Anglais: *see* La Société des Anglais. **2.** Syndicat des Pièces interchangeables (SPI), Liège, Belgium. Formed in 1898 by *Neumann frères, *Janssen fils & Cie and *Dumoulin fils & Cie, this co-operative venture sought to produce sporting guns based on standardised parts. The basic components were

made by *Fabrique Nationale d'Armes de Guerre, but they were finished in a variety of styles by the individual partners.

Syracuse Forging Company, also known as the Syracuse Arms Company, Syracuse, New York State. This business was formed in 1887 to make *Baker-patent exposed-hammer double-barrelled shotguns. It is said to have traded until the factory was destroyed by fire c. 1902, then was succeeded in 1903 by the Baker Gun & Forging Company. The chronology of this change remains obscure.

Syrett – **1.** Benjamin Syrett. This government arms inspector, working in the late 1890s, accepted military stores marked 'BS'. **2.** H. Syrett, operating c. 1905, accepted guns and equipment for the US Army marked 'HS'. Care is necessary to distinguish them from weapons accepted by H. *Saunders, Horace *Scott, Harrison *Shaler, Harris *Smith and Howard *Stockton, all of whom used 'HS' marks. Possibly a misrepresentation of W. Syrett (below). **3.** W. Syrett, an arms inspector working for the US government c. 1905, accepted items marked 'WS'. Possibly a misrepresentation of H. Syrett (above). *See also* US arms inspectors' marks.

T

'T', 't' – 1. Found as 'T' on the receivers of British No. 4 ★Lee-Enfield rifles fitted for telescope sights (No. 4 Mark 1 [T]). **2.** As 't'; associated with German small-arms ammunition made after 1940 by ★Dynamit of Troisdorf/Rheinland.
'TA', 'ta' – 1. A superimposition-type monogram, with the letters equally dominant. Correctly 'AT' (q.v.); used by Alois ★Tomiška of Pilsen, Czechoslovakia. **2.** As 'ta'; a mark allotted in 1940 to Dürener Metallwerke AG of Berlin-Borsigwalde, to identify small-arms ammunition made for the German armed forces. **3.** A superimposition-type 'TA' monogram, with neither letter dominant; customarily found on a shield. Probably Spanish; see 'IA'.
Ta'as Military Industries. See Israeli Military Industries.
'TAB'. See Theodore A. ★Belknap.
Tabatière. A ★Snider-like lifting-block conversion system adopted by the French in 1867. More than 340,000 guns had been altered when the Franco-Prussian War began in 1870. Known colloquially as 'à Tabatière' ('like a snuff-box') the breech-block opened to the right (unlike the leftward Snider type) and was cut down behind the breech to serve as a loading tray. The original breech-block was prone to open on firing if the parts had worn, so a retaining catch, or *Bouton-Arrêt*, was added in 1868. The 17.8mm-calibre Tabatière-type firearms included the Mle 1867 infantry rifle, the Mle 1867 dragoon rifle and an Mle 1867 cavalry carbine, but obsolete cap-lock muskets were also altered during the Franco-Prussian War. Most common was the Mle 1822 T.bis, but adaptions of Napoleonic An IX flintlocks are known.
Tabuk. A name applied to an indigenous copy of the AKM-type ★Kalashnikov assault rifle, made by the Iraqi state firearms factory. See also 'Al Quds.
'TAC'. A superimposition-type monogram, sometimes encircled, with no letters prominent. Found on ★Smith & Wesson-type break-open and swinging-cylinder revolvers made in Eibar, Spain, by ★Trocaola, Aranzabal y Cia.
Taden. Designed by Reginald Turpin ('T'), the Armament Design Establishment ('AD') and Enfield ('EN'), this was a tripod-mounted belt-fed ★Bren-type sustained-fire machine-gun developed in Britain for the experimental .280 cartridge. Successful enough in its original chambering, the Taden was unsatisfactory when converted for the 7.62mm T65E3 round. It was replaced in the mid-1950s by another Bren-based design known as the X11, but this was unable to challenge the FN ★MAG in the elimination trials.
Taft-Pierce Manufacturing Company. See Johnson automatic rifles.
Tait. See Adams & Tait.
Taittoperä, or TP. The Finnish term for 'folding butt', applied as a suffix in the designations of some ★Kalashnikov-type assault rifles made by ★Valmet and ★Sako-Valmet.
Taiyo Juki, Miroku, Japan. Maker of the ★Bobcat gas-powered BB pistol, apparently dating from the 1970s. Guns of this type may be found with the marks of ★Precise Imports Corporation of Suffren, New York State.
Take Down Model. See Special Model.

Talcott. George Talcott, a US Army lieutenant, accepted ★Hall and other firearms in the 1830s; they bore a cursive 'GT'. See also US arms inspectors' marks.
'Tally-Ho' [The]. A brandname found on shotgun ammunition made by Eley-Kynoch shortly after the First World War for William ★McCall & Sons of Dumfries.
Talon Safari. A brandname associated with bolt-action rifles made by ★McMillan Gunworks from 1988 onward. Embodying a strengthened ★Signature action, the guns are chambered specifically for magnum ammunition, ranging from .300 H&H to .458 Winchester. A Talon Safari Super Magnum, with a fibreglass stock, has been made for big-bore Weatherby Magnums (.378–.460) and .416 Rigby; it weighs about 10lb empty.
Talvenheimo. Niilo Talvenheimo, Finland. Designer of the m/39 ★Mosin-Nagant rifle.
Tamar [The]. Associated with British shotgun ammunition loaded by the ★Cornwall Cartridge Works of Liskeard.
Tambeur. Bernard Tambeur. A member of the London gun trade, perhaps also a gunmakers' agent, listed in 1866–68 at 21 Bartlett's Buildings.
Tanfoglio. Giuseppe Tanfoglio, or Armi G. Tanfoglio, Gardone Val Trompia, Brescia, Italy. Maker of the .22-calibre GT-22 and 6.35mm GT-25 automatic pistols, and a range of guns based on the ČZ275..
Tang. Wen-Li Tang, People's Republic of China. This engineer has been credited with the design of the Type 63 and Type 68 automatic rifles.
Tanne. This German brandname, often accompanied by a picture of a fir tree, has been used by Albrecht ★Kind.
Tanner. André Tanner, Fulenbach. A Swiss gunmaker, best known for target rifles.
Tanque. This compact automatic pistol was made in Eibar, Guipúzcoa, Spain, by ★Ojanguren y Vidosa: 6.35mm, six rounds, hammer fired.
Tansley. George A. Tansley. An engineer employed by ★Colt's Patent Fire Arms Manufacturing Company, patentee of grip-safety system (US no. 891,510 of 23 June 1908), which withdrew the firing pin into the slide when an operating lever was pivoted. This was combined with a similar system developed by Carl ★Ehbets and fitted to the .45 M1911 ★Government Model pistol.
Tantal. A designation applied to light automatic weapons based on the ★Kalashnikov, offered by ★Zakłady Metalowe Łucznik of Poland in 5.45mm and 5.56mm.
TargAire Pistol Company. Recorded by Eldon Wolff in *Air Guns* (1958) as a 'maker of current spring guns' in Chicago, Illinois. Nothing else is known about the business and it is assumed that trading had ceased by the early 1960s.
Target, Target... – 1. K-32 Target. A short-lived and rarely encountered ★Smith & Wesson swing-cylinder revolver, based on the ★Military & Police Model, this chambered the .32 S&W Long cartridge and had an adjustable back sight. Fewer than 100 were made in 1940. *See also* Mexican Model. **2.** Target Bulldog. A variant of the

*Charter Arms *Bulldog .357 Magnum and .44 Magnum revolver with a 6in heavy barrel, a shrouded ejector, adjustable target-type sights and special squared walnut grips. **3.** Target Kit Gun. Introduced by *Smith & Wesson in 1982, as the Model 651, this swing-cylinder revolver was a variant of the .22 Magnum rimfire *Service Kit Gun with a 4in barrel and adjustable sights. **4.** Target Model, or New Model Double Action Target Revolver. Made in the USA from the mid-1890s until 1908, this was a variant of the *Colt New Army Model, having chequered walnut grips and a special flat-top frame with adjustable sights. **5.** Target Model. Dating from 1987, this variant of the *Smith & Wesson Model 422 (an internal-hammer .22 rimfire *blow-back) had an unusually low-mounted barrel, adjustable sights and wood grips. The Model 622 of 1990 was a variant with a stainless-steel slide. See also Field Model. **6.** Target Products Company, Jackson, Michigan, USA. A maker of a BB pistol in the late 1940s. **7.** Target Stainless, or Model 624. This *Smith & Wesson swing-cylinder revolver was introduced in 1985, chambering the .44 S&W Special cartridge. A long barrel, micro-adjustable back sights and target-style Goncalo Alves grips are standard.

Targeteer. A slide-cocking ball-firing air pistol, designed by Charles *Lefever in 1936, which was made in the USA by *Daisy in 3mm calibre during 1937–40 (fixed back sight) and 1946–52 (adjustable sight).

Targetmaster, guns made by the *Remington Arms Company. **1.** Model 41A Targetmaster (1936–39) was a single-shot .22 rimfire target rifle made on the basis of the Model 33, with a half-stock and a straight-comb pistol-grip butt. **2.** Model 510A Targetmaster (1939–41, 1945–62) was a single-shot successor to the Model 41A, with a special loading platform and a streamlined self-cocking bolt. **3.** Targetmaster Pump Action. A name given by *AMAC in the 1980s to imported slide-action *Erma rimfire rifles.

Targetsman. Introduced in 1955 by *Colt's Patent Fire Arms Manufacturing Company, and made by the Firearms Division of Colt Industries until 1977, this was a variant of the *Huntsman with a 6.5in barrel, an adjustable back sight and an anatomical, or thumb-rest-style, left grip. Production amounted to about 65,000 guns.

Tarrassa arms factory. Industrias de Guerra de Cataluña, Tarrassa, made 1916-pattern *Mauser short rifles during the Spanish Civil War (1936–39).

Taschenpistole... – 1. A generic term used for any compact pocket pistol (cf. Westentaschenpistole). **2.** Taschen-Pistole, or TP. Introduced in 1961 by Carl *Walther Sportwaffenfabrik GmbH, this .25-calibre personal-defence pistol was little more than a modernised Modell 9 (patented in 1920–21!). It was discontinued in 1977 after only about 15,000 had been made. **3.** Taschenpistole mit Hahn, or TPH. Offered in .22 LR rimfire and 6.35mm Auto from October 1968 onward, this replaced the TP. It is mechanically similar to the Polizei-Pistole and has a similarly-raked grip. The rimfire variant lacks the loaded-chamber indicating pin of the centrefire gun, but otherwise the two are identical. The standard blued finish can be replaced by polished black and oakleaf or arabesque engraving.

Tatham. Henry Tatham the Younger. Son of Henry Tatham of Tatham & Egg, born in 1804, this London 'Gunmaker & Sword Cutler' began trading on his own account from 24 Pall Mall in 1825, but had moved to 37 Charing Cross by 1834. There he remained until his death in 1860. Additional premises in Opera Arcade were listed in 1857–58 only. Tatham's marks have been reported on self-cocking *pepperboxes from the mid-nineteenth century.

Tatler. John Tatler, sometimes listed as 'Tatlor', accepted *Colt, *Savage and *Starr *cap-lock revolvers for the Federal government during the early years of the American Civil War in 1861–62. They were marked 'JT'. See also Jerome *Towne, Josiah *Tatnall and US arms inspectors' marks.

Tatnall. Josiah Tatnall, a captain in the army, accepted *cap-lock revolvers made by the *Massachusetts Arms Company prior to the Civil War, his work (identified by JT) apparently being confined to 1858–59. This distinguishes it from the subsequent efforts of John *Tatler and Jerome *Towne. See also US arms inspectors' marks.

Tatra. A 6.35mm-calibre automatic pistol of unknown provenance, based on the *FN-Browning of 1905: six rounds, hammer fired.

Tauler, Madrid. This gun dealer, formerly an officer in the Guardia Civil, sold a variety of handguns to Spanish police forces. They included compact 6.35mm six-shot hammer-fired Browning-type pocket pistols made by *Gabilondo y Urresti, and a variety of Llama-brand Colt-Browning adaptations made by *Gabilondo y Cia. Most bear a kneeling-archer mark, registered in Spain on 13 December 1933 (no. 96,730) and may also display 'TAULER MARK P' on the left side of the slide.

Taunton – 1. Usually found as 'The Taunton'. A brand-name used on shotgun cartridges handled in south-west England by George *Hinton of Taunton. **2.** 'Taunton Demon' [The]. A brandname found on British shotgun cartridges sold by *Luckes of Taunton.

Taurus – 1. A brandname applied to the Hungarian-made *Telly LP 27 rifle by *Relum Ltd, its British importers. **2.** Forjas Taurus SA, Porto Alegre, Brazil. Perhaps best known for its *Smith & Wesson-type revolvers, Taurus has also made a range of automatic pistols. Based for the most part on *Beretta products, they include the .22-calibre PT-22 and the 6.35mm PT-25. Taurus purchased Amadeo *Rossi SA in 1998, but the effects on the two product-lines is not yet clear. It is assumed that production of at least some of the Smith & Wesson-style Taurus and Rossi revolvers will continue once rationalisation has been completed.

'Taxidermist' [The]. Found on shotgun cartridges loaded by the *Chamberlain Cartridge Company of Cleveland, Ohio, USA.

Taylor – 1. Driffield, Yorkshire. A mark of this type has been reported on shotgun cartridges made prior to 1914 by *Kynoch Ltd, possibly for sale by the successors of the gunmaker William Taylor (listed in Middle Street, Driffield, in 1854–57). **2.** Daniel Taylor, a lieutenant in the US Army, sometimes listed as 'Tyler', working prior to 1850, accepted muskets made by *Starr; these were marked 'DT'. See also US arms inspectors' marks. **3.** H.F. 'Ben' Taylor. Co-patentee with David *Theobald of the Theoben gas-ram, or gas-piston, system. **4.** Leslie Bown Taylor. Co-patentee with Charles *Gardner of an automatic loading port for air rifles (British Patent 2863/06 of 1906) and with Edward *Parsons of an SMLE-type training air rifle (British Patent 5495/06 of 1906). The patents list his profession as managing director and his home as West Hill, Selly Oak, Birmingham, Warwickshire, England. **5.** William P. Taylor, employed by the Federal government during the Civil War, accepted guns and accoutrements, marking them 'WPT'. See also US arms inspectors' marks. **6.** Taylor, Sherrard & Company, Lancaster, Texas. Working in the Confederate

States of America during the American Civil War, successor to *Tucker & Son, this business made a few sets of revolver parts before failing. The work was completed by *Clark, Sherrard & Company.

'Tayside' [The]. A mark found on shotgun cartridges sold in Scotland by *Gow of Dundee.

'TBH'. A mark found on US military firearms and accessories inspected by Thomas B. *Hawks.

T-Bolt. A rimfire rifle made by FN Herstal SA of Herstal-lèz-Liège in 1965–74. It was distinguished by a pivoting-bar straight-pull action with the bolt handle at the rear right side of the receiver. Standard .22 LR cartridges could be fed from the magazine, but Short or Long rounds could be loaded individually into the chamber if required. A deluxe T-2 version had a better stock, with chequering on the pistol grip and fore-end. However, the T-Bolt was replaced in the mid-1970s by a rimfire version of the *A-Bolt.

'TCS', 'T.C.S.', 'T...C...S'. *Headstamps associated with the products of T.C. *Sage of Middletown, Connecticut.

'TDA'. Usually encountered in a double-line oval cartouche. Associated with the products of Thermodynamic Associates, Inc., which included revolvers.

'Teal' [The]. Found on shotgun cartridges loaded by the *Chamberlain Cartridge Company of Cleveland, Ohio.

Teat-fire. These cartridges had a tiny tube, or 'teat', of fulminate priming compound, projecting backward from the base. Unfortunately, if force was used to overcome fouling in the chamber, the teat could be crushed and the fulminate ignited. Teat-fire cartridges had a short production life.

Teck. See panel, below.

'Ted Williams'. A brandname used on sporting guns and accessories sold in the USA by *Sears, Roebuck & Company.

Teham. P.A. Teham, sometimes listed as 'Tetham' or even 'Tatham', a US arms inspector working shortly before 1910,

accepted guns and accessories marked 'PAT'. *See also* US arms inspectors' marks.

Tell – 1. A brandname used on German shotgun cartridges, made in the Durlach factory of *Rheinisch-Westfälische Sprengstoff prior to 1914. **2.** A trademark used by A.L. *Frank of Hamburg prior to 1918. It will be found on a variety of firearms, from blank-firers to multi-barrel shotguns and combination rifles. Most of the guns were purchased from manufacturers in Suhl. **3.** A trademark used on spring-airguns made by Oscar Will of Zella-Mehlis, Thüringen, Germany, but possibly only after 1919 (cf. previous entry). **4.** A brandname and trademark associated with Wilhelm Foss (*see* Venuswaffenwerk), successor to Oskar Will. A cursive version of Tell was registered in Germany on 4 August 1925, as trademark no. 337,292, but the original pattern may date from the early 1900s.

'Tellow'. Found on spring-airguns made in Germany by Oscar *Will of Zella-Mehlis, 1919–22. This variant may have been confined to a market (Switzerland, perhaps?) where 'Tell' was already in use.

Telly. Often misrepresented as 'Jelly', this name graces a series of spring-airguns made in Budapest, Hungary, from the late 1950s onward. The guns, including barrel- and underlever-cocking patterns, have been exported by *Artex and are distributed in Britain by *Relum.

Tempered Dart. Airgun projectiles made in Britain by *Lanes Brothers of Bermondsey, apparently only prior to the First World War.

Tempest – 1. Usually found as 'The Tempest' on shotgun cartridges loaded and sold in England by *Garrett of Evesham. **2.** A lifting-barrel spring-air .177 or .22 pistol introduced by *Webley & Scott Ltd in 1979 to replace the *Junior, with which it shares similar operation.

Temple & Company. This London entrepreneur was,

TECK

Offered by H. *Krieghoff GmbH as a 12-, 16- or 20-bore over/under shotgun, a Double Rifle (in chamberings from 7x65R to 9.3x74R) or a combination gun with an optional free-floating rifle barrel. The rifled barrel of the combination guns may chamber cartridges ranging from .22 Hornet to 9.3x74R. All Tecks are built on a classic *box-lock action. Ejectors can be fitted if required, and the frame may be aluminium alloy instead of steel.

The earliest Teck was a self-cocker with a safety catch on the tang, but now a variety of trigger systems can be obtained, including a *Handspanner*, or manual-cocking feature. A small fixed back sight is fitted to the tip of the quarter-rib, and a ventilator, or bore evacuator, is

often fitted between the muzzles. The *Ulm patterns are essentially deluxe versions of the Teck.

The Teck Bergstutzen, built on the standard Teck action, is a short-barrelled *Double Rifle customarily chambered for ammunition ranging from .22 Hornet to 5.6x52R in the lower barrel, and .243 Winchester to 9.3x74R in the upper barrel.

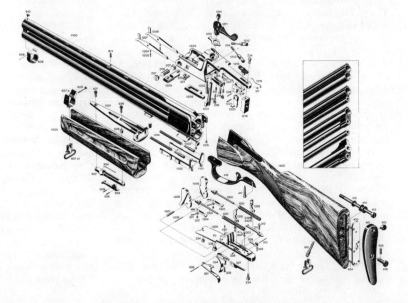

An exploded view of the Krieghoff Teck sporting gun, offered in a variety of rifle/shotgun combinations.

briefly, the British licensee of the *Nordenfelt machine-gun in the mid-1880s.

Ten... – **1.** 'Ten Shots Quick'. An advertising slogan associated with the .32 automatic pistols made by the *Savage Arms Company from 1907 onward, arising from their unusually large magazine capacity. **2.** 'Ten Star'. A name found on shotguns handled in the USA by the H. & D. *Folsom Arms Company, possibly imported from Europe. This particular name may have been intended for the Texan market, Texas having being admitted as the tenth state of the Union in 1846.

'TER', encircled, accompanied by stars and circles (customarily two and four respectively). Associated with revolvers made in the USA by Thomas E. *Ryan.

Tercerole, Tercerola, Terzerole. A term of Spanish origin, customarily attached to a short-barrelled carbine; often with a bellmouth muzzle.

Terling. K. Terling, Zella-Mehlis, Thüringen. Listed in 1920 as a gunmaker.

Terni arms factory. *See* Fabbrica d'Armi.

Terrible. A Browning-type pocket pistol made in Spain by Hijos de Calixto *Arrizabalaga, Eibar: 6.35mm, six shots. It was named after a Spanish warship.

Terrier. A *Suicide Special revolver made by J. *Rupertus Patent Pistol Manufacturing Company of Philadelphia, Pennsylvania, USA, in the late nineteenth century.

Terrific. A name associated with a revolver made in Belgium prior to 1914 by A. *Bertrand.

Terror. A brandname associated with a .38-calibre single-action *Bull Dog-type revolver made in the USA by *Forehand & Wadsworth, c. 1880.

Terry – **1.** James William Terry. An English gunmaker listed at 24 Great Prescot Street, London E., in 1845–50. H.J. Blanch, writing in *Arms & Explosives* in 1909, records him as William J. Terry. **2.** William Terry. Co-proprietor of the Birmingham based *Calisher & Terry gunmaking business, and designer of the Terry Carbine. His British patents included 812/55 of 12 April 1855, granted to protect a proprietary nipple and combustible cartridge design, and 843/56 of 7 April 1856 for the breech-loading carbine. **3.** Terry Carbine. A cap-lock breech-loader embodying a distinctive bolt-action system patented in 1856 by William Terry. The breech cover, pivoted to the breech-bolt, was pulled outward and rotated to disengage the locking lugs, allowing the bolt to be pulled back to give access to the chamber. A carbine of this type was recommended for British Army service on 23 August 1858. However, although patterns were *sealed in December 1858, November 1860 and March 1861, the Terry carbine was never entirely satisfactory. Sporting guns were made to an identical design in the 1860s, but never in large quantities.

Terssen rifle. Credited to the commandant of the Manufacture d'Armes de l'État in Liège, this lifting-block conversion was unique to Belgium. It was adopted as a temporary measure, but was not perpetuated once problems with the *Albini-Braendlin had been overcome and the *Comblain rifles were available in quantity. The Terssen was locked by a sliding bolt in the breech-block entering a recess in the rear face of the receiver. Rotating the operating handle withdrew the bolt into the block. Individual patterns included the Mle 1777–1868 infantry rifle and the Mle 1848–68 short rifle.

Teschner. Georg Teschner, Frankfurt an der Oder. This German gunmaker specialised in hammerless drop-barrel shotguns and combination rifle-shotguns, usually locked by the trigger guard or a rotary underlever. Teschner also developed a unique system of classifying bore sizes, which gained popularity in some parts of Europe. This ranged from Teschner calibre 0 (ten-bore) to 8 (28-bore). The business was sold to Wilhelm *Collath in the 1890s.

Tesching. A German name for a light sporting rifle, usually with a minimal stock.

Tesco. A brandname associated with guns and cartridges made in Germany by Georg *Teschner of Frankfurt an der Oder, and his successor, Wilhelm *Collath.

Tett. H.G. Tett, Coventry, Warwickshire. The marks of this English gunsmith have been reported on shotgun ammunition made by *Eley Bros. prior to 1914.

'Teuf-Teuf'. Found on a small 6.35mm semi-automatic pistol, sometimes mistakenly identified as Belgian owing to proof marks. Actually the guns were made in Spain by *Arizmendi y Goenaga of Eibar. The shape of the barrel shroud (which is virtually cylindrical) and the presence of a typically Spanish patent number ('45067') are noteworthy.

'Teutonia'. Found on shotgun cartridges made in Germany prior to 1914 by *Munitionswerke Schönebeck.

Tex. A 4.5mm break-barrel spring-air pistol, also known as the vz. 086, made by Prešne Strojírentsví of Uherský Brod, Czechoslovakia. Exported by *Omnipol and *Merkuria, it has been distributed in Britain by *Edgar Brothers.

Texas... – **1.** Texas Bull-Dog. A name associated with a revolver made in Belgium prior to 1914 by *Deprez. **2.** 'Texas Ranger'. Found on a single-action six-shot .380 'Western'-style revolver made in Spain, but often marked by Fabrique d'Armes Réunies of Liège. Some guns also bear 'MODEL 1929'.

'TFJ'. Used on US military firearms and accessories inspected by Thomas F. *Jewell.

Thacker & Company, Worcester, Worcestershire, England. Maker of guns and fishing tackle, this business distributed shotgun ammunition marked with its own name. The cartridges seem to have been supplied by *Kynoch Ltd.

Thälmann. VEB Fahrzeug- und Waffenfabrik 'Ernst Thälmann', Meininger Strasse, Suhl. This state-run organisation controlled the production and distribution of firearms and airguns made in the Suhl district of what was the German Democratic Republic (DDR). Thälmann dates from 1958/59, when an attempt was made to rationalise production; only the brandnames of *Haenel, *Merkel and *Simson were retained thereafter. The Haenel name was restricted to airguns, which ranged from bolt-action trainers to a pneumatic target rifle of surprising sophistication. Merkel and Simson were used on sporting guns.

Thalson Import Company, San Francisco, California, USA. A distributor of sporting rifles, including Czechoslovakian-made *Mausers imported in the 1950s.

'Thames Arms Co.' Found on *Suicide Special revolvers made by the *Hopkins & Allen Arms Company of Norwich, Connecticut, USA, in the late nineteenth century.

Thayer & Company Ltd. Listed as a member of the London gun trade by H.J. Blanch, in *Arms & Explosives* in 1909, Thayer may have been a merchant or agent. Premises were occupied in 1878 at 1 Leadenhall Street, London E.C.

'Th.B.', usually accompanied by crossed pistols. This distinctive trademark, a variation of the 'E.G.' of Eisenwerk Gaggenau, Baden, Germany, was used by Theodor *Bergmann during 1895–1905.

The... Most entries of this type are listed under the other part of their names (e.g. 'The Ansonia' will be 'Ansonia' [The]). Typical examples are The British Bull Dog, a compact large-calibre revolver; The Defender and The Huntsman, US-made knife pistols; The Mousetrap, a shotgun invented by Theophilus *Murcott of London; and The Woodsman, a .22 rimfire semi-automatic pistol made by *Colt's Patent Fire Arms Manufacturing Company.

Theale Royal Ordnance Factory. Maker of British 9mm Mark II, Mark IIS, Mark V and Mark 6 *Sten submachine-guns during the Second World War.

Théate. E. Théate, later '…& Cie', Liège. A maker of revolvers, sporting rifles and shotguns, active in Belgium from the 1870s until 1961.

Theobald. David R. Theobald. Co-patentee with H.F. *Taylor of the gas-ram system used in the *Theoben rifle.

Theoben Engineering, Anglia Works, Burrell Road, St Ives, Cambridgeshire. This business was formed in 1981 by H.F. 'Ben' *Taylor and D.R. *Theobald to exploit a unique gas-ram design. This was applied successfully in the *Sirocco rifle, and since has been licensed with great success to gunmakers including *Weihrauch.

Theodorovič. Wasa Theodorovič (Austria-Hungary). *See* Roth-Steyr.

Thermostabil (TS). A free-floating barrel assembly associated with guns (especially the *Ultra) made by H. *Krieghoff GmbH of Ulm/Donau. It dates from the 1990s.

Thieme – 1. Thieme y Edeler, Eibar, Guipúzcoa, Spain. This gunmaking business, possibly with German connections (*see* Thieme & Schlegelmilch) is associated with the *Sivispacem Parabellum pocket pistol. Trading seems to have ceased by the early 1920s. **2.** Thieme & Schlegelmilch, Nimrod-Gewehr-Fabrik, Suhl in Thüringen, Gothaer Strasse 18 (1940). This gunmaking partnership was listed in the *Deutsches Reichs-Adressbuch* for 1900–30, owned by Ernst Schlegelmilch. Then it was sold to Alfred Funk, noted as the 'proprietor' in the directories for 1938–41. Trading ceased at the end of the Second World War. Best known for sporting rifles, shotguns and combination guns, Thieme & Schlegelmilch has been linked with 6.35mm *Browning-type pistols dating from the 1920s, which, it is assumed, were imported from Spain. Among its trademarks and brandnames were Feldmann and Parva.

Thistle – 1. A brandname applied to *Mayer & Grammelspacher Diana Model 23 spring-air rifles sold in Scotland in the late 1920s by *Clyde's Game & Gun Mart of Glasgow. **2.** Usually found as 'The Thistle' on shotgun cartridges made after the First World War for Alex *Martin & Company of Glasgow by *Eley-Kynoch.

Thivillier, 4 rue des Armuriers, Saint-Étienne, France. Listed in 1951 as a gunmaker.

'Th. K', 'TH. K.' Trademarks used by Theodor *Kommer of Zella-Mehlis, found on the grips of 6.35mm and 7.65mm semi-automatic pistols dating from the early 1920s. The guns are similar to the FN-Browning blowbacks, but have a distinctive dismantling system; the earliest are marked 'D.R.G.M.', whereas later guns display 'D.R.P. ANG.'

Thomas – 1. Fritz Thomas, Zella-Mehlis in Thüringen. A maker of hunting and sporting equipment prior to 1939. **2.** John Thomas, 66 & 67 Slaney Street, Birmingham, Warwickshire, England (1879–84). Best known for his self-extracting revolver, the subject of British Patent 779/69 of 1869, Thomas had worked for *Tipping & Lawden prior to 1877. He was also granted British Patent 324/70 of 1870; 3091/71 of 1871 for the Wedge Fast drop-down-barrel

action; 3578/74 of 1874 (jointly with Thomas Tipping Lawden) for a drop-barrel and hinged-breech-block action; and 3291/76 of 1876 (also with Lawden) for another drop-barrel action. **3.** Thomas et Juquel aîné, rue Saint-Denis 14, Saint-Étienne, France. Listed in 1879 as a distributor of, and agent for, arms and ammunition.

Thommen. Ernst Thommen, Switzerland. *See* Hämmerli.

Thomson. Benjamin Thomas Lindsay Thomson, an 'Engineer' living at 4 Altenburg Gardens, Clapham Common, Surrey, was granted patents in collaboration with John *Wallace to protect improvements made in the *Giffard gas-gun. The subject of British Patents 4205/91 of 1891 and 1724/92 of 1892, these included an internal hammer. Thomson is believed to have been the works manager of the Giffard Gun & Ordnance Company.

Thompson – 1. Albert H. Thompson, working for the Federal government during the American Civil War, accepted arms and equipment marked 'AHT'. *See also* US arms inspectors' marks. **2.** Alexander Thompson. The son of John Thompson, this gunmaker began trading c. 1820 from Drummond Street, Edinburgh. By 1840, he was also using the 3 South St Andrew Street workshop once operated by his father, and had closed the Drummond Street shop in favour of a new one at 16 Union Place. By 1850, however, the South St Andrew Street address had also been abandoned. Trading as Alexander Thompson & Son from 1863 onward, with a branch in Aberdeen, the company introduced pinfire breech-loading shotguns in 1865. A move to 95 Princes Street in 1868 was followed by one to 3 Hanover Street in 1876, but operations ceased in 1880. **3.** John Taliaferro Thompson, born in Kentucky in 1860, was a member of the Board of Officers appointed to test potential US Army handguns in 1899. A captain in the US Army Ordnance Corps, Thompson inspected a variety of firearms during 1895–1902. They included .38 and .45-calibre *Colt revolvers, and some of the earliest 1900-pattern *Colt-Browning pistols. He used a 'JTT' mark. Thompson was also one of the co-principals of the Thompson-LaGarde Wound Ballistics Board of 1904. After commanding the Small Arms Division of the Ordnance Department and, ultimately, serving as Assistant Chief of Ordnance during the First World War, Thompson retired to devote his time to the *Auto-Ordnance Corporation. He died in 1940. **4.** William Philips Thompson, Thompson & Company. This patent agency acted for inventors such as George *Gunn, Jacob *Mayer and *Mayer & Grammelspacher (*see* British Patents 3299/86 of 1886, 11,750/95 of 1895 and 4315/15 of 1915). Thompson's activities began prior to 1879, but he entered a nominal partnership with Alfred Julius *Boult in the early 1890s. He returned to solitary practice in 1897, and retired in 1908; operations were continued by his sons and heirs as Thompson & Company. The patent specifications list the chambers at 6 Lord Street in Liverpool, 6 Bank Street in Manchester, 118 New Street in Birmingham, and in Bradford. Thompson also ran the Agency for Foreign Patent Solicitors. **5.** Thompson Auto Rifle. This delayed-blowback design was promoted by the *Auto-Ordnance Corporation in the USA and *BSA Guns Ltd in Britain. It relied on the friction created between two different metals as they slid over each other to hold the breech closed until pressure had dropped sufficiently (*see* Blish Principle). Unfortunately, the lock was marginal, the breech leaked gas and ejection was too violent. The earliest guns were tested by the US Army in May 1920 with promising results, but by 1925, the Thompson Auto Rifle PC (or M1922) was being challenged by the *Garand and *Pedersen designs. Although a .30 Thompson Automatic Rifle was tested against the .30 primer-actuated M1924 Garand, .276 Tl Pedersen and .256 Bang in 1928, work was abandoned. **6.** Thompson & Boult, Britain. *See* William Philips Thompson. **7.** Thompson Brothers, Bridgwater, Somerset. Supplier of guns and ironmongery, this business also distributed shotgun cartridges under the brandname Ruby. They were made by *Eley Bros. prior to the First World War. **8.** Thompson/Center Arms, Farrington Road, Rochester, New Hampshire. Formed as the K.W. Thompson Tool Company immediately after the Second World War, this engineering business moved to Rochester in 1962. Gun parts were already being made in quantity when the designer of the Contender single-shot pistol, Warren Center, joined Thompson in 1965. Break-open Contenders, operated by a lever doubling as the trigger guard, have since been made in a bewildering variety of chamberings (.17 Bumblebee to .45/410), and are regarded among the finest examples of their type. Current examples incorporate a dual rim-/centrefire firing pin protected by US Patent 4,615,133, and sometimes also a detachable internal choke protected by no. 4,008,538. Carbine derivatives are available, alongside a variety of black-powder handguns (including the Patriot) and longarms. **9.** Thompson-Ramo-Woolridge, Inc., Cleveland, Ohio, USA. Maker of 319,160 7.62mm M14 rifles for the US government in 1962–64. **10.** Thompson & Son of Edinburgh entered a *Lancaster-patent 12-bore breech-loading shotgun in *The Field* trials of 1866 by. **11.** Thompson submachine-gun: *see* panel, below.

Thonon & Cie, Liège, Belgium. A gunmaking business active between the world wars. The marks will be found on sporting rifles and shotguns, some of the finest quality.

Thorn – 1. Henry A.A. Thorn was the manager of the gunmaking business of Charles William *Lancaster. As Lancaster grew older, Thorn became more responsible for day-to-day operations, and he purchased the business when Lancaster died in 1878. He continued to trade under the name Charles Lancaster (sometimes including '...& Co.' in the early 1880s) from 151 New Bond Street and 2 Little Bruton Street, London, making a range of sporting guns and rifles. These included a distinctive multi-barrel self-cocking pistol patented by Thorn c. 1880. **2.** William Thorn was a gunmaker, and possibly a gunmakers' agent, trading in 1874–76 from 4 Pall Mall, London S.W.

THOMPSON SUBMACHINE-GUN

Thompson (10)

This legendary weapon was developed secretly during the First World War by engineers employed by the Auto-Ordnance Corporation of New York, formed by John T. *Thompson and his backers to exploit patents granted to John B. *Blish. The principal feature of the gun was a 'hesitation lock', which depended on the friction generated by two surfaces of differing material sliding over each other to delay the opening of the breech. Drum magazines gave a capacity of fifty .45 ACP rounds.

A series of experimental guns, developed by Auto-Ordnance employees *Payne and *Eickhoff, was followed by the perfected Model 1921. Then a single series of 15,000 guns was made in Hartford, Connecticut, by *Colt's Patent Fire Arms Manufacturing Company. Sales were slow, and guns were revised periodically and re-marked to camouflage their origins. The most popular were the Model 1928 and the improved M1928A1, used in small numbers by the US armed forces.

More guns were made after 1940, principally to satisfy the demands of the British purchasing commision, but the entry of the USA into the war in December 1941 forced a review of the basic design. Trials showed the bronze locking piece to be superfluous, and the simplified blowback M1 pattern was substituted. No fewer than 1,387,134 M1928A1, M1 (hammer and firing pin) and M1A1 (fixed firing pin) Thompsons were made by the Savage Arms Company in Utica, New York State, in 1941–44. Production continues for the modern-day Auto-Ordnance Corporation of West Hurley, New York.

The history of the 'Tommy Gun', including the abortive BSA-Thompsons and a host of copies, will be found in Tracie L. Hill's *Thompson: the American Legend* (Collector Grade Publications, 1996).

This long-barrelled modern derivative of the .45 M1A1 Thompson machine-gun is still being marketed by Auto-Ordnance.

Thorneycroft. This Cavalry Rifle was made in Britain in small numbers at the beginning of the twentieth century, as a result of lessons learned from war in South Africa.

Thornton – 1. O.A. Thornton, a government arms inspector working c. 1910, accepted arms and equipment marked 'OAT'. **2.** William A. Thornton, a captain in the US Army Ordnance Corps, accepted a variety of firearms from the 1840s until the beginning of the American Civil War. They included *cap-lock muskets and pistols; cap-lock revolvers made by the *Massachusetts Arms Company (*Beaumont-Adams type), *Colt's Patent Fire Arms Manufacturing Company, E. *Remington & Sons, and the *Savage Revolving Fire Arms Company; and a few *Joslyn breech-loading carbines dating from 1861/62. Thornton's mark was 'WAT'. *See also* US arms inspectors' marks.

Thorsen – 1. Theodor M. Thorsen, Philadelphia, Pennsylvania, and Camden, New Jersey, USA. A patentee of three gun-related devices between 1902 and 1907, and possibly a partner in Thorsen & Cassady. **2.** Thorsen & Casady, Chicago, Illinois, USA. Distributors of the *Challenge airgun in the late nineteenth century.

Thorssin. J. Thorssin & Son, Alingsås. This Swedish engineering company, based near Göteborg, made a few examples of the *Hamiltonpistol in 1901–03. It was unsuccessful.

'THR'. Found on US military firearms and accessories. *See* T.H. *Rogers.

Three... – 1. Three Barrel Gun Company [The], Moundsville, West Virginia, USA. This business was founded by Frank *Hollenbeck to make multi-barrel guns in 12, 16- and 20-bore, and a variety of rifle chamberings from .22 centrefire to .30-30. Sales were slow, however, and the business was reorganised c. 1908 as the *Royal Gun Company. **2.** Three Crowns [The]. This trademark and brandname are associated with shotgun cartridges loaded in Britain by the *Hull Cartridge Company.

Thuer – 1. Frederick Alexander Thuer, Hartford, Connecticut, USA. Born in Germany, Thuer emigrated to the USA shortly before the American Civil War. He was responsible for the first cartridge conversion of cap-lock *Colt revolvers, and also for the Colt pivoting-barrel No. 3 cartridge derringer. **2.** Thuer Conversion. Patented in the USA on 15 September 1868 (no. 82,258), this was applied to about 5,000 Colt cap-lock revolvers in 1869–70. An auxiliary ring was placed in the frame, behind a shortened cylinder loaded (from the front) with tapered copper-case cartridges. The hammer-nose struck a firing pin in the breech-ring, and an ejecting arm, when activated, automatically expelled the contents of the nearest chamber. The Thuer conversion was too complicated to succeed and was superseded by the simpler *Richards type. **3.** Thuer Model [Derringer]. Also known as the Model No. 3 or Third Model, distinguishing it from two earlier *National-type guns, this was made by *Colt's Patent Fire Arms Manufacturing Company, in accordance with a patent granted to F.A. Thuer in 1871. A small .41-calibre single-shot pocket pistol with a spur trigger and a barrel that swung laterally to load, the Thuer derringer was popular: production during 1871–1912 amounted to about 45,000 guns, and 112,000 were made in 1959–63, when the basic design was revived as the Fourth Model. Some of these guns were concealed in books and bookends, hung in picture frames or sold in cased pairs. *See also* Lady Model and Lord Model.

Thumann. A. Thumann & Company. A merchanting business and gunmakers' agency, operating from 6 Fen-church Buildings, London E.C., in 1883, and from 11 Great St Helen's in 1894.

Thunder. A 6.35mm-calibre Browning-pattern pocket pistol with a six-round box magazine, made by Martin A. *Bascaran of Eibar, Guipúzcoa, Spain. It was similar to the 6.35mm *Martian.

Thunderbolt – 1. Associated with a push-in-barrel-cocking air pistol made by Produsit Ltd. **2.** Made in rifle, carbine and shotgun form by the *Whitney Arms Company, c. 1865–69, this was patented in 1862–65 by the *Howard family. The lever-action guns were remarkable for their tubular receivers; rifles customarily chambered .56-46 Spencer cartridges, whereas the carbines often accepted .44 Long rimfire ammunition.

Thunderer – 1. A name associated with a large-bore centrefire revolver sold in Belgium prior to 1914 by H. *Ortmann. **2.** A .41 version of the *Colt *Lightning, originally named by Benjamin *Kittredge & Company of Cincinatti. About 167,000 .38-calibre Lightnings and .41 Thunderers were made between 1877 and 1909.

Thüringer Waffenhaus. *See* Albin *Metzner.

'Thurland' [The]. This mark is associated with British shotgun cartridges sold by *Knight of Nottingham.

Tibbenham. F. Tibbenham Ltd, Ipswich, Suffolk. Allocated the manufacturer's code 'S 111', this participant in the *Monotype Scheme made grips, butts and carrying handles for the British *Bren Gun during the Second World War.

Tickner. William Tickner, Bishops Waltham, Hampshire. The name of this distributor of guns, ammunition and sporting goods has been reported on shotgun cartridges (origins unknown) sold as The Sportsman.

Tientsin arsenal. A maker of *Arisaka rifles under Japanese supervision, c. 1944. The guns seem to have been assembled from largely sub-contracted parts.

Tiesing. Frank Tiesing of New Haven, Connecticut, was the co-designer (with Eli Whitney the Younger and Charles Gerner) of the breech-loading shotgun protected by US Patents 93,149 of 27 July 1869 and 113,470 of 4 April 1871. Among his later designs were 'breech-loading firearms' (114,230 of 25 April 1871 with Gerner, and 191,197 of 22 May 1877 alone); and the 'magazine firearms' protected by 191,196 of 22 May 1877, 193,574 of 24 July 1877, 206,367 of 23 July 1878, 208,128 of 17 September 1878, 222,749 of 16 December 1879, 226,809 of 20 April 1880, and 238,988 of 15 March 1881. Tiesing also received US Patent 204,863, granted on 11 June 1878 to protect a lever-action rifle with a tubular magazine, and became involved in work on the *Kennedy lever-action rifle. This led to grants of US Patents 225,664 of 16 March 1880, with 'W. and Samuel V. Kennedy'; and 235, 829 of 21 December 1880 with Samuel Kennedy alone. Then Tiesing and Kennedy patented a bolt-action rifle with a five-round box magazine (US no. 235,829 of 31 December 1880). Most of these 'co-patents' were assigned to Eli Whitney.

Tiffany Grips. Cast from white metal to the designs of John Ward, and often plated, most of these decorative accessories dated from the 1860s. The most popular patterns were eagle-and-justice, a Civil War battle scene, the US eagle, and the Mexican eagle and snake. Colt revolvers were the favoured recipients, but other patterns survive.

Tiger – 1. An Austrian *Mauser-pattern sporting rifle, made by Karl *Dschulnigg of Salzburg in the 1960s, this was similar to the *Chamois, with the exception of a hog's-back comb and squared *Bavarian-style cheek-piece. **2.**

Usually encountered as 'The Tiger'; used in Britain by *Lisle of Derby on *Kynoch-made shotgun cartridges dating prior to 1914. **3.** Found on *Suicide Special revolvers made in the late nineteenth century by the *Crescent Arms Company of Norwich, Connecticut; by *Ely & Wray of Springfield, Massachusetts; and by *Johnson, Bye & Company and/or *Iver Johnson of Worcester and Fitchburg, Massachusetts, USA. **4.** Associated with shotguns handled in the USA by the H. & D. *Folsom Arms Company, possibly imported from Europe. **5.** A European air pistol, probably made in Italy, distributed in the USA in the 1980s by *Firearms Import & Export Corporation.

Tikkakoski. *See* panel, below.

Tilbury & Jeffries, Parsons' Garage, Littlehampton Road, Worthing, Sussex. The marks of this partnership have been reported on shotgun cartridges, possibly from Europe, which were distributed as The *Highdown. It is assumed that they date from between the world wars.

Tilney. Robert Tilney & Son, Beccles, Suffolk. The marks of this East Anglian gunsmithing business, first listed at 17 Smallgate Street in 1868, and trading as '...& Son' from c. 1890, have been found on sporting guns and shotgun ammunition sold as Tilney's Special. Most examples were made by *Nobel prior to the First World War.

Tily & Brown, Farnham and Guildford, Surrey. The

marks of this English sporting-goods business have been reported on guns and ammunition, including shotgun cartridges made by *Remington for sale as The Farnford.

'Times' [The]. A brandname found on shotgun cartridges made in Britain by *Eley Bros. prior to 1914 and sold by H.J. *Hussey Ltd of London.

Ti-Men. A lever-action spring-air BB Gun made by Productos *Mendoza SA and also known as the Modelo V-45. Apparently the name is an abbreviated form of the Spanish for 'Little Mendoza'.

Tinkham. Edward M. Tinkham, working at the beginning of the twentieth century, accepted .38 *Colt revolvers marked 'EMT'. *See also* US arms inspectors' marks.

Tipping... – **1.** Thomas Tipping-Lawden, Birmingham, Warwickshire. Tipping-Lawden was granted British Patent 368/61 of 13 February 1861, jointly with Thomas Jones, for a breech-loading mechanism suited to cap-lock and pinfire ignition; he also received British Patent 1648/62 of 31 May 1862 to protect a drop-down-barrel action for sporting and cane guns. **2.** Tipping & Lawden. Caleb and Thomas Tipping-Lawden registered their partnership in Birmingham in 1837, trading from 40 (later 40 & 41) Constitution Hill until a move to 18 Buckingham Street occurred in 1860. However, representation was maintained in London from 37 Cheapside (1837–40); at 18 Pancras

OY TIKKAKOSKI AB (TIKKA)

This Finnish engineering business, founded in 1893, began to make firearms only after Finland had gained independence from Russia following the revolution of 1917. Best known for sporting guns, the *Suomi submachine-guns, and replacement barrels for *Parabellum pistols and *Mosin-Nagant rifles, Tikkakoski ceased production at the end of the Continuation War between Finland and Russia in 1944. However, work began again in the early 1960s, when a modified Mauser-action sporting rifle (the Model 55) appeared.

This formed the basis for the first generation of rifles, made in standard, deluxe and Super Sporter guise, and in chamberings ranging from .17 Remington to .308 Winchester. Next came the Model 65, embodying a variant of the 1955-type action strengthened to handle magnum

ammunition. These guns were also made in different forms, and in chamberings as diverse as .25-06 Remington and .300 Winchester Magnum. A sniper rifle, known as the Tikka 65 Master, was made with a fluted extra-rigid barrel set in a synthetic cycolac stock; a muzzle weight and a replaceable cheek-piece insert were also standard.

The Tikka 55 and 65 patterns remained in production until 1989, when they were replaced by an improved design originally advertised as the Models 558 (standard) and 658 (magnum). However, only prototypes had been made before the patterns were changed and reintroduced as 590 and 690. These can be recognised by the squared contours of the action, made for Tikkakoski by Sako. The Tikka 595 Master, generally comparable to the 590, has a special

butt plate equipped with rods and spacers to adjust the rake and length of pull.

Tikkakoski has also offered shotguns (Model 77); a combination rifle-shotgun (Model 77K) with a 12-bore smoothbore above a rifled barrel chambering cartridges ranging from .222 Remington to 7x65R; and a purpose-built combination gun, the Model 07, with a simplified lock mechanism and an exposed hammer. Tikka has also advertised the Model 512-S 12-bore shotgun and an associated Double Rifle (c. 1992–97), made on machinery sold by Sako-Valmet to Marocchi of Italy. This rifle, an improved form of the Valmet 412-S, chambered a variety of rounds from 7x65R to 9.3x74R.

This box-lock Tikka m/07 has a rifle barrel beneath a smoothbore .410 shotgun.

Lane (1842); at 9 Dyer's Buildings, Holborn (1843); at 20 Bartlett's Buildings (subsequently at 26) in 1844–54; and finally, after a break, from 17 Woodstock Street in 1871–77. Tipping & Lawden was finally bought by P. *Webley & Son in 1877. Pistols, revolvers, air canes and possibly airguns had been made during the preceding forty years. Tipping & Lawden also produced the multi-barrel derringer pistols patented by Christian Sharps, apparently licensed by Sharps' executors. British-made guns of this type are often surprisingly well decorated and will be found in a variety of finishes. Work on them is believed to have stopped c. 1881.

Tirol – 1. Associated with spring-air and gas-powered rifles made by, or possibly for, Richard Mahrholdt of Innsbruck. **2.** Tirol Arms Company, Austria. See Richard *Mahrholdt. **3.** Tiroler Jagd- und Sportwaffenfabrik, Kufstein in Tirol. Occasionally suggested as a maker of the *Tirol-brand airguns, this Austrian machinery and woodworking business has often been confused with Richard Mahrholdt. **4.** Tirolerschaft. See Stock. **5.** Tiroler Waffenfabrik, Austria. See Richard *Mahrholdt.

Tisan. A small Browning-type automatic pistol made by Santiago *Salaberrin in Eibar, Guipúzcoa, Spain: 6.35mm, six rounds, hammer fired.

Titan – 1. A brandname associated with sporting guns and accessories made in Suhl, Germany, by Imman *Meffert. See also Hubertus. **2.** Associated with a small Browning-type 6.35mm hammer-fired pocket pistol made in Spain, by *Retolaza Hermanos of Eibar, Guipúzcoa.

Titanic. A small Browning-type automatic pistol made in Eibar, Guipúzcoa, Spain, by *Retolaza Hermanos: 6.35mm or 7.65mm, six rounds, hammer fired. The slide may also be marked 'Model 1914'.

'Tivvy' [The]. A brandname found on shotgun ammunition sold in south-west England by *Heal of Tiverton.

Tiwa. Another of the many unattributable Browning-type pocket pistols made in the Eibar district: 6.35mm, six rounds, hammer fired.

'TJC'. A superimposition-type cursive monogram, with the 'J' slightly dominant. Found on the grips of revolvers made in the USA during the late nineteenth century; significance unknown. See also 'KT'.

'TJL', 'TJS'. Found on US military firearms and accessories. See T.J. *Lovett, and T.J. *Smith and T.J. *Stevenson.

'TK', 'T.K.' – 1. A superimposition-type monogram with neither letter prominent. Used by Theodor *Kommer of Zella-Mehlis, Germany, on the butt plates of sporting guns and the grips of semi-automatic pistols. **2.** An encircled cursive linear monogram, with 'T' slightly dominant. Probably interpreted more accurately as 'KJ' (q.v.); found on revolvers made in Spain prior to 1914. **3.** A 6.35mm Tula-Korovin pocket pistol, made in large quantities by the *Tula ordnance factory, c. 1925–40. It was designed by Sergey *Korovin and sometimes is listed as the TOZ (owing to the 'TO3' cyrillic factory mark moulded into its grips).

'TKL'. An unidentified Civil War-period arms inspector's mark, reportedly found on Joslyn carbines made for the Federal Army in 1862.

'TL', 'T.L.', 'T. & L.' See Tipping & Lawden.

'TMH'. Found on US military firearms and accessories. See Thomas M. *Hervey.

TNI, Tentara National Indonesia. A property mark applied by the Indonesian Army since the 1950s.

Tokagypt. A name given to a 9mm Parabellum version of the *Tokarev 48.M pistol, made in Hungary from 1958 onward (by FÉG) for the Egyptian Army. Unlike the handguns supplied by Beretta, subsequently made in Egypt as the Helwan, Tokagypt examples are not customarily marked in Arabic. However, the state insignia will be found on the left side of the slide.

Tokarev – 1. Fedor V. Tokarev, one of the Soviet Union's premier gun designers, was born in Egorlykskaya in 1871 and entered the local engineering school in 1885. There he was taught by Andrey Chernolikhov, designer of the 6-line (.6-calibre) *cap-lock cossack rifle of the 1850s. Then Tokarev joined the army as an armourer, serving until seconded to the Oranienbaum officers' school in 1907. There he produced his first automatic-rifle design and immediately was sent to the Sestroretsk ordnance factory as assistant to V.G. *Fedorov. Active duty in the First World War was followed by a return to gun design after the 1917 revolution, culminating in the development of the Maxim-Tokarev (MT) light machine-gun. Then came a submachine-gun, the Tokarev pistol (below) and the first of a series of rifles that culminated in official adoption. Fedor Tokarev effectively ceased work after the Second World War, but enjoyed a lengthy retirement; he died as recently as 1968. **2.** Nikolay Fedorovich Tokarev (1899–1972), the son of Fedor Tokarev, is credited with the design of the quadruple mount for the standard Soviet Maxim machine-gun (PM) in 1931, and the ZPU mount for three PV-1 aircraft guns in 1941. **3.** Tokarev pistol, or Tula-Tokarev (TT). This was a 7.62mm copy of the *Colt-Browning, lacking adequate manual safety features, but with a cleverly packaged lock mechanism that could be removed on a subassembly (this clearly inspired Charles Petter, designer of the SACM and SIG pistols). It was introduced in the Red Army in 1930, after trials with a variety of unsuccessful submissions by *Korovin, *Prilutskiy and others, but encountered so many teething troubles that it was revised, then re-introduced in 1933 with locking ribs that ran entirely around the barrel. Production was quite slow initially, and the venerable Nagant gas-seal revolver was put back into production as an expedient. However, during the Second World War, the problems were largely solved and large numbers of Tokarevs were made. Work continued well into post-war days, although the Tokarev was supplemented after 1951, then replaced by the smaller *Makarov (PM). Pistols of this type have been made in many Soviet-bloc and satellite countries, including Hungary (as the Pisztoly 48.M), the People's Republic of China (Type 51) and Yugoslavia (Model 57). **4.** Tokarev rifle: see panel, p. 520.

Tokyo... – 1. Tokyo Juki, Tokyo, Japan. A maker of 7.7mm Type 99 *Arisaka rifles, c. 1943/44. **2.** Tokyo Rifle Laboratory and Tokyo Rifle Company Ltd (Japan). This business was founded in 1952 by Kensuke Chiba, Japan's premier designer of pneumatic airguns, and made the early Sharp Tiger, Veteran and Victory rifles. It was succeeded in 1953 by the Tokyo Rifle Manufacturing Company, and in 1955 by the Tokyo Rifle Company Ltd.

Toledo... – 1. Toledo Arms Co[mpany]. A *Suicide Special revolver made by the *Hopkins & Allen Arms Company of Norwich, Connecticut, USA, in the late nineteenth century. **2.** Toledo Firearms Co[mpany]. A *Suicide Special revolver made by *E.L. Dickinson of Springfield, Massachusetts, USA, in the late nineteenth century. **3.** Toledo Works. See Charles *Reeves & Company.

Tolley – 1. F. & W. Tolley. This English gunmaking business was listed at 1 Conduit Street, London W., in 1883–84,

TOKAREV RIFLES

Tokarev (4)

These were the outcome of a series of trials with gas- and recoil-operated rifles undertaken in the Soviet Union in the 1920s and 1930s. The first Tokarev to see success was the 1930 model, perhaps 100 being made for troop trials. This was followed by a variety of rifles and carbines, until the design of the gas piston and the tilting-block breech had been completed. On 26 February 1939, therefore, the *Samozariadniya vintovka Tokareva* (SVT-38) was adopted for service, and series production began in Izhevsk. Among the most distinctive features were the position of the cleaning rod, carried in a channel on the right side of the two-piece stock, and a six-port muzzle brake.

The first guns were delivered in October 1939, but combat experience during the Winter War with Finland (1940–41) soon showed their weaknesses. The original introduction was cancelled in favour of the improved Model 1940 (SVT-40), which was formally approved on 13 April 1940. The cleaning rod lay under the barrel, a sheet-metal fore-end was fitted, and the stock was fluted beneath the back sight to improve grip. Eventually a simplified two-port muzzle brake replaced the six-port design.

The 1940-pattern rifles were much better than their predecessors, although not without their faults. The magazines were badly made, parts broke too readily, and they were deemed to be too complicated for the rank-and-file. Consequently Tokarev rifles were confined largely to elite units, NCOs and marines. A few selective-fire versions (AVT-40) were made, usually distinguished by a sturdier stock and an additional selector; and a large number of sniper rifles (SNT-40) appeared before it became clear that they lacked the accuracy of the 1891/30 Mosin-Nagants.

Carbine derivatives of the basic design (SKT-40) were made in small numbers, perhaps for cavalry or mechanised forces, but most guns of carbine length were so-called Partisan Guns, cannibalised from damaged full-length examples. The Tokarev is usually derided in Western literature as a failure. However, production in 1941 alone reached 1,070,000, and it is clear that it was made in far greater numbers than any semi-automatic rifle used during the Second World War, with the exception of the US M1 Garand.

Comparatively little has been written about these fascinating rifles, although David N. Bolotin's *Soviet Small-Arms and Ammunition* (Finnish Arms Museum Foundation/Handgun Press, 1992), and John Walter's *Rifles of the World* (Krause Publications, second edition, 1998) give a few details.

The 7.62x54R Tokarev rifle was made in surprisingly large numbers during the Second World War, but was ultimately abandoned in favour of the bolt-action Mosin-Nagant when the dislocated Russian industry failed to cope with its complexities. This is an example of the supposedly perfected SVT 40.

but is probably a misprint of J. & W. Tolley (below). **2.** Henry Tolley & Company. A British gunmaking business trading in 1890–91 from 65–66 Weaman Street, Birmingham, Warwickshire. **3.** James & William Tolley, Birmingham, Warwickshire. Listed in local directories from 1859 onward, as gun-, pistol and rifle makers, this partnership traded from St Mary's Row until c. 1877, then from Loveday Street. A 12-bore *Lefaucheux-type pinfire breech-loading shotgun was entered in *The Field* trials in 1866. London directories list J. & W. Tolley at 1 Conduit Street, London W., from 1885 until a move to 59 New Bond Street took place in 1895, which suggests that the business maintained a London office for some years. Work continued until the First World War and possibly later.

Tomes – 1. William James Tomes. Recorded as a gunmaker, living at 28 Church Street, Soho, London, in 1863–64. **2.** Tomes & Company. A gunmaking business trading from 98 High Holborn, London W.C., in 1884–85. **3.** Tomes, Melvain & Company. A distributor of cap-lock revolvers made in the 1860s by the *Bacon Manufacturing Company of Norwich, Connecticut, USA.

Tomiška. *See* panel, facing page.

Tomma. A repeating pistol, with a four-barrel block similar to that of the Menz *Regnum. A few guns were made for the 7.65mm Auto cartridge, but most chambered the 6.35mm version. Some were produced in Germany, and others, noticeably cruder, were made in Belgium prior to 1914 by Manufacture d'Armes 'HDH' of Liège.

'Tommy Gun'. A nickname applied to the *Thompson submachine-gun, deriving from General John T. Thompson, its most enthusiastic promoter. *See also* Auto-Ordnance Corporation and John B. *Blish.

Tonks. Joseph Tonks, Boston and Malden, Massachusetts, USA. The city directories place this maker of New England-style spring-air Gallery Guns at 37 High Street, Boston, in 1854–57, 49 Union Street in 1857–73, and 45 & 49 Union Street in 1873–75. Then Tonks moved to Malden, where he began a career as a gun designer. His breech-loading designs were protected by US Patents 254,727 and 254,728 of 7 March 1882; 282,429 of 31 July 1883 (jointly with Andrew E. *Whitmore); 333,795 of 5 January 1886; and 435,334 of 26 August 1890.

Tool guns. Occasionally pistols have been built into tools, particularly hammers and wrenches. Most have had the handles or hafts altered to conceal a single barrel chambered for a small rim- or centrefire cartridge. Pivoting-bar or button triggers release spring-loaded strikers, although a few slam-fire designs are known. There is no evidence that tool guns were made in quantity, or that established gunsmiths were involved. The *Buco pistol, however, took the form of a small telescope. Some details will be found in John Walter's *Secret Firearms* (1997), and Lewis Winant's *Firearms Curiosa* (1955).

Top... – **1.** Top Hit. This was a *Mauser-pattern sporting rifle made in Austria by Karl *Dschulnigg of Salzburg in the 1960s, usually with a radial magazine floor-plate latch. **2.** Top Score, Top-Score, Topscore. A spring-air pistol made in the USA by, or more probably for, *Healthways; also known as *Sharpshooter. **3.** Top Single. Applied to a variant of the *Krieghoff K-80 12-bore over/under shotgun with one barrel in the upper position. *See also* Unsingle. **4.** Top Snap. Associated with single-barrel box-lock hammerless shotguns made by Iver *Johnson in the early 1900s.

Torch pistols. *See* Flashlight pistols.

Torino arms factory. *See* Fabbrica d'Armi.

Tornado. A Hungarian-made *Telly barrel-cocking spring-air rifle distributed in Britain by *Relum Ltd.

Torpedo. A 5mm Sheridan-type airgun slug made in Germany by *Bimoco, as the Bimoco-Sheridan-Torpedo.

Torre Annunziata arms factory. *See* Fabbrica d'Armi.

'Torro' [The]. A mark reportedly found on shotgun cartridges loaded by the *Schultze Gunpowder Company, incorporating components supplied by *Eley Bros. The name reputedly celebrates bullfighting.

Toschi. R. Toschi & fils, Liège, Belgium. A gunmaking business operating from 1919 until 1941 or later, known for shotguns of the highest quality.

Tournaire, 4 rue Arago, Saint-Étienne, France. Listed in 1951 as a gunmaker.

Tower Bull Dog. A revolver made in Britain by P. *Webley & Sons, c. 1882–87. Apparently it was a variant of the No. 2 *Bull Dog – a double-action solid-frame design chambering .320, .380 or .450 centrefire ammunition – with its frame extended rearward to give a prawled

backstrap not unlike that of the Colt *Lightning.

Tower's Safety Police. A *Suicide Special revolver made by the *Hopkins & Allen Arms Company of Norwich, Connecticut, USA, in the late nineteenth century.

Towl. Joseph Towl, Bridge Street, Boston, Lincolnshire (1834–68). The marks of this English country gunmaker have been reported on *pepperboxes and cap-lock revolvers dating from the mid-nineteenth century.

Towlson. John Fox Towlson, High Street, Marlborough, Wiltshire. The marks of this English gunmaker (trading 1841–55) have been reported on self-cocking *pepperboxes.

Town... – **1.** Town & Country. An airgun marketed in the immediate post-1945 period by the *Crosman Arms Company of Fairport, New York State. **2.** Town & Country Junior. A simplified version of the Crosman *Town & Country (above), marketed in 1949–53 as the Models 109 and 110 in .177 and .22 respectively.

Towne. Jerome Towne, a Federal government arms inspector, working in 1863 during the Civil War, accepted arms and equipment marked 'JT' – although these may be difficult to distinguish from items inspected by Josiah *Tatnall. *See also* John *Tatler and US arms inspectors' marks.

Townsend. James Townsend. Trading from 11 & 12 Sand Street, Birmingham, Warwickshire, in 1845–71, Townsend was the predecessor of Townsend & Williams. He was granted English Registered Design no. 2052 in 1849, to protect an airgun-valve design, and made 'improved air guns, canes, and Patent Staff walking sticks...'

Toyo Juki, Hiroshima, Japan. A maker of 7.7mm Type 99 *Arisaka rifles from 1941 until the factory was destroyed in 1945 by the first atomic bomb.

Toz, TOZ, T.O.Z. Marks associated with the products of the *Tula arms factory (*Tulskii Oruzheinyi Za'vod*), but specifically with the 6.35mm TOZ, or *TK, pistol designed

---

ALOIS TOMIŠKA

Born in Pardubice on 13 February 1867, Alois Tomiška was apprenticed to a gunsmith before starting out on his own in Vienna, then the capital of the Austro-Hungarian empire. He specialised in mounts for optical sights, and is credited with the development of one of the first successful double-action trigger systems to be incorporated in a semi-automatic pistol. The *Little Tom was developed prior to 1918 by *Wiener Waffenfabrik, and after the First World War by Tomiška's own workshop in Pilsen.

Subsequently the inventor worked for Česká Zbrojovka; he died in Prague on 29 December 1946. Tomiška undoubtedly deserves much of the credit for the first successful combination of a double-action trigger and an auto-loading pistol. Customarily given to Fritz *Walther on the basis of the *Polizei-Pistole of 1929, this overlooks the commercial success of the Little Tom prior to

1918. However, the charge that Walther first purchased, then deliberately suppressed Tomiška's German patents in 1922 has never been proven satisfactorily. *See also* Fox.

Alois Tomiška designed one of the first double-action trigger systems to be applied successfully to a semi-automatic pistol. This 7.65mm Little Tom was made by Wiener Waffenfabrik soon after the First World War.

by Sergey ★Korovin and a more recent series of bolt-action sporting/target rifles.

'TP' – 1. Usually encountered as 'Mod. TP' on the slides of single-action German ★Taschen-Pistolen made by Carl ★Walther Waffenfabrik and its successors. **2.** Associated with the TP-70, a 6.35mm pocket pistol made in Germany by ★Korriphila-Präzisionsmechanik GmbH of Ulm to the designs of Edgar Budischowsky. **3.** A multi-barrel survival pistol (alternatively designated TP-82), developed as part of the Soviet cosmonauts' ★SONAZ kit.

'TPH'. Usually encountered as 'Mod. TPH' on the slides of double-action ★Taschenpistolen [mit] Hahn, made in Germany by Carl ★Walther Sportwaffenfabrik.

'TPM'. A mark found on US military firearms and accessories. *See* T.P. ★Maroney.

'TR', 'T&R', 'T. & R.' – 1. A monogram, 'T' within 'R', usually encircled. Found on ★Melior pistols made by T. ★Robar of Liège. **2.** A superimposed-type cursive monogram found on the grips of Belgian .44-calibre ★Frontier revolvers: *see* 'FR'. **3.** 'T&R' or 'T. & R.', encircled or in a decorative cartouche. Applied by the distributors ★Turner & Ross to revolvers made in the USA by the ★Hood Firearms Company and the ★Hopkins & Allen Arms Company of Norwich, Connecticut. They date from the late nineteenth century.

Tracker. A .177 or .22 sidelever-cocking spring-and-piston air rifle introduced by ★Webley & Scott in 1983. Based on the Viscount, it has also been marketed as the ★Barnett Spitfire.

Tracy. Henry Tracy, or Tracey, a government arms inspector working until c. 1850, accepted arms and equipment marked 'HT'. *See also* US arms inspectors' marks.

Trademarks and brandnames. *See* p. 572.

Tradewinds, Inc., Tacoma, Washington, USA. Importer of ★Krico bolt-action rifles and other firearms from the late 1950s onward.

Trail Rider. Rifles made by the ★Remington Arms Company. *See* Nylon series.

Training Rifles. A name given to a range of Japanese military rifles made toward the end of the Second World War, some salvaged from cannibalised ★Arisaka actions, and others made of the cheapest and poorest materials imaginable. Some were capable of firing ball ammunition (although the margins of safety would have been minimal), but others were restricted to either blanks or nothing at all.

Tramps Terror. Associated with a ★Suicide Special revolver made by ★Johnson, Bye & Company and/or ★Iver Johnson of Worcester and Fitchburg, Massachusetts, in the late nineteenth century.

Transfer-bar safety. A name customarily given to an addition in the lockwork of revolvers made after the implementation of the US Gun Control Act of 1968, ensuring that the hammer (or a striker propelled by the hammer) could reach the primer of a chambered cartridge only in the final stages of a deliberate trigger pull.

Tranter. William Tranter, Birmingham, Warwickshire. Born in 1816, Tranter rose to become one of the leading nineteenth-century English gunmakers. He was apprenticed to Isaac ★Hollis, and subsequently worked for, or with, several other gunmakers. Listed in 1841 at 29¹/₂ Whittall Street, 'Successor to R. Dugard' and in St Mary's Row in 1849 as a partner in Hollis, Sheath & Tranter, Tranter alone was occupying the St Mary's Row premises from the early 1850s until 1875. A steam-powered workshop was maintained in nearby Loveday Street until the 1860s. Tranter was granted a registered design for a pepperbox and a gunlock in October 1849,

following it with self-cocking revolvers and a safety mechanism (British Patent 212/53 of January 1853), then with a breech-loading rifle, a double-action revolver and projectiles (2921/53 of December 1853). Then came British Patent 1913/56 of 1856, protecting, among many other ideas, the well-known double-trigger revolver. British Patent 2067/62 of July 1862 protected the lockwork of a revolver, a rammer and a method of rifling; 1862/63 of July 1863 was granted for a breech-loading revolver; 1889/65 of July 1865 described a drop-barrel sporting gun and a cartridge-conversion system for ★cap-lock revolvers. Patent 2113/66 of August 1866 was granted for a bolt-action breech-loading rifle and another drop-barrel sporting gun; 2228/67 of 1867 improved Tranter's bolt-action rifle and cartridge revolver; and 285/68 of January 1868 improved the revolver still further. British Patents 3622/68 and 3557/69, granted in November 1868 and December 1869, protected a variety of sporting guns. Then William Tranter obtained British Patent 2509/71 (September 1871) for a rod-type extractor suited to revolvers and a swinging rifle breech-block. Patent 3171/79 of July 1879 protected a self-extracting revolver; 1881/82 of April 1882 and 6787/84 of April 1884 described drop-barrel sporting guns. Tranter's last British Patent, 3049/87 of February 1887, was granted three years before his death to protect his perfected bolt-action magazine rifle.

Trap... – 1. Trap, ★Concorde Trap or ★Daytona Trap. Over/under shotguns made by ★Società Armi Bresciane of Gardone Val Trompia in 20-bore (Concorde) and 12-bore (Daytona), usually with an anatomical pistol grip, a beavertail fore-end and a single trigger. Barrels are customarily 760 or 810mm long. The Trap SL is similar, but has side-locks. **2.** 'Trap and Game'. Accompanied by a setter dog and a flying clay pigeon, this mark will be found on shotgun cartridges sold in England in the 1950s by Steven ★Smith of Ashton-under-Lyme. The headstamp reveals the manufacturer to have been the ★Midland Gun Company. **3.** Trap Gun. The range of firearms of this type extends from guns built into man- and animal traps to simple drop-weight alarms. Although few can be truly classed as handguns, an important exception was the ★Game-Shooter.

'Trapdoor Springfield'. A nickname associated with the single-shot lifting-block rifles designed by Erskine S. ★Allin and made by ★Springfield Armory. *See* Springfield-Allin rifles and carbines.

Trapmaster. The .38 ★Crosman gas-powered shotgun, usually marketed as part of a similarly-named shooting kit.

Traux. Feno H. Traux, an army lieutenant, accepted ★High Standard pistols on behalf of the US government shortly after the USA declared war on Japan in December 1941. They are marked 'FHT'. *See also* US arms inspectors' marks.

Treago. A.C. Treago, sometimes listed as 'Treego', a captain in the US Army, accepted .45 ★Smith & Wesson M1917 revolvers during the First world War. They were marked 'ACT'. *See also* US arms inspectors' marks.

Treeby – 1. Thomas William Gardener Treeby, living in 1858 in Westbourne Terrace Villas, Westbourne Square, Paddington. A member of the London gun trade, listed in 1861–62 at 319 Oxford Street, Treeby was granted British Patents 1552/55 of 11 July 1855, 2629/55 of 21 November 1855 and 1306/58 of 9 June 1858 to protect 'improvements in revolving firearms...', then received no. 2310/58 of 1858 for a single-shot breech-loading rifle. **2.** Treeby Chain Gun. Made in small numbers c. 1854–58, in handgun and long-arm guise, this was distinguished by an endless chain of cartridge chambers dangling beneath the receiver. Most guns were *cap-locks, with a manually-retracted hammer-like striker, but apparently some self-cocking examples were made. Most guns also had a barrel that could be slid over the mouth of each chamber to improve the gas seal.

'Trelawney' [The]. Found on British shotgun cartridges loaded by the *Cornwall Cartridge Works of Liskeard.

Trevor Stampings Ltd, Bridge Street East, Welwyn Garden City, Hertfordshire. A maker of magazines for the 9mm *Sten Gun in the Second World War. The regional code 'S 114' may have been used instead of the company name. *See also* British military manufacturers' marks.

Tribuzio. Catello Tribuzio, Turin. Designer of the *Lampo repeating pistol, patented in Italy in 1899, and maker of sporting guns and rifles prior to the First World War.

Trident – 1. A name given to modified *Colt-type *double-action revolvers made by *Società Armi Bresciane. The standard guns have 62.5 or 75mm barrels, chamber .32 S&W or .38 Special cartridges, and have round-butt wooden grips. They weigh about 650gm. **2.** Trident Super. An enlarged version of the *SAB Trident revolver with 100mm or 150mm ventilated-rib barrels and adjustable back sights. The grips are customarily squared; weight is 720–850gm. **3.** Trident Match, or Match 900. Destined for target shooting, this *SAB revolver has a heavy squared 150mm barrel, an anatomical Neoprene grip and an adjustable competition-type back sight. It weighs about 1kg.

Triebel – 1. Chr. Triebel, Suhl in Thüringen. This German gunmaking business was trading in 1930 under the ownership of Richard Triebel, which suggests an earlier origin – perhaps prior to the First World War. **2.** Chr. Friedr. Triebel, Suhl in Thüringen, Backstrasse 14. Founded in 1800, this specialist gunmaking business was still being listed in 1941 and is assumed to have ceased trading at the end of the Second World War. The proprietor was Richard Friedr. Triebel. **3.** Fritz Triebel, Zella St Blasii and Zella-Mehlis in Thüringen. Listed in local directories for 1913–22 as a gunmaker, and in the 1939 edition of the *Deutsches Reichs-Adressbuch* as a specialist gun-stock maker (these entries may cover two generations with the same fore-name). **4.** A. & W. Triebel, Zella-Mehlis in Thüringen, Germany. Listed as master gunsmiths in the 1919–20 directories. **5.** Karl & Otto Triebel, Suhl in Thüringen. Master gunsmiths listed in German directories in 1930. **6.** K. & W. Triebel, Suhl in Thüringen. The *Deutsches Reichs-Adressbuch* for 1914 lists this gunsmithing business, perhaps a predecessor of Karl & Otto Triebel (above). **7.** Triebel & Kerner, Suhl in Thüringen. Listed as a gunmaker, period unknown.

Triomphe... – 1. A small Browning-type pocket pistol made in Spain by *Apaolozo Hermanos of Eibar: 6.35mm, six rounds, hammer fired. **2.** Triomphe Française. A 6.35mm six-shot *Browning-type pocket pistol made in France prior to 1940 by *Manufacture d'Armes des Pyrénées, possibly for *SFM of Paris.

Triple... – 1. Triple Action Safety Lock. Designed in 1906 by John *Murphy, this was applied to the Hopkins & Allen *Safety Police revolver. As the trigger was pressed, an eccentric pin altered the arc in which the hammer fell to strike the firing pin instead of resting on the frame. **2.** Triple-B. An air-powered shotgun; *see* Ye-Wha. **3.** Triple Lock. A sobriquet bestowed on the *Smith & Wesson .44 *Hand Ejector revolver, owing to the addition of a third locking point in the mechanism.

Triumph – 1. Usually found as 'The Triumph'; associated

with shotgun cartridges sold in northern Scotland by *Donaldson of Grantown-on-Spey. The name was accompanied by a trademark in the form of a hand holding a dagger. The name is also found on shotgun cartridges, made by *Eley-Kynoch, for sale by P.D. *Malloch of Perth. **2.** An airgun pellet made in Britain by *Lane Brothers to the 1929 patent of John B. Lane. The Japanese *Silver Jet was essentially a copy of the original Triumph design. **3.** A five-shot double-action *Merwin, Hulbert & Company revolver, chambered for the .38 S&W cartridge, but otherwise similar to the *Double Action Army pattern. It was made by *Hopkins & Allen in the mid-1880s, later examples often displaying a folding hammer.

Trojan. A *Suicide Special revolver made by the *Hood Firearms Company of Norwich, Connecticut, USA, in the late nineteenth century.

Trombon, Trombone – 1. Usually as 'Trombon'. A nickname applied to the *Carabine à Répétition Browning, made by *Fabrique Nationale d'Armes de Guerre. **2.** As 'Trombone'. A brandname applied to the *Daisy Model 107 pump-action BB Gun, made in the USA in the 1950s. The Trombone Repeater, also known as the Model 107, was a variant of the *Buck Jones Special made with a 500-, 450- or 375-ball magazine during 1959–62.

Trommelmagazin. 'Drum magazine' in German; this term was applied to the spring-powered feed units issued during the First World War with the *Parabellum pistol (TM. 08) and *Mondragon rifle (TM. für FSK). Once thought to have been based on the designs of Tatarek and von Benkö, they are more accurately attributed to Friedrich *Blum. *See also* Allgemeine Elektrizitäts- Gesellschaft, Gebr. *Bing and Vereinigte Automaten-Fabriken.

Tronchon-Robert, rue Badouillère 12 and (later) 16, Saint-Étienne, France. Listed in 1879–92 as a gunmaker.

Trooper. Made by *Colt's Patent Fire Arms Manufacturing Company and the Firearms Division of *Colt Industries in 1953–69, this .22 rimfire or .357 Magnum/.38 Special revolver was based on the *Police Positive Special, but had adjustable sights and a heavy barrel. The Trooper Mark III appeared in 1969, with internal improvements and an ejector-rod shroud/ventilated-rib barrel; and the Trooper Mark V followed in 1980 with a better trigger mechanism and a ventilated-rib barrel. Work ceased in 1986. *See also* Magnum Model and Lawman Mark III.

Trowbridge. Frank C. Trowbridge. A partner in the *Hexagon Air Rifle Company of Detroit, Michigan.

True Fit. *See* A True Fit.

Tru-Flyte. Rifling used by the *Crosman Arms Company of Fairport, New York State, USA, on some of its pneumatic and gas-powered BB Guns.

Trulock. Edward Trulock & Son, 9 Dawson Street, Dublin. This Irish gunmaking business displayed *pepper-box-type 'revolving pistols' at the Great Exhibition held in London in 1851.

Trumpf. *See* panel, p. 524.

Truncheon guns. Occasionally guns may be found disguised as blackjacks and truncheons, often intended to appeal to mid-nineteenth-century policemen. Most pre-1850 products are cap-locks, including a sizeable number of English-made folding-trigger underhammers marked 'DAY'S PATENT' (granted in 1823 to John Day of Barnstaple, Devon), but a few cartridge guns are also known.

Trust. Made by, or perhaps for, Fabrique d'Armes de *Grande Précision of Eibar, Guipúzcoa, Spain, this 6.35mm

TRUMPF

A three-barrel combination gun introduced prior to 1939 by *Krieghoff, and now made by the company in Ulm/Donau with two shotgun barrels above a central rifle (which may be free-floating), or two rifles above a central shotgun.

The 12-, 16- or 20-bore shotgun barrels (both of the same calibre) will be accompanied by rifles chambered for cartridges from .22 Hornet to 9.3x74R. Double rifle barrels (restricted to .30-06, 8x57 and 9.3x74R) are accompanied by a single 20-bore shotgun. The *box-lock action has a sliding safety catch on the left side of the top lever, while a cocking slide on the tang switches between the upper right and lower central barrels. A non-selective single trigger mechanism is optional.

The Trumpf-L, introduced in the late 1980s, is a lightened version of the standard Trumpf with 550mm barrels instead of the standard 650mm length. The shotgun barrels are chambered only for 12- or 16-bore cartridges.

A Krieghoff leaflet advertising the short version of the Trumpf, the Trumpf-L.

pocket pistol had a six-round box magazine and a hammer-type firing mechanism.

'Trusty Servant' [The]. A mark used by *Hammond Bros. of Winchester on shotgun ammunition.

Tryon. Edward K. Tryon [& Company], Philadelphia, Pennsylvania, USA. A gunmaker/distributor active in 1837–68, succeeded by his son (Edward K. Tryon Jr. & Company, c. 1868–1905), then by Edward K. Tryon Company, Inc., from 1905 onward. Tryon marks have been reported on a variety of sporting guns and rifles, ranging from *cap-locks made in Philadelphia to the products of *Colt, *Remington and *Winchester.

TS. See Thermostabil.

TT, T.T. Associated with the Soviet 7.62mm Tula-Tokarev pistol, designed by Fedor *Tokarev and made in the *Tula arms factory from the mid-1930s until the early 1950s. See also TOZ.

'TTCO'. A floriated superimposition-type monogram; see 'JJCO.'

'TTH', 'TTSL'. Associated with US military firearms and accessories. See Thomas T. *Holmes and Theodore T.S. *Laidley respectively.

Turbite. See Lane's Turbite.

Tucker – **1.** George F. Tucker, an arms inspector employed by the Federal government during the Civil War, accepted arms and equipment marked 'GFT'. See also US arms inspectors' marks. **2.** Tucker & Son, Weatherford, Texas, Confederate States of America. Successor to Tucker, Sherrard & Company, this business made about 100 *Navy Model Colt copies with round barrels. Operations were succeeded by *Taylor, Sherrard & Company. **3.** Tucker, Sherrard & Company, Lancaster, Texas. This Confederate gunmaking business accepted a contract to make 3,000 Colt-type revolvers during the American Civil War, but deliveries had not even begun when Labon Tucker with-drew to form Tucker & Son.

Tula ordnance factory, Tula, RSFSR (Russia). Originally founded in 1648 to make gun barrels, Tula became a gun manufactory when Tsar Peter I signed an appropriate decree on 15 February 1712. Flint- and *caplock muskets, rifle-muskets and pistols were produced in quantity before the factory re-equipped to make the *Berdan II rifle in the early 1870s. Copies of the *Smith & Wesson *New Model Russian revolvers were made from c. 1882 until the adoption of the *Nagant gas-seal pattern in 1895, although production of the latter did not begin in Tula until 1901. Other products have included *Mosin-Nagant rifles, *Tokarev pistols and 6.35mm automatic pistols made under the designation TK. Edged weapons, sporting guns and ammunition have also been made.

Tulle arms factory. The manufacture of firearms began in Tulle in 1646, and a state-owned factory (Manufacture d'Armes de Tulle) was erected there in 1690.

Tulloch. William Tulloch & Company. This English gunmaking business traded from Broad Street House, New Broad Street, London E.C., from 1898 until 1900 and probably later.

Turbiaux. Jacques Edmond Turbiaux, a French gunsmith, was responsible for the turret-type palm pistol covered by US Patent 273,644 of 6 March 1883. Subsequently the gun was marketed as the *Protector.

Turin arms factory. See Fabbrica d'Armi.

Turnbull. William Turnbull, a government arms inspector, accepted firearms and accoutrements in the 1840s. They were marked 'WT'. See also US arms inspectors' marks.

Turner – 1. D.A. Turner, a government arms inspector, accepted .45 M1911 pistols made by *Colt's Patent Fire Arms Manufacturing Company. Dating from c. 1915, they bore 'DAT' markings. See also US arms inspectors' marks. **2.** Thomas Turner. An English gun-barrel maker listed in Birmingham directories at 5 Aston Road (1834–37), and thereafter as a gun- and pistol maker at 8 Fisher Street (1838–90). Well known as a maker of cap-lock rifles, Turner was succeeded in 1890 by his sons, Thomas and James S. Turner. Business continued until 1899 or later. **3.** Thomas Turner. A gunmaker trading from 19 Brook Street, London W., in 1884–91, and from 17 New Bond Street, London W., in 1892–93. Possibly the elder son of Thomas Turner (above). **4.** Thomas Turner, Reading, Berkshire, England. Turner was listed at 3 Middle Row in 1843–51 and 63 Market Place in 1869. His marks have been reported on a variety of sporting guns, self-cocking *pepperboxes and cap-lock revolvers. **5.** Turner & Ross, Boston, Massachusetts, USA. Best known as a distributor of metalware and consumer goods, active in 1873–85, this partnership also handled firearms. *Czar-brand revolvers made by *Hopkins & Allen, the *Whitney Arms Company and possibly others are among those that have been identified.

Turney. Henry Turney. A London gunmaker listed in 1847–49 at 3 Ebenezer Terrace, Commercial Road, Limehouse; at 2 Jamaica Terrace, Limehouse, from 1850 until 1862; at 11 Hales Terrace, West India Dock Road (1863–67); at 11 Jamaica Terrace in 1868–69; and lastly at 9 Pennyfields, Poplar, in 1870–71.

'Turnover' [The]. An English-made *cap-lock *pepperbox, the work of Joseph *Lang of London.

Turpin. Harold Turpin was the co-designer with Reginald *Shepherd of the British *Sten Gun.

Tuttle. S.L. Tuttle. This US government arms inspector, working in the mid-1890s, accepted guns and equipment marked 'SLT'. See also US arms inspectors' marks.

'TV', 'TWB'. Marks found on US military firearms and accessories. See Thomas *Valentine and Thomas W. *Booth.

'Tweed' [The]. A mark found on shotgun cartridges sold in Scotland by *Forrest & Son of Kelso.

Twelve... – 1. 'Twelve Twenty' [The]. A brandname found on shotgun cartridges sold by Charles *Lancaster & Company of London. **2.** 'Twelve-Two' [The]. A brandname associated with 12-bore shotgun cartridges loaded for *Holland & Holland of London. They had 2in cases.

Twentieth Century. A single-shot break-open BB Gun made in the USA by *Daisy in 1901–08. It was designed by Clarence *Hamilton and others. The Twentieth Century Repeater was variant with a magazine for 350 balls; small quantities were made between 1902 and 1912.

'Twenty Cartridge' [The]. Associated with 20-bore shotgun cartridges sold by Charles S. *Rosson of Norwich. See also 'Sixteen Cartridge'.

'TWH'. A mark found on US military firearms and accessories. See Thomas W. *Hafer and T.W. *Holmes.

Twigg. John Twigg. The marks of this London gunmaker have been reported on self-cocking *pepperboxes dating from the middle of the nineteenth century.

Twining. Nathan C. Twining, a US Navy lieutenant, accepted .38 revolvers made by *Colt's Patent Fire Arms Manufacturing Company and .236 *Lee-patent rifles made by the *Winchester Repeating Arms Company. They bore an 'NCT' stamping. See also US arms inspectors' marks.

Two-Bit Special. This brandname will be found on a .25 automatic pistol made in the USA by *Steel City Arms.

'TWR'. Found on US military firearms and accessories. See Thomas W. *Russell.

Tycoon. A sheath-trigger revolver made by *Johnson & Bye of Worcester, Massachusetts, USA, in calibres ranging from .22 to .44. A version of the *Favorite, it was introduced c. 1873.

Tyler – 1. D. Waldo Tyler, an inspector employed by the Federal government during the American Civil War, accepted arms and equipment marked 'DWT'. **2.** J.B. Tyler. This government arms inspector, working early in the twentieth century, accepted .38 *Colt revolvers and other ordnance stores marked 'JBT'. See also US arms inspectors' marks for both entries. **3.** Philos Tyler, USA. See American Machine Works. **4.** P.S. Tyler, Boston, Massachusetts, USA. Co-designer with Francis E. *Boyd of the breech-loading shotguns protected by US Patents 73,494 and 88,540 of 21 January 1868 and 6 April 1869 respectively.

Type Française. A generic French-language term reserved for *Velo-Dog-type revolvers chambering a special 6mm rimfire cartridge instead of the customary 5.5mm centrefire version.

Typhoon. A lifting-barrel .177 and .22 spring-air pistol made in Britain by *Webley & Scott Ltd as a replacement for the *Premier. See also Hurricane.

Tyrol – 1. Offered by Société Anonyme Continentale pour la Fabrication des Armes à Feu *Lebeau-Courally in 7x65R only, this single-barrel break-open design had a lock on the left side with a matching side-plate on the right. The octagonal barrel is locked in the frame by a double-bite slide and a double Greener (Kersten) crossbolt. An ejector and a set trigger can be fitted to order. Fine English scroll-and-bouquet engraving is customary, with oak leaves on the fences and trophy heads in the panels. **2.** Tyrol Brand. See Tirol Brand.

Tyrolean stock. See Stock.

Tyson. John Tyson, USA: see DuBiel.

U

'U'. Customarily encircled. A *headstamp found on cartridges made by the *Union Metallic Cartridge Company.

'ua'. A codemark allocated in 1940 to Osnabrücker Kupfer- und Drahtwerke AG, a maker of German small-arms ammunition components.

UAS. *See* Universal-Abzug-System.

UB – 1. Associated with British small-arms and parts made by the Shirley factory of *BSA Guns Ltd c. 1955–64. **2.** An abbreviation of *Universalny Berezin*, applied to the 12.7mm aircraft machine-gun developed by Mikhail *Berezin. *See also* UBK, UBS and UBT.

Ubel. Christopher Ubel, or Uebel. Reportedly a US based maker of spring-air *Gallery Guns, c. 1860–70.

Uberti. Aldo Uberti & C. SNC, Via G. Carducci, Ponte Zanano/Brescia. An Italian maker of reproduction Winchester, Colt and other guns.

UBK, UBS, UBT. Applied to Soviet *Berezin UB 12.7mm aircraft machine-guns adapted for wing mounting (UBK); for synchroniser gear to fire through a propeller arc (UBS); or for ring tracks to provide an observer's gun (UBT).

'UE'. Associated with guns and components made in Britain by the *Royal Small Arms Factory and *Royal Ordnance plc, Enfield Lock, prior to 1988, and by Royal Ordnance plc, King's Meadow, Nottingham, thereafter.

'UF'. Found on guns and components made by in Britain by the *Royal Small Arms Factory, Fazakerly, c. 1955–60.

Uhlinger. William Uhlinger, Philadelphia, Pennsylvania. A maker, or perhaps simply a distributor, of inexpensive *Suicide Special revolvers named Grant (q.v.).

Uhlman. A. Uhlman, Stettin. A maker of volute-spring Gallery Guns working in the 1850s.

Ulm – 1. Made by H. *Krieghoff GmbH of Ulm/Donau, Germany, in chamberings ranging from 7x65R to 9.3x74R, this *Double Rifle is similar to the *Teck, but is the maker's finest product. The *side-locks are detachable, double triggers are standard, and there is a safety slide on the upper tang; the back sights are usually mounted on quarter-ribs. **2.** Ulm Bergstutzen. Identical mechanically to the standard *Krieghoff rifle of this type, chambering the same ammunition as the *Teck Bergstutzen, this has short barrels of differing calibre. **3.** Ulm Primus. A high-quality version of the standard *Krieghoff Ulm rifle, with exquisite engraving and excellent woodwork. **4.** Ulm Trap (Ulm-T). A 12-bore shotgun version of the basic Krieghoff over/under design, with a single non-selective trigger mechanism.

Ulrich. C.F. Ulrich, using a 'CFU' mark, accepted .38 *Colt and *Smith & Wesson revolvers on behalf of the US Navy in 1905–06. *See also* US arms inspectors' marks.

Ulster – 1. Normally as 'The Ulster' on shotgun cartridges sold in Northern Ireland by *Cambridge & Company of Carrickfergus. **2.** Ulster Bull Dog. A brandname associated with revolvers made in England by P. *Webley & Son. **3.** Ulster Volunteer Force (UVF). This paramilitary force was raised in northern Ireland, shortly before the First World War, to contest a grant of Home Rule threatened by the British government. Apparently single-shot 1871-pattern Mauser, ex-Italian Mo 1870–87 *Vetterli and *Steyr-made 1904-type Mannlicher rifles were bought in Germany, probably from *Spiro of Hamburg. They often bore 'FOR GOD AND ULSTER', or 'U.V.F.' and the Red Hand of Ulster (the badge of the O'Neill family) on a shield.

Ultimate. Used by the *Colt Custom Gun Shop from 1988 onward, distinguishing hand-finished versions of standard production guns, with special sights and grips, a high-quality finish and hand-honed trigger components.

Ultra – 1. Introduced by H. *Krieghoff GmbH in 1985, this features a *box-lock secured by a slide in the frame engaging two lumps on the underside of the barrel-block. Configurations include an over/under *Double Rifle chambered for cartridges ranging from 7x65R to 9.3x74R; a 12- or 20-bore over/under shotgun; and a two-barrel combination gun with a 12- or 20-bore smoothbore upper barrel (Ultra-12, Ultra-20). The frame is normally aluminium alloy. The box-lock contains two hammers, and has a manual *Kickspanner* cocking slide/safety catch on the upper tang. Rifles are usually fitted with a two-trigger unit, although the optional Ultra-B has a selector under the receiver to switch the front, or set, trigger to the smoothbore, or upper, barrel. **2.** Ultra Bergstutzen. Distinguished by short barrels, this has a large-calibre barrel above a smaller one. The chambering is basically the same as for the *Teck Bergstutzen. **3.** Ultra S, Ultra Bergstutzen S and Ultra Bockdoppelbüchse S. Identical to the standard guns in all other respects, these have additional side-plates extending backward to provide more space for decoration. **4.** Ultra-20 Bockdoppelbüchse TS. Dating from 1996, this gun, also made with as *Bockbüschflinte* with a 20-bore shotgun barrel, amalgamates a special free-floating heat-stable barrel assembly – Thermostabil (TS) – with a three-point radial adjustment system to regulate the point of impact. **5.** The Model 300 Ultra was a Mauser-type bolt-action rifle offered in the USA by *Harrington & Richardson in 1967–82, in chamberings from .22-250 to .308 Winchester. It had a roll-over comb and Williams ramp sights. The actions came from *Fabrique Nationale. **6.** Or Kodiak Ultra. Also known as the Model 101, this bolt-action sporting rifle was built in the USA in 1960–73 by the *Kodiak Manufacturing Company on a *Mauser action. The stock had a roll-over comb. **7.** Ultra Carbine. Also known as the Model 301, this was a version of the *Harrington & Richardson *Ultra sporting rifle (above) with a full-length stock and a simple folding-leaf back sight. **8.** Ultra-Hi Products, Florence Avenue, Hawthorne, New Jersey, USA. A manufacturer of BB-firing Kentucky Rifles, introduced in 1977. **9.** Ultra-Light Arms, Inc., Granville, West Virginia. A maker of modified *Mauser-type Model 20 bolt-action rifles from 1987 to date. There are three basic versions: the short-action Model 20 (.17 Remington to .300 Savage), the intermediate Model 24 (.25-06 Remington to .30-06) and the long Model 28 (.264 Winchester to .338 Winchester

Magnum). **10.** Ultra Medalist. Made by ★Harrington & Richardson in 1968–73, on an FN ★Supreme Mauser action, this 'varmint' or bench-rest rifle had a heavy barrel, a roll-over comb and a semi-beavertail fore-end. *See* Ultra 300 (above).

Umarex. Umarex Sportwaffen GmbH & Co. KG, Arnsberg. German sporting-goods and firearms distributor. Licensee of the Mauser banner trademark, and owner since 1994 of ★Walther.

Umbrella guns. *See* Cane guns.

'U.M.C.Co.' An abbreviation of ★Union Metallic Cartridge Company, found in the headstamps of a wide variety of US-made ammunition.

'UN'. A mark found on US military firearms and accessories. *See* Urban ★Niblo.

Unceta y Compañía, Guernica, Spain. *See* panel, below.

Uncle Dan, or Uncle Dan Grade. A brandname associated with box-lock shotguns made in the USA in 1903–06 by D.M. ★Lefever, Sons & Company of Bowling Green, Ohio.

Undercover, Undercoverette. Revolvers made in the USA by ★Charter Arms. Once marketed as the 'smallest and lightest steel-frame revolver made in the USA', the Undercover is basically a diminutive Police Bulldog (q.v.) chambered for either .32 S&W Long or .38 Special ammunition. P-suffix guns have a spurless Pocket Hammer. The Undercoverette, intended specifically for women, had a special narrow butt. It was substituted for the 1.8in-barrelled Undercover (c.1977–82), but then the patterns were merged. However, the '-ette' suffix has recently reappeared.

Underwater pistols. It is generally thought that a conventional firearm cannot be fired under water, although tests have shown that, while operating pressures rise greatly, many guns have sufficient safety margins to survive such harsh treatment. The Russians and others have designed guns to work specifically under water. *See* V.G. Simonov.

Underwood-Elliott-Fisher Company, Hartford, Connecticut, USA. A maker of 542,620 ★M1 Carbines during 1942–44.

Undetectable pistols. The increasing use of synthetic components has led to fears that an 'undetectable' gun would evade X-ray surveillance equipment. The first to receive this label was the Austrian ★Glock, even though it has many steel components (including the barrel) and cannot pass even the most primitive of X-ray systems undetected. However, plastics technology may advance to a point where a material will be strong enough to make gun barrels or sufficiently resilient to replace metal springs. Teamed with caseless ammunition, this could bring the undetectable gun much closer to reality.

Uneedem. A tradename associated with shotgun cartridges made by, or perhaps for, J.V. ★Needham of Birming-ham. Accompanied by an illustration of a bounding rabbit, the mark is a play partly on the promoter's name, but also on the claim, 'You need them'.

'Unequalled' [The], or 'Michie's Unequalled'. This brandname will be found on shotgun ammunition handled in Scotland by G.M. ★Michie of Stirling. Apparently it was made

UNCETA Y COMPAÑÍA

Guernica, Spain. Successor to ★Esperanza y Unceta in 1926, itself succeeded by ★Astra–Unceta SA in the 1960s. Production of the Astra 200, Astra 300 and Astra 400 pistols continued alongside the 900-series of Mauser C/96 adaptations introduced in 1927 specifically for sale in the Far East. Sales routed into China, initially by way of Japanese trading houses, were very successful; eventually, in 1931, Astra China Company Ltd was founded in Shanghai. After 1931, however, the Republican government in Spain introduced the first of a series of restrictions on gunmaking, when all handguns accepting military-type ammunition were confiscated, and all export orders were subject to official approval.

When the Civil War began in 1936, Guernica was occupied by the Republican forces. Production in the Astra factory slowed perceptibly (the owners had Nationalist sympathies) and, eventually, an order was given to move the production facilities to Bilbao. On 25 April 1937, however, the Nationalist Air Force mounted the now-notorious raid on Guernica; within a week, the area had been retaken by the Nationalist Army, and the Astra factory resumed work.

Handguns were made for the Germans during the Second World War (mostly Astra 600, but including a few thousand 900-series pistols), until the advent of laws prohibiting selective-fire handguns in Spain and the liberation of France brought military production to an end. Guns marked 'Union' were made for ★Seytre and possibly also for Tómas de ★Urizar. Those bearing 'Unique' were produced for Manufacture d'Armes des Pyrénées Françaises.

Unceta y Cia of Guernica made pistols under the Astra name. This is a 7.63mm Modelo F from the early 1930s, shown attached to its German-inspired holster-stock. Guns of this type were extremely popular in the Far East, especially in selective-fire form.

from ★Eley, or possibly Belgian, components prior to 1914.

Union – 1. Union (Seytre). Associated with M. Seytre of Saint-Étienne, a wholesaler of guns, ammunition and accessories, c. 1920–39. Virtually all of the pistols were purchased from ★Manufacture d'Armes des Pyrénées or in Spain, the latter often being ★Llama-type copies of the locked-breech ★Colt-Browning. The mark will also be found on 6.35mm six-shot and 7.65mm nine-shot ★Browning-type blowbacks made prior to 1940 by ★Manufacture d'Armes des Pyrénées. The slides of the smaller guns may be marked '*Fabrique à St. Étienne*' in addition to 'Union'. **2.** Found on Browning-type semi-automatic pistols made in Spain by ★Esperanza y Unceta of Guernica: 6.35mm, six rounds, hammer fired. Made for M. ★Seytre of Saint-Étienne (above). **3.** Found on small Browning-type semi-automatic pistols made by ★Unceta y Compañía of Guernica: 6.35mm or 7.65mm, six rounds, hammer fired. Apparently they were made for ★Seytre of Saint-Étienne in the late 1920s, although sometimes they are associated with Tómas de ★Urizar of Barcelona. **4.** Found on the ★Gross- and Gwyn & Campbell-pattern carbines made in the USA by the ★Cosmopolitan Arms Company during the American Civil War. **5.** A ★Suicide Special revolver made by the ★Hopkins & Allen Arms Company of Norwich, Connecticut, USA, in the late nineteenth century. **6.** Fábrica de Armas 'Union', Eibar, Guipuzcoa, Spain. Maker of pocket pistols marked ★Rival. **7.** Union Arms Co. A ★Suicide Special revolver made in the USA in the 1880s by the ★Whitney Arms Company of Whitneyville, Connecticut. **8.** Union Arms Company. A distributor of cap-lock revolvers made in the USA by the ★Bacon Manufacturing Company and the ★Whitney Arms Company during the American Civil War. **9.** Union Cap & Chemical Company, East Alton, Illinois. A manufacturer of ammunition, making its first rimfires in 1907. Among the distinctive marks was a small target superimposed on a Maltese Cross. **10.** Union-France: *see* Union (Seytre). **11.** Union Hill Models. Named after a famous North American shooting range (cf. Creedmoor, What Cheer), the No. 8 (new) and No. 9 (new) ★Marlin-made ★Ballards were introduced in 1884 to compete in the medium-price target-rifle market. They normally had half-octagon barrels and pistol-grip butts; the No. 8 had a double set trigger, whereas the No. 9 had a single trigger. **12.** Union Jack. A ★Suicide Special revolver made in the USA by the ★Hood Firearms Company of Norwich, Connecticut. It dates from the late nineteenth century. **13.** Union Metallic Cartridge Company, Boston, Massachusetts, and Bridgeport, Connecticut. Founded in 1866 to produce powder flasks and metallic-case cartridges, this business became one of the leading US ammunition makers, eventually being purchased by ★Hartley & Graham and merged in 1902 with the ★Remington Arms Company to form ★Remington–UMC. The earliest ★headstamps comprised 'U', usually within a circle; later examples read 'U.M.C.Co.', then 'REM–UMC'. Some cartridges made shortly after the Second World War were stamped 'MEDICUS' (possibly the name of a dealer). **14.** Union Repeating Gun. Patented in Britain in 1866, by Wilson ★Ager, this was the subject of a design-infringement suit fought in New York in 1861 between Edward Nugent and William Palmer. A prototype was tested successfully in October 1861, and the first ten guns were bought by the Federal Army; purchases during the American Civil War exceeded sixty. They fired .58-calibre combustible paper cartridges from special capped cylinders

fed into a hopper on top of the breech, which gave the sobriquet, 'Coffee Mill Gun'. As the operating handle rotated, each cylinder was fed into the breech, fired, extracted and dropped down through the action into a receiving tray, from which it could be retrieved and reloaded. **15.** Union Switch & Signal Company, Swissvale, Pennsylvania. A subsidiary of the Westinghouse Air Brake Company, US&S contracted to make .45 M1911A1 ★Colt-Browning pistols during the Second World War; 55,000 guns were made in 1943. Their slides bore an 'SS' within 'U' trademark, ahead of 'U.S. & S. CO.' above the address. *See also* Winchester.

Unique – 1. A tradename associated with ★Manufacture d'Armes des Pyrénées, usually applied to its sturdy ★blowback pistols. Most of the guns were given numerical designations originally, but those that survived 1945, and new models, received alpha-numeric identifiers. Pre-1945 pistols included the Kriegsmodell, made under German supervision during the Vichy period. Derived from the ★FN-Brownings, the MAP guns had slides that enveloped the barrels; newer guns, however, have open-topped slides. The 7.65mm or 9mm Short Unique Bcf (or Bcf-66) had the front sight on the slide, mounted on a bridge over the barrel, although most other guns had their sights at the muzzle. They included the 7.65mm Unique C and C-2, the latter with an open-top slide; the rimfire Unique D (.22 LR) and Unique E (.22 Short), with short or long barrels identified by -1 and -2 suffixes respectively. The Unique L, a modernised C, was offered in .22 LR rimfire (Lr), 7.65mm Auto and 9mm Short; the Unique R and its rimfire equivalent, Mle Rr, were similar, but had longer butts and larger-capacity magazines. *See also* Mikros. **2.** A Browning-type pocket pistol made in Guernica, Spain, by ★Unceta y Compañía for Manufacture d'Armes des Pyrénées Françaises of Hendaye: 6.35mm, six rounds, hammer fired. Often marked 'Model 1924'. **3.** A ★Suicide Special revolver made by C.S. ★Shatuck of Hatfield, Massachusetts, USA, in the late nineteenth century. **4.** Or Shatuck Unique: a .22 or .32 rimfire pocket pistol, made by C.S. ★Shatuck in accordance with a patent granted to Oscar ★Mossberg. Its four-barrel block tipped down to load and was fired by a slider-actuated rotary striker.

United... – 1. United Merchandising, Inc.: *see* Marlin. **2.** United States Cartridge Company, Lowell, Massachusetts, USA. Founded in 1869 by General Benjamin F. Butler and associates, this was run by Butler until his death in 1893, then by his son, Paul, until 1918. Control passed to the National Lead Company, which had gained a half-share in the business in 1910. Capacity was considerable: during the First World War, under contract to the British, Dutch, French and Italian governments, in addition to the US authorities, the Bridgeport factory made more than 2.26 billion items. The principal ★headstamp mark was 'US', often encircled. Trading ceased in 1929. **3.** United States Machine-Gun Company [The], Boston, Massachusetts, and Meridan, Connecticut. This agency was formed by William Haskell to promote ★Berthier machine-guns and automatic rifles, securing a 7,000-gun contract once the weapon had been provisionally adopted by the army in 1917. However, unable to raise suitable capital, the business soon failed. The US government cancelled the rifle contract in November 1918, and a few unsatisfactory post-war prototypes did nothing to change the situation. Trading ceased in 1922, when Berthier took his ideas to ★Vickers in Britain. *See also* Vickers-Berthier. **4.** United States Revolver Company [The], Fitchburg, Massachusetts, USA. The name of this non-existent business was used by Iver *Johnson on simplified *US DA revolvers made in 1910–13. **5.** United States Supply Company, Medley, Florida. This wholesaler and distributor of sporting equipment has handled the Russian *Baikal air rifle, marketed as the Universal/Baikal Model 22.

Unity Heating Ltd, Welwyn Garden City, Hertfordshire. Maker of box magazines for the British .303 *Bren Gun during the Second World War, often marking them with the code 'S 365' instead of the company name.

Universal – 1. Usually encountered as 'The Universal' on shotgun cartridges made by *Eley Bros. prior to the acquisition of the company by Explosives Trades Ltd in 1918, and thereafter by *Eley-Kynoch Ltd. They will be found with various dealers' names, including John H.B. *North and Charles *Smith & Sons of Newark. **2.** A convertible semi-automatic pistol designed by Augustin *Nečaš and made in Czechoslovakia by Zbrojovka Brno. It was offered in .22 LR rimfire and .22 Short rimfire for normal and rapid-fire competitions respectively. There were three basic models: Sport, Precision and Super Rapid. **3.** 'Universal-Abzug-System' (UAS); known in English as the Universal Trigger System (UTS). A patented operating mechanism incorporated since the 1980s in shotguns, Double Rifles and combination guns made by H. *Krieghoff GmbH of Ulm/Donau. **4.** Universal machine-gun: see panel, below. **5.** Universal Trigger System (UTS): see Universal-Abzug-System.

Unknown Spanish semi-automatic pistols. In addition to the many brandnames linked with individual manufacturers, large numbers of unattributed brandnames exist. They include Asiatic, Aurora, Automatic Pistol, Cow Boy (sometimes misleadingly marked '*Fabrication Française*'), Defense, Dewaf, Handy, Hudson, Joha, Olympia, Radium, Rayon, Tatra, Tiwa and Zaldun. Most are listed separately.

'UN-QUALITY'. Found on US *M1 Carbine receivers made for *Quality Hardware by the *Union Switch & Signal Company.

Unsingle. Applied to a variant of the *Krieghoff K-80 12-bore over/under shotgun with one barrel in the lower position. See also Top Single.

Unwin & Rogers, Sheffield, England. Some of the best-known *knife pistols were made by Unwin & Rodgers from the 1850s onward. The earliest were single-barrel cap-locks with two folding blades beneath a grip of wood, staghorn or chequered gutta-percha. The barrel lay along the top of the grip, and the trigger folded up beneath it. Cap-lock models often had a scissors-type ball mould and a rammer in slots in the grip, being held by friction. Later guns (especially those made by Joseph *Rodgers after 1867) accepted small-calibre rim- or centrefire ammunition. Most guns had a small lidded trap in the butt for bullets or spare .22 Short cartridges. Unwin & Rodgers also made a few twin-barrel knife pistols under the name *Self-Protector.

'UOR'. Comprising a superimposed 'OR' monogram within 'U': a mark found on small-arms used by the

UNIVERSAL MACHINE-GUN

Universal (4)

A term applied to any machine-gun that can be adapted to undertake a variety of tasks without altering the gun. The solution is usually found in the provision of a selection of mounts, including a light bipod and tripods of varying size or complexity. While lightweight multi-purpose guns were developed during the First World War, the first of this configuration to encounter success was the German MG. 34 *Einheitsmaschinengewehr*, introduced in the late 1930s, although the MG. 42 of 1943 proved the concept more efficiently.

Modern guns of this type include the *MAG, made by FN Herstal SA in Belgium, and used throughout the world (including Britain, where it serves as the L7 series). The US M60 and the Soviet PK/PKM series are other good examples of the genre. *See also* General-purpose machine-gun.

A German MG3 general-purpose machine-gun, with its tripod and periscope sight (top), and a British 7.62x51 British L7A2 'Jimpy' on its tripod (bottom). The sling on the British gun suggests universality of purpose!

Republica Oriental del Uruguay.

U.O.S. A mark found on 6.35mm *Browning-type revolvers, allegedly made in Italy by Ufficio Scambi Commerciale after 1945, but more probably in the 1920s. The guns may have been imported from Spain, perhaps from *Ojanguren y Marcaido.

'UP', or 'U' and 'P' separated by a vertical arrow – **1.** Found on British military firearm components used during wartime in unproved (i.e., not tested) condition. **2.** With crossed pennants. A military proof mark used by the authorities in the Union of South Africa until independence was gained from Britain in 1960.

Upirov. The co-designer with *Paramonov and *Ochnev of the TP-82 multi-barrel survival pistol issued as part of the Soviet/Russian *SONAZ kit.

'UPS'. A mark found on US military firearms and accessories. *See* Urial P. *Strong.

Upton – **1.** Upton Machine Company, St Joseph, Michigan, USA. This washing-machine maker acquired the *American Tool Works in 1912 and began making *Sterling BB guns. Initially these had 'ATW' marks, although Upton sold some under its own name as the *American Dart Rifle. Sterlings sold after c. 1922 may also display Upton's name. Many guns were made for *Sears, Roebuck & Company in 1912–27, and the ATW machinery was sold to Sears when Upton returned to washing-machine manufacture. Subsequently Sears sold it to the *All-Metal Products Company. **2.** Upton Repeater. A 1,000-shot lever-action BB Gun, a simplified version of the 1911 *Sterling, made by the Upton Machine Company in 1922–27. **3.** Upton Single-Shot. A minor variant of the lever-action *Sterling BB Gun, made in 1922–27 by the Upton Machine Company. **4.** Upton Special. Also known as the *Sterling Special, this BB Gun was made by the Upton Machine Company in 1922–27.

'Ural'. A brandname found on Soviet/Russian sporting rifles; *see also* 'Vostok'.

Urizar. Tómas de Urizar of Barcelona, Spain, was a distributor of guns made in Eibar and elsewhere – identified by the many brandnames that still cause confusion. They include *Celta, *Continental, *Ermua, *Express (generally made by *Garate, Anitua y Compañía), *Imperial, *J. Cesar, *Le Dragon, *Le Secours, *Phoenix (may be marked 'Victoria Arms Co.'), *Premier, *Princeps, *Principe, *Puma and *Venus. Guns marked 'Continental' and 'Princeps' may also be marked by Fabrique d'Armes de Grande Précision.

'URO', consisting of a superimposed 'RO' monogram within 'U': *see* 'UOR'.

Urrejola y Cia, Eibar, Spain, made *Ruby-pattern semi-automatic pistols for the French during the First World War.

Urry. George Frederick Urry of Sparkhill, Birmingham, England, appears to have been the company secretary of Lincoln *Jeffries & Company. His name appears on three British patents for airgun loading-plugs, granted jointly with Lincoln Jeffries: 20,733/06 and 21,324/06, from 70 Durham Road; and 25,939/07 from 140 Grove Road, Sparkhill.

'US', 'U.S.', US... – **1.** A code associated with the products of the British *Sterling Engineering Company Ltd, in NATO days. **2.** A property mark applied by the US government (particularly by the US Army) to virtually any piece of military equipment. The marks on firearms may be accompanied by a flaming bomb, dates of acceptance, manufacturers' marks or inspectors' initials. *See also* US arms inspectors' marks. **3.** Accompanied by a star, usually as 'U★S'. A mark applied to the products of Joseph *Rodgers

of Sheffield, England. **4.** Encircled. Found on handguns made by the 'US Revolver Company', a name used by Iver *Johnson. **5.** Usually, but not always, encircled. A *headstamp mark associated with the *United States Cartridge Company. It may take the form of a monogram resembling a dollar sign ('$'). **6.** U.S. Arms Co. *Suicide Special revolvers made in the 1880s in Norwich, Connecticut, by the *Bacon Manufacturing Company, the *Hood Firearms Company and the *Crescent Arms Company. **7.** US arms inspectors' marks. These provide an excellent method of identifying US military firearms, and also of dating components whose age may not be apparent. Most of the marks consist of two, three or (rarely) four plain or cursive initials stamped into metalwork or (notably on wood) within a rectangular cartouche. The inclusion of inspectors' initials in US markings is particularly helpful to collectors, and many inspectors and their marks are listed individually. **8.** US Carbine 22: *see* AMAC. **9.** U.S. Machine Gun Company, Meriden, Connecticut. *See* United States Machine-Gun Company. **10.** 'U.S. Pistol Co.' Found on two patterns of *Suicide Special revolver made in Norwich, Connecticut, by the *Crescent Arms Company and the *Hood Firearms Company in the late nineteenth century. **11.** 'U.S. Property'. Found on war material, including small-arms, supplied by the USA to Britain during the Second World War, under Lend-Lease. **12.** U.S. Repeating Arms Company, New Haven, Connecticut, USA. The modern successor to the *Winchester Repeating Arms Company. **13.** 'U.S. Revolver Co.' A spurious name used on revolvers made by Iver *Johnson prior to 1914. **14.** *See also* United States.

'U.S.C.Co.' Used in the headstamps of ammunition made by the *United States Cartridge Company of Lowell.

USDA, or U.S. Double Action. Made by Iver *Johnson in 1910–13, this was a simplified form of the company's standard revolver, in .22, .32 and .38, which lacked the *Hammer-the-Hammer safety system. The guns were marked 'United States Revolver Company'.

'USMC', or 'US' over 'MC'. A property mark applied to weapons and equipment by the US Marine Corps.

'USN', 'U.S.N.', often over an anchor. A property mark applied by the US Navy, taking many forms.

'U' containing 'SS'. A mark found on the slides of .45 M1911A1 *Government Model pistols made for the US armed forces by the *Union Switch & Signal Company.

'U.S. & S. CO.' Found on .45 M1911A1 *Government Model pistols made for the US forces during the Second World War by the *Union Switch & Signal Company.

Uter. Franz Uter, Heidersbach bei Suhl in Thüringen. A gunmaker active in Germany, apparently late in the nineteenth century.

'Utility' [The]. Found on shotgun cartridges loaded in Britain by, or perhaps for, E.J. *Churchill of London.

UTS. *See* Universal-Abzug-System.

'UVF', 'U.V.F.' *See* Ulster Volunteer Force.

'U y E'. A superimposition-type monogram. Correctly 'E y A'; a mark used by *Esperanza y Unceta of Guernica.

Uzi. A 9x19mm blowback submachine-gun designed in 1949–53 by Major Uziel Gal, an Israeli Army officer, on the basis of work begun in Czechoslovakia. The Uzi has been made in large numbers by *Fabrique Nationale d'Armes de Guerre, Israeli Military Industries and others. It has a magazine that runs up through the pistol grip and an overhung bolt mechanism. Compact Mini- and Micro-Uzi derivatives have also been offered in recent years.

V

'**va'**. This mark was used after 1940 by Kabel- und Metallwerke Neumeyer AG of Nürnberg on small-arms ammunition components produced for the German armed forces.

Vacher, Saint-Étienne, France. Listed in 1933 as a gun-maker. Still trading in 1951 at 20 rue Jean-Baptiste David.

'**VAF' above 'C'.** Said to have been applied to *Parabellum drum magazines (TM. 08) made in 1917–18 by *Vereinigte Automaten-Fabriken of Köln.

'**VAL'.** A mark found on US military firearms and accessories. *See* Viotto A. *Luukkonen.

'**Valeka' [The].** A brandname associated with shotgun cartridges made in Scotland by *Nobel Explosives Ltd of Glasgow prior to 1918 and the purchase by Explosives Trades Ltd.

Valentine – 1. Charles Valentine inspected .38-calibre *Colt revolvers and Krag-Jørgensen Philippine Constabulary rifles in the early 1900s, using a 'CV' mark. **2.** Henry E. Valentine, working for the Federal government during the American Civil War, accepted arms and equipment marked 'HEV'. **3.** Thomas Valentine, employed by the Federal government, accepted arms and equipment in 1863 during the Civil War. The items bore a cursive 'TV', but the down-curled tail of the 'T' has led to the erroneous identification of P. Valentine. *See also* US arms inspectors' marks.

Valle Susa di Guglielminotti (FAVS) [Fabbrica Armi Valle Susa...], Villarfochardio/Torino, Italy. FAVS made sporting rifles in the 1960s based on refurbished military-surplus *Mauser actions. Most had slender three-quarter-length stocks and a double-trigger mechanism, which supposedly was optional. The company also produced a range of *Diana-type spring-air rifles, including barrel- and underlever-cocking patterns, and may also have been responsible in the 1950s for the *Vittoria range; *see also* Nadir. Apparently trading ceased c. 1972.

Valmet Oy, Jyväskylä, Finland. Once the state-owned engineering works, also renowned as a maker of firearms, Valmet produced the successful m/58 (*Kalashnikov) assault rifle prototype for the Finnish Army, which was adopted officially as the m/62 after a handful of fm/58 prototypes and a few hundred m/60 field-trial guns had been made. Variations of the *Rynnakkokiväärit* – and the essentially similar m/78 light machine-gun – were made until the business was amalgamated with *Sako in 1987 to become Sako-Valmet. The individual variations have included the m/62, m/62-TP (folding-butt), m/71, m/76 (in a variety of forms), and an m/76B, or m/82, *bullpup. The m/71 rifle and m/78 machine-gun had the front sight on the barrel and the rear sight on the receiver, directly above the chamber, whereas the others had the front sight on the gas tube and the back sight on the bolt cover. With the exception of the original 7.62mm m/62, all the Valmet Kalashnikovs have been offered in 5.56x45 and 7.62x39. Semi-automatic guns were usually distin-

guished by an S-suffix. The *Galil rifle is a simple adaptation of the Valmet-type Kalashnikov.

Valtions... – 1. Valtions Kiväritedhas (VKT), Jyväskyla, Finland. The state rifle factory was best known for making *Mosin-Nagant rifles and *Lahti pistols prior to 1940. **2.** Valtions Metallitehdas Oy (Valmet), Helsinki, Finland. This was the state-owned metalworking factory, founded shortly after Finland became independent in 1917. A simple barrel-cocking spring-air rifle – the Aries – was made in small numbers in the early 1960s alongside pistols, submachine-guns and automatic rifles. *See also* Valmet Oy.

Vampir. Also known as *Zielgerät 1229*, this was an early infra-red night sight, made in Germany during the Second World War. *See* Haenel and Sights, infra-red.

Van Amburgh. C.J. Van Amburgh, working for the US government c. 1910, accepted .30 *Colt 'Potato Digger' machine-guns for the army. They were marked 'CJV'. *See also* US arms inspectors' marks.

Vandenburgh Volley Gun. This US-made Battery Gun was tested unsuccessfully in Britain in 1862.

Van Zuylen. *See* Zuylen.

Varmint – 1. Used generically for any firearm (normally, but not exclusively, a rifle) and cartridge specifically developed for the hunting of animals classed as pests (e.g. squirrels, groundhogs, foxes, etc). The rifles are intended to be used at long range against small targets, and often have features derived from target-shooting practice: heavy free-floating barrels, flat-bottom fore-ends and high-comb butts. They are almost always used with optical sights and lack open, or 'iron', alternatives. **2.** Varmint Special. The *Remington M700 VS, or BDL VS, bolt-action rifle, made since 1967, has been chambered for cartridges ranging from .22-250 to .308 Winchester. It has a heavy 24in barrel, lacks open sights and weighs 9lb. Among the derivatives of the basic design have been the VLS (Varmint, Laminated Stock), announced in 1995, with a 26in barrel and a wood-laminate stock. **3.** Varmint Synthetic. A variant of the *Remington M700 *Varmint Special rifle, dating from 1992. Offered only in .220 Swift, .22-250, .223 Remington and .308 Winchester, it has an aluminium bedding block running the length of the blacked receiver, and a composite stock containing Kevlar, fiberglass and graphite. The M700 VS SSF (Varmint Special, Synthetic Satin Finish) appeared in 1994. It has a non-reflective finish and a 26in fluted barrel. **4.** Varmint Ultra, or Kodiak Ultra Varminter. Names associated with a rifle made in the USA by the *Kodiak Manufacturing Company (it was also known as the Model 102). Dating from c. 1965–73, it had a heavy barrel, but lacked sights.

Varney. A.L. Varney, Watertown, Massachusetts, USA. Patentee of the breech-loading firearms protected by US Patents 88,530 and 88,531 of 30 March 1869 (for a breech-block that lifted up and forward), and 95,395 of

28 September 1869 for a tilting-block design propped closed by a sliding rod.

Vassal, 13 rue Franklin, Saint-Étienne, France. Listed in 1951 as a gunmaker.

'VB'. *See* Vickers-Bethier and Vivens-Bessière.

'VB' over 'G', within a triangle, beneath a pelican. Used by Vincenzo ★Bernardelli of Gardone Val Trompia, Italy, on pistols, revolvers, shotguns and sporting rifles.

'V.C.' [The]. Found on shotgun cartridges made in Britain by ★Eley Bros. prior to the acquisition of the company by Explosives Trades Ltd in 1918.

'VCS', 'V.C.S.' Trademarks associated with V.C. ★Schilling of Suhl, Thüringen, Germany.

'VD', 'V.D.', 'V-D'. Marks indicating a ★Velo-Dog revolver, usually accompanied by the calibre identifier: '5.5mm' or '5.75mm' for standard centrefire ammunition; '6mm' for the ★Type Française rimfires.

VEB Fahrzeug- & Waffenfabik. The East German state-run firearms business. *See* Ernst ★Thälmann.

Vectis [Spencer's]. *See* F.P. ★Spencer.

Vedder. Ewald Vedder, Sömmerda. Listed in Germany in 1941 as a retailer of sporting guns and ammunition.

Veisey & Son, 105 Moor Street, Birmingham, Warwickshire. The marks of this English gunmaker – known to have been working in 1868 – have been reported on self-cocking ★pepperboxes, which suggests that trading began at least fifteen years prior to the earliest-known directory entry.

Vejprty. *See* Weipert.

Vektor Engineering, South Africa. *See* Lyttelton Engineering Pty, Ltd.

'Velm' [The]. Found on shotgun ammunition marked by Alex ★Martin & Company of Glasgow, but actually made by ★Eley-Kynoch. It is assumed that the cartridges date from 1920–39.

'Velocity' [The]. A shotgun cartridge made in Britain by ★Eley-Kynoch Ltd.

Velo-Dog. *See* panel, below.

'Velogrant' [The]. Found on shotgun cartridges sold in Britain by ★Grant & Lang of London.

Velo-Mith. Associated with improved ★Velo-Dog guns made in Spain, including enclosed-hammer ★Browning-revolvers styled on the 1900-model FN-Browning pistol. The principal characteristic is the break-open auto-ejecting construction; most have folding triggers. Makers include ★Crucelegui Hermanos, ★Garate Hermanos, ★Ojanguren y Marcaido (OM) and ★Retolaza Hermanos of Eibar.

Velox – 1. 'Velox Sporting Rifle'. A brandname used by Daniel ★Fraser & Company on large-calibre sporting rifles, including single-shot dropping-block, two-shot 'double' and magazine-fed bolt-action patterns. The chamberings ranged from .303 to .577. **2.** Usually found as 'The Velox' on shotgun cartridges sold in south-west England prior to the First World War by Edwinson ★Green of Gloucester.

Ventilated rib. A barrel rib (q.v.) in which the rib is held away from the barrel by a series of supports, allowing air to circulate beneath it. The purpose is to cool the barrel to prevent heat rising and disturbing the sight line. Although widely used on thin-barrelled shotguns, ventilated ribs are much less common on sporting rifles.

'Ventracta' [The]. Found on shotgun cartridges sold in Britain by Joseph ★Lang & Sons of London.

Venus – 1. A German brandname, associated with Carl ★Walther, Oskar ★Will and the ★Venuswaffenwerk. **2.** A

VELO-DOG REVOLVER

A generic term, apparently emanating from France, applied to compact firearms originally marketed for cyclists who wanted to defend themselves against animals with something more deadly than a simple ★Scheintod 'frightener'.

The guns chambered the unique centrefire 5.5mm Velo-Dog cartridge (or sometimes the comparable 6mm 'Type Française' rimfire), which had an unusually long straight case. Consequently, the revolvers can be identified by a long small-diameter cylinder. Guns of this type were made in large numbers prior to 1920, when the growing popularity of the small ★Browning semi-automatic pistol swept them all away.

Belgian manufacturers included L. ★Ancion-Marx (L.A.M.), Auguste ★Francotte et Cie (AF), ★Henrion, Dassy et Heuschen (HDH), ★Lepage et Cie, and ★Manufacture Liégeoise d'Armes à Feu (ML); French makers included Charles ★Galand et Cie and ★Manufacture Française d'Armes et

Cycles (MFAC); Friedrich ★Pickert made them in Zella St Blasii in Germany; and Francisco ★Arizmendi (FA), Francisco ★Arizmendi y Goenaga (FAG), ★Crucelegui Hermanos, ★Retolaza Hermanos and others produced examples in Eibar, Spain. The ★Tula small-arms factory also seems to have made guns of this type in Russia, identified by displayed-eagle grip motifs accompanied by 'I.T.O.Z.' in Cyrillic (*Imperatorskiy Tukskiy Oruzheinyi Zavod,* 'Imperial Tula Ordnance Factory').

Few appear to have used specific brandnames, although Crucelegui Hermanos made the Velo-Brom.

The ready availability of ammunition persuaded some gunmakers to chamber larger revolvers for the Velo-Dog cartridges. While some of these were conventional, there were oddities: Francotte and others made Velo-Dog revolvers in the style of the 1900-model ★FN-Browning semi-automatic pistol (*see also* Browning-revolver), and Henrion, Dassy et

Heuschen made a ten-shot break-open simultaneous-ejector gun with a folding trigger. HDH also produced a huge twenty-shot variant with superimposed barrels and two concentric rows of chambers, the barrels and cylinder assembly opening around a lateral pivot at the top rear of the frame. Another oddity was ★L'Explorateur-Mitraille, apparently made in France.

Velo-Dog revolvers from a catalogue issued in 1909 by the Belgian gun dealer L. Ancion-Marx. Note the unusually long cylinders, which distinguish Velo-Dogs from many otherwise essentially similar guns.

small Browning-type semi-automatic pistol made in Spain (probably in Eibar) for the distributor/wholesaler Tómas de ★Urizar of Barcelona: 6.35mm Auto or 7.65mm, six rounds, hammer fired. **3.** Venuswaffenwerk, Zella St Blasii and Zella-Mehlis in Thüringen, Germany. *See* Oskar ★Will. **4.** 'Venuswaffenwerk vormals Oskar Will', Inhaber Wilh. Foss, Zella-Mehlis in Thüringen, Germany. Foss bought out Will in 1920/21 and continued airgun production. Many of the guns were marketed initially under the ★Tell brand, although a 'VWW' monogram was adopted in the mid-1920s. A bolt-action training rifle, the ★Mars, was developed in 1935/36 to compete with the Haenel ★Sportmodell; production of the Mars is said to have been continued in the German Democratic Republic in 1948–53, but by then the production machinery may have been transferred to the former ★BSW factory in Suhl.

Venzedor. A Spanish Browning-type pocket semi-automatic pistol made by Casimir ★Santos of Eibar: 6.35mm, six rounds, hammer fired.

Vercar, VerCar, Ver-Car. Marks associated with Manufacture d'Armes Verney-Carron et Cie of Saint-Étienne, found on 6.35mm ★Browning-type pistols either made in Spain or, perhaps, by ★Manufacture d'Armes des Pyrénées. They will also be encountered on ammunition, shotguns and sporting rifles.

Verdiell, 16 rue de Champagne, Saint-Étienne, France. Listed in 1951 as a gunmaker.

Vereinigte... – 1. Vereinigte Automaten-Fabriken, Pelzer & Co., Köln, Germany. This maker of vending machinery, formed in 1899 by amalgamating Allgemeine Automatengesellschaft and Deutsche Kolonial-Kakao-Gesellschaft, was eventually liquidated in 1932 after several changes of ownership. It was recruited in 1917 to make drum magazines for the ★Parabellum pistol (TM. 08), but no surviving examples have yet been found. They are said to have been marked 'VAF' above 'C' (for Cöln). **2.** Vereinigte Köln-Rottweiler Pulverfabriken, Köln and Rottweil/Neckar, Germany. A manufacturer of propellant and ammunition, including the shotgun cartridges marketed under the ★Rottweil brand.

Vergueiro. *See* Mauser-Vergueiro.

Veritable Mosser Superior. A small Browning-type auto-loading pistol usually attributed to ★Gabilondo y Compañía of Elgoeibar, Guipúzcoa, Spain: 6.35mm, six rounds.

Verminkiller. A name applied by distributors to a German pointed-nose diabolo airgun pellet manufactured in 4.5mm and 5.5mm by ★Haendler & Natermann from 1978.

Verney – 1. E. Verney, rue Badouillère 34, Saint-Étienne, France. Listed in 1879 as a gunmaker. **2.** Verney-Carron frères, rue de Foy 4, Saint-Étienne, France. Listed in 1879 as a gunmaker. At the time, premises were also being occupied at rue des Archers 2 in Lyon, and rue Cannebière 46 in Marseille. The 1892 directories list the Saint-Étienne premises as rue de la République 27. Still trading in 1932 as Verney-Carron et Cie and, in the early 1950s, from 17 cours Fauriel. In addition to its good-quality shotguns, Verney-Carron handled the 6.35mm ★Ver-Car pistol. These handguns seem to have been purchased in Spain, or possibly from Manufacture d'Armes des Pyrénées Françaises. Verney-Carron still trades in Saint-Étienne, making good-quality sporting guns and a riot gun, which fires small spherical containers of CS gas and dye.

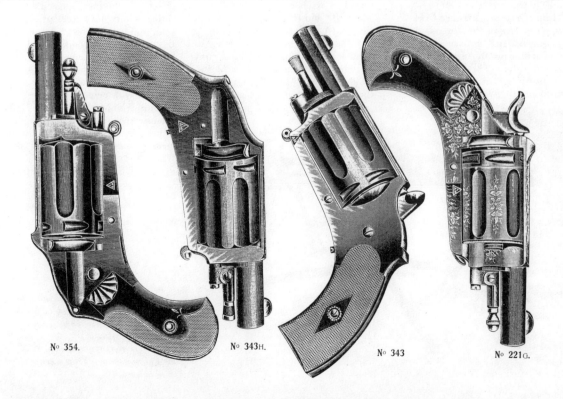

Nᵒ 354.   Nᵒ 343H.   Nᵒ 343   Nᵒ 221G.

Verot, 36 cours Fauriel, Saint-Étienne, France. Listed in 1951 as a gunmaker.

Verrier-Varence, rue Roanelle 29, Saint-Étienne. Listed in 1879 as a distributor of, and agent for, arms and ammunition.

Vervier. Ernest Vervier, Belgian engineer: *see* Fabrique Nationale d'Armes de Guerre.

Veselý – 1. Josef Veselý , Czechoslovakian-born British gun designer. In addition to work on submachine-guns and post-war airguns, this employee of ★BSA Guns Ltd also designed the 7.62mm X16 sustained-fire machine-gun. Apparently this elegant belt-feed conversion of the ★Bren Gun worked satisfactorily, but political pressure to adopt the FN-designed MAG was too strong. Among Veselý's British airgun patents, usually sought in conjunction with Roger David ★Wackrow, were 930,124 and 930,125 of 5 January 1961, for the optical-sight system of the ★Merlin; 937,658, sought in May 1959, for the O-ring piston-head of the improved ★Meteor; 937,659, sought on 17 May 1960, for a sight clamp; 941,711, sought on 19 May 1959, for the barrel-block used in the ★Meteor and ★Mercury; 945,362 (19 May 1959) for a method of making air cylinders from a single sheet; and 1,111,082, sought on 15 January 1965, which described a

modified ★Airsporter trigger unit. **2.** Veselý submachine-gun. The first 'machine carbine' of this pattern, the V-40 of 1941, was followed by improved V-42 and V-43 (para-troop) models before the project was finally cancelled in 1945. The guns were made by ★BSA Guns Ltd, eight being delivered for trials in September 1944 alone.

Vesta – 1. A Browning-type pocket pistol made by Hijos de A. ★Echeverria in Eibar, Guipúzcoa, Spain, in at least two patterns: (a) 6.35mm, six rounds, striker fired, often marked 'Model 1912'; (b) 7.65mm, nine rounds, hammer fired. **2.** Based on the ★FN-Browning of 1905, this Spanish semi-automatic pistol was made in Eibar by ★Garate, Anitua y Compañía: 6.35mm, six rounds, hammer fired. Some guns are marked 'Model 1924', and some will be found with the safety lever in the rear of the receiver. The earliest guns may have been made for Garate, Anitua by Hijos de A. ★Echeverria.

Vest Pocket, Vest-Pocket – 1. A name associated with a 6.35mm semi-automatic pistol, similar to the ★Menta, made in Germany in the 1920s by August ★Menz of Suhl. **2.** Solid-framed double-action revolvers, made in the USA by ★Harrington & Richardson, c. 1890–1910, with spurless hammers and barrels less than 2in long. **3.** Vest Pocket Hammerless Model. A tiny .25

VICKERS GUN

Vickers (6)

Developed in Britain in the early twentieth century, this was simply a ★Maxim Gun with the locking mechanism reversed so that the toggle broke downward. The 'Gun, Machine, Vickers, .303-inch Mark I' was introduced on 26 November 1912 and only declared obsolete in 1968.

There was only a single Land Service pattern. The Mark I★ (1918) was an Air Service gun with louvres cut in an otherwise-standard barrel

jacket. The Mark II (June 1917) was similar to the Mark I★, but had a smaller barrel casing and lacked the fusee spring box on the left side of the receiver. The Mark II★ (1927), another Air Service gun, was essentially a Mark II with an extended cocking lever; Mark III guns had extended flash-hiders. Marks II★ and III could feed from the left (A-suffix) or right (B-suffix).

The Marks IV A and IV B were water-cooled armoured-vehicle guns introduced 'for the record' in May 1930; modified Mark I examples, they had new mounting plates,

trunnion blocks and barrel casings, and could be fitted with butts. The Air Service Mark V was little more than a Mark III with a top cover that hinged laterally instead of transversely. Marks VI A and VI B (both introduced in 1934) were vehicle guns with strengthened dovetail mountings, alloy fusee spring covers and fluted barrel casings. The Marks VI★ A and VI★ B, conversions of Mark I Land Service guns for use in armoured vehicles, had fluted barrel casings and trunnion blocks adapted to connect with vehicle cooling systems. The Mark VII was a modified Mk VI with an improved mounting dovetail, integral with the ejection-tube sleeve; its barrel casing was customarily plain.

The US Army also used Vickers Guns in quantity. With the exception of changes necessary to feed rimless cartridges, the .30 M1915 Vickers machine-gun was

Left: *A British .303 Vickers Mark I, fitted with a panoramic dial sight, on the standard Mark IVB tripod. The can contained water for the cooling system.*

Right: *The pre-1914 commercial version of the Vickers Gun, which was exported only in small numbers.*

ACP semi-automatic pistol made by ★Colt's Patent Fire Arms Manufacturing Company. *See* Hammerless Pocket Model. **4.** Vest Pocket Pistol, USA. *See* E. ★Remington & Sons and J. ★Stevens. **5.** *See also* Westentaschenmodell and Westentaschenpistole.

Veteran. A pneumatic rifle designed by Kensuke ★Chiba and made in Japan by the ★Sharp Rifle Company, 1952–60.

Vetterli – **1.** Friedrich Vetterli, also known as Frédéric Vetterli. Born in 1822, Vetterli was apprenticed to a Swiss gunmaker, but subsequently worked in Paris and Saint-Étienne, where he learned the merits of production by machine at first hand. Today he is remembered as the inventor of the Vetterli rifle, adopted in Switzerland and Italy. Vetterli (who had designed a wedge-type breech-block in 1849) joined ★Schweizerische Industrie-Gesellschaft in 1865, and soon developed a metallic-cartridge gun by combining a bolt system inspired by the ★Dreyse with a tube magazine adapted from the ★Henry rifles tested throughout Europe in the 1860s. Vetterli's design was adopted in Switzerland in 1869 and, in a simplified single-shot form, by Italy in 1870. Subsequently Friedrich Vetterli continued to experiment with guns and ammunition until his death in 1882. **2.** Vetterli-Bertoldo

rifle. A name applied to the Mo 1882 magazine rifles made for the Italian Navy in the 1880s. Unlike the later Vitali conversions, which had detachable box magazines, Bertoldo fitted an under-barrel tube. **3.** Vetterli-Ferraciú rifle. Made only in small numbers, c. 1890, this conversion of the Italian Mo 1882 ★Vetterli-Bertoldo navy rifle accepted a detachable box magazine. **4.** Vetterli rifle. Designed by Friedrich ★Vetterli in the mid-1860s, this bolt-action rifle was used only in Switzerland and Italy. The first trials were undertaken by the Swiss in 1867, the perfected tube-magazine gun being adopted on 1 August 1869. Adoption in Italy followed in 1870, although originally these guns were all single-loaders. The rifles remained in service for more than twenty years, being replaced in front-line service in the 1890s by the ★Schmidt-Rubin in Switzerland and the Mannlicher-★Carcano in Italy. Total production of Swiss Vetterli rifles, short rifles and carbines exceeded 350,000, the largest single component being 128,060 M1869 rifles. The best source of detailed information about these guns is *Handfeuerwaffen System Vetterli* (Stocker-Schmidt, Zürich, 1988) by Schneider, am Rhyn, Krebs, Reinhart and Schiess. **5.** Vetterli-Vitali rifle. This name has been widely applied to a box-magazine conversion of the sin-

---

identical to the British .303 Mark I. Four thousand were ordered from Vickers in 1916, but issues were delayed until the autumn of 1917. By the end of the First World War, nearly 10,000 Land Service Vickers Guns had been delivered by Vickers and the US licensee, ★Colt's Patent Fire Arms Manufacturing Company; Colt had also delivered about 900 aircraft guns.

The 11mm-calibre US M1918 Vickers Gun chambered French Gras cartridges, loaded with incendiary bullets for use against observation balloons and aircraft.

These guns were converted from 7.62x54 examples ordered from Colt in 1915 by the Russians, which had remained in store in Hartford since the 1917 Revolution.

The British 'Gun, Machine, Vickers, .5-inch Mark I' (introduced 'for the record' in 1933) was a selective-fire Land Service gun, which could feed from either side. The Mark II of 1932 was a vehicle gun with an angled pistol grip; the Mark III was a water-cooled Naval Service gun modified from Mark I examples, with changes in the action

and a stronger buffer spring to increase the cyclic rate from 450 to about 700rds/min.

Made only in small numbers, the Vickers .5 Mark IV (1933) had a narrow dovetail plate and mounting base to allow it to be exchanged with .303 vehicle guns. Mark V vehicle guns were similar, but had detachable ejection tubes and reinforced mounts. With the exception of the .303 Mark I Land Service and .5 Mark III Naval Service patterns, all .303 and .5 Vickers machine-guns were declared obsolete in August 1944.

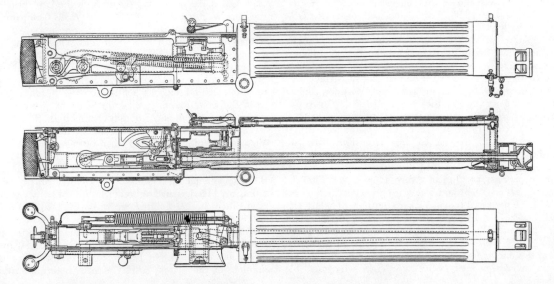

gle-shot Italian *Vetterli, adopted in 1887. Large numbers of these obsolete guns were converted in the state arsenals until the adoption of the *Mannlicher-Carcano rifle in 1891. Many of the Vetterlis, however, survived to be converted again (to 6.5mm) during the First World War.

Veyron, rue Villeboeuf 27, Saint-Étienne, France. Listed in 1892 as a gunmaker.

'VGO'. See Vickers-Berthier.

Vici. This 6.35mm pistol, undoubtedly made in Spain (probably in Eibar), often bears misleading marks that cause it to be classified as Belgian. The left side of the frame, for example, may display 'Pistolet Automatique Breveté' and 'Herstal (Liège) Belgique'. The shallow slide reciprocates on rails cut on the inside of the frame, doubtless inspired by the 1900-pattern *FN-Browning.

Vickers – 1. John Vickers was the recipient of several US Patents, including 35,667 of 17 June 1862 ('cartridge cases for revolving firearms'), and 47,775 of 16 May 1865 and 57,448 of 21 August 1866 for 'revolving firearms'. All were assigned to Lucius *Pond. **2.** Vickers Ltd. Formed in 1911 to succeed *Vickers, Sons & Maxim Ltd, this business flourished prior to 1918, making a wide range of items, from machine-guns to entire warships. Shortly after the First World War, Vickers became embroiled in the supply of *Luger pistols to the Netherlands Indies Army. Large quantities of DWM-made parts were shipped to Britain, apparently clandestinely. They were assembled and proved in the Crayford factory, then returned to the Netherlands where – allegedly – most were rejected and sent to *Fabrique Nationale d'Armes de Guerre for attention. Shortly afterward, Vickers merged with Sir W.G. Armstrong, Whitworth & Company Ltd to form Vickers-Armstrongs Ltd. In addition to machine-guns, which were made throughout this period, Vickers produced .22 *Martini-action rifles and shotguns. A licence was also obtained to make the light machine-gun designed by Adolphe *Berthier. **3.** Vickers-Armstrongs Ltd. Formed in 1927 to succeed *Vickers Ltd, following a merger with Sir W.G. Armstrong, Whitworth & Company Ltd, this powerful combine continued to make everything from small-arms and tanks to aircraft and warships. In addition to *Vickers(-Maxim) and *Vickers-Berthier machine-guns, interest was shown in *Pedersen rifles. Box magazines for the British .303 *Bren Gun were made in a factory in Bathwick Hill, Bath, during the Second World War. These were often marked with the code 'S 121' instead of the company name. See also British military manufacturers' marks. **4.** Vickers-Berthier. This machine-gun (with a distinctive top-mounted box magazine) was based on patents granted to Adolphe *Berthier, rights having been acquired by Vickers in 1918. A .303 version developed in 1925–31 was tested extensively in Britain during the early 1930s, where it was expected to win the army trials until the *ZGB appeared. The Vickers-Berthier ground gun (VB) and the Vickers Gas Operated (VGO), a derivative destined for airborne use, enjoyed limited success: the Indian Army adopted the .303 I. Mark I VB in 1935, and a few others went to Iraq in 1936. The perfected Indian Vickers-Berthiers (I. Mark III and I. Mark IIIB) were made in small numbers in *Ishapore in 1939–42, but were superseded by the *Bren Gun. The VGO, displaced from air service, was put to good use during the Second World War on vehicles. **5.** Vickers Gas Operated (VGO): see Vickers-Berthier. **6.**

Vickers Gun: see panel, pp. 534/35. **7.** Vickers, Sons & Company. Formed in Sheffield c. 1823, the steelmaker Naylor, Hutchinson, Vickers & Company became Vickers, Sons & Company in 1867. Within twenty years of this change, it was producing naval guns and armour plate, growing to such prominence by the 1890s that it could build and arm entire battleships. Realising the potential of the machine-gun invented by Hiram S. *Maxim, Vickers was instrumental in the formation in 1884 of the *Maxim Gun Company Ltd. **8.** Vickers, Sons & Maxim Ltd succeeded the *Maxim-Nordenfelt Gun & Ammunition Company Ltd in November 1897, trading until reorganised as Vickers Ltd in 1911. The intervening period saw a grant of Maxim machine-gun licences to, among others, *Deutsche Waffen- und Munitions-fabriken, and the development of the *Vickers Gun. VS&M continued to make firearms in the Crayford (Maxim) and Erith (Nordenfelt) factories.

'Victa' [The]. Found on British-made *Kynoch shotgun ammunition sold by *Lisle of Derby prior to 1914.

Victor – 1. A Belgian .450 auto-extracting revolver, probably made in Liège, perhaps by *Francotte, in the late nineteenth century. The barrel and five-chamber cylinder could be rotated, then pulled forward off a stationary star-plate. Essentially similar to the American *Merwin & Hulbert design, it relied on two locking points immediately ahead of the cylinder. **2.** Generally encountered as 'The Victor' on shotgun cartridges handled in Britain by *Cogswell & Harrison of London. **3.** A small Browning-type 6.35mm semi-automatic pistol made in Spain in the 1920s by Francisco *Arizmendi of Eibar: six rounds, hammer or striker fired. Often marked 'Fabrique d'Armes de Précision'. **4.** A tradename associated with rimfire cartridges made by, or possibly for, *Brown & Brothers of New York. **5.** A single-shot cartridge derringer, based on the *Thuer-patent Colt No. 3, made by John *Marlin of New Haven, Connecticut, USA. **6.** A *Suicide Special revolver made by the *Harrington & Richardson Arms Company of Worcester, Massachusetts, USA, in the late nineteenth century. **7.** A break-open BB Gun, a sheet-metal version of the original *Atlas, made by the Atlas Gun Company in 1899–1906. **8.** Victor Special. A brand-name associated with shotguns made in the USA prior to the First World War by the *Crescent Arms Company of Norwich, Connecticut

Victoria – 1. Usually encountered as 'The Victoria' on shotgun cartridges retailed by the *Army & Navy Co-Operative Society Ltd and its successor, *Army & Navy Stores Ltd of London, but probably made by *Eley prior to 1900. **2.** A blowback semi-automatic pistol, copied from the FN-Browning, made in Spain by Esperanza y Unceta in 6.35mm and 7.65mm chamberings. The earliest guns were marked 'Model 1911 Automatic Pistol Victoria Patent', but by 1914 had been renamed 'Astra' (q.v.). **3.** A *Suicide Special revolver made by the *Hood Firearms Company of Norwich, Connecticut, USA, in the late nineteenth century. **4.** Victoria Small Arms Company [The]. This London promotional agency occupied offices in 29a Gillingham Street and 226 Strand in 1900–05. Its activities are unknown.

Victory – 1. Victory MC-5. A sophisticated exchangeable-barrel (Multi-Calibre) semi-automatic pistol designed in Britain in the 1980s by David Smith, and made in small numbers by the Victory Arms Company before the entire project was sold to Magnum Research, Inc., of Minneapolis. The '5' referred to the number of different chamberings: 9mm Parabellum, .38 Super, .40 S&W, .41 AE and .45 ACP. Several barrel lengths were also offered. **2.** A pneumatic rifle, designed by Kensuke *Chiba and made by the *Sharp Rifle Company of Tokyo, Japan, in 1952–62. **3.** The Victory. A Spanish Browning-type pocket pistol made in Eibar by M. *Zulaica y Compañía: 6.35mm, seven rounds, hammer fired. The slide may display 'Model 1914'. **4.** Victory Arms Company, Brixworth, Northamptonshire, England. Maker of the Victory MC-5 pistol (above) in 1987–88. The project was transferred to the USA, and the British promoter ceased operating.

Vielle. Paul-Marie-Eugène Vieille, a French government chemist, is generally credited with the perfection of the first small-calibre military cartridge to be loaded with smokeless propellant, adopted in France in March 1887. *See also* Lebel.

Vigneron. A 9mm submachine-gun made in Belgium by La Précision Liégeoise SA of Herstal. It dates from the 1950s.

Vignoul. Rodolphe Vignoul, Liège, Belgium. A specialist metal stamper, renowned for the manufacture of gun parts, Vignoul supplied large quantities of sights in the 1870s to Ludwig *Loewe & Co., sight-bases to Gebr. *Mauser & Co., barrel bands to *Dreyse, and gun bolts to makers in Suhl. Work seems to have ended in the 1880s.

Viking Sport Arms AB. *See* FFV-Viking.

Vilimeč. A. Vilimeč, Kdyně, Czechoslovakia. Maker of the 6.35mm *Slavia pistol.

Villa. A diabolo-type airgun pellet with a markedly basal waist, made in Britain by *Cox & Son of Birmingham in the early twentieth century. *See also* Aston.

Villebonnet, 61 rue Liogies, Saint-Étienne, France. Listed in 1951 as a gunmaker.

Villemagne, place Chavanelle 35, Saint-Étienne, France. Listed in 1879 as a gunmaker, and again, as Villemagne fils, in 1892.

Villevieille, Saint-Étienne, France. Listed in 1933 as a gunmaker.

Vincent. Frank Vincent invented an experimental .410-calibre pneumatic shotgun and a similar .22 rifle, about 100 being made in the USA c. 1953–56. He died in 1971.

Vincitor. A Browning-type semi-automatic pistol made by M. Zulaica y Compañía of Eibar, Guipúzcoa, in two calibres: (a) 6.35mm, six rounds, striker fired; (b) 7.65mm, seven rounds, hammer fired, often marked 'Model 1914'.

'Vipax' [The]. A mark found on shotgun cartridges sold in England by Charles *Rosson of Derby and Charles S. *Rosson of Norwich.

Viper – 1. A .38 Special double-action revolver made in 1977–84 by the Firearms Division of *Colt Industries. It had an alloy frame and a 4in barrel. **2.** Also known as the Model 522, this .22 LR rimfire auto-loading rifle was introduced by the *Remington Arms Company in 1993. It has a matt-black synthetic receiver set in a synthetic half-stock, a detachable box magazine, a magazine safety and a manual hold-open.

Virginia Arms Company. A brandname associated with shotguns made in the USA prior to 1920 by the *Crescent Arms Company of Norwich, Connecticut.

'VIS', in a downward-pointing triangular border. Found on the grips of Polish 9mm *Radom, or VIS-35, pistols.

Originally the mark was to have read 'WiS', honouring the designers *Wilniewczyc and Skrzpinski, but was changed by the government so that it alluded to the Latin word for 'force'.

Viscount – 1. A sidelever-cocking air rifle produced by *Webley & Scott of Birmingham, introduced to replace the Osprey in 1982. Made in .177 and .22, the Viscount was loaded through a rotary tap. A deluxe version had a better stock, a ventilated butt pad and swivels; the Stingray was an all-black version, first exhibited in 1987; and the Tracker (sold in the USA as the *Barnett Spitfire) was a short-barrel version with a muzzle weight and an optical sight. A Cammo Tracker (*sic*) appeared in 1986, with a camouflage-painted stock, but was made only in small numbers. **2.** *See* Mark X.

Vitali. Giuseppe Vitali, born in Bergamo in 1845, was an Italian Army officer. He is best remembered for a box-magazine conversion applied to the Italian Army Vetterli rifles from 1887 onward (*see* Vetterli-Vitali). He was also responsible for a series of repeating and auto-loading pistols developed from 1885 until shortly before he died in 1921.

Vite. A compact Spanish semi-automatic pistol, based on the *FN-Browning of 1905, made by *Esperanza y Unceta in Guernica: 6.35mm, six or eight rounds, striker fired. 'Model 1912' or 'Model 1913' may appear on the slide.

Vittoria. Found on a range of Italian barrel-cocking spring-air rifles dating from the 1950s, possibly made by Valle Susa di Guglielminotti.

Vittum. Francis J. Vittum, a US gun patentee. *See* Ely & Wray.

Vivario. N. Vivario-Plomdeur, Passage Lemonnier, Liège. This Belgian gun dealer was advertising in 1845 as a furnisher of '*Armes de Guerre, de Luxe & d'Exportations pour Touts Pays*' ('Firearms, military, deluxe and [for] export to all countries'). He was a shareholder in *Fabrique Nationale d'Armes de Guerre, formed in 1889, and remained active until the beginning of the twentieth century.

Vivens-Bessières. French designer of rifle grenades (V-B), which, by virtue of an axial passage, could be fired from a cup discharger with a conventional ball cartridge. *See* Lebel.

Vixen. A name applied to an adapted *Weihrauch HW35E spring-air rifle marketed by Norman *May & Company in the early 1980s. Extensive revisions were made to the piston system, but the quantities involved seem to have been very small.

'V.L. & A.', 'V.L. & D.' Marks associated with sporting guns, accessories and ammunition handled by Von *Lengerke & Antoine and Von Lengerke & Detmold.

Vladimirov. Semen Vladimirov. Designer of the Soviet 14.5mm *KPV and *PKP machine-guns, and also partly responsible for transforming the 7.62mm *ShKAS machine-gun into the 20mm *ShVAK cannon.

'VLB'. *See* V.L. *Bennett.

'VNS'. Found on components for the No. 4 *Lee-Enfield rifle made in Britain during the Second World War by Viners Ltd. This company was allocated the area code 'N79', but often used its initials instead.

Voere, or Voere-Austria. A trademark and brandname associated with *Voetter & Companie and its successors.

Voetter & Co., Schwarzwalder Jagd- und Sportwaffenfabrik, Vöhrenbach/Schwarzwald, Germany. This engineering company was founded in 1945 by Erich Voetter and partner, trading as Koma-Werke in Fürtwangen. The business was registered with the local authorities on 9 April 1948. Production of a few inexpensive airguns began in this era, and continued after 1955, when the company adopted its present name. A move to Vöhrenbach took place in 1958, and airgun production finally ceased in 1967, after about 750,000 had been made. Voetter & Co. has also offered *Mauser-type sporting rifles since the 1950s. The Repetierbüchse 2155 had a Kar. 98k-type action and a walnut stock with either a *Bavarian-style cheek-piece and a hog's-back comb or a *Monte Carlo pattern Chamberings ranged from .22-250 Remington to 9.3x62. The Repetierbüchse 2165 (in standard or magnum forms) had an improved bolt mechanism with the safety catch on the upper tang. The Voere 2175 (Light, Medium or Special) had a Bavarian-style walnut half-stock and a pivoting safety that protruded from the stock behind the bolt handle. Chamberings ranged from .222 Remington to 9.3x64. An associated Austrian company, Tiroler Jagd- und Sportwaffenfabrik of Kufstein/Tirol, was formed in 1965. By 1985, Voetter was employing eighty people. Voere rifles have been distributed in the USA by *KDF, Inc., and Kleingunther's.

Vogelsang and Rebholz. Designers of the shortened action embodied in the M1889/96 Swiss 7.5mm *Schmidt-Rubin infantry rifle.

Voino Techniki Zavod (VTZ). The Yugoslavian state-owned arms factory in Kragujevač (now part of Serbia) was equipped initially by *Fabrique Nationale d'Armes de Guerre shortly after the First World War, and made *FN-Browning pistols and *Mauser-type rifles for many years. The beginning of the pro-Communist era, after the Second World War, eventually led to the factory being renamed Zavodi *Crvena Zastava, or ZCZ. It is still making an assortment of pistols, *Mauser rifles, *Kalashnikov assault rifles and heavy support weapons.

Volcanic – 1. A pump-up pneumatic rifle was developed in 1973–75 by the *National Volcanic Corporation, but its production status remains unknown. **2.** Volcanic Repeating Fire Arms Company, New Haven, Connecticut, USA. This business traded in 1855–57, being succeeded by the *New Haven Arms Company. It promoted distinctive lever-action repeating carbines and pistols firing self-contained ammunition derived from Walter *Hunt's original *Volition Ball.

Volition Ball. A self-contained 'rocket ball' cartridge patented in the USA by Walter *Hunt.

Volkmann. Peter Volkmann became a member of the Vienna gunmakers' guild in 1842. He made bellows-type airguns in Austria in the middle of the nineteenth century alongside sporting guns and rifles.

Volks... Names applied to some of the 'last-ditch' firearms developed in Germany in 1944–45. – **1.**

VULCAN MINI-GUN

Vulcan (4)

As early as 1890, a Gatling Gun driven by an electric motor had sustained a cyclic rate of 1,500rds/min and had even been improved to an unprecedented 3,000rds/min by 1903. These demonstrations failed to convince military observers of their value, owing to the prodigious rate at which ammunition was consumed. In 1944, however, motorising an 1883-pattern .45-70 Gatling Gun taken from the Aberdeen Proving Ground Museum showed that a rate of 5,000rds/min was possible.

The practicable maximum for a single-barrel gun had been established at about 2,000rds/min by the Russian *ShKAS and the experimental Hungarian *Kiraly aircraft guns, but only at the expense of considerable complexity.

The US Army turned the powered Gatling project over to *General Electric, under the codename Vulcan. The .60-calibre T45 of 1949 was followed by the improved .60 T62, before efforts were diverted into 20mm designs.

The perfected 20mm M61 was adopted in 1956, to be followed by the M139; the success of the large-calibre weapons inspired development of 7.62 and 5.56mm Mini-Guns in the 1960s. These proved effective in airborne gunships. Rates of fire can reach the 10,000rds/min of the six-barrel 5.56mm Vulcan Mini-Gun.

The electrically-driven General Electric/Vulcan 5.56x45 Mini-Gun is an awesome weapon, capable of spectacularly high rates of fire...but difficult to keep supplied with sufficient ammunition.

Volksgewehr ('People's Rifle'). A term associated with the VG 1-5, a gas-delayed blowback semi-automatic rifle designed by *Barnitzke for *Gustloff-Werke. **2.** Volkskarabiner ('People's Carbine'). This is usually reserved for a simplified version of the *Mauser Kar. 98k, often half-stocked. The most primitive patterns lacked magazines and had crude slab-sided butts. **3.** Volkspistole ('People's Pistol'). A variety of guns was developed to satisfy this requirement, including a Webley-type revolver offered by Deutsche-Werke of Erfurt. A pressed-metal variant of the Walther Polizei Pistole, the locked-breech Mauser Gerät 040, and a gas-delayed blowback credited to Barnitzke were among the pistols.

Volunteer. A brandname associated with shotguns made in the USA prior to the First World War by the *Crescent Arms Company of Norwich, Connecticut.

Vom Hofe & Scheinemann. This German gunmaking partnership, based in Berlin, built sporting rifles on 1898-pattern *Mauser actions from c. 1927 onward. Ernst-August vom Hofe continued business after the withdrawal of his partner in 1931, developing the 6.2x73 Super Express (Belted) cartridge soon afterward. This was replaced in 1933 by a 7x73 version. A move to Karlsruhe took place in 1936. The introduction of the 5.6x61 Super Express cartridge was accompanied by the first Vom Hofe Super Express rifles, built on Oberndorf-made *Mauser actions and barrels supplied by Christoph *Funk and *Triebel-Gewehrfabrik of Suhl. In 1955, Walter *Gehmann of Karlsruhe succeeded to the business of vom Hofe, who had died some years earlier.

Von... – **1.** Von Dreyse: see Dreyse. **2.** P. Von Frantzius, Chicago. A retailer of sporting guns and ammunition active prior to the First World War. **3.** Von Lengerke and Antoine, Chicago, Illinois, USA. Opened in 1891 as a retail sporting-goods store by Oswald von Lengerke and Charles Antoine, in Bosler's Harness shop, 246 South Wabash Avenue. Moved in 1894 to premises of their own at 271 South Wabash, then to the corner of Wabash and Van Buren, in 1896, selling bicycles, tents, camping gear, fishing tackle, etc. The store was destroyed by fire in 1915. Subsequent moves were made to Palmer House, 130–132 South Wabash, then to 33 South Wabash in 1924. Acquired in 1928 by Abercrombie & Fitch, but trading continued under the original name. Finally to 9 North Wabash (1941–77). Filed Chapter 11 bankruptcy petition, 1975; sold and closed, 1977. **4.** Von Lengerke & Detmold, New York City. Established in 1889 to sell sporting goods, including guns and ammunition, from 349 Fifth Avenue. Acquired in 1928 by Abercrombie & Fitch.

Vorgrimmler. Ludwig Vorgrimmler is credited with developing the roller-locking system invented by Wilhelm *Stähle until it could be embodied satisfactorily in the *CETME rifles.

Voronkov. Vasiliy Efimovich Voronkov (1899–1976), an employee of the Kovrov machine-gun factory from 1922 until his retirement as a research engineer in 1960, was the co-perfector with Mikhail Goryunov of the Soviet SG, or Goryunov, machine-gun after the death of its originator, Petr *Goryunov. Voronkov became better known as a designer of motorcycles in the 1950s.

Voss. L. Voss, location unknown (but probably in Prussia). Maker of a volute-spring *Gallery Gun in the 1850s.

Vostok. Sometimes listed as 'Vostock', this brandname was applied to sporting guns, including spring-air rifles, made in the Soviet/Russian *Izhevsk ordnance factory and exported by *Raznoexport V/O. See also Baikal.

Voytier, rue Badouillère 10 and (later) 16, Saint-Étienne, France. Listed in 1879–92 as a gunmaker.

'V.R.', beneath a crown. Found on British weapons: the mark of Queen Victoria (1837–1901). See also Cyphers, imperial and royal.

'VR' and 'P', with a crown and crossed pennants. A military proof mark used in Britain during the reign of Queen Victoria (1837–1901). See also British military proof marks.

VS, or VS SSF. See Varmint Special and Varmint Synthetic.

'V.S.M.' Used by *Vickers, Sons & Maxim Ltd on charger-loading conversions of Long *Lee-Enfield rifles made in Britain during 1911–12.

VSS. This identified the silenced carbine developed in the USSR by *Seryukov and *Kraskov.

VTZ. See Voino Techniki Zavod.

Vulcan – **1.** Usually found as 'The Vulcan' on shotgun cartridges manufactured in Britain by *Eley Bros., prior to the acquisition of the company by Explosives Trades Ltd in 1918. **2.** A break-barrel .177 or .22 spring-air rifle introduced by *Webley & Scott in July 1979. **3.** Vulcan Arms Company. A brandname associated with shotguns manufactured by the *Crescent Arms Company of Norwich, Connecticut, USA. Apparently they date prior to 1917. **4.** Vulcan Mini-Gun: see panel, facing page.

Vulcain. A compact Spanish 6.35mm Browning-inspired pocket pistol, probably made in Eibar: five rounds, hammer fired.

'VWW', often in monogram form. A trademark adopted in the 1930s by *Venuswaffenwerke W. Foss, vorm. Oskar Will, of Zella-Mehlis, Thüringen, Germany.

'W' – 1. Beneath a star, sometimes in an oval cartouche. Found on British rifle barrels worn by cordite erosion. **2.** Beneath a distinctive squared crown. Found on weapons issued to the navy and colonial-protection forces of the German Empire: the mark of Kaisers Wilhelm I (1871–88) and Wilhelm II (1888–1918). *See also* Cyphers, imperial and royal. **3.** Sometimes cursive, beneath a crown. Found on weapons issued in the Netherlands: the marks of King Willem III (1849–90) and Queen Wilhelmina (1890–1948). *See also* Cyphers, imperial and royal. **4.** Beneath a crown. Found on Prussian weapons: the mark of Kings Wilhelm I (1861–88) and Wilhelm II (1888–1918). *See also* Cyphers, imperial and royal. **5.** Roman or fraktur, beneath a crown. Found on the weapons of Württemberg: the mark of King Wilhelm (1891–1918). *See also* Cyphers, imperial and royal. **6.** A ★headstamp mark applied to cartridges made by, and sometimes also on behalf of, the ★Winchester Repeating Arms Company. It may be found on .41 rimfire cartridges, ★Flobert primer-propelled ammunition and industrial tool blanks.

'WA', 'wa' – 1. Usually as 'WA'; associated with ★Lee-Enfield rifle and a few other small-arms components made by the Australian government 'feeder' factory in ★Wellington. **2.** As 'wa': allocated in 1940 to the Leipzig lamp-making factory of Hugo Schneider AG (later Hasag Eisen- und Metallwerke GmbH) for use on signal pistols, small-arms and ammunition components supplied to the German armed forces. **3.** A monogram with an angular 'A' superimposed on 'W'. Found on revolvers made in the USA by Dan ★Wesson Arms. **4.** Usually as 'W.A.': found in the headstamps of ammunition sold in the USA by ★Western Auto Stores.

'WAC'. A concentric-type monogram with all three letters equally dominant. Found on semi-automatic pistols made by the ★Warner Arms Company.

'WACD'. A concentric-type monogram with all four letters of equal significance. Correctly 'WDAC' (q.v.); used by the ★Warner-Davis Arms Corporation.

Wackerhagen. Edward R. Wackerhagen. Founder of ★Sheridan Products, Inc., and co-designer, with Irwin ★Krause, of the Sheridan pneumatic rifle.

Wackes. Hugo Wackes, Suhl in Thüringen, Germany. Listed in 1930 and 1939 as a gunsmith.

Wackrow. Roger David Wackrow. An employee of ★BSA, associated with the company in development work undertaken on sights, airguns and automatic rifles. Much of Wackrow's earliest work was done in collusion first with Claude Perry, then with Josef ★Veselý. Typical of Wackrow's British airgun patents are 1,219,302, sought on 18 March 1968 to protect the forged air cylinder of the ★Mercury, and 1,423,153 (sought on 1 December 1972 with Roger Cranston and Harold Jones) for the mechanism of the Scorpion pistol. British Patent no. 1,428,027 was sought on 6 April 1973 to protect the ill-fated BSA recoilless air rifle.

Waco. A Spanish 6.35mm-calibre Browning-type pistol made in Eibar by Sociedad Española de Armas y Municiones (★SEAM): 6.35mm Auto. Made for Tómas de ★Urizar.

'WADC'. *See* 'WACD'.

Wade. *See* Boult & Wade.

Wadsworth. Henry C. Wadsworth. Co-designer with Sullivan ★Forehand of the revolvers protected by US Patents 162,162 of April 1875 and 193,367 of 24 July 1877. *See* Forehand & Wadsworth.

Waffen... – 1. Waffen-Frankonia, Würzburg. This wholesaler has handled large numbers of Mauser-pattern sporting rifles, usually built on refurbished military actions. In 1965, therefore, the company was advertising the ★Favorit (standard and de luxe) and the ★Favorit Safari. **2.** Waffen-Glaser, Switzerland: *see* Walter ★Glaser. **3.** Waffen-Schmidt. A wholesaling business active in Suhl in 1935–45, handling, among other things, sporting guns and shooting accessories. **4.** Waffen-Versand-Haus. A wholesale agency founded in the 1930s by Karl Menz, specialising in guns, ammunition and accessories. Listed in 1941 at Schleusinger Strasse 122, it ceased trading in 1945.

Waffenfabrik... – 1. Waffenfabrik Neuhausen, Switzerland: *see* 'SIG'. **2.** Waffenfabrik von Dreyse, Germany: *see* Dreyset and Rheinische Metallwaaren- & Machinenfabrik.

Waffenwerke Mehlis, Mehlis and Zella-Mehlis in Thüringen, Germany. Listed in 1914 as a gunmaker, owned by Valentin ★Bader.

Wagner – 1. A. Wagner, Zella-Mehlis in Thüringen, Germany. Listed in 1930 as a maker of weapons. Possibly the same as August Wagner (below). **2.** August Wagner, Zella-Mehlis in Thüringen, Germany. Listed in 1920–30 as a gun-barrel maker. **3.** Edmund Wagner, Zella-Mehlis in Thüringen, Germany. Listed in 1939 as a master gunsmith. **4.** Ernst Fritz Wagner & Co., Suhl in Thüringen. A maker (wholesaler?) of weapons and ammunition listed in the 1930 edition of the *Deutsches Reichs-Adressbuch*. **5.** Franz Wagner, Zella-Mehlis in Thüringen, Germany. Listed in 1930 as a master gunsmith and gun-stocker. **6.** Fritz Wagner, Suhl in Thüringen, Germany. Listed as a weapons maker, 1930. **7.** Wilhelm Wagner, Zella-Mehlis in Thüringen, Germany. Listed in 1930 as a gun-stock maker.

Wagonmaster Slide Action. A name given by AMAC (q.v.) to an Erma lever-action rifle imported into the USA from Germany.

'Wagria'. A brandname found on spring-air guns made in Germany in 1954–59 by Maschinen- und Apparatebau 'Wagria' GmbH & Co. of Ascheberg/Holstein. *See* Aerosport, Rapid and Scout.

Wah arms factory. The principal Pakistani small-arms factory, currently making ★Heckler & Koch rifles under licence.

Wahl – 1. Albin Wahl, Zella-Mehlis, Thüringen, Germany. This gunsmith, active in the 1920s, was responsible for the 6.35mm ★Stern, or AWZ, pistols. He was still listed in 1939, but as a gun-barrel drawer. **2.** E. Wahl, Zella St Blasii in Thüringen, Germany. Listed in 1900 as a gunmaker. **3.** Kurt

& Kuno Wahl, Zella-Mehlis in Thüringen, Germany. Listed in 1939 as master gunsmiths. **4.** Wilhelm Wahl, Zella St Blasii and Zella-Mehlis in Thüringen, Germany. Listed in 1914–20 as a gun-stock maker and wholesaler.

Walam. A brandname associated with an automatic pistol made by ★FÉG of Budapest.

Walch. John Walch and the Walch Fire Arms Company, New York City. Inventor and manufacturer of ★cap-lock revolvers protected by US Patent 22,905 of 8 February 1859. The guns were made in ten- and twelve-shot guise, with two charges in each chamber. Each was activated by a separate hammer.

Waldheil. This brandname will be found on shotgun cartridges made in Germany by ★Munitionswerke Schönebeck prior to 1914.

Waldman. A Spanish Browning-type pocket automatic made in Eibar by F. ★Arizmendi y Goenaga: (a) 6.35mm, six rounds, striker fired; (b) 7.65mm, seven rounds, hammer striker fired. These guns may also be marked 'Model 1913'. *See also* Walman.

Walker – 1. George A. Walker, Boston, Massachusetts. Patentee of the breech mechanism incorporated in the ★Bedford & Walker air pistol. *See also* Augustus ★Bedford; the basic pistol appears to have been a ★Quackenbush design. **2.** Henry Walker, sometimes listed as 'Walke', a commander in the US Navy, accepted single-shot ★Remington pistols in the years immediately after the American Civil War. They bore simple 'HW' stamps. *See also* US arms inspectors' marks. **3.** Linus Walker. A gun designer employed by the ★Remington Arms Company, responsible for modifying the action of the Remington-Hepburn rifle. **4.** Michael Walker. A designer employed by the ★Remington Arms Company, credited with much of the development work on the 720-series bolt-action rifles introduced shortly after the Second World War. **5.** W.A. Walker, Jr, a government arms inspector working in 1905, accepted .38 ★Colt revolvers and other ordnance stores marked 'WAW'. *See also* US arms inspectors' marks. **6.** Walker Colt. This was a large and cumbersome six-shot cap-lock revolver, made for Samuel ★Colt by Eli ★Whitney in 1847–48. The name commemorated Captain Samuel Walker of the US Army, who had played a vital role in its promotion, but who had been killed in the Mexican-American War.

Walking... – 1. 'Walking Beam'. A nickname applied by the ★Whitney Arms Company to a ring-trigger revolver designed by Fordyce ★Beals. Patented in 1856, it used an oscillating bar to rotate the cylinder. **2.** Walking-stick guns: *see* Cane guns.

Wall. Howard Wall Ltd, Hackney Road, London E2. A maker of box magazines for the British .303 ★Bren Gun during the Second World War, often marked with the code 'S 123' instead of the company name. *See also* British military manufacturers' marks.

Wallace. John Stewart Wallace, resident in Cliftonville Avenue, Belfast, where he earned his living as a 'Timber Merchant', seems to have been a shareholder and director of the ★Giffard Gun & Ordnance Company. He became a member of Parliament in 1892, and his interest in firearms ceased. *See* British Patents 10,456/90 of 1890, 4205/91 of 1891 and 1724/92 of 1892, the last two being obtained in collusion with ★Benjamin Thomas Lindsay Thomson.

Wallenberg. H.E. Wallenberg, using an 'HEW' mark,

accepted equipment for the US Army c. 1905. *See also* US arms inspectors' marks.

Wallis – 1. John Wallis. Son of W.R. Wallis, owner of Manton & Company of Calcutta, John Wallis began trading on his own account in 1859. His business was based at 116 Jermyn Street, London S.W., until 1864. *See also* Samuel ★Nock. **2.** R.J. Wallis. Recorded as a gunmaker, Wallis could be found at 3 Waterloo Road, London, from 1892 onward, trading as R.J. Wallis & Company after 1893.

Walls, Ltd, Birmingham. A maker of magazines for the British 9mm ★Sten Gun during the Second World War. The regional code 'M 260' may have been used instead of the company name. *See also* British military manufacturers' marks.

Walman. A compact automatic pistol, based on the 1910-type ★FN-Browning, made in Spain by F. ★Arizmendi y Goenaga of Eibar: (a) 6.35mm, six rounds, striker fired; (b) 7.65mm, seven rounds, striker fired, often marked 'Model 1914'; (c) 7.65mm, nine rounds, striker fired. *See also* Waldman.

Walnut Hill. A famous American rifle range, and also used as a brandname by the ★Stevens Arms & Tool Company.

Walsrode. A brandname associated with Walsrode Pulverfabriken.

Walter, Walters – 1. George Walter, also known as Walters. A gunmaker recorded at 7 Guildford Place, Spitalfields, London, in 1836–57. **2.** William Walter, using a 'WW' mark, accepted ★Remington and ★Pettengill ★cap-lock revolvers during the American Civil War. *See also* Wallace ★Whitney and US arms inspectors' marks. **3.** Walters, Britain: *see* Weatherhead, Walters & Company. **4.** *See also* Walther

'Waltham' [The]. Found on shotgun cartridges made by F. ★Joyce & Comany Ltd of London, prior to 1907.

Walther – 1. Carl Walther, Zella St Blasii, Zella-Mehlis in Thüringen, Germany. Founded in 1886, and listed in 1914 as a gun- and weapon maker, then in 1920–39 as a gunmaker under the ownership of Fritz, Georg and Erich Walther. Manufacturer of a range of pistols (below); rifles and shotguns were also made prior to 1945. *See* panel, pp. 542/43. **2.** Carl Walther Sportwaffenfabrik, Ulm/Donau, Germany. Walther offered bolt-action sporting rifles built on refurbished ★Mauser actions between 1955 and 1974, before they were replaced by the JR pattern. The Model A had a double set trigger; the Model B was similar, but had a single trigger. Chamberings ranged from 6.5x57mm to .375 H&H Magnum. The only pocket pistols produced since the end of the Second World War have been the TP and the TPH, each made in .22 and 6.35mm, but a range of target pistols (OSP, GSP) has been offered alongside the P1, P88 and their derivatives. Walther has also become known for airguns, ranging from simple barrel-cockers made in the early 1950s to the most sophisticated recoilless target guns of the 1990s. **3.** E. Walther, Heidersbach bei Suhl in Thüringen. Listed as a maker of hunting weapons, probably in the early 1920s. **4.** Fritz Walther (1889–1966), son of Carl ★Walther, was the presiding genius behind the success of the Walther firearms firm, responsible for pistols such as the PP/PPK and the P.38, in addition to many of the post-war airguns and target guns. **5.** Lothar K. Walther, Zella-Mehlis in Thüringen. Founded in 1925, listed in 1930 as a precision gunmaker and in 1939 as a weapon maker. Subsequently specialised in barrel inserts for Luger and other pistols. **6.** Walther pistols: *see* panel, pp. 542/43.

'Wantage' [The]. Found on shotgun cartridges sold in

WALTHER

Walther (1 & 6)

Carl Walther (1860–1915) was apprenticed to a gunsmith before founding a gunmaking business of his own in Zella St Blasii in 1886, initially making target rifles. However, the success of the Browning-designed blowback pistols being made by *Fabrique Nationale d'Armes de Guerre inspired Walther to design a rival, but his first attempt, the *Venus-Pistole, was a failure. Not until Walther had been joined by his eldest son, Fritz (1889–1966), was progress made.

The Walther-Selbstladepistole Modell 1 was patented on 22 November 1911 (DRP 256606), although introduction dates as early as 1908 have been misleadingly claimed in Walther's sales literature. About 31,000 of these little pistols had been sold when the First World War began. DRP 271863, granted in January 1913, protected a variety of loaded-chamber indicators, but neither the 6.35mm Model 2 nor the 7.65mm Model 3 pistol had been made in quantity before the Walther company outgrew its facilities in 1915. The old factory was sold to Oskar *Will.

The 7.65mm Model 4 was accepted by the German armed forces as a *Behelfspistole, but the 1918 Armistice stopped pistol production in Zella St Blasii – where a workforce of seventy-five in 1915 had grown to nearly 500. Subsequently Walther manufactured optical-instrument components until production of the Models 4, 5 and 7 resumed in 1920/21. During the intervening period, the villages of Zella St Blasii and Mehlis had united, forming the town of Zella-Mehlis.

German Patent 365,265 of May 1921 protected an improved striker mechanism 'for guns with closed frames', resulting in the 6.35mm Model 9, the first successful *Westentaschenpistole. The advent of the 7.65mm Model 8 allowed work on pre-war designs to stop in the mid-1920s. A toggle-lock shotgun, subsequently licensed to Heinrich *Ortgies, dated from this era; and an experimental toggle-lock pistol was made in accordance with patents granted in 1916–19 to August

*Menz. The Heeresmodell signal pistol was patented on 22 December 1926 (DRP 506,011).

Fritz Walther had taken the first steps to perfecting a new double-action blowback pistol by 1927, although it has been alleged (but never proved) that he had purchased the rights to Alois *Tomiška's Little Tom pistol simply to allow the patents to elapse. The single-action Sportpistole, derived from the Model 8, appeared in 1926/27, but then came the Polizei-Pistole (PP, q.v.), protected by DRP 578,765 of 7 November 1930. The compact Kriminalpolizei-Pistole (PPK) – perhaps initially known as the Polizei-Pistole, Kurz – made its debut in the early 1930s, eventually being selected as the *Ehrenwaffe des Politischen Leiters* (Honour Weapon of the Political Leadership).

Made in several guises, the .22 rimfire Olympia-Pistole not only helped gain all the medals in the 1936 Olympic Standard Pistol competition, but also, in its post-war *Hämmerli-modified forms, was still winning trophies in the 1980s.

The success of the PP/PPK series encouraged Walther to enter the military market. The first stage was the Militärische Pistole of 1934, an enlarged PP chambering the 9mm Parabellum cartridge, but this was soon replaced by a locked-breech design. The development history of the latter remains obscure, but apparently most of the work was undertaken by Fritz *Barthelmes. Patents were sought in the mid-1930s (e.g. DRP 721,102 of 27 October 1936 for the locking-block and actuator pin) and enclosed-hammer Armee-Pistolen were made in small numbers before a much-modified exposed-hammer Walther pistol was accepted by the *Heereswaffenamt* on 26 February 1940. Production of the Pistole 38 began immediately in Zella-Mehlis, to be followed by Waffenfabrik *Mauser in Oberndorf and Spreewerke of Berlin. Occupied facilities in Belgium and Czechoslovakia contributed many of the parts.

Production of pistols and rifles continued throughout the Second World War, although external finish of the guns declined. The company developed simplified guns during this period, including a sophisticated

rotary-barrel locked-breech pistol and a stamped-metal version of the Polizei-Pistole. Post-1940 Walther products may be identified by the letter codes 'ac' or 'qve', the latter dating only from the end of 1944.

The period immediately before the Second World War was thus the apogee of the Walther operations in Zella-Mehlis. Walther also made small quantities of *Bergmann-system submachine-guns, the sophisticated SLD signal pistol for the *Kriegsmarine*, and a series of semi-experimental military rifles. The unsuccessful Gew. 41 (W), with a *Bang-type muzzle-cup actuator, eventually gave way to the crude, but efficient, Gew. 43; the latter was still being made when the fighting ceased, production totalling at least 400,000. However, Walther's entrant in the *Maschinenkarabiner* competition of 1940–42 was overlooked in favour of the rival *Haenel submission.

The US Army reached Zella-Mehlis on 12 April 1945, and work in the Walther factory ceased. Shortly afterward, Fritz Walther and his family transferred to the American occupation zone, and work on mechanical calculators began again in Heidenheim an der Brenz, a small village in Württemberg. Small factories had soon been built in Niederstötzingen and Gerstetten; the Olympia-Pistole was licensed to *Hämmerli on 31 March 1950 to provide a small royalty income; and rights to the Polizei-Pistolen were sold to Manufacture de Machines du Haut-Rhin (Manurhin) in France.

Eventually, in 1950, Walther purchased an old cavalry barracks in Ulm/Donau and – with a workforce of only six men – began to make the air rifles protected by DRP 824,160 of 4 July 1950. The success of the LG51 (rifle) and the LP53 (pistol) led to the LG55 and the LGV, spring-and-piston designs that were superseded eventually by a recoilless single-stroke pneumatic designated LGR. The pneumatic was based on German Patent 1,164,279 of July 1961, which protected the Präzisions-Luftpistole Modell 2. The LGR was the prototype for a range of similar rifles, but has now been overtaken by pre-charged pneumatic and gas-powered designs.

The Allies allowed work to

The Walther P88 is the first of the company's locked-breech handguns to abandon the Barthelmes-Walther pin-operated tilting-block locking system in favour of the simpler Colt-Browning tipping barrel.

recommence on the P.38 in 1954, and a starting pistol – the Übungspistole 1 (UP 1) – appeared in 1955. The first new Pistolen 38 left the Ulm production line in 1957, although Manurhin assembled a few thousand guns for export to Portugal during the same period. Renamed Pistole 1 in 1963, the old P.38 has provided the basis for a series of successful commercial variants. The P38k and the P4 are conventional-looking guns, identical to the P.38/P1 apart from shorter barrels, but the P5 and the P5A1 have barrel-enveloping slides.

However, difficulties encountered in mass-producing a pre-war design, together with the preference of German police for *Heckler & Koch designs and the Austrian-developed *Glock, forced Walther to develop the P88. This embodies a Browning-style tipping barrel instead of the Barthelmes block, and has become just one of many similar designs competing in the military/police market.

The firearms business continued to grow rapidly throughout the 1960s. Although the TP pocket pistol was comparatively unsuccessful, the PP, PPK, PPK/S and the perfected TPH sold surprisingly well. Then Walther perfected two rapid-fire pistols (the OSP and GSP), successfully re-entering international competition.

Walther's pistol exploits have rather overshadowed the successful production of full-bore and rimfire rifles. During the Zella-Mehlis days, Walther had made a range of rimfire rifles, including an effective semi-automatic rifle introduced in the early 1930s. Production of the Kleinkalibergewehre (KK series) began again in the mid-1950s, the range being extended to include the KJS, KKJ, KKM, KKS and other sub-variants. Some of these guns were sporters chambering .22

Hornet or 5.6x45 Vierling ammunition, whereas others were destined for specialist UIT/ISU competitions. The target-shooting adaptations of the rimfire system were very successful, although they encountered much opposition in Germany from the similar products of J.G. *Anschütz and latterly *Feinwerkbau–Westinger & Altenburger. The .22 rimfire UIT BV (*Blockverschluss*, 'block-lock') rifle of 1986 was touted as a replacement for the bolt-action Walthers, but lasted in production for only four years.

From c. 1955 into the 1970s, Walther stocked and barrelled commercial Mauser-type bolt-actions, offering the Model A sporting rifle in chamberings from 6.5x57 and .270 Winchester to .30-06 and 9.3x63. These guns are rarely seen, particularly the full-stocked *stutzen*, and were replaced by the Jagd-Repetier-Gewehr, or JR, (1974–78) in chamberings from 7x64 to 9.3x64.

The obsolescence of the P1 threw Walther's fortunes into sharp relief, and the failure of the expensive WA-2000 sniper rifle heralded a decline. The once-large and powerful gunmaking business became a shadow of its former self, greatly hindered by the early death of Karl-Heinz Walther (1922–83). Eventually, it was purchased in 1994 by Umarex Sportwaffen GmbH & Co. KG of Arnsberg;

work continues today, albeit on a reduced scale.

Current handguns range from historically-significant guns such as the PP and the P.38, through tried-and-tested GSP and OSP competition pistols, to the ultra-modern P99 (licensed to Smith & Wesson). However, only two rimfire rifles are being made (KK100 and KK200 series), and the gas-powered competition guns have been abandoned in favour of pneumatics. This group contains the single-stroke LPM1 and LG210, alongside the pre-charged LP300 and LG300

Surprisingly, for such a long-lived and important gunmaker, very little has been written about Walther in English. Outstanding among the studies of individual guns has been *The P.38 Pistol*, by Warren H. Buxton (two volumes, 1978, 1984), but most other books have been pictorial catalogues. Among the most useful are *Walther PP and PPK, 1929–1945*, and *Walther*, Volumes II and III, by Jim Rankin (published privately, 1974–81), and W.H.B. Smith's *Mauser, Walther & Mannlicher Firearms* (combined edition, 1971). Information on specific topics can be found in a variety of articles (e.g. 'Hämmerli-Walther Olympia-Pistolen', by Douglas Robertson, in *Gun Collector's Digest*, no. IV, 1985; and 'Walther Airguns', by John Walter, in the British periodical *Guns Review*, January–March and May 1982).

south-east England by *Kent & Son of Wantage.

Wänzl – 1. Franz Wänzl. A gunsmith trading in St Margarethen near Vienna, Wänzl promoted a breech-loading transformation of the Austro-Hungarian Lorenz rifle-musket. The swinging-block breech, similar to many of its day (cf. Snider) was fitted to a few hundred cap-lock conversions in the winter of 1866 and was adopted officially on 5 January 1867. **2.** Wänzl rifle. The Austro-Hungarian M1867 Wänzl, often known as the M1863/67, was made on the basis of the cap-lock Lorenz rifle-musket. Wrought-iron or steel barrels were used, depending on the manufacturing pattern (1854 or 1862 respectively); 1862-type guns also had smaller lock plates. Converted by gunmaking establishments in Ferlach, as well as in Werndl's factory in Steyr, the Wänzl chambered a 13.9x33mm rimfire cartridge, which was originally defined as 6¹/₃ linie or '6 linie 4 punkt'. The mechanism was operated by thumbing back the hammer to half-cock, raising the breech-block, inserting a new cartridge and pressing it forward into the chamber. As the cocked hammer flew forward to hit the striker, it drove a sliding bar into the back face of the breech-block to lock the mechanism at the instant of discharge. Wänzl conversions were also applied to old Jäger-Stutzen, creating the M1867 short rifle, or *Stutzer*. These had heavy octagonal barrels, with the muzzle crowns turned down to accept a sword-bladed socket bayonet. The Ordinäre Stutzer of 1853 had been rifled originally with four grooves and sighted to 1,000 schritt, while the pillar-breech Dornstutzer of 1854 had had a heavy ramrod and sights graduated to 1,200 schritt. All the guns had key-retained barrels. Trigger guards ended in a finger-spur, while the back sights were distinctive curved-leaf 'grasshopper' patterns. The Extra-Corps-Gewehre M1854/67 and M1862/67 were Wänzl conversions of the cap-locks of 1854 and 1862. They were used by gendarmerie, sappers, pioneers and ancillary troops.

Ward – 1. Henry Ward. An English gunmaker, listed at 55 Rupert Street, Coventry Street, London W., in 1876; then, as Ward & Sons, at 1 Basinghall Street (1877–79) and 66 Colman Street, E.C. (1880). The 1880 directory notes premises in Birmingham, which after 1882 are named specifically as 2 St Mary's Row and Bath Street. **2.** H.A. Ward. An English gunmaker, listed in Birmingham, Warwickshire, trading successively in Russell Street (1883–93), Weaman Street (1894–97) and 27 Loveday Street from 1898 onward. **3.** John Ward, USA: see Tiffany Grips. **4.** Montgomery Ward & Company. This business was founded in Chicago, Illinois, in 1872 by Aaron Montgomery Ward (1844–1913), rising to become the first of the USA's great mail-order businesses. Ward's partners soon withdrew, but he replaced them with his brother-in-law, George R. Thorne, and in 1889 the business became a private-stock corporation. Soon overhauled by *Sears, Roebuck & Company, thanks to the latter's advertising skills, Ward diversified into retail operations, and by 1930 had 556 stores across the USA. The business merged with the Container Corporation in 1968, forming Marcor, Inc., and Marcor was acquired by Mobil Oil in 1974; the mail-order operations ceased in 1985, three years before Montgomery Ward & Company re-acquired the independence it retains. Ammunition sold by mail-order, or through retail outlets, may be marked 'EP', 'MW' or 'Cleanfire'. **5.** William Ward. The co-patentee with Bethel *Burton of a bolt-action magazine rifle. **6.** Ward-Burton rifle. This combined a turning-bolt action patented in 1859–68 by Bethel Burton with an extractor designed by William Ward. At least 1,000 .50-70 rifles were made in *Springfield Armory in 1871–72, but the single-shot infantry rifle (despite its good features) failed to challenge the Springfield-Allin and was promptly abandoned. Ward-Burton carbine No. 97 was tested concurrently for cavalry use, but with a similar lack of success; it had a tube magazine beneath the barrel.

Warenhaus für Armee- und Marine, Berlin and Berlin-Charlottenburg, Germany. This business was formed c. 1880 to sell uniforms and military equipment, trading until finally renamed Armee- u. Marinehaus, Inh. Deutscher-Offizier-Verein c. 1911. Its marks have been found on rifles and ammunition.

Warnant – 1. Jean Warnant, Hognée and Liège, Belgium. A maker and patentee of lockwork for revolvers active in the 1870s, Warnant received three relevant British Patents: 5031/76 of 1878 (jointly with Michael Kaufmann), plus 5504/81 and 5520/81 of 1881 (with Bled & Richoux). He also designed a lever ejector, patented in the USA on 8 July 1884 and subsequently exploited by *Colt. **2.** L. & J. Warnant Frères, Hognée, Belgium. Maker of a 6.35mm-calibre automatic pistol. Warnant also made double-barrelled shotguns on the 'Ch. Levé' system, said to have been patented in France c. 1926. The barrels were pushed forward when the eared top lever was pulled upward, and if the selector was set accordingly, this allowed two cartridges held in separate elevators to rise in the front of the standing breech to be chambered on the closing stroke. **3.** Warnant System. A name applied, often generically, to low-power rimfire, or *Flobert-type, *saloon guns characterised by a breech-block pivoted on pins or bolts projecting laterally from the barrel. Lifting the block gave access directly to the chamber. The breeches of some guns could be locked by rotating a knob on the right side; others were retained simply by the blade of the hammer as it fell. Some guns extracted automatically, others did not. Very popular prior to 1914, the Warnant design was not suited to high-power ammunition; however, it was exceptionally easy to make.

Warner – 1. Frank C. Warner, a civilian employee of the US Navy Bureau of Ordnance, accepted Plymouth *cap-lock rifles, *Remington rolling-block pistols and carbines, and *Whitney cap-lock revolvers dating from the end of the American Civil War in 1865. They were marked 'FCW'. *See also* US arms inspectors' marks. **2.** James Warner, Springfield, Massachusetts, USA. Warner invented a 'revolving firearm' with a hammer-rotated cylinder, protected by US Patent 8229 of 15 July 1851. He made about 10,000 .28- and .31-calibre pocket revolvers under his own name, after the failure of the *Springfield Arms Company in the early 1860s. A .30 rimfire version of the cap-lock pocket revolver was also produced in small numbers, but infringed the Rollin *White patent. However, work continued virtually until Warner died in 1870. **3.** Warner Arms Company [The], Brooklyn, New York, and Norwich, Connecticut. This US gunmaking business, best known for the *Infallible automatic pistol, was merged eventually with N.R. *Davis in 1917. *See also* Davis-Warner Corporation. **4.** Warner carbine. Made to James *Warner's US Patents (41,732 of February 1864 and 45,660 of December 1864), this embodied a breech-block that swung laterally up and to the right to expose the chamber. Four thousand brass-frame Warners were purchased on behalf of the Federal government. The original .50-calibre version had a thumb-piece adjacent to the hammer, which had to be pressed before the breech-block could be opened, whereas the later guns (mostly chambered for the .56-50 *Spencer cartridge), made by the *Greene Rifle Works, had a sliding breech-block catch on the left side of the frame. **5.** Warner & Swazey Optical Company, Cleveland, Ohio, USA. Manufacturer of optical sights, adopted by the US Army prior to the First World War. Ambrose Swazey of Cleveland received US Patent 677,288 of 25 June 1901, and 820,998 of 22 May 1906 for prismatic optical sights, assigning them to the company. The US Army's first 'telescopic musket sights' (6x M1908, 5,2x M1913) were made by Warner & Swazey.

'Warren Arms Company'. A name found on shotguns handled in the USA by the H. & D. *Folsom Arms Company, possibly imported from Europe.

Warrilow. J.B. Warrilow. This English gunmaker traded in Chippenham, Wiltshire, in 1891–93.

Warrior. A British sidelever-cocking spring-air pistol designed by Frank *Clarke and Edward *Anson, and the subject of British Patent 351,268 (1931). US Patent 538,057 was essentially similar. Several thousand pistols were made by *Accles & Shelvoke in 1932–33.

Washburn. H.C. Washburn, working for the US government, accepted *Colt revolvers and ordnance stores marked 'HCW'. *See also* US arms inspectors' marks.

Washington – 1. Washington 38. A name associated with a revolver sold in Belgium prior to c. 1910 by Ch. *Clément. **2.** Washington Arms Company, Washington, D.C. A maker of small single-shot *cap-lock pistols and six-shot double-action *pepperboxes in the mid-nineteenth century. The 'manufacturer's' name may hide one of the better-known gunmakers in the New England area.

Wasp. A diabolo-type airgun pellet manufactured by the *Eley Division of Imperial Metal Industries, London. *See also* Pylarm.

Wassner. George W. Wassner, a government arms inspector working in 1939, accepted .45 M1911A1 pistols made by *Colt's Patent Fire Arms Manufacturing Company. They bore 'GWW'. *See also* US arms inspectors' marks.

'Wasters' [The]. A mark found on shotgun ammunition made, or perhaps simply assembled, in Britain by the *Normal Powder Company of Hendon.

'WAT'. Found on US military firearms and accessories. *See* William A. *Thornton.

Watch pistol. *See* Leonard *Woods.

Waters – 1. Asa H. Waters & Company, Milbury, Massachusetts, USA. Active 1843–56, this gunmaking business made Joslyn rifles and carbines under sub-contract to William *Freeman of New York. **2.** Frank Waters. Designer of the British *Sterling Automatic Rifle, eventually exploited in a modified form by Chartered Industries of Singapore.

Watkin. Henry S.S. Watkin, a colonel in the British Army, was the superintendent of the *Royal Small Arms Factory, Enfield, in 1899–1905. He was the recipient of several British Patents, including 14,163/01 of 11 July 1901, protecting a double-pull trigger system, a bayonet attachment and a front-sight protector. Subsequently elements of these were incorporated in the SMLE rifle (see *Lee-Enfield). Three other British Patents were granted jointly with Joseph J. *Speed: 14,162/01 of 11 July 1901, for a charger-loading system with a guide on the bolt head; 6743/03 of 23 March 1903 for a back sight; and 6744/03 of 23 March 1903, protecting a barrel-attachment method and

the manual safety mechanism of the SMLE. Watkin was also renowned for his work in other fields, developing a depression rangefinder, a position finder and a clinometer for artillery use.

Watson – 1. Edward Watson, Batavia, New York. Patentee (US 798,469 of 29 August 1905) of an ejector mechanism for shotguns. Assigned to the *Baker Gun & Forging Company. **2.** James R. Watson [& Company Ltd]. Registered in London in 1892, at 35 Queen Victoria Street, this company acquired the *Arms & Ammunition Manufacturing Company Ltd (James Watson may have been one of its shareholders), in 1904. *See also* Argles. **3.** John Watson. An English gunmaker trading from 17 Whittall Street, Birmingham, in 1900. **4.** Thomas W. Watson. London directories list this gunmaker at 4 Pall Mall in 1878–94 (as Watson Bros. after 1885), then at 29 Old Bond Street from 1895 until the First World War or later. **5.** William Watson & Son. This gunmaking business was established in London at 313 High Holborn in 1868, and moved to 308 High Holborn in 1882. The style became Watson & Hancock in 1886, but work seems to have ceased c. 1891. It is possible that James R. *Watson began trading on his own account after that date.

Watts – 1. W.H. Watts. A gunmaker listed at 54a Marshall Street, London W., in the 1880s. **2.** Watts Locke, Britain. *See* William Watts *Locke & Company Ltd.

'WAW'. Found on US military firearms and accessories. *See* W.A. *Walker, Jr.

Waygood Otis Ltd, Falmouth Road, London SE1. Best known for lifts and hoisting equipment, this engineering business made drum magazines for the British .303 *Bren Gun during the Second World War, often using the code 'S 292' instead of the company name. *See also* British military manufacturers' marks.

'Wayland' [The]. Found on shotgun cartridges sold in Britain by *Golding of Watton.

'wb', 'WB' – 1. As 'wb': a codemark used after 1940 by Hugo Schneider AG of Berlin-Köpenick, on small-arms ammunition components made for the German armed forces. **2.** As 'WB': *see* William *Bradbury, Waldemar *Broberg and William *Brown.

'W B Ltd', in three lines, separated by short horizontal bars. Found on parts for the British No. 4 *Lee-Enfield rifle made during the Second World War by *Wilkinsons Ltd of Bradford, Yorkshire, England. *See also* 'WL'.

'wc', 'WC' – 1. A superimposition-type monogram, with 'C' within 'W'. Correctly 'CW' (q.v.); used prior to 1919 by Waffenfabrik Carl *Walther of Zella St Blasii. **2.** As 'wc': a code allotted during the Second World War to the Meuselwitz/Thüringen factory of Hugo Schneider AG. It will be found on small-arms ammunition parts.

'WCA'. A concentric-type monogram with all three letters equally dominant. Correctly 'WAC' (q.v.); used by the *Warner Arms Company.

'WCAD'. A concentric-type monogram with all four letters of equal significance. Correctly 'WDAC' (q.v.); used by the *Warner-Davis Arms Corporation.

'WCC', 'W C C', 'W.C.C.', 'W.C.Co.' Marks associated with ammunition made in the USA by the *Western Cartridge Company of East Alton.

'WCO'. Found on US military firearms and accessories. *See* Warren C. *Odell.

'WCDA'. *See* 'WCAD'.

'WCW'. An unidentified Civil War-period inspector's

mark, found on *Sharps & Hankins carbines made for the Federal Army in 1863–65.

'WD', 'W.D.', 'wd' – 1. As 'WD' (majuscule): the British War Department property mark, invariably accompanied by a broad arrow. **2.** As 'wd' (minuscule): found on small-arms ammunition components made for the German armed forces during the Second World War, by Hugo *Schneider AG in Taucha bei Leipzig.

'WDAC', 'WDCA'. A concentric-type monogram with all four letters of equal significance. A trademark used on semi-automatic pistols manufactured by the *Warner-Davis Arms Corporation.

'WDN', 'WDW'. Found on US military firearms and accessories. *See* Wiiliam D. *Nicholson and W.D. *Whiting respectively.

'we'. Used from 1940 onward by the Langwiesen factory of Hugo *Schneider AG, found on German small-arms ammunition components.

Weatherby, Inc., South Gate, California, USA. Founded by Roy Weatherby, and renowned for its proprietary magnum cartridges, this gunmaking business built sporting rifles on *FN-Mauser actions in 1949–58, prior to the appearance of the Weatherby Mark V rifle credited to Weatherby and Fred Jennie. They were chambered for cartridges ranging from .220 Rocket to .375 H&H Magnum. A list of individual patterns may be found in *Rifles of the World* by John Walter (Krause Publications, second edition, 1998).

Weatherhead & Walters, or Weatherhead, Walters & Company, Irongate, Derby. The marks of this English provincial gunmaking business – active from 1828 until 1857 or later – have been reported on sporting guns and self-cocking *pepperboxes dating from the mid-nineteenth century. The partnership succeeded J.G.S. Weatherhead, at the same address in 1818–21.

Weaver – 1. G.T. Weaver, an inspector employed by the US government, accepted .38 *Colt revolvers and other ordnance stores in the 1890s, marking them 'GTW'. *See also* US arms inspectors' marks. **2.** W.R. Weaver Company, El Paso, Texas. A US optical-sight maker.

Webber. George Webber of Chicago, Illinois, USA, patented a single-shot .32 centrefire 'squeezer' pistol on 7 May 1905 (US Patent 788,866). It consisted of a tube forming the barrel and breech, a hemispherical rubber palm rest and a sliding operating collar. The gun was held in the hand with the rubber pad against the base of the thumb, and the muzzle projecting between the index and second fingers. Squeezing the fingers inward slid the collar down the tube, cocking and ultimately releasing the striker to fire the gun. The barrel unscrewed from the breech to load. The Webber pistol was made only in very small quantities.

Weber – 1. Casimir Weber, Zürich, Bahnhofplatz. Founded in 1807 by Jean Frey, succeeded in 1847 by Casimir Weber the Elder, and in 1895 by Casimir the Younger. Active until the First World War or later. A distributor of guns and ammunition. **2.** Michael Weber, Zürich, Switzerland. A manufacturer of surgical instruments and an airgun patentee: *see* British Patent 3376/77 of 1877, protecting a gun cocked by a ratchet-pattern trigger guard.

Webley – 1. P. Webley & Son, Birmingham, Warwickshire, England. The origins of this well-known gunmaking business date back to 1838, although Philip Webley & Son was formed only in 1859. After successfully marketing revolvers and other firearms, Webley acquired

Tipping & Lawden in 1877. Webley was listed in London directories at 82–89 Weaman Street, Birmingham, in 1884; at 60 Queen Victoria Street, London, and Birmingham in 1888–89; in Birmingham only in 1890–93; and at 78 Shaftesbury Avenue, London, and Birmingham in 1894–98. The business bought W. & C. *Scott & Sons in 1897, and became the Webley & Scott Revolver & Arms Company Ltd (below). **2.** Webley-Fosbery, Webley Government and Webley-Green revolvers: *see* panel, facing page. **3.** Webley & Scott Revolver & Arms Company Ltd. In 1897, P. Webley & Son amalgamated with W. & C. Scott & Son and Richard Ellis & Sons to form the Webley & Scott Revolver & Arms Company Ltd, which at various times traded from 89–91 Weaman Street, Slaney Street, Lancaster Street and 13 St Mary's Row in Birmingham. Sales offices were also maintained in London, initially at 78 Shaftesbury Avenue, then (after 1907) at 55 Victoria Street. The company became Webley & Scott Ltd in 1906. **4.** Webley & Scott Ltd. Several revisions in its ownership have occurred since 1906, and at present Webley & Scott is part of the Harris & Sheldon Group. The works in Weaman Street was demolished in 1959, and the business was moved to new premises in Park Lane, Handsworth. Webley & Scott is best known for cartridge revolvers and semi-automatic pistols – including the .25-calibre *Hammerless Pocket Model and *Pocket Model – but has also produced an extensive range of airguns. *See* panel, p. 548. Webley & Scott made Pistols, Revolver, .455 No. 1 Mk VI for the British armed forces in 1940–41, and also supplied commercial .38 Mark IV guns from stock. Codes 'M 264' (Birmingham) and 'M 265' (Stourbridge) were allocated to replace the company name where appropriate. *See also* British military manufacturers' marks. **5.** Webley-Whiting. A term sometimes used to describe the semi-automatic pistols made by Webley & Scott Ltd of Birmingham in accordance with patents granted to William J. *Whiting prior to 1914. These protected a breech-block that ran diagonally back and down during recoil to break the lock between the barrel and the slide. An experimental pattern made in 1904 was followed by the perfected Model 1909 exposed-hammer version (9mm Short), and the .38 High Velocity variants of 1910 and 1913 (9mm Browning Long) with enclosed hammers. All had barrels projecting from short slides, safety levers set into the backstraps and butts that were notably square to the axis of the bore. The large .455 Mark I (1912) and Mark I No. 2 (1915) pistols were purchased in small numbers for service with the Royal Navy, the Royal Artillery and the Royal Flying Corps. The No. 2 had a distinctive rotary back sight on the top of the slide, ahead of the hammer, and a modified safety catch. **6.** Webley-Wilkinson. A name given to revolvers made by P. Webley & Sons from 1878, firstly for the sword-cutler Henry Wilkinson & Son, then for the Wilkinson Sword Company. The original guns were .476-calibre derivatives of the Webley-Pryse, but those produced after 1892 were essentially long-barrel versions of the Webleys used by the British Army. However, they were finished differently, had 'prawled' (humped) backstraps, barrels of 6–7.5in, and often adjustable sights. Wilkinson was also responsible for the 'Revolver Transformer', marketed prior to 1914, which allowed individual guns to be adapted to fire small-calibre ammunition. *See also* panel, facing page.

Webster – 1. B. Webster & Company [The Southern Armoury], London. This business was founded in 1887 by Bertram Webster and George E. Greene, apparently as an off-

WEBLEY REVOLVERS

Webley (2 & 6)

The original guns were single-action *cap-locks, patented by James Webley on 29 March 1853 (British Patent 743/53) and introduced commercially shortly before the Crimean War (1853–56). Known as the Longspur, owing to the extended hammer that facilitated cocking, the guns were offered in a range of sizes. They had open-top frames, and thus were not especially durable compared with rivals from *Adams.

After James Webley died, his brother, Philip, progressed to solid-frame and double-action designs of his own, and the company was best known in the 1870s for short-barrel large-calibre *Bulldog and *Royal Irish Constabulary (RIC) designs. These were marketed under a variety of names, apparently in chamberings as large as .577. More advanced technically were the break-open auto-ejectors based on several patents, the earliest design being credited to Edward N. Wood, although the first to be successful was the so-called Webley-Pryse. This embodied a cylinder-locking bolt patented by Charles *Pryse the Younger in November 1876 (British 4421/76).

The Webley Improved Government Revolver (W.G.) of 1882 embodied patents granted to Michael Kaufmann, protecting a trigger mechanism with only five parts (British Patent 4302/80 of 1880) and a three-piece transverse locking bolt (3313/81 of 1881). Changes made to the gun included the substitution of an improved stirrup-fastener patented in March 1885 by Henry Webley and John Carter (British Patent 4070/85 of 1885). However, these elegant large-calibre weapons with flared-heel butts are sometimes credited to Edwinson *Green, a Cheltenham gunmaker who claimed to have had a hand in their design and subsequently pursued high-profile litigation with Webley over alleged patent infringements. The case was found for Webley, but the suspicion remains that there was more substance to Green's case than his protagonist admitted.

Hard on the heels of the Webley Government Revolver, or Model 1886 (incorporating a cylinder-pin ferrule patented by William

A typical Revolver, Webley, .455-inch Mark V, introduced in the British Army in 1913. The bird's-head butt was replaced on the Mark VI by a prawled, or hump-back, version, improving grip considerably.

*Whiting), came the greatest success, when the British Army adopted the 'Pistol, Breech-Loading, Revolver, Webley (Mark 1)'. Sealed on 8 November 1887, nominally of .442 calibre, this gun would accept the .476 Enfield cartridges as well as the .455 Webley type standardised in 1899! This break-open auto-ejector replaced the unsuccessful Enfield (Owen *Jones) pattern and remained the official British service handgun until the approval of the FN-Browning semi-automatic in 1957.

The revolver proceeded through a series of Marks: the Mark II of 1894, with a modified hammer and a better barrel latch; the Mark III of October 1897, with a new barrel and cylinder assembly; the Mark IV, sealed on 21 July 1899 during the Boer War, and characterised by better grades of steel and a few minor detail changes; and the Mark V, sealed on 9 December 1913 (the last of the pre-war patterns), with a strengthened cylinder to withstand ammunition loaded with smokeless propellant. There was also a range of 'starred' sub-variants, customarily indicating in-service modifications to approximate the latest *Sealed Pattern.

The .455 Mark VI Webley, sealed on 5 May 1915 and known after 1926 as the 'Pistol, Revolver, No. 1 Mk VI' was displaced in British service by the .38-calibre government developed Enfield (approved on 2 June 1932), which was little more than a slightly simplified Webley. The Webley & Scott Revolver & Arms Company and its successor, Webley & Scott Ltd, had always marketed .32 and .38-calibre revolvers commercially

and continued to make them in competition with the government products.

When the Second World War began, ironically, substantial quantities of the Webley & Scott revolver were impressed into service alongside the .38 Enfield. Records show that orders totalling 105,066 'Pistols, Revolver, Webley, .38 Mk IV' were placed between May 1940 and November 1944; approved retrospectively in 1945, these guns were not declared obsolete until June 1963. They were similar to the Enfields, but had a commercial-grade finish and Bakelite grips bearing the maker's trademark.

Production of .32- and .38-calibre revolvers continued in Birmingham into the 1960s, the last revolvers to have been made in quantity in Britain. Their demise reduced the once-great Webley & Scott to a mere producer of airguns and occasional importer of shotguns. However, the revolver-making activities of Webley and Webley & Scott have been chronicled most ably by Taylerson, Andrews and Firth in *The Revolver, 1818–1865* (Herbert Jenkins, 1968); by A.W.F. Taylerson in *The Revolver, 1865–1888* (Herbert Jenkins, 1966) and *The Revolver, 1889–1914* (Barrie & Jenkins, 1970); and by Gordon Bruce and Christian Reinhart in *Webley Revolvers* (Stocker-Schmidt, 1988).

WEBLEY AIRGUN

After dabbling unsuccessfully in the market prior to 1914, as the 1910 patent to William John *Whiting testifies, Webley & Scott quickly established itself in the mid-1920s, when the Mark I pistol was produced to the patents of Douglas Vaughan *Johnstone and John William *Fearn (beginning with British no. 219,872 of 1923). The gun was a great success and was followed by the essentially similar Junior, Senior and Premier. The modern Hurricane, Tempest and Typhoon are little more than minor improvements on the original design, testimony to its efficiency.

The pistols established Webley & Scott's claim to being the principal British manufacturer of spring-air pistols. The company also introduced the Mark I rifle in 1927, following it with the Mark 2 *Service (or New Service) possibly the finest pre-1939 British air rifle. It was developed in 1932/33 by Albert Edward *Statham. Neither was made in sufficient quantity to

wrest the laurels from *BSA Guns Ltd, and despite the introduction of the Mark 3 rifle in 1946, the *Airsporter of 1948 regained the lead for BSA. The two companies have enjoyed similar rivalry throughout the 1960s and 1970s, with the Webley *Hawk, *Osprey and *Vulcan attempting to challenge the BSA *Merlin, *Meteor,

The Webley Tempest spring-and-piston pistol, introduced in 1979, is the lineal successor to the Johnstone & Fearn design first patented in 1923.

*Mercury and *Airsporter. Webley's patents are listed under the names of the designers: Fearn, Johnstone, Smallwood, Statham and Whiting.

---

shoot of the London Armoury Company. In addition to cartridge guns, it imported large numbers of cheap push-in-barrel pistols from Belgium (*see* Dare Devil Dinkum) and marketed a range of projectiles under such brandnames as *Armoury and *Butts. Premises were occupied at 41 Newington Butts, London SE11, in 1922, and at 31–33 Newington Causeway in 1931–39 (after Greene had died). There was also a warehouse at the Elephant & Castle, but subsequently the company was owned by *Collins Bros. and traded from New Kent Road in south-east London. **2.** William Webster. This lock filer, originally an employee of the Forsyth Patent Gun Company, started a business of his own in 1818 at 8 George Street, Princes Street, London. After trading briefly as Webster & Company, he eventually settled at 2 St James's Place, Hampstead Road, in 1851. Webster is believed to have died at the age of seventy in 1854.
Wedge Frame. A *cap-lock revolver made by P. *Webley & Son.
Wegner. Louis Wegner, Zella St Blasii and Zella-Mehlis in Thüringen, Germany. Listed in 1900 as a gun- and weapon maker, subsequently as a wholesaler of guns and and a maker of tools. Listed in 1914 as a gun- and weapon maker, and in 1920 as a wholesaler (when owned by Franz Wegner).
Wegria, Wegria-Charlier. A name applied to a 6.35mm semi-automatic pistol, originating in Belgium prior to 1914, which unwisely combined the trigger lever with the grip-safety mechanism set into the backstrap of the butt. Most guns have 'WS' monograms moulded into the grips, but the significance of this is unknown, as apparently they were made by *Charlier et Cie.
'WEH'. A mark found on US military firearms and accessories. *See* W.E. *Hosmer and William E. *House.

Weihrauch – **1.** A. Weihrauch, Zella-Mehlis in Thüringen, Germany. Listed in 1930 as a gun-stock maker. **2.** Hermann Weihrauch, Zella St Blasii and Zella-Mehlis in Thüringen, Germany. Founded in 1899. Listed in 1900–20 as a master gunsmith and gunmaker. Listed in 1930–39 as a gun- and bicycle-component maker, under the control of Hermann Weihrauch the Elder, Hermann Weihrauch the Younger and Otto Weihrauch. In addition to hunting and sporting guns, Weihrauch became famous for bicycles during the Weimar Republic. Firearms were made until the end of the Second World War, when the company was allotted the code letters 'eea' (in 1941), and is assumed to have made machine-gun parts and signal pistols. Plans to produce air rifles were made in 1938/39, but were suspended when the war began. The Weihrauch family, like the Walthers, were able to flee from Eastern Germany before the area became part of the Soviet occupation zone, and their company was re-established in 1948. **3.** Hermann Weihrauch KG, Mellrichstadt/Bayern. The end of the Second World War caused the closure of the pre-war Weihrauch business in Zella-Mehlis, but operations were re-established in Bavaria in 1948, when production of bicycle components began again. Air rifles appeared two years later; finally, in 1960/61, handguns and rifles were added to the product range, including a number of revolvers made under the *Arminius brandname (associated before 1945 with Frederich *Pickert of Zella-Mehlis). Recently, however, emphasis has reverted to airguns (particularly the HW 35 and HW 55 rifles, and HW 70 pistol) owing to the introduction of a new German law controlling firearms. The workforce numbered 210–220 in the 1980s, when the business was managed by Hans-Hermann Weihrauch. The trademark 'HWM' ('M' for Mellrichstadt) replaced the pre-war 'HWZ' ('Z' for Zella-Mehlis), although a few guns made for Albrecht ★Kind were marked 'Gecado'. **4.** O. Weihrauch, Zella-Mehlis in Thüringen, Germany. Listed in 1920–30 as a weapon maker. **5.** Oskar Weihrauch, Zella-Mehlis in Thüringen. Listed in 1939 as a master gunsmith. Possibly the same as the preceding entry.

Weipert. One of the leading gunmaking centres in Bohemia (once part of the Austro–Hungarian empire; subsequently incorporated in Czechoslovakia as 'Vejprty') with lengthy traditions, Weipert experienced a period of decline in the nineteenth century, in the face of competition from newer and more progressive gunmakers who were prepared to mechanise. However, excessive demands made on the Steyr facilities of ★Werndl, then ★Österreichische Waffenfabriks-Gesellschaft brought a new lease of life to the craftsmen in the Weipert district, who thereafter made parts on a sub-contract basis. The adoption of the straight-pull ★Mannlicher rifle by the Austro-Hungarian Army, in 1886, led to the establishment of a manufacturing co-operative answering directly to Steyr. Led by Rudolf Harnisch, members of the scheme included Gustav ★Bittner, Gustav ★Fückert, Wenzel Morgenstern, Eduard Schmidl and Elias Schwab. Eventually, however, the OEWG management decided to build a subsidiary factory of its own in Weipert, and the influence of the individual gunmakers waned once again. Even though a proof house was established in the town in 1889, the influence of the local traditions had waned greatly by 1918.

Weisbach. Karl Weisbach, Mehlis and Zella-Mehlis in Thüringen. Listed in German directories as a weapon maker and wholesaler, 1900–20.

Weisheit, Weissheit, Weißheit. A.R. Weisheit, Mehlis and Zella-Mehlis in Thuringen, Germany. Listed in 1914–39 as a gun- and weapon maker. The 1930 *Deutsches Reichs-Adressbuch* notes A.R. Weissheit as a retailer of guns and ammunition, but this is believed to have been a mis-printed form of Weisheit. The 1941 edition lists Aug. Rich. Weisheit of Zella-Mehlis in Thüringen as a maker of hand-guns and sporting guns, but trading ceased at the end of the Second World War.

Weiss, Weiß – 1. Aug. Weiss, Suhl in Thüringen, Germany. A gunmaker, or possibly two generations of gun-makers, trading in 1914–30. Then the younger man may have been recruited by ★Mauser to supervise pistol production. **2.** F. Weiss, Suhl in Thüringen. Trading as a gun-smith, 1920. **3.** Fritz Weiss, Suhl in Thüringen. Listed in 1939 as a gunsmith. Probably the same as F. Weiss (above). **4.** H. Weiss, Heidersbach bei Suhl in Thüringen, Germany. A gunmaker active prior to 1914. **5.** Herm. Weiss, Suhl in Thüringen, Germany. A gunmaker listed in the 1930 *Deutsches Reichs-Adressbuch*. Possibly the same as the preceding entry. **6.** Max Weiss, Goldlauter be Suhl in Thüringen. This German gunmaking business is said to have been active in the early 1920s, but trading may have been short-lived. **7.** O. Weiss, Zella-Mehlis in Thüringen. Listed in the early 1930s as a retailer of guns and ammunition.

Weisser. August Weisser. Co-patentee with Helmut ★Liebmann of an underlever-cocking airgun. *See* J.G. ★Anschütz.

Wel... – 1. Wel-Cheroot. About 4½in long, this was an enlarged Wel-Woodbine (below) made in the form of a small cigar. It contained a single .22 Short rimfire cartridge activated by a lanyard, which was revealed by biting off the end of the cigar. Pulling the lanyard released the firing pin from the ball-bearing 'sear'. A few Wel-Cheroots are believed to have been issued in 1945 to the OSS, but no records of their use exist. **2.** Welgun. Dating from 1943, this British 9mm sub-machine-gun was designed by the Special Operations Executive at Welwyn. A return spring concentric with the barrel pulled the bolt forward during the reloading stroke, but proved to be vulnerable to barrel heat. Production was com-paratively small. **3.** Welpen. Among the clandestine weapons produced in Britain during the Second World War was the '.22 Experimental Firing Device, Hand Held, Welpen' of 1941, a single-shot pistol disguised as a fountain pen. Only about 100 were made in the Welwyn research establishment in Hertfordshire before the project was abandoned in favour of the smaller ★Enpen. **4.** Welrod. A silenced pistol devel-oped in Britain by the SOE research establishment at Welwyn during the Second World War. The earliest guns were 7.65mm single-shot Mark 1 examples, but a magazine was soon added. The cartridge was ineffective, so the origi-nal introduction was cancelled in favour of the 9mm Mark 1, chambering standard British submachine-gun ammunition (which was essentially the same as 9mm Pist. Patr. 08 [9mm Parabellum] that could be found in occupied Europe). The 9mm pistol had a six-round magazine. BSA Guns Ltd was to have begun production of the improved 9mm Mark 2A in 1944, but the war in Europe ended before work could begin in earnest. **5.** Wel-Wand. A gun developed by the British SOE research establishment at Welwyn during the Second World War. **6.** Wel-Woodbine. Taking its name from the well-known British cigarette, which provided disguise, the gun was little more than a 3x¼in tube containing a 1in .177-calibre barrel. A detachable breech chamber was held by two tiny cross-pins. The hardened-steel projectile was fired by a pellet of priming composition, activated by a spring-loaded striker. Wel-Woodbines were rolled inside cigarette papers, care being taken to reflect the appropriate theatre of opera-tions in the design. The muzzles were disguised with a plug of charred tobacco to suggest that they had already been lit. The gun was activated by biting off the filter tip, severing the safety wire, then pressing the thumbnail on to a small trigger protruding through the cigarette paper. The tiny gun could even be reloaded by driving out the cross-pins holding the breech, inserting a new bullet and propellant-pellet, then replacing the breech and inserting a new cork-tip safety wire.

Welch – 1. Jabez Bloxham Welch, Butcher Row, Banbury, Oxfordshire (1829–52). The marks of this English provincial gunmaker have been reported on sporting guns and ★pepperboxes. **2.** W.W. Welch Company, Norfolk, Connecticut. A gunmaking business active in the USA dur-ing the American Civil War, Welch received several Federal government contracts for 1861-pattern rifle-mus-kets (1862–64). Seventeen thousand had been delivered by the time hostilities ceased.

'Welcome' [The]. This name was associated with shot-gun cartridges sold by ★Lacey of Stratford-upon-Avon prior to 1914.

'Wellesley' [The]. Associated with shotgun cartridges sold in India by ★Rodda & Company of Calcutta, appar-ently made in Birmingham by ★Kynoch prior to 1914. Sir Arthur Wellesley became the Duke of Wellington.

Wellington ['Feeder' Factory], Maughan Street, Wellington, New South Wales, Australia. This was estab-lished in 1942 to supply a few SMLE components to the ★Orange factory. Its products were marked 'WA'.

Wells – 1. A. Wells & Company, Progress Works, Stirling Road, Walthamstow, London. A maker of magazines for the British 9mm *Sten Gun during the Second World War. The regional code 'S 125' may have been used instead of the company name. *See also* British military manufacturers' marks. **2.** George Wells, a lieutenant in the US Navy, accepted single-shot *cap-lock pistols prior to the American Civil War. They were marked 'GW'. *See also* George *Wright and US arms inspectors' marks. **3.** J.H. Wells. A member of the London gun trade recorded in 1891–92 at 6 Wells Street, Oxford Street. **4.** Joseph P. Wells, working for the Federal government during the American Civil War, accepted guns and equipment marked 'JPW'. *See also* US arms inspectors' marks. **5.** Wells Fargo Colt. Among the most sought-after variations of the .31 *Pocket revolver, this had a short barrel and lacked the rammer. Allegedly the first consignments were delivered to Wells, Fargo & Company, the stagecoach operator, but the story may be apocryphal. **6.** Wells Fargo Commemorative. The Model 5994 lever-action spring-airgun made in the USA by *Daisy to commemorate the 100th anniversary of the founding of Wells, Fargo & Company.

Weltersbach. Wilhelm Weltersbach, Solingen, Bimerichter Strasse 11, 1939. Founded in 1882 and registered with the authorities on 2 August 1910, this cutlery manufacturer has been linked with a knife pistol sold under the name Bazar (q.v.). There is, however, no evidence that Weltersbach did anything other than supply the knife components.

Welwyn. This was the principal research establishment of the Special Operations Executive, which was responsible for British clandestine activities during the Second World War. It produced a variety of sabotage equipment and guns, such as the *Wel-Cheroot, *Welrod, *Wel-Wand and *Wel-Woodbine.

Wen-Li Tang. *See* Tang.

Werder – 1. Johann-Ludwig Werder, director of the

WERDER RIFLE

Werder (2)

Pressing the front trigger of the Werder rifle dropped the breech-block automatically and kicked the spent case out of the breech; a new cartridge was inserted, and the spur of the operating lever was pulled back to raise the block. The speed of this action earned the *Rückladungsgewehr M/1869, System Werder* the sobriquet *Blitzgewehr* (Lightning Rifle) during the Franco-Prussian War of 1870–71.

About 1,000 Liège-made rifles, with a single barrel band, were tried against Steyr-made Werndls in 1868, and the perfected two-band M/69 was approved on 18 April 1869. About 125,000 were made by the *Amberg manufactory, assisted by sub-contractors, and about 20,000 came from the *Handfeuerwaffen-Productionsgenossenschaft in Suhl. Maschinenfabrik 'Landes' of München, and Auguste Francotte & Cie of Liège each made about 4,000 M/1869 carbines, adopted on 1 July 1869, 600 others being converted in Amberg from 1868-pattern trials rifles. Apparently Francotte also made a Werder gendarmerie rifle, a variant of the standard carbine that accepted a socket bayonet.

An improved *Aptierte M/1869* (Altered M1869) chambered for the 11mm Mauser cartridge, or Reichspatrone, gained Royal approval on 5 June 1875; by 1 November 1876, Amberg had produced 124,540 rifles by rechambering the old barrels and

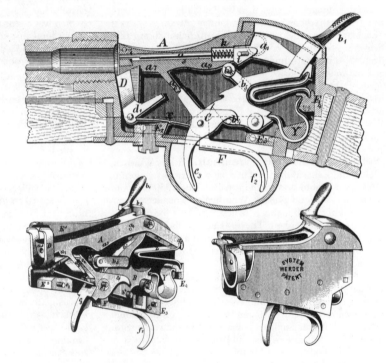

fitting new 1871-pattern back sights. Converted rifles were known to be comparatively weak, so the strengthened M/1869, *neues Muster* (new Pattern) was substituted on 21 July 1875.

The chamber, barrel, sights and nose-cap duplicated those of the 1871-pattern bolt-action Mauser. The rifles were assembled in Amberg from actions made by Maschinenfabrik Augsburg and barrels purchased from *Österreichische Waffenfabriks-Gesellschaft of Steyr. The Bavarian

The single-shot 11mm Werder rifle, the 'Bavarian Lightning', was used in small numbers during the Franco-Prussian War of 1870–71. These sectional drawings show its complexity; the action was operated by a combination of the front trigger and the lever protruding from the top of the receiver.

Army finally approved the Mauser in August 1877, surviving Werder rifles being relegated to foot artillerymen; they had been withdrawn into store by 1882.

Cramer-Klett'schen Établissements in Nürnberg, patented a block-action breech mechanism in Bavaria in June 1868. **2.** Werder rifle: *see* panel, facing page.

Werndl – 1. Josef Werndl, son of gunmaker Leopold Werndl, was born on 26 February 1831. Apprenticehip in the family workshop was followed by a peripatetic career as a journeyman gunsmith in Prague, Vienna, Suhl and the USA, before he returned to his native Austria. Experience of mass-production in the Remington and Colt factories in North America convinced Werndl that a fortune could be made in gunmaking only by following this lead. Succeeding to his father's operations in 1853, Josef Werndl enlarged the factory and installed steam-driven machinery in his search of lasting success. In company with his factory superintendent, Carl ★Holub, Werndl visited the USA in 1863 to see at first hand how the industry had coped with the unprecedented demand for firearms during the Civil War, and how the design of firearms had evolved to meet the need for increased firepower. Inspired by the American experience, Werndl and Holub returned to Austria determined to make guns that were completely interchangeable. A group of small workshops along the banks of the Steyr river was purchased – including a saw mill, an iron foundry and a grindery. Machinery was ordered from Pratt & Whitney in the USA, and Greenwood & Batley in Britain, and series production began. Switching from producing small parts for guns to making complete guns was risky, but the gamble proved worthwhile: the business was employing 3,000 people by 1866. When work on the first 100,000 ★Werndl rifles began in earnest in 1867, weekly production capacity was rated at 5,000 guns. Werndl's operations were reconstituted as ★Österreichische Waffenfabriks-Gesellschaft, founded in Vienna on 1 August 1869; the founder, by then a rich and much-honoured man, died in Steyr on 29 April 1889. **2.** Leopold Werndl. This gunmaker, the father of the better-known Josef Werndl (above), established a workshop in the village of Oberletten an der Steyr in the Oberdonau region in 1834. A flourishing business had been built by the 1840s, making components for firearms and edged weapons; as many as 500 workers were employed in workshops in Oberletten and Steyr. Werndl retired in 1853, being succeeded by his son, Josef, and died two years later. **3.** Werndl-Holub rifle. A prototype of this drum-breech rifle was submitted to the Austro-Hungarian authorities after the rifle trials of 1866 had begun. A 'dirty tricks' campaign was mounted to reverse the acceptance of the Remington ★Rolling Block rifle, which had won the trials, and the Werndl-Holub rifle was approved on 28 July 1867 as the *Infanterie- und Jägergewehr Modell 1867*. A carbine was also made in quantity. The subsequent production order ensured the prosperity of Werndl's Steyr manufactory. Prolonged service showed that the breech-shoe, or receiver, was not as strong as it could have been, and that the leaf springs enclosed in the drum unit soon became brittle. The back-sight leaf was too weak, and few people liked the clumsy external hammer. The improved, or 1873-pattern, Werndl (made as a rifle, a carbine or an ★Extra-Corps-Gewehr) had a stronger receiver and significant changes in the breech drum. Coil springs replaced leaves, and the hammer was mounted inside the lock plate. An improved cartridge was adopted in December 1878, although the M. 1877 rifles and carbines remained unchanged, apart from chambering and sighting arrangements.

Werner – 1. Alfred Werner, Suhl in Thüringen, Germany.

A gunsmith active in 1939. **2.** C.G. Werner. Working in Rochester, New York State, in 1857–64, first from 2 Buffalo Street, then 43 Front Street, Werner made New York-pattern spring-air Gallery Guns. They were stocked in oak and customarily had revolving-cylinder magazines. Apparently C.G. Werner was succeeded by Otto Werner in 1865. **3.** Charles Werner, Buffalo Street and Front Street, Rochester, New York State. A maker of shotguns, target rifles and revolving rifles listed in 1857–65. **4.** Charles F. Werner, Main Street, Orange, New Jersey. This gunsmith is believed to have been the son of Charles Werner (above), listed from 1867 until 1870. **5.** Daniel Werner, St Louis, Missouri. Designer of a breech-loading firearm patented in the USA on 6 October 1868 (no. 82,908). This took the form of a knife pistol with double barrels that sprang forward from the standing breech when a catch was released. **6.** E. Werner, Suhl in Thüringen, Germany. Listed in 1930 as a gun-part maker. **7.** Friedrich Werner Waffenschmiede, Suhl in Thüringen. A German gunmaker operating in 1920. **8.** George W. Werner, Lancaster, Pennsylvania. Patentee of a gun-lock (US no. 468,853 of 16 February 1892), this gunsmith is believed to have made double-barrelled shotguns. **9.** Hugo Werner, Suhl in Thüringen. Listed in 1930 as a gunmaker. **10.** J. Rob. Werner, Zella-Mehlis in Thüringen, Germany. Trading in 1930 as a retailer of guns and ammunition, but possibly also maintaining repair facilities. **11.** Oscar Werner, Heidersbach bei Suhl, Germany. A maker of sporting guns in the 1920s, specialising in over/under shotguns 'with and without ejector'. **12.** Otto A. Werner, Suhl in Thüringen, Germany. A gunmaking business listed prior to 1900. Fate unknown. **13.** Otto F. Werner, Rochester, New York State, USA. This gunsmith was listed at 5 South Paul Street in 1866/67, and at 24 Front Street in 1874/75; trading then ceased. Otto Werner made small single-shot drop-barrel pistols, according to Robert E. Gardner in *Small Arms Makers* (1963). **14.** Rob. Werner, Suhl in Thüringen, Germany. A gun-part maker listed in directories in the early 1930s. **15.** Wilhelm Werner, Zella-Mehlis in Thüringen, Germany. Listed in 1939 as a master gunsmith.

'WES'. A mark found on US military firearms and accessories. *See* W.E. ★Strong.

Wesson – 1. Dan Wesson Arms, Monson, Massachusetts. Founded in 1968, this gunmaking business specialises in revolvers (protected by a range of US Patents) with a detachable barrel within a shroud, and also a series of innovative Pistol Pacs and Hunter Pacs: *see* panel, p. 552. **2.** Daniel Baird Wesson: *see* panel, p. 552. **3.** Edwin Wesson, Grafton and Northborough, Massachusetts, and Hartford, Connecticut. Established in Grafton in 1835 as a gunsmith and rifle maker, Wesson rapidly gained a reputation for the quality of his cap-lock target and sporting rifles. He moved to Northborough, in 1842, and to Hartford in 1848, making cap-lock revolvers in accordance with patents granted in 1839 to Daniel ★Leavitt, and Stevens and Miller. Edwin Wesson was granted US Patent 5146 of 5 June 1847, protecting a multi-barrel volley gun, and 6669 of 28 August 1849, protecting a 'revolving firearm' operated by bevel gears, approved several months after his sudden death the previous January. Wesson's heirs and assignees elected to produce the gun, which was made by the ★Massachusetts Arms Company as the Wesson & Leavitt, but this was challenged successfully by Samuel ★Colt, and the resulting lawsuit virtually bankrupted the Massachusetts Arms Company. Control of Edwin Wesson's business passed to a syndicate of

DANIEL BAIRD WESSON

Wesson (2)

Born on 18 May 1825 in Worcester, Massachusetts, Wesson was apprenticed to his elder brother, Edwin, in 1843. When Edwin died unexpectedly in Hartford, Connecticut, in January 1849, Daniel Wesson attempted to perpetuate the business. Its failure led to the formation of the *Wesson Rifle Company, but when this also failed Wesson returned to making *cap-lock rifles with his other brothers, Franklin and Martin.

In October 1850, with the fraternal partnership at an end, Daniel Wesson returned to Massachusetts, working first as superintendent of the *Leonard Pistol Works in Charlestown (although actually the Leonard pepperboxes were made under contract by *Robbins & Lawrence), then for *Allen, Brown & Luther in Worcester. This move was short-lived, however, as the first partnership between Smith and Wesson was formed at the end of 1852. Prior to this, Wesson claimed to have been employed by Parry W. *Porter to improve the Porter turret repeater, patented in the USA on 18 July 1851.

Wesson seems to have met Horace *Smith while working for Allen, Brown & Luther. He was particularly keen to develop a cartridge with the fulminate igniter placed in the case head, separated from the charge by a disc, and some of the earliest 'Norwich' Smith & Wesson pistols took this form. However, the manufacturing techniques of the day could not cope with Wesson's demands, and a reversion to a *Hunt-style rocket ball was made. When this project failed and the initial partnership with Smith ended, Wesson continued to to develop self-contained metallic-case cartridges. In 1856, therefore, Smith and Wesson renewed their partnership.

Daniel Wesson received a wide range of US Patents. They included US Patent 72,434 of 17 December 1867, protecting an automatically-retracting ejector; and 78,847 of 9 June 1868 for hammers that retracted automatically to half-cock as the breech of the double-barrelled

The Triple Lock Smith & Wesson revolver, with its yoke-mounted cylinder and auxiliary locking system, was the culmination of work begun by Daniel B. Wesson in the 1880s and continued by his son, Joseph, into the twentieth century.

sporting gun opened. Subsequently guns of this type were made by the *Wesson Firearms Company. US Patent 114,374 of 2 May 1871 protected the detachable lock of a double-barrelled gun.

The first of the revolver patents to be granted in the USA in Wesson's name alone (previous protection had been sought jointly with Horace Smith) was no. 136,348 of 25 February 1873. Then came an extraction mechanism protected by 158,874 of 19 January 1875, incorporated in the *New Model Russian revolver, which allowed the cylinder to be removed without tools. US Patent 186,509 of 23 January 1877, protecting a revolver, was followed by two patents granted jointly with James *Bullard and assigned to Smith & Wesson. The first, 187,689 of 20 February 1877, protected an improved retainer for revolver cylinders; 198,228 of 18 December 1877 protected a rebounding hammer.

US Patent 202,388 of 16 April 1878 was granted for a 'Firearm Lock'; 217,562 of 15 July 1879 protected a magazine firearm. These were followed by a series of patents protecting revolvers or their components: 222,167 and 222,168 of 2 December 1879, 227,009 of 25 May 1880, and 285,862 of 2 October 1883. US Patent 289,875 was granted on 11 December 1883 to protect a gun-lock safety attachment; 323,837 was obtained jointly with Joseph H. Wesson (q.v.)

for a 'revolving firearm'; and two patents granted on 4 August 1885 (323,838 and 323, 839) protected safety-lock systems.

Locking devices were featured in US Patent 323,873, obtained jointly with John S. Landers on 4 August 1883, and in 361,100 of 12 April 1887. Then came the revolving firearms protected by 371,523 of 11 October 1887, 401,087 of 9 April 1889, and 429,397 of 3 June 1890. US Patent 421,798 was granted on 18 February 1890 to protect a 'barrel catch for firearms', and 611,826 of 4 October 1898 (jointly with Joseph H. Wesson) depicted a 'cylinder stop for revolving firearms'.

Daniel Wesson continued to patent improvements well into his seventies, receiving protection for 'revolving firearms' (615,117 of 29 November 1898 and 689,260 of 17 December 1901) and 'Firearm hammer construction' (US Patent 684,331 of 8 October 1901). He died in Springfield on 4 August 1906, to be succeeded by his sons, Walter and Joseph.

local businessmen, who had advanced him large sums of money, and an agreement was concluded with Thomas *Warner not only to finish work in progress, but also to continue to make the 1,000 rifles of the Wesson & Smith contract. This resulted in the formation of the Wesson Rifle Company. **4.** Franklin Wesson, Worcester and Springfield, Massachusetts. An elder brother of Daniel B. Wesson (above), this gunmaker began trading on his own account after the failure of the partnership formed in Hartford in 1850 with his brothers. Premises were occupied in Worcester in 1854–62, then Wesson left for Manchester Street in Springfield. Operations continued until 1872, when Wesson moved back to Worcester, but finished c. 1880. Franklin Wesson was granted US Patents 25,926 and 36,925 (25 October 1859 and 11 November 1862 respectively) to protect the drop-barrel breech-loading rifle made in small numbers during the Civil War in carbine form. He also received US Patent 92,918 of 20 September 1869, for a double-barrelled 'rotating' pistol with a spring bayonet in a housing between the barrels. Derringers and the Pocket Rifle, a long-barrel pistol, were made in accordance with US Patent 103,694, granted on 31 March 1870 to protect a pistol with a barrel that pivoted around a longitudinal rod. A distinctive barrel-latch protruded beneath the frame, ahead of the sheath trigger. US Patent 115,916 of 13 June 1871, protecting Wesson's 'revolving firearm', and 193,060 of 10 July 1877 (obtained jointly with C.N. Cutter) described a 'Breech-loading firearm'. **5.** Joseph Hayes Wesson, Springfield, Massachusetts. Born in Springfield in 1850, Wesson was educated as an engineer and returned to his father's business in 1880. Within a year, he had been granted his first patent (US no. 243,183 of 21 June 1881), protecting a 'gun lock'. Among the many other patents granted to Joseph Wesson were 251,750 of 3 January 1882 for a revolving firearm; 323,837 of 4 August 1885, jointly with Daniel B. Wesson (above), for a 'cylinder stop for revolving firearm'; and 635,705 of 24 October 1899, jointly with J.L. Hobbs, for a 'revolving firearm safety device'. These were followed by 702,607 of 17 June 1902, 708,437 of 2 September 1902 and 743,784 of 10 November 1903 (all protecting revolvers or their components), then by 811,807 of 6 February 1906 and 818,721 of 24 April 1906 for 'firearms'. US Patent 923,915 of 8 June 1908 protected a 'revolver-frame clamp', assigned to Smith & Wesson, and 839,911 of 1 January 1907 was granted for a 'magazine pistol'. Several patents were granted to improve the Belgian *Clément pistol, made under license by *Smith & Wesson from 1913 onward. A US Patent of 6 December 1910 protected a thumb-bar safety (suitable only for right-handed firers); another, of 13 December 1910, protected an improved finger-lever safety set into the front grip-strap; and a third, of 30 July 1912, was granted for a recoil-spring disconnector that greatly eased the cocking process. One of Joseph H. Wesson's last designs was the *Half-Moon Clip, patented shortly after the US Army entered the First World War. His health had already begun to fail, however, and he died in April 1920. **6.** Wesson carbine. Only 151 of these Franklin *Wesson designs were purchased by the Federal government, being ordered in July 1863 from Benjamin *Kittredge & Company of Cincinnati, Ohio. However, Kittredge is known to have supplied hundreds more to individual regiments in such states as Illinois and Kentucky. The distinctive frame had two separate trigger apertures. The front trigger released the barrel, which tipped forward and

down to elevate the breech. **7.** Wesson Firearms Company, Stockbridge Street, Springfield, Massachusetts. This was formed on 27 May 1867 by Daniel *Wesson, the first directors being Horace *Smith, J.W. *Storrs and Cyrus E. Buckland. The principal product was a 12-bore drop-barrel shotgun (patented by Daniel *Wesson, John *Blaze and John *Stokes), opened by pushing forward on a thumb-lever above the breech. Only a little over 200 guns had been sold by 1871, when all of the stock and the assets of the company were bought back by Daniel Wesson. **8.** Wesson Firearms Company, Springfield and Worcester, Massachusetts. Maker of the derringer pistols and Pocket Rifles patented by Franklin Wesson (above). It is thought that the trading style post-dates Wesson's return to Worcester in 1872. **9.** Wesson & Harrington. This partnership was formed by Franklin Wesson and his nephew, Gilbert Harrington, a one-time employee of *Ballard & Fairbanks, to make an auto-ejecting pocket revolver patented by Harrington c. 1874. Harrington bought his uncle's share of the business and with the factory manager, William *Richardson, formed *Harrington & Richardson in 1874. **10.** Wesson & Leavitt revolvers. These mechanically-rotated .31 and .40 cap-locks, based on the manually-operated *Leavitt pattern, were manufactured by the *Massachusetts Arms Company in accordance with patents granted to Daniel *Leavitt in 1837, and Edwin Wesson in 1850. About 2,000 were made. **11.** Wesson Rifle Company, Hartford, Connecticut. Formed to complete the work of Edwin Wesson, under the supervision of Thomas *Warner, this gunmaking business was short-lived. Its assets were sold at auction on 22 November 1849 to a group of businessmen in Chicopee Falls, Massachusetts, who wished to exploit the Wesson & Leavitt revolver. *See* Massachusetts Arms Company. **12.** Wesson & Smith, Hartford, Connecticut. A partnership of Edwin Wesson, Daniel B. Wesson and Thomas Smith, created to make 1,000 cap-lock rifles (said to have been for the US Dragoons). This order, if it existed, does not seem to have been met.

Westentaschen... – 1. Westentaschenmodell (WTM). These waistcoat-pocket-model guns were introduced in Germany by J.P. *Sauer & Sohn to compete with the *Mauser *WTP. There were two types. **2.** Westentaschenpistole (WTP). This German-language term (vest-pocket pistol, or waistcoat-pocket pistol) was used by *Mauser-Werke for its two tiny 6.35mm automatic pistols.

Western, Western... – 1. 'Western', 'Western & Co.' Marks found on a gas-powered revolver made in the USA by, or for, *Healthways, Inc. *See also* Spring & Western. **2.** Western Arms & Cartridge Company, Chicago, Illinois, USA. One of the best known of all North American ammunition makers, this business was acquired the *Winchester Repeating Arms Company after the Second World War. **3.** Western Arms Company, New York City. A distributor of cap-lock revolvers made by the *Bacon Manufacturing Company and the *Whitney Arms Company during the American Civil War. **4.** Western Arms Corporation, Los Angeles, California, USA. Distributors of firearms and ammunition, including muzzle-loaders made in Belgium in the mid-1950s by *Dumoulin. **5.** Western Auto Stores. A distributor of guns and ammunition bearing 'W.A.' marks. *See* Marlin. **6.** Western Boy. A name associated with a revolver made in Belgium prior to 1914 by A. *Bertrand and possibly also *Deprez. **7.** 'Western Bul Dog'. A mark encountered on six-shot double-action revolvers, chambered for the .44 S&W Russian cartridge and based on the Webley *Bulldog. Made in Belgium prior to 1914, but rarely (if ever) signed, the guns have bird's-head butts. **8.** Western Bulldog. A *Suicide Special revolver made in the USA by the *Hopkins & Allen Arms Company of Norwich, Connecticut; it dates from the late nineteenth century. **9.** Western Cartridge Company, East Alton, Illinois. This cartridge manufacturer produced its first rimfires in 1908. Among the company's tradenames has been Diamond, a simple diamond shape sufficing as a trademark. *Headstamps have included 'W.C.C.', 'W.C.Co.' and 'WESTERN'. It was purchased by Olin and merged eventually with the cartridge-making facilities of the *Winchester Repeating Rifle Company to form the *Winchester-Western Division of Olin Corporation. **10.** Western Field. A US brandname associated with guns and sporting goods sold by *Montgomery, Ward & Company. **11.** Western Spring, USA. *See* Spring & Western.

'Westgate' [The]. Associated with shotgun cartridges sold by Jewson of Halifax.

Westinger – **1.** Karl Westinger, an employee of Mauser-Werke AG, is best remembered for the perfected selective-fire system applied to the Mauser C96 pistol in 1936. This replaced the essentially similar, but less successful Nickl type. Westinger was also involved in the design of the recoilless air rifles made by Westinger, Alternburger & Co. (below). Among the relevant German patents are 1,132,827, sought on 31 December 1959, although final acceptance was delayed until 23 March 1967. Protecting the basic sidelever cocking mechanism, the papers name the inventors as Ernst Altenburger, Karl Westinger and Ernst Trumpelmann. German Patent 1,140,489 was sought on 24 February 1961 by Ernst Altenburger, Karl Westinger and Edwin Wöhrstein. Provisionally accepted on 29 November 1962, and finally on 14 September 1967, it protected the basic Feinwerkbau recoil-suppressing system with the barrel and receiver running on tracks in the frame. Patents 1,147,142 (sought on 18 July 1961, finally accepted in June 1968) and 1,150,906 (26 July 1961, 7 March 1968) protected modifications to 1,140,489. They were granted to Westinger, Altenburger and Wöhrstein. German Patent 1,181,590 (sought on 7 January 1960, accepted on 8 July 1965) protected the back sight of the LP 65. It was filed on behalf of Westinger, Altenburger and Wöhrstein. Patent 1,183,407 was sought on 7 January 1960 and granted in August 1965 to protect the safety system embodied in the recoilless Feinwerkbau guns. The designers are named as Karl Westinger, Ernst Altenburger and Ernst Trumpelmann. German Patent 1,578,289, sought by Edwin Wöhrstein on 18 August 1967 and accepted on 28 September 1972, protected an improved back sight for airguns. British Patent 981,122, sought on 19 January 1962, and US Patent 3,247,836 of 1964 were amalgamations of most of the pre-1962 master patents sought in Germany. Protection was also sought in Belgium, France, India, Italy, Austria, Switzerland and Spain. **2.** Westinger & Altenburger KG (Feinwerkbau), Oberndorf am Neckar, Württemberg. This German engineering company was founded on 1 April 1949 by two ex-*Mauser employees. After concentrating for some years on precision machinery, production of the first truly successful recoilless air rifles began. Developed in the 1950s, these were protected eventually by a German Patent sought on 31 December 1959 and granted in July 1962. The patent specifications name the inventors as Ernst Altenburger, Karl Westinger and Ernst Trumpelmann, *see* preceding entry. The

resulting Feinwerkbau LG 150 (essentially similar to the LG 100) appeared in January 1963 and immediately caused a sensation; during its production life, until December 1968, it swept away the bulk of its competition with the possible exception of the *Anschütz 250, and was a catalyst in the elevation of airgun shooting to a major international sport. It was replaced by the LG 300 in May/June 1972. The success story continued unabated until the appearance of the Walther LGR in 1974. Once the Walther began to challenge the supremacy of the Feinwerkbau LG 300 series, Westinger & Altenburger admitted defeat and introduced its first single-stroke pneumatic rifle in 1984. The LP 65 recoilless pistol was introduced in November 1965, and the improved LP 80 in 1979; no gun, including the Walther LP 2 and LP 3, was able to loosen the hold of these weapons at international level until the Italian *Air Match and *FAS appeared in the mid-1980s. Now, however, pre-charged pneumatics and guns powered by carbon dioxide are generally favoured. Although target rifles have always been the cornerstone of Westinger & Altenburger's reputation, a spring-air sporting rifle was introduced in 1973 in response to demands from the USA. Known universally as the Feinwerkbau Sport, it will also be found with the marks of leading distributors, such as *Air Rifle Headquarters and *Beeman in the USA, and *ASI in Britain. The runaway success of the airguns persuaded Westinger & Altenburger to produce a series of .22 rimfire target rifles. An entry has even been made into the replica-shooting sport, with a modern version of the *Rogers & Spencer cap-lock revolver. The influence of Westinger & Altenburger has spread worldwide: the Korean *Yew-Ha target rifle, for example, was a shameless copy of the LG 300.

Westley Richards. *See* Richards.

'Westminster' [The]. Found on shotgun ammunition loaded by the *Schultze Gunpowder Company, the cases and caps being supplied by *Eley Bros. The name refers to a district of London near Schultze's headquarters in Gresham Street, and was perpetuated by *Eley-Kynoch until 1940.

Weston. William Weston, 7 Royal Colonnade and 7 New Road, Brighton, Sussex. This English provincial gunmaker occupied the same premises from 1825 until 1866, the street name changing in 1844. His marks have been reported on sporting guns and self-cocking *pepperboxes dating from the 1850s.

West Point. A brandname used in the USA by *Cotter & Company. *See also* Marlin.

'Westro' [The]. A mark found on shotgun cartridges loaded in Britain by the *Cogschultze Ammunition & Powder Company Ltd in 1911–14.

Wetmore. William W. Wetmore, Lebanon, New Hampshire, and Windsor, Vermont, USA. Active from 1876 until 1895 or later, Wetmore spent part of his career working for *Winchester. Relevant US 'magazine firearm' patents include 190,264 of 1 May 1877 (assigned to T.G. *Bennett); 206,202 of 23 July 1878; 213,538 of 25 March 1879 and 219,886 of 23 September 1879 (both assigned to the Winchester Repeating Arms Company); 220,734 of 21 October 1879 and 223,409 of 6 January 1880 (jointly with Joseph L. Sweeney); 224,366 of 10 February 1880 (with T.G. Bennett); 310,103 of 30 December 1884 (assigned to Winchester); and 548,410 of 22 October 1895 (also assigned to Winchester). US Patent 223,662 was granted on 20 January 1880 for an improved 'Firearm Lock'.

Wettkampfkugel. Associated with a flat-head diabolo

airgun pellet made in Germany by *Haendler & Natermann.

'WF', 'wf', 'W&F' – **1.** Found as 'wf' on German military small-arms ammunition made in 1940–44 in the Kielce (Poland) factory of Hugo Schneider AG. **2.** As 'W&F', a monogram with both letters of equal dominance, 'F' superimposed on 'W'. Correctly 'F&W' (q.v.); used in the USA by *Forehand & Wadsworth.

'WFW'. A mark found on US military firearms and accessories. *See* W.F. *Wilbur.

'WG', 'W.G.', 'wg' – **1.** As 'WG' or 'W.G.', sometimes encircled. Found on revolvers, shotguns and sporting rifles made in Liège prior to the First World War by W. *Grah. **2.** A 'wg' codemark was used by Hugo Schneider AG of Altenburg in Thüringen on German small-arms ammunition components made during the Second World War.

'WGÖ'. A vertical superimposition-type monogram, with the letter 'W' dominant, accompanied by 'STEYR' in a banner. Correctly 'ÖWG' (q.v.); associated with Österreichische Waffenfabriks-Gesellschaft.

'WGP'. Found on US military firearms and accessories. *See* Walter G. *Penfield.

'wh', 'WH' – **1.** As 'wh': dating from 1940, this code identified German small-arms ammunition components made in the Eisenach factory of Hugo Schneider AG during the Second World War. **2.** Found as 'WH' on US military firearms and accessories. *See* Wescom *Hudgins.

W. & H. A *Suicide Special revolver made by *Wesson & Harrington of Worcester, Massachusetts, in the late nineteenth century.

Whaley's of North London Ltd, Hornsey Road, London N19. This gunsmithing company, founded in 1950, offered a greatly modified version of the Crosman pump-up pneumatic rifle, developed by Adam Whaley in 1978/79 (apparently in conjunction with Peter Marshall) and marketed as the Whaley-Crosman 761 XL Super.

'What Cheer'. This brandname, derived from the name of a renowned rifle range, was used on *Peabody-Martini target rifles.

Wheeler – **1.** Austin Kent Wheeler, Grand Rapids, Michigan, USA. A 'Wholesale Merchant' and partner with William Matthews *Butts in the *Rapid Rifle Company. Austin Wheeler was also co-patentee with Butts, William Henry Calkins and Charles Augustus Lindberg of a spring-air BB Gun protected by British Patent 24,688/98 of 1898. An otherwise comparable US Patent, 614,532 of 1898, merely credits Calkins and Lindberg (who may have been the actual designers). **2.** Charles Wheeler. A London gunmaker recorded at 41 Royal Street, Lambeth, in 1844–54. **3.** E.C. Wheeler, working from the American Civil War on into the 1880s, accepted a variety of firearms. They included *Springfield and *Ward-Burton single-shot rifles, *Spencer repeaters and *Remington *cap-lock revolvers, all marked 'ECW'. *See also* US arms inspectors' marks. **4.** Henry Wheeler. Co-patentee with George *Fox of a shotgun with a laterally-pivoting breech (US Patent 196,749 of 6 November 1879). The guns were made by the *American Arms Company of Boston. Wheeler was also co-recipient with George *Fox of US Patent 422,930 of 11 March 1890, granted to protect a firing system for a revolver. **5.** William Wheeler, Devizes, Wiltshire. This English country gunmaker traded successively from Little Brittox (1841–51), 4 Sidmouth Street (1854–59) and 56 New Park Street (1866). His marks have been found on sporting guns and *pepperboxes dating from the 1850s.

'WHH'. Found on US military firearms and accessories. *See* W.H. *Hayden.

Whip pistols. These uncommon weapons usually consist of nothing other than a short tubular barrel/breech assembly that can be detached from the body of the whip when required. Cap-lock and cartridge versions have been reported, and are normally fired by a combination of a retractable spring-loaded striker and a rocking bar or button trigger. Individual construction varies greatly. No individual gunmaker has been identified as specialising in this particular weapon, although many surviving examples seem to display Birmingham proof marks.

Whiscombe. John Whiscombe, Birmingham, Warwickshire. A British maker of custom airguns on a 'private' basis, renowned for double-cylinder airguns, in which both chambers provide power (cf. Giss system, where only one of the two is the power piston). Some have been made by combining two BSA *Mercury actions, but Whiscombe progressed to design the JB-1 Titan exchangeable-barrel pneumatic rifle. Announced in 1989, this was to be made in China until production problems apparently brought an otherwise promising project to a premature end.

Whistler – **1.** A *Suicide Special revolver made by the *Hood Firearms Company of Norwich, Connecticut, USA, in the late nineteenth century. **2.** Edward Whistler. A London silversmith, pawnbroker and 'Dealer in Guns & Pistols', Whistler appears to have begun trading on his own account in 1856, from No. 11 Strand, then continued from 1875 as Edward Whistler & Company. Trading finally ceased in 1957.

Whitcomb. B.R. Whitcomb, using a 'BRW' mark, inspected and accepted weapons on behalf of the US government at the end of the nineteenth century. *See also* US arms inspectors' marks.

White, White... – **1.** A.A. White, a government inspector working in the early 1900s, accepted arms and equipment marked 'AAW'. *See also* US arms inspectors' marks. **2.** Edward White. A gunmaker listed in 1844–88 at 3 Worcester Street, Old Gravel Lane, London. Then he may have died, at the age of 78. **3.** George A. White, using a 'GAW' mark (sometimes mistakenly identified as 'CAW'), accepted ordnance stores on behalf of the US Army in 1875. *See also* US arms inspectors' marks. **4.** H.P. White Laboratories Inc., USA. Henry Packard White was one of the USA's foremost ballisticians. The laboratory he founded helped to perfect the chamber insert that allowed the *Garand rifle to handle 7.62x51 ammunition. **5.** Henry D. White, a US government inspector working at the end of the nineteenth century, accepted arms and equipment marked 'HDW'. *See also* US arms inspectors' marks. **6.** John White. The co-designer with Willard *Ellis of the *Plant revolver, protected by US Patents 24,726 of 12 July 1859 and 39,318 of 25 August 1863. **7.** Joseph Chester White. Co-founder with Samuel Merrill of the *White-Merrill Arms Company, formed to promote the .45-calibre *White-Merrill pistol in the US Army trials of 1906–07. He was granted US Patents 717,958 (6 March 1903) to protect the original pistol – a delayed blowback depending on the interaction of the extended hammer with the bolt – and 888,560 of 26 May 1908 to protect the finalised locked-breech gun, which dropped the barrel to release three circumferential lugs from the inside of the half-length slide and had a 'one-hand' cocking spur beneath the trigger guard. Subsequently he became interested in automatic rifle design and continued work until the 1920s. **8.** Rollin C. White (1817–92), USA. Patentee of a revolver with a bored-through cylinder, US no. 12,648 of 3 April 1855. The idea had occurred previously to Eli *Whitney, who had, however, omitted to make a specific claim for the chamber design. Subsequently rights were acquired by *Smith & Wesson, but White was left with the task of pursuing infringers. Eventually he lost interest and retired from the firearms business, going on to produce the White steam car. **9.** Rollin White Arms Company, Lowell, Massachusetts, USA. *Smith & Wesson-type revolvers were made legitimately until the assets of the insolvent company were acquired by the *Lowell Arms Company, after which they were regarded as transgressions. **10.** White & Bates, Birmingham, Warwickshire. The marks of this English gunmaking business have been reported on self-cocking *pepperboxes dating from the middle of the nineteenth century. **11.** White House. A name associated with a revolver sold in Belgium prior to c. 1910 by Ch. *Clément. **12.** White Jacket. A *Suicide Special revolver made by the *Hopkins & Allen Arms Company of Norwich, Connecticut, USA, in the late nineteenth century. **13.** White-Merrill Arms Company, Boston, Massachusetts. This promotional agency was formed in 1905 to exploit patents granted to Samuel Merrill and J. Chester White. These protected a recoil-operated .45-calibre pistol. One gun was submitted to the US Army in 1906, marked 'PAT. APP'D FOR'; another, with a slide-retracting spur beneath the trigger guard, followed in 1907. Neither gun was sufficiently well made to impress the testers, and the design soon faded into obscurity. **14.** White Star. A *Suicide Special revolver made by the *Harrington & Richardson Arms Company of Worcester, Massachusetts, USA, in the late nineteenth century. Probably named after the well-known Anglo-American shipping line.

Whitehead. Thomas Whitehead. A gun-lock maker operating from 115 Halfpaved Court, Dorset Street, London, in 1832–34, then from 117 Dorset Street, Fleet Street, until 1852.

Whitehouse. John E. Whitehouse & Son. Gunmakers trading in Oakham, Rutland, in 1908–14, and probably later. John Whitehouse was responsible for the White-house Patent Target Apparatus, and the business's marks have been reported on shotgun cartridges sold under the names Quorn and Rutland. They were probably loaded using components supplied by *Eley Bros.

Whiteley. Robert H.K. Whiteley, a captain in the US Army, inspected a variety of firearms from the 1830s until the 1870s. They included single-shot *cap-lock pistols, *Sharps breech-loading carbines, and cap-lock revolvers made by *Colt, *Savage and *Starr. All were marked 'RHKW'. *See also* US arms inspectors' marks.

Whiting – 1. Nathaniel Whiting, active on behalf of the Federal government during the early days of the American Civil War, accepted weapons marked 'NW'. **2.** W.D. Whiting, a commander in the US Navy, working shortly after the Civil War, accepted barrels and components for the Remington single-shot pistol. These were marked 'WDW'. *See also* US arms inspectors' marks. **3.** William John Whiting. 'Bill' Whiting, as he was usually known, was responsible for many of the improvements made in the revolvers produced first by the *Webley & Scott Revolver & Arms Company Ltd, then by its successor, Webley & Scott Ltd. The patents granted from 1886 and 1910 chart Whiting's rise from a 'Tool Maker' to 'Director of the Webley & Scott Revolver & Arms Company' in 1905. He

designed the so-called *Webley-Whiting semi-automatic pistol and a selection of airguns, eventually rising to become works manager of the Birmingham factory. Among his patents were British no. 15,802/00 of 1900, 7218/05 of 1905 and 4213/10 of 1910, all of which protected airguns. Whiting's home address was given successively as Sutton Coldfield, near Birmingham; Mona Terrace, Bracebridge Street, Aston juxta Birmingham (1888); 53 Douglas Road, Handsworth; and 153 Linwood Road, Birmingham.

Whitmore – 1. Andrew E. Whitmore, Ilion, New York State, and Boston, East Boston and Springfield, Massachusetts. Active from 1868 until the 1890s, Whitmore is best known as the designer of the earliest double-barrelled hammer shotguns made by E. *Remington & Sons. These were protected by US Patents 117,843 of 8 August 1871 and 122,775 of 16 April 1872; pushing forward on the top lever withdrew a sliding bolt from engagement with lugs under the breech. He was also co-designer with William *Mason of the first hammerless shotguns made by Colt. Whitmore's other US Patents included 153,509 of 28 July 1874; 238,821 of 15 March 1881 (assigned to William H. *Davenport); 262,521 of 8 August 1882; 282,429 of 31 July 1883 (with Joseph *Tonks); 282,941 of 7 August 1883; and 386,184 of 17 July 1888 – all for 'breech-loading firearms'. US Patent no. 433,262 of 29 July 1890 protected a breakdown shotgun action. He was also granted US Patents 185,881 of 2 January 1877, for a revolver, and 266,245 of 17 October 1882 for a 'Firearm Lock'. **2.** Thomas Whitmore & Company. This English gunmaking business was listed at 24 Little Tower Street, London, in 1871.

Whitney – 1. Eli Whitney, Whitneyville, Connecticut. Regarded almost universally as one of the pioneers of series-production by machinery, Whitney accepted a contract to make 1,000 Colt *Walker revolvers in 1847. **2.** Eli Whitney the Younger. The co-designer, with Charles *Gerner and Frank *Tiesing, of the breech-loading shotgun protected by US Patent 93,149 of 27 July 1869. The gun had a drop-barrel action operated by a lever ahead of the trigger guard. **3.** Wallace Whitney, working for the Federal government toward the end of the Civil War, accepted Amoskeag *cap-lock rifle-muskets marked 'WW'. *See also* William *Walter and US arms inspectors' marks. **4.** Whitney Arms Company, New Haven, Connecticut, USA. The earliest Whitney revolver was a crude brass-framed gun with a manually-rotated cylinder. Eventually Eli Whitney produced a ring-trigger revolver protected by US Patent 11,447 of 1 August 1854, with the frame made 'all in one piece, with a top bar, not only to strengthen the frame, but also to serve as a foil with a comb of the hammer to strike against to prevent battering the cones [nipples]'. This was soon abandoned in favour of the so-called *Walking Beam pattern patented by Fordyce Beals in September 1856. After making copies of the *Navy Colt, Whitney produced the .36 six-chamber cap-lock usually known as the Belt (or Navy) Revolver. Federal purchases during the Civil War amounted to 11,200 for the army, 5,700 for the navy and 800 for the New Jersey State Militia. Total production approached 33,000. A few shotguns were made on the *Howard-pattern action, then on the better-known *Phoenix (or Whitney-Phoenix) design. Pinfire double-barrelled shotguns were also built, before production was switched to a centrefire drop-barrel breech-loader patented in 1869 by Eli Whitney the Younger, Charles Gerner and Frank

Tiesing. The first guns (1869–70) lacked the auxiliary guard for the barrel-release catch, but this was soon added. The Whitney was cheap, but not successful enough to stay in production later than 1875. After making a range of cartridge rifles, the Whitney Arms Company was acquired in 1888 by *Winchester. **5.** Whitneyville Armory. A *Suicide Special revolver made by the *Whitney Arms Company in the late nineteenth century.

Whittier. Otis Whittier, Enfield, New Hampshire. This gunmaker, active in the USA during 1829–42, patented a 'revolving firearm' on 30 May 1837 (US no. 216). A few guns of this type were completed as rifles and shotguns.

Whitworth – 1. Whitworth & Company Ltd. First listed in 1866 at 28 Pall Mall, London S.W., this business had become Joseph Whitworth & Company by 1871. The London directory for 1879 lists it as Sir Joseph Whitworth & Company Ltd, at 44 Chorlton Street, Manchester, and (from 1880 until 1887) at 24 Great George Street, London S.W. The London office moved to 2 Victoria Mansions for 1888 only. **2.** Whitworth Express Rifle, African Model. Made only in .375 H&H and .458 Winchester Magnum, this *Interarms sporting rifle had an *Express sight and an English-style stock. It was introduced in the mid-1970s.

'WHL'. Found on US military firearms and accessories. *See* W.H. *Lyndon.

'WHM' – 1. Often in monogram form, accompanied by a rabbit and a corn stook. A trademark associated with William H. *Mark, found on shotgun ammunition and accessories sold in Britain. **2.** Found on US military firearms and accessories. *See* W.H. *Morley.

Wholesale Arms & Ammunition Trading Company [The]. A gun merchant operating from 40 St Andrew's Hill, London E.C., in 1894–98.

'WHR', 'WHS'. Marks found on US military firearms and accessories. *See* William H. *Roberts and William H. *Russell, and W.H. *Soderholm.

Wicker. C.H. Wicker, a government inspector, accepted arms and equipment marked 'CHW' c. 1905. *See also* US arms inspectors' marks.

Wickliffe. This US dropping-block rifle, based on the *Stevens No. 44½, was patented in 1978 by Triple-S Development Company, Inc., of Wickliffe, Ohio. The Model 76 was announced in 1976 in standard and deluxe grades, chambered for cartridges ranging from .22 Hornet to .45-70, but production ceased in 1981.

Wide Awake. *Suicide Special revolvers made in the USA by the *Forehand & Wadsworth Arms Company of Worcester, Massachusetts, and the *Hood Firearms Company of Norwich, Connecticut. They date from the late nineteenth century.

Widmer. C. Widmer, Rorschacherstr. 52, Zürich. The name of this retailer of guns and ammunition has been reported on *Einsteckläufe* (sub-calibre adaptors) made for the Luger, as well as on Swiss sporting rifles.

Wiegand. H. Wiegand, Mehlis in Thüringen, Germany. Listed in 1914 as a gun-stock maker.

Wiener... – 1. Wiener-Neustadt armoury. This Austro-Hungarian small-arms depot converted ex-Russian 1891-pattern *Mosin-Nagants to chamber Austrian 8x50R ammunition during the First World War. **2.** Wiener Waffenfabrik. This Viennese gunmaking company produced the 6.35mm and 7.65mm *Little Tom pistols in accordance with the designs of Alois *Tomiška.

Wiggett. J. Wiggett & Sons. An English gunmaking busi-

ness trading from 74 Bath Street, Birmingham, Warwickshire, in 1881–82.

Wilbraham. Joseph Wilbraham. Blanch, writing in *Arms & Explosives* in 1909, notes that this English gunmaker was listed variously in 1854–60 at 4 or 5 Pavilion Terrace, Battersea, London. Howard Blackmore's *A Dictionary of London Gunmakers, 1650–1850* has him at 280 Strand in 1851–54, and 404 Strand in 1854–56.

Wilbur. W.F. Wilbur, working in 1905 as a government inspector, accepted military equipment marked 'WFW'. *See also* US arms inspectors' marks.

Wilcox. Henry W. Wilcox accepted 1860- or Army-pattern .44 *Colt *cap-lock revolvers during the American Civil War, marking them 'HWW'. *See also* US arms inspectors' marks.

Wild. Hermann Wild. An employee of J.G. *Anschütz, Wild was an inventor of hydraulic and pneumatic recoil-suppressing systems. Among them was German Patent 1,287,479 (accepted provisionally in February 1966), which protected the mechanism of the LG250.

Wilder. John Wilder, using a 'JW' mark, inspected and accepted a variety of *cap-lock and breech-loading rifles acquired by the Federal Army during the Civil War, and by the US Army in the immediate post-war years. *See also* John *Williamson and US arms inspectors' marks.

Wildburger. Designer of the earliest metallic-case ammunition to reach service in the Austro-Hungarian 'Common Army', for the 11mm *Werndl-Holub rifle. Weaknesses in the cartridge case and an unnecessarily large primer led to replacement by a *Roth-type case within a few years of introduction.

'Wildfowler' – 1. As 'The Wildfowler': a mark found on 12-bore shotgun ammunition distributed by T.W. *Murray & Company of Cork; origins unknown, possibly *Eley-Kynoch. **2.** A mark identifying shotgun cartridges loaded from *Eley-Kynoch components by T. *Page-Wood of Bristol. Perhaps also supplied elsewhere (e.g. to Ireland).

Wilhelm – 1. J. Wilhelm, Zella-Mehlis in Thüringen, Germany. Listed in 1930 as a master gunsmith. **2.** O. Wilhelm, Zella-Mehlis in Thüringen. Listed in 1930 as a gun-barrel maker.

Wilkes – 1. John Wilkes, the successor to gunmakers Wilkes & Harriss (below) in 1895, continued to trade from 1 Lower James Street, London W., into the twentieth century. **2.** Joseph Wilkes, Birmingham, Warwickshire. Listed by Bailey and Nie in *English Gunmakers* successively at 4 New Summer Street (1846–54), Colmore Place (1855–58), Alma Street, Aston New Town (1859), and 1 Lench Street (1860–72), Joseph Wilkes made airguns until he moved from Alma Street – an address maintained by John Wilkes (perhaps a brother) until 1875. **3.** Wilkes & Harriss. This gunmaking partnership was trading from 1 Lower James Street, West London, in 1894. In 1895, however, it became John Wilkes (above).

Wilkinson – 1. James Wilkinson & Son. Founded in Ludgate Hill, London, in 1818, this gunmaking business moved to 27 Pall Mall in 1829, trading until 1889, when it became the *Wilkinson Sword Company Ltd. London directories record additional premises at 18 St Mary Axe (1850–52), and King's Road and Sydney Street, Chelsea from 1888 onward. Wilkinson's marks have been found on a variety of sporting guns, including self-cocking *pepperboxes dating from the mid-nineteenth century. **2.** Wilkinson Arms, Parma, Idaho, USA. Maker of the Diana automatic pistol in .22 and .25. **3.** 'Wilkinson Arms Company' [The]. A brandname found on shotguns handled in the USA prior to 1917 by the H. & D. ★Folsom Arms Company, possibly imported from Europe. **4.** Wilkinson Revolver Transformer: *see* Webley-Wilkinson revolvers panel, p. 547. **5.** Wilkinson Sword Company Ltd [The]. Formed c. 1889 by James Wilkinson & Son and German interests – Rudolf Kirschbaum of Weyersberg, Kirschbaum & Co. was one of the first directors – this business grew to become Britain's best-known sword cutler. It was also responsible for commissioning the Webley-Wilkinson revolvers and made the Revolver Transformer (above).

Will – **1.** Bruno Will, Zella St Blasii and Zella-Mehlis in Thüringen, Germany. Listed in 1914–20 as a gunmaker. **2.** Julius Will, Zella St Blasii and Zella-Mehlis in Thüringen. Listed in 1900–14 as a gun- and weapon maker and wholesaler. Julius Will was the younger brother of Oskar Will; in 1925, his products were quoted as being solely airguns. He was still listed in 1930–39, but as a maker of guns and weapons. **3.** Oskar Will, Zella St Blasii and Zella-Mehlis in Thüringen. The operations of this German metalworking and gunmaking business began in Zella in 1844. Listed prior to 1914 as a gunmaker specialising in 'air-, target- and hunting guns, Hirschfängern, hunting knives, etc. Ammunition. Complete shooting outfits', Oskar Will the Younger was one of the best known of the airgun makers active in Germany prior to 1914. Production included a vast number of crude bolt-action *Mauser-Verschluss* (Mauser-action) airguns made, apparently, to the patents of Adalbert ★Kempe, alongside barrel-cocking guns bearing model numbers in the 1700 range; work on these continued into Foss's days, as the Modell 1708 (a repeater based on the Mauser-Verschluss gun) did not appear until 1932. Oskar Will was granted several new patents prior to the First World War, including British no. 12,793/96 of 1896, for a break-action airgun, and 22,205/05 of 1905 for a modification of the basic design. His home address was given as 39a Kleine Bahnofstrasse in 1905, but this had become 17 Kleine Bahnofstrasse by 1912. Will was also responsible for cartridge weapons ranging from single-shot pistols to magazine rifles and double-barrel shotguns. However, the business was sold c. 1923 to Dipl.-Ing. Wilhelm ★Foss, who continued to trade until 1945 under the Venuswaffenwerk banner. The 1925 edition of the *Deutsches Reichs-Adressbuch* lists Foss's specialities as airguns and shooting-gallery equipment. A cursive form of the ★Tell trademark (no. 337,292) was registered in August 1925 to 'Venuswaffenwerk Oscar Will, Inhaber Wilh. Foss'. **4.** Will & Köhler, Schmalkalden in Thüringen. Listed in 1925 as a maker of airguns, pistols and flare guns.

Willcox. *See* Johnsons & Willcox.

Willen, Jones & Sons Ltd, Birmingham, Warwickshire, England. A maker of magazines for the British 9mm ★Sten Gun during the Second World War. The regional code 'M 136' may have been used instead of the company name. *See also* British military manufacturers' marks.

Williams – **1.** Benjamin Williams, New York City, USA. This inventor was granted US Patent 150,120 in April 1874 to protect his 'improvements in revolver design'. Subsequently these were exploited by ★Merwin, Hulbert & Company. **2.** David Marshall 'Marsh' Williams ['Carbine' Williams]. The high cost of using .30 M1906 ammunition for training was realised long before the Second World War, and the US Army had taken steps to develop barrel inserts as early as 1928. These, however, had not been successful, and

a suitable sub-calibre conversion was still being sought when, early in the 1930s, Williams approached the Ordnance Board with his patented floating-chamber system, which had already proved its worth in several rifles and the Colt Ace conversion. Subsequently an efficient prototype was demonstrated to the Ordnance Board which, much impressed, made some examples of its own (as the T2) in 1935–36. Williams is best known, however, as the 'designer' of the ★M1 Carbine (although only the short-stroke piston system was his work), and the American press gave him the nickname 'Carbine'. **3.** Frederick Williams. An English gunmaker listed at 32–33 Weaman Street, Birmingham, from 1893 until 1900 or later. **4.** Henry Williams. This gunmaker began trading from 3 Little Prescot Street, London E., in 1854. Then he moved to 10 Chamber Street in 1861, and was at 4 Wellclose Square by 1872. Trading seems to have ceased c. 1880. **5.** Isaiah Williams. A British patent agent; *see also* Micheloni. **6.** Ted Williams. A brandname associated with guns and sporting goods sold in the USA by ★Sears, Roebuck & Company. *See also* J.C. ★Higgins. **7.** Walter Frederick Williams. This English gunmaker was the co-designer with Arthur Henry ★Hill of the ★Hill & Williams air rifle, protected by British Patents 25,222/05 of 1905 and 19,519/07 of 1907. The patent specifications record Williams' address as 82 Wills Street, Aston Manor, Warwickshire. **8.** Williams & Powell. A gunmaking business trading from 25 South Castle Street, Liverpool, in 1881–92. Its marks have been reported on self-cocking ★pepperboxes dating from the 1850s. *See also* Jeremiah ★Patrick, Liverpool. **9.** *See also* ★Townsend & Williams.

Williamson – **1.** David Williamson. The designer of the ★teat-fire cartridge chambered in the ★Moore revolver, protected by a patent granted on 5 January 1864. Williamson also designed the combination extractor/cartridge retainer found on Moore revolvers, protected by patents granted on 17 May and 5 June 1864. Another patent, granted on 2 October 1866, protected a single-shot convertible cartridge/cap-lock derringer. **2.** E.A. Williamson accepted ★Spencer carbines on behalf of the Federal government, marking them 'EAW'. They date from 1864–65 only. **3.** John Williamson, a captain in the US Army, accepted a variety of military stores prior to 1850; all bore 'JW'. *See also* John ★Wilder and US arms inspectors' marks. **4.** Robert Williamson. This English gunmaker was listed at 42 Prince's Street, Leicester Square, London, in 1865–66. **5.** Thomas Williamson & Son[s] of Bridgnorth, Shropshire, made a 12-bore ★Lefaucheux-type breech-loading pinfire shotgun entered by Mr Joyner in the trials undertaken by *The Field* in 1866. The business first entered the directories in 1797, trading from 'Back of Castle' Street in 1834, Waterloo Terrace (by 1841), then High Street (by 1855). A branch was also maintained in Bull Ring, Ludlow, Shropshire, from the mid-1850s. The trading style became '…& Son' (occasionally listed in the plural) some time after 1863. **6.** William Williamson. Based at 61 Gracechurch Street, London E.C., in 1878–90, this gunmaker also maintained premises at 153 ★Minories in 1879–84. **7.** Williamson Brothers. This gunmaking business retained as its London agent William J. Cummings of 4 Guildhall Chambers, 54 Basinghall Street, E.C., in 1868. The directories record a move on the business's own account to 27 Finsbury Pavement in 1869 (Cummings had been dismissed) and to 42 and 44A Cannon Street in 1872 or 1873. The trading style became

Williamson & Company in 1875, but operations seem to have ceased shortly afterward.

'William Tell'. Found on spring-airguns made in Zella-Mehlis by Oskar ★Will and possibly also the ★Venuswaffenwerke, then sold by ★Clyde's Game & Gun Mart of Glasgow in the 1920s.

Willison. Archibald G. Willison. A gunmaker listed in 1873–74 at 9 Railway Approach, London Bridge.

Willoughby. *See* Nagy-Willoughby.

'Wilmont Arms Company'. A name found on shotguns handled in the USA by the H. & D. ★Folsom Arms Company, possibly imported from Europe.

Wilshire Arms Company. A brandname associated with shotguns made by the ★Crescent Arms Company of Norwich, Connecticut, prior to 1917. *See also* 'Wiltshire Arms Company'.

Wilsker & Companie (Wischo KG), Erlangen, Bavaria. The status of this business, now trading from Dresdener Strasse in Erlangen, has been the subject of some dispute. Smith, in *Gas, Air and Spring Guns* (1957), credits it with the production of airguns during the 1950s, but the specifications and illustrations look so similar to those of the BSF products that Wilsker was probably acting simply as an export and distribution agency.

Wilson – 1. This mark will be found on a small 6.35mm semi-automatic pistol, undoubtedly made in Spain (most probably in Eibar). Individual guns customarily bear marks suggesting French or Belgian origins; the left side of the frame, for example, may display *'Pistolet Automatique Cal. 6,35 Wilson Patent – Deposé'*. The shallow slide reciprocates on rails cut on the inside of the frame (cf. Vici), and a lenticular ejection port is cut through the right frame wall. **2.** Alfred Wilson. This English gunmaker was listed at 20 Little Alie Street, London E., from 1875 until 1887. **3.** Archibald Wilson. An English gunmaker trading from 6 Princes Street, Drury Lane, London, in 1834–36, then from 141 Drury Lane until 1850. **4.** Charles E. Wilson, working for the Federal government during the American Civil War, inspected weapons and equipment marked 'CEW'. *See also* US arms inspectors' marks. **5.** Edward Wilson, Bridge Street, Horncastle, Lincolnshire. Listed in 1861–68 variously as a maker of guns, archery equipment and fishing tackle, Wilson entered a 12-bore ★Lefaucheux-type breechloading pinfire shotgun in *The Field* trials of 1866. **6.** F.E. Wilson, sometimes listed as Willson. A government inspector, working in the early 1900s, Wilson accepted arms and equipment marked 'FEW'. However, his work is very difficult to distinguish from that of F.E. ★Wyman. *See also* US arms inspectors' marks. **7.** Henry J. Wilson. A gunsmith, or possibly a gun merchant, trading in 1888 from 134 Cheapside, London E.C. **8.** John Wilson. A gunmaker of 6 Edward Street, York Road, King's Cross, recorded in the London directories for 1856. Apparently he began trading in Bishopsgate Street in 1841, but little else is known about this retailer, or distributor, of air canes, mentioned by Eldon Wolff in *Air Guns* (1958). **9.** Russell C. Wilson accepted .22 ★High Standard pistols on behalf of the US government in 1941, marking them 'RCW'. *See also* US arms inspectors' marks. **10.** Thomas Wilson & Company. This gunmaking business began operating in 1869 from 15 Cockspur Street, London S.W. By 1870/71, it had moved to 2 East India Avenue, London E.C., and 5 Lime Street. Appropriate marks have been found on Snider rifles, Wilson being granted a tenth share of royalties after settling a patent-

infringement claim. **11.** Wilson & Mathieson Ltd, Leeds, Yorkshire. A maker of box and drum magazines for the British .303 ★Bren Gun during the Second World War, often marking them with 'N 90' instead of the company name. *See also* British military manufacturers' marks.

Wiltshire Arms Company. A name found on shotguns handled in the USA prior to the First World War by the H. & D. ★Folsom Arms Company, but possibly imported from Europe. *See also* Wilshire.

Winans. Ross Winans (1796–1877) of Baltimore, Maryland, USA, was renowned as a maker of railway locomotives and rolling stock, first for the Baltimore & Ohio Railroad, then in partnership with Joseph Gillingham. He retired from railway work in 1860, but is said to have designed and built the so-called Confederate Steam Gun in the early days of the American Civil War.

Winchester – 1. Oliver Fisher Winchester (1810–80), a one-time shirt manufacturer and President of the ★New Haven Arms Company, bought what became the Winchester Repeating Arms Company (next entry) in 1865. **2.** Winchester Repeating Arms Company, New Haven (1865–66, 1873 to date) and Bridgeport (1966–73), Connecticut. The convoluted history of this long-established gunmaker has been the subject of innumerable books (*see* Bibliography), particularly those that have concerned individual gun types, but a good overview may be gained from Harold F. Williamson's *Winchester. The Gun that Won the West* (A.S. Barnes, 1962). Some details of the shotguns are given below, and details of the rifles will be gleaned from the panel on pp. 560/61. However, the company has also dabbled in handguns. Winchester was given a contract for 100,000 .45 M1911 ★Colt-Browning pistols for the US armed forces during the First World War. No guns are known to have been made, as the order was cancelled immediately after the 1918 Armistice. The company's contribution to the history and distribution of the airgun remains a mere flirtation with the importation of Mayer & Grammelspacher Diana guns in 1973. These were given new model designations in the 300 and 400 series. Winchester maintained representation in Britain in the late nineteenth century, first from 54 King William Street (1884), then from 118 Queen Victoria Street in 1884–87. The directories record a move to 114 Queen Victoria Street in 1888, but this is thought to have been the original office renumbered. **3.** Winchester shotguns. The first shotguns to bear Winchester's name were Model 1879 10- and 12-bore hammer doubles bought in England, mostly from C.G. ★Bonehill and W. & C. ★Scott & Sons. They were offered in grades ranging from de luxe Match Gun to plain class D. The first slide-action shotgun was the 12-bore exposed-hammer Model 1893, designed by John M. ★Browning. A tube magazine lay beneath the barrel. The M1893 was not particularly successful, and only 34,000 had been made when it was superseded by the Model 1897 (12- and 16-bore). When work ceased in 1957, more than 1,000,000 1897-type guns had been made. The lever-action Model 1887 shotgun was designed by John ★Browning, about 65,000 10- and 12-bore examples being made during 1887-1901 in a variety of patterns. The 10-bore Model 1901 was little more than the 1887 pattern strengthened for smokeless ammunition. It was discontinued in 1919 after fewer than 14,000 had been made. The auto-loading Winchester Model 11 shotgun was the work of Thomas ★Bennett, but only about 83,000

WINCHESTER RIFLES

Winchester (4)

The success of the Winchester Repeating Arms Company was based on a lever-action rifle, the Model 1866 Yellow Boy, an adaptation of the 1860-patent *Henry rimfire rifle. The principal improvement was the receiver-side loading gate patented by Nelson A. King.

The M1866 was superseded by the M1873, with a receiver of wrought-iron instead of bronze. The principal chambering was a centrefire .44-40, but the Winchester was still a comparatively weak toggle-locked design. However, more than 720,000 had been made when work finally ceased c. 1924.

Next came the M1876, based on a patent granted to Luke Wheelock (US no. 111,500 of 31 January 1871), which had been embodied in a rifle submitted unsuccessfully to the US Army trials of 1872–73.

The changes allowed long-case ammunition, such as .40-60 and .50-95 WCF, to be chambered safely. Yet while sales were buoyant throughout the 1870s, the inability of the Winchesters to compete with the single-shot *Sharps, and *Remington buffalo-hunting and long-range target rifles seemed an insurmountable barrier.

Salvation came in the form of John Browning, whose improved locking system, which relied on a locking block that slid vertically in the receiver, was incorporated in the M1886 lever-action rifle.

Introduced concurrently with the M1885 single-shot dropping-block rifle, adapted from a gun patented in October 1879 (US no. 220,271) by John *Browning, the new M1886 lever-action was a great success. Chamberings had ranged from .33 Winchester to .50-110 Express by the time work ceased in 1936. A similar locking mechanism was incorporated in the M1892 (short-case centrefire cartridges) and M1894 (long-case centrefire cartridges), production of the latter, which is still under way, far exceeding 7,000,000.

Chamberings were restricted initially to .32-40, .38-55 and .44-40, although rounds as diverse as .219 Zipper and .32 Winchester Special have also been used. However, the most popular option has proved to be .30-30, introduced in 1895.

Ejection changed from vertical to lateral with the advent of the M94 Angle Eject in 1983, allowing optical sights to be mounted above the centreline of the receiver.

Primarily intended as a military weapon, a guise in which it was unsuccessful – with the exception of 'desperation sales' to Russia during

the First World War – the Model 1895 was a Browning design with a detachable box magazine beneath the receiver. It could chamber cartridges such as 7x57, .30-03, .30-06 and .303 British.

Among other lever-action rifles have been a variety of guns introduced between the world wars, and the streamlined Model 88 (1955–73), a hammerless design handling cartridges ranging from .243 to .358 Winchester.

If the lever-action Winchester can be said to have made and then perpetuated the company's fortunes, post-1945 success has been based equally on a variety of shotguns and the Model 70 bolt-action rifle. The latter owed its inception to the Model 54, developed in the early 1920s by a team headed by Thomas *Johnson, although the first bolt-action Winchester was a single-shot .22 M1900 rimfire patented by John *Browning in August 1899 (US no. 632,094), and a range of similar guns had been marketed prior to the First World War.

The Model 1873, derived from the Model 1866 Yellow Boy, with an iron frame instead of bronze, was one of a long line of lever-action sporting rifles that survives today in the form of the Browning-inspired Model 94.

of this comparatively unsuccessful design had been made when work ceased in 1925. The Model 12, however, designed by Thomas C. *Johnson, was outstandingly successful: nearly 2,000,000 had been made when production ended in 1963. **4.** Winchester rifles: *see* panel, above.

Windage adjustment. *See* Drift adjustment.

Windsor. Associated with Diana-type *Mayer & Grammelspacher spring-airguns sold in the 1920s by *Clyde's Game & Gun Mart of Glasgow. They appear to be identical with the *Clyde.

Winfield Arms Company – 1. Usually as 'Winfield Arms Co.': found on *Suicide Special revolvers made by the *Crescent Arms Company of Norwich, Connecticut, USA, in the late nineteenth century. **2.** Usually as 'Winfield

Arms Company': a brandname associated with shotguns made in the USA prior to 1917 by the *Crescent Arms Company of Norwich, Connecticut.

Winkler. Benedikt Winkler, Ferlach, Austria. This gunsmith made sporting rifles incorporating refurbished military *Mauser actions. Most were fitted with a double set trigger and a magazine floor-plate latch; they were often ornately decorated.

Winoca Arms Company. A brandname associated with shotguns made in the USA prior to the First World War by the *Crescent Arms Company of Norwich, Connecticut.

Winslow Arms Company, Camden, South Carolina, USA. This gunmaking business produced *Mauser-type sporting rifles from 1962 until the late 1980s under such

The Model 54 was superseded in 1936 by the superb Model 70. Designed by Edwin Pugsley, Leroy Crockett, Albert Laudensack and a team of company engineers, the M70 has since been made in a bewildering variety of styles (e.g. African, Alaskan, Featherweight, Varmint and Westerner) and, even though Winchester has changed hands several times during its lifetime, still spearheads the company's activities.

However, major changes have been made during the life of the M70, and collectors recognise three distinct patterns. Many details were changed in 1964, to reduce production costs, but the new guns were badly made and poorly finished. Although some of the changes were seen to be beneficial, a new variant appeared in 1968. This embodied a guide slot in the bolt head that mated with a rib in the right side of the receiver, restoring the smooth stroke of pre-1964 guns.

Like its immediate predecessors, this variant of the Model 70 has been made in a tremendous profusion of sub-varieties, ranging from the African Rifle (.458 Winchester Magnum only, 1970–84), by way of the Laredo Long-Range Hunter (7mm Remington and .300 Winchester Magnum, 1996) to the Win-Tuff Sporter of 1992–95.

Winchester has made military weapons, including British .303 P/14 (★Enfield) rifles and their US Army equivalent, the .30 M1917; 235,530 of the former and 465,980 of the latter had been made by 11 November 1918. About 300,000 1895-pattern lever-action rifles were delivered to Russia prior to 1917, and .44-40 Model 1894 guns served the armed forces of Britain and France in this era.

The blowback auto-loading rifles designed by Thomas ★Johnson in the early 1900s were also successful; the lineal successor to the .22 rimfire M1903, the Model 63, remained in production until 1958. Centrefire guns were less popular, although 70,000 .351 M1907 rifles were made.

The ★M1 Carbine was a Winchester submission to the US Army in 1941, although only 828,060 of more than 6,000,000 guns were made in New Haven. Large quantities of M1 ★Garand (513,580, 1940–45) and M14 rifles (356,500, 1959–64) were also made.

Unfortunately, changes of ownership have not always been accompanied by improvements in fortune. Although Winchester had swallowed many companies in the nineteenth century – including ★Burgess, ★Fogerty, ★Robinson and ★Whimey – and had entered a partnership with the Western Cartridge Company, fortunes declined after the Olin Corporation took control. Eventually Olin sold the business to the ★US Repeating Rifle Company in 1983.

Winchester rifles, important in hunting, sport and war, have been studied in great detail. Among the many books that have chronicled them – either together or individually – are *The Winchester Single-Shot Rifle*, by John Campbell (Mowbray, 1995); *Winchester '73 & '76*, by David F. Butler (Winchester Press, 1970); *Winchester 94. The First Hundred Years*, by Robert C Renneberg (Krause Publications, 1991; and *Winchester Slide-action Rifles*, by Ned Schwing (two volumes, Krause publications, 1992 and 1993). Particularly good guides to the richness and diversity of the company's history are given by Harold Wllliamson in *Winchester. The Gun that Won the West* (Barnes, 1962), and Herbert G. House in *Winchester Repeating Arms Company* (Krause Publications, 1996). A handy list of individual rifle models will be found in John Walter's *Rifles of the World* (Krause Publications, second edition, 1998).

---

names as Bushmaster and Plainsmaster. Customarily distinguished by the outlandish design of their stocks, the actions were purchased from ★Fabrique Nationale and Zavodi ★Crvena Zastava.

Winter. Gustav Winter & Co., Suhl in Thüringen, Germany. According to 1920s directories, a manufacturer of hunting and sporting guns, automatic pistols and munitions of all types – but probably little more than an agent, despite a claim to 'export to all countries'.

'Winton' [The]. This mark will be found on shotgun cartridges sold by Howard ★Davis of Winchester and his successor, B.E. Chaplin.

Wirsing – 1. A.F. Wirsing, Cincinnati, Ohio, USA. A gunsmith working at 53 Sycamore Street between 1862 and 1865, and probably succeeded – possibly briefly – by the partnership of Wirsing and Schemann. **2.** Wirsing & Schemann, Cincinnati, Ohio, USA. Presumed to be a successor to the business of A.F. Wirsing, but probably short-lived. New York-pattern spring-air Gallery Guns were made and distributed in 1865–70.

Wirth & Companie, Frankfurt am Main. This German patent solicitor worked for Michael ★Weber in connection with British Patent 3376/77 of 1877.

Wischo. A German trademark and brandname used in between 1955 and 1980 by ★Wilsker & Co. of Erlangen, the principal exporter of ★BSF spring-airguns. It was often associated with guns sold in the USA.

Wissler Instrument Company, St Louis, Missouri,

USA. This maker of levels, theodolites and other surveying equipment also built *Benjamin airguns until Wissler died in 1926. Then the factory was acquired by Aloys *Spack.

Withers & Grant, Rugby, Warwickshire. The marks of this English gunmaking business, probably founded c. 1855–58, have been reported on sporting guns and *pepperboxes dating from the 1850s.

Witkop. M. Witkop. This government arms inspector, working c. 1910, accepted equipment for the US Army marked 'MW'. *See also* US arms inspectors' marks.

Witte. Otto Witte, Berlin. A German patentee of improvements in air-pistol design, mentioned in *Die Waffenschmied* in 1883.

Wittmann. K. Wittmann, Zella-Mehlis in Thüringen, Germany. Listed in 1930 as a master gunsmith.

Witton – 1. Applied to a brand of diabolo airgun pellet made in Britain by *Kynoch Ltd of Witton, Birmingham. **2.** David William Witton. A merchant first listed in Fenchurch Street, London, c. 1812, Witton was successively a partner in Lacy & Witton (1815–33) and Lacy & Reynolds (1837–52). When Lacy retired in 1852, Witton succeeded to the business, moving to 21 Great St Helen's in 1854. By 1857, David William Witton and Thomas Wilson Witton were operating as 'Witton Brothers', from 21 Great St Helen's and Dunning's Alley, Bishopsgate Street Without, until 1869. **3.** Joseph Sergeant Witton. A gunmaker listed at 82 Old Broad Street in 1841–50, but subsequently a partner in Witton & Daw (below). His marks have been found on sporting guns, *pepperboxes and caplock revolvers dating from the middle of the nineteenth century. **4.** Thomas Wilson Witton, Witton Brothers, Britain: *see* David William Witton (above). **5.** Witton Cast Steel Cannon & Small Arms Factory. This agency was recorded in 1874–78 occupying offices at 23 Abchurch Lane, London E.C. It is believed to be the Witten Company of Witten an der Ruhr, Germany. **6.** Witton, Daw & Company succeeded Joseph Sergeant Witton (above) in 1851, trading from 57 Threadneedle Street, London E.C., until 1853, then as Witton & Daw (at the same address) until 1860. Then the business passed to George H. *Daw.

Wittwer, Schemmer & Mahrholdt GmbH, or Suhler Waffengesellschaft, Suhl in Thüringen. This gunmaking business advertised in the 1920s as sole agent in Germany for *Manufacture Liégeoise d'Armes à Feu, but does not seem to have survived for more than a few years. Owing to the absence of the company from the 1930 *Deutsches Reichs-Adressbuch*, it is assumed that the onset in 1929 of the Depression had already accounted for it.

'Wizard' [The]. Associated with shotgun ammunition, perhaps emanating from Belgium or Germany, distributed by James *Matthews of Ballymena. *See also* Hawk, Kingfisher and Swift.

'wj'. Used by Hugo Schneider AG of Oberweissbach on German military small-arms ammunition components made after 1940.

'WJH', 'WJO'. Marks used on US military firearms and accessories by W.J. *Hines and W.J. *Ober respectively.

'wk', 'WK' – 1. Found as 'wk' on German military small-arms ammunition components produced in the Schlieben factory of Hugo Schneider AG. The mark dates from 1940. **2.** Used on US military firearms and accessories by William *Kennedy.

'WL', 'W.L.' Found on components for the British No. 4 *Lee-Enfield rifle made during the Second World War by *Wilkinsons Ltd. This company was also allocated the area code 'N85', but often used its initials instead.

WLAR, Winchester Light-Weight Military Rifle. This was a .224-calibre automatic rifle created for the *Winchester Repeating Arms Company by Ralph *Clarkson to challenge the AR-15 in 1958–59. Only a few guns were made, as the ArmaLite was preferred.

'WLJ'. A superimposition-type monogram, with 'L' and 'J' on the arms of the dominant 'W'. Correctly 'LJW' (q.v.); used by L. & J. *Warnant Frères of Hognée.

'WLM', or 'WLM' over '260'. Found on components for the No. 4 *Lee-Enfield rifle produced in Britain during the Second World War by *Walls Ltd. This company was also allocated the area code 'M260', but often used its initials instead.

'WM', 'wm' – 1. A monogram, possibly to be read as 'MW'. A trademark associated with the products of *Patronen-Hülsen-Fabriken Bitschweiler. Its significance is unknown. **2.** A superimposition-type 'WM' monogram with both letters equally prominent, usually on a shield. Found on the grips of pistols and the butt plates of sporting rifles made by *Waffenfabrik Mauser AG, generally prior to 1909. It was replaced by the better-known 'banner' trademark. **3.** Usually encountered as 'wm' (minuscule); this post-1940 mark was applied by Hugo Schneider AG of Dermbach in Thüringen to small-arms ammunition components made for the German armed forces. **4.** Found as 'WM' on US military firearms and accessories. *See* William *Maynadier.

'WMH'. A monogram, correctly 'WHM', found on sporting guns and shotgun ammunition. *See* William H. *Mark.

'WMM'. A mark used on US military firearms and accessories by W.M. *Mills.

Wm. Tell – 1. *See also* 'Tell' and 'William Tell'. **2.** A *Suicide Special revolver made by the *Lee Arms Company of Wilkes-Barre, Pennsylvania, USA, in the late nineteenth century.

'WN', 'WNJ'. Used on US military firearms and accessories by Walter *North and W.N. *Jeffers respectively.

'WÖG'. A vertical superimposition-type monogram, with 'W' dominant, accompanied by 'STEYR' in a banner. Correctly 'ÖWG' (q.v.); associated with Österreichische Waffenfabriks-Gesellschaft.

Wolf – 1. A brandname found on shotgun cartridges made in Germany by *Wolff & Co. of Walsrode prior to 1911. **2.** Adalbert Wolf, Zella-Mehlis in Thüringen, Germany. Listed in 1939 as a master gunsmith. **3.** Albert Wolf, Suhl in Thüringen. Listed as a gunsmith in 1930 and 1939. Possibly the son of, and successor to, Albert Wilhelm Wolf (below). **4.** Albert Wilhelm Wolf, Suhl in Thüringen. Listed as a gunmaker immediately after the First World War, although the business may have failed by 1925. Possibly the son of Julius Wolf (below). **5.** Ernst, Max & Otto Wolf, Zella-Mehlis in Thüringen, Germany. Listed in 1939 as specialist gun-stock makers. **6.** Ewald Wolf, Suhl in Thüringen, Germany. A gunsmith trading in 1939. **7.** Fritz Wolf, Zella-Mehlis in Thüringen, Germany. Working in 1930 as a gun-stock maker. **8.** Fritz Wolf, Rob. Sohn, Zella-Mehlis in Thüringen. Listed in 1939 as a gun-stock maker. **9.** Julius Wolf, Zella St Blasii and Zella-Mehlis in Thüringen. Founded in 1879, this gunmaking workshop seems to have disappeared by the beginning of the First World War. **10.** R. Wolf, Zella-Mehlis in Thüringen, Germany. Listed in 1920 as a gun-stock maker.

Wolff – 1. J. Wolff, Zella-Mehlis in Thüringen, Germany.

Listed in 1930 as a master gunsmith. **2.** Wolff & Company. This ammunition manufacturer was responsible for shotgun cartridges marketed in Germany prior to 1911, under the names *Sonnenmarke and *Wolf. **3.** Wolff & Anschütz, Zella-Mehlis. Founded immediately after the First World War, this gun- and tool-distributing partnership soon failed. Few other details are known.

Wolloms & Company. A British gunmaking business operating from 239 Tottenham Court Road, London, in 1867–72.

Wolverine Arms Company. A brandname associated with shotguns made prior to 1917 by the *Crescent Arms Company of Norwich, Connecticut, USA.

Wonder – 1. A *Suicide Special revolver made by the *Hopkins & Allen Arms Company of Norwich, Connecticut, USA, in the late nineteenth century. **2.** A short-body airgun pellet made in Britain by *Cox & Son of Aston, Birmingham, with a medial waist.

Wood – 1. Edson L. Wood, a government arms inspector, accepted .45 M1911A1 pistols made by *Colt's Patent Fire Arms Manufacturing Company. Dating from 1940, they bear 'ELW' marks. *See also* US arms inspectors' marks. **2.** J. Wood, 194 School Hill, High Street, Lewes, Sussex. This English provincial gunmaker was listed in local directories in 1850, but had been superseded by his widow, Ann, by 1858. His marks have been reported on *pepperboxes. **3.** J.A. Wood, a government inspector, accepted firearms and accoutrements in the 1870s, although his 'JAW' mark may be difficult to distinguish from a similar stamping applied thirty years later by J.A. *Woodward. *See also* US arms inspectors' marks. **4.** John & William Wood, 79 Market Street and 74 King Street, Manchester, Lancashire (1844–55). The marks of this English gunmaking partnership have been reported on *pepperboxes.

5. Joseph Wood, Spurrier Gate, York, England. This name has been found on sporting guns and self-cocking *pepperboxes. The business was founded by Joseph Wood the Elder prior to 1815, became Joseph Wood & Son in 1828/29, and was run by Joseph Wood the Younger from about 1850 to 1867 or later. **6.** Stephen W. Wood was responsible for the break-open revolver made by the *Connecticut Arms Company, protected by US Patents granted on 1 March 1864 and 16 January 1866. He also developed revolvers experimentally for the *Winchester Repeating Arms Company. **7.** William S. Wood, using a 'WSW' mark, accepted firearms on behalf of the Federal Army during the American Civil War. *See also* US arms inspectors' marks. **8.** *See also* Woods.

Woodbury. J.G. Woodbury, a government arms inspector working in the early 1900s, accepted weapons marked 'JGW'. *See also* US arms inspectors' marks.

'Woodcock' [The]. A mark used on shotgun cartridges made in the USA by the *Chamberlain Cartridge Company of Cleveland, Ohio.

Woodman. Charles Woodman inspected and accepted .45 *Schofield *Smith & Wesson revolvers on behalf of the US government in the mid-1870s, marking them 'CW'. *See also* US arms inspectors' marks.

Woods – 1. Alfred Woods. An English gunmaker occupying premises at 3 Waterloo Road, London S.E., in 1890. **2.** Edmund Woods & Son. Listed in the London directories in 1864, trading from 36 Bow Street, W.C., this gunmaking business had become simply Edmund Woods by 1871. Additional premises were used at 38 Lime Street, E.C., 46 Waterloo Road, S.E., and 38 Russell Street, W.C., until 1881. Then 46 Waterloo Road was used alone until 1889; 68 Waterloo Road was occupied in 1890–91. **3.** Leonard Woods of St Louis, Missouri, patented a single-shot watch gun on 16

WOODSMAN

Made by Colt's Patent Fire Arms Manufacturing Company, from 1915 until 1943, then again from 1946 to c. 1977, although the Woodsman name was adopted only in 1927, this target/sporting pistol was designed by John *Browning. A similar series of pistols was made in Belgium after the Second World War by *Fabrique Nationale d'Armes de Guerre.

Characterised by a raked grip, a fixed barrel and a half-length reciprocating slide, Colt-made guns were chambered only for the .22 LR rimfire cartridge. Total production has been estimated as 690,000 Woodsman pistols of all types. About 54,000 'pre-1927' guns were made, initially with ultra-slender barrels. They were followed by the first named series, 112,000 being made prior to 1948, when a slide stop and a hold-open were added, the butt-heel magazine release became a push-button, and plastic grips replaced wood.

After another 146,000 guns had been made, Colt reverted in 1955 to the butt-heel magazine catch that lasted until production ended in 1977. Most of the guns made after 1960 had walnut grips. The Sport model, introduced in 1933, allied a 4.5in barrel with fixed sights; the Target version had a 6.5in barrel and adjustable sights.

The Woodsman Match Target, made c. 1938–44, was easily recognised by a slab-sided 6.5in barrel, milled from bar stock, and a one-piece walnut grip. The trigger mechanism was finished by hand, but, thanks to a high price in a depressed market, production was never large. Guns purchased by the US armed forces during the Second World War customarily had elongated plastic grips and ordnance inspectors' marks.

This .22 FN-Browning Challenger pistol, made in the 1970s, is a modernised European variant of the original Colt Woodsman.

September 1913 (US no. 1,073,312). This contained a single central barrel (masquerading as the winder stem) and had a simple hammer mechanism. It was loaded by unscrewing the barrel, and fired by pressing back the slider above the barrel to activate the hammer. Subsequently Woods produced a repeating .22 Short rimfire version (patented in the USA in August 1915) with a seven-shot cylinder, but there is no evidence that it was ever made in quantity. **4.** *See also* Wood.

Woodsman. *See panel, p. 563.*

Woodstock, Wood Stock. Lever-action spring-air BB Guns made in the USA by *Daisy, with a wooden stock instead of the synthetic form customarily associated with guns of this type and age.

Woodward – 1. James Woodward & Sons. This gunmaking business was formed by the dissolution of the partnership between Charles Moore and James Woodward (formed in 1843), and began trading from 64 St James's Street, London, in 1872. It was still operating when the First World War began. **2.** J.A. Woodward, using a 'JAW' mark, accepted guns and equipment for the US Army in the early 1900s. A similar mark was used by J.A. *Wood thirty years earlier. *See also* US arms inspectors' marks.

Woodgate – 1. Herbert Ferdinand Woodgate, an officer in the South Wales Borderers, was the co-designer with William Griffiths of the *Griffiths & Woodgate rifle. This was the subject of British Patents 21,282/91 of 5 December 1891 and 16,730/92 of 19 September 1892, but subsequently Woodgate received 20,792/94 of 30 October 1894 (in his own name) to protect an improved turning-bolt recoil-operated rifle.

Woodsmaster. A series of rifles made by *Remington-UMC and the *Remington Arms Company. **1.** Model 81A Woodsmaster. An auto-loading rifle made in accordance with patents granted to John *Browning, introduced in 1936 to replace the Model 8A. It chambered .300 Savage cartridges in addition to Remington's proprietary ammunition, and was superseded eventually by the Model 740 in 1950. **2.** Model 740A Woodsmaster. Made in huge numbers in 1952–63, this gas-operated replacement for the Model 81A relied on lugs on the rotating bolt locking into the barrel extension. Chamberings were restricted initially to .30-06 and .308 Winchester, but .280 Remington was added in 1957. The Model 740ADL (1955–63) was a deluxe version with chequering on the pistol grip and fore-end; the 740BDL offered select-grade woodwork and a special squared-back receiver. **3.** Model 742A Woodsmaster. Dating from 1960–80, this was an improved 740A, chambering cartridges ranging from .243 Winchester to .30-06. It could be identified by its decorative skip-line chequering, with a fleur-de-lys border on the butt and foliate edging on the fore-end. The Model 742ADL had hand-cut chequering and better-quality woodwork; the Model 742BDL rifle had basketweave chequering and a Monte Carlo butt; and the Model 742 carbine (1962–80), made only in .30-06 and .308, had a short barrel. The Model 742D *Peerless and 742F *Premier rifles (1961–80) had scroll engraving and gold-inlaid game scenes respectively.

Woodworth. A.L. Woodworth, a government arms inspector, working from 1905 until the early 1930s, accepted .38 *Colt revolvers and other military stores identified by 'ALW'. *See also* US arms inspectors' marks.

Woody. George A. Woody, a lieutenant-colonel in the US Army Ordnance Corps, accepted .45 M1911A1 *Colt-Browning pistols in the 1930s. They were customarily marked 'GAW'. *See also* US arms inspectors' marks. Woody

is also known for the design of a trigger fitted to *Springfield-type International Match Rifles.

Worcester Metallic Cartridge Company, Worcester, Massachusetts. A short-lived ammunition maker, founded to capitalise on the American Civil War, but unable to withstand competition in peacetime.

Worden. G.E. Worden. This government inspector, working in 1905, accepted arms and equipment marked 'GEW'. *See also* US arms inspectors' marks.

Worsley. Samuel L. Worsley, a Federal government inspector working during the Civil War, accepted guns marked 'SLW'. *See also* US arms inspectors' marks.

Worthington Arms Company. A brandname associated with shotguns made prior to 1917 by the *Crescent Arms Company of Norwich, Connecticut, USA.

Wotkyns. G.L. Wotkyns, a US Army officer, inspected and accepted *Colt pistols in the mid-1920s. They were marked 'GLW'. *See also* US arms inspectors' marks.

'WP' – 1. As a monogram, usually in an oval. A private proof mark used by the *Winchester Repeating Arms Company. **2.** Found on US military firearms and accessories. *See* William *Page and William *Prince.

'WPP', 'WPT'. Marks used on US military firearms and accessories by W.P. *Pulcifer and William P. *Taylor.

'W.R.A. Co.', 'W R A CO'. Found on the products of the *Winchester Repeating Arms Company of New Haven, including cartridge *headstamps, from c. 1884 until the merger with the *Western Cartridge Company.

Wrage. Hans Wrage & Co. GmbH, Hamburg. Distributor of the Alpina air pistols in 1968–76.

'WR & Co.' A mark associated with Westley *Richards & Company of Birmingham, Warwickshire.

Wright – 1. Arthur C. Wright, Worcester, Massachusetts. Patentee of a 'firearm' (US no. 625,009 of 16 May 1899). Apparently this was a feature of a revolver made by *Harrington & Richardson. **2.** Charles Wright, Barnsley, Yorkshire. The marks of this English gunmaker have been reported on self-cocking *pepperboxes dating from the middle of the nineteenth century. **3.** Charles Wright, or Charles Wright & Company. This gunmaker was recorded in London in the 1841 census at Gloster Buildings, St Georges, but was operating from 1 Fenchurch Street, London E.C., in 1853–58, and at 376 Strand in 1859–62. **4.** G.E. Wright & Company. An English gunmaking business trading at 9 and 11 Wilson Street, London E.C., from 1900 until the First World War or later. **5.** George Wright, an arms inspector working in the early 1850s, accepted single-shot *cap-lock pistols for the US Army. Marked 'GW', they can be distinguished from the work of George *Wells by the absence of navy marks. *See also* US arms inspectors' marks. **6.** James Wright. A gunsmith at 9 Castle Court, Berners Street, London W., in 1881–85. **7.** Sheffield H. Wright, working on behalf of the Federal government, accepted *cap-lock rifle-muskets during the American Civil War. They were stamped 'SHW'. *See also* US arms inspectors' marks.

Wrist. *See* Butt.

'WRS'. Used on US military firearms and accessories by W.R. *Shipley.

'WS', 'W.S.', W&S' – 1. A superimposition-type 'WS' monogram, with neither letter dominant. Found on grip-trigger semi-automatic pistols made in Belgium prior to 1914, allegedly by *Charlier et Cie of Liège. *See also* Wegria-Charlier. **2.** As 'W&S', sometimes cursive, and often accompanied by a winged-bullet trademark. Associated with the products of ★Webley & Scott Ltd of Birmingham, England. **3.** A 'WS' superimposition-type monogram, with the letter 'S' slightly dominant. Found on a ★Smith & Wesson-type break-open revolver made in Spain, or possibly Belgium, prior to 1914. Significance unknown. **4.** Found as 'WS' on US military firearms and accessories. *See* W. ★Syrett.

'WSS'. A superimposition-type monogram with 'W' placed centrally on two overlapping letters 'S'. Correctly 'SSW' (q.v.); used by ★Steyr-Solothurn Waffen AG.

'WSW'. Found on US military firearms and accessories. *See* William S. ★Wood.

'WT'. Associated with US military firearms and accessories. *See* William ★Turnbull.

WTM. *See* Westentaschenmodell.

WTP. *See* Westentaschenpistole.

Wunler. E.L. Wunler, working on behalf of the US Navy, accepted .38 ★Colt revolvers in 1903; they were marked 'ELW'. The date and style of the guns distinguishes them from .45 Colt pistols accepted many years later by Edson L. ★Wood. *See also* US arms inspectors' marks.

Würthrich. W. Würthrich, Lützelflüh, Switzerland. A modern gunmaker, specialising in re-creations of the ★Heeren action marketed from 1977 onward in a variety of chamberings. The guns have a special extractor, patented in Switzerland (no. 458,125) to overcome one of the perceived weaknesses of the Heeren prototypes.

Württembergische Metallwarenfabrik. Geislingen-Stiege, Germany. A maker of parts for the MP43 during the Second World War. These were marked 'awt'.

Würz. Hugo Würz, Suhl in Thüringen, Germany. Operating in the late 1930s as a gunsmith.

Würzinger. An experimental Austrian breech-loading rifle submitted to the Austro-Hungarian rifle trials of 1866, where it competed against the American ★Peabody and ★Remington rolling-block rifles. It was eliminated in testing undertaken at the end of September 1866.

Wüst. Ernst Wüst, Vacha. Listed in Germany in 1941 as a retailer of sporting guns and ammunition.

'WW', 'W-W' – 1. Usually found as 'W-W' in the head-stamps of cartridges made by the Winchester-Western Division of the Olin Corporation. *See* Western Cartridge Company and Winchester Repeating Arms Company. **2.** Found as 'WW' on US military firearms and accessories. *See* William ★Walter and Wallace ★Whitney.

'WWF'. A linear monogram with a small 'W' above a large 'W', the tail of the latter forming the stem of 'F'. Found on the grips of ★Little Tom pistols made by ★Wiener Waffenfabrik.

'WWG', 'W.W.G.', often with an encircled elephant. A trademark associated with W.W. ★Greener Ltd of Birmingham. It will be found on a range of products, from bayonets to shotguns. It will also be found on rimfire conversions of .303 Lee-Enfield rifles made by W.W. ★Greener Ltd of Birmingham in 1918–19, and also on components for the No. 4 ★Lee-Enfield rifle made during the Second World War. Greener was allocated the area code 'M94', but often used initials instead.

'WWK'. Found on M1889 Colt revolvers accepted for service in the US Navy in the early 1890s. *See* W.W. ★Kimball.

'WWS'. Associated with marks applied to US military firearms and accessories by W.W. ★Street.

Wyatt – 1. Kenneth W. Wyatt. The designer, jointly with Elmer R. ★Imthurn, of the .45 Wyatt-Imthurn Target Luger pistol protected by US Patent 3,039,366 of 14 December 1959. The patent was assigned to the ★Cascade Cartridge Company, but only about fifty guns were made. The fixed magazine was loaded through the top of the open action. **2.** William Wyatt, Romsey, Hampshire. The marks of this English country gunmaker have been reported on self-cocking ★pepperboxes dating from the 1850s. **3.** Wyatt-Imthurn Target Luger, USA: *see* Kenneth L. Wyatt (above).

Wyman. F.E. Wyman, a government arms inspector working in 1909–10, accepted ★Colt revolvers marked 'FEW'. *See also* US arms inspectors' marks.

Wyoming Saddle Gun. A name given to half-stock carbines embodying a Sharps action modified by Frank ★Freund of Cheyenne, Wyoming. A few guns featuring hand-made Freund-Sharps actions, with notably elongated flat-sided receivers, were made before the project was abandoned in the early 1880s.

X

'X'. Beneath a crown, above a number. A mark applied by an inspector in the *London Small Arms Company Ltd factory. *See also* British military inspectors' marks.

'xa'. Found on German small-arms ammunition components made during the Second World War by Busch-Jaeger, Lüdenscheider Metallwerke AG, of Lüdenscheid in Westfalen.

Xcelsior. *See* Excelsior.

'XL', 'X.L.', 'X-L' – 1. Generally encountered as 'The X.L.' on shotgun cartridges sold in England by *Gale of Barnstaple, and *Leech & Sons of Chelmsford. **2.** A brandname used by *Hopkins & Allen of Norwich, Connecticut, USA, on *Suicide Special revolvers introduced in 1871–75: .22 XL No. 1, .32 Short No. 2, .32 Short No. 2¹/₂, .32 Long No. 3, .38 Short No. 4, .38 Long No. 5, .38 No. 6, and .41 No. 7. With the exception of the .38 No. 6, which fired centrefire ammunition, all were rimfires; apart from the seven-chamber No. 1, virtually all of the guns were five-shot. **3.** A single-shot cartridge derringer, based on the *Thuer-patent Colt No. 3, made by *Hopkins & Allen of Norwich and its successor, *Forehand & Wadsworth,

until the late 1880s. **4.** A single-shot cartridge derringer, based on the *Thuer-patent Colt No. 3, made by John *Marlin of New Haven, Connecticut, USA. **5.** Found in the *headstamps of Extra Long [Range] ammunition made in the USA by the *Federal Cartridge Company. **6.** XL DA. These double-action revolvers were made in the USA in the 1880s by *Hopkins & Allen, with trigger guards and folding-spur hammers. They included .32 Short XL DA No. 3, .32 and .38 XL DA No. 6, and the .32 and .38 XL Bulldog. The five-shot No. 3 DA chambered rimfire ammunition; the others were six-shot centrefire guns.

X-Pert. A brandname associated with *Suicide Special revolvers made by the *Hopkins & Allen Arms Company of Norwich, Connecticut, USA, in the late nineteenth century.

'XR', 'X-R'. Marks found in the *headstamps of Xtra Range rimfire cartridges manufactured for *Sears, Roebuck & Company.

XXX Standard. A *Suicide Special revolver made by the *Marlin Fire Arms Company of New Haven, Connecticut, USA, in the late nineteenth century.

Y

'Y', 'y' – 1. Associated, as 'y', with small-arms components made under contract to the German armed forces during the Second World War by the Nagytetený subsidiary of the Hungarian state munitions factory, Jagdpatronen-, Zündhütchen- und Metallwarenfabrik AG, Budapest. 2. Found on US military firearms and accessories. See Jonathan *Young.

'ya'. A codemark allocated in 1940 to Sächsische Metallwarenfabrik August Wellner Söhne AG of Aue/Sachsen, for use on German small-arms ammunition.

YakB. A four-barrelled powered machine-gun developed in the USSR by Yakushev and *Borzov.

Ybarzabal, Eibar, Spain. Active in the middle of the nineteenth century, this gunmaker was responsible for large quantities of cap-lock rifle-muskets. Subsequently many were fitted with *Berdan-type breech-loading conversion units.

Ydeal – 1. A mark found on the grips of Czechoslovakian *Ideal pistols, probably made in Spain. See also Singer. 2. A small Spanish 6.35mm or 7.65mm Browning-type automatic pistol made in Eibar by Francisco *Arizmendi: six rounds, striker fired.

Ye Bishop's Gate. See Charles *Riggs & Company.

Yellow... – 1. 'Yellow Seal'. Found on shotgun ammunition made in Birmingham in the *Mullerite Cartridge Works. The name refers to the colour of the case-crimp disc. See also 'Green Seal', 'Grey Seal' and 'Red Seal'. 2. 'Yellow Wizard' [The]. Used on shotgun cartridges made in Britain by Frank *Dyke & Company of London.

Yeoman, Yeomans – 1. Usually found as 'The Yeoman' on shotgun cartridges loaded by the *Schultze Gunpowder Company, apparently often on the basis of components supplied by *Eley Bros. The mark was used by *Eley-Kynoch until the Second World War began. 2. Horace Yeomans [& Company]. This gunmaking business is believed to have been formed by the son of J. Yeomans (below), trading from 42 Great Tower Street, London E., in 1865, and 35 Upper East Smithfield from 1866 until 1870. 3. J. Yeomans & Son. An English gunmaking business first listed at 67 Chamber Street, London E., in 1837. Yeomans the Elder died in 1851, and entries for 1853–56 list Mrs Elizabeth Yeomans at Tenter Street West, then Elizabeth Yeomans & Son until 1864. Additional premises at 7 Mildred's Court, Poultry, were listed in 1864 only. Thereafter the business was continued by Horace Yeomans & Company (above).

'Ye-Wha', Republic of Korea. This mark, which may be the manufacturer's name, may be found on a pneumatic shotgun known as the Model Triple-B Dynamite and a recoilless rifle copied from the Feinwerkbau 300.

Yokosuka navy arsenal. Maker of the 'Special Navy Rifle' for service in the last days of the Second World War. Based on the *Arisaka, the 7.7mm gun had a cast-iron receiver and a bolt with lugs that locked directly into the barrel.

You Bet. A *Suicide Special revolver made by the *Hopkins & Allen Arms Company of Norwich, Connecticut, USA, in the late nineteenth century.

Young – 1. D. Young & Company. This patent agency occupied chambers at 11 & 12 Southampton Buildings, London W.C., when it acted for John Miller *Epensheid in connection with British Patent 21,235/02 of 1902; a sub-agent named George Harrison was also involved in the work, presumably one of Young's employees. 2. Jonathan Young, a gunner in the US Navy, accepted *Whitney *cap-lock revolvers in the years immediately prior to the American Civil War. They were marked 'Y' or 'JY'. See also US arms inspectors' marks. 3. Young America. Made by J.P. *Lindsay, this US cap-lock pistol contained two charges, one on top of the other, which were fired from a single barrel by two hammers. 4. Young America. A small double-action .22- or .32-calibre revolver offered by *Harrington & Richardson of Worcester, Massachusetts, USA, sometimes with a spurless Safety Hammer. 5. Young America Bulldog. This was a five-shot .32-calibre *Harrington & Richardson revolver with a 2in barrel, made from the 1890s until 1908 or later. 6. Young American: see Young America.

Z

'Z', 'z' – 1. Within a concentric-circle motif representing a rifled barrel. A trademark found on pistols, rifles and machine-guns made by *Československá Zbrojovka of Brno and its successor, *Zbrojovka Brno. **2.** As 'z': a mark associated with small-arms ammunition made under German supervision by Waffenwerke Brünn AG of Povaška Bystrica during the Second World War.

Zabala Hermanos SA, Eibar, Guipúzcoa, Spain. A maker of sporting and target spring-airguns.

Zacharie – 1. Rue de l'Huerton 4, Saint-Étienne, France. Listed in 1892 as a distributor of, and agent for, arms and ammunition. **2.** Zacharie aîné, place Chavanelle 23, Saint-Étienne, France. Listed in 1879 as a distributor of, and agent for, arms and ammunition. **3.** Zacharie père et fils, rue de Lyon 112, Saint-Étienne, France. Listed in 1879 as a distributor of, and agent for, arms and ammunition.

Zakłady Metalowe Łucznik. The Polish state firearms factory, best known for a selection of *Mauser rifles and Wilniewczyk/Skrzpinski Radom pistols, has also made a selection of *Kalashnikov derivatives. These have ranged from the 7.62mm PMK and PMK-M, to the KA-90 Tantal and the KA-96 Beryl assault rifles. A range of accessories is also produced, including the 40mm Pallad grenade launcher.

Zaldun. A Spanish 6.35mm Browning-type automatic pistol made by an unknown gunmaker, probably in Eibar.

Zamacola. S. Zamacola SA [Sucesores de], Eibar, Guipúzcoa, Spain. A maker of spring-airguns.

Zanoletti. Attilio Zanoletti, Armigas-Comega SpA (also known as Costruzione Armigas or Costruzione Meccaniche Gardonese), Via Valle Inzino, Brescia, Italy. Maker of *Armigas-brand gas-powered rifles, Zanoletti began trading in February 1961 and registered in Brescia in March of the same year. Trading ceased in the 1980s.

Zastava, Zastava Arms. See Zavodi *Crvena Zastava.

Zauch. George Zauch, a government arms inspector working in 1905, accepted guns and equipment marked 'GZ'. See also US arms inspectors' marks.

Zavatero, rue de l'Heurton 24, Saint-Étienne, France. Listed in 1892 as a gunmaker. Still listed in 1933 as Zavattero et Cie, and in 1951 as Zavaterro (trading from 24 rue Jean-Claude Tissot).

Zavodi Crvena Zastava (Red Banner Works), Yugoslavia, Serbia. See Crvena Zastava.

'ZB', 'zb' – 1. Usually as 'ZB': an abbreviation applied to the products of *Československá Zbrojovka of Brno, Czechoslovakia. They included the vz. 24 *Mauser-action rifle and its derivatives, and ZB vz. 26 light machine-gun (derived from the *Praga), which was adopted by the Czechoslovakian Army in 1926. Improvements in the bolt and gas system created the vz. 27, but this was soon superseded by a vz. 30 with a stronger piston and a better gas regulation system. Later patterns included the 7.9mm ZB 53 and the 15mm ZB

60. Brno-designed machine-guns sold in large numbers to Bulgaria, China, Portugal and Turkey; others were made under licence in Romania and Yugoslavia. **2.** As 'zb': a code allocated in 1940 to distinguish the German small-arms ammunition components made by Kupferwerk Ilsenburg AG of Ilsenburg/Harz.

'Z-BER'. Found on British small-arms with components damaged beyond economic repair and fit only for scrap.

'Z-BLR'. Found on British small-arms with components damaged beyond local repair.

Zbrojovka... – 1. Zbrovojka Brno, a Czechoslovakian gunmaking business: see Československá Zbrojovka. **2.** Zbrojovka Praga, Prague. This Czechoslovakian gunmaking business was founded in 1918 by A. Nowotny. It employed the *Holek brothers, František *Myška and Karel *Krnka, making the 6.35mm and 7.65mm Praga pistols and a series of experimental light automatic weapons until the work (which included the perfected *Praga M-24 light machine-gun) was transferred to *Československá Zbrojovka of Brno. The Praga company was taken over by its principal creditor, the Industrial Bank, and liquidated in 1926.

ZCZ. See Zavodi *Crvena Zastava.

'ZE'. A part-superimposition monogram with slight prominence given to 'Z'. Correctly 'EZ' (q.v.); associated with Eduard *Zehner of Suhl.

Zehna. A compact 6.35mm-calibre pocket pistol, based on the *FN-Browning of 1906, made in Suhl by Eduard *Zehner. It is thought that the gun dates from the early 1920s, and that it formed the basis for the later *Haenel pattern; the earliest examples (usually marked 'Zehna' above 'D.R.G.M.') have their barrels retained by a lateral pin, whereas later guns rely on the recoil-spring rod, and display 'D.R.P.a.' and the manufacturer's name in the slide mark.

Zehner – 1. Ad. Zehner, Suhl, Thüringen, Germany. This man was listed in 1939 as a gunsmith. **2.** Eduard Zehner, Suhl in Thüringen, Germany. A maker of sporting guns and rifles, this gunsmith is also renowned as the designer of the 6.35mm *Zehna semi-automatic pistol. His business may have been sold to *Haenel c. 1925, but details are lacking. **3.** Emil Zehner, Suhl in Thüringen. This German 'gunsmith' is recorded in the 1914 *Deutsches Reichs-Adressbuch* as a specialist screw maker. Business continued into the post-war period (it was owned in 1920 by Wilhelm Zehner), but there is no evidence to suggest an involvement in gunmaking after 1919. Operations were still being listed in 1939 as 'metalworking', but it is supposed that trading ceased in 1945. Zehner is believed to have marked his guns with 'E.Z.' or an 'EZ' monogram. **4.** Heinz Zehner, Suhl in Thüringen. Designer of the earliest *Sauer semi-automatic pistol, patented in Germany in 1912.

Zeiss. Carl Zeiss, Jena. A leading manufacturer of optical equipment, including optical sights, gunmakers' tools, bore sighters, etc.

'Zenit'. This mark will be found on a spring-air pistol, cocked by a top lever, made in Germany by *Moritz & Gerstenberger c. 1937–40. *See also* Krone.

Zenith. Applied to *Langenhan-made spring-airguns advertised in Germany in Gustav *Genschow catalogues published in the mid-1920s.

Zentrum. A single-shot block-action target pistol made by M. *Neumann of Suhl prior to 1940.

Zero. A brandname applied to diabolo-type airgun pellets sold in the early 1980s by *Sussex Armoury.

'ZF', 'Z F'. Found on British small-arms with components damaged beyond local repair, but capable of being repaired at an approved factory.

'ZGB'. This Czechoslovakian light machine-gun was a .303-calibre variant of the *ZB vz. 27, made for trials in Britain from 1931 onward. The last major sub-variant, the ZGB Improved Model 4 of 1934, was virtually a prototype of the *Bren Gun. It lacked the barrel fins of the original ZGBs, and the back sight was on the receiver behind the magazine; the rate of fire was slowed. Sixty Brno-made Improved Model 4 machine-guns arrived in Britain early in 1935 to facilitate field trials.

'Zi-Di', 'ZIDI'. Marks associated with *Ziegenhahn & Diem of Suhl.

Ziegenhahn – 1. Alfred Ziegenhahn, Suhl in Thüringen, Germany. This gunmaking business was founded in 1922, trading independently until absorbed into the partnership of Ziegenhahn & Diem (below). 2. Ziegenhahn & Diem, Suhl in Thüringen, Germany. A partnership of Alfred Ziegenhahn and Heinrich Diem, trading from c. 1935 until the end of the Second World War, this business manufactured sporting guns and target pistols that often bore the trademark 'Zi-Di'. Apparently the factory was absorbed after 1946 by the state-owned firearms industry of the German Democratic Republic; *see* Ernst *Thälmann.

Zieh- und Stanzwerk Schedetal. *See* Schedetal and Haendler & Natermann.

Zielgewehr, Zielkarabiner. Applied to pre-1918 conversions of German *Mauser military rifles and carbines for practice use. They chambered a special 5.5m rimfire cartridge.

'Zig-Zag'. A nickname applied to a German *Mauser revolver and the US-made Remington-Elliott derringer. *See* W.H. *Elliott and E. *Remington & Son.

Zimmermann – 1. Carl Zimmermann, Mehlis and Zella-Mehlis in Thüringen. Founded in 1857, this gunmaker also made hunting accessories. Listed in 1900 under the heading *Waffen* (Weapons) in the *Deutsches Reichs-Adressbuch*, he seems to have ceased trading at the end of the First World War. Details are lacking. 2. Friedrich Zimmermann, Arnstadt in Thüringen. Listed in Germany in 1941 as a maker of sporting-gun parts. 3. Fritz Zimmermann, Albrechts bei Suhl in Thüringen. Listed in 1940–41 as a maker of gun parts. 4. Karl Zimmermann, Ulm/Donau. Employed by *Anschütz, this engineer was the co-patentee of recoilless air rifles with Heinrich *Liebmann. 5. R. Zimmermann, Suhl in Thüringen, Germany. A specialist barrel-blank maker active in the late 1930s.

Zimmerstutzen. *See* Saloon Gun.

Zink – 1. Carl Zink, Zella St Blasii and Zella-Mehlis. A gunmaking business founded in 1871; operations may not have survived into the twentieth century. 2. Fritz Zink, Suhl and Zella-Mehlis in Thüringen. Possibly the son of (and successor to) Carl Zink, this gunmaking business made sporting rifles and shotguns until 1939 or later.

Zip. A cheap break-barrel spring-air pistol manufactured in Italy by *Mondiale; distributed in Britain by Gunmark during 1976/77.

'ZJC'. A cursive superimposition-type monogram. Correctly 'JCZ' (q.v.); used briefly by *Jihočeská Zbrojovka of Prague, Czechoslovakia.

Zögner. Richard Zögner, Suhl in Thüringen. Listed in 1930 and 1939 as a gunsmith.

Zoli. A. Zoli & Co. SNC, Gardone Val Trompia, Brescia, Italy. A manufacturer of shotguns, sporting rifles and an automatic pistol.

Zöller. Gebr. Zöller, Zella St Blasii in Thüringen, Germany. Listed in directories of 1900 as a master gunsmith and gunmaker.

Zonda. A .22 LR rimfire semi-automatic pistol made in Argentina by Hispano-Argentina Fábrica de Automoviles SA.

'ZS', 'Z & S'. A mark associated with Zieh- und Stanzwerk *Schedetal AG.

Zschocke. Fr. Zschocke, Suhl, Thüringen. Apparently established in the 1870s, this German gunmaking business was being operated by 1914 as Fr. Zschockes Nachfolger, Paul Stadelmann. It seems to have failed c. 1923.

Zulaica. M. Zulaica y Compañía, Eibar, Guipúzcoa, Spain. A maker of *Ruby-pattern semi-automatic pistols for the French Army during the First World War. Also distributor of pistols bearing *Royal, The *Victory and *Vincitor brandnames.

Zulu. A name applied in the USA to 12-bore shotguns converted from French *Tabatière breech-loaders, purchased in Europe after the Franco-Prussian War of 1870–71.

Zündnadelgewehr (Needle gun). *See* panel, pp. 570/71.

Zurch, or 'Zurich', New York City. Robert E. Gardner (*Small Arms Makers*, 1963) lists this gunmaker at 106 East Houston Street in 1850–61, but Eldon Wolff (*Air Guns*, 1958) reports that no such place existed in the city and speculates that Zurch may have owned a shooting arcade – and that, consequently, *Gallery Guns bearing his name were actually made by a New York gunsmith named John Zuendorff.

Zürich Zeughaus. A maker of 1,500 1869-pattern *Vetterli rifles for the Swiss government, 1869–74.

Zuylen [van]. Prosper van Zuylen. A gun merchant listed in directories of 1857 at 8 Catherne Court, Tower Hill, London E..

'ZV'. Czechoslovak-made spring-air rifles have been reported with the designations 'ZV3' and 'ZV4', but their maker has not been identified.

'ZVP'. Encountered on an inexpensive break-barrel spring-air pistol exported by *Omnipol of Prague during the 1960s. *See also* 'ZV', as it was probably made by the same company.

ZÜNDNADELGEWEHR

This Prussian needle gun was the work of Johann Dreyse (1787–1867), a gunsmith who had trained with Samuel Pauly in Paris prior to 1814. Dreyse embarked on a gun of his own after returning to Thüringia, although experiments undertaken in partnership with Kaufmann Collenbusch stretched over several years. From this era came a variety of single-shot pistols, loaded from the muzzle, but fired by a needle igniter

These were comparatively primitive, and not until Dreyse developed the first of his breech-loading rifles in 1833 (locked by what was effectively a door bolt) was progress made. The Prussian Army undertook field trials with Dreyse *Zundnadelgewehre* in 1836–39 and adopted the weapon for infantry service on 4 December 1840.

Made in the Dreyse factory in Sommerda, the M1841 rifle was long and cumbersome, with three barrel bands and a small cheek-piece on the butt. The needle catch had to be retracted from the back of the bolt before the mechanism could be opened, but reloading was easier than recharging a muzzle-loading musket. M1841 rifles that survived the Franco-Prussian War (1870–71)

were relegated to the Landwehr in August 1872.

The M1849 sharpshooter's rifle (with a barrel held by keys instead of bands) was accepted in December 1851, but replaced by the M1854 *Jägerbuchse* (or *Pikenbuchse*), adopted on 22 March 1855, which had a distinctive rod bayonet beneath the barrel. Next came the M1860 *Füsiliergewehr*, adopted on 4 August 1860, with its barrel held by keys instead of bands; the M1865 *Jägerbüchse* (16 March 1866) was similar, but had an additional set trigger within a spurred guard.

Adopted on 28 July 1862, the M1862 infantry rifle was a refinement of the original 1841 pattern, with a shorter action, whereas the short-barrelled *Pioniergewehre u/M* (16 November 1865) and M1869 (25 January 1869) were issued to the pioneers. There were also two cavalry carbines, the models of 1855 and 1857, but these had an unsuccessful shortened action and were made only in small quantities.

Dreyse-type rifles were used in many of the states that supplied contingents to the Prussian Army, often converted from old muskets. The bolt action also inspired a legion of copies, even though the Dreyse cartridge was ballistically

inferior to any small-calibre rifle-musket. Alterations were made to the ammunition in 1847 and 1855, reflected in wholesale changes of back sights, but it continued to rely on poorly-shaped bullets set in papier mâché sabots that engaged the rifling. In addition, the needle had to pass through the charge before reaching the primer that had been set in the sabot base.

Tests with *Chassepot rifles showed the Prussians that the Dreyse was greatly inferior in muzzle velocity, trajectory height and potential accuracy. A short-term solution was found in a bolt head designed by Johannes Beck, a foreman armourer in the Spandau factory. Adopted on 10 March 1870, before the war with France began, this is easily distinguished by a large screw head on the bolt body, ahead

Dreyse needle guns, such as the 1865-pattern Zündnadelbüchse (below), were used extensively during the Franco-Prussian War. The engraving (right), by the renowned artist C. Röchling, shows men armed with the 1862-pattern infantry rifle – identifiable by its barrel bands.

of the operating handle.

The Beck Transformation allowed more powerful cartridges to be used, but only a few guns (converted M1862 infantry rifles and M1865 Jägerbüchsen) reached the troops during the Franco-Prussian War. The conversion programme ended soon afterward, owing to progress with the 1871-pattern *Mauser cartridge rifle.

The last Dreyse infantry rifles had been withdrawn by 1877; others remained in the hands of second-line troops into the 1880s, but most were either scrapped or sold as surplus to the major arms dealers of the day.

The best guide to Dreyse needle guns is *Das Zündnadelgewehr. Eine militärtechnische Revolution im 19. Jahrhundert* (Rolf Wirtgen [ed.], 1990), although John Walter's *The German Rifle* (Arms & Armour Press, 1979) and *Rifles of the World* (Krause Publications, second edition, 1998) present concise identification details.

Trademarks

THE MARKS granted to protect the rights of manufacturers and distributors – and to assure purchasers of merchantable quality – provide some of the best ways of identifying guns, ammunition and accessories if they can be read correctly. Trademarks have their origins in the masons' marks of the Middle Ages and in the marks applied by guild members thereafter, which helped to differentiate the work of individuals in an era where literacy was an exception instead of the rule.

Where firearms are concerned, trademarks (except in the form of initials) were rare prior to the American Civil War of 1861–65, but after that they became increasingly common. This was entirely due to the perfection in the 1870s of a moulding process that allowed gutta-percha to be used to make grips for pistols and revolvers.

The result was a proliferation of decoration and the embodiment of marks and monograms in the basic designs. The complexity was limited only by the skills of the mould maker, which were often exceptionally high. Dogs' heads, birds, flowers, impressive scrolls and delicate chequering were among the many designs that each manufacturer guarded jealously – and their rivals just as eagerly copied. Consequently, although it is usually easy to link a design with a particular manufacturer, grips commissioned by distributors could grace a variety of inexpensive rimfire revolvers with different origins.

Trademark acts have been passed in most European countries, although registry in Germany did not begin until 1874; Britain followed in 1877, and many Spanish marks were registered originally as patents. In the USA, uniquely, first use of a mark often guarantees legal protection; prior to the Lanham Act of 1946, which made important changes, registration conferred only minor additional advantages.

The first international agreement protecting 'Industrial Property' was signed in Paris in 1883, the Paris Convention being modified many times thereafter until, by the time of the meeting in Lisbon in 1958, more than eighty countries had subscribed. The Arrangement for the International Registration of Trademarks was signed in Madrid in 1891. Although some international consensus exists, however, intra-national views vary appreciably.

Protection for marks in Germany, prior to 1945 at least, was granted for ten years. At the end of that period, unless the renewal was prompt, anyone was free to register the same mark. There are a few cases where gun-related marks have changed hands three times or more. Some countries, notably the USA (and Britain, to a lesser extent), deem protection to have ended once a name is classed as generic.

Trademarks found on firearms may be divided into several categories. The easiest to identify are those accompanied by a name: the well-known Mauser and Walther 'banners' for example. Next comes the group accompanied by abbreviations, then the marks composed of *monograms (interlocking initials). Marks consisting of an illustration and an abbreviation are usually easy to read, and can be identified if the abbreviations can be linked with a specific manufacturer. However, in some cases, this is impossible; in others, a range of possibilities may exist.

Monograms range from the simple and easily read (normally the situation with recent designs) to the complex and confusing (common with many nineteenth-century patterns). The latter group is usually due to the zeal with which pre-1900 lettering was decorated: tendrils, floriation and hatching often make the letter forms difficult to detect. Brandnames are customarily easily read, and as easily identified. However, very little research among brandname registries – tedious, but potentially very useful – has yet been undertaken by the gun-collecting fraternity and, consequently, many names are still difficult to date precisely.

Many 'word', 'abbreviation' and 'monogram' marks and brandnames have been listed separately, but typical marks are shown on the following pages. *See also* Monograms and National markings.

1. *Abercrombie & Fitch*. 2 & 3. *Accuracy International*. 4. *Air Arms*. 5. *Air Match*. 6, 7 & 8. *J.G. Anschütz*. 9 & 10. *Arizmendi (Norica Arms Company)*. 11. *Astra-Unceta*. 12. *Auto Ordnance*, 13. *Azanza y Arrizabalaga*. 14. *Baikal*. 15 & 16. *Fritz Barthelmes*. 17. *C. & T. Bascaran*. 18 & 19. *Bayerische Sportwaffenfabrik*. 20. *Beeman*. 21 & 22. *Bernardelli*. 23. *Benelli*. 24–27. *Beretta*. 28. *Berlin-Suhler-Werke*. 29. *Bersa*. 30. *Bildstein, Mommer & Co*. 31–36. *Birmingham Small Arms/BSA*. 37. *Bolte & Anschütz*. 38. *Browning Arms Company*. 39. *California Industrial Company (Calico)*. 40–42. *Česká Zbrojovka*. 43 & 44. *Charter Arms*. 45–48. *Colt's Patent Fire Arms Manufacturing Company/Colt Industries (47 is the mark of the Colt Custom Gun Shop)*. 49. *Daewoo*. 50. *Daisy*. 51. *Dansk Industri Syndikat (Madsen)*. 52. *Deutsche Waffen- & Munitionsfabriken*. 53 & 54. *G.C. Dornheim*. 55 & 56. *Echave y Arizmendi*. 57. *Bonifacio Echeverria*. 58. *Edgar Bros*.

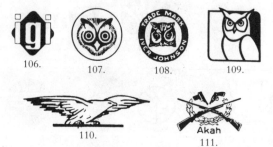

59–62. *Eidgenössische Waffenfabrik, Bern.* 63. *Eley IMI.* 64 & 65. *Industrias El Gamo.* 66. *Ensign Arms Company.* 67 & 68. *Erma-Werke.* 69. *FAIR.* 70. *FAS.* 71 & 72. *Fabrique Nationale d'Armes de Guerre.* 73. *FIE Corporation.* 74. *Fiocchi.* 75. *Forehand & Wadsworth.* 76–78. *Luigi Franchi.* 79–81. *A.L. Frank.* 82. *Renato Gamba.* 83. *General Electric (found on Vulcan Miniguns).* 84 & 85. *Gustav Genschow (now used by Dynamit Nobel).* 86. *Gerstenberger & Eberwein.* 87 & 88. *Grünig & Elmiger.* 89. *Gustloff-Werke.* 90 & 91. *Haendler & Natermann.* 92. *Haenel.* 93. *Hämmerli.* 94–100. *Harrington & Richardson.* 101. *F.W. Heym.* 102. *Hopkins & Allen.* 103. *Husqvarna.* 104. *Israeli Military Industries.* 105 & 106. *Italguns.* 107–109. *Iver Johnson.* 110. *Armas Juaristi.* 111. *Albrecht Kind.*